IT TAKES A WIZARD

ART BY
Sean Lam

STORY BY
Thomas R. Hart

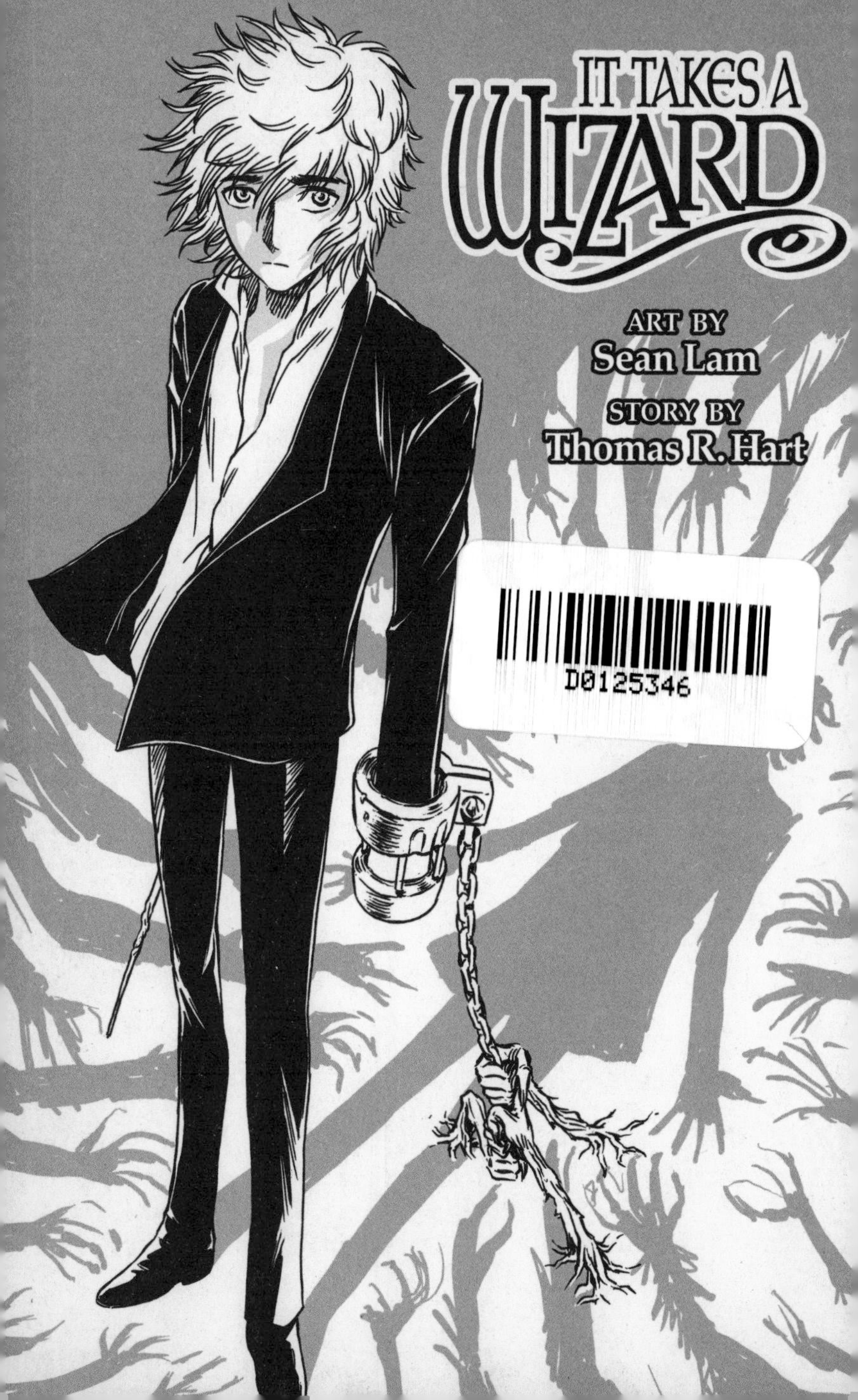

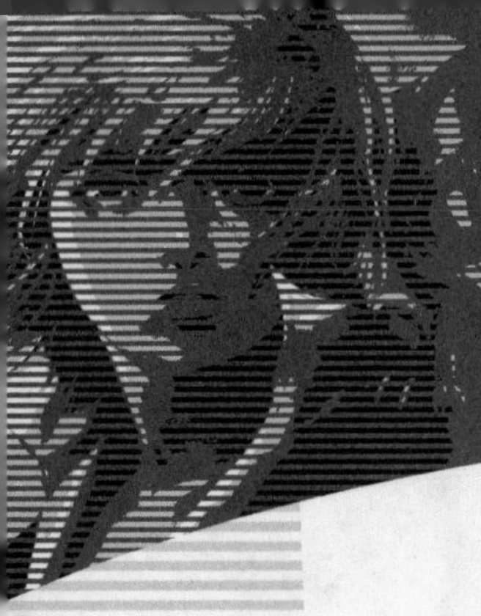

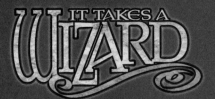

It Takes a Wizard

story by Thomas R. Hart art by Sean Lam

STAFF CREDITS

original concept	**Jason DeAngelis**
lettering	**Nicky Lim**
toning	**Ludwig Sacramento**
book layout	**Adam Arnold**
cover design	**Nicky Lim**
editor	**Adam Arnold**
Publisher	**Jason DeAngelis**
	Seven Seas Entertainment

This is a work of fiction. Names, characters, places, and incidents are the products of the author's imagination or are used fictitiously. Any resemblance to actual events, locales, or persons, living or dead, is entirely coincidental.

Visit us online at www.gomanga.com

ISBN: 978-1-934876-34-3

Printed in Canada

First Printing: July 2009

10 9 8 7 6 5 4 3 2 1

TABLE OF CONTENTS

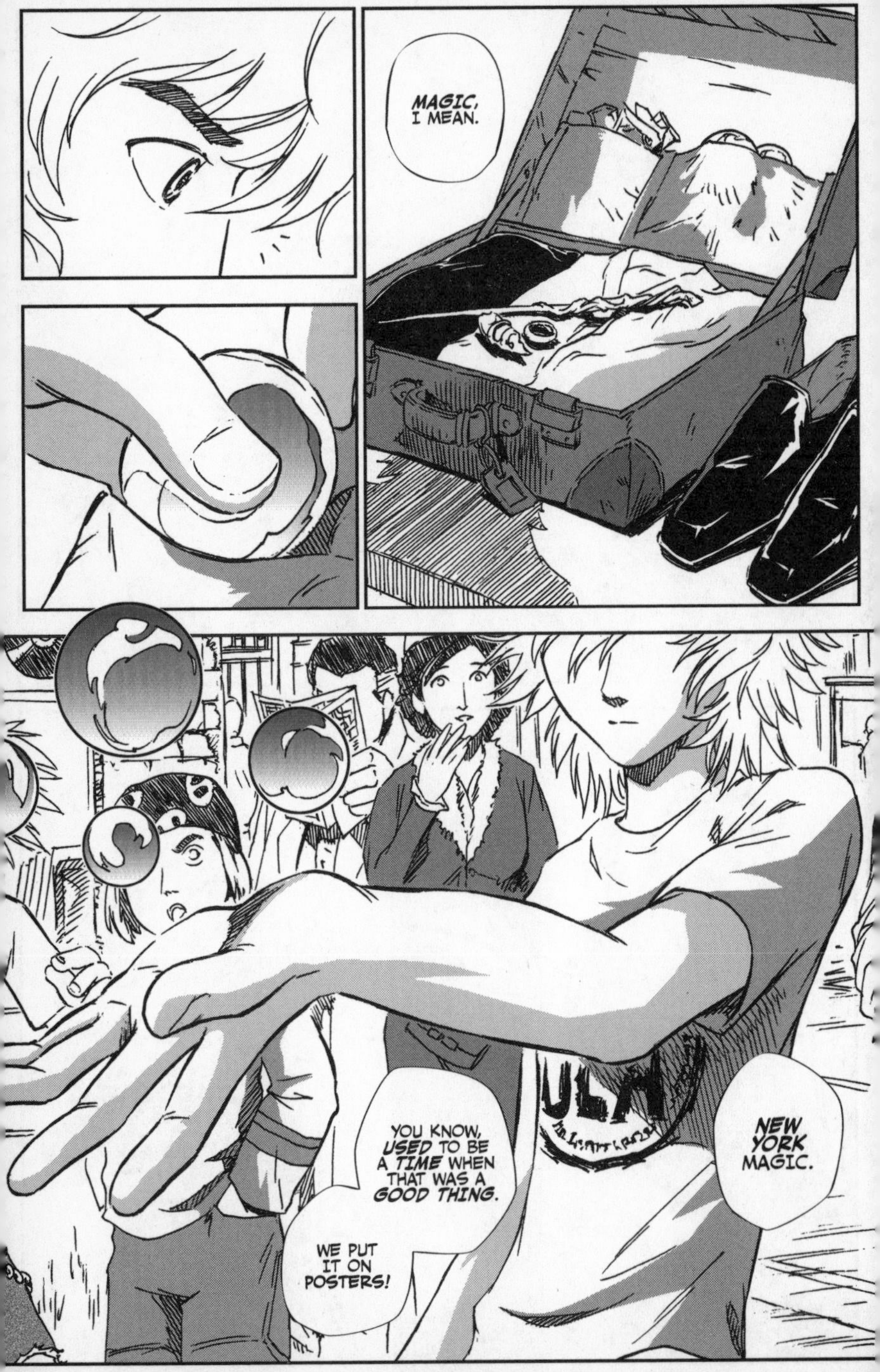
MAGIC, I MEAN.
NEW YORK MAGIC.
YOU KNOW, USED TO BE A TIME WHEN THAT WAS A GOOD THING.
WE PUT IT ON POSTERS!

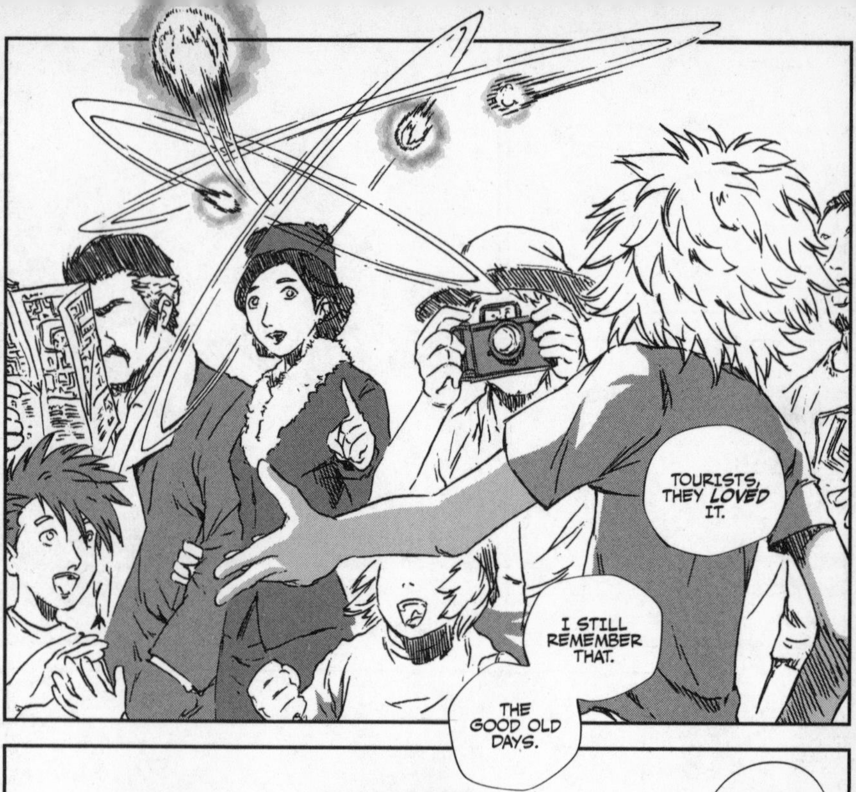
TOURISTS, THEY *LOVED* IT.
I STILL REMEMBER THAT.
THE GOOD OLD DAYS.
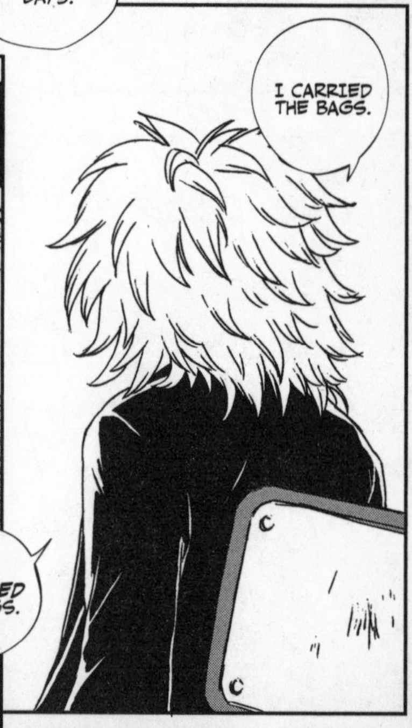
I CARRIED THE BAGS.
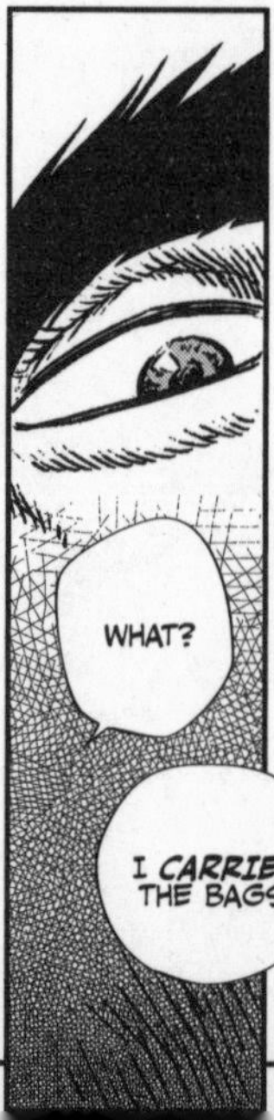
WHAT?
I *CARRIED* THE BAGS.
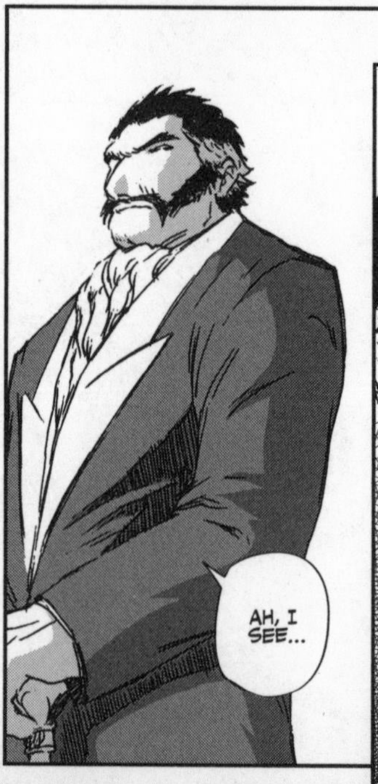
AH, I SEE...

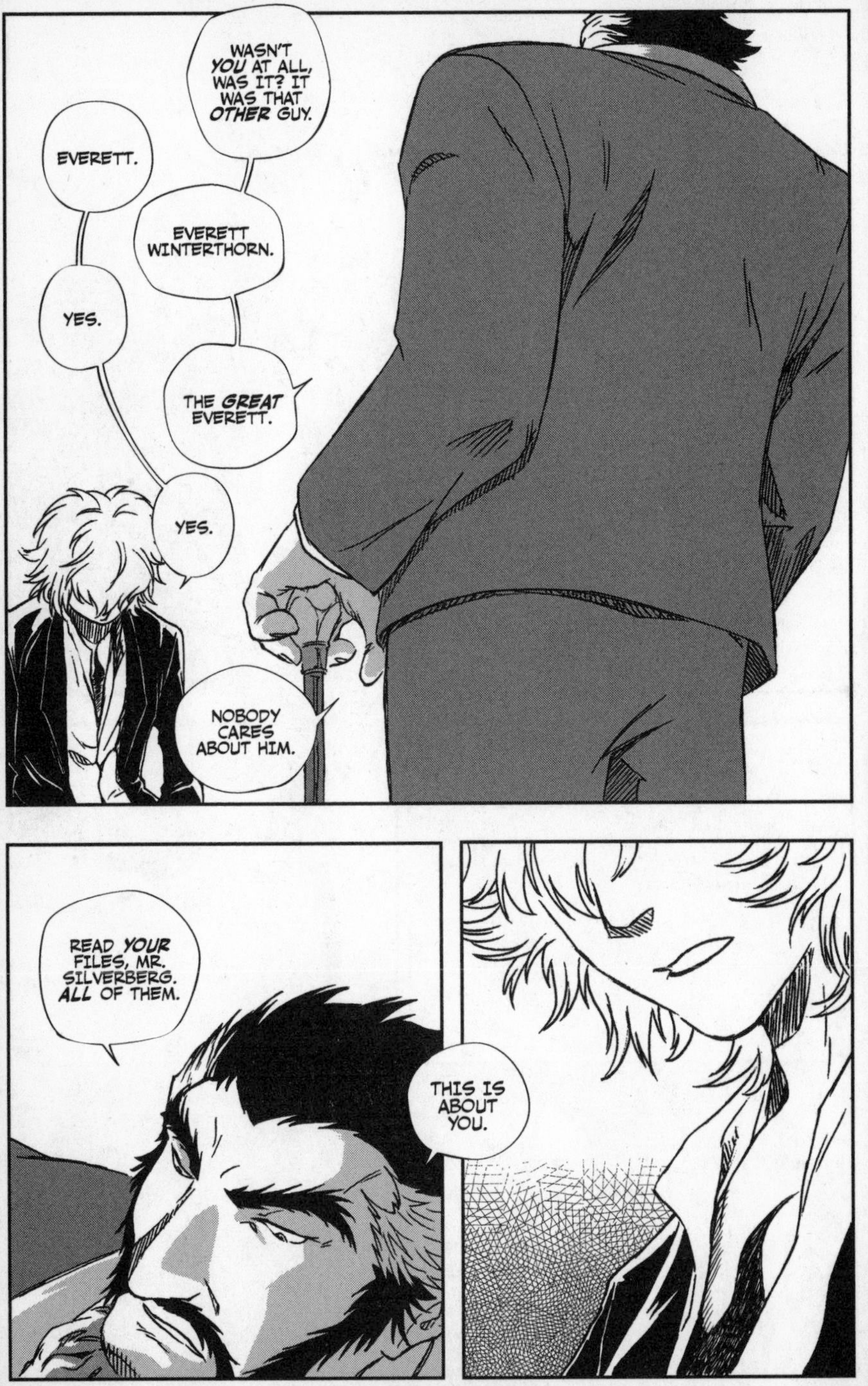
WASN'T YOU AT ALL, WAS IT? IT WAS THAT OTHER GUY.
EVERETT.
EVERETT WINTERTHORN.
YES.
THE GREAT EVERETT.
YES.
NOBODY CARES ABOUT HIM.
READ YOUR FILES, MR. SILVERBERG. ALL OF THEM.
THIS IS ABOUT YOU.

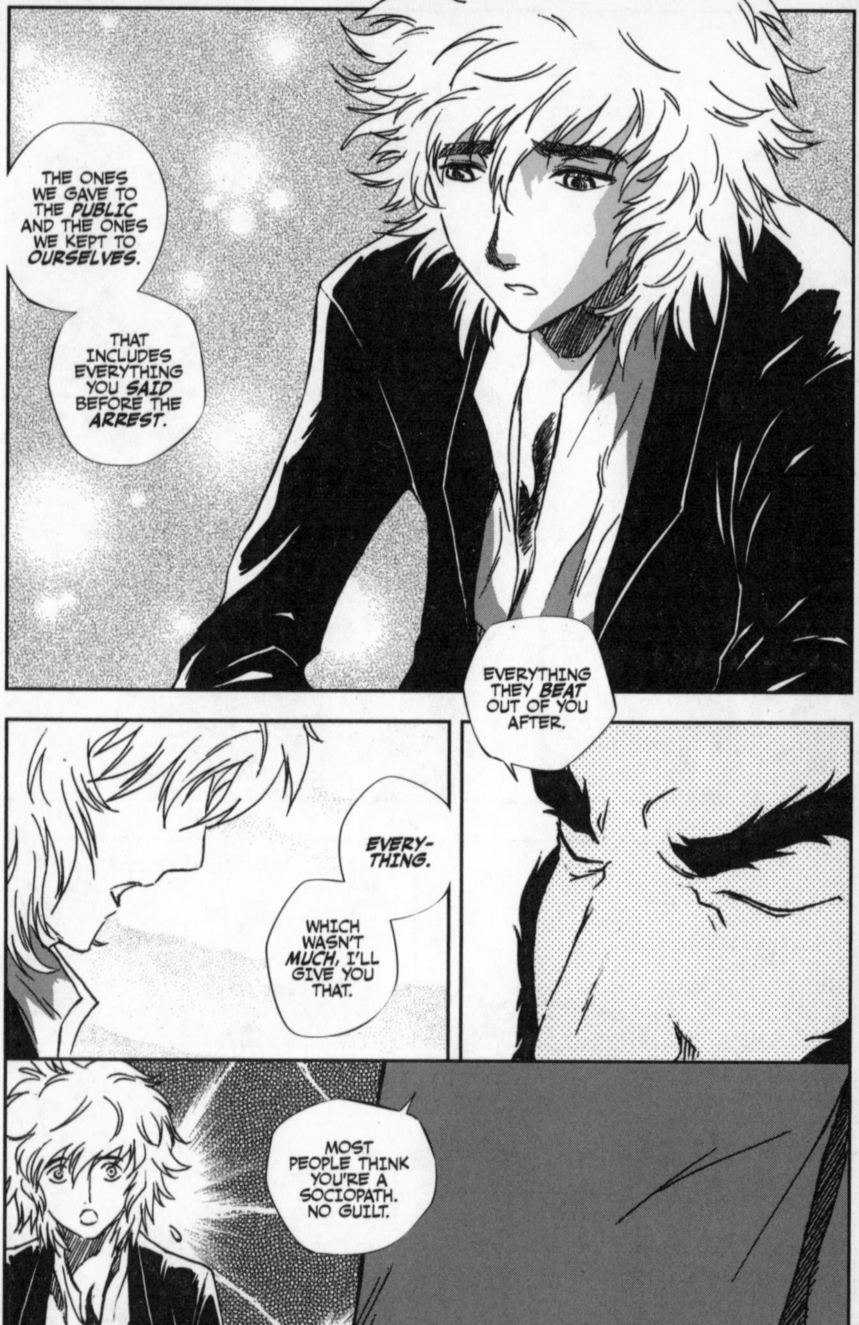
THE ONES WE GAVE TO THE *PUBLIC* AND THE ONES WE KEPT TO *OURSELVES*.
THAT INCLUDES EVERYTHING YOU *SAID* BEFORE THE *ARREST*.
EVERYTHING THEY *BEAT* OUT OF YOU AFTER.
EVERY-THING.
WHICH WASN'T *MUCH,* I'LL GIVE YOU THAT.
MOST PEOPLE THINK YOU'RE A SOCIOPATH. NO GUILT.

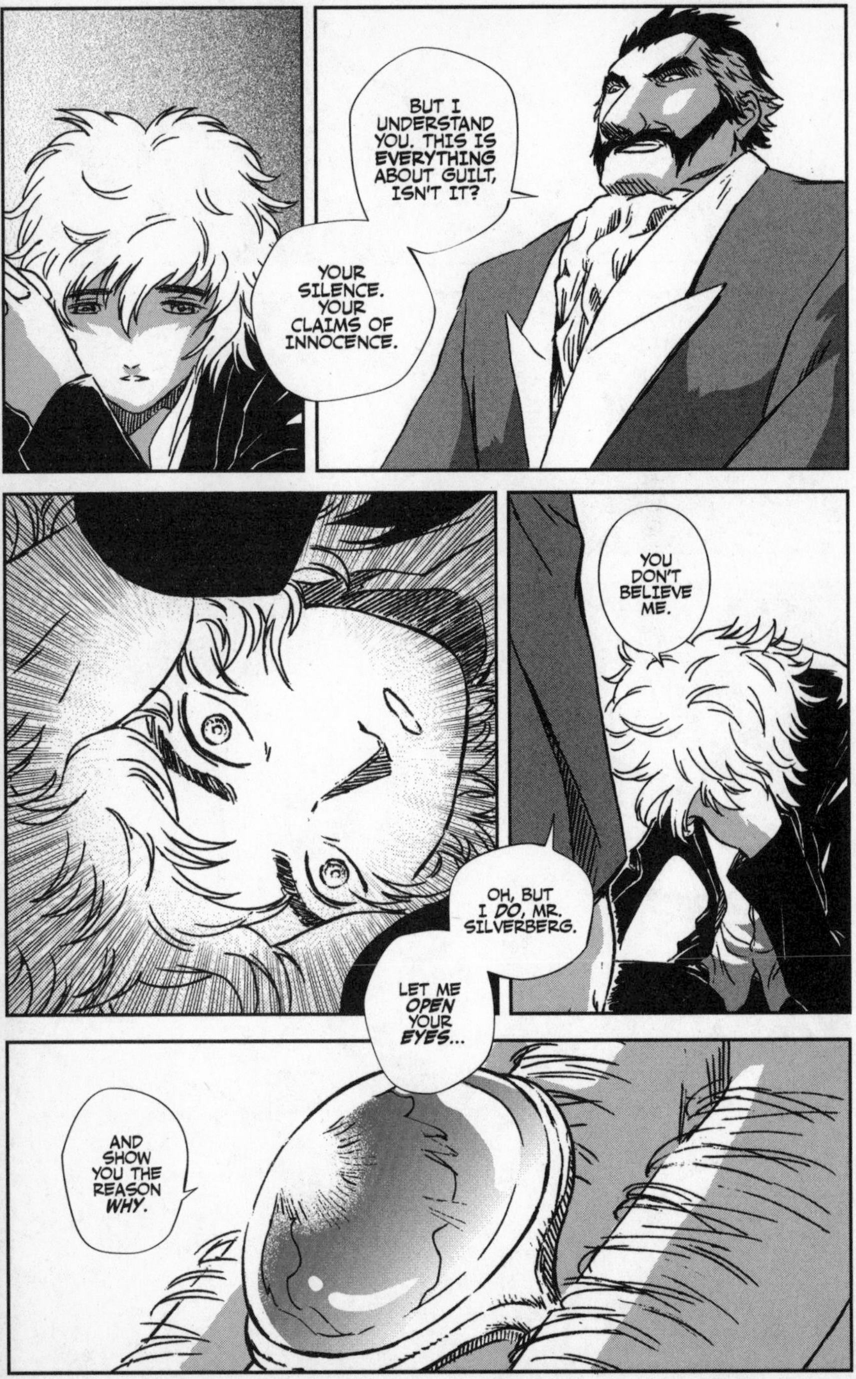
BUT I UNDERSTAND YOU. THIS IS EVERYTHING ABOUT GUILT, ISN'T IT?
YOUR SILENCE. YOUR CLAIMS OF INNOCENCE.
YOU DON'T BELIEVE ME.
OH, BUT I *DO*, MR. SILVERBERG.
LET ME *OPEN* YOUR *EYES*...
AND SHOW YOU THE REASON *WHY*.

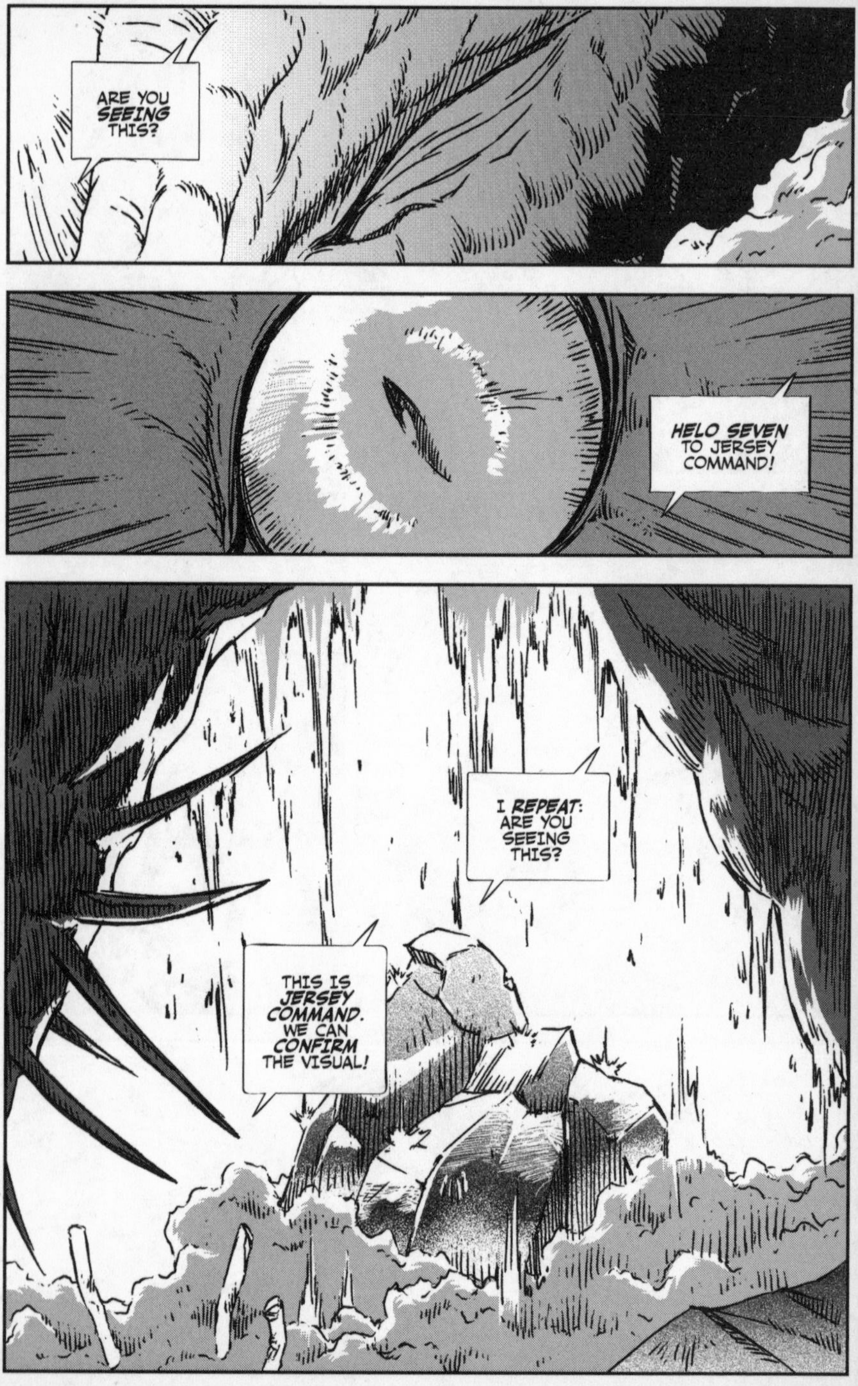
ARE YOU SEEING THIS?
HELO SEVEN TO JERSEY COMMAND!
I REPEAT: ARE YOU SEEING THIS?
THIS IS JERSEY COMMAND. WE CAN CONFIRM THE VISUAL!

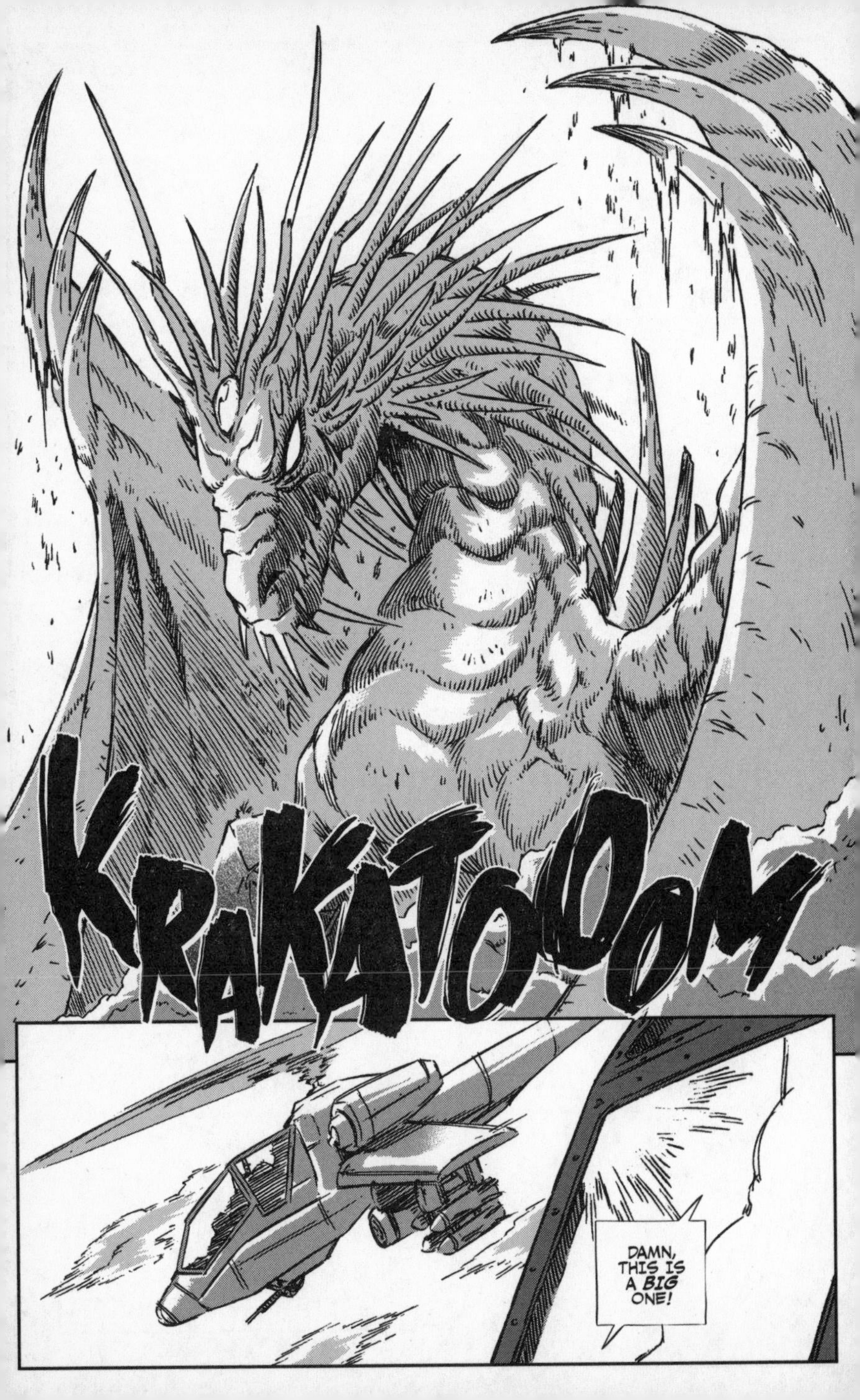
KRAKATOOOOM
DAMN, THIS IS A *BIG* ONE!

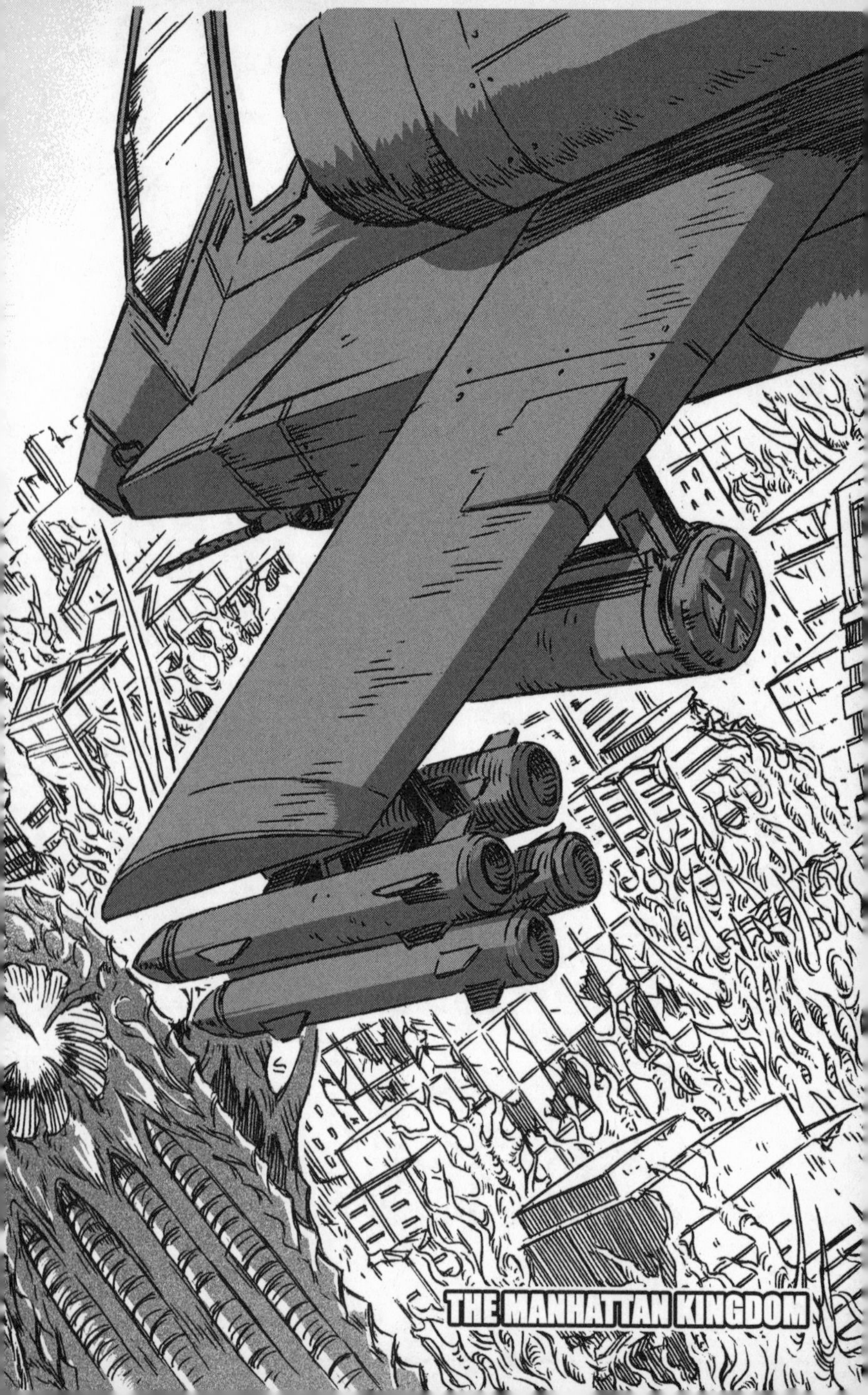
THE MANHATTAN KINGDOM

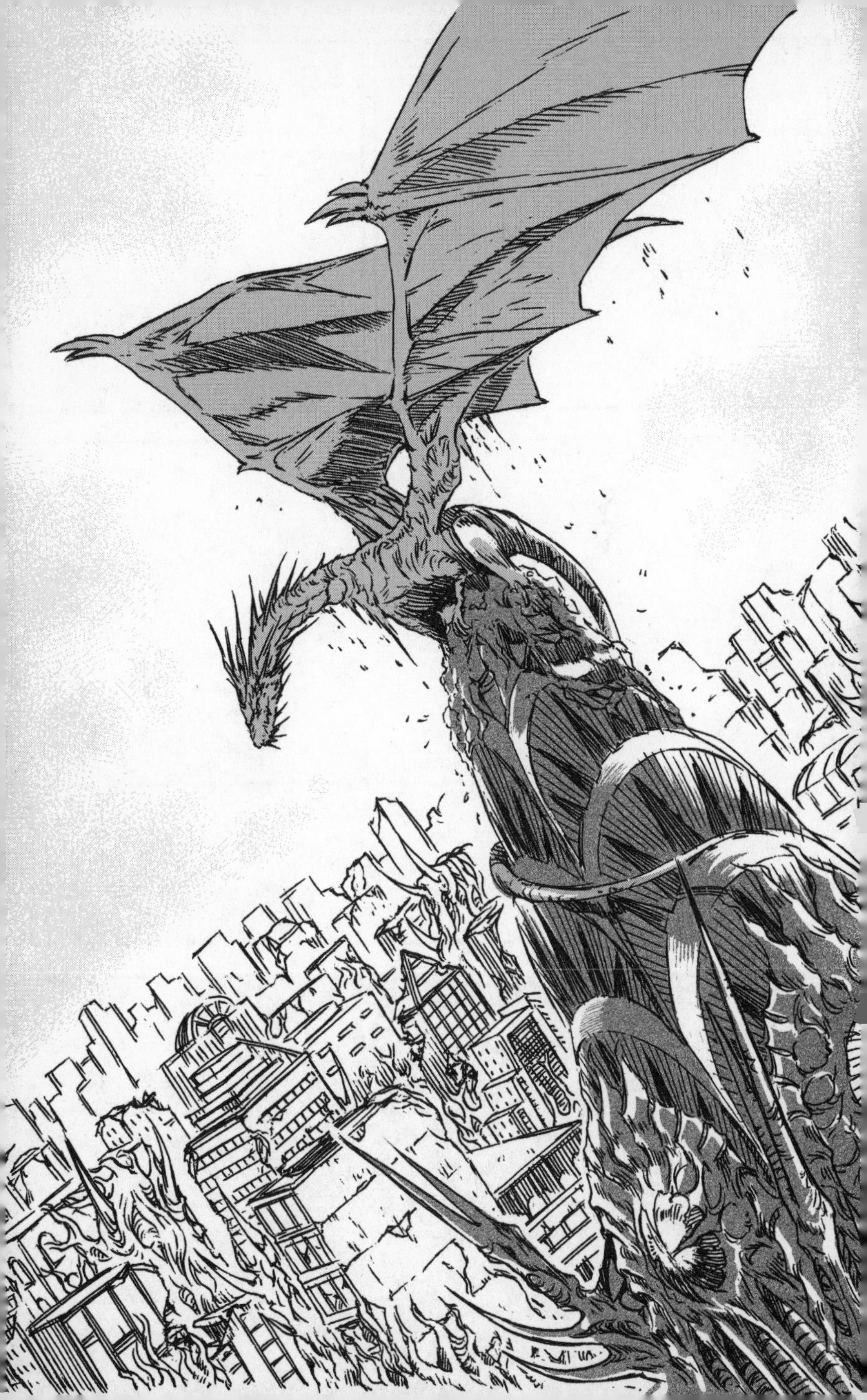

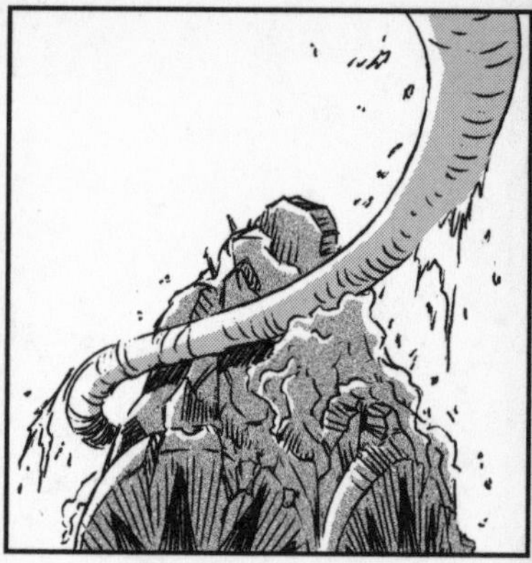

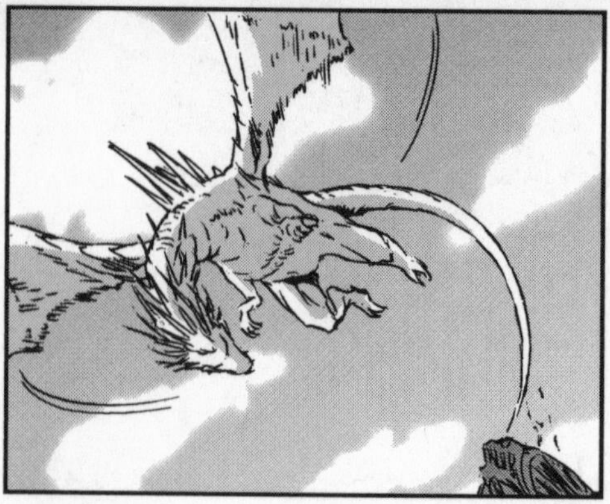

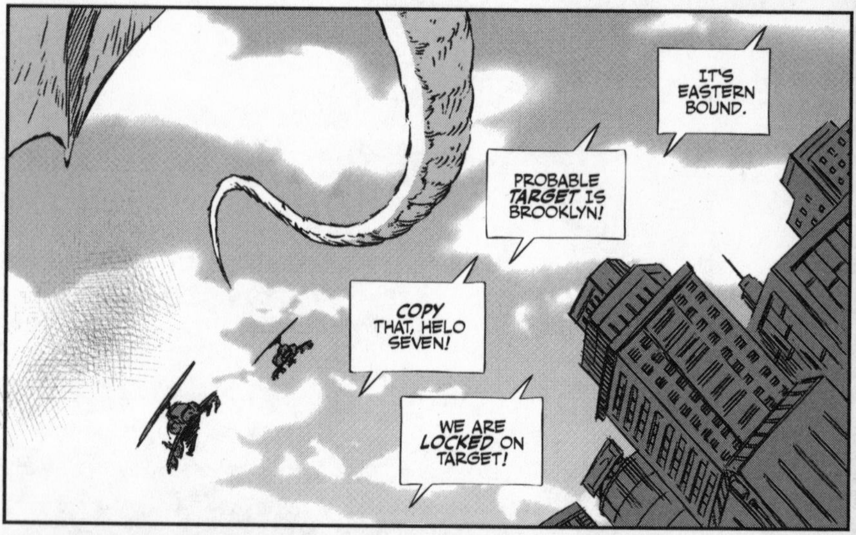
IT'S EASTERN BOUND.
PROBABLE *TARGET* IS BROOKLYN!
COPY THAT, HELO SEVEN!
WE ARE *LOCKED* ON TARGET!

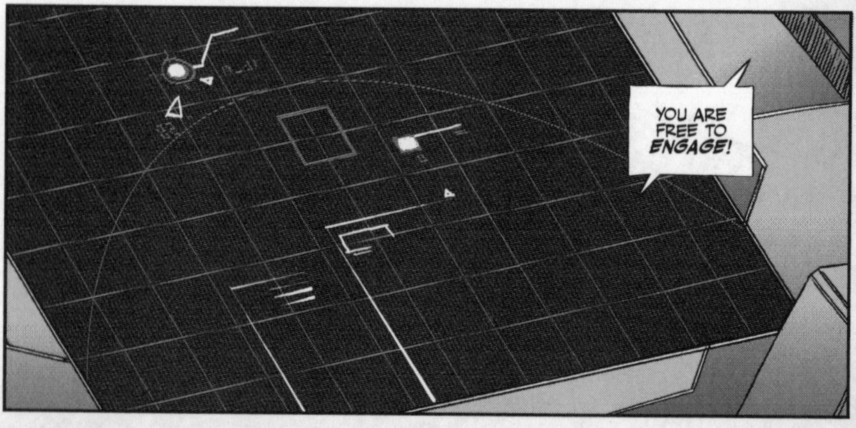
YOU ARE FREE TO *ENGAGE!*

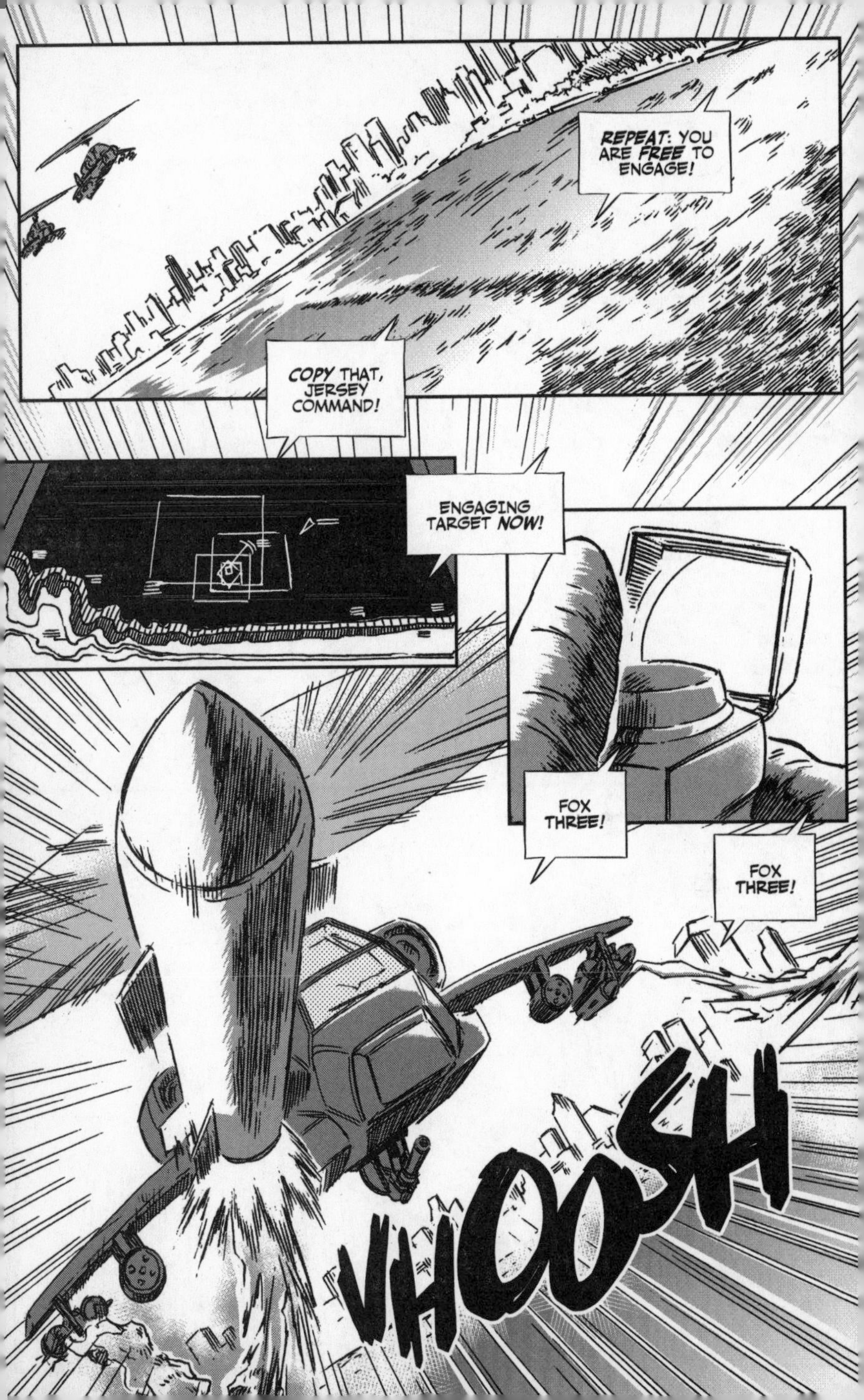
REPEAT: YOU ARE FREE TO ENGAGE!
COPY THAT, JERSEY COMMAND!
ENGAGING TARGET NOW!
FOX THREE!
FOX THREE!
WHOOSH

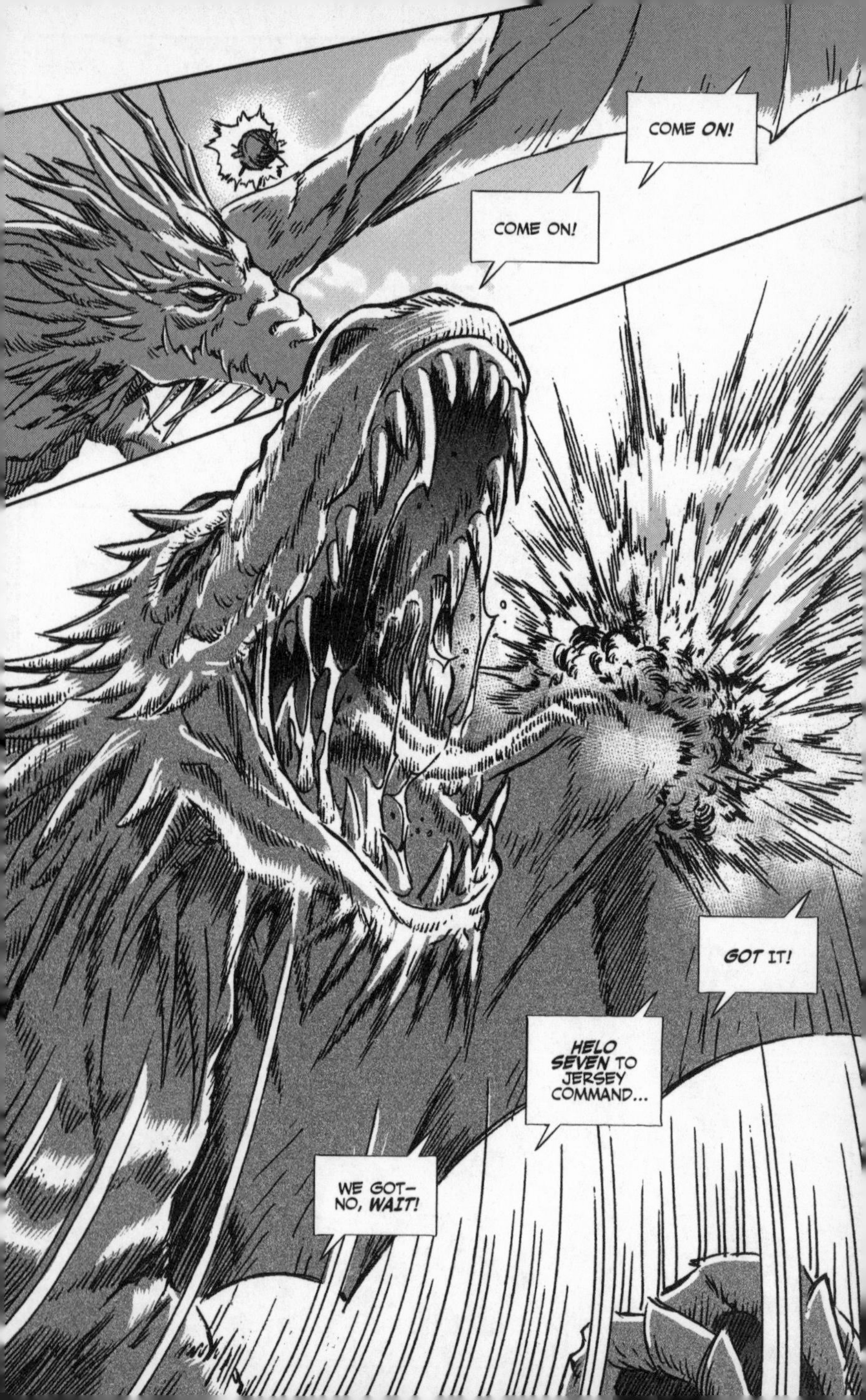
COME ON!
COME ON!
GOT IT!
HELO SEVEN TO JERSEY COMMAND...
WE GOT— NO, WAIT!

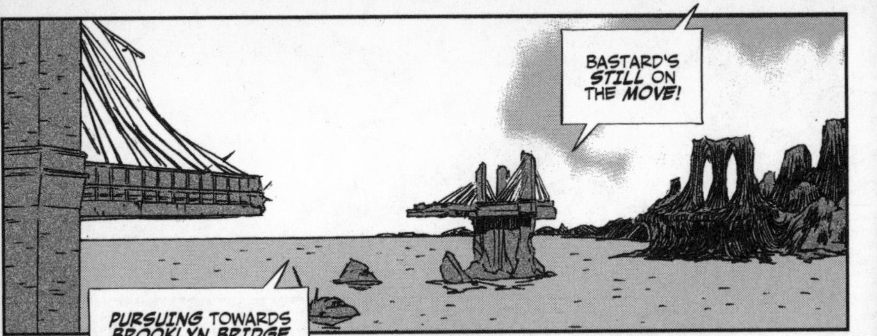
BASTARD'S STILL ON THE MOVE!
PURSUING TOWARDS BROOKLYN BRIDGE CHECKPOINT!

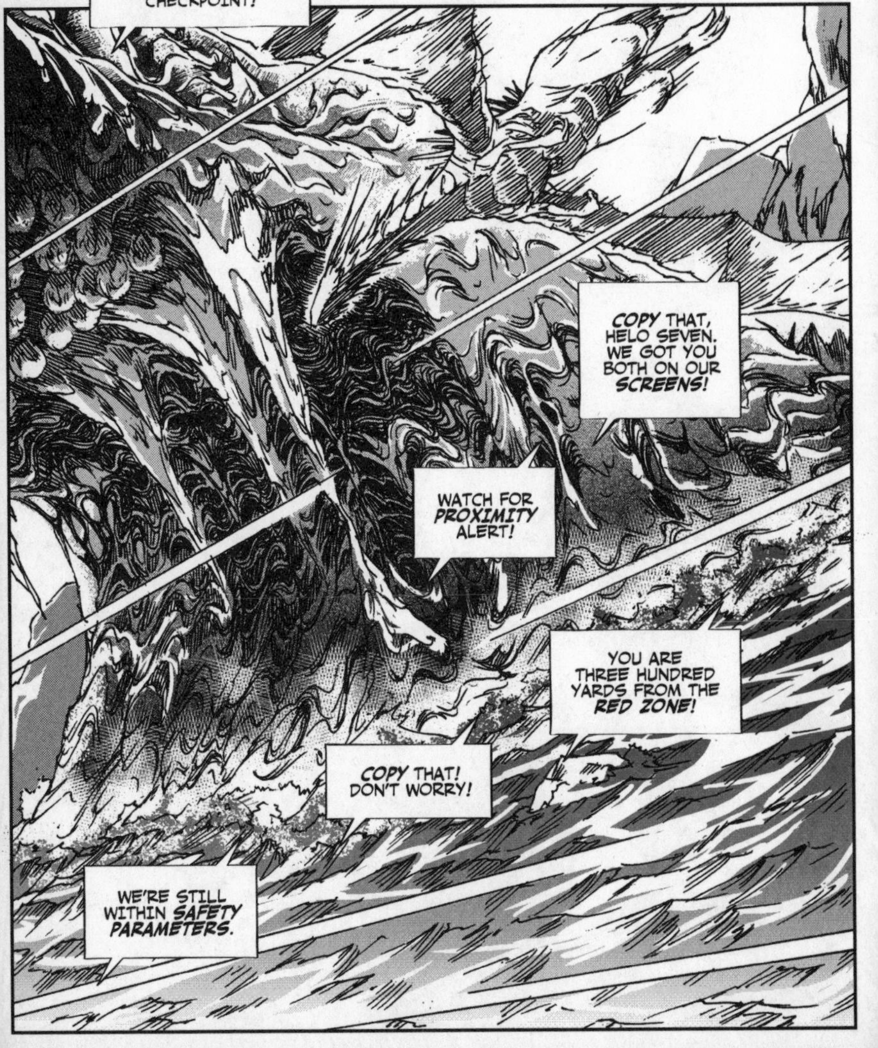
COPY THAT, HELO SEVEN. WE GOT YOU BOTH ON OUR SCREENS!
WATCH FOR PROXIMITY ALERT!
YOU ARE THREE HUNDRED YARDS FROM THE RED ZONE!
COPY THAT! DON'T WORRY!
WE'RE STILL WITHIN SAFETY PARAMETERS.

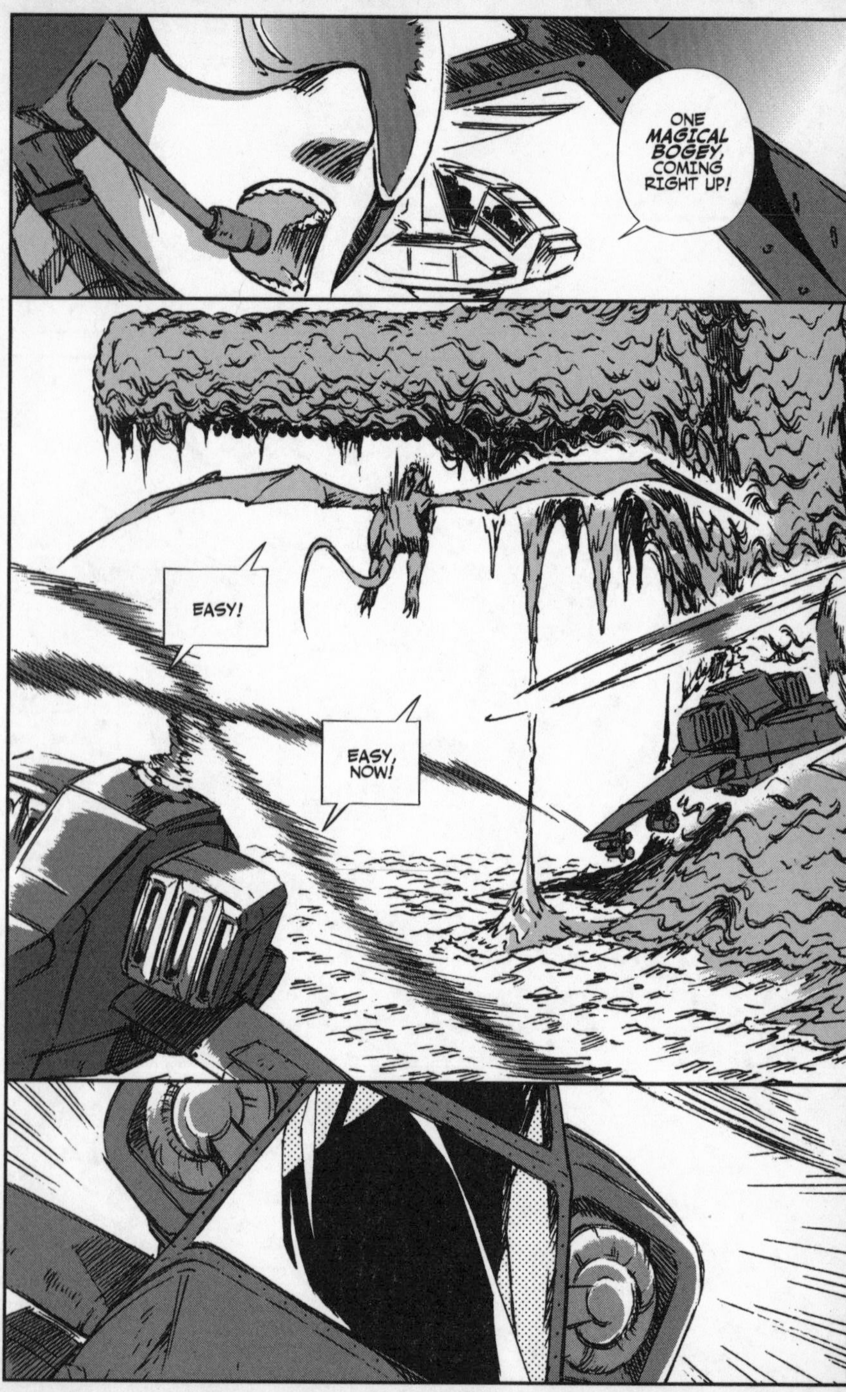
ONE *MAGICAL BOGEY*, COMING RIGHT UP!
EASY!
EASY, NOW!

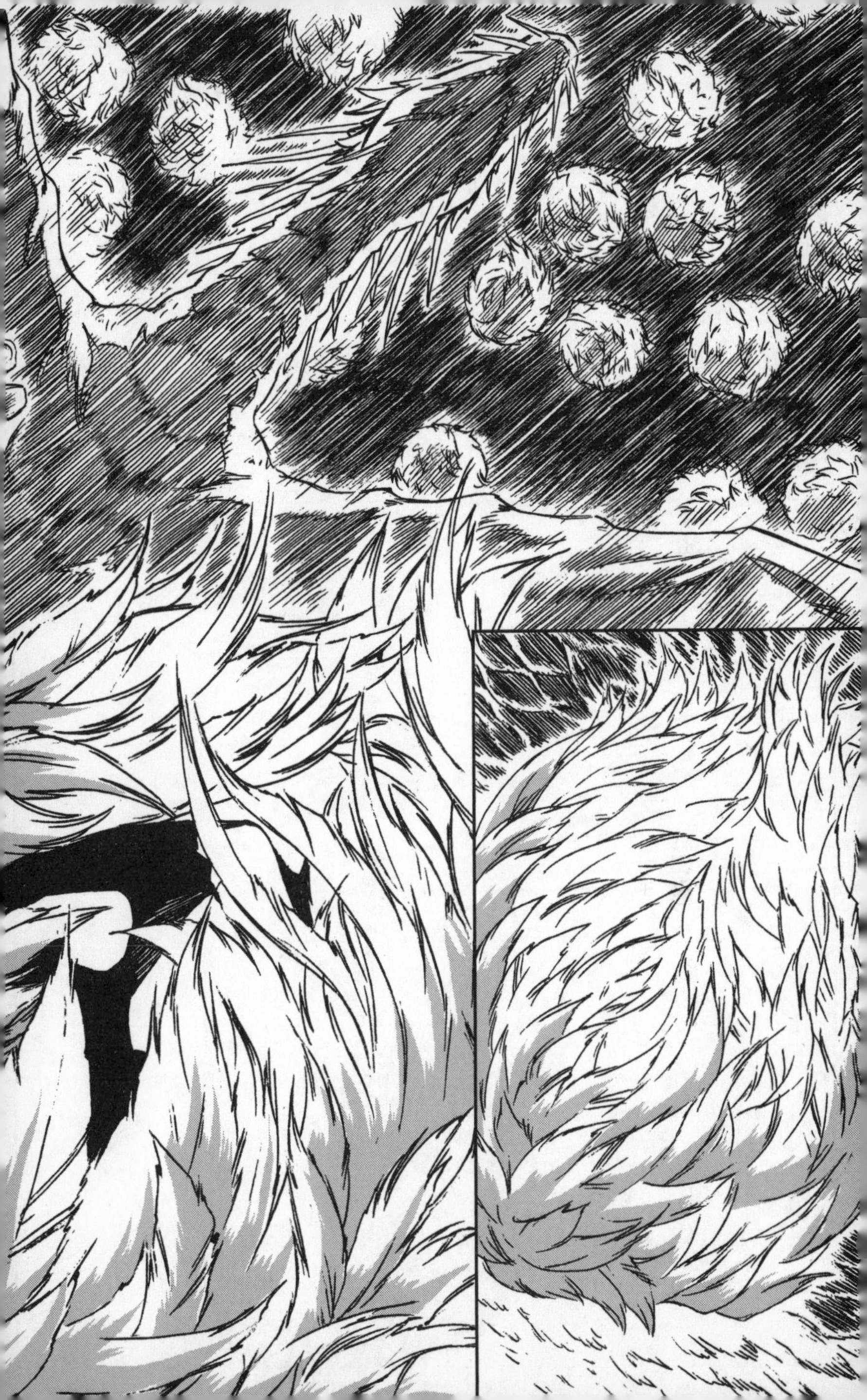

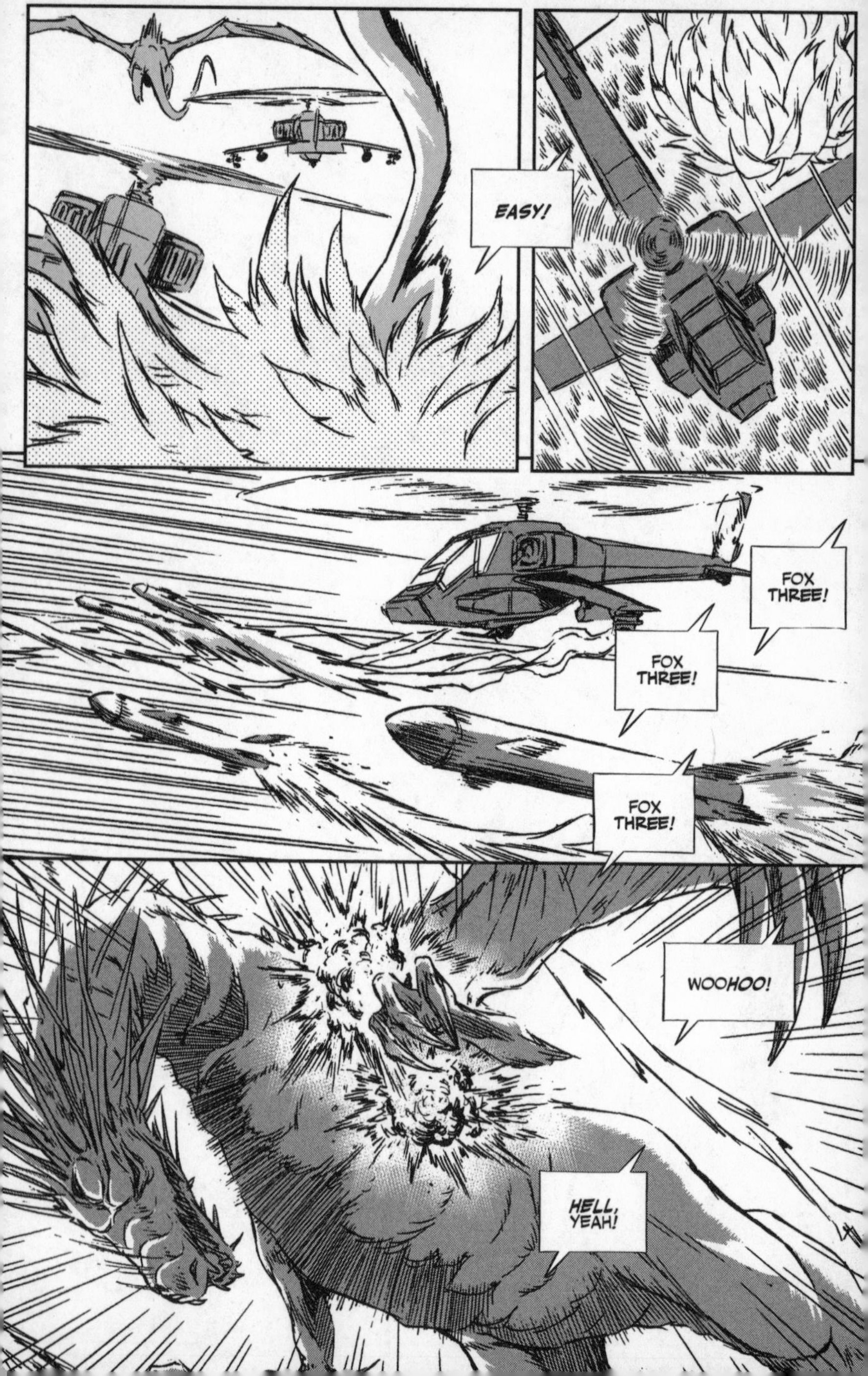
EASY!
FOX THREE!
FOX THREE!
FOX THREE!
WOOHOO!
HELL, YEAH!

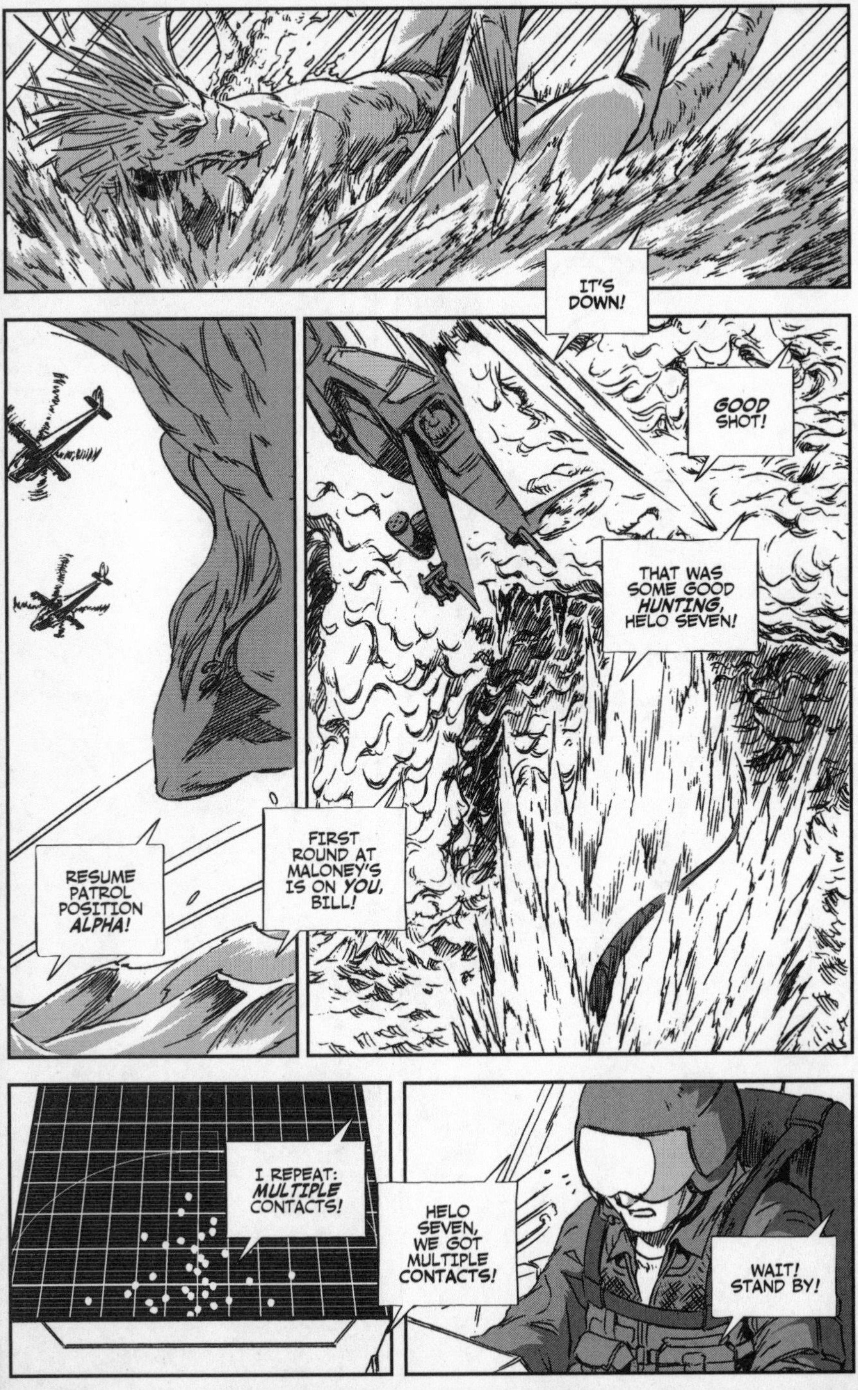
IT'S DOWN!
GOOD SHOT!
THAT WAS SOME GOOD *HUNTING*, HELO SEVEN!
FIRST ROUND AT MALONEY'S IS ON *YOU*, BILL!
RESUME PATROL POSITION *ALPHA*!
HELO SEVEN, WE GOT MULTIPLE CONTACTS!
WAIT! STAND BY!
I REPEAT: *MULTIPLE* CONTACTS!

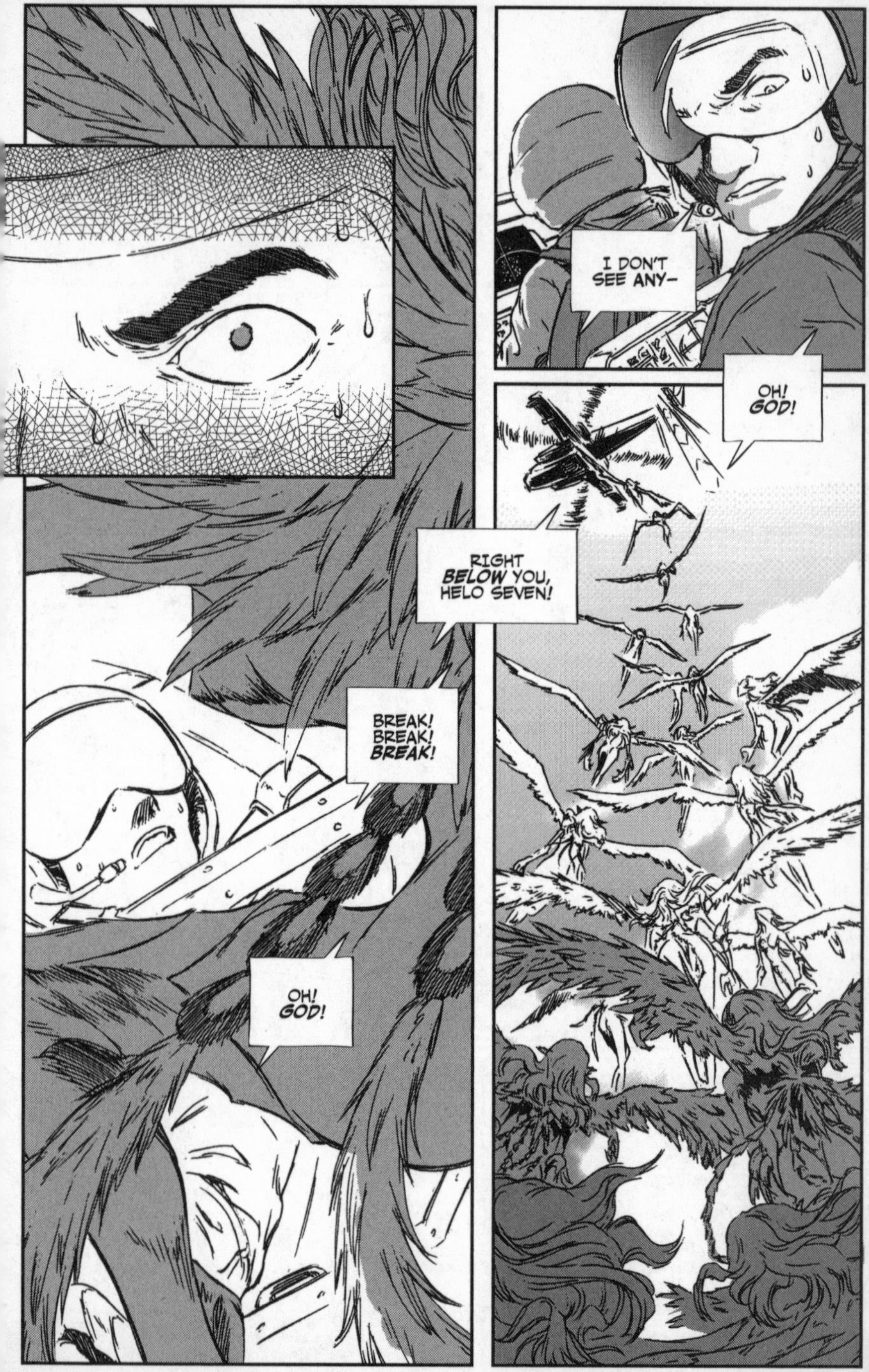
I DON'T SEE ANY–
OH! GOD!
RIGHT BELOW YOU, HELO SEVEN!
BREAK! BREAK! BREAK!
OH! GOD!

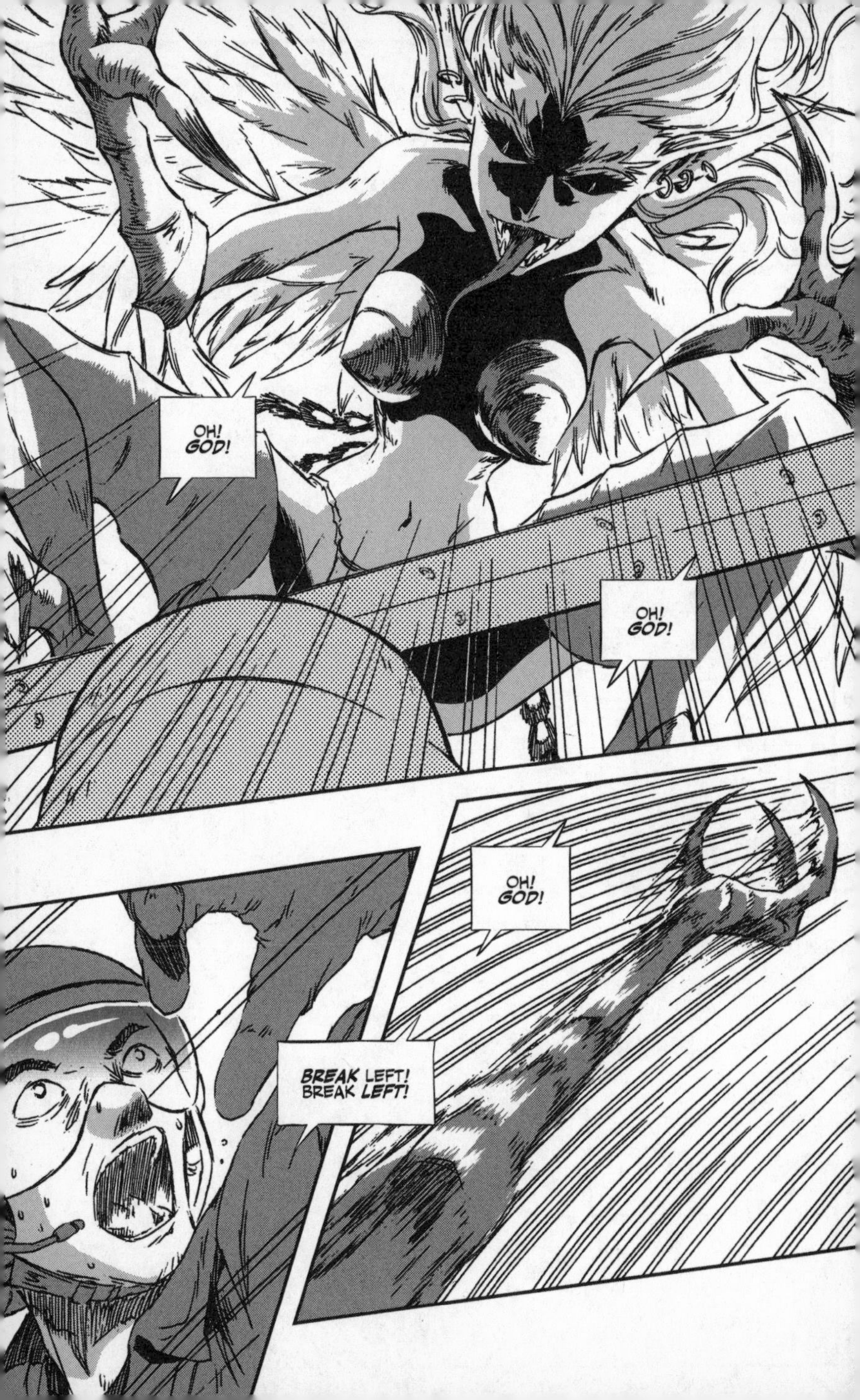
OH! GOD!
OH! GOD!
OH! GOD!
BREAK LEFT! BREAK LEFT!

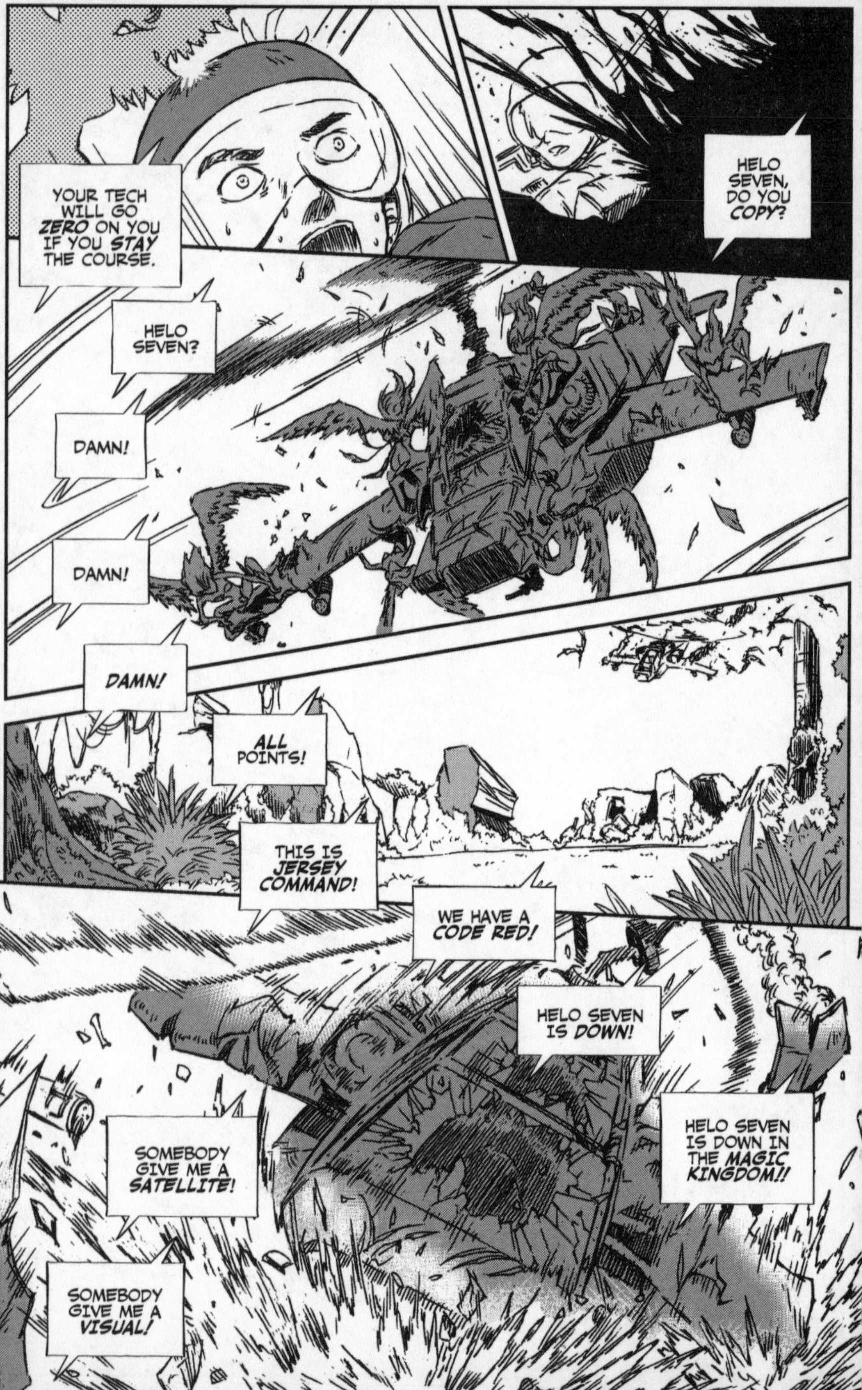
YOUR TECH WILL GO ZERO ON YOU IF YOU STAY THE COURSE.
HELO SEVEN, DO YOU COPY?
HELO SEVEN?
DAMN!
DAMN!
DAMN!
ALL POINTS!
THIS IS JERSEY COMMAND!
WE HAVE A CODE RED!
HELO SEVEN IS DOWN!
HELO SEVEN IS DOWN IN THE MAGIC KINGDOM!!
SOMEBODY GIVE ME A SATELLITE!
SOMEBODY GIVE ME A VISUAL!

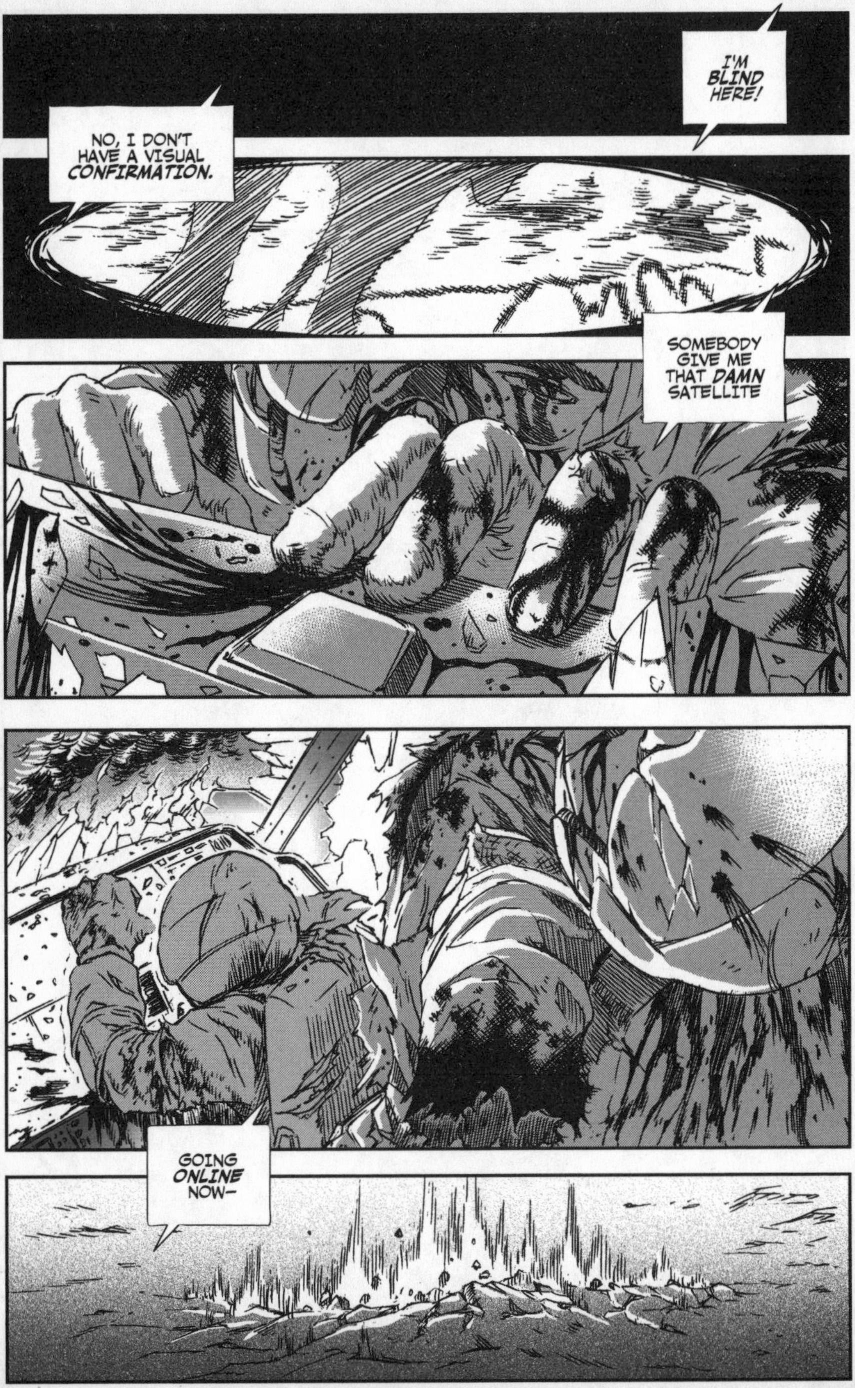
I'M BLIND HERE!
NO, I DON'T HAVE A VISUAL CONFIRMATION.
SOMEBODY GIVE ME THAT DAMN SATELLITE
GOING ONLINE NOW–

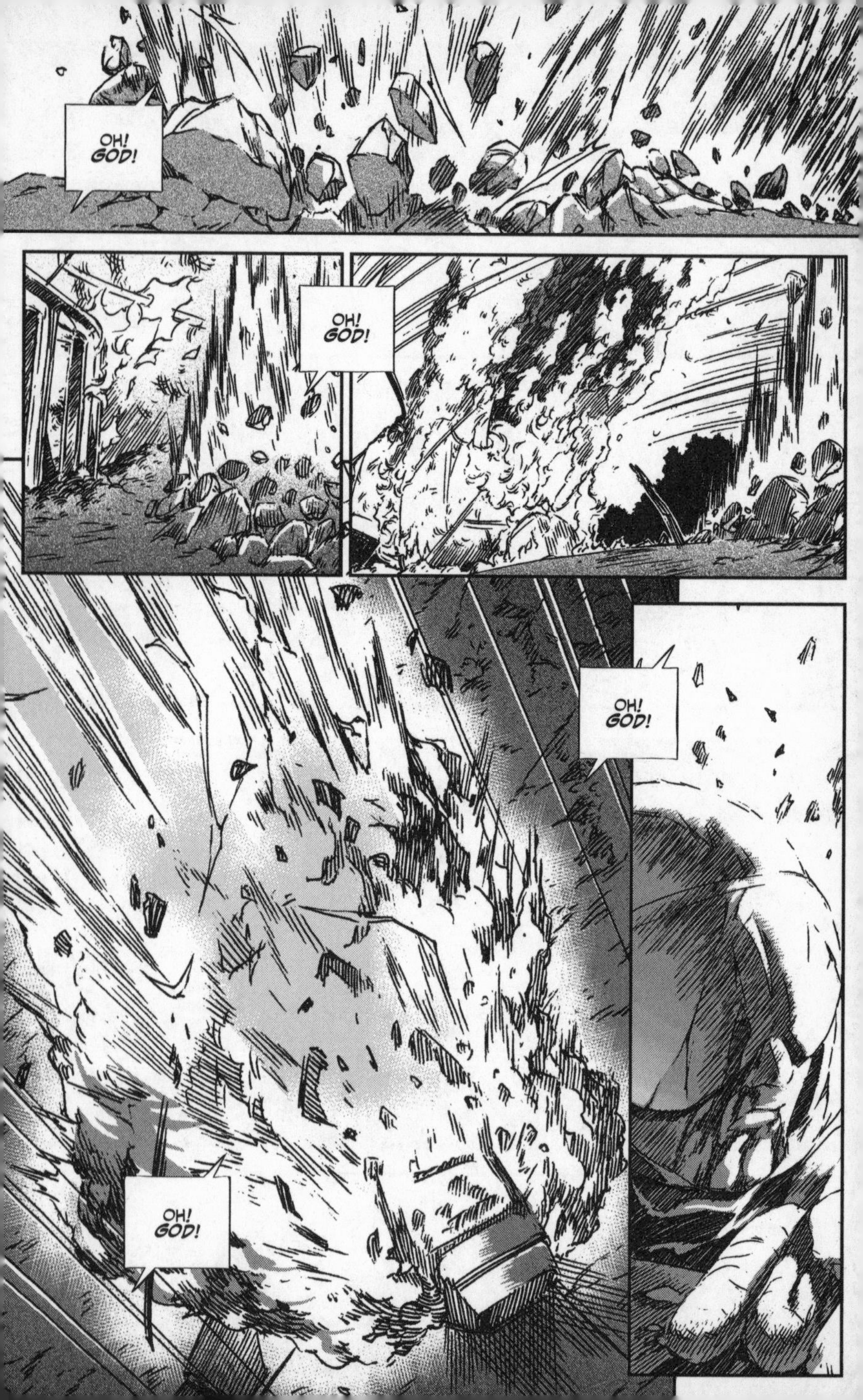
OH! GOD!
OH! GOD!
OH! GOD!
OH! GOD!

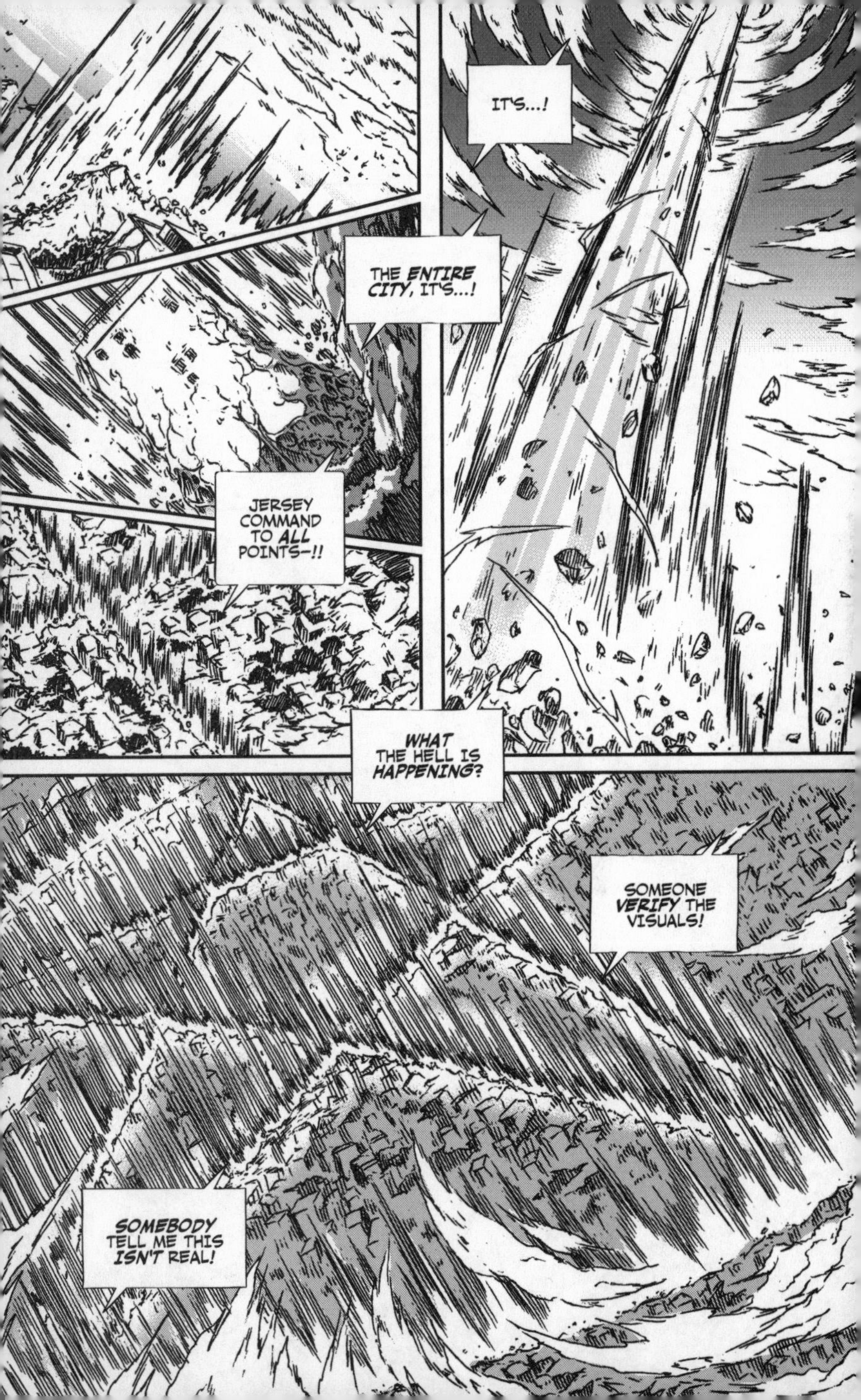
IT'S...!
THE ENTIRE CITY, IT'S...!
JERSEY COMMAND TO ALL POINTS-!!
WHAT THE HELL IS HAPPENING?
SOMEONE VERIFY THE VISUALS!
SOMEBODY TELL ME THIS ISN'T REAL!

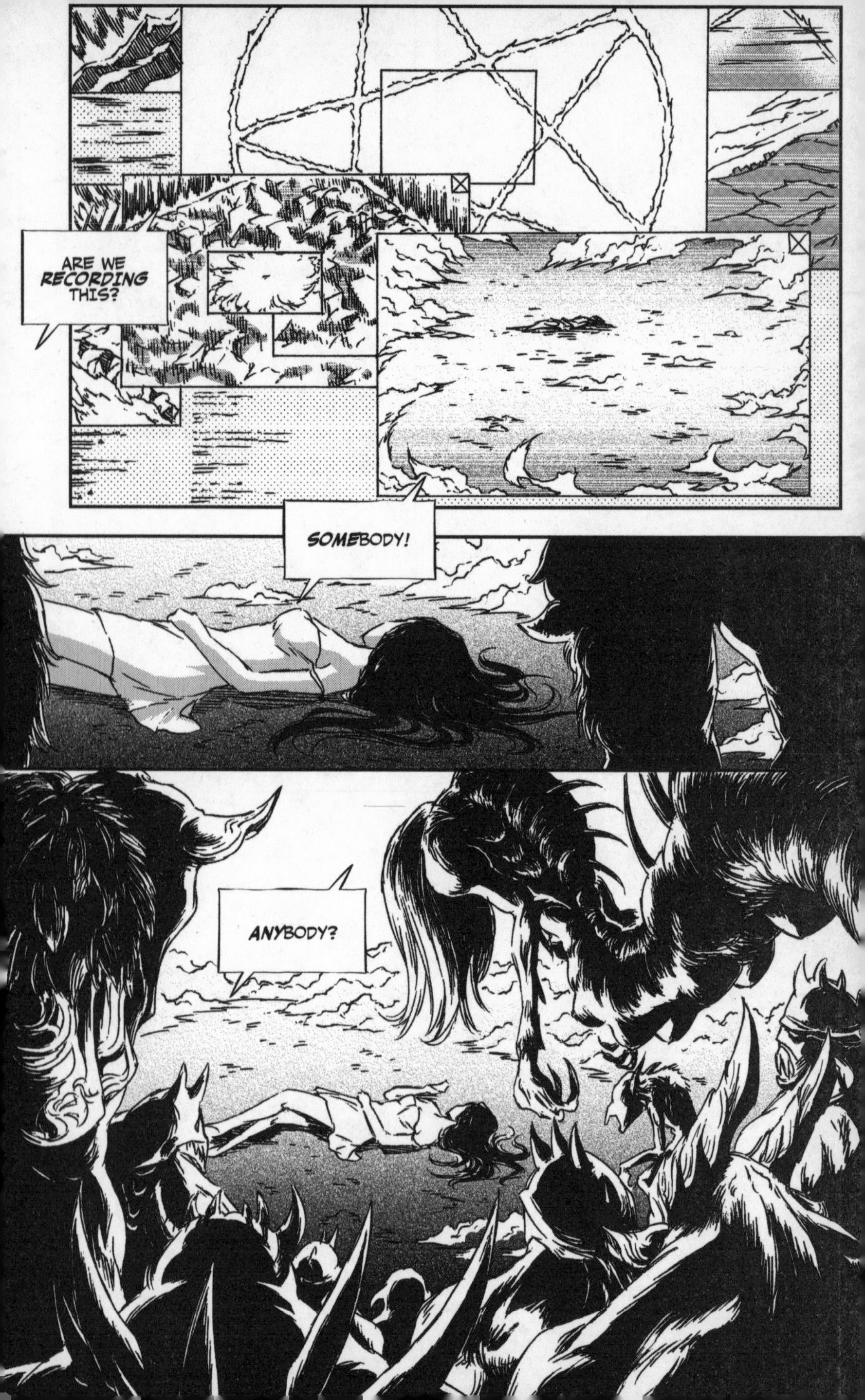
ARE WE RECORDING THIS?
SOMEBODY!
ANYBODY?

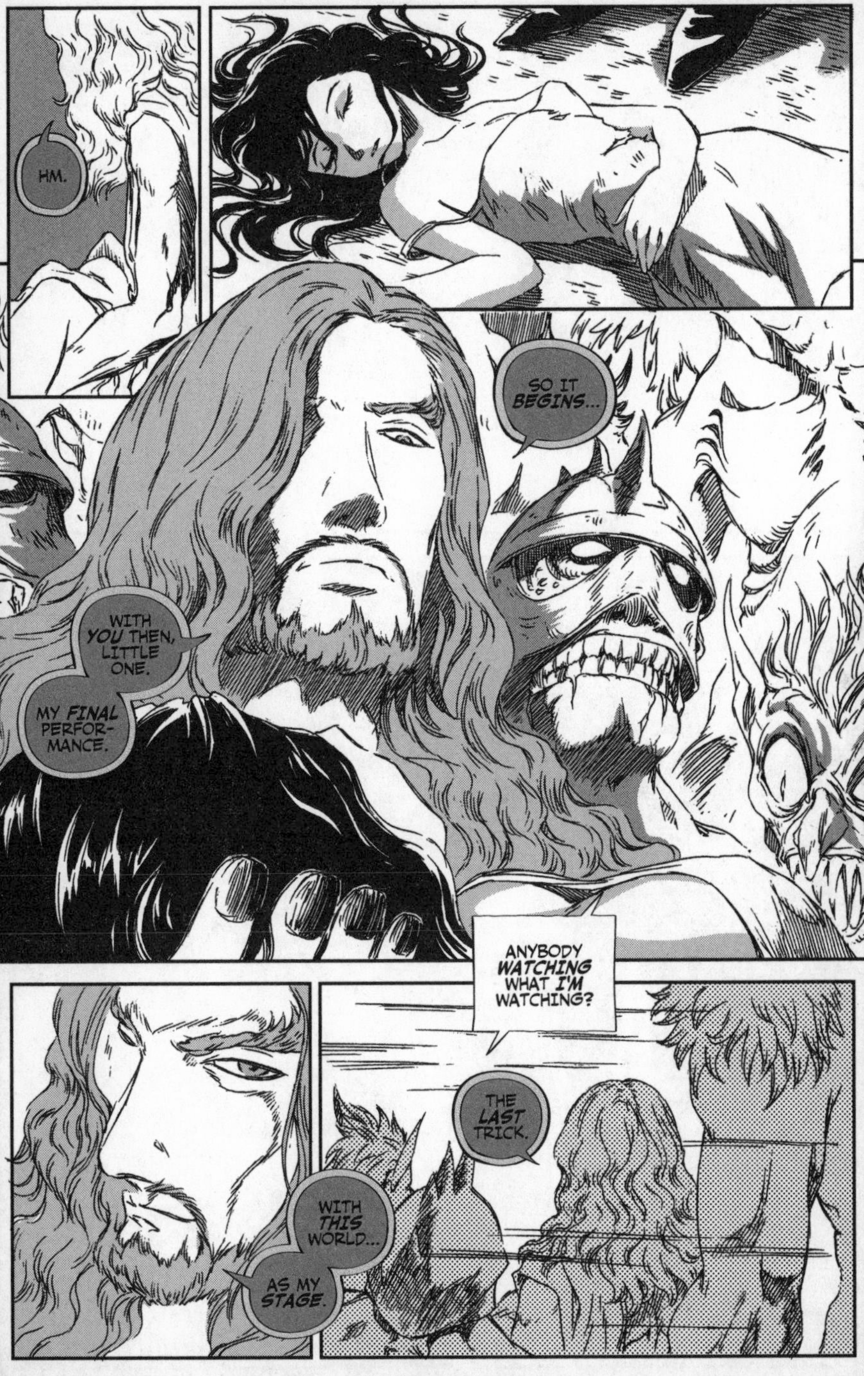
HM.
SO IT BEGINS...
WITH YOU THEN, LITTLE ONE.
MY FINAL PERFORMANCE.
ANYBODY WATCHING WHAT I'M WATCHING?
THE LAST TRICK.
WITH THIS WORLD...
AS MY STAGE.

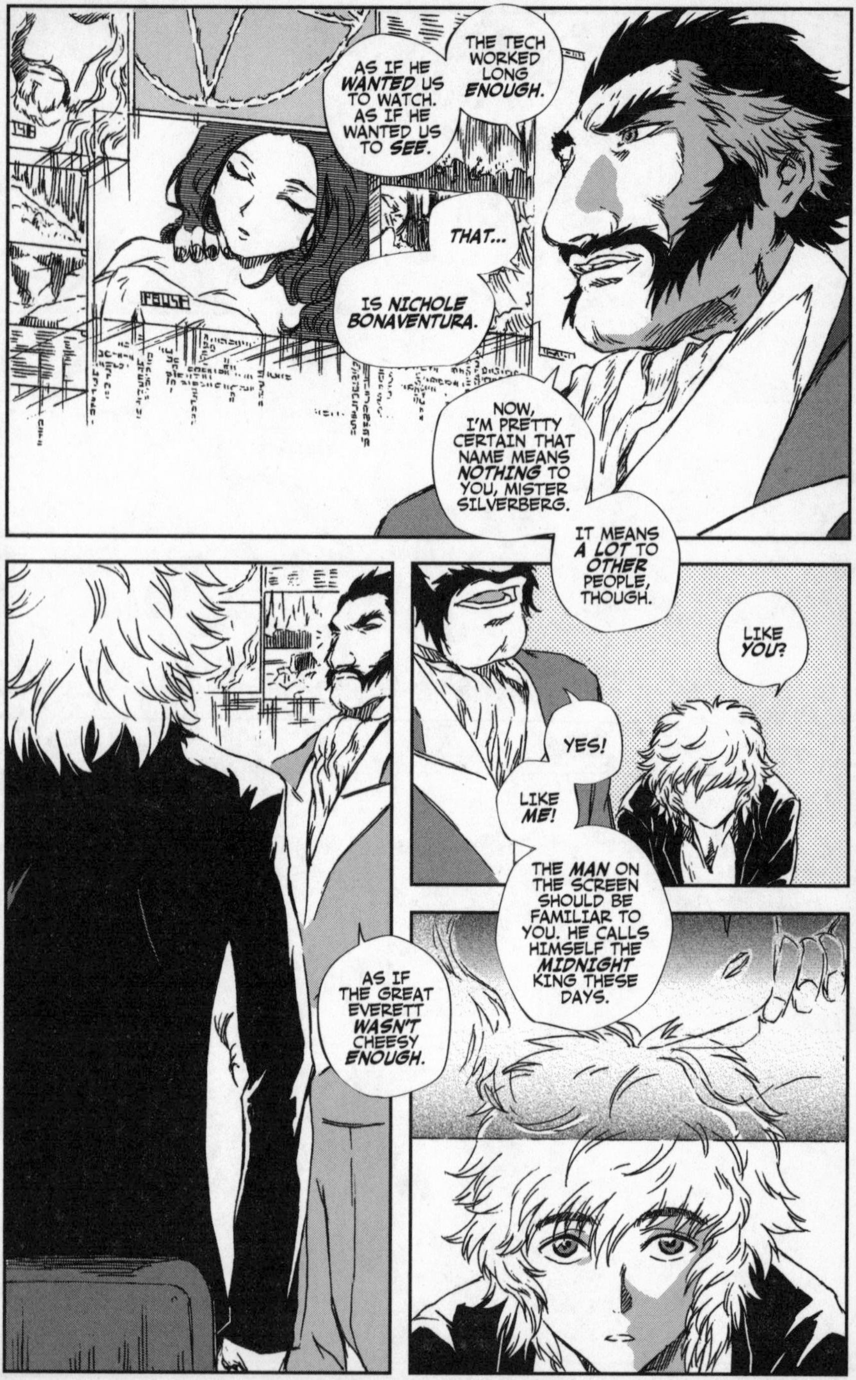

THE TECH WORKED LONG ENOUGH.
AS IF HE WANTED US TO WATCH. AS IF HE WANTED US TO SEE.
THAT...
IS NICHOLE BONAVENTURA.
NOW, I'M PRETTY CERTAIN THAT NAME MEANS NOTHING TO YOU, MISTER SILVERBERG.
IT MEANS A LOT TO OTHER PEOPLE, THOUGH.
LIKE YOU?
YES!
LIKE ME!
THE MAN ON THE SCREEN SHOULD BE FAMILIAR TO YOU. HE CALLS HIMSELF THE MIDNIGHT KING THESE DAYS.
AS IF THE GREAT EVERETT WASN'T CHEESY ENOUGH.

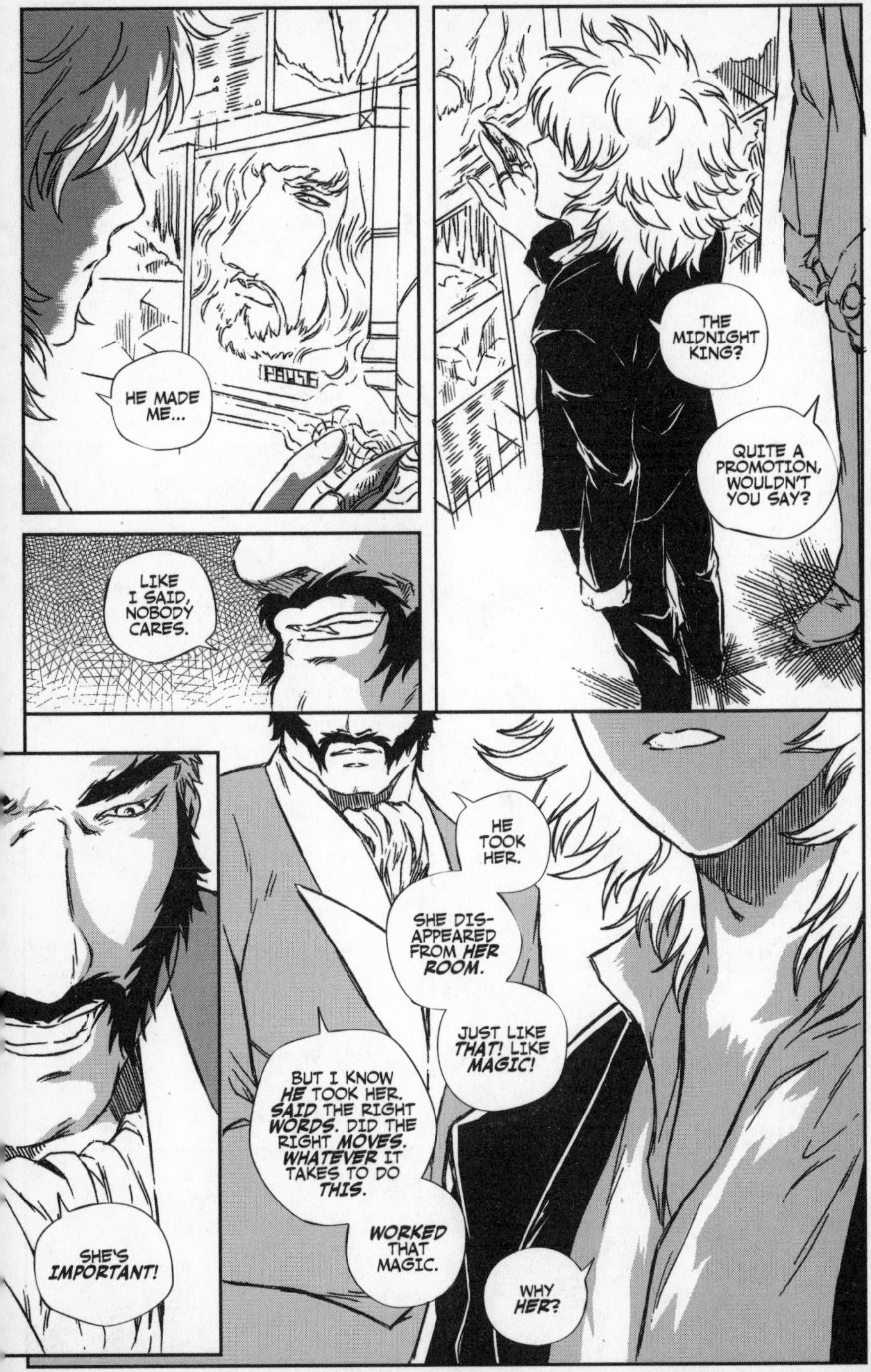
HE MADE ME...
THE MIDNIGHT KING?
QUITE A PROMOTION, WOULDN'T YOU SAY?
LIKE I SAID, NOBODY CARES.
HE TOOK HER.
SHE DIS-APPEARED FROM HER ROOM.
JUST LIKE THAT! LIKE MAGIC!
BUT I KNOW HE TOOK HER. SAID THE RIGHT WORDS. DID THE RIGHT MOVES. WHATEVER IT TAKES TO DO THIS.
WORKED THAT MAGIC.
WHY HER?
SHE'S IMPORTANT!

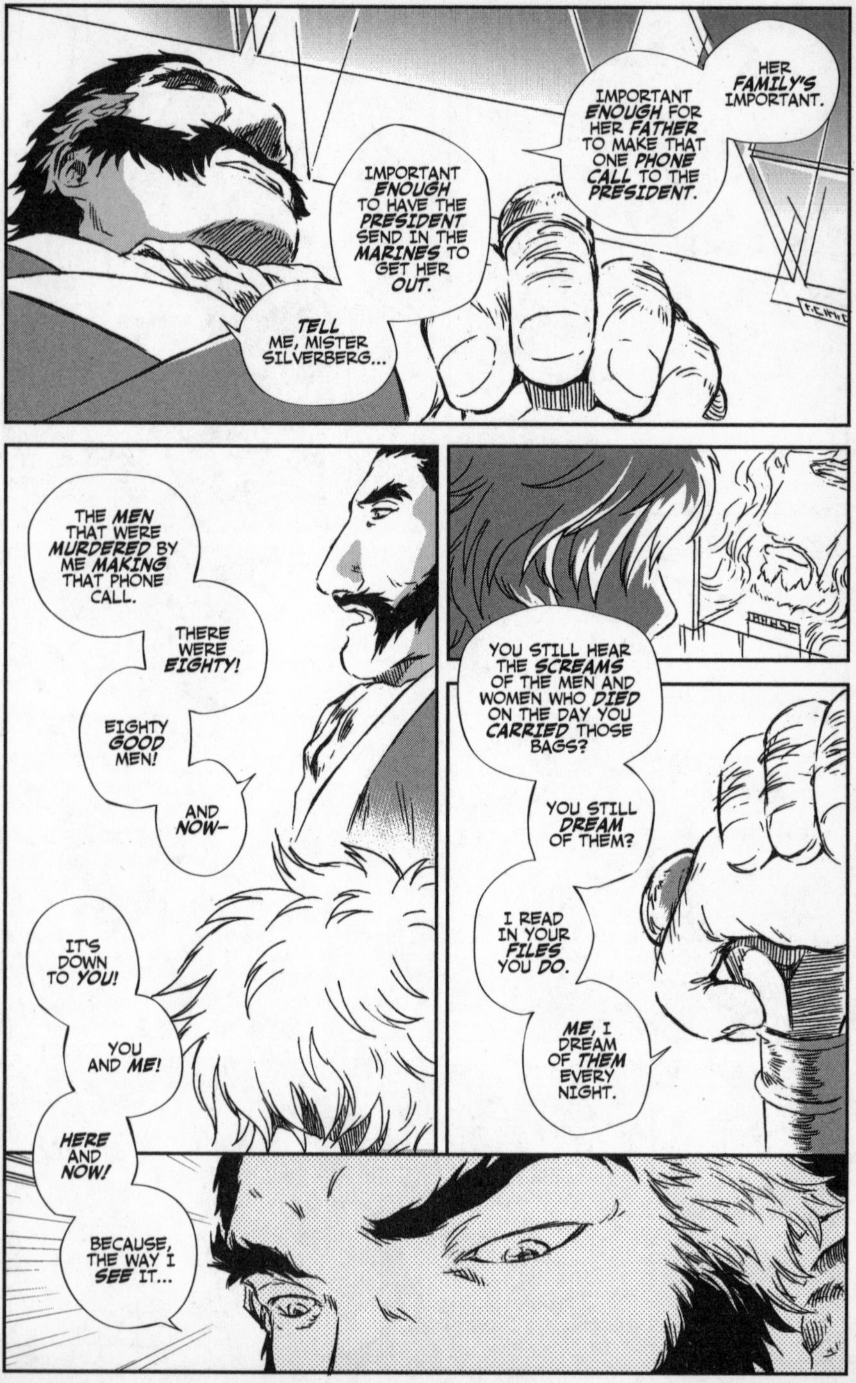
HER FAMILY'S IMPORTANT.
IMPORTANT ENOUGH FOR HER FATHER TO MAKE THAT ONE PHONE CALL TO THE PRESIDENT.
IMPORTANT ENOUGH TO HAVE THE PRESIDENT SEND IN THE MARINES TO GET HER OUT.
TELL ME, MISTER SILVERBERG...
YOU STILL HEAR THE SCREAMS OF THE MEN AND WOMEN WHO DIED ON THE DAY YOU CARRIED THOSE BAGS?
YOU STILL DREAM OF THEM?
I READ IN YOUR FILES YOU DO.
ME, I DREAM OF THEM EVERY NIGHT.
THE MEN THAT WERE MURDERED BY ME MAKING THAT PHONE CALL.
THERE WERE EIGHTY!
EIGHTY GOOD MEN!
AND NOW–
IT'S DOWN TO YOU!
YOU AND ME!
HERE AND NOW!
BECAUSE, THE WAY I SEE IT...

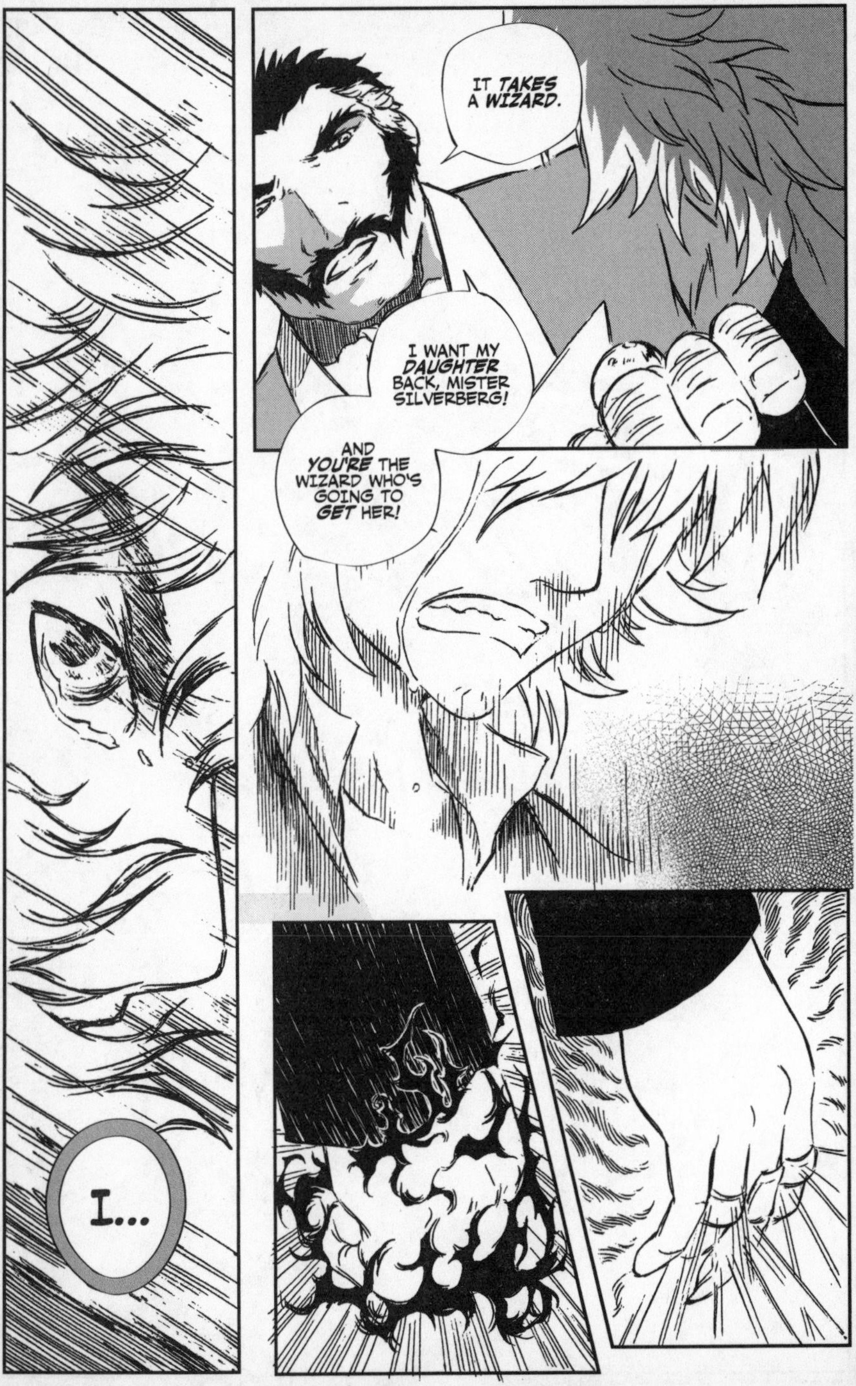
IT TAKES A WIZARD.
I WANT MY DAUGHTER BACK, MISTER SILVERBERG!
AND YOU'RE THE WIZARD WHO'S GOING TO GET HER!
I...

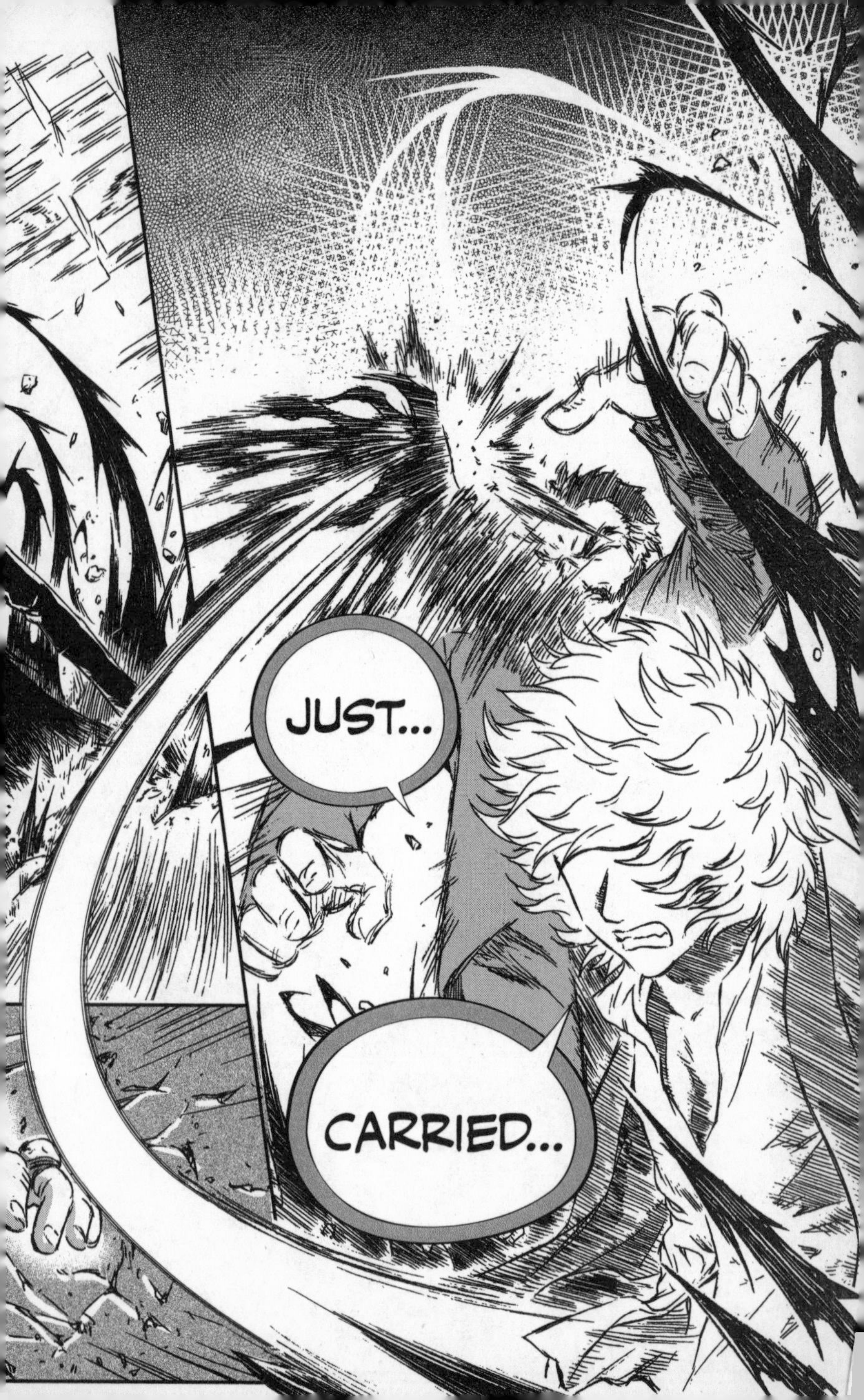
JUST...
CARRIED...

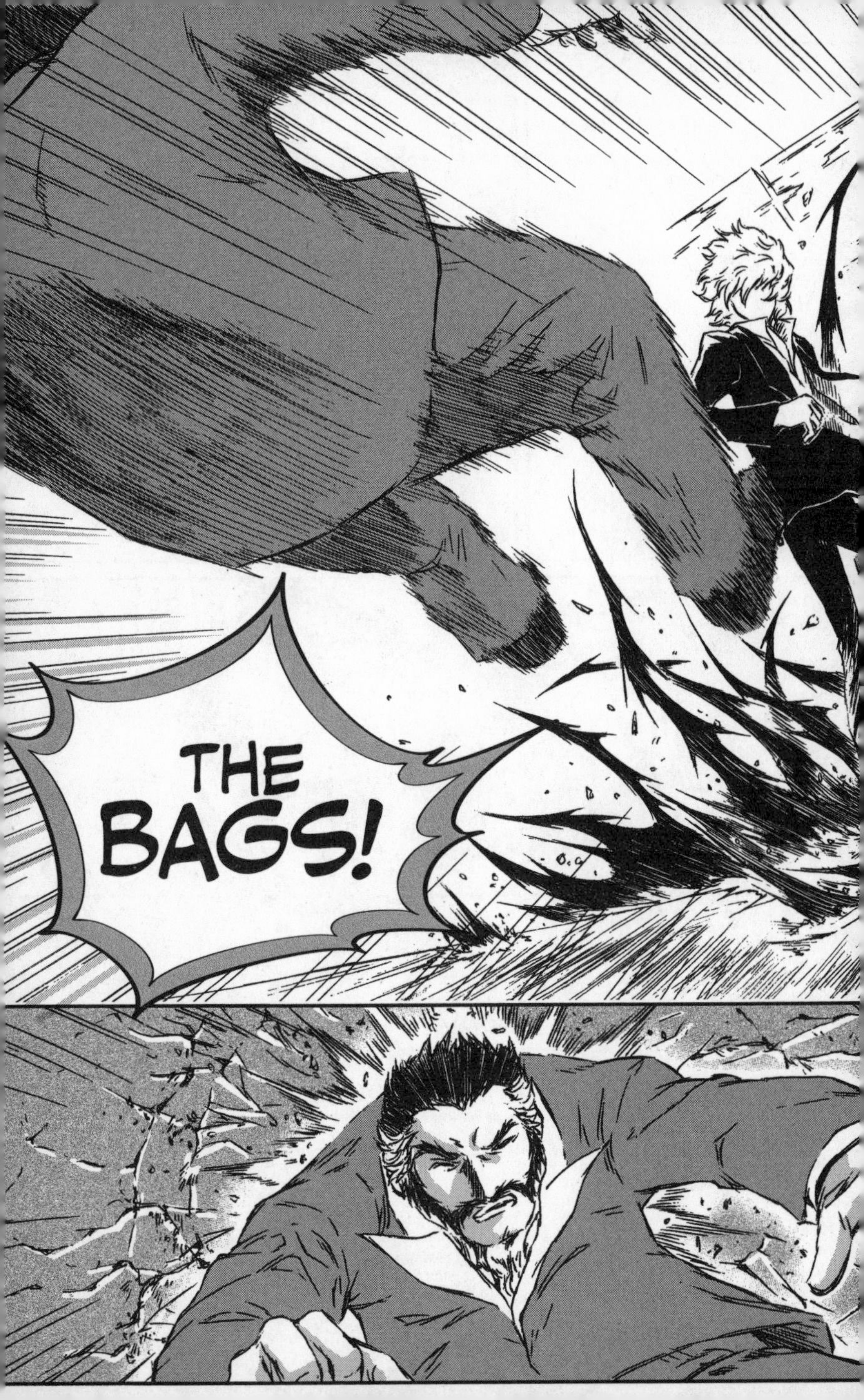
THE BAGS!

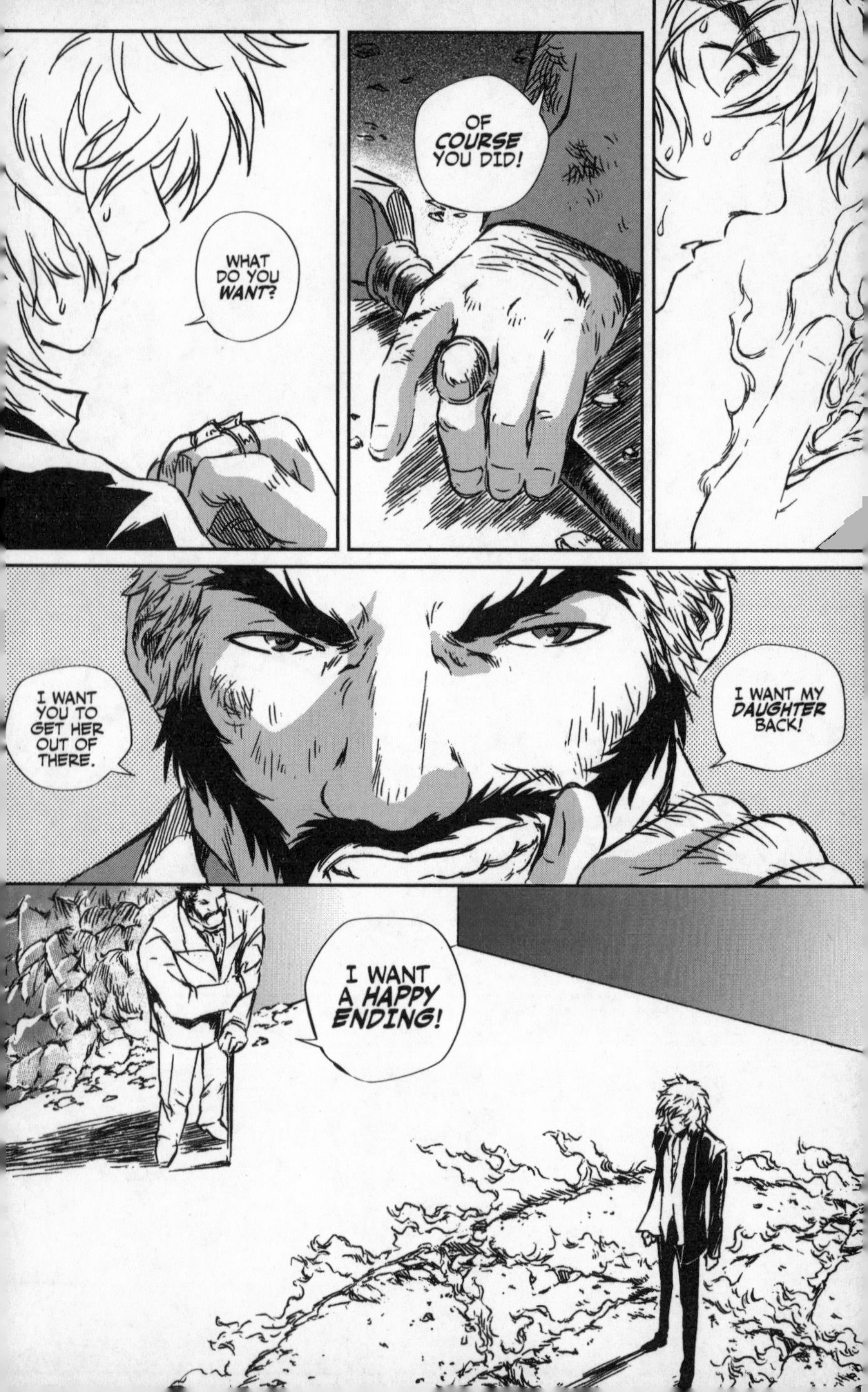
OF COURSE YOU DID!
WHAT DO YOU WANT?
I WANT MY DAUGHTER BACK!
I WANT YOU TO GET HER OUT OF THERE.
I WANT A HAPPY ENDING!

CHAPTER
2

END OF THE TUNNEL

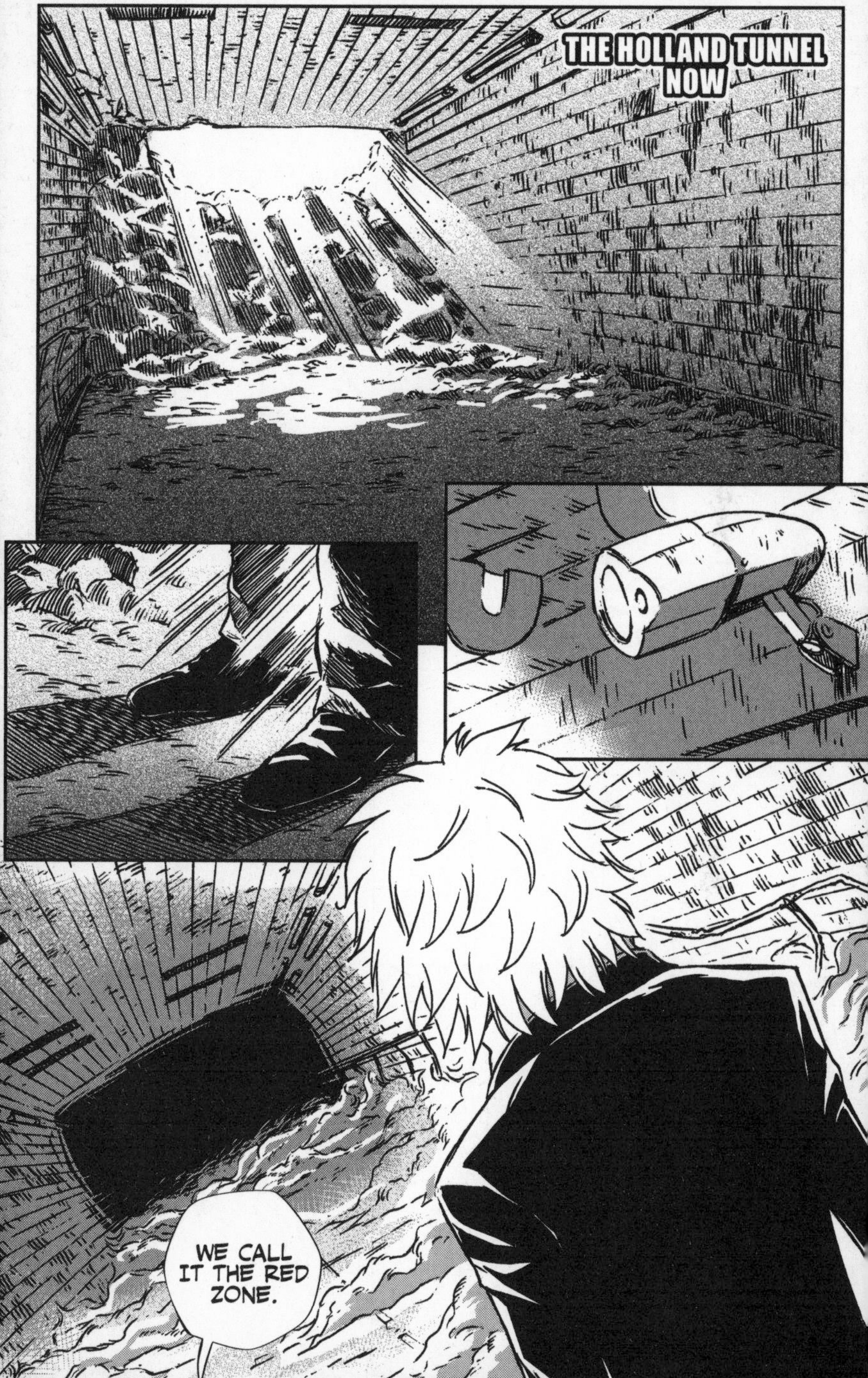
THE HOLLAND TUNNEL
NOW
WE CALL IT THE RED ZONE.

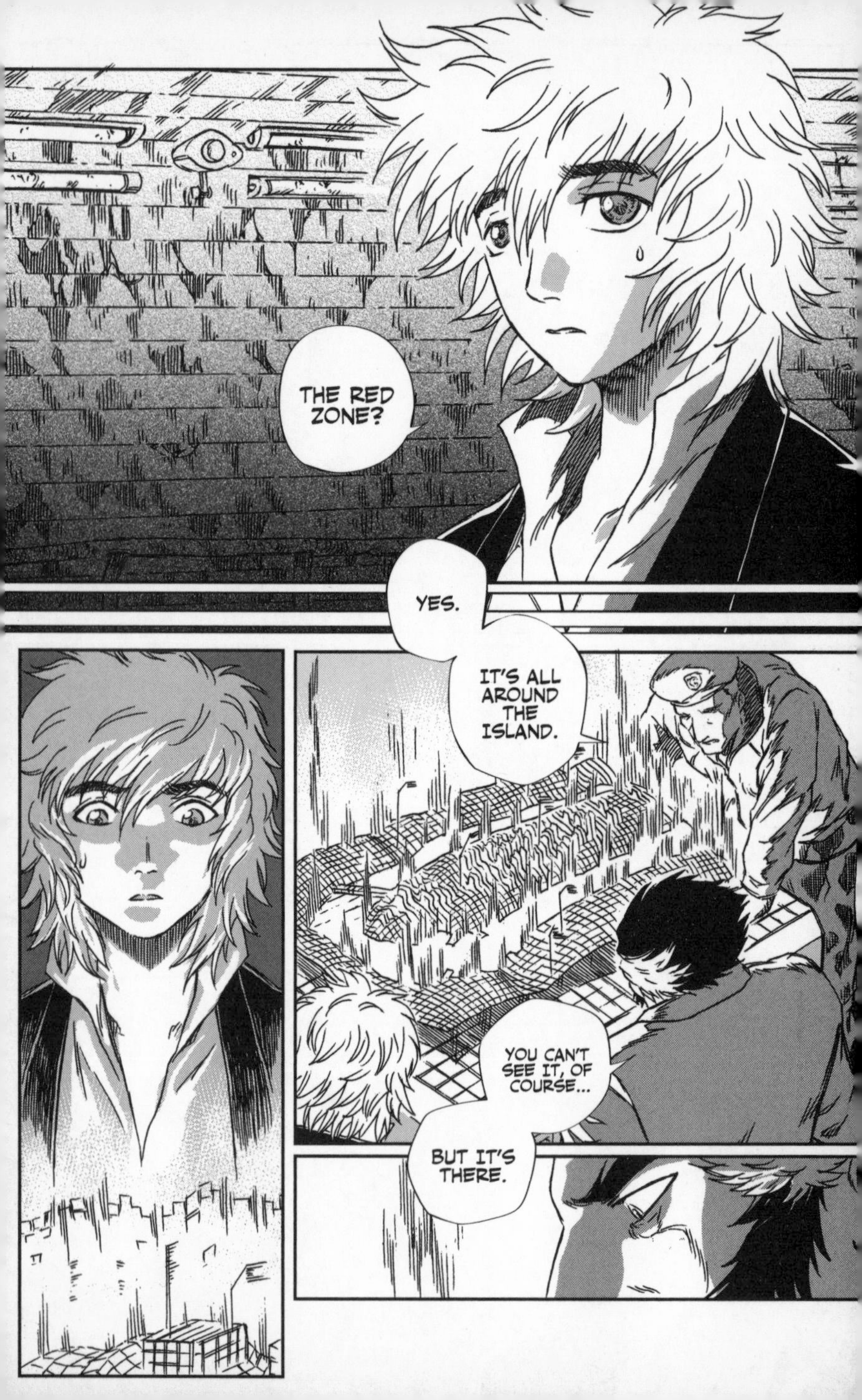
THE RED ZONE?
YES.
IT'S ALL AROUND THE ISLAND.
YOU CAN'T SEE IT, OF COURSE...
BUT IT'S THERE.

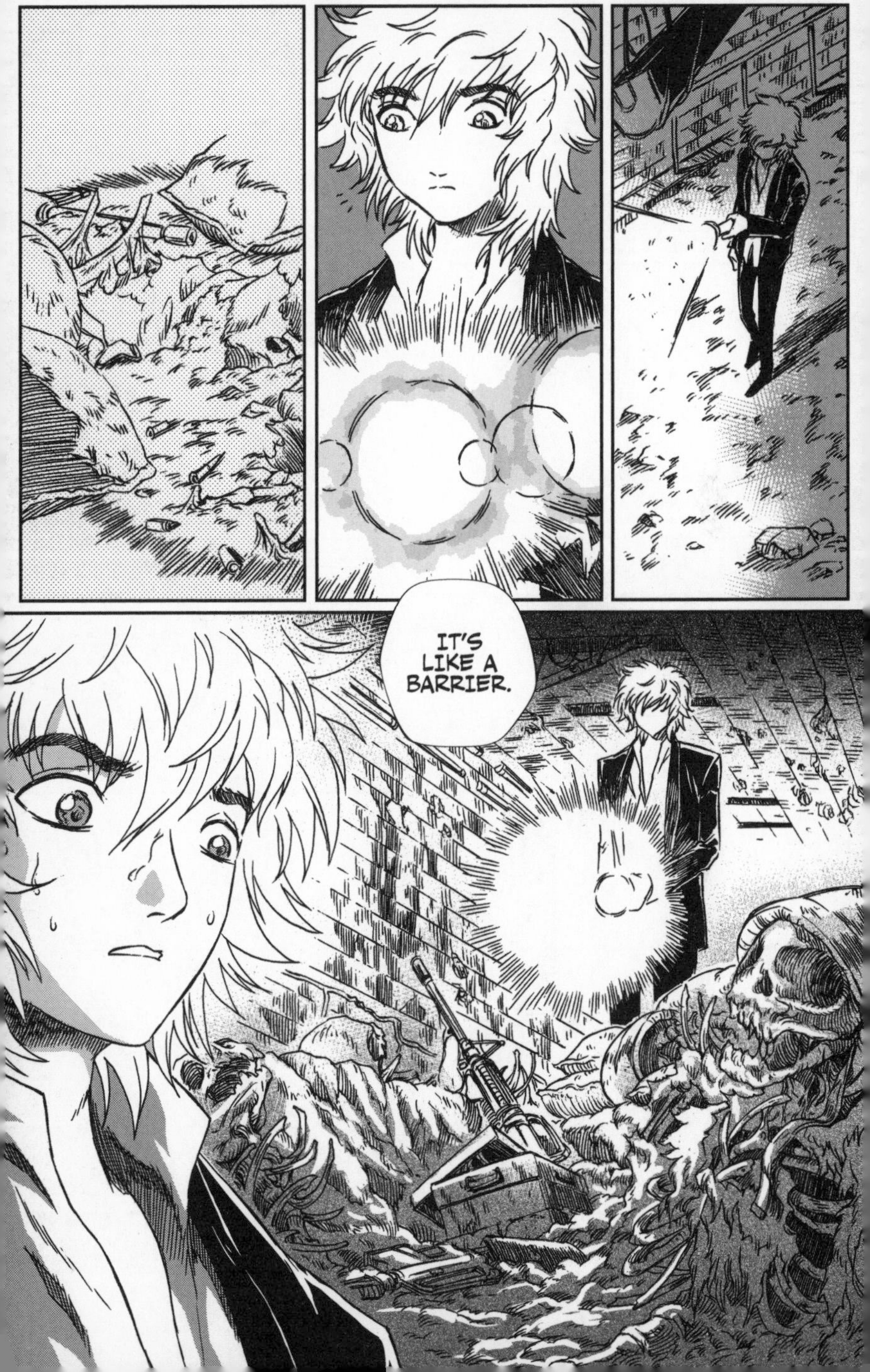
IT'S LIKE A BARRIER.

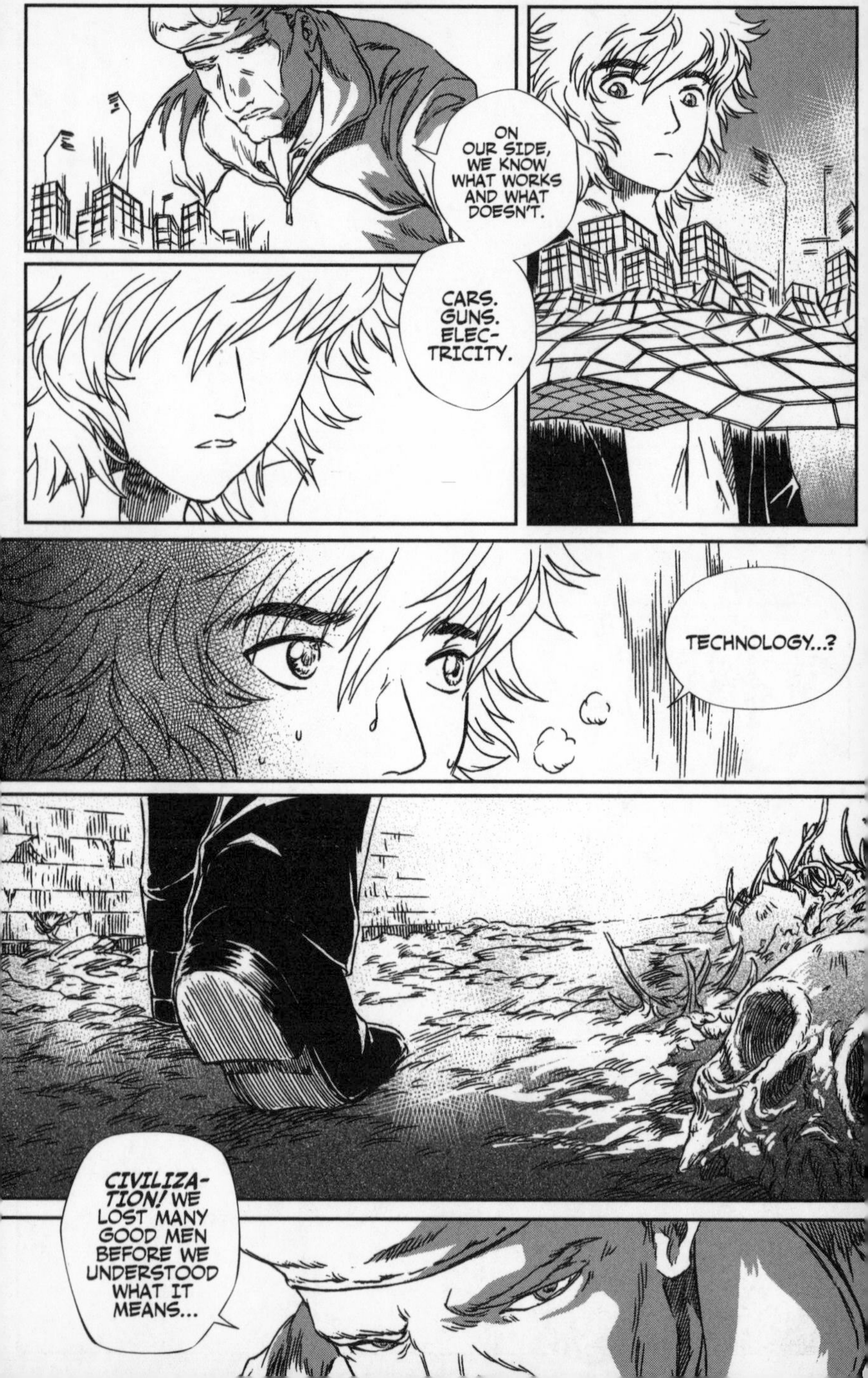
ON OUR SIDE, WE KNOW WHAT WORKS AND WHAT DOESN'T.
CARS. GUNS. ELEC-TRICITY.
TECHNOLOGY...?
CIVILIZA-TION! WE LOST MANY GOOD MEN BEFORE WE UNDERSTOOD WHAT IT MEANS...

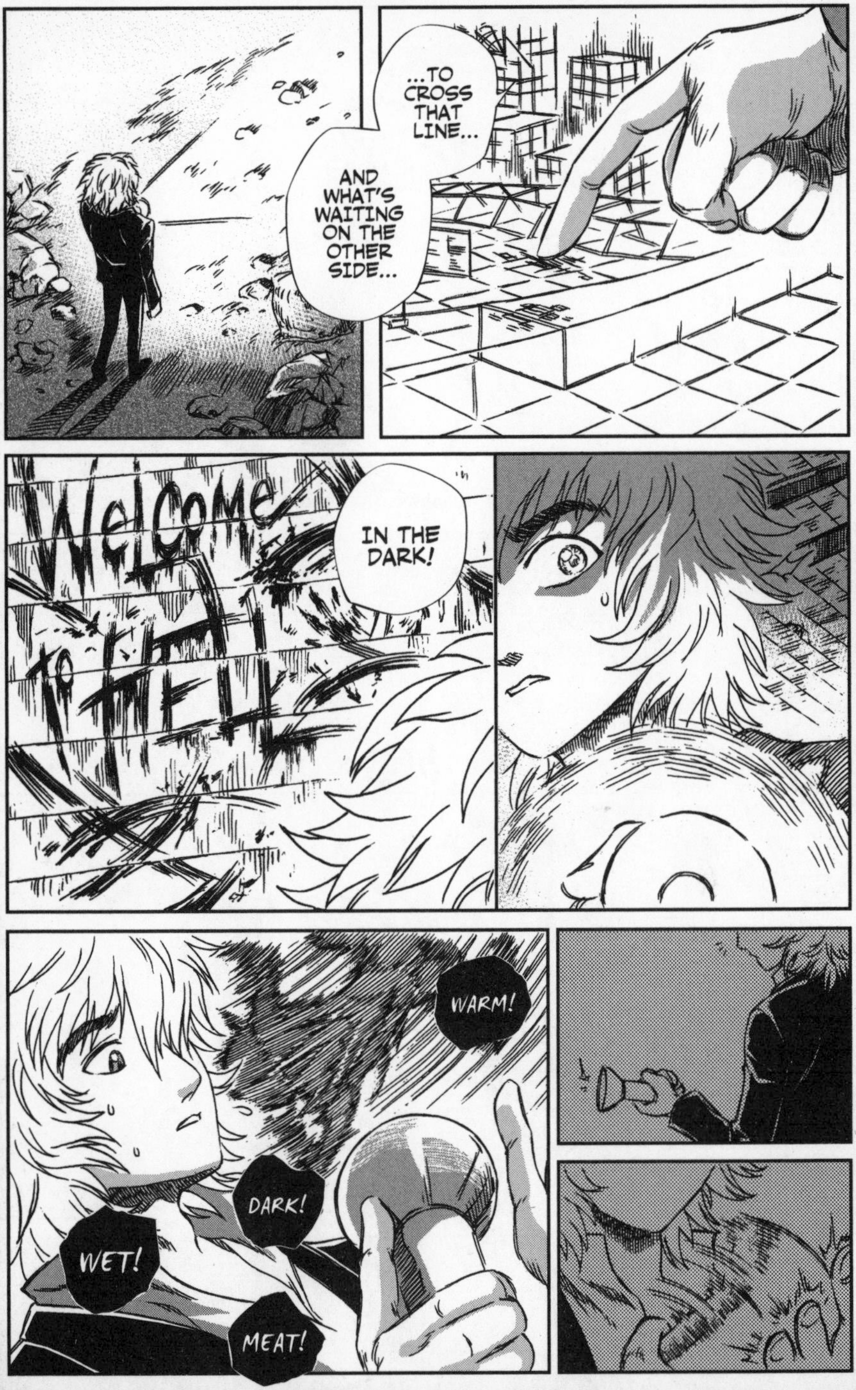
...TO CROSS THAT LINE...
AND WHAT'S WAITING ON THE OTHER SIDE...
IN THE DARK!
Welcome to HELL
WARM!
DARK!
WET!
MEAT!

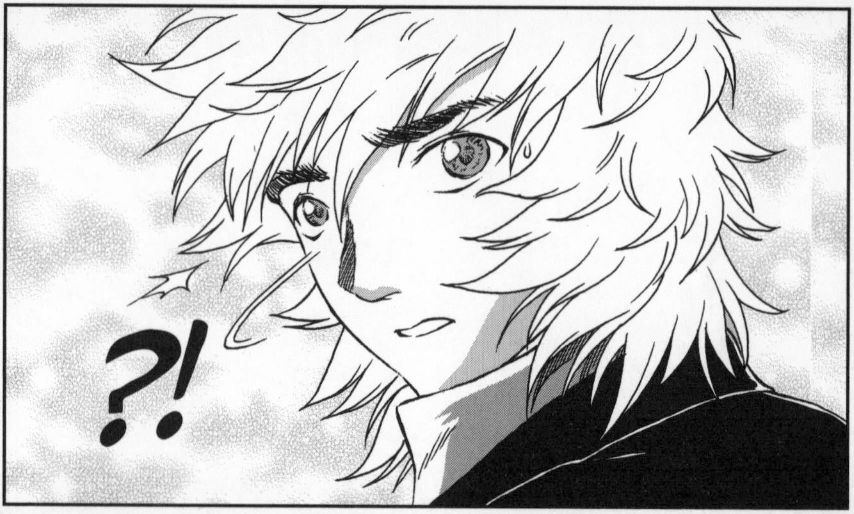
?!

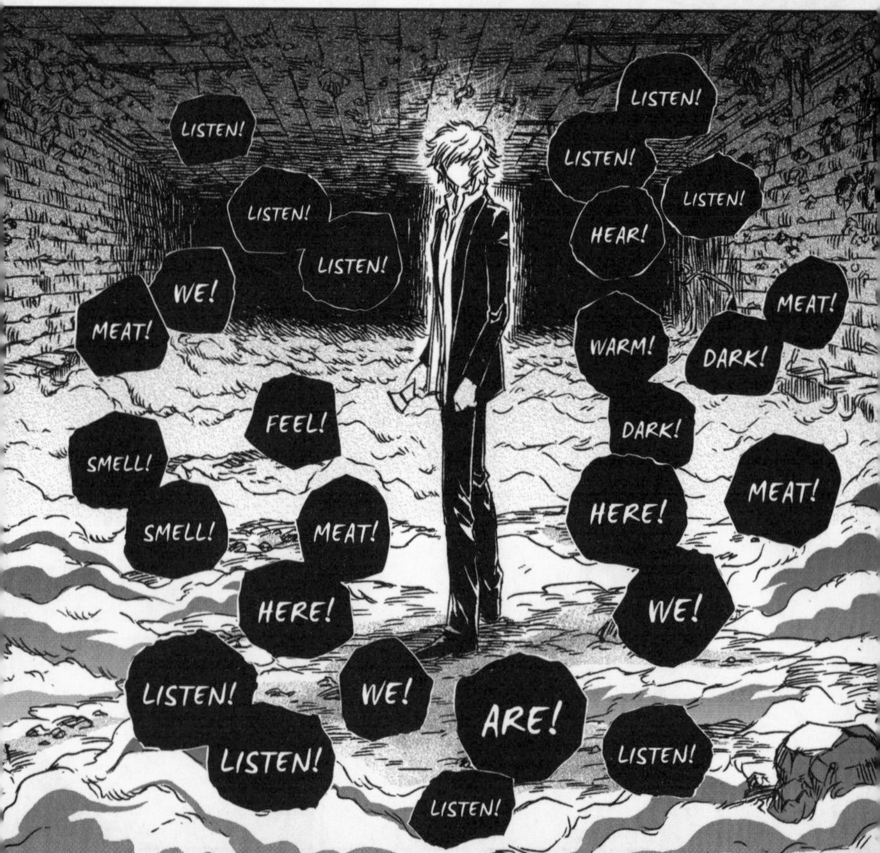
LISTEN!
LISTEN!
LISTEN!
HEAR!
MEAT!
DARK!
WARM!
DARK!
MEAT!
HERE!
WE!
LISTEN!
LISTEN!
LISTEN!
LISTEN!
WE!
MEAT!
FEEL!
SMELL!
MEAT!
SMELL!
HERE!
ARE!
WE!
LISTEN!
LISTEN!
LISTEN!

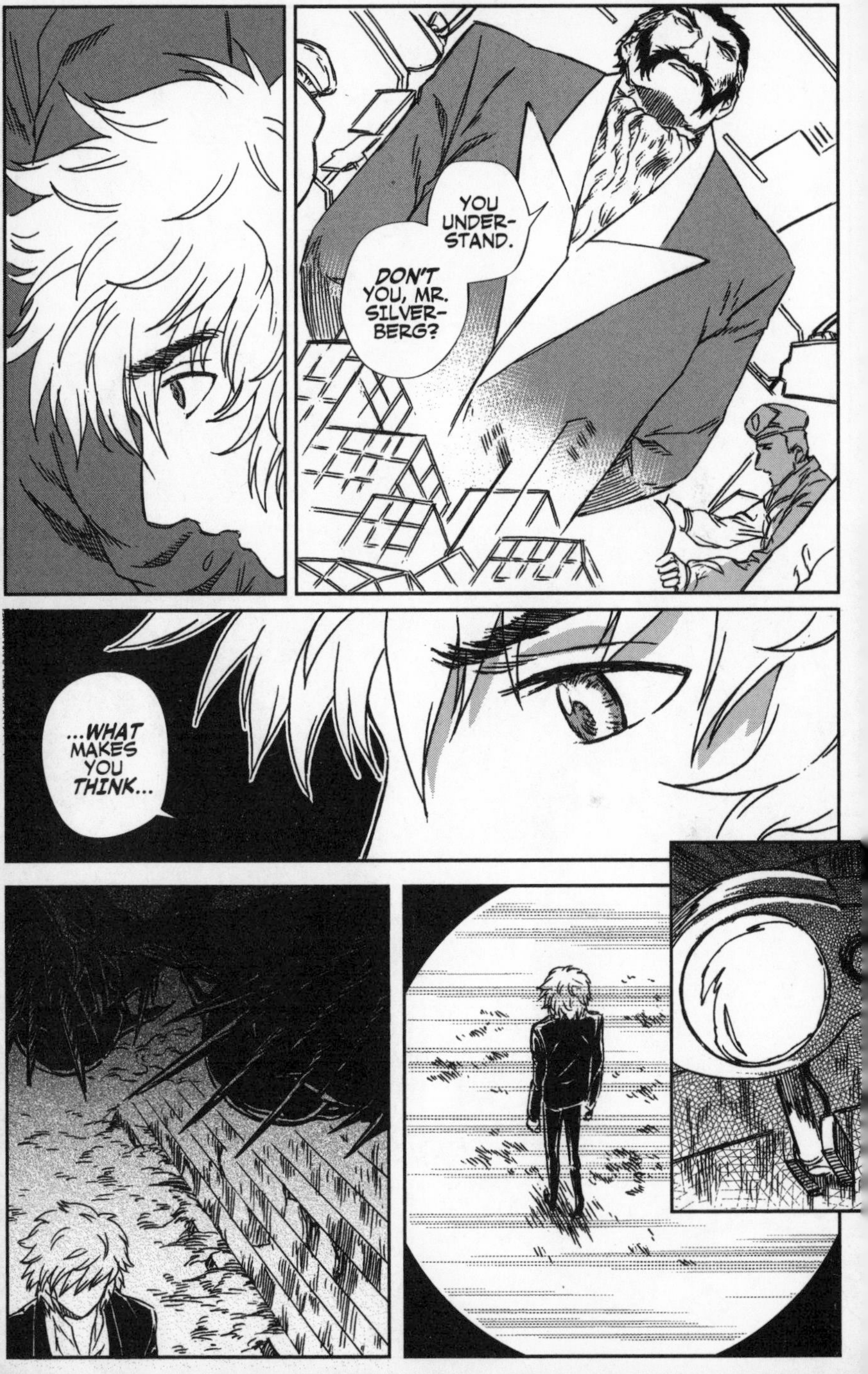
YOU UNDER-STAND.
DON'T YOU, MR. SILVER-BERG?
...WHAT MAKES YOU THINK...

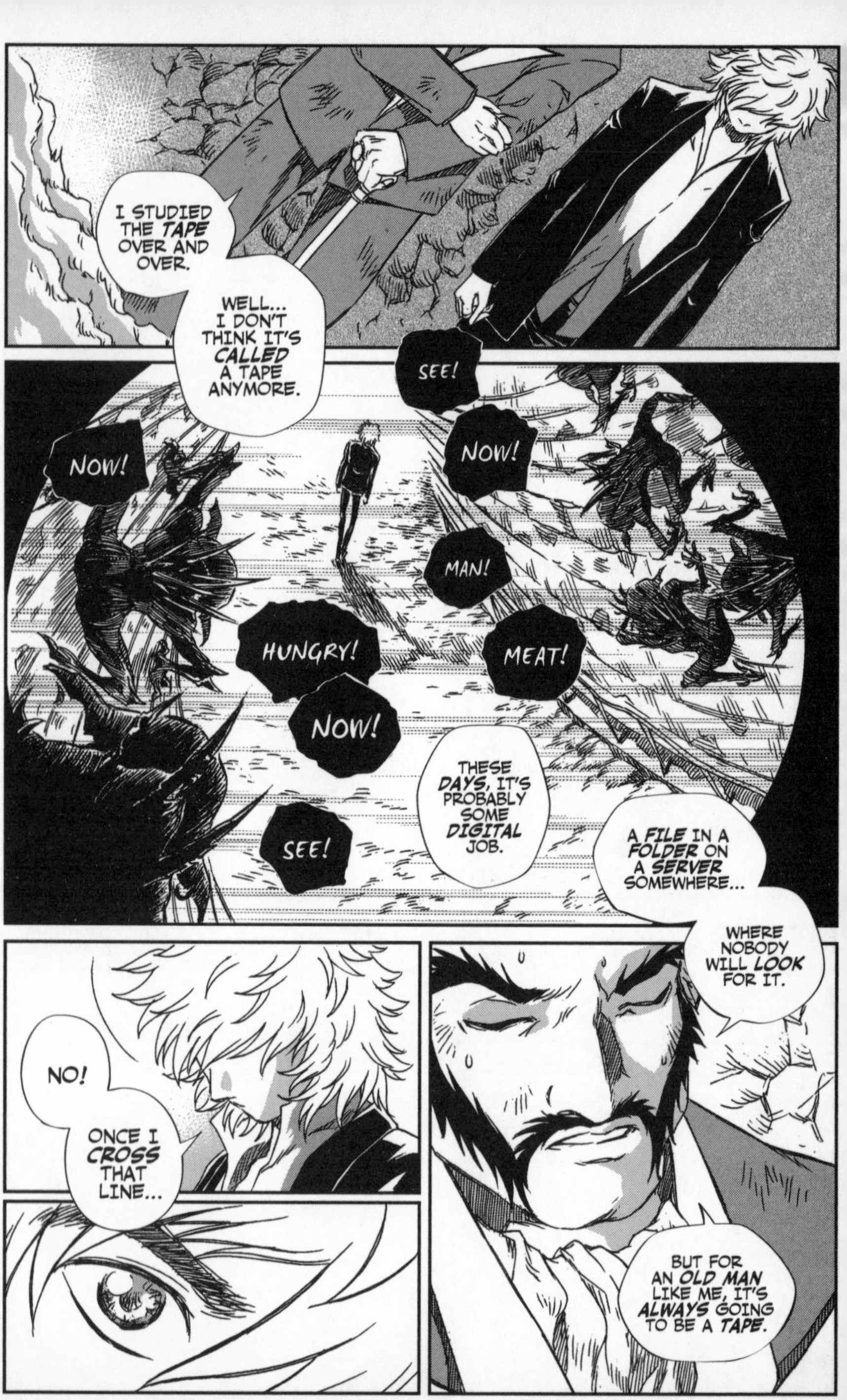
I STUDIED THE TAPE OVER AND OVER.
WELL... I DON'T THINK IT'S CALLED A TAPE ANYMORE.
SEE!
NOW!
MAN!
MEAT!
NOW!
HUNGRY!
NOW!
SEE!
THESE DAYS, IT'S PROBABLY SOME DIGITAL JOB.
A FILE IN A FOLDER ON A SERVER SOMEWHERE...
WHERE NOBODY WILL LOOK FOR IT.
BUT FOR AN OLD MAN LIKE ME, IT'S ALWAYS GOING TO BE A TAPE.
NO!
ONCE I CROSS THAT LINE...

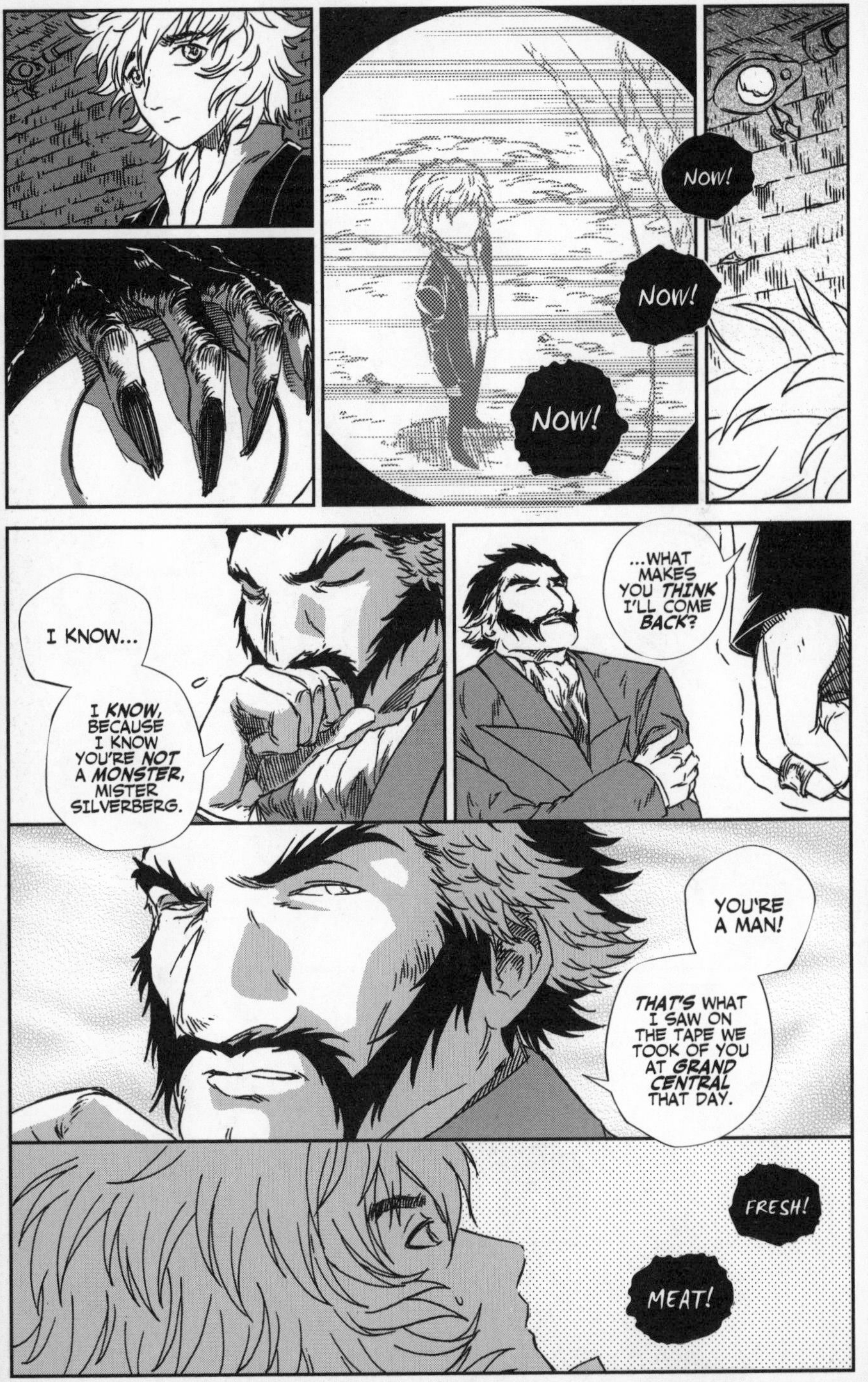
NOW!
NOW!
NOW!
...WHAT MAKES YOU *THINK* I'LL COME *BACK*?
I KNOW...
I *KNOW*, BECAUSE I KNOW YOU'RE *NOT* A *MONSTER*, MISTER SILVERBERG.
YOU'RE A MAN!
THAT'S WHAT I SAW ON THE TAPE WE TOOK OF YOU AT *GRAND CENTRAL* THAT DAY.
FRESH!
MEAT!

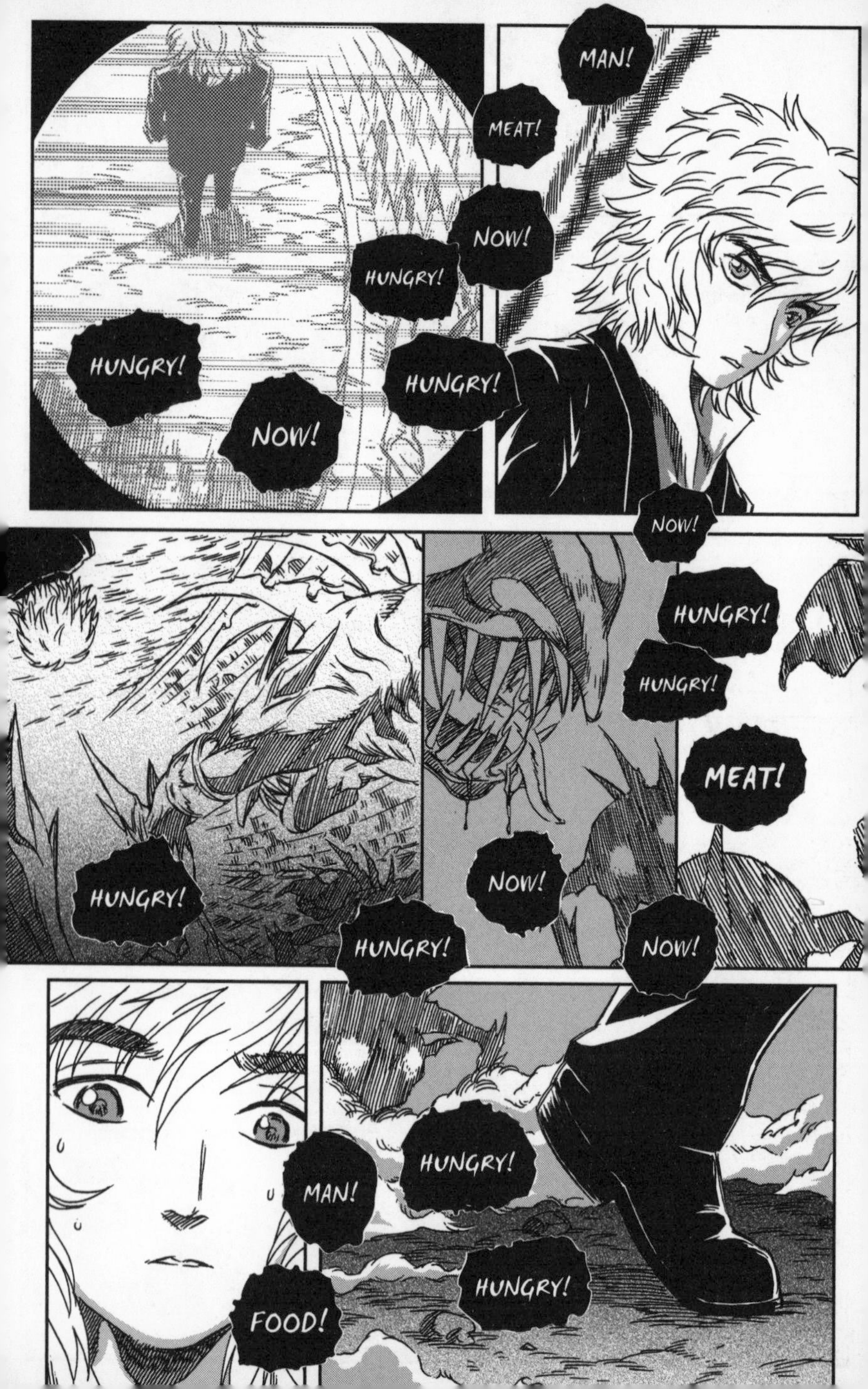
MAN!
MEAT!
NOW!
HUNGRY!
HUNGRY!
HUNGRY!
NOW!
NOW!
HUNGRY!
HUNGRY!
MEAT!
NOW!
NOW!
HUNGRY!
HUNGRY!
HUNGRY!
MAN!
HUNGRY!
FOOD!

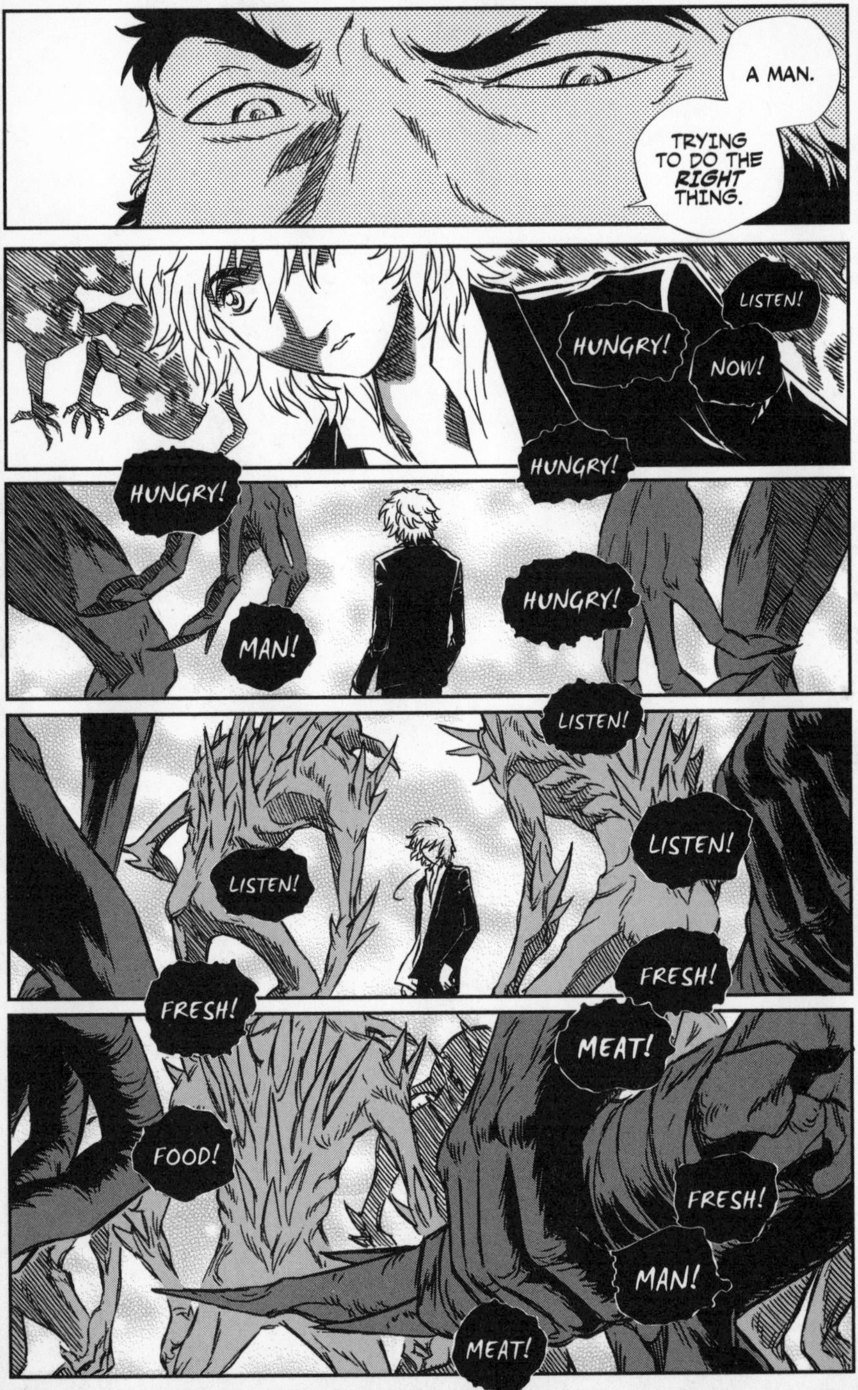
A MAN.
TRYING TO DO THE *RIGHT* THING.
LISTEN!
NOW!
HUNGRY!
HUNGRY!
HUNGRY!
HUNGRY!
MAN!
LISTEN!
LISTEN!
LISTEN!
FRESH!
FRESH!
MEAT!
FRESH!
FOOD!
MAN!
MEAT!

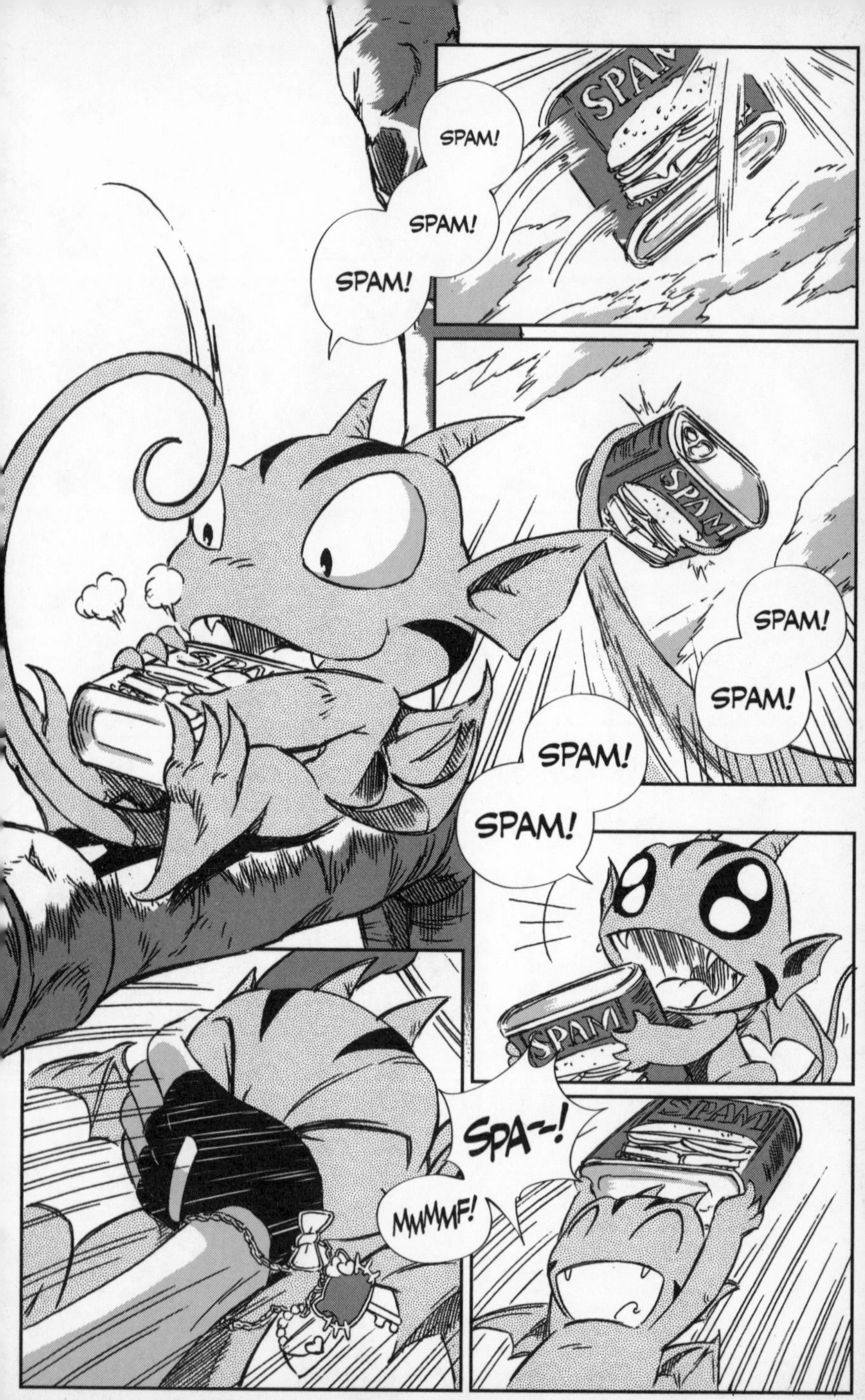
SPAM!
SPAM!
SPAM!
SPAM!
SPAM!
SPAM!
SPAM!
SPA--!
MWMMF!

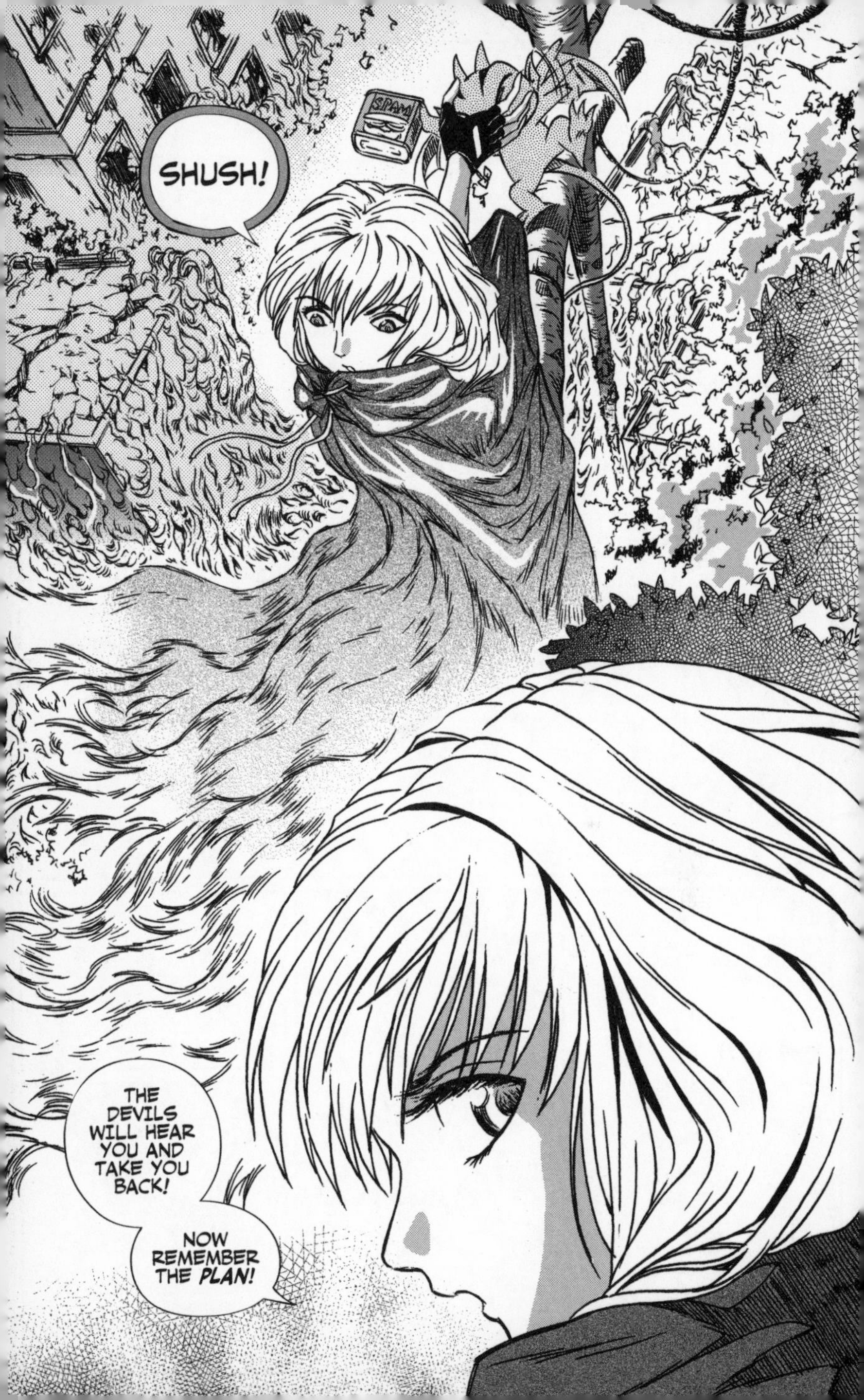
SHUSH!
THE DEVILS WILL HEAR YOU AND TAKE YOU BACK!
NOW REMEMBER THE PLAN!

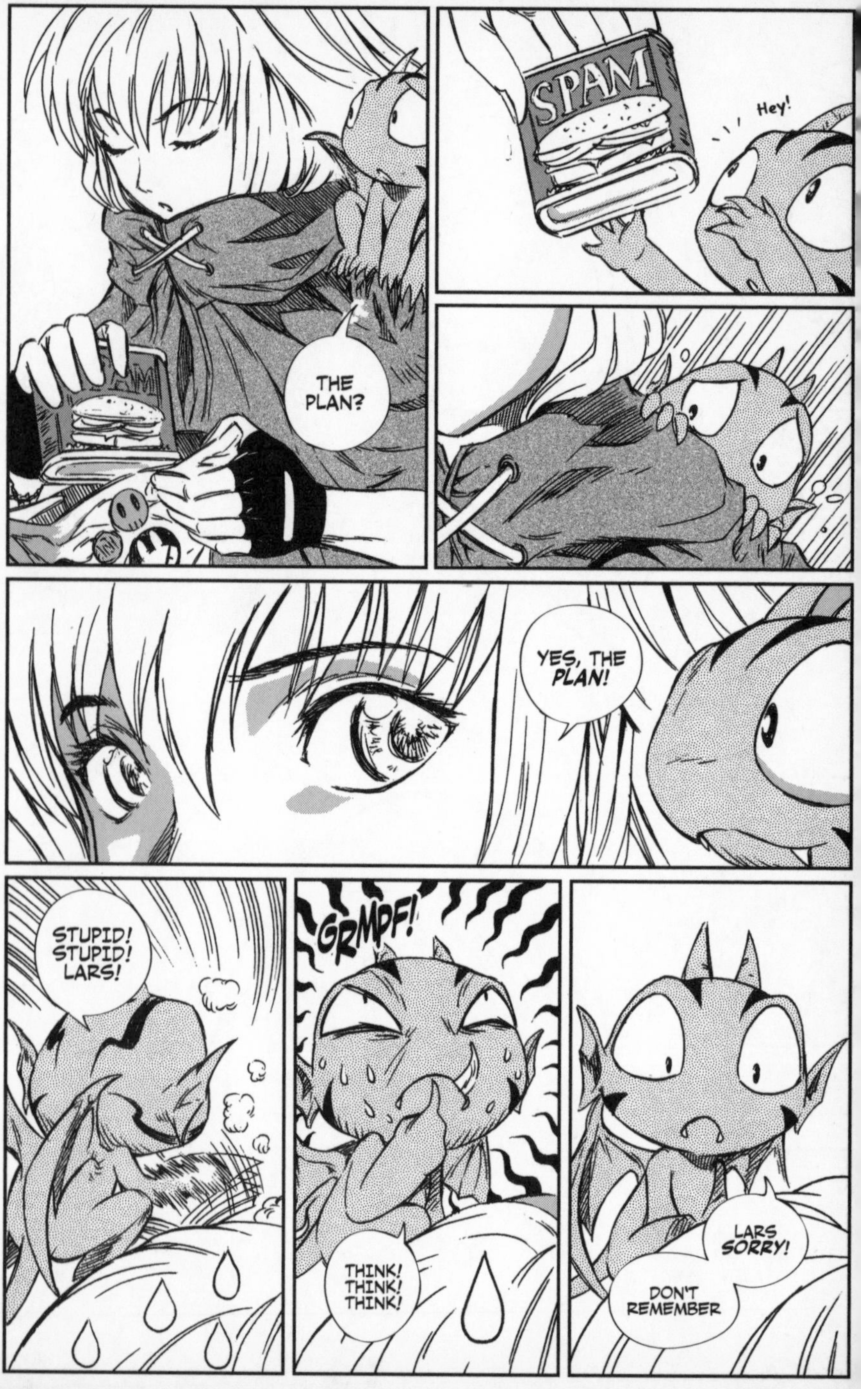
THE PLAN?
SPAM
Hey!
YES, THE PLAN!
STUPID! STUPID! LARS!
GRMPF!
THINK! THINK! THINK!
LARS SORRY!
DON'T REMEMBER

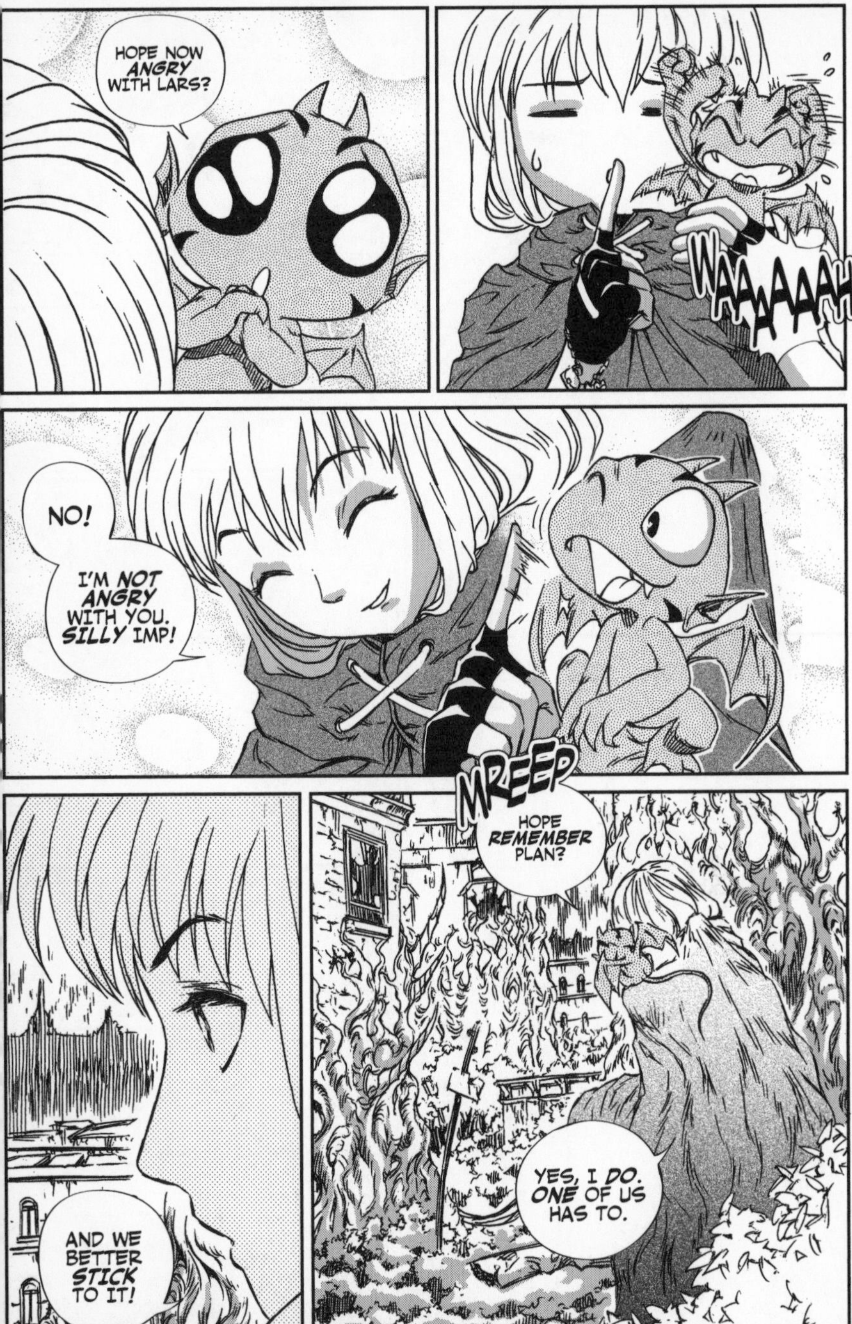
WAAAAAAH!
HOPE NOW ANGRY WITH LARS?
NO!
I'M NOT ANGRY WITH YOU. SILLY IMP!
MREEP
HOPE REMEMBER PLAN?
YES, I DO. ONE OF US HAS TO.
AND WE BETTER STICK TO IT!

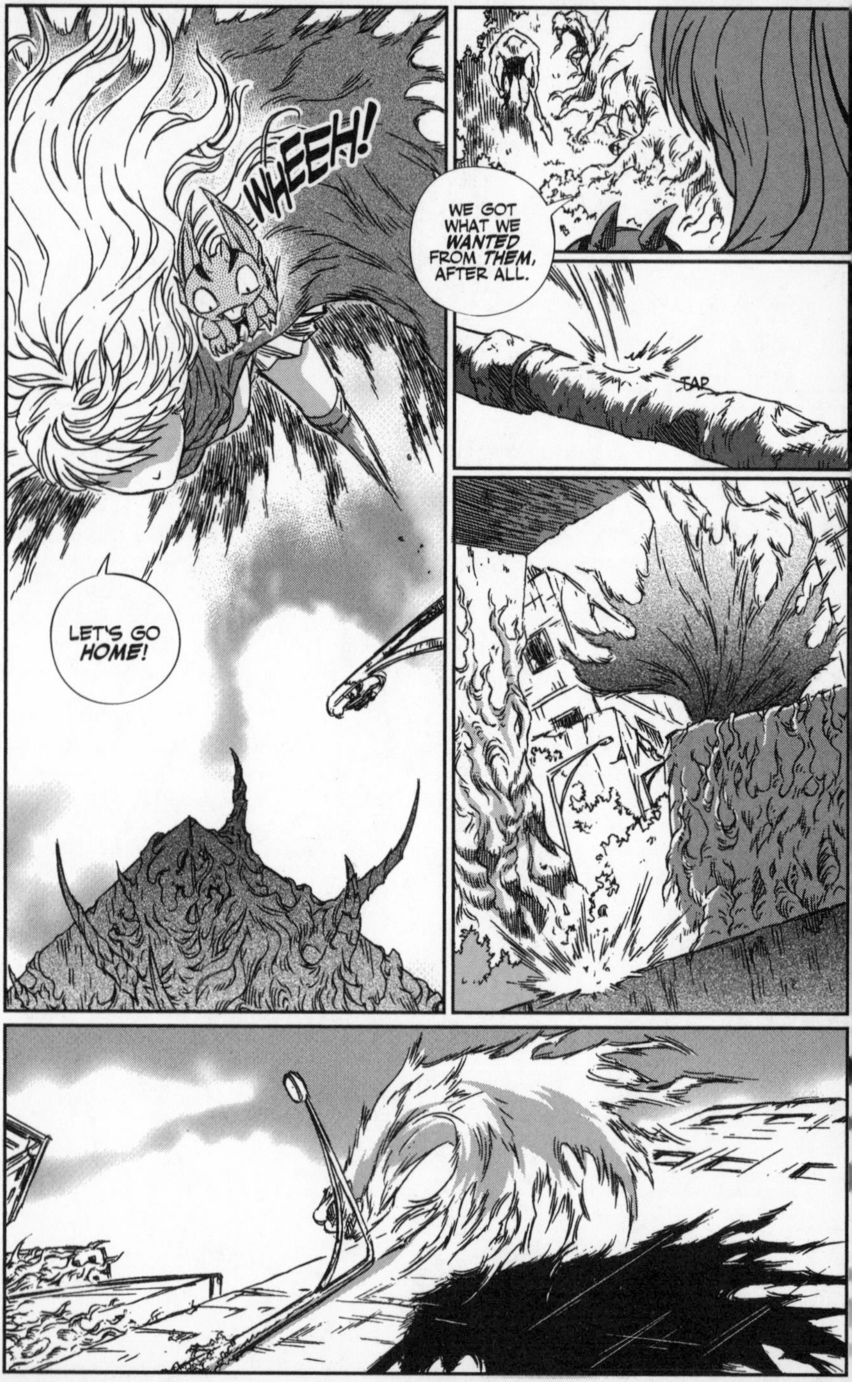
WE GOT WHAT WE WANTED FROM THEM, AFTER ALL.
TAP
WHEEEH!
LET'S GO HOME!

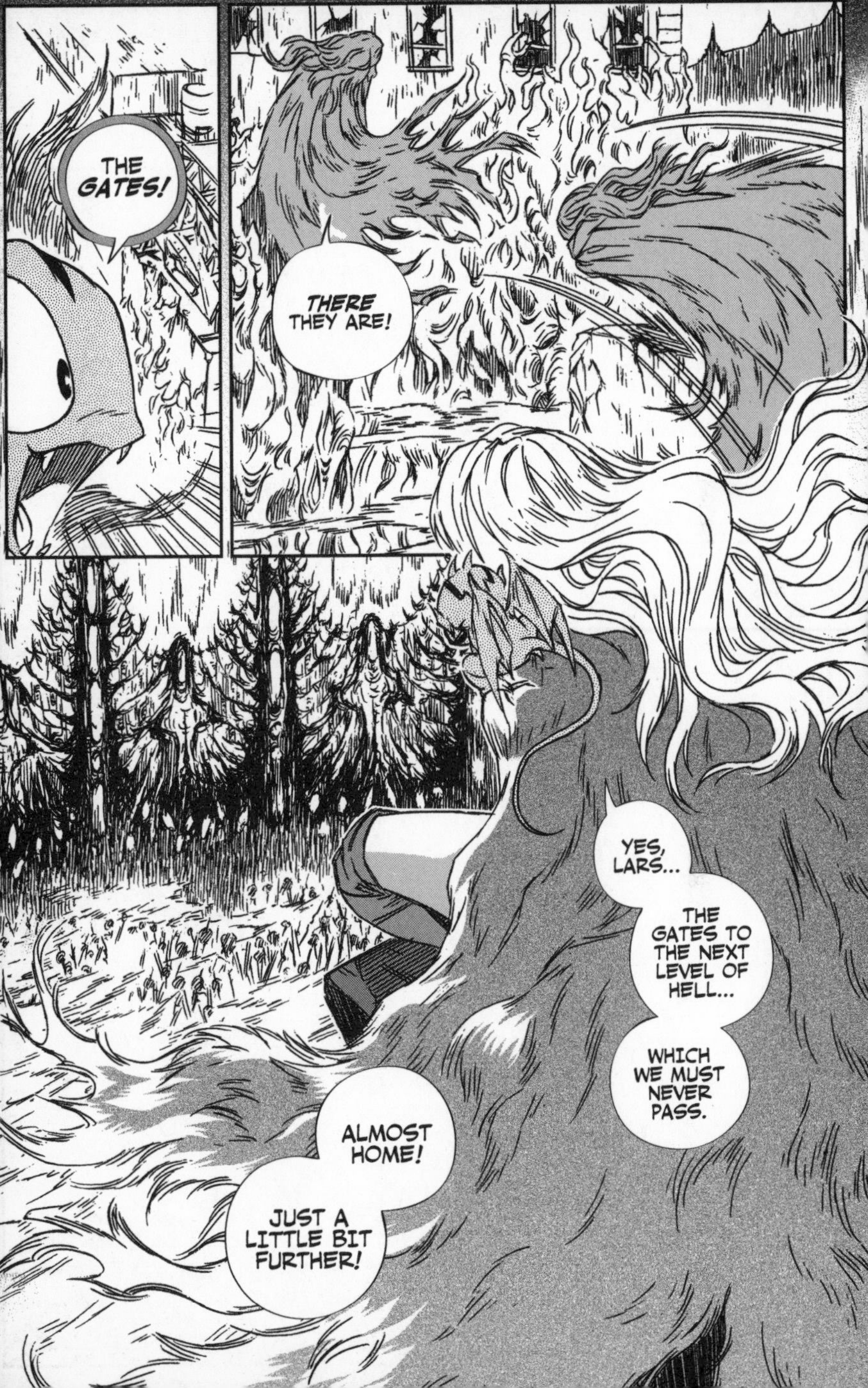
THERE THEY ARE!
THE GATES!
YES, LARS...
THE GATES TO THE NEXT LEVEL OF HELL...
WHICH WE MUST NEVER PASS.
ALMOST HOME!
JUST A LITTLE BIT FURTHER!

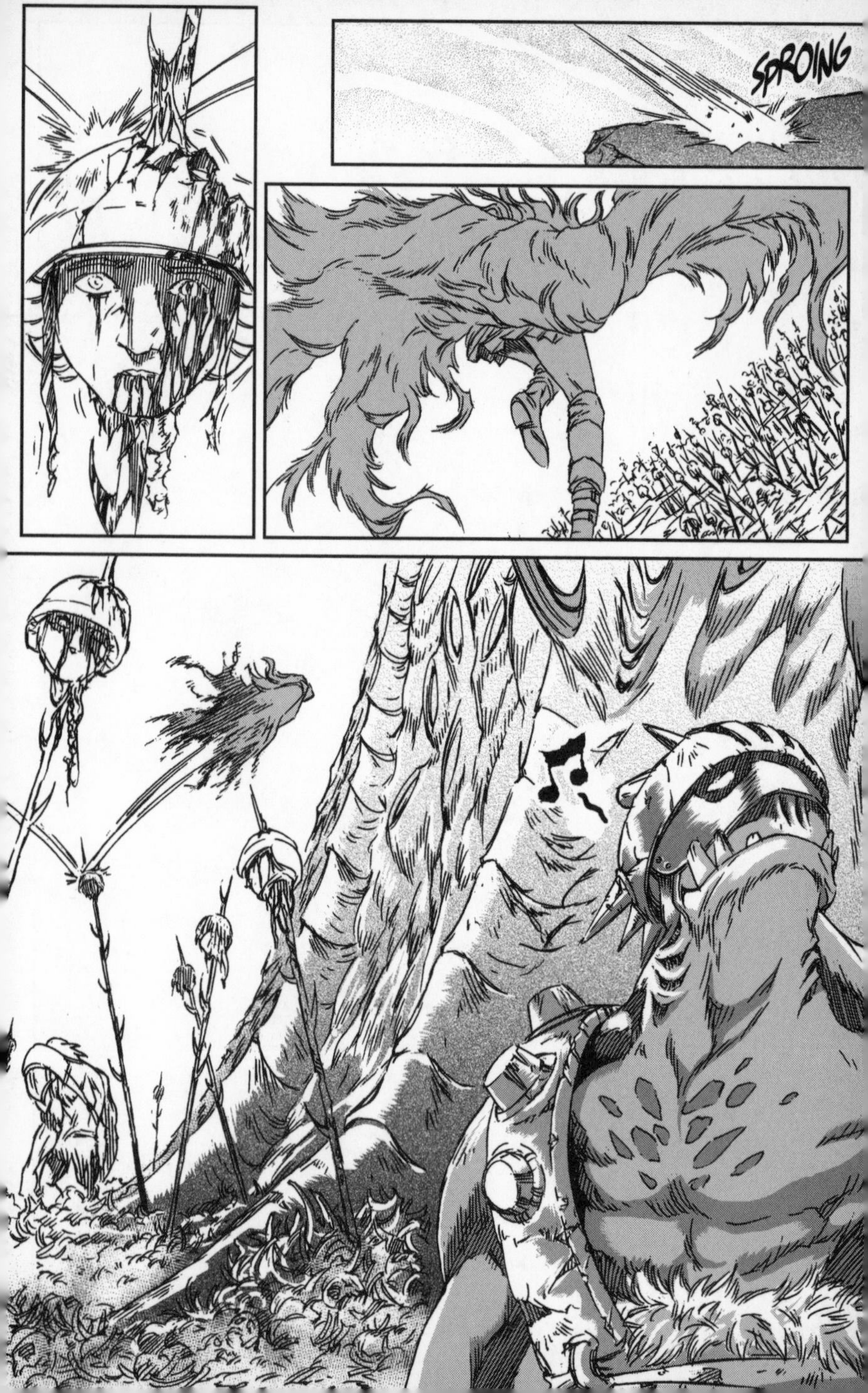
SPROING

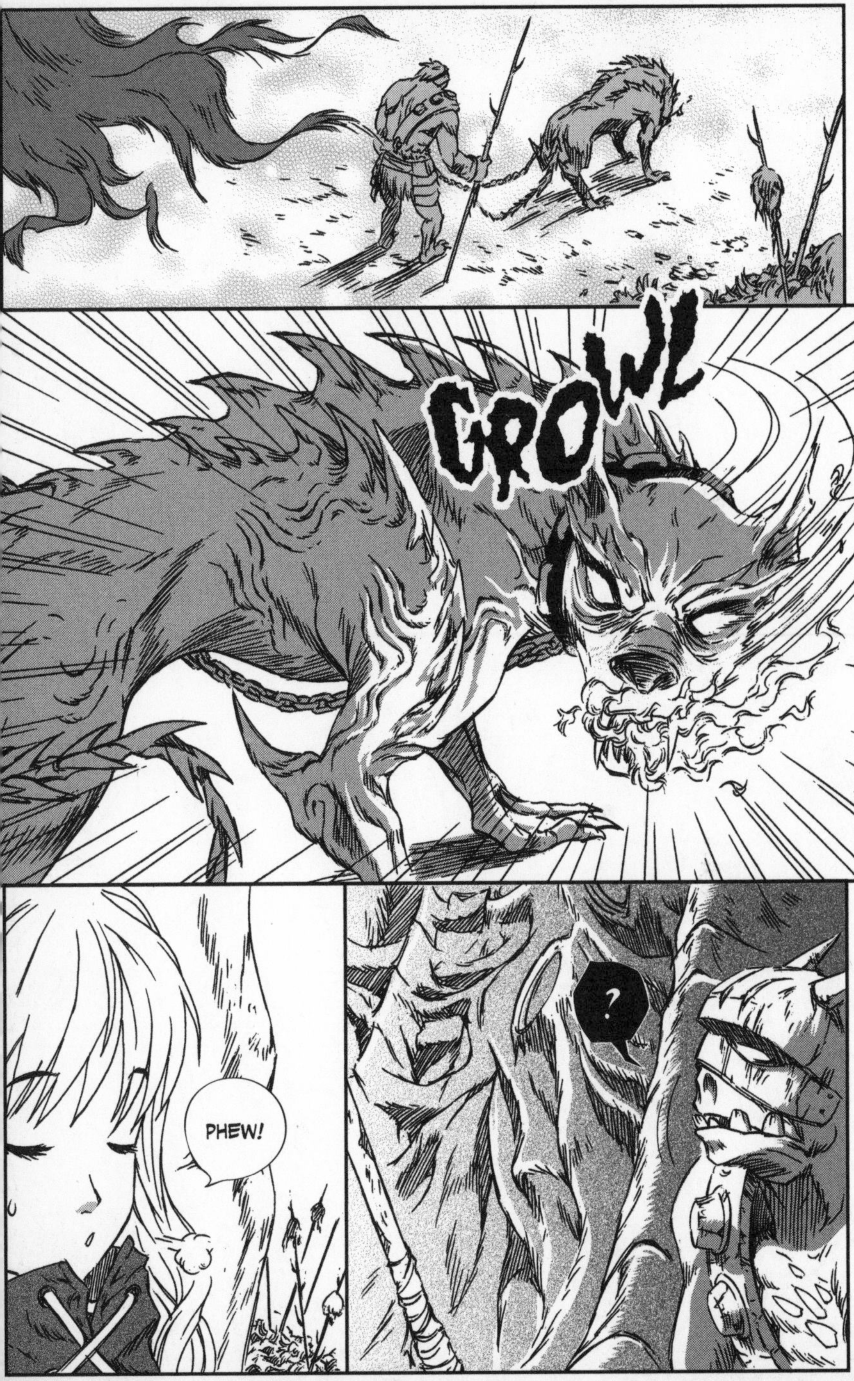
GROWL
?
PHEW!

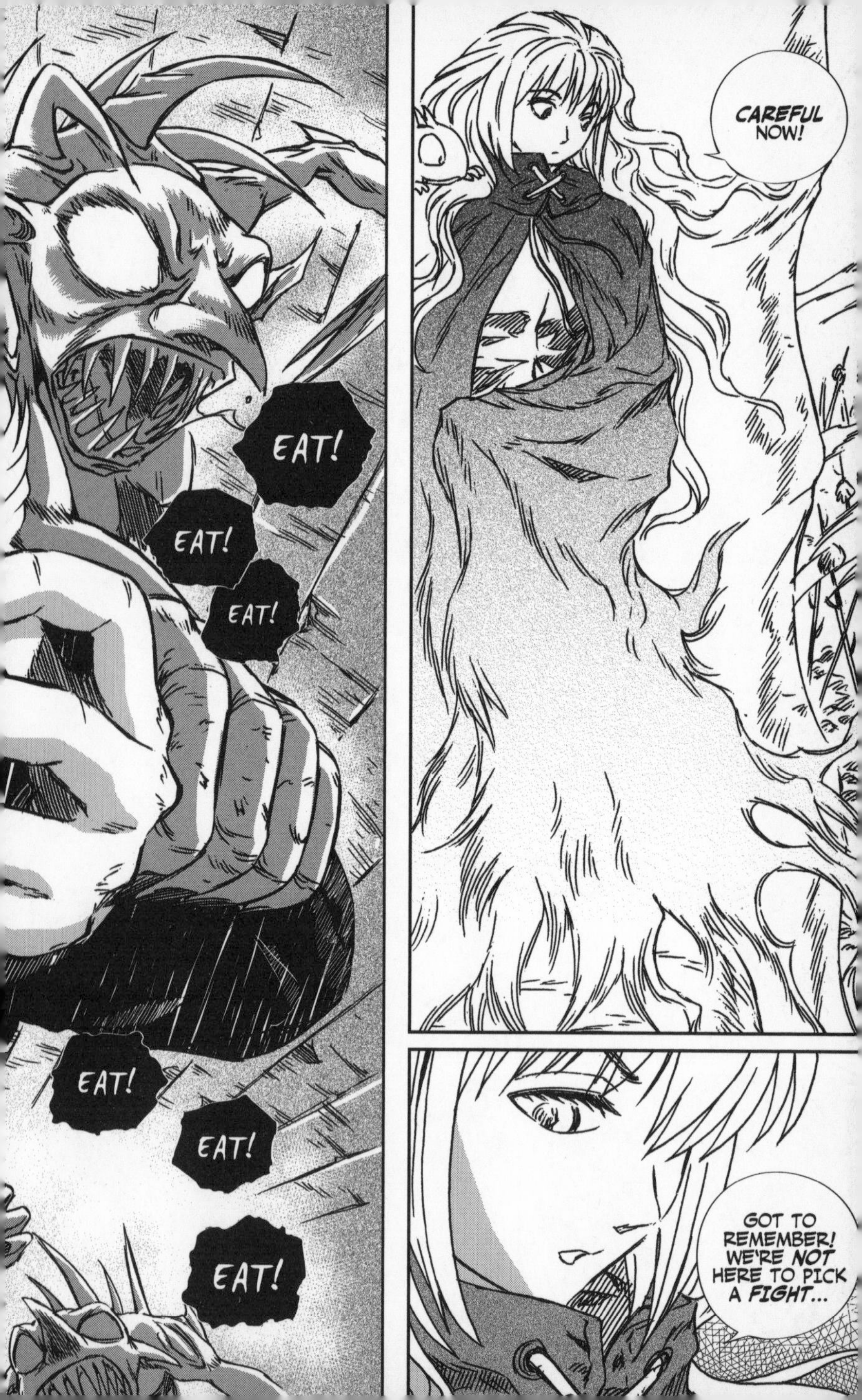
CAREFUL NOW!
GOT TO REMEMBER! WE'RE NOT HERE TO PICK A FIGHT...
EAT!
EAT!
EAT!
EAT!
EAT!
EAT!

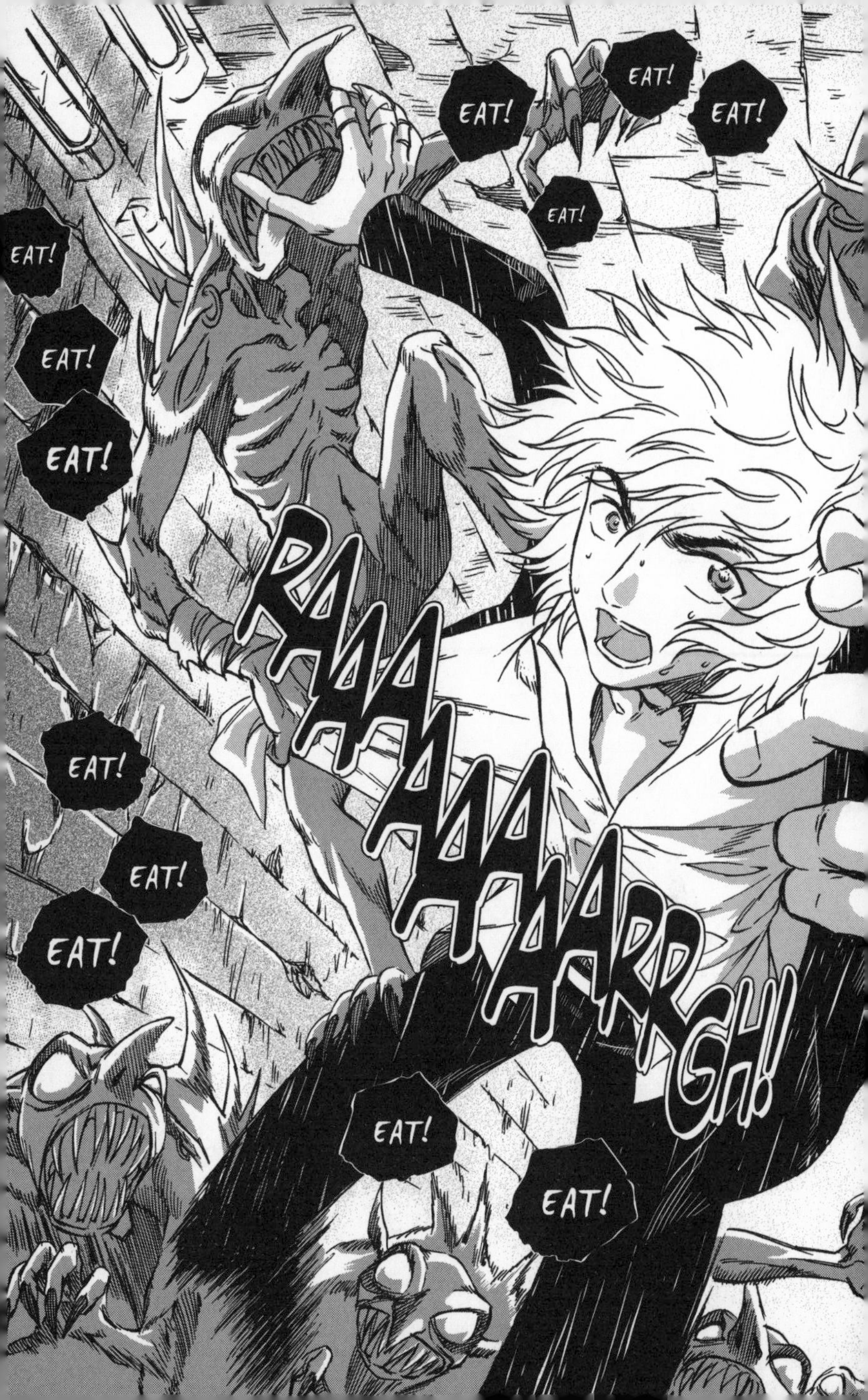
EAT!
EAT!
EAT!
EAT!
EAT!
EAT!
EAT!
RAAAAAAAAAARRGH!
EAT!
EAT!
EAT!
EAT!
EAT!

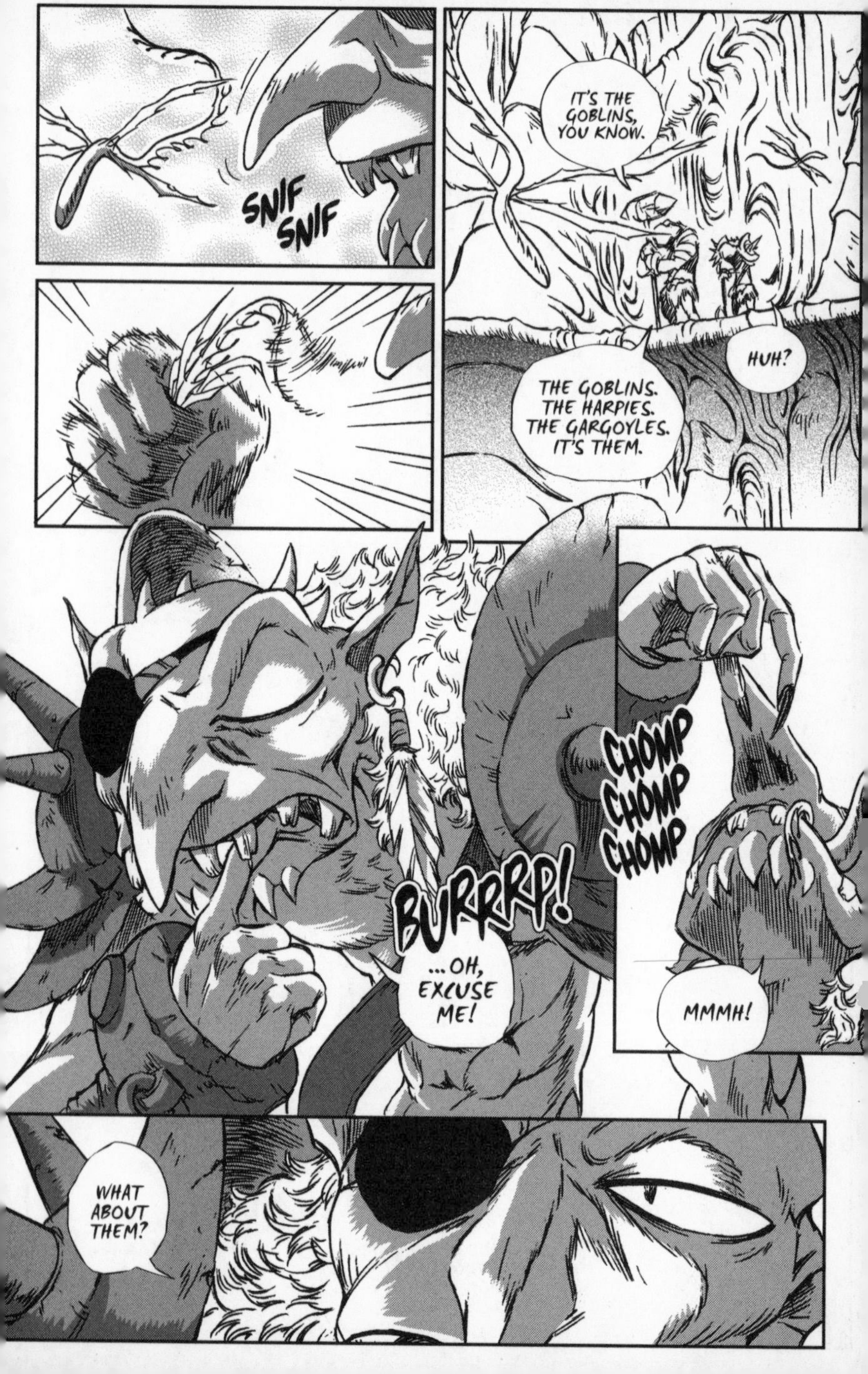
IT'S THE GOBLINS, YOU KNOW.
HUH?
THE GOBLINS. THE HARPIES. THE GARGOYLES. IT'S THEM.
SNIF SNIF
CHOMP CHOMP CHOMP
MMMH!
BURRRP!
...OH, EXCUSE ME!
WHAT ABOUT THEM?

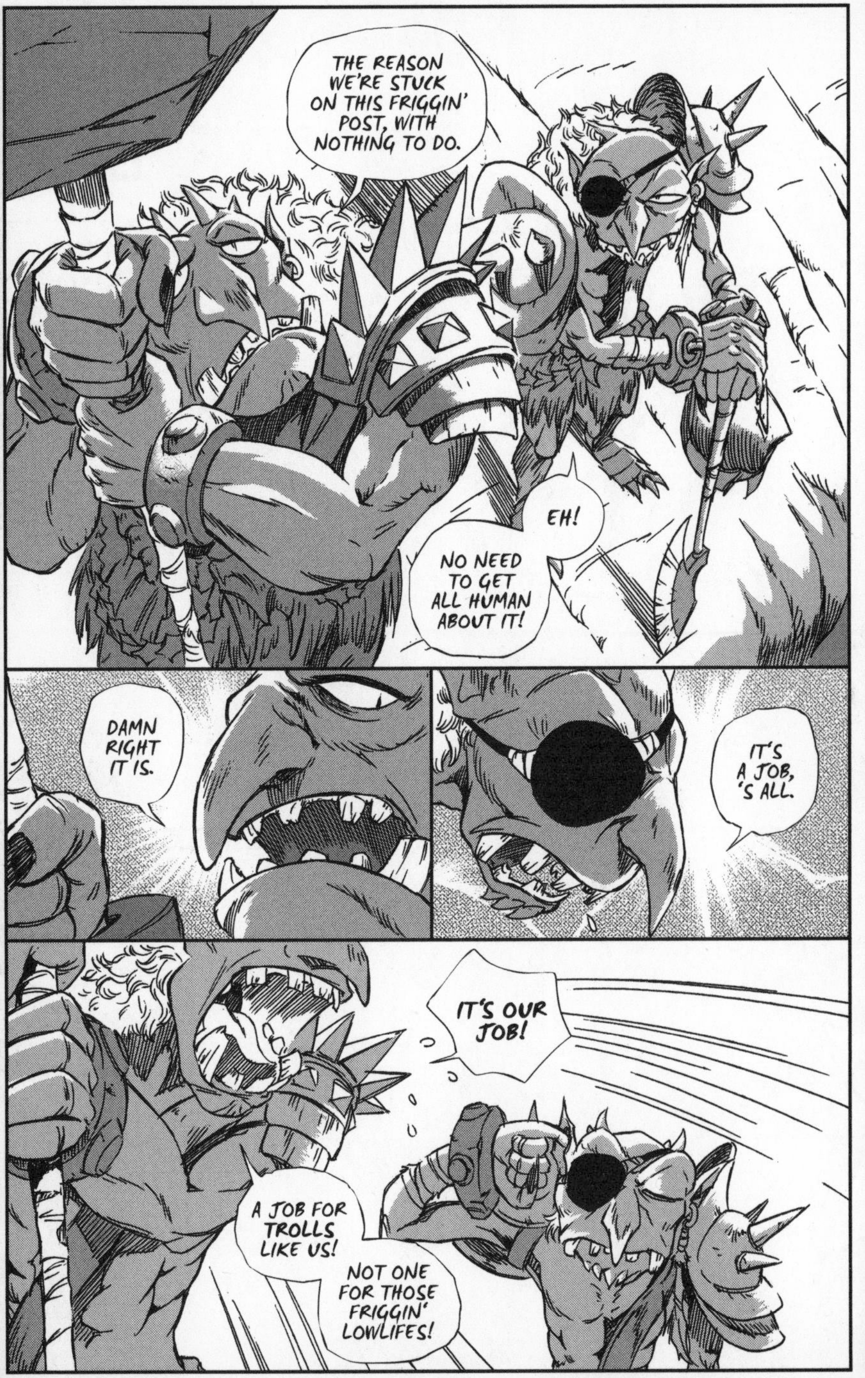
THE REASON WE'RE STUCK ON THIS FRIGGIN' POST, WITH NOTHING TO DO.
EH!
NO NEED TO GET ALL HUMAN ABOUT IT!
DAMN RIGHT IT IS.
IT'S A JOB, 'S ALL.
IT'S OUR JOB!
A JOB FOR TROLLS LIKE US!
NOT ONE FOR THOSE FRIGGIN' LOWLIFES!

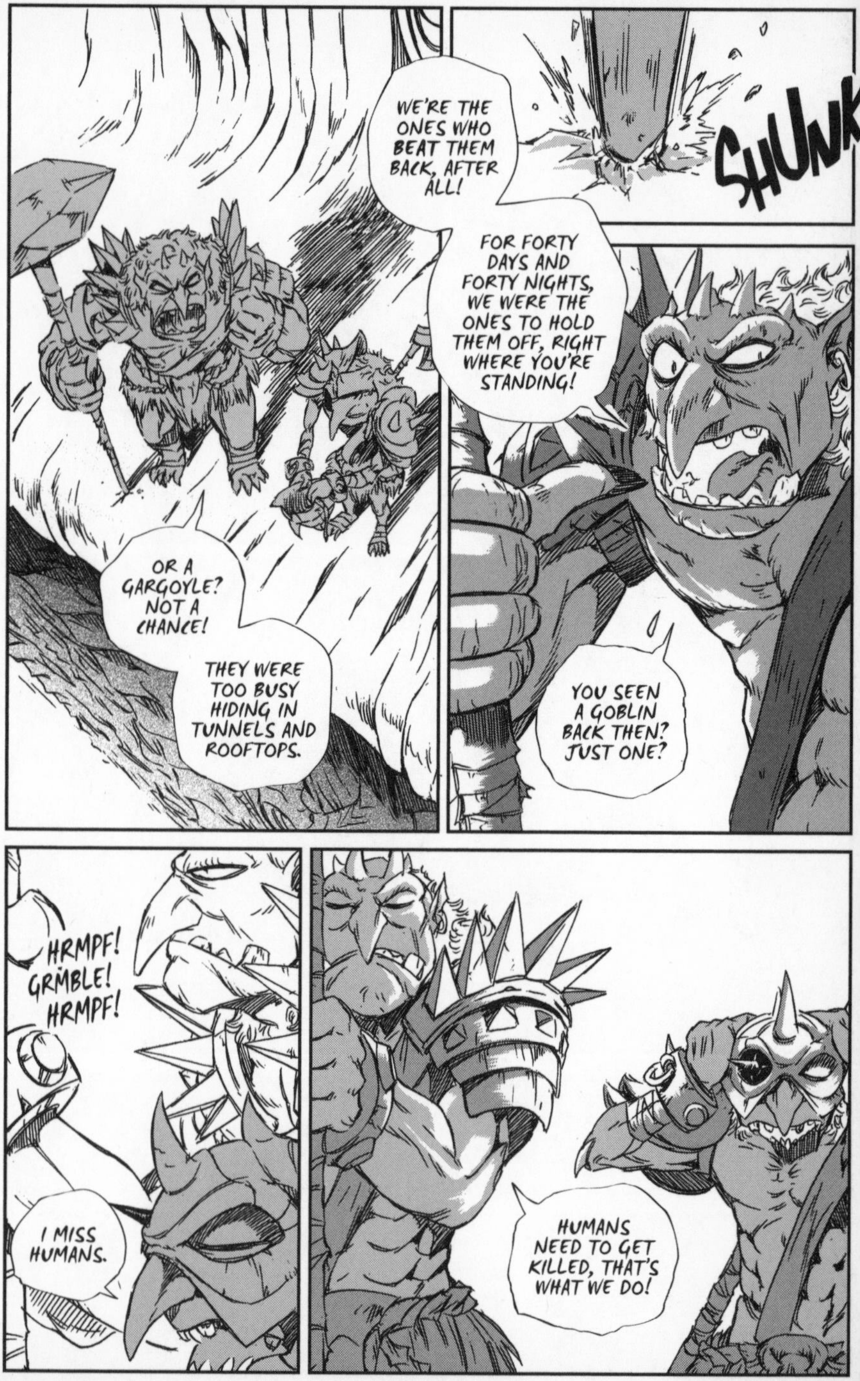
SHUNK
FOR FORTY DAYS AND FORTY NIGHTS, WE WERE THE ONES TO HOLD THEM OFF, RIGHT WHERE YOU'RE STANDING!
YOU SEEN A GOBLIN BACK THEN? JUST ONE?
OR A GARGOYLE? NOT A CHANCE!
THEY WERE TOO BUSY HIDING IN TUNNELS AND ROOFTOPS.
WE'RE THE ONES WHO BEAT THEM BACK, AFTER ALL!
HUMANS NEED TO GET KILLED, THAT'S WHAT WE DO!
HRMPF! GRMBLE! HRMPF!
I MISS HUMANS.

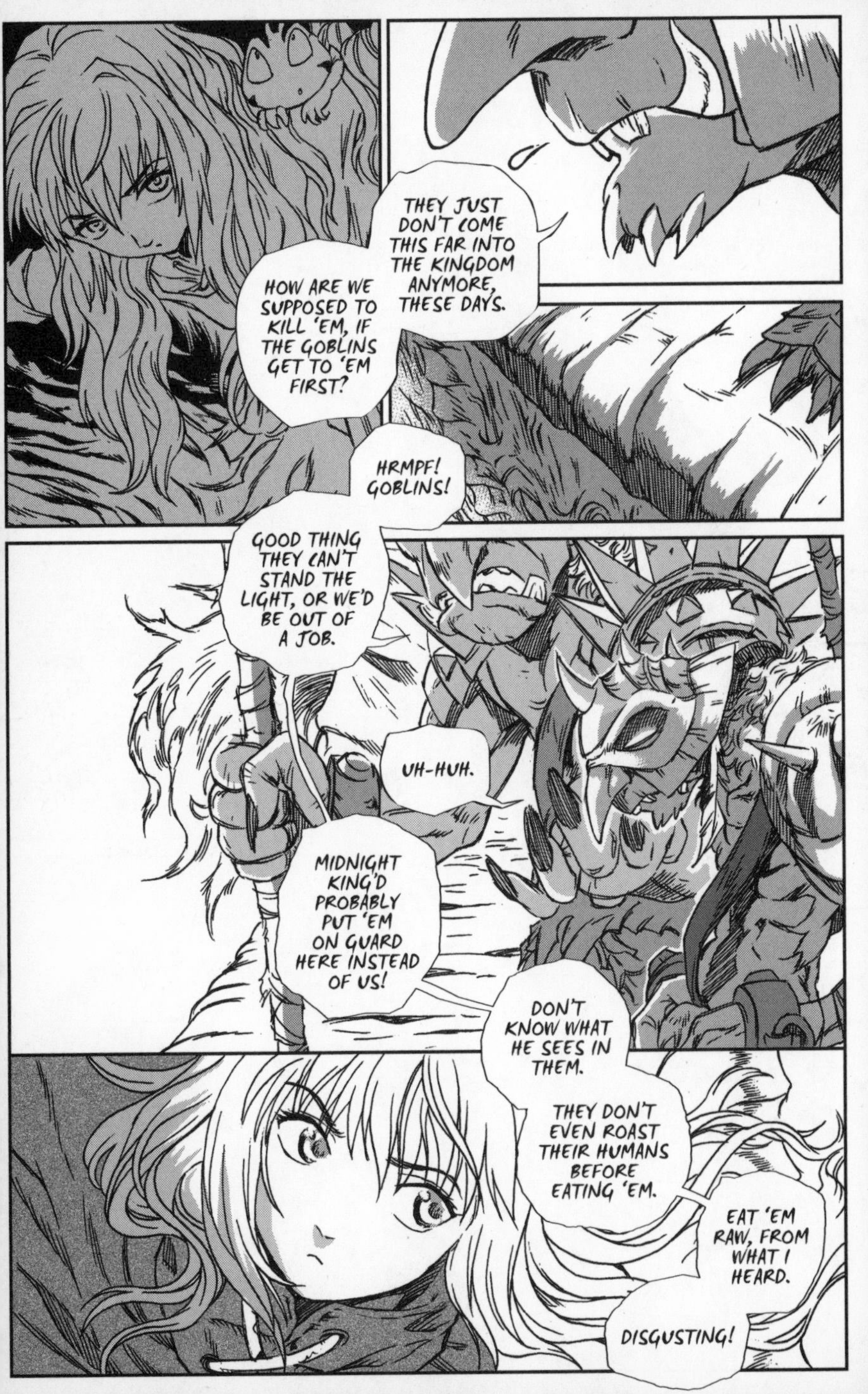
THEY JUST DON'T COME THIS FAR INTO THE KINGDOM ANYMORE, THESE DAYS.
HOW ARE WE SUPPOSED TO KILL 'EM, IF THE GOBLINS GET TO 'EM FIRST?
HRMPF! GOBLINS!
GOOD THING THEY CAN'T STAND THE LIGHT, OR WE'D BE OUT OF A JOB.
UH-HUH.
MIDNIGHT KING'D PROBABLY PUT 'EM ON GUARD HERE INSTEAD OF US!
DON'T KNOW WHAT HE SEES IN THEM.
THEY DON'T EVEN ROAST THEIR HUMANS BEFORE EATING 'EM.
EAT 'EM RAW, FROM WHAT I HEARD.
DISGUSTING!

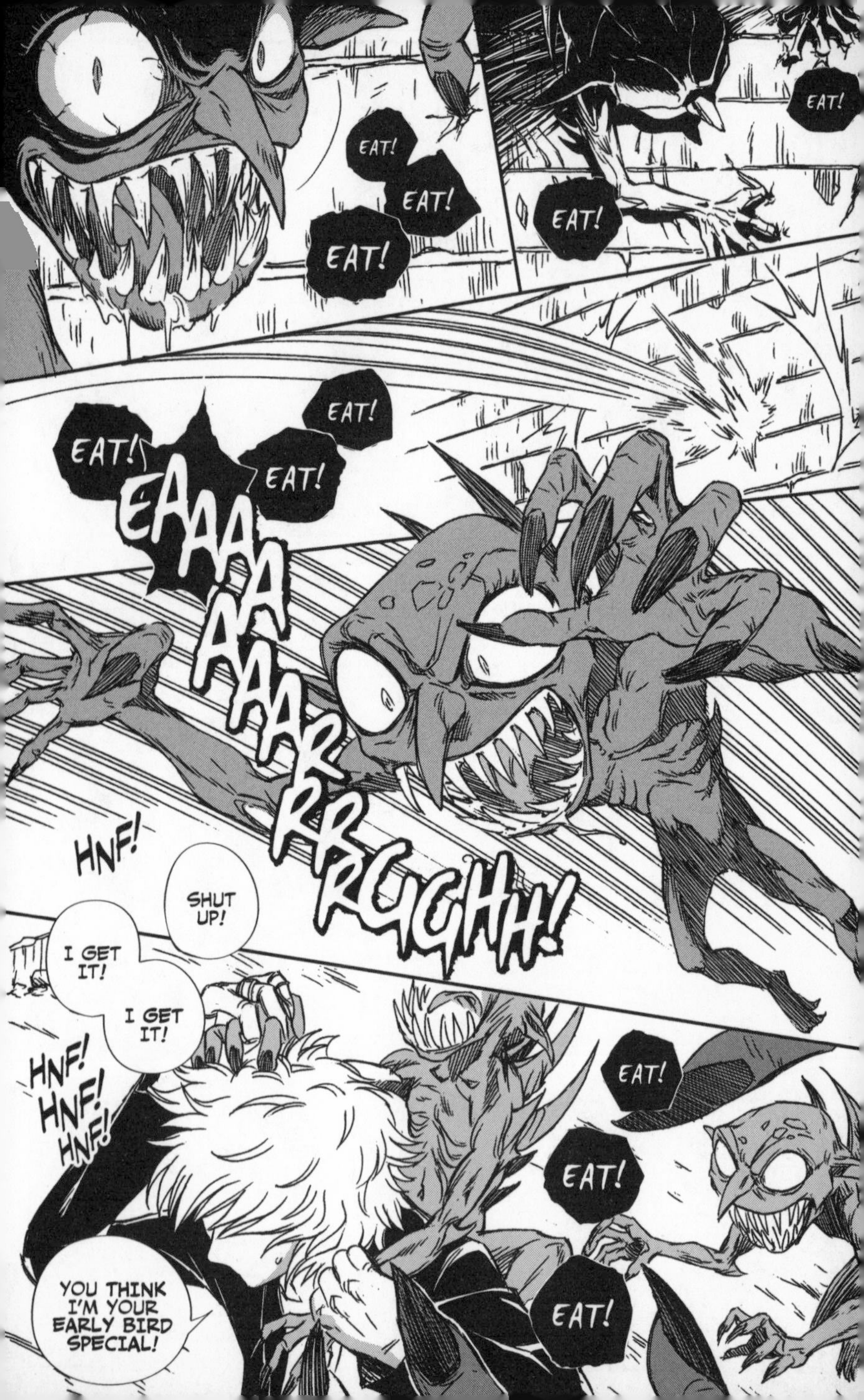
EAT!
EAT!
EAT!
EAT!
EAT!
EAT!
EAT!
EAT!
EAAAAAAAARRRRGHH!
EAT!
EAT!
EAT!
HNF!
SHUT UP!
I GET IT!
I GET IT!
HNF! HNF! HNF!
YOU THINK I'M YOUR EARLY BIRD SPECIAL!

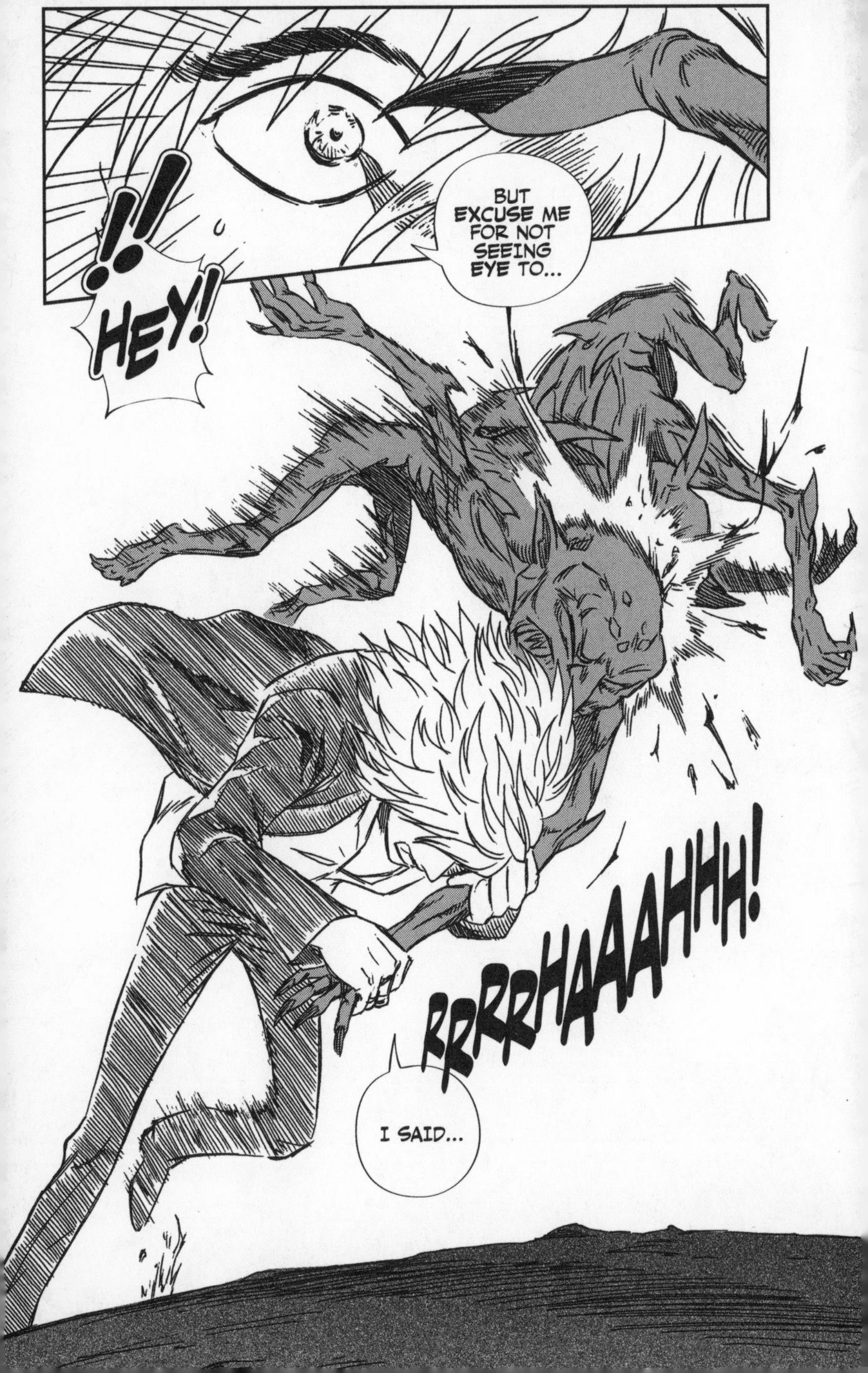

BUT EXCUSE ME FOR NOT SEEING EYE TO...
!!
HEY!
RRRRHAAAAHHH!
I SAID...

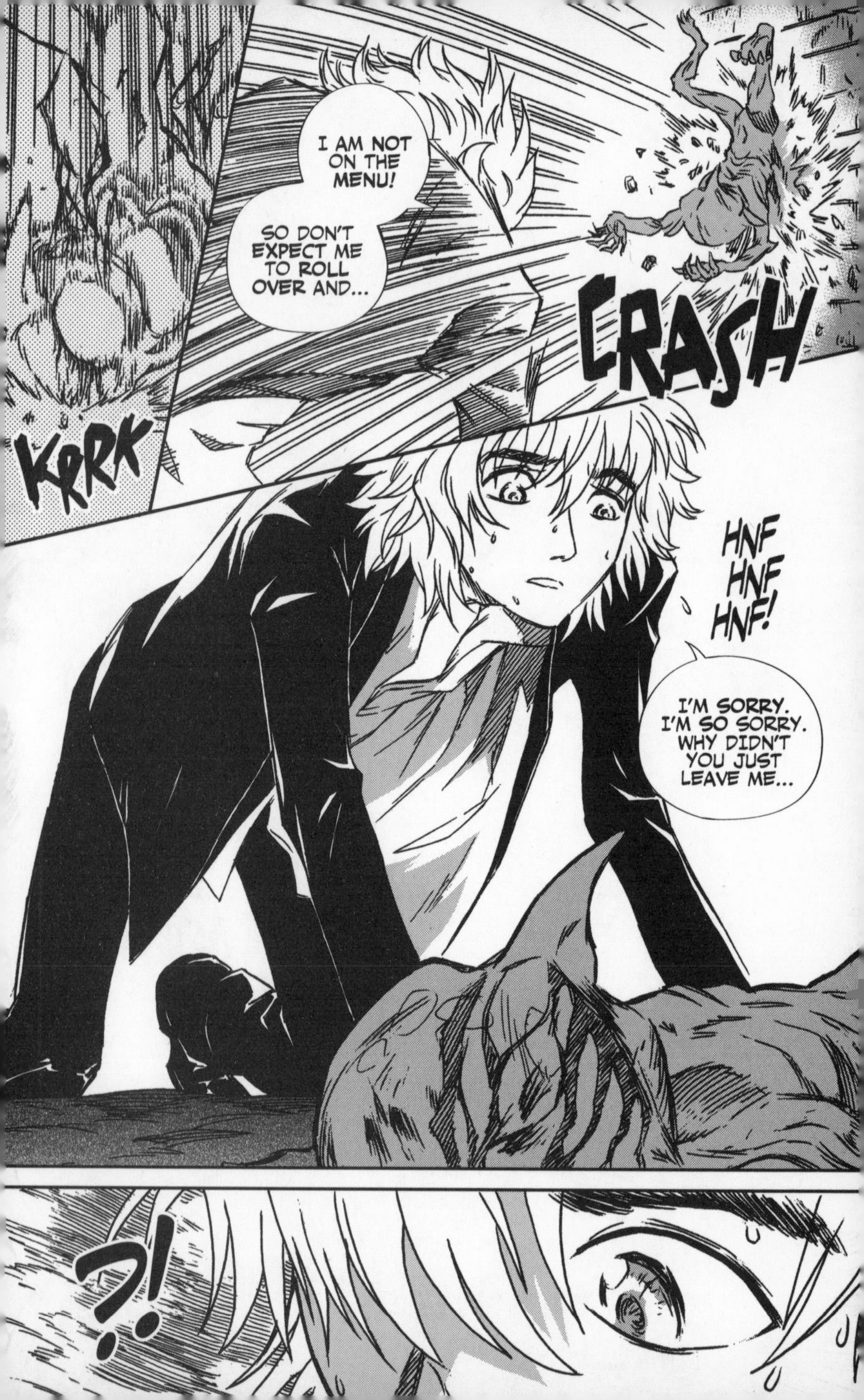
I AM NOT ON THE MENU!
SO DON'T EXPECT ME TO ROLL OVER AND...
CRASH
KRRK
HNF HNF HNF!
I'M SORRY. I'M SO SORRY. WHY DIDN'T YOU JUST LEAVE ME...
?!

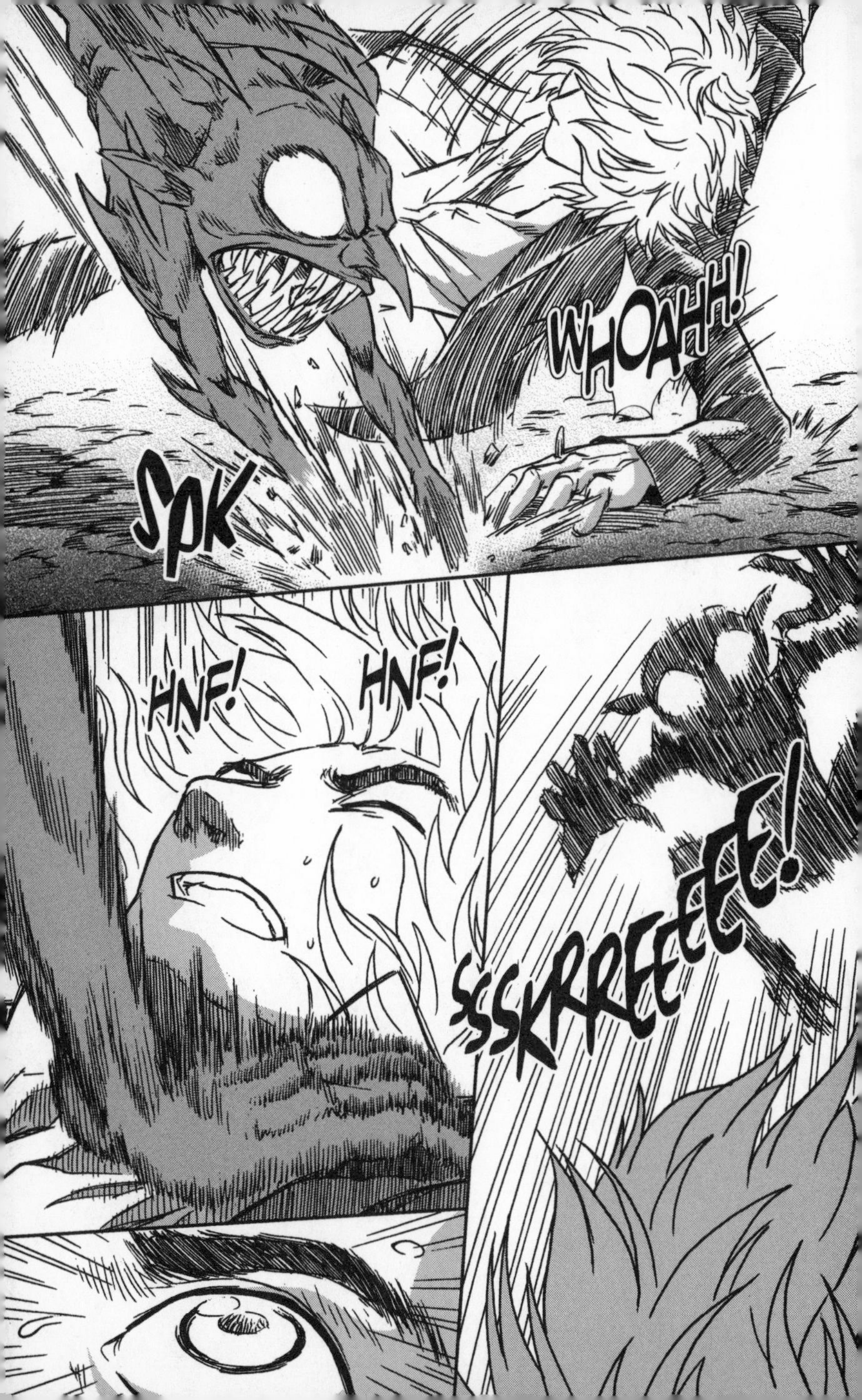
WHOAHH!
SPK
SSSKRREEEEE!
HNF!
HNF!

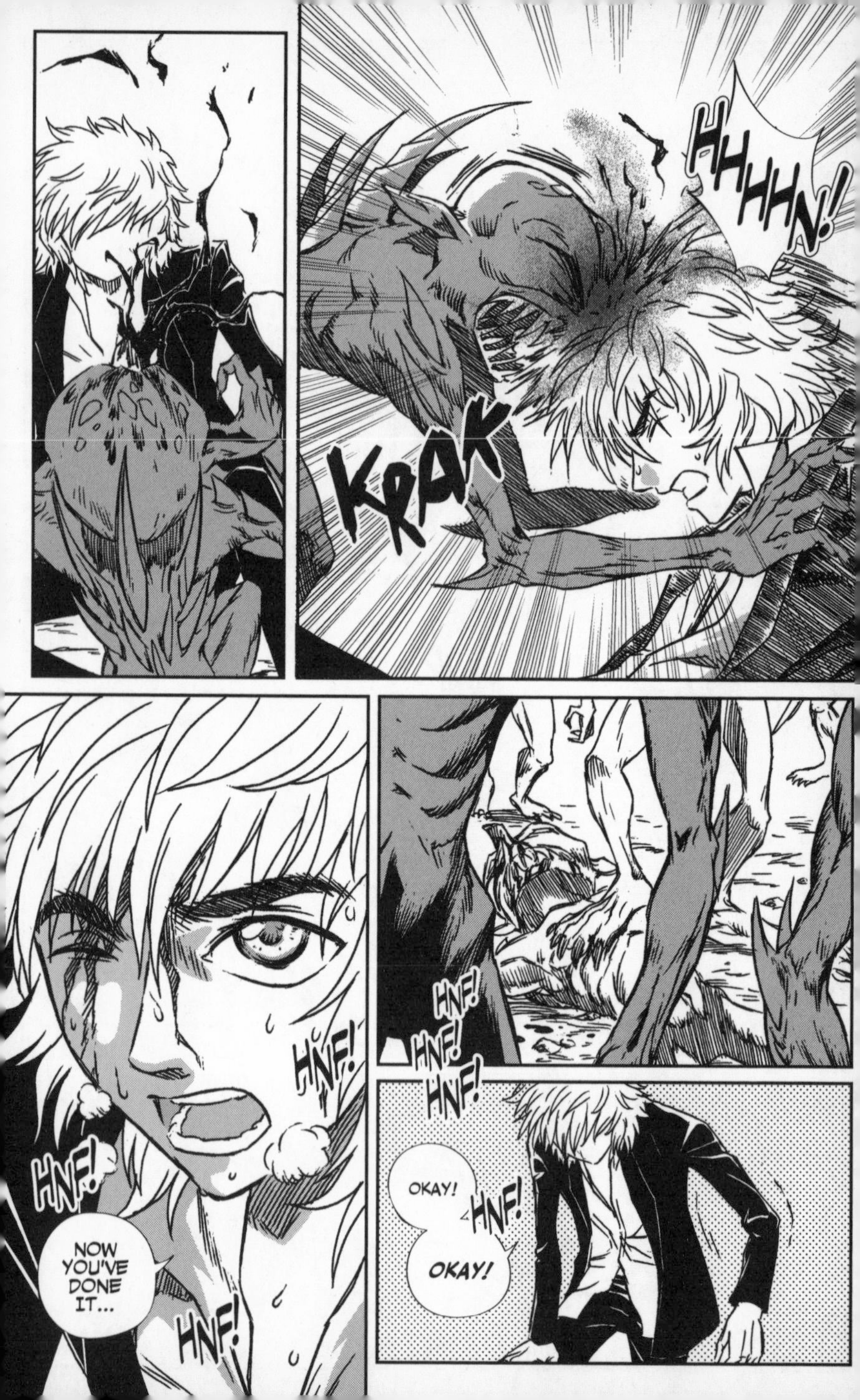
HHHHN!
KRAK
HNF!
HNF!
HNF!
OKAY!
HNF!
OKAY!
HNF!
HNF!
NOW YOU'VE DONE IT...
HNF!

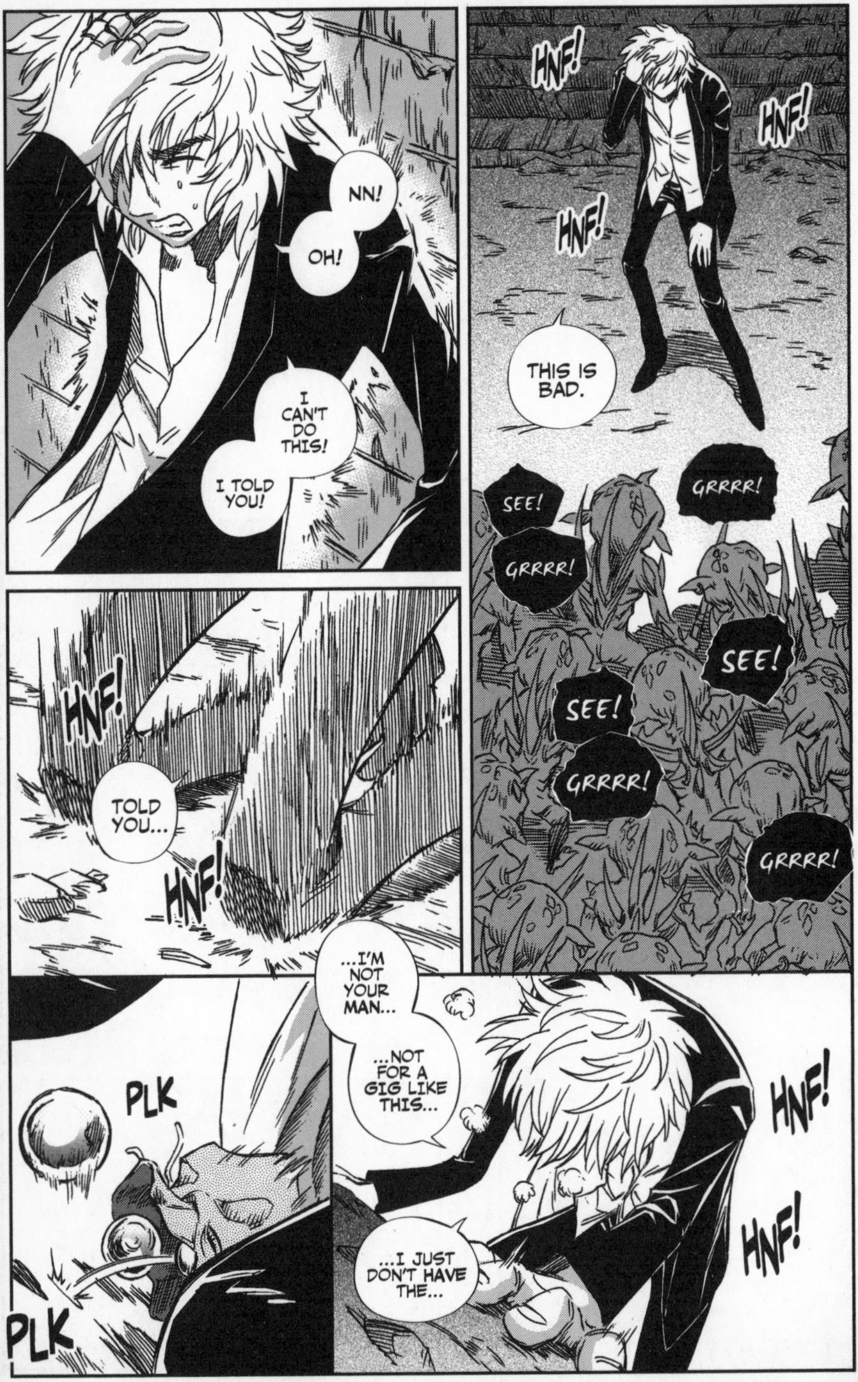
HNF!
HNF!
HNF!
THIS IS BAD.
SEE!
GRRRR!
GRRRR!
SEE!
SEE!
GRRRR!
GRRRR!
NN!
OH!
I CAN'T DO THIS!
I TOLD YOU!
HNF!
TOLD YOU...
HNF!
...I'M NOT YOUR MAN...
...NOT FOR A GIG LIKE THIS...
HNF!
HNF!
...I JUST DON'T HAVE THE...
PLK
PLK

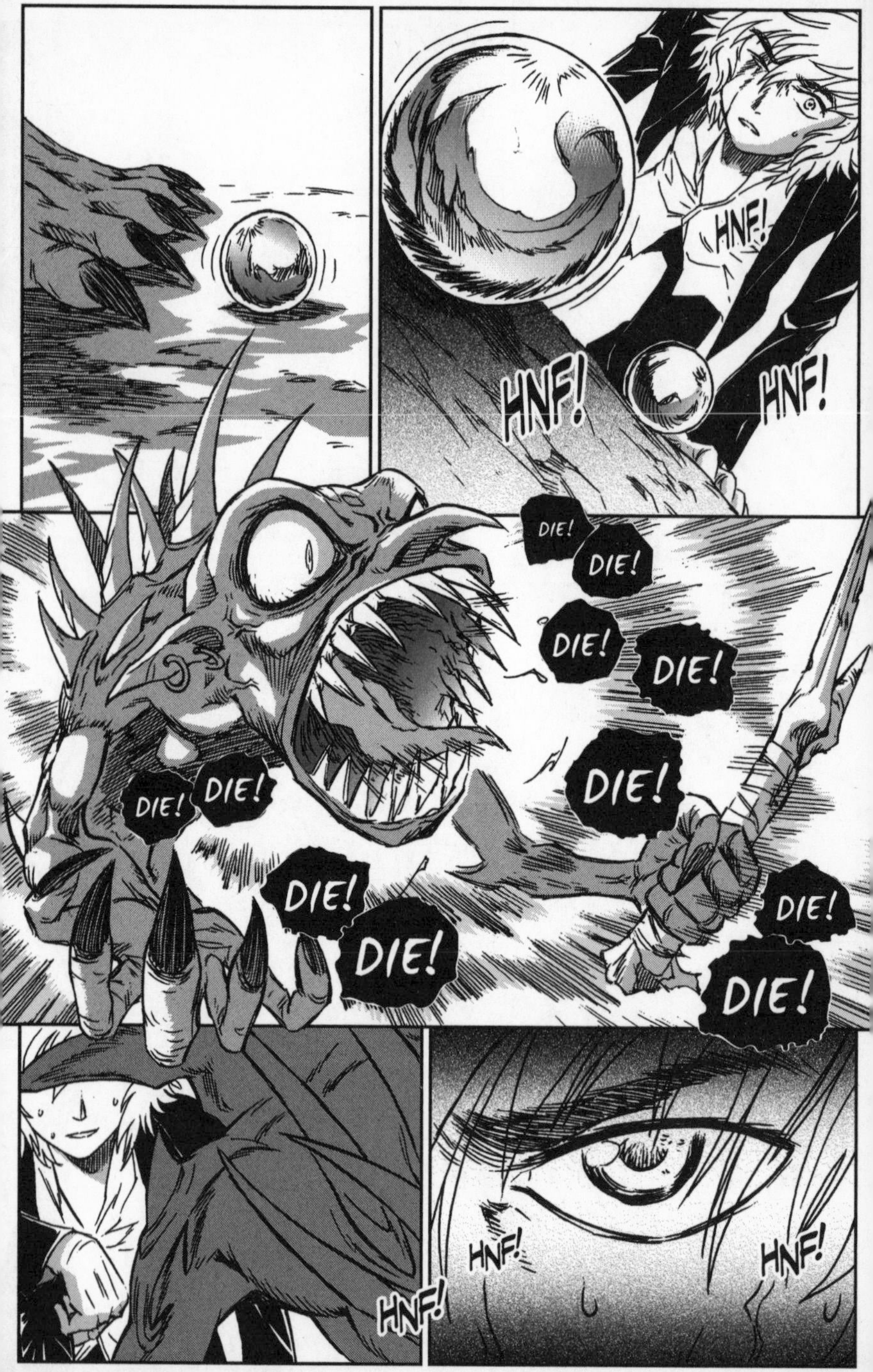
HNF!
HNF!
HNF!
DIE!
DIE!
DIE!
DIE!
DIE!
DIE!
DIE!
DIE!
DIE!
DIE!
DIE!
DIE!
HNF!
HNF!
HNF!

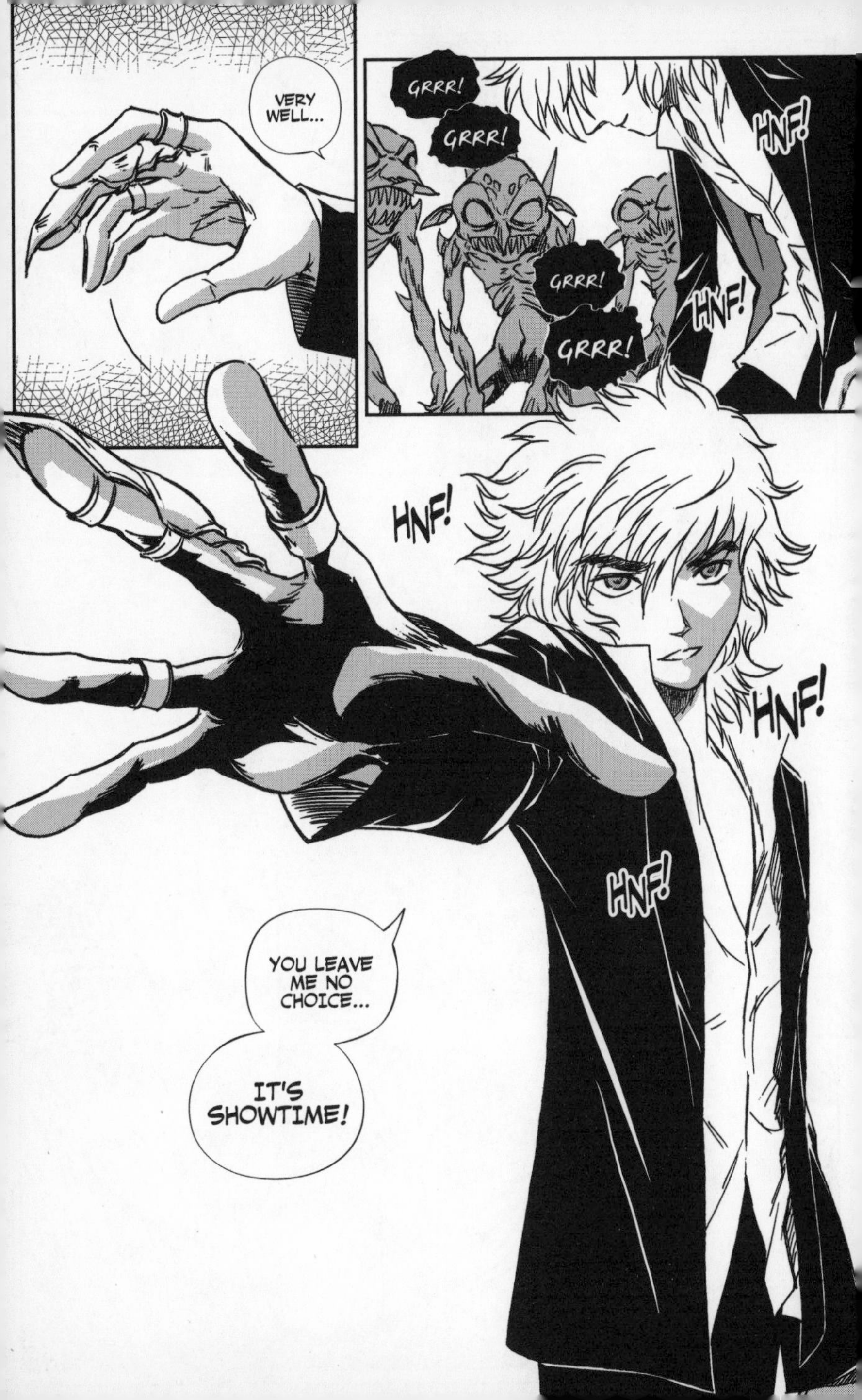
HNF!
GRRR!
GRRR!
HNF!
GRRR!
GRRR!
VERY WELL...
HNF!
HNF!
HNF!
YOU LEAVE ME NO CHOICE...
IT'S SHOWTIME!

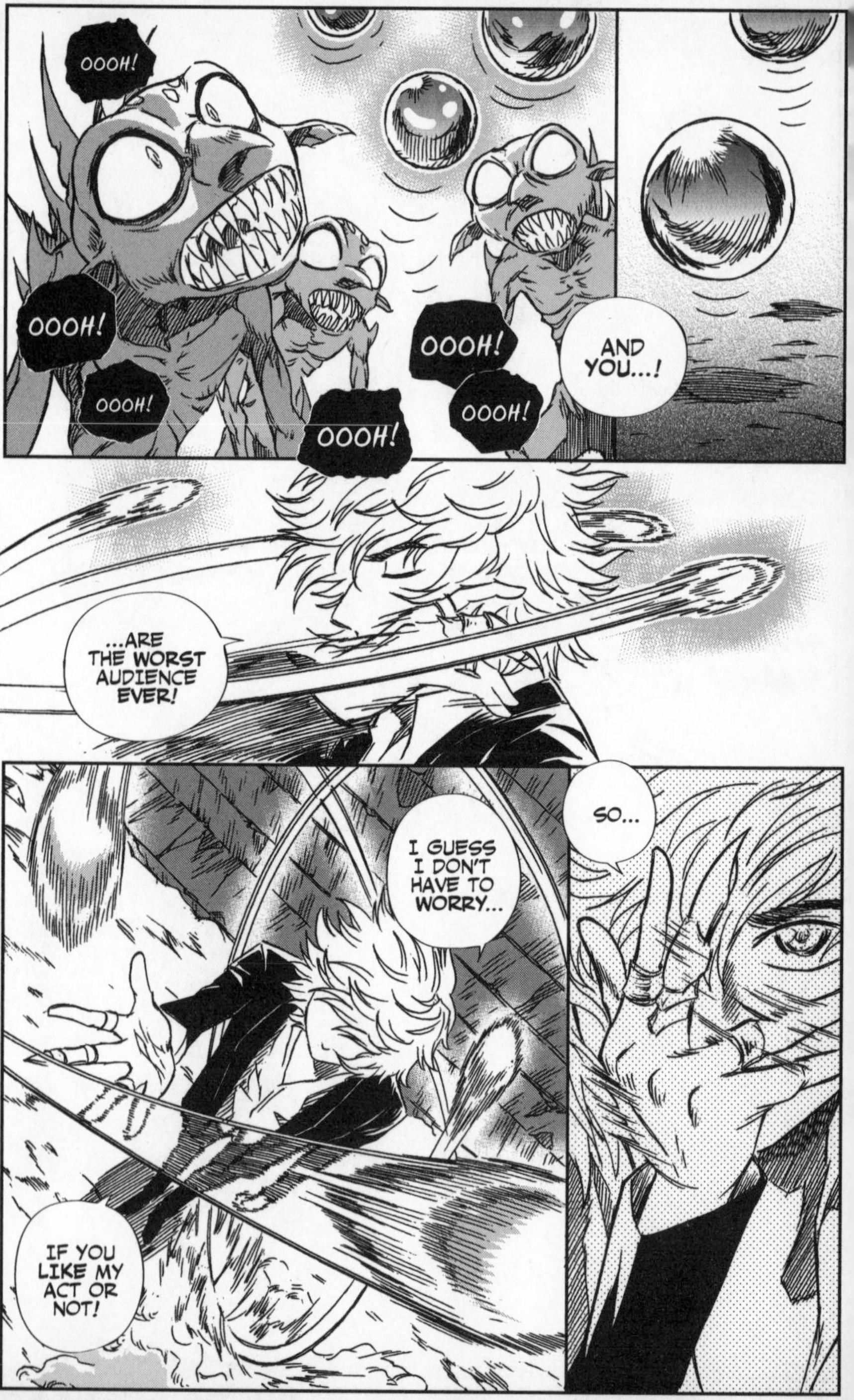
OOOH!
OOOH!
OOOH!
OOOH!
OOOH!
OOOH!
OOOH!
AND YOU...!
...ARE THE WORST AUDIENCE EVER!
SO...
I GUESS I DON'T HAVE TO WORRY...
IF YOU LIKE MY ACT OR NOT!

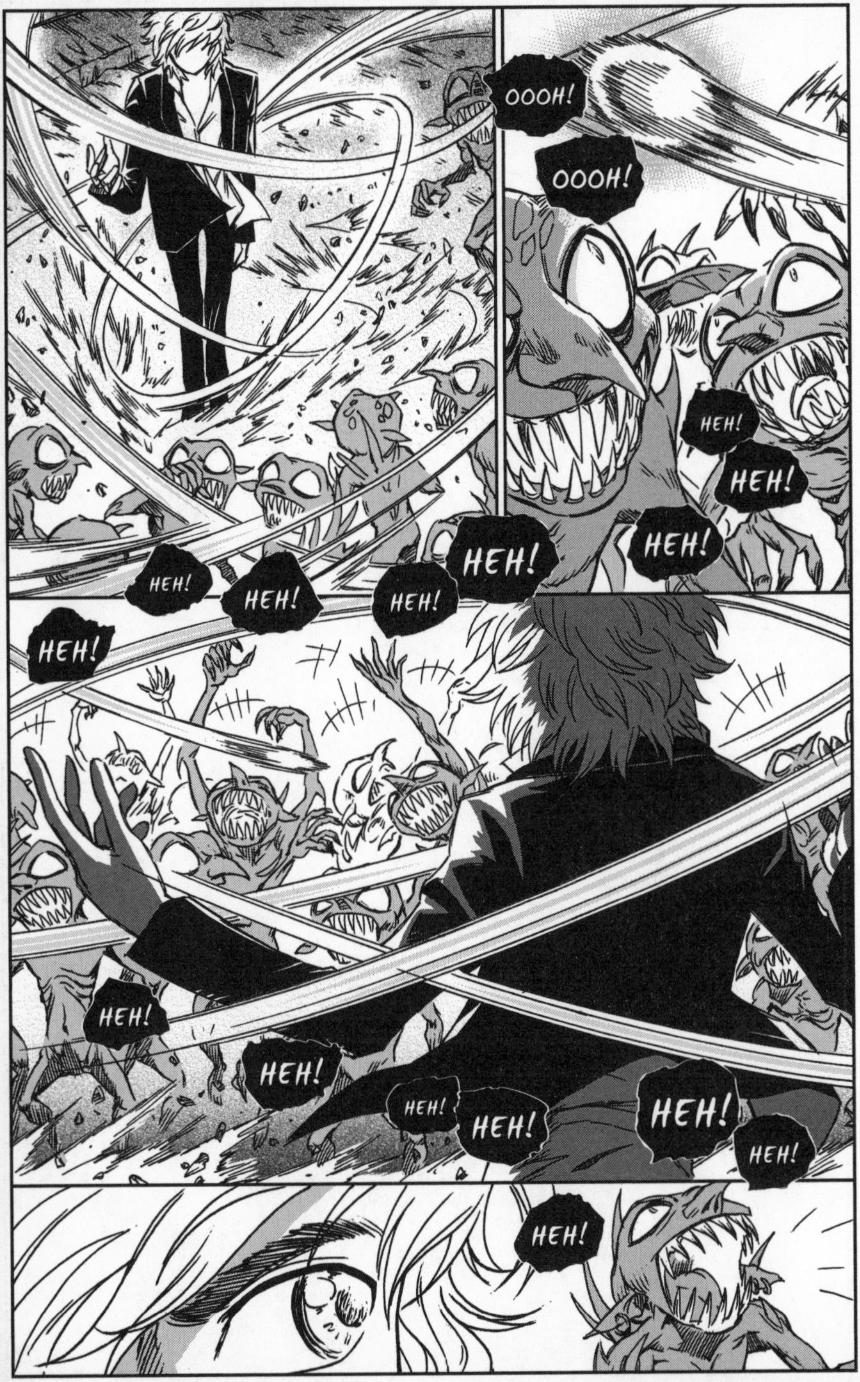
OOOH!
OOOH!
HEH!
HEH!
HEH!
HEH!
HEH!
HEH!
HEH!
HEH!
HEH!
HEH!
HEH!
HEH!
HEH!
HEH!
HEH!
HEH!

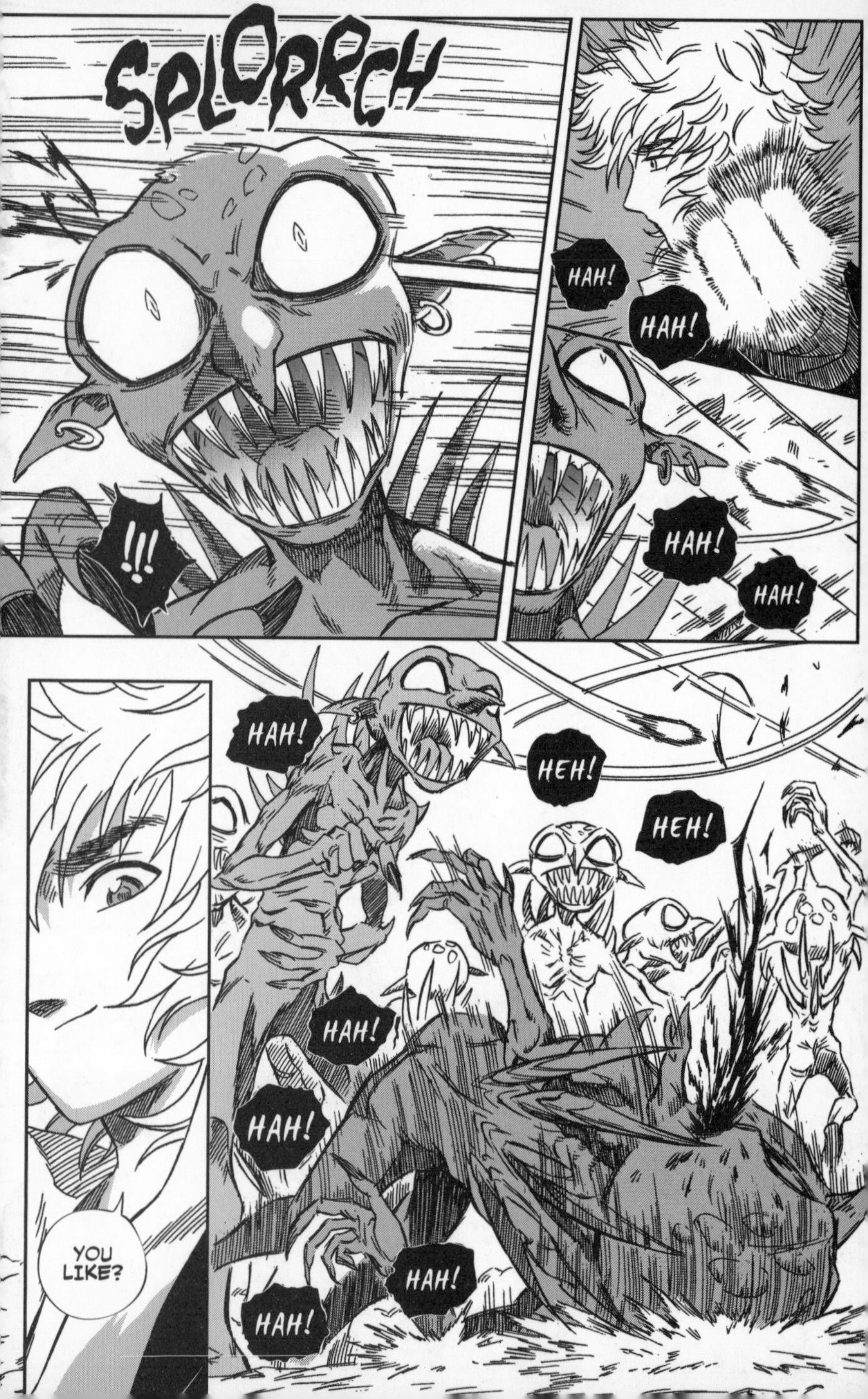
HAH!
HAH!
HAH!
HAH!
SPLORRCH
!!!
HAH!
HEH!
HEH!
HAH!
HAH!
HAH!
HAH!
YOU LIKE?

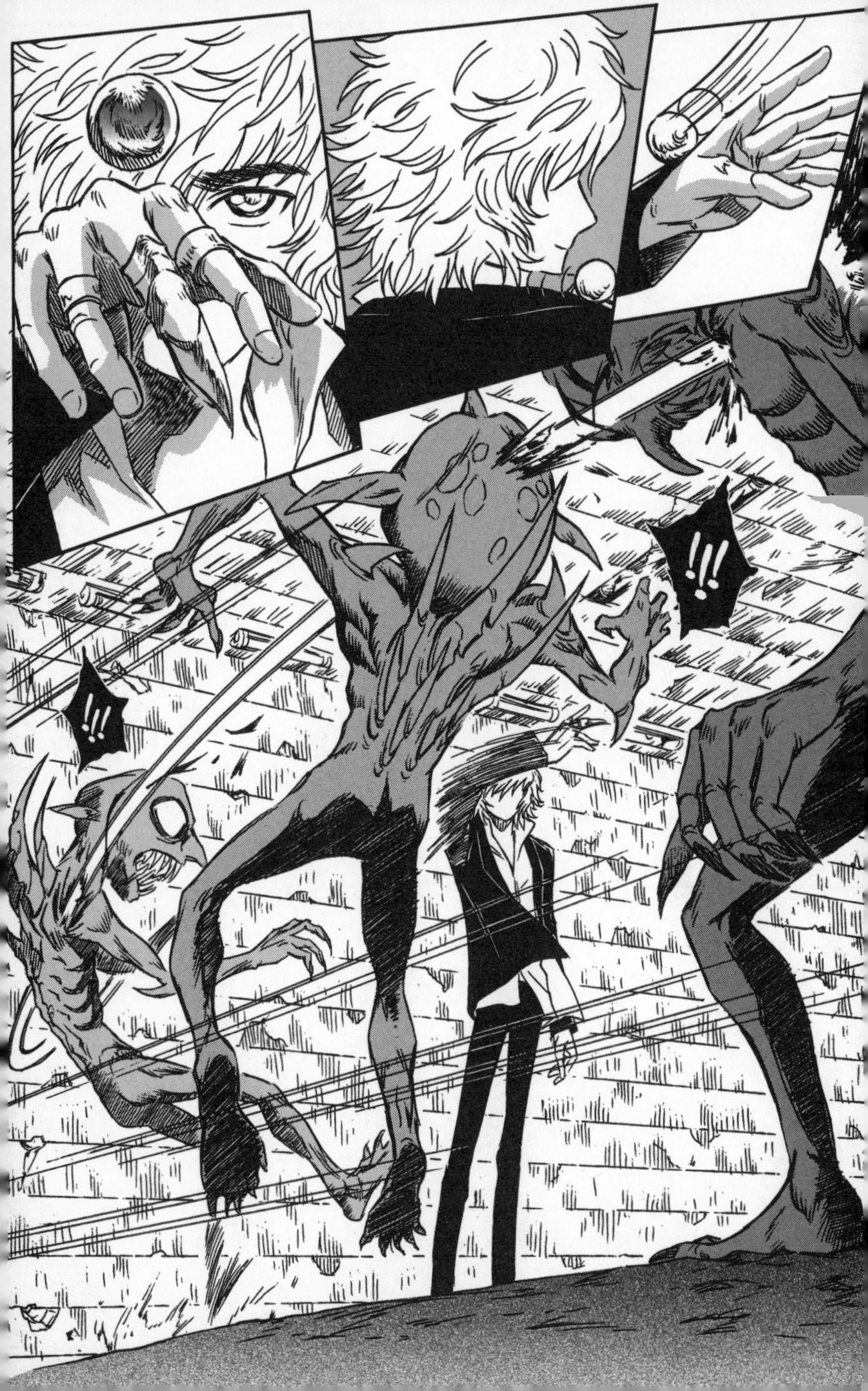
!!!
!!!

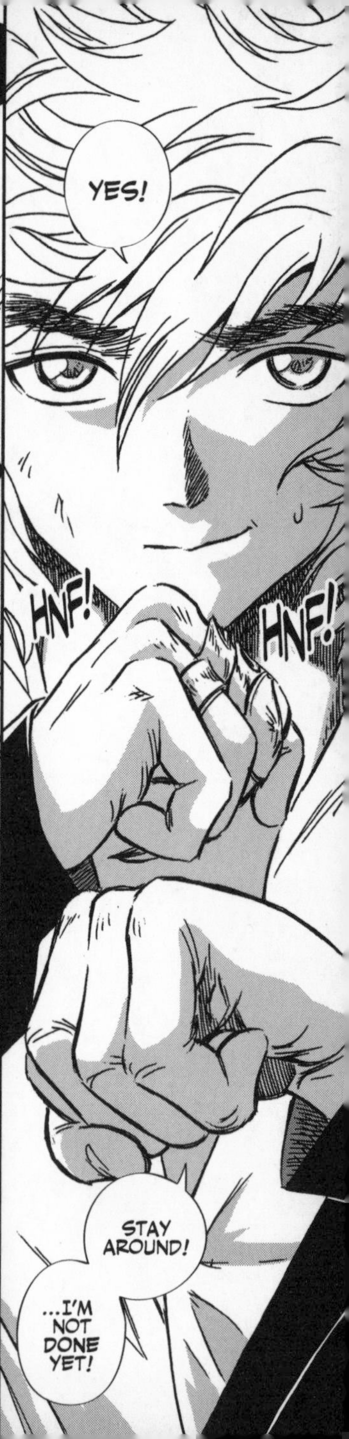
YES!
HNF!
HNF!
STAY AROUND!
...I'M NOT DONE YET!
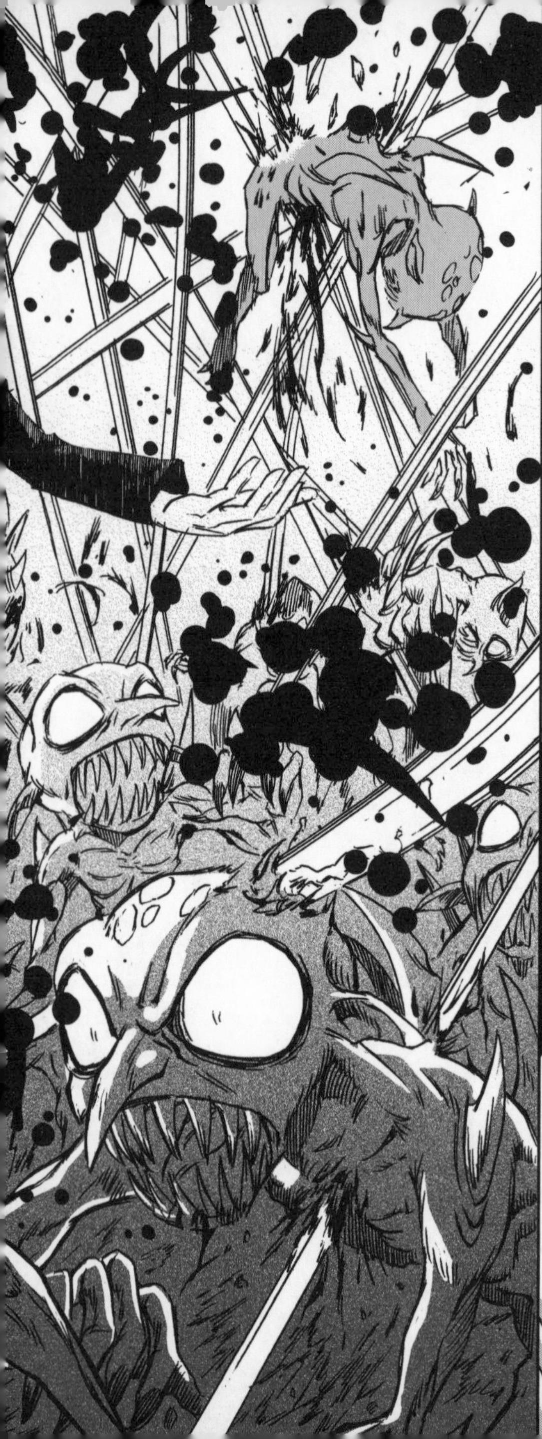

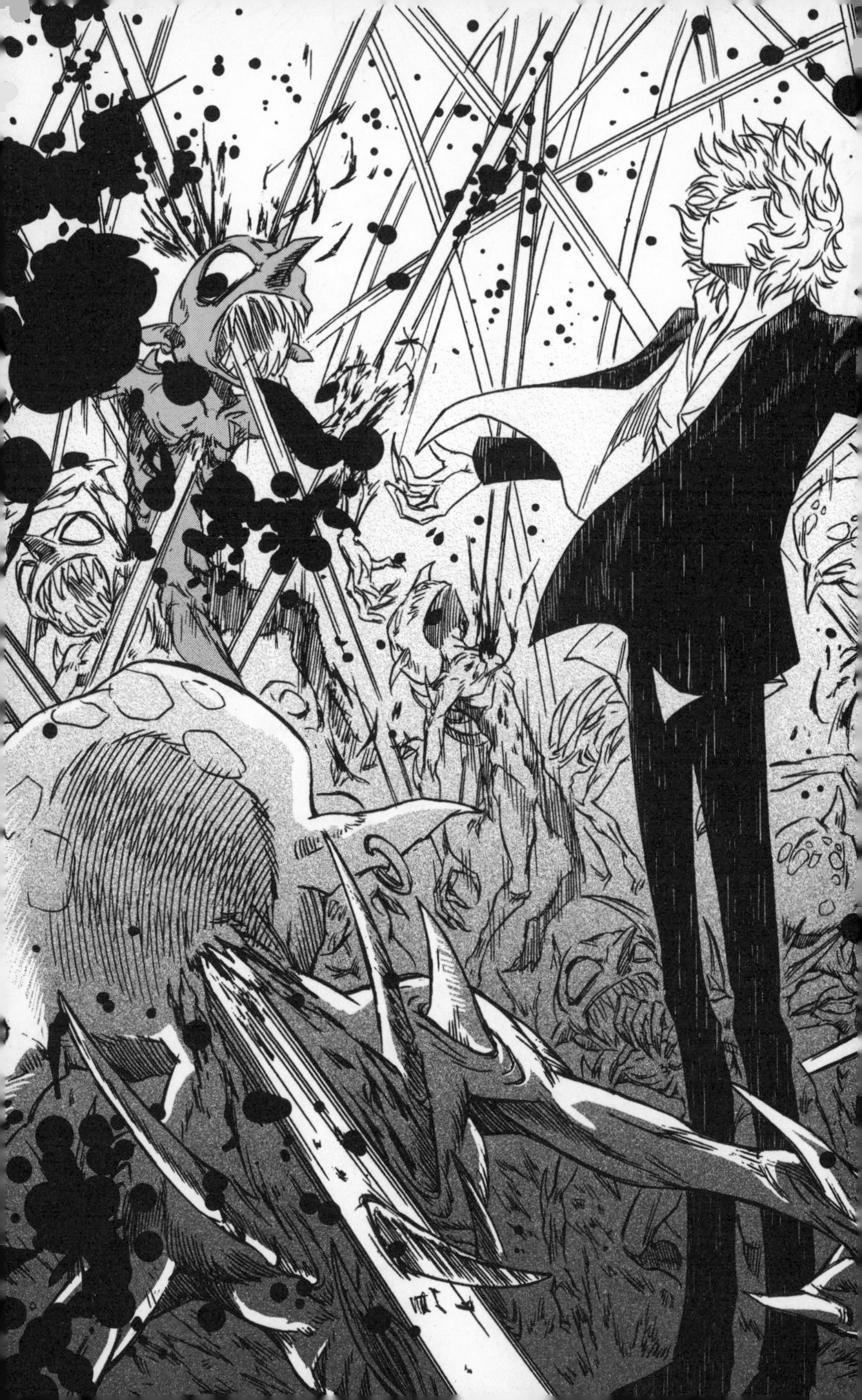

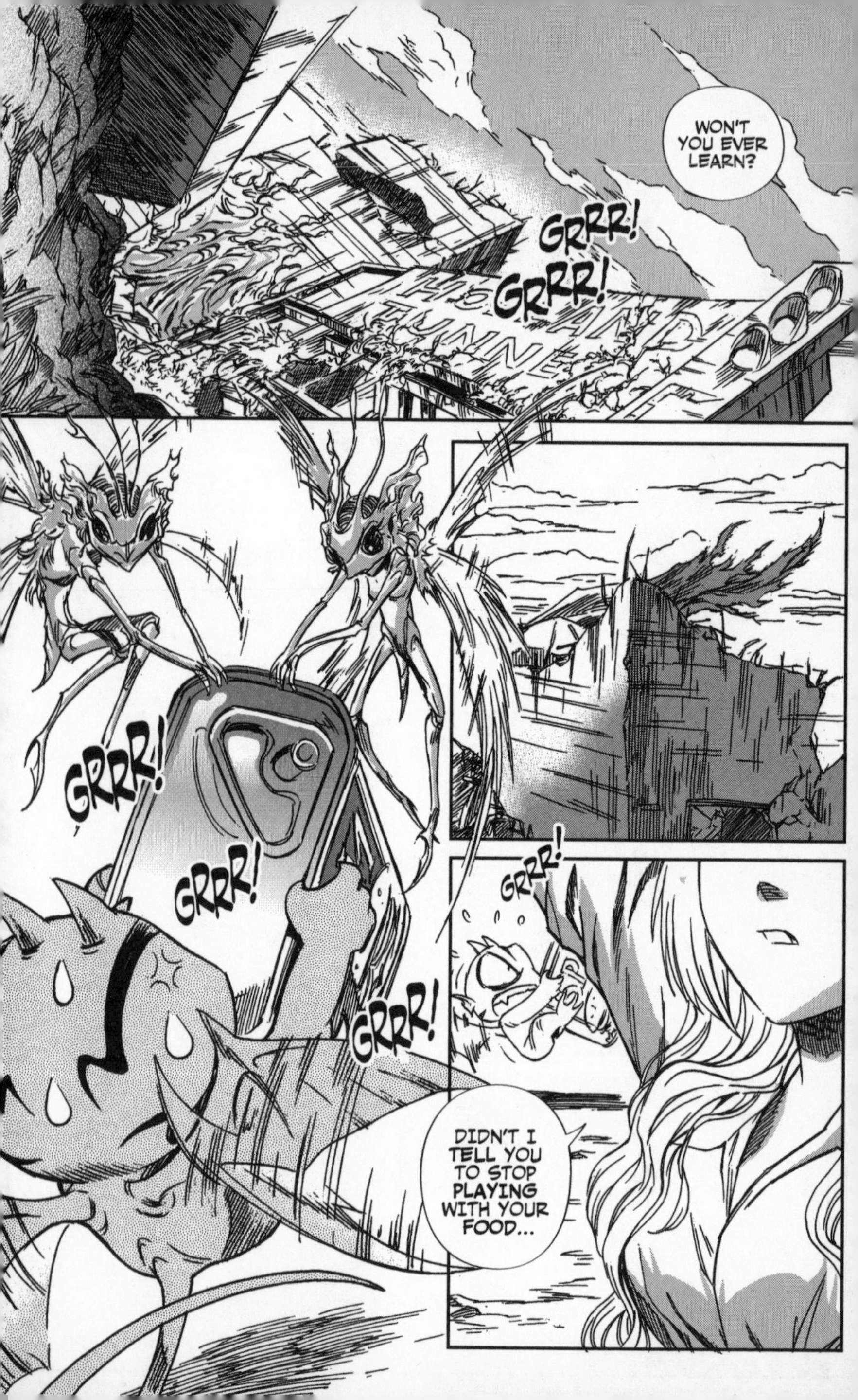
WON'T YOU EVER LEARN?
GRRR!
GRRR!
GRRR!
DIDN'T I TELL YOU TO STOP PLAYING WITH YOUR FOOD...
GRRR!
GRRR!
GRRR!

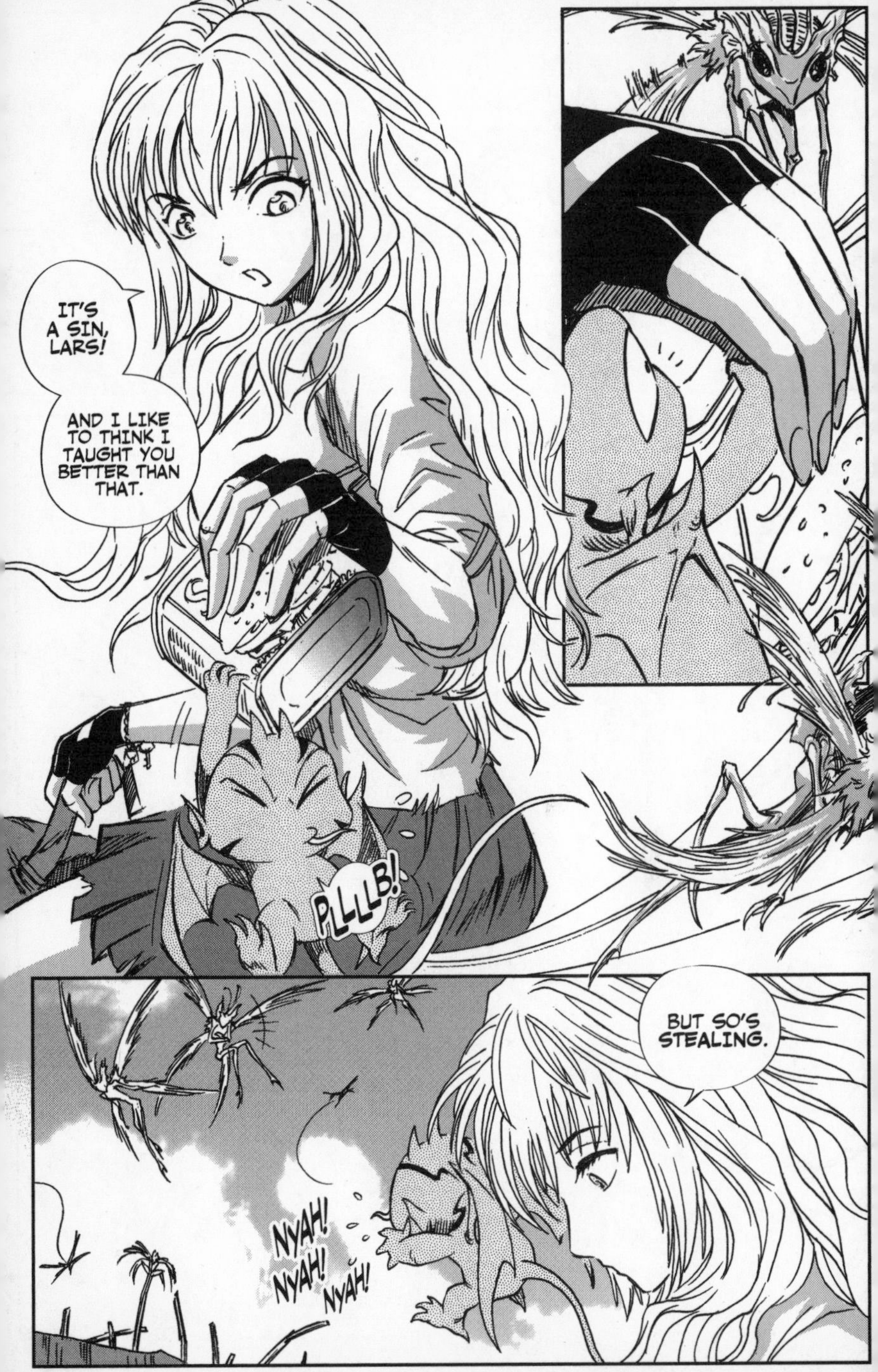
IT'S A SIN, LARS!
AND I LIKE TO THINK I TAUGHT YOU BETTER THAN THAT.
PLLLLB!
BUT SO'S STEALING.
NYAH! NYAH! NYAH!

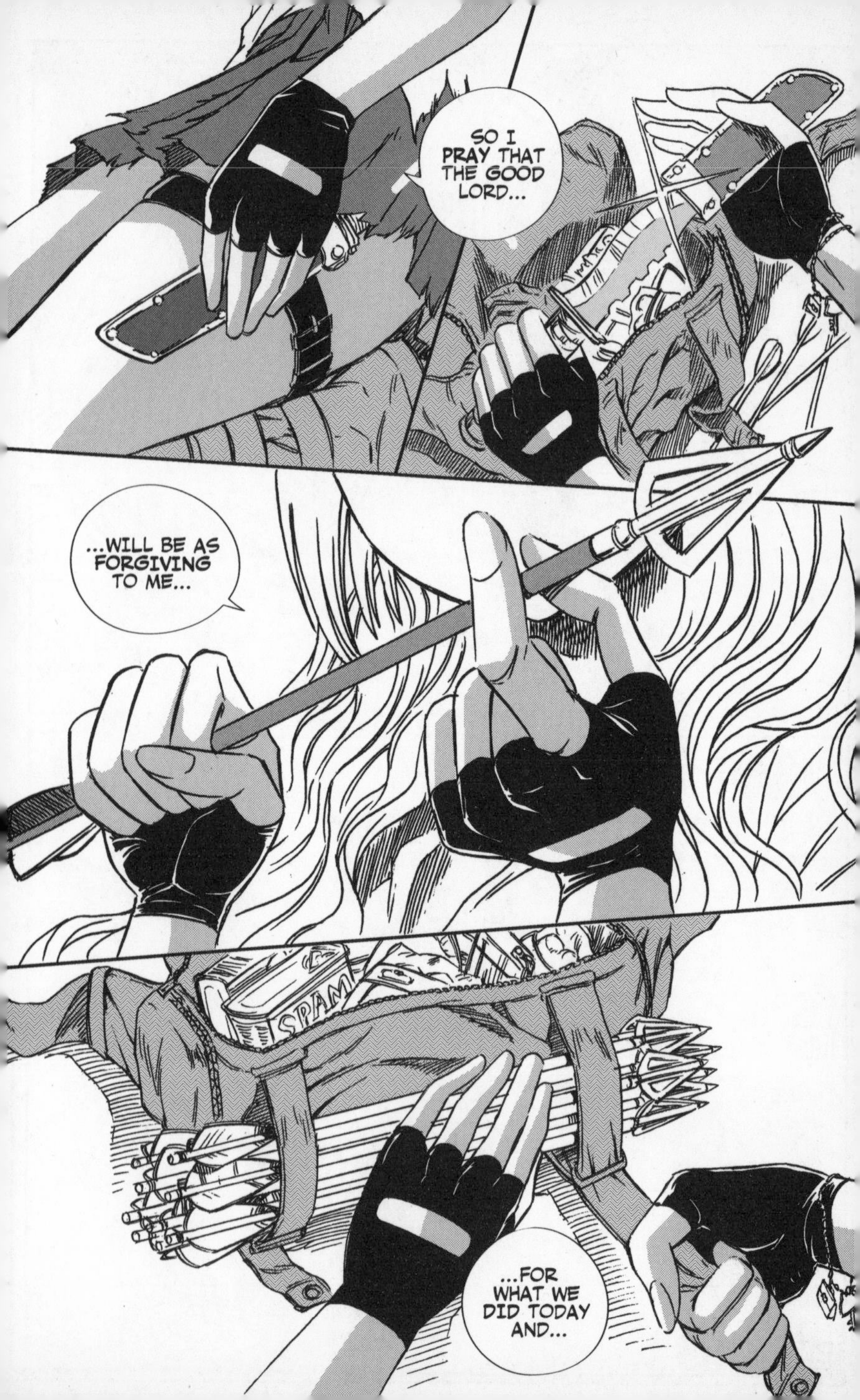
SO I PRAY THAT THE GOOD LORD...
...WILL BE AS FORGIVING TO ME...
SPAM
...FOR WHAT WE DID TODAY AND...

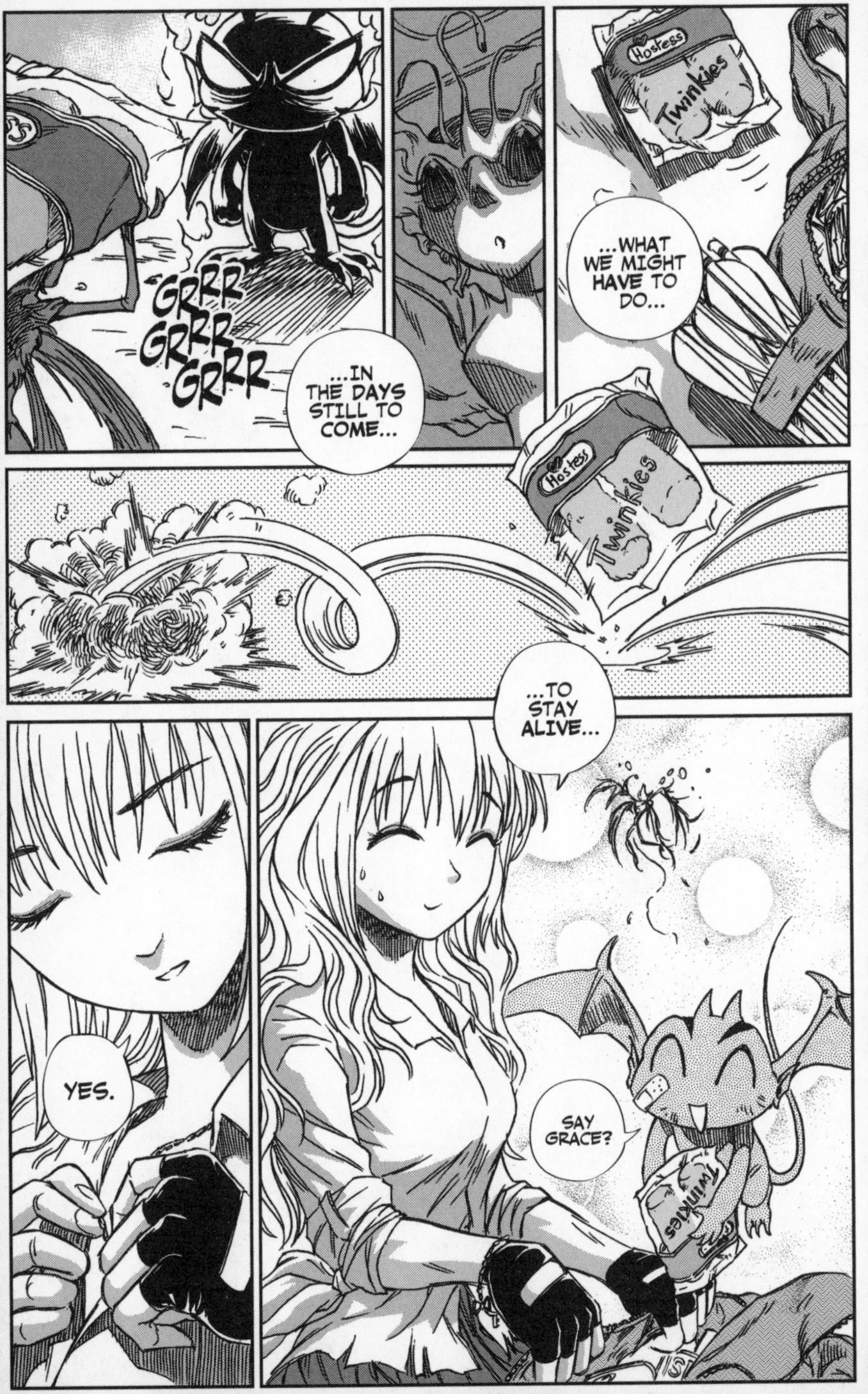
Hostess
Twinkies
...WHAT WE MIGHT HAVE TO DO...
...IN THE DAYS STILL TO COME...
GRRR GRRR GRRR
Hostess
Twinkies
...TO STAY ALIVE...
SAY GRACE?
Twinkies
YES.

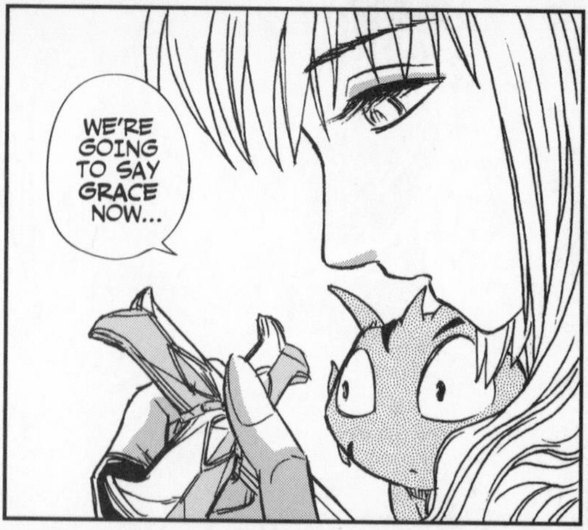
WE'RE GOING TO SAY GRACE NOW...

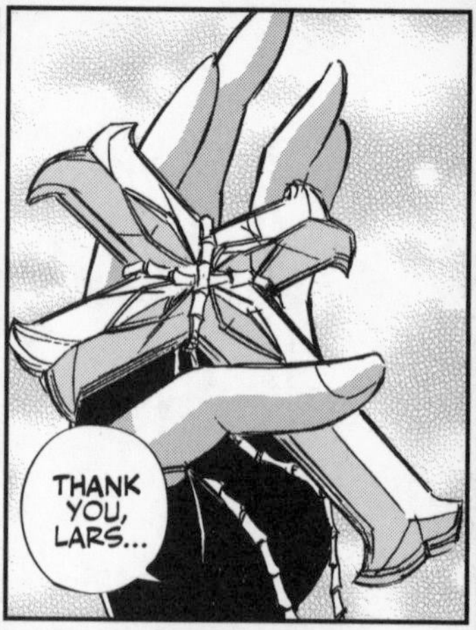
THANK YOU, LARS...

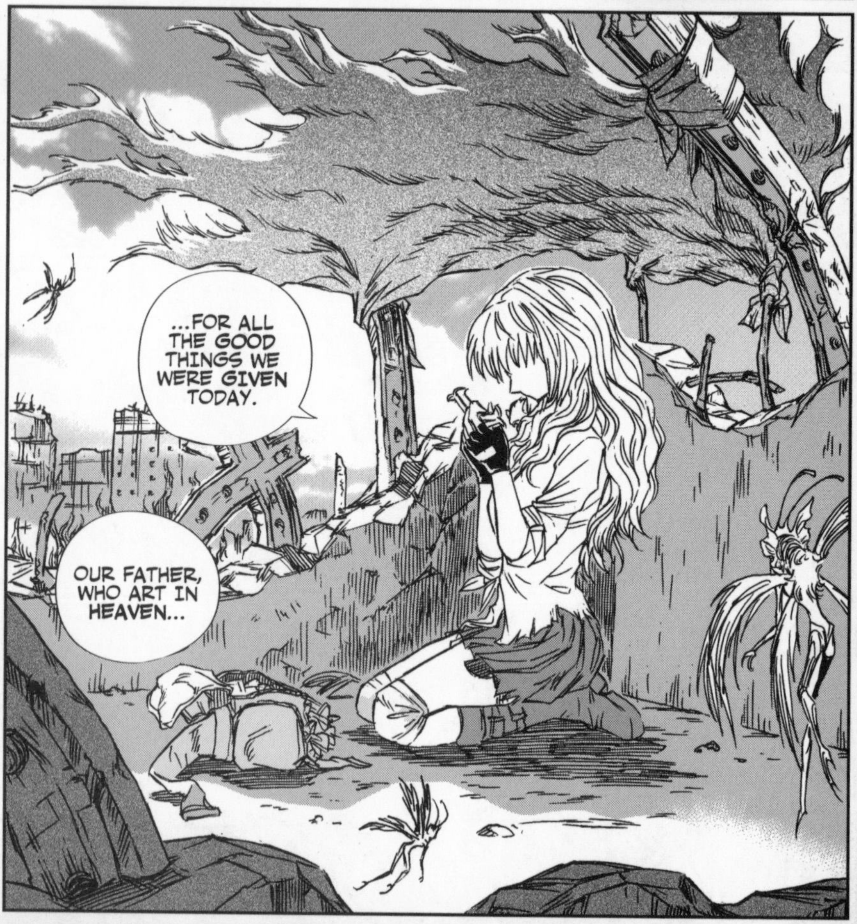
...FOR ALL THE GOOD THINGS WE WERE GIVEN TODAY.
OUR FATHER, WHO ART IN HEAVEN...

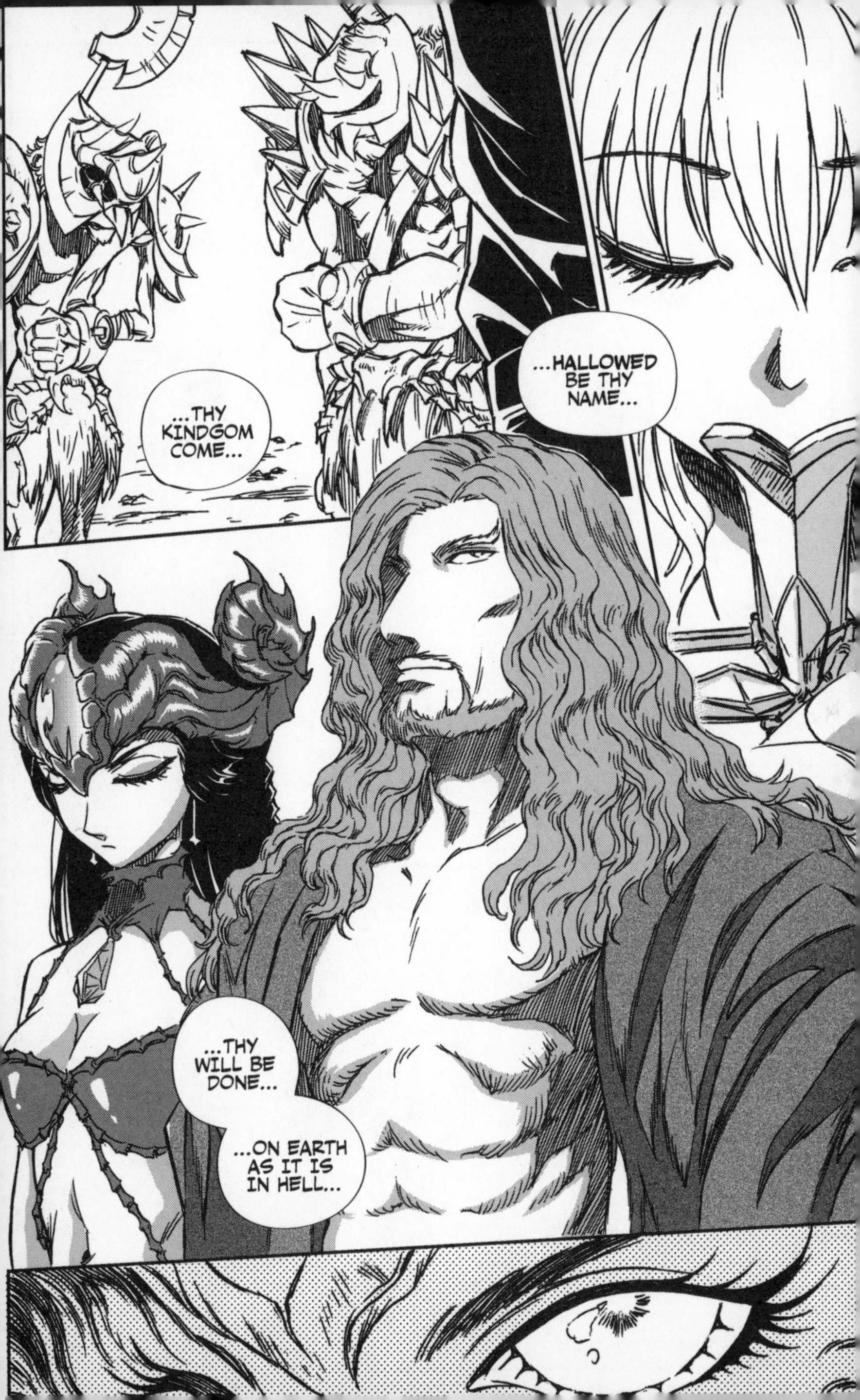
...HALLOWED BE THY NAME...
...THY KINDGOM COME...
...THY WILL BE DONE...
...ON EARTH AS IT IS IN HELL...

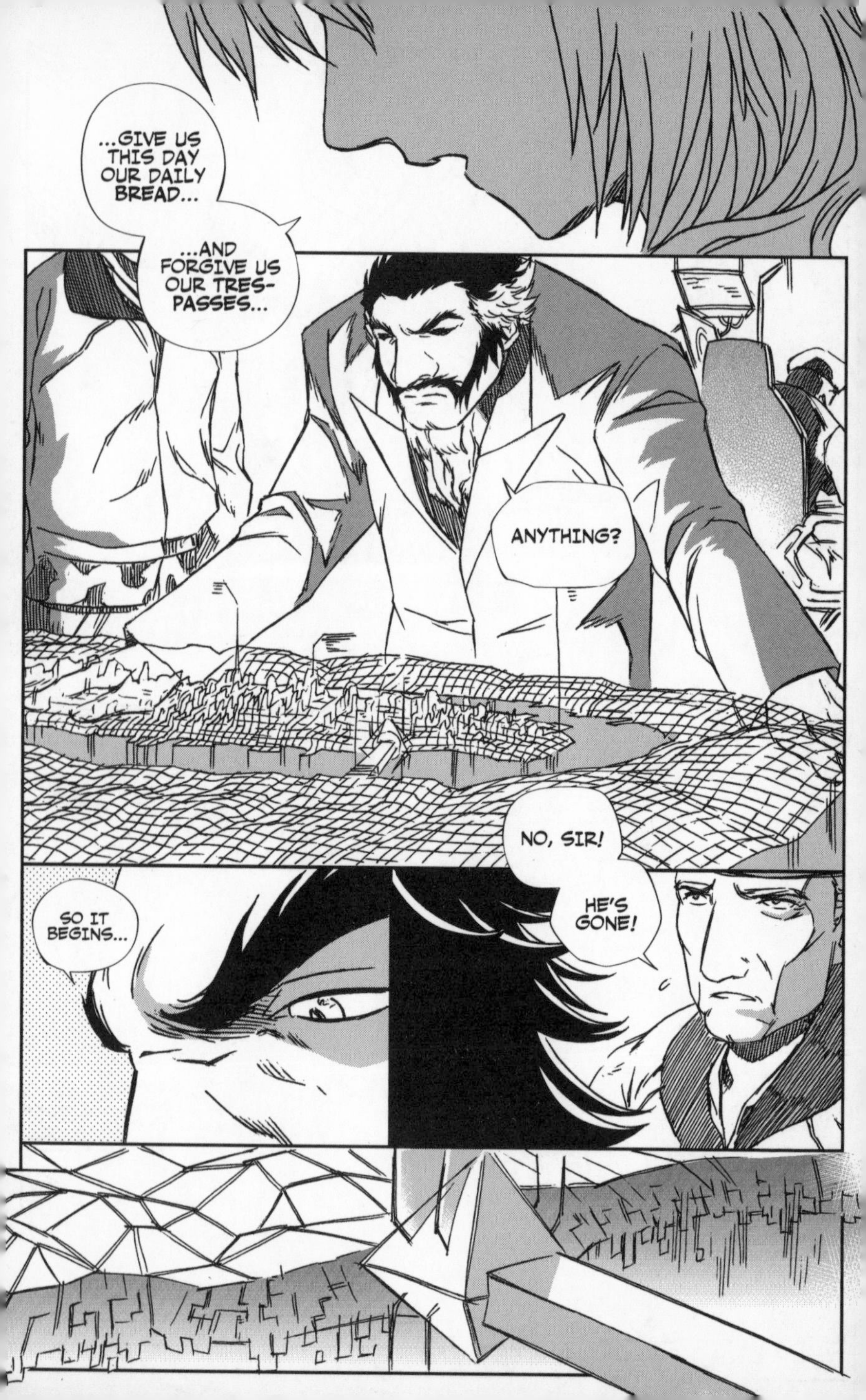
...GIVE US THIS DAY OUR DAILY BREAD...
...AND FORGIVE US OUR TRES-PASSES...
ANYTHING?
NO, SIR!
HE'S GONE!
SO IT BEGINS...

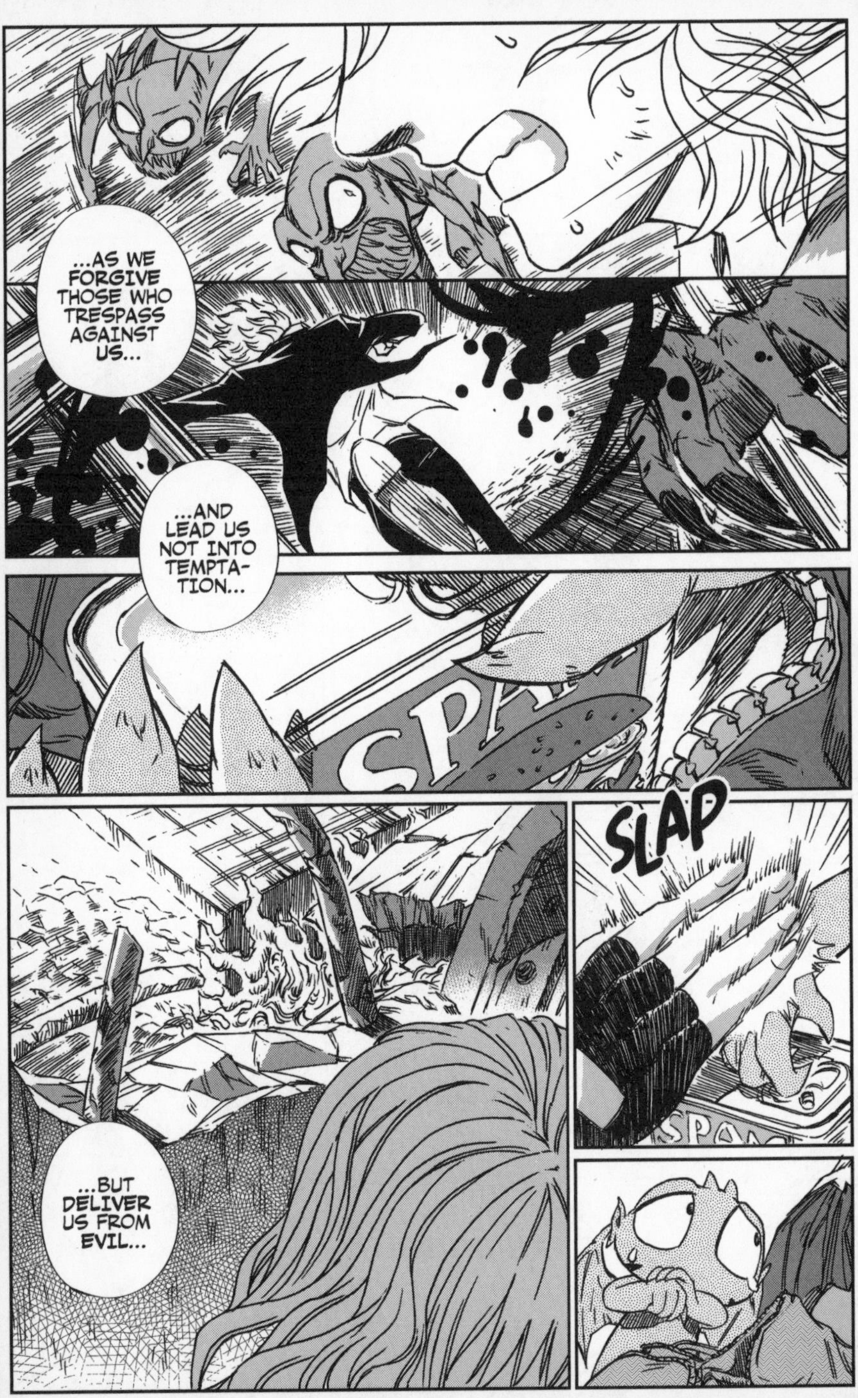
...AS WE FORGIVE THOSE WHO TRESPASS AGAINST US...
...AND LEAD US NOT INTO TEMPTA-TION...
SPA
...BUT DELIVER US FROM EVIL...
SLAP
SPA

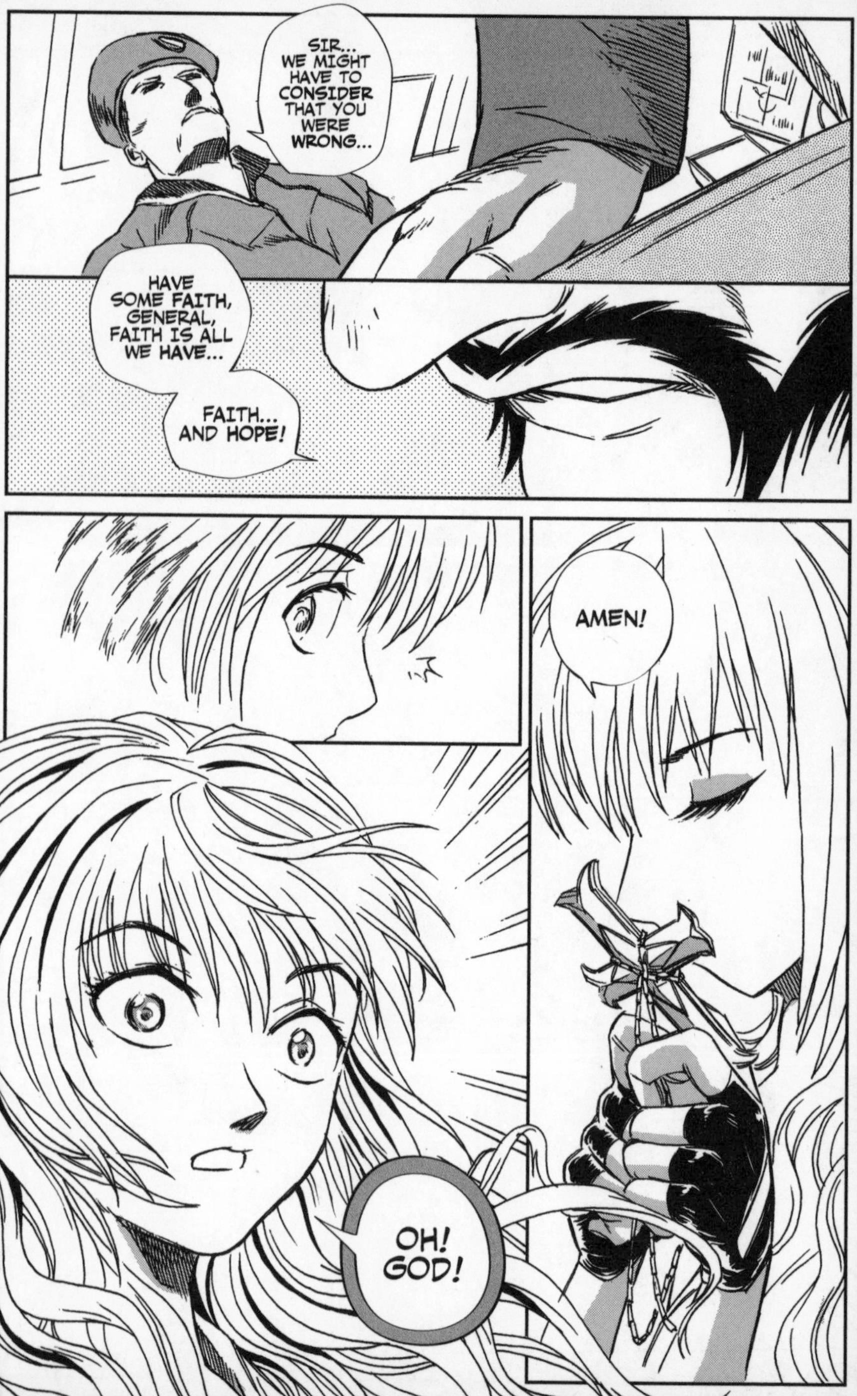
SIR... WE MIGHT HAVE TO CONSIDER THAT YOU WERE WRONG...
HAVE SOME FAITH, GENERAL, FAITH IS ALL WE HAVE...
FAITH... AND HOPE!
AMEN!
OH! GOD!

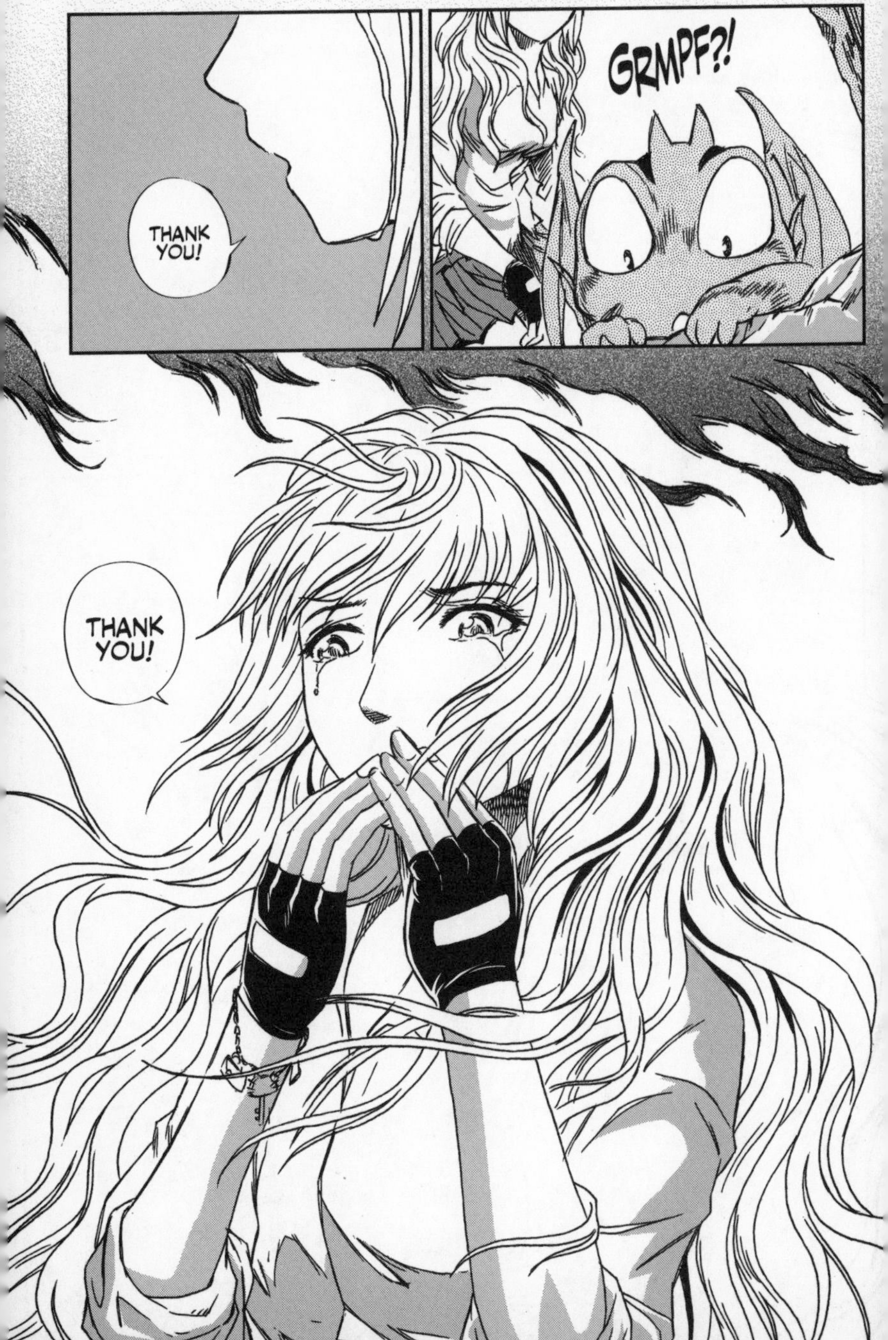
GRMPF?!
THANK YOU!
THANK YOU!

CHAPTER 3

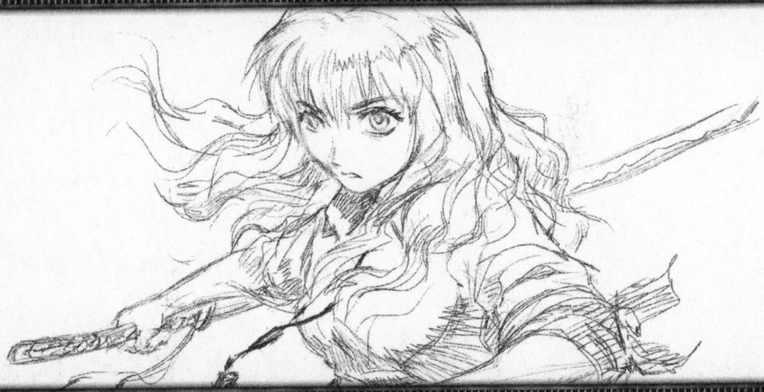

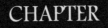

HOPE IN HELL

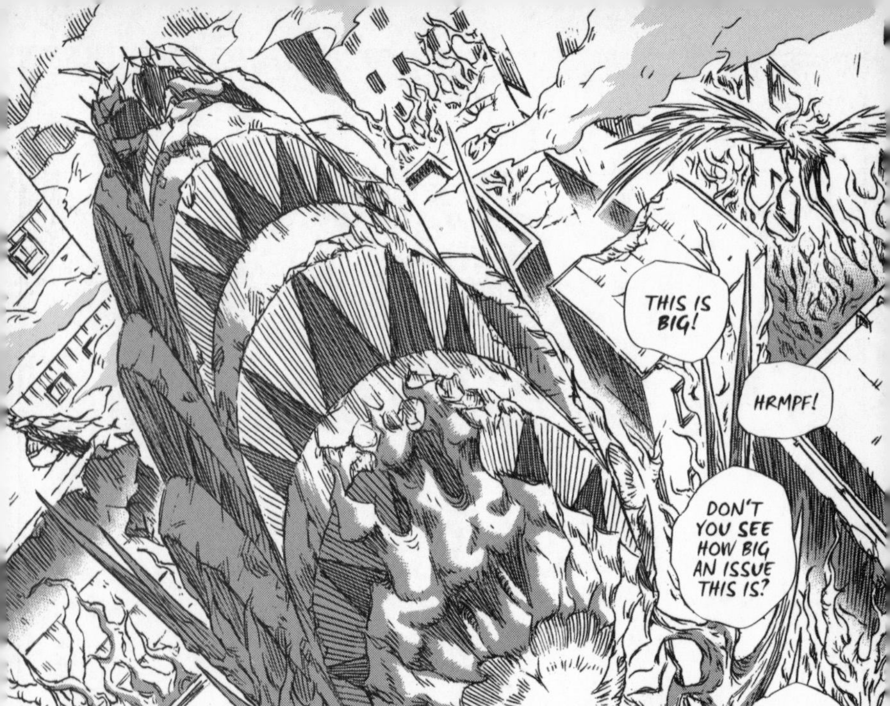
THIS IS BIG!
HRMPF!
DON'T YOU SEE HOW BIG AN ISSUE THIS IS?
HRMPF!
NO.
NO, I DON'T SEE THAT!
GUILDENFANG, WOULD YOU JUST...
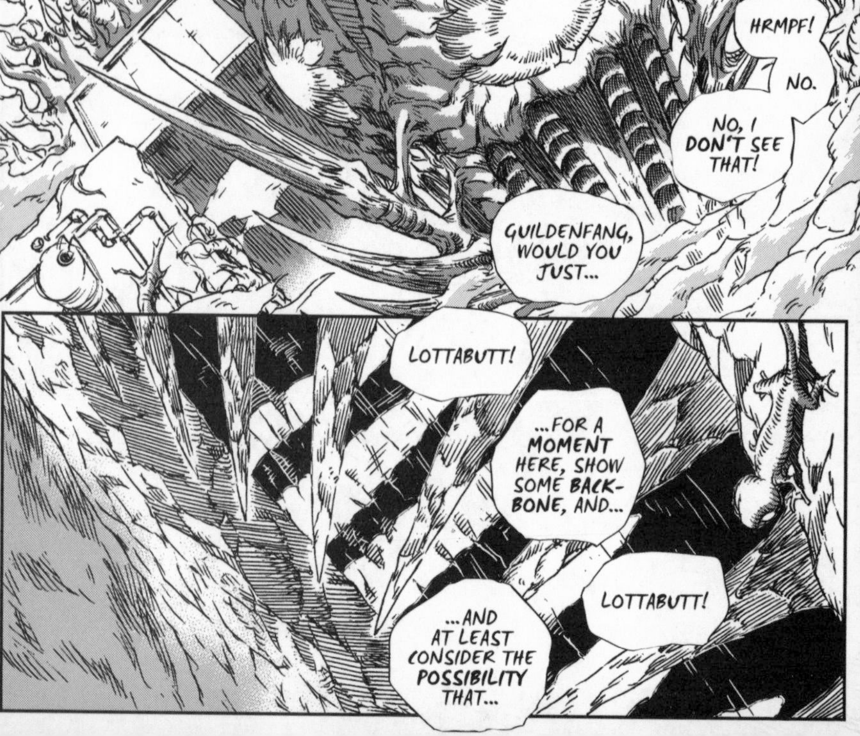
LOTTABUTT!
...FOR A MOMENT HERE, SHOW SOME BACK-BONE, AND...
LOTTABUTT!
...AND AT LEAST CONSIDER THE POSSIBILITY THAT...

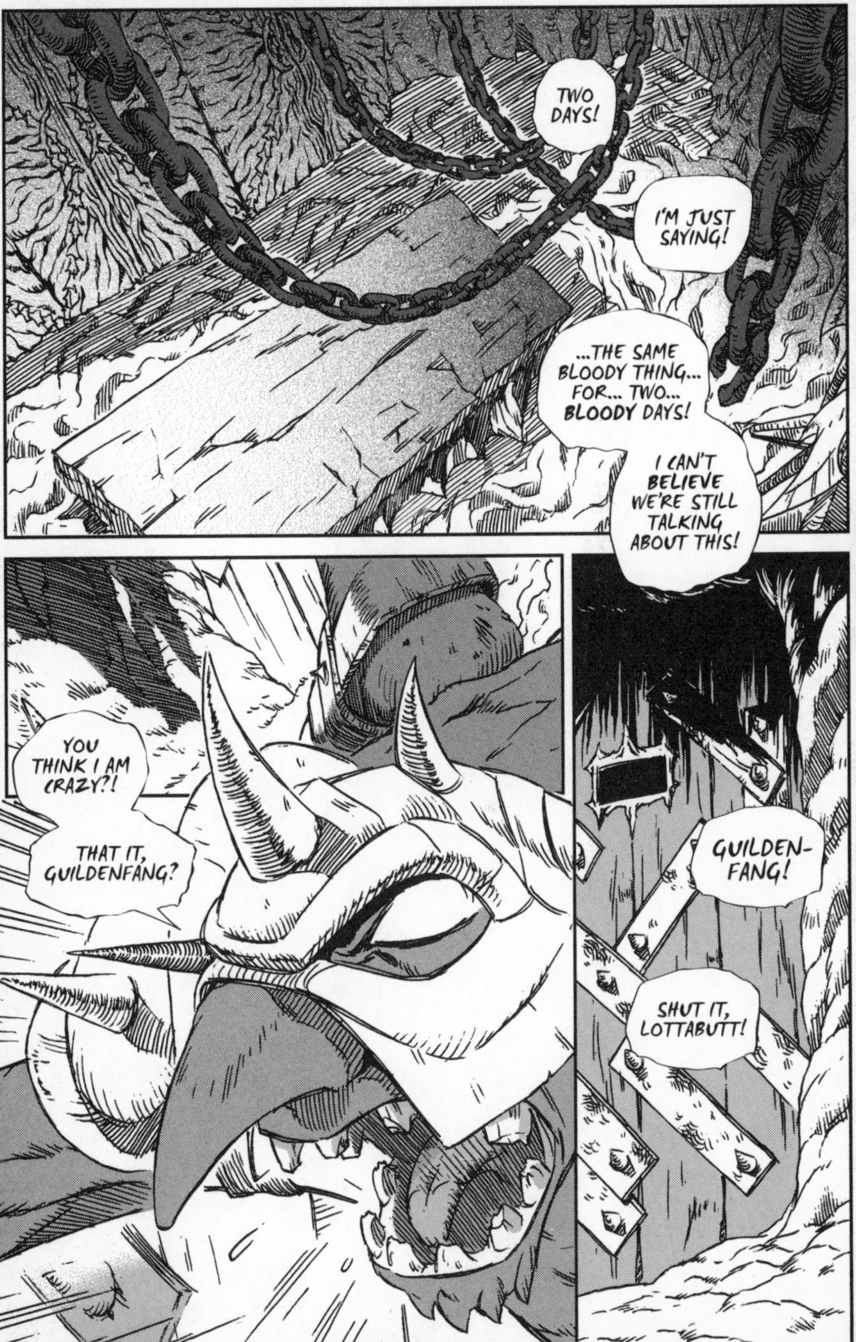
TWO DAYS!
I'M JUST SAYING!
...THE SAME BLOODY THING... FOR... TWO... BLOODY DAYS!
I CAN'T BELIEVE WE'RE STILL TALKING ABOUT THIS!
YOU THINK I AM CRAZY?!
THAT IT, GUILDENFANG?
GUILDEN-FANG!
SHUT IT, LOTTABUTT!

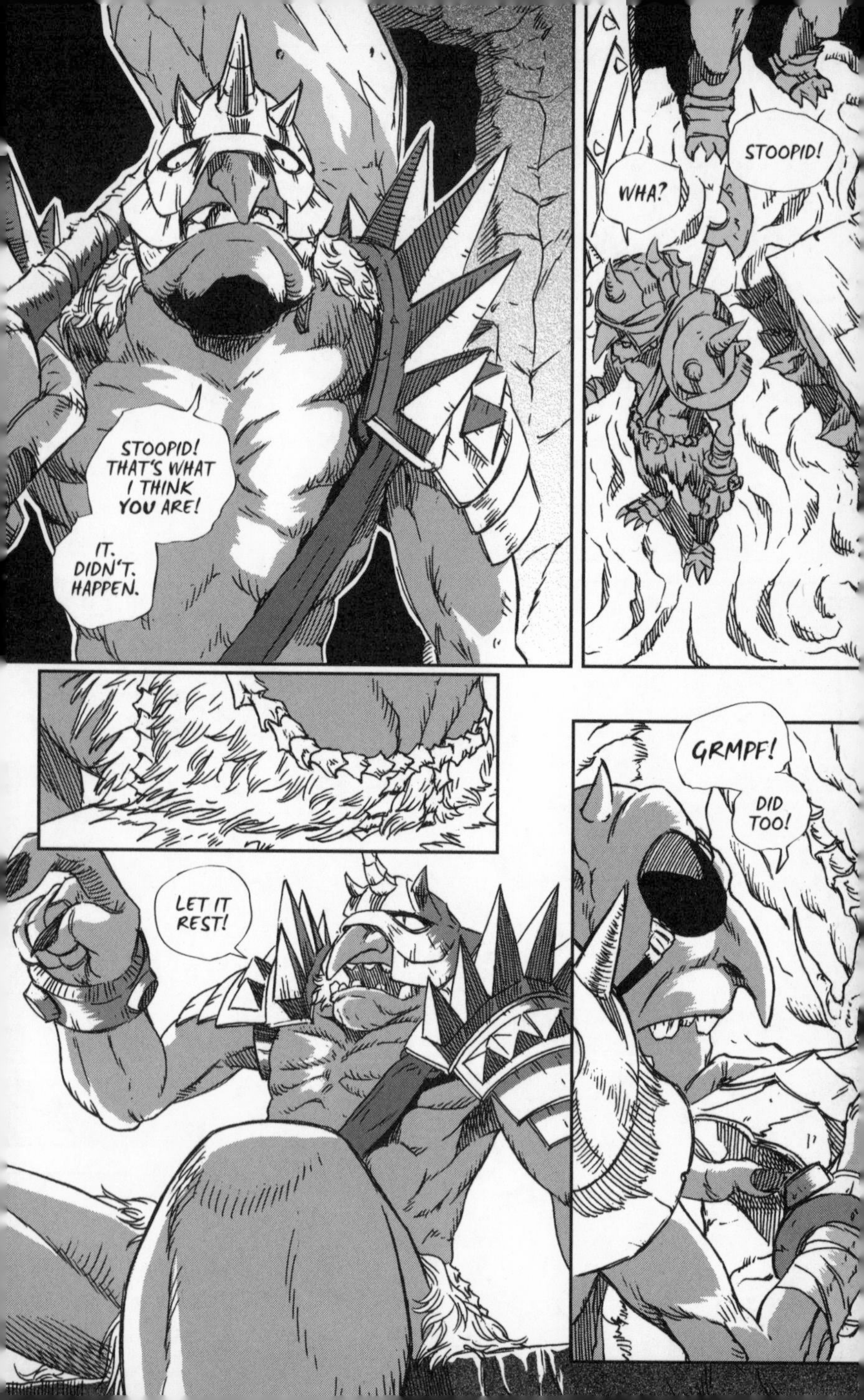
STOOPID!
WHA?
STOOPID! THAT'S WHAT I THINK YOU ARE!
IT. DIDN'T. HAPPEN.
GRMPF!
DID TOO!
LET IT REST!

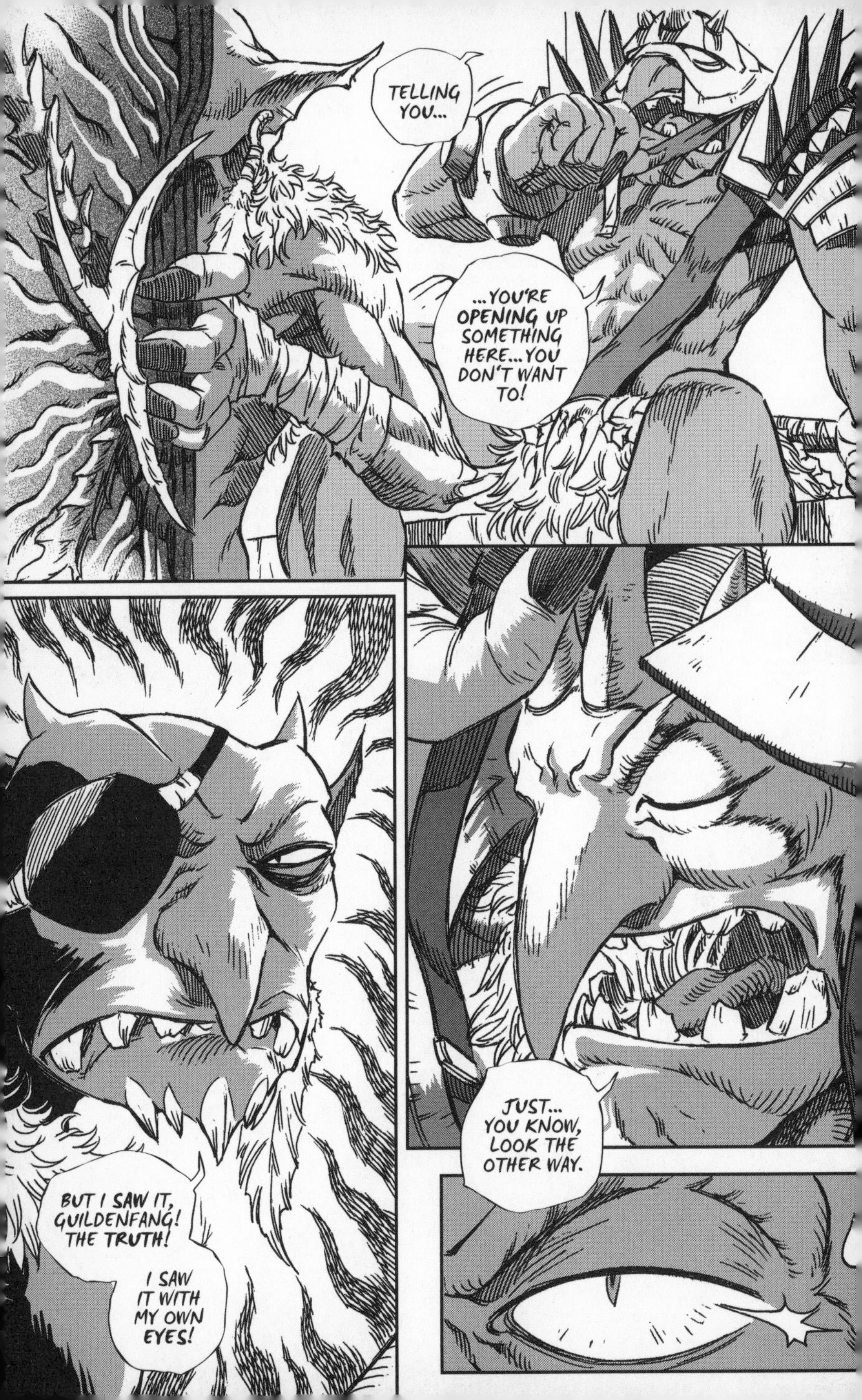
TELLING YOU...
...YOU'RE OPENING UP SOMETHING HERE...YOU DON'T WANT TO!
JUST... YOU KNOW, LOOK THE OTHER WAY.
BUT I SAW IT, GUILDENFANG! THE TRUTH!
I SAW IT WITH MY OWN EYES!

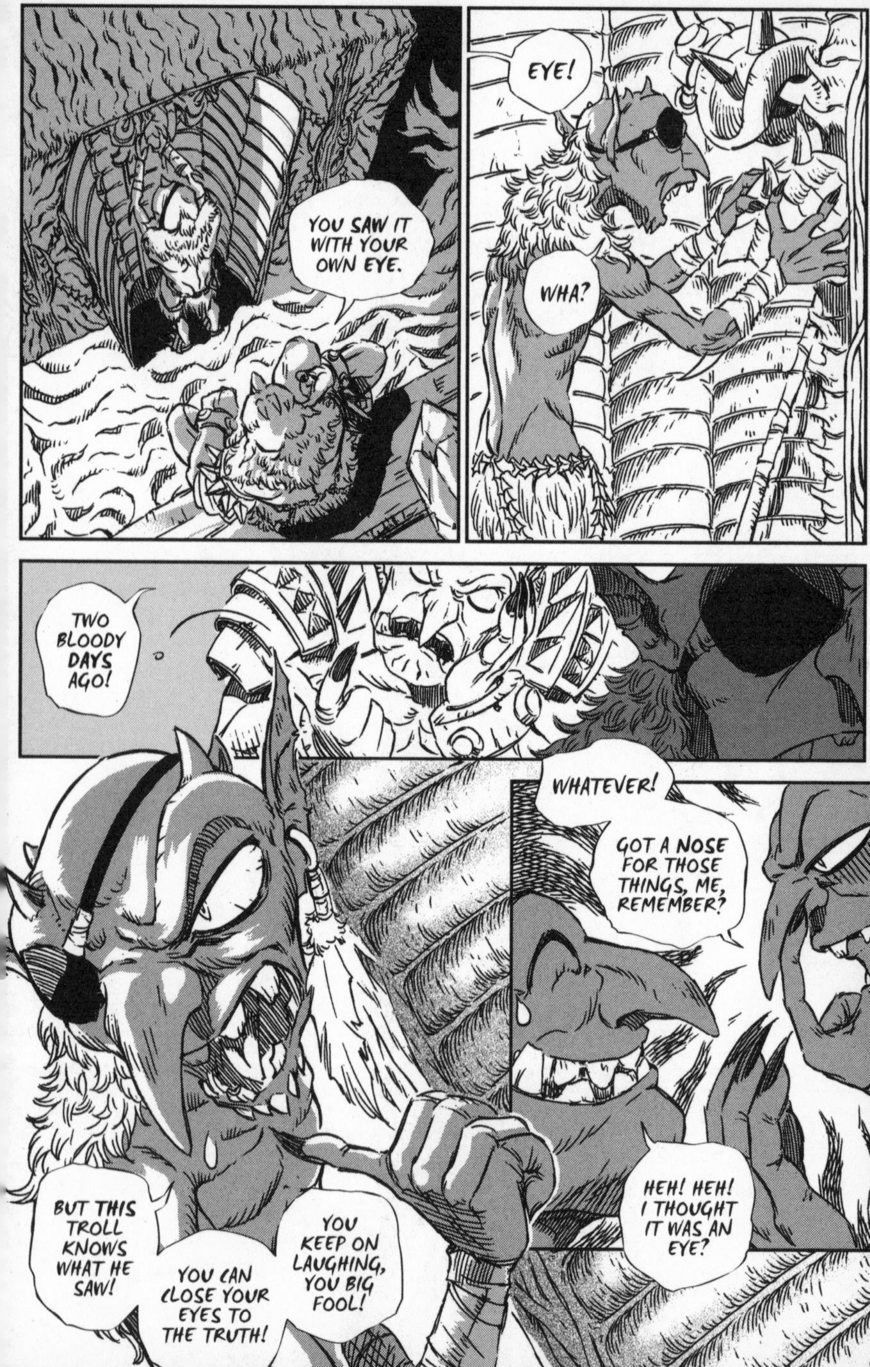
YOU SAW IT WITH YOUR OWN EYE.
EYE!
WHA?
TWO BLOODY DAYS AGO!
BUT THIS TROLL KNOWS WHAT HE SAW!
YOU CAN CLOSE YOUR EYES TO THE TRUTH!
YOU KEEP ON LAUGHING, YOU BIG FOOL!
WHATEVER!
GOT A NOSE FOR THOSE THINGS, ME, REMEMBER?
HEH! HEH! I THOUGHT IT WAS AN EYE?

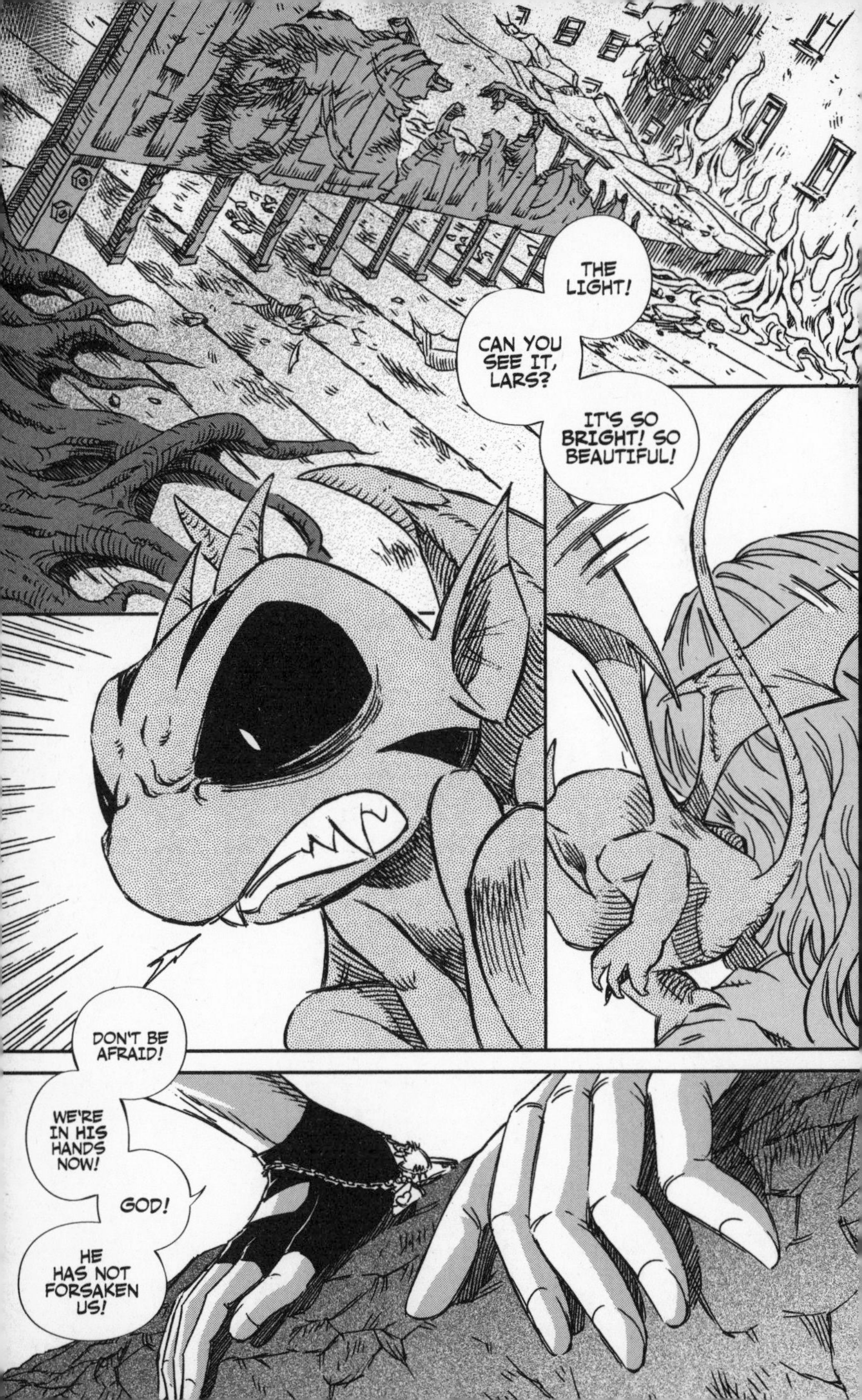
THE LIGHT!
CAN YOU SEE IT, LARS?
IT'S SO BRIGHT! SO BEAUTIFUL!
DON'T BE AFRAID!
WE'RE IN HIS HANDS NOW!
GOD!
HE HAS NOT FORSAKEN US!

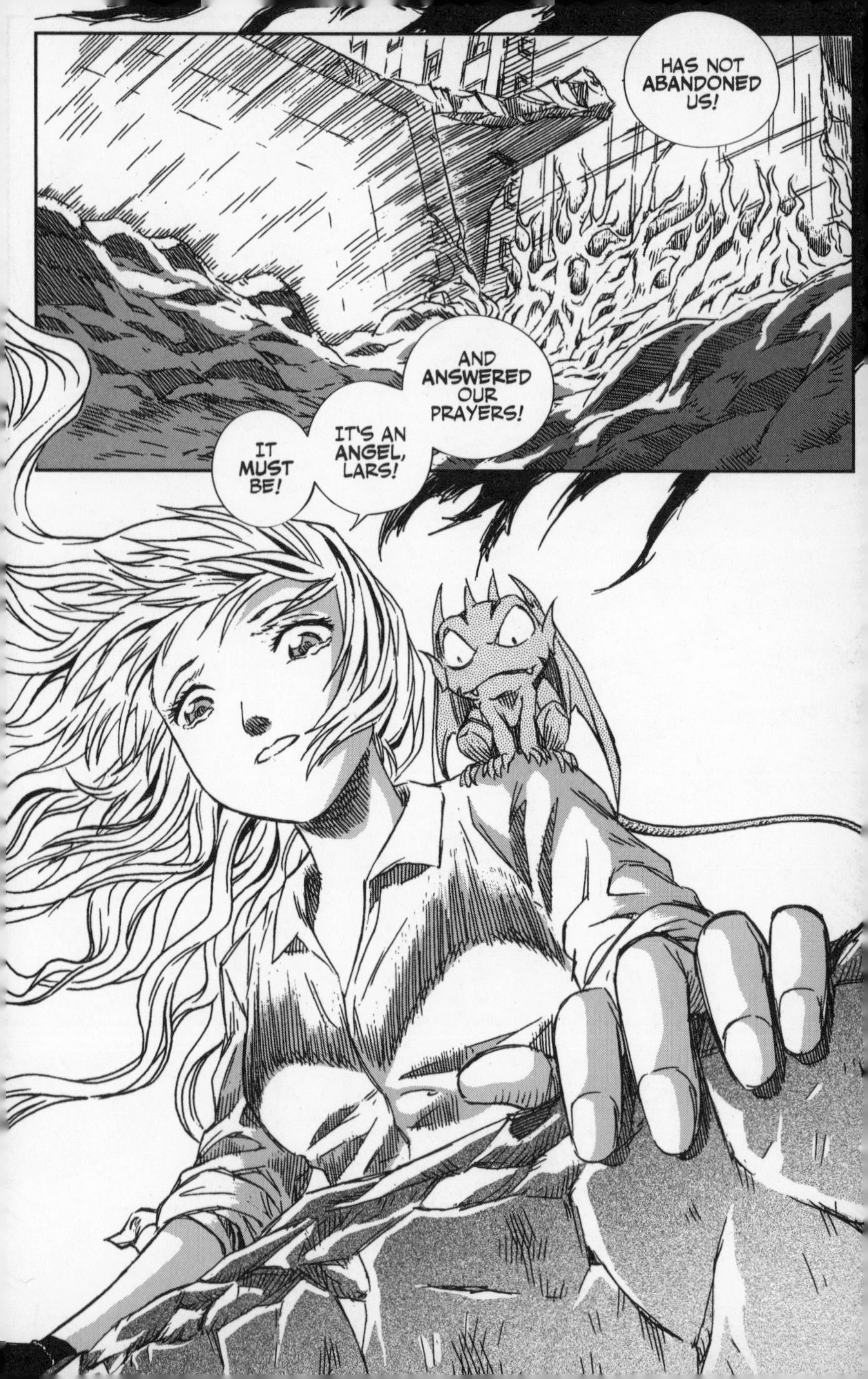
HAS NOT ABANDONED US!
AND ANSWERED OUR PRAYERS!
IT'S AN ANGEL, LARS!
IT MUST BE!

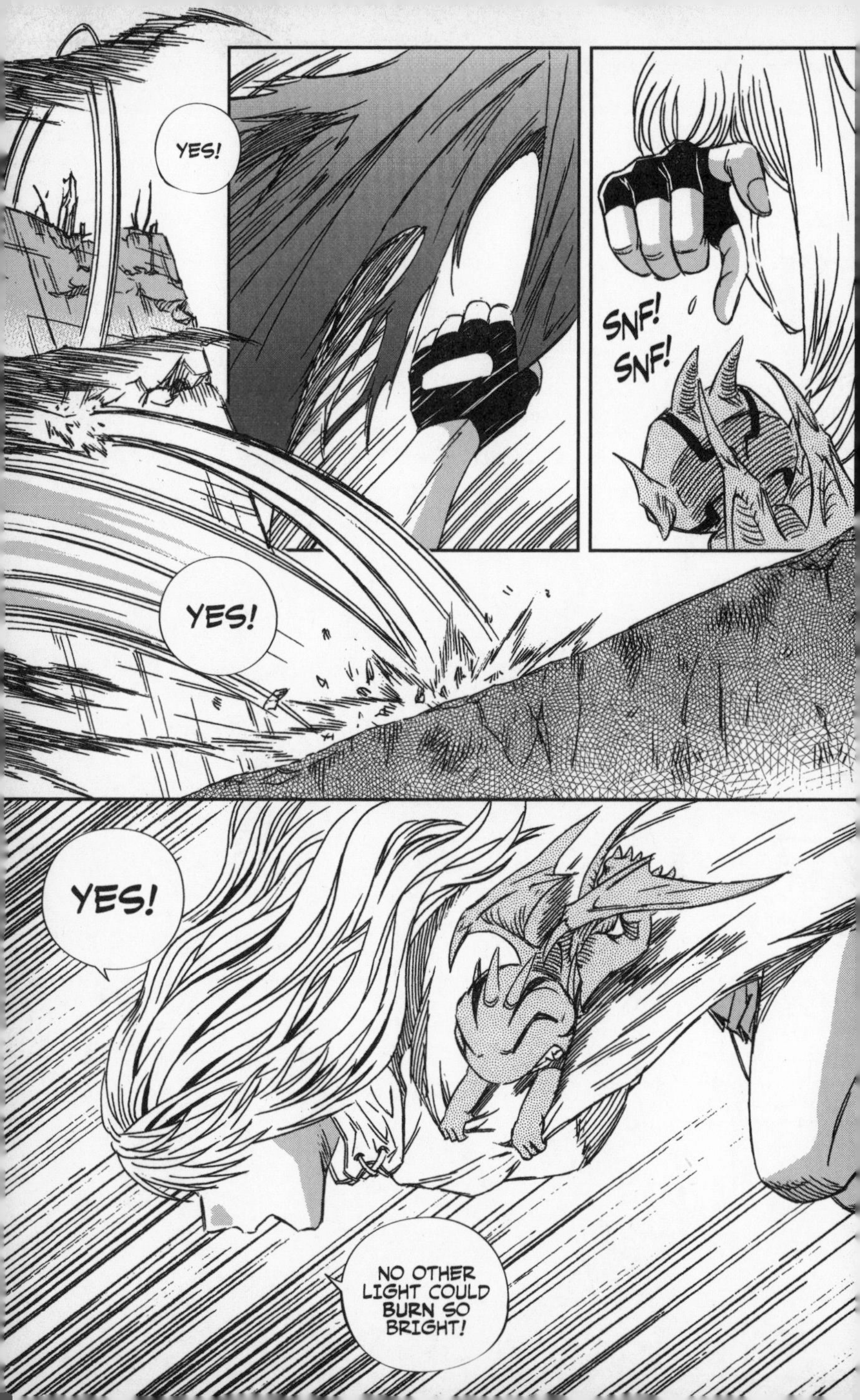
SNF! SNF!
YES!
YES!
YES!
NO OTHER LIGHT COULD BURN SO BRIGHT!

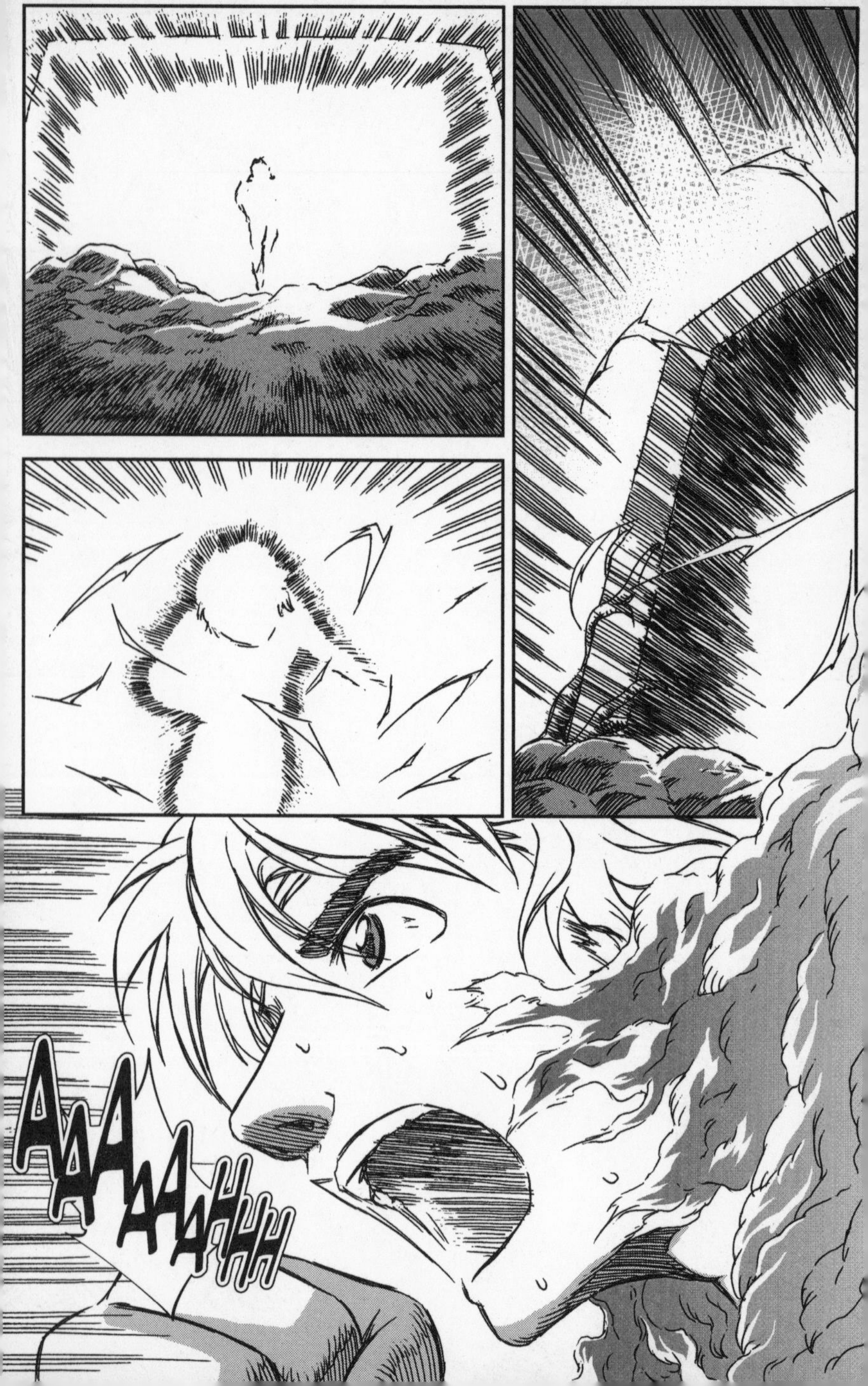
AAAAAAAHHHH

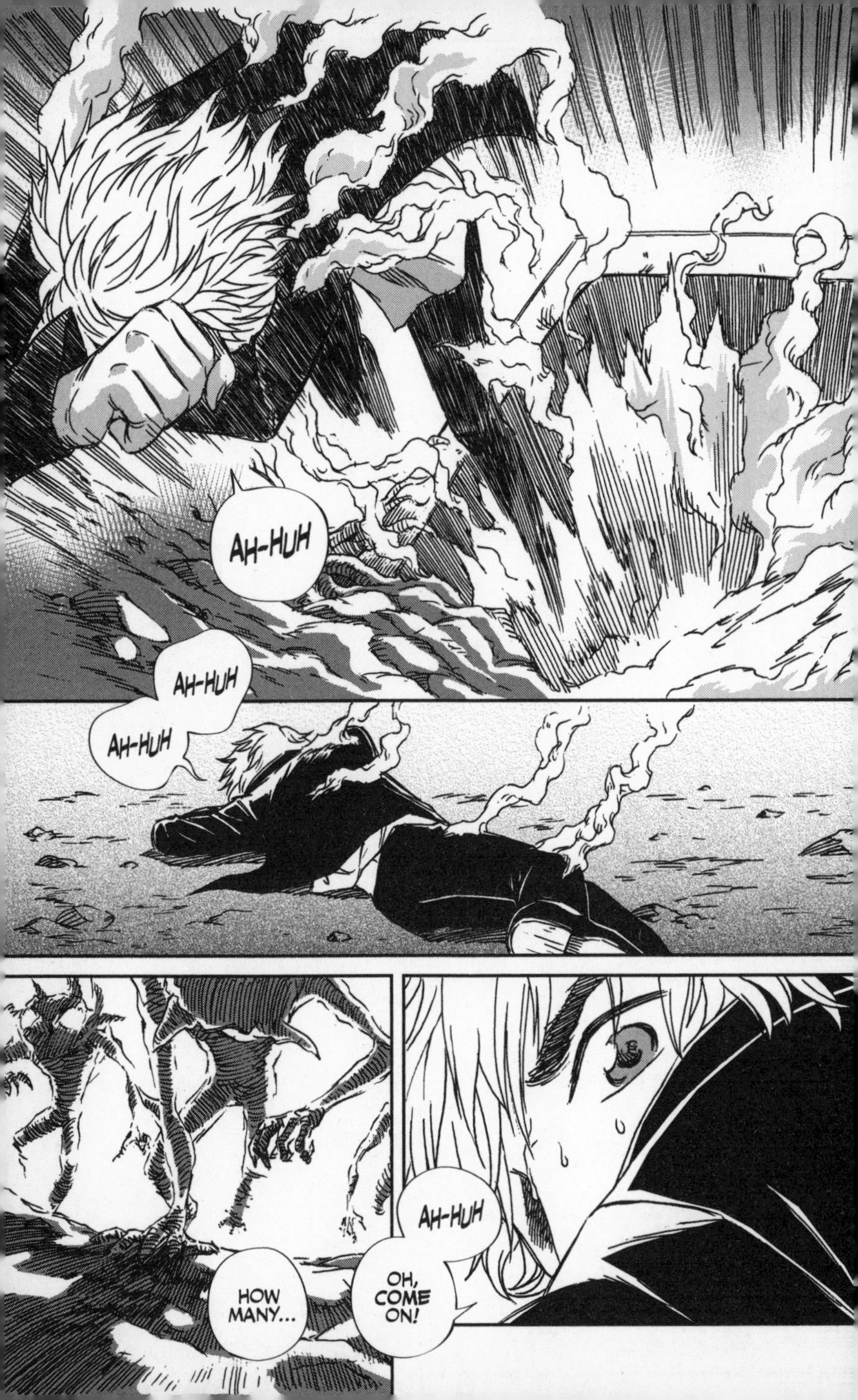
AH-HUH
AH-HUH
AH-HUH
AH-HUH
OH, COME ON!
HOW MANY...

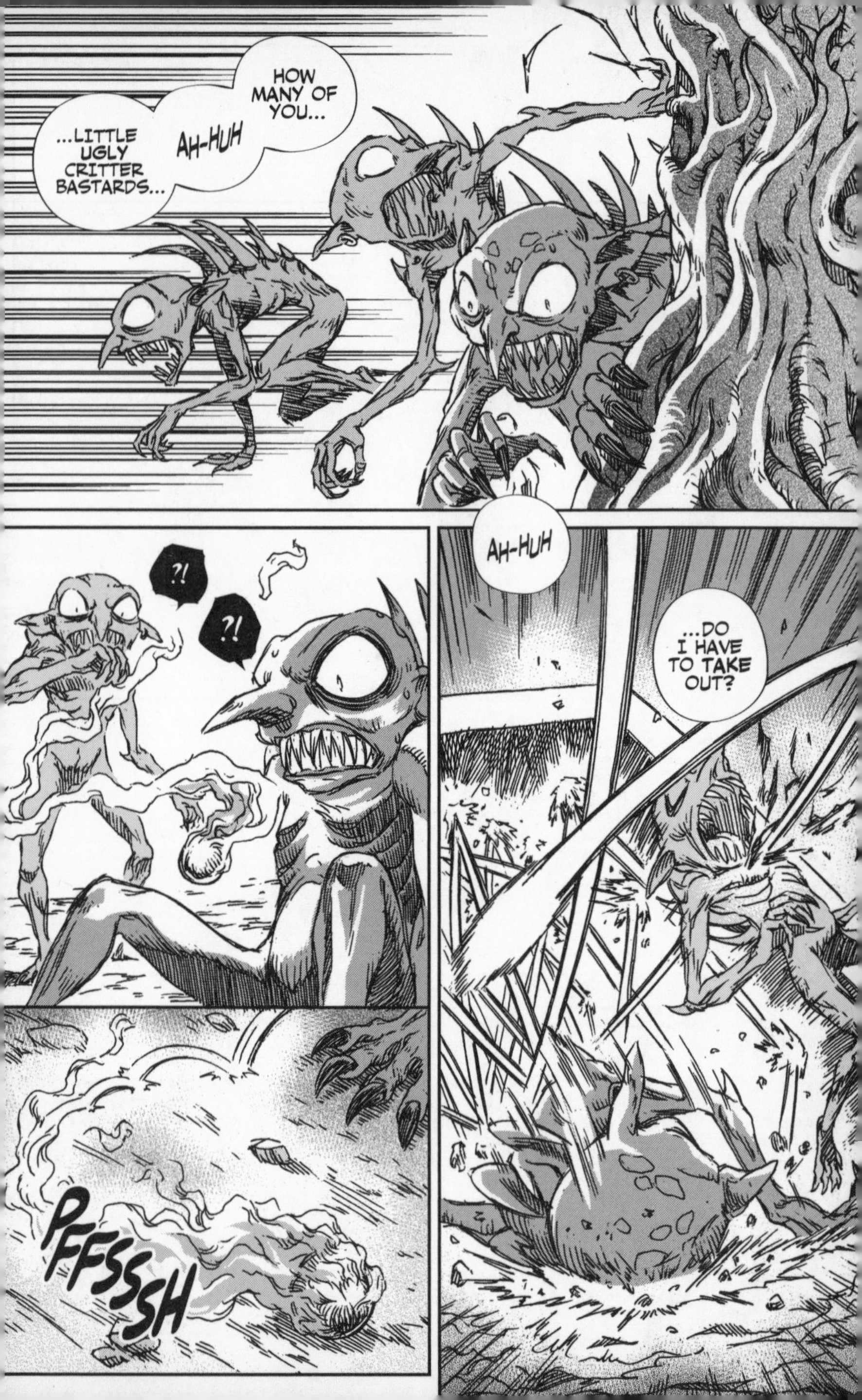
HOW MANY OF YOU...
AH-HUH
...LITTLE UGLY CRITTER BASTARDS...
AH-HUH
...DO I HAVE TO TAKE OUT?
?!
?!
PFFSSSH

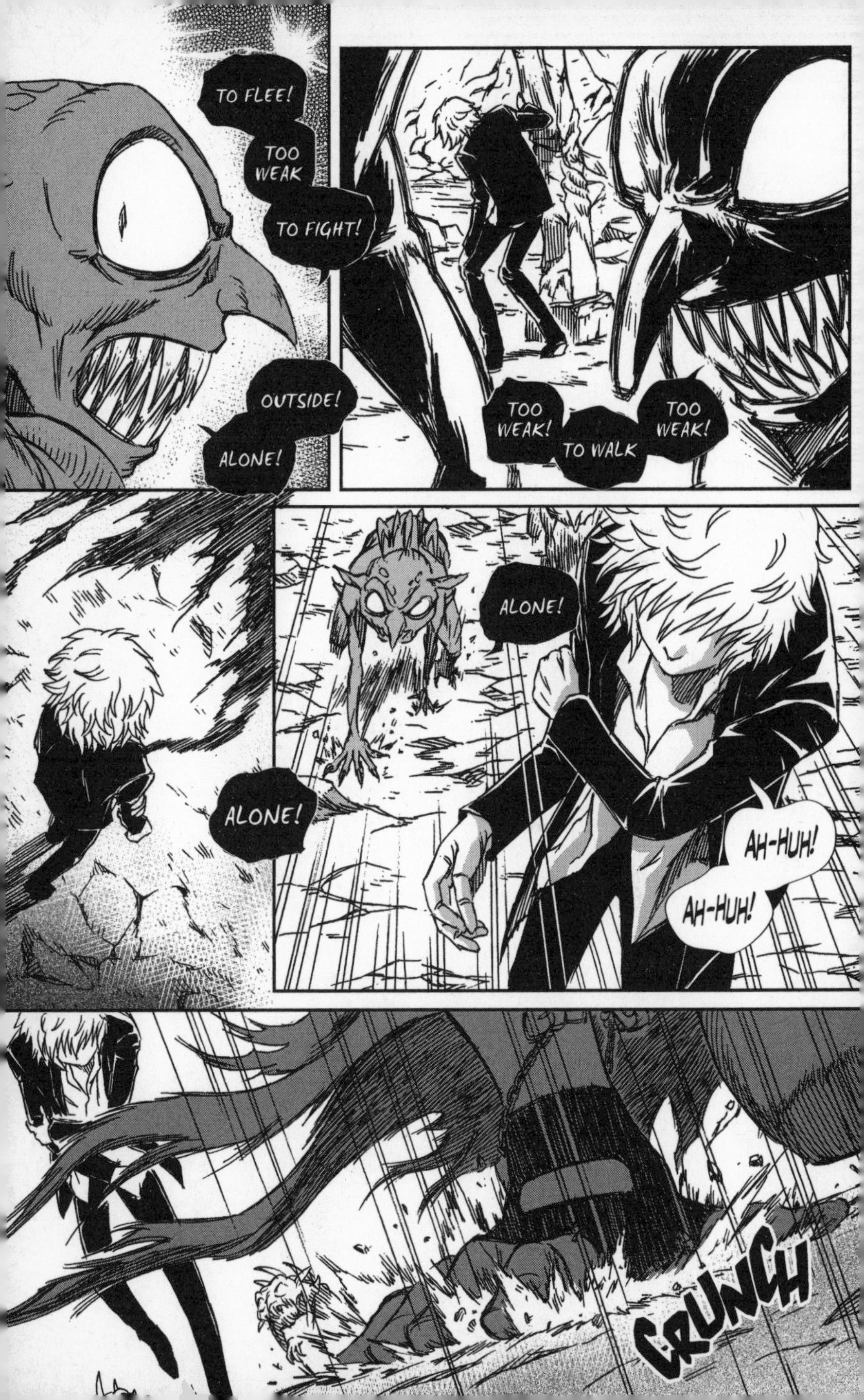
TO FLEE!
TOO WEAK
TO FIGHT!
OUTSIDE!
ALONE!
TOO WEAK!
TO WALK
TOO WEAK!
ALONE!
ALONE!
AH-HUH!
AH-HUH!
CRUNCH

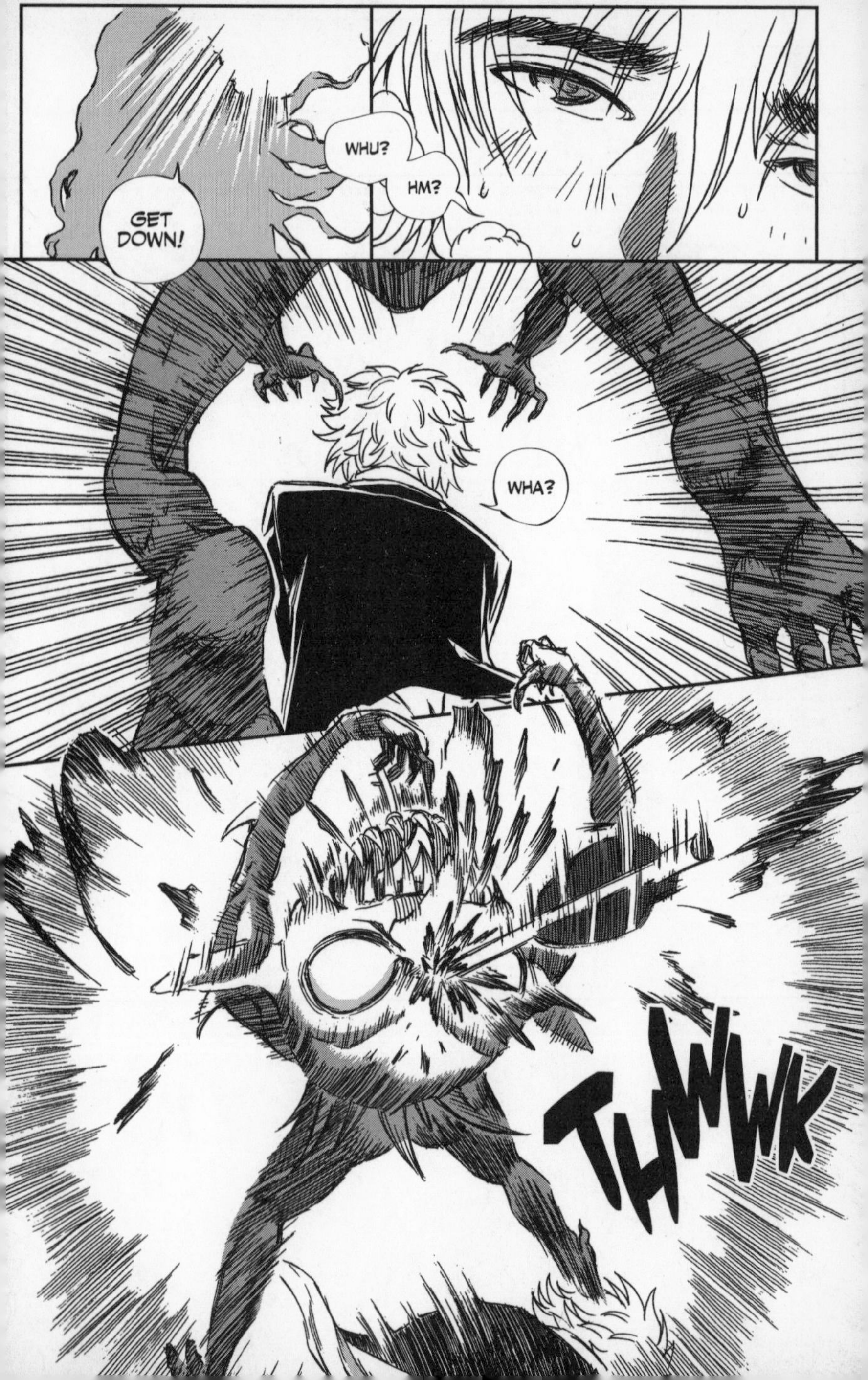
WHU?
HM?
GET DOWN!
WHA?
THWWK

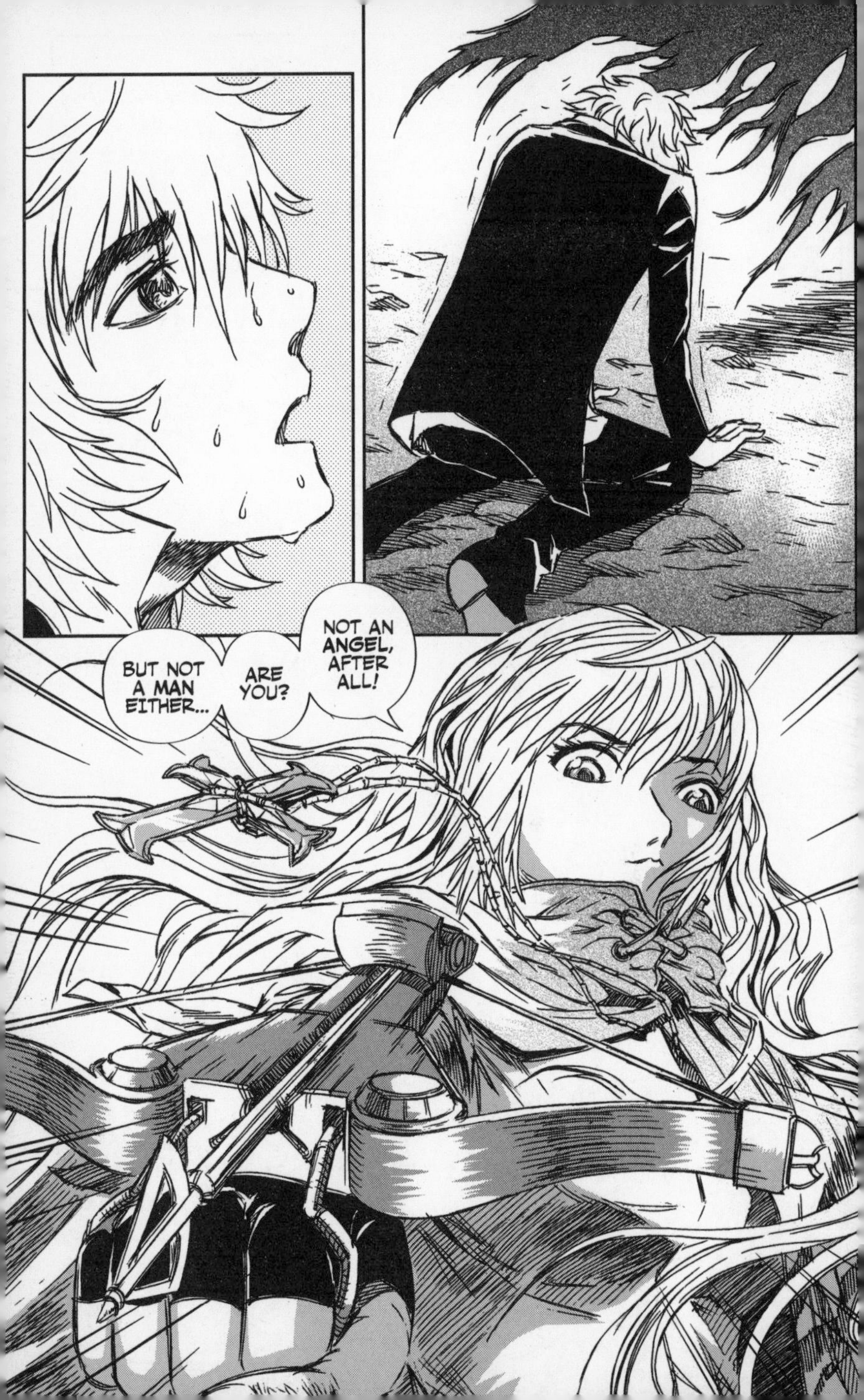
NOT AN ANGEL, AFTER ALL!
ARE YOU?
BUT NOT A MAN EITHER...

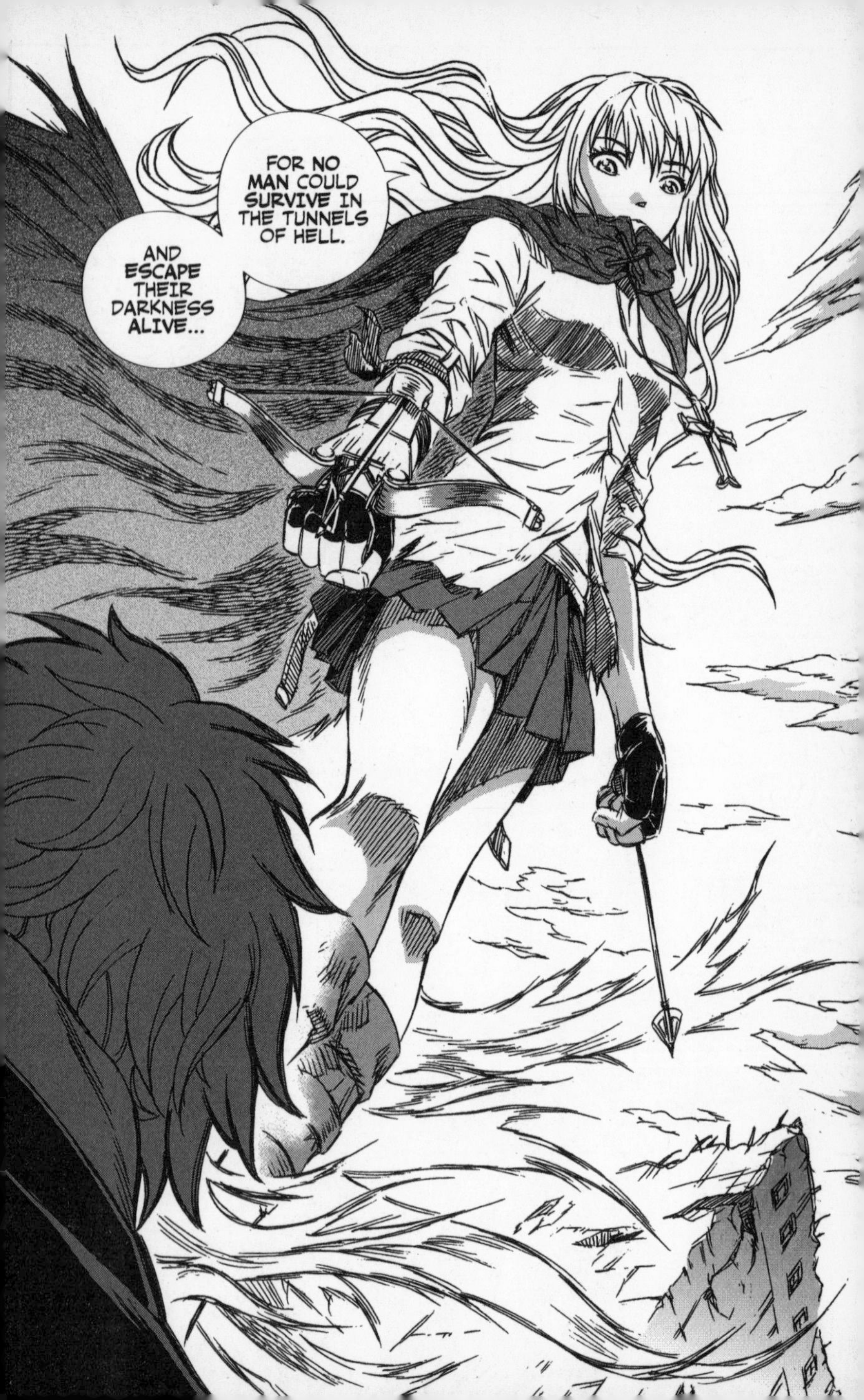
FOR NO MAN COULD SURVIVE IN THE TUNNELS OF HELL.
AND ESCAPE THEIR DARKNESS ALIVE...

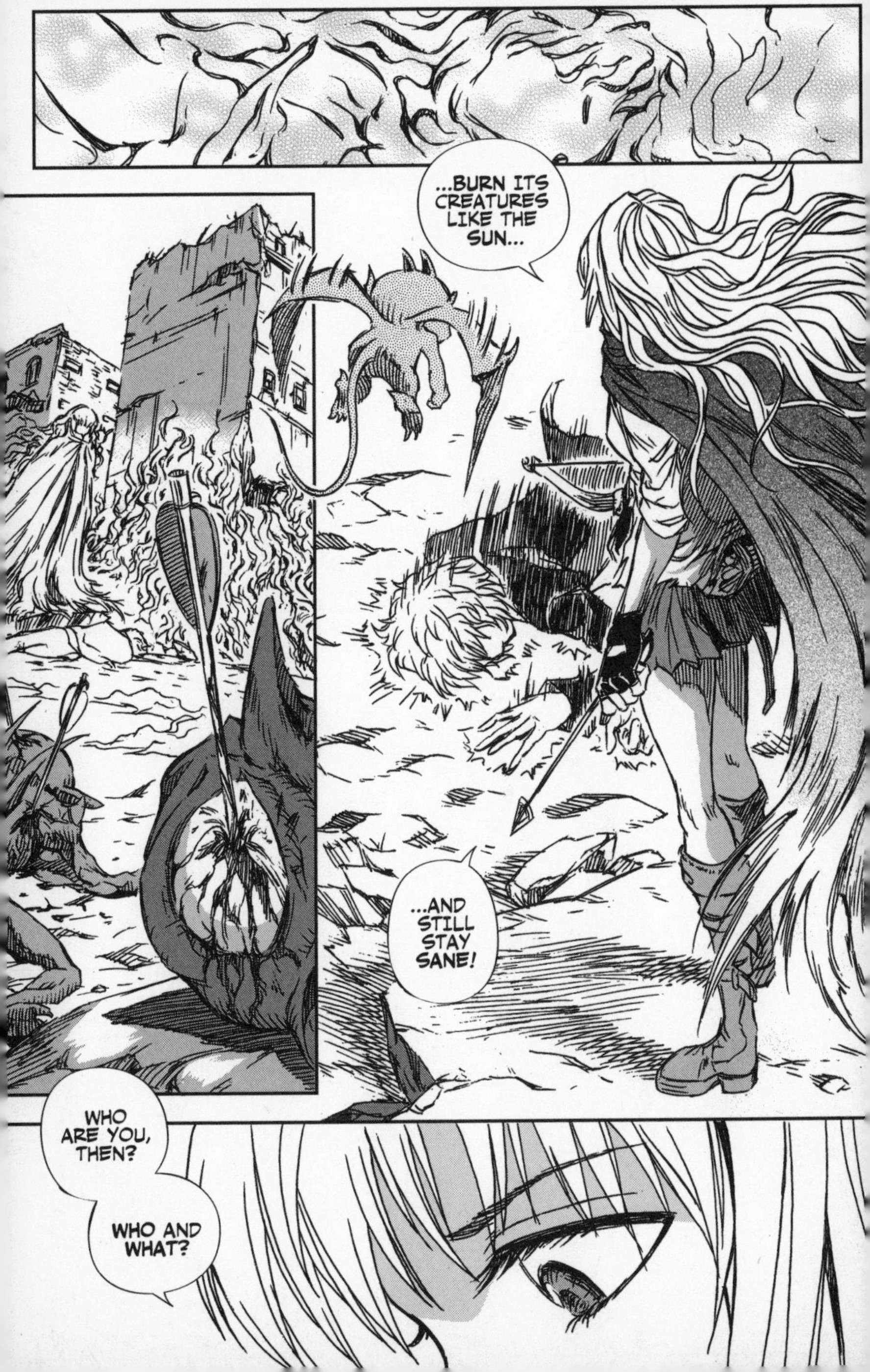
...BURN ITS CREATURES LIKE THE SUN...
...AND STILL STAY SANE!
WHO ARE YOU, THEN?
WHO AND WHAT?

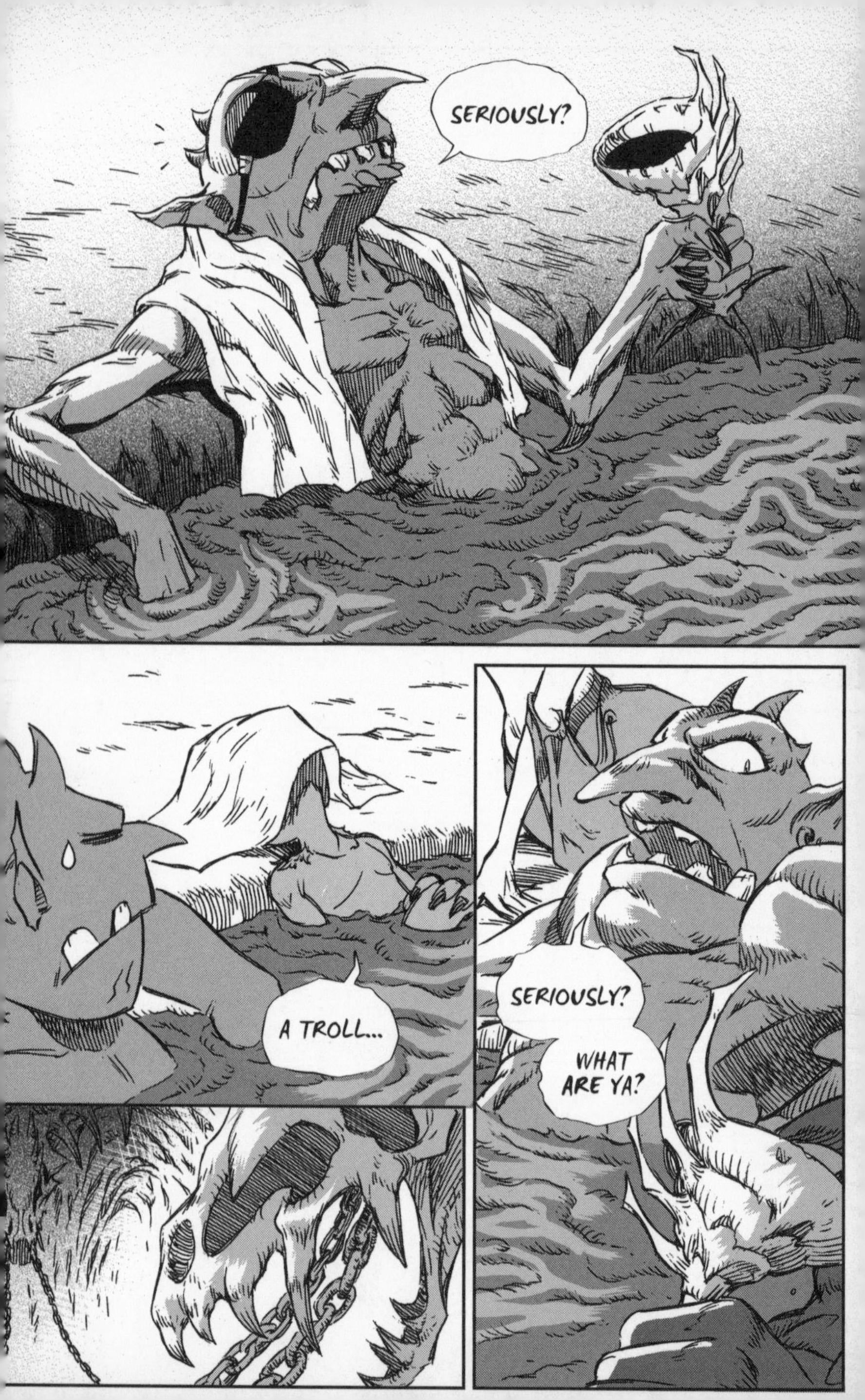
SERIOUSLY?
A TROLL...
SERIOUSLY?
WHAT ARE YA?

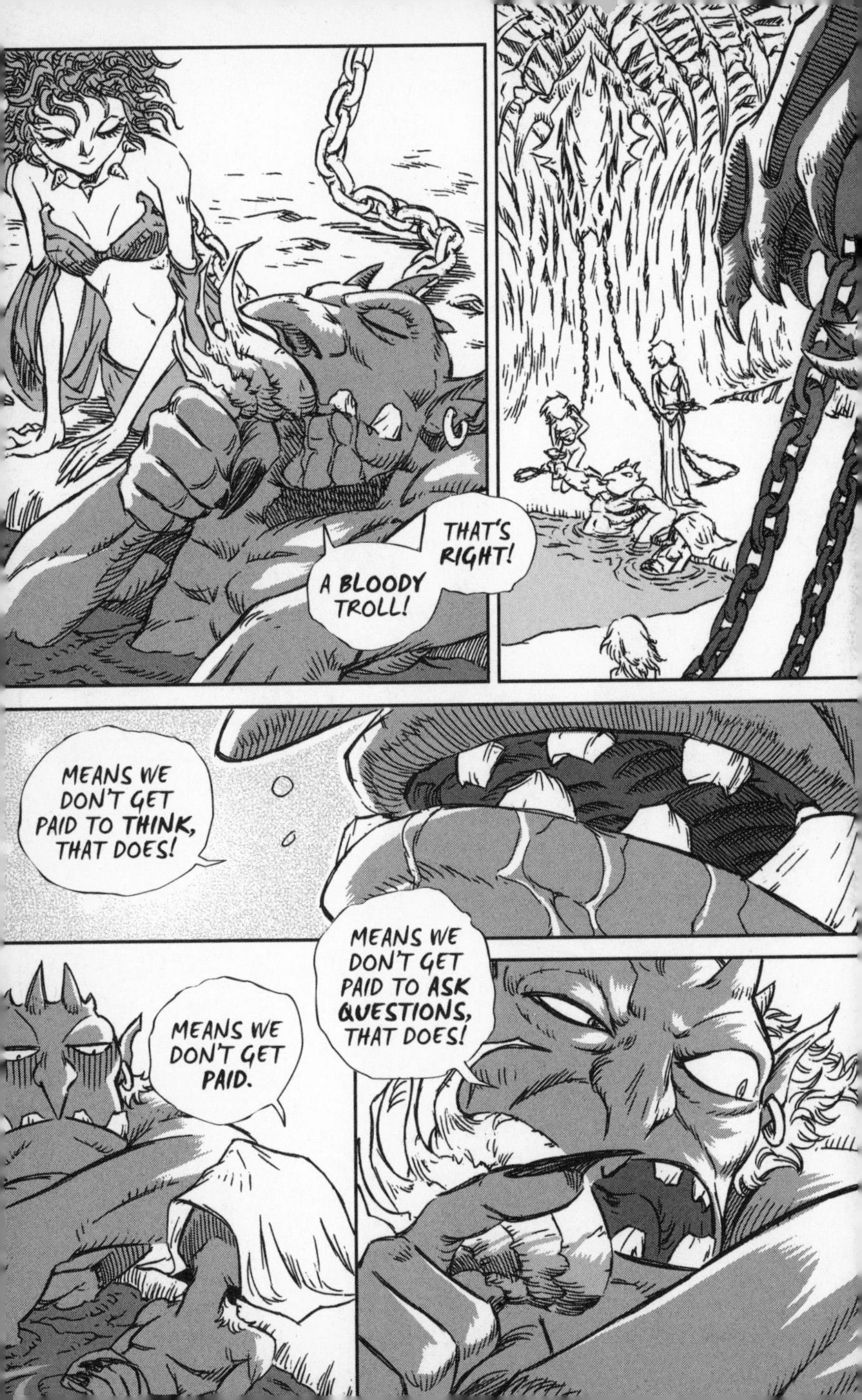
THAT'S RIGHT!
A BLOODY TROLL!
MEANS WE DON'T GET PAID TO THINK, THAT DOES!
MEANS WE DON'T GET PAID TO ASK QUESTIONS, THAT DOES!
MEANS WE DON'T GET PAID.

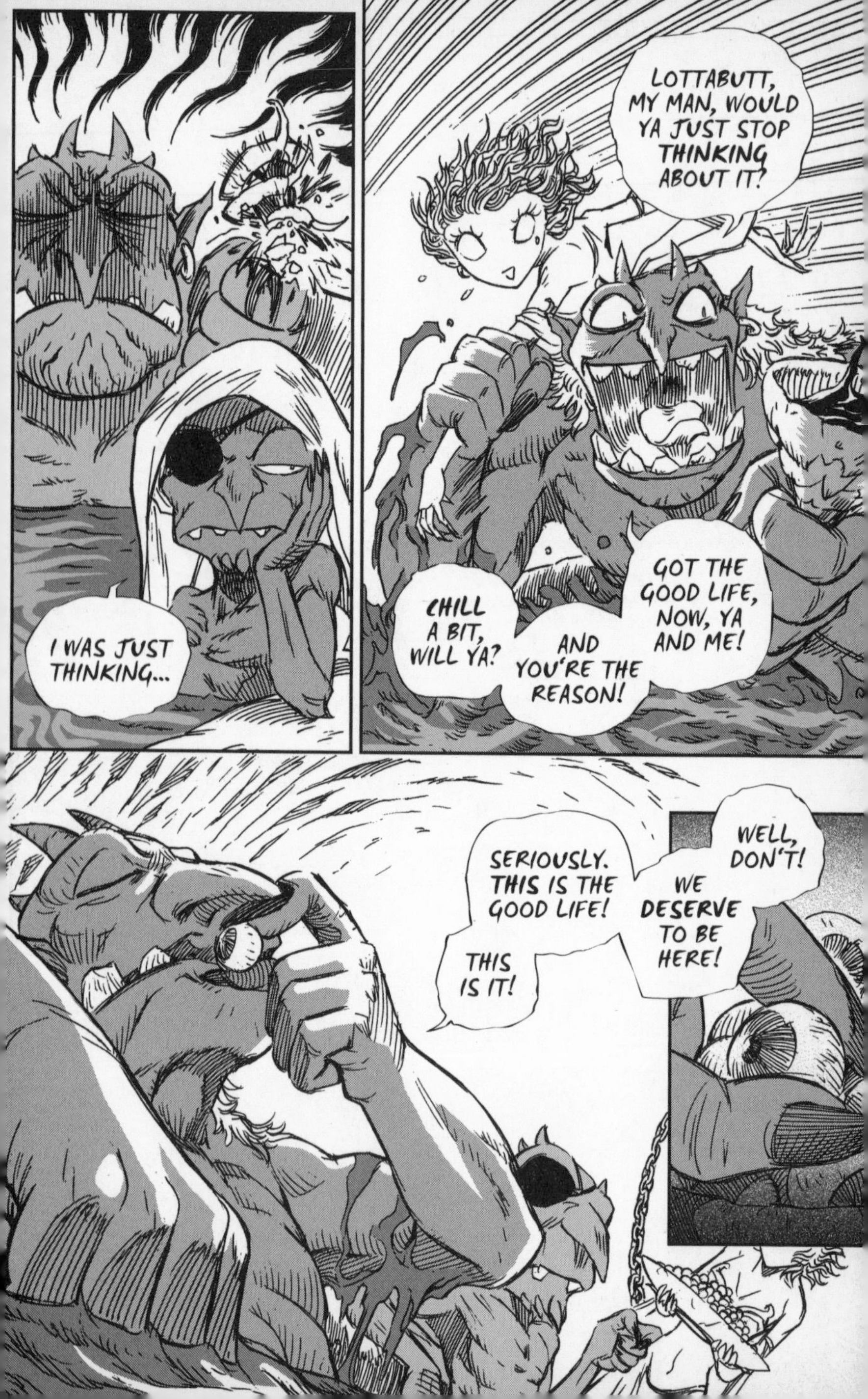
I WAS JUST THINKING...
LOTTABUTT, MY MAN, WOULD YA JUST STOP THINKING ABOUT IT?
CHILL A BIT, WILL YA?
AND YOU'RE THE REASON!
GOT THE GOOD LIFE, NOW, YA AND ME!
SERIOUSLY. THIS IS THE GOOD LIFE!
THIS IS IT!
WELL, DON'T!
WE DESERVE TO BE HERE!

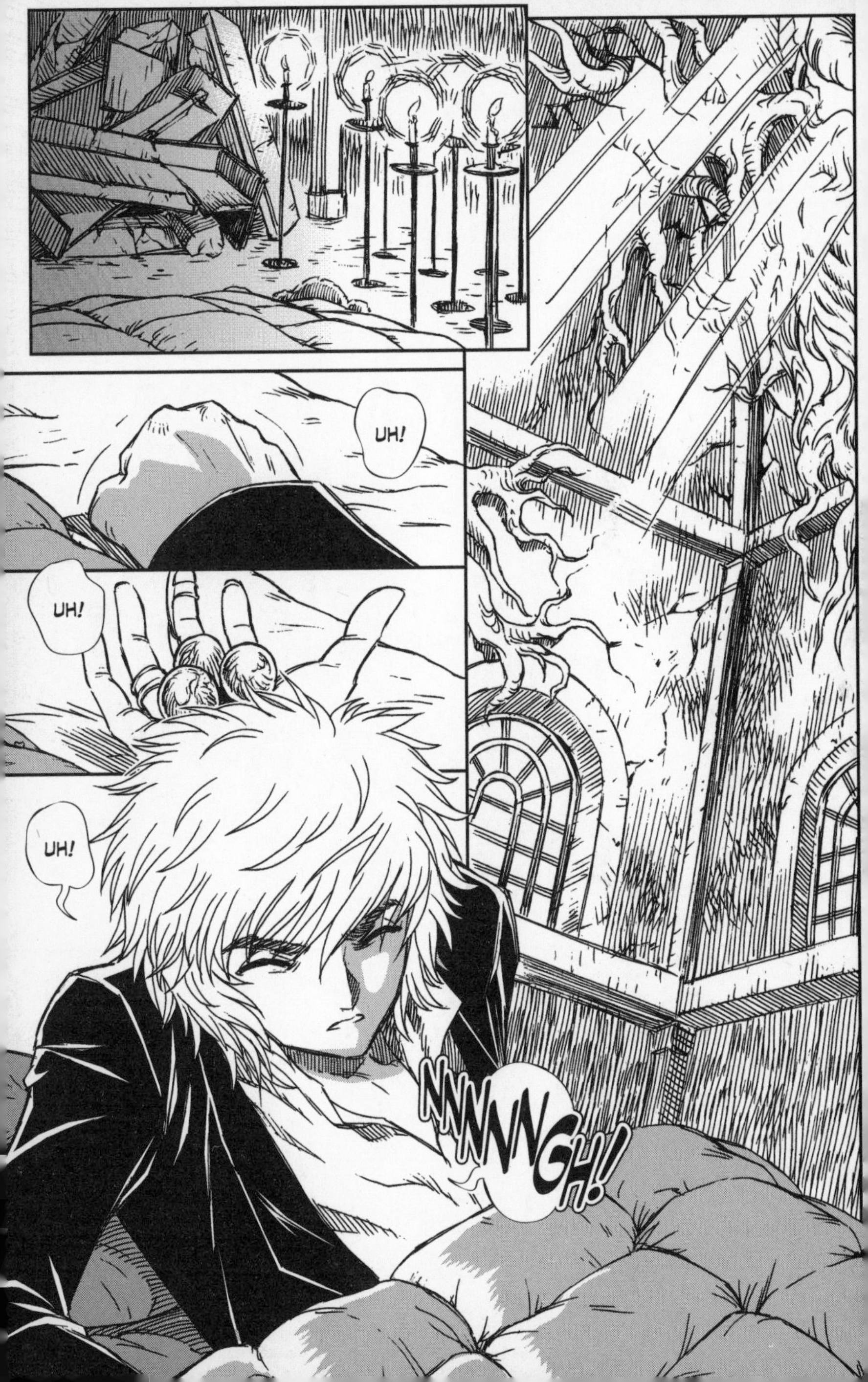
UH!
UH!
UH!
NNNNNGH!

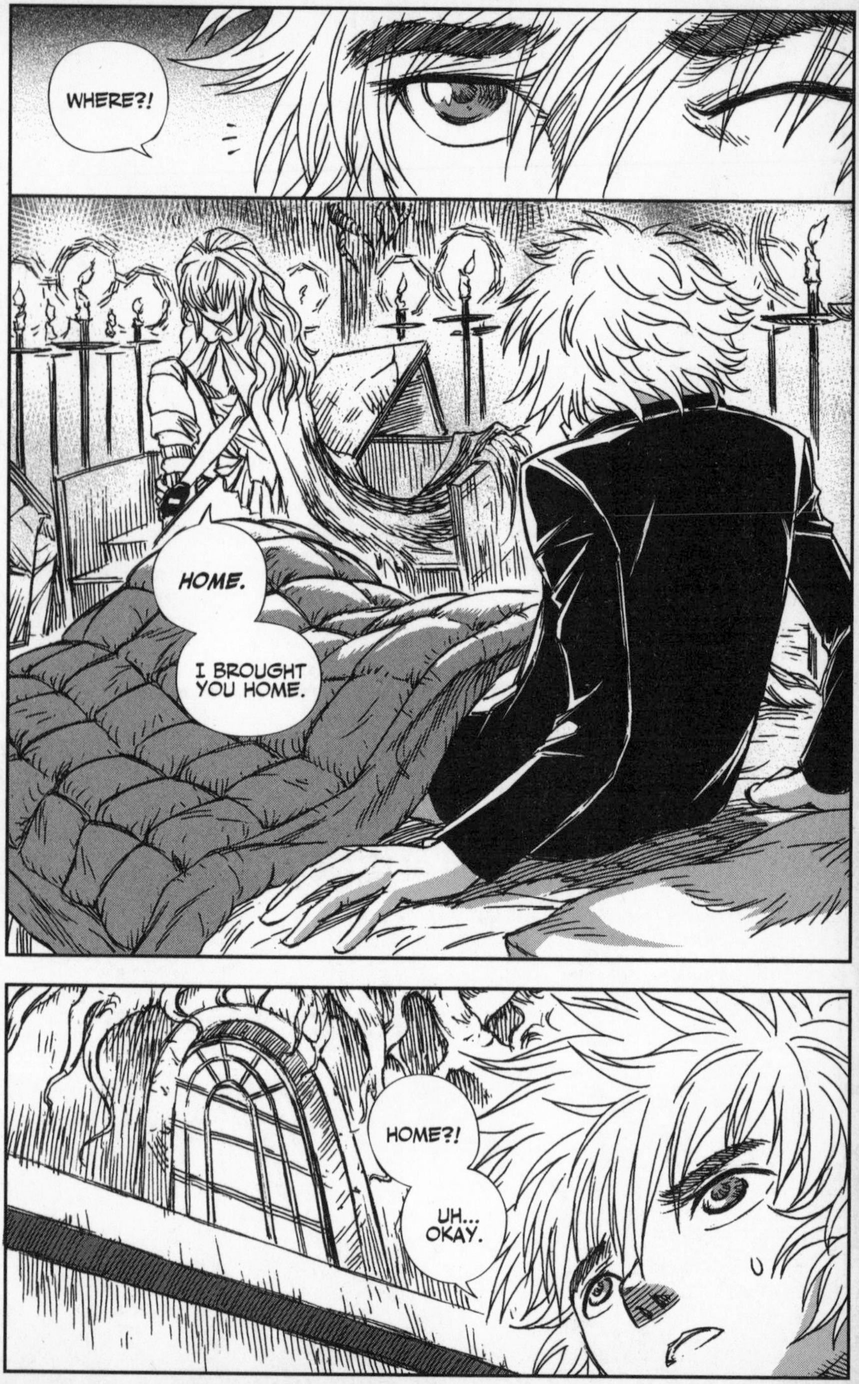
WHERE?!
HOME.
I BROUGHT YOU HOME.
HOME?!
UH... OKAY.

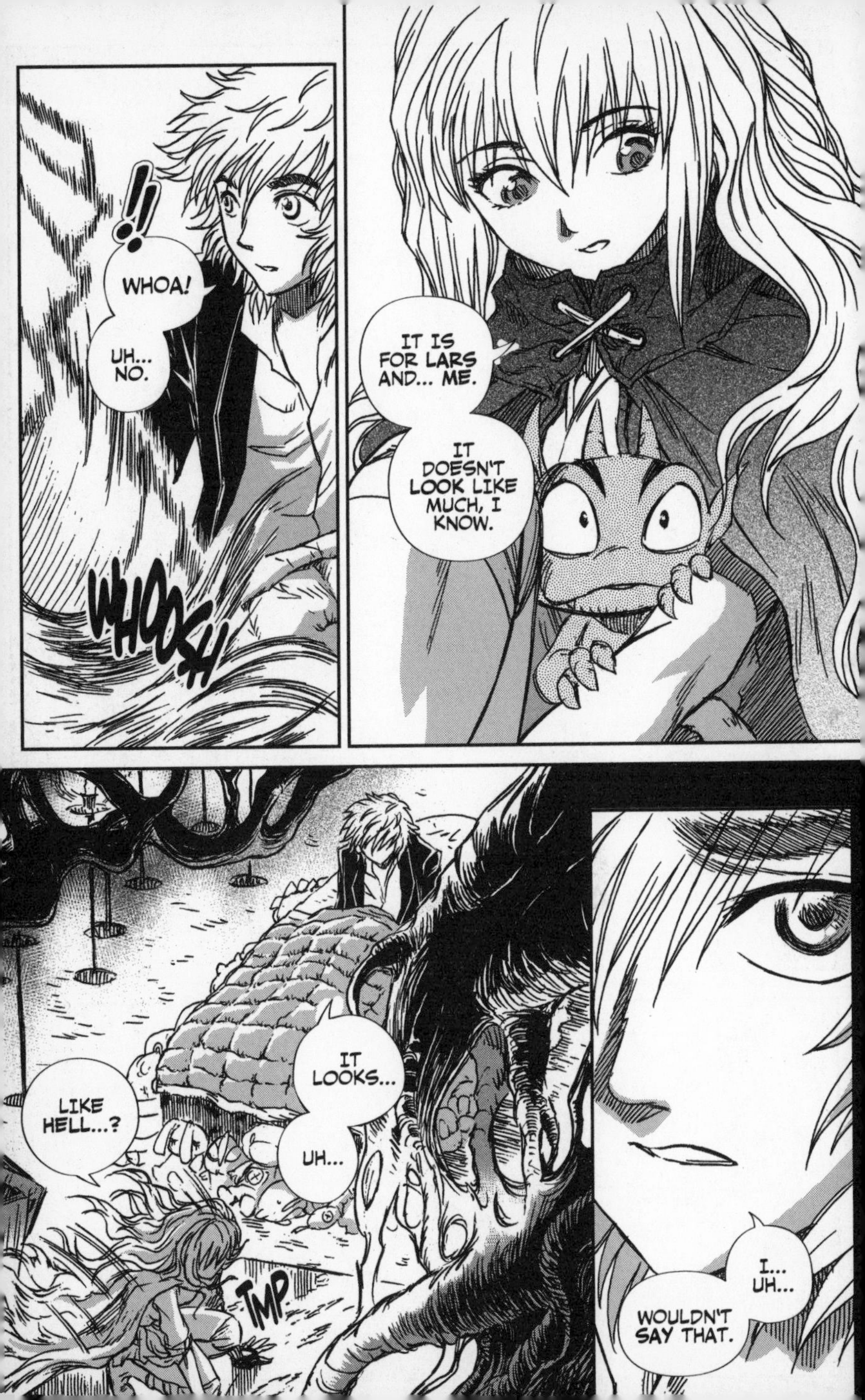
IT IS FOR LARS AND... ME.
IT DOESN'T LOOK LIKE MUCH, I KNOW.
!!
WHOA!
UH... NO.
WHOOSH
I... UH...
WOULDN'T SAY THAT.
IT LOOKS...
UH...
LIKE HELL...?
TMP

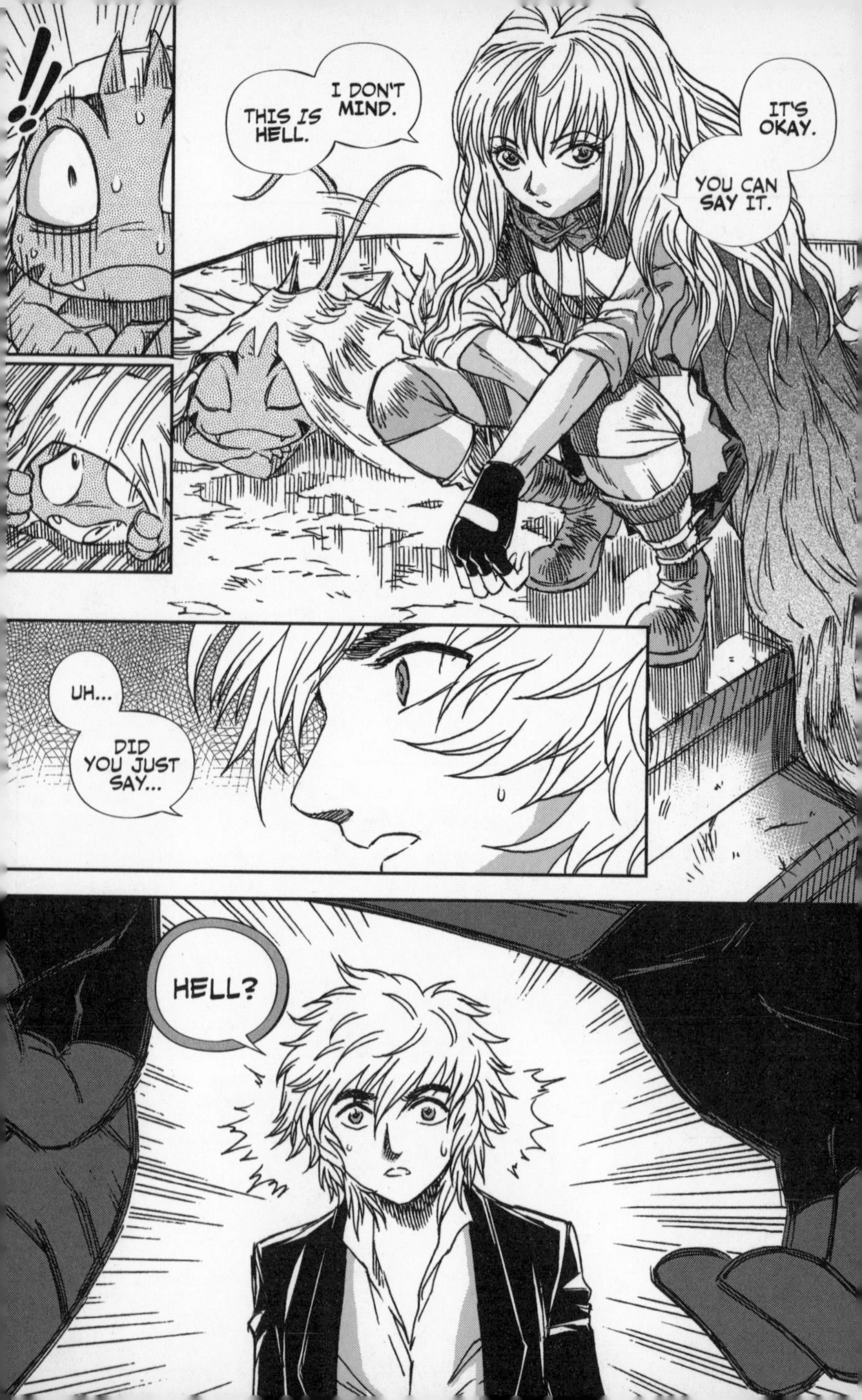
IT'S OKAY.
YOU CAN SAY IT.
I DON'T MIND.
THIS *IS* HELL.
!!
UH...
DID YOU JUST SAY...
HELL?

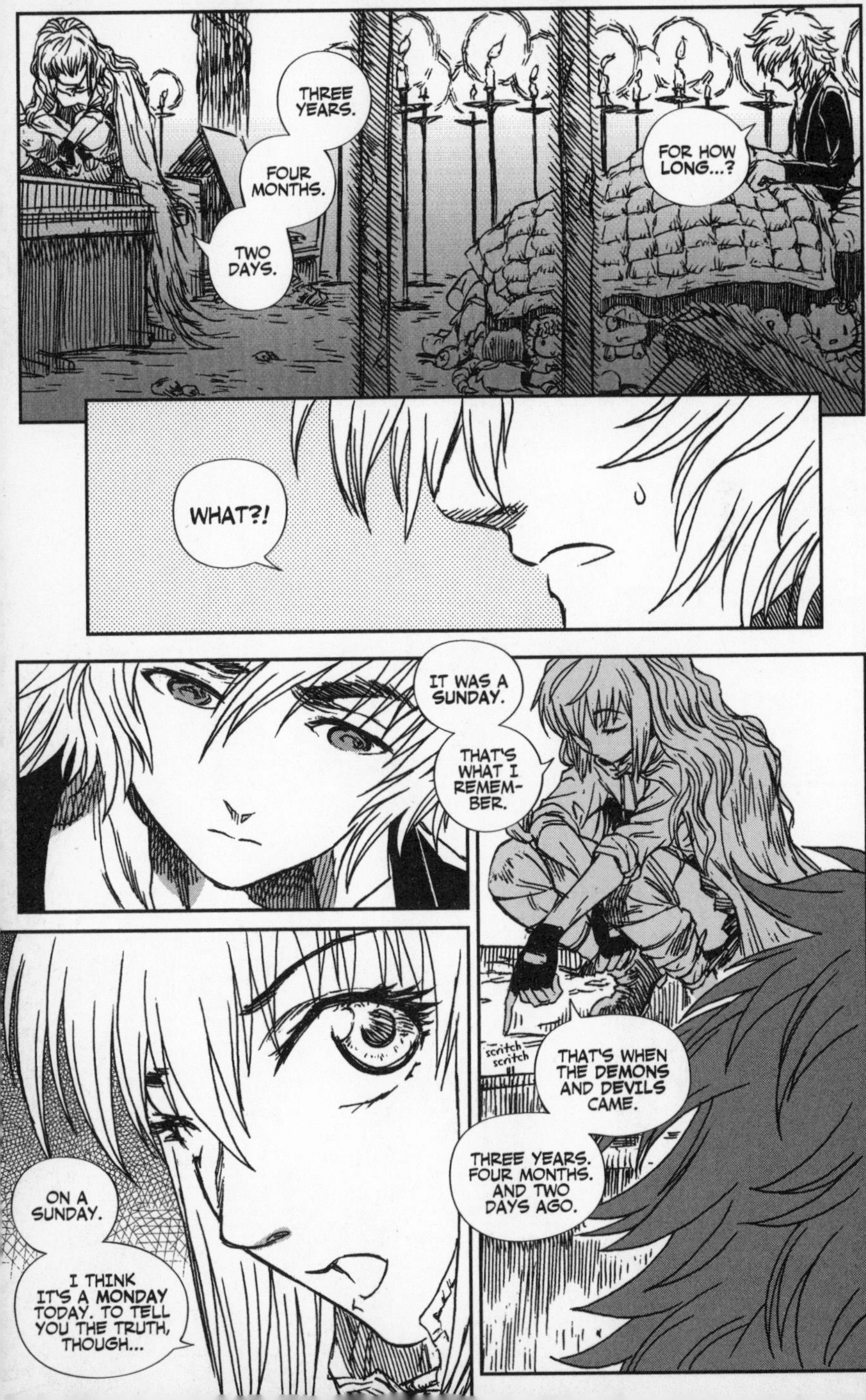
FOR HOW LONG...?
THREE YEARS.
FOUR MONTHS.
TWO DAYS.
WHAT?!
IT WAS A SUNDAY.
THAT'S WHAT I REMEMBER.
scritch scritch
THAT'S WHEN THE DEMONS AND DEVILS CAME.
THREE YEARS. FOUR MONTHS. AND TWO DAYS AGO.
ON A SUNDAY.
I THINK IT'S A MONDAY TODAY. TO TELL YOU THE TRUTH, THOUGH...

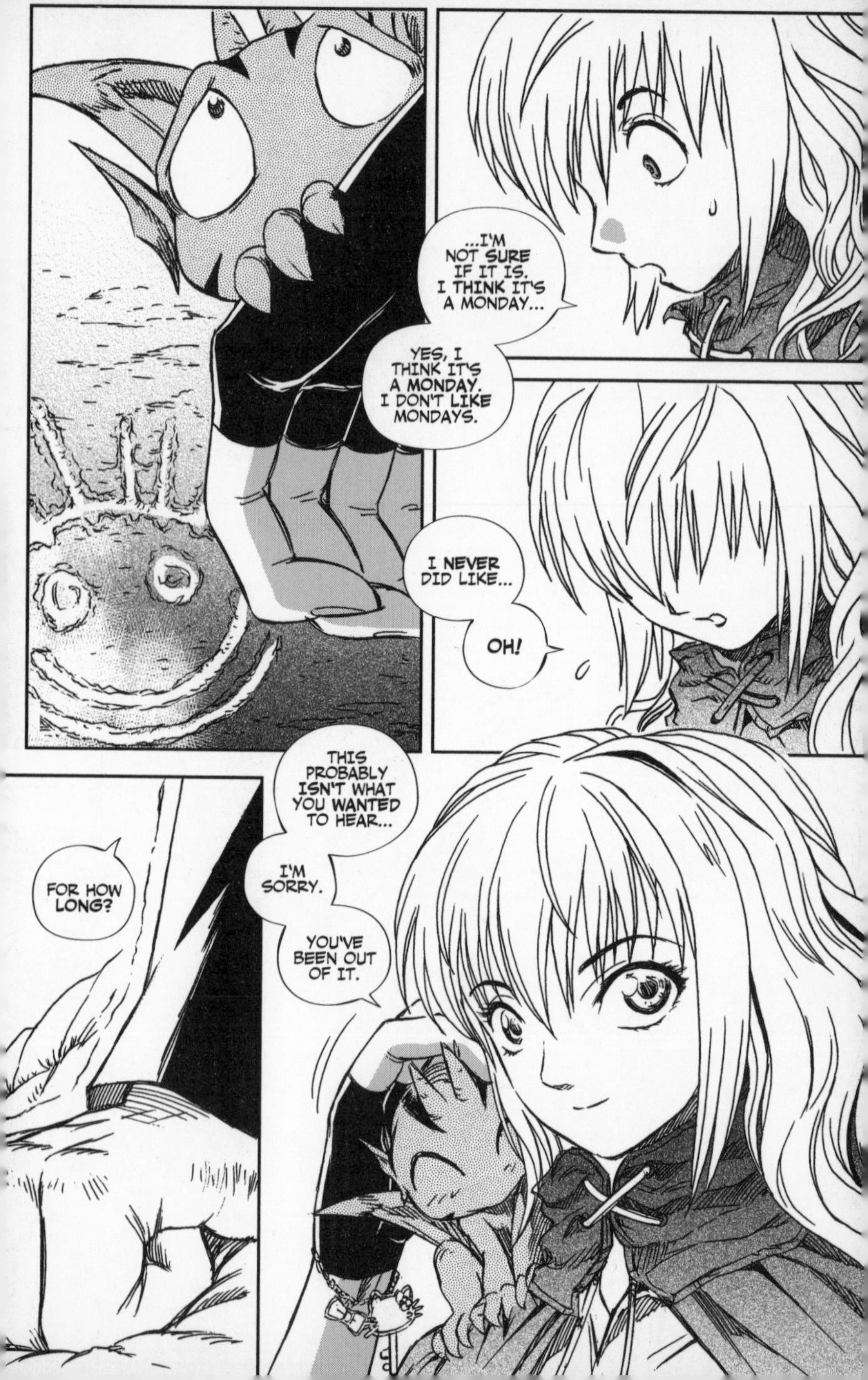
...I'M NOT SURE IF IT IS. I THINK IT'S A MONDAY...
YES, I THINK IT'S A MONDAY. I DON'T LIKE MONDAYS.
I NEVER DID LIKE...
OH!
THIS PROBABLY ISN'T WHAT YOU WANTED TO HEAR...
I'M SORRY.
YOU'VE BEEN OUT OF IT.
FOR HOW LONG?

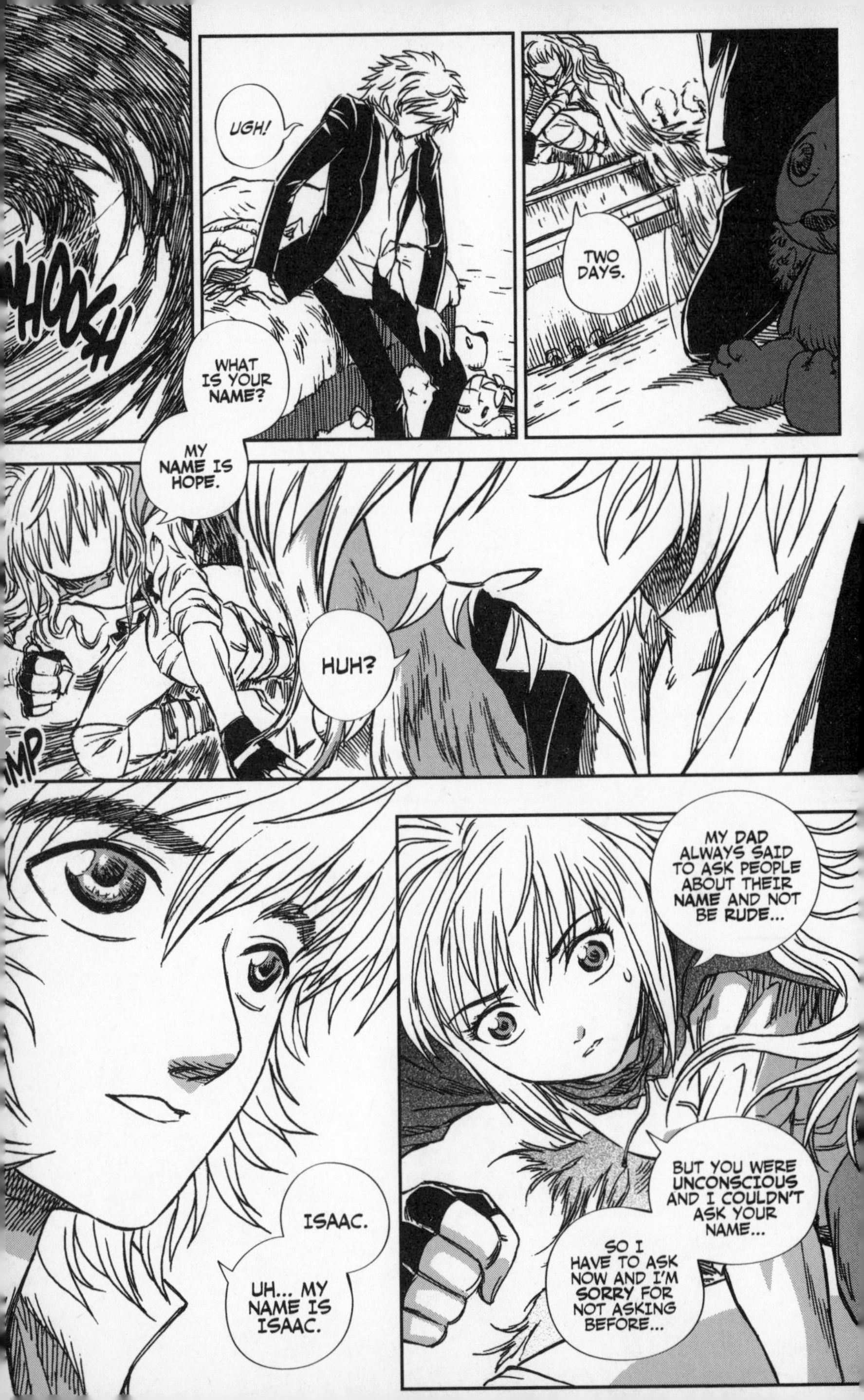
TWO DAYS.
UGH!
WHAT IS YOUR NAME?
WHOOSH
MY NAME IS HOPE.
HUH?
MY DAD ALWAYS SAID TO ASK PEOPLE ABOUT THEIR NAME AND NOT BE RUDE...
BUT YOU WERE UNCONSCIOUS AND I COULDN'T ASK YOUR NAME...
SO I HAVE TO ASK NOW AND I'M SORRY FOR NOT ASKING BEFORE...
ISAAC.
UH... MY NAME IS ISAAC.

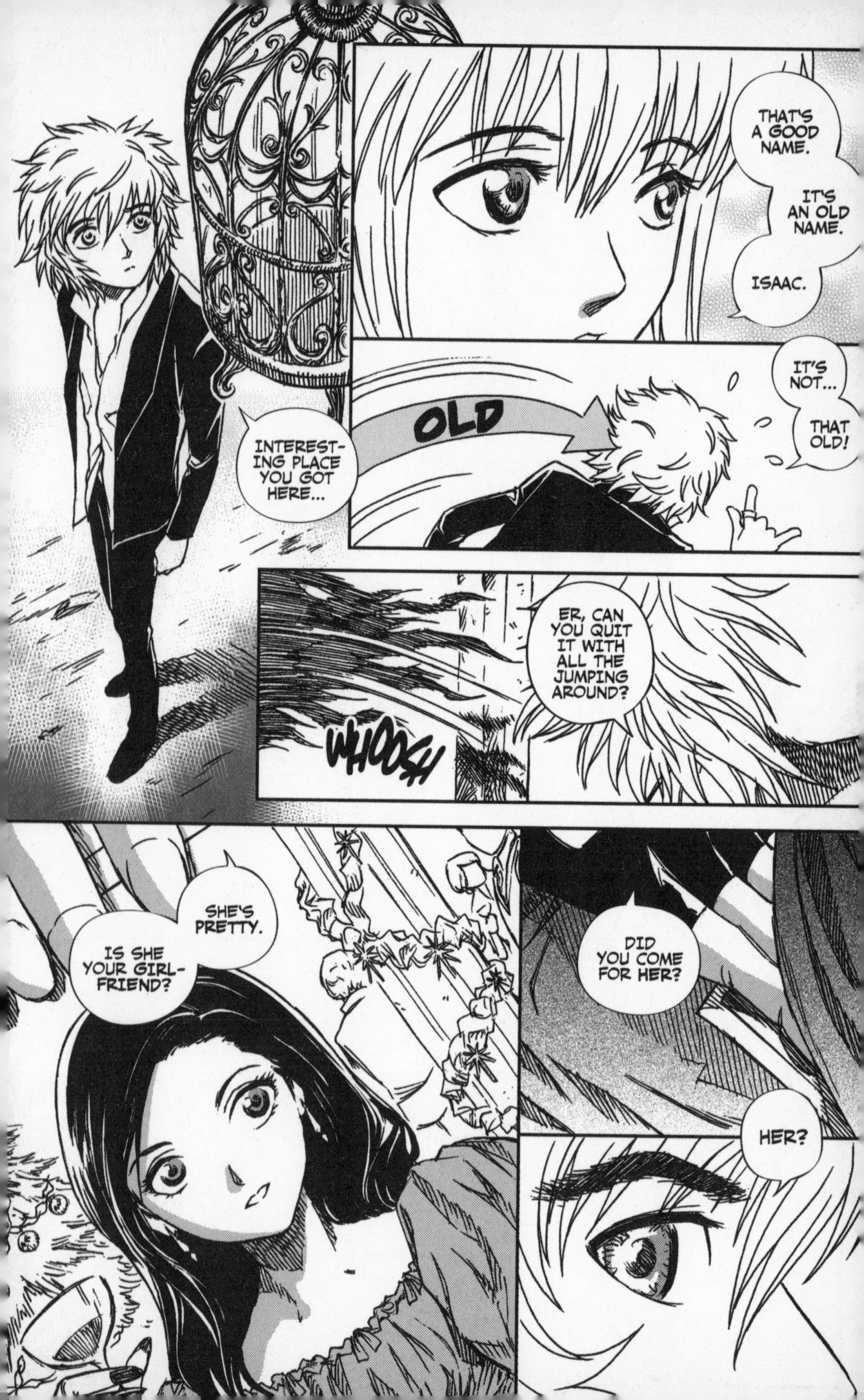
INTERESTING PLACE YOU GOT HERE...
THAT'S A GOOD NAME.
IT'S AN OLD NAME.
ISAAC.
OLD
IT'S NOT...
THAT OLD!
ER, CAN YOU QUIT IT WITH ALL THE JUMPING AROUND?
WHOOSH
SHE'S PRETTY.
IS SHE YOUR GIRL-FRIEND?
DID YOU COME FOR HER?
HER?

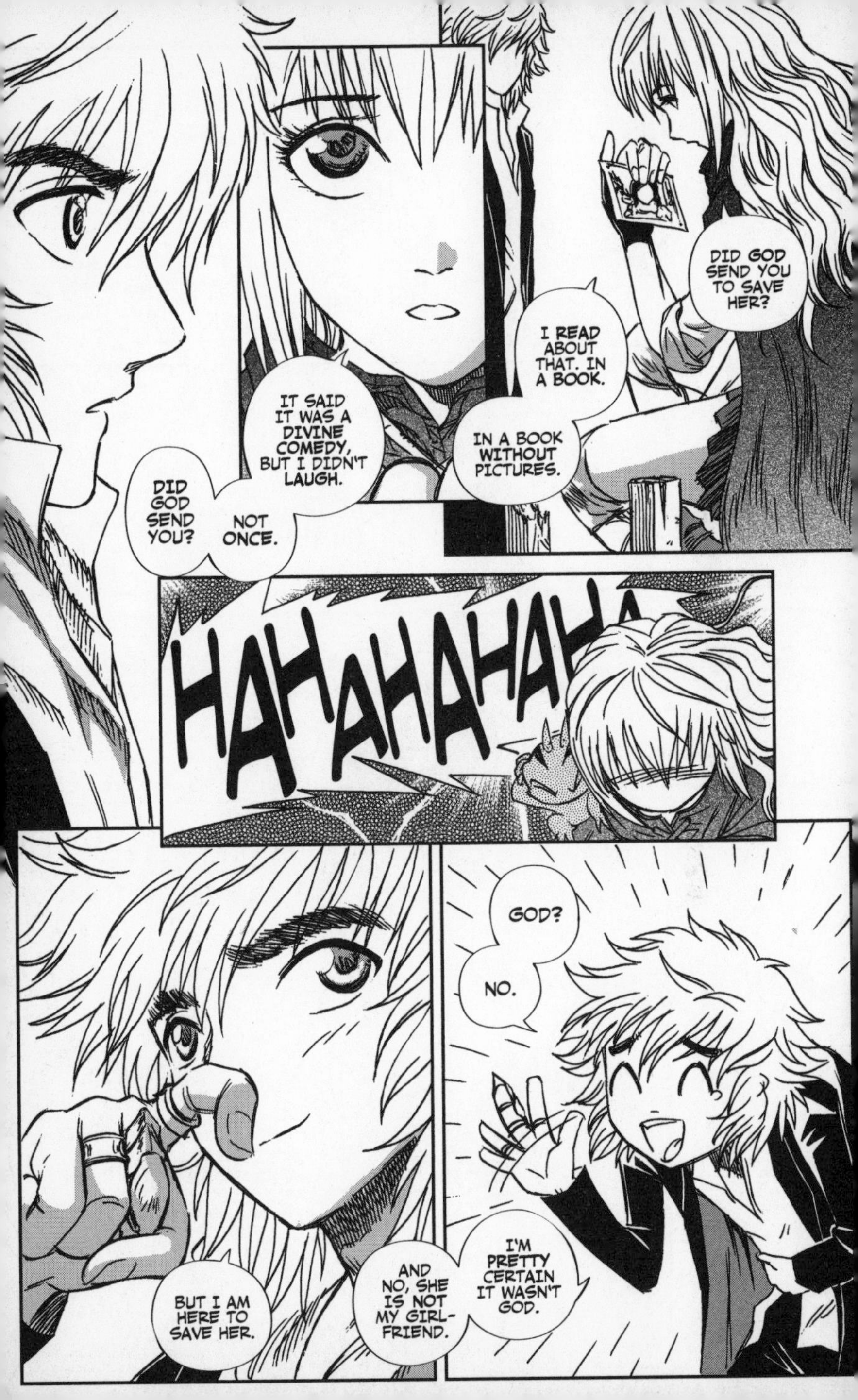

DID GOD SEND YOU TO SAVE HER?
I READ ABOUT THAT. IN A BOOK.
IN A BOOK WITHOUT PICTURES.
IT SAID IT WAS A DIVINE COMEDY, BUT I DIDN'T LAUGH.
NOT ONCE.
DID GOD SEND YOU?
HAHAHAHAHAHA
GOD?
NO.
I'M PRETTY CERTAIN IT WASN'T GOD.
AND NO, SHE IS NOT MY GIRL-FRIEND.
BUT I AM HERE TO SAVE HER.

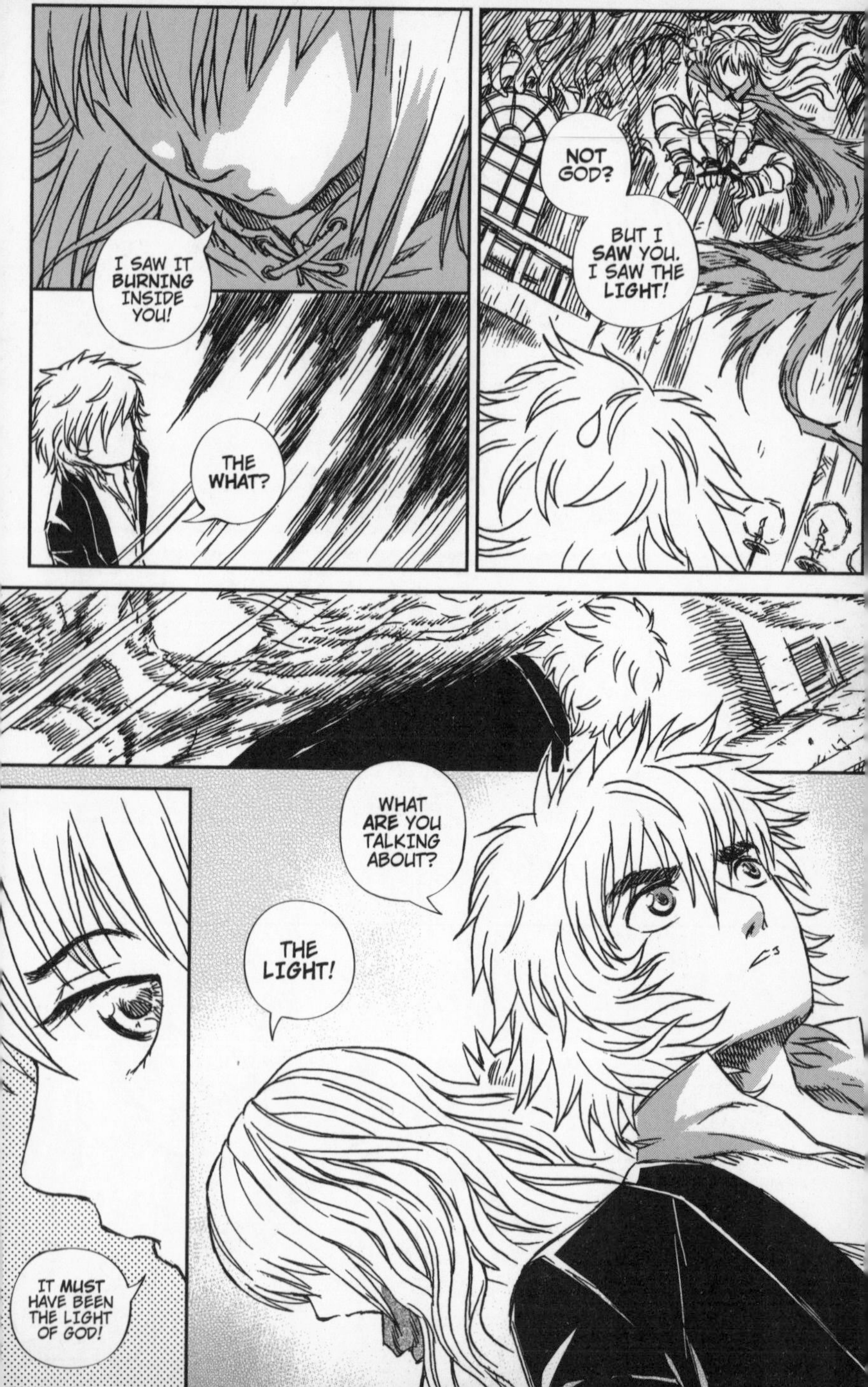
NOT GOD?
BUT I SAW YOU. I SAW THE LIGHT!
I SAW IT BURNING INSIDE YOU!
THE WHAT?
WHAT ARE YOU TALKING ABOUT?
THE LIGHT!
IT MUST HAVE BEEN THE LIGHT OF GOD!

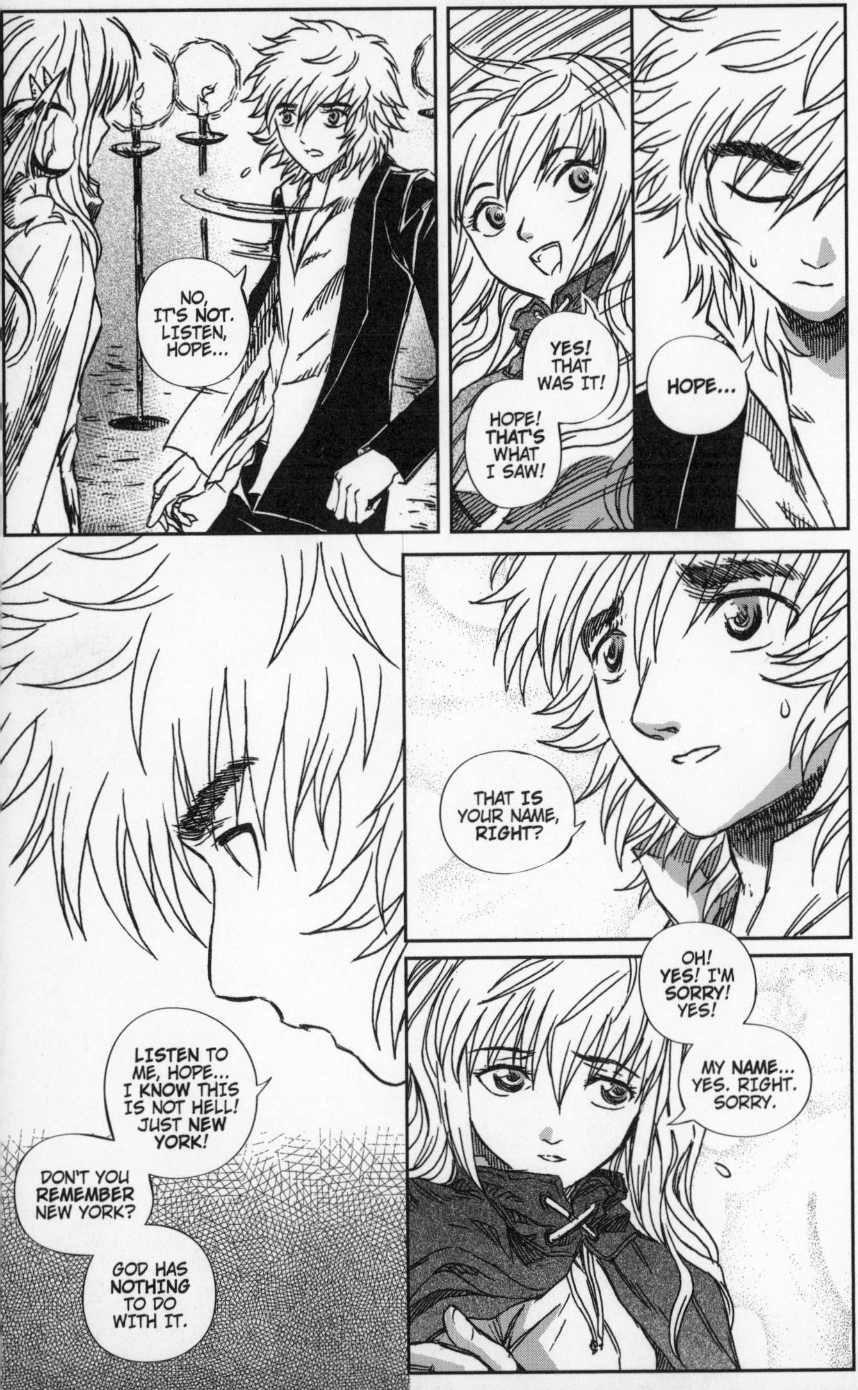
HOPE...
YES! THAT WAS IT!
HOPE! THAT'S WHAT I SAW!
NO, IT'S NOT. LISTEN, HOPE...
THAT IS YOUR NAME, RIGHT?
OH! YES! I'M SORRY! YES!
MY NAME... YES. RIGHT. SORRY.
LISTEN TO ME, HOPE... I KNOW THIS IS NOT HELL! JUST NEW YORK!
DON'T YOU REMEMBER NEW YORK?
GOD HAS NOTHING TO DO WITH IT.

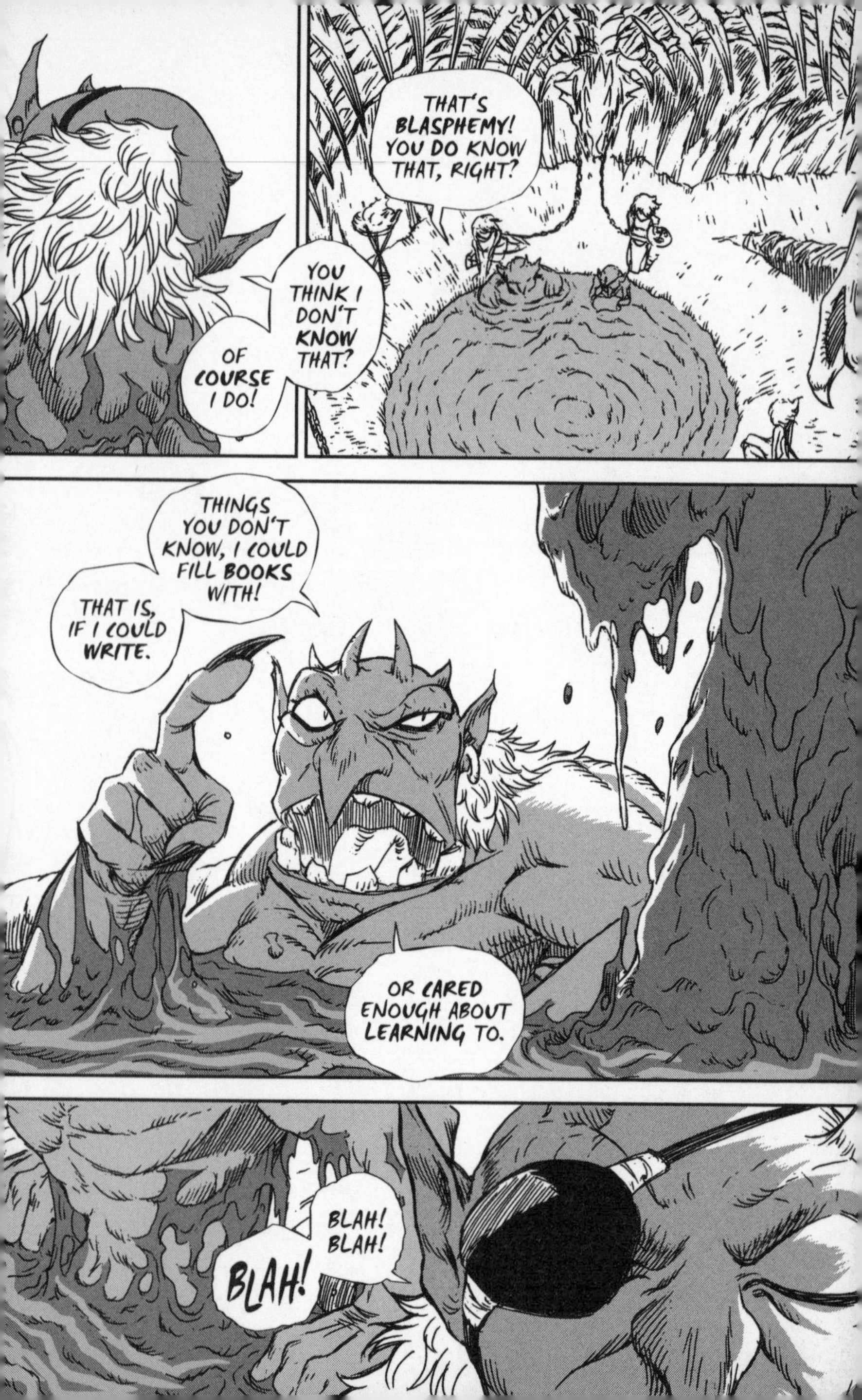
THAT'S BLASPHEMY! YOU DO KNOW THAT, RIGHT?
YOU THINK I DON'T KNOW THAT?
OF COURSE I DO!
THINGS YOU DON'T KNOW, I COULD FILL BOOKS WITH!
THAT IS, IF I COULD WRITE.
OR CARED ENOUGH ABOUT LEARNING TO.
BLAH! BLAH!
BLAH!

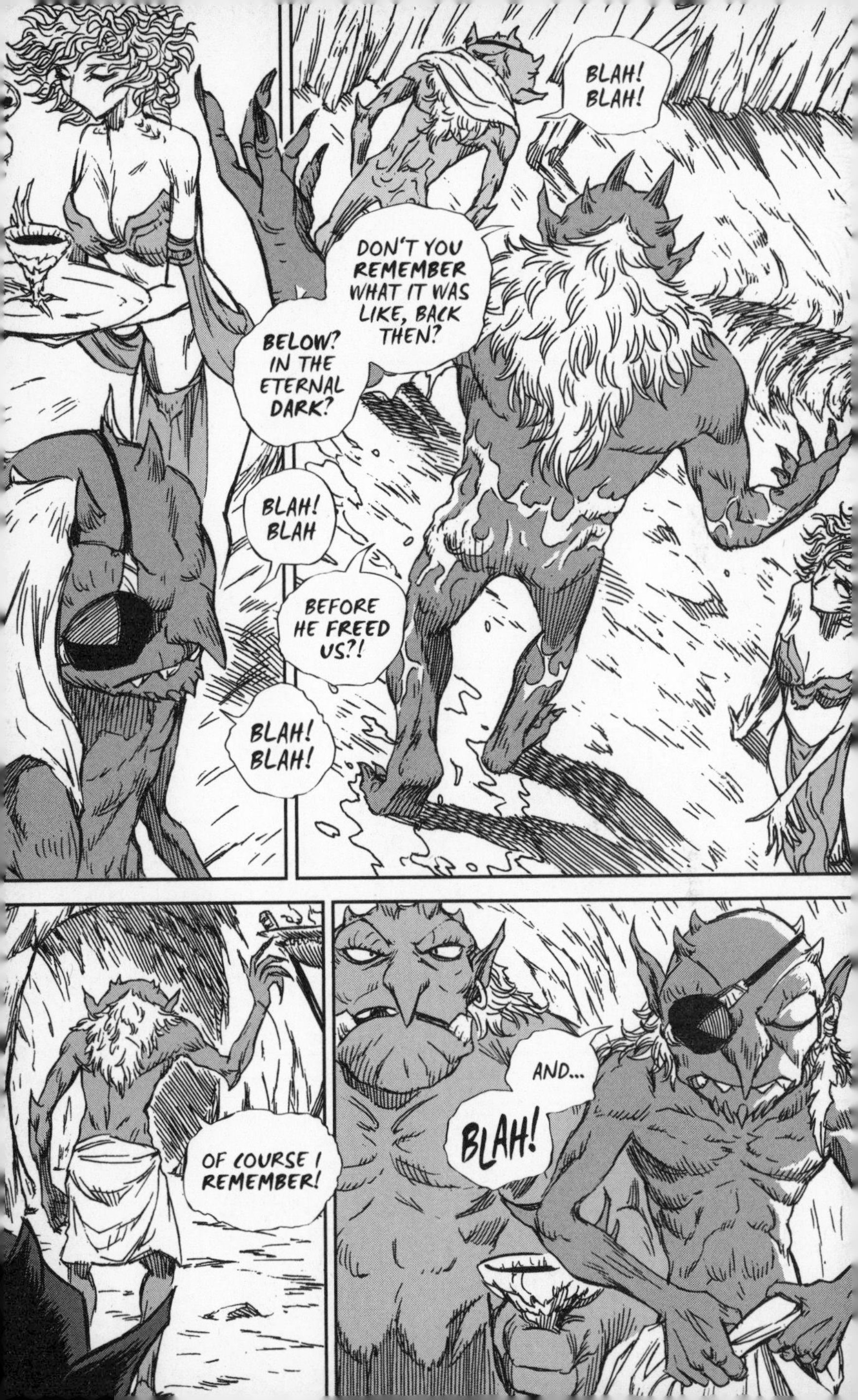
BLAH! BLAH!
DON'T YOU REMEMBER WHAT IT WAS LIKE, BACK THEN?
BELOW? IN THE ETERNAL DARK?
BLAH! BLAH
BEFORE HE FREED US?!
BLAH! BLAH!
OF COURSE I REMEMBER!
AND...
BLAH!

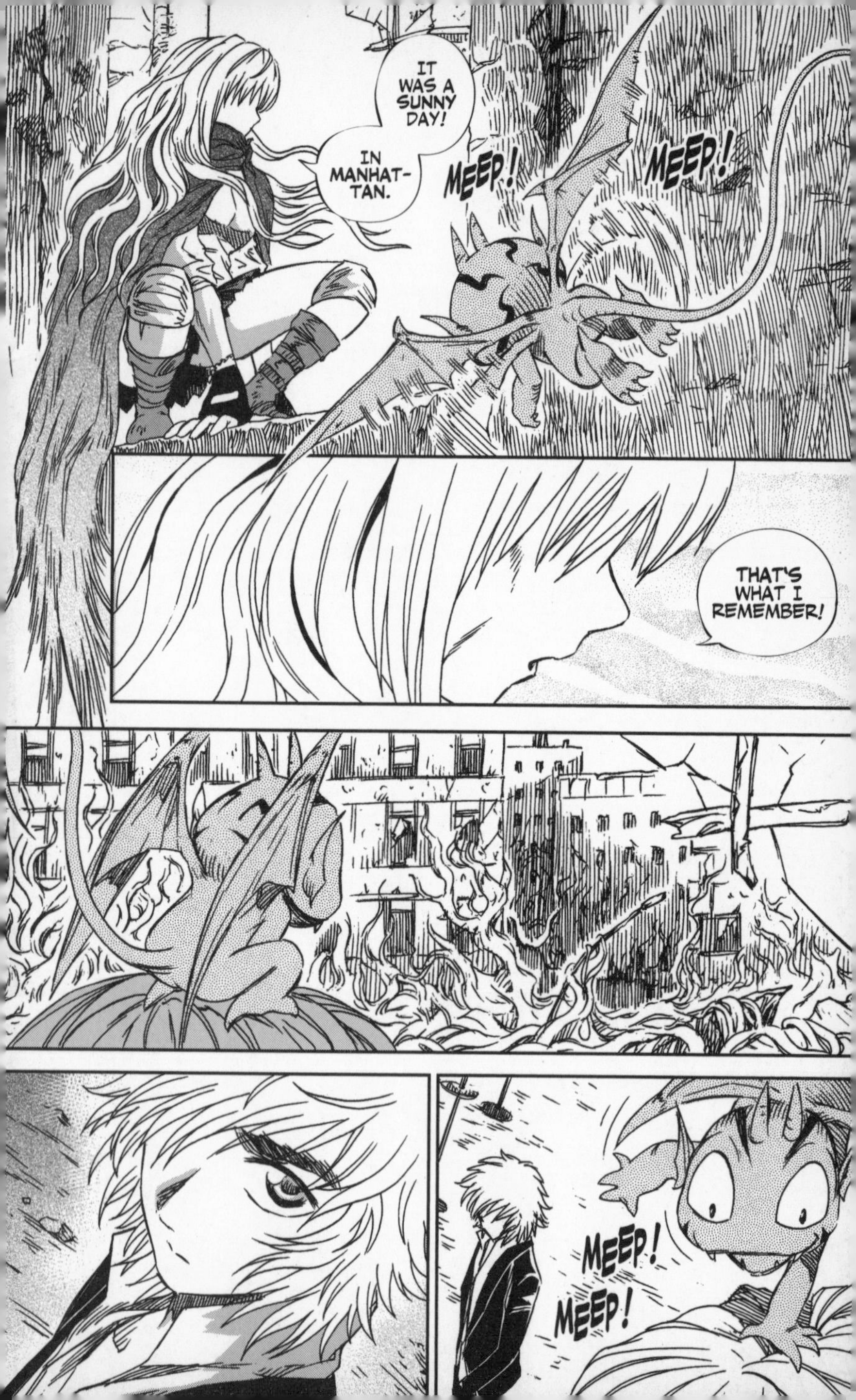
MEEP!
MEEP!
IT WAS A SUNNY DAY!
IN MANHAT-TAN.
THAT'S WHAT I REMEMBER!
MEEP!
MEEP!

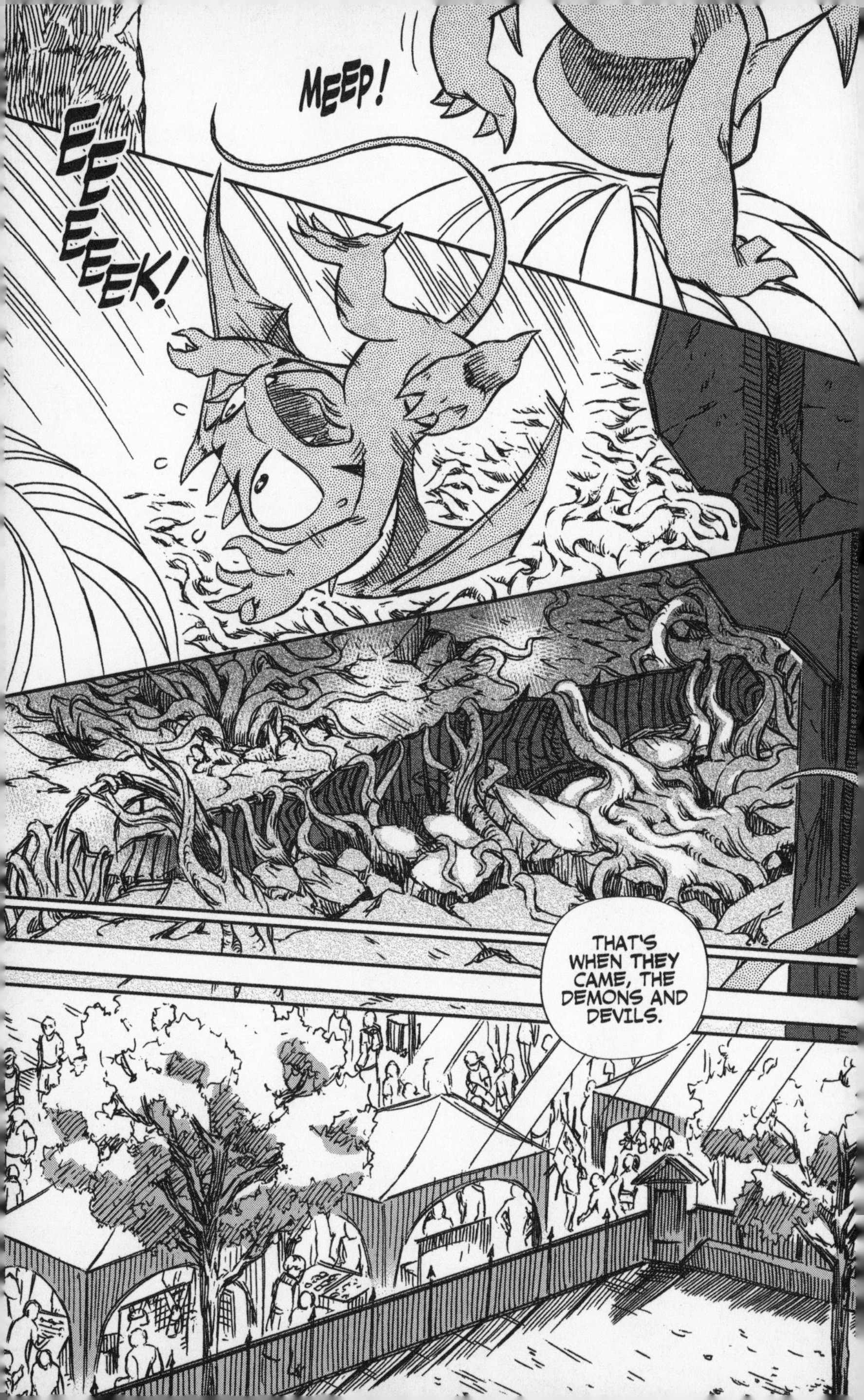
MEEP!
EEEEEEK!
THAT'S WHEN THEY CAME, THE DEMONS AND DEVILS.

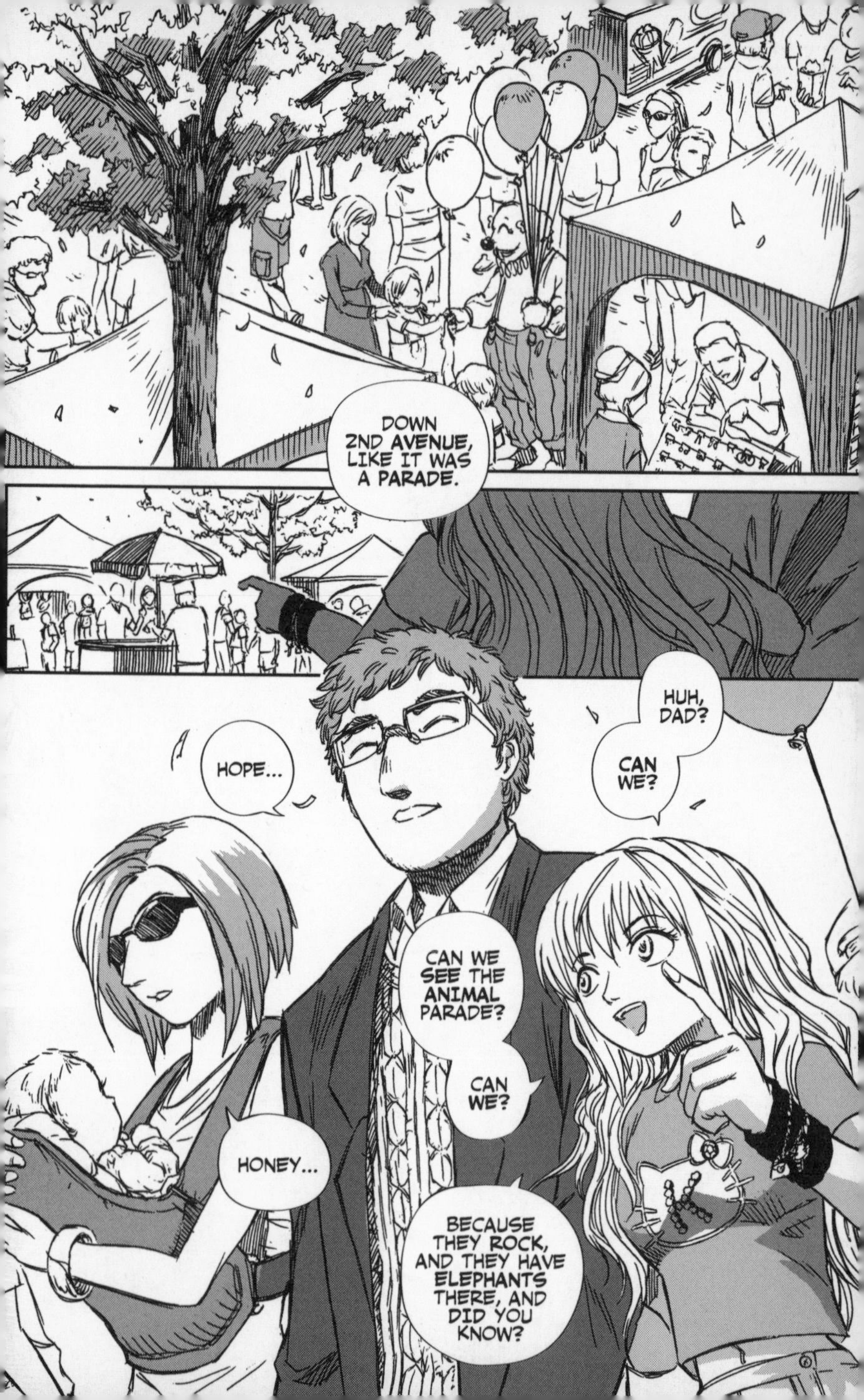
DOWN 2ND AVENUE, LIKE IT WAS A PARADE.
CAN WE SEE THE ANIMAL PARADE?
CAN WE?
BECAUSE THEY ROCK, AND THEY HAVE ELEPHANTS THERE, AND DID YOU KNOW?
HUH, DAD?
CAN WE?
HOPE...
HONEY...

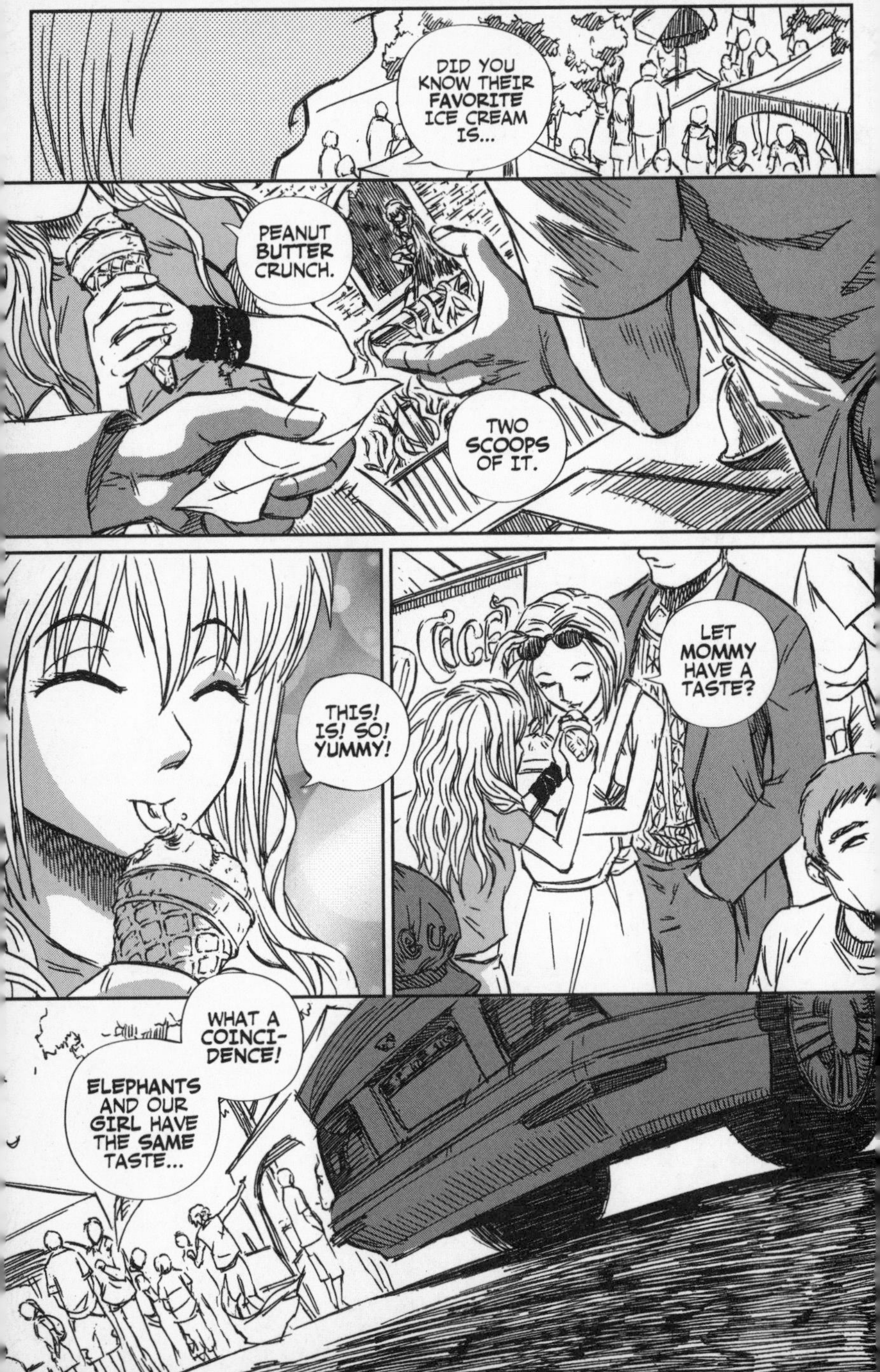
DID YOU KNOW THEIR FAVORITE ICE CREAM IS...
PEANUT BUTTER CRUNCH.
TWO SCOOPS OF IT.
LET MOMMY HAVE A TASTE?
THIS! IS! SO! YUMMY!
WHAT A COINCI-DENCE!
ELEPHANTS AND OUR GIRL HAVE THE SAME TASTE...

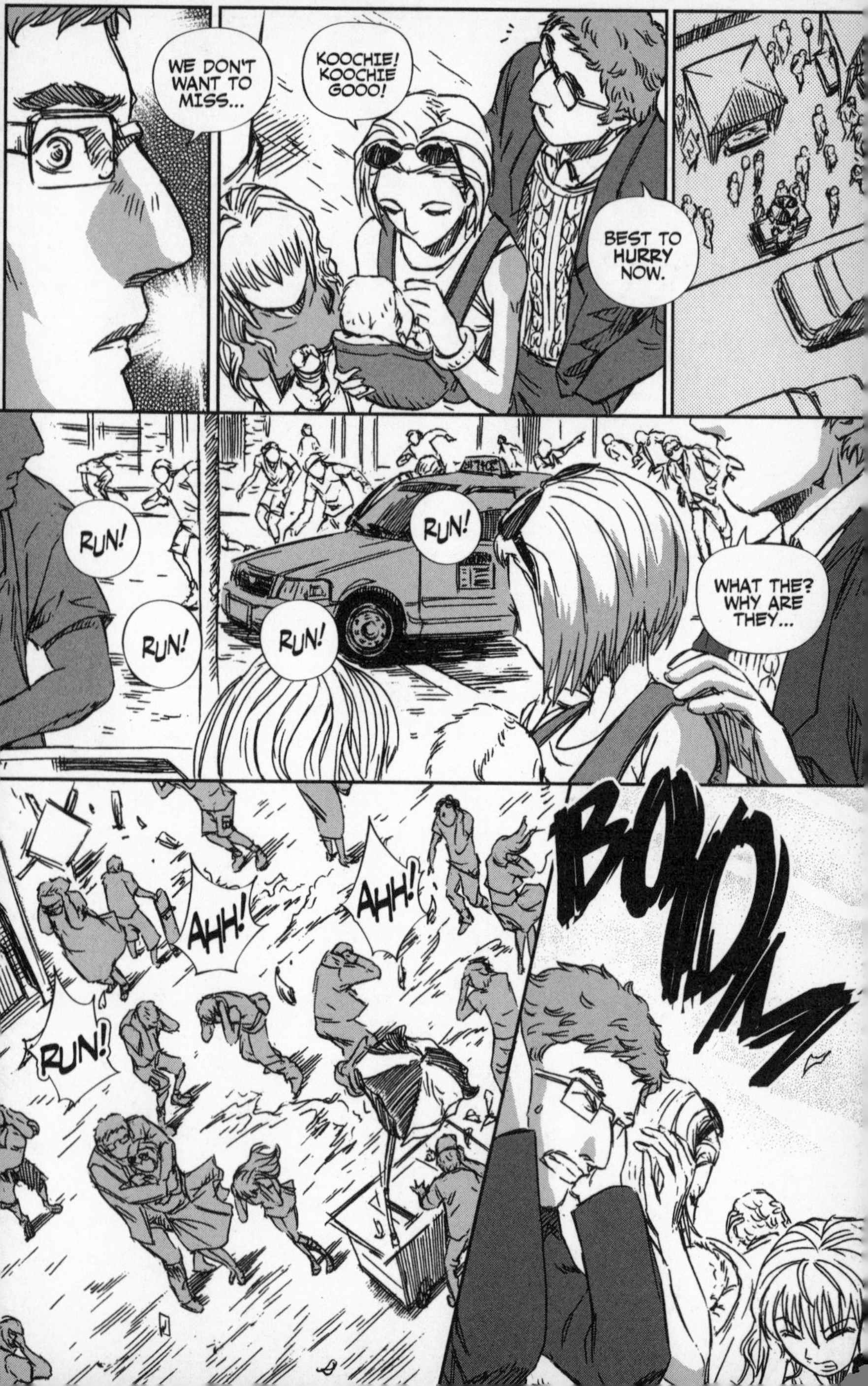
KOOCHIE! KOOCHIE GOOO!
BEST TO HURRY NOW.
WE DON'T WANT TO MISS...
WHAT THE? WHY ARE THEY...
RUN!
RUN!
RUN!
RUN!
BOOM
AHH!
AHH!
RUN!

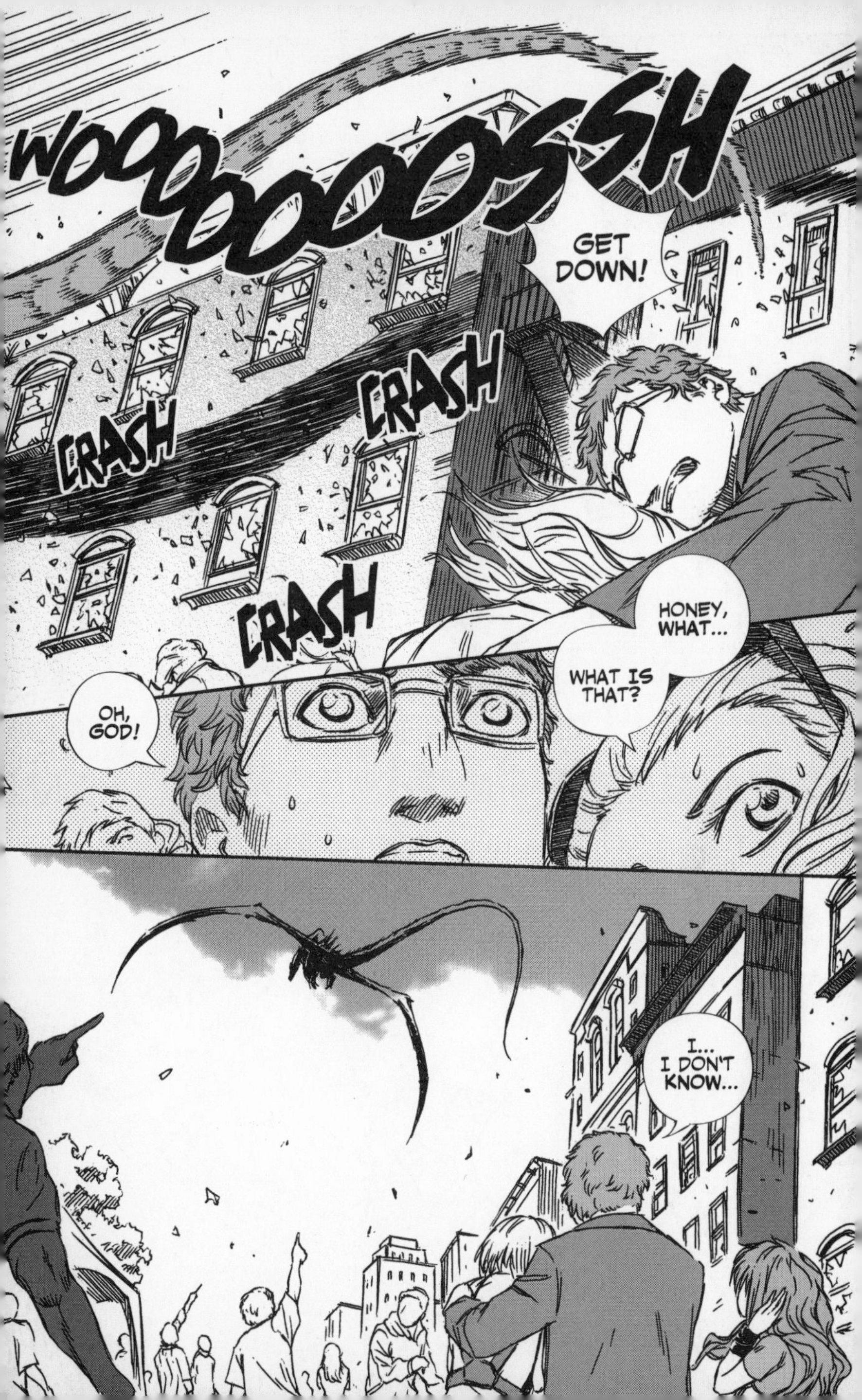
WOOOOOOOSSH
GET DOWN!
CRASH
CRASH
CRASH
HONEY, WHAT...
WHAT IS THAT?
OH, GOD!
I... I DON'T KNOW...

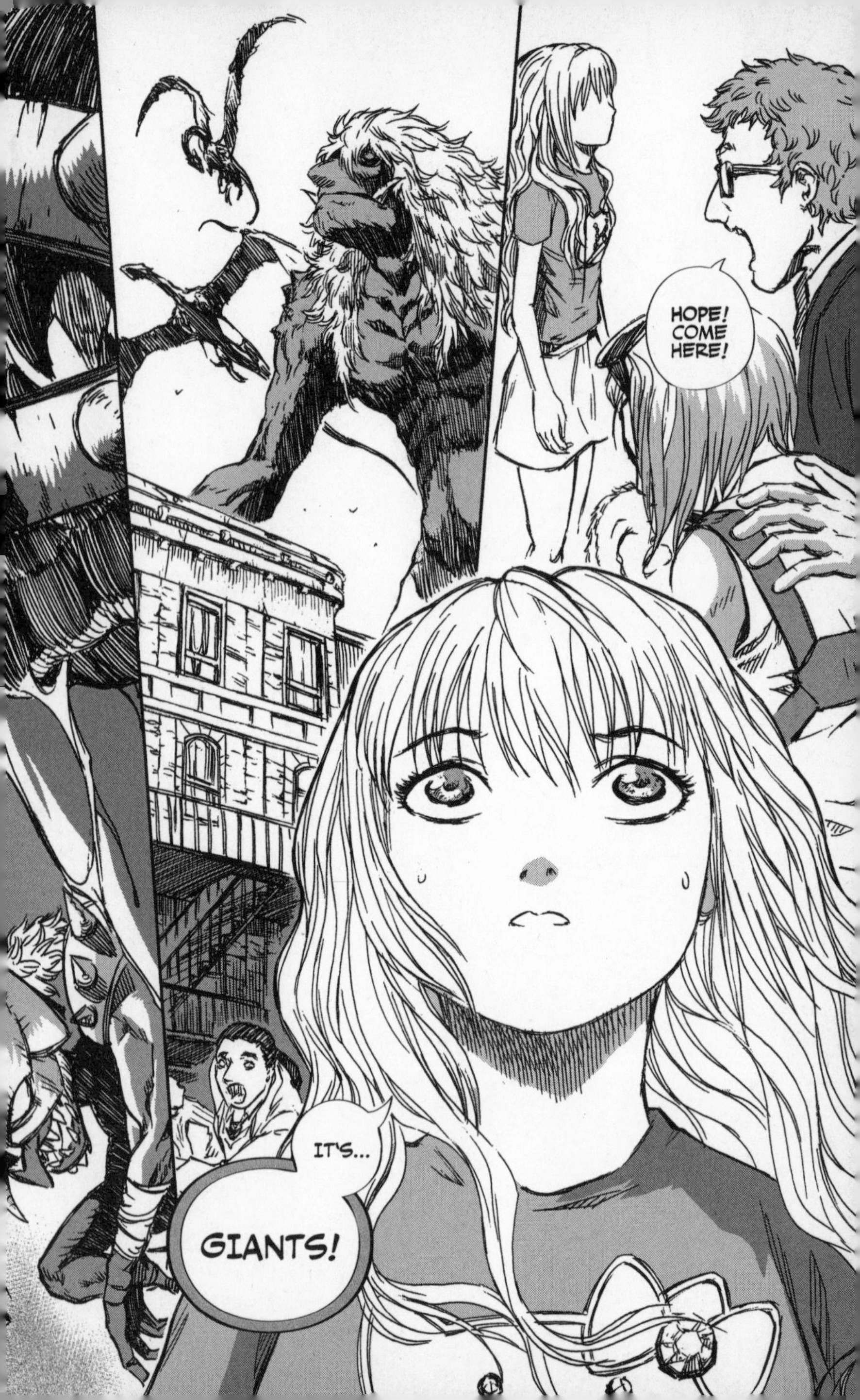
HOPE! COME HERE!
IT'S...
GIANTS!

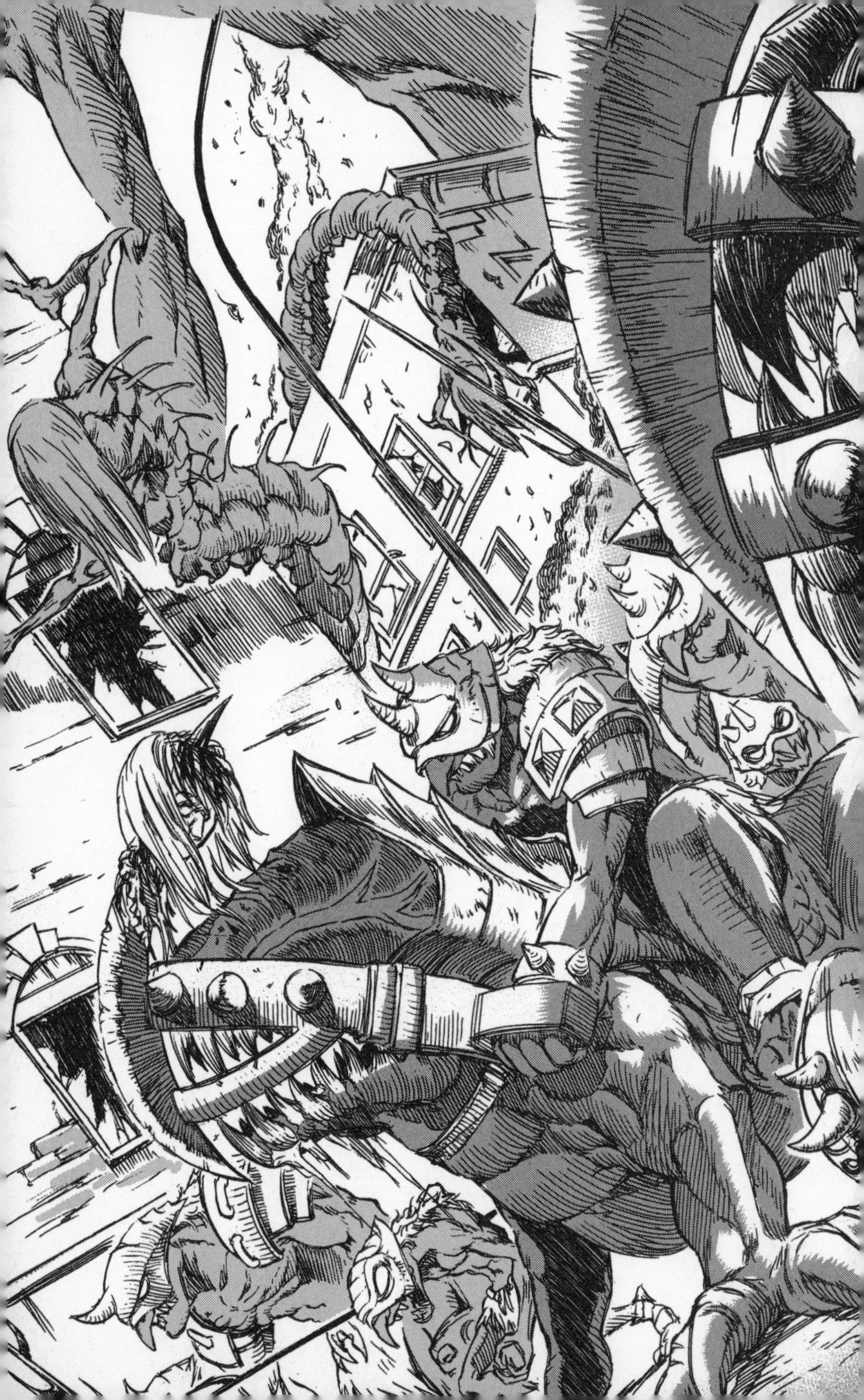

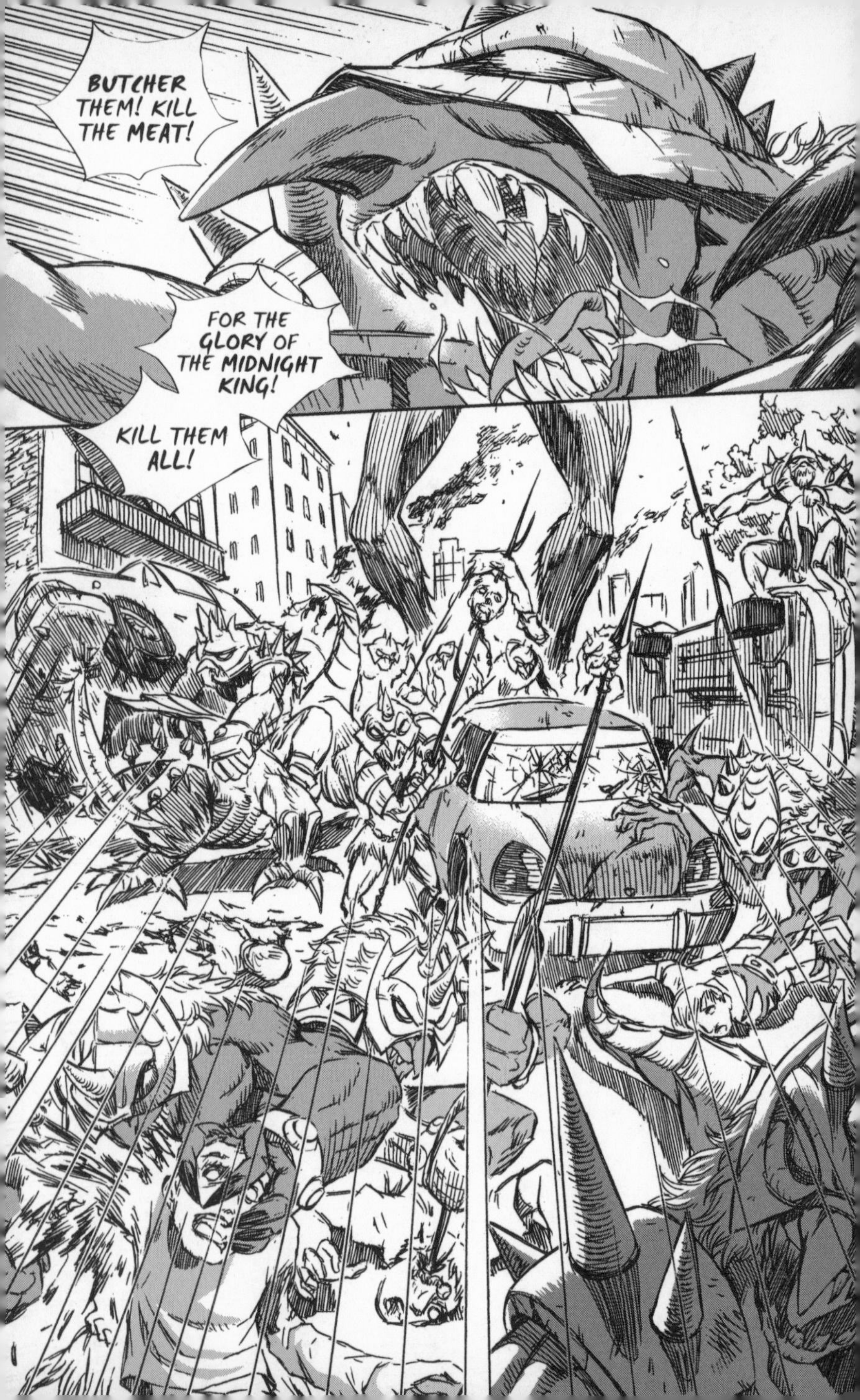
BUTCHER THEM! KILL THE MEAT!
FOR THE GLORY OF THE MIDNIGHT KING!
KILL THEM ALL!

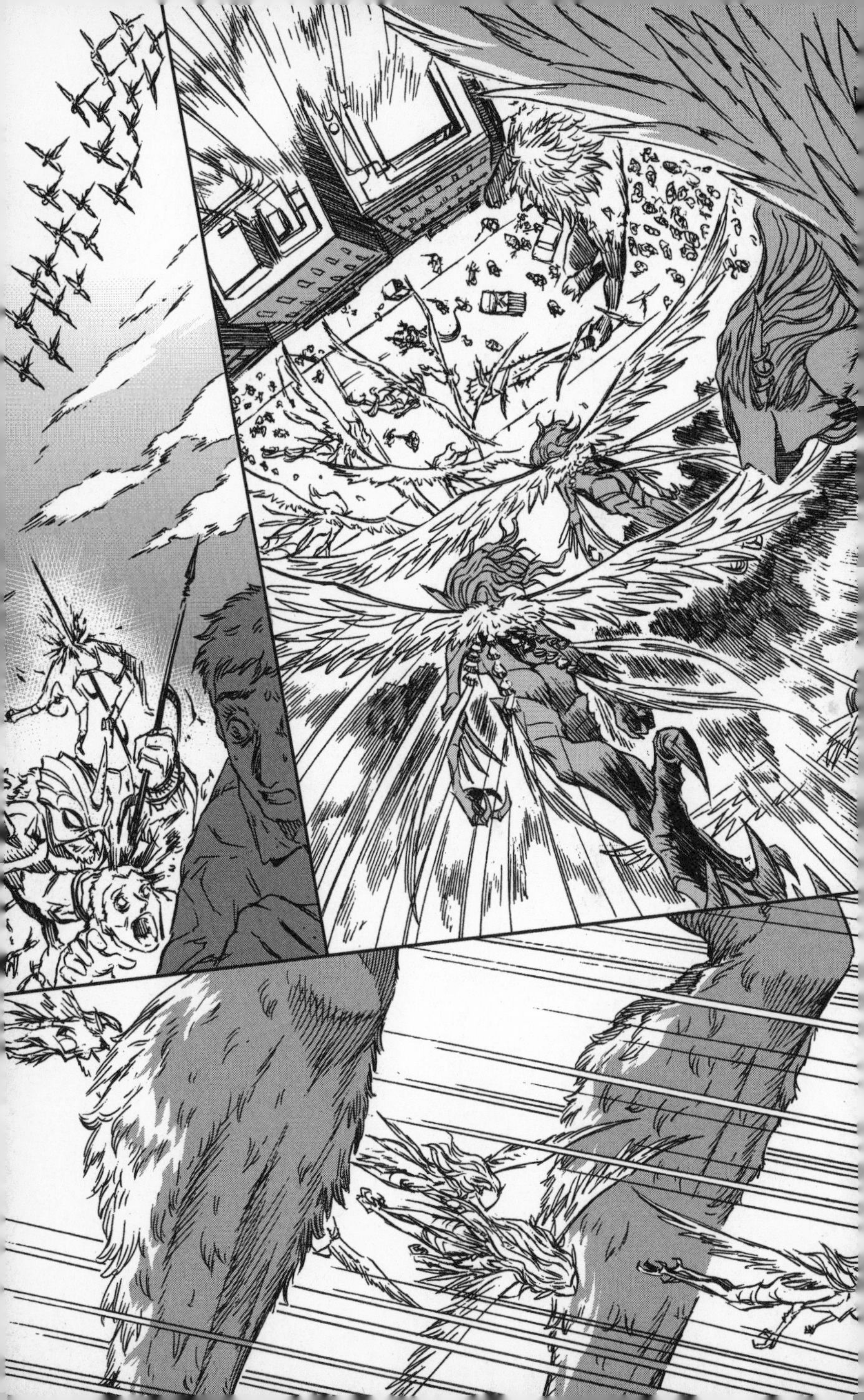

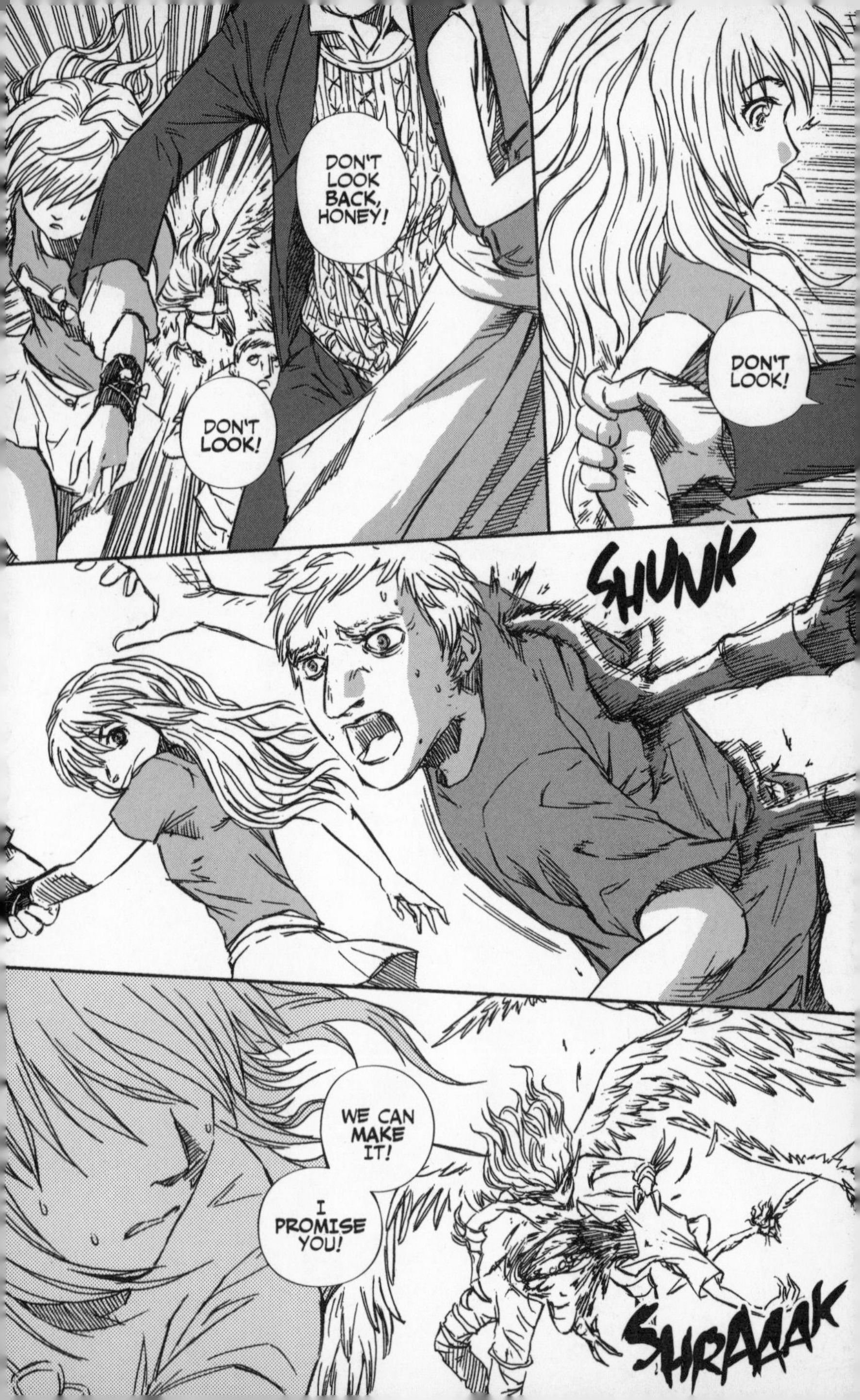
DON'T LOOK!
DON'T LOOK BACK, HONEY!
DON'T LOOK!
SHUNK
WE CAN MAKE IT!
I PROMISE YOU!
SHRAAAK

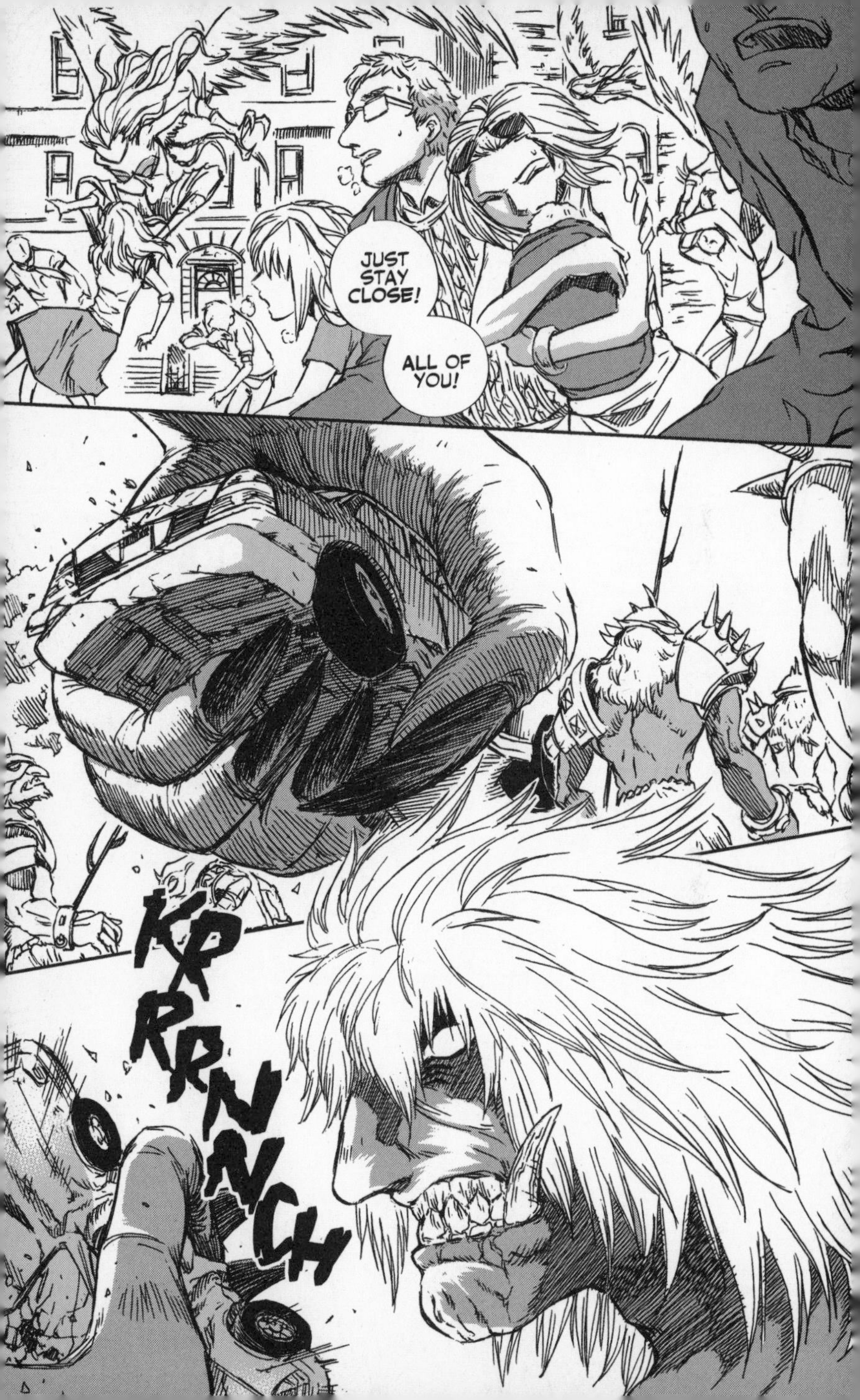
JUST STAY CLOSE!
ALL OF YOU!
KRRRNNCH

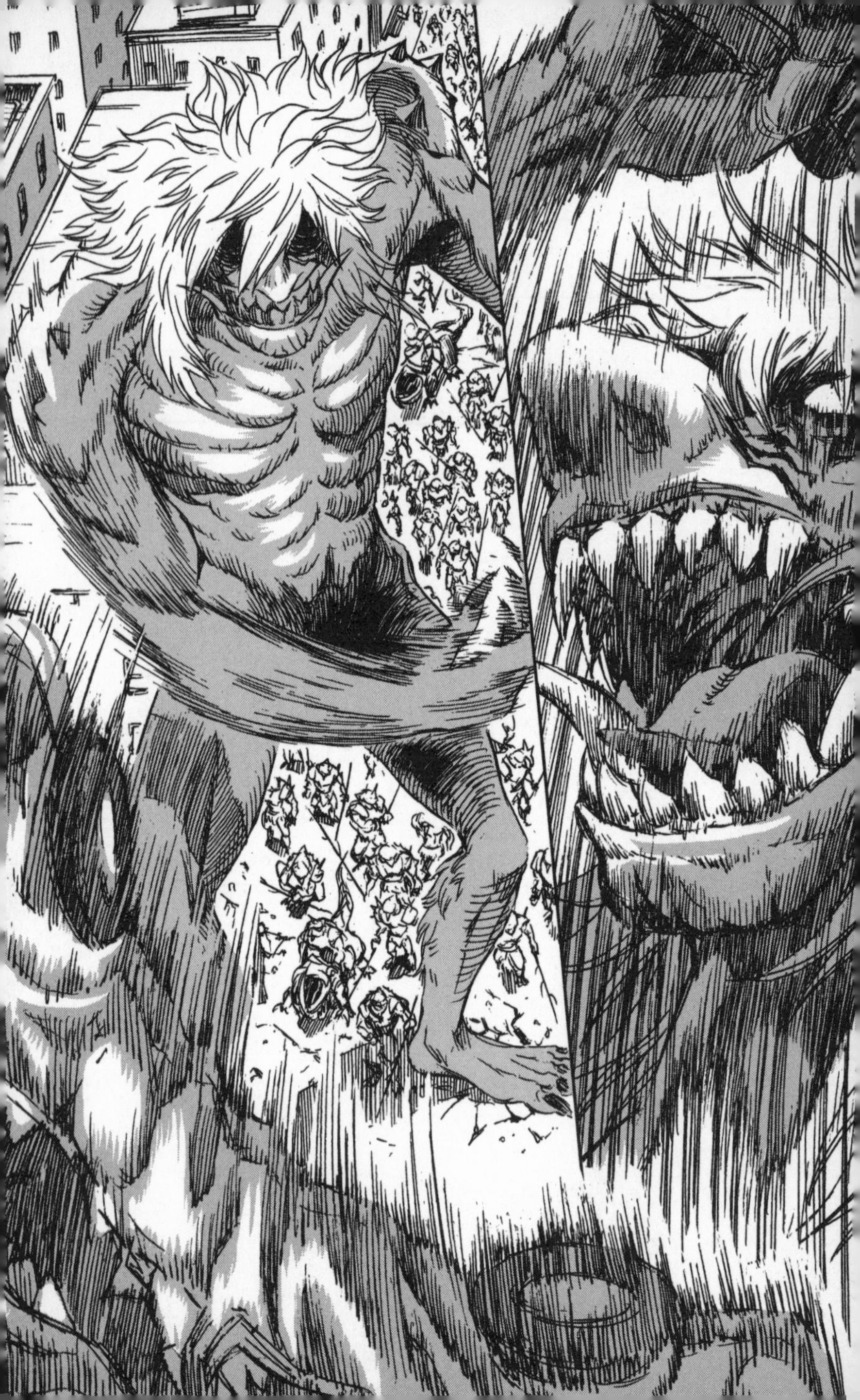

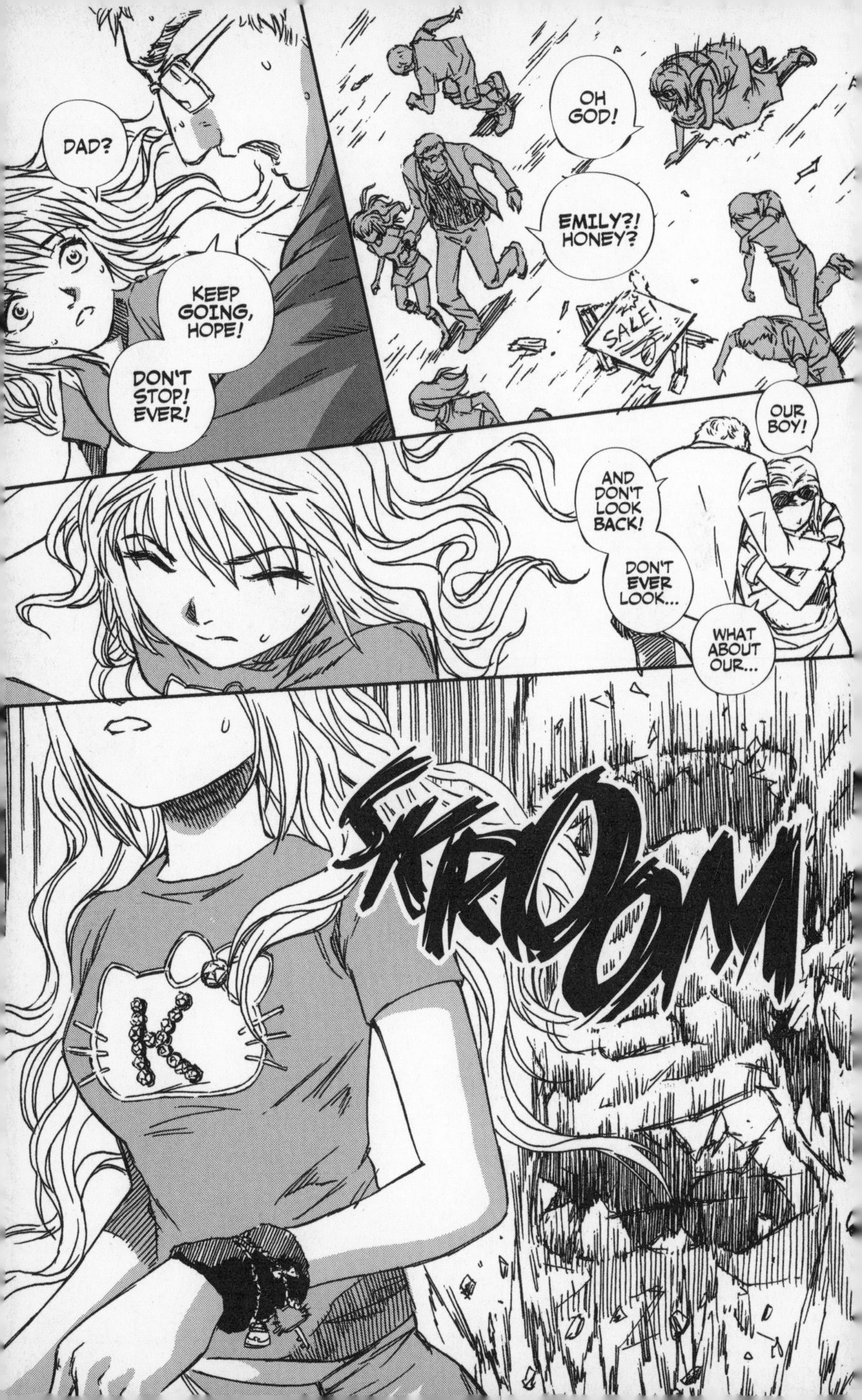
DAD?
KEEP GOING, HOPE!
DON'T STOP! EVER!
OH GOD!
EMILY?! HONEY?
SALE!
AND DON'T LOOK BACK!
DON'T EVER LOOK...
OUR BOY!
WHAT ABOUT OUR...
KROOM

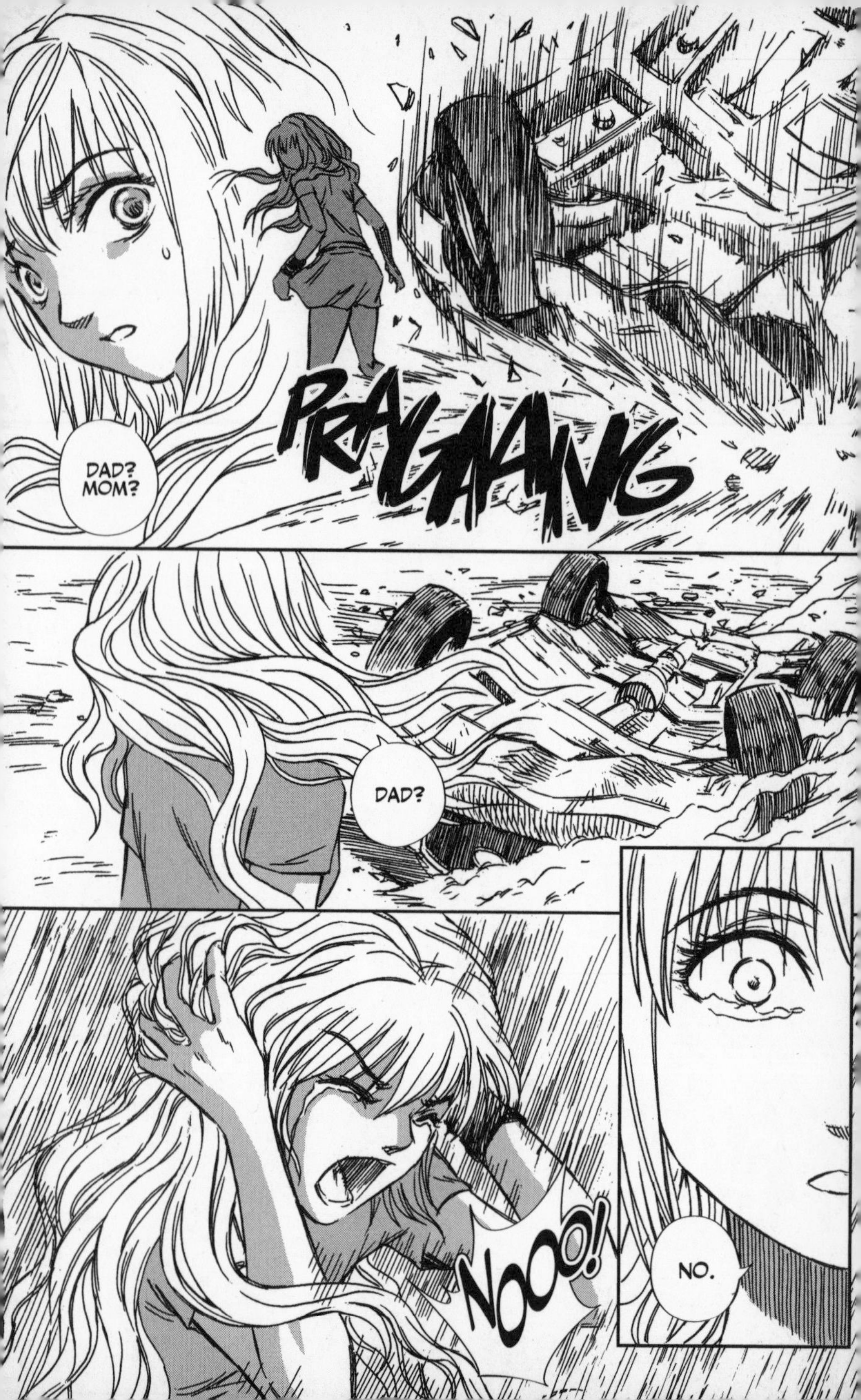
PRAGAAANG
DAD? MOM?
DAD?
NO.
NOOOO!

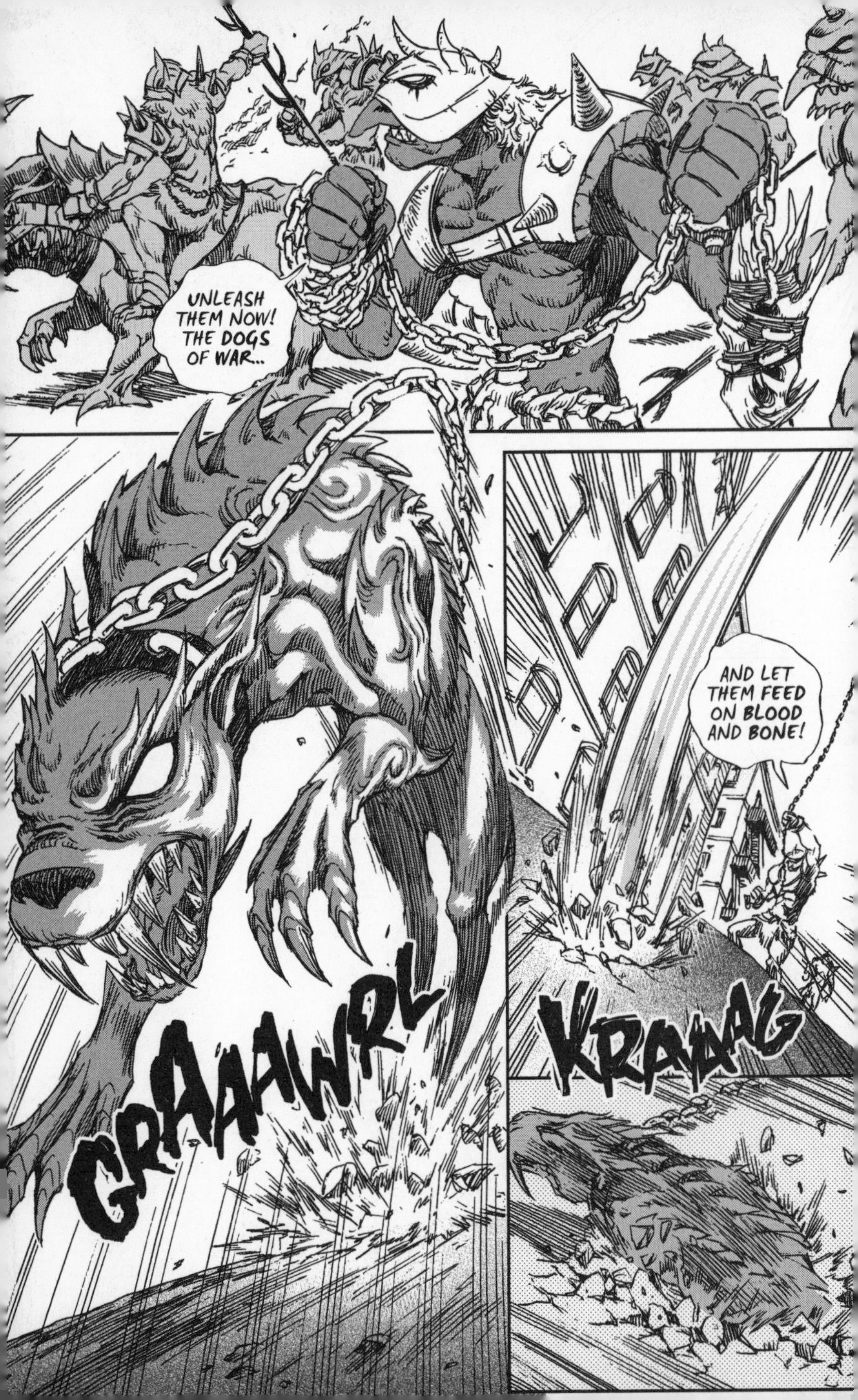
UNLEASH THEM NOW! THE DOGS OF WAR...
GRAAAWRL
AND LET THEM FEED ON BLOOD AND BONE!
KRAAAG

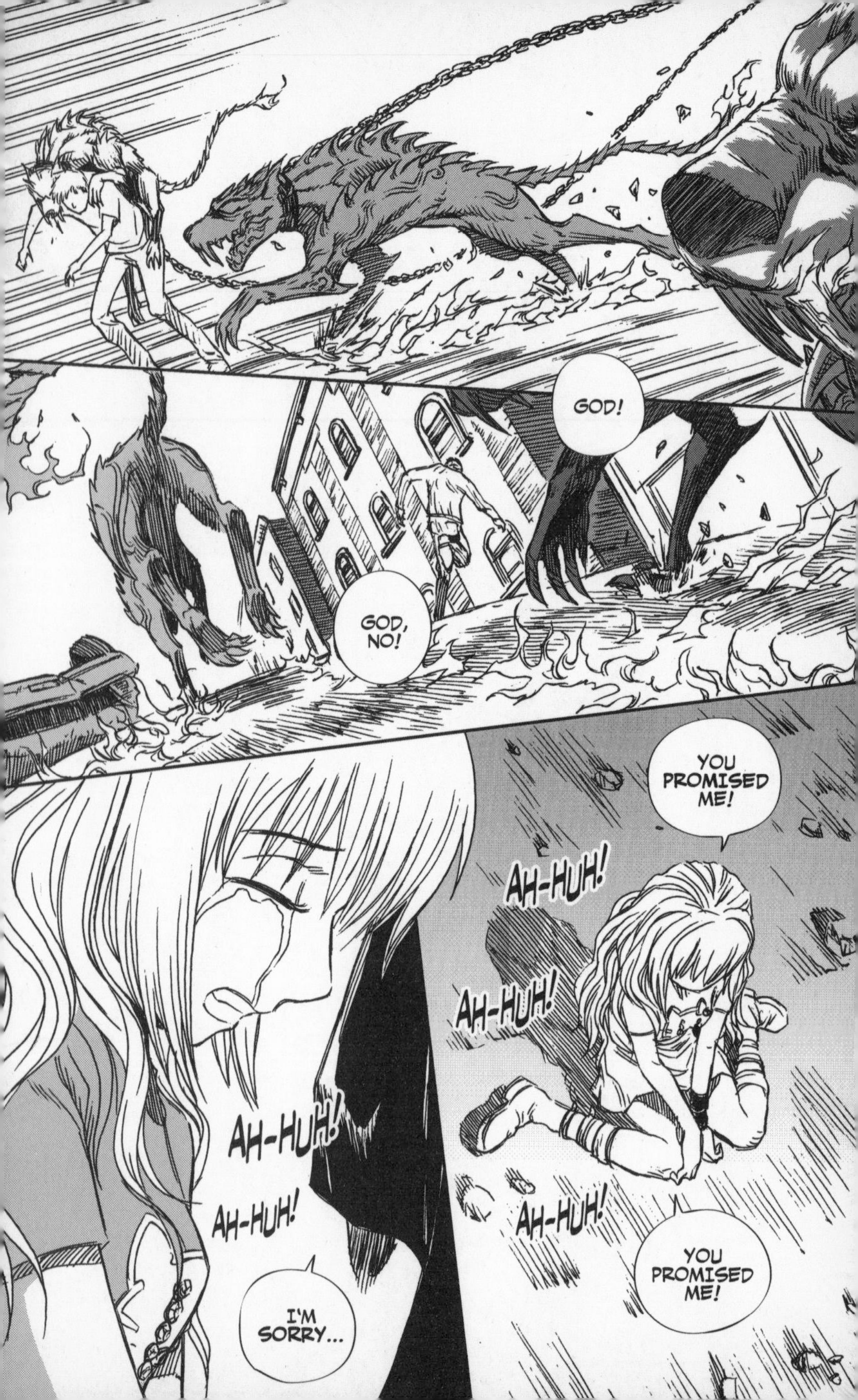
GOD!
GOD, NO!
YOU PROMISED ME!
AH-HUH!
AH-HUH!
AH-HUH!
AH-HUH!
AH-HUH!
YOU PROMISED ME!
I'M SORRY...

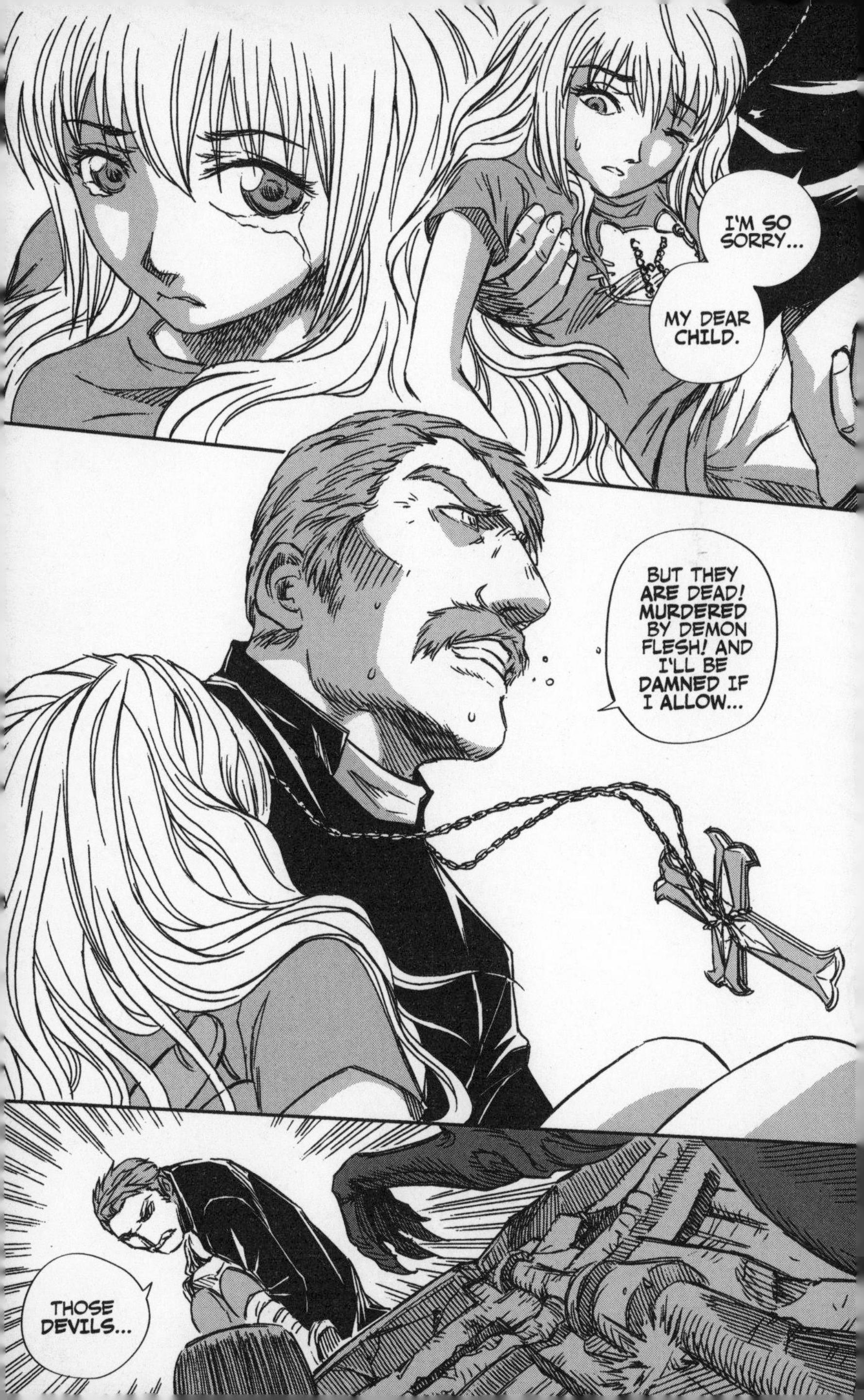
I'M SO SORRY...
MY DEAR CHILD.
BUT THEY ARE DEAD! MURDERED BY DEMON FLESH! AND I'LL BE DAMNED IF I ALLOW...
THOSE DEVILS...

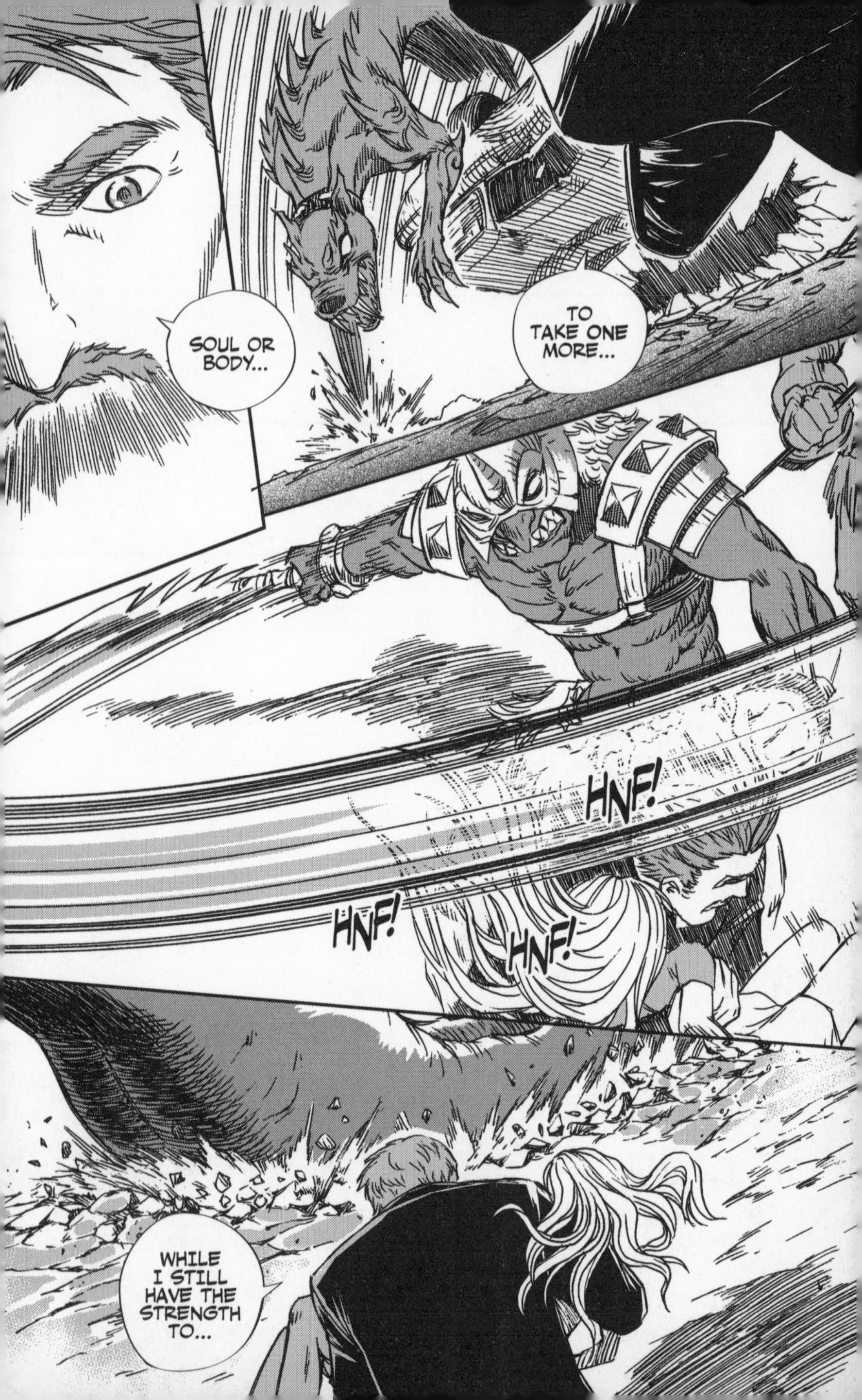
TO TAKE ONE MORE...
SOUL OR BODY...
HNF!
HNF!
HNF!
WHILE I STILL HAVE THE STRENGTH TO...

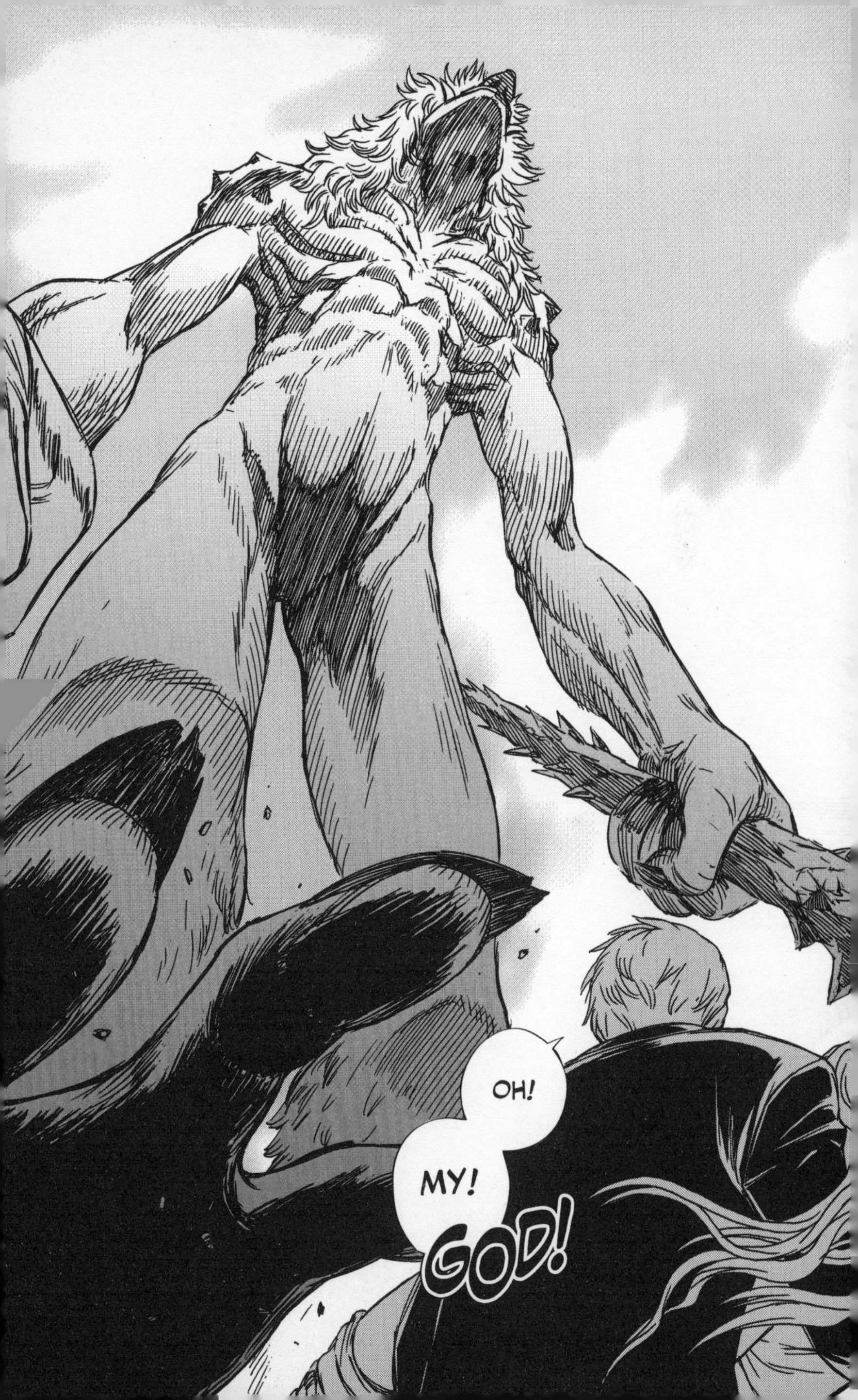
OH!
MY!
GOD!

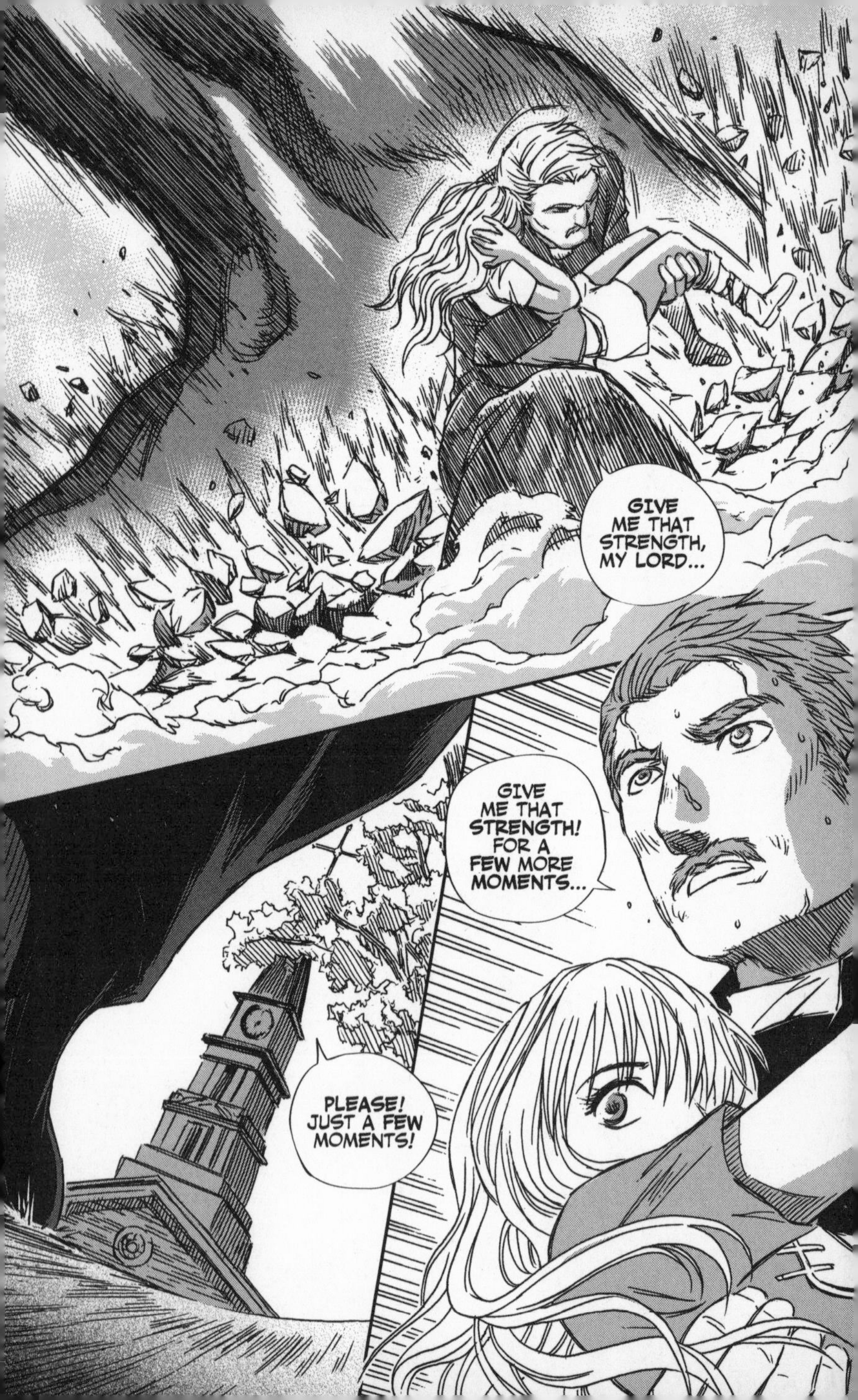
GIVE ME THAT STRENGTH, MY LORD...
GIVE ME THAT STRENGTH! FOR A FEW MORE MOMENTS...
PLEASE! JUST A FEW MOMENTS!

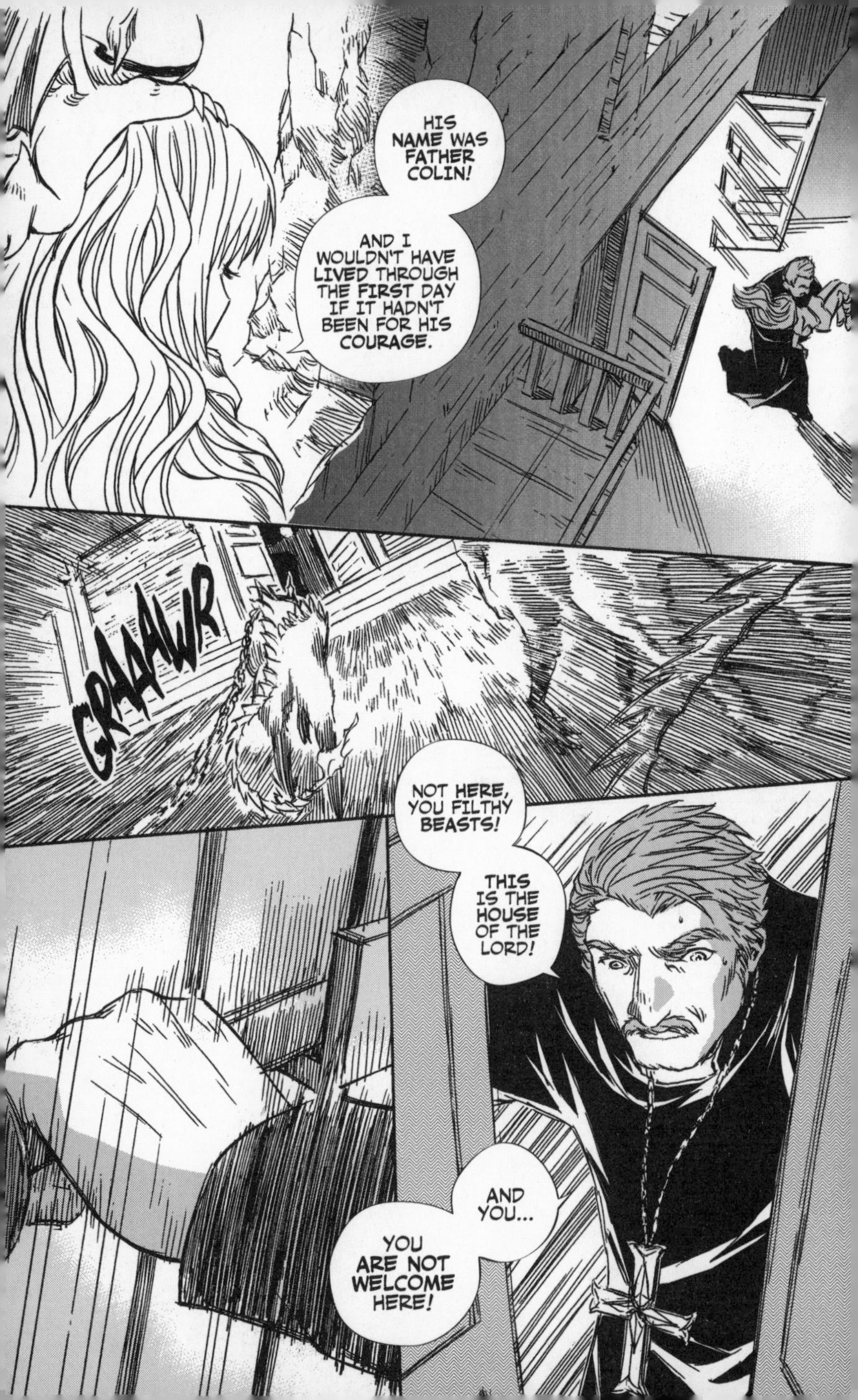
HIS NAME WAS FATHER COLIN!
AND I WOULDN'T HAVE LIVED THROUGH THE FIRST DAY IF IT HADN'T BEEN FOR HIS COURAGE.
GRAAAWR
NOT HERE, YOU FILTHY BEASTS!
THIS IS THE HOUSE OF THE LORD!
AND YOU...
YOU ARE NOT WELCOME HERE!

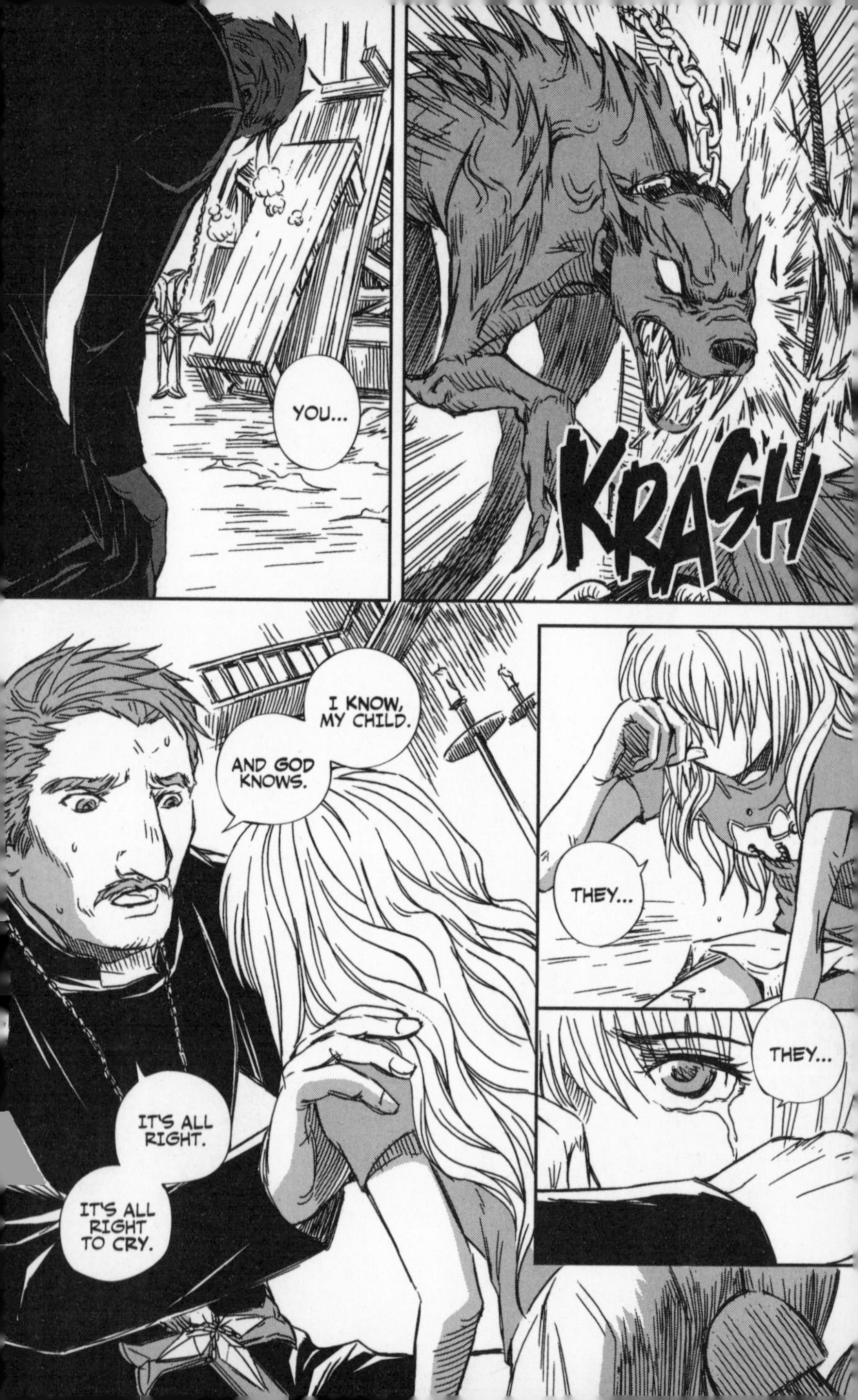
KRASH
YOU...
THEY...
THEY...
I KNOW, MY CHILD.
AND GOD KNOWS.
IT'S ALL RIGHT.
IT'S ALL RIGHT TO CRY.

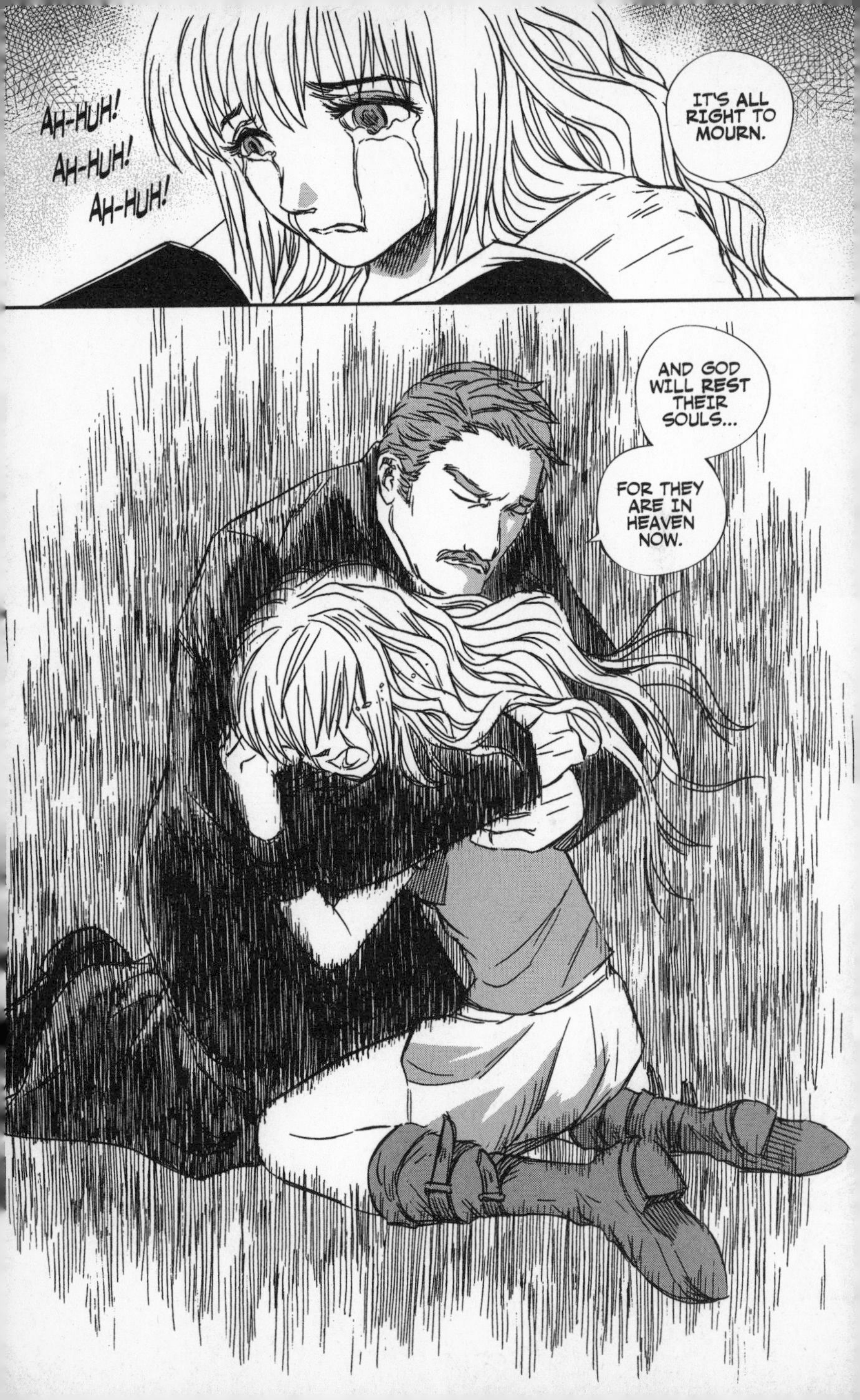
IT'S ALL RIGHT TO MOURN.
AH-HUH! AH-HUH! AH-HUH!
AND GOD WILL REST THEIR SOULS...
FOR THEY ARE IN HEAVEN NOW.

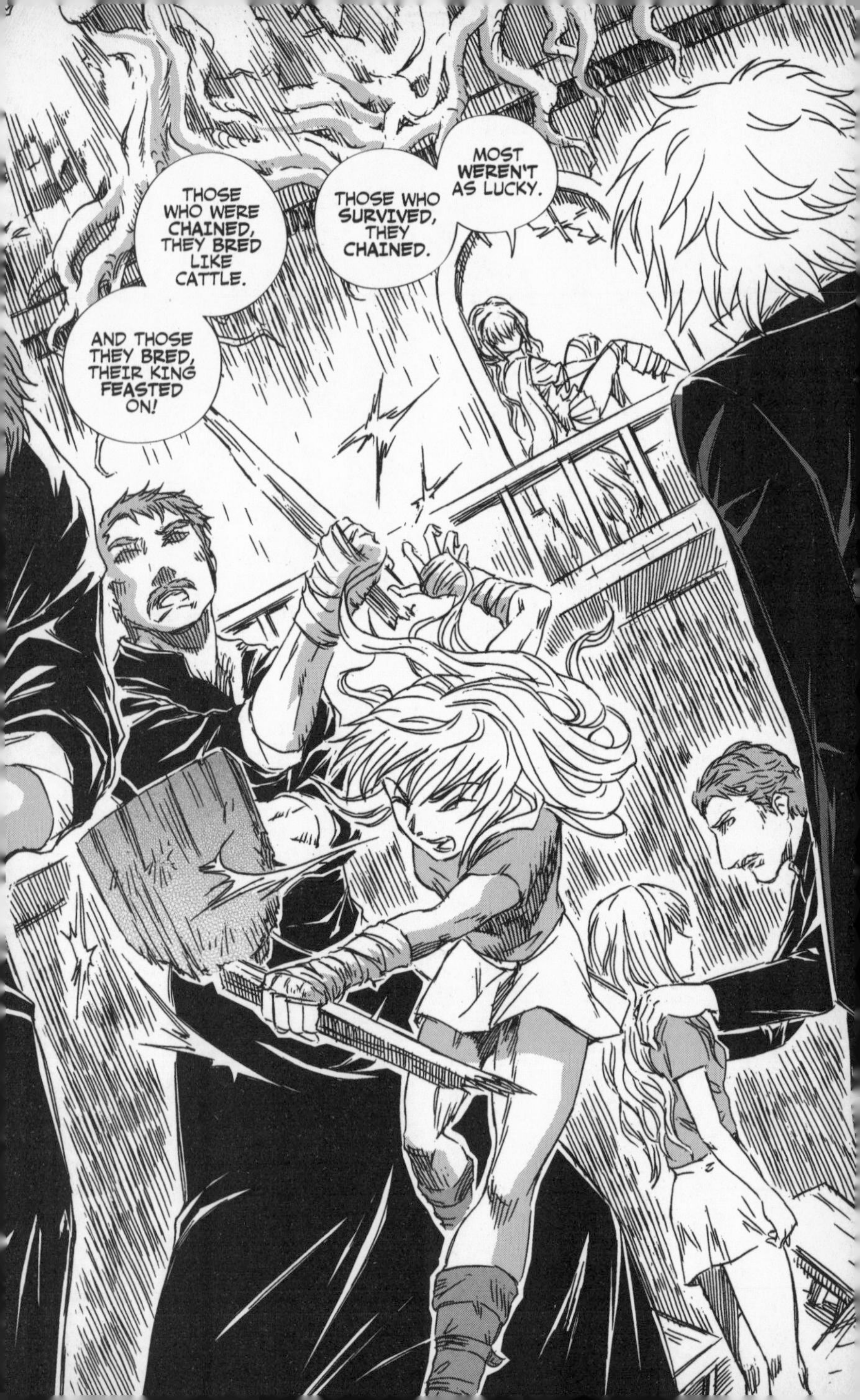
MOST WEREN'T AS LUCKY.
THOSE WHO SURVIVED, THEY CHAINED.
THOSE WHO WERE CHAINED, THEY BRED LIKE CATTLE.
AND THOSE THEY BRED, THEIR KING FEASTED ON!

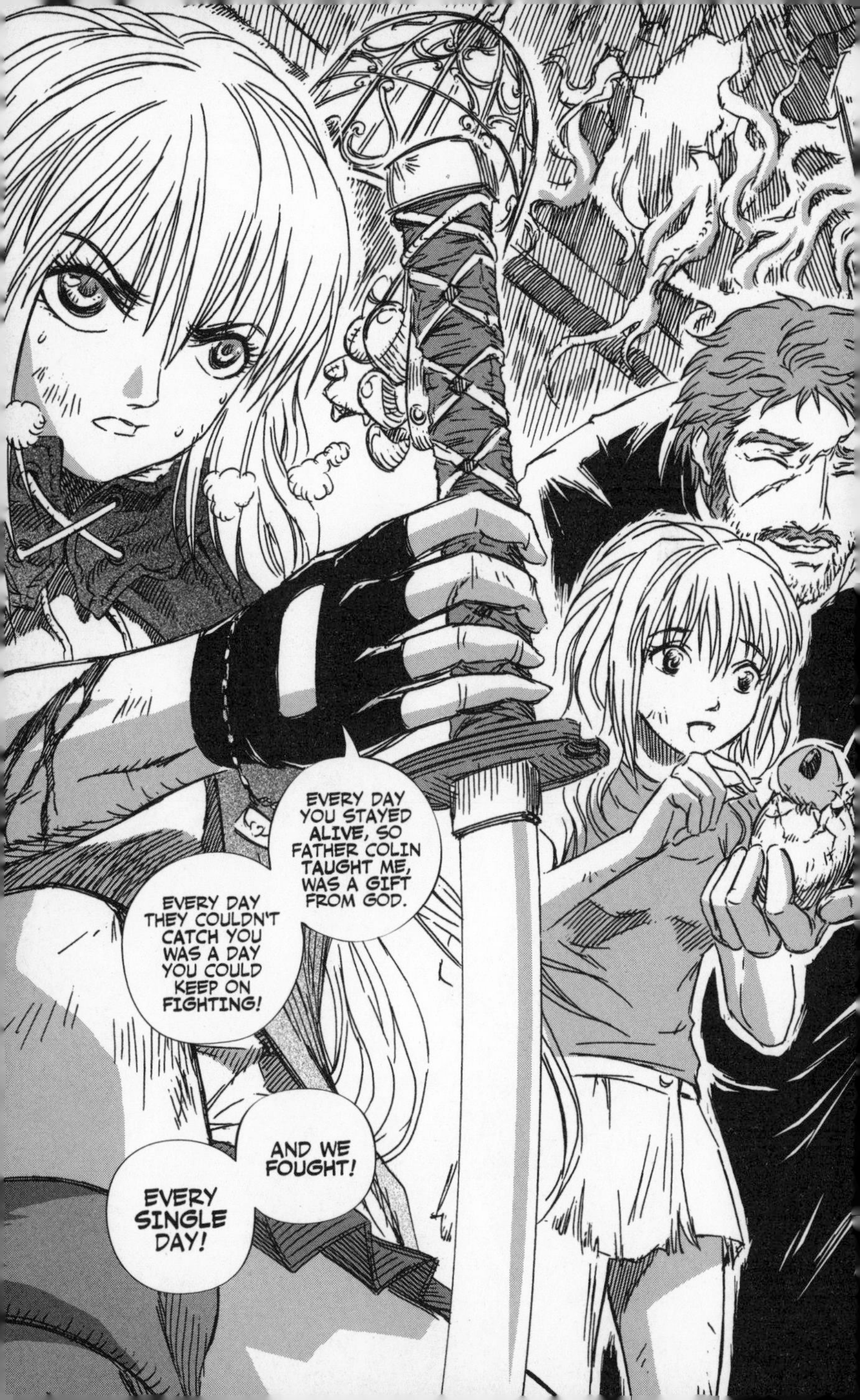
EVERY DAY YOU STAYED ALIVE, SO FATHER COLIN TAUGHT ME, WAS A GIFT FROM GOD.
EVERY DAY THEY COULDN'T CATCH YOU WAS A DAY YOU COULD KEEP ON FIGHTING!
AND WE FOUGHT!
EVERY SINGLE DAY!

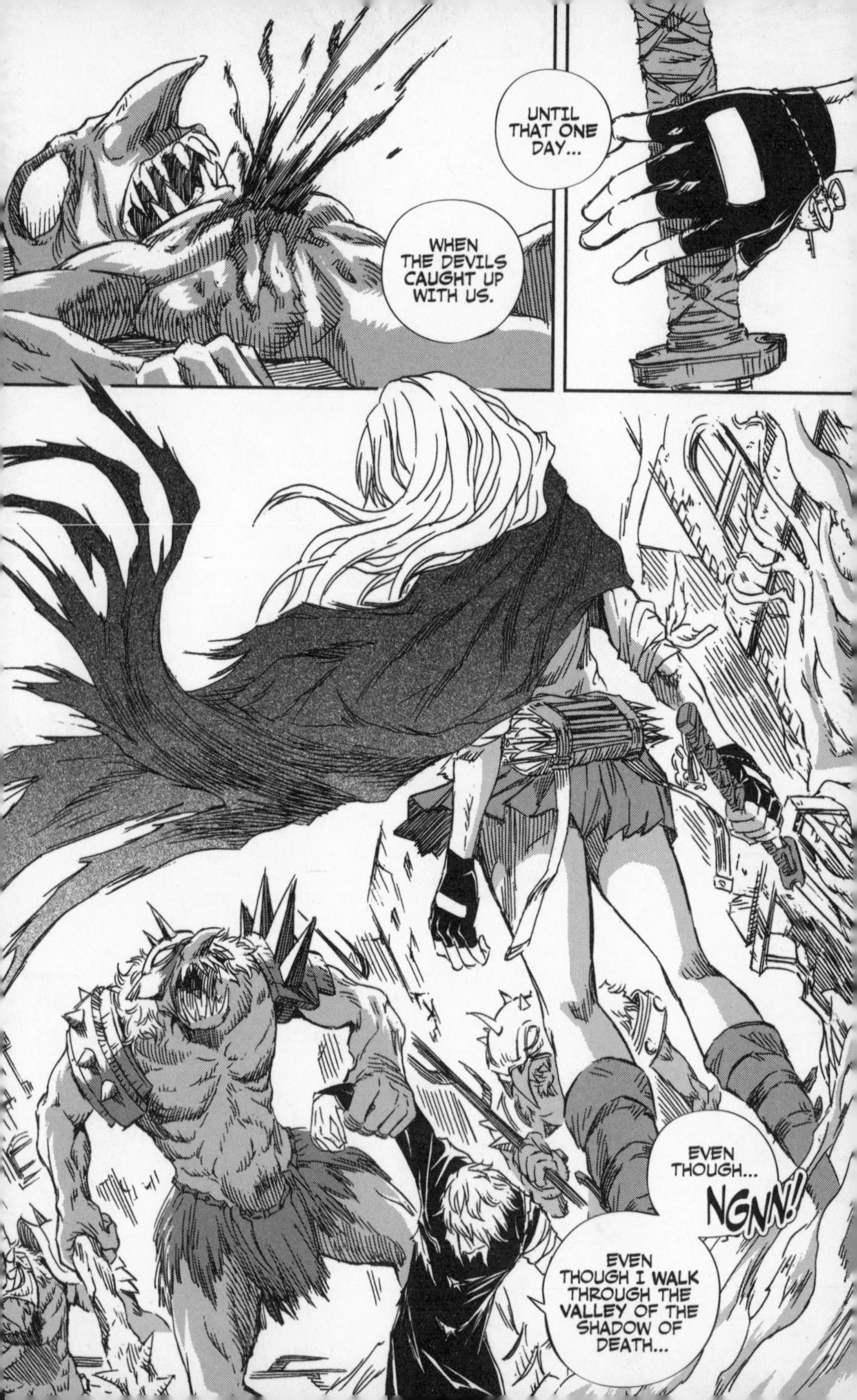
UNTIL THAT ONE DAY...
WHEN THE DEVILS CAUGHT UP WITH US.
EVEN THOUGH...
NGNN!
EVEN THOUGH I WALK THROUGH THE VALLEY OF THE SHADOW OF DEATH...

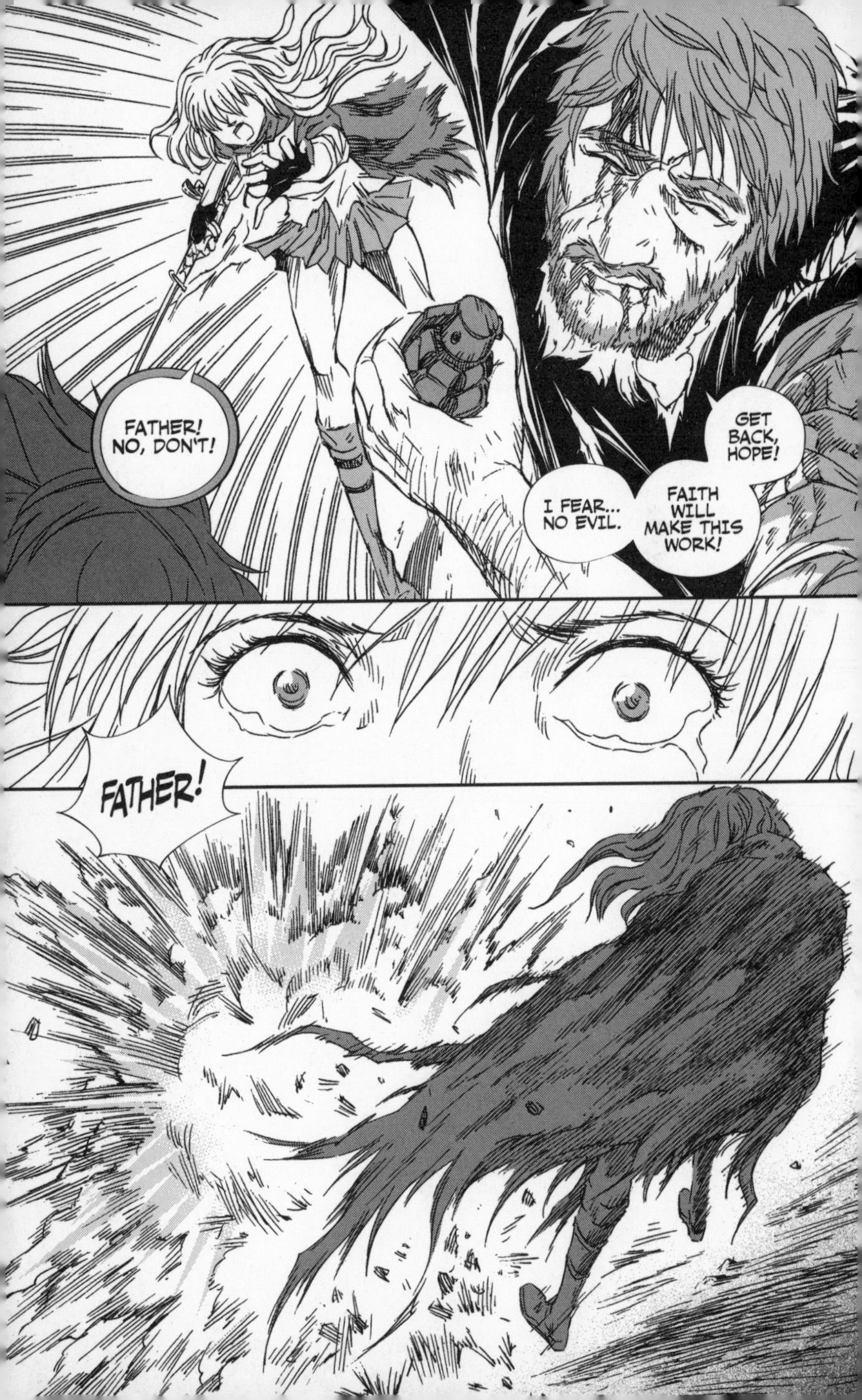
GET BACK, HOPE!
FAITH WILL MAKE THIS WORK!
I FEAR... NO EVIL.
FATHER! NO, DON'T!
FATHER!

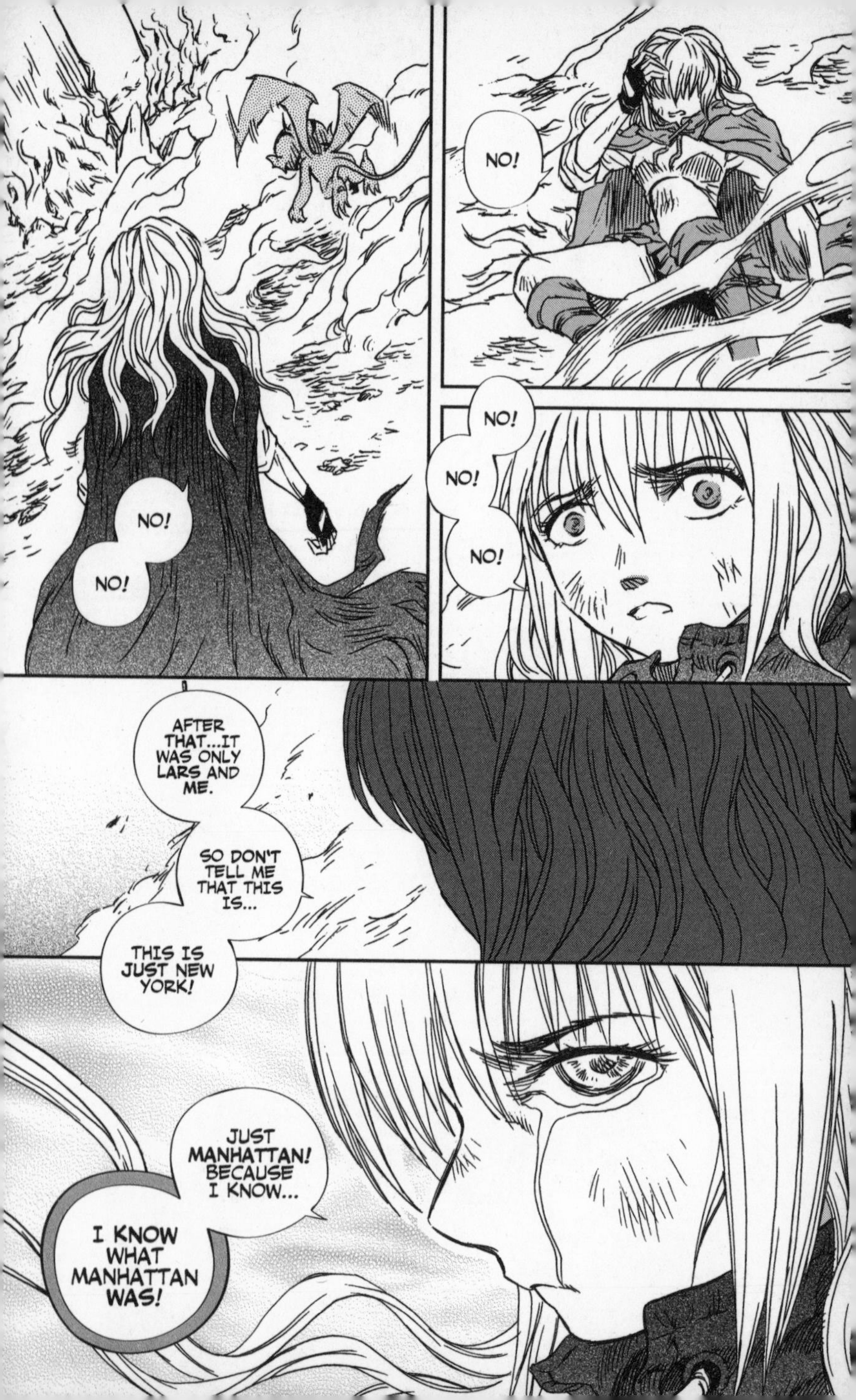
NO!
NO!
NO!
NO!
NO!
NO!
AFTER THAT...IT WAS ONLY LARS AND ME.
SO DON'T TELL ME THAT THIS IS...
THIS IS JUST NEW YORK!
JUST MANHATTAN! BECAUSE I KNOW...
I KNOW WHAT MANHATTAN WAS!

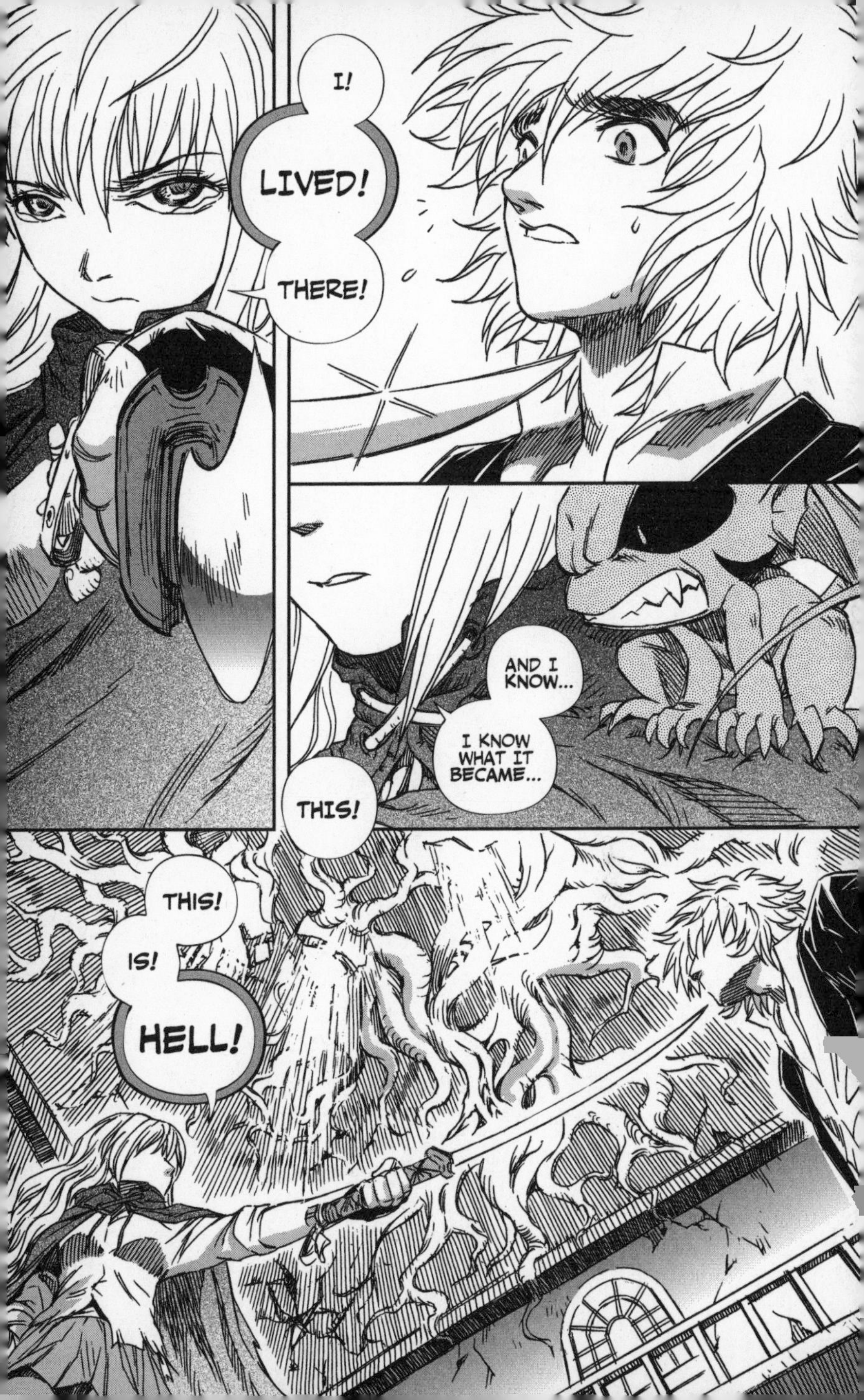
I!
LIVED!
THERE!
AND I KNOW...
I KNOW WHAT IT BECAME...
THIS!
THIS!
IS!
HELL!

CHAPTER

4

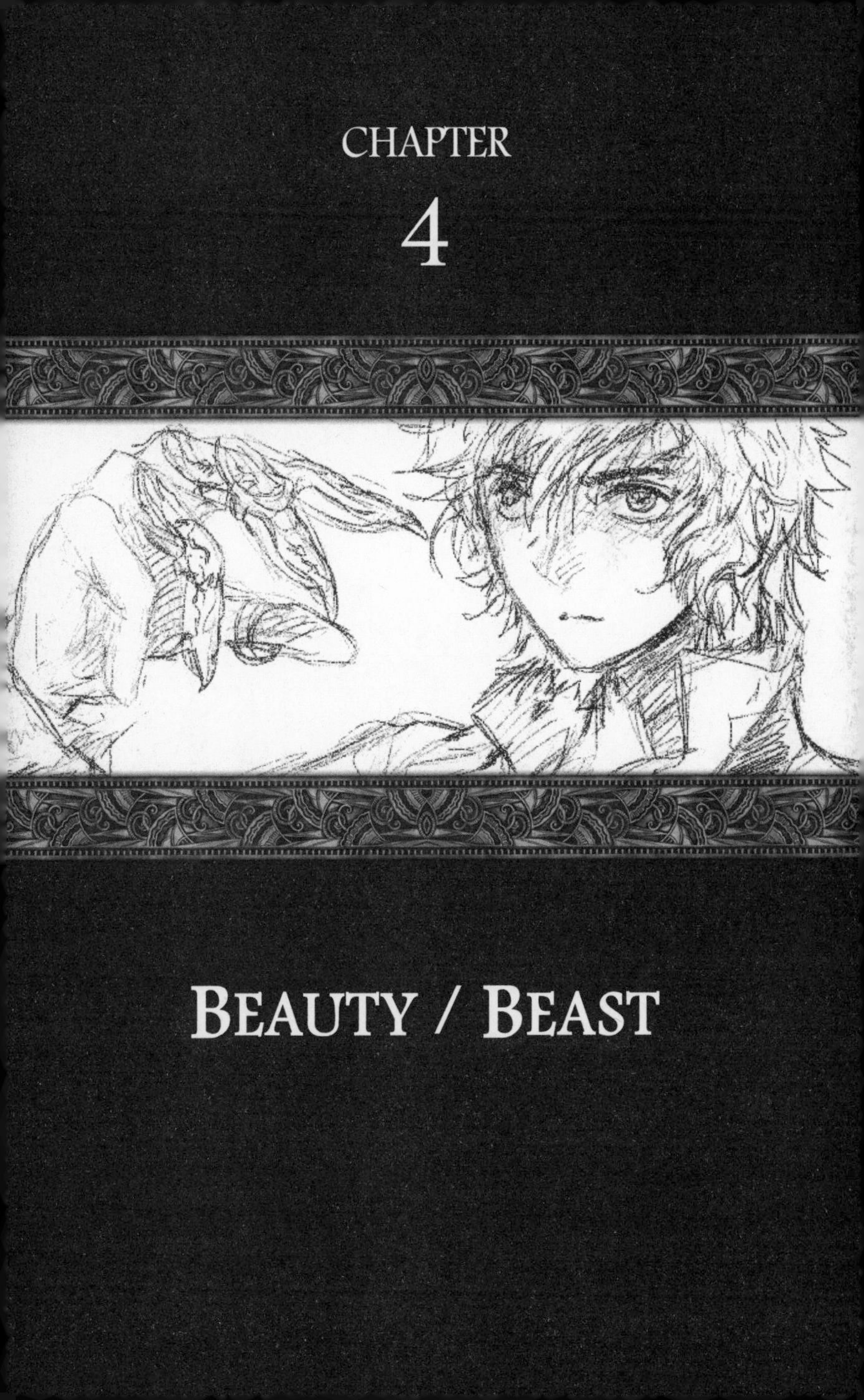

BEAUTY / BEAST

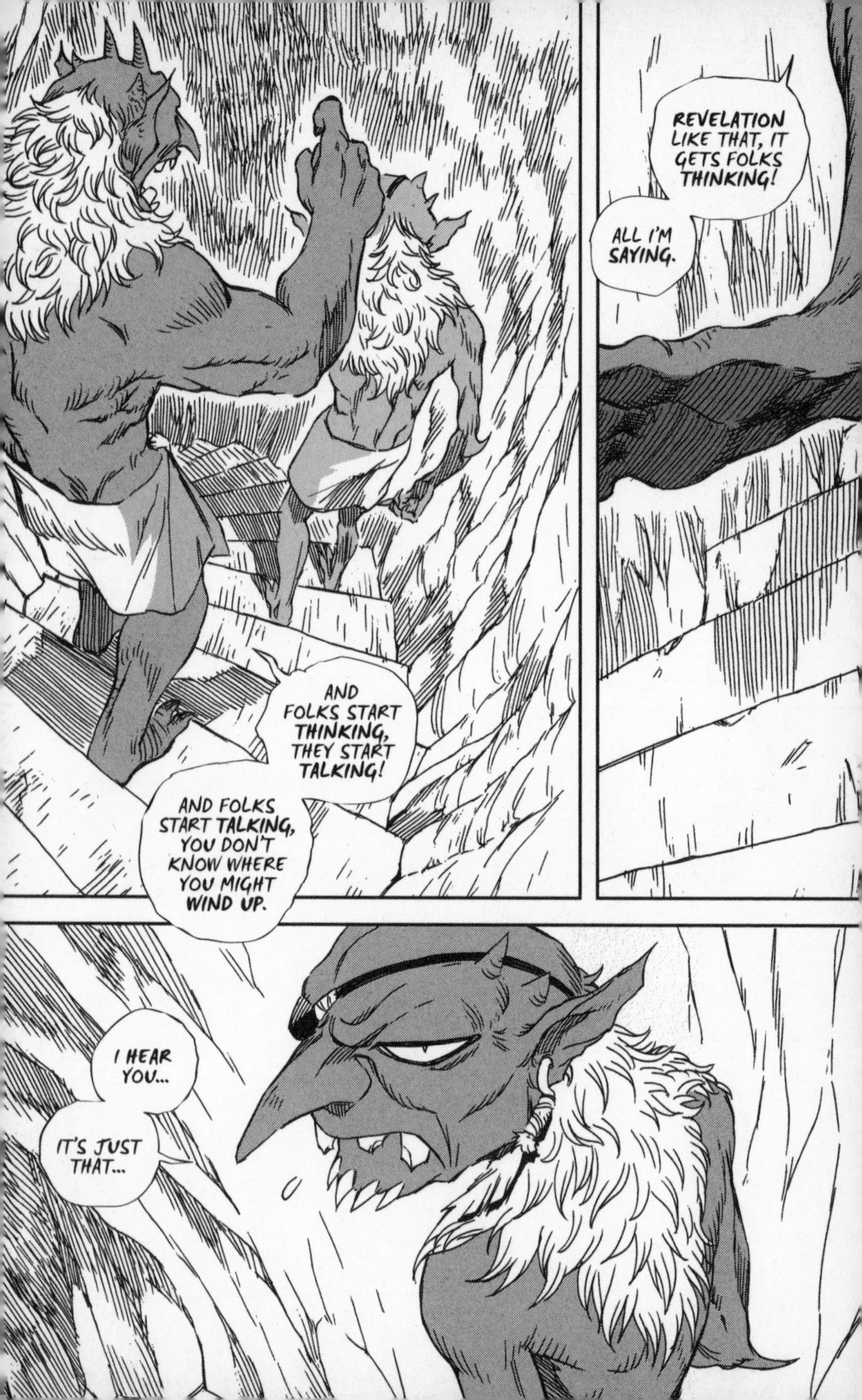
REVELATION LIKE THAT, IT GETS FOLKS THINKING!
ALL I'M SAYING.
AND FOLKS START THINKING, THEY START TALKING!
AND FOLKS START TALKING, YOU DON'T KNOW WHERE YOU MIGHT WIND UP.
I HEAR YOU...
IT'S JUST THAT...

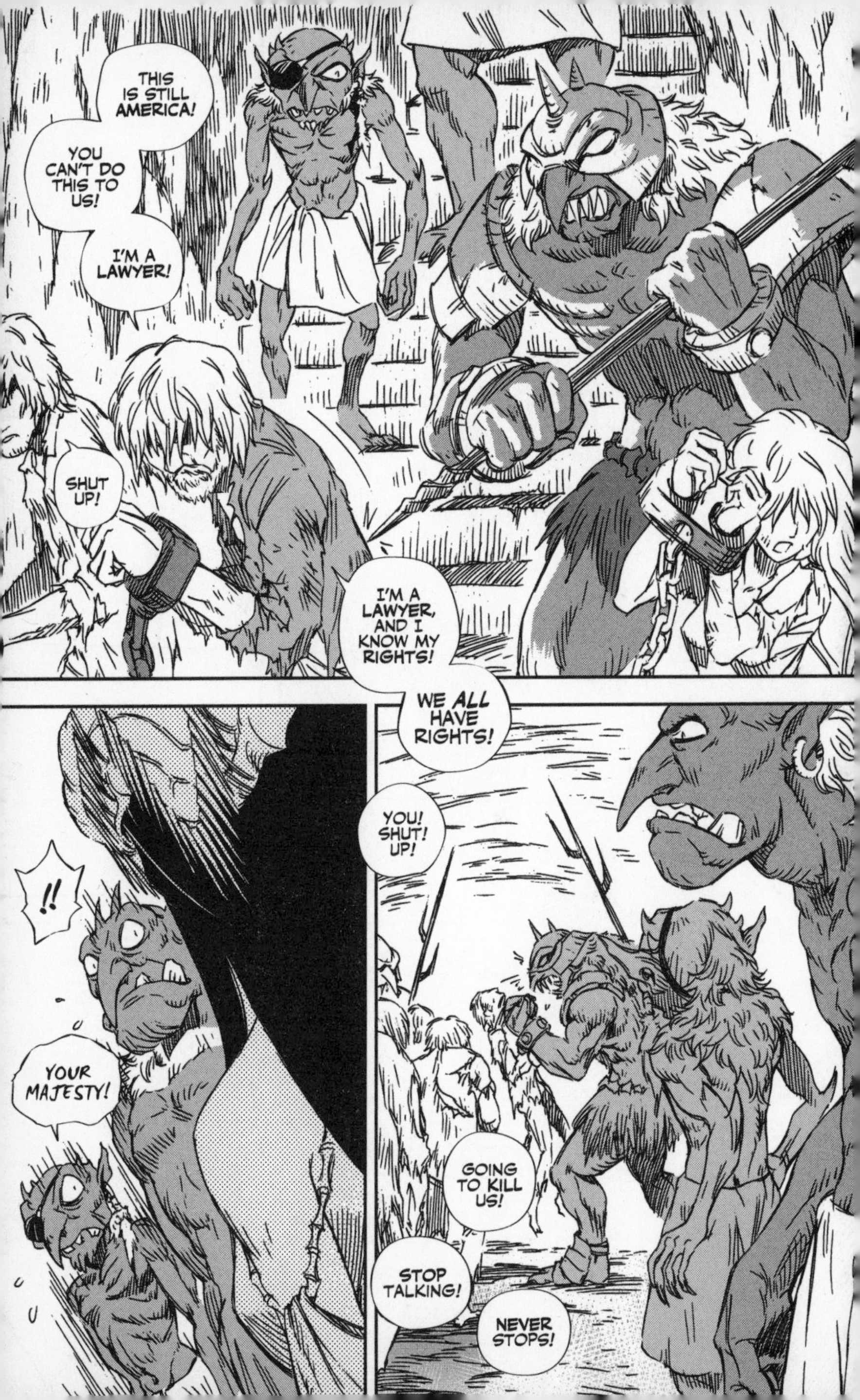
THIS IS STILL AMERICA!
YOU CAN'T DO THIS TO US!
I'M A LAWYER!
SHUT UP!
I'M A LAWYER, AND I KNOW MY RIGHTS!
WE ALL HAVE RIGHTS!
YOU! SHUT! UP!
GOING TO KILL US!
STOP TALKING!
NEVER STOPS!
!!
YOUR MAJESTY!

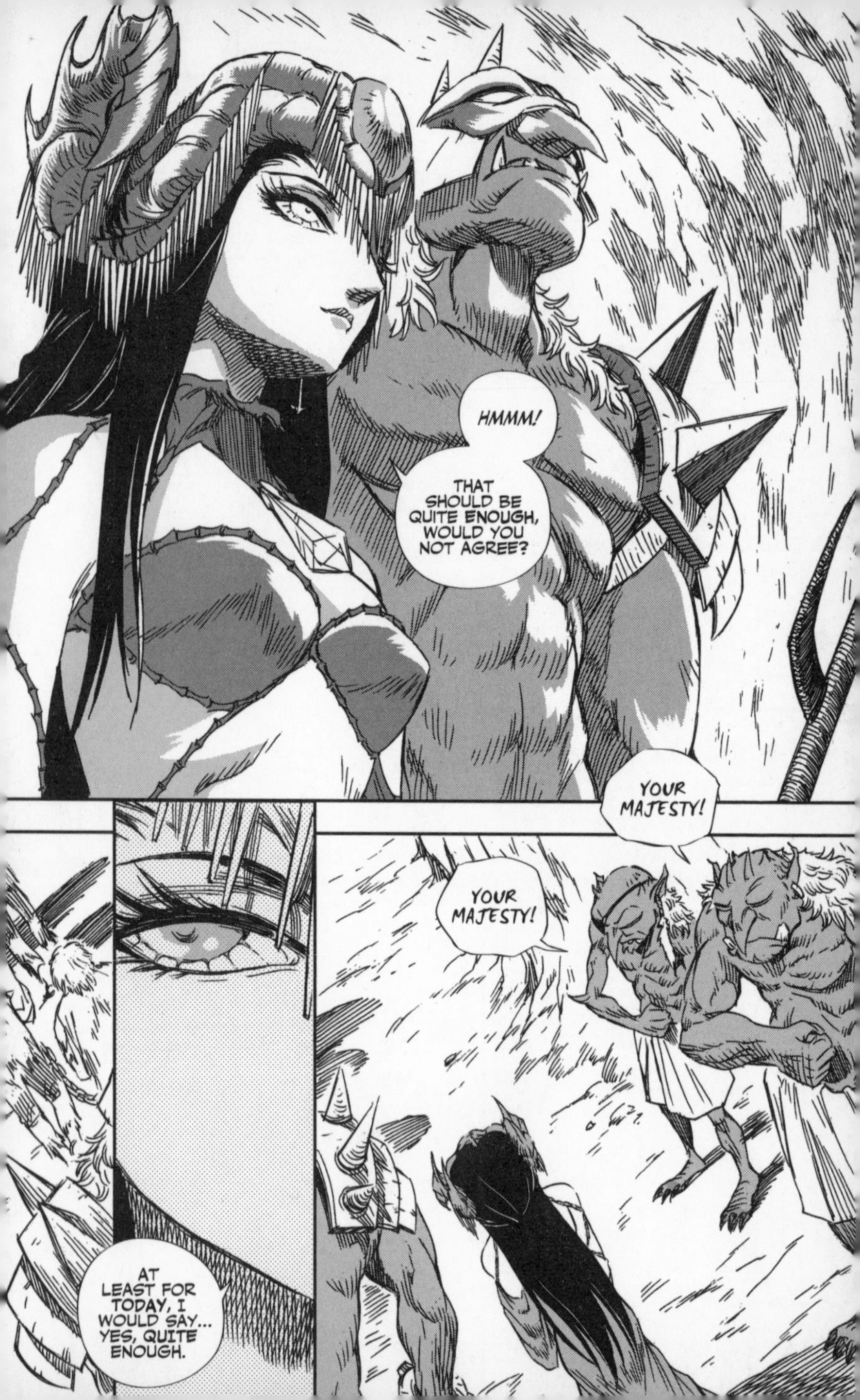
HMMM!
THAT SHOULD BE QUITE ENOUGH, WOULD YOU NOT AGREE?
YOUR MAJESTY!
YOUR MAJESTY!
AT LEAST FOR TODAY, I WOULD SAY... YES, QUITE ENOUGH.

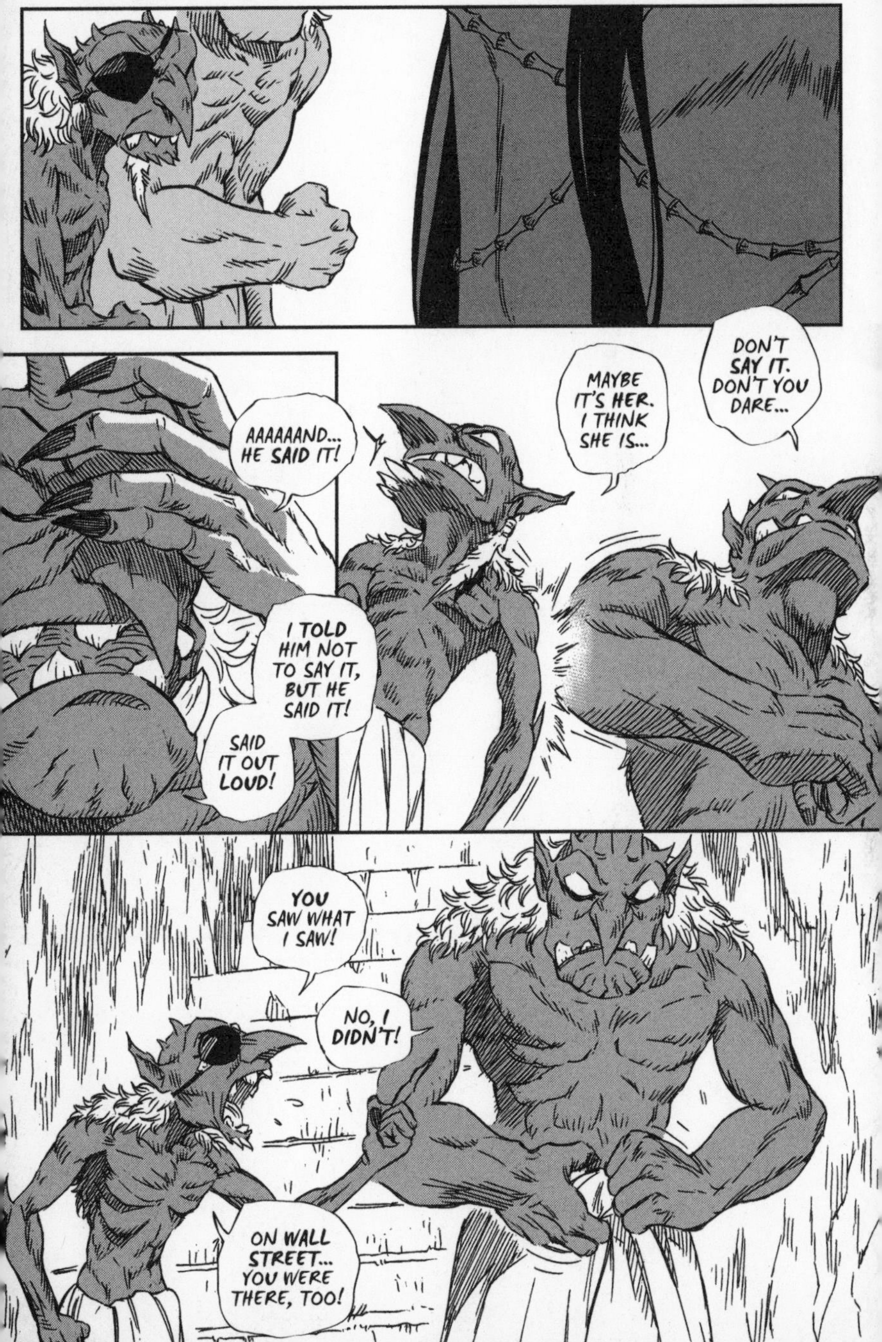
DON'T SAY IT. DON'T YOU DARE...
MAYBE IT'S HER. I THINK SHE IS...
AAAAAAND... HE SAID IT!
I TOLD HIM NOT TO SAY IT, BUT HE SAID IT!
SAID IT OUT LOUD!
YOU SAW WHAT I SAW!
NO, I DIDN'T!
ON WALL STREET... YOU WERE THERE, TOO!

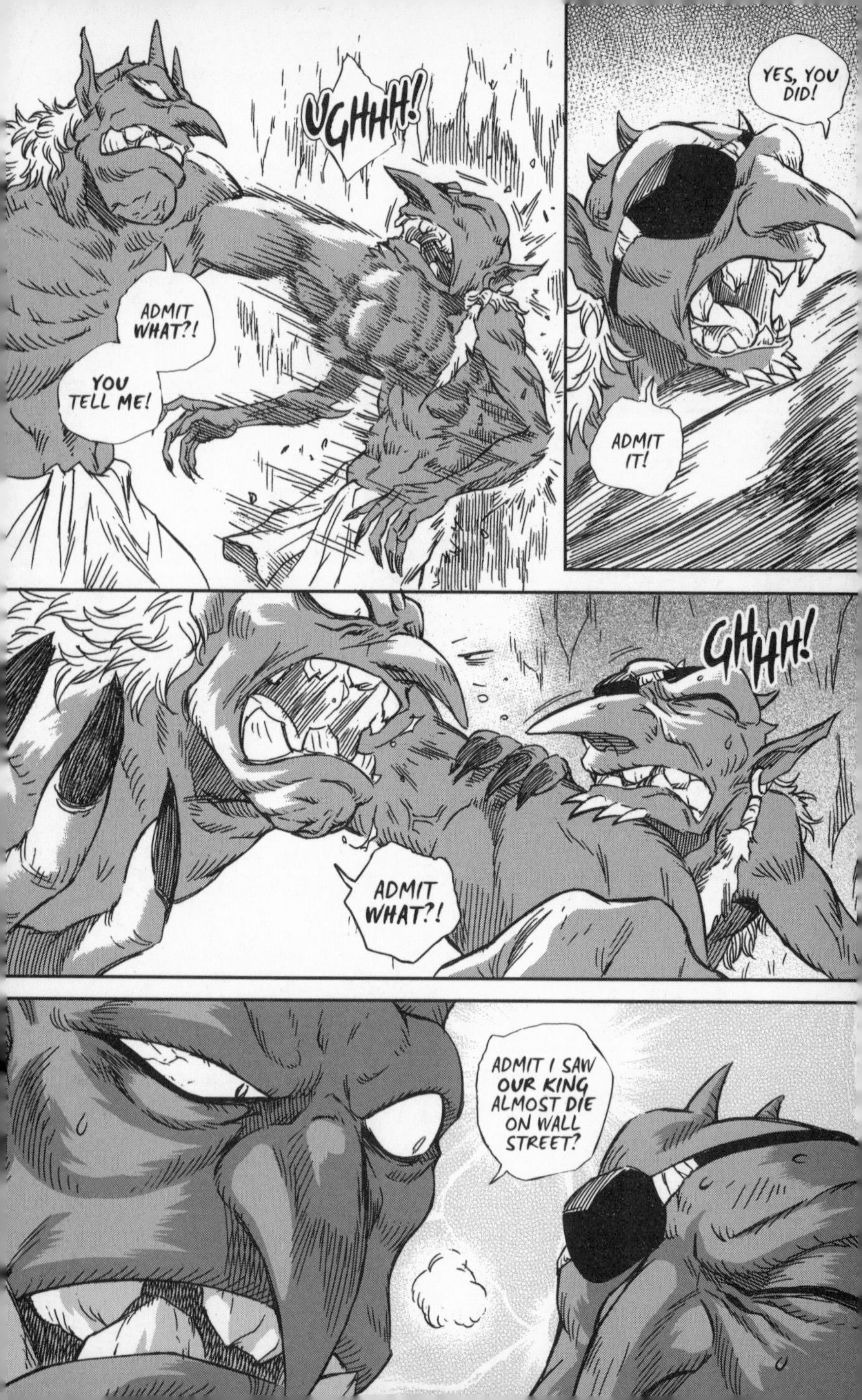
YES, YOU DID!
ADMIT IT!
UGHHH!
ADMIT WHAT?!
YOU TELL ME!
GHHH!
ADMIT WHAT?!
ADMIT I SAW OUR KING ALMOST DIE ON WALL STREET?

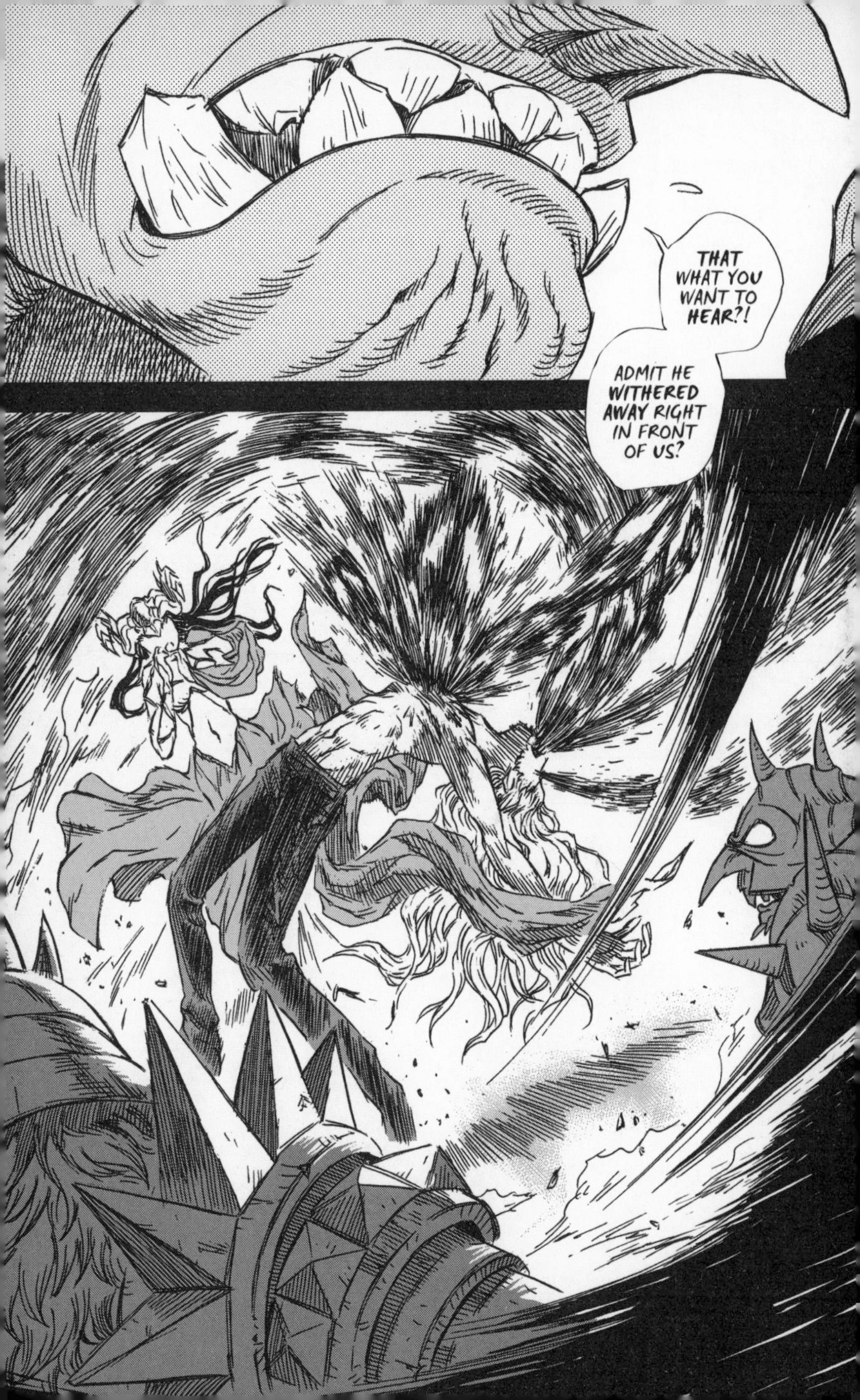
THAT WHAT YOU WANT TO HEAR?!
ADMIT HE WITHERED AWAY RIGHT IN FRONT OF US?

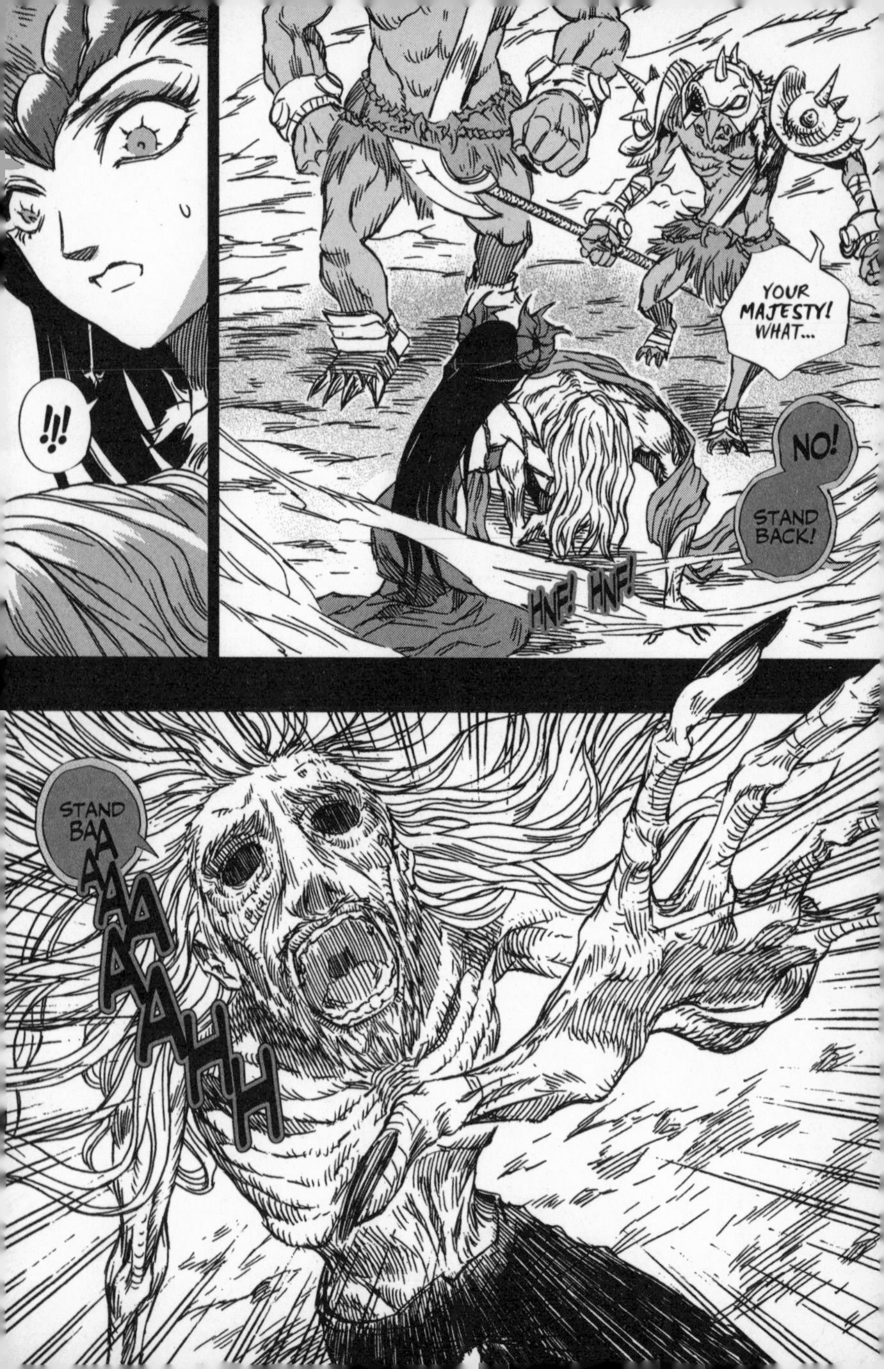
YOUR MAJESTY! WHAT...
NO!
STAND BACK!
HNF! HNF!
!!!
STAND BAAAAAAAAHHH

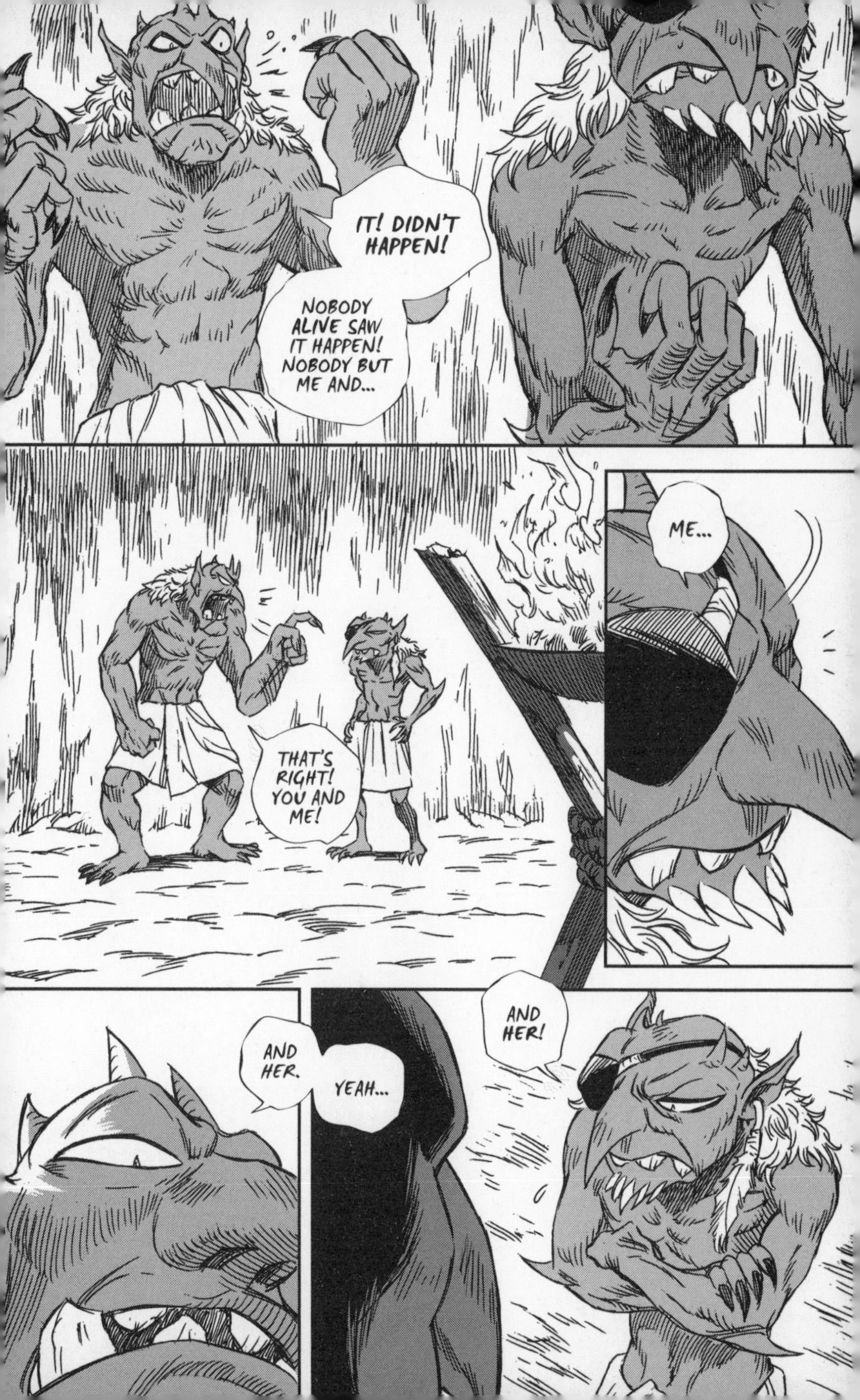
IT! DIDN'T HAPPEN!
NOBODY ALIVE SAW IT HAPPEN! NOBODY BUT ME AND...
THAT'S RIGHT! YOU AND ME!
ME...
AND HER.
YEAH...
AND HER!

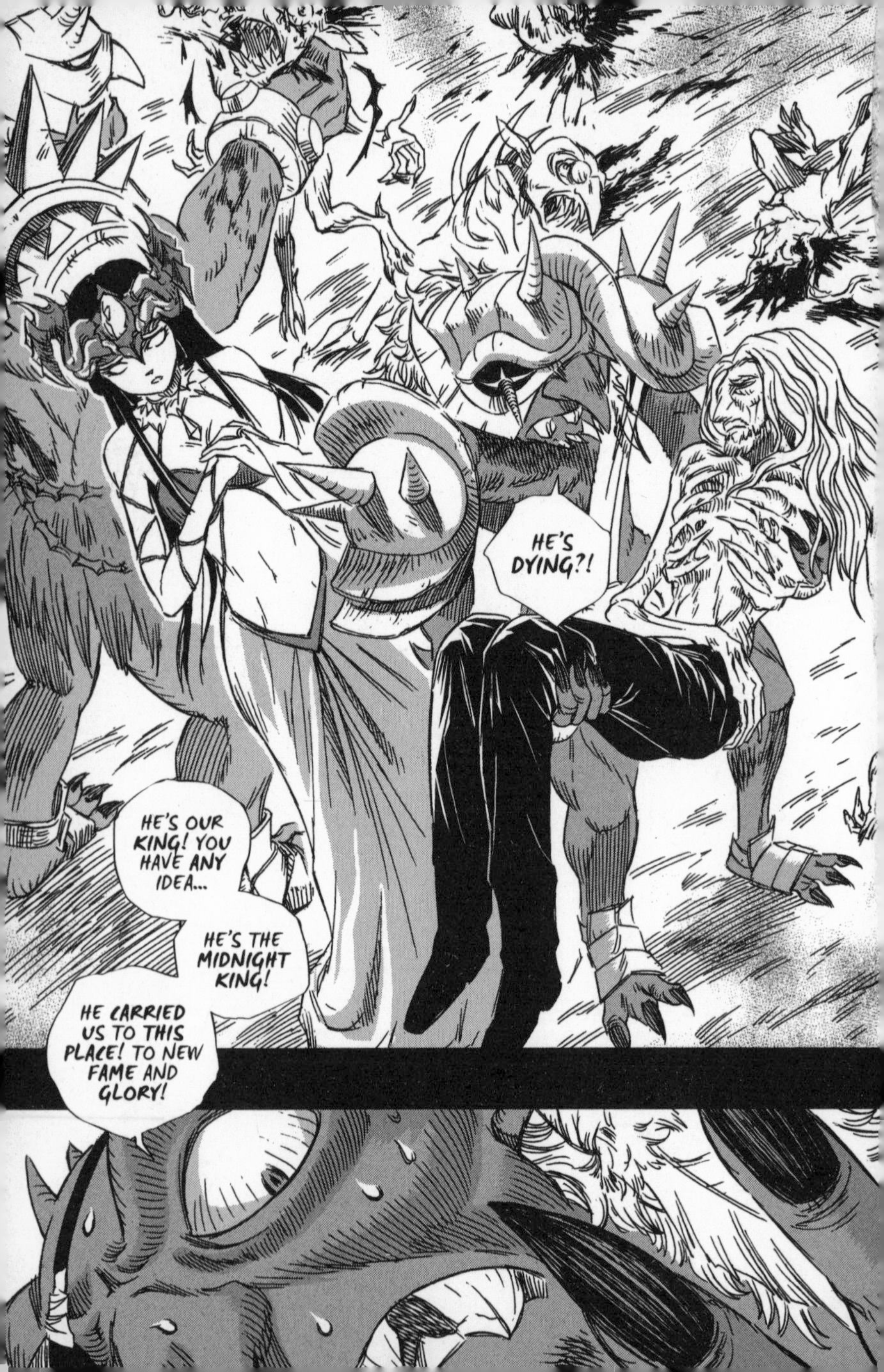
HE'S DYING?!
HE'S OUR KING! YOU HAVE ANY IDEA...
HE'S THE MIDNIGHT KING!
HE CARRIED US TO THIS PLACE! TO NEW FAME AND GLORY!

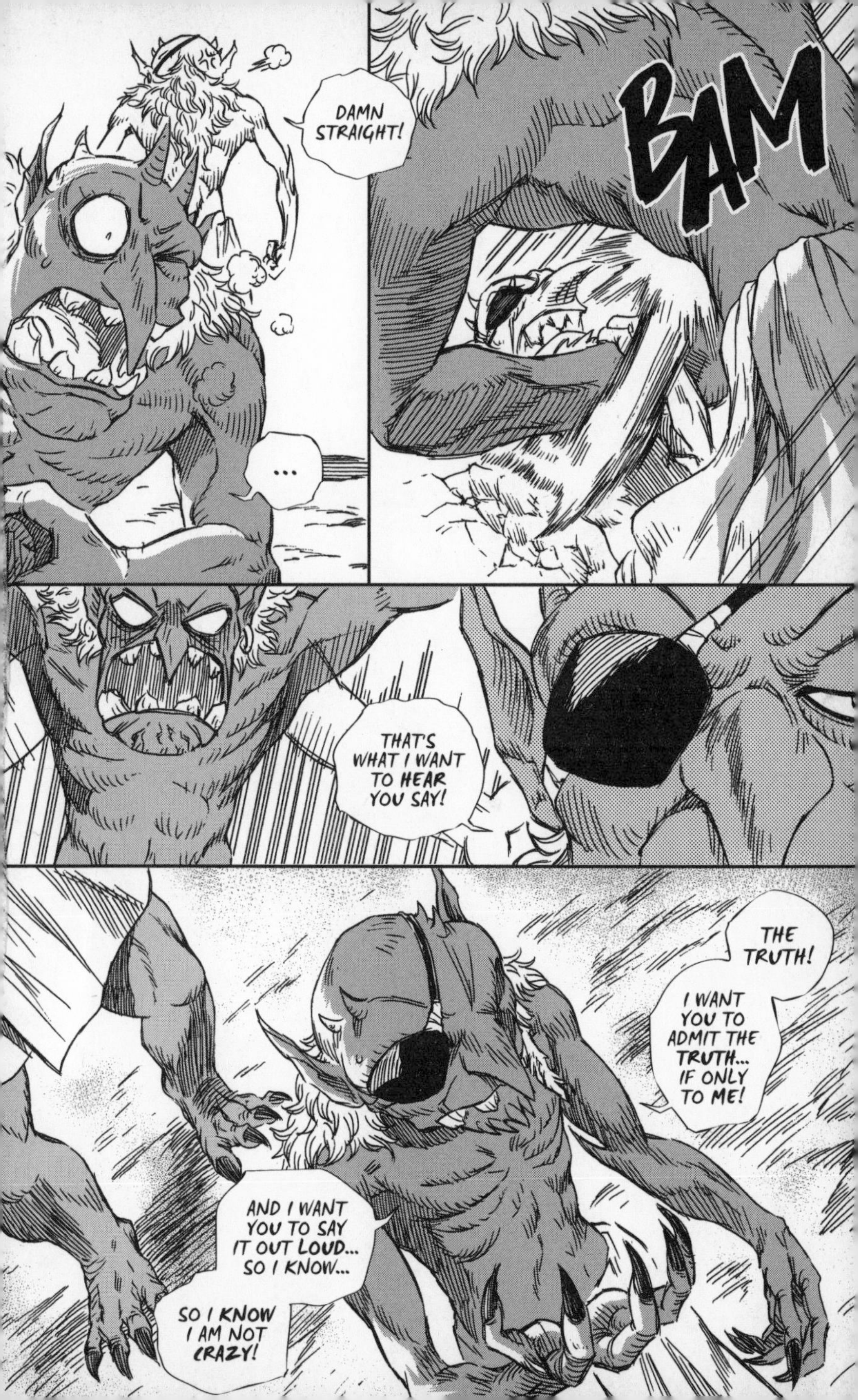
DAMN STRAIGHT!
...
BAM
THAT'S WHAT I WANT TO HEAR YOU SAY!
THE TRUTH!
I WANT YOU TO ADMIT THE TRUTH... IF ONLY TO ME!
AND I WANT YOU TO SAY IT OUT LOUD... SO I KNOW...
SO I KNOW I AM NOT CRAZY!

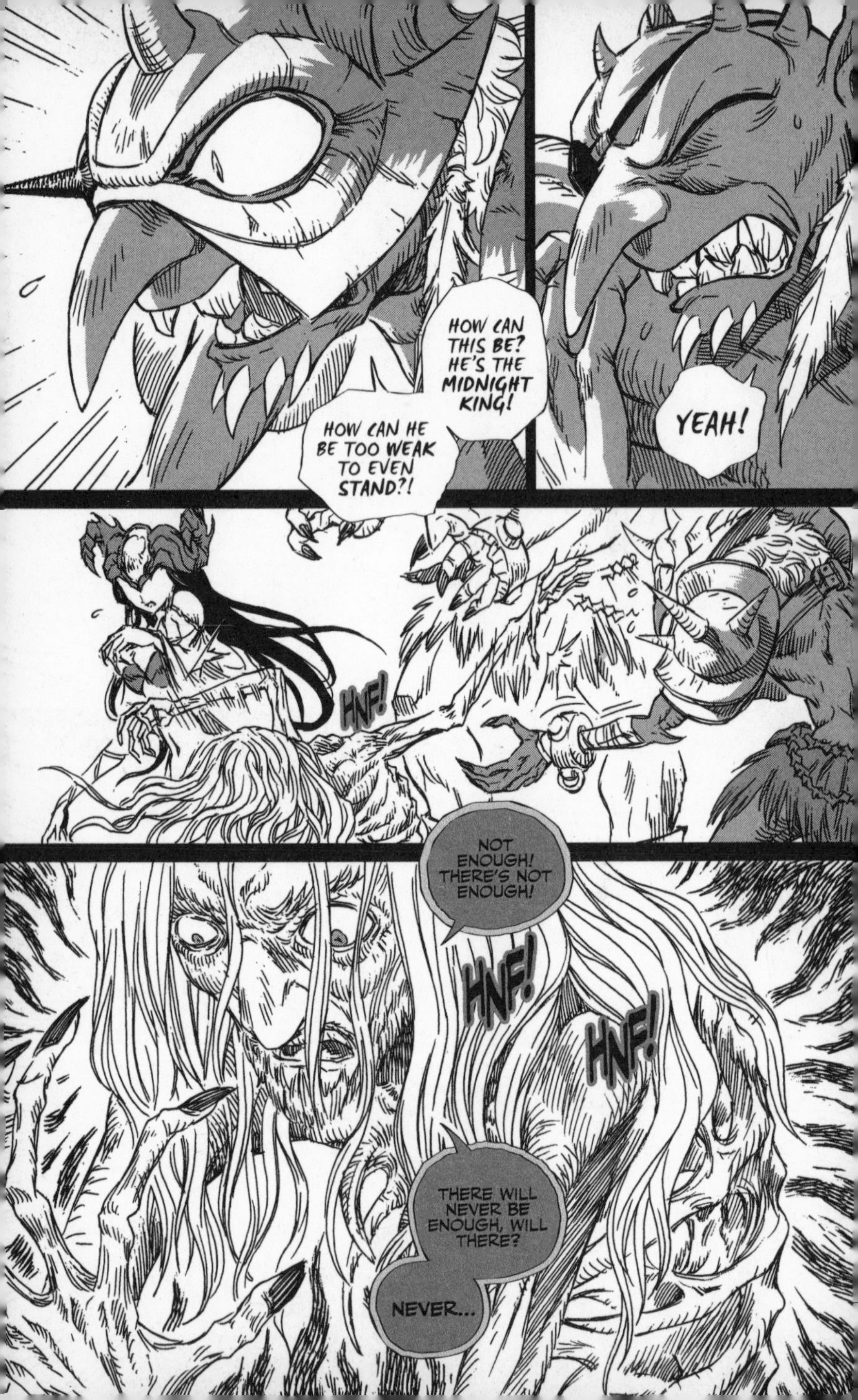
HOW CAN THIS BE? HE'S THE MIDNIGHT KING!
HOW CAN HE BE TOO WEAK TO EVEN STAND?!
YEAH!
HNF!
NOT ENOUGH! THERE'S NOT ENOUGH!
HNF!
HNF!
THERE WILL NEVER BE ENOUGH, WILL THERE?
NEVER...

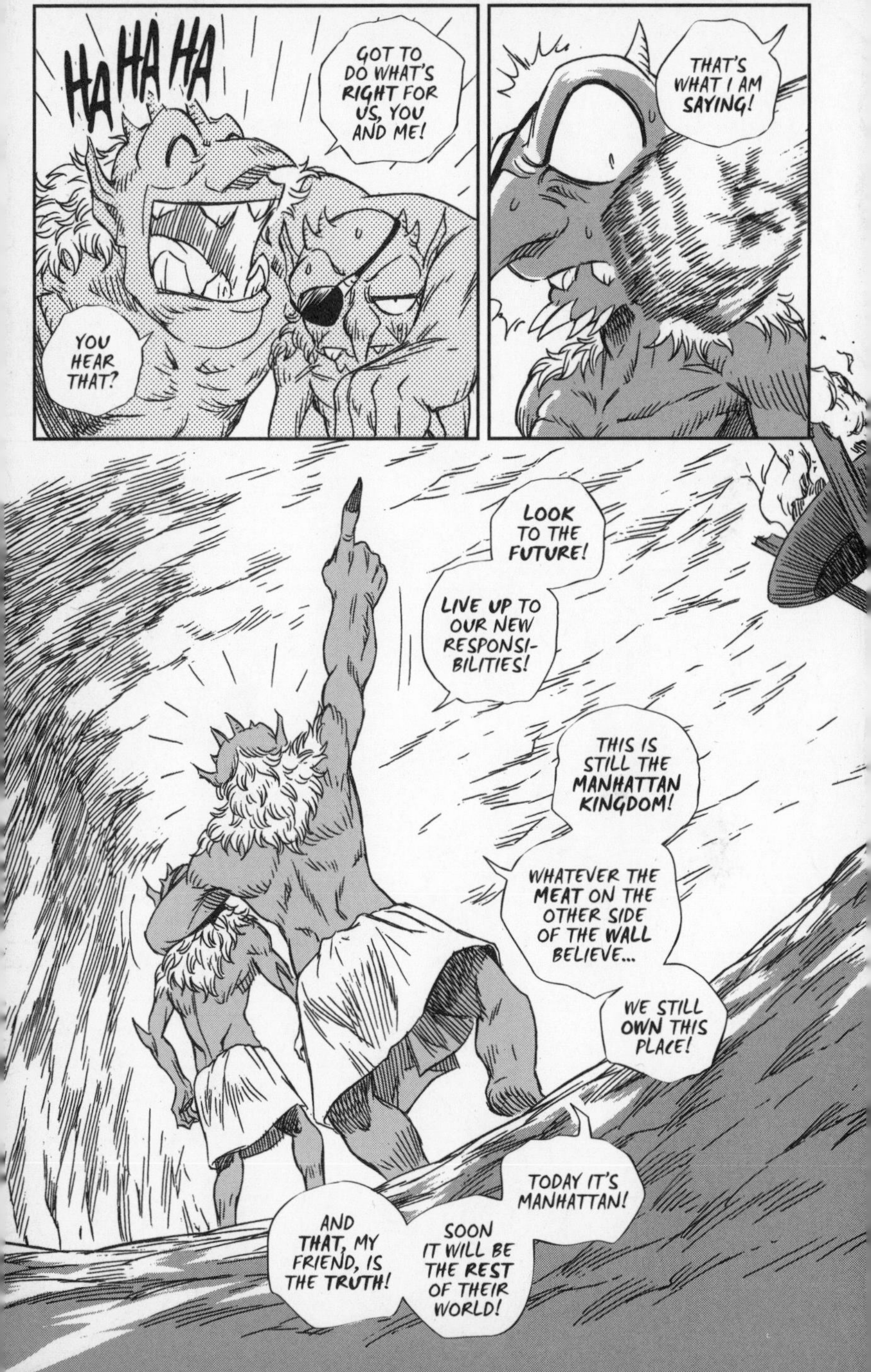
HA HA HA
YOU HEAR THAT?
GOT TO DO WHAT'S RIGHT FOR US, YOU AND ME!
THAT'S WHAT I AM SAYING!
LOOK TO THE FUTURE!
LIVE UP TO OUR NEW RESPONSI-BILITIES!
THIS IS STILL THE MANHATTAN KINGDOM!
WHATEVER THE MEAT ON THE OTHER SIDE OF THE WALL BELIEVE...
WE STILL OWN THIS PLACE!
TODAY IT'S MANHATTAN!
SOON IT WILL BE THE REST OF THEIR WORLD!
AND THAT, MY FRIEND, IS THE TRUTH!

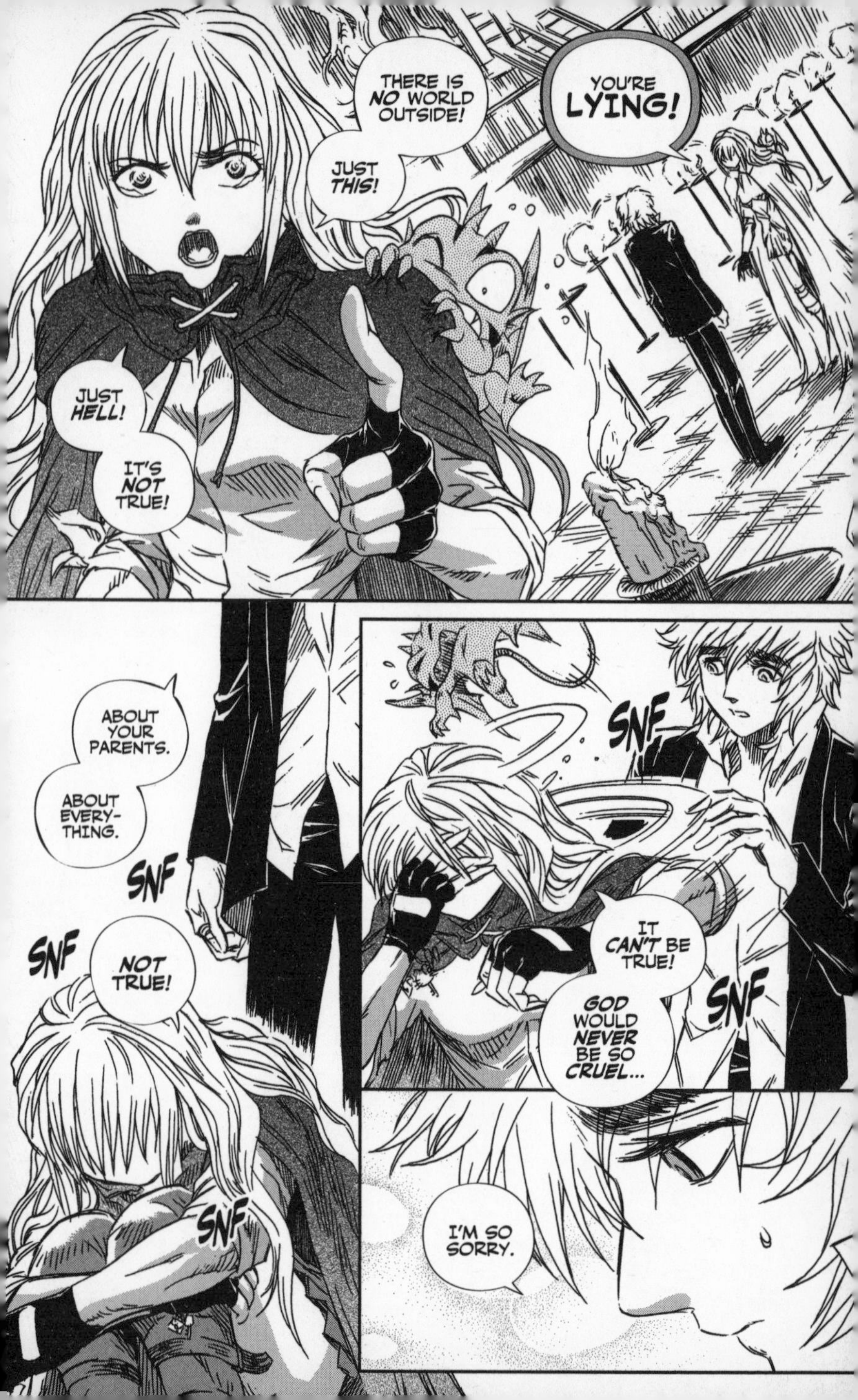
YOU'RE LYING!
THERE IS NO WORLD OUTSIDE!
JUST THIS!
JUST HELL!
IT'S NOT TRUE!
SNF
IT CAN'T BE TRUE!
GOD WOULD NEVER BE SO CRUEL...
SNF
I'M SO SORRY.
ABOUT YOUR PARENTS.
ABOUT EVERY-THING.
SNF
SNF
NOT TRUE!
SNF

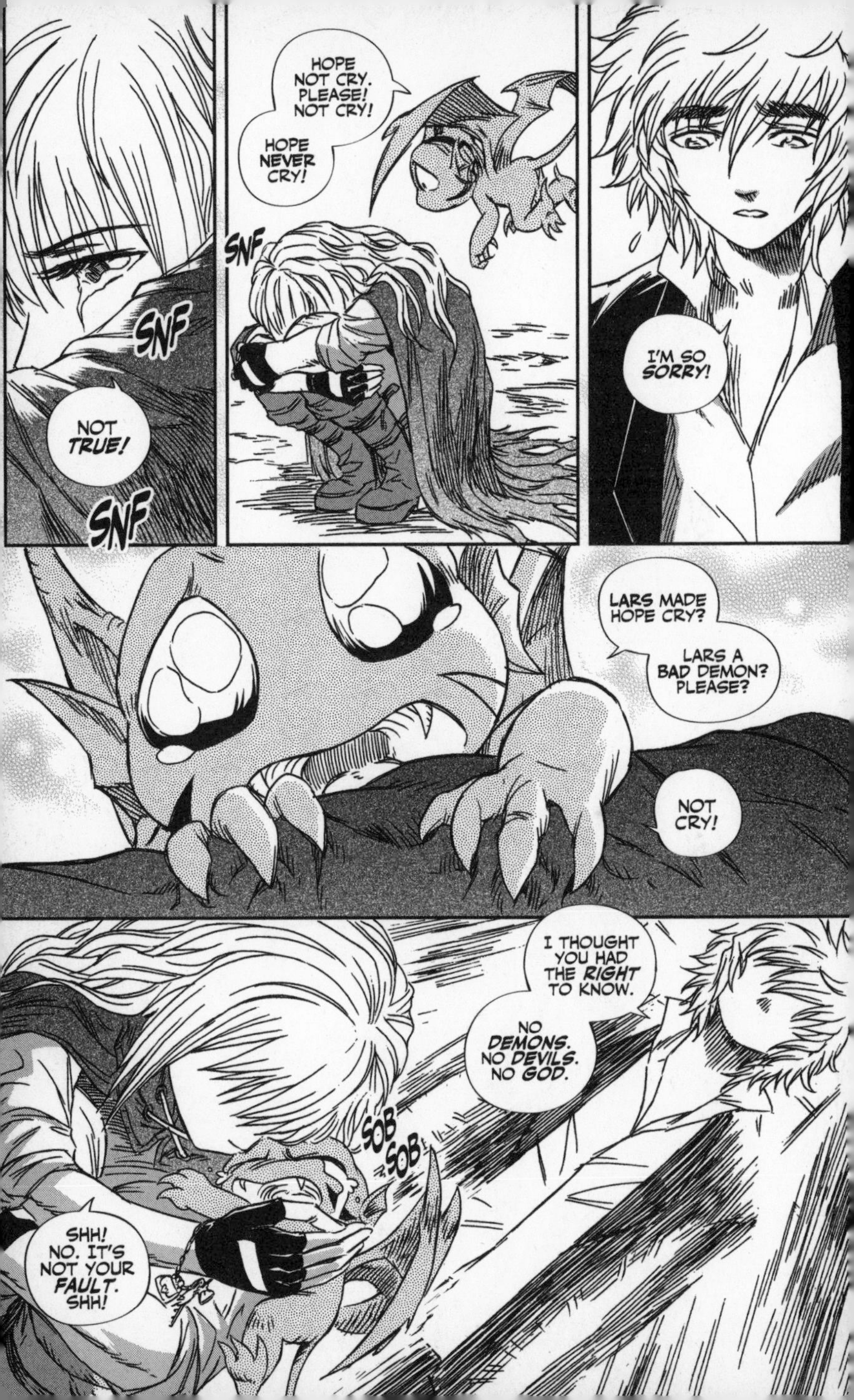
I'M SO SORRY!
HOPE NOT CRY. PLEASE! NOT CRY!
HOPE NEVER CRY!
SNF
SNF
NOT TRUE!
SNF
LARS MADE HOPE CRY?
LARS A BAD DEMON? PLEASE?
NOT CRY!
I THOUGHT YOU HAD THE RIGHT TO KNOW.
NO DEMONS. NO DEVILS. NO GOD.
SOB SOB
SHH! NO. IT'S NOT YOUR FAULT. SHH!

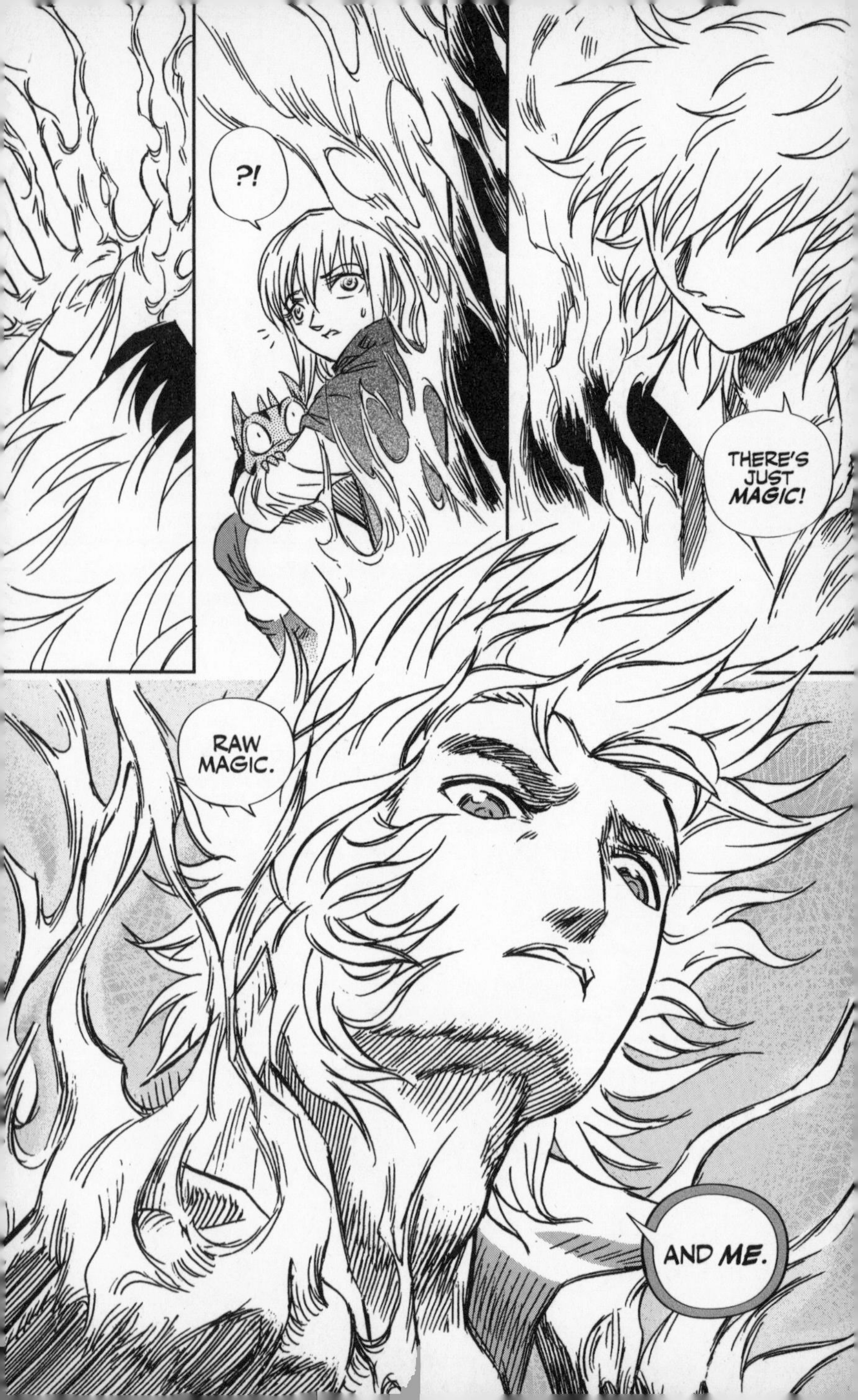
?!
THERE'S JUST MAGIC!
RAW MAGIC.
AND ME.

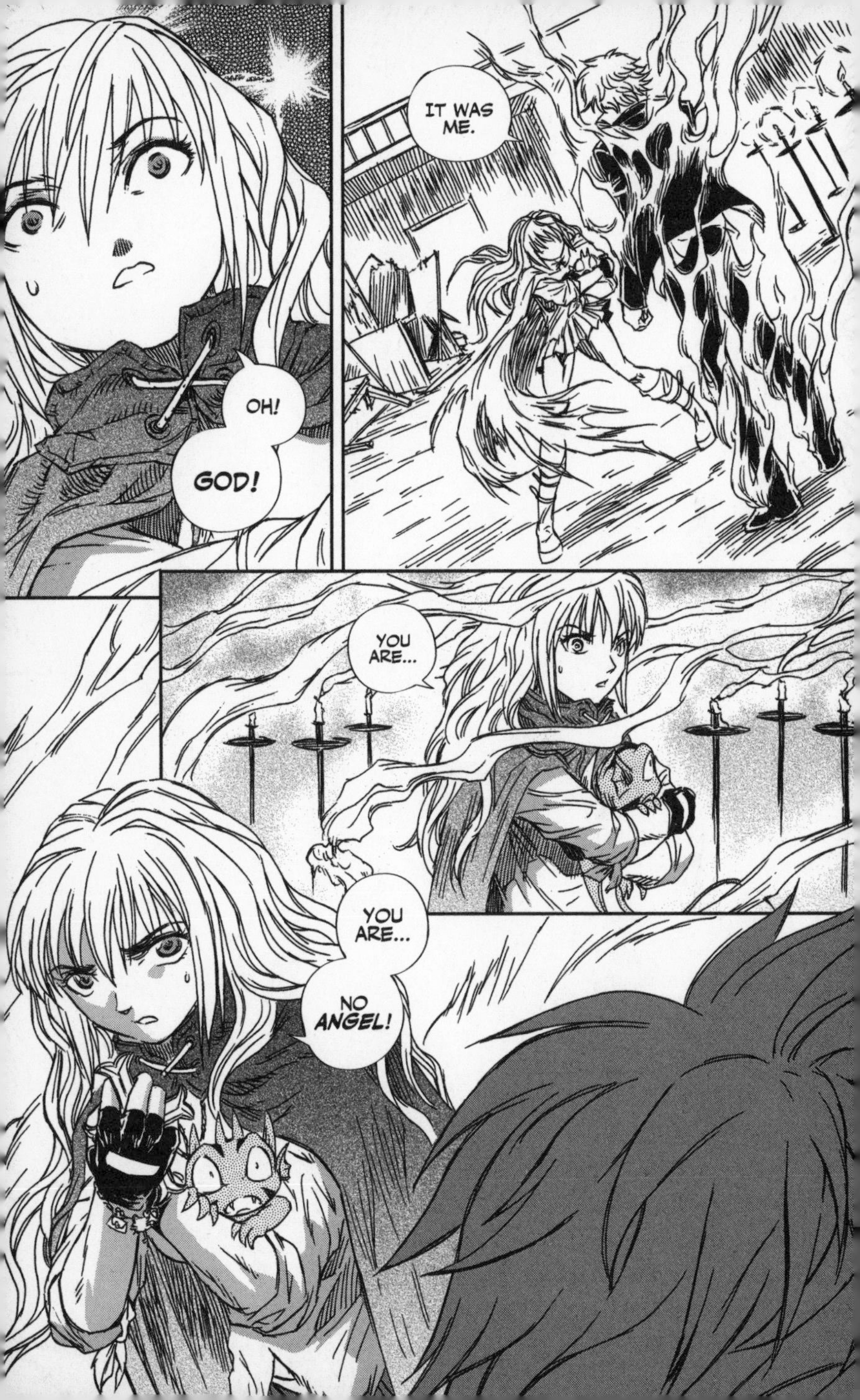
IT WAS ME.
OH!
GOD!
YOU ARE...
YOU ARE...
NO ANGEL!

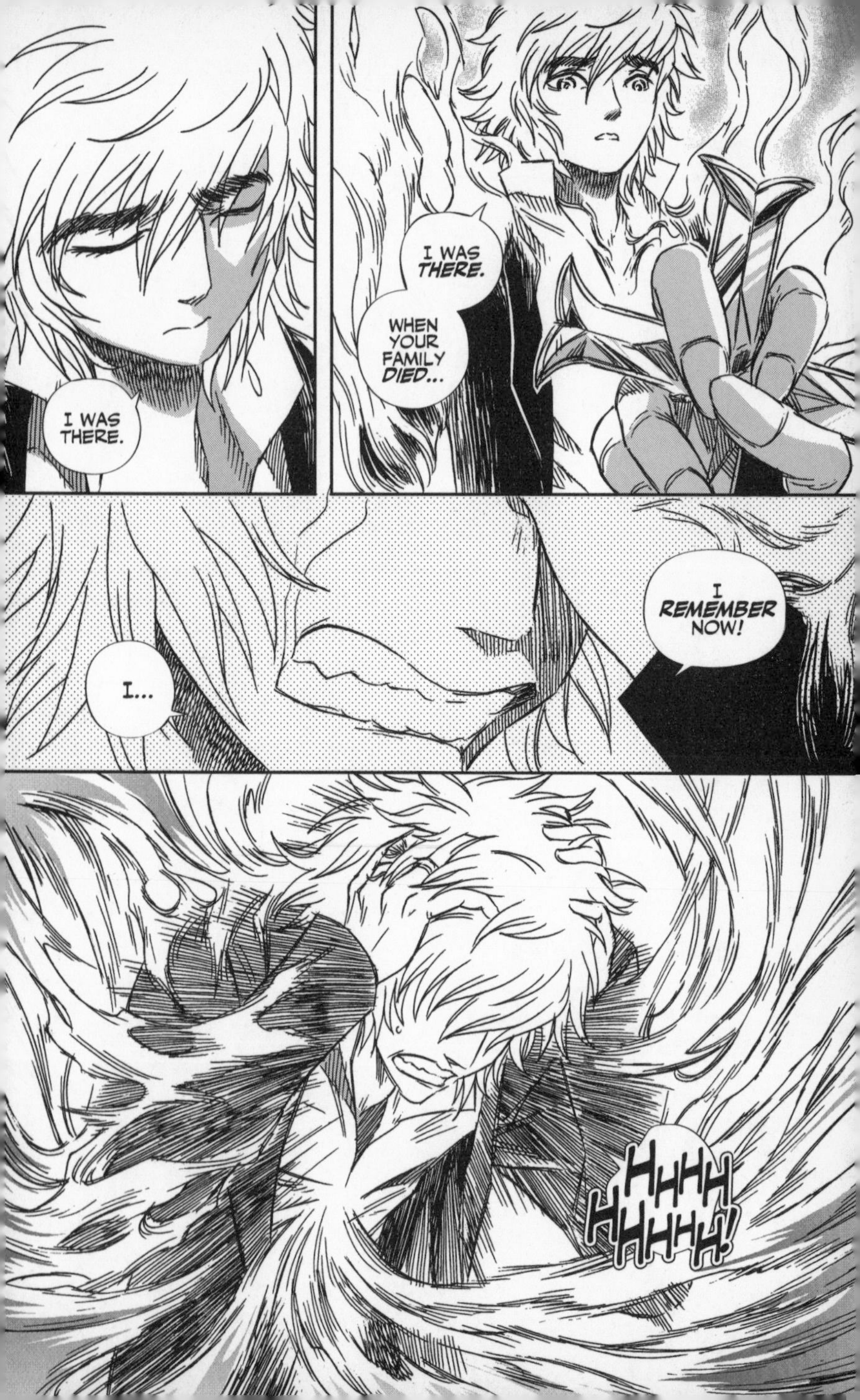
I WAS *THERE.*
WHEN YOUR FAMILY *DIED...*
I WAS THERE.
I *REMEMBER* NOW!
I...
HHHH HHHHH!

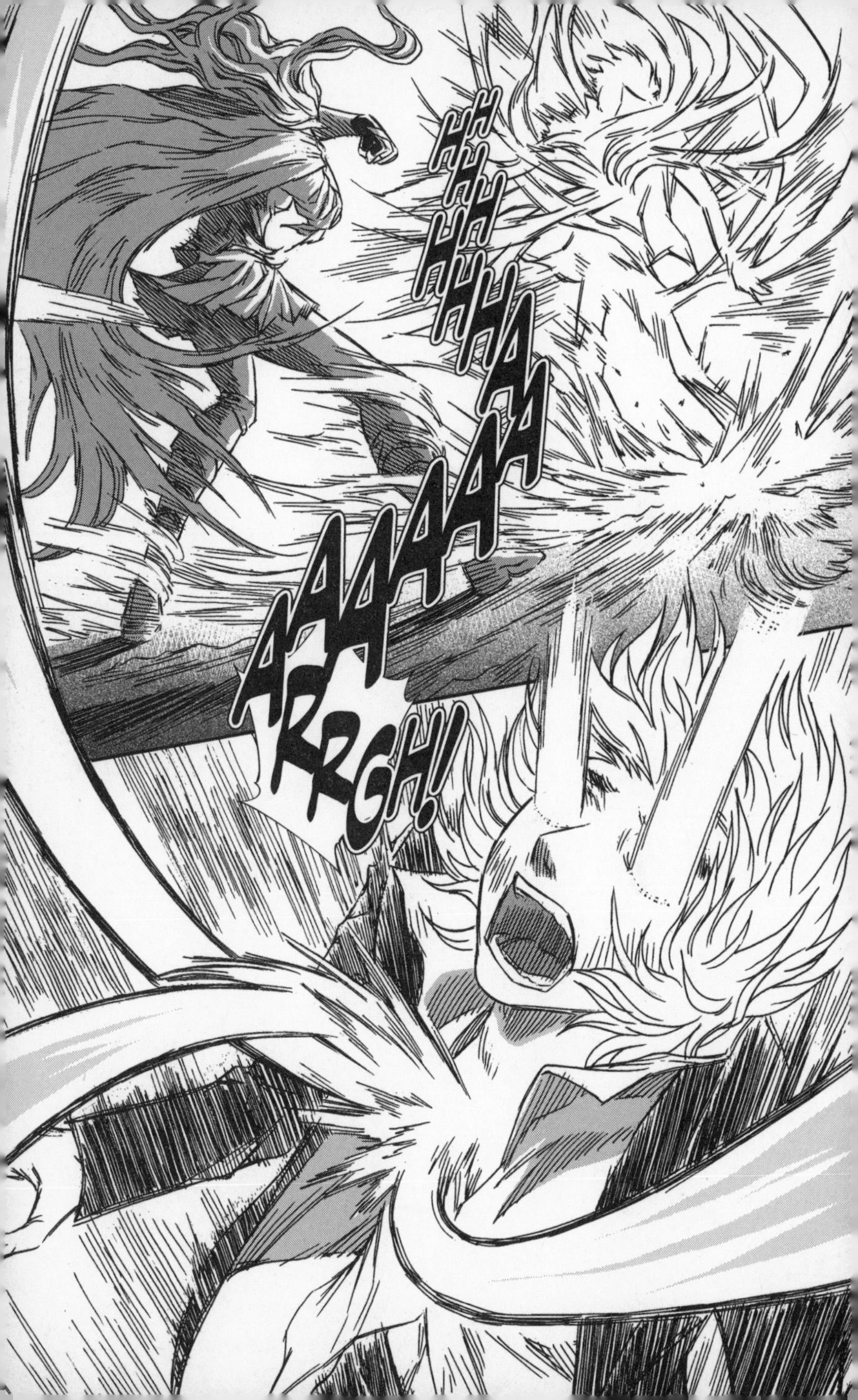
HHHHHHHHHAAAAAAAAAARRRGH!

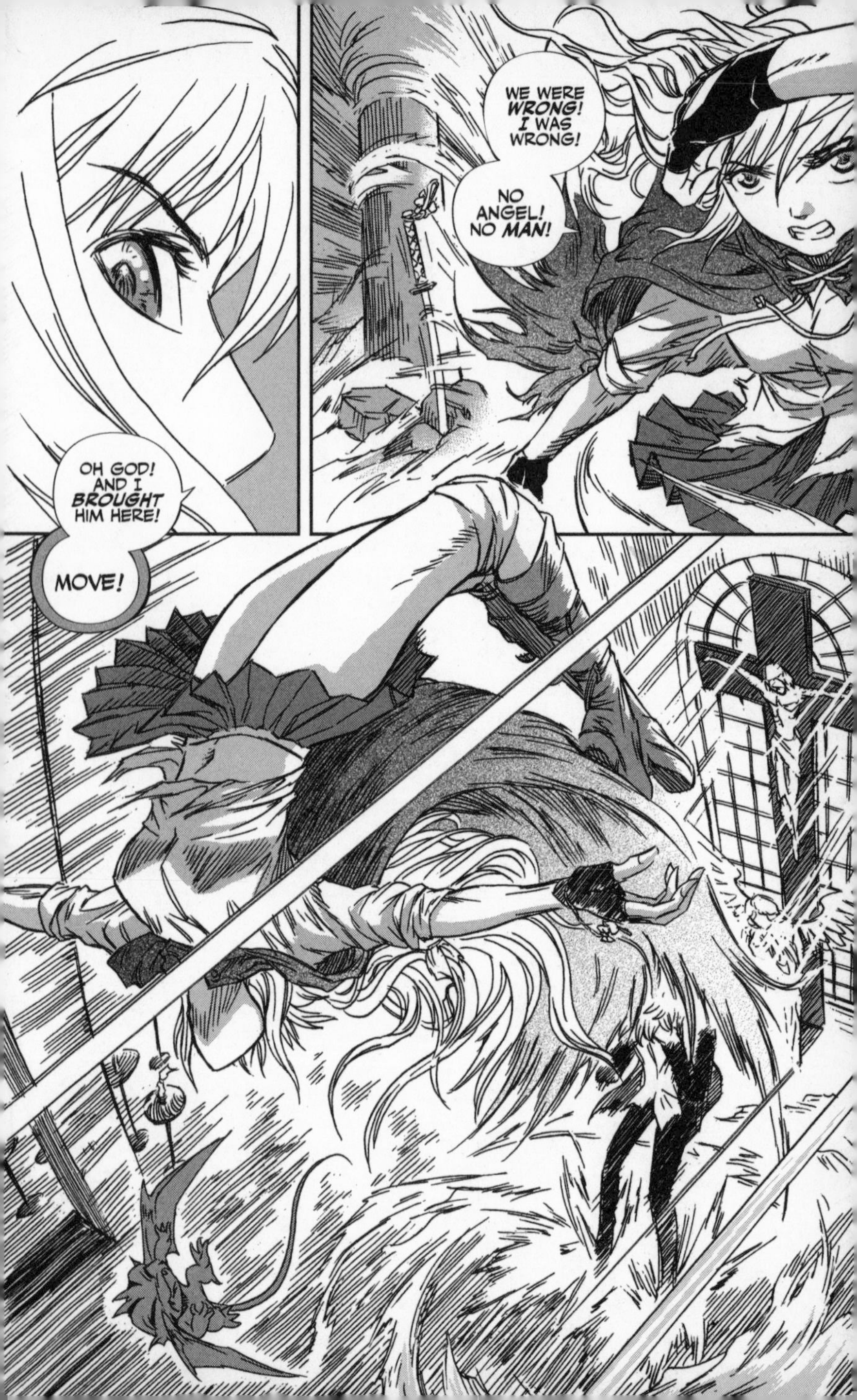
WE WERE WRONG! I WAS WRONG!
NO ANGEL! NO MAN!
OH GOD! AND I BROUGHT HIM HERE!
MOVE!

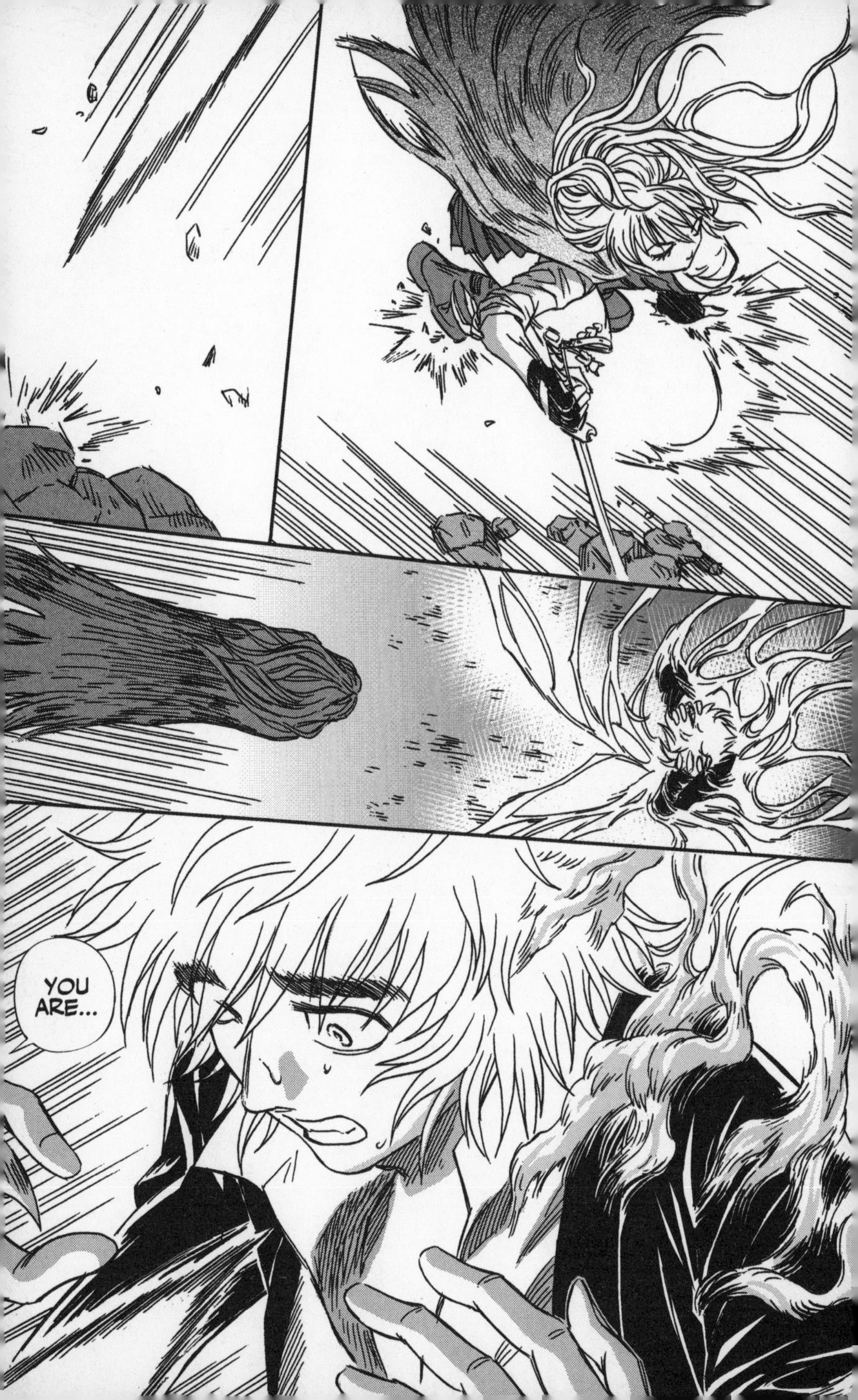
YOU ARE...

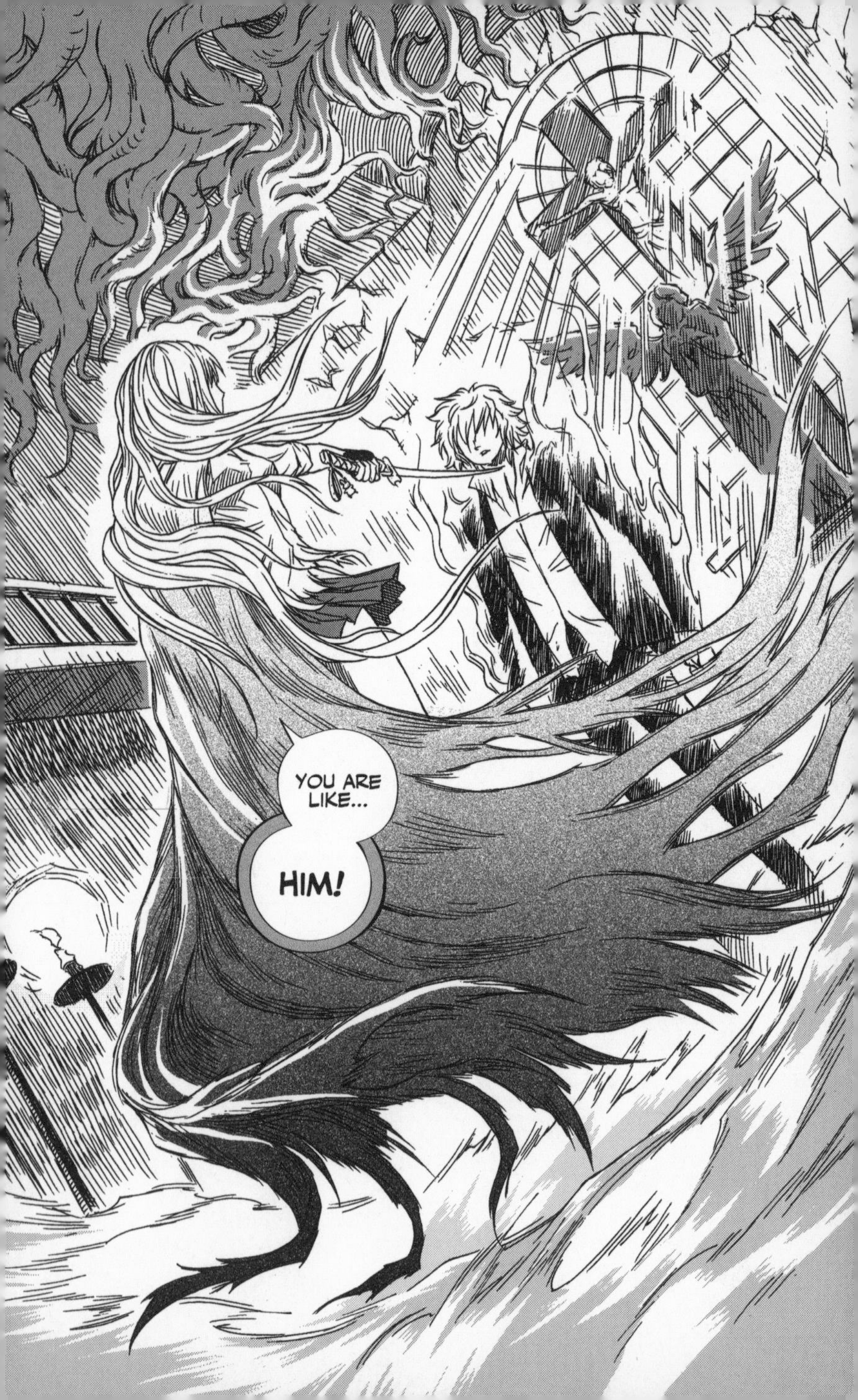
YOU ARE LIKE...
HIM!

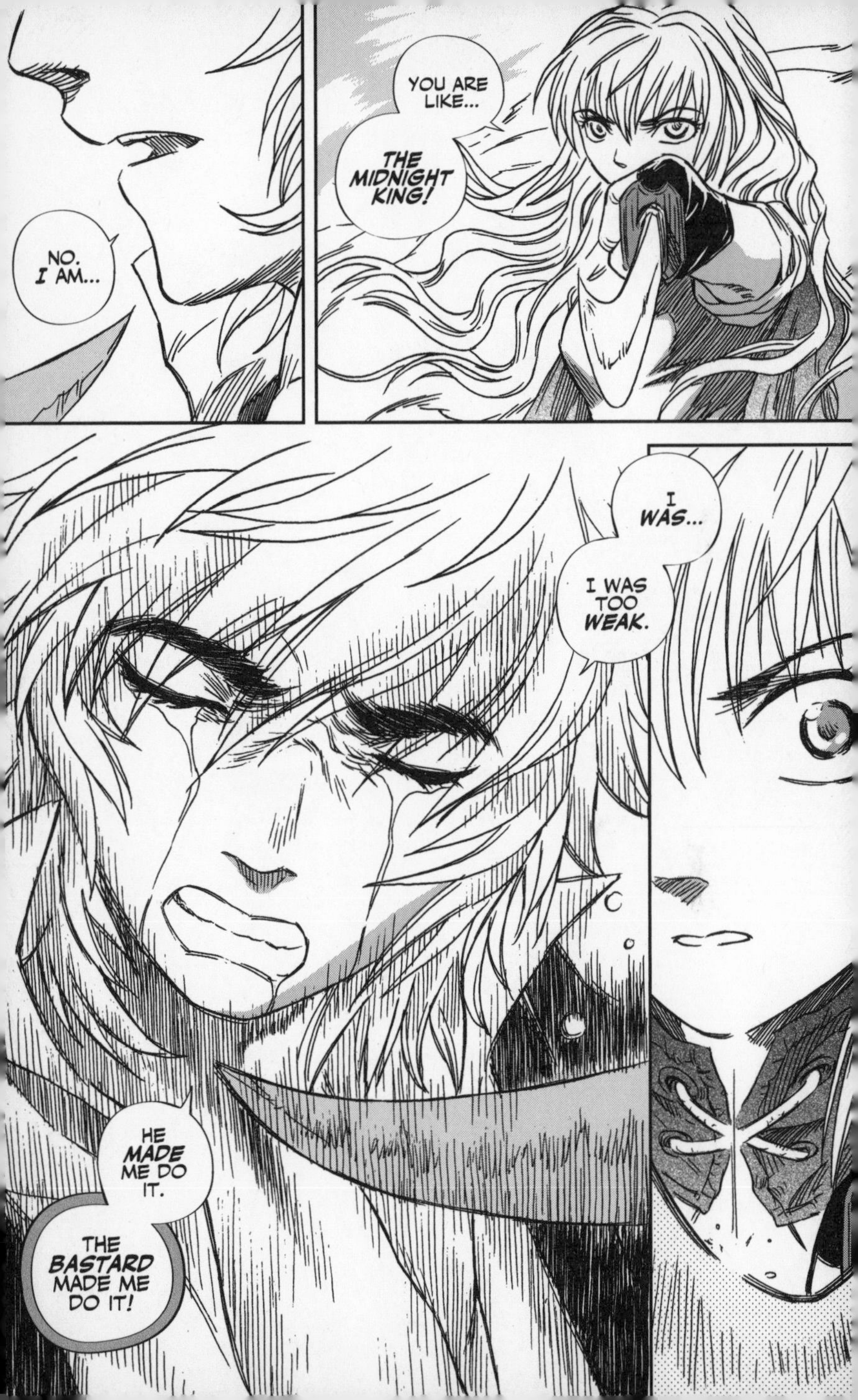
YOU ARE LIKE...
THE MIDNIGHT KING!
NO. I AM...
I WAS...
I WAS TOO WEAK.
HE MADE ME DO IT.
THE BASTARD MADE ME DO IT!

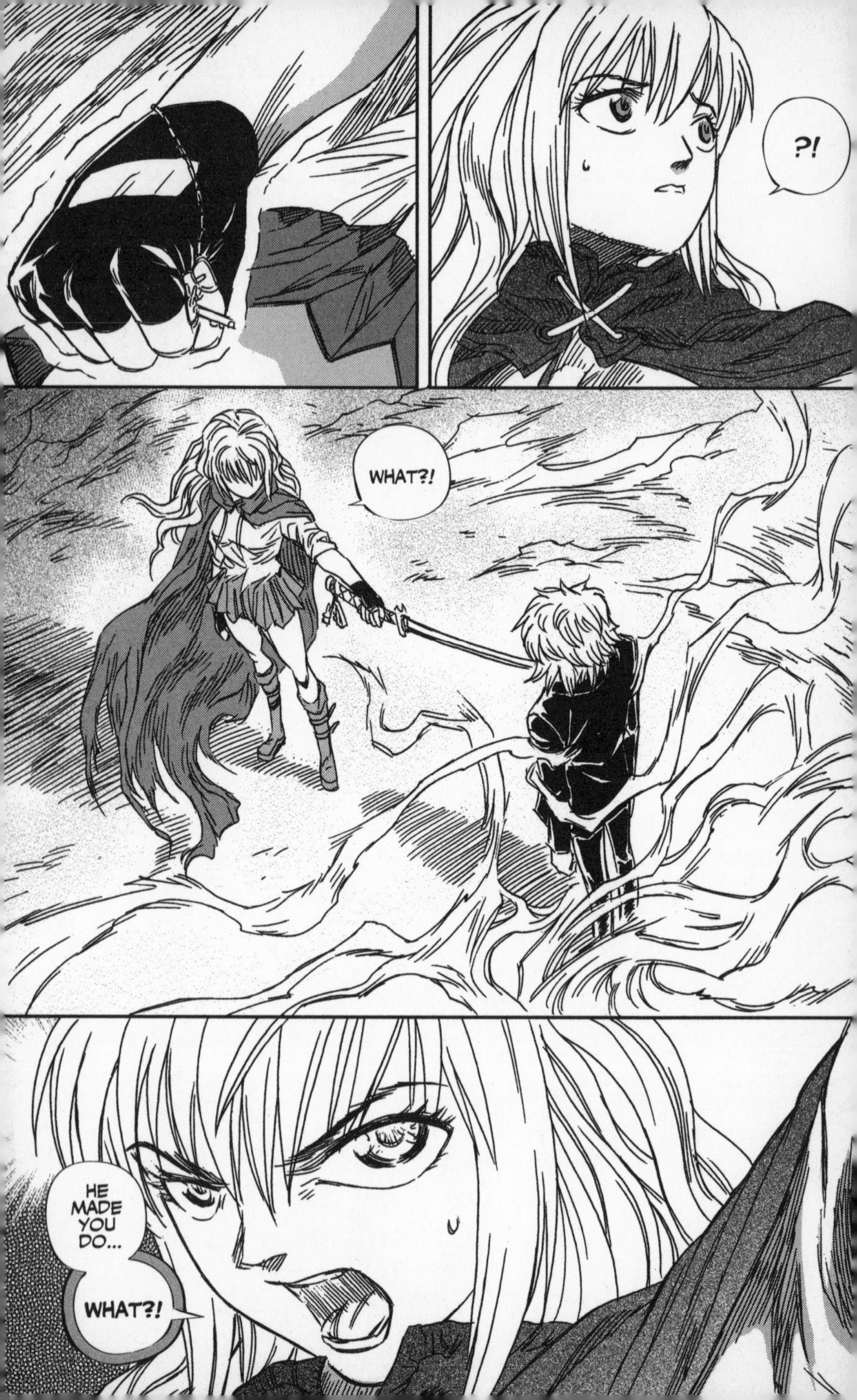
?!
WHAT?!
HE MADE YOU DO...
WHAT?!

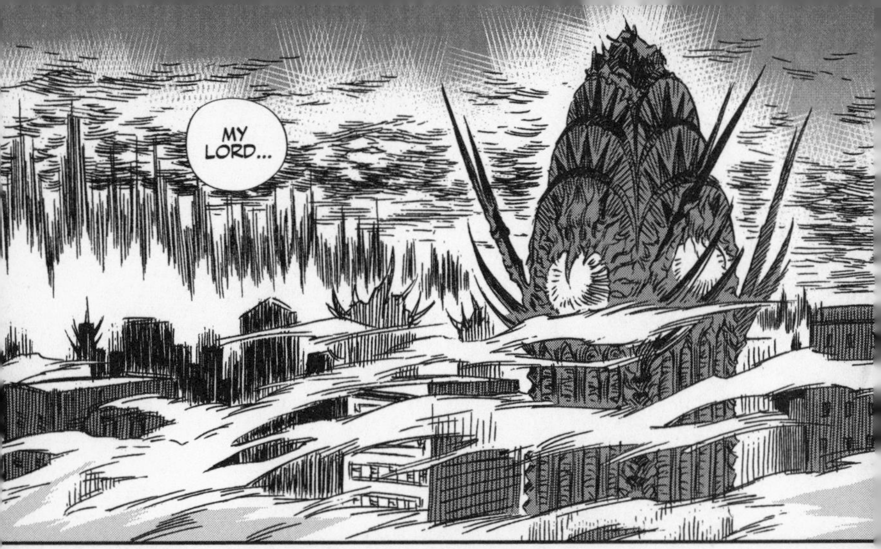
MY LORD...
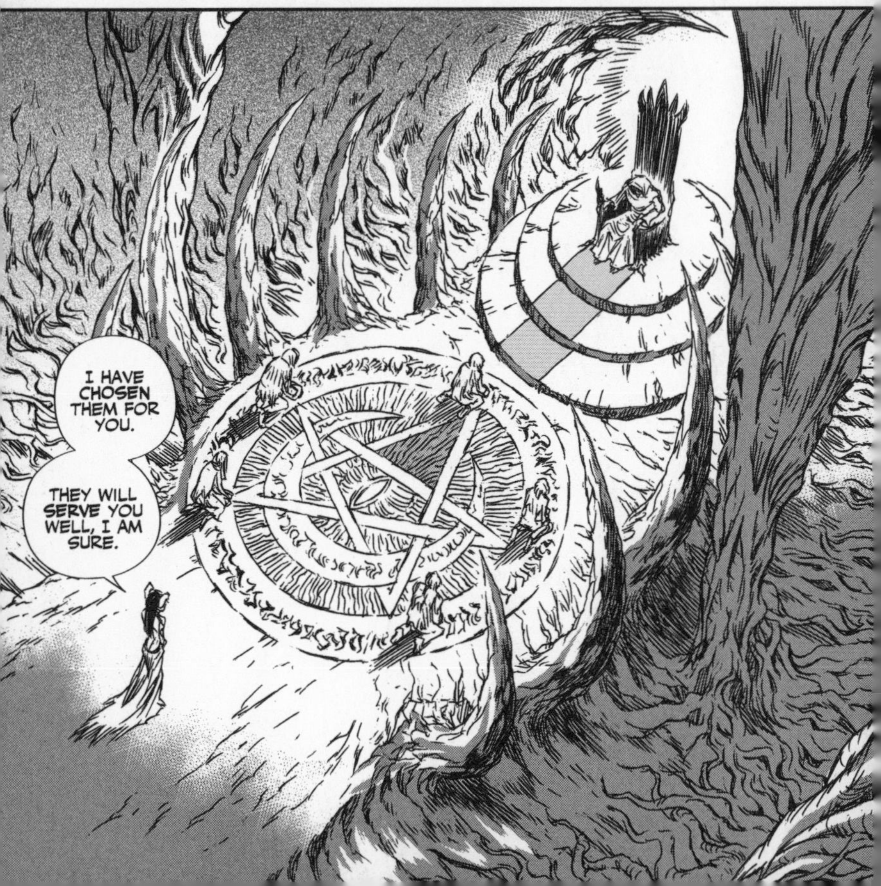
I HAVE CHOSEN THEM FOR YOU.
THEY WILL SERVE YOU WELL, I AM SURE.

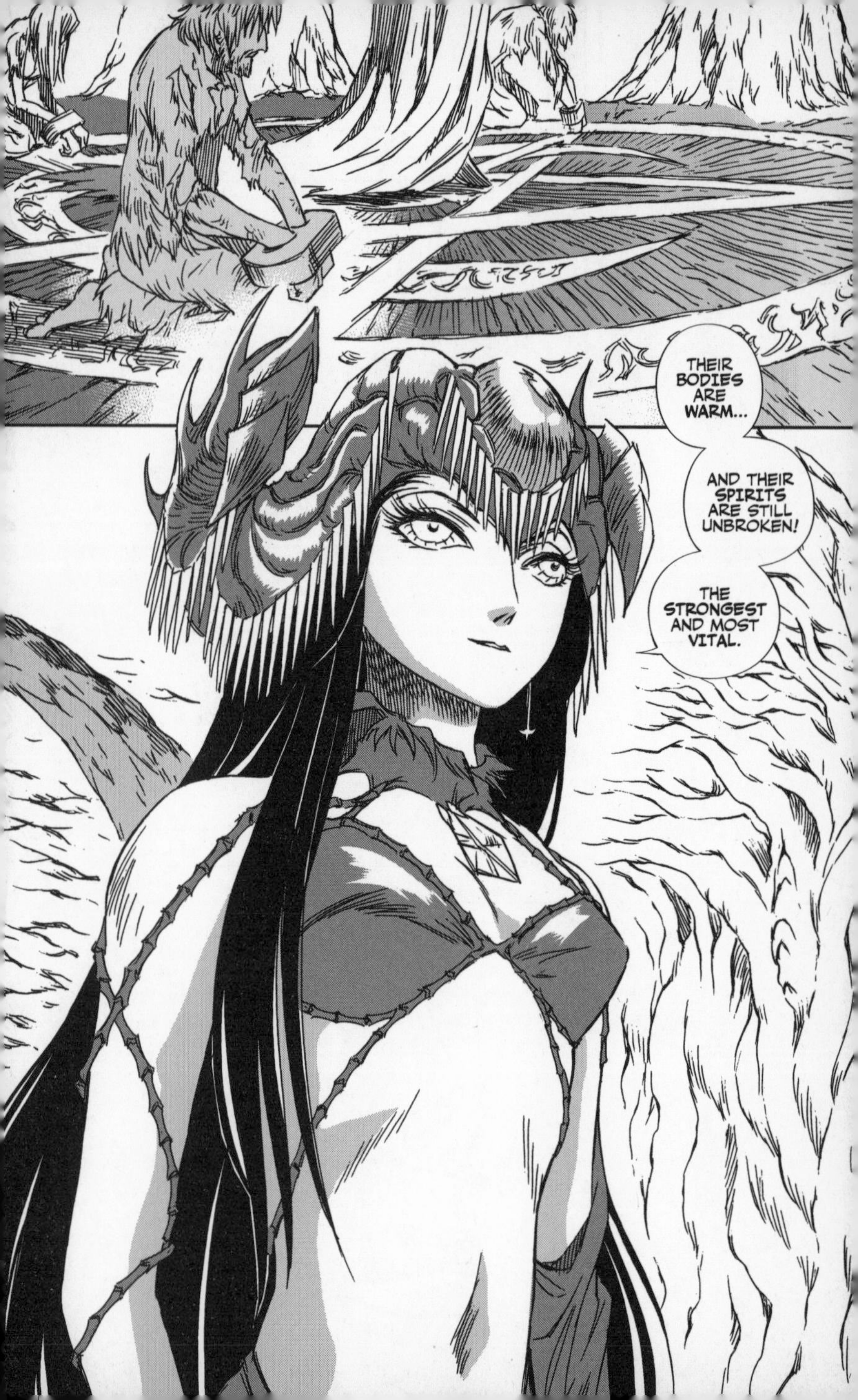
THEIR BODIES ARE WARM...
AND THEIR SPIRITS ARE STILL UNBROKEN!
THE STRONGEST AND MOST VITAL.

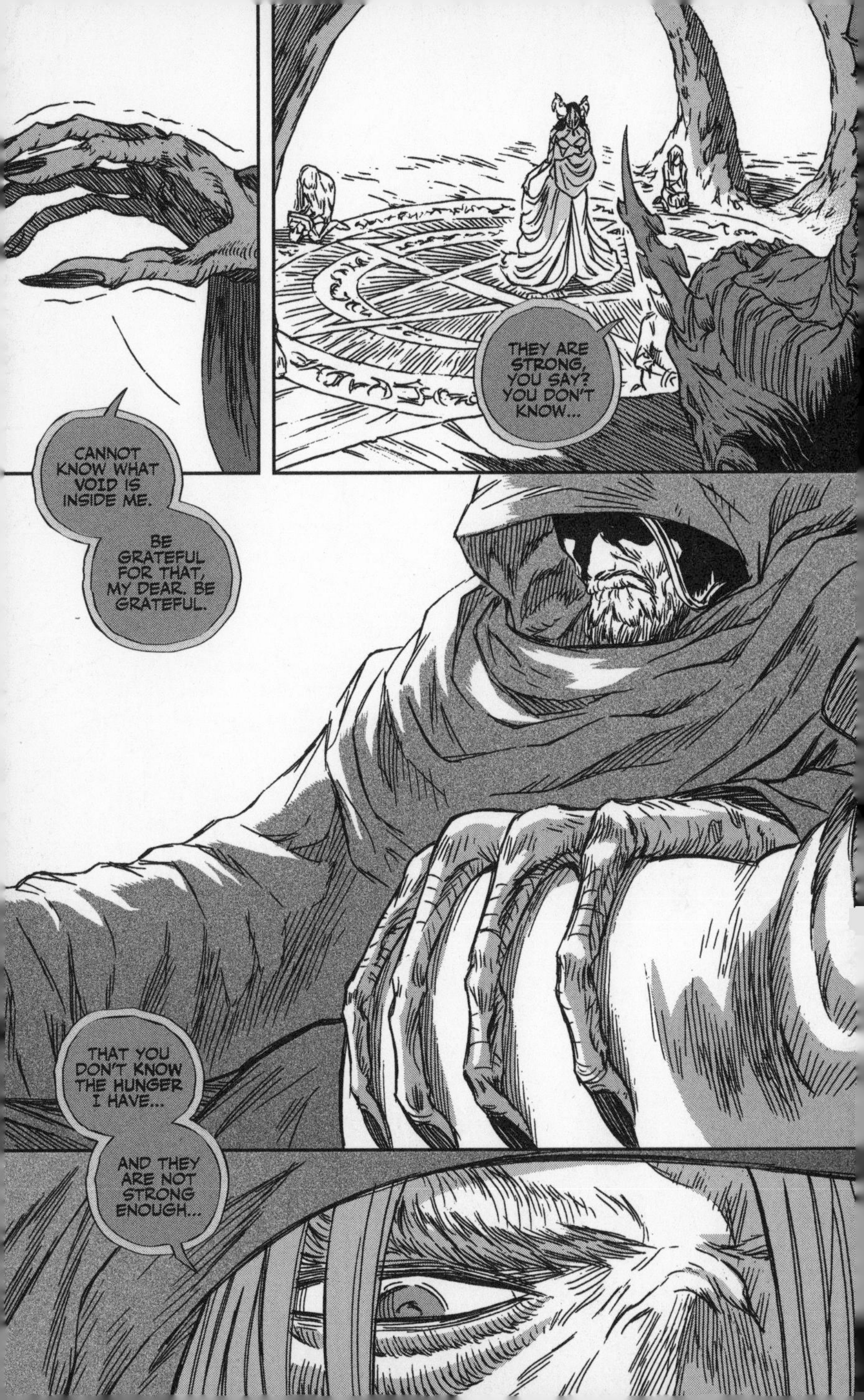
THEY ARE STRONG, YOU SAY? YOU DON'T KNOW...
CANNOT KNOW WHAT VOID IS INSIDE ME.
BE GRATEFUL FOR THAT, MY DEAR. BE GRATEFUL.
THAT YOU DON'T KNOW THE HUNGER I HAVE...
AND THEY ARE NOT STRONG ENOUGH...

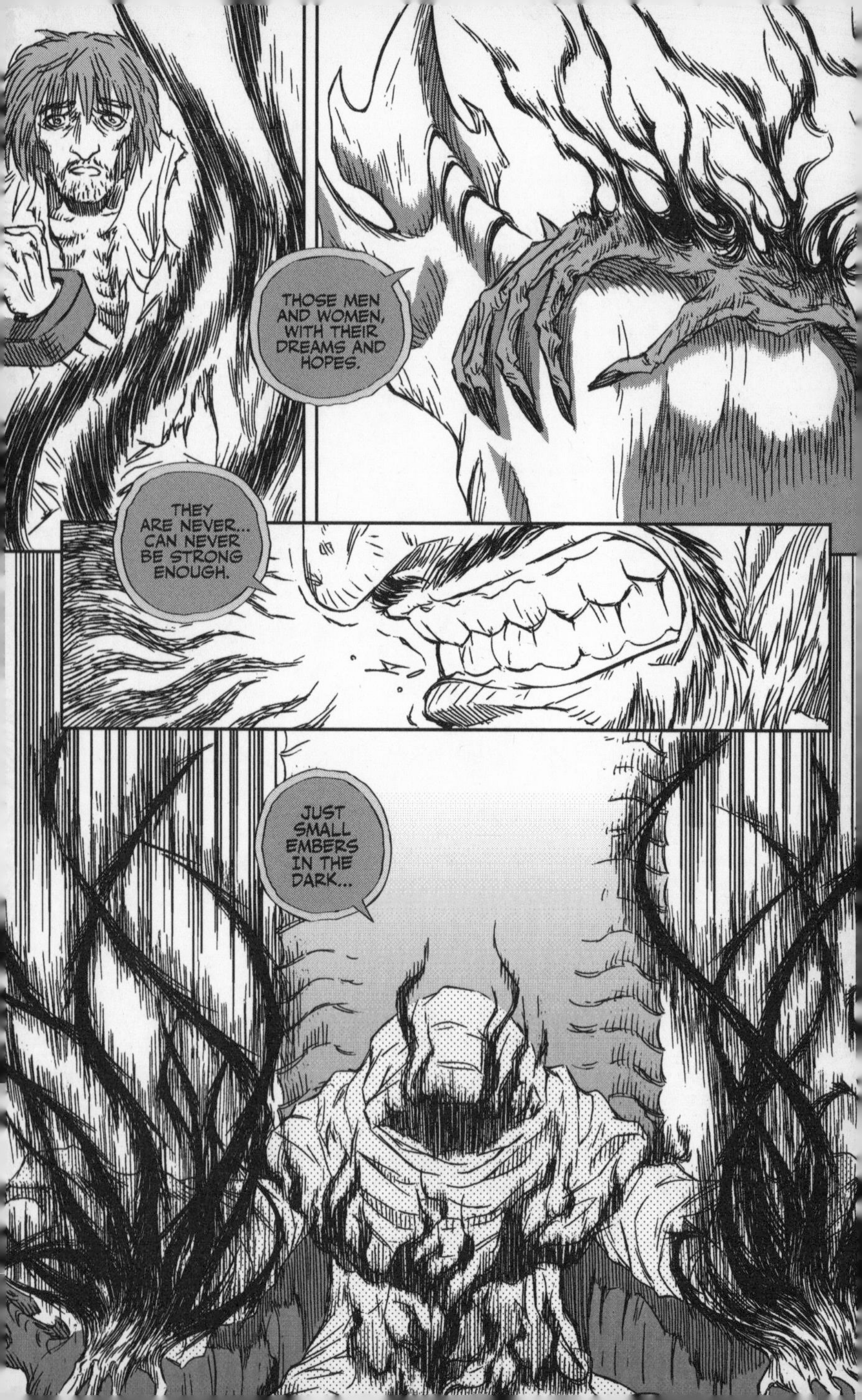
THOSE MEN AND WOMEN, WITH THEIR DREAMS AND HOPES.
THEY ARE NEVER... CAN NEVER BE STRONG ENOUGH.
JUST SMALL EMBERS IN THE DARK...

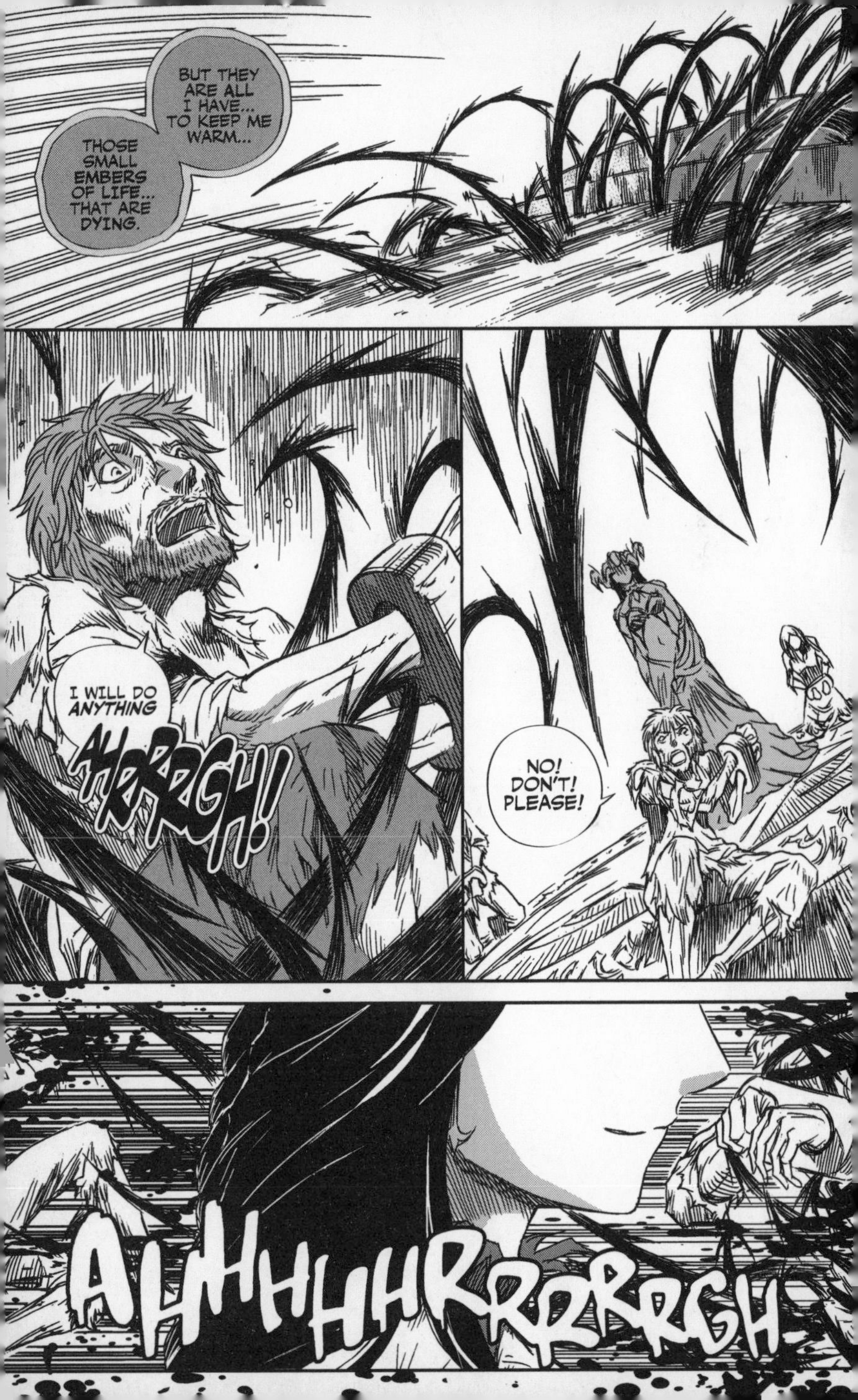
BUT THEY ARE ALL I HAVE... TO KEEP ME WARM...
THOSE SMALL EMBERS OF LIFE... THAT ARE DYING.
NO! DON'T! PLEASE!
I WILL DO *ANYTHING*
AHRRGH!
AHHHHHRRRRRGH

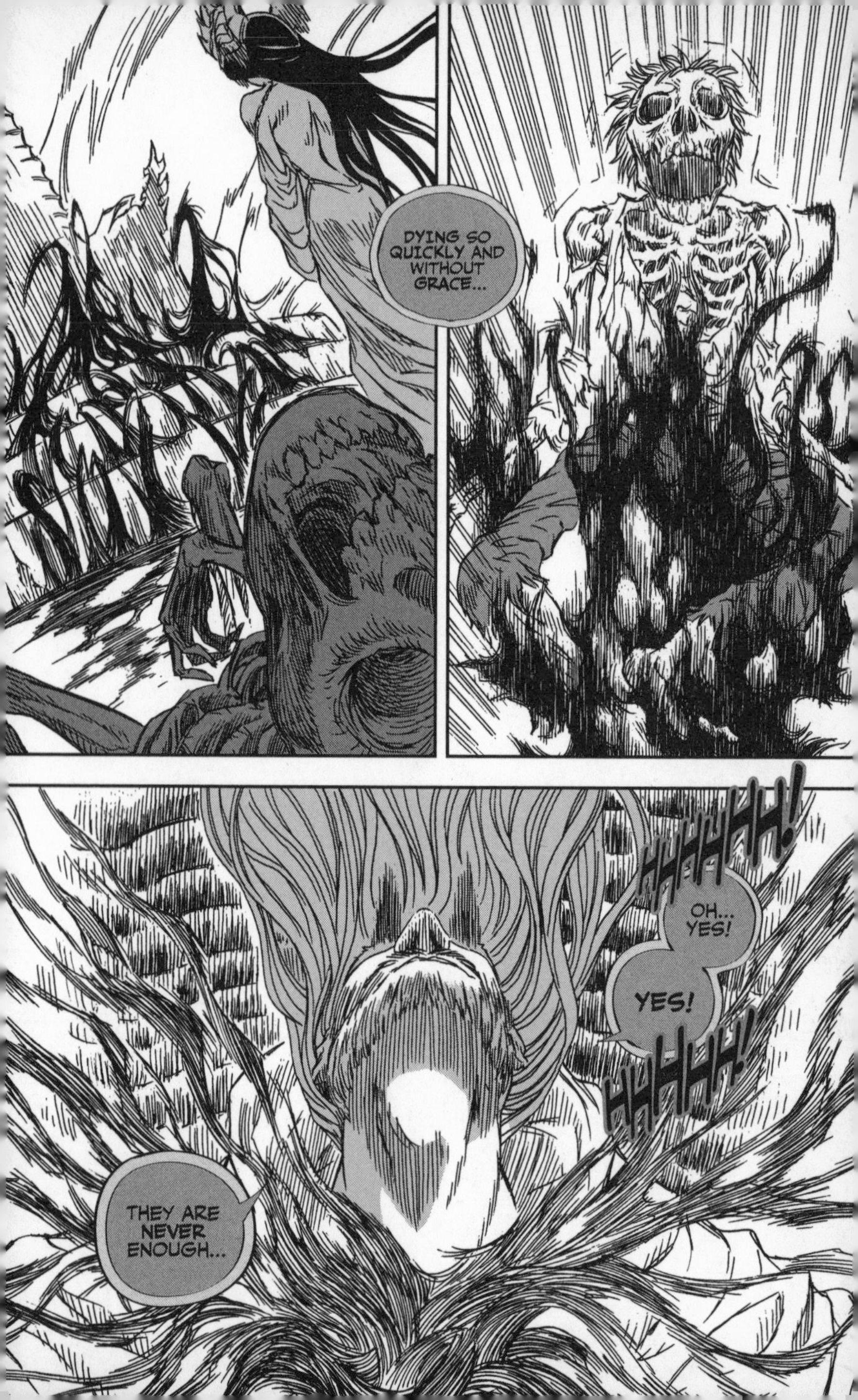
DYING SO QUICKLY AND WITHOUT GRACE...
HHHHHH!
OH... YES!
YES!
HHHHH!
THEY ARE NEVER ENOUGH...

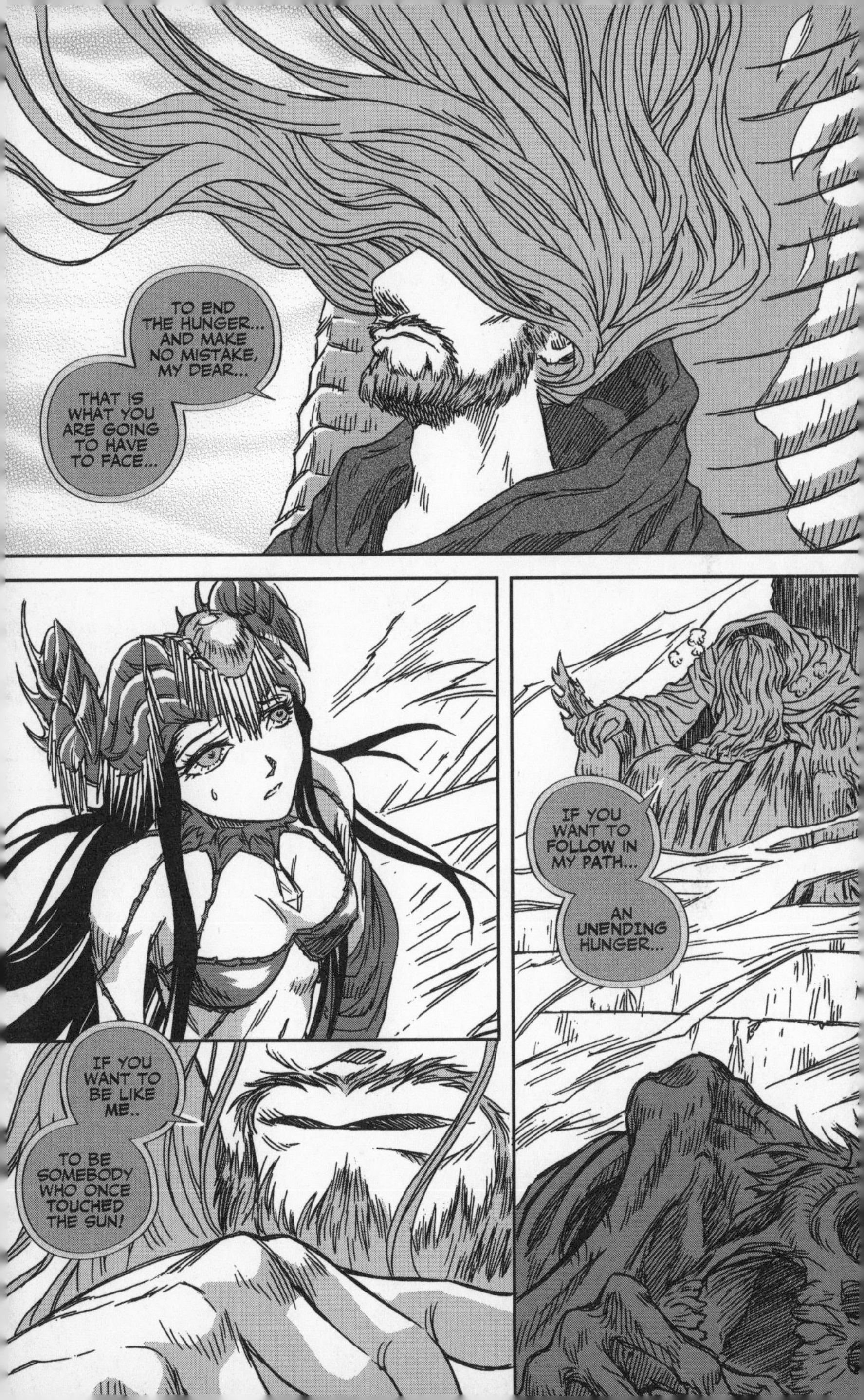
TO END THE HUNGER... AND MAKE NO MISTAKE, MY DEAR...
THAT IS WHAT YOU ARE GOING TO HAVE TO FACE...
IF YOU WANT TO FOLLOW IN MY PATH...
AN UNENDING HUNGER...
IF YOU WANT TO BE LIKE ME..
TO BE SOMEBODY WHO ONCE TOUCHED THE SUN!

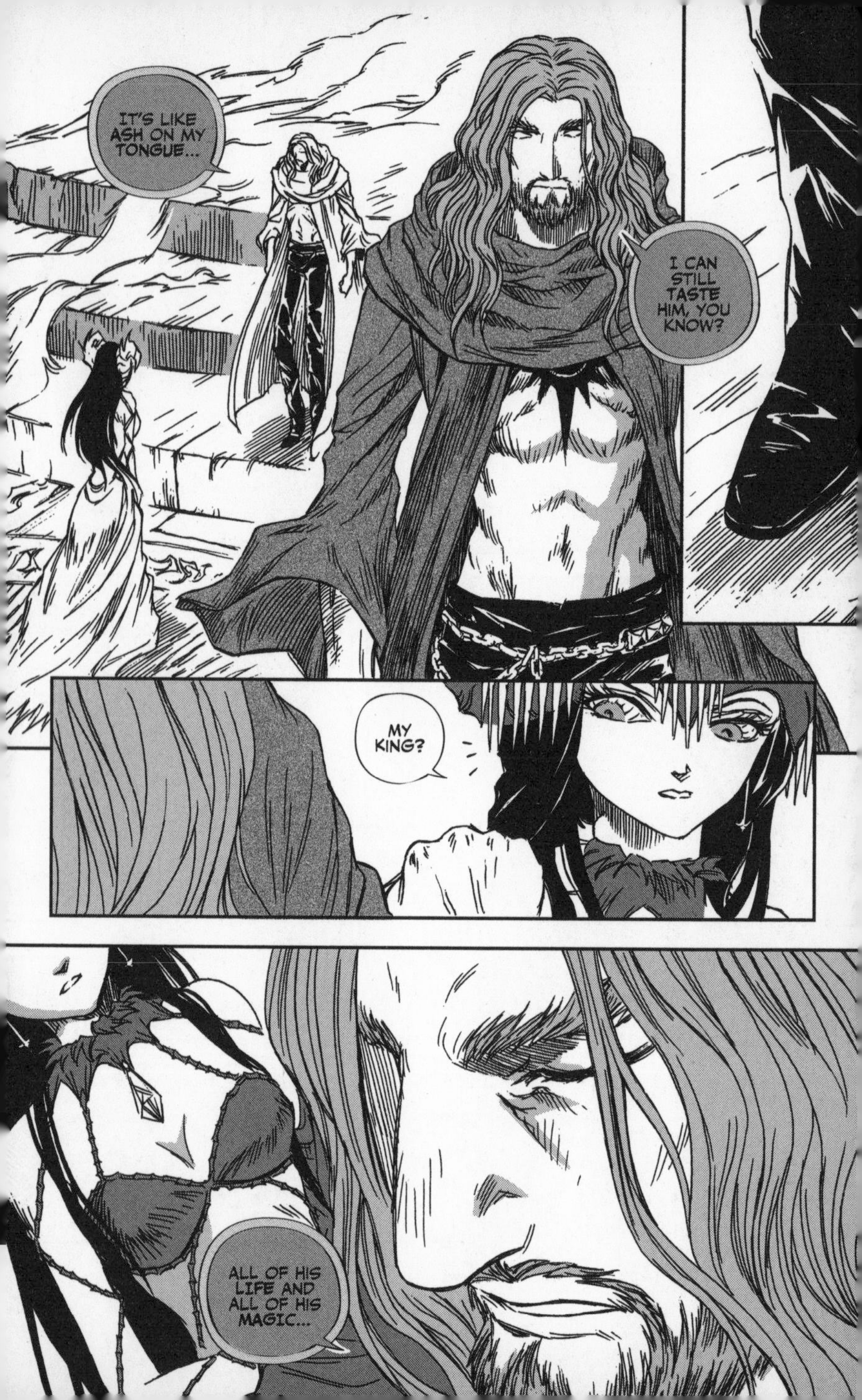
IT'S LIKE ASH ON MY TONGUE...
I CAN STILL TASTE HIM, YOU KNOW?
MY KING?
ALL OF HIS LIFE AND ALL OF HIS MAGIC...

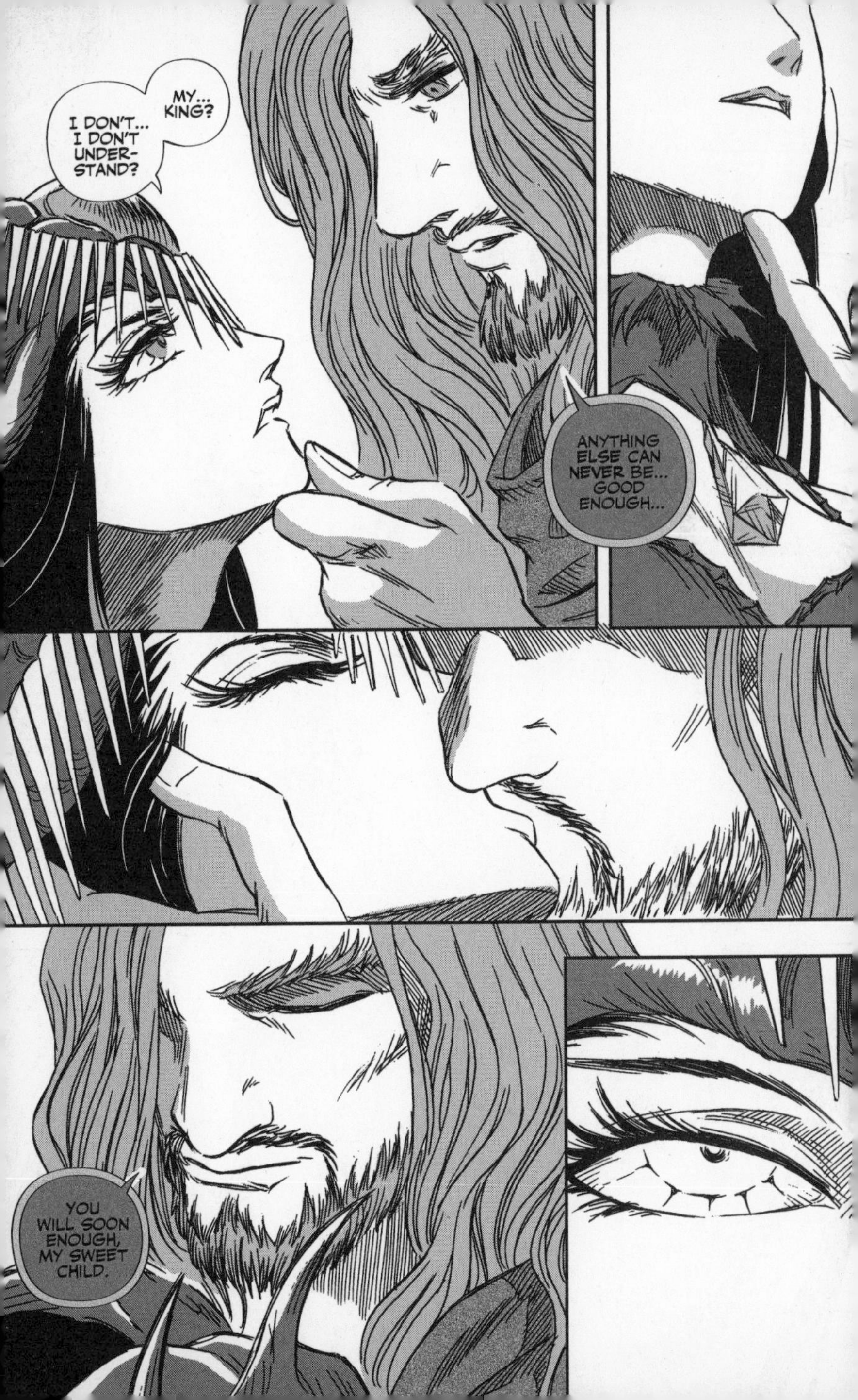
MY... KING?
I DON'T... I DON'T UNDER-STAND?
ANYTHING ELSE CAN NEVER BE... GOOD ENOUGH...
YOU WILL SOON ENOUGH, MY SWEET CHILD.

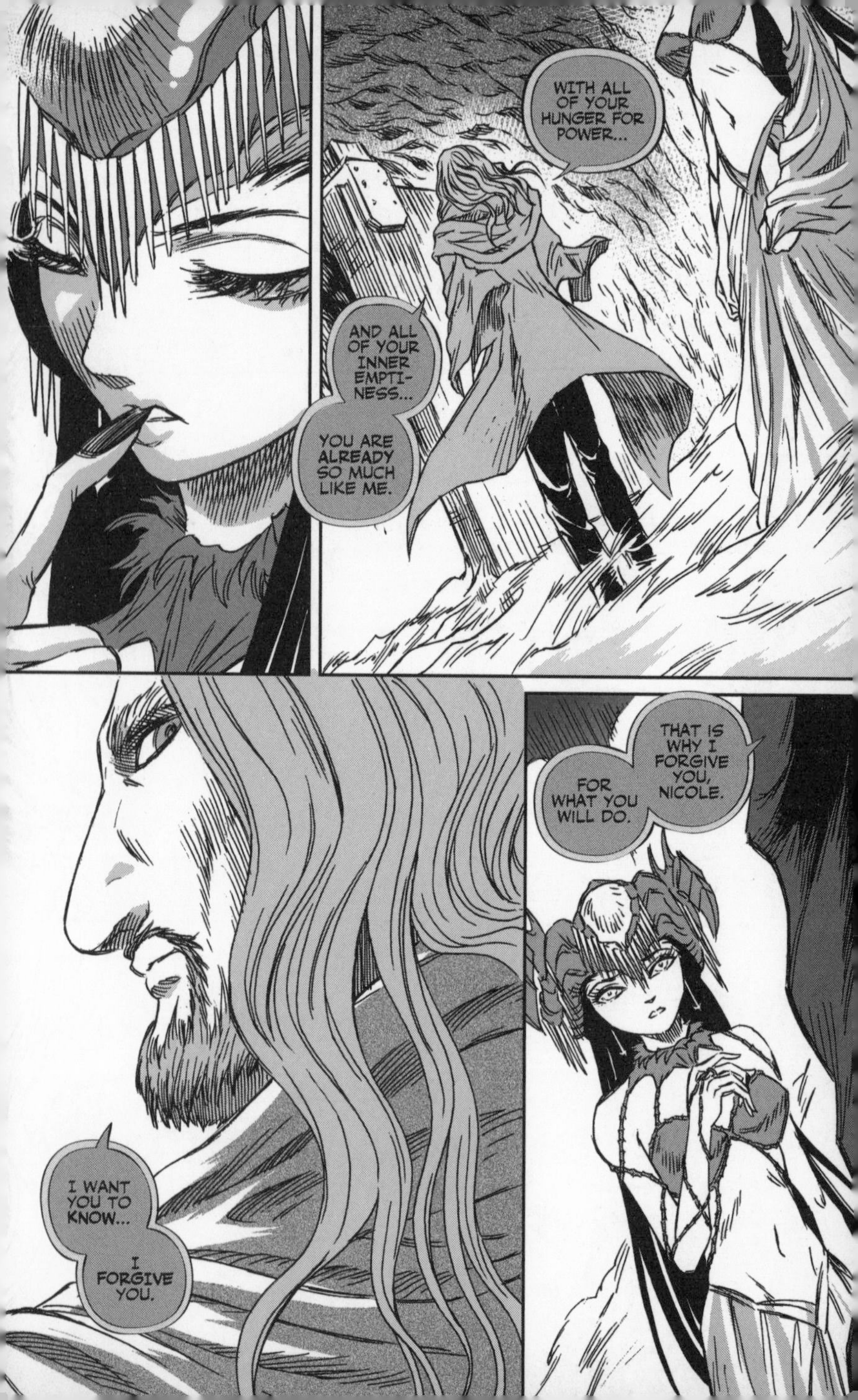
WITH ALL OF YOUR HUNGER FOR POWER...
AND ALL OF YOUR INNER EMPTI-NESS...
YOU ARE ALREADY SO MUCH LIKE ME.
THAT IS WHY I FORGIVE YOU, NICOLE.
FOR WHAT YOU WILL DO.
I WANT YOU TO KNOW...
I FORGIVE YOU.

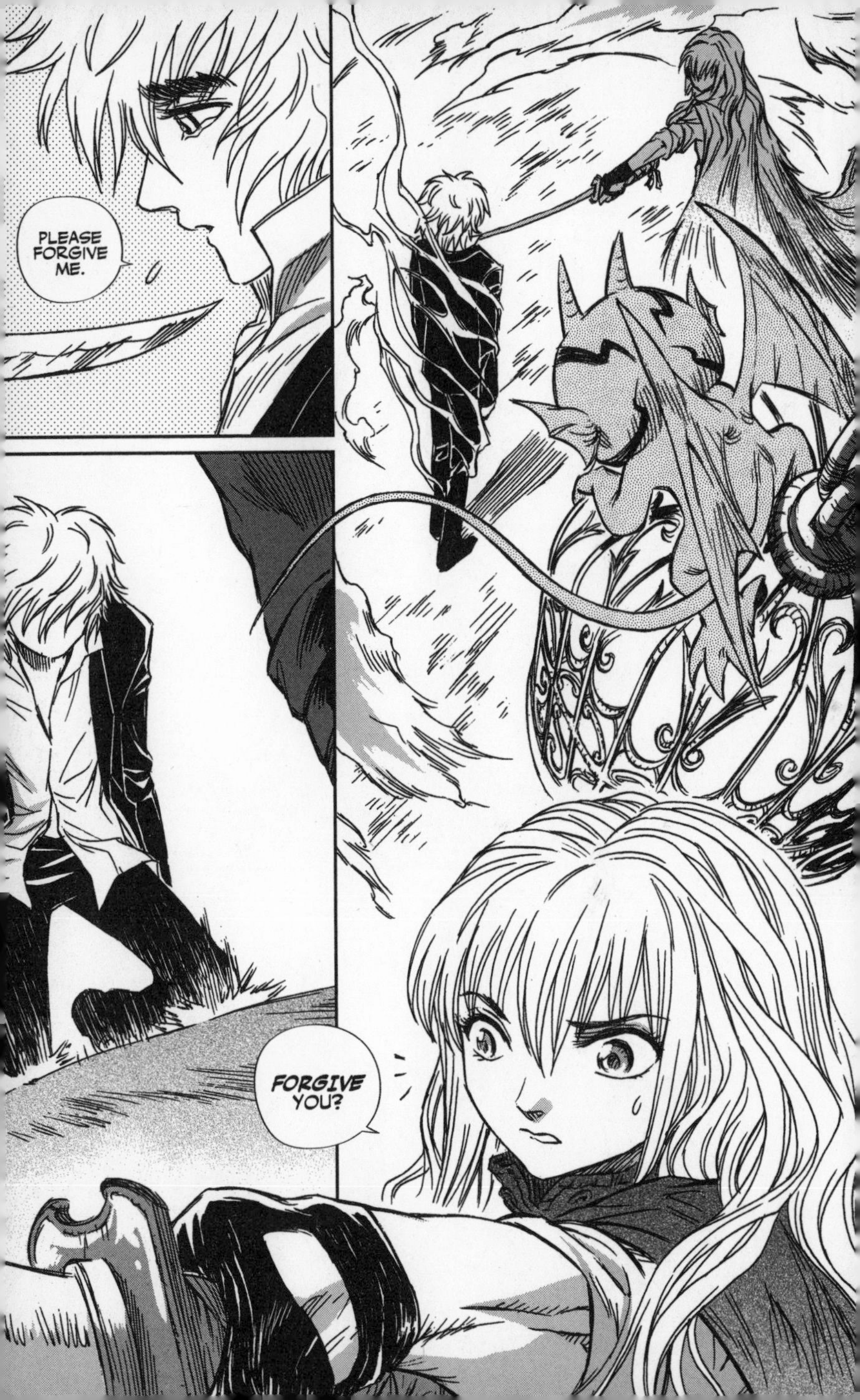
PLEASE FORGIVE ME.
FORGIVE YOU?

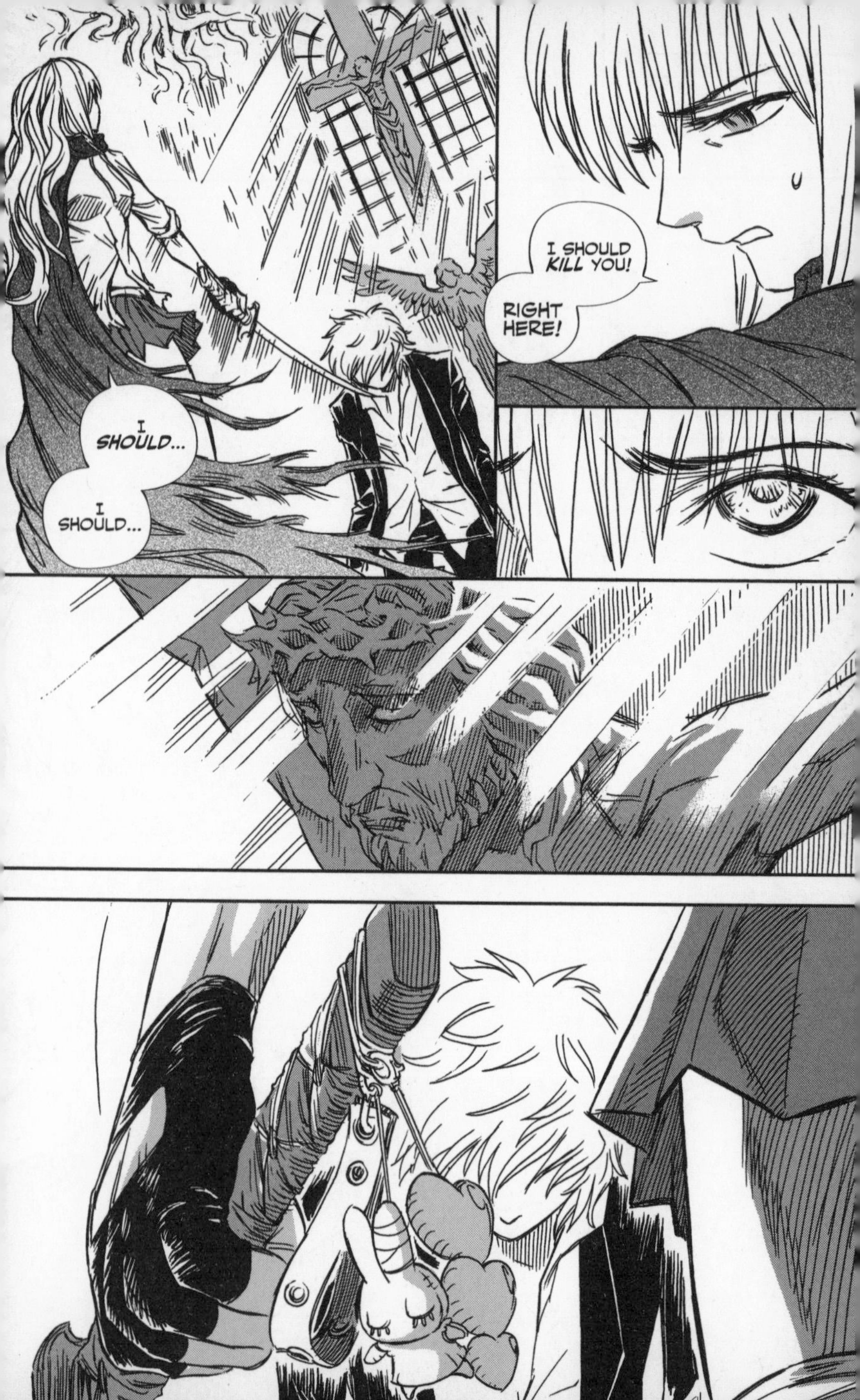
I SHOULD KILL YOU!
RIGHT HERE!
I SHOULD...
I SHOULD...

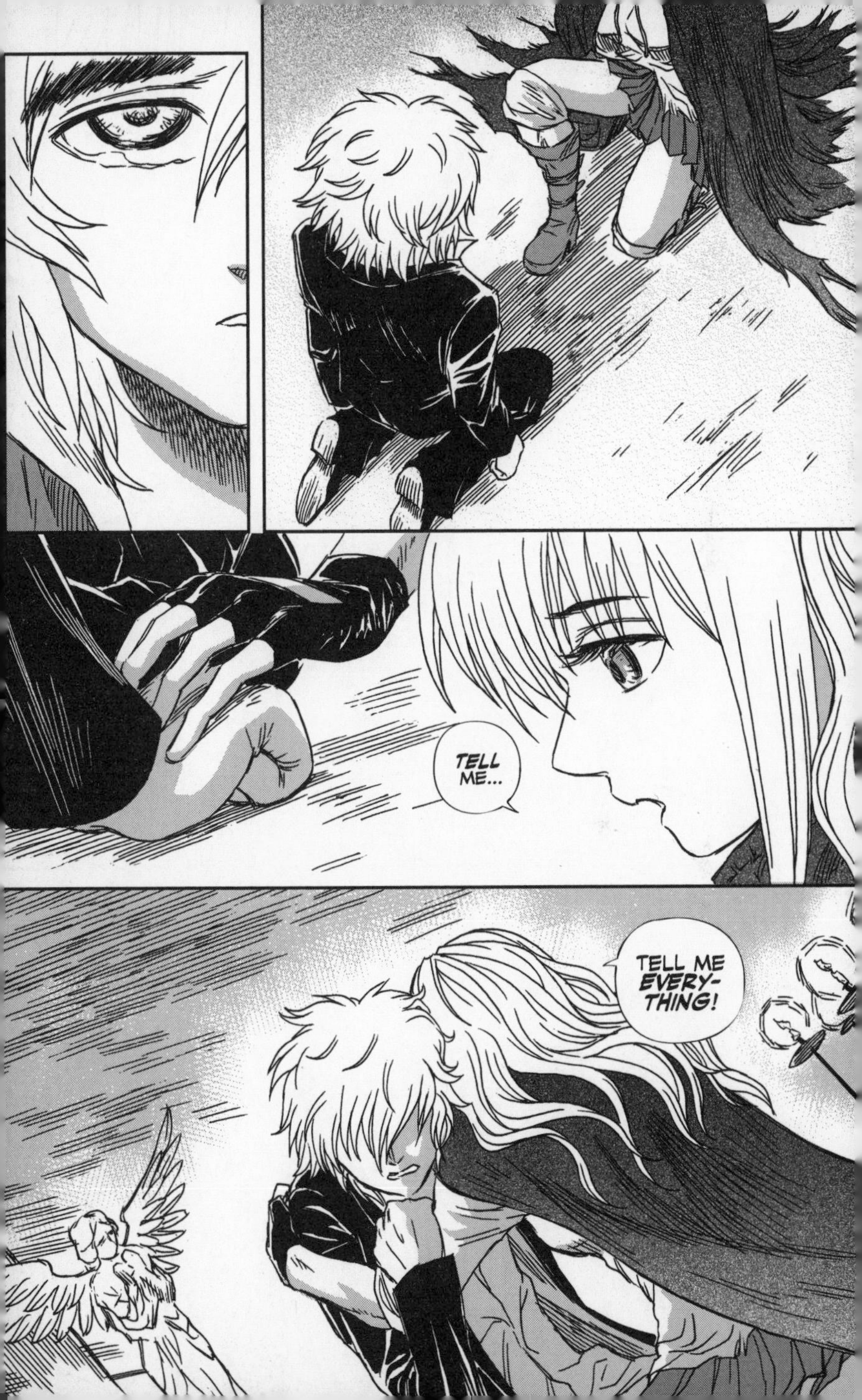
TELL ME...
TELL ME EVERY-THING!

CHAPTER

5

BLOOD OF EDEN

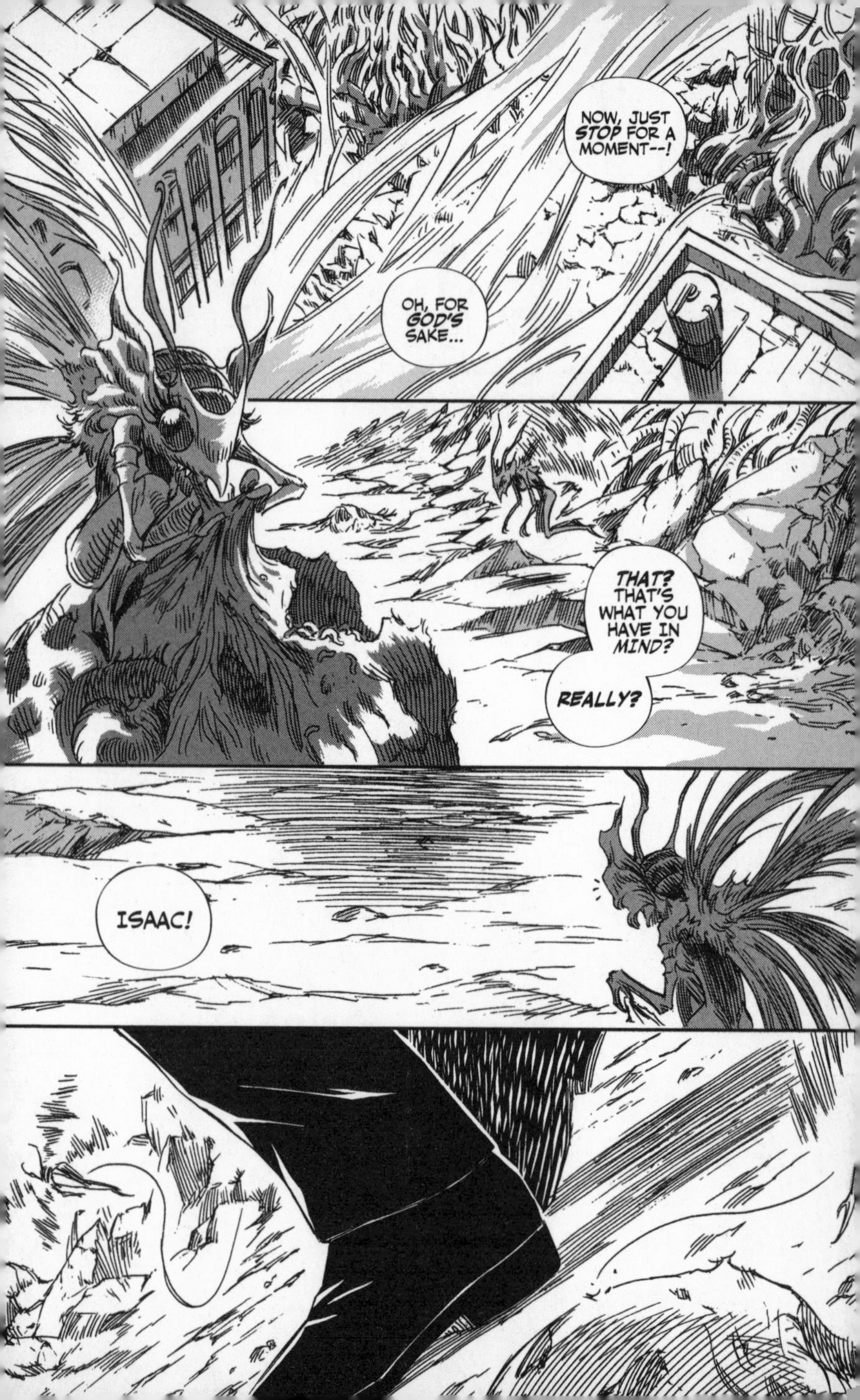
NOW, JUST STOP FOR A MOMENT--!
OH, FOR GOD'S SAKE...
THAT? THAT'S WHAT YOU HAVE IN MIND?
REALLY?
ISAAC!

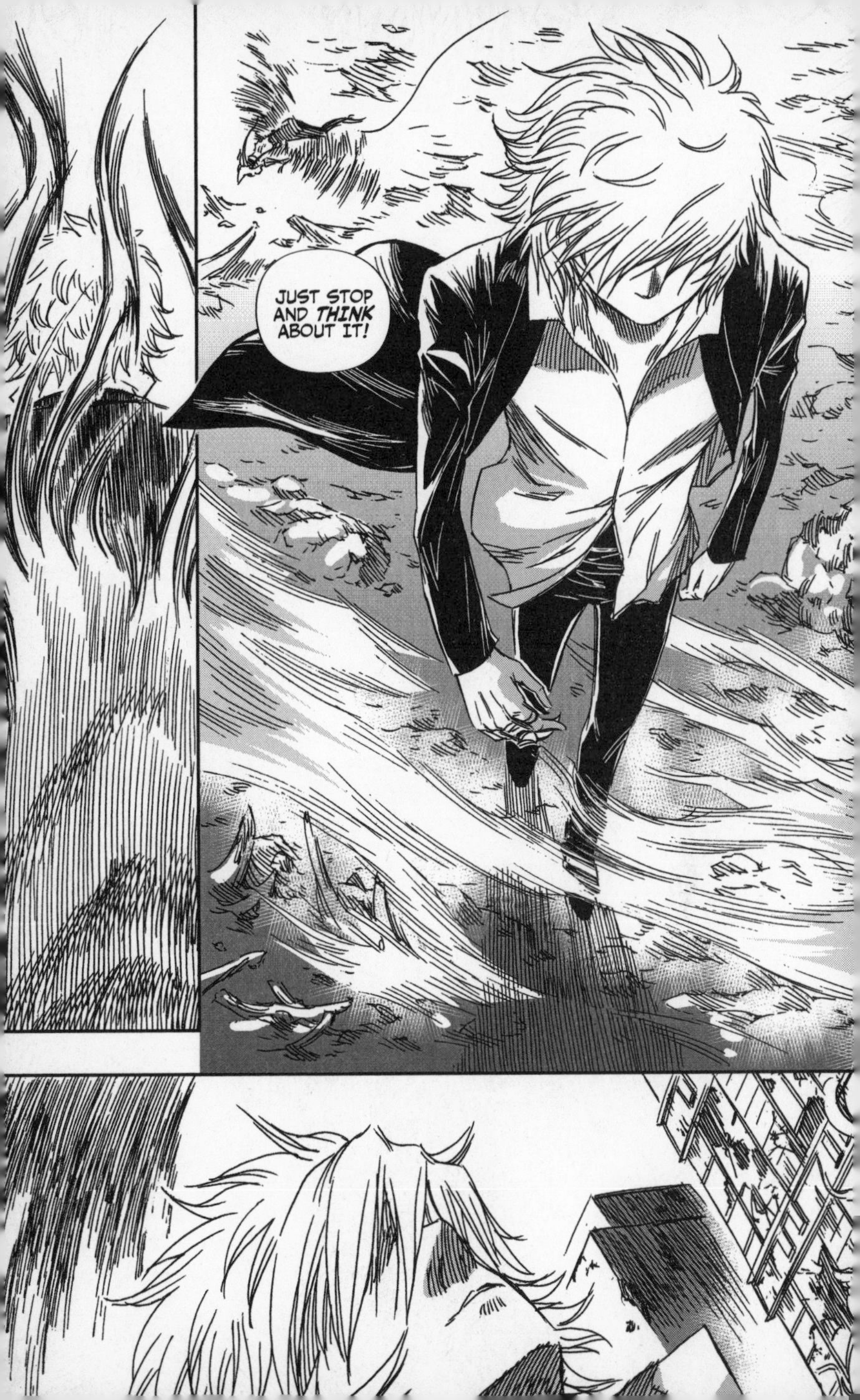
JUST STOP AND *THINK* ABOUT IT!

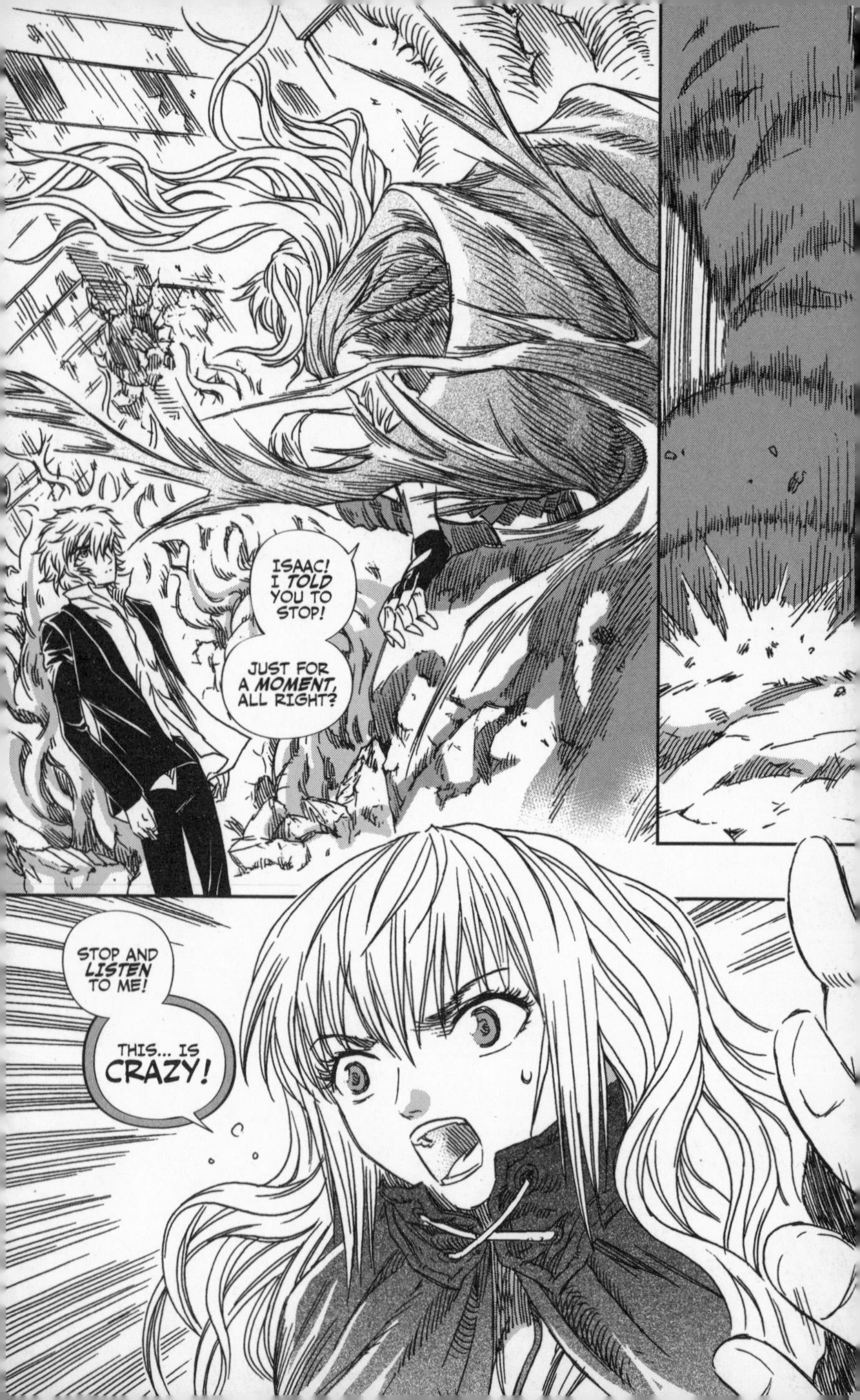
ISAAC! I TOLD YOU TO STOP!
JUST FOR A MOMENT, ALL RIGHT?
STOP AND LISTEN TO ME!
THIS... IS CRAZY!

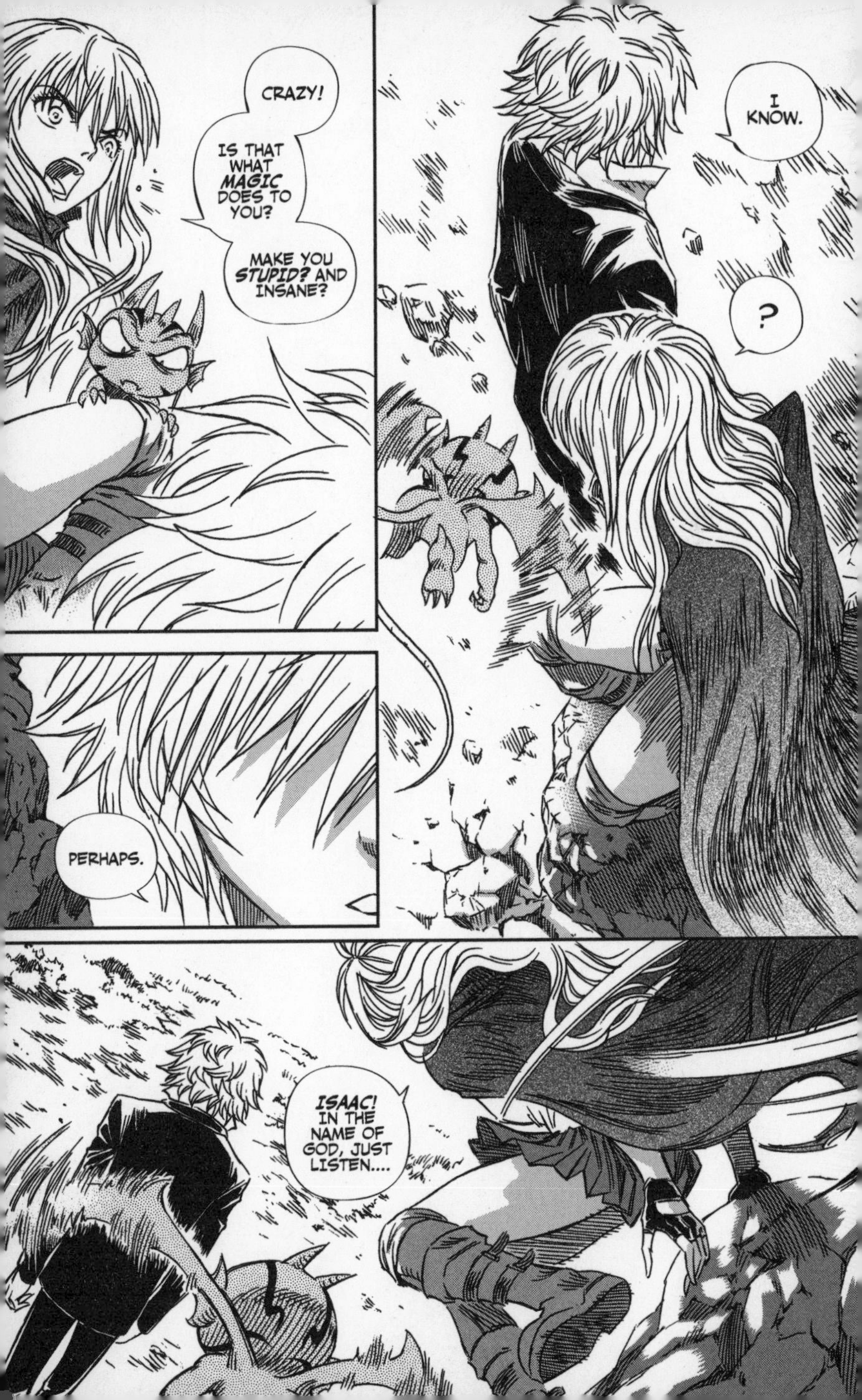
CRAZY!
IS THAT WHAT *MAGIC* DOES TO YOU?
MAKE YOU *STUPID?* AND INSANE?
PERHAPS.
I KNOW.
?
ISAAC! IN THE NAME OF GOD, JUST LISTEN....

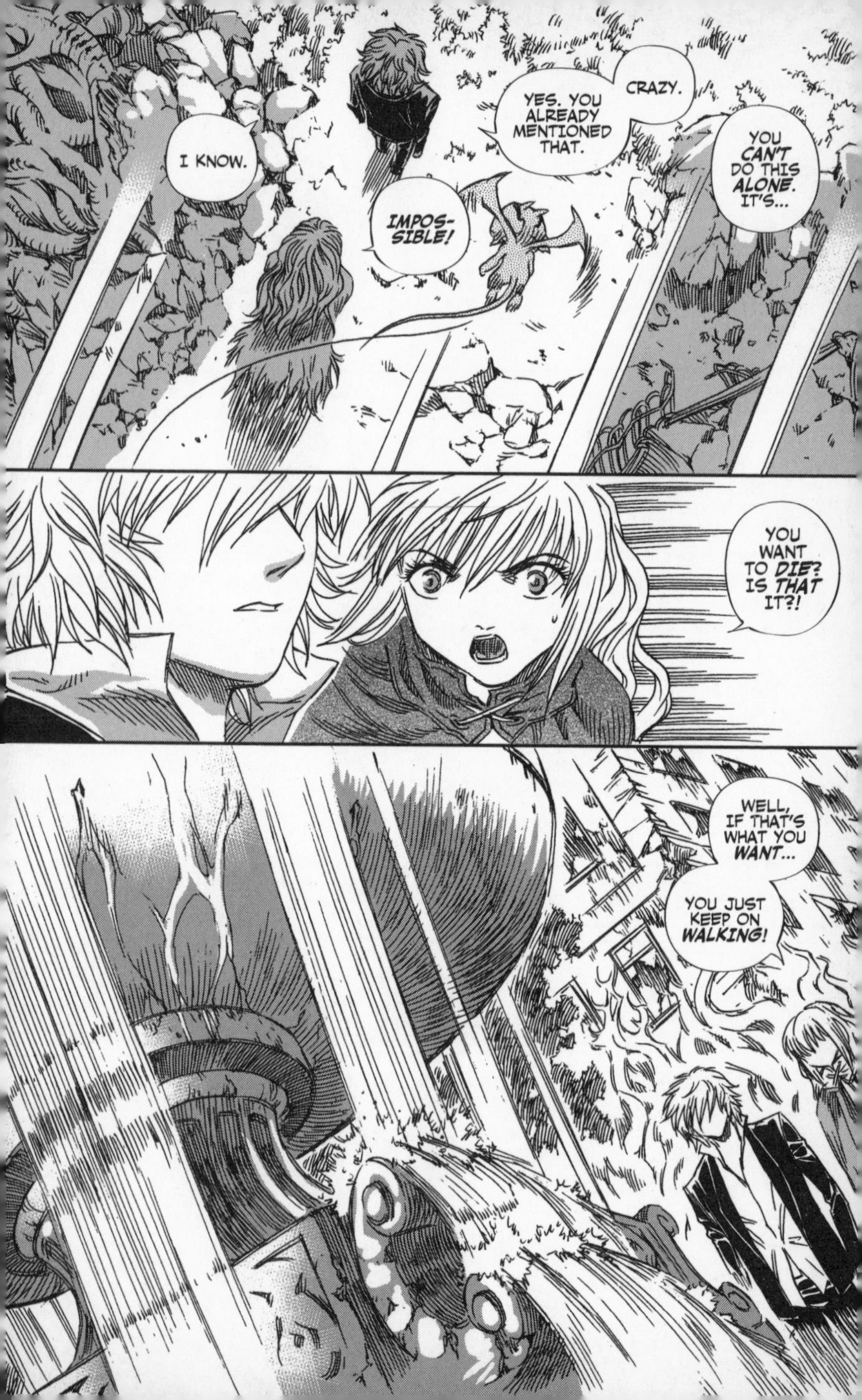
YOU *CAN'T* DO THIS *ALONE*. IT'S...
CRAZY.
YES. YOU ALREADY MENTIONED THAT.
IMPOSSIBLE!
I KNOW.
YOU WANT TO *DIE*? IS *THAT* IT?!
WELL, IF THAT'S WHAT YOU *WANT*...
YOU JUST KEEP ON *WALKING*!

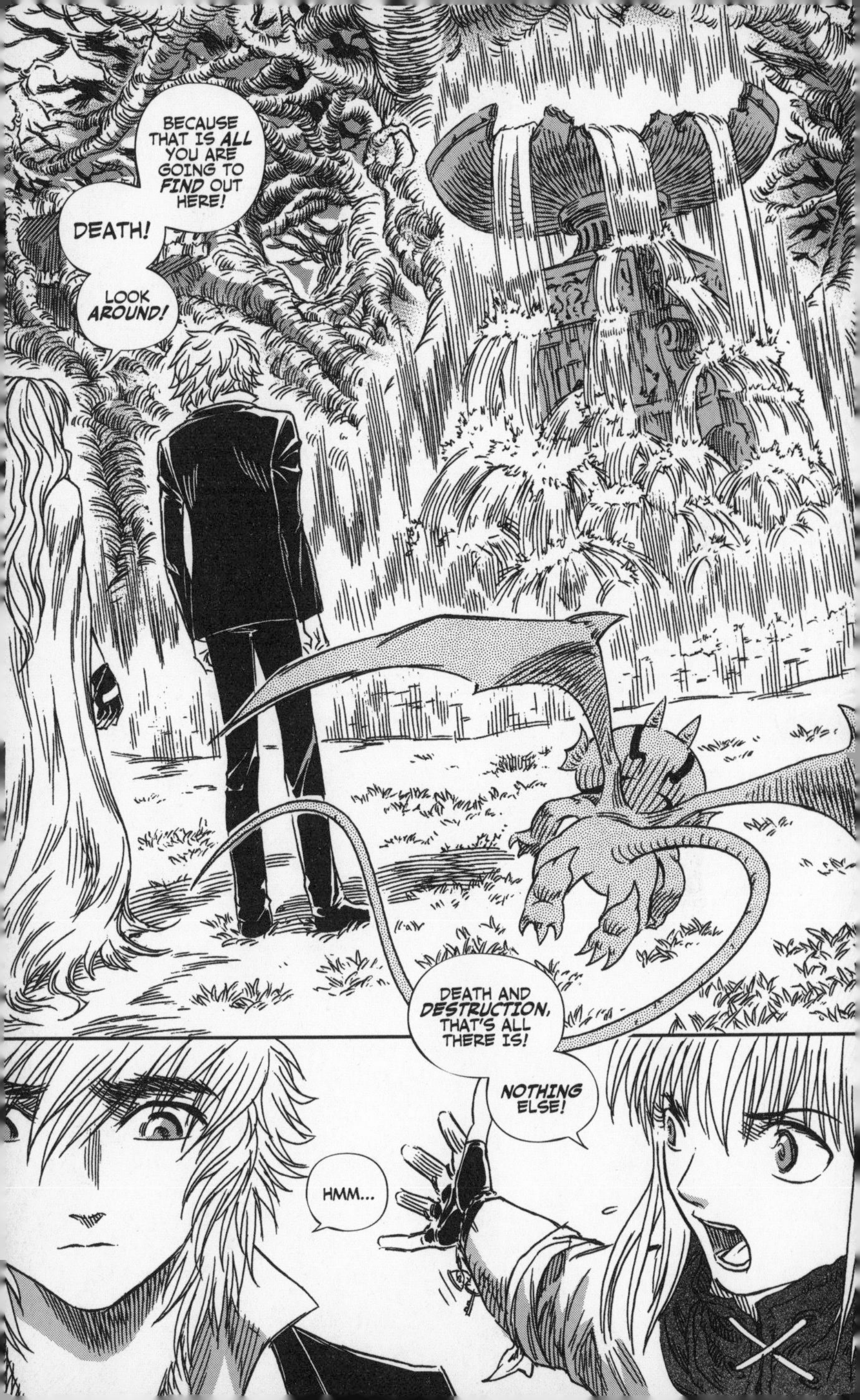
BECAUSE THAT IS ALL YOU ARE GOING TO FIND OUT HERE!
DEATH!
LOOK AROUND!
DEATH AND DESTRUCTION, THAT'S ALL THERE IS!
NOTHING ELSE!
HMM...

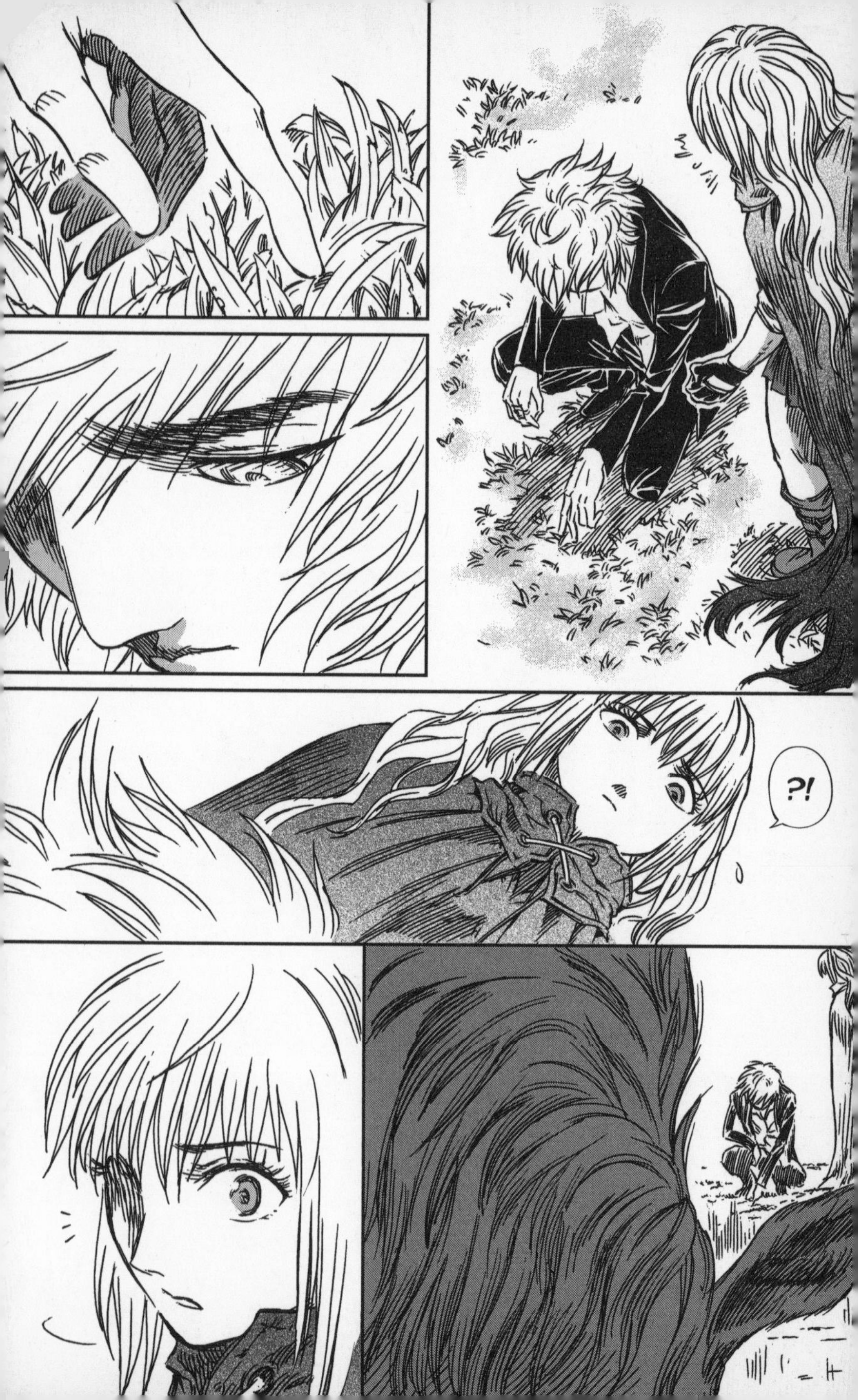
?!

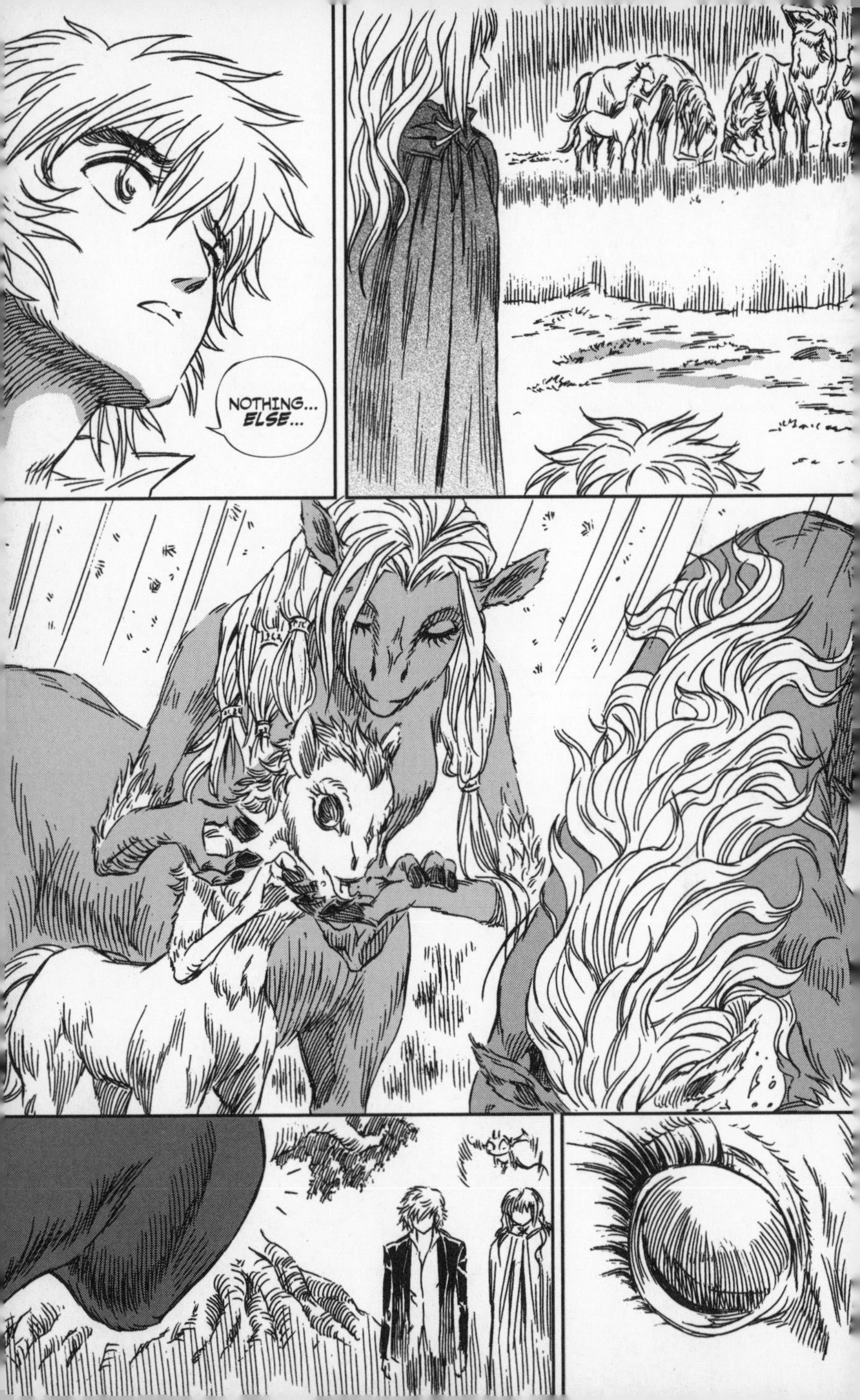
NOTHING... ELSE...

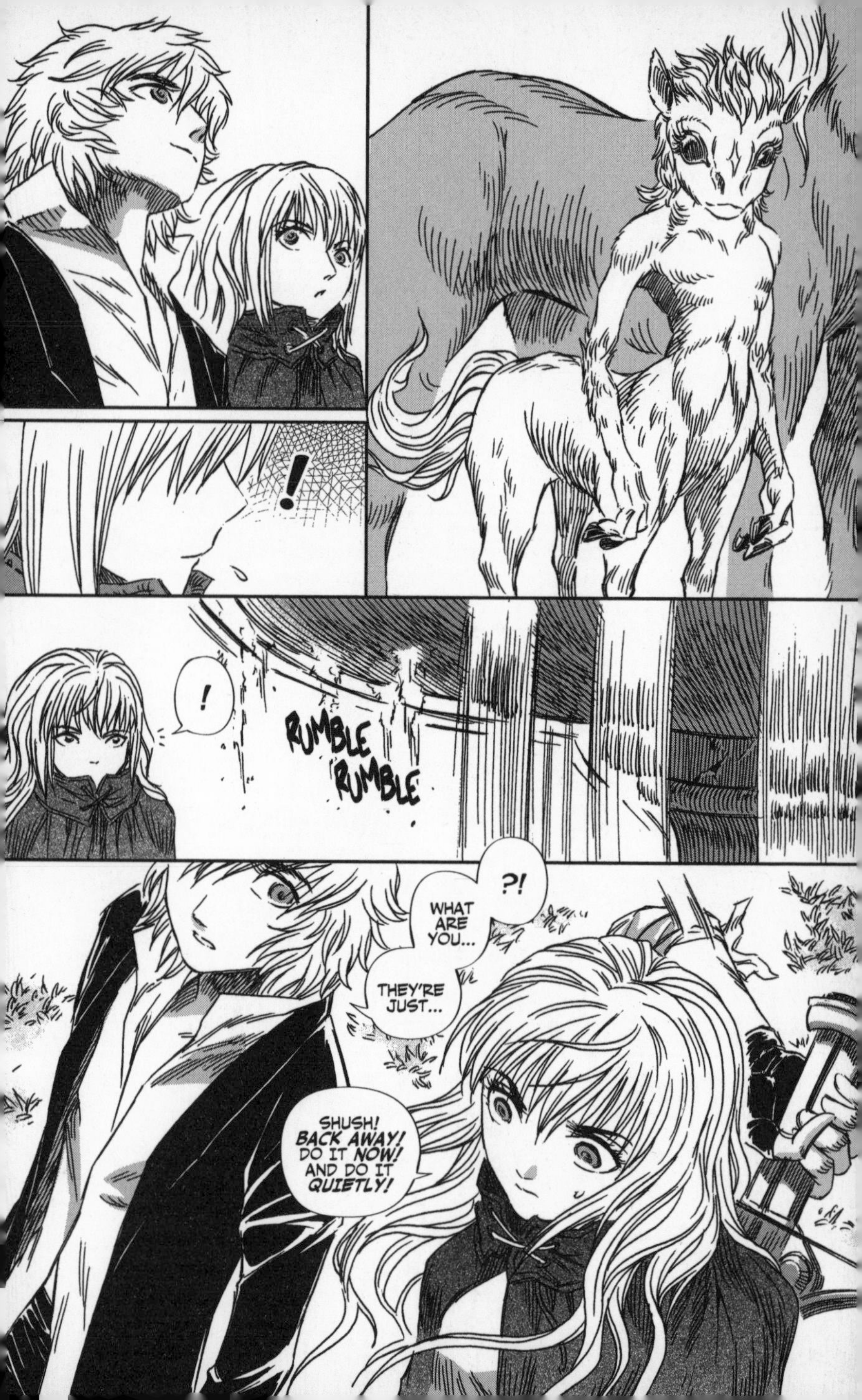
!
!
RUMBLE RUMBLE
?!
WHAT ARE YOU...
THEY'RE JUST...
SHUSH! BACK AWAY! DO IT NOW! AND DO IT QUIETLY!

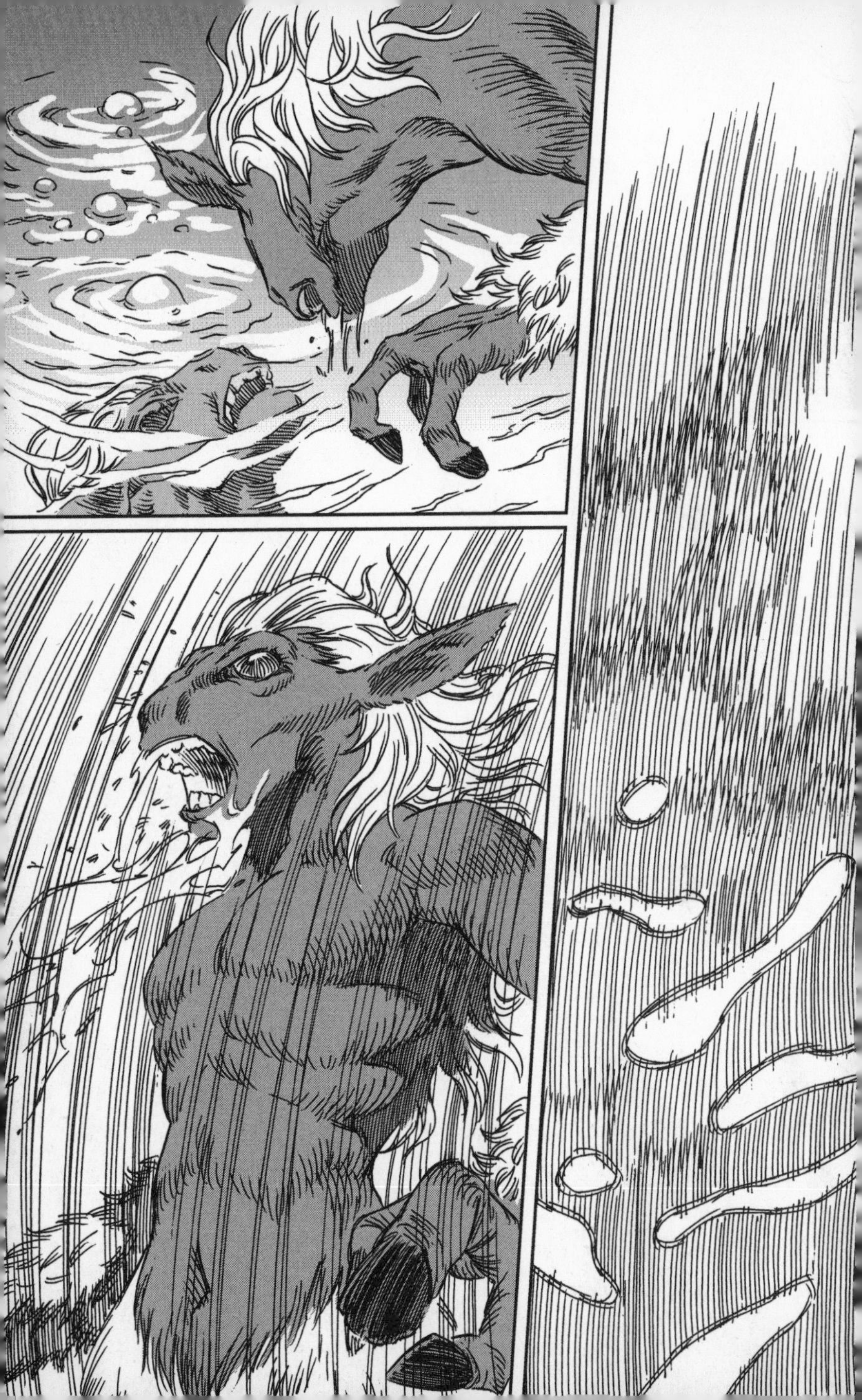

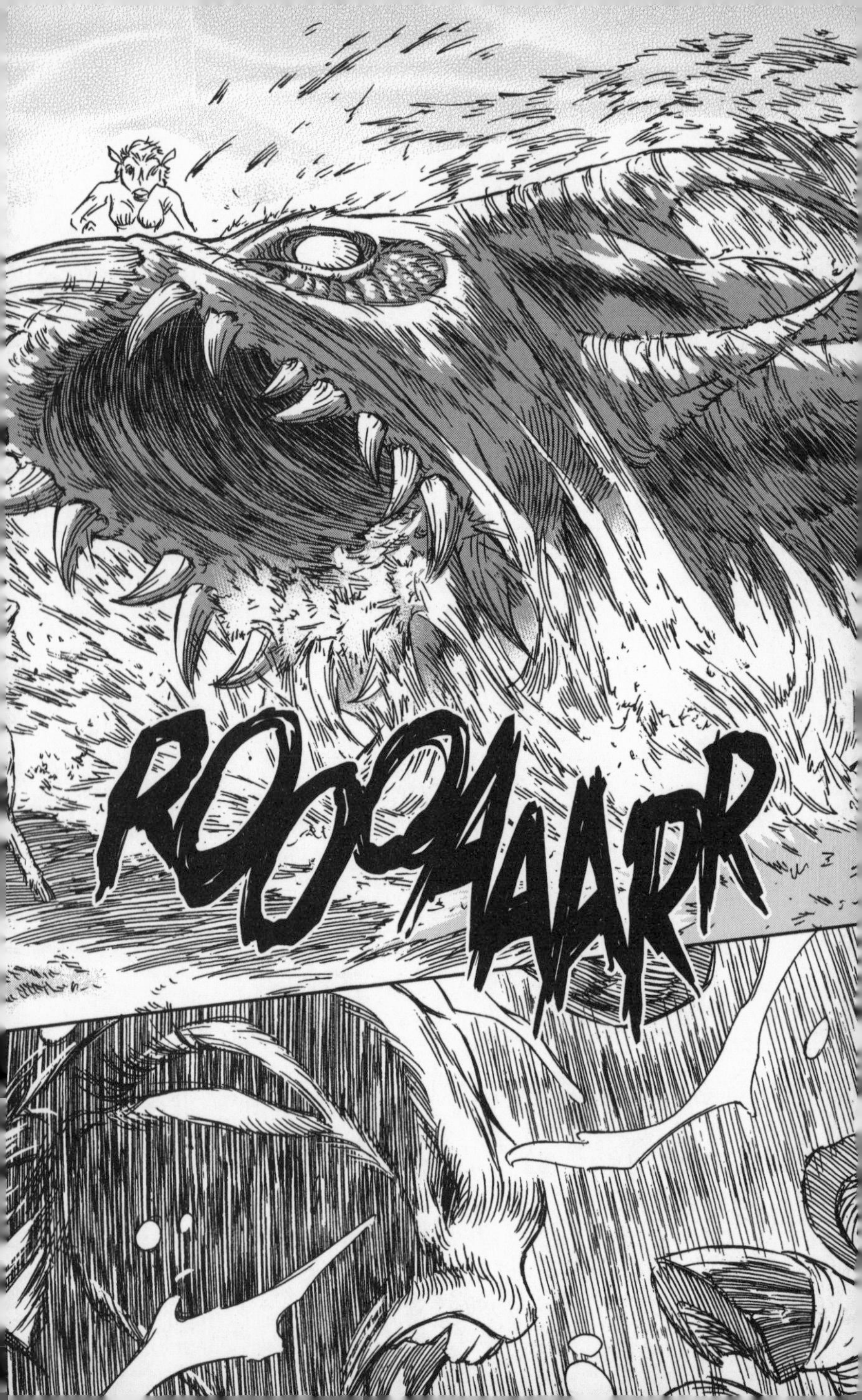
ROOOAAARR

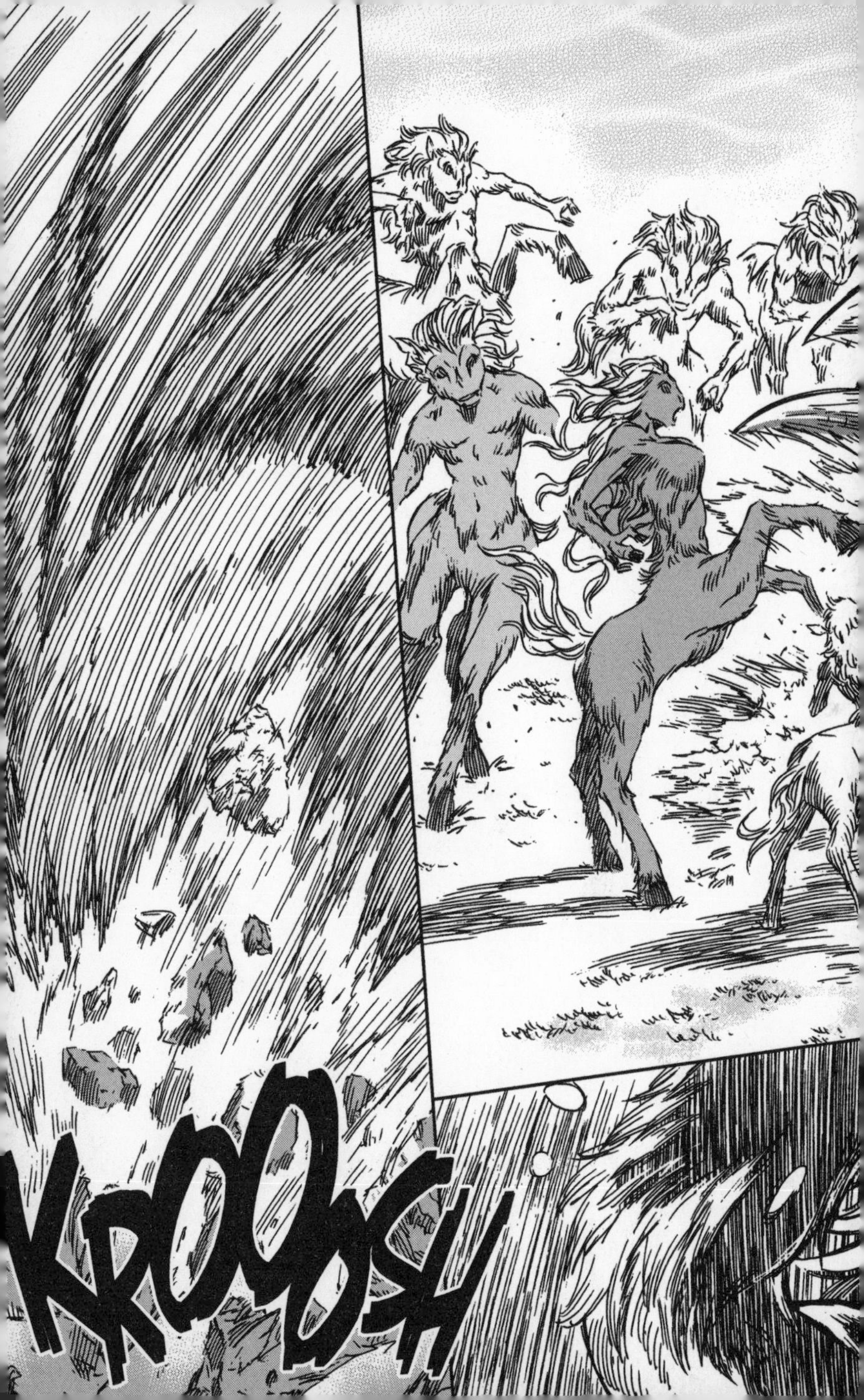
KROOSH

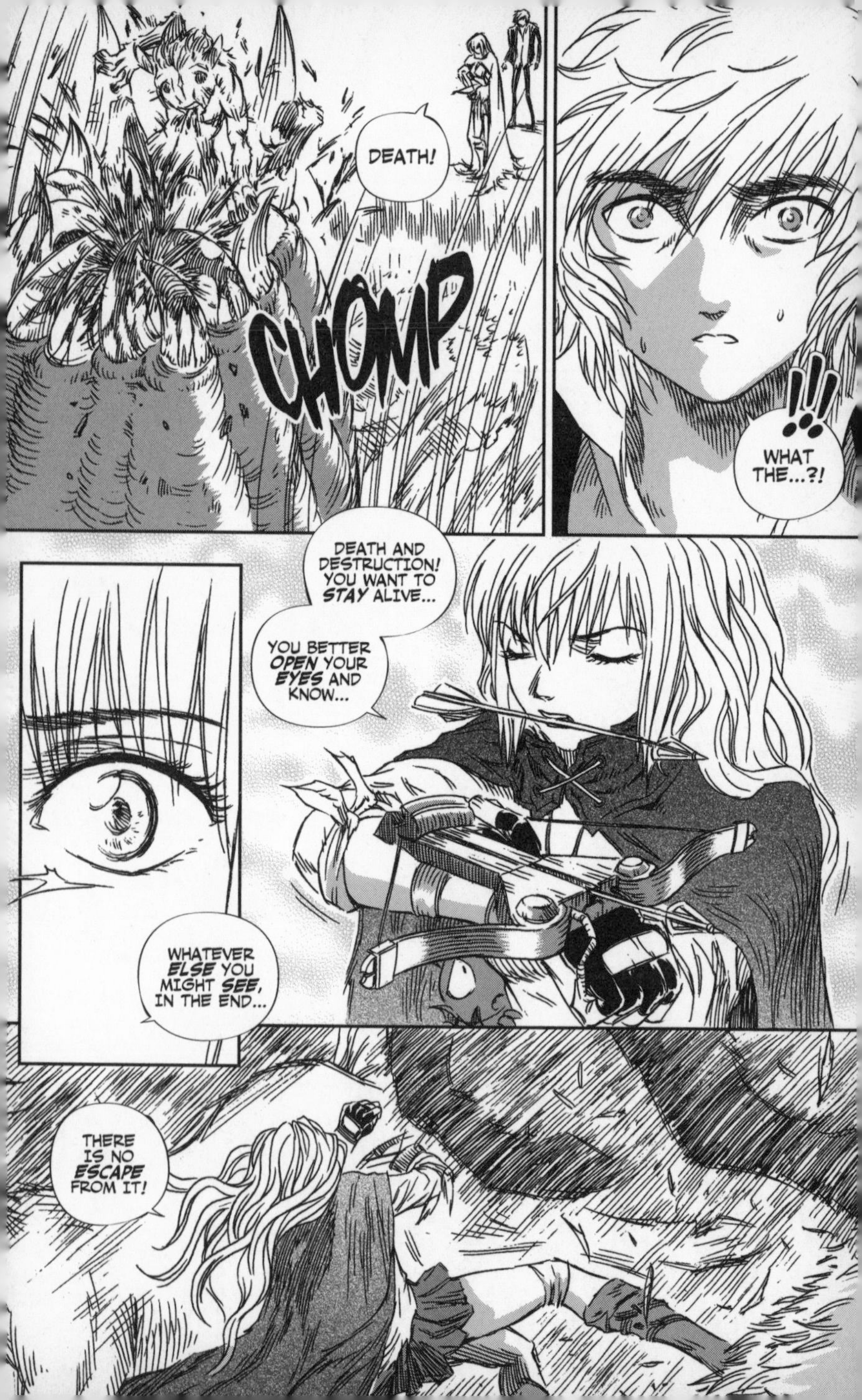
DEATH!
CHOMP
!!
WHAT THE...?!
DEATH AND DESTRUCTION! YOU WANT TO STAY ALIVE...
YOU BETTER OPEN YOUR EYES AND KNOW...
WHATEVER ELSE YOU MIGHT SEE, IN THE END...
THERE IS NO ESCAPE FROM IT!

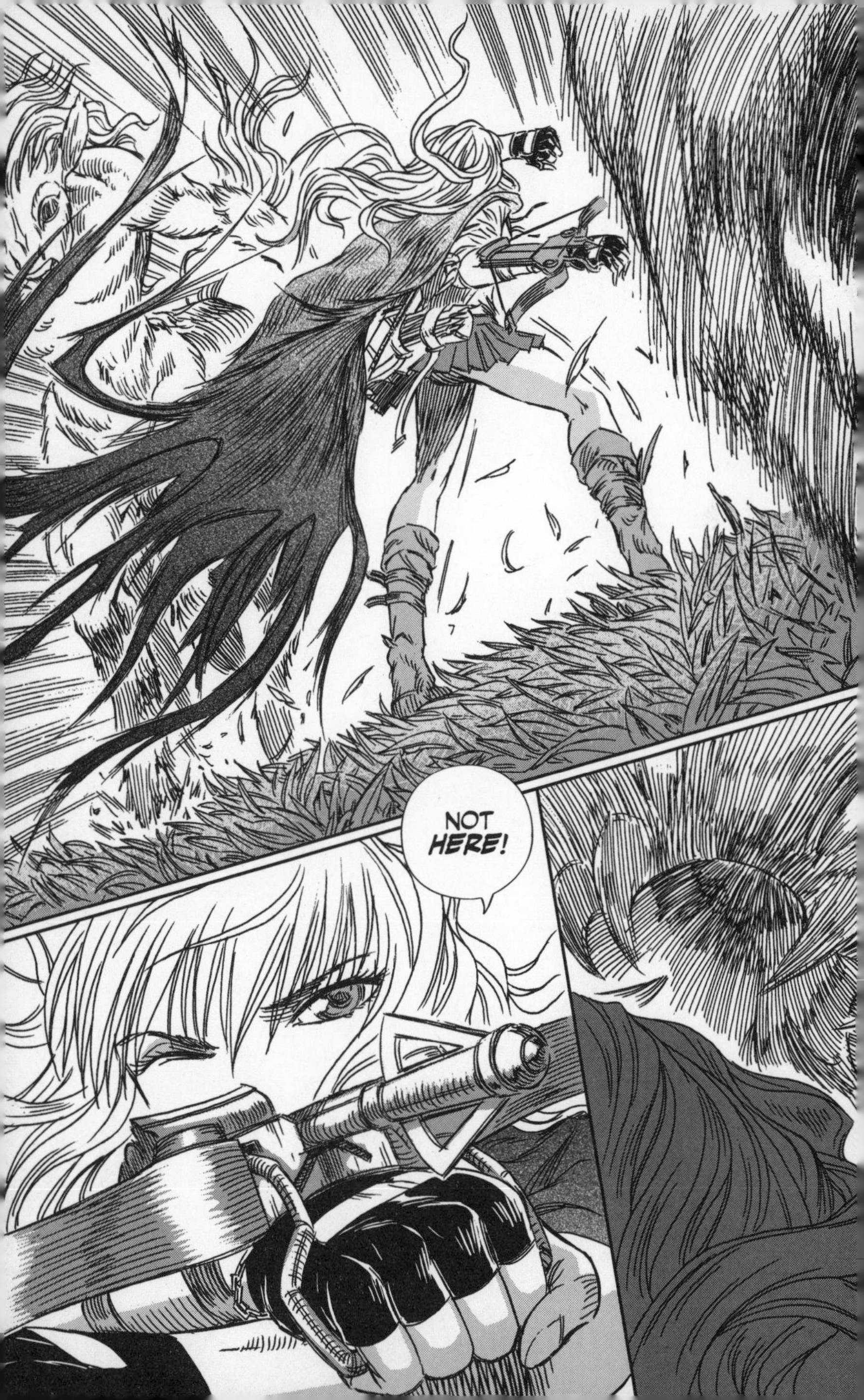
NOT HERE!

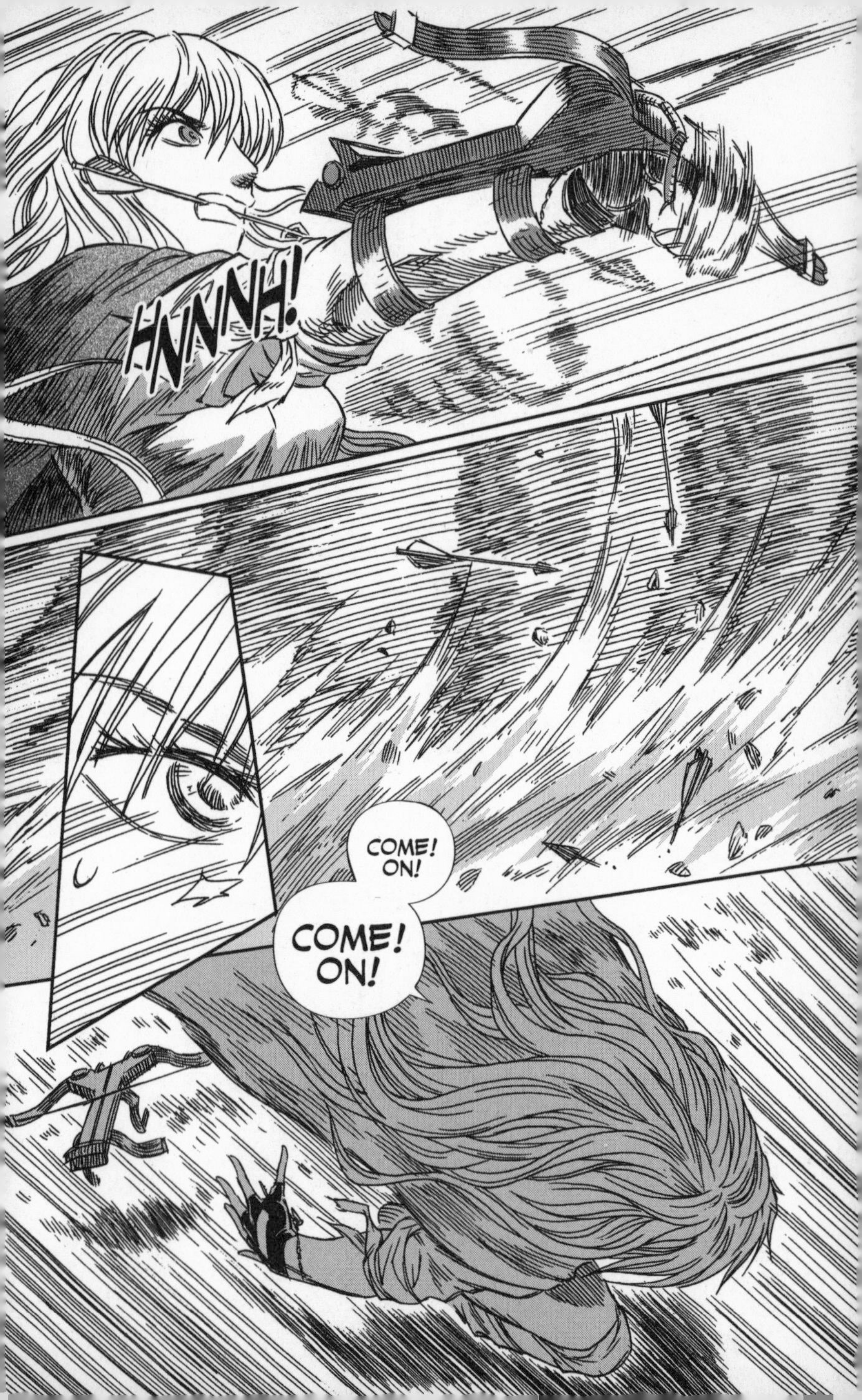
HNNNH!
COME! ON!
COME! ON!

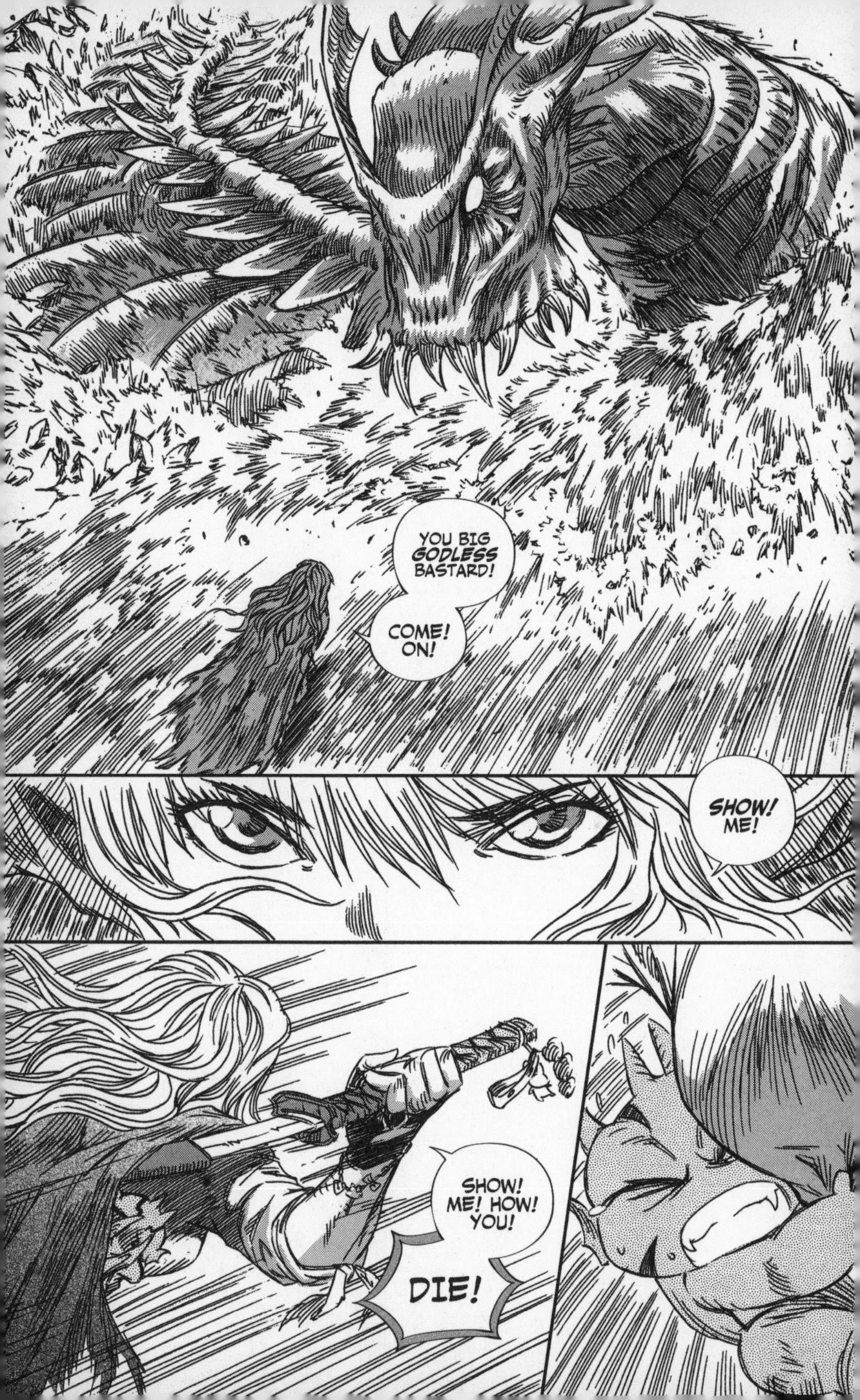
YOU BIG GODLESS BASTARD!
COME! ON!
SHOW! ME!
SHOW! ME! HOW! YOU!
DIE!

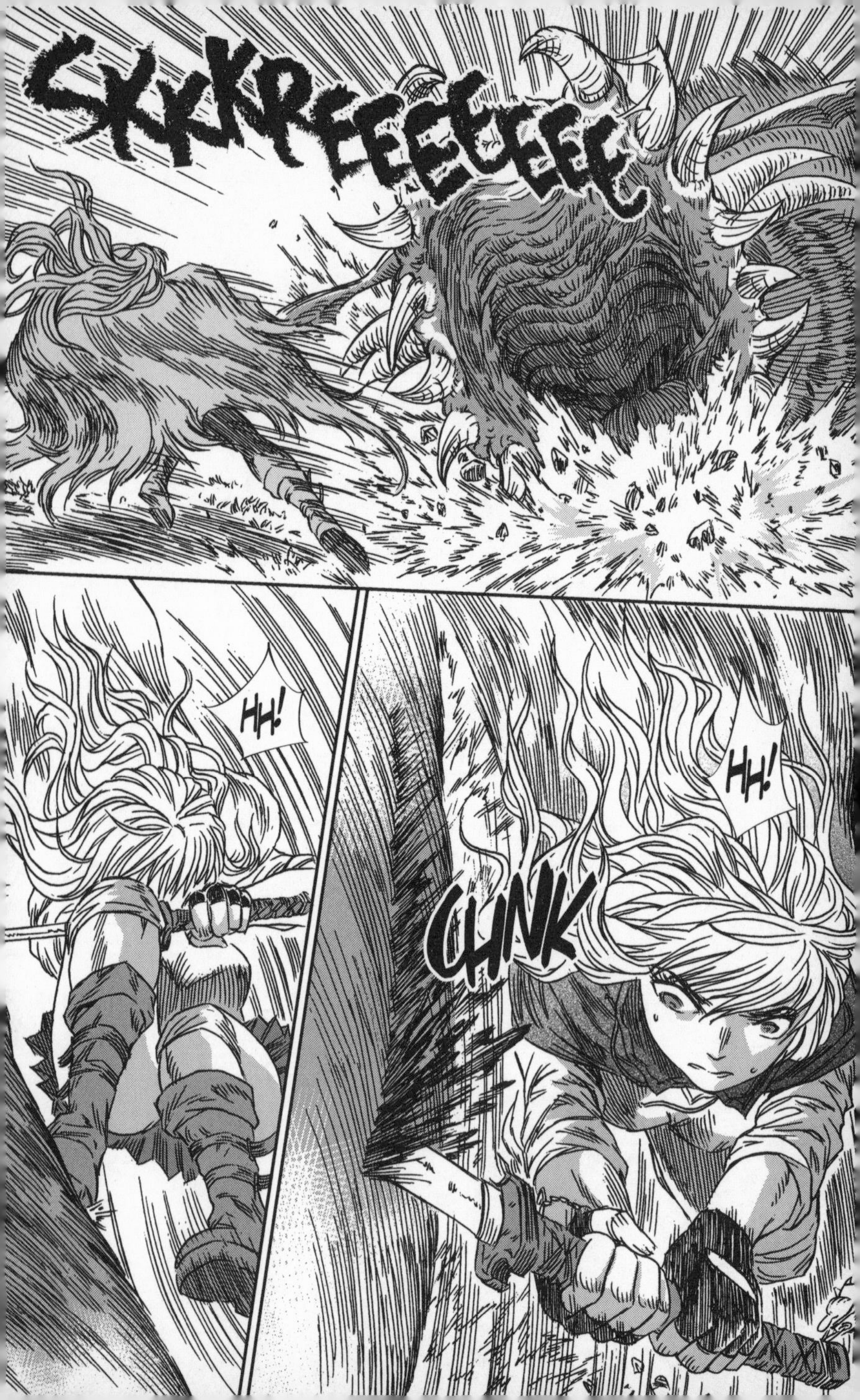
SKKKREEEEEEEE
HH!
CHNK
HH!

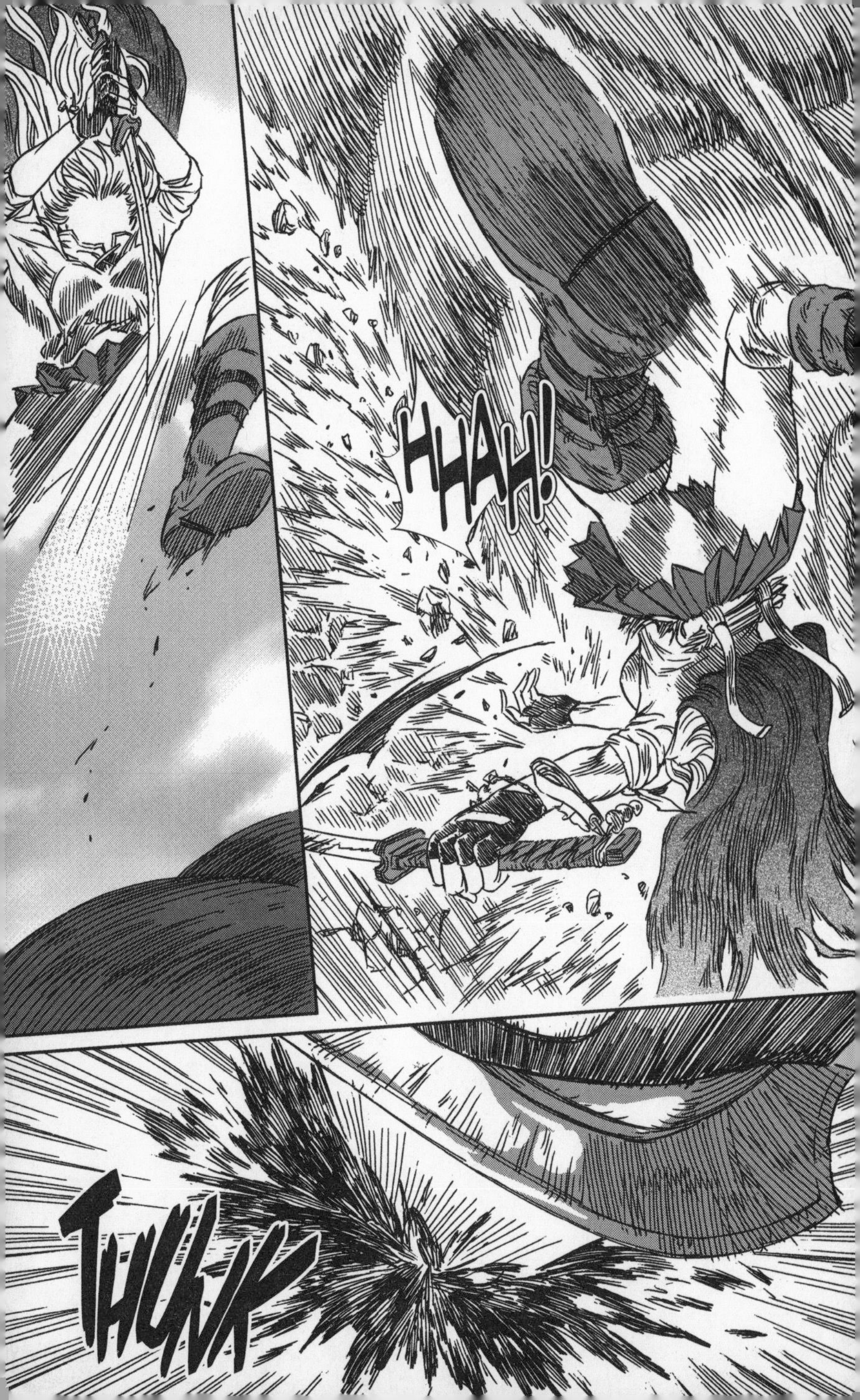
HHAH!
THUNK

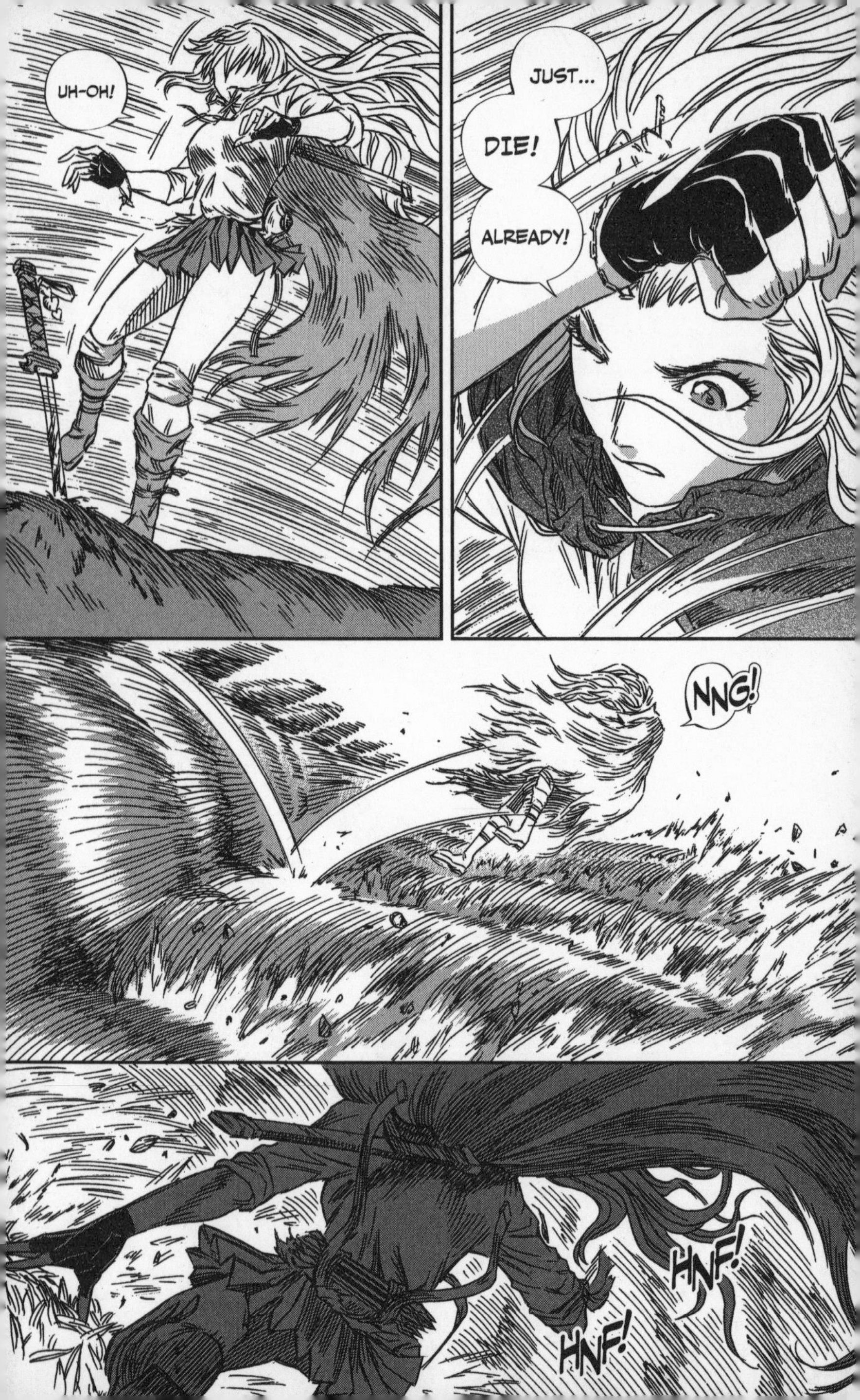
JUST...
DIE!
ALREADY!
UH-OH!
NNG!
HNF!
HNF!

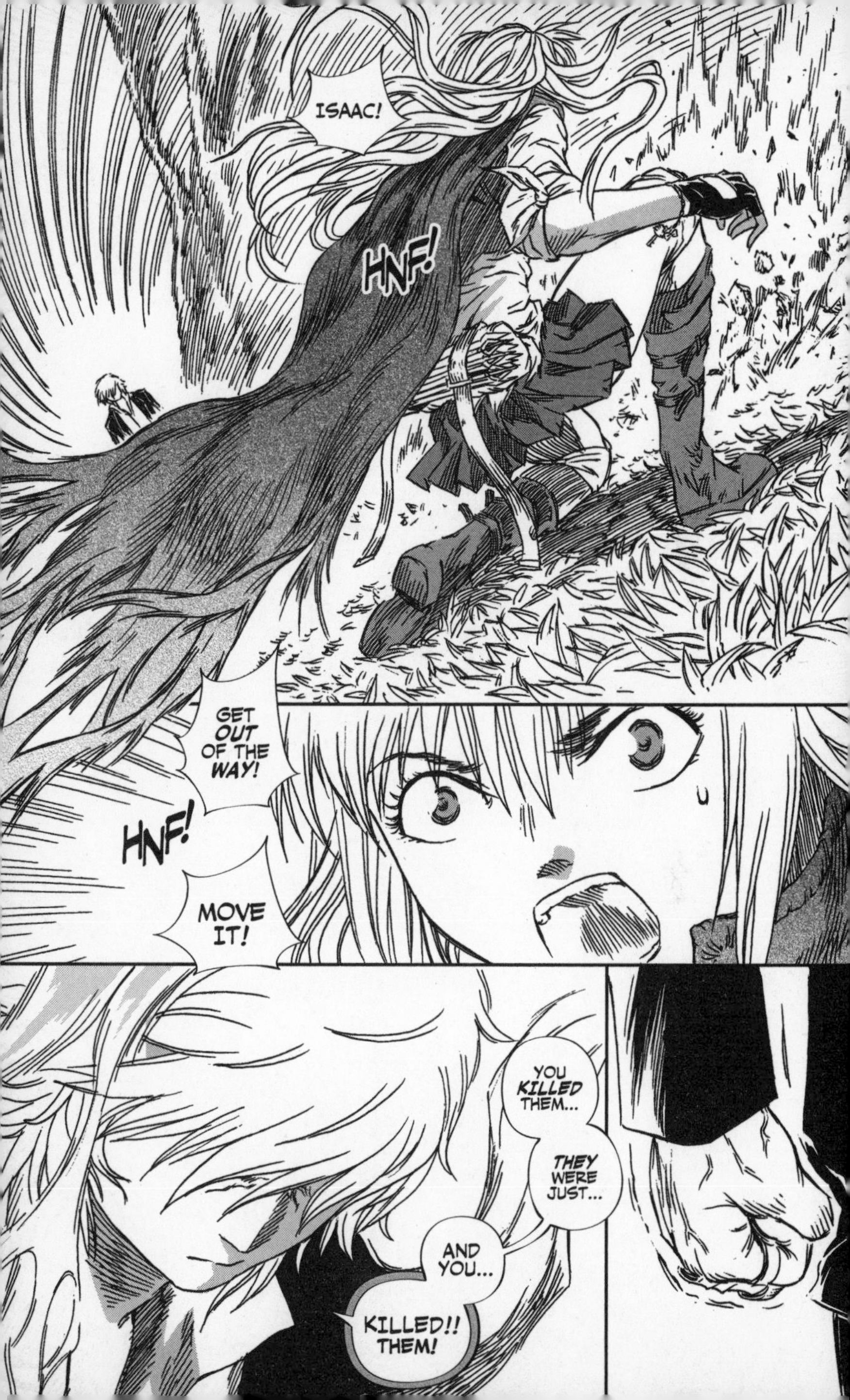
ISAAC!
HNF!
GET OUT OF THE WAY!
HNF!
MOVE IT!
YOU KILLED THEM...
THEY WERE JUST...
AND YOU...
KILLED!! THEM!

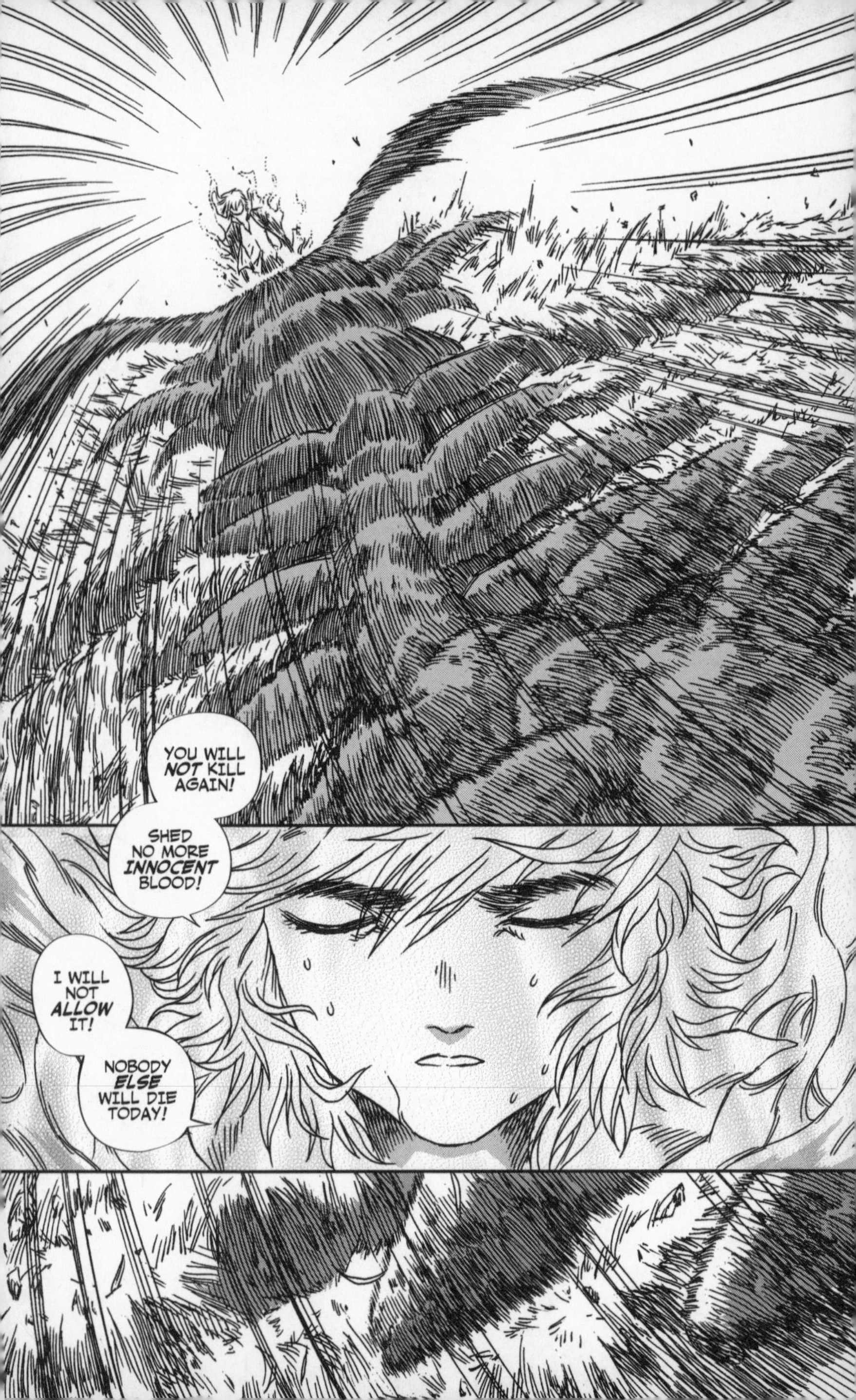
YOU WILL *NOT* KILL AGAIN!
SHED NO MORE *INNOCENT* BLOOD!
I WILL NOT *ALLOW* IT!
NOBODY *ELSE* WILL DIE TODAY!

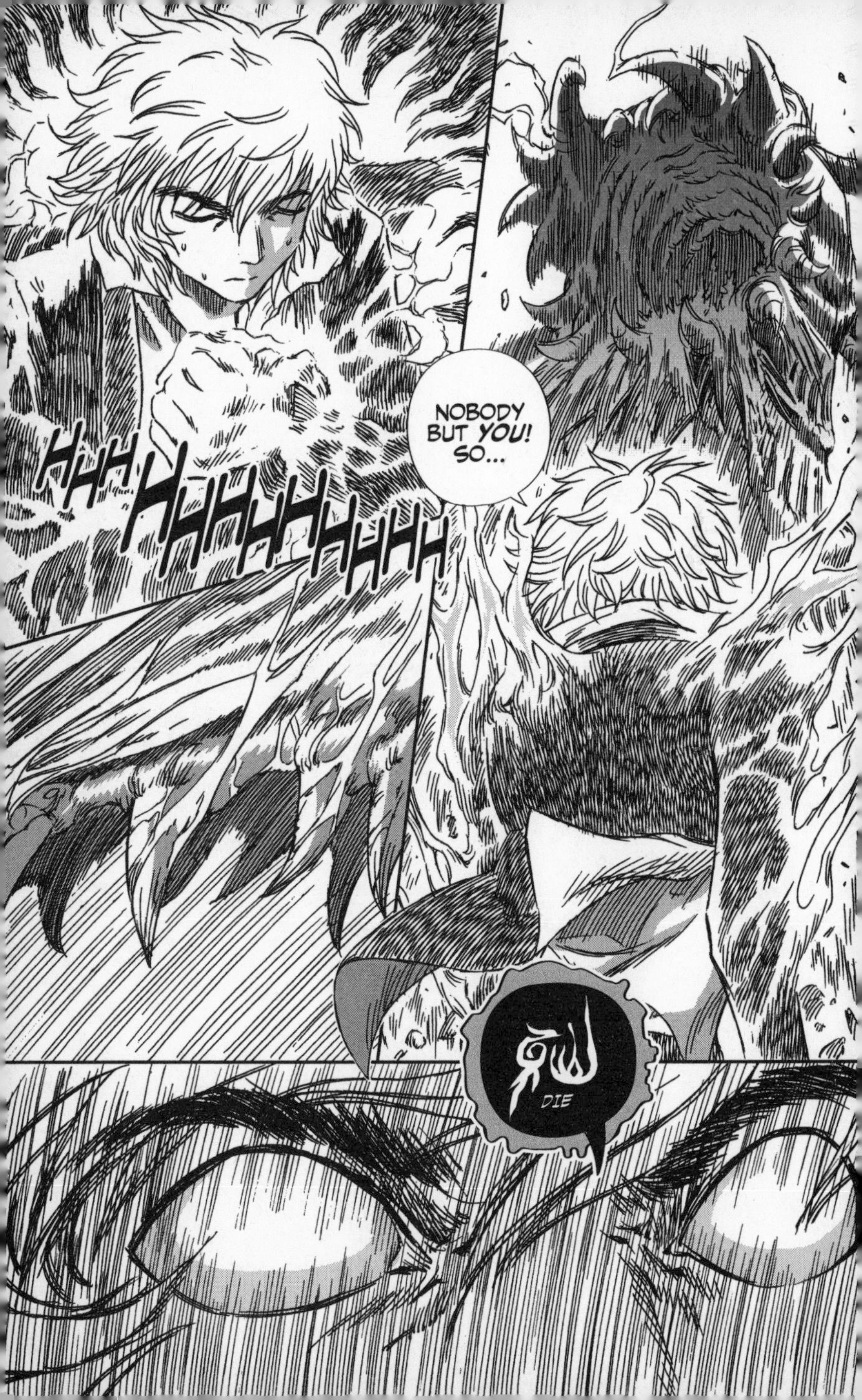
NOBODY BUT YOU! SO...
HHHHHHHHHHHHHHHH
DIE

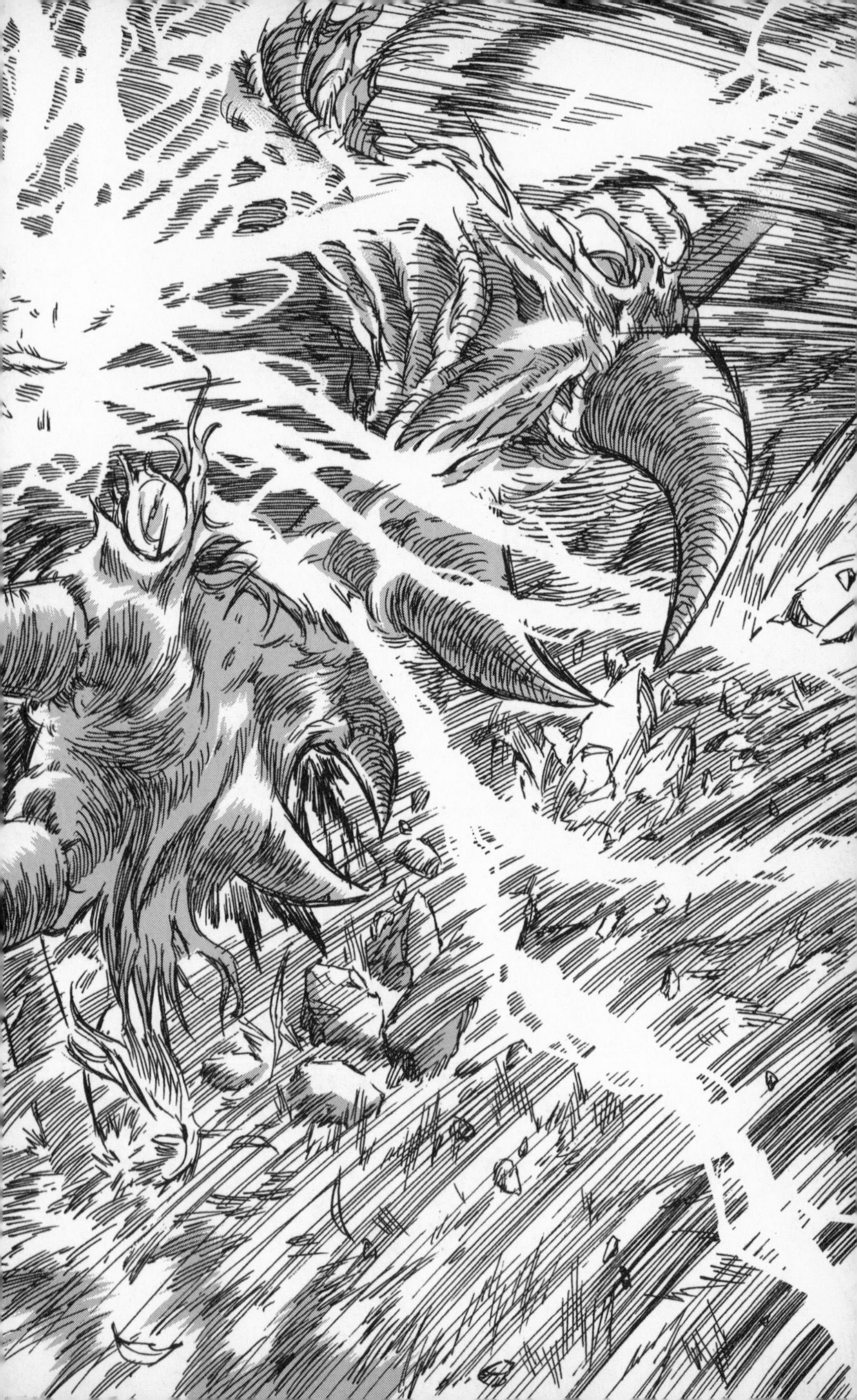

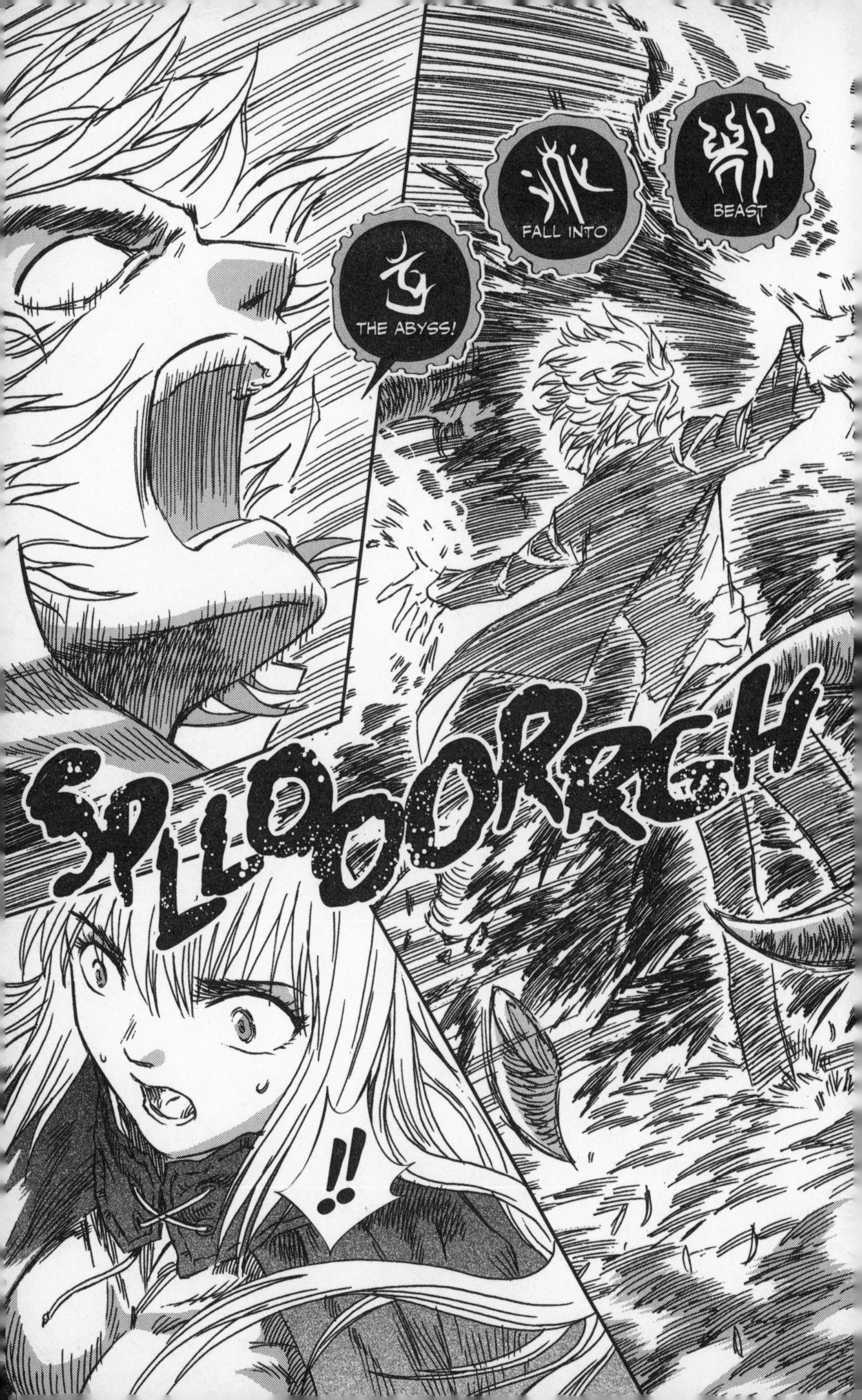
BEAST
FALL INTO
THE ABYSS!
SPLLOOORRGH
!!

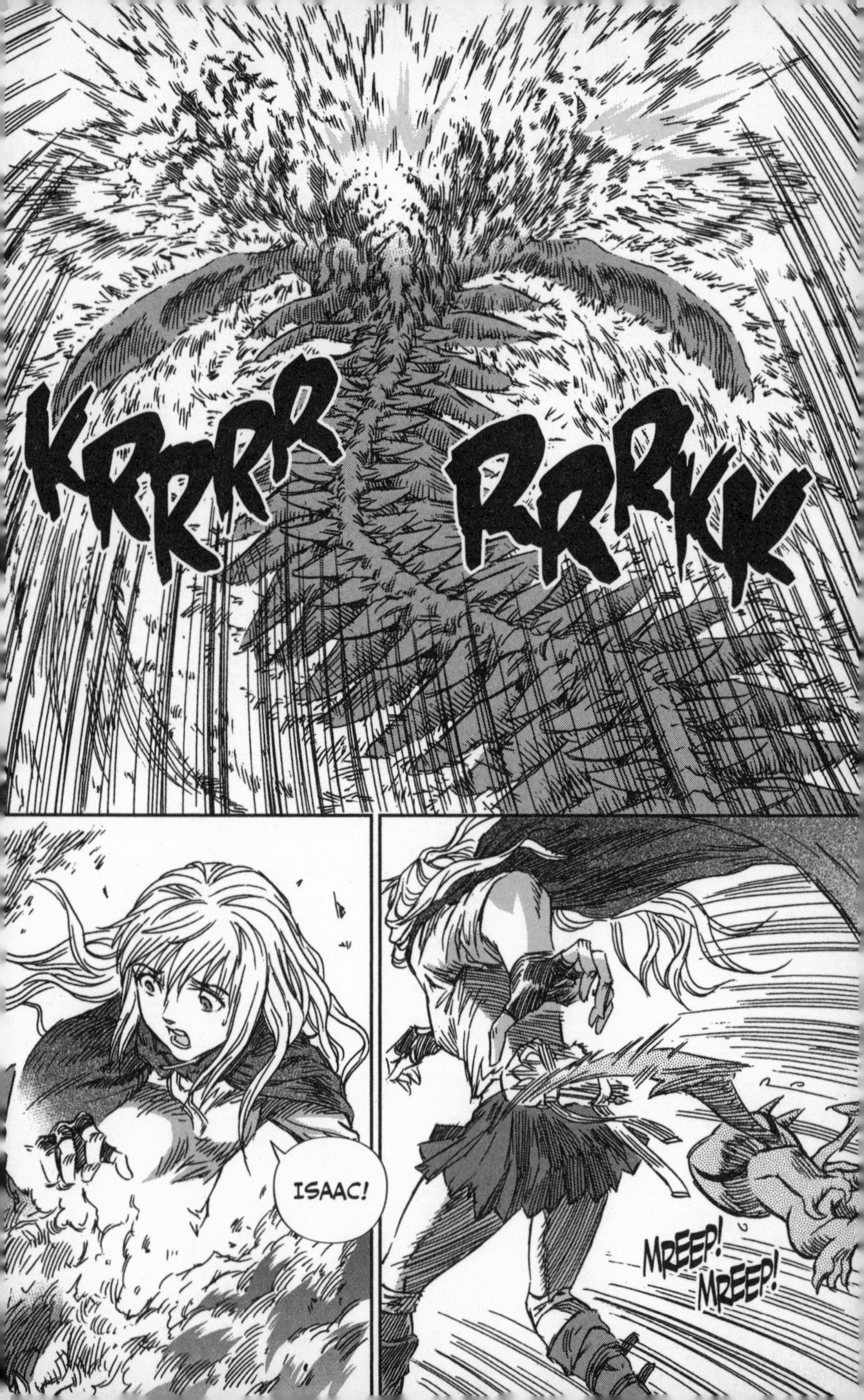
KRRRR RRRKK
MREEP! MREEP!
ISAAC!

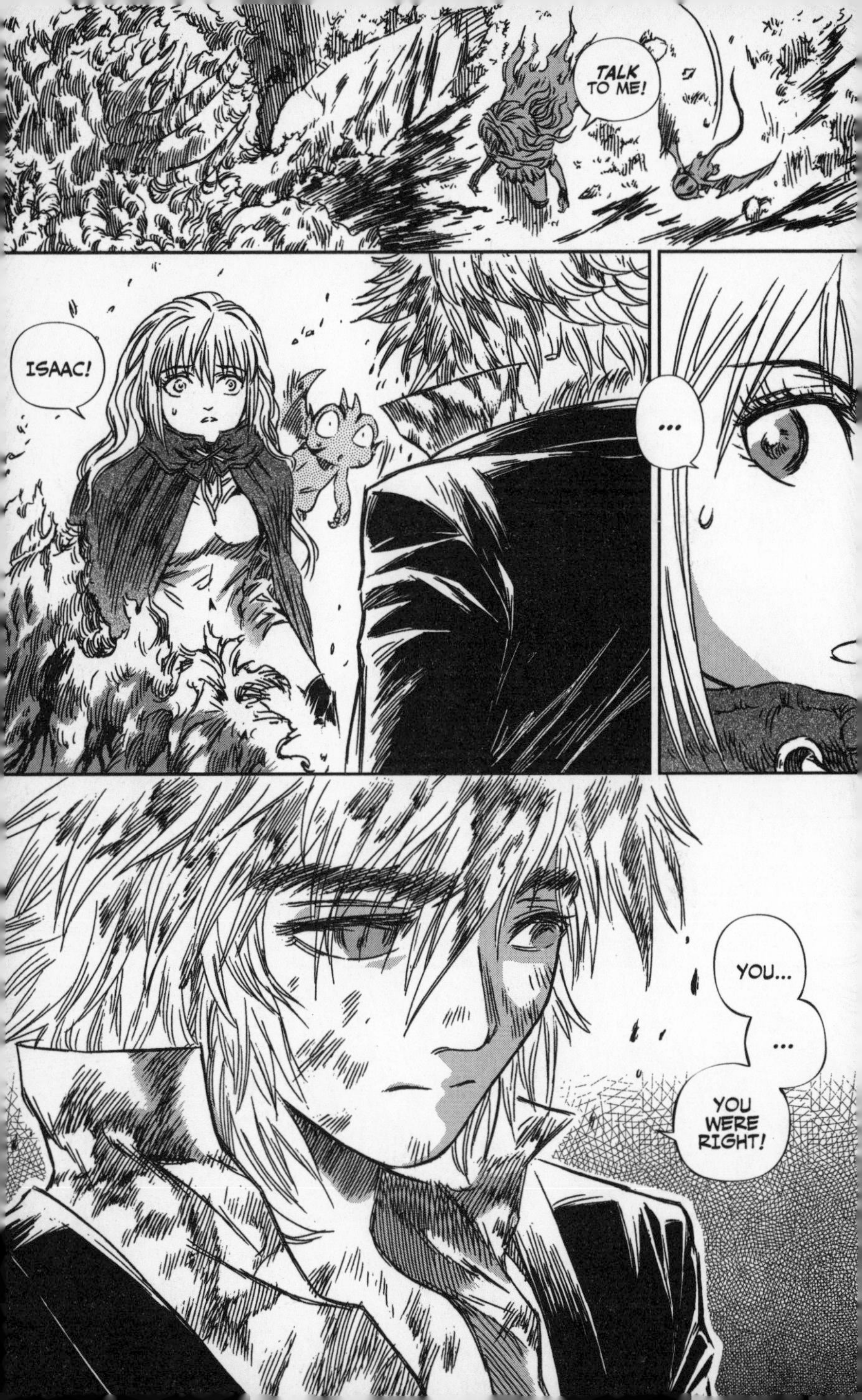
TALK TO ME!
...
ISAAC!
YOU...
...
YOU WERE RIGHT!

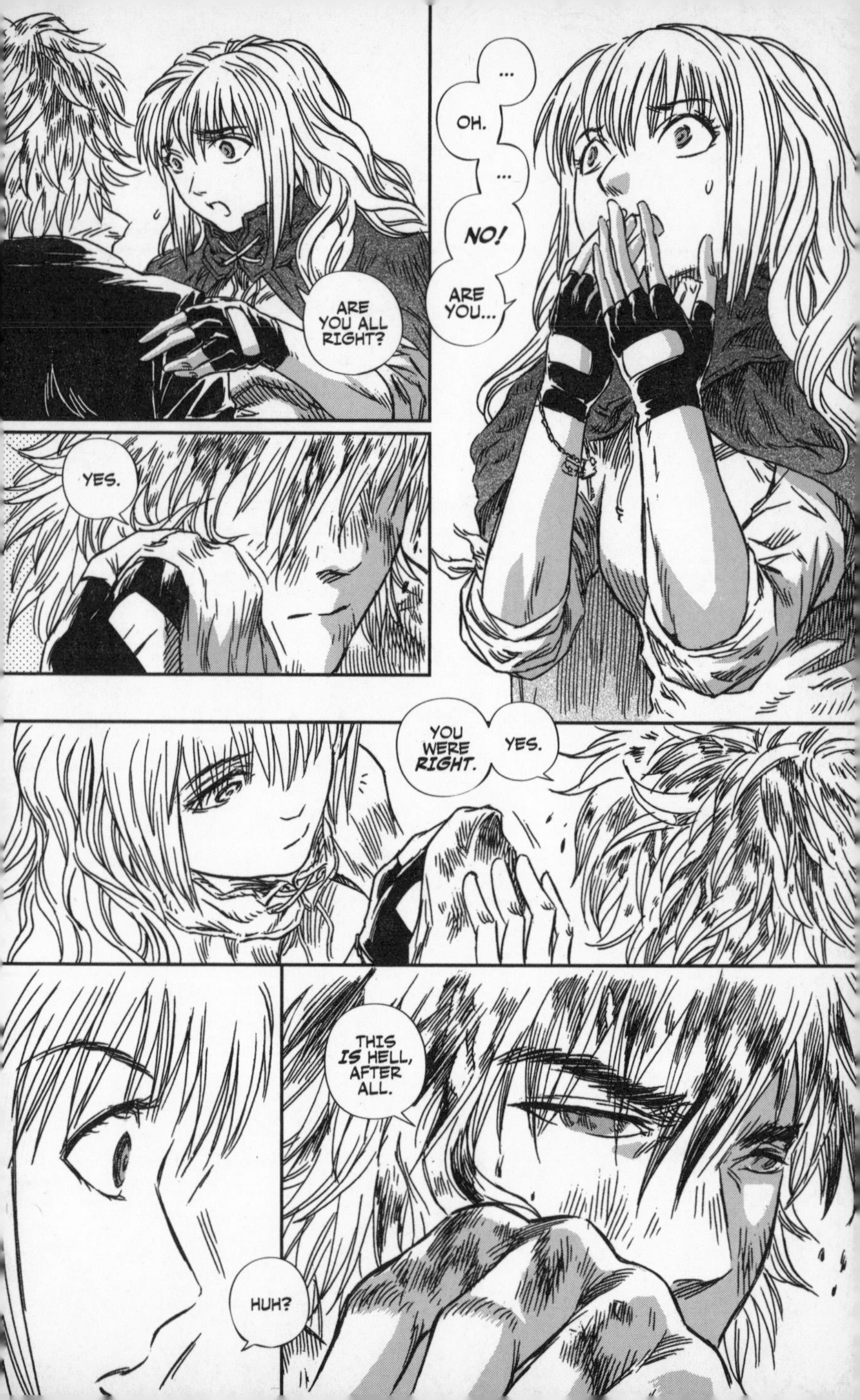
...
OH.
...
NO!
ARE YOU...
ARE YOU ALL RIGHT?
YES.
YES.
YOU WERE RIGHT.
THIS IS HELL, AFTER ALL.
HUH?

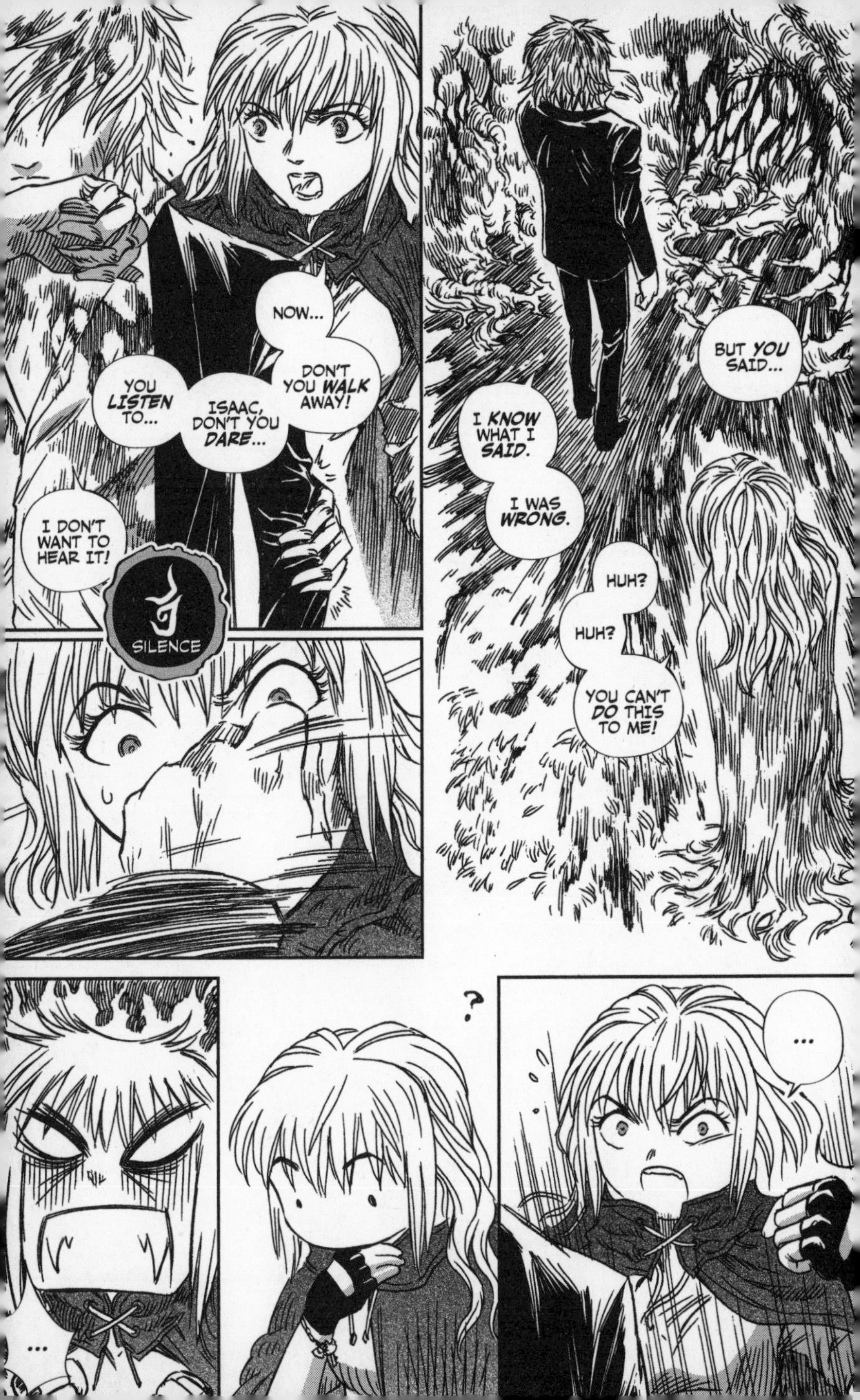
BUT YOU SAID...
I KNOW WHAT I SAID.
I WAS WRONG.
HUH?
HUH?
YOU CAN'T DO THIS TO ME!
NOW...
DON'T YOU WALK AWAY!
ISAAC, DON'T YOU DARE...
YOU LISTEN TO...
I DON'T WANT TO HEAR IT!
SILENCE
...
?
...

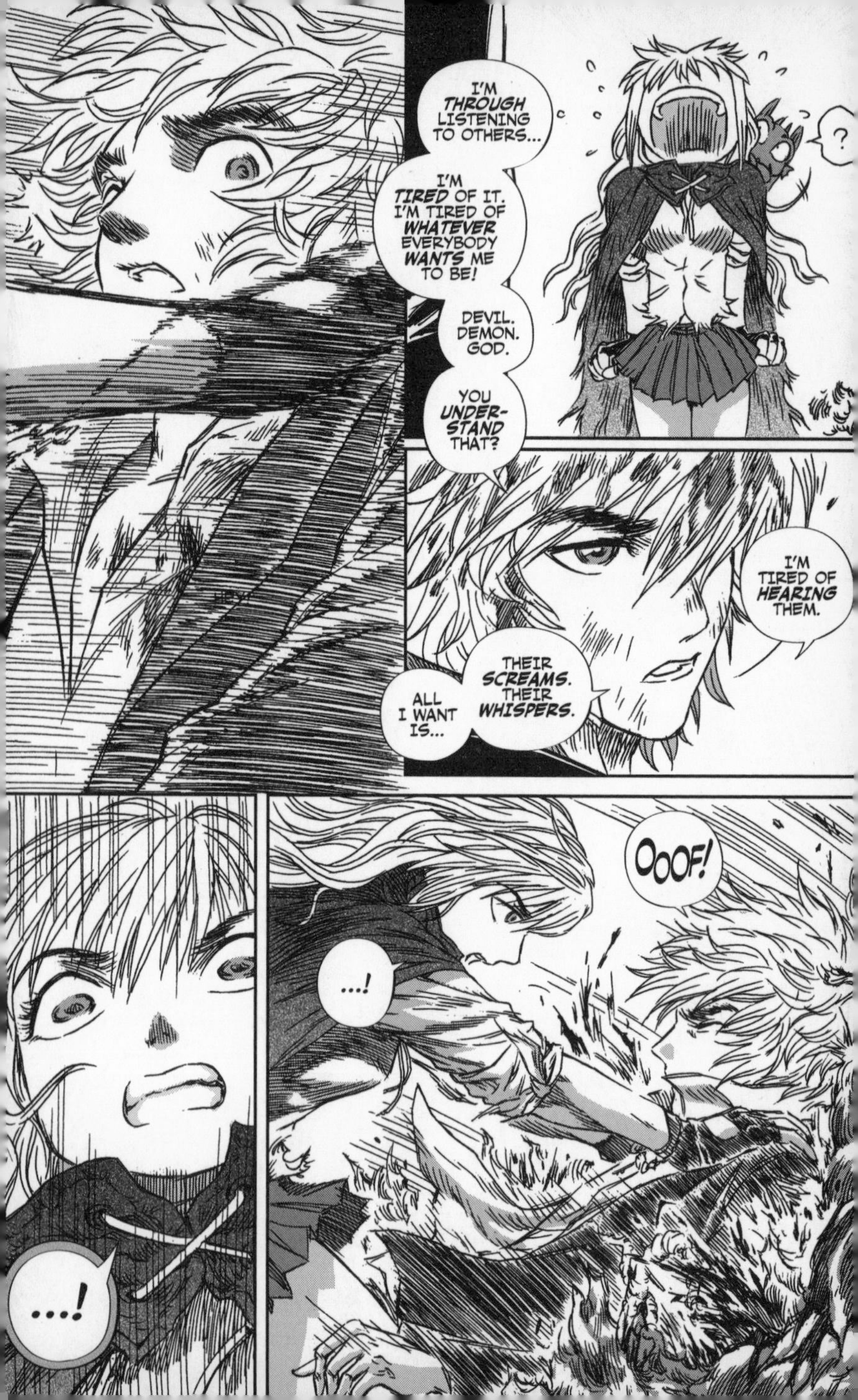
I'M THROUGH LISTENING TO OTHERS...
?
I'M TIRED OF IT. I'M TIRED OF WHATEVER EVERYBODY WANTS ME TO BE!
DEVIL. DEMON. GOD.
YOU UNDERSTAND THAT?
I'M TIRED OF HEARING THEM.
THEIR SCREAMS. THEIR WHISPERS.
ALL I WANT IS...
HEY!
OOOF!
...!
...!

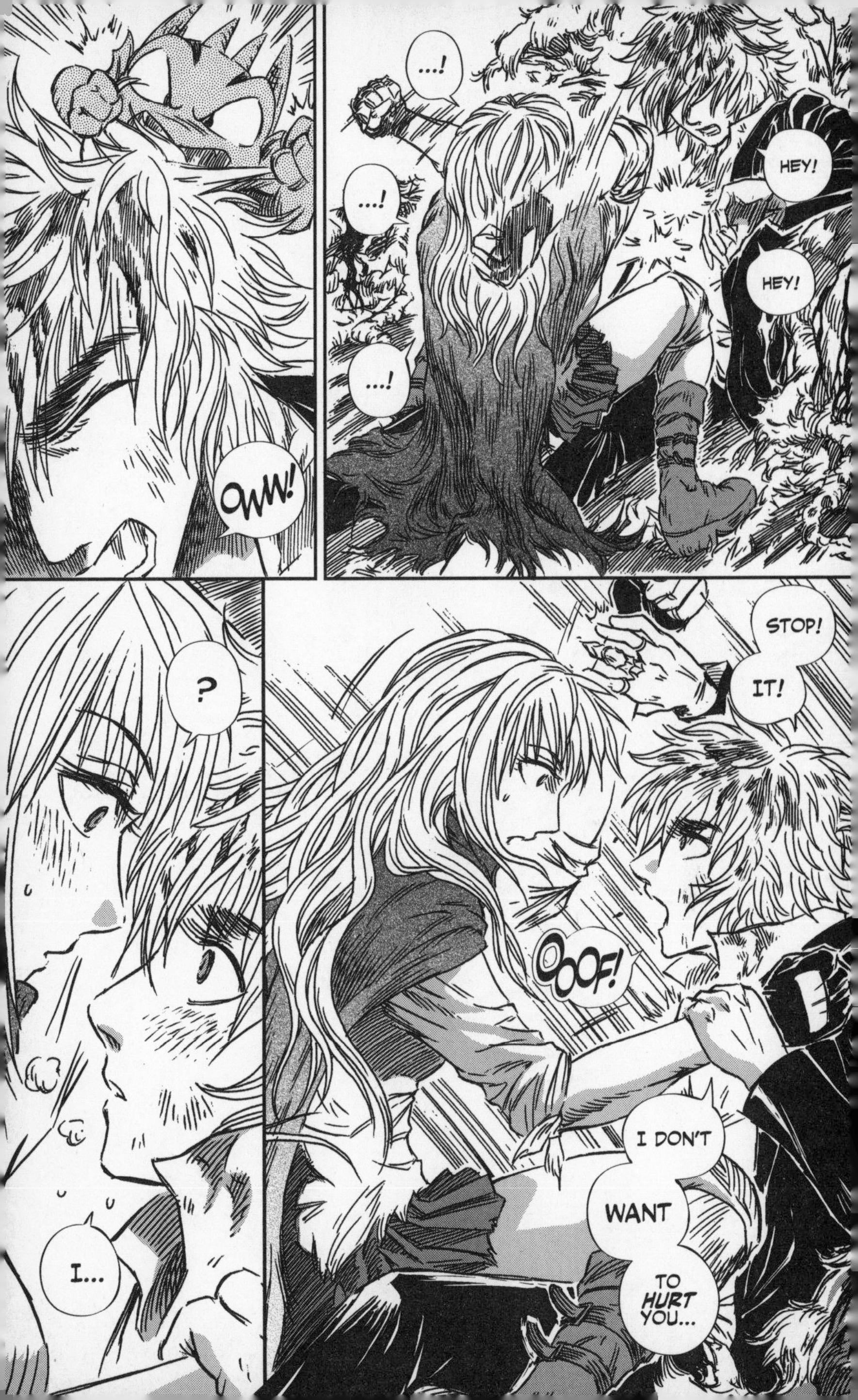
HEY!
HEY!
...!
...!
...!
OWW!
STOP! IT!
OOOF!
I DON'T WANT TO HURT YOU...
?
I...

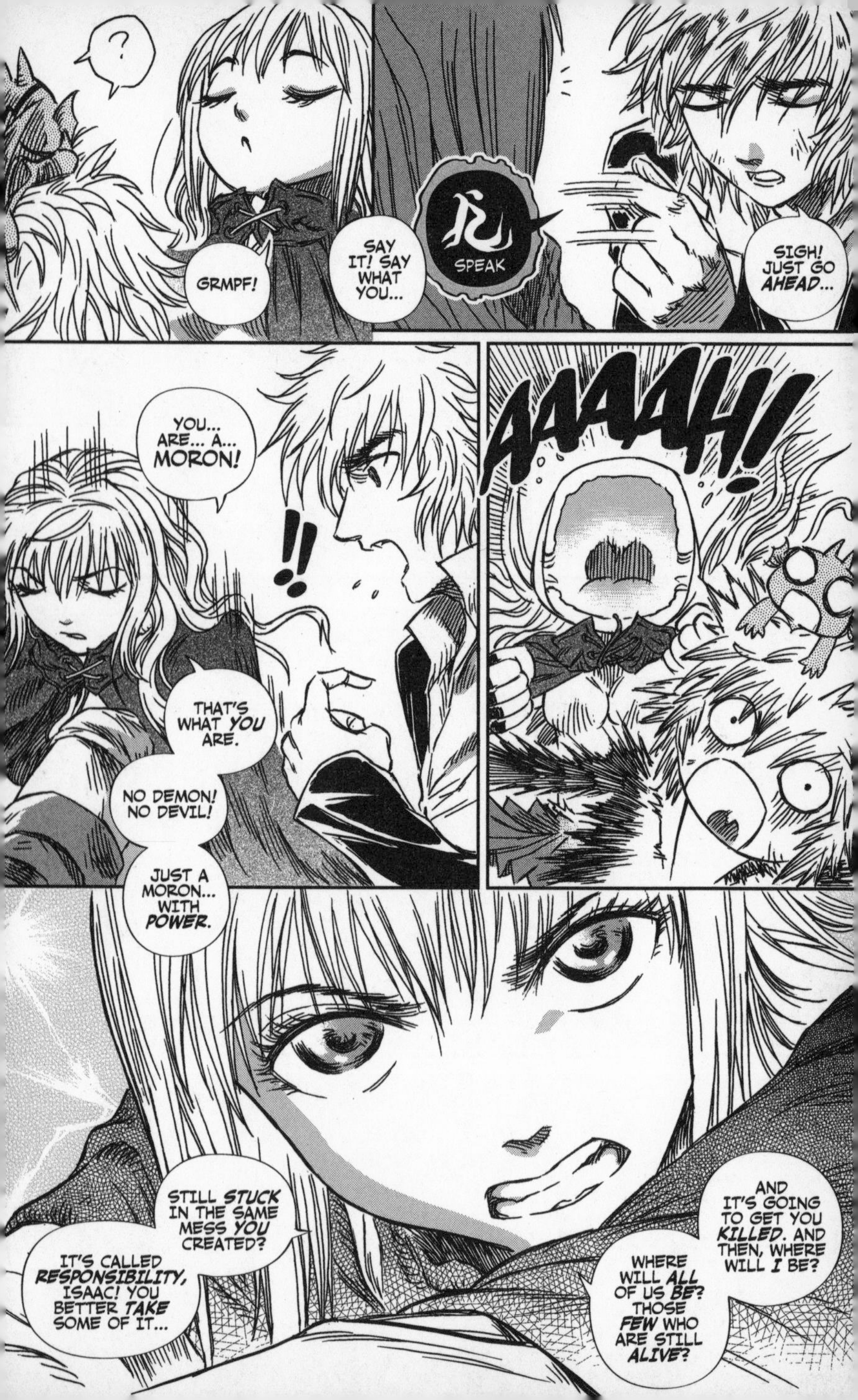
?
GRMPF!
SAY IT! SAY WHAT YOU...
SPEAK
SIGH! JUST GO AHEAD...
YOU... ARE... A... MORON!
!!
THAT'S WHAT YOU ARE.
NO DEMON! NO DEVIL!
JUST A MORON... WITH POWER.
AAAAH!
STILL STUCK IN THE SAME MESS YOU CREATED?
IT'S CALLED RESPONSIBILITY, ISAAC! YOU BETTER TAKE SOME OF IT...
AND IT'S GOING TO GET YOU KILLED. AND THEN, WHERE WILL I BE?
WHERE WILL ALL OF US BE? THOSE FEW WHO ARE STILL ALIVE?

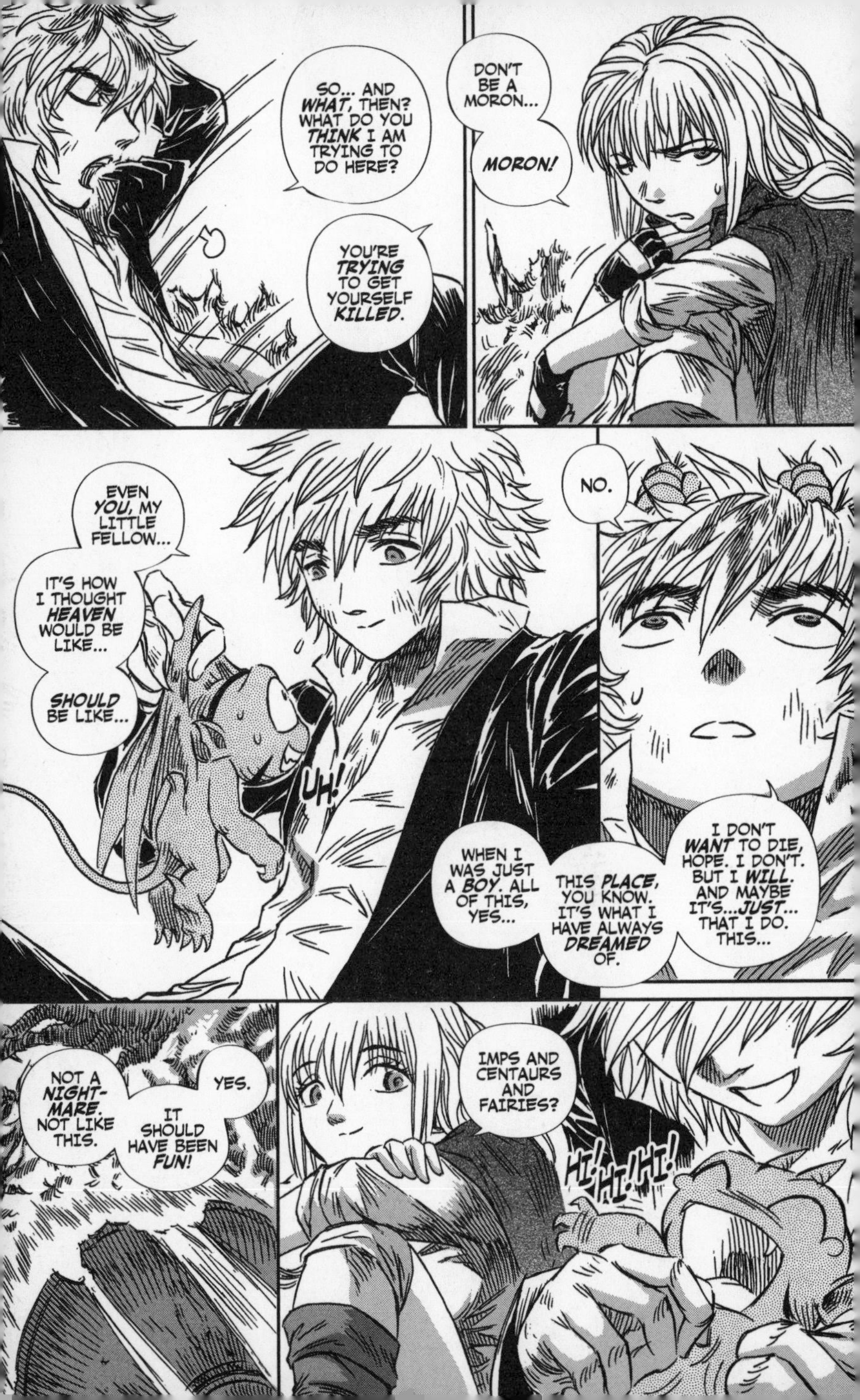
DON'T BE A MORON...
MORON!
SO... AND WHAT, THEN? WHAT DO YOU THINK I AM TRYING TO DO HERE?
YOU'RE TRYING TO GET YOURSELF KILLED.
NO.
I DON'T WANT TO DIE, HOPE. I DON'T. BUT I WILL. AND MAYBE IT'S...JUST... THAT I DO. THIS...
THIS PLACE, YOU KNOW. IT'S WHAT I HAVE ALWAYS DREAMED OF.
WHEN I WAS JUST A BOY. ALL OF THIS, YES...
EVEN YOU, MY LITTLE FELLOW...
IT'S HOW I THOUGHT HEAVEN WOULD BE LIKE...
SHOULD BE LIKE...
UH!
IMPS AND CENTAURS AND FAIRIES?
HI! HI! HI!
YES.
NOT A NIGHT-MARE. NOT LIKE THIS.
IT SHOULD HAVE BEEN FUN!

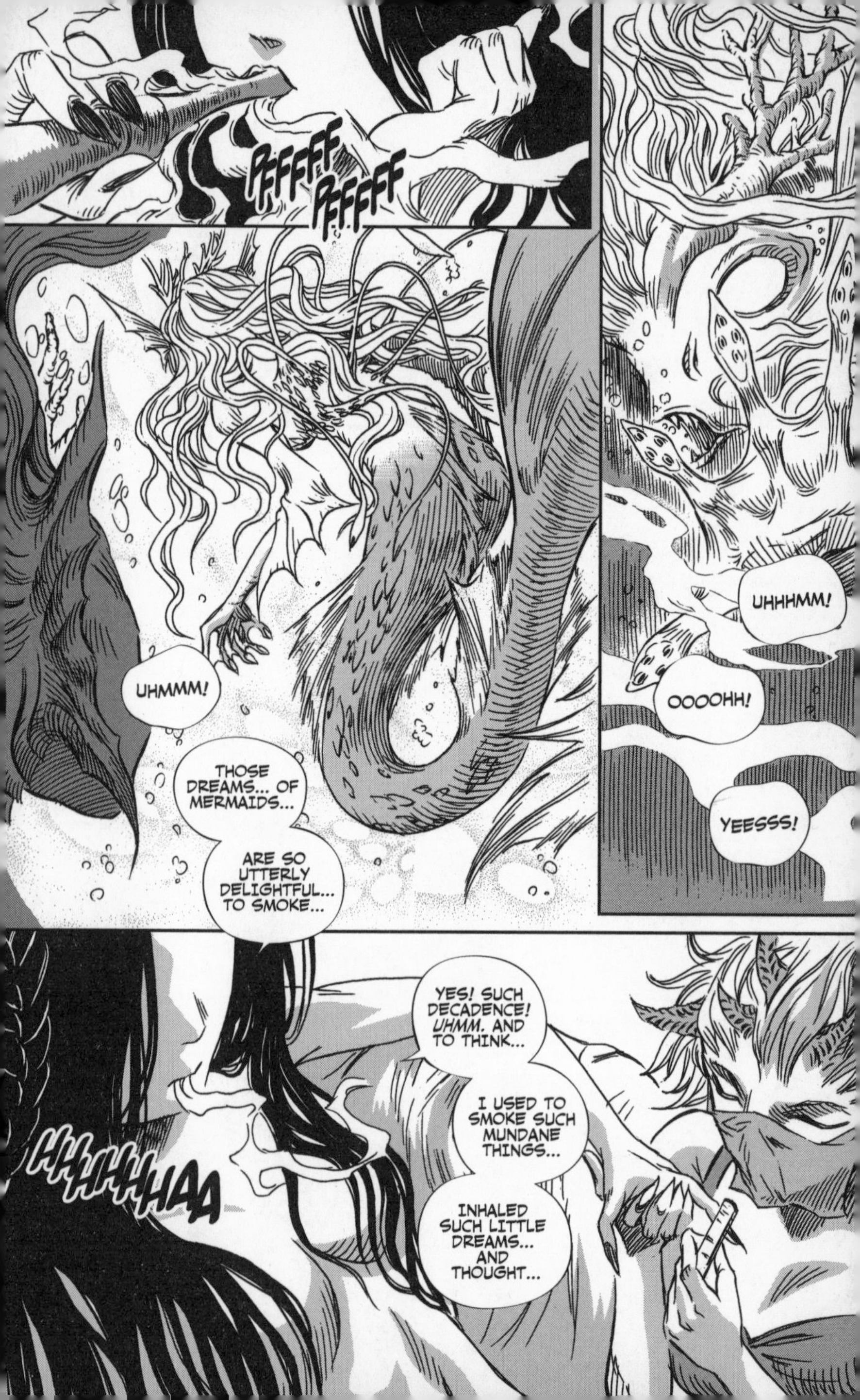
UHHHMM!
OOOOHH!
YEESSS!
PFFFFF PFFFFF
UHMMM!
THOSE DREAMS... OF MERMAIDS...
ARE SO UTTERLY DELIGHTFUL... TO SMOKE...
YES! SUCH DECADENCE! UHMM. AND TO THINK...
I USED TO SMOKE SUCH MUNDANE THINGS...
INHALED SUCH LITTLE DREAMS... AND THOUGHT...
HHHHHHAA

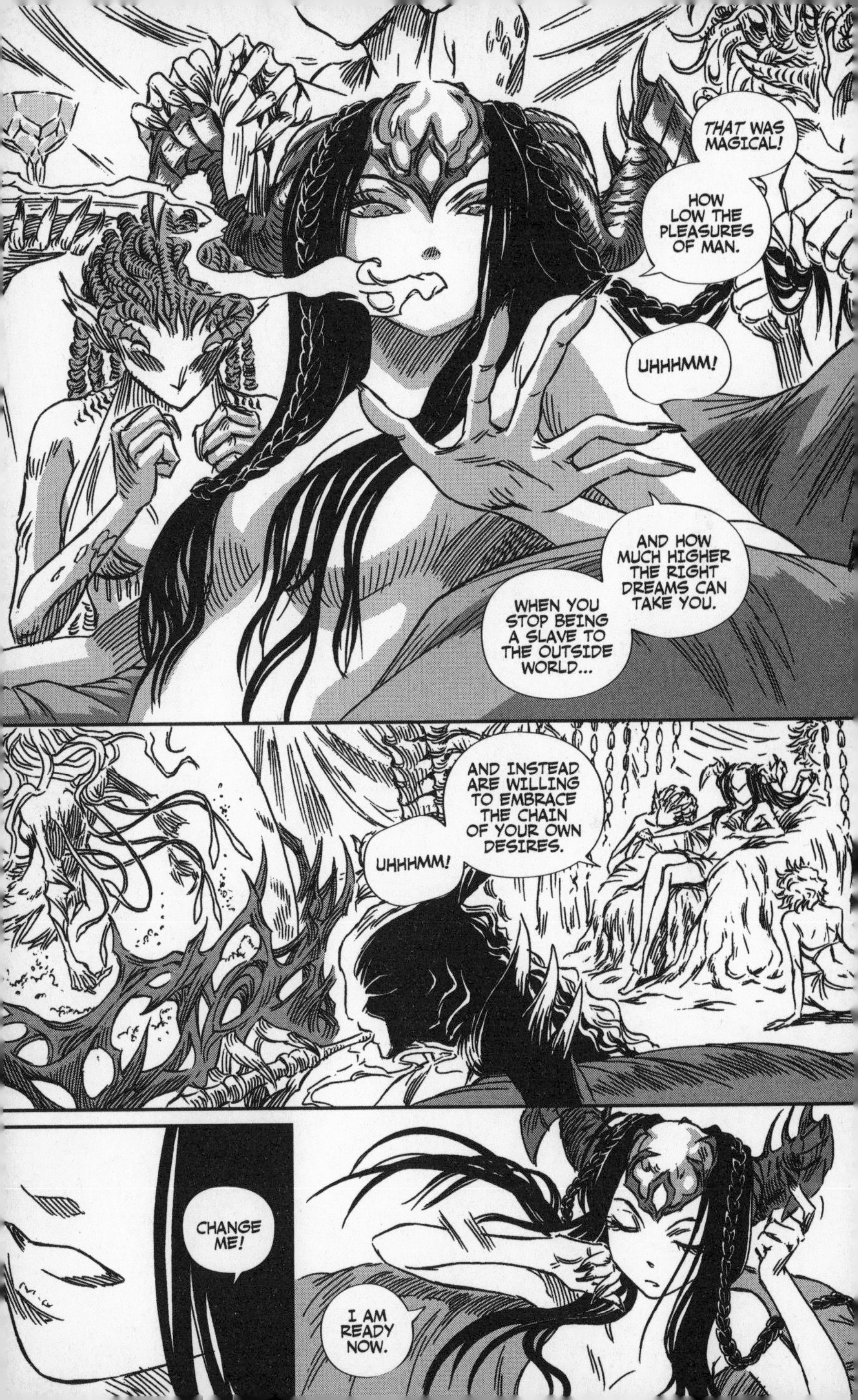
THAT WAS MAGICAL!
HOW LOW THE PLEASURES OF MAN.
UHHHMM!
AND HOW MUCH HIGHER THE RIGHT DREAMS CAN TAKE YOU.
WHEN YOU STOP BEING A SLAVE TO THE OUTSIDE WORLD...
AND INSTEAD ARE WILLING TO EMBRACE THE CHAIN OF YOUR OWN DESIRES.
UHHHMM!
CHANGE ME!
I AM READY NOW.

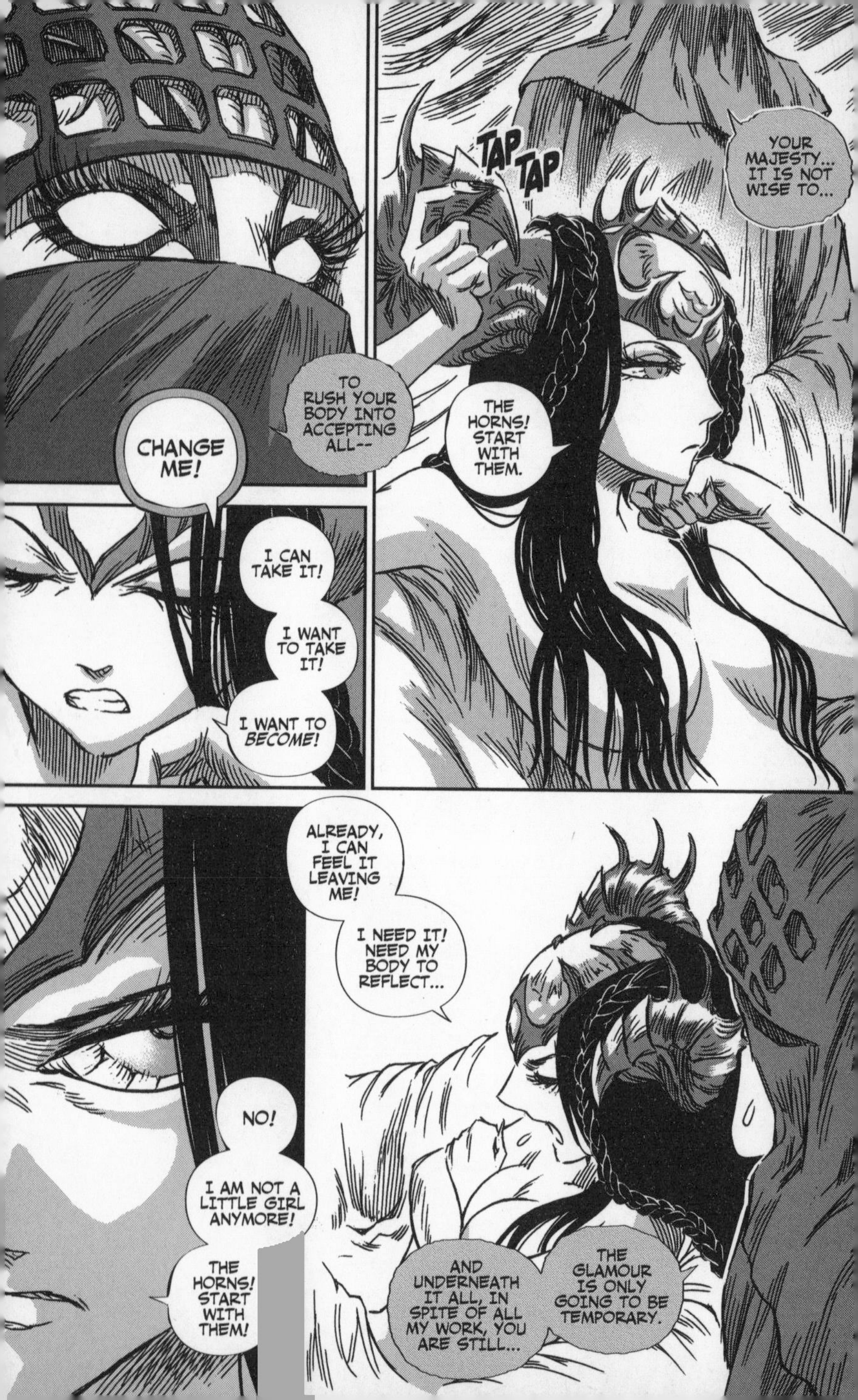
TAP TAP
YOUR MAJESTY... IT IS NOT WISE TO...
THE HORNS! START WITH THEM.
TO RUSH YOUR BODY INTO ACCEPTING ALL--
CHANGE ME!
I CAN TAKE IT!
I WANT TO TAKE IT!
I WANT TO *BECOME*!
THE GLAMOUR IS ONLY GOING TO BE TEMPORARY.
ALREADY, I CAN FEEL IT LEAVING ME!
I NEED IT! NEED MY BODY TO REFLECT...
AND UNDERNEATH IT ALL, IN SPITE OF ALL MY WORK, YOU ARE STILL...
NO!
I AM NOT A LITTLE GIRL ANYMORE!
THE HORNS! START WITH THEM!

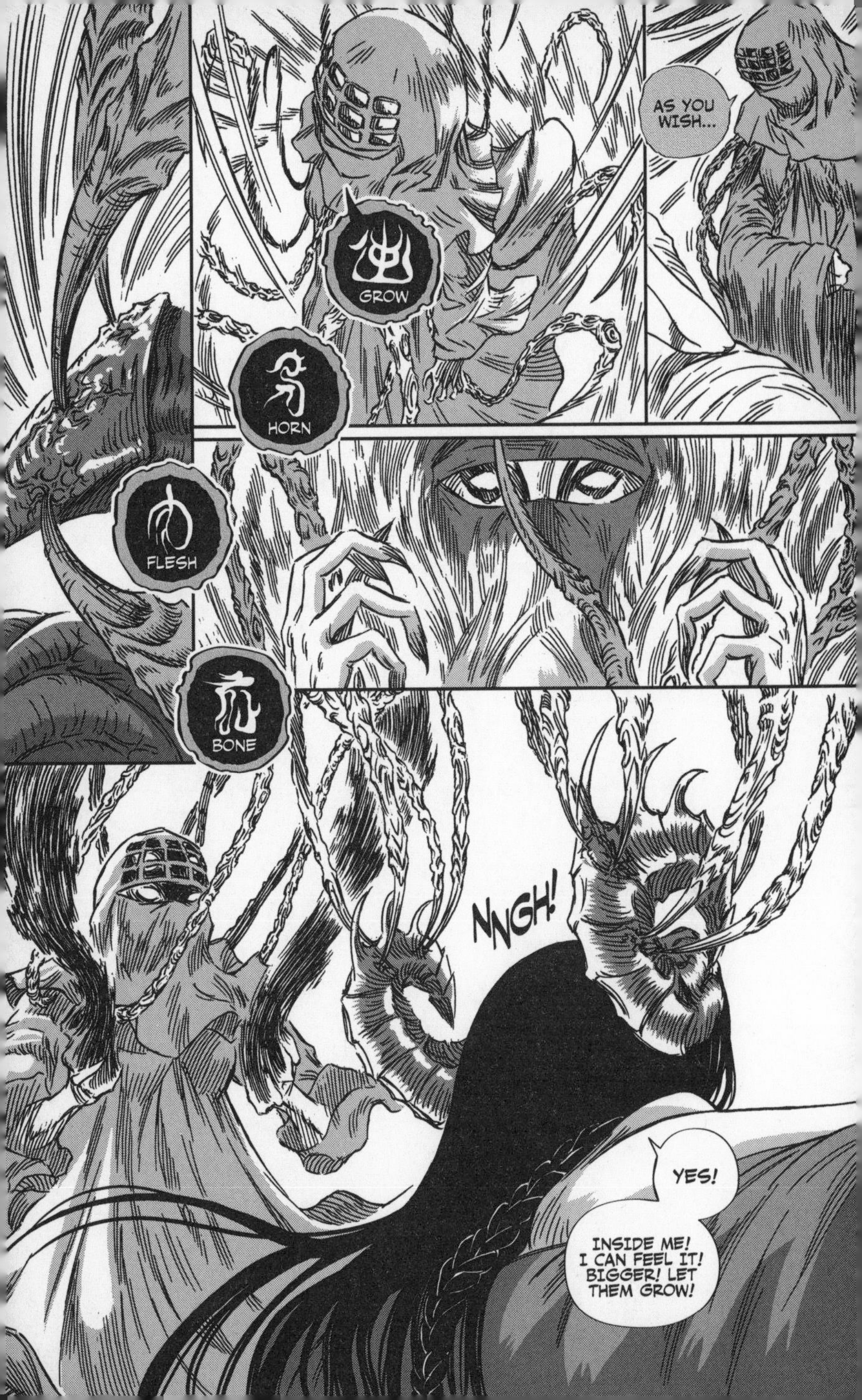
AS YOU WISH...
GROW
HORN
FLESH
BONE
NNGH!
YES!
INSIDE ME! I CAN FEEL IT! BIGGER! LET THEM GROW!

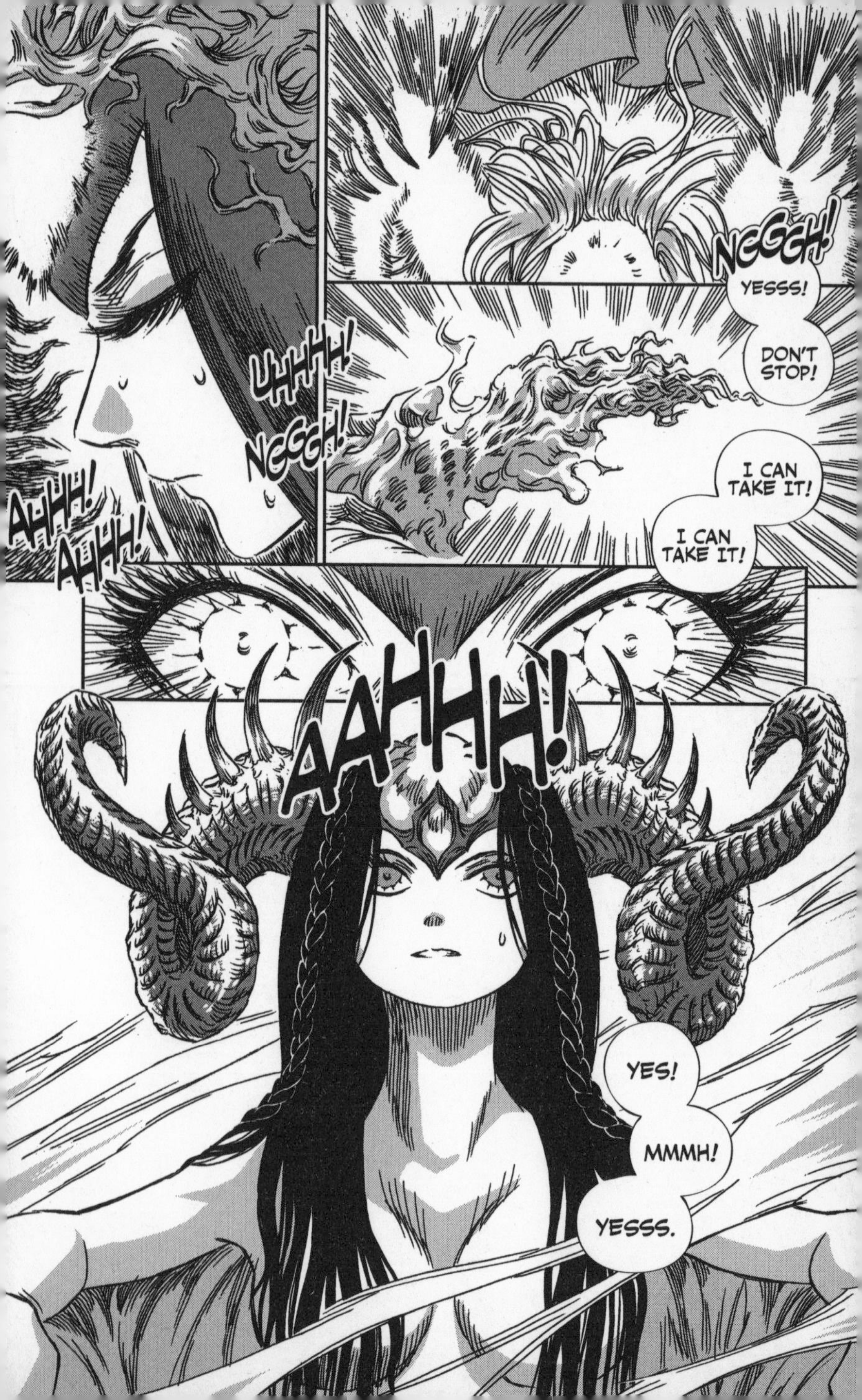
NGGGH!
YESSS!
DON'T STOP!
I CAN TAKE IT!
I CAN TAKE IT!
UHHHH!
NGGGH!
AHHH!
AHHH!
AAHHHH!
YES!
MMMH!
YESSS.

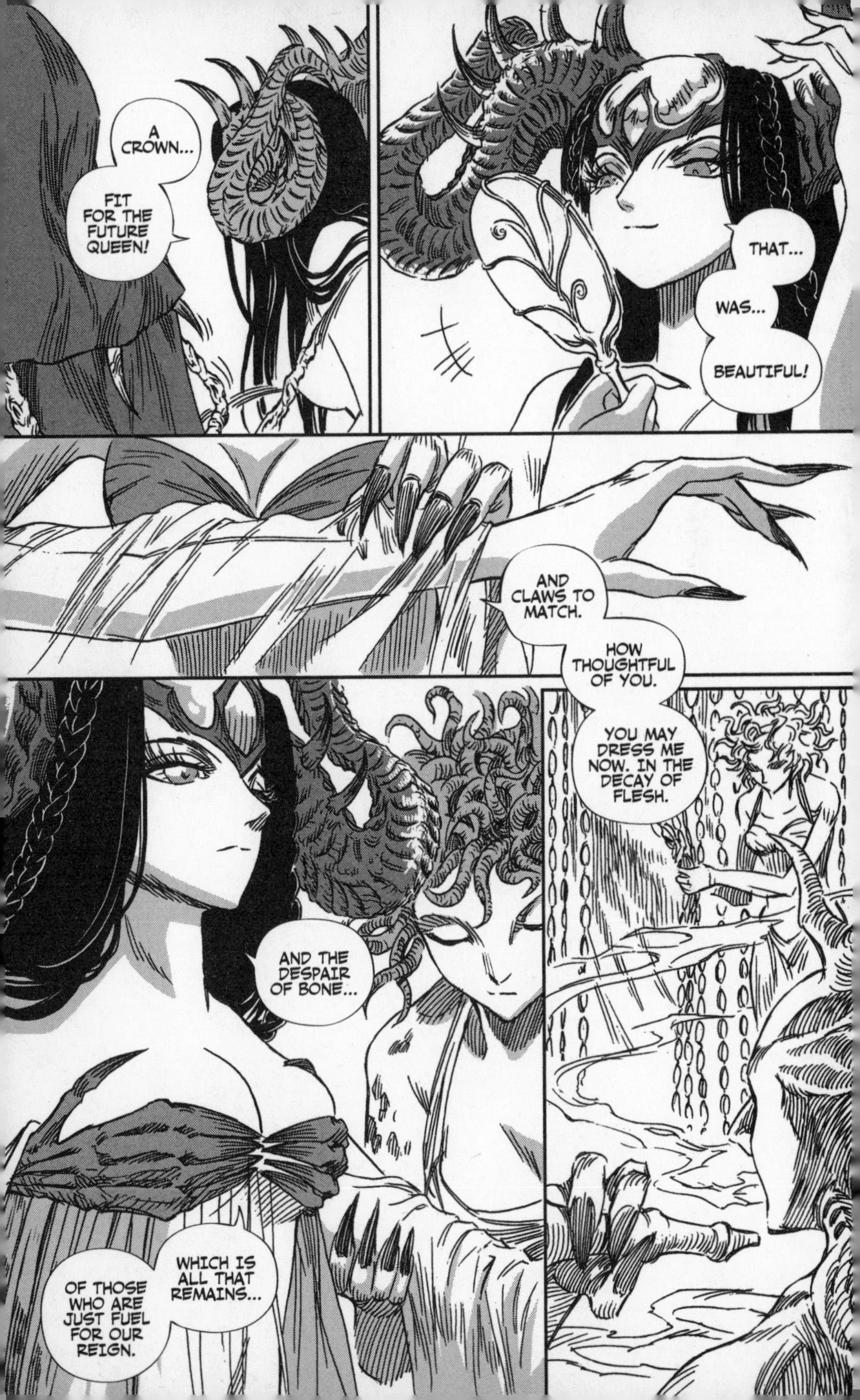
THAT...
WAS...
BEAUTIFUL!
A CROWN...
FIT FOR THE FUTURE QUEEN!
AND CLAWS TO MATCH.
HOW THOUGHTFUL OF YOU.
YOU MAY DRESS ME NOW. IN THE DECAY OF FLESH.
AND THE DESPAIR OF BONE...
WHICH IS ALL THAT REMAINS...
OF THOSE WHO ARE JUST FUEL FOR OUR REIGN.

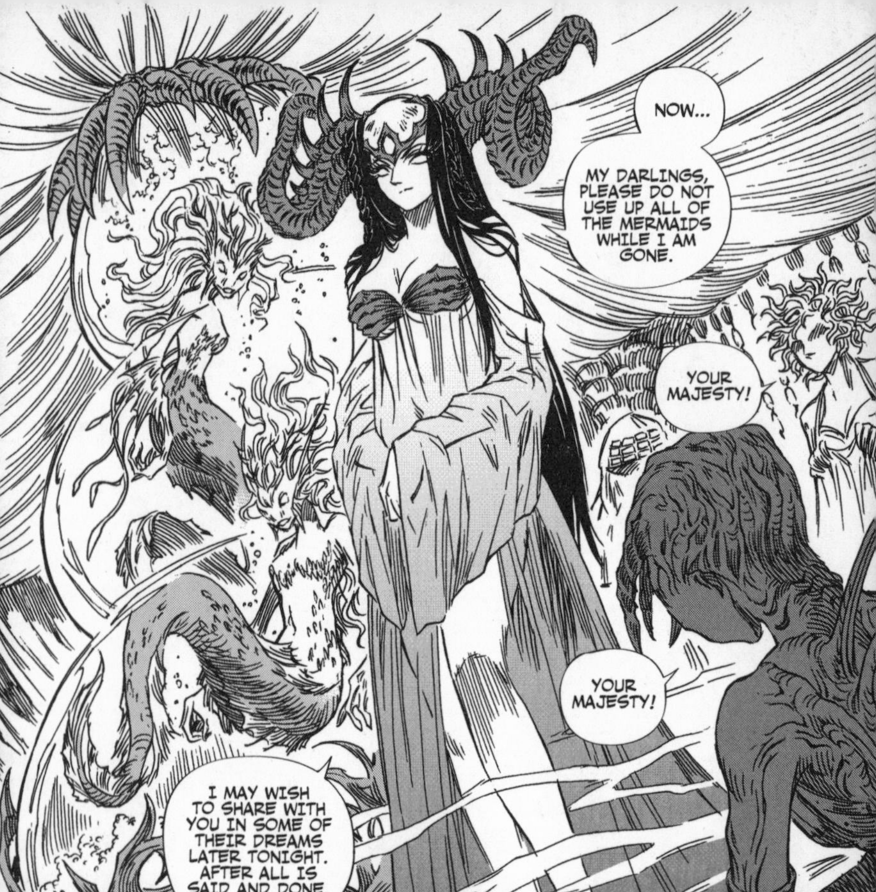
NOW...
MY DARLINGS, PLEASE DO NOT USE UP ALL OF THE MERMAIDS WHILE I AM GONE.
YOUR MAJESTY!
YOUR MAJESTY!
I MAY WISH TO SHARE WITH YOU IN SOME OF THEIR DREAMS LATER TONIGHT. AFTER ALL IS SAID AND DONE.
IF I SO CHOOSE.

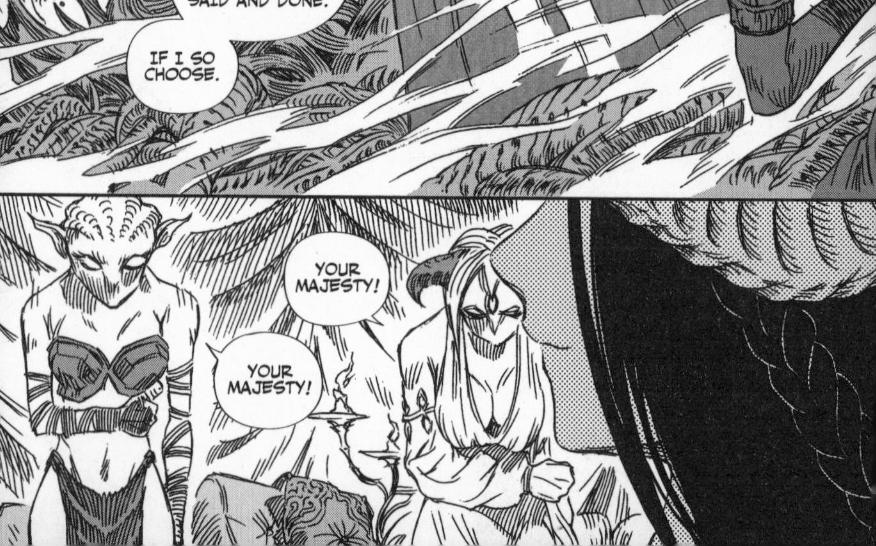
YOUR MAJESTY!
YOUR MAJESTY!

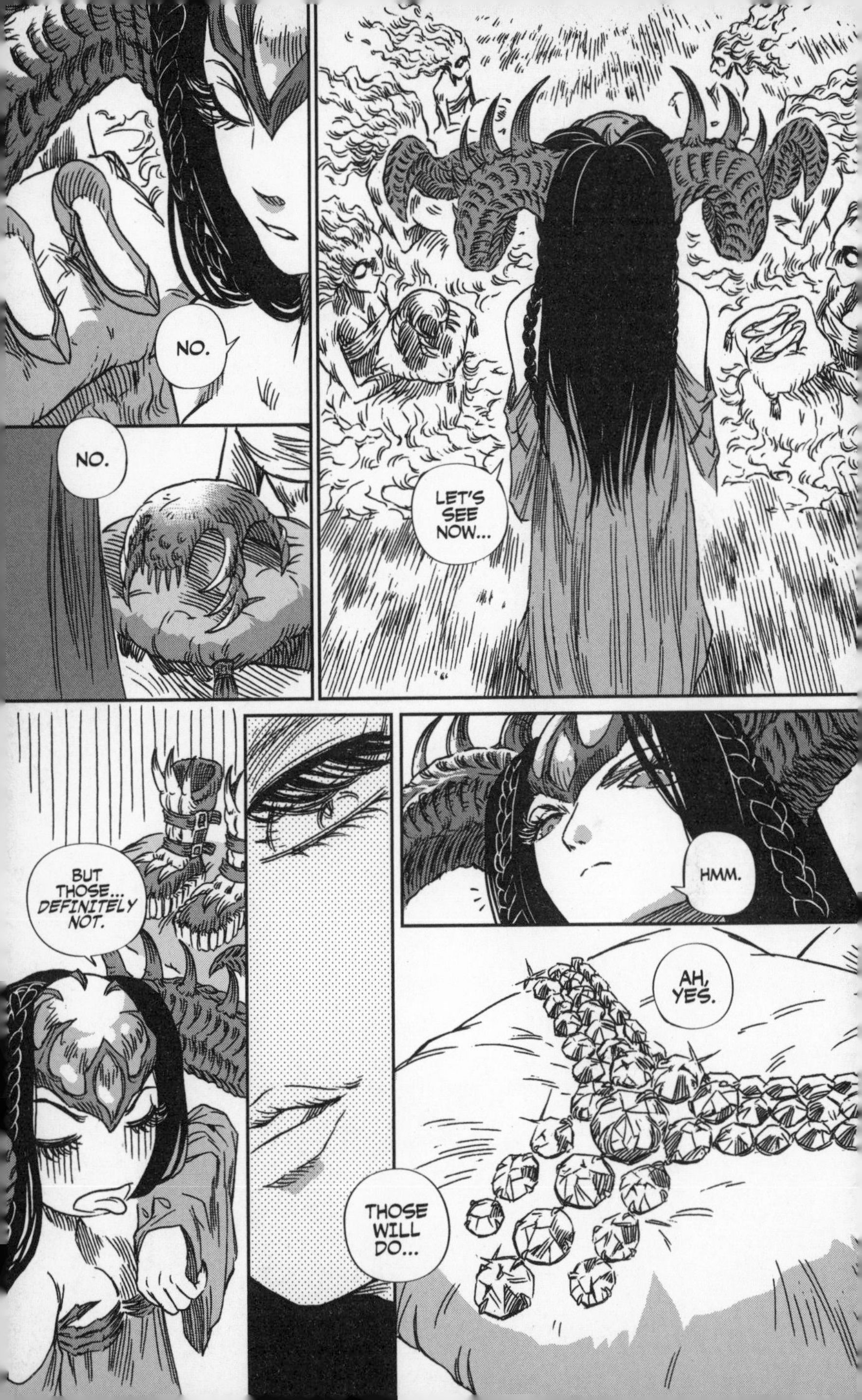
NO.
NO.
LET'S SEE NOW...
BUT THOSE... DEFINITELY NOT.
HMM.
AH, YES.
THOSE WILL DO...

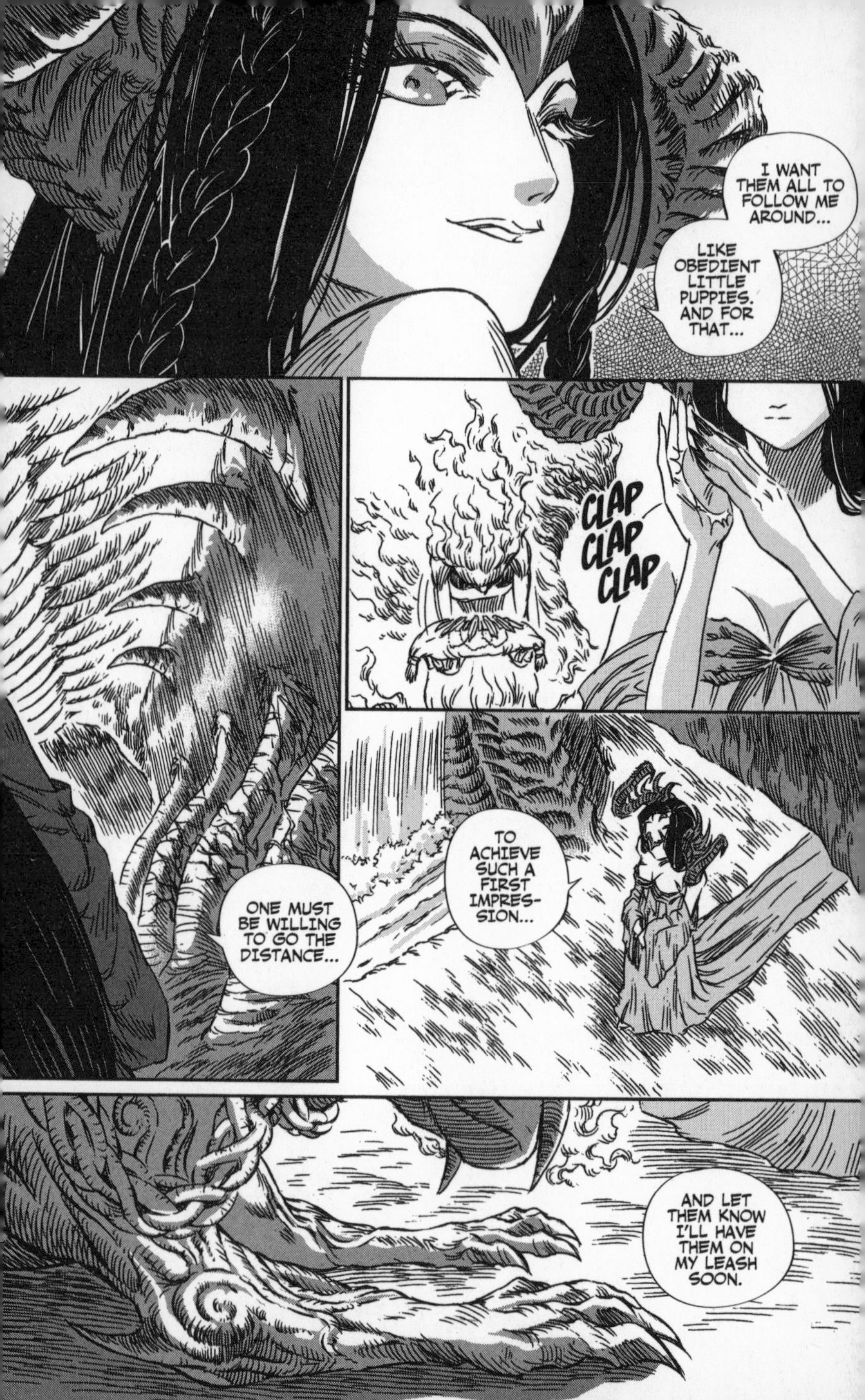
I WANT THEM ALL TO FOLLOW ME AROUND...
LIKE OBEDIENT LITTLE PUPPIES. AND FOR THAT...
CLAP CLAP CLAP
TO ACHIEVE SUCH A FIRST IMPRES-SION...
ONE MUST BE WILLING TO GO THE DISTANCE...
AND LET THEM KNOW I'LL HAVE THEM ON MY LEASH SOON.

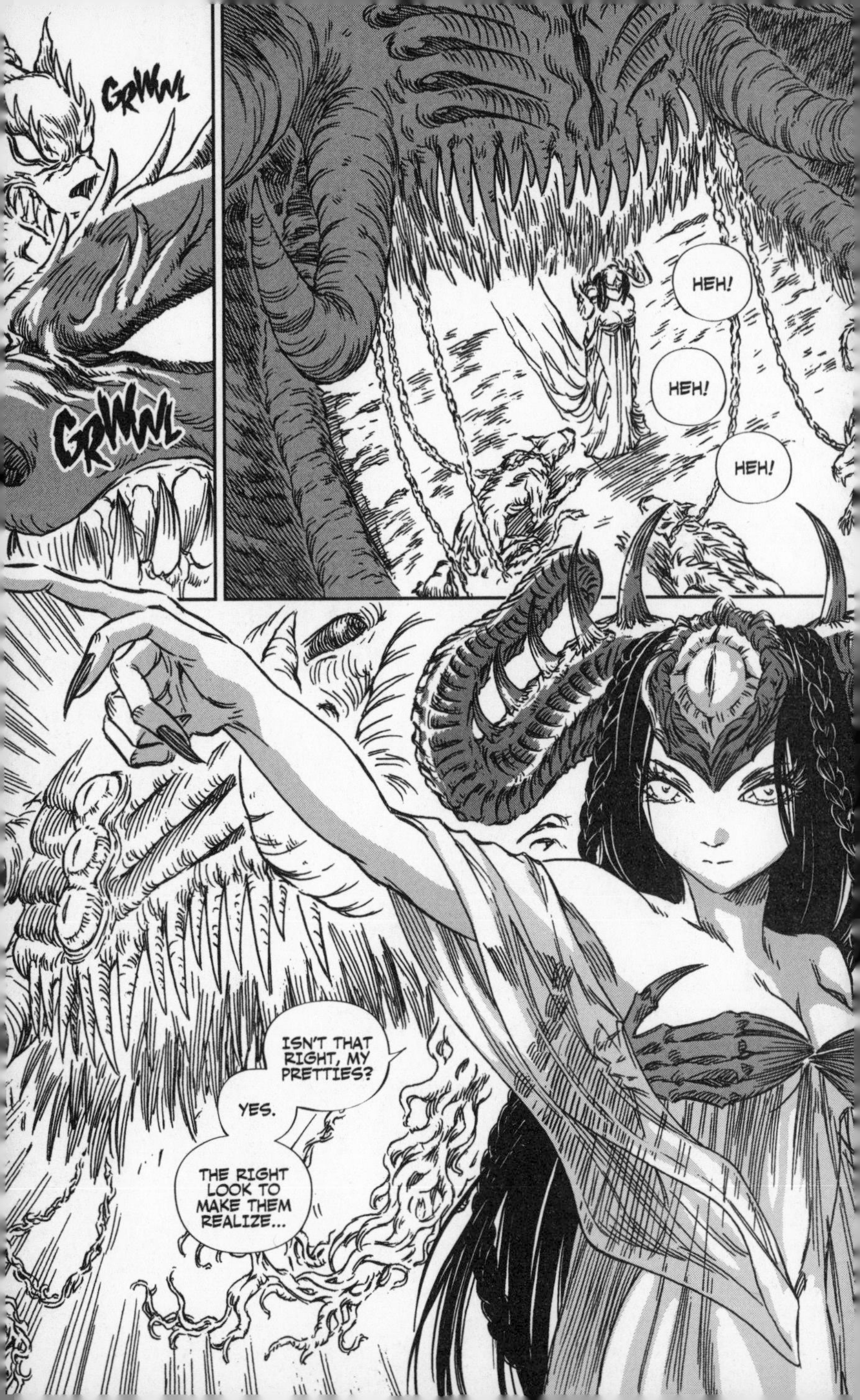
HEH!
HEH!
HEH!
GRWWL
GRWWL
ISN'T THAT RIGHT, MY PRETTIES?
YES.
THE RIGHT LOOK TO MAKE THEM REALIZE...

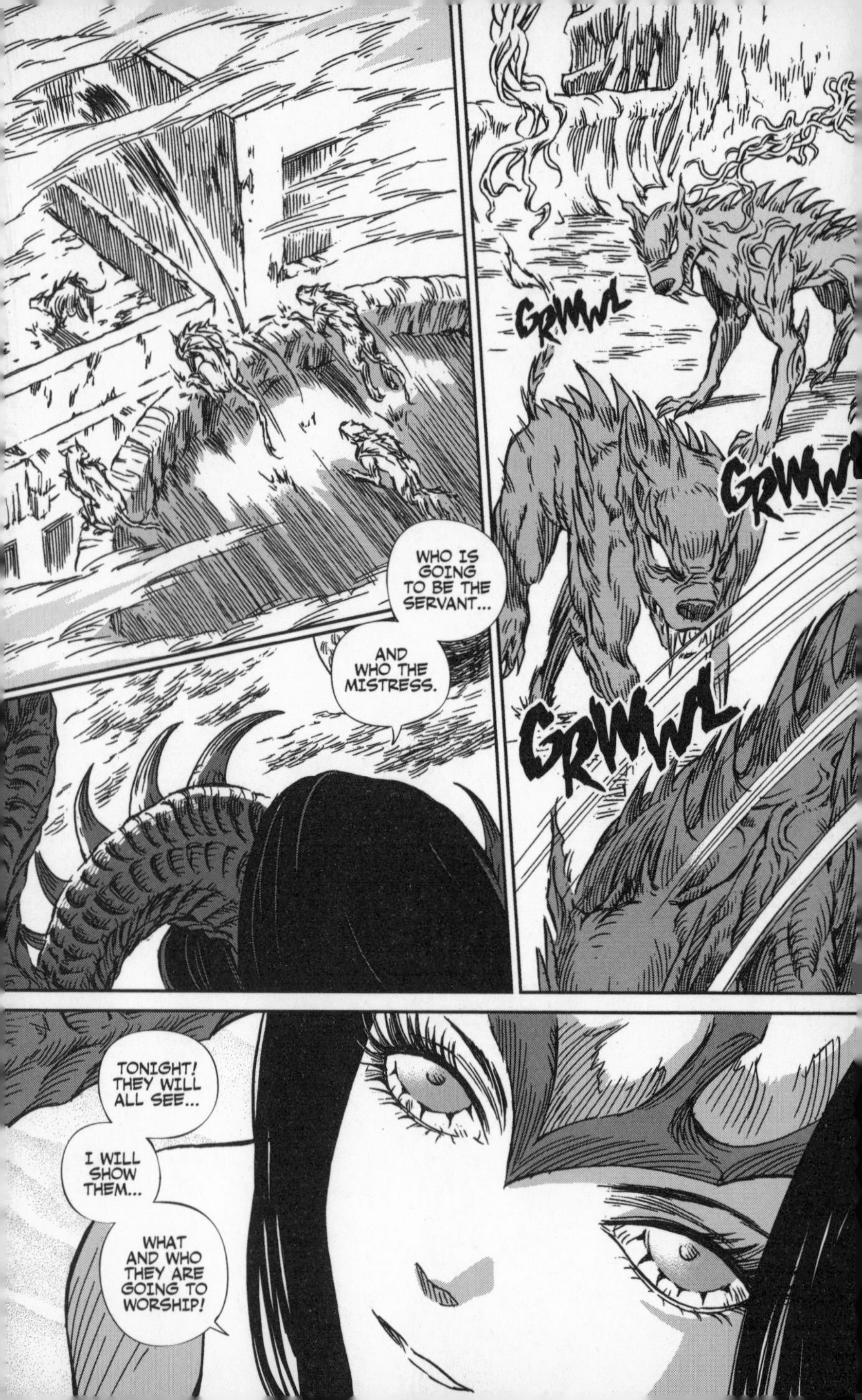
GRWWL
GRWWL
GRWWL
WHO IS GOING TO BE THE SERVANT...
AND WHO THE MISTRESS.
TONIGHT! THEY WILL ALL SEE...
I WILL SHOW THEM...
WHAT AND WHO THEY ARE GOING TO WORSHIP!

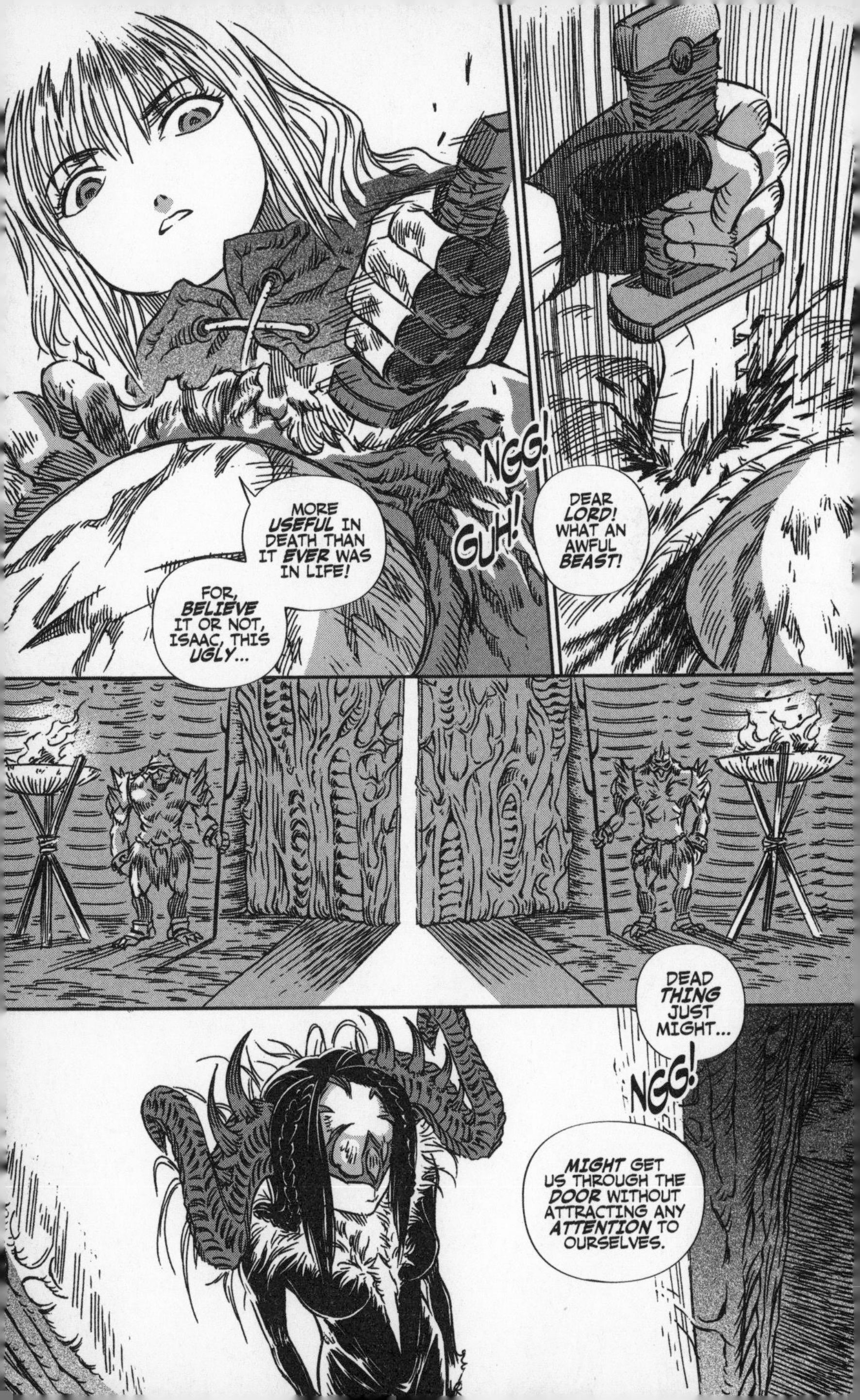
NGG!
GUH!
DEAR LORD! WHAT AN AWFUL BEAST!
MORE USEFUL IN DEATH THAN IT EVER WAS IN LIFE!
FOR, BELIEVE IT OR NOT, ISAAC, THIS UGLY...
DEAD THING JUST MIGHT...
NGG!
MIGHT GET US THROUGH THE DOOR WITHOUT ATTRACTING ANY ATTENTION TO OURSELVES.

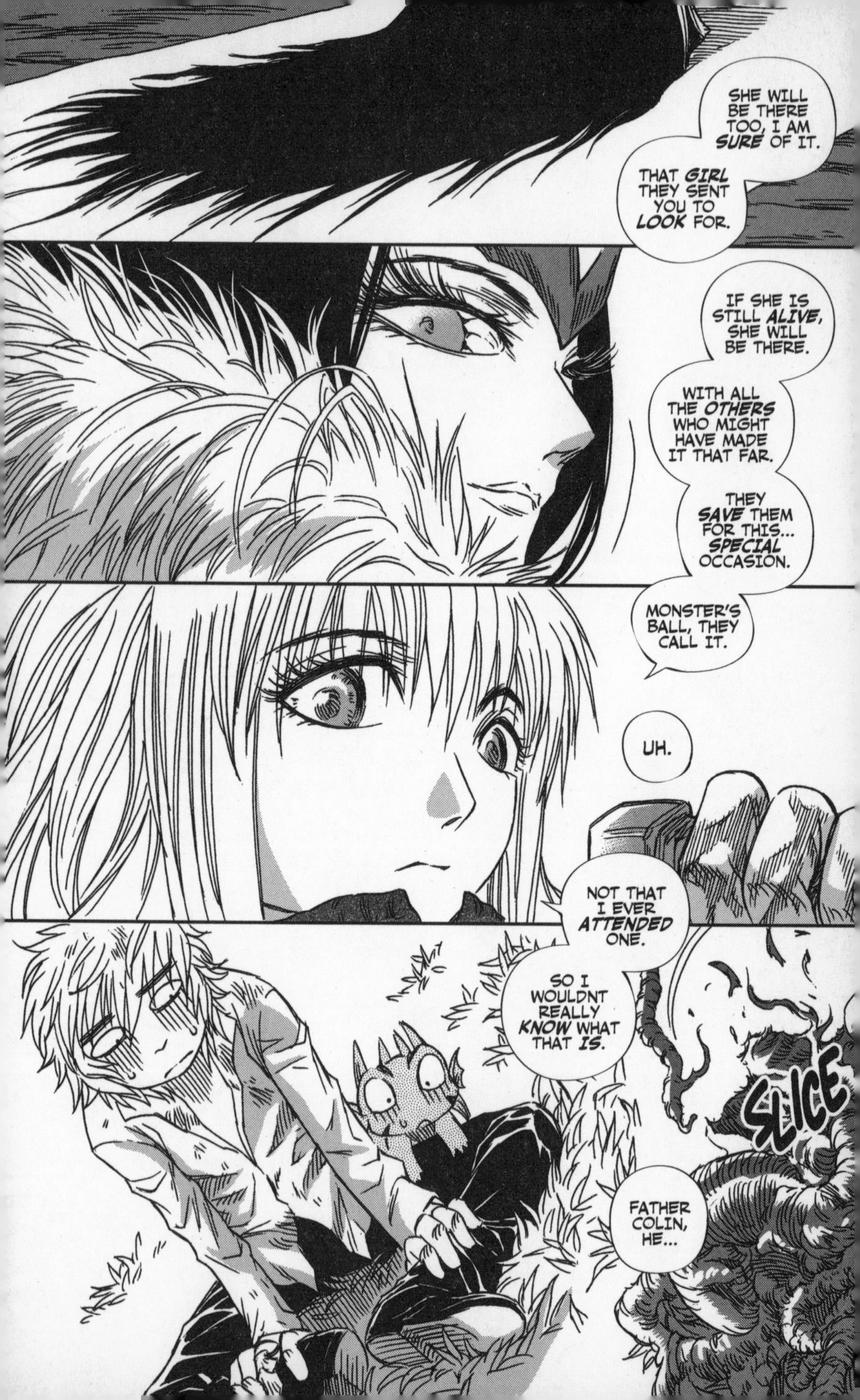
SHE WILL BE THERE TOO, I AM SURE OF IT.
THAT GIRL THEY SENT YOU TO LOOK FOR.
IF SHE IS STILL ALIVE, SHE WILL BE THERE.
WITH ALL THE OTHERS WHO MIGHT HAVE MADE IT THAT FAR.
THEY SAVE THEM FOR THIS... SPECIAL OCCASION.
MONSTER'S BALL, THEY CALL IT.
UH.
NOT THAT I EVER ATTENDED ONE.
SO I WOULDNT REALLY KNOW WHAT THAT IS.
SLICE
FATHER COLIN, HE...

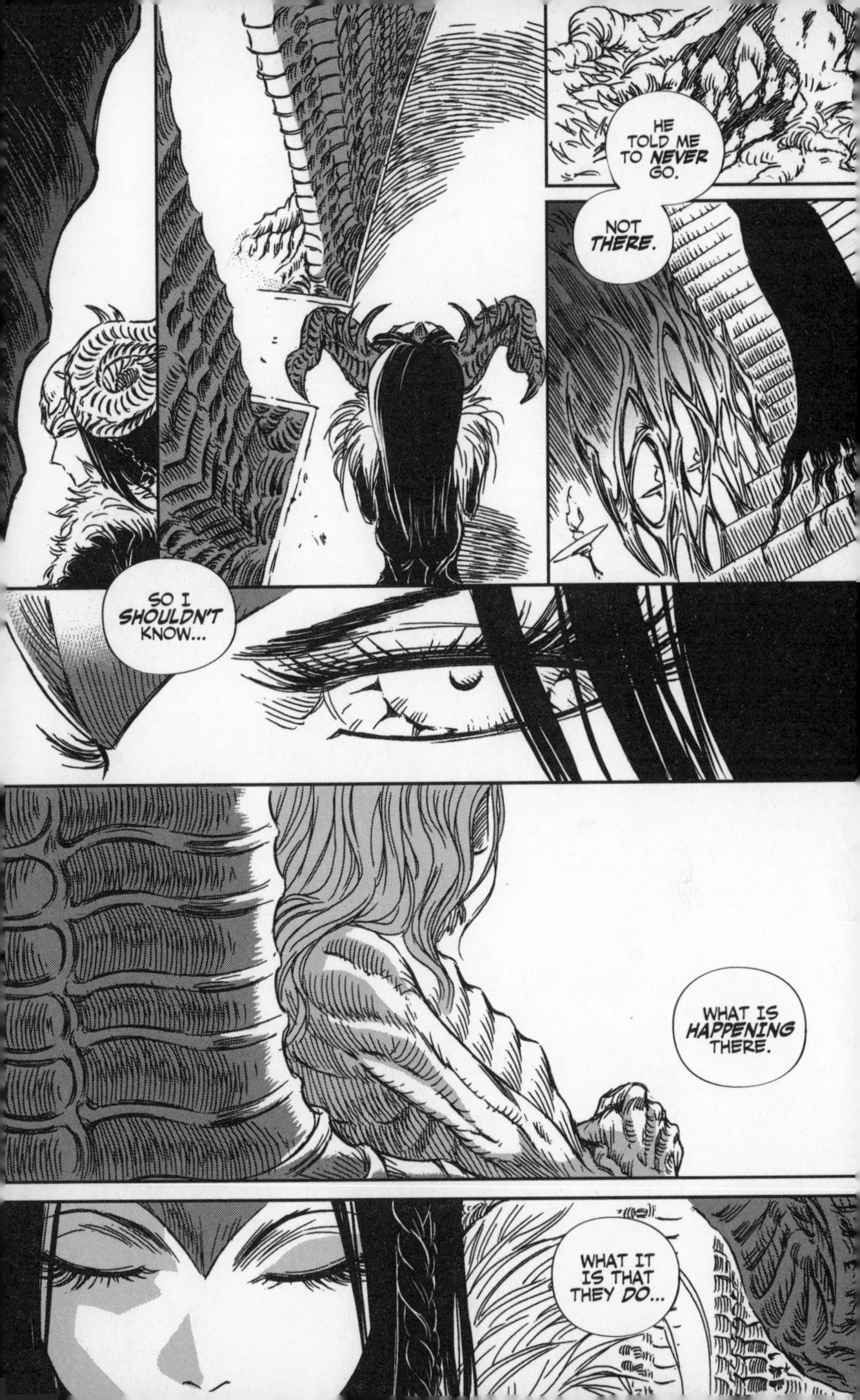
HE TOLD ME TO NEVER GO.
NOT THERE.
SO I SHOULDN'T KNOW...
WHAT IS HAPPENING THERE.
WHAT IT IS THAT THEY DO...

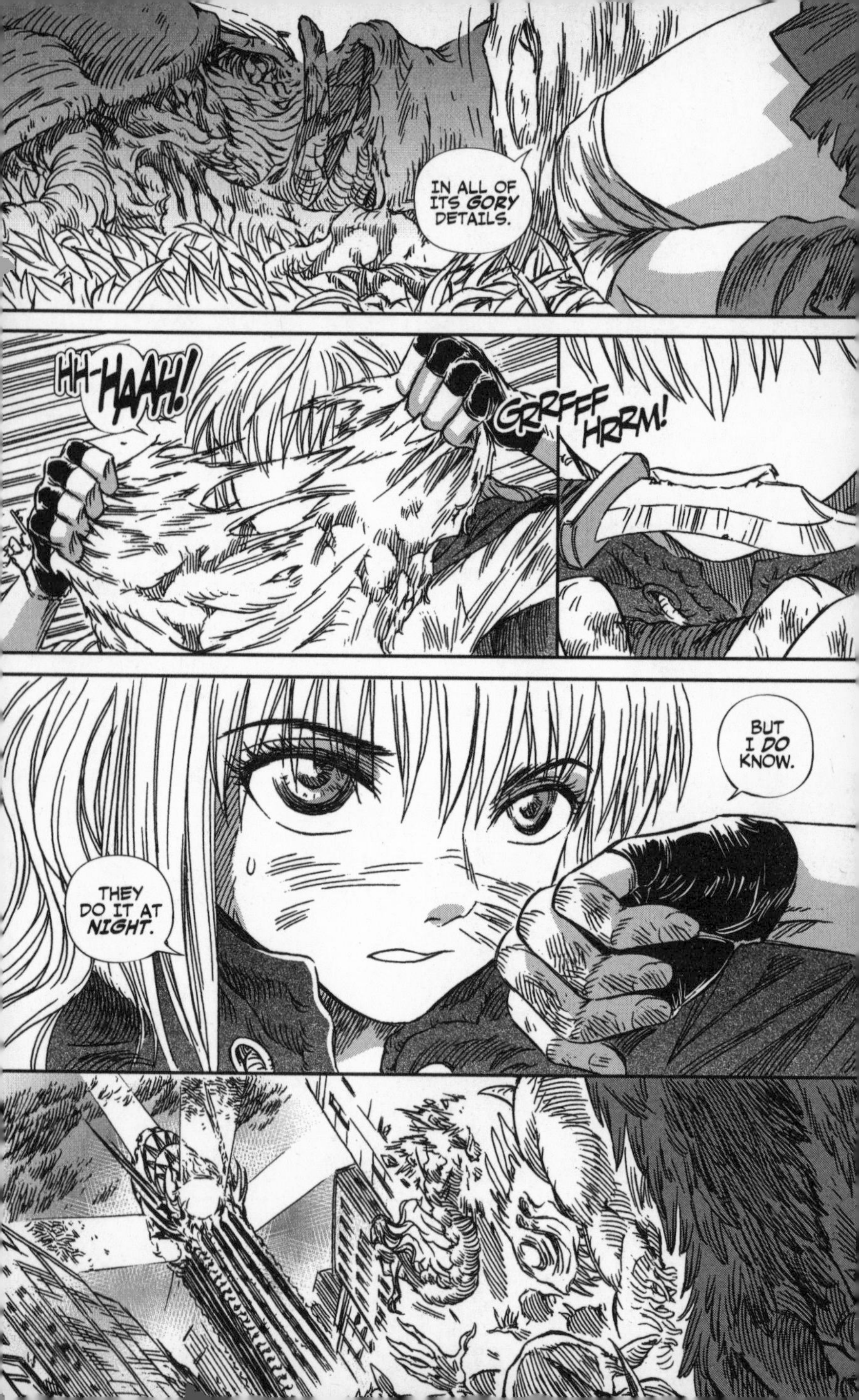
IN ALL OF ITS GORY DETAILS.
GRRFFF HRRM!
HH-HAAH!
BUT I DO KNOW.
THEY DO IT AT NIGHT.

CHAPTER
6

MONSTER'S BALL

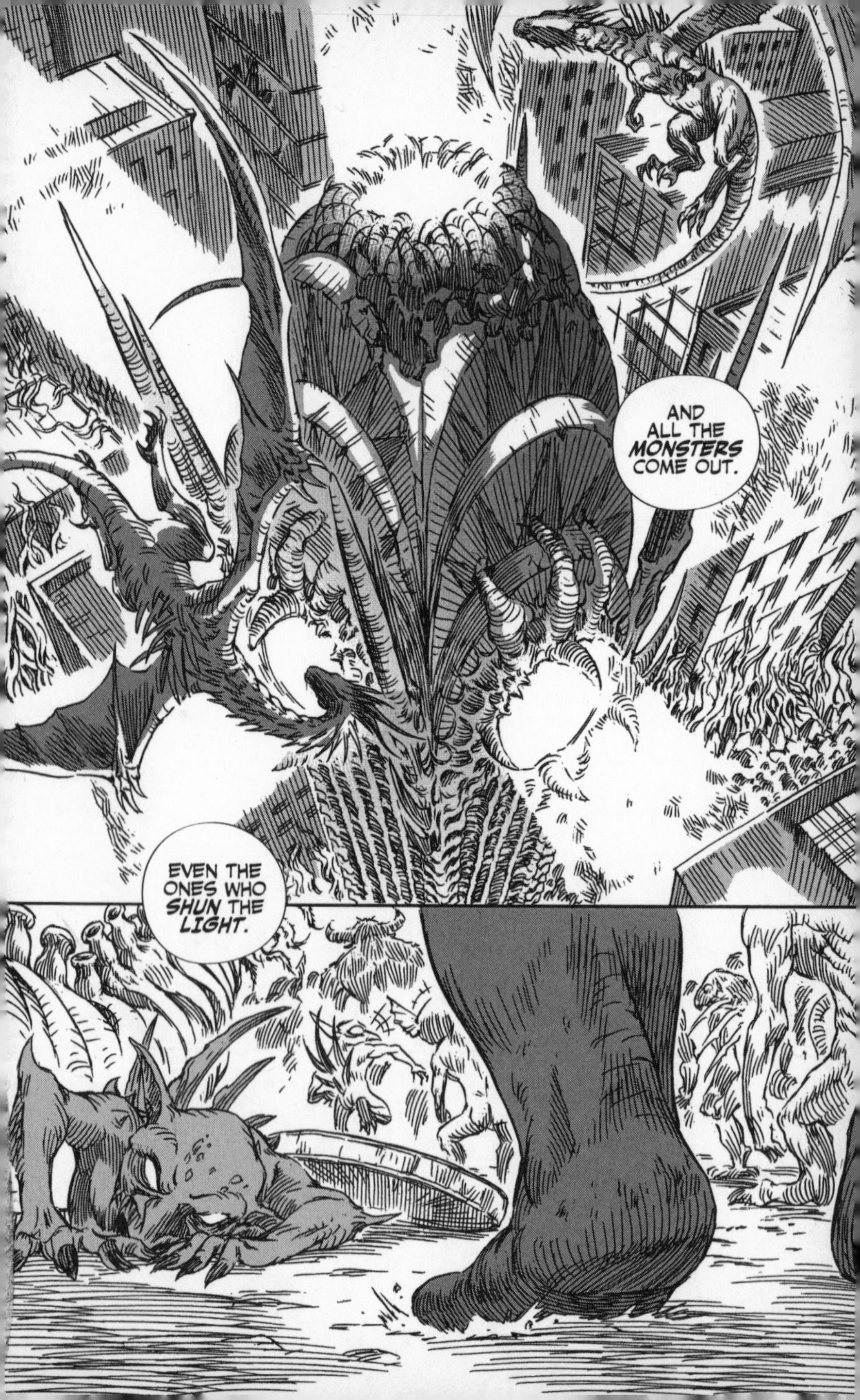
AND ALL THE MONSTERS COME OUT.
EVEN THE ONES WHO SHUN THE LIGHT.

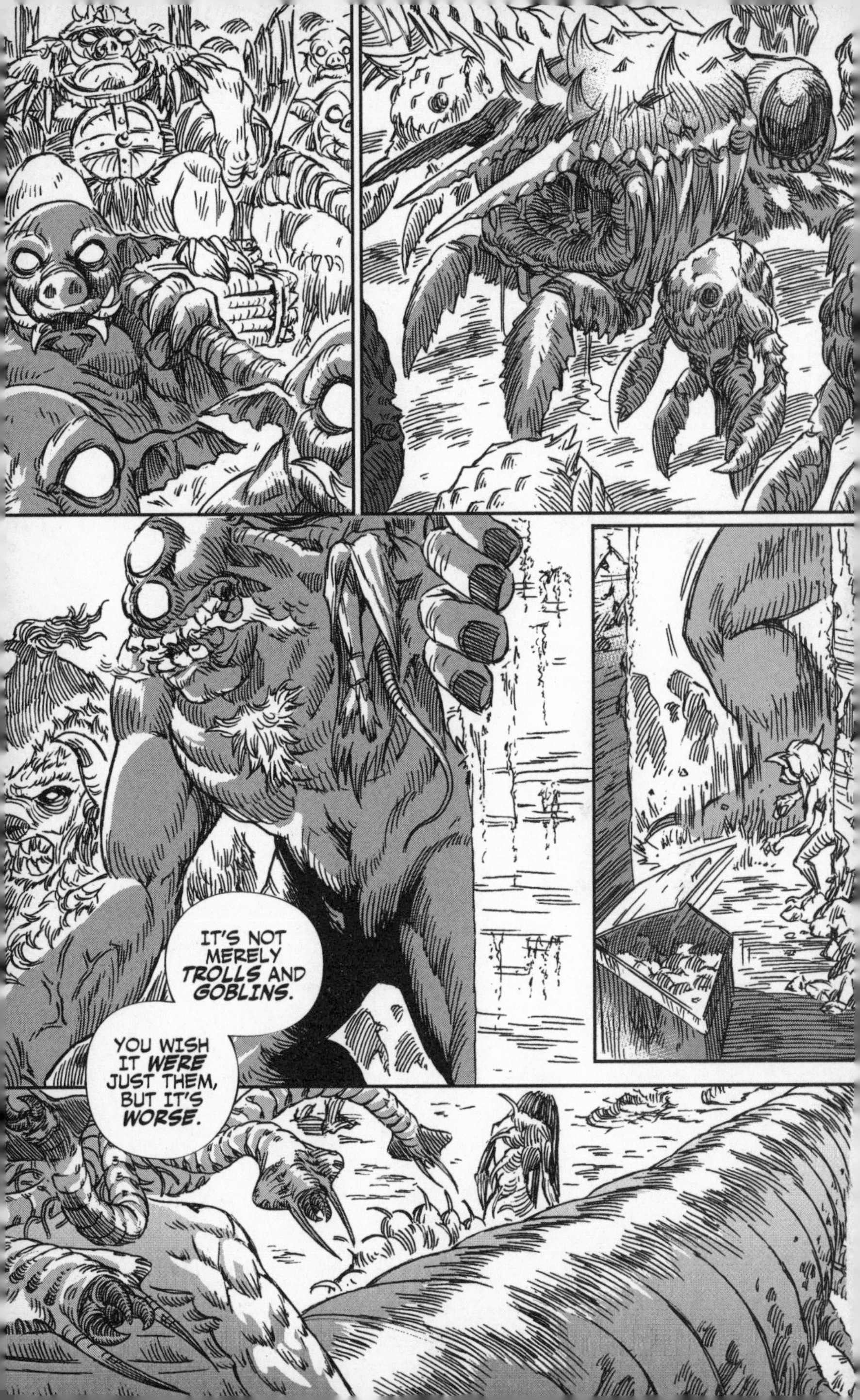
IT'S NOT MERELY TROLLS AND GOBLINS.
YOU WISH IT WERE JUST THEM, BUT IT'S WORSE.

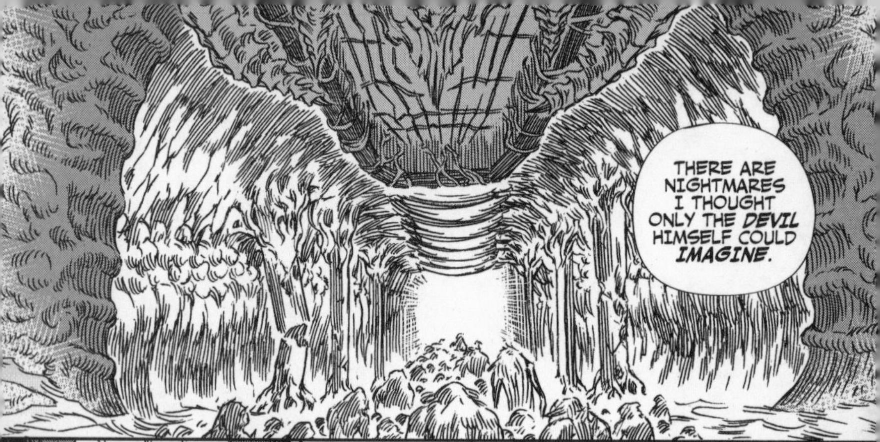
THERE ARE NIGHTMARES I THOUGHT ONLY THE *DEVIL* HIMSELF COULD *IMAGINE*.

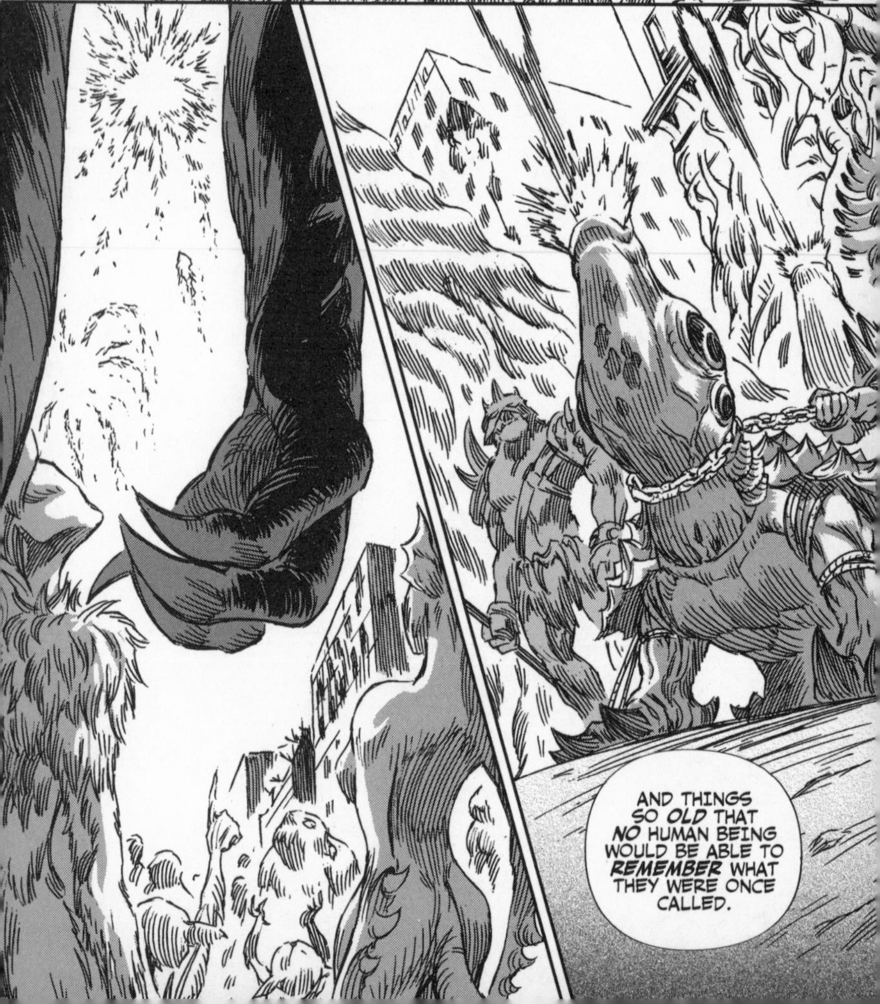
AND THINGS SO *OLD* THAT *NO* HUMAN BEING WOULD BE ABLE TO *REMEMBER* WHAT THEY WERE ONCE CALLED.

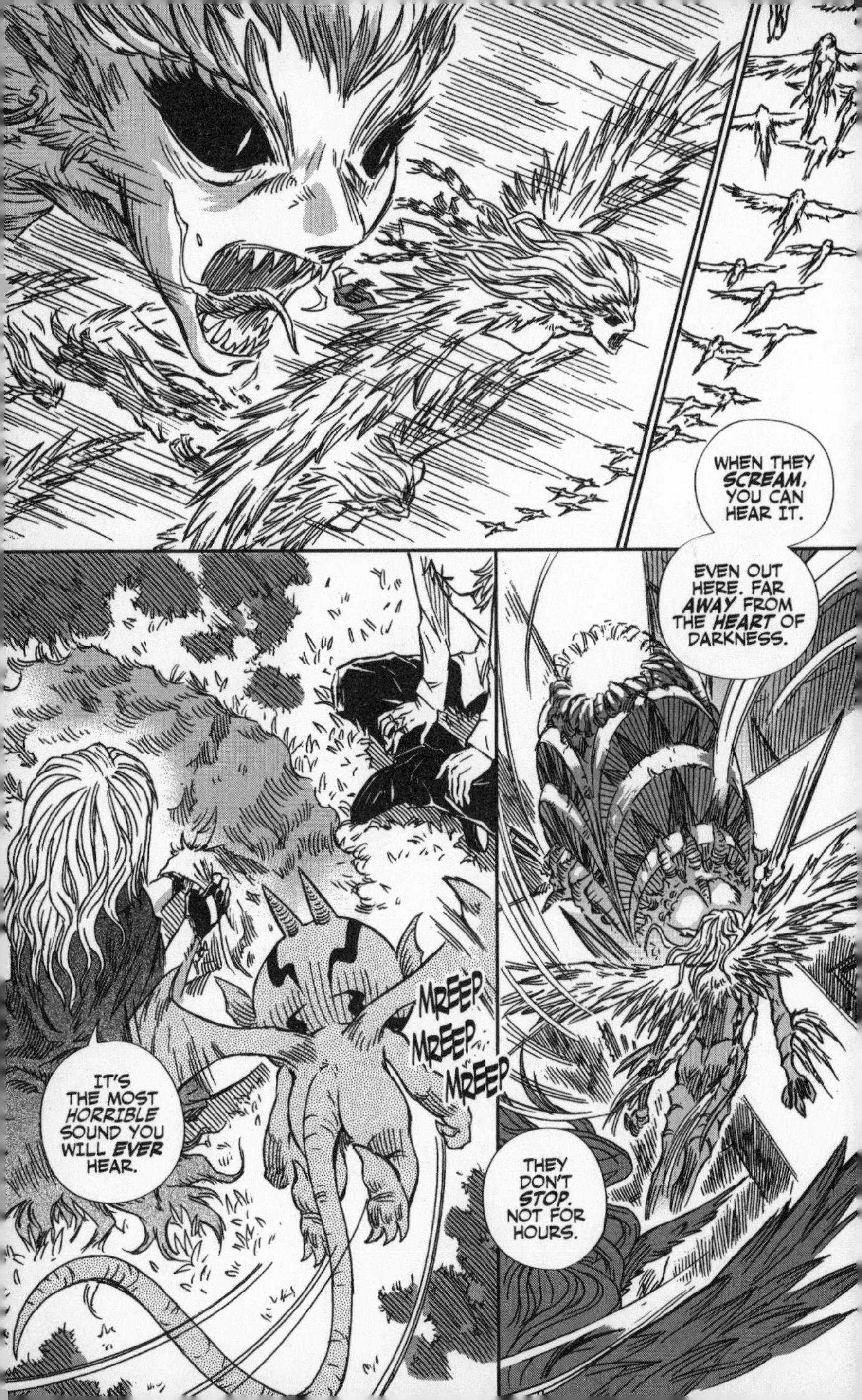
WHEN THEY SCREAM, YOU CAN HEAR IT.
EVEN OUT HERE. FAR AWAY FROM THE HEART OF DARKNESS.
IT'S THE MOST HORRIBLE SOUND YOU WILL EVER HEAR.
MREEP MREEP MREEP
THEY DON'T STOP. NOT FOR HOURS.

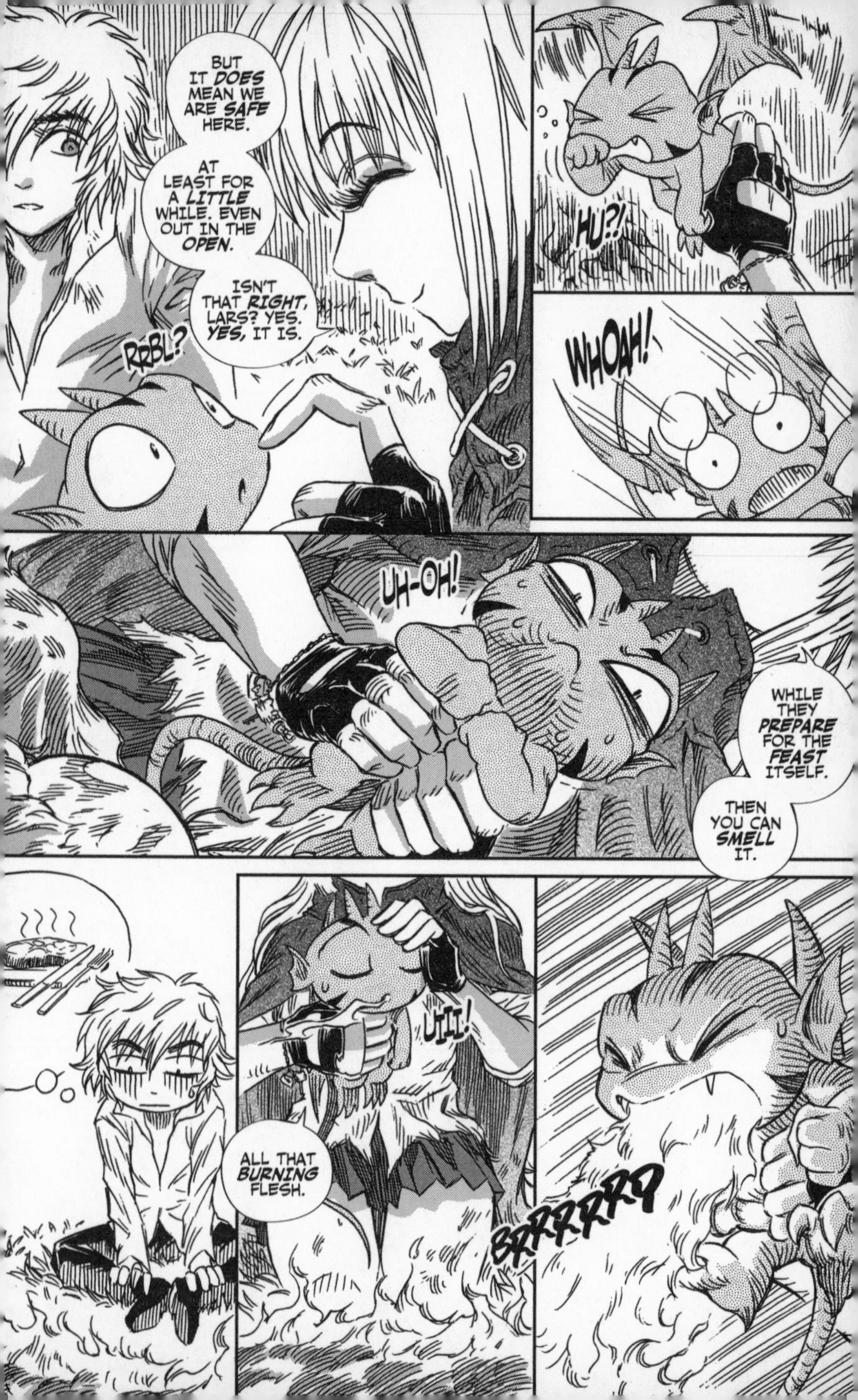
BUT IT *DOES* MEAN WE ARE *SAFE* HERE.
AT LEAST FOR A *LITTLE* WHILE. EVEN OUT IN THE *OPEN*.
ISN'T THAT *RIGHT*, LARS? YES. *YES,* IT IS.
RRBL?
HU?!
WHOAH!
UH-OH!
WHILE THEY *PREPARE* FOR THE *FEAST* ITSELF.
THEN YOU CAN *SMELL* IT.
ALL THAT *BURNING* FLESH.
UIII!
BRRRRRRQ

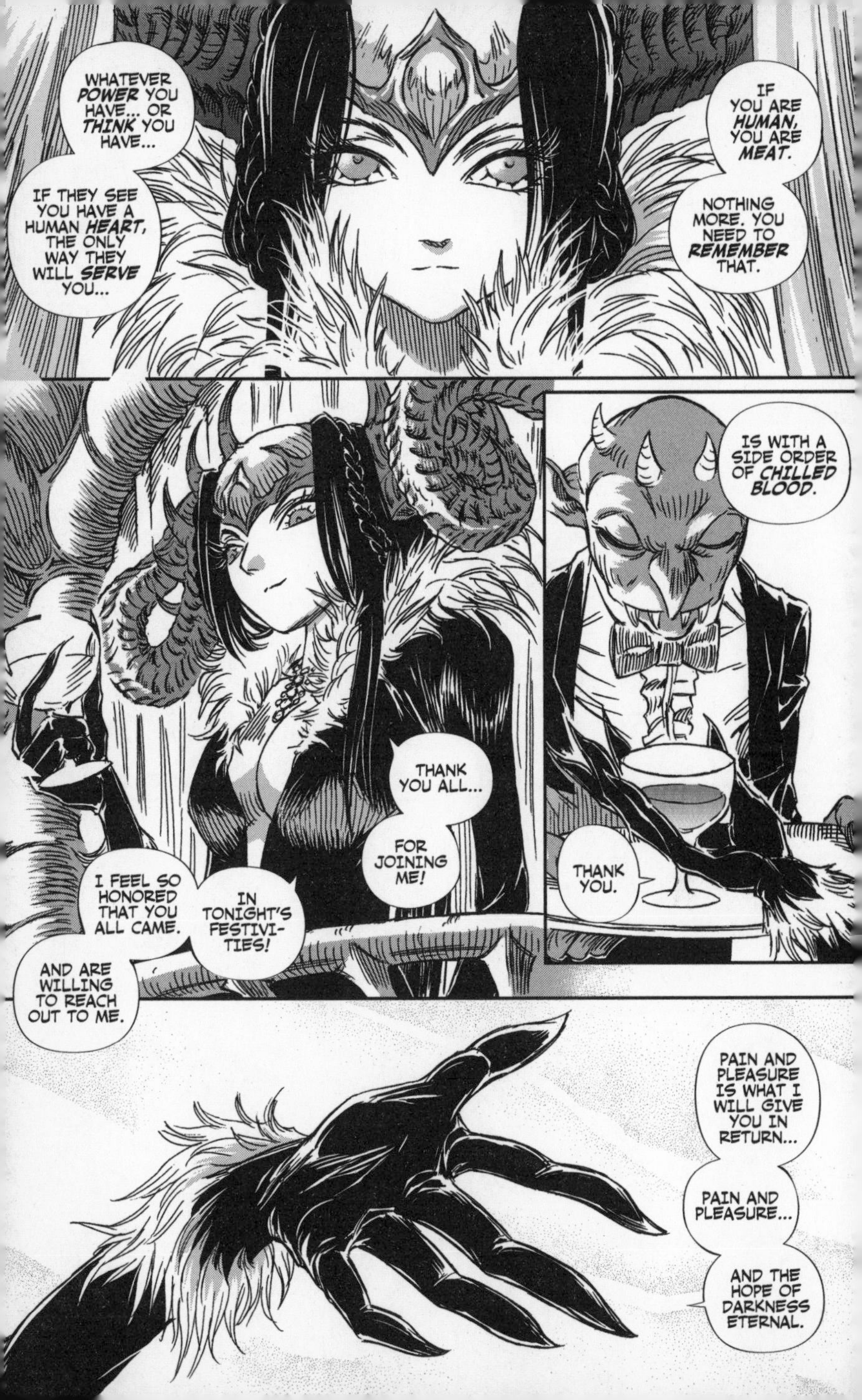
IF YOU ARE HUMAN, YOU ARE MEAT.
NOTHING MORE. YOU NEED TO REMEMBER THAT.
WHATEVER POWER YOU HAVE... OR THINK YOU HAVE...
IF THEY SEE YOU HAVE A HUMAN HEART, THE ONLY WAY THEY WILL SERVE YOU...
IS WITH A SIDE ORDER OF CHILLED BLOOD.
THANK YOU.
THANK YOU ALL...
FOR JOINING ME!
IN TONIGHT'S FESTIVI-TIES!
I FEEL SO HONORED THAT YOU ALL CAME.
AND ARE WILLING TO REACH OUT TO ME.
PAIN AND PLEASURE IS WHAT I WILL GIVE YOU IN RETURN...
PAIN AND PLEASURE...
AND THE HOPE OF DARKNESS ETERNAL.

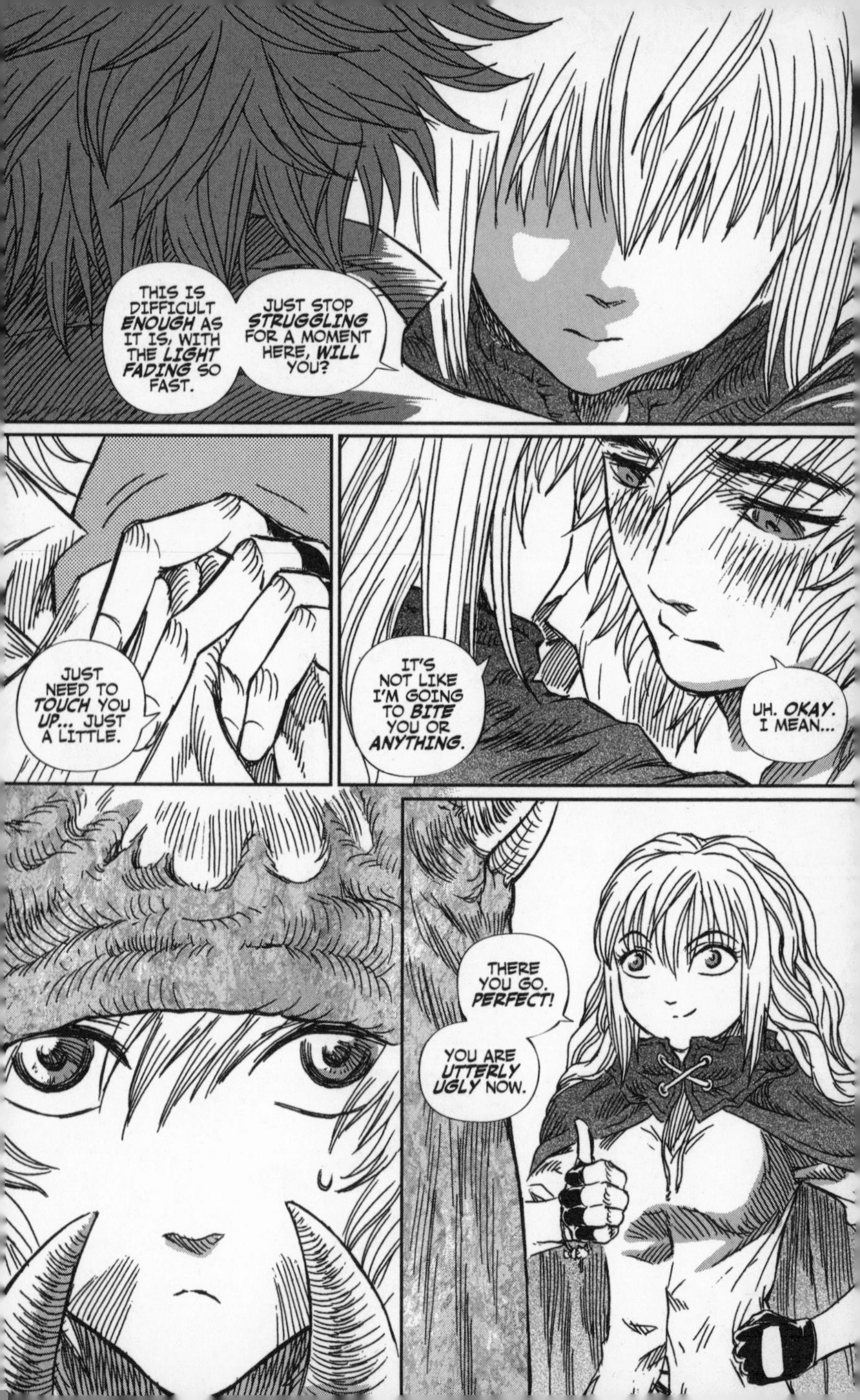
THIS IS DIFFICULT ENOUGH AS IT IS, WITH THE LIGHT FADING SO FAST.
JUST STOP STRUGGLING FOR A MOMENT HERE, WILL YOU?
JUST NEED TO TOUCH YOU UP... JUST A LITTLE.
IT'S NOT LIKE I'M GOING TO BITE YOU OR ANYTHING.
UH. OKAY. I MEAN...
THERE YOU GO. PERFECT!
YOU ARE UTTERLY UGLY NOW.

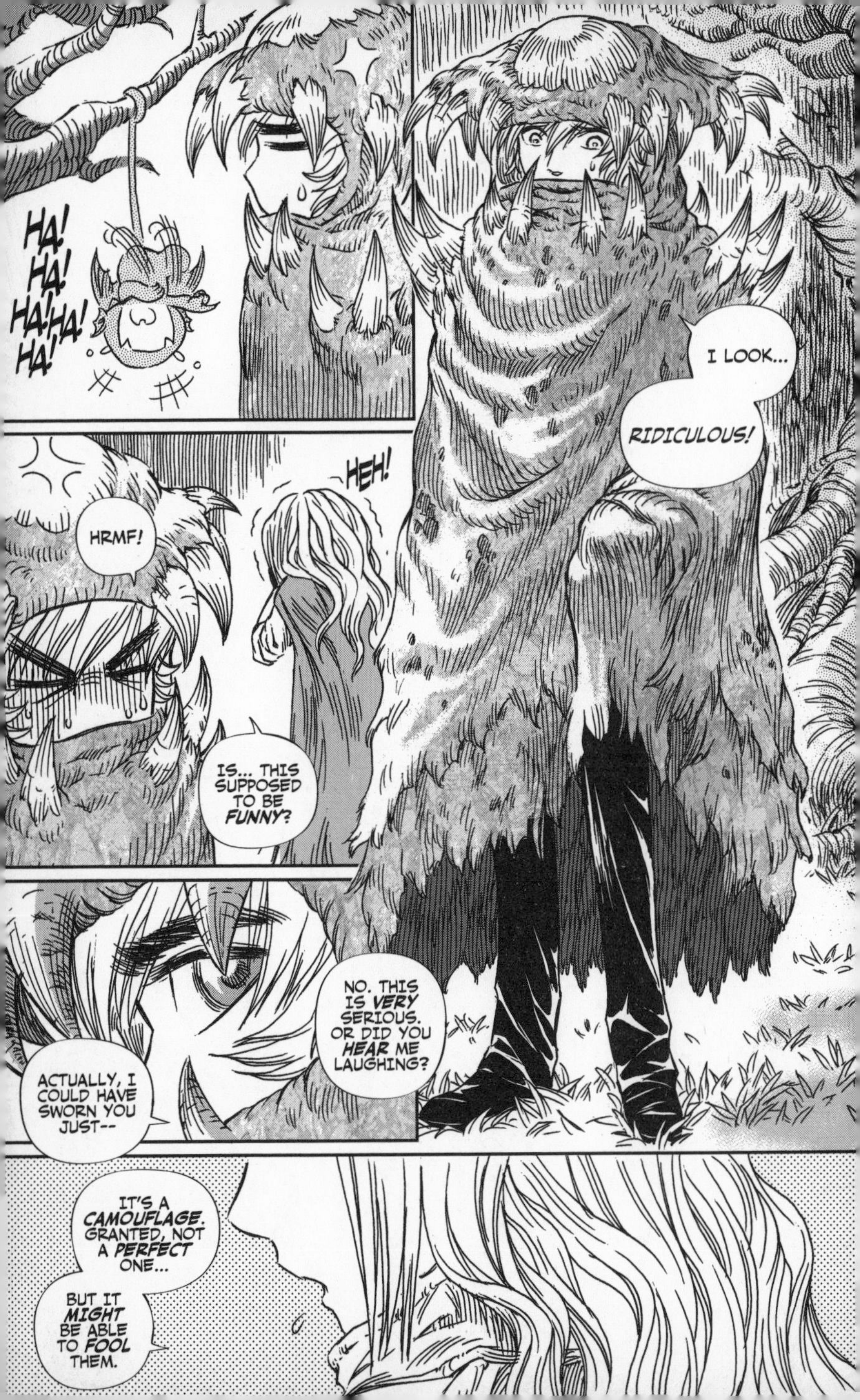

I LOOK...
RIDICULOUS!
HA! HA! HA! HA! HA!
HEH!
HRMF!
IS... THIS SUPPOSED TO BE FUNNY?
NO. THIS IS VERY SERIOUS. OR DID YOU HEAR ME LAUGHING?
ACTUALLY, I COULD HAVE SWORN YOU JUST--
IT'S A CAMOUFLAGE. GRANTED, NOT A PERFECT ONE...
BUT IT MIGHT BE ABLE TO FOOL THEM.

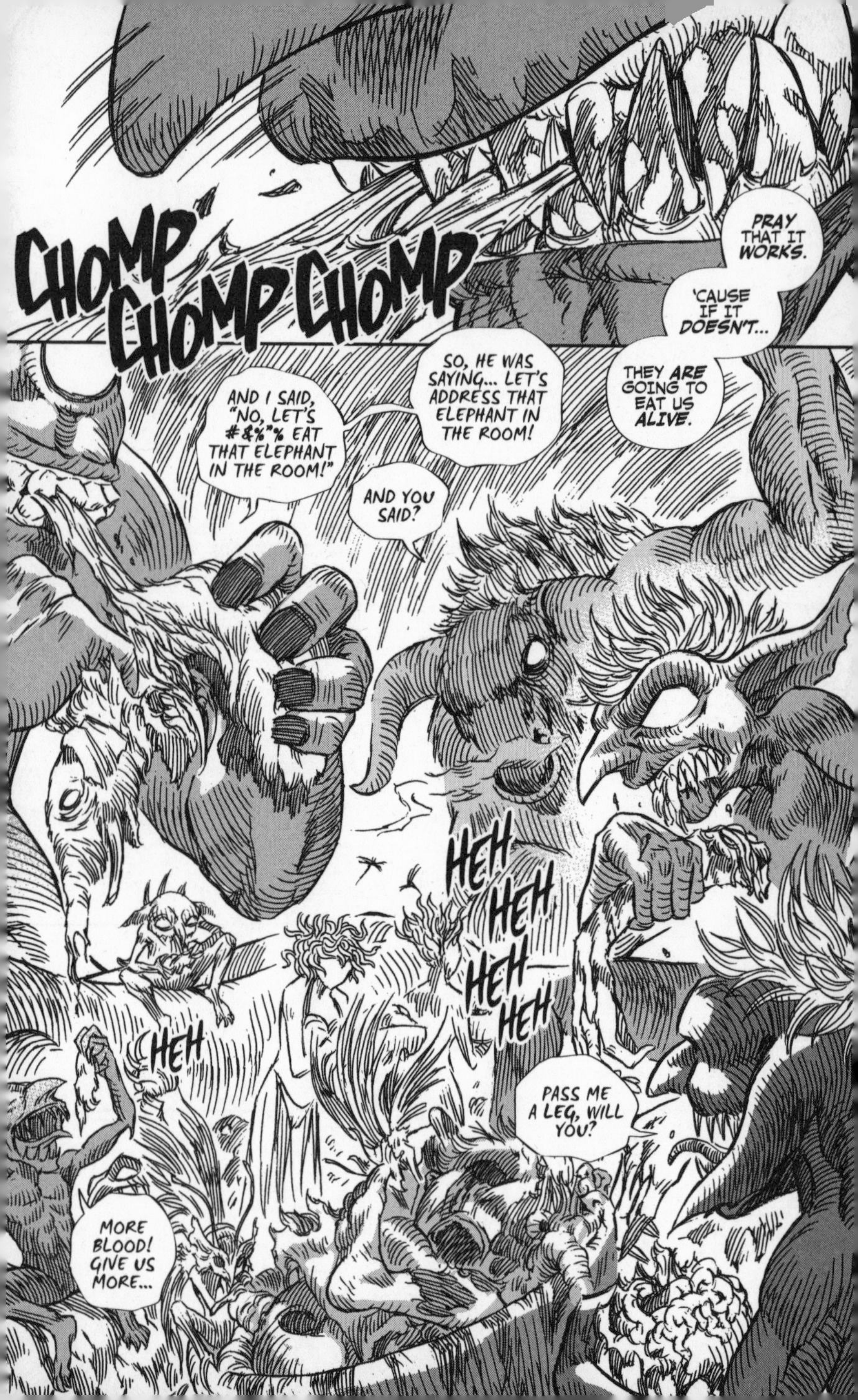
PRAY THAT IT WORKS.
'CAUSE IF IT DOESN'T...
THEY ARE GOING TO EAT US ALIVE.
CHOMP CHOMP CHOMP CHOMP
SO, HE WAS SAYING... LET'S ADDRESS THAT ELEPHANT IN THE ROOM!
AND YOU SAID?
AND I SAID, "NO, LET'S #&%"% EAT THAT ELEPHANT IN THE ROOM!"
HEH HEH HEH HEH
PASS ME A LEG, WILL YOU?
HEH
MORE BLOOD! GIVE US MORE...

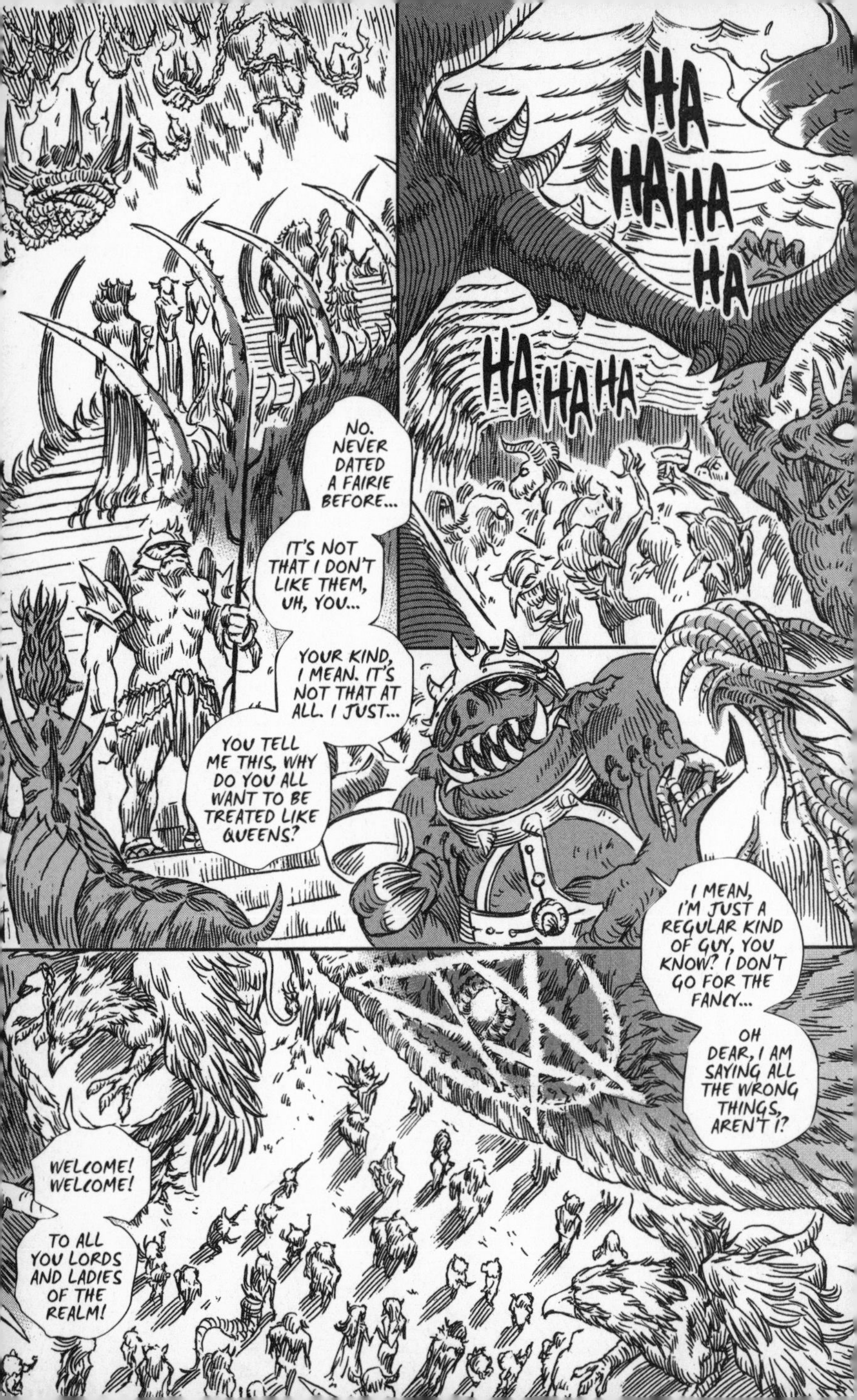
NO. NEVER DATED A FAIRIE BEFORE...
IT'S NOT THAT I DON'T LIKE THEM, UH, YOU...
YOUR KIND, I MEAN. IT'S NOT THAT AT ALL. I JUST...
YOU TELL ME THIS, WHY DO YOU ALL WANT TO BE TREATED LIKE QUEENS?
HA HA HA HA HA
HA HA HA
I MEAN, I'M JUST A REGULAR KIND OF GUY, YOU KNOW? I DON'T GO FOR THE FANCY...
OH DEAR, I AM SAYING ALL THE WRONG THINGS, AREN'T I?
WELCOME! WELCOME!
TO ALL YOU LORDS AND LADIES OF THE REALM!

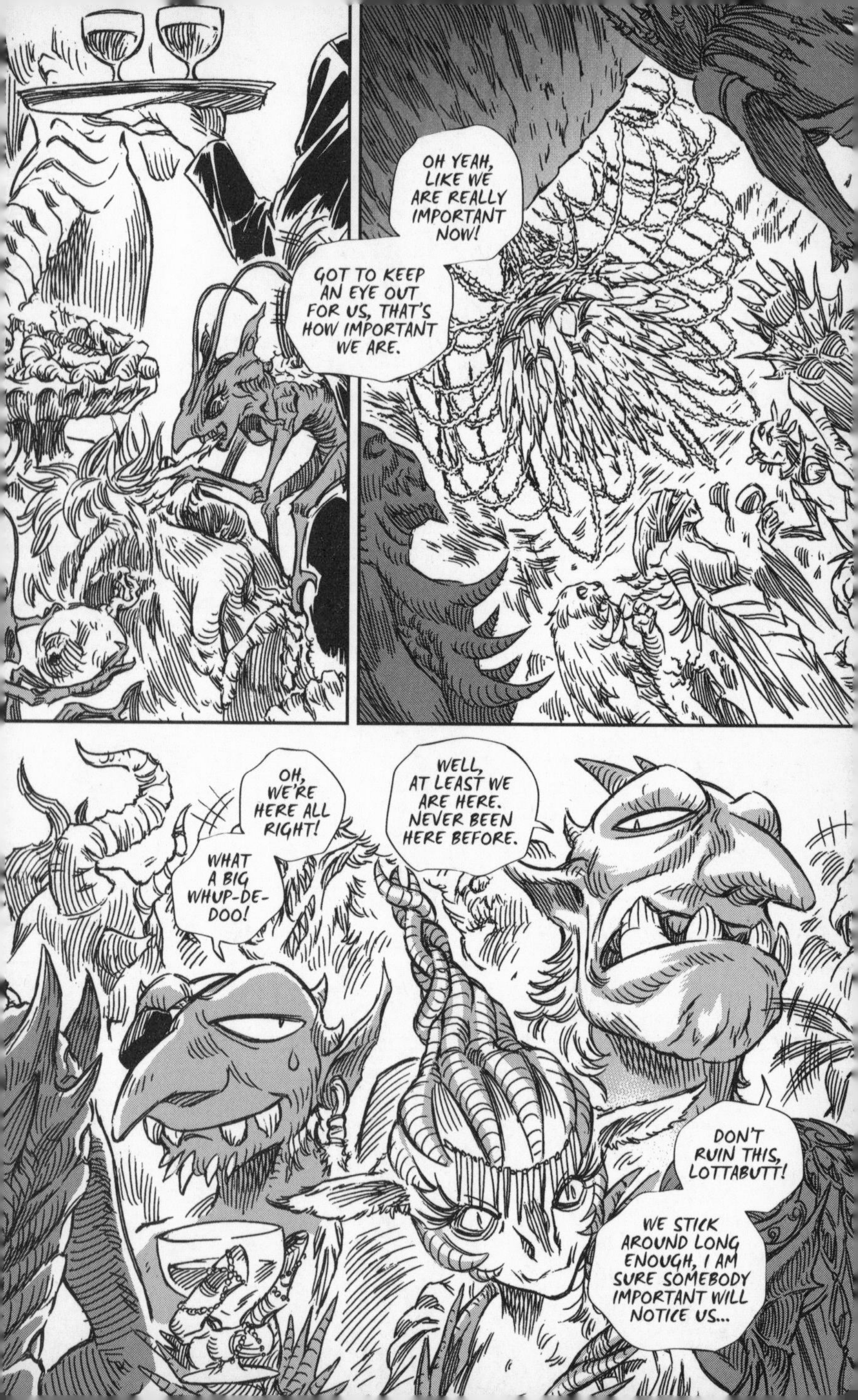
OH YEAH, LIKE WE ARE REALLY IMPORTANT NOW!
GOT TO KEEP AN EYE OUT FOR US, THAT'S HOW IMPORTANT WE ARE.
WELL, AT LEAST WE ARE HERE. NEVER BEEN HERE BEFORE.
OH, WE'RE HERE ALL RIGHT!
WHAT A BIG WHUP-DE-DOO!
DON'T RUIN THIS, LOTTABUTT!
WE STICK AROUND LONG ENOUGH, I AM SURE SOMEBODY IMPORTANT WILL NOTICE US...

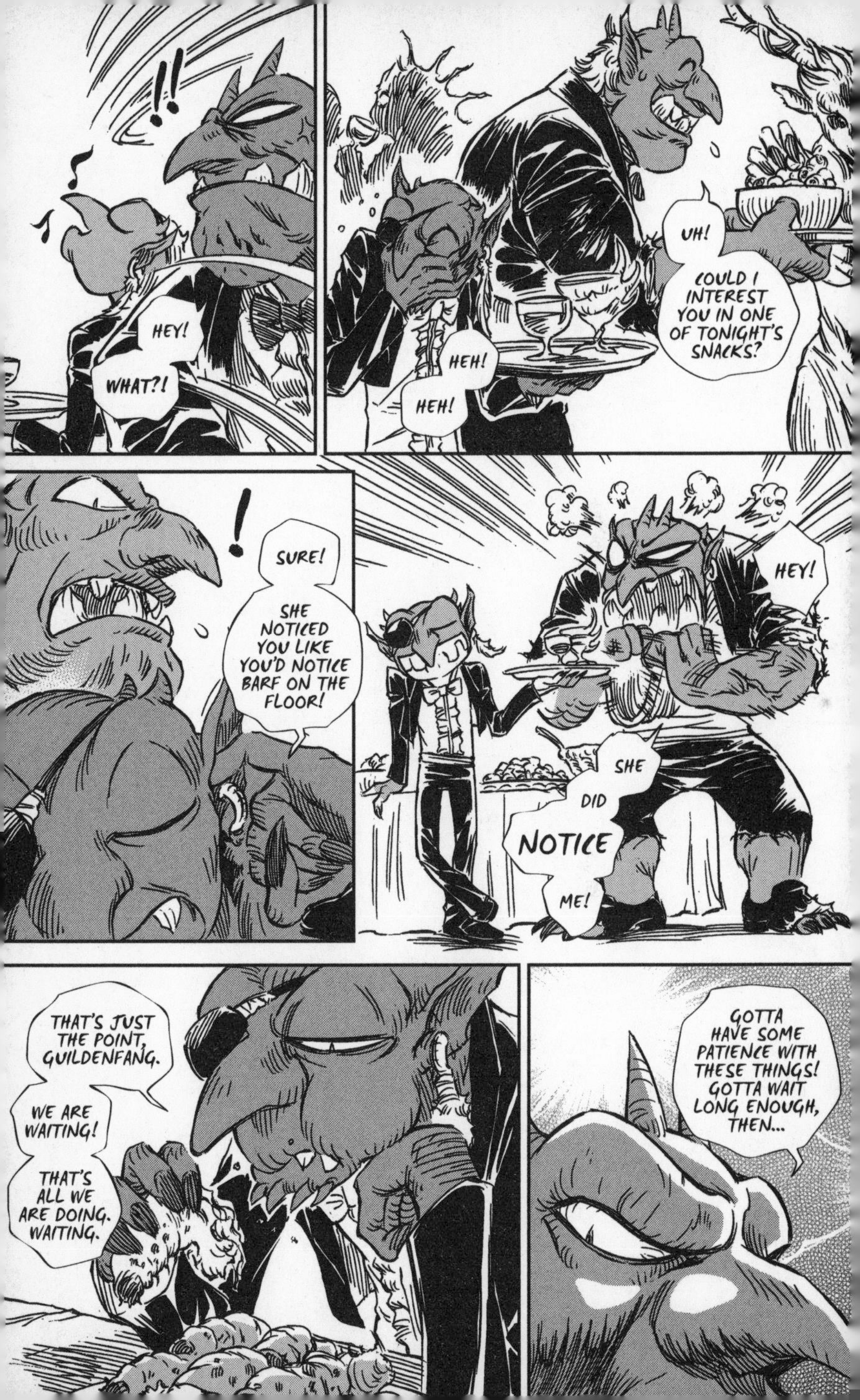
!!
HEY!
WHAT?!
UH!
COULD I INTEREST YOU IN ONE OF TONIGHT'S SNACKS?
HEH!
HEH!
!
SURE!
SHE NOTICED YOU LIKE YOU'D NOTICE BARF ON THE FLOOR!
HEY!
SHE DID NOTICE ME!
THAT'S JUST THE POINT, GUILDENFANG.
WE ARE WAITING!
THAT'S ALL WE ARE DOING. WAITING.
GOTTA HAVE SOME PATIENCE WITH THESE THINGS! GOTTA WAIT LONG ENOUGH, THEN...

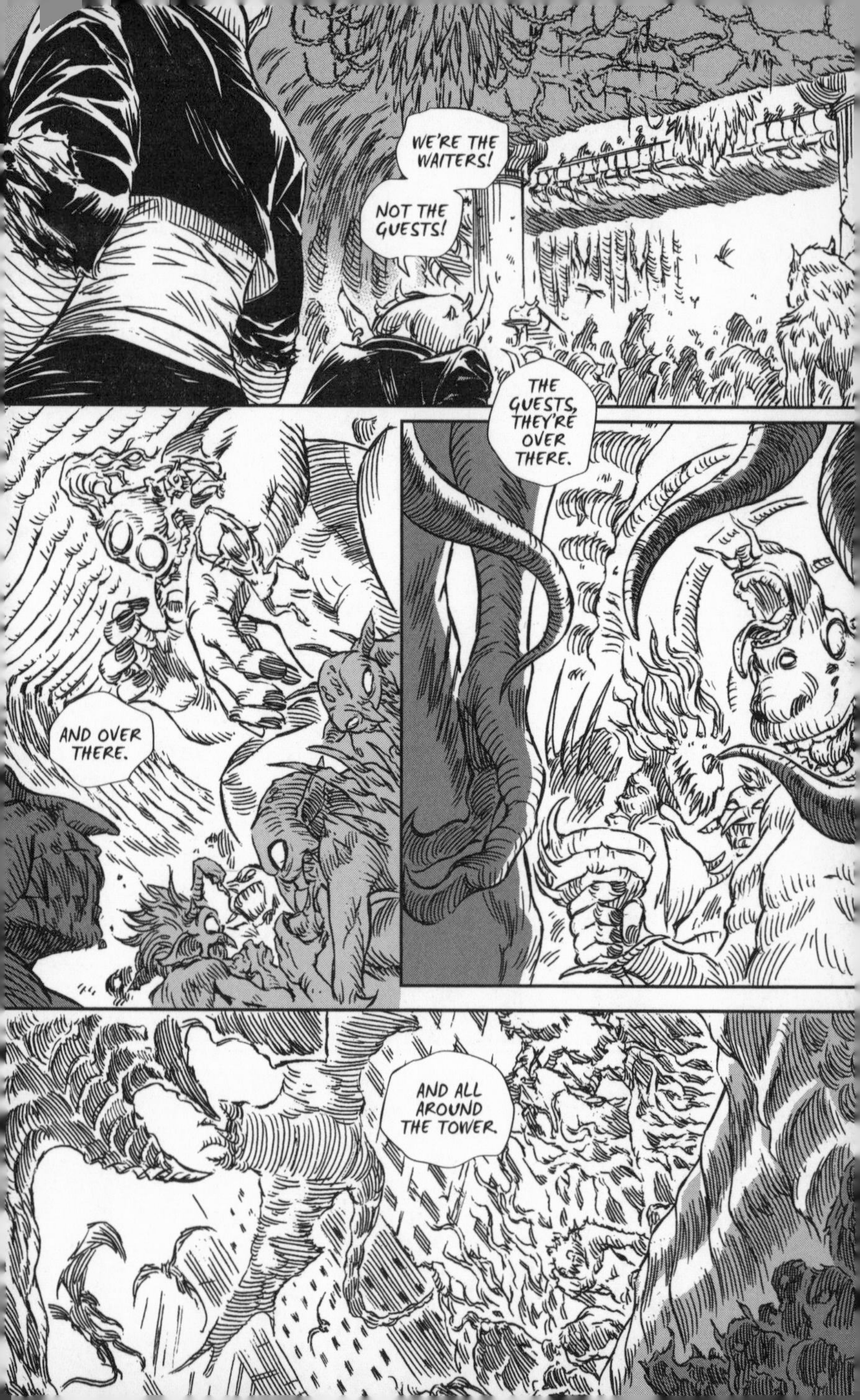
WE'RE THE WAITERS!
NOT THE GUESTS!
THE GUESTS, THEY'RE OVER THERE.
AND OVER THERE.
AND ALL AROUND THE TOWER.

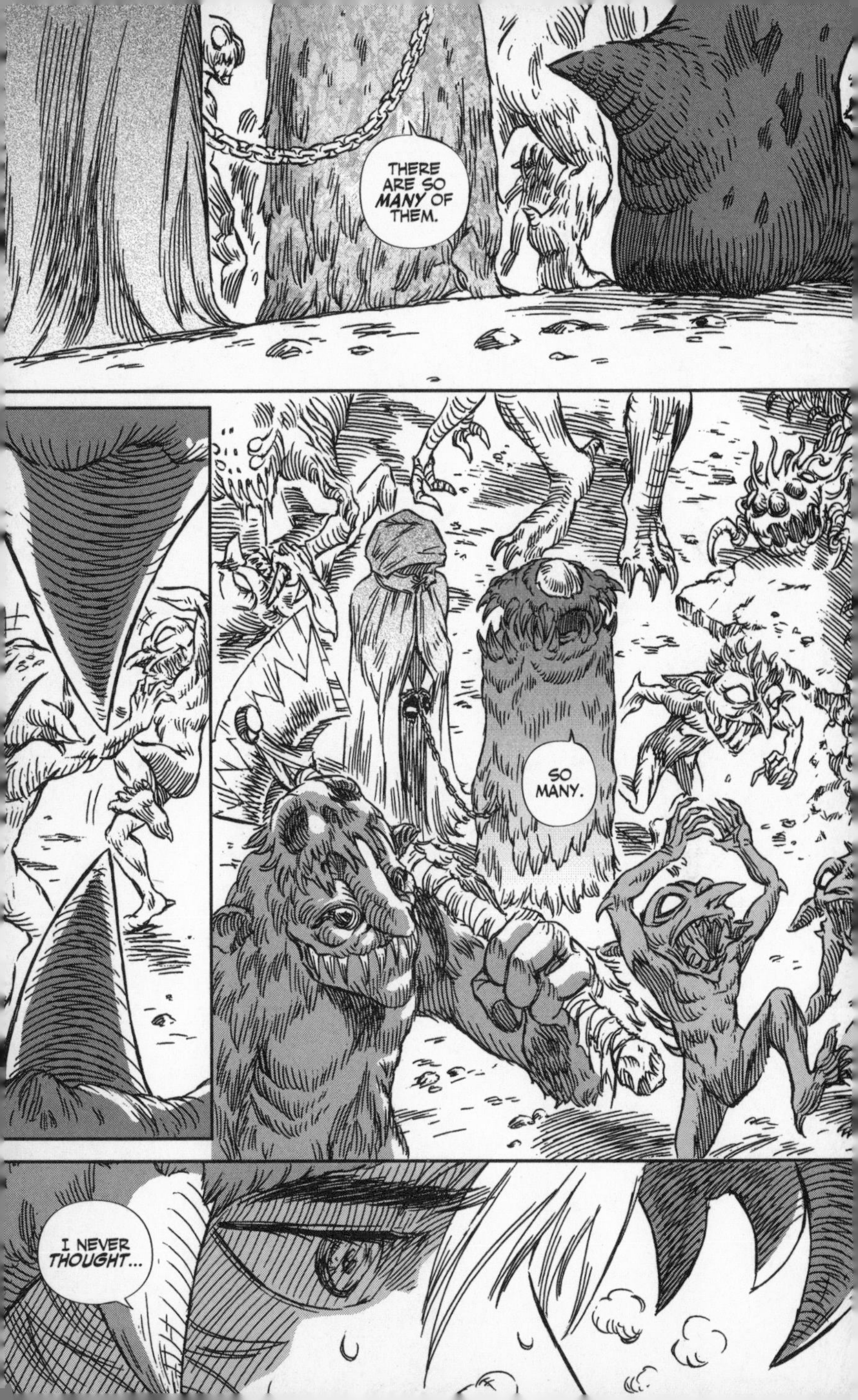
THERE ARE SO MANY OF THEM.
SO MANY.
I NEVER THOUGHT...

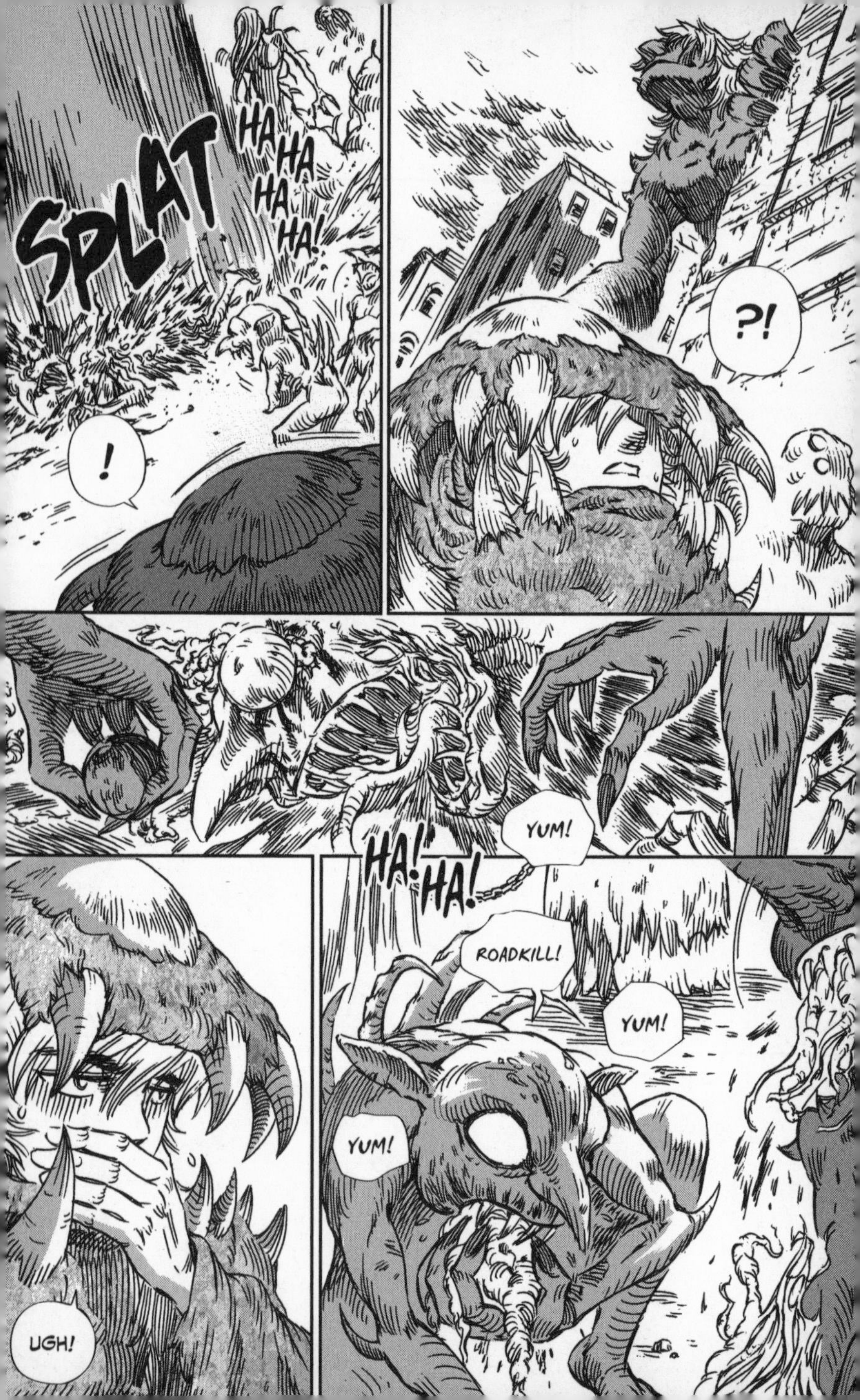
?!
SPLAT
HA HA HA HA!
!
YUM!
HA! HA!
ROADKILL!
YUM!
YUM!
UGH!

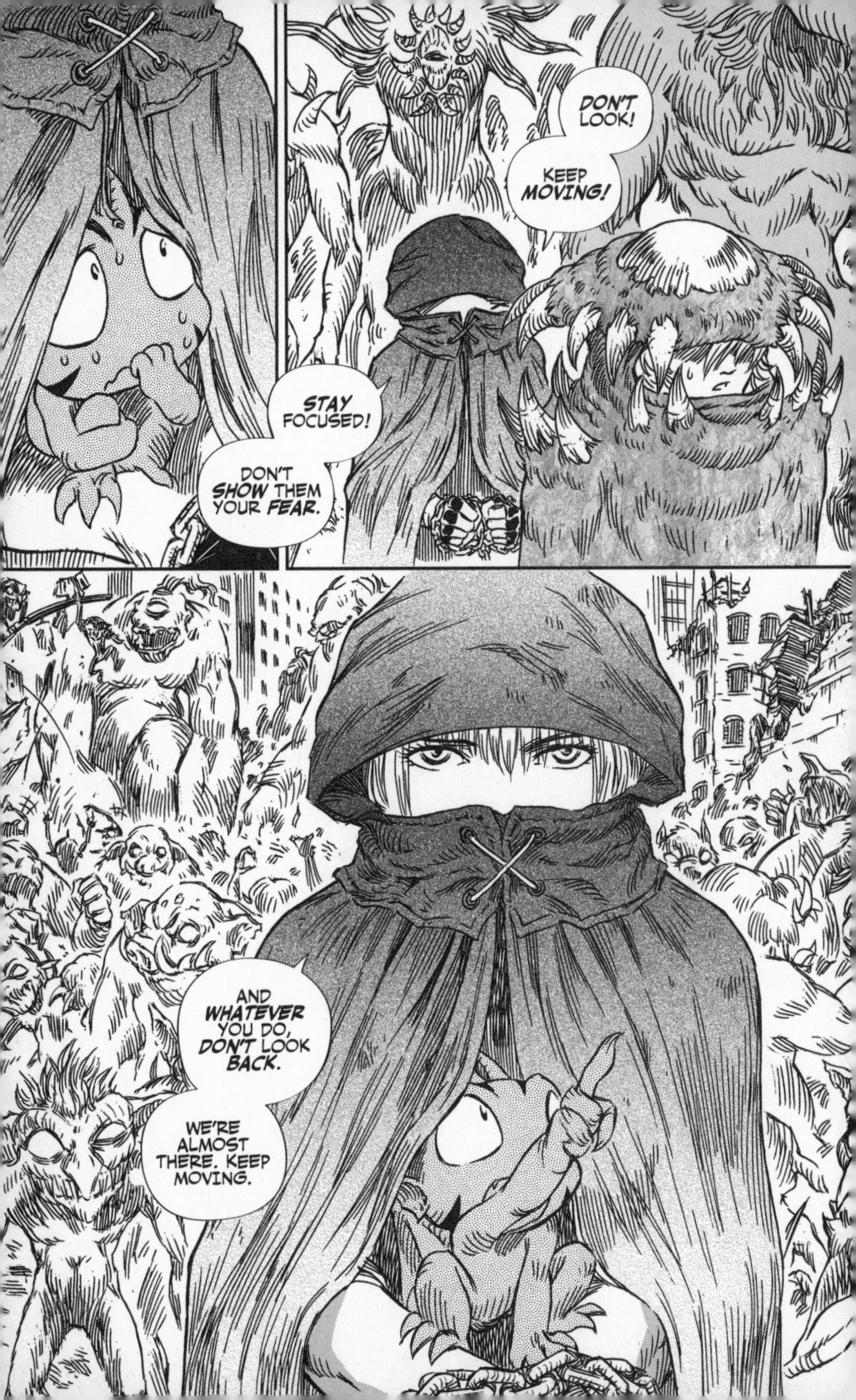
DON'T LOOK!
KEEP MOVING!
STAY FOCUSED!
DON'T SHOW THEM YOUR FEAR.
AND WHATEVER YOU DO, DON'T LOOK BACK.
WE'RE ALMOST THERE. KEEP MOVING.

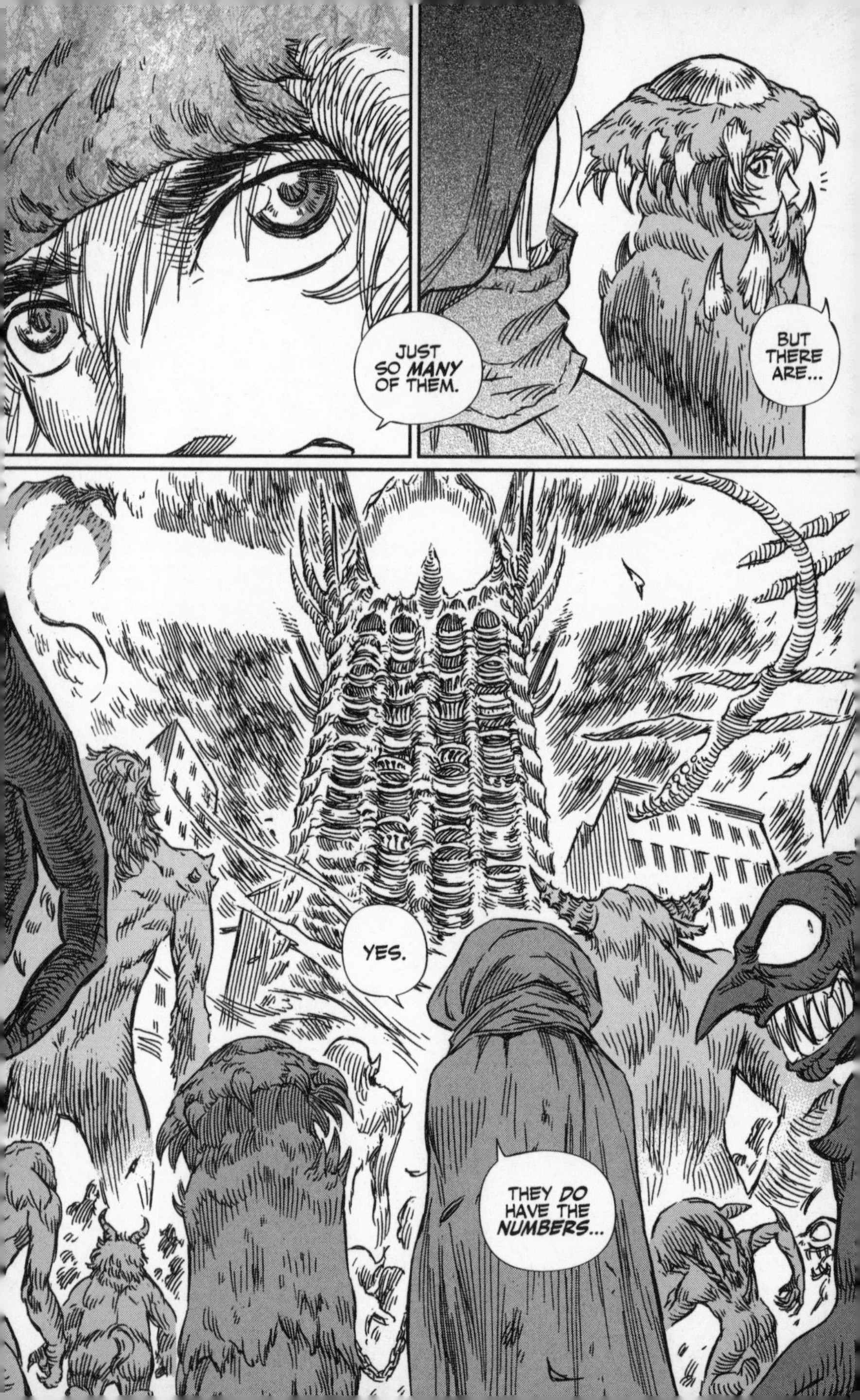
BUT THERE ARE...
JUST SO MANY OF THEM.
YES.
THEY DO HAVE THE NUMBERS...

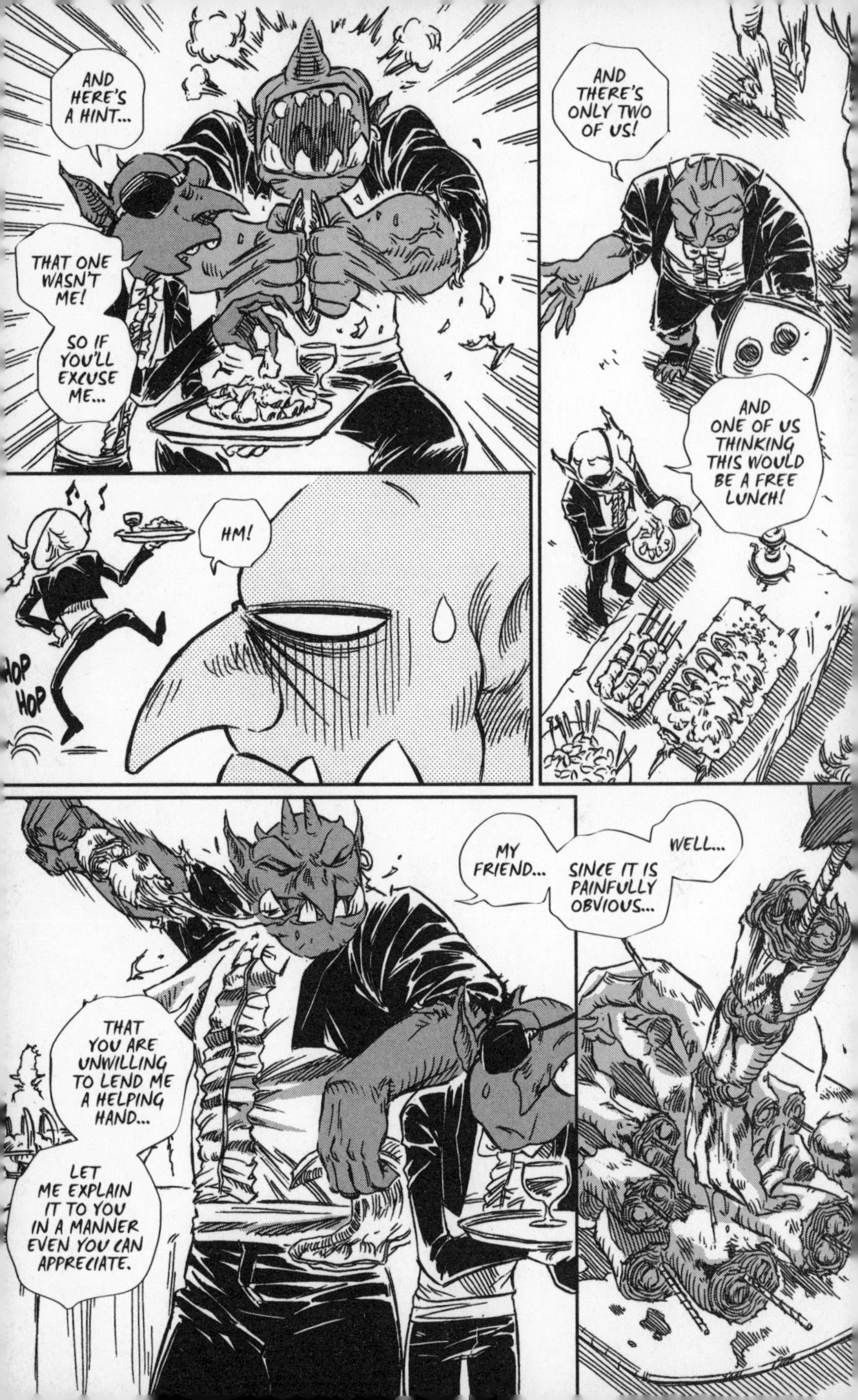
AND THERE'S ONLY TWO OF US!
AND ONE OF US THINKING THIS WOULD BE A FREE LUNCH!
AND HERE'S A HINT...
THAT ONE WASN'T ME!
SO IF YOU'LL EXCUSE ME...
HM!
HOP HOP
WELL...
MY FRIEND...
SINCE IT IS PAINFULLY OBVIOUS...
THAT YOU ARE UNWILLING TO LEND ME A HELPING HAND...
LET ME EXPLAIN IT TO YOU IN A MANNER EVEN YOU CAN APPRECIATE.

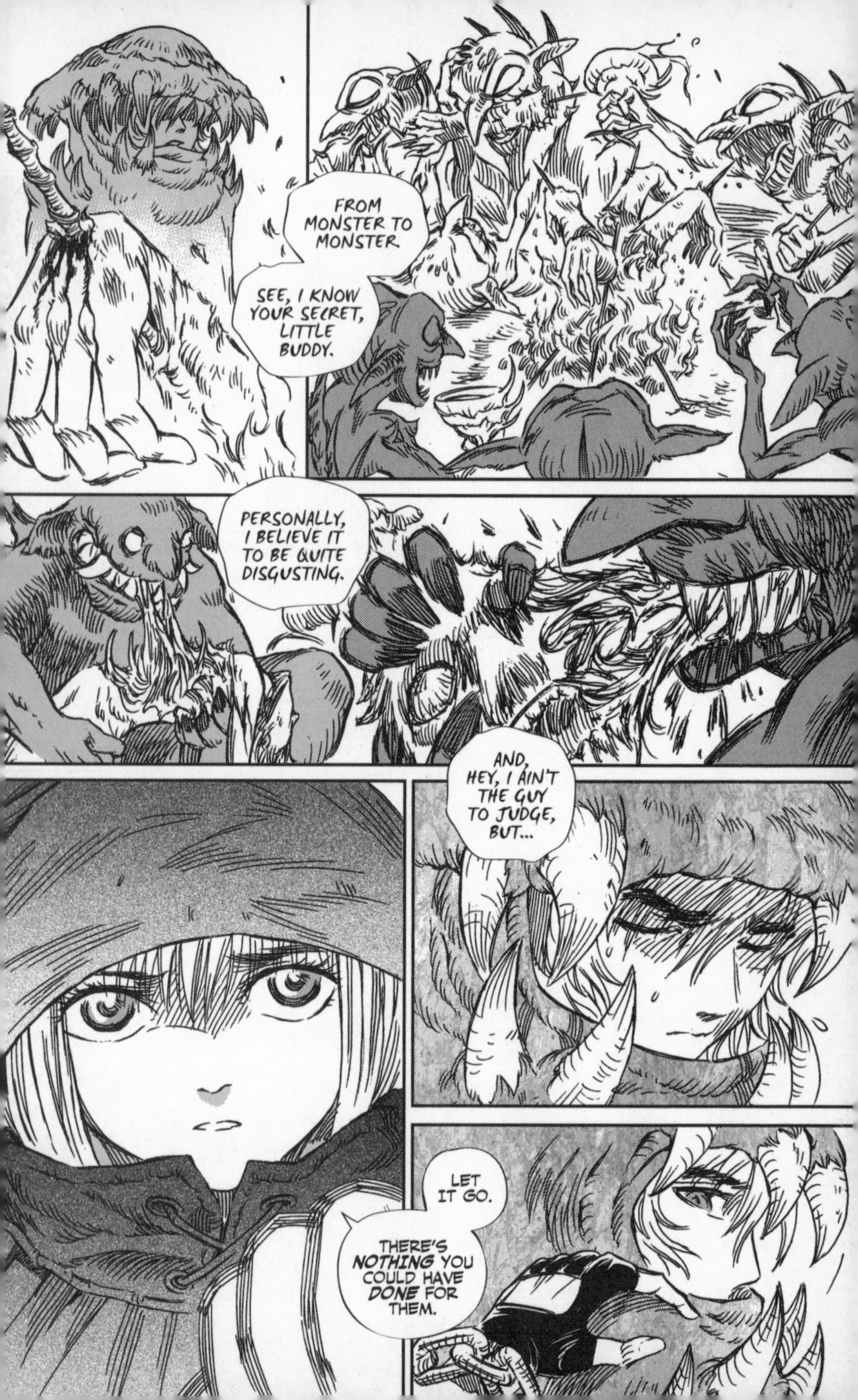
FROM MONSTER TO MONSTER.
SEE, I KNOW YOUR SECRET, LITTLE BUDDY.
PERSONALLY, I BELIEVE IT TO BE QUITE DISGUSTING.
AND, HEY, I AIN'T THE GUY TO JUDGE, BUT...
LET IT GO.
THERE'S *NOTHING* YOU COULD HAVE *DONE* FOR THEM.

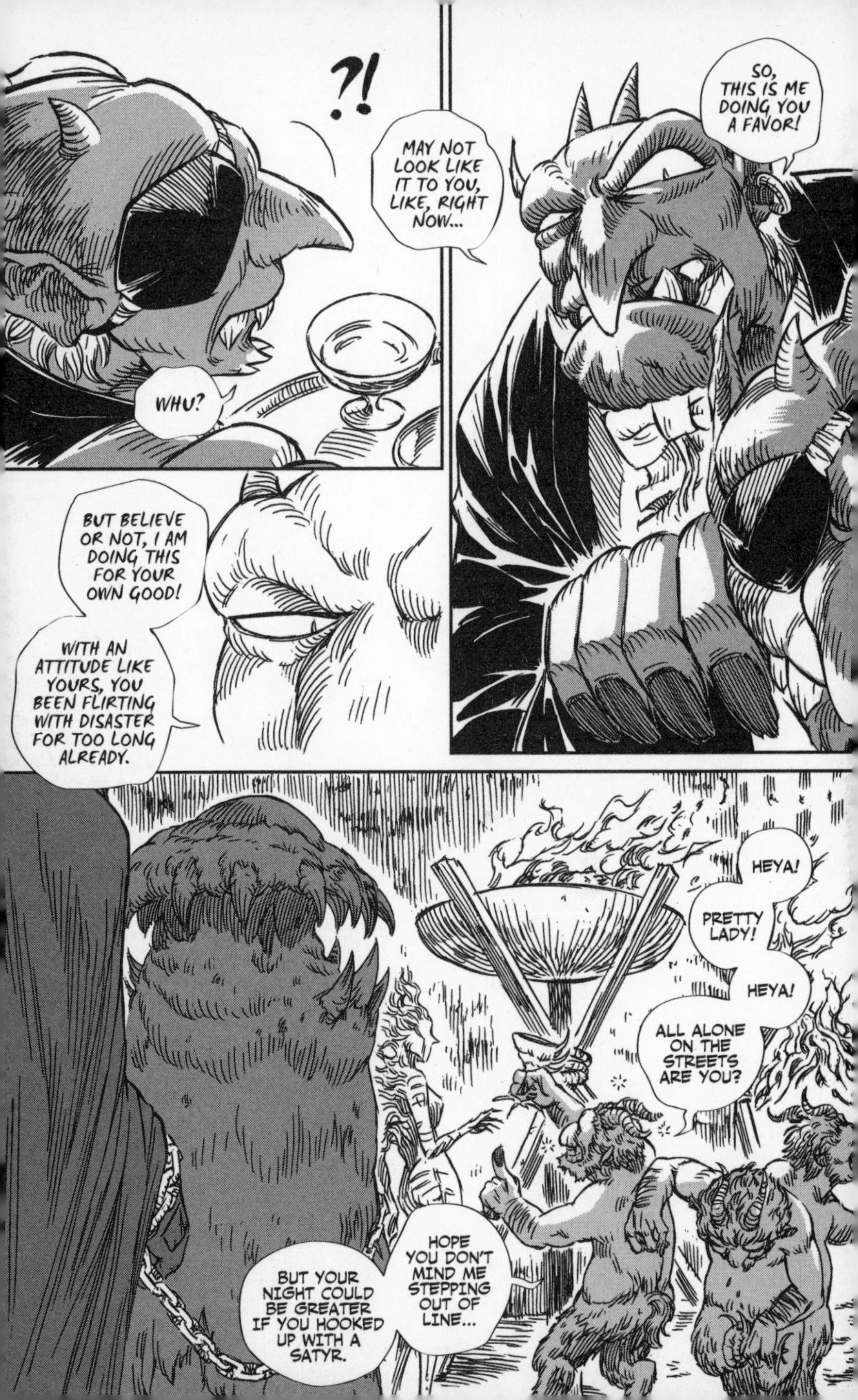
SO, THIS IS ME DOING YOU A FAVOR!
MAY NOT LOOK LIKE IT TO YOU, LIKE, RIGHT NOW...
?!
WHU?
BUT BELIEVE OR NOT, I AM DOING THIS FOR YOUR OWN GOOD!
WITH AN ATTITUDE LIKE YOURS, YOU BEEN FLIRTING WITH DISASTER FOR TOO LONG ALREADY.
HEYA!
PRETTY LADY!
HEYA!
ALL ALONE ON THE STREETS ARE YOU?
HOPE YOU DON'T MIND ME STEPPING OUT OF LINE...
BUT YOUR NIGHT COULD BE GREATER IF YOU HOOKED UP WITH A SATYR.

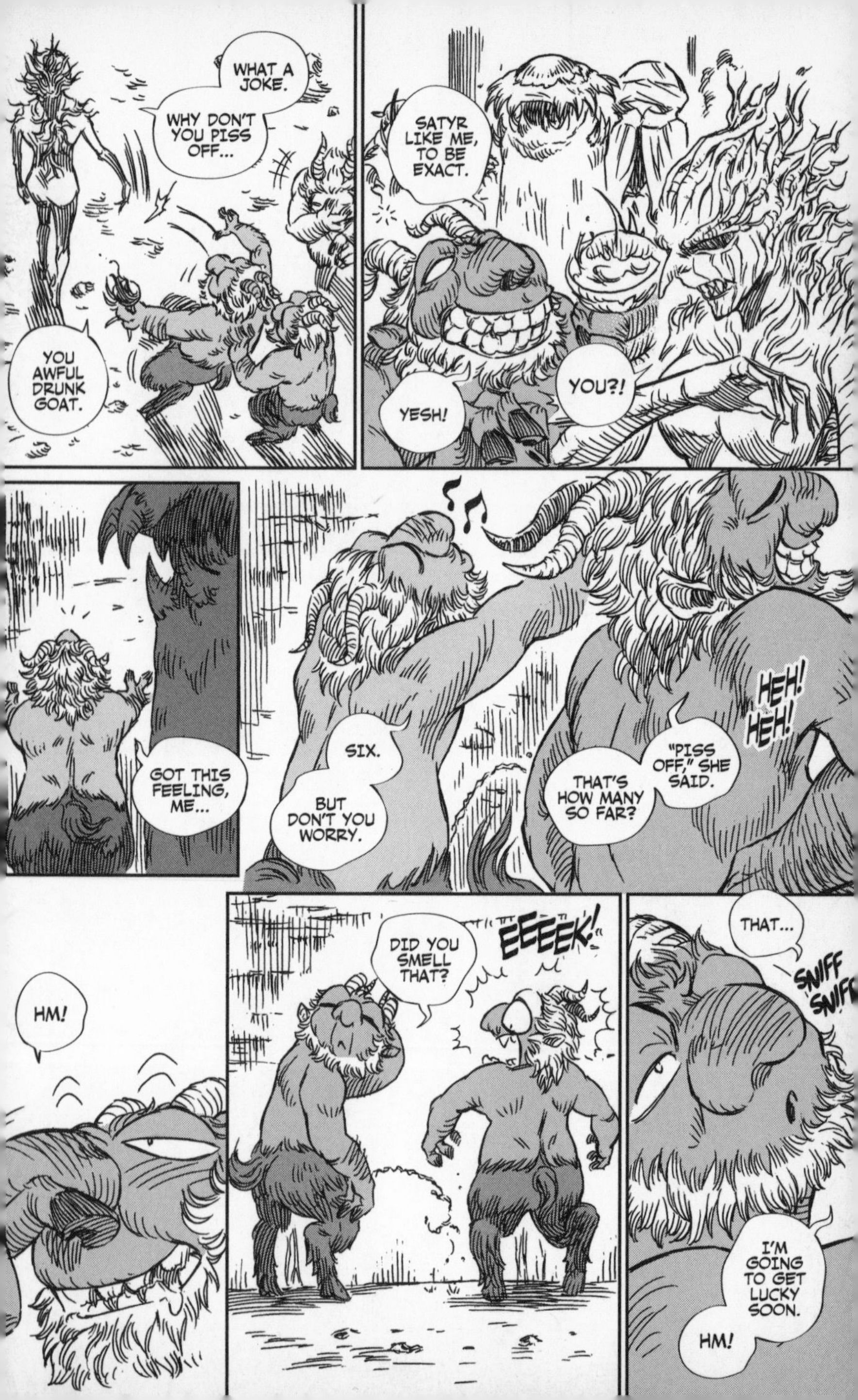

SATYR LIKE ME, TO BE EXACT.
YOU?!
YESH!
WHAT A JOKE.
WHY DON'T YOU PISS OFF...
YOU AWFUL DRUNK GOAT.
HEH! HEH!
"PISS OFF," SHE SAID.
THAT'S HOW MANY SO FAR?
SIX.
BUT DON'T YOU WORRY.
GOT THIS FEELING, ME...
THAT...
SNIFF SNIFF
I'M GOING TO GET LUCKY SOON.
HM!
EEEEK!
DID YOU SMELL THAT?
HM!

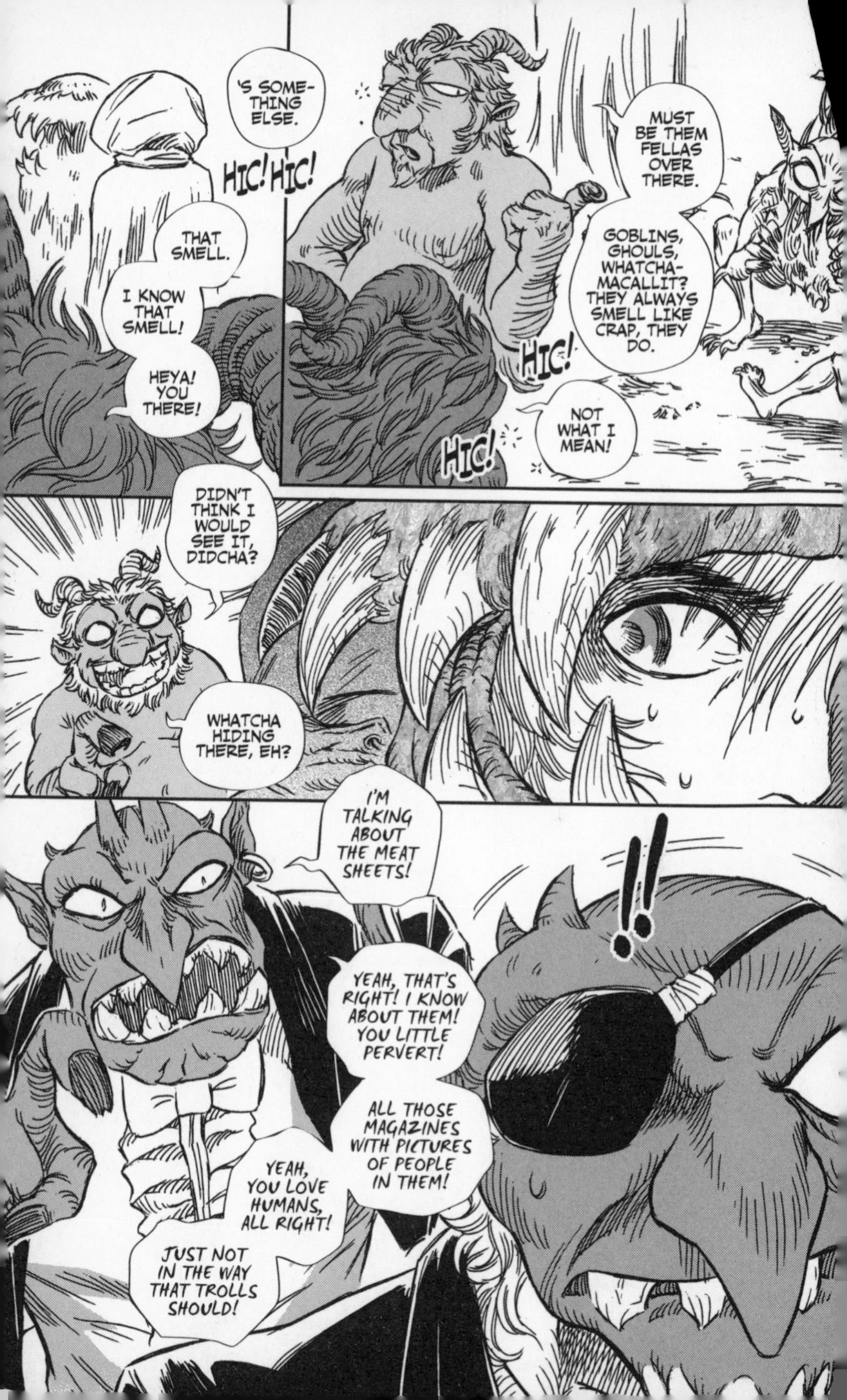
MUST BE THEM FELLAS OVER THERE.
GOBLINS, GHOULS, WHATCHA-MACALLIT? THEY ALWAYS SMELL LIKE CRAP, THEY DO.
HIC!
NOT WHAT I MEAN!
HIC!
'S SOME-THING ELSE.
HIC! HIC!
THAT SMELL.
I KNOW THAT SMELL!
HEYA! YOU THERE!
DIDN'T THINK I WOULD SEE IT, DIDCHA?
WHATCHA HIDING THERE, EH?
!!
I'M TALKING ABOUT THE MEAT SHEETS!
YEAH, THAT'S RIGHT! I KNOW ABOUT THEM! YOU LITTLE PERVERT!
ALL THOSE MAGAZINES WITH PICTURES OF PEOPLE IN THEM!
YEAH, YOU LOVE HUMANS, ALL RIGHT!
JUST NOT IN THE WAY THAT TROLLS SHOULD!

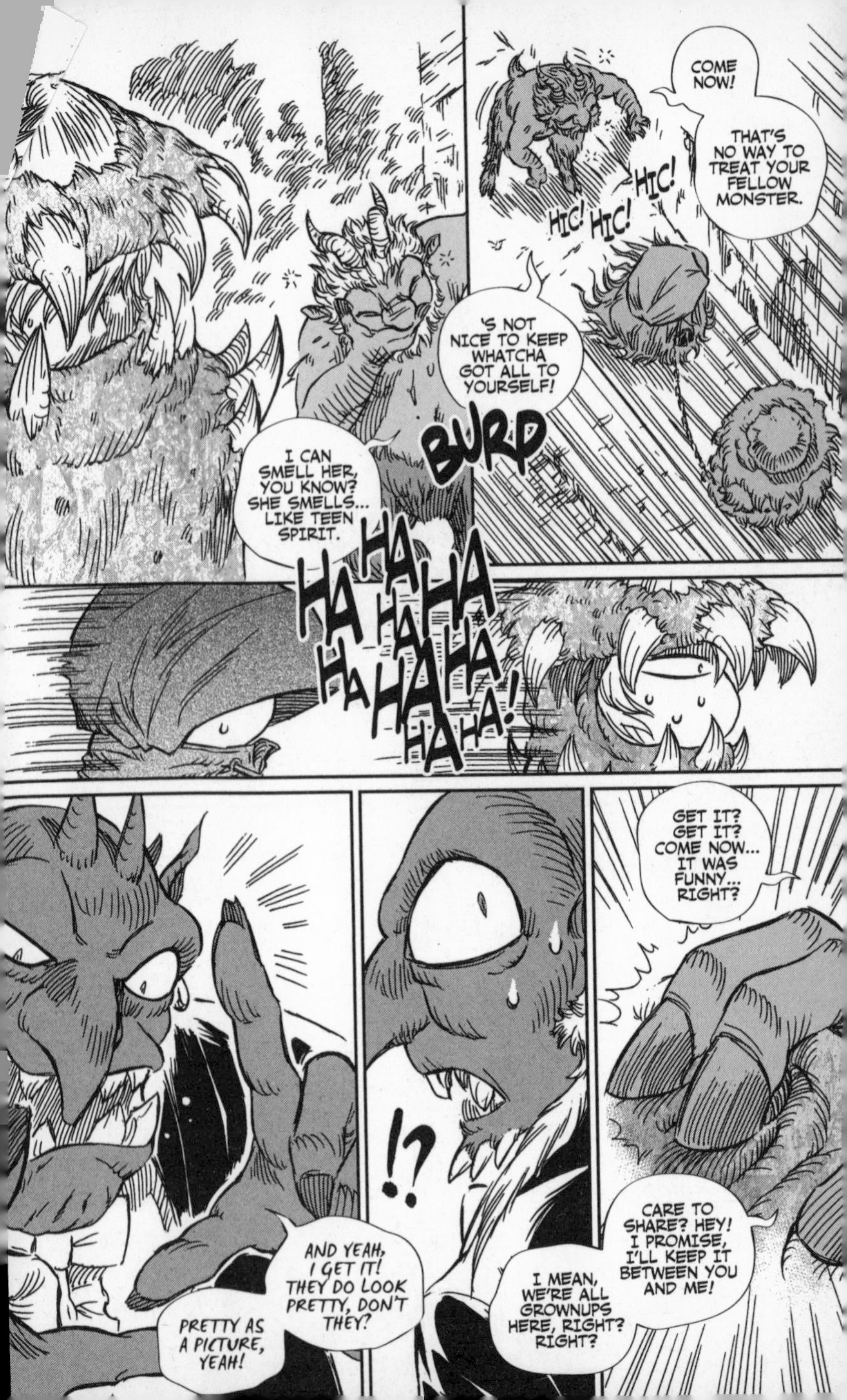
COME NOW!
THAT'S NO WAY TO TREAT YOUR FELLOW MONSTER.
HIC! HIC! HIC!
'S NOT NICE TO KEEP WHATCHA GOT ALL TO YOURSELF!
BURP
I CAN SMELL HER, YOU KNOW? SHE SMELLS... LIKE TEEN SPIRIT.
HA HA HA HA HA HA HA HA HA HA HA HA HA HA!
GET IT? GET IT? COME NOW... IT WAS FUNNY... RIGHT?
CARE TO SHARE? HEY! I PROMISE, I'LL KEEP IT BETWEEN YOU AND ME!
I MEAN, WE'RE ALL GROWNUPS HERE, RIGHT? RIGHT?
!?
AND YEAH, I GET IT! THEY DO LOOK PRETTY, DON'T THEY?
PRETTY AS A PICTURE, YEAH!

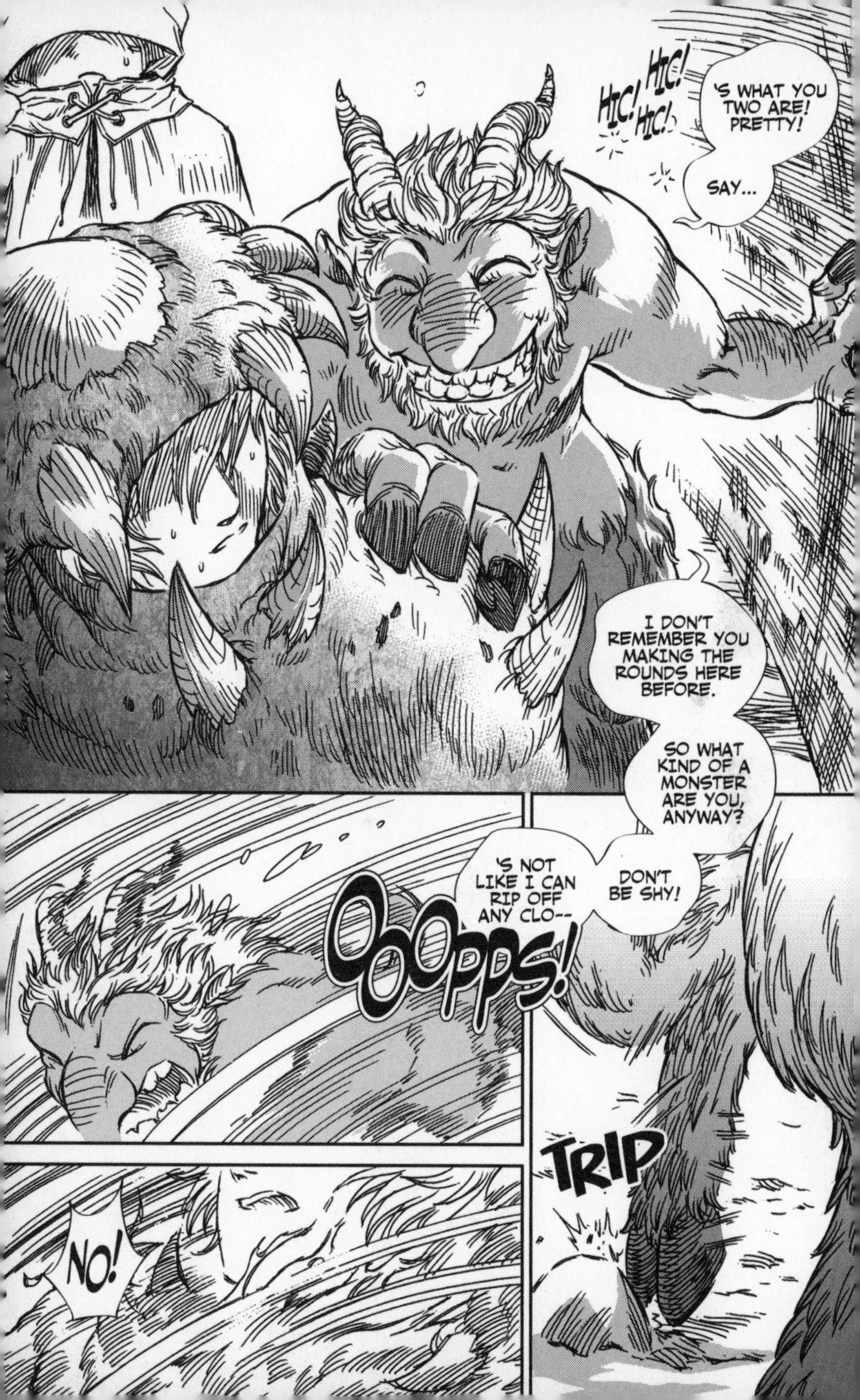
HIC! HIC! HIC! HIC!
'S WHAT YOU TWO ARE! PRETTY!
SAY...
I DON'T REMEMBER YOU MAKING THE ROUNDS HERE BEFORE.
SO WHAT KIND OF A MONSTER ARE YOU, ANYWAY?
DON'T BE SHY!
'S NOT LIKE I CAN RIP OFF ANY CLO--
OOOOPPS!
TRIP
NO!

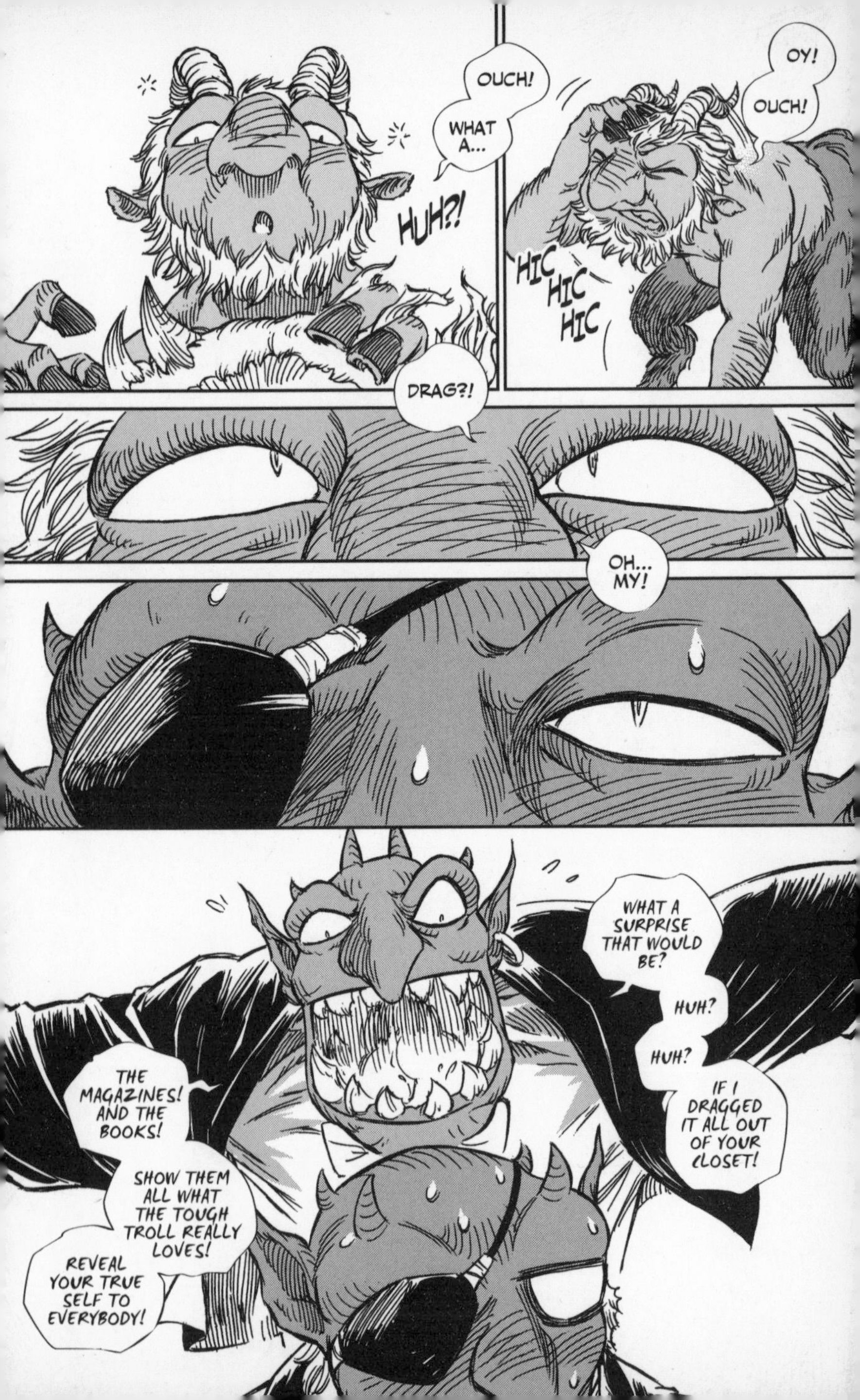
OY!
OUCH!
HIC HIC HIC
OUCH!
WHAT A...
HUH?!
DRAG?!
OH... MY!
WHAT A SURPRISE THAT WOULD BE?
HUH?
HUH?
IF I DRAGGED IT ALL OUT OF YOUR CLOSET!
THE MAGAZINES! AND THE BOOKS!
SHOW THEM ALL WHAT THE TOUGH TROLL REALLY LOVES!
REVEAL YOUR TRUE SELF TO EVERYBODY!

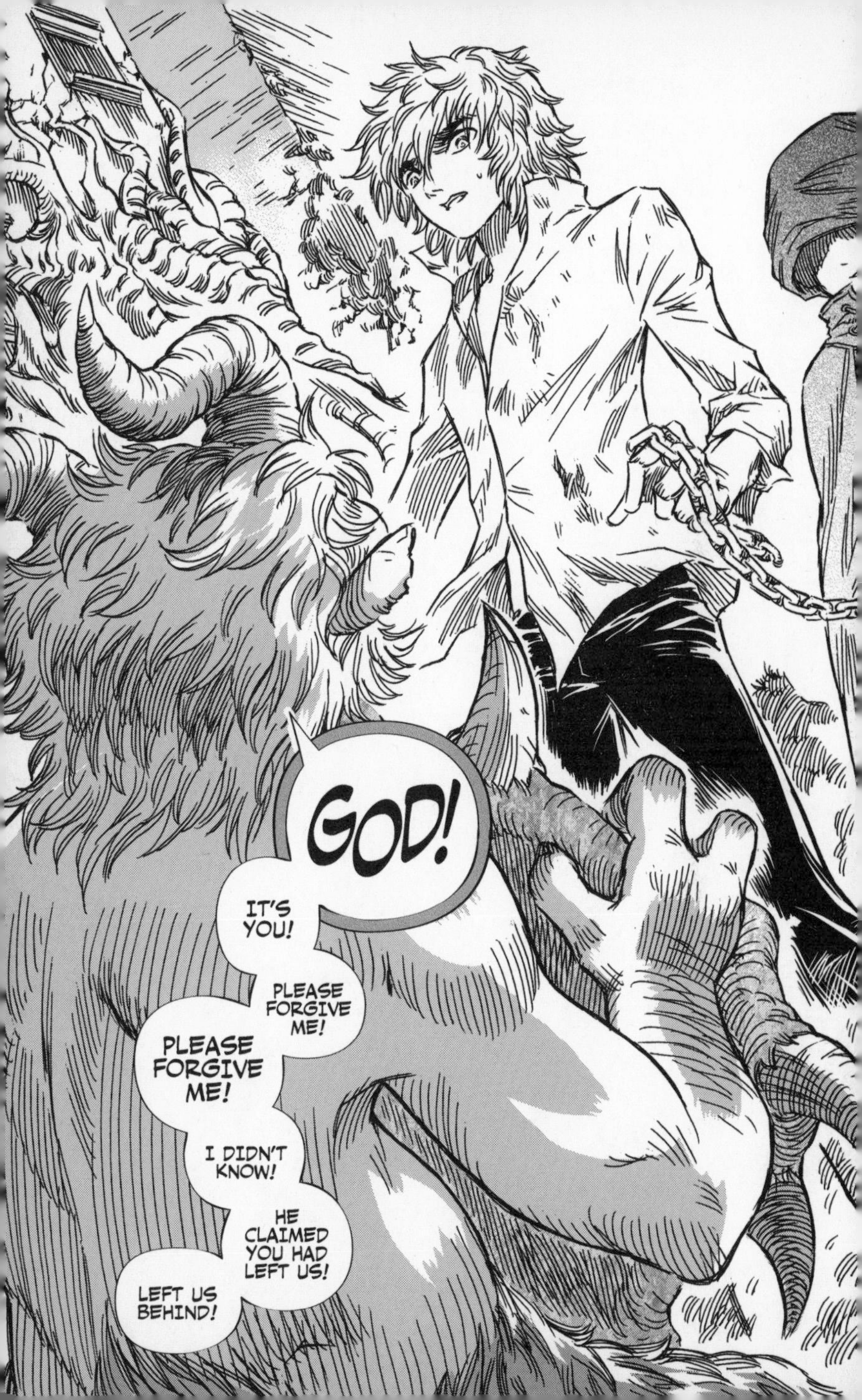
GOD!
IT'S YOU!
PLEASE FORGIVE ME!
PLEASE FORGIVE ME!
I DIDN'T KNOW!
HE CLAIMED YOU HAD LEFT US!
LEFT US BEHIND!

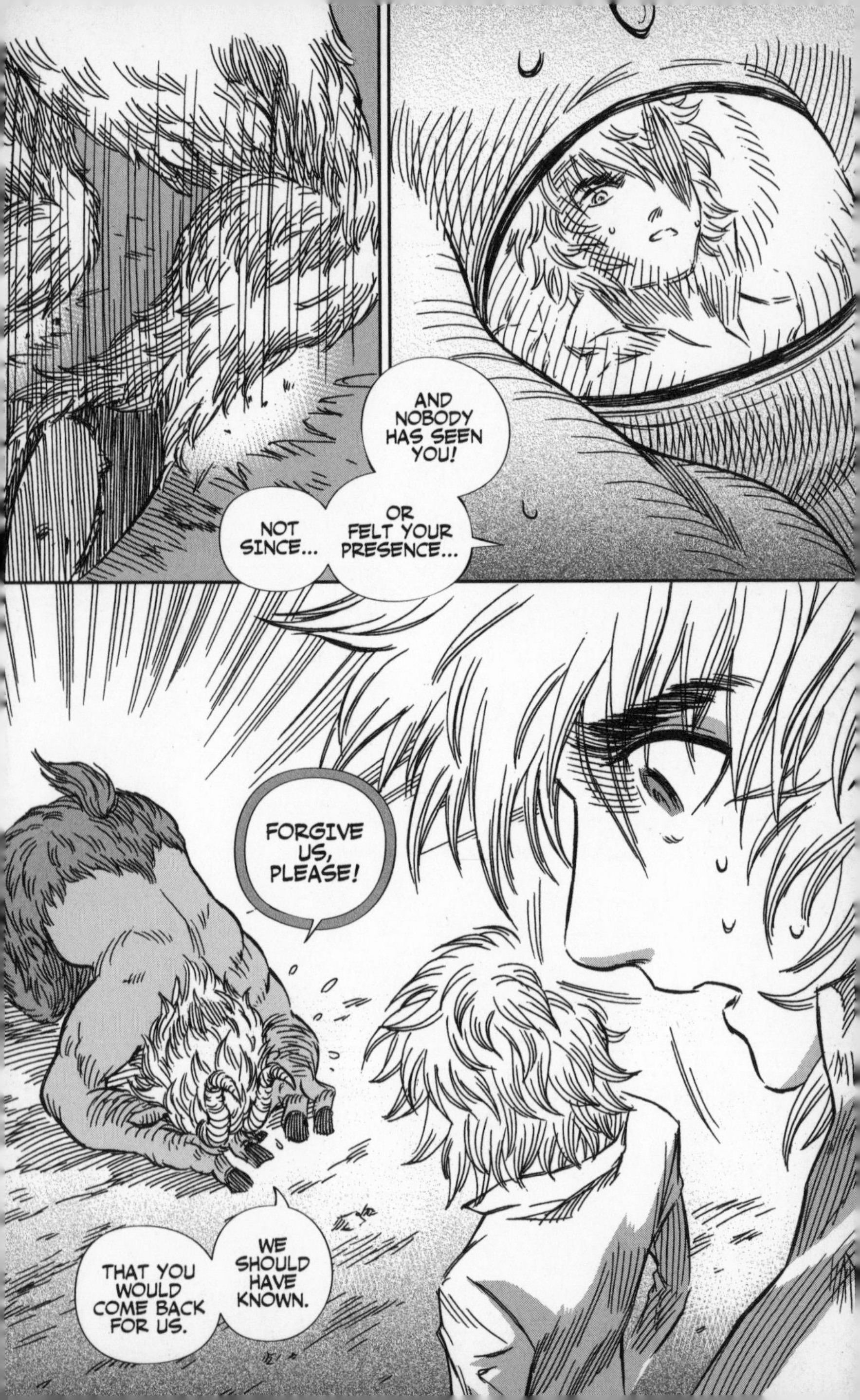
AND NOBODY HAS SEEN YOU!
OR FELT YOUR PRESENCE...
NOT SINCE...
FORGIVE US, PLEASE!
WE SHOULD HAVE KNOWN.
THAT YOU WOULD COME BACK FOR US.

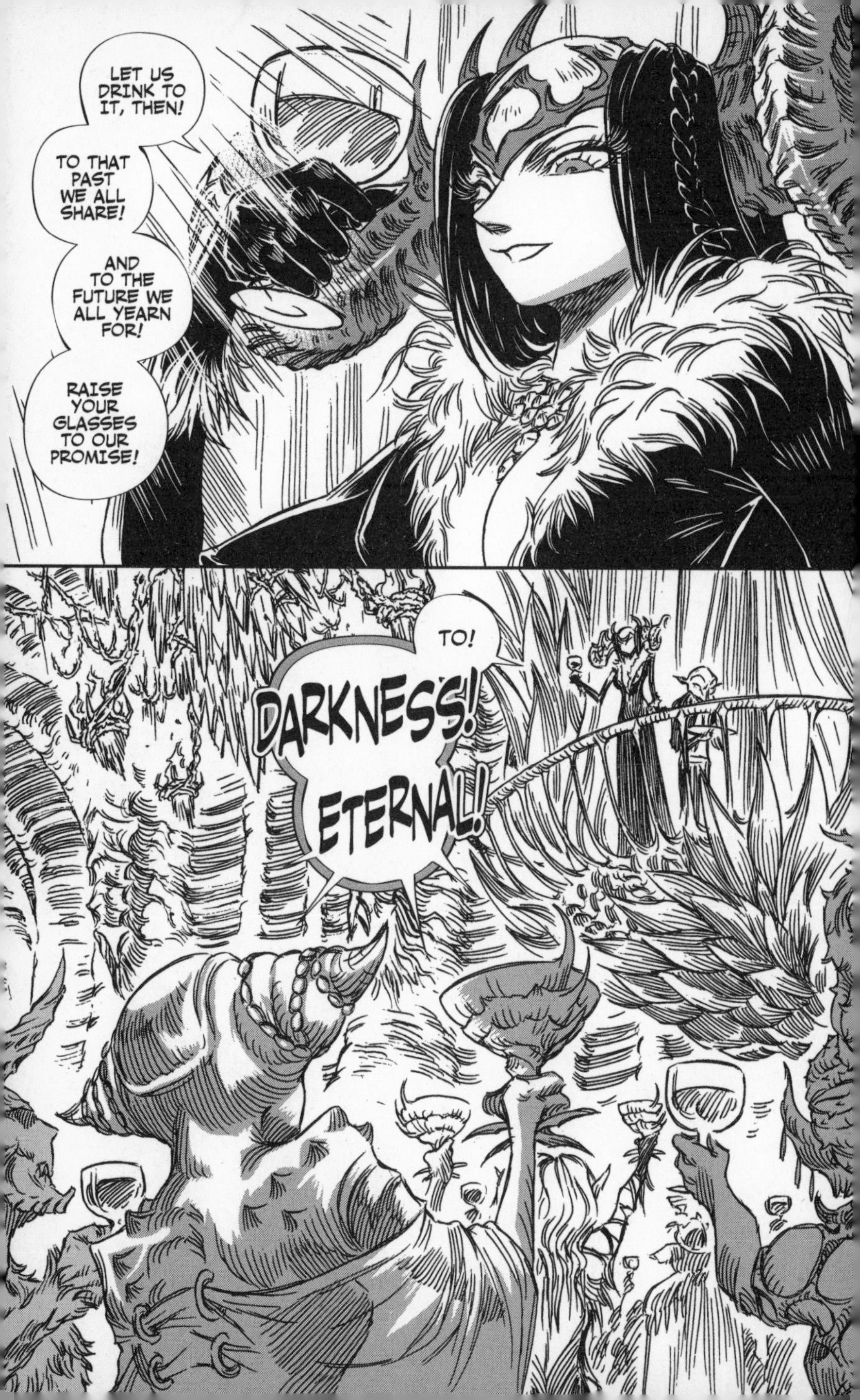
LET US DRINK TO IT, THEN!
TO THAT PAST WE ALL SHARE!
AND TO THE FUTURE WE ALL YEARN FOR!
RAISE YOUR GLASSES TO OUR PROMISE!
TO!
DARKNESS! ETERNAL!

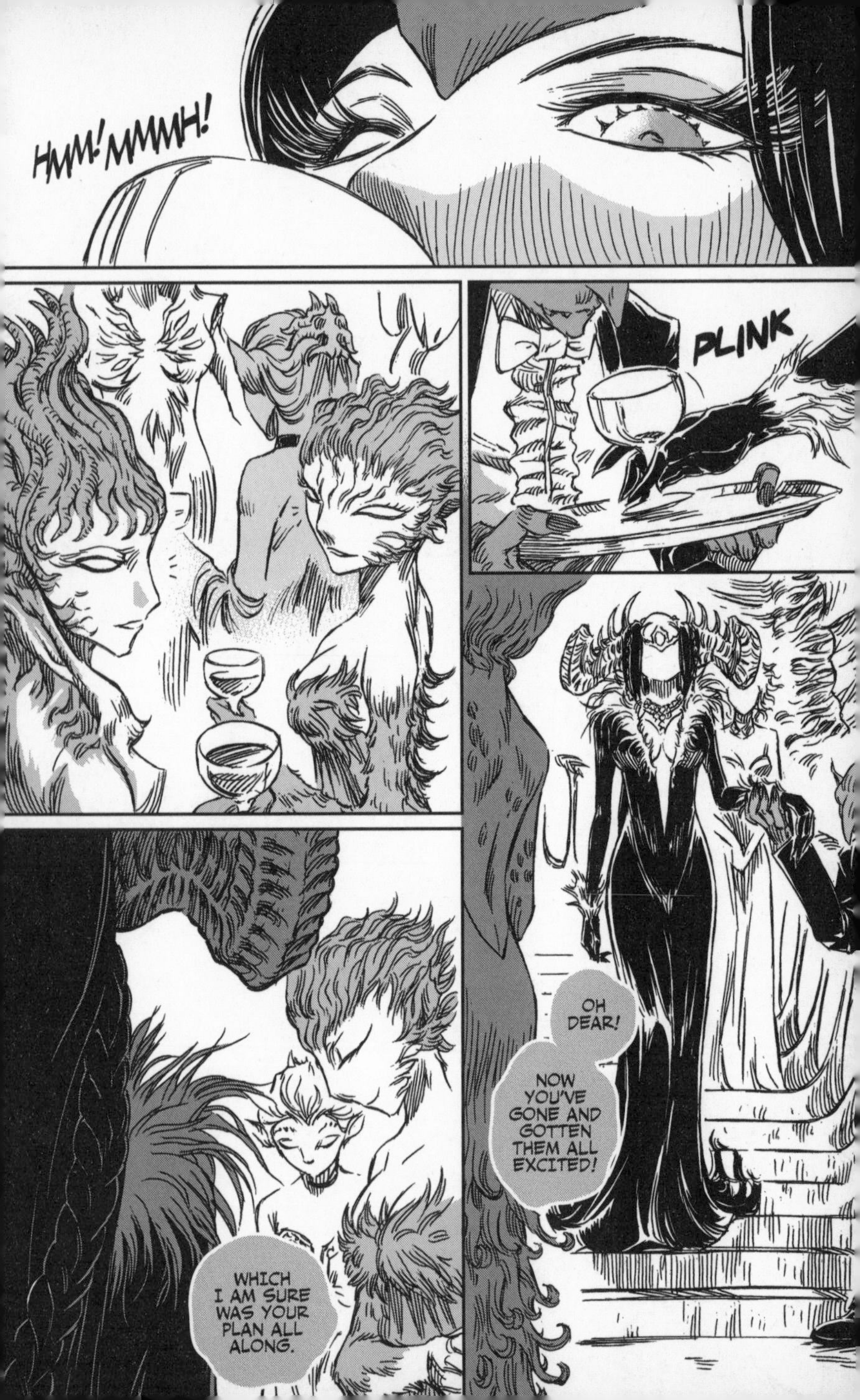
HMM!MMMH!
PLINK
OH DEAR!
NOW YOU'VE GONE AND GOTTEN THEM ALL EXCITED!
WHICH I AM SURE WAS YOUR PLAN ALL ALONG.

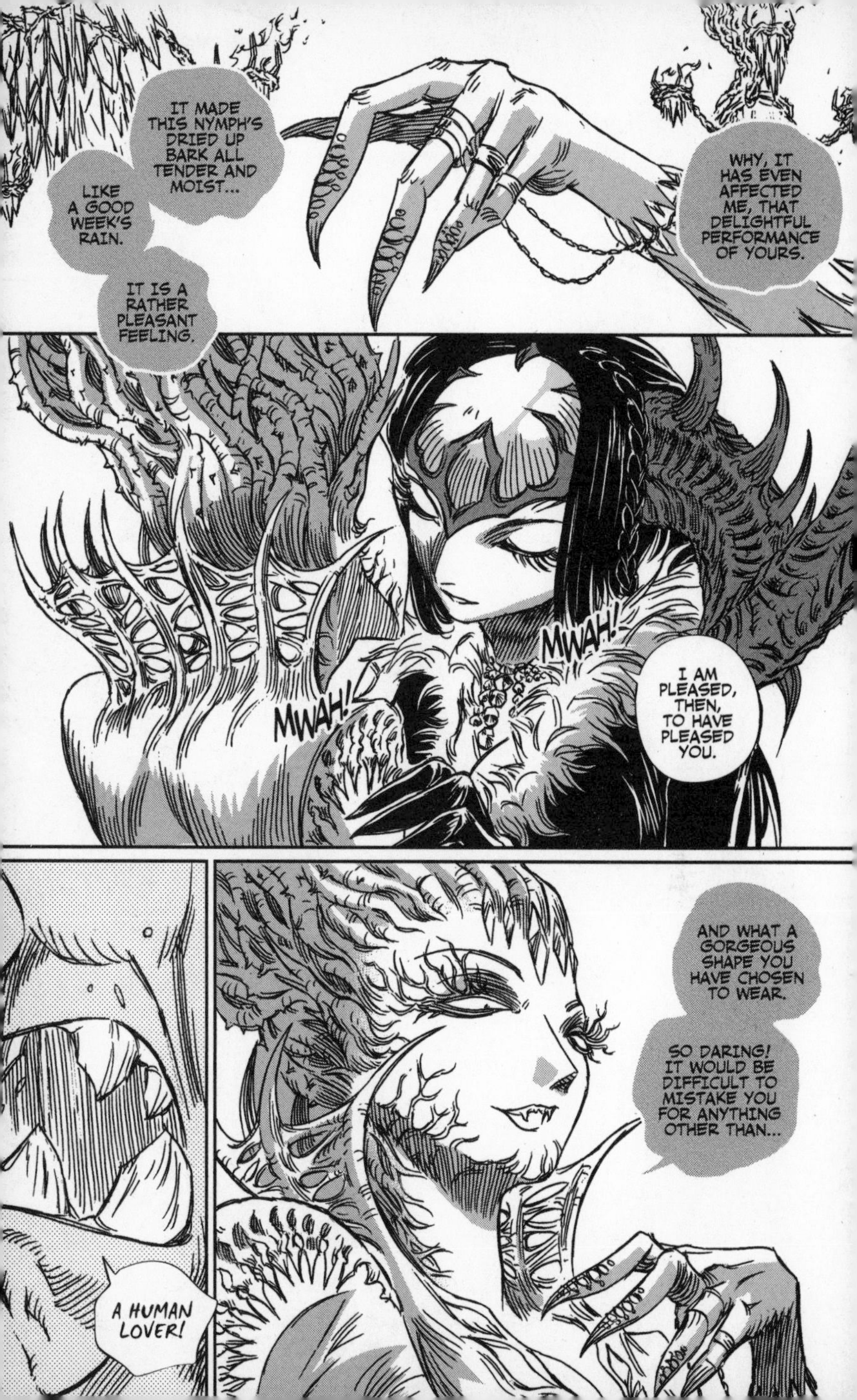
WHY, IT HAS EVEN AFFECTED ME, THAT DELIGHTFUL PERFORMANCE OF YOURS.
IT MADE THIS NYMPH'S DRIED UP BARK ALL TENDER AND MOIST...
LIKE A GOOD WEEK'S RAIN.
IT IS A RATHER PLEASANT FEELING.
MWAH!
MWAH!
I AM PLEASED, THEN, TO HAVE PLEASED YOU.
AND WHAT A GORGEOUS SHAPE YOU HAVE CHOSEN TO WEAR.
SO DARING! IT WOULD BE DIFFICULT TO MISTAKE YOU FOR ANYTHING OTHER THAN...
A HUMAN LOVER!

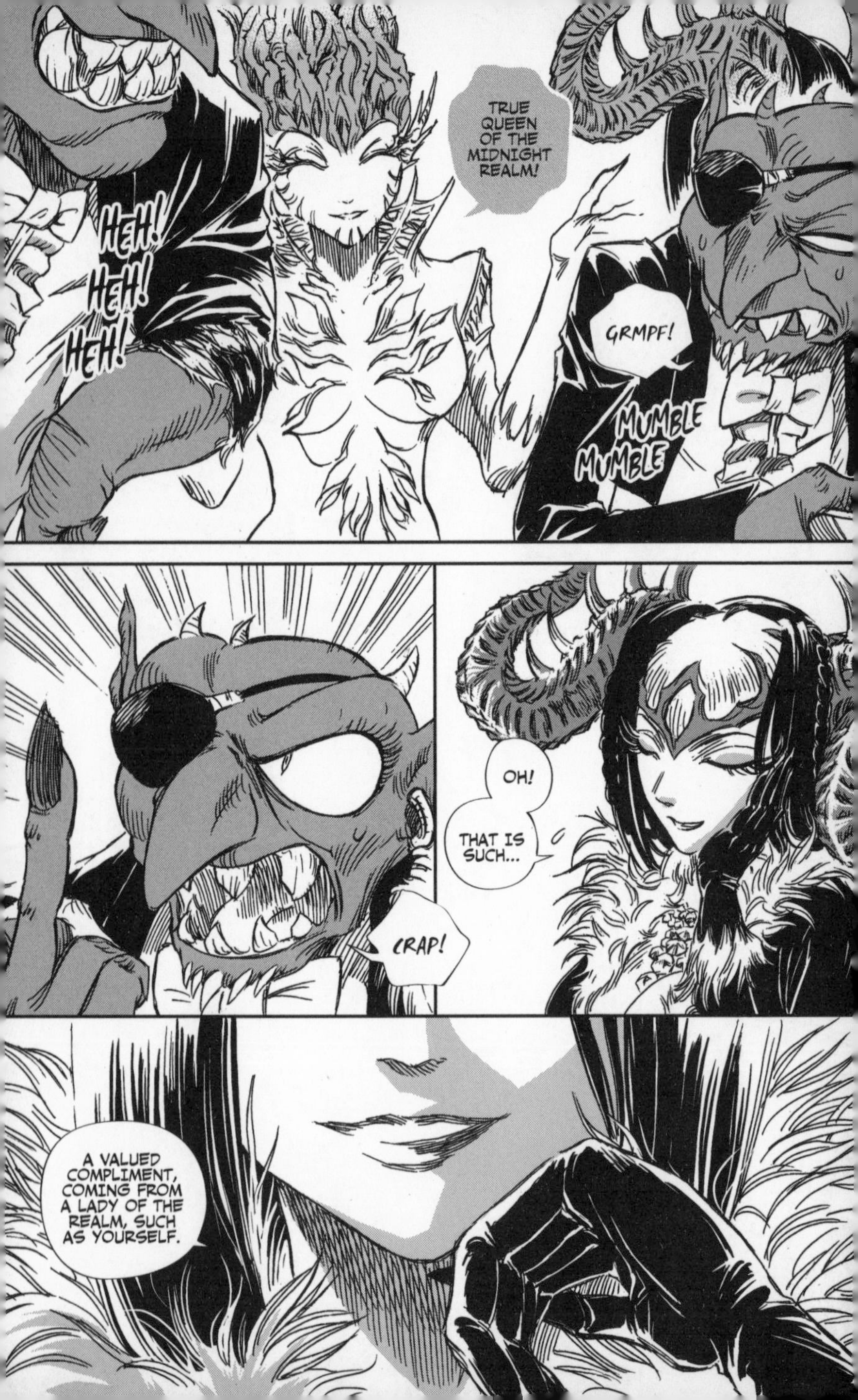
TRUE QUEEN OF THE MIDNIGHT REALM!
HEH! HEH! HEH!
GRMPF!
MUMBLE MUMBLE
OH!
THAT IS SUCH...
CRAP!
A VALUED COMPLIMENT, COMING FROM A LADY OF THE REALM, SUCH AS YOURSELF.

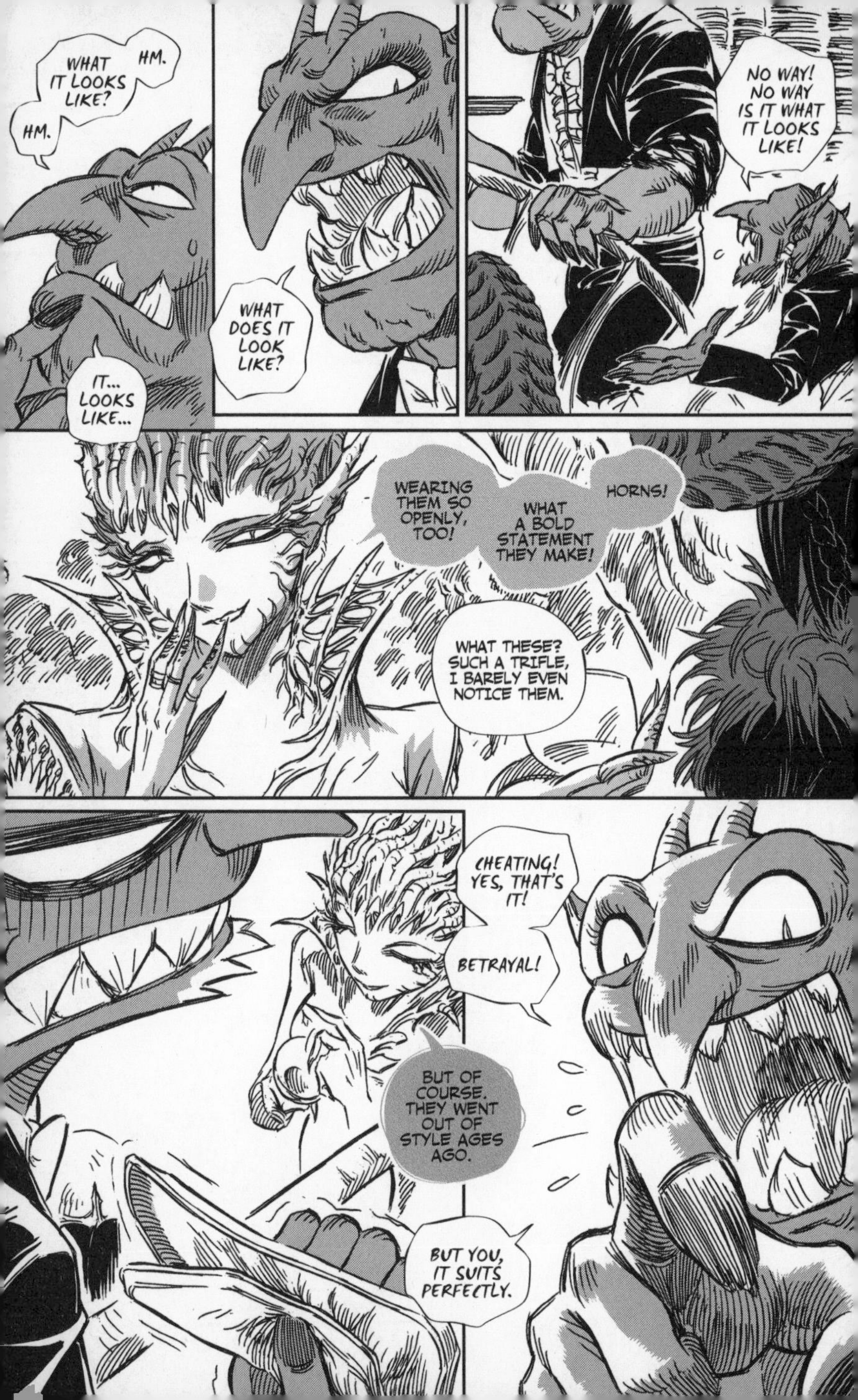
NO WAY! NO WAY IS IT WHAT IT LOOKS LIKE!
WHAT DOES IT LOOK LIKE?
HM.
WHAT IT LOOKS LIKE?
HM.
IT... LOOKS LIKE...
HORNS!
WHAT A BOLD STATEMENT THEY MAKE!
WEARING THEM SO OPENLY, TOO!
WHAT THESE? SUCH A TRIFLE, I BARELY EVEN NOTICE THEM.
CHEATING! YES, THAT'S IT!
BETRAYAL!
BUT OF COURSE. THEY WENT OUT OF STYLE AGES AGO.
BUT YOU, IT SUITS PERFECTLY.

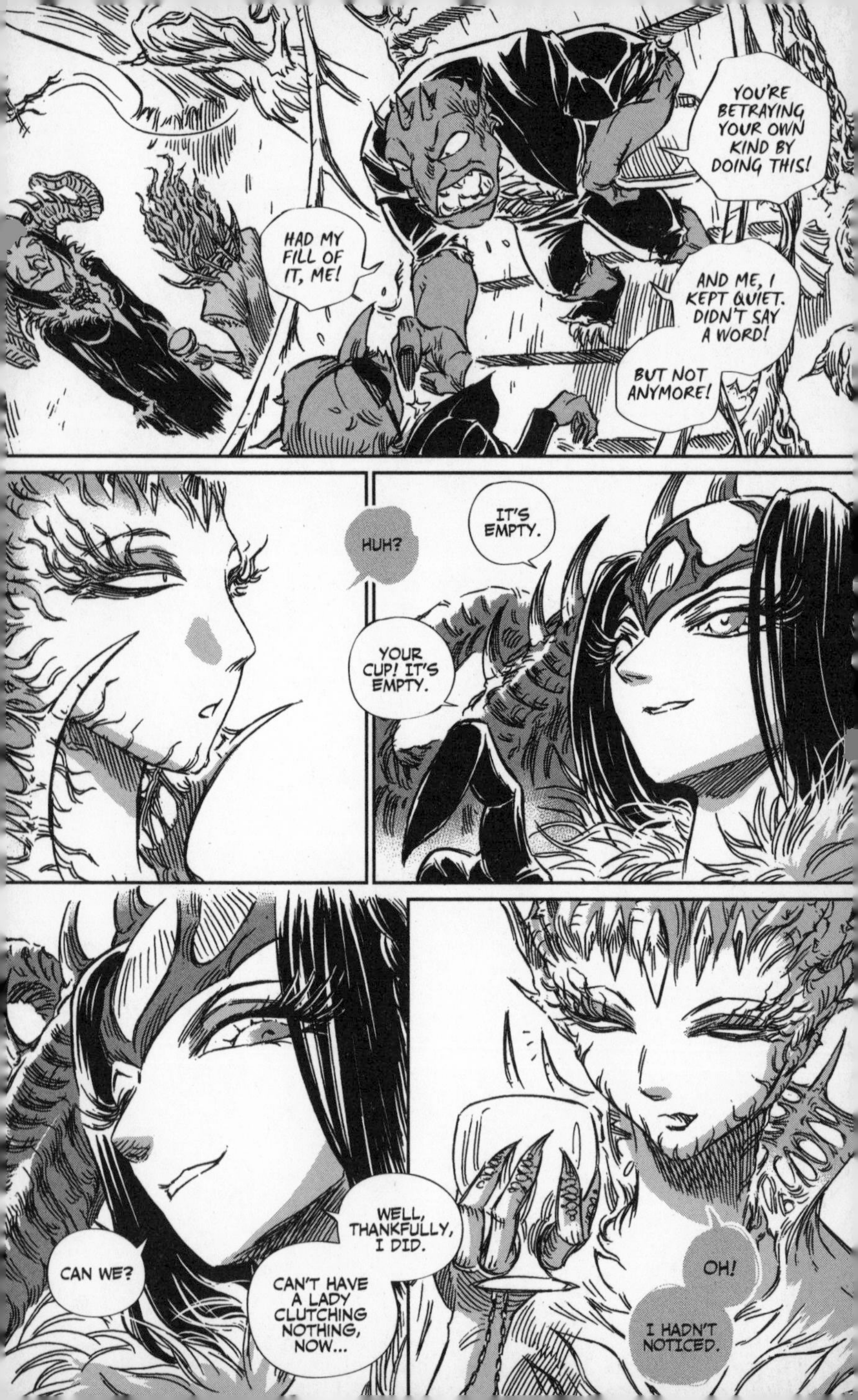
YOU'RE BETRAYING YOUR OWN KIND BY DOING THIS!
HAD MY FILL OF IT, ME!
AND ME, I KEPT QUIET. DIDN'T SAY A WORD!
BUT NOT ANYMORE!
IT'S EMPTY.
HUH?
YOUR CUP! IT'S EMPTY.
OH!
I HADN'T NOTICED.
WELL, THANKFULLY, I DID.
CAN'T HAVE A LADY CLUTCHING NOTHING, NOW...
CAN WE?

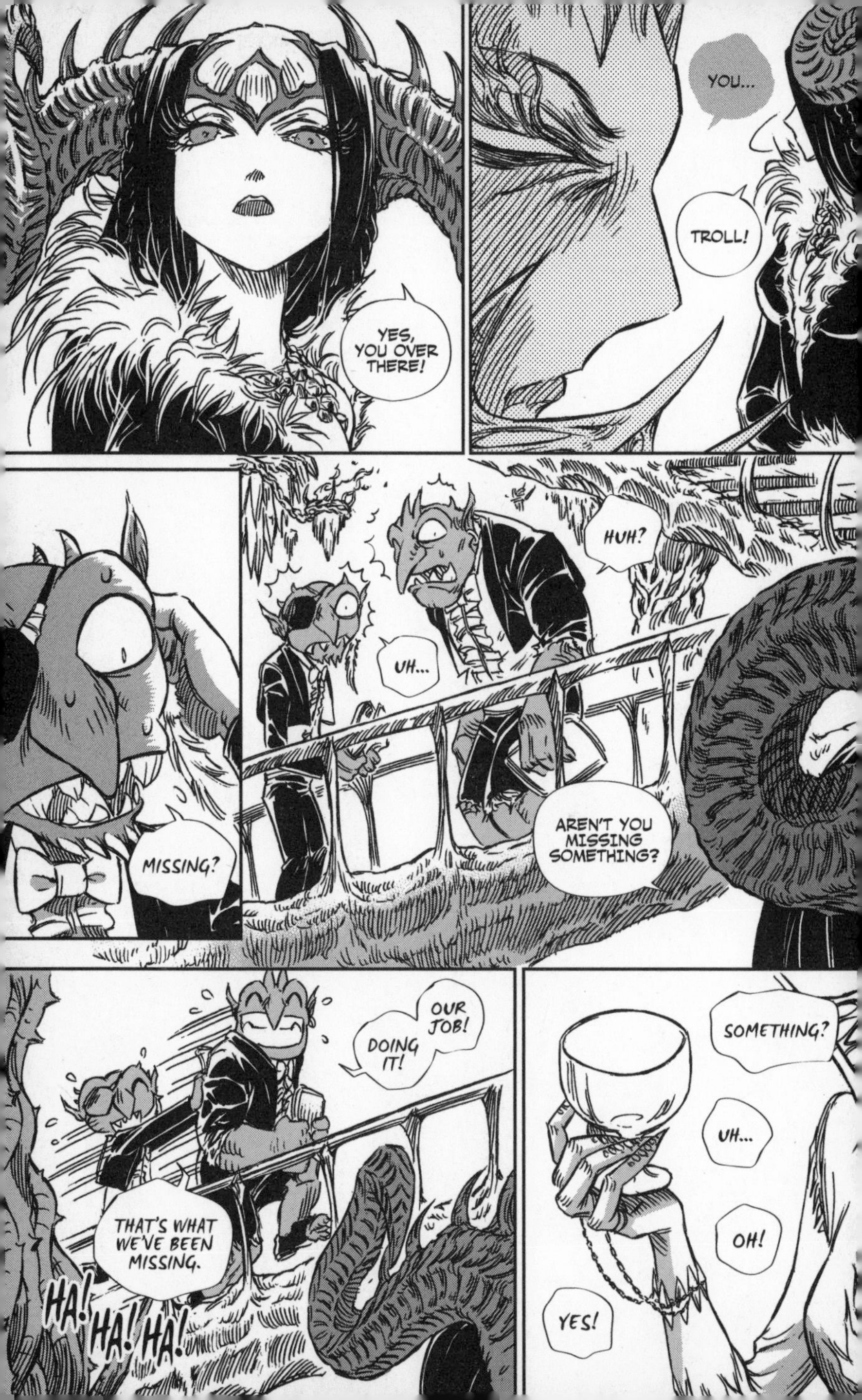
YOU...
TROLL!
YES, YOU OVER THERE!
HUH?
AREN'T YOU MISSING SOMETHING?
UH...
MISSING?
SOMETHING?
UH...
OH!
YES!
OUR JOB!
DOING IT!
THAT'S WHAT WE'VE BEEN MISSING.
HA! HA! HA!

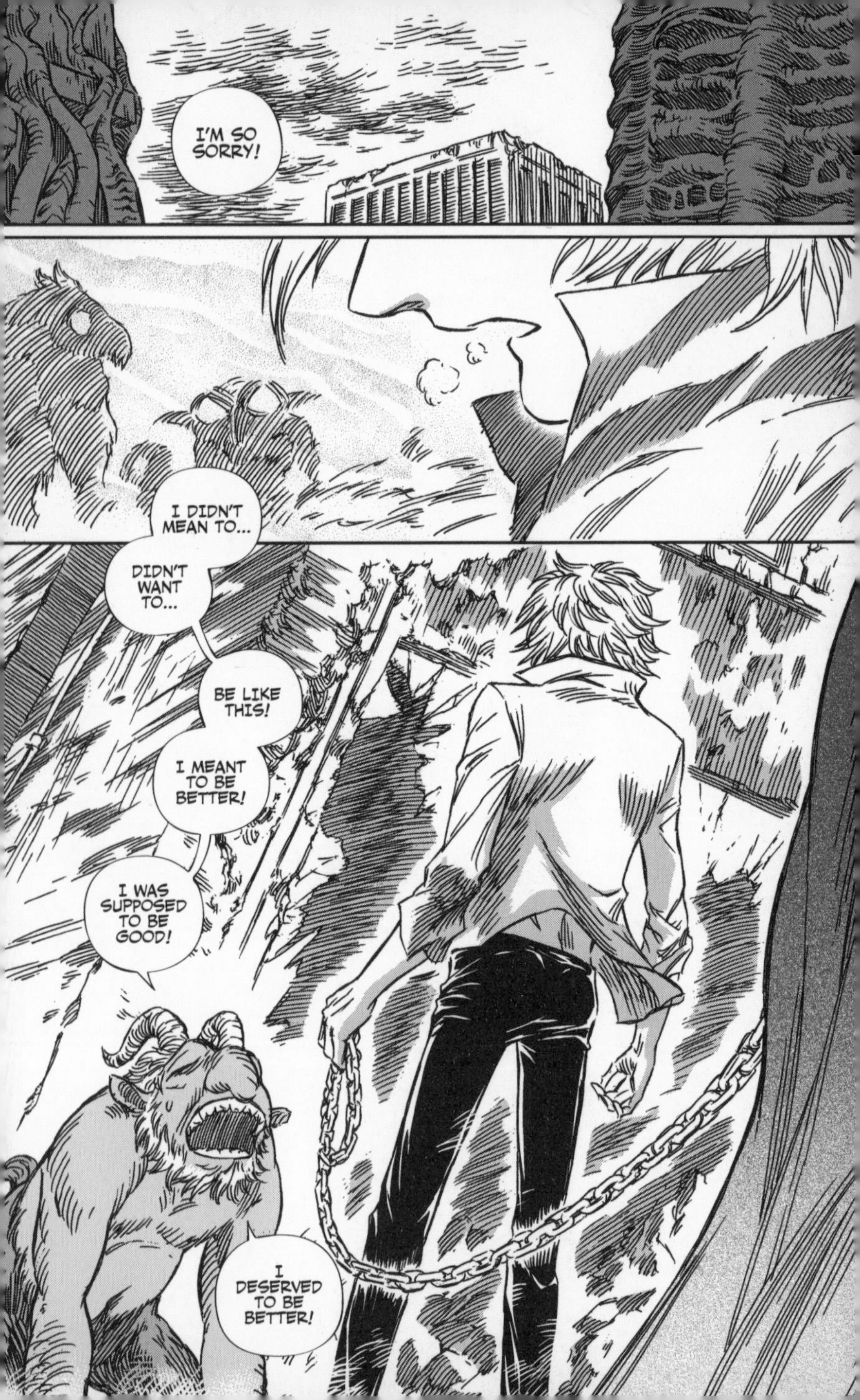
I'M SO SORRY!
I DIDN'T MEAN TO...
DIDN'T WANT TO...
BE LIKE THIS!
I MEANT TO BE BETTER!
I WAS SUPPOSED TO BE GOOD!
I DESERVED TO BE BETTER!

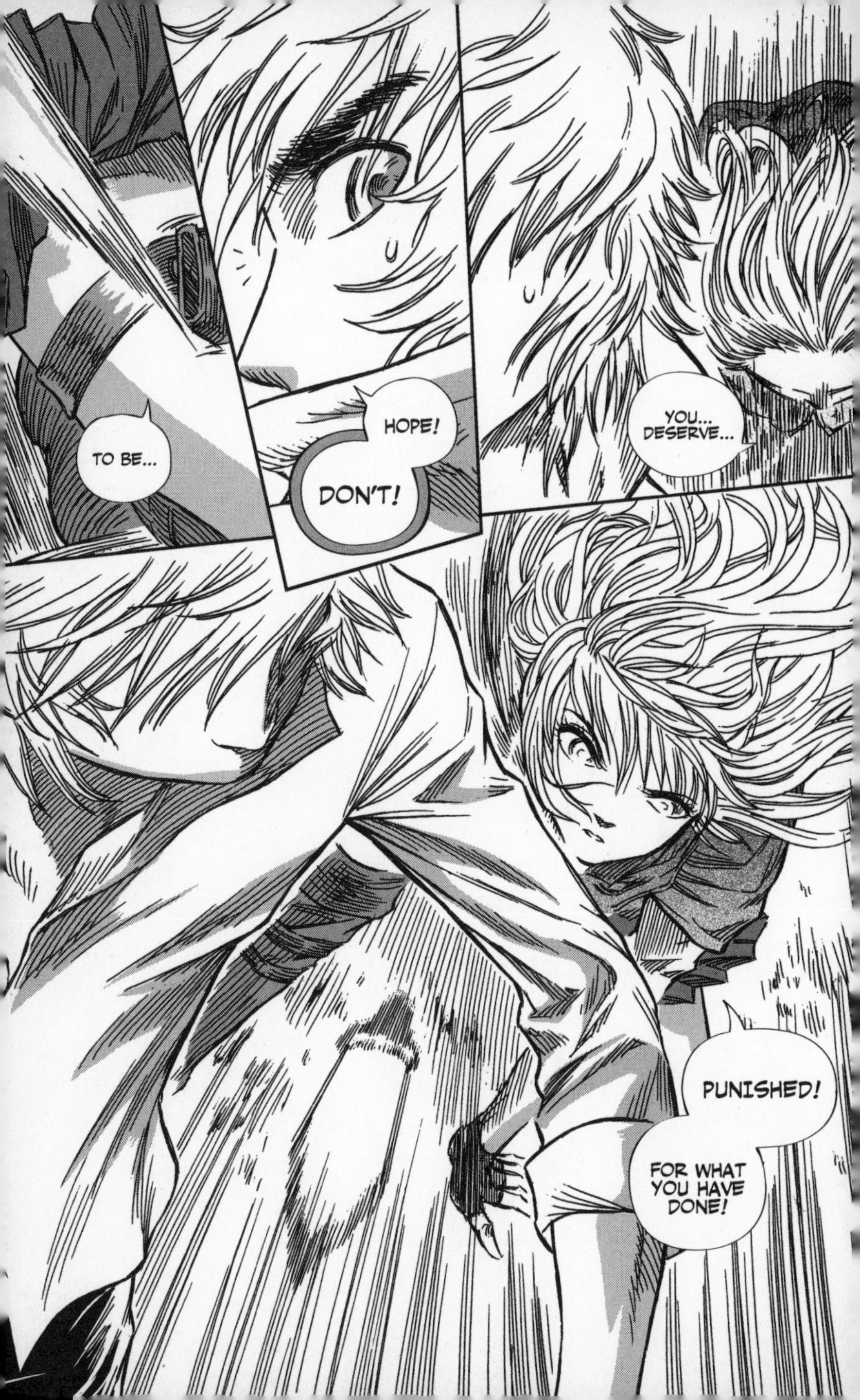
YOU... DESERVE...
HOPE!
DON'T!
TO BE...
PUNISHED!
FOR WHAT YOU HAVE DONE!

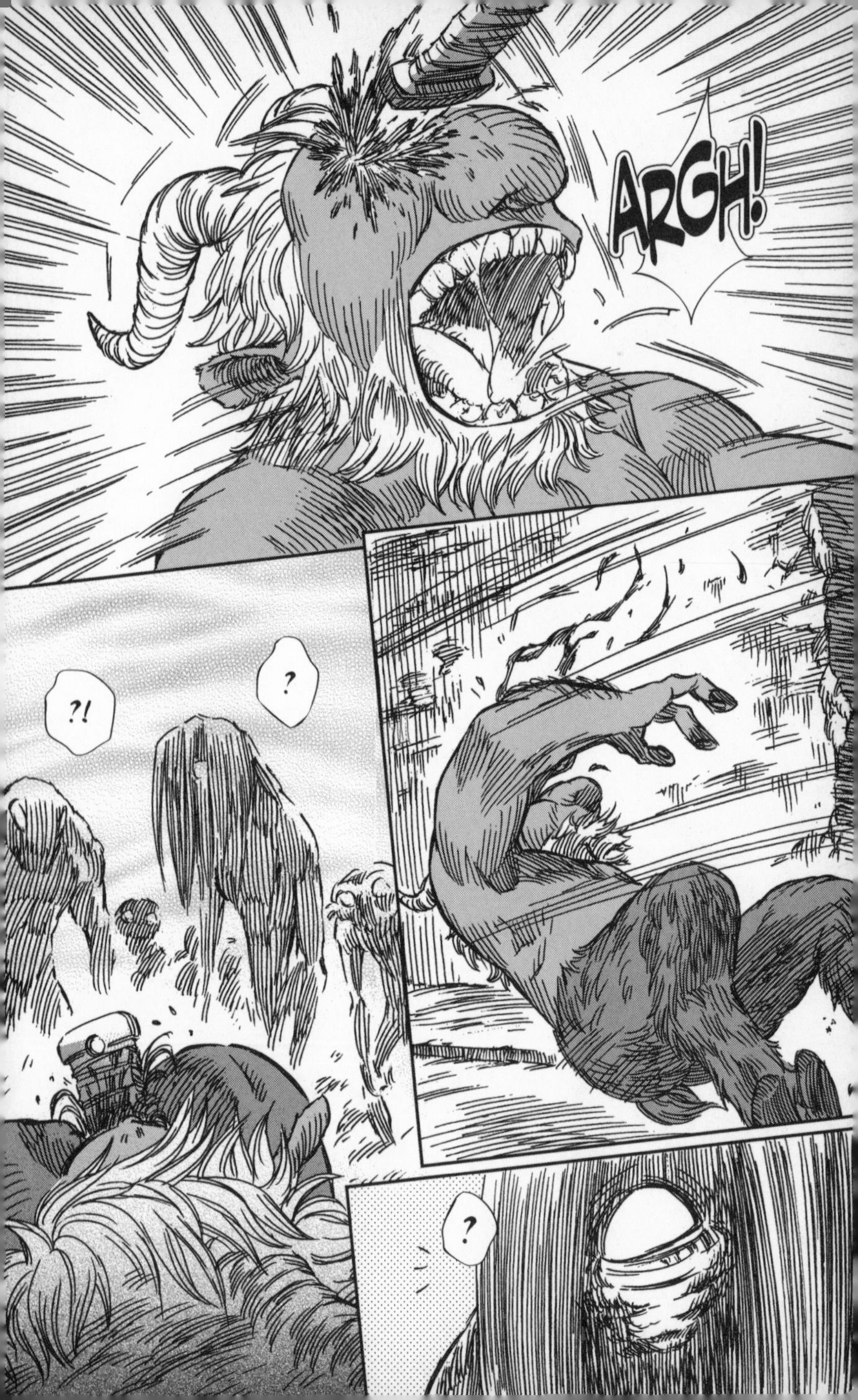
ARGH!
?
?!
?

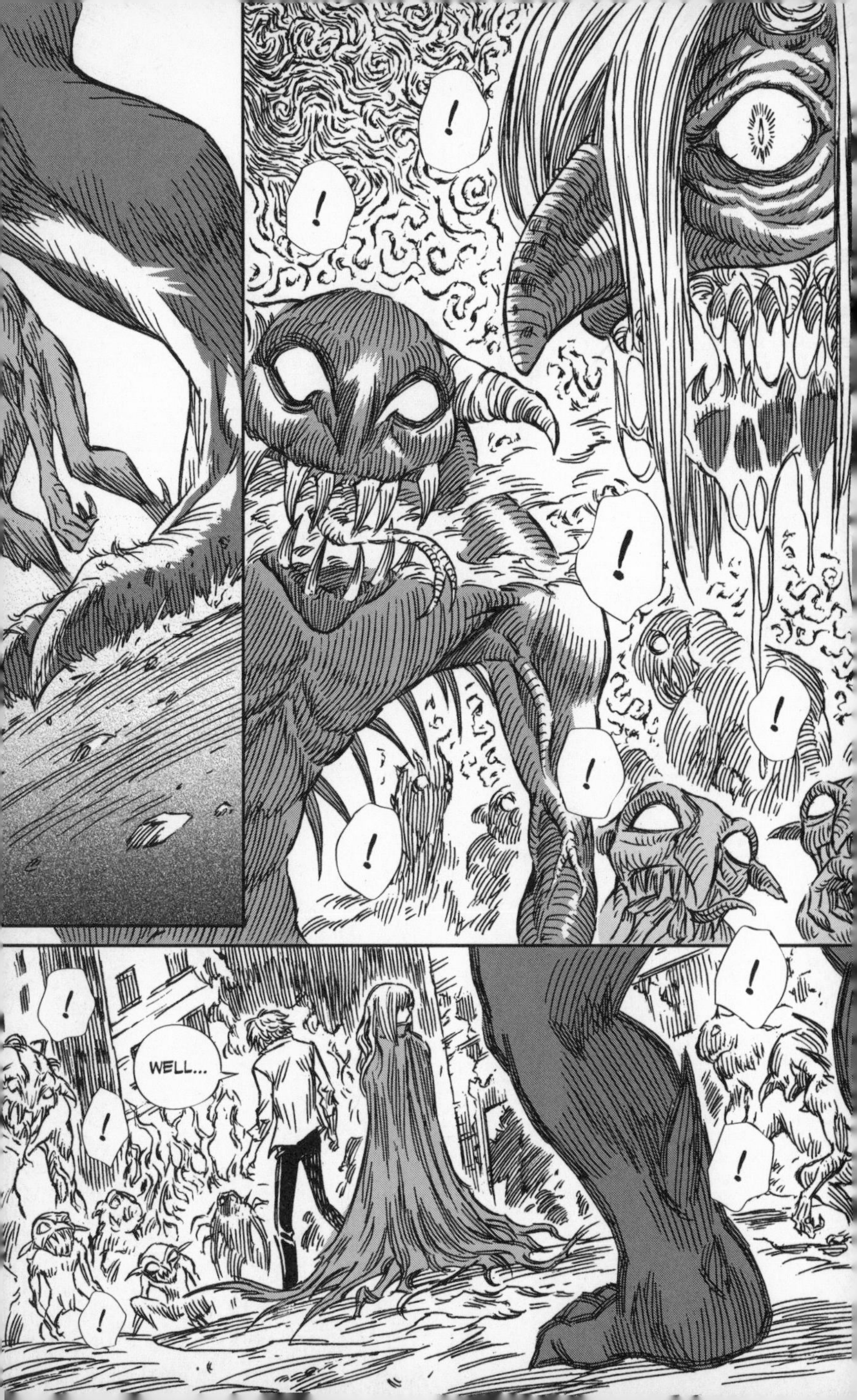
!
!
!
!
!
!
!
!
!
WELL...
!
!
!

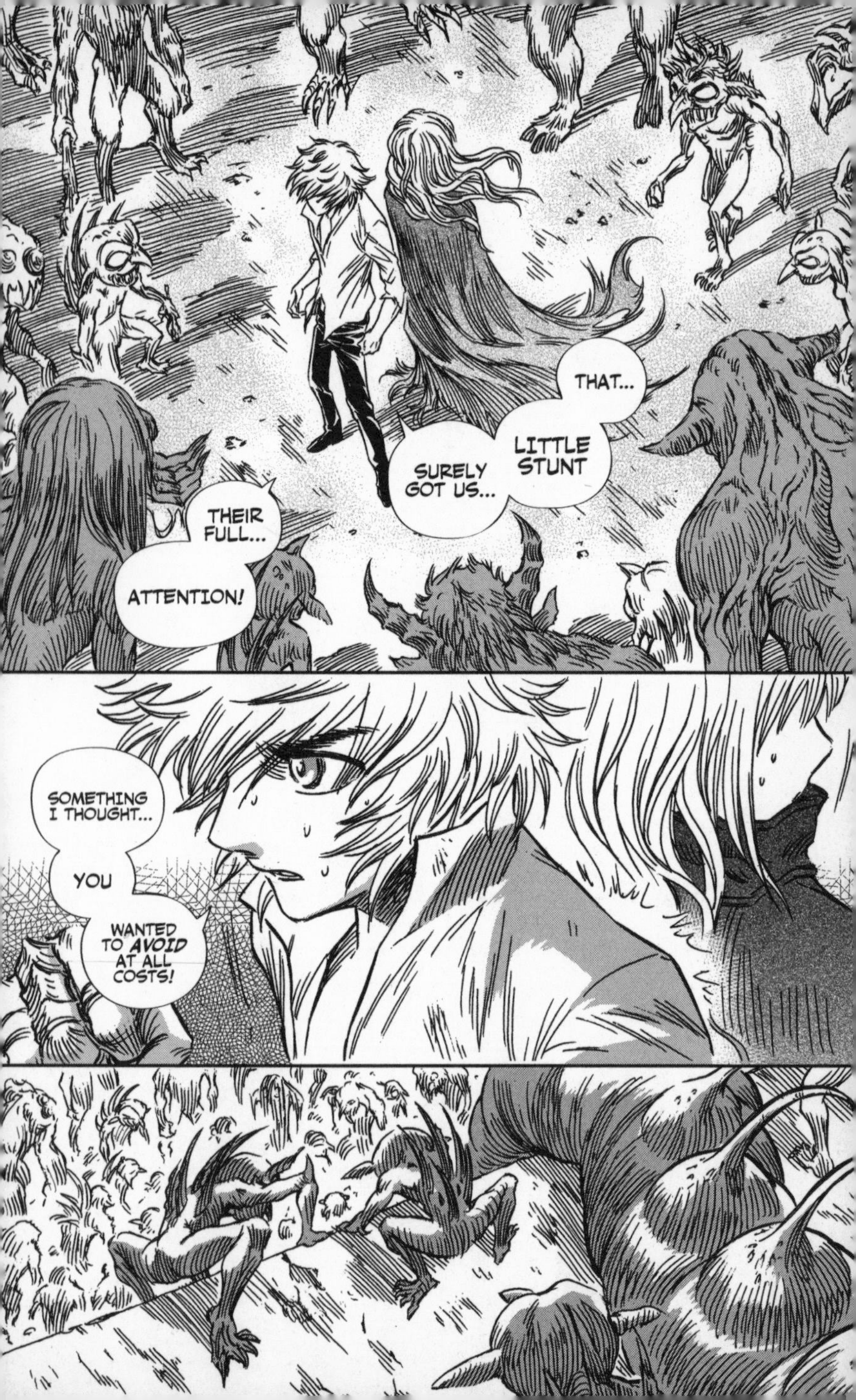
THAT...
LITTLE STUNT
SURELY GOT US...
THEIR FULL...
ATTENTION!
SOMETHING I THOUGHT...
YOU
WANTED TO AVOID AT ALL COSTS!

CHAPTER
7

EVE OF DESTRUCTION

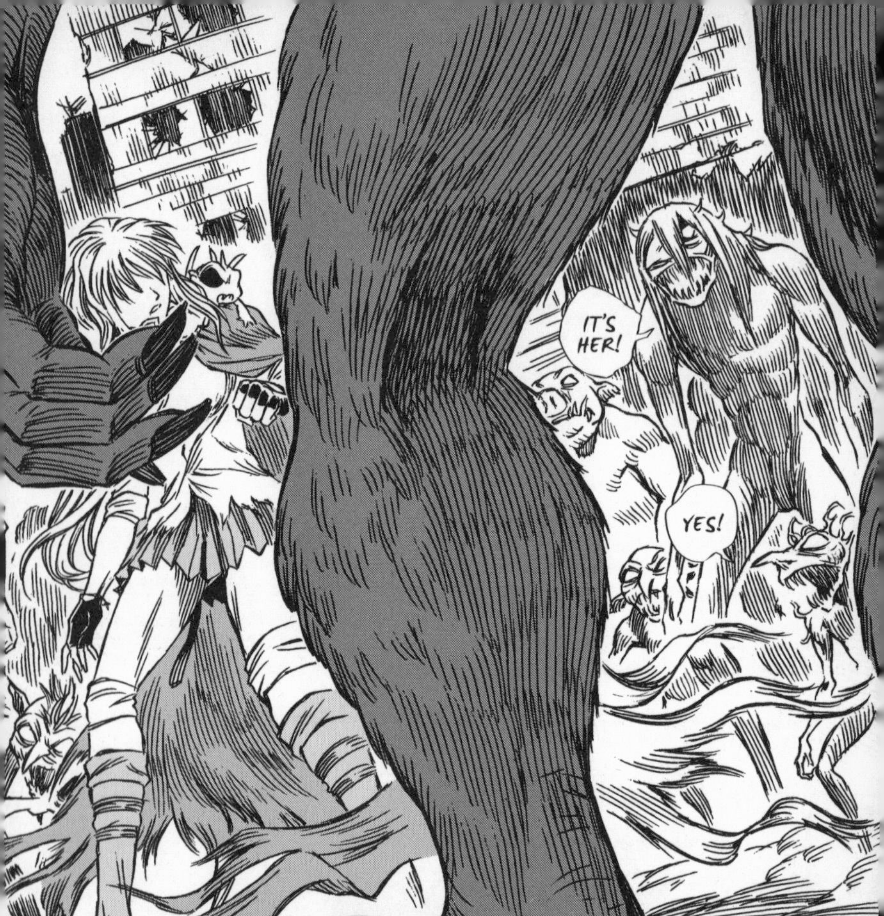
IT'S HER!
YES!
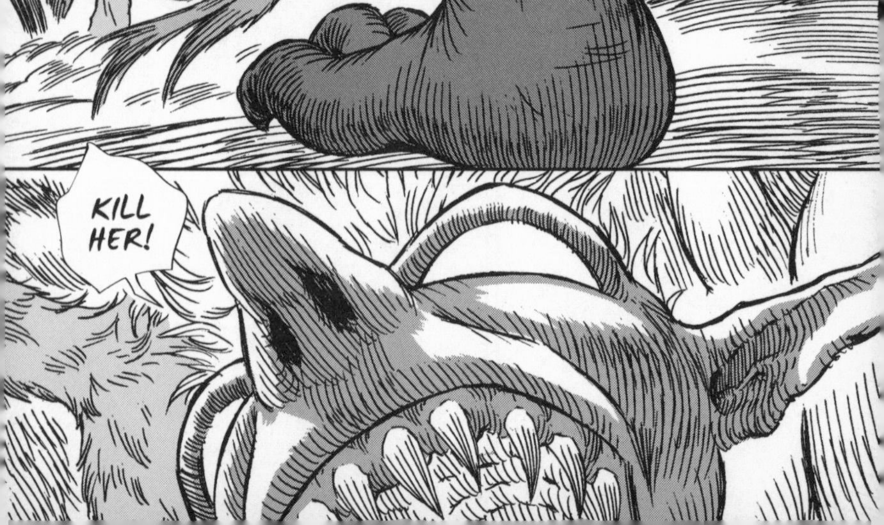
KILL HER!

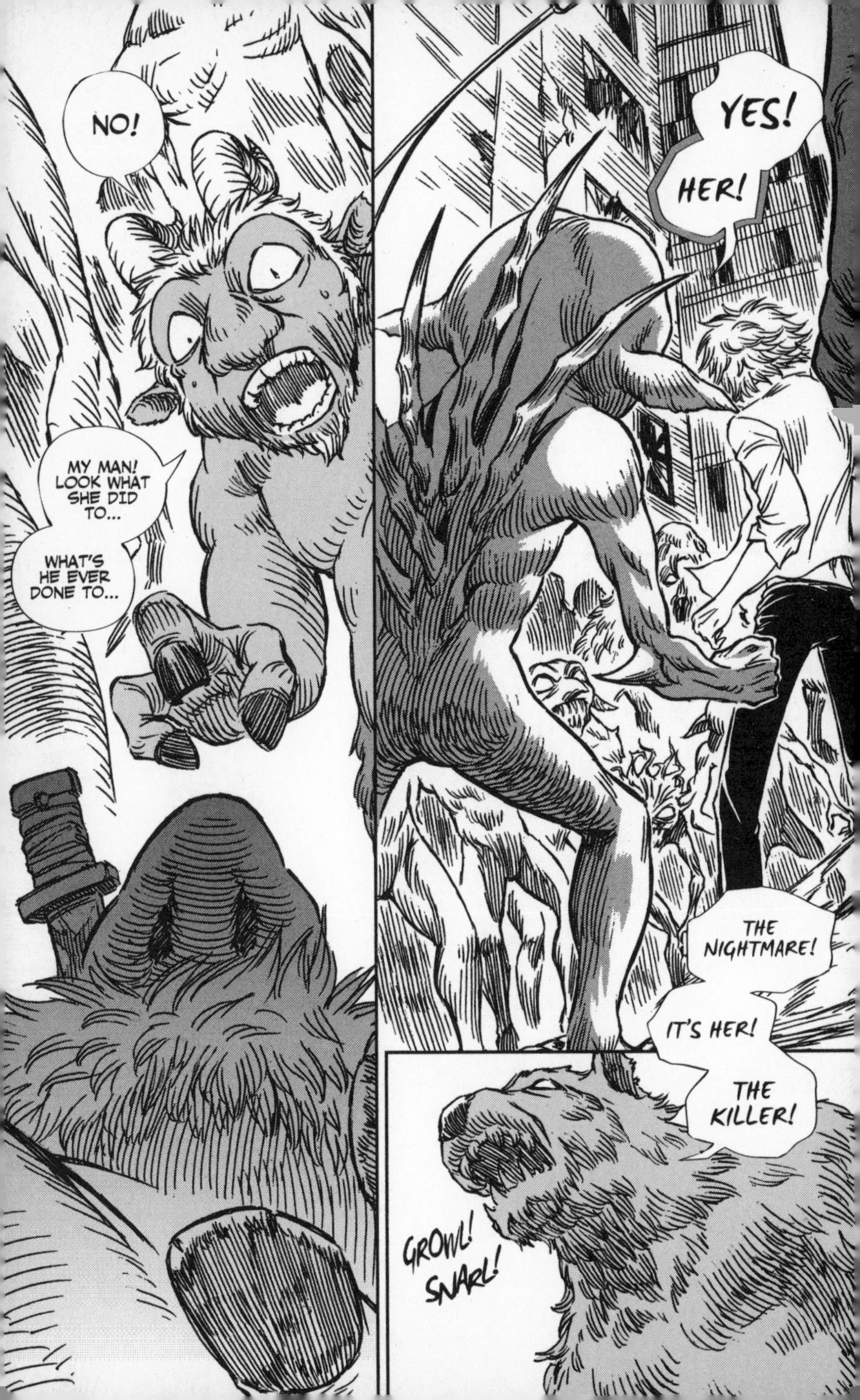
NO!
MY MAN! LOOK WHAT SHE DID TO...
WHAT'S HE EVER DONE TO...
YES!
HER!
THE NIGHTMARE!
IT'S HER!
THE KILLER!
GROWL!
SNARL!

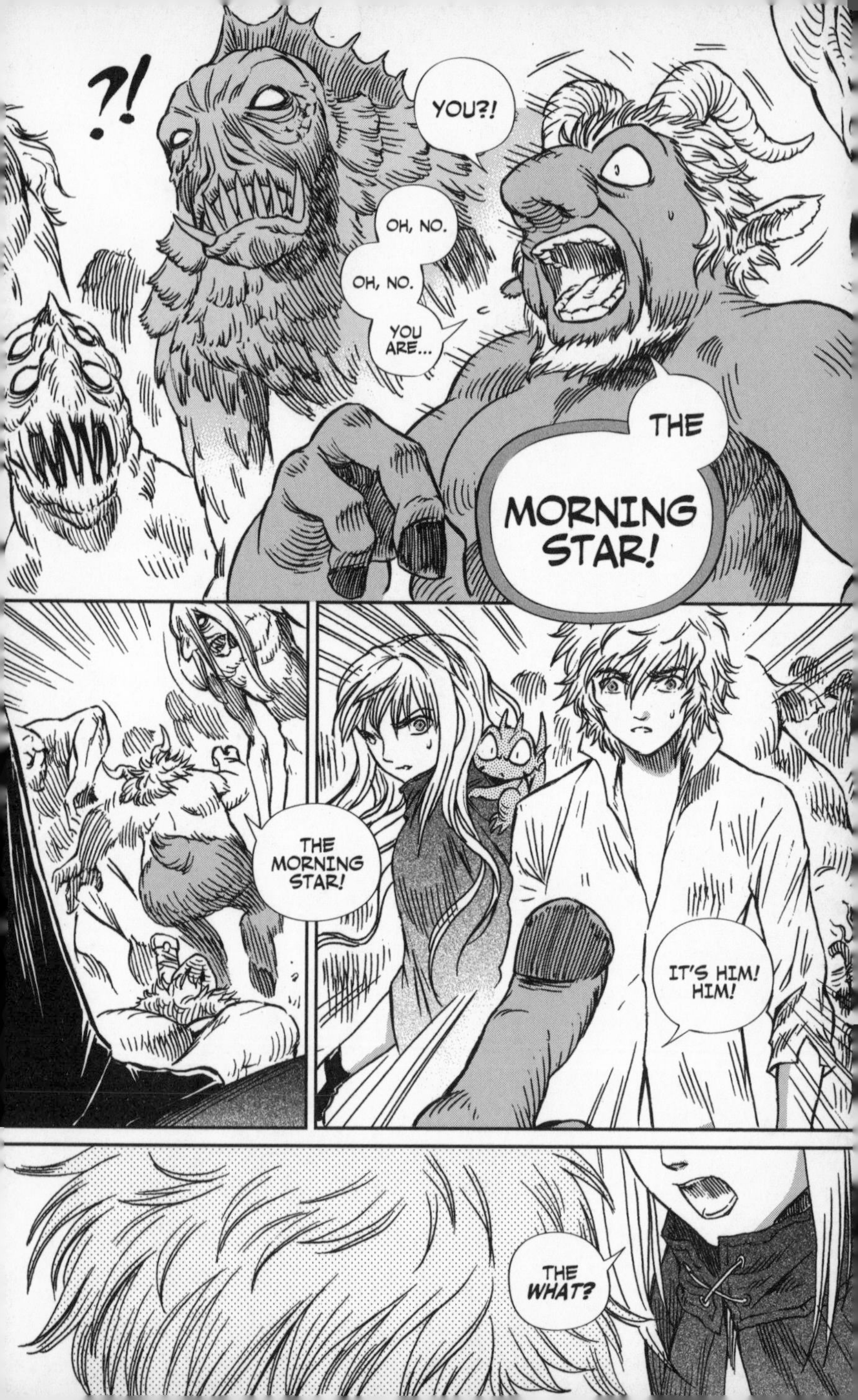
YOU?!
OH, NO.
OH, NO.
YOU ARE...
THE MORNING STAR!
?!
IT'S HIM! HIM!
THE MORNING STAR!
THE WHAT?

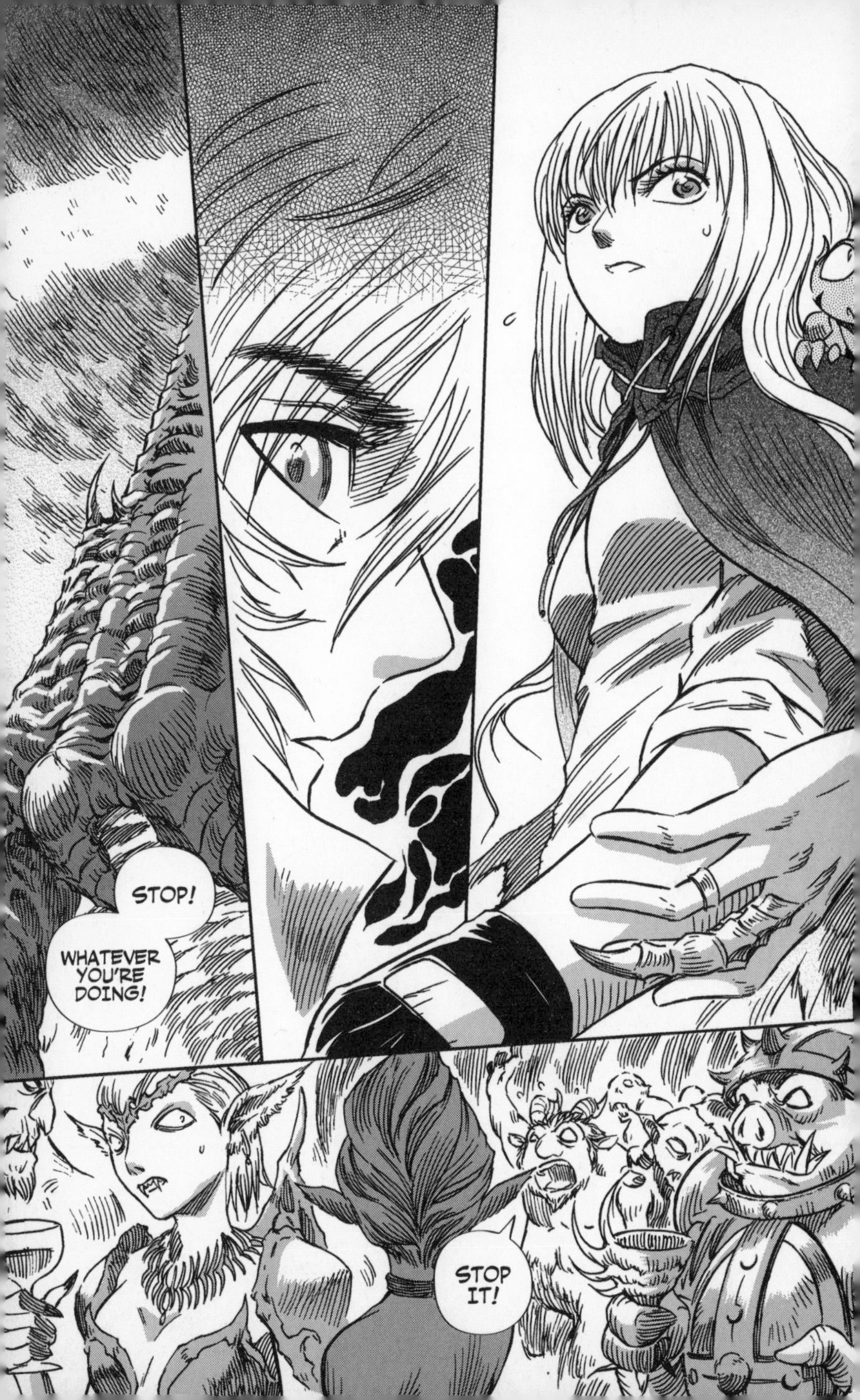
STOP!
WHATEVER YOU'RE DOING!
STOP IT!

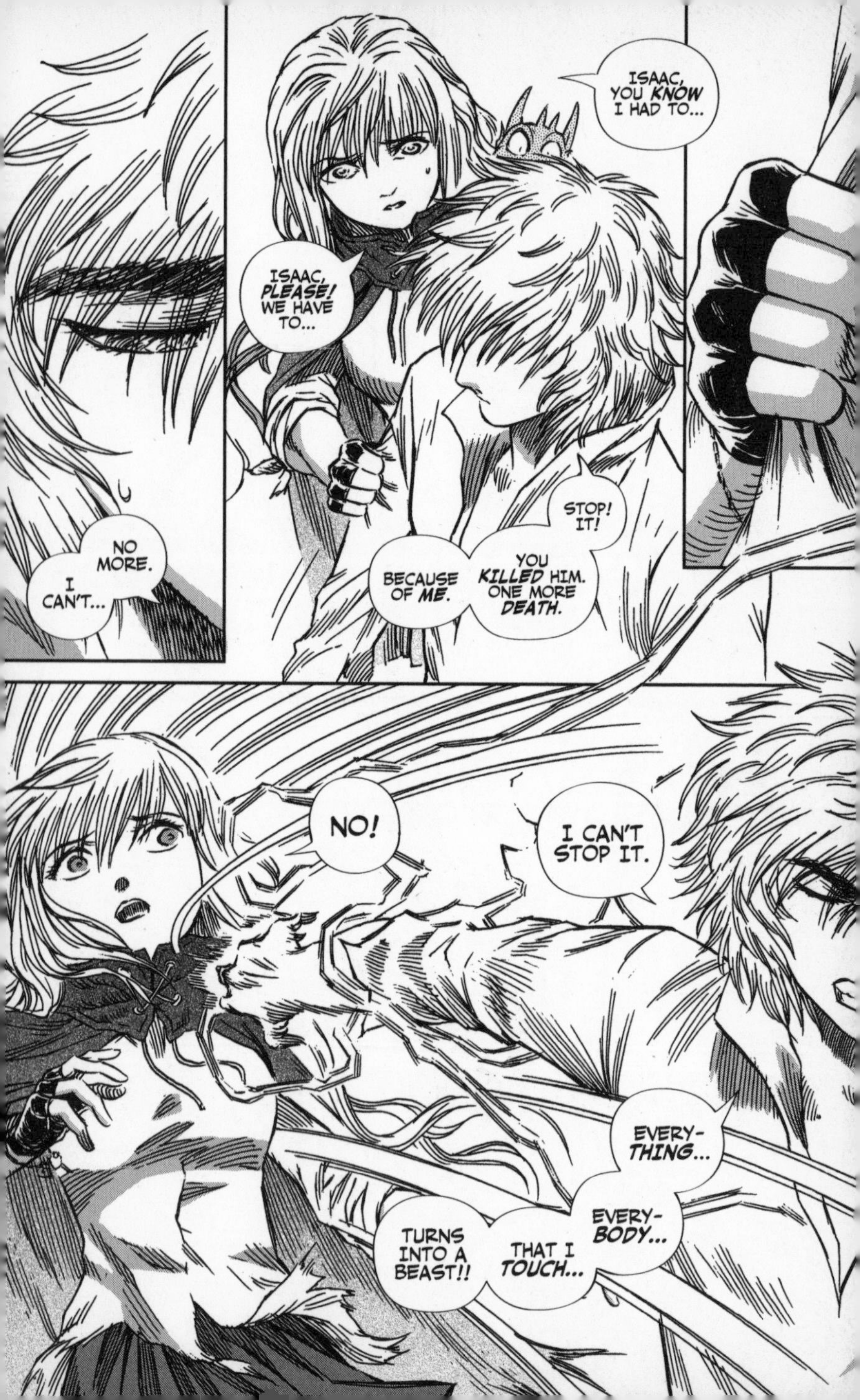
ISAAC, YOU KNOW I HAD TO...
ISAAC, PLEASE! WE HAVE TO...
STOP! IT!
YOU KILLED HIM. ONE MORE DEATH.
BECAUSE OF ME.
NO MORE.
I CAN'T...
I CAN'T STOP IT.
NO!
EVERY-THING...
EVERY-BODY...
THAT I TOUCH...
TURNS INTO A BEAST!!

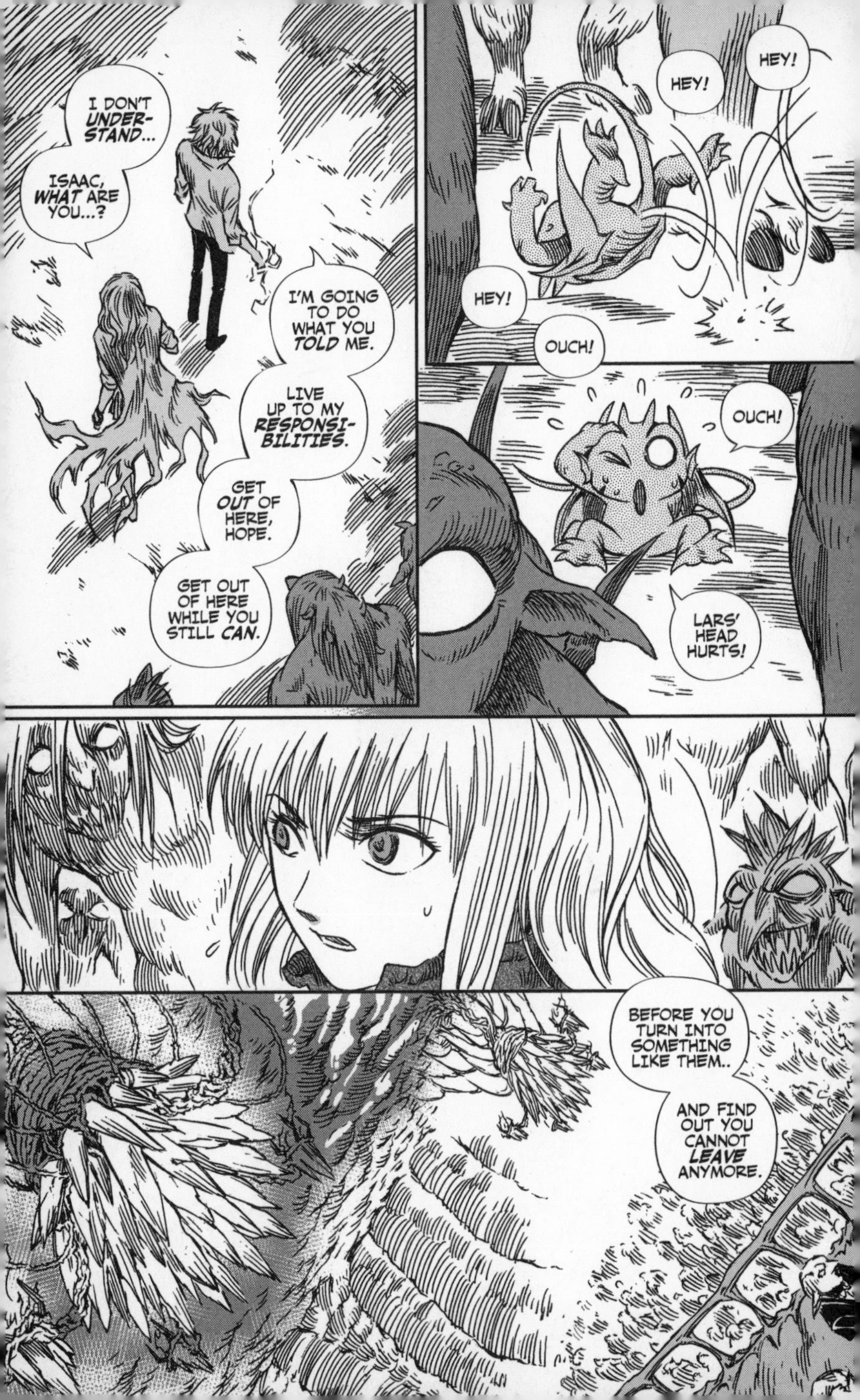
HEY!
HEY!
HEY!
OUCH!
OUCH!
LARS' HEAD HURTS!
I DON'T UNDER-STAND...
ISAAC, WHAT ARE YOU...?
I'M GOING TO DO WHAT YOU TOLD ME.
LIVE UP TO MY RESPONSI-BILITIES.
GET OUT OF HERE, HOPE.
GET OUT OF HERE WHILE YOU STILL CAN.
BEFORE YOU TURN INTO SOMETHING LIKE THEM..
AND FIND OUT YOU CANNOT LEAVE ANYMORE.

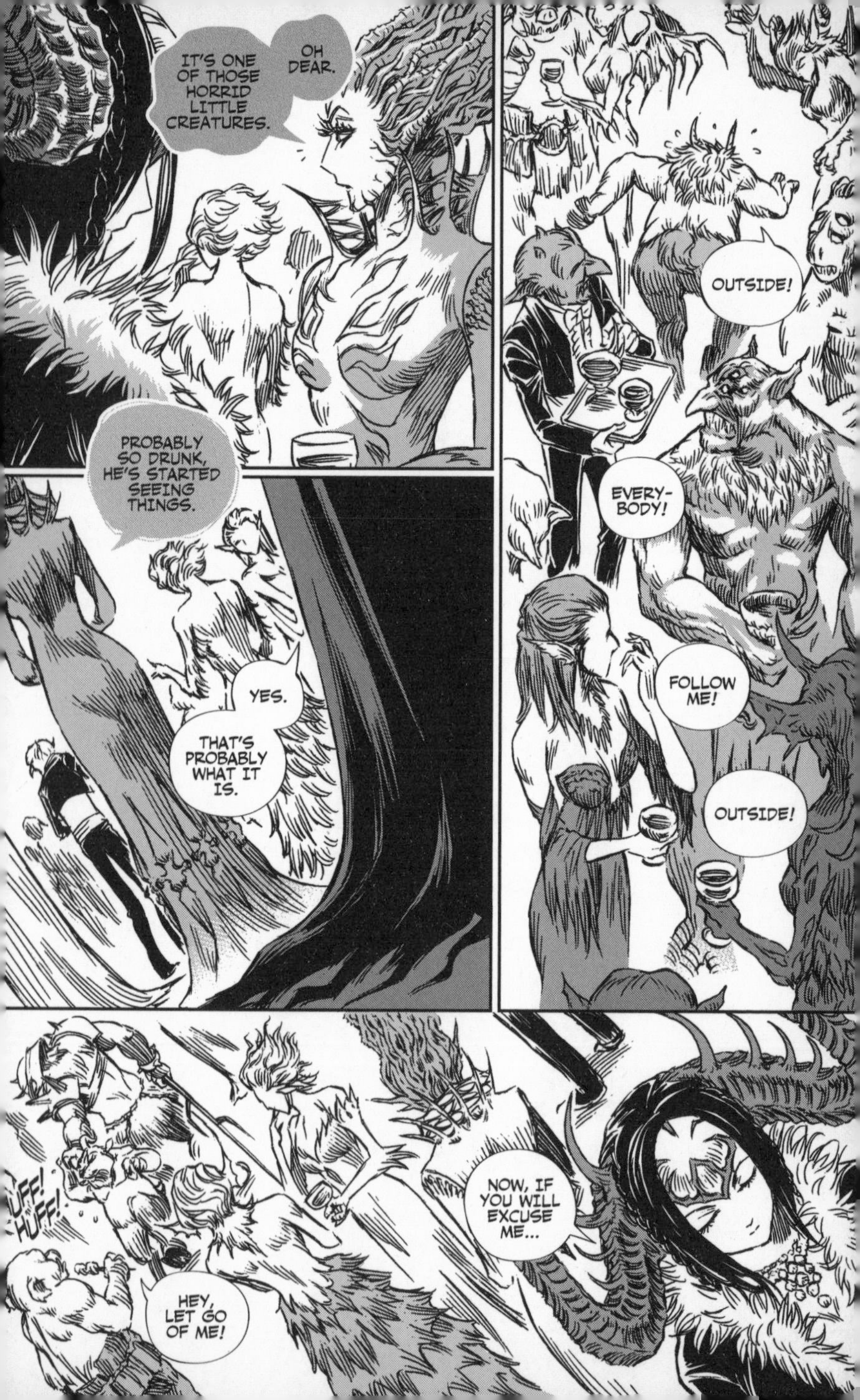
OH DEAR.
IT'S ONE OF THOSE HORRID LITTLE CREATURES.
PROBABLY SO DRUNK, HE'S STARTED SEEING THINGS.
YES.
THAT'S PROBABLY WHAT IT IS.
OUTSIDE!
EVERY-BODY!
FOLLOW ME!
OUTSIDE!
HUFF! HUFF!
HEY, LET GO OF ME!
NOW, IF YOU WILL EXCUSE ME...

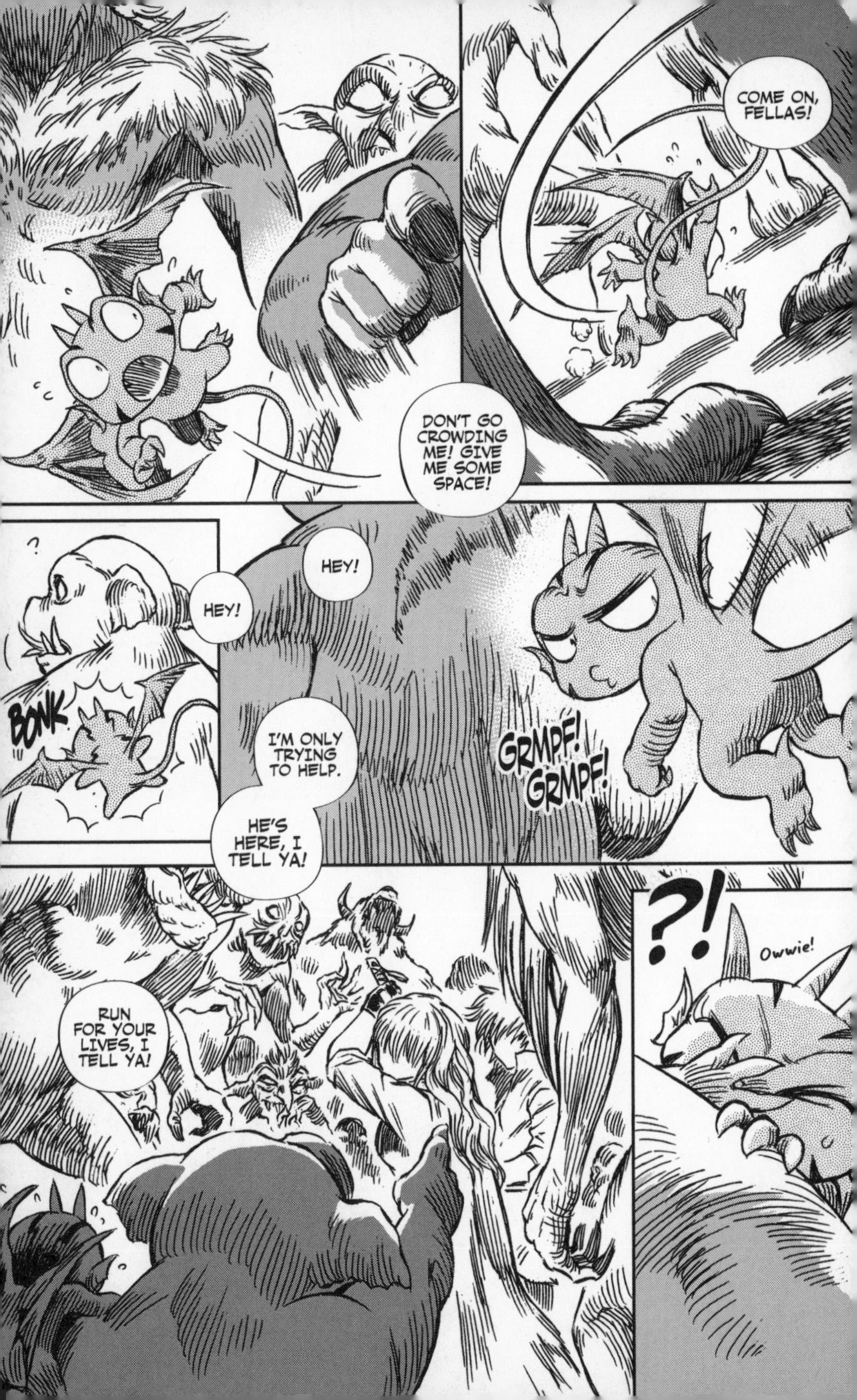
COME ON, FELLAS!
DON'T GO CROWDING ME! GIVE ME SOME SPACE!
HEY!
HEY!
GRMPF! GRMPF!
I'M ONLY TRYING TO HELP.
BONK
HE'S HERE, I TELL YA!
?!
Owwie!
RUN FOR YOUR LIVES, I TELL YA!

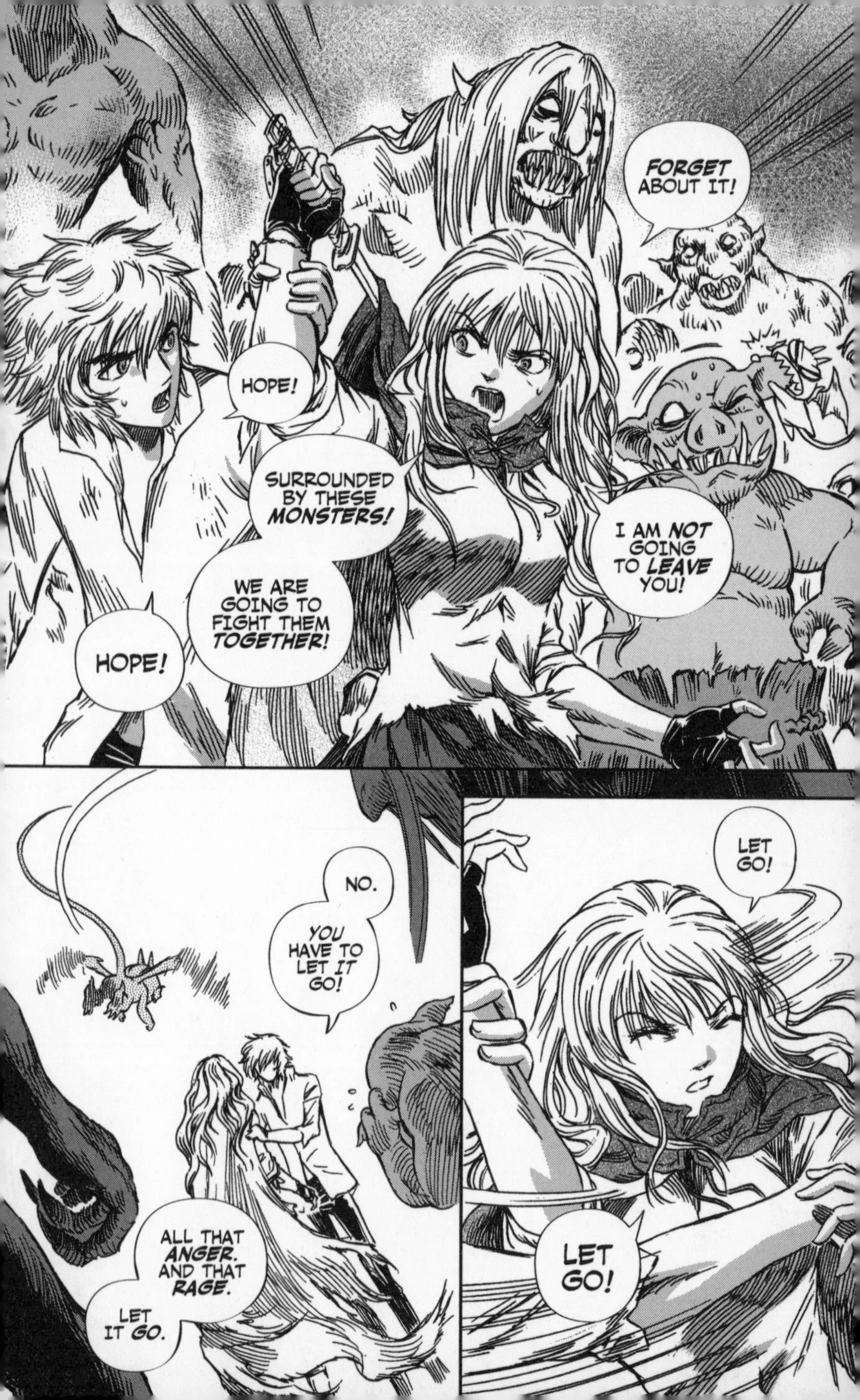
FORGET ABOUT IT!
I AM NOT GOING TO LEAVE YOU!
HOPE!
SURROUNDED BY THESE MONSTERS!
WE ARE GOING TO FIGHT THEM TOGETHER!
HOPE!
LET GO!
LET GO!
NO.
YOU HAVE TO LET IT GO!
ALL THAT ANGER. AND THAT RAGE.
LET IT GO.

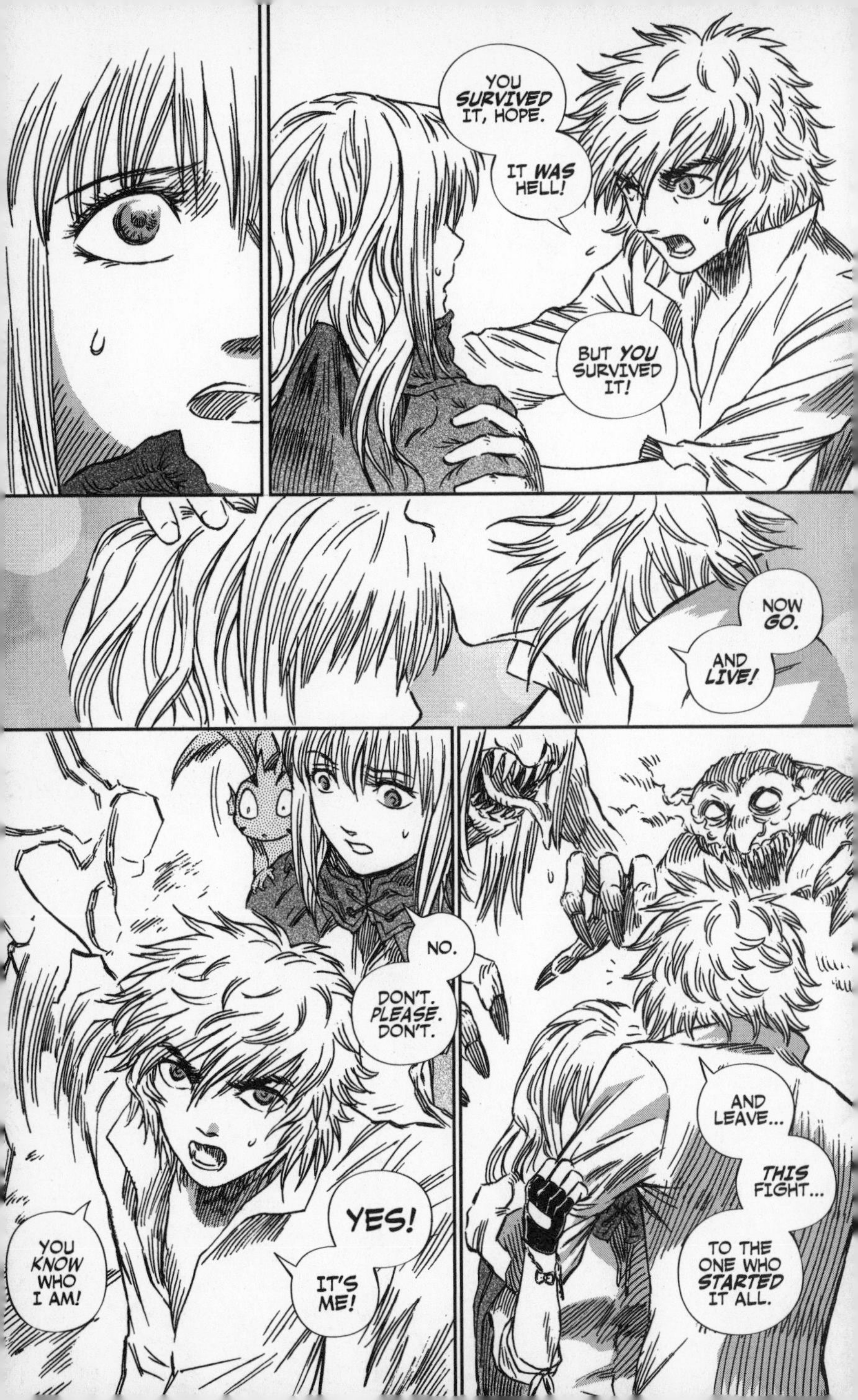
YOU *SURVIVED* IT, HOPE.
IT *WAS* HELL!
BUT *YOU* SURVIVED IT!
NOW *GO.*
AND *LIVE!*
NO.
DON'T. *PLEASE.* DON'T.
YES!
IT'S ME!
YOU *KNOW* WHO I AM!
AND LEAVE...
THIS FIGHT...
TO THE ONE WHO *STARTED* IT ALL.

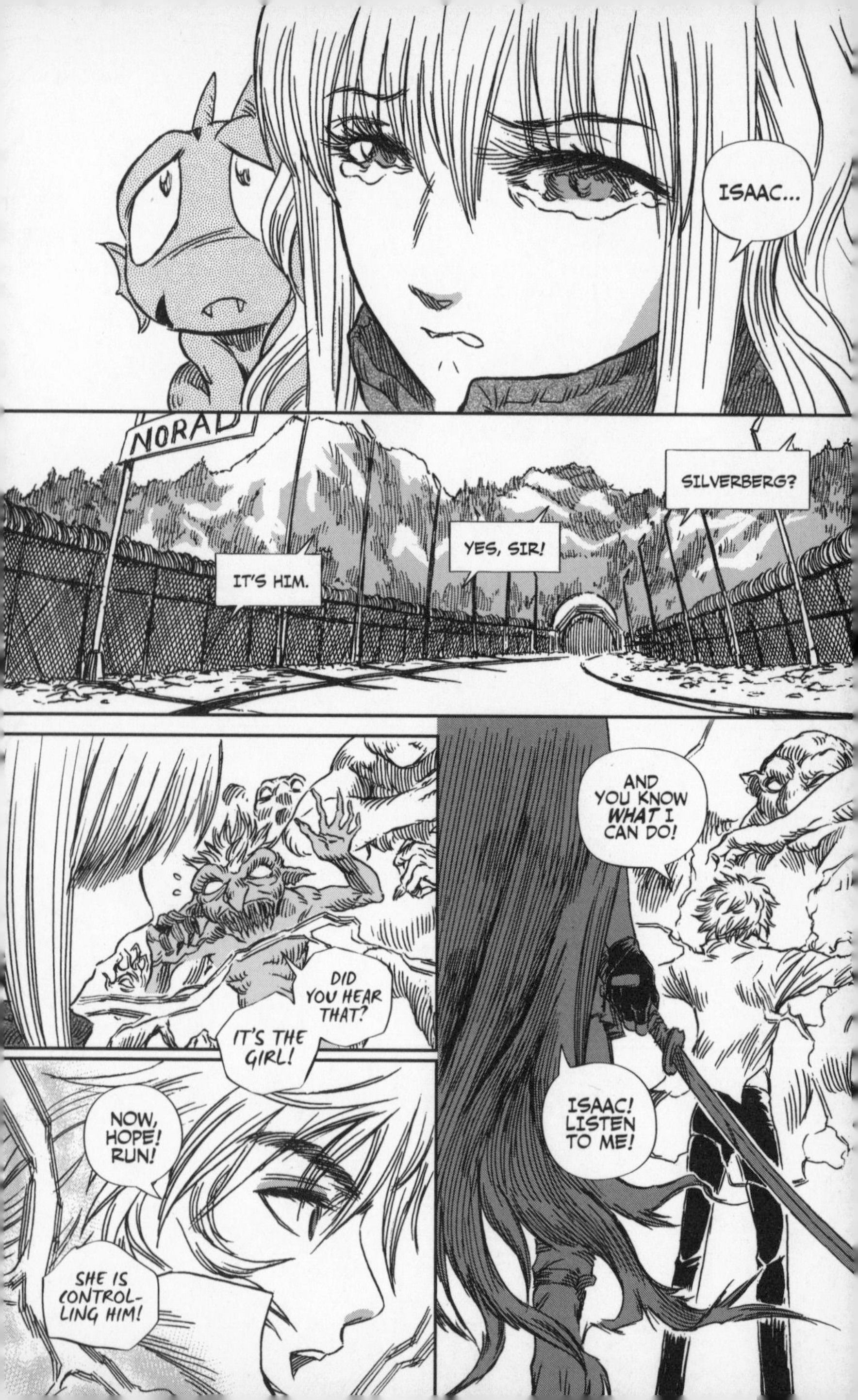
ISAAC...
SILVERBERG?
YES, SIR!
IT'S HIM.
NORAD
AND YOU KNOW *WHAT* I CAN DO!
ISAAC! LISTEN TO ME!
DID YOU HEAR THAT?
IT'S THE GIRL!
NOW, HOPE! RUN!
SHE IS CONTROL-LING HIM!

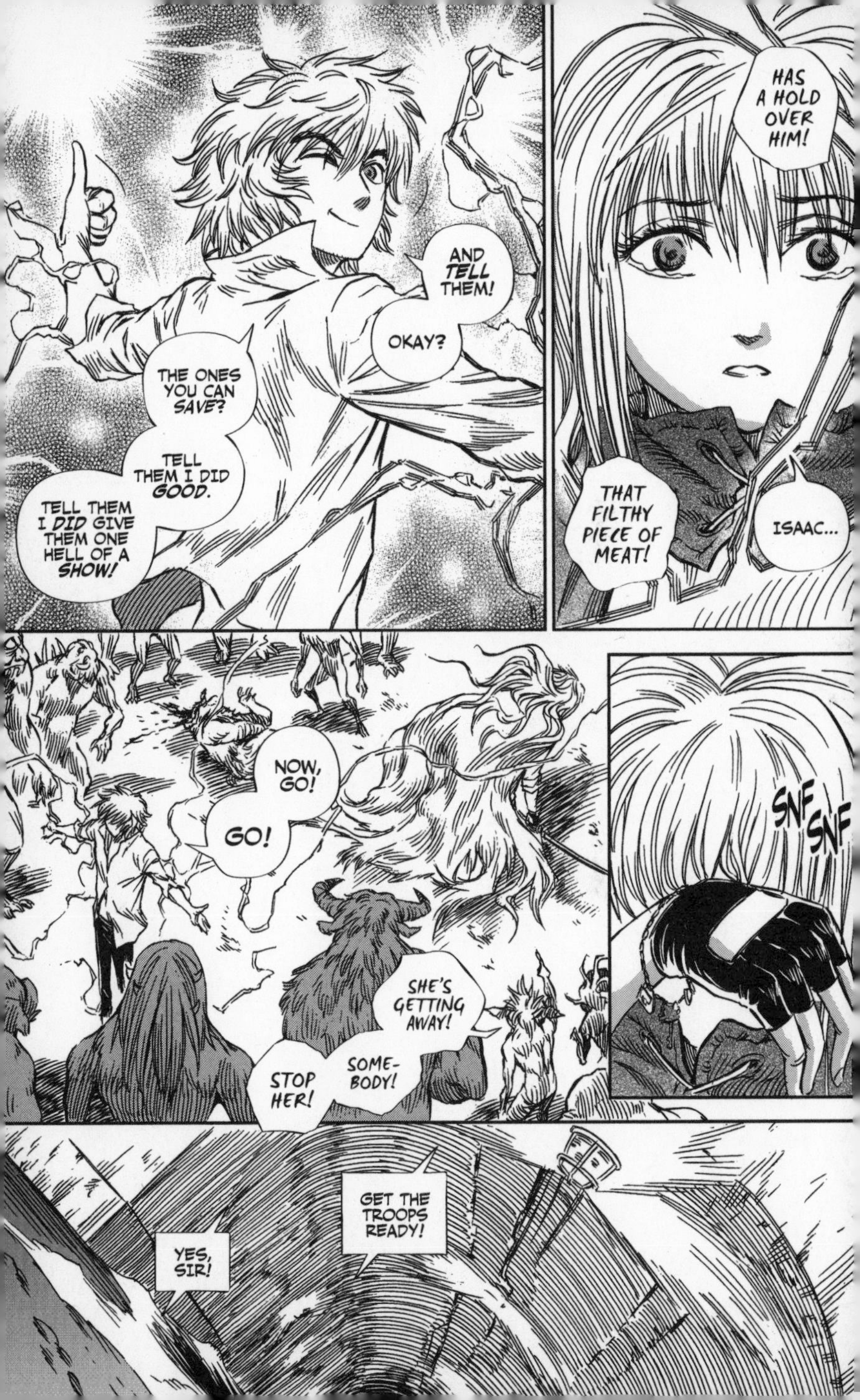
HAS A HOLD OVER HIM!
THAT FILTHY PIECE OF MEAT!
ISAAC...
AND *TELL* THEM!
OKAY?
THE ONES YOU CAN *SAVE*?
TELL THEM I DID *GOOD*.
TELL THEM I *DID* GIVE THEM ONE HELL OF A *SHOW!*
SNF SNF
NOW, GO!
GO!
SHE'S GETTING AWAY!
SOME-BODY!
STOP HER!
GET THE TROOPS READY!
YES, SIR!

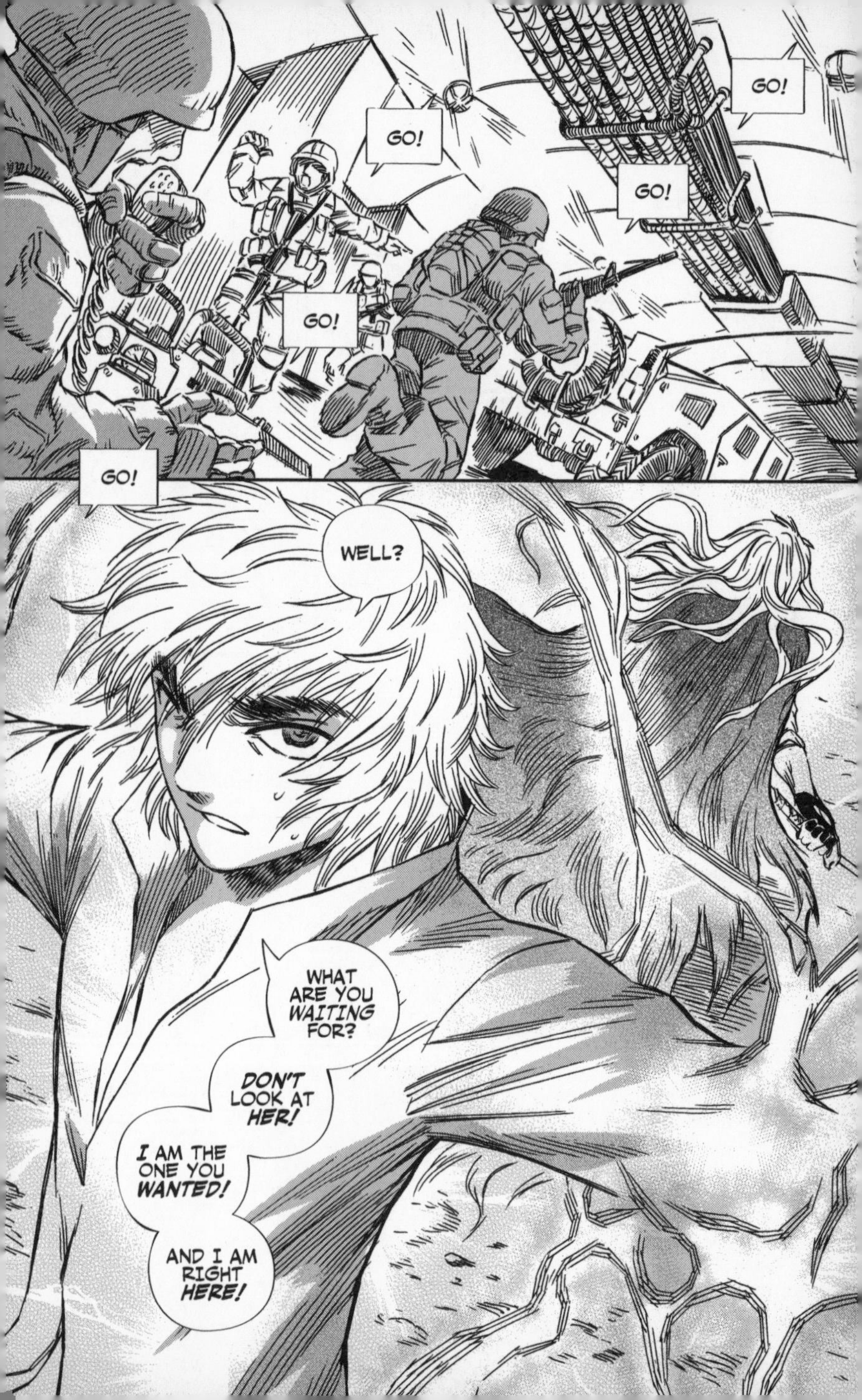
GO!
GO!
GO!
GO!
GO!
WELL?
WHAT ARE YOU *WAITING* FOR?
DON'T LOOK AT *HER!*
I AM THE ONE YOU *WANTED!*
AND I AM RIGHT *HERE!*

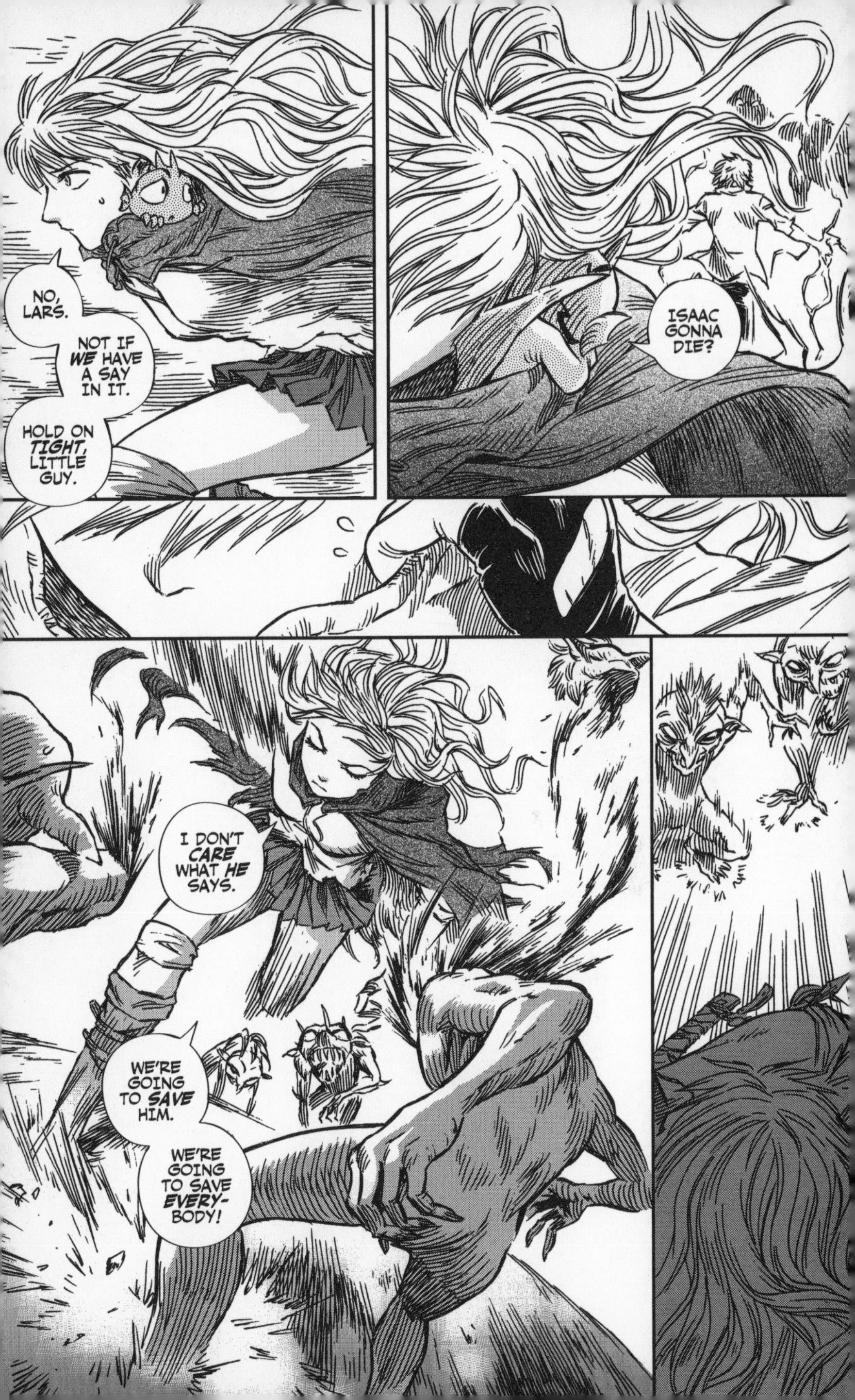
ISAAC GONNA DIE?
NO, LARS.
NOT IF WE HAVE A SAY IN IT.
HOLD ON TIGHT, LITTLE GUY.
I DON'T CARE WHAT HE SAYS.
WE'RE GOING TO SAVE HIM.
WE'RE GOING TO SAVE EVERY-BODY!

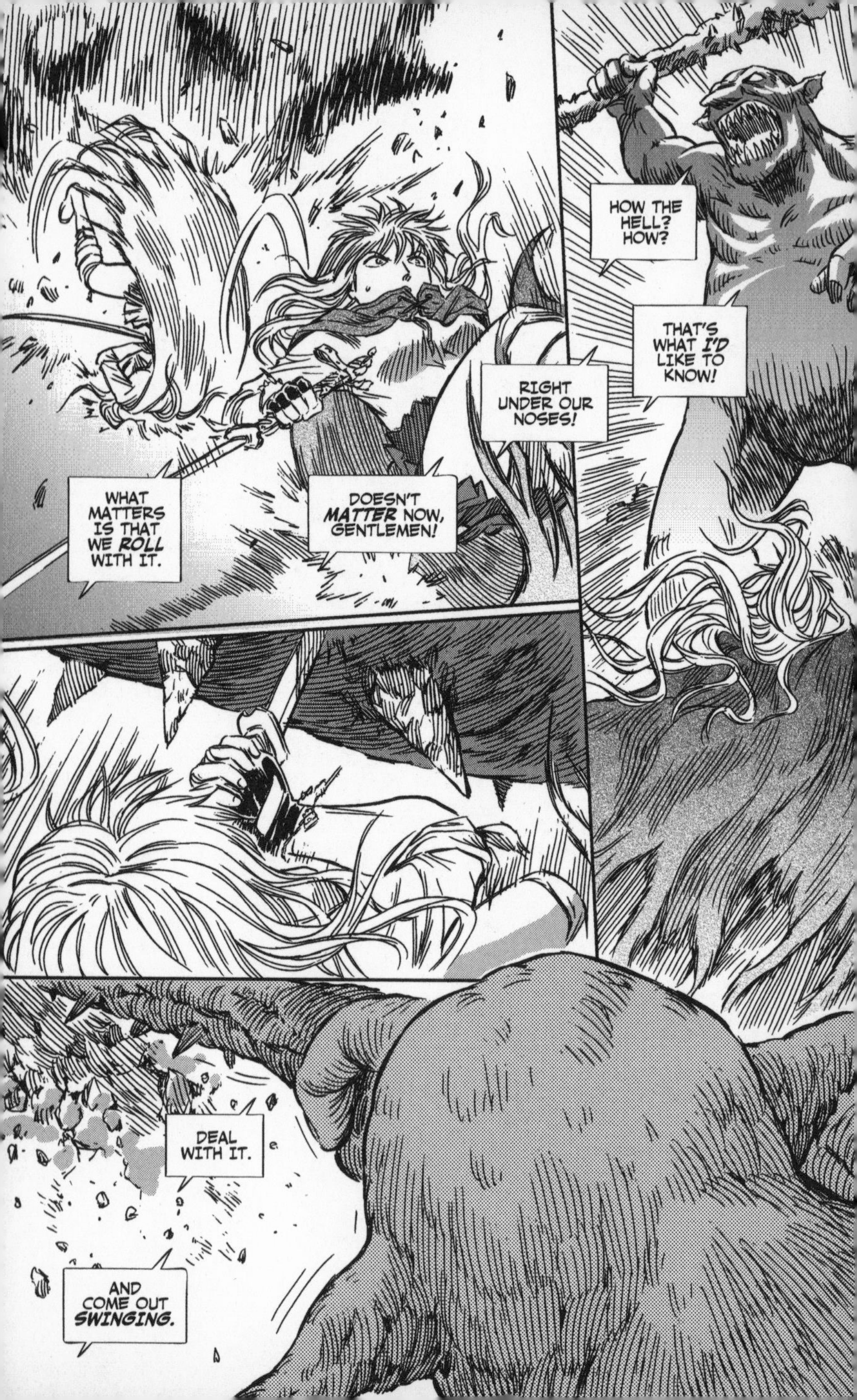
HOW THE HELL? HOW?
THAT'S WHAT I'D LIKE TO KNOW!
RIGHT UNDER OUR NOSES!
DOESN'T MATTER NOW, GENTLEMEN!
WHAT MATTERS IS THAT WE ROLL WITH IT.
DEAL WITH IT.
AND COME OUT SWINGING.

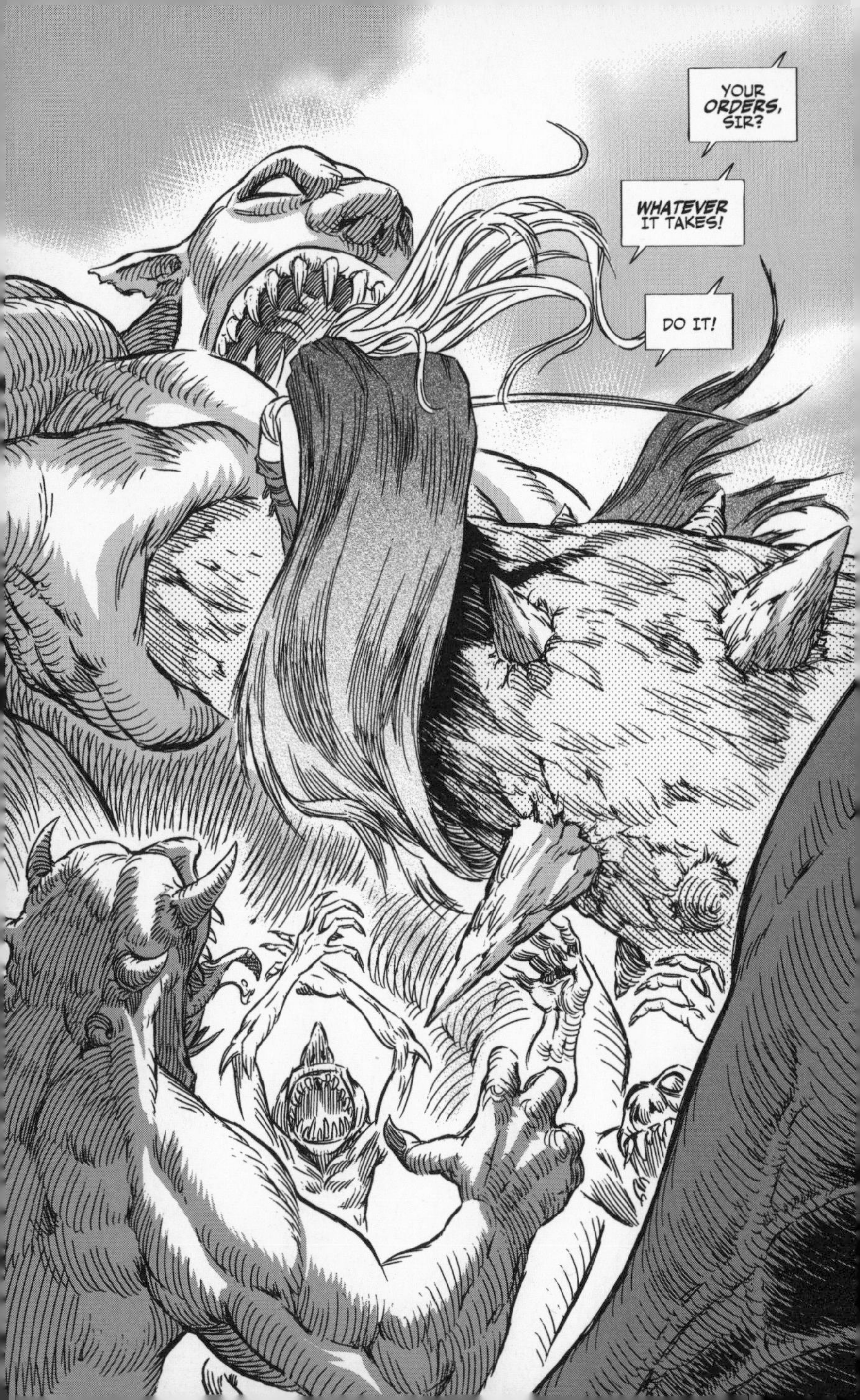
YOUR ORDERS, SIR?
WHATEVER IT TAKES!
DO IT!

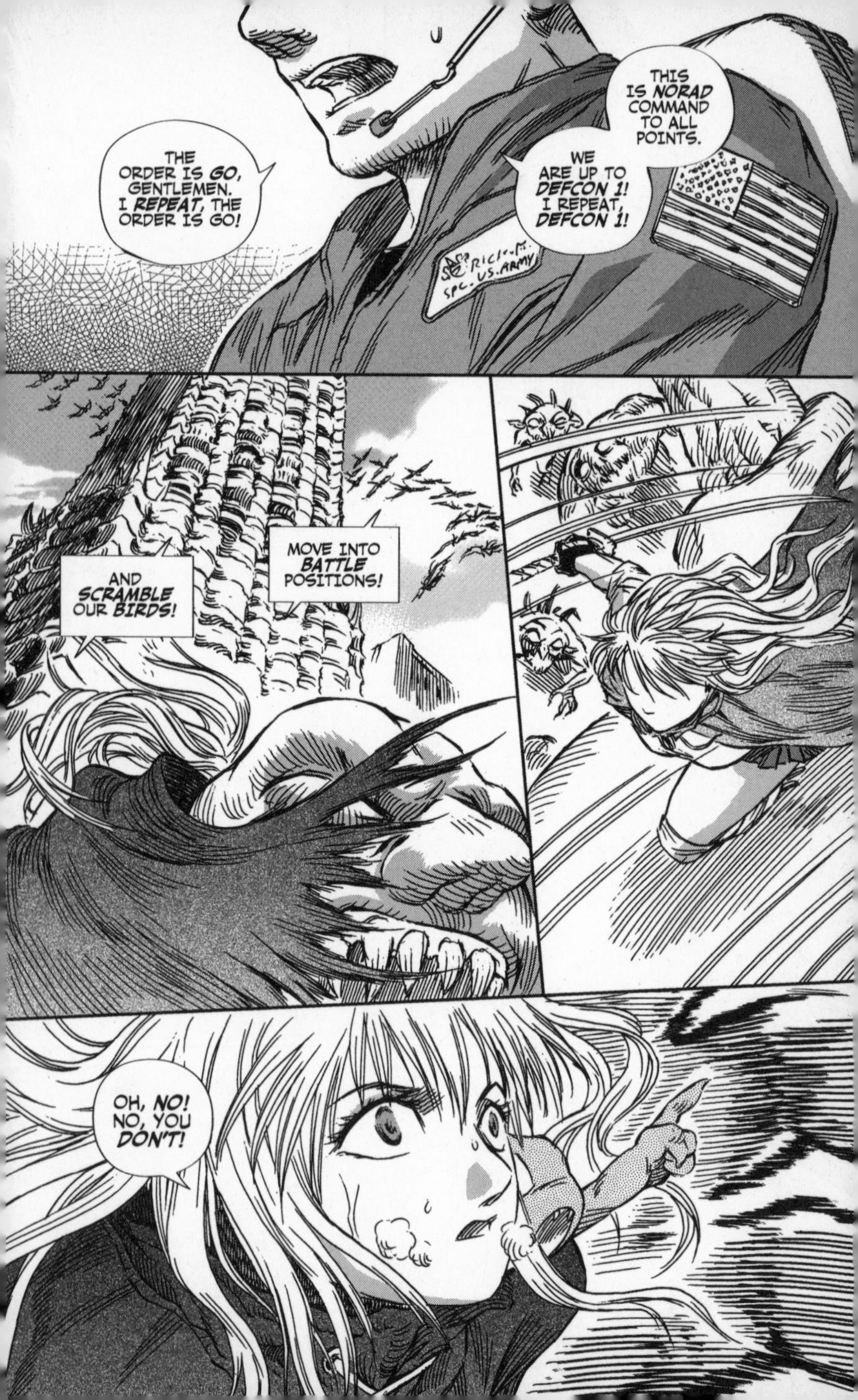
THIS IS NORAD COMMAND TO ALL POINTS.
WE ARE UP TO DEFCON 1! I REPEAT, DEFCON 1!
THE ORDER IS GO, GENTLEMEN. I REPEAT, THE ORDER IS GO!
MOVE INTO BATTLE POSITIONS!
AND SCRAMBLE OUR BIRDS!
OH, NO! NO, YOU DON'T!

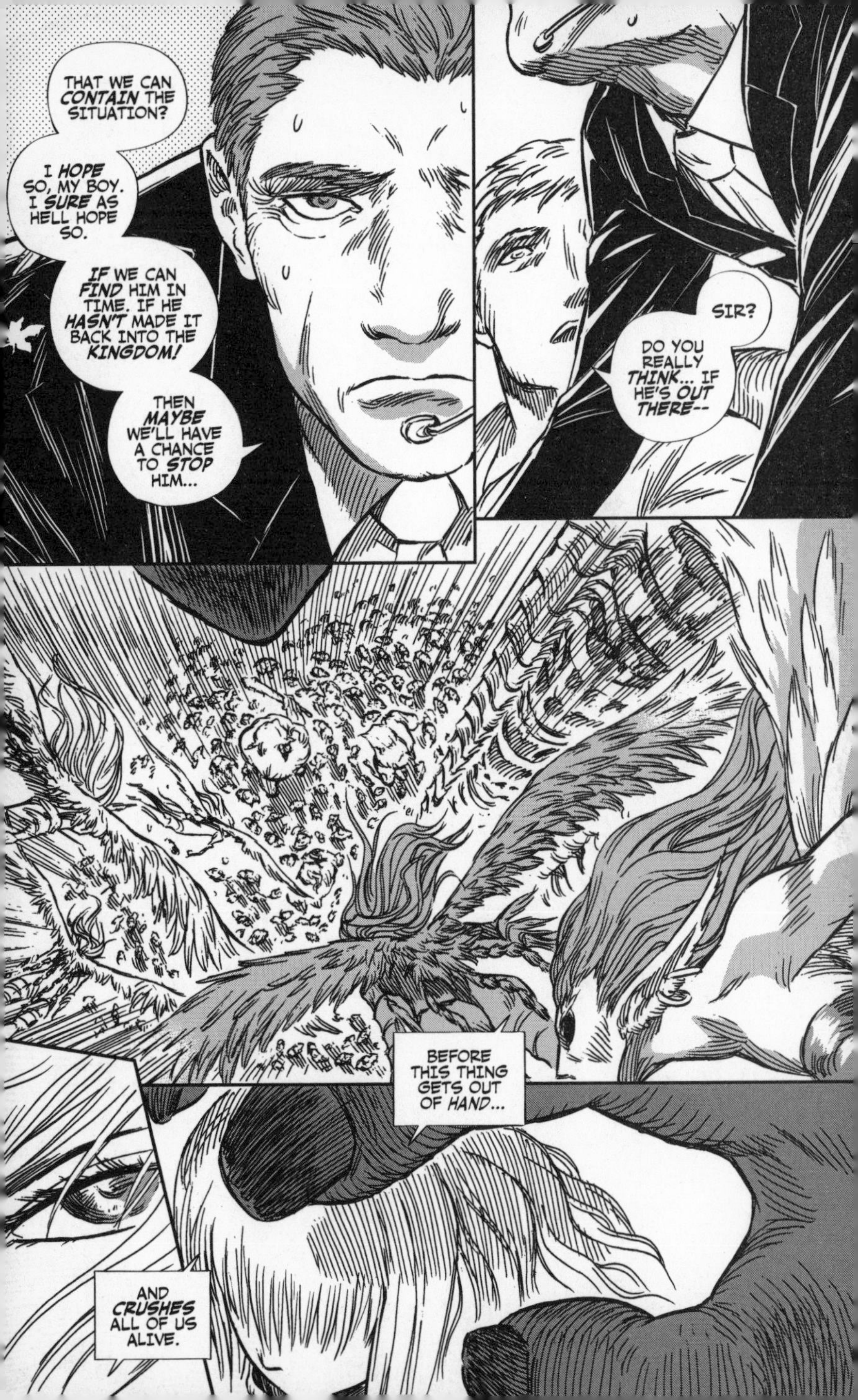
SIR?
DO YOU REALLY THINK... IF HE'S OUT THERE--
THAT WE CAN CONTAIN THE SITUATION?
I HOPE SO, MY BOY. I SURE AS HELL HOPE SO.
IF WE CAN FIND HIM IN TIME. IF HE HASN'T MADE IT BACK INTO THE KINGDOM!
THEN MAYBE WE'LL HAVE A CHANCE TO STOP HIM...
BEFORE THIS THING GETS OUT OF HAND...
AND CRUSHES ALL OF US ALIVE.

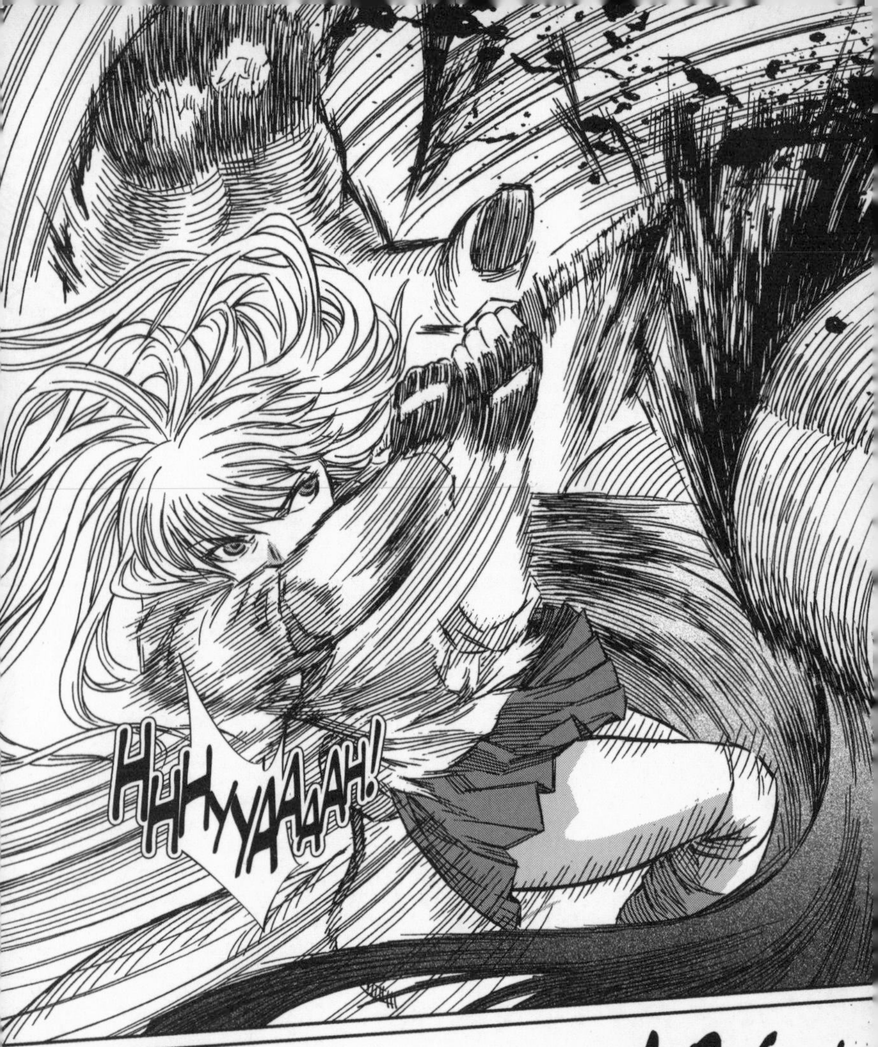
HHHYYAAAAH!
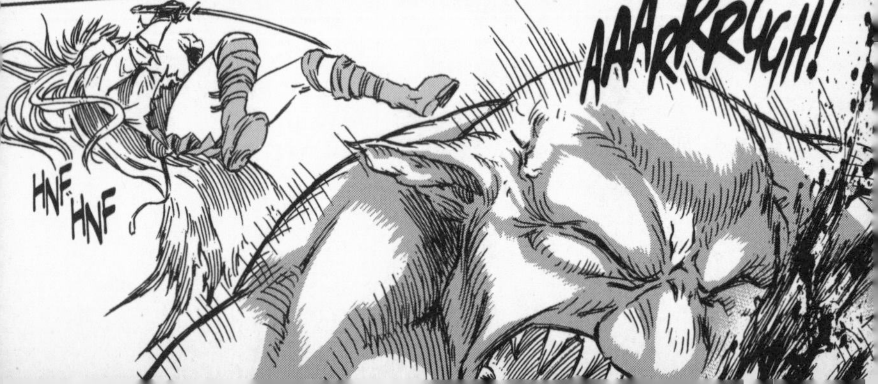
AAARRRGGH!
HNF HNF

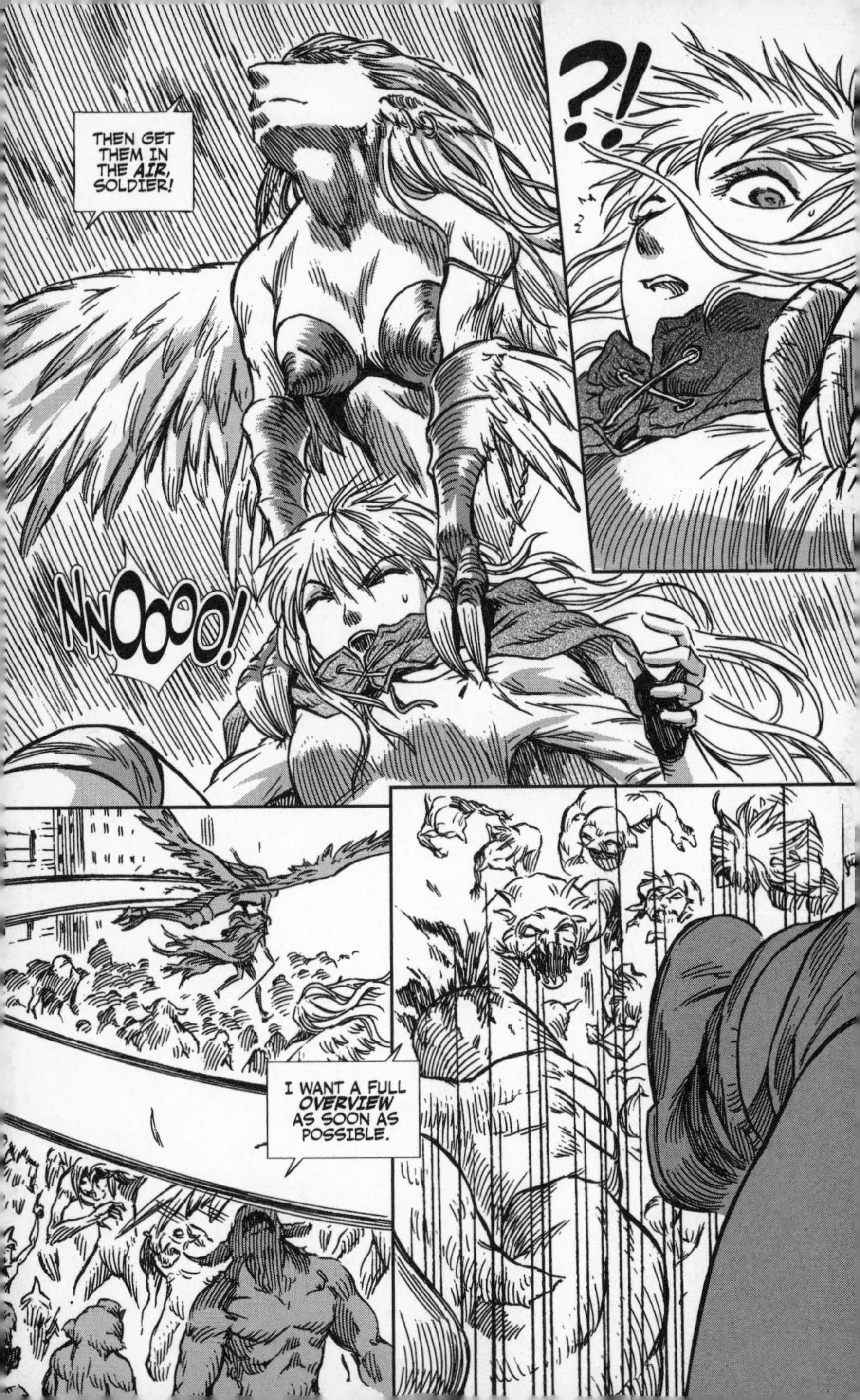
?!
THEN GET THEM IN THE AIR, SOLDIER!
NNOOOO!
I WANT A FULL OVERVIEW AS SOON AS POSSIBLE.

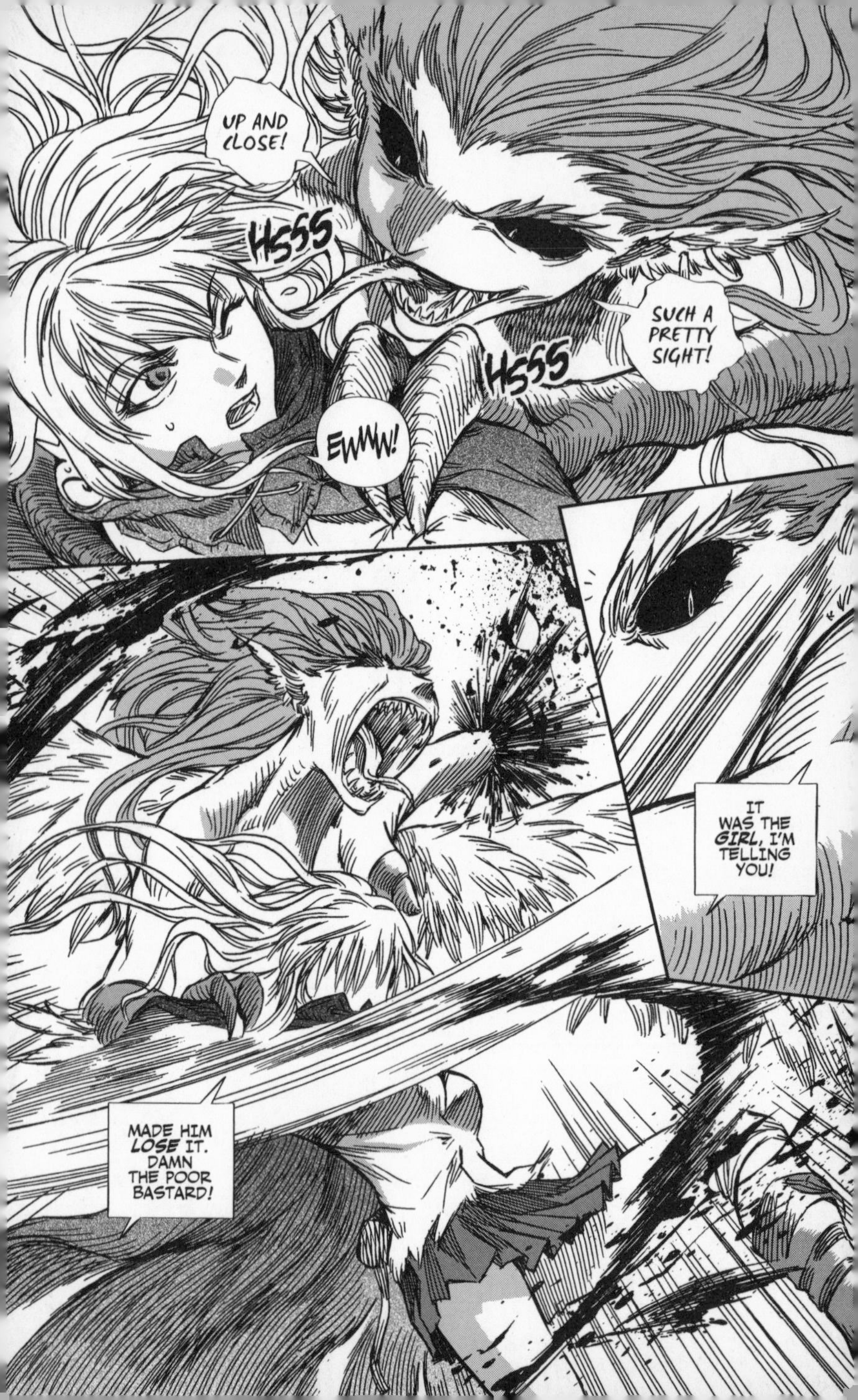
UP AND CLOSE!
HSSS
SUCH A PRETTY SIGHT!
HSSS
EWWW!
IT WAS THE GIRL, I'M TELLING YOU!
MADE HIM LOSE IT. DAMN THE POOR BASTARD!

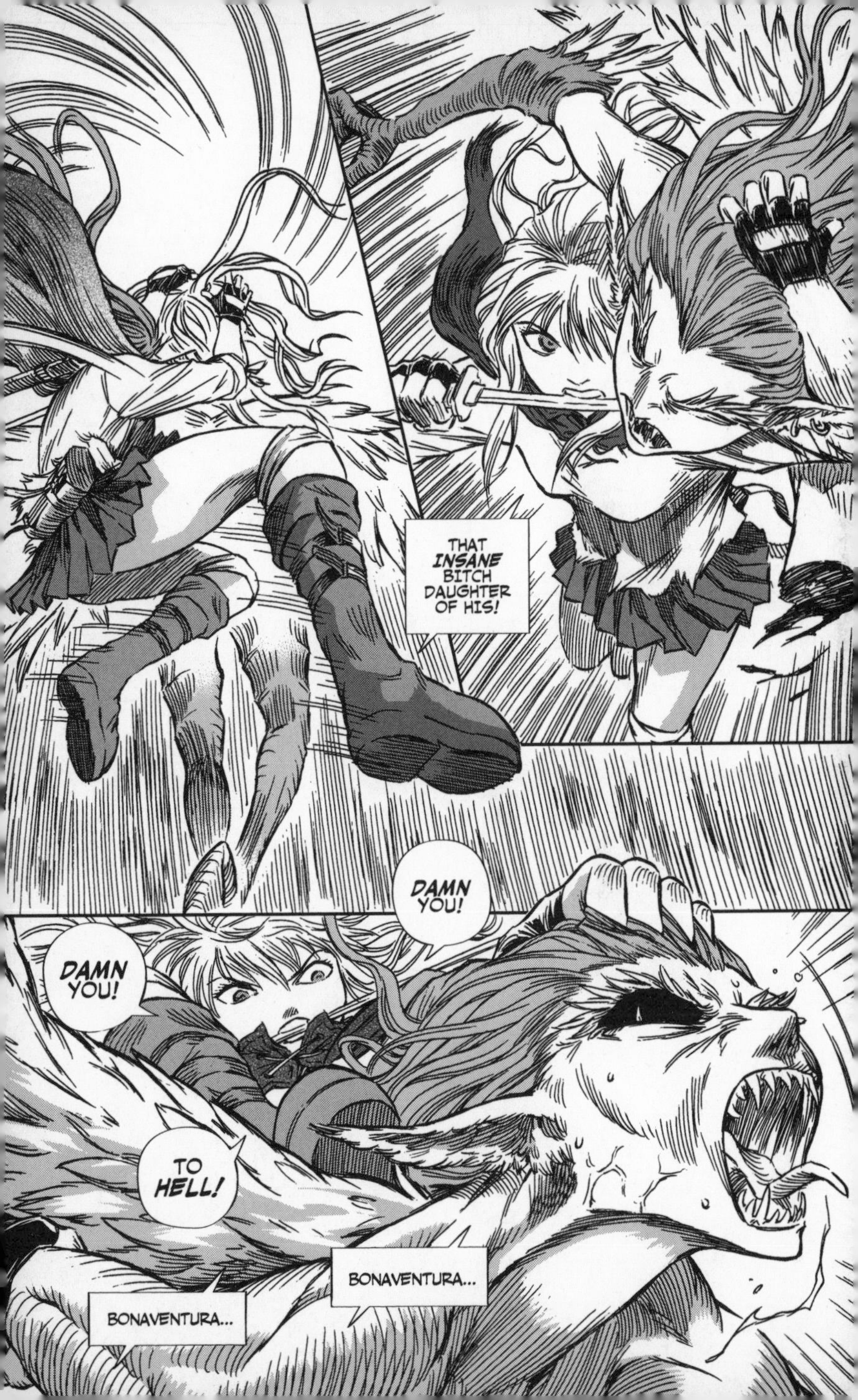
THAT INSANE BITCH DAUGHTER OF HIS!
DAMN YOU!
DAMN YOU!
TO HELL!
BONAVENTURA...
BONAVENTURA...

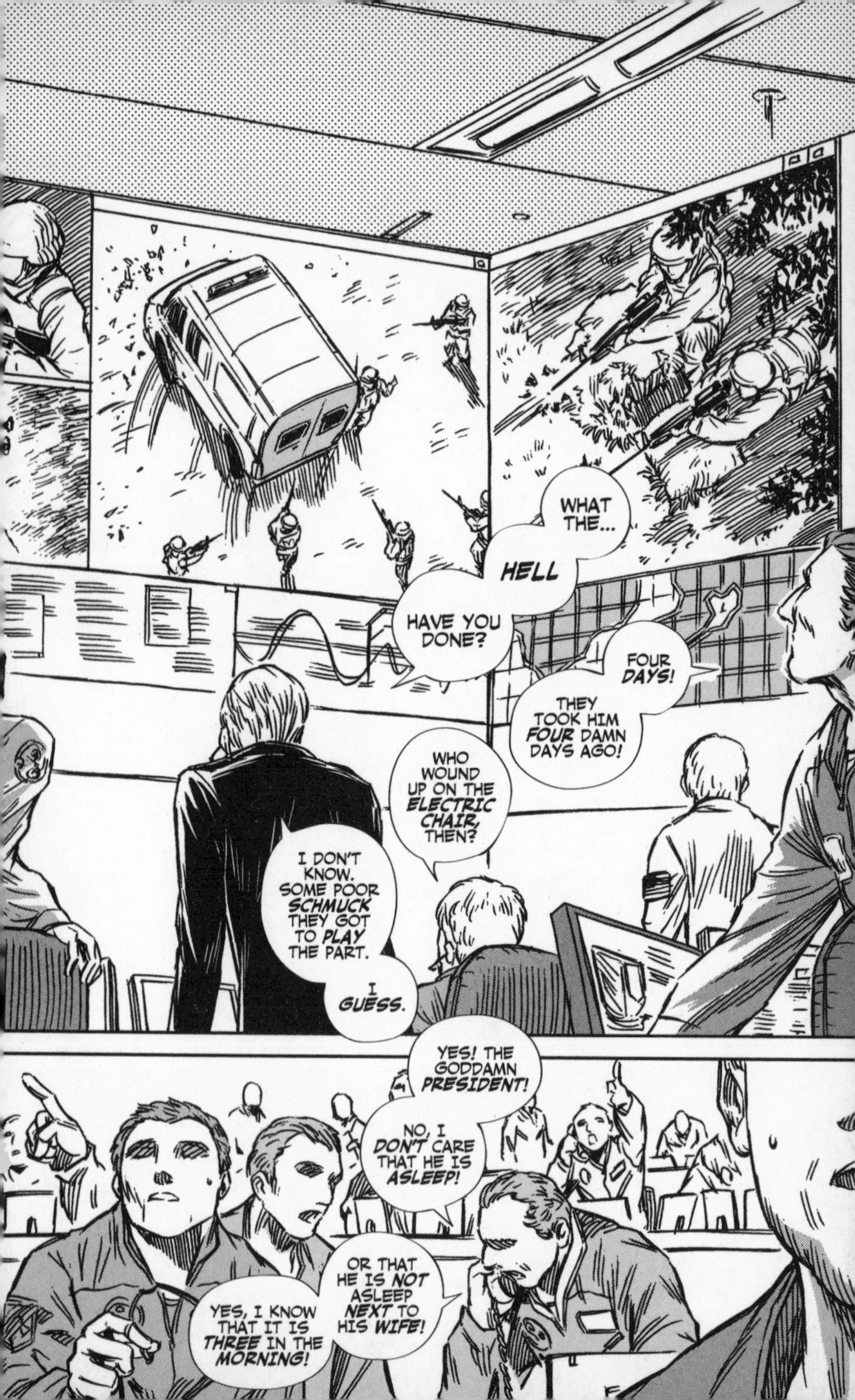
WHAT THE...
HELL
HAVE YOU DONE?
FOUR DAYS!
THEY TOOK HIM FOUR DAMN DAYS AGO!
WHO WOUND UP ON THE ELECTRIC CHAIR, THEN?
I DON'T KNOW. SOME POOR SCHMUCK THEY GOT TO PLAY THE PART.
I GUESS.
YES! THE GODDAMN PRESIDENT!
NO, I DON'T CARE THAT HE IS ASLEEP!
OR THAT HE IS NOT ASLEEP NEXT TO HIS WIFE!
YES, I KNOW THAT IT IS THREE IN THE MORNING!

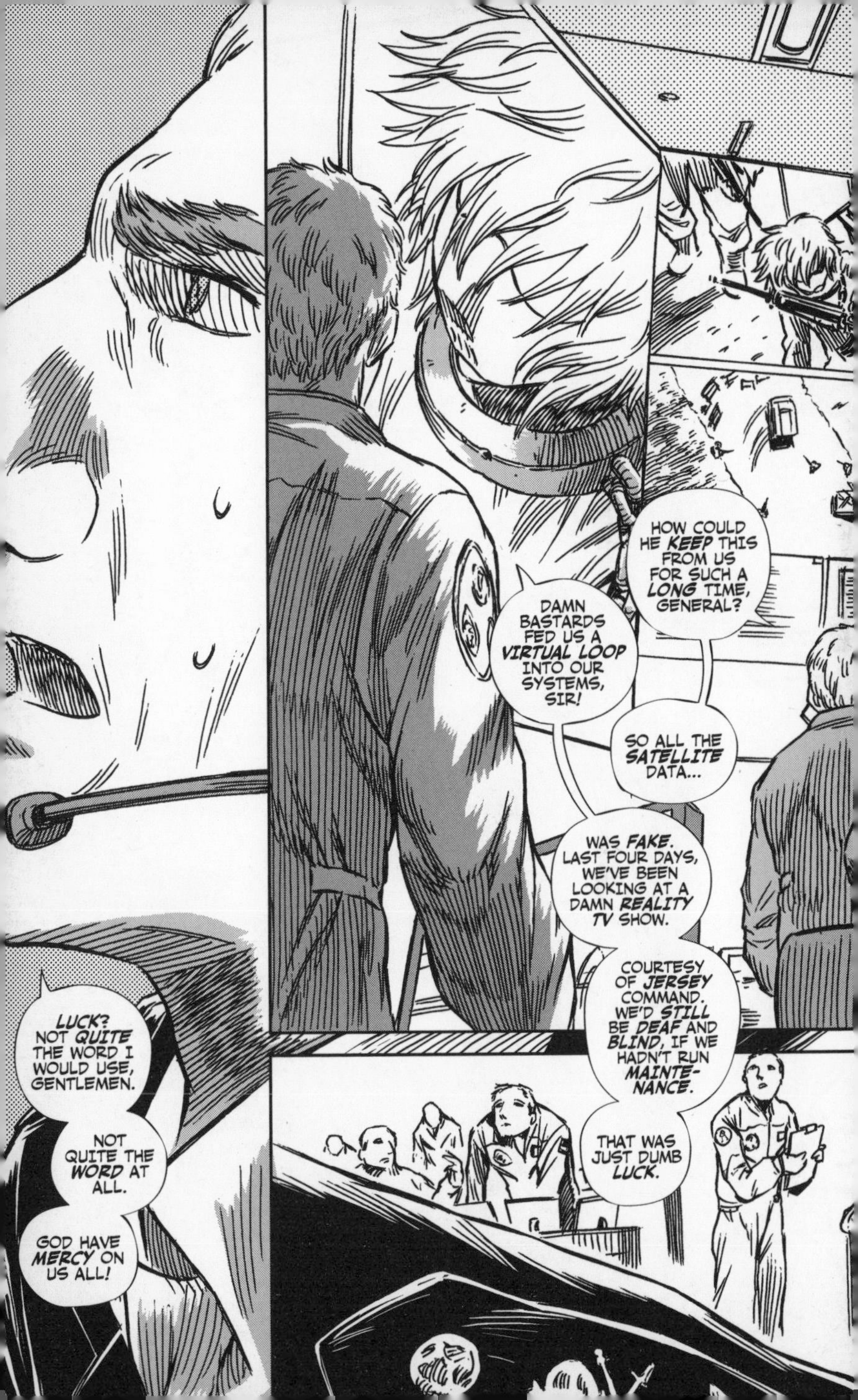
HOW COULD HE KEEP THIS FROM US FOR SUCH A LONG TIME, GENERAL?
DAMN BASTARDS FED US A VIRTUAL LOOP INTO OUR SYSTEMS, SIR!
SO ALL THE SATELLITE DATA...
WAS FAKE. LAST FOUR DAYS, WE'VE BEEN LOOKING AT A DAMN REALITY TV SHOW.
COURTESY OF JERSEY COMMAND. WE'D STILL BE DEAF AND BLIND, IF WE HADN'T RUN MAINTE-NANCE.
THAT WAS JUST DUMB LUCK.
LUCK? NOT QUITE THE WORD I WOULD USE, GENTLEMEN.
NOT QUITE THE WORD AT ALL.
GOD HAVE MERCY ON US ALL!

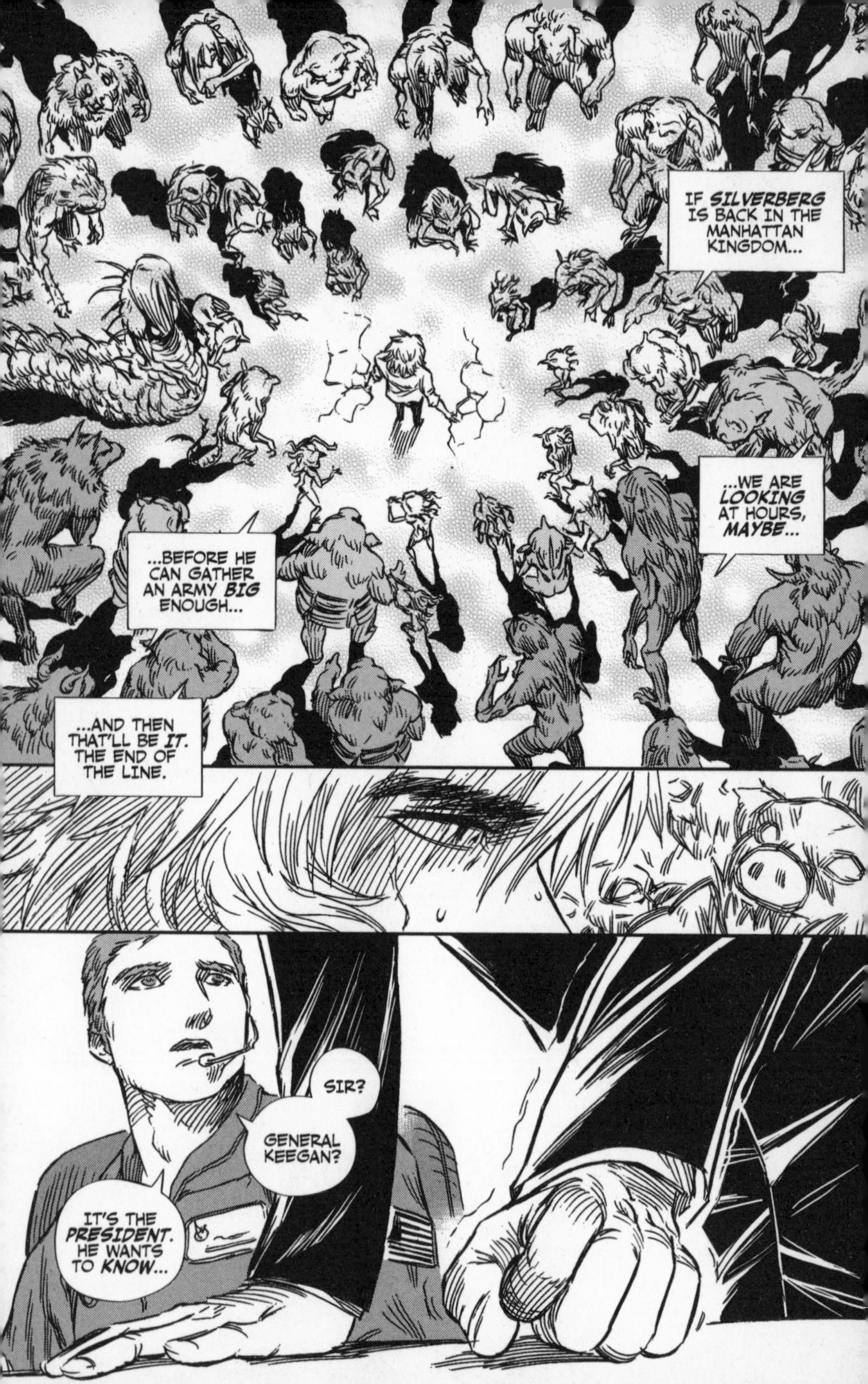
IF *SILVERBERG* IS BACK IN THE MANHATTAN KINGDOM...
...WE ARE *LOOKING* AT HOURS, *MAYBE*...
...BEFORE HE CAN GATHER AN ARMY *BIG* ENOUGH...
...AND THEN THAT'LL BE *IT*. THE END OF THE LINE.
SIR?
GENERAL KEEGAN?
IT'S THE *PRESIDENT*. HE WANTS TO *KNOW*...

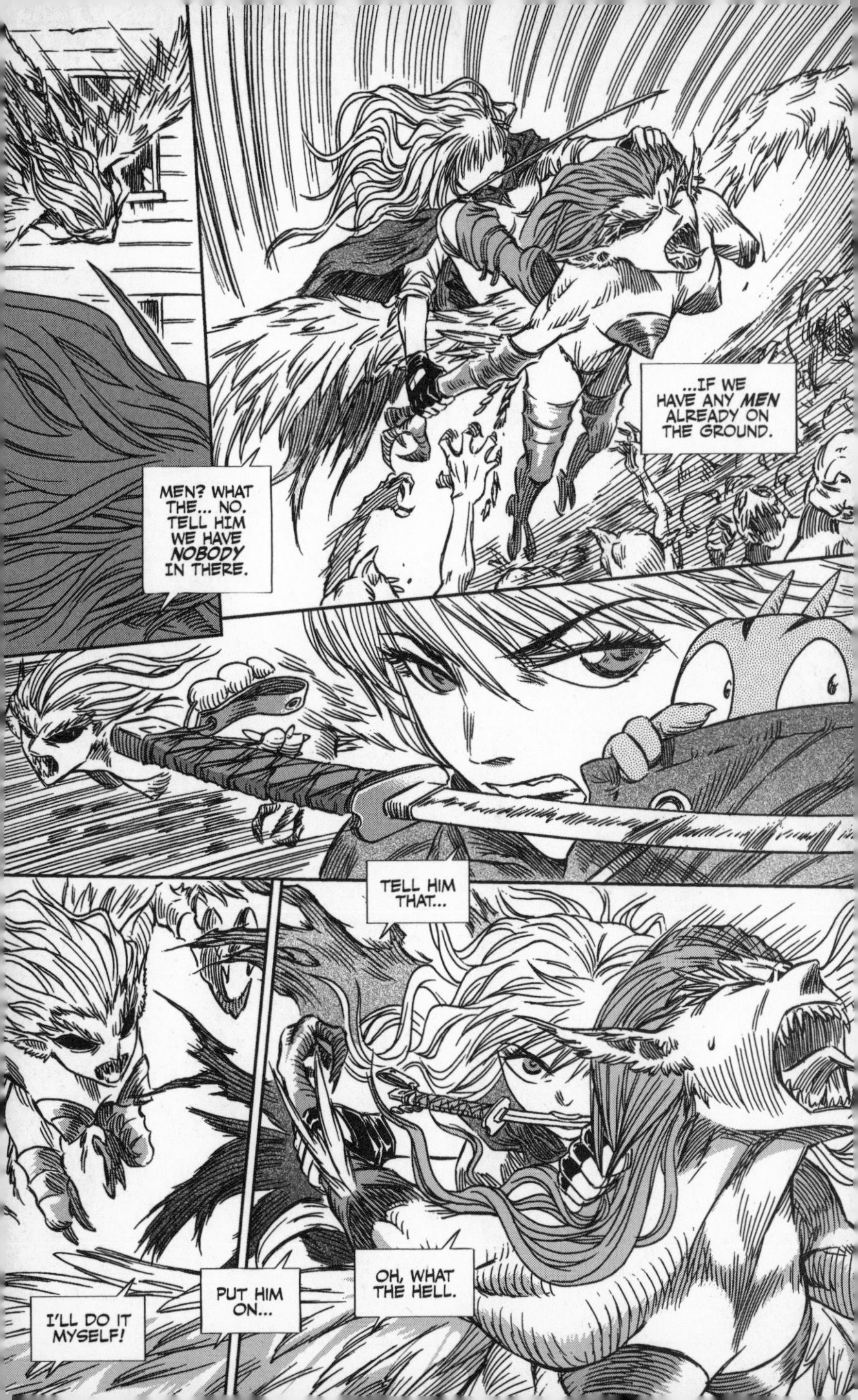
...IF WE HAVE ANY *MEN* ALREADY ON THE GROUND.
MEN? WHAT THE... NO. TELL HIM WE HAVE *NOBODY* IN THERE.
TELL HIM THAT...
OH, WHAT THE HELL.
PUT HIM ON...
I'LL DO IT MYSELF!

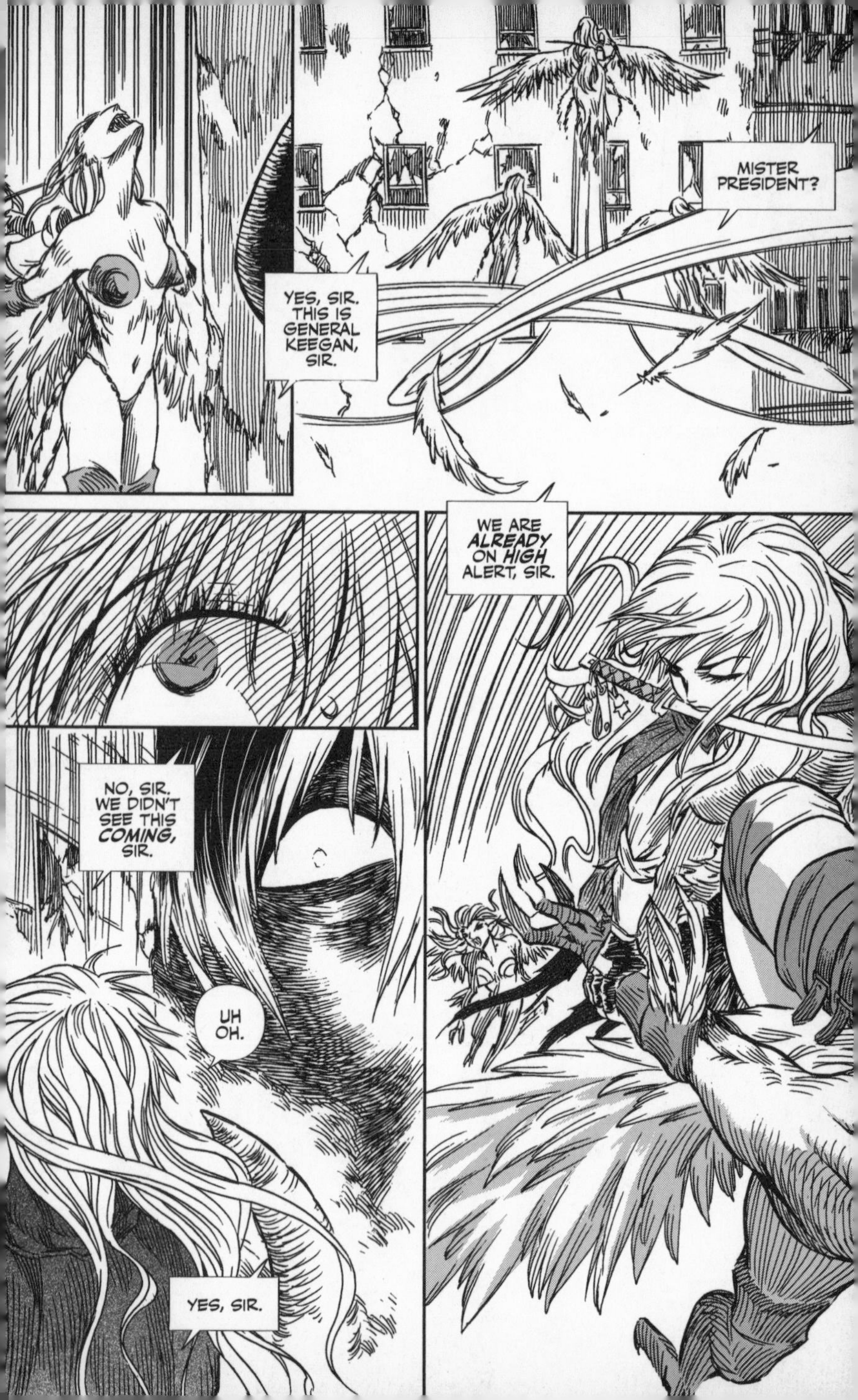
MISTER PRESIDENT?
YES, SIR. THIS IS GENERAL KEEGAN, SIR.
WE ARE *ALREADY* ON *HIGH* ALERT, SIR.
NO, SIR. WE DIDN'T SEE THIS *COMING*, SIR.
UH OH.
YES, SIR.

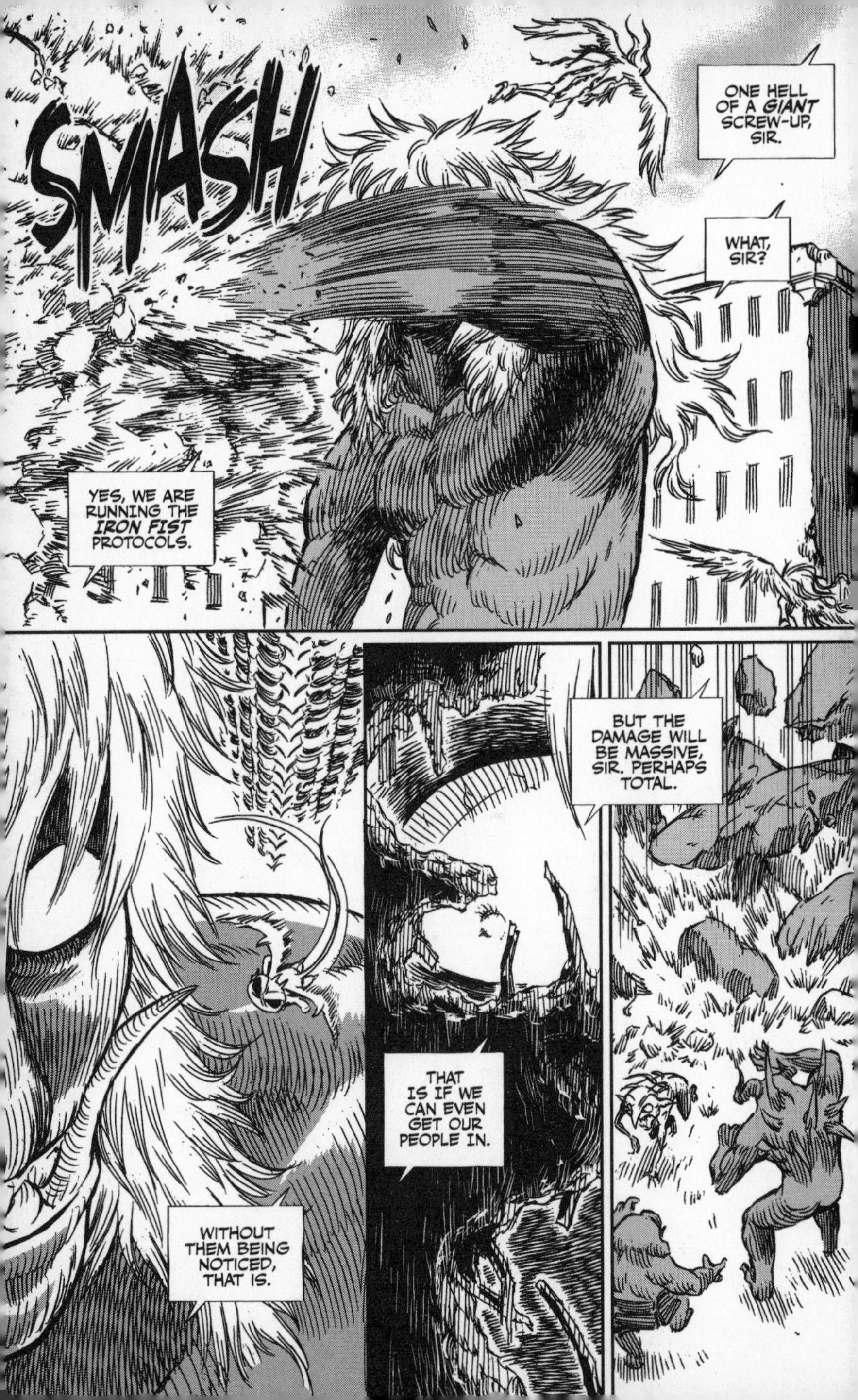
ONE HELL OF A *GIANT* SCREW-UP, SIR.
WHAT, SIR?
SMASH
YES, WE ARE RUNNING THE *IRON FIST* PROTOCOLS.
BUT THE DAMAGE WILL BE MASSIVE, SIR. PERHAPS TOTAL.
THAT IS IF WE CAN EVEN GET OUR PEOPLE IN.
WITHOUT THEM BEING NOTICED, THAT IS.

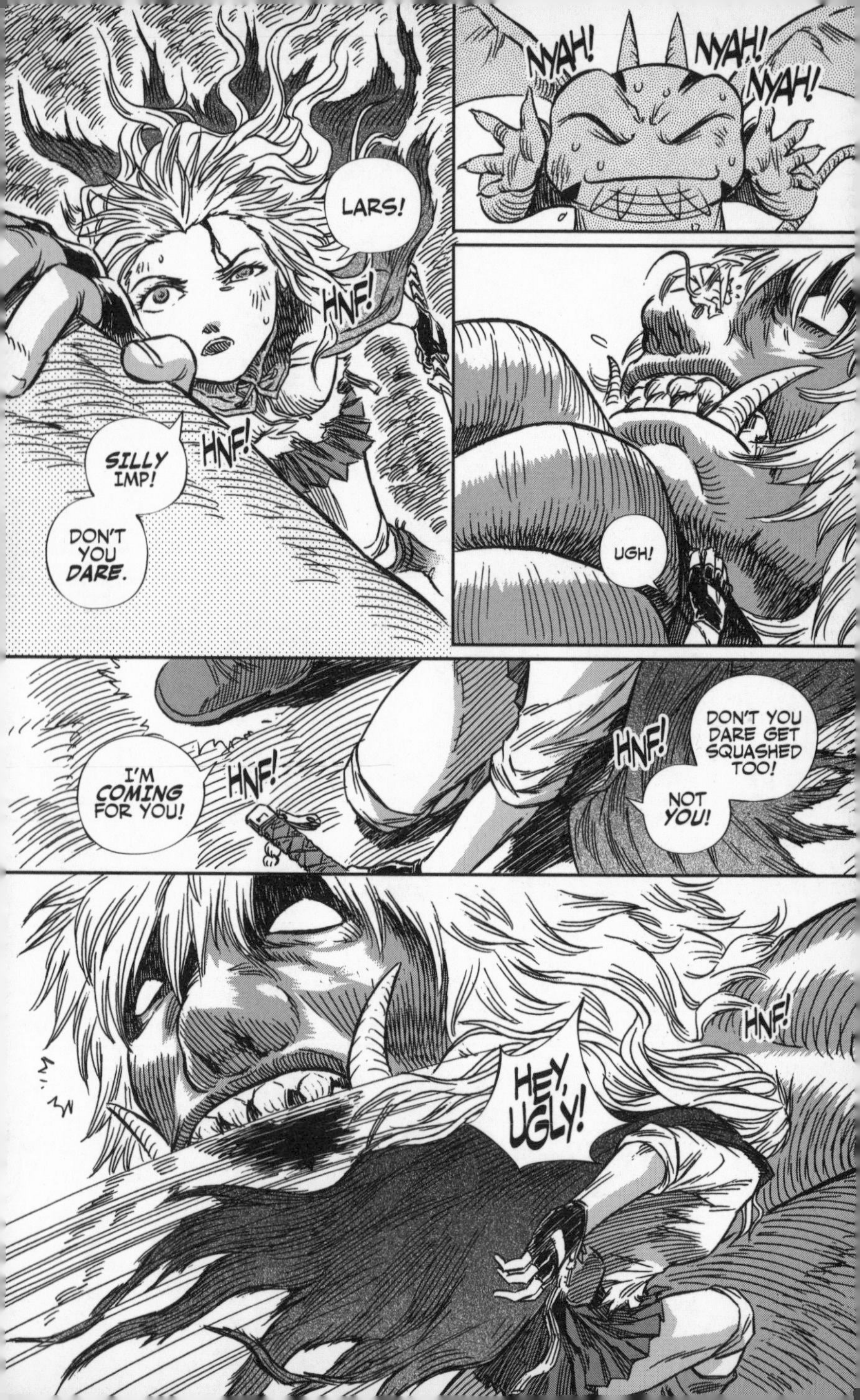
NYAH!
NYAH!
NYAH!
UGH!
LARS!
HNF!
HNF!
SILLY IMP!
DON'T YOU DARE.
HNF!
DON'T YOU DARE GET SQUASHED TOO!
NOT YOU!
HNF!
I'M COMING FOR YOU!
HNF!
HEY, UGLY!

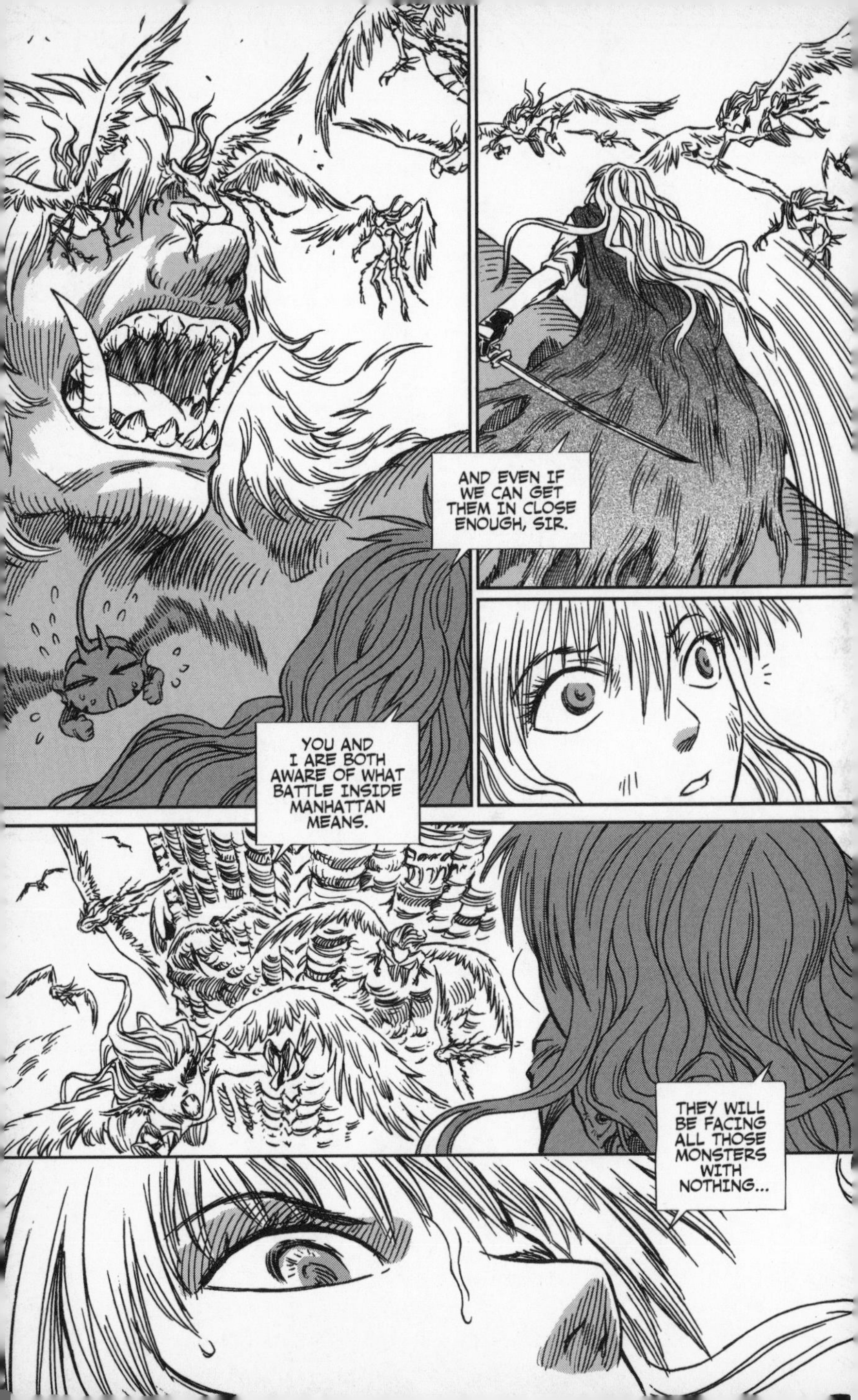
AND EVEN IF WE CAN GET THEM IN CLOSE ENOUGH, SIR.
YOU AND I ARE BOTH AWARE OF WHAT BATTLE INSIDE MANHATTAN MEANS.
THEY WILL BE FACING ALL THOSE MONSTERS WITH NOTHING...

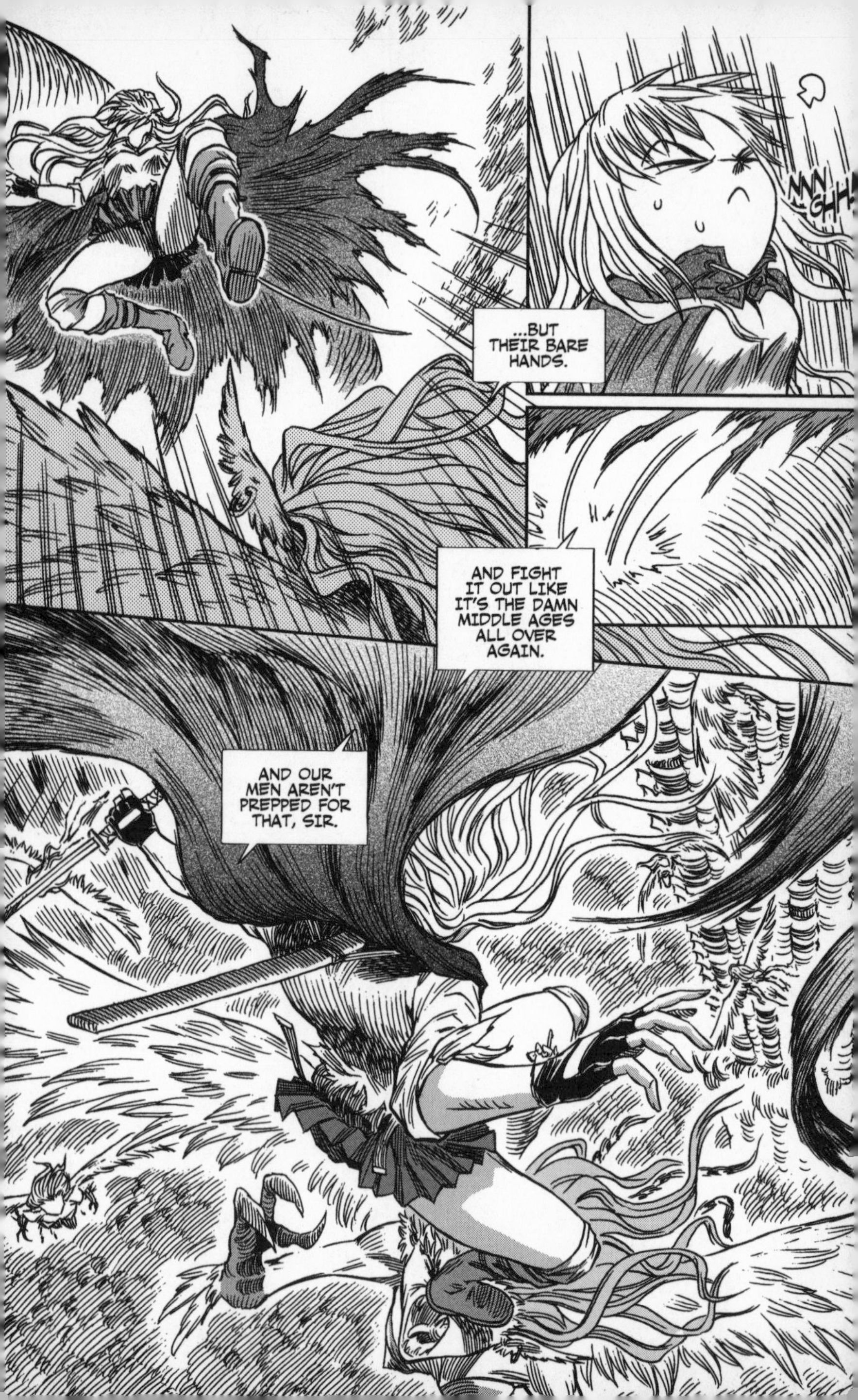
NNN GHH
...BUT THEIR BARE HANDS.
AND FIGHT IT OUT LIKE IT'S THE DAMN MIDDLE AGES ALL OVER AGAIN.
AND OUR MEN AREN'T PREPPED FOR THAT, SIR.

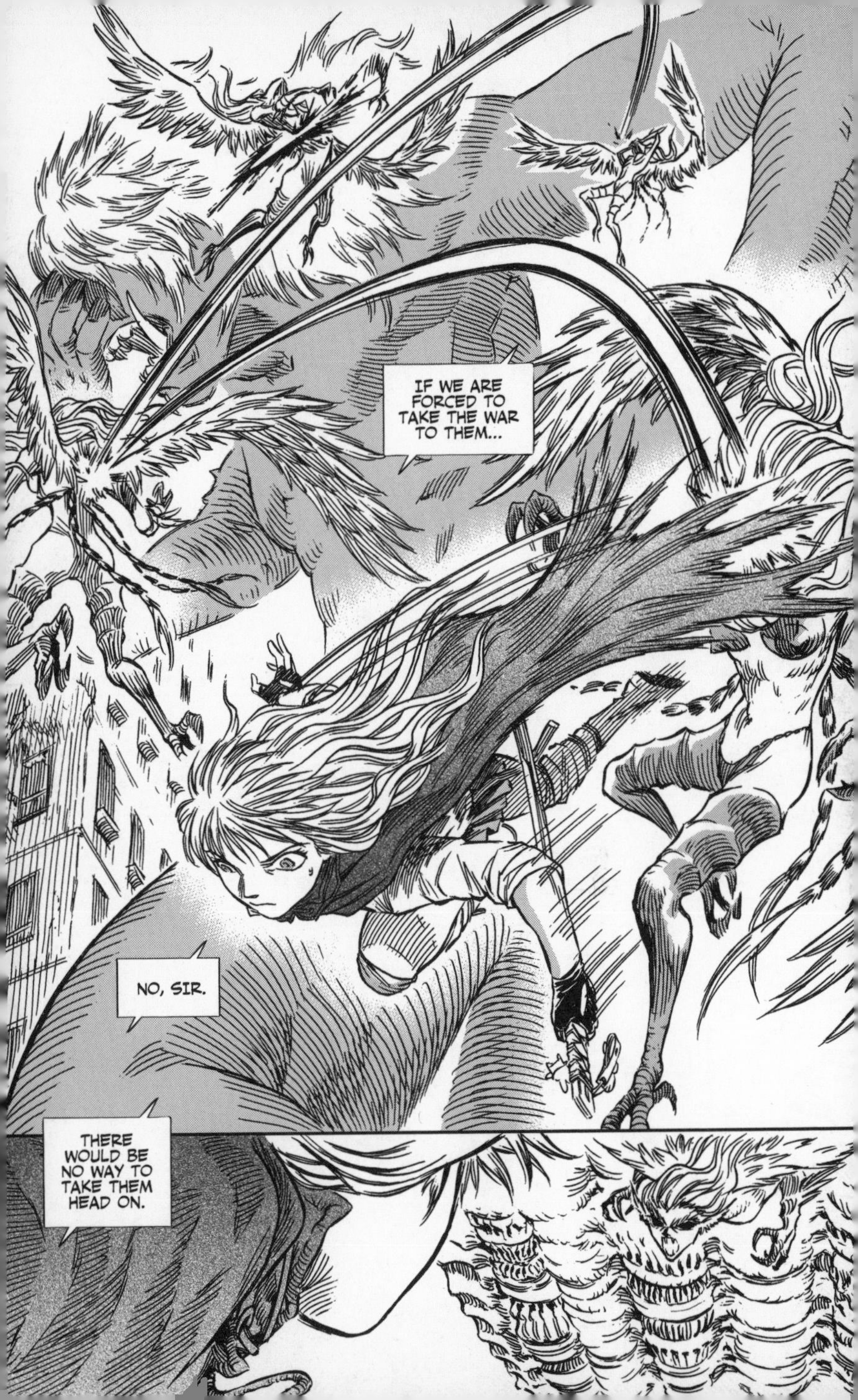
IF WE ARE FORCED TO TAKE THE WAR TO THEM...
NO, SIR.
THERE WOULD BE NO WAY TO TAKE THEM HEAD ON.

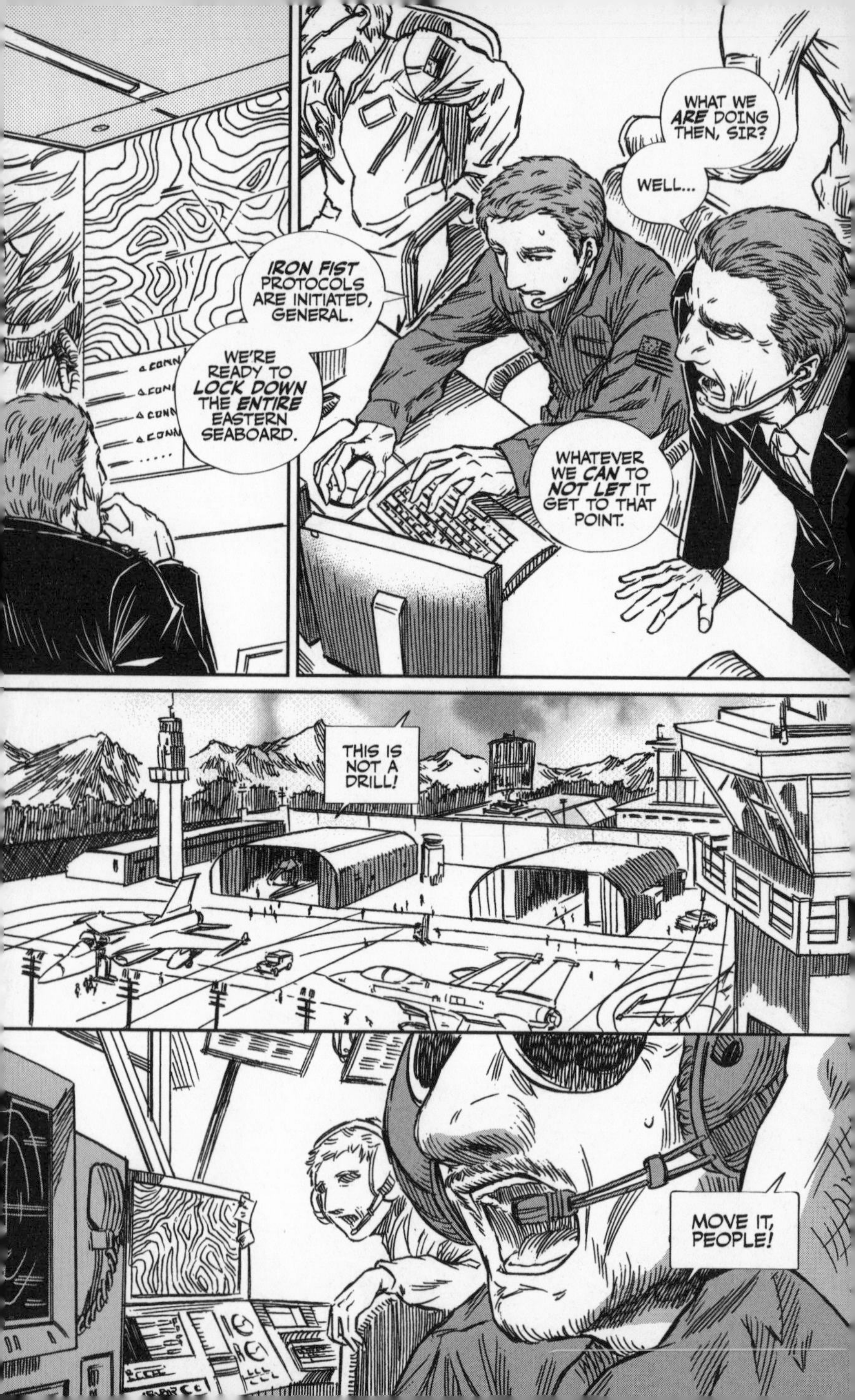
IRON FIST PROTOCOLS ARE INITIATED, GENERAL.
WE'RE READY TO LOCK DOWN THE ENTIRE EASTERN SEABOARD.
WHAT WE ARE DOING THEN, SIR?
WELL...
WHATEVER WE CAN TO NOT LET IT GET TO THAT POINT.
THIS IS NOT A DRILL!
MOVE IT, PEOPLE!

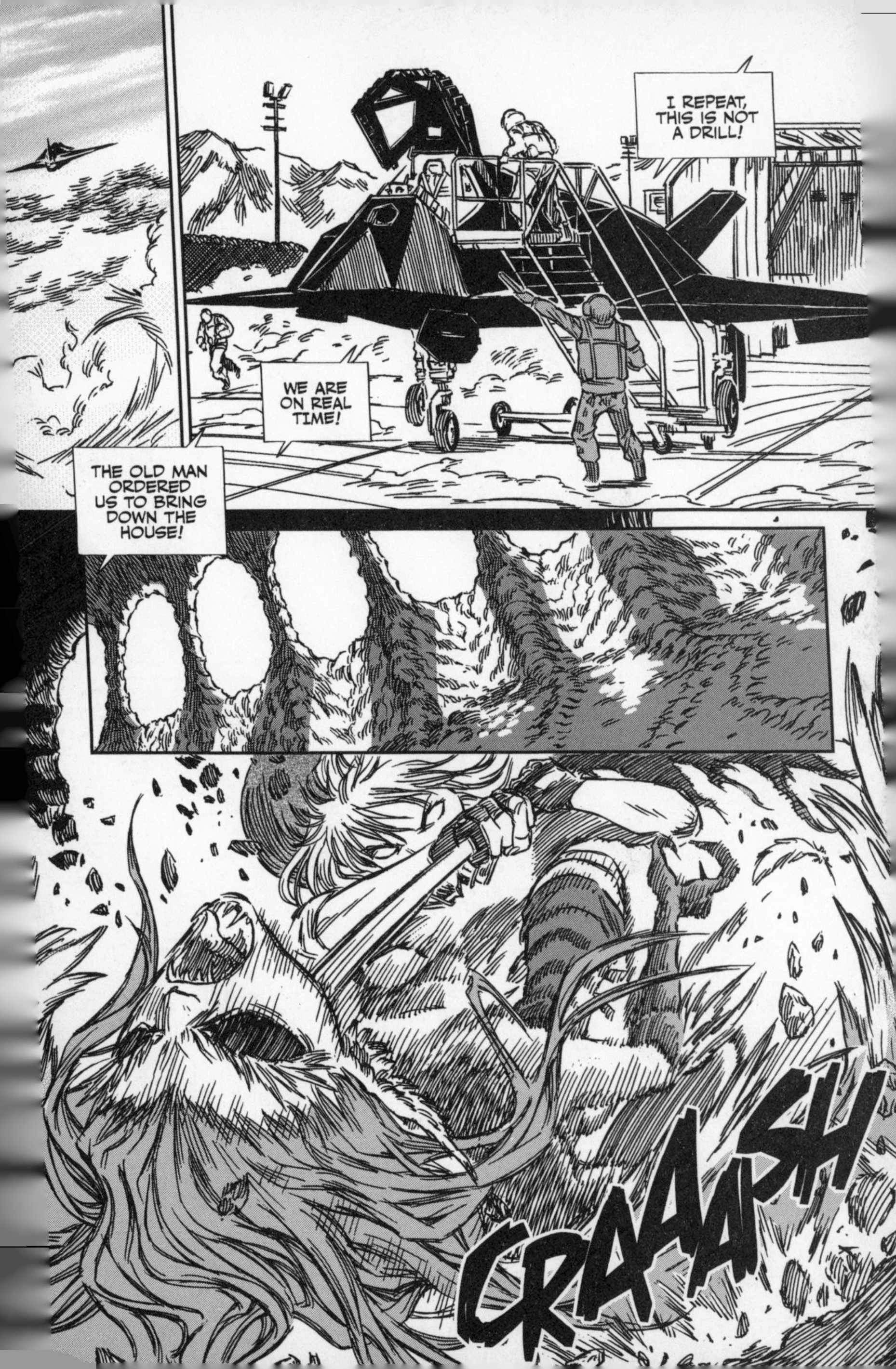
I REPEAT, THIS IS NOT A DRILL!
WE ARE ON REAL TIME!
THE OLD MAN ORDERED US TO BRING DOWN THE HOUSE!
CRAAASH

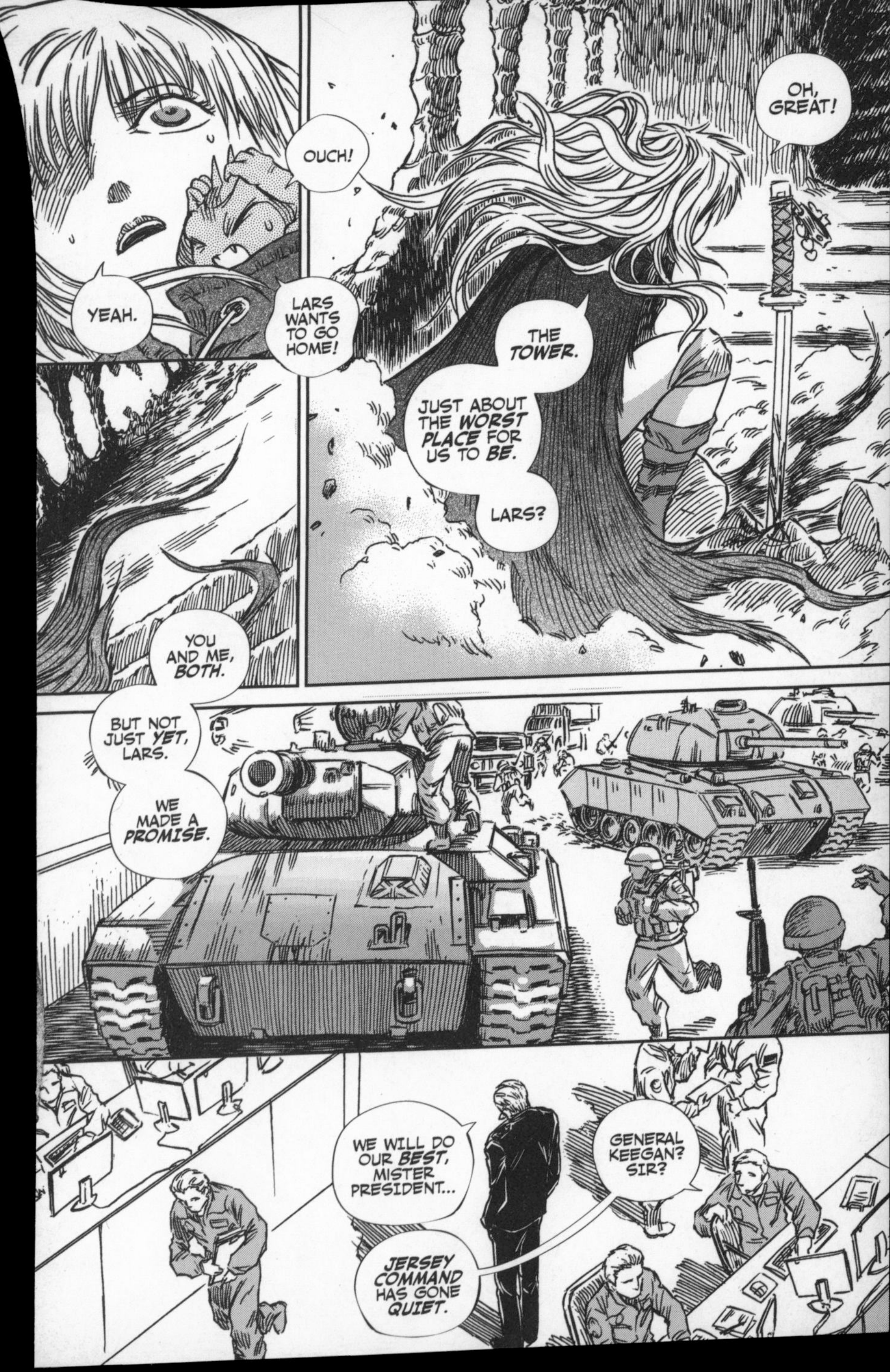
OH, GREAT!
THE *TOWER*.
JUST ABOUT THE ***WORST PLACE*** FOR US TO ***BE***.
LARS?
OUCH!
YEAH.
LARS WANTS TO GO HOME!
YOU AND ME, ***BOTH***.
BUT NOT JUST ***YET***, LARS.
WE MADE A ***PROMISE***.
GENERAL KEEGAN? SIR?
JERSEY COMMAND HAS GONE ***QUIET***.
WE WILL DO OUR ***BEST***, MISTER PRESIDENT...

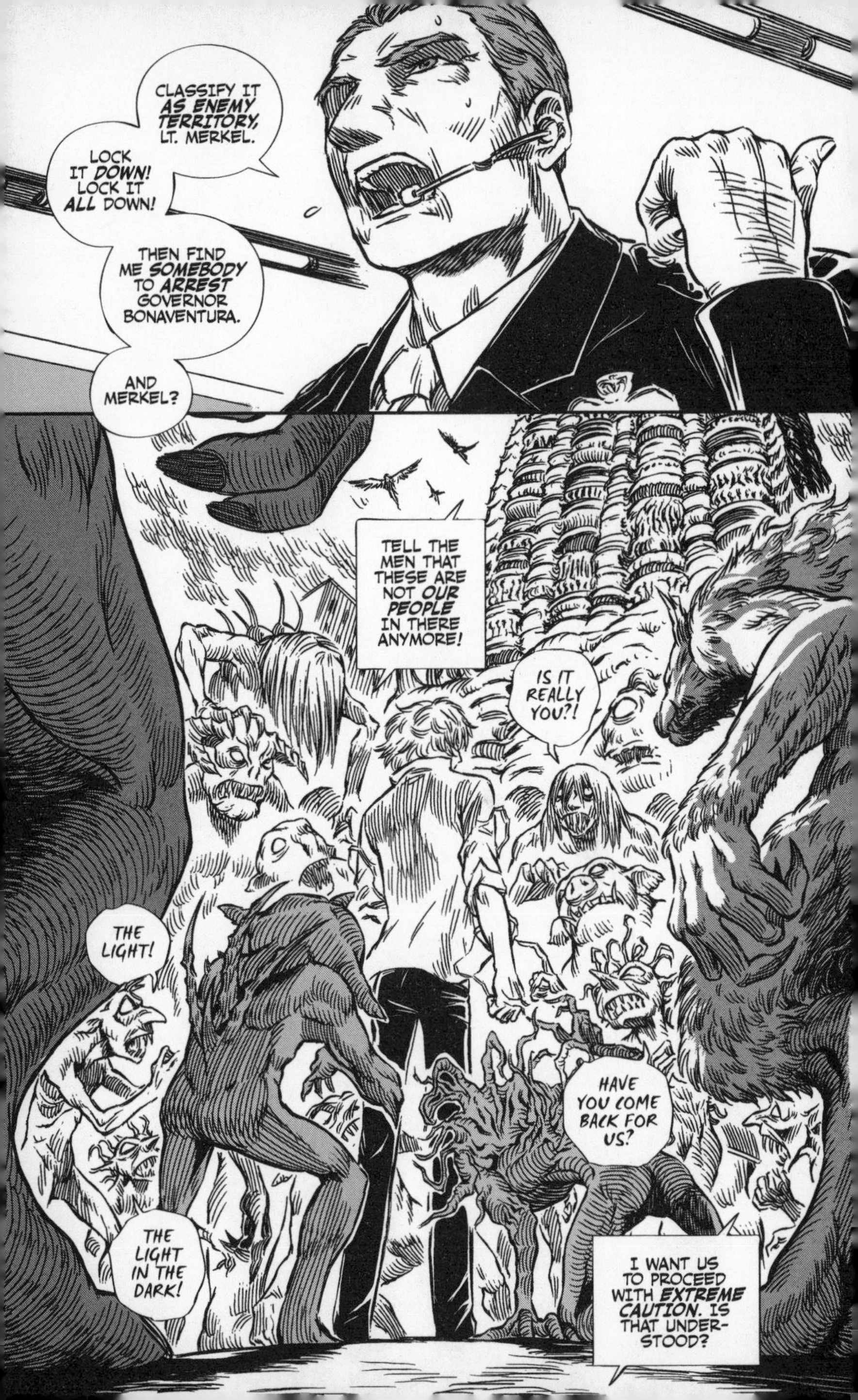
CLASSIFY IT *AS ENEMY TERRITORY,* LT. MERKEL.
LOCK IT *DOWN!* LOCK IT *ALL* DOWN!
THEN FIND ME *SOMEBODY* TO *ARREST* GOVERNOR BONAVENTURA.
AND MERKEL?
TELL THE MEN THAT THESE ARE NOT *OUR PEOPLE* IN THERE ANYMORE!
IS IT REALLY YOU?!
THE LIGHT!
HAVE YOU COME BACK FOR US?
THE LIGHT IN THE DARK!
I WANT US TO PROCEED WITH *EXTREME CAUTION.* IS THAT UNDER-STOOD?

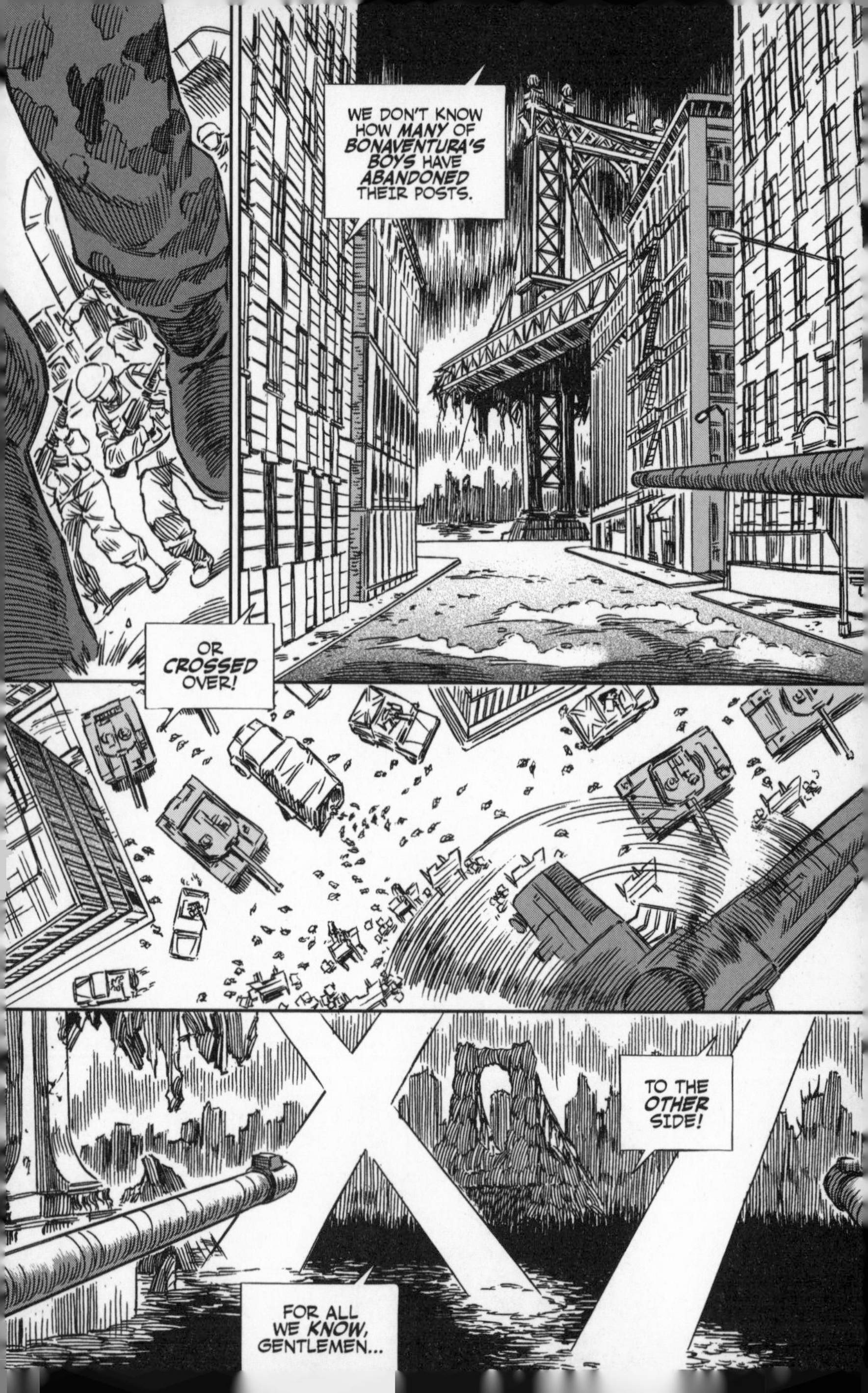
WE DON'T KNOW HOW MANY OF BONAVENTURA'S BOYS HAVE ABANDONED THEIR POSTS.
OR CROSSED OVER!
TO THE OTHER SIDE!
FOR ALL WE KNOW, GENTLEMEN...

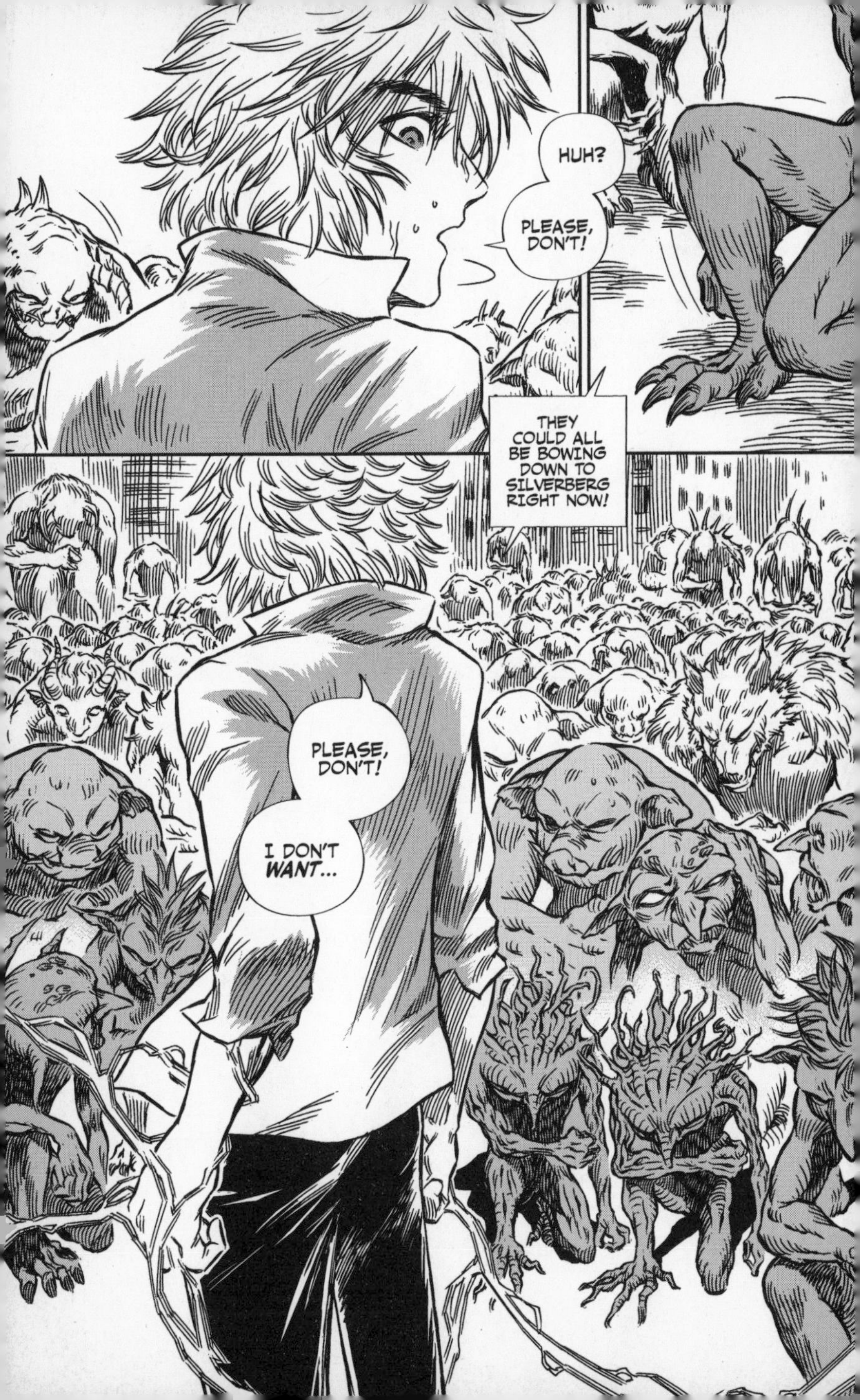
HUH?
PLEASE, DON'T!
THEY COULD ALL BE BOWING DOWN TO SILVERBERG RIGHT NOW!
PLEASE, DON'T!
I DON'T *WANT*...

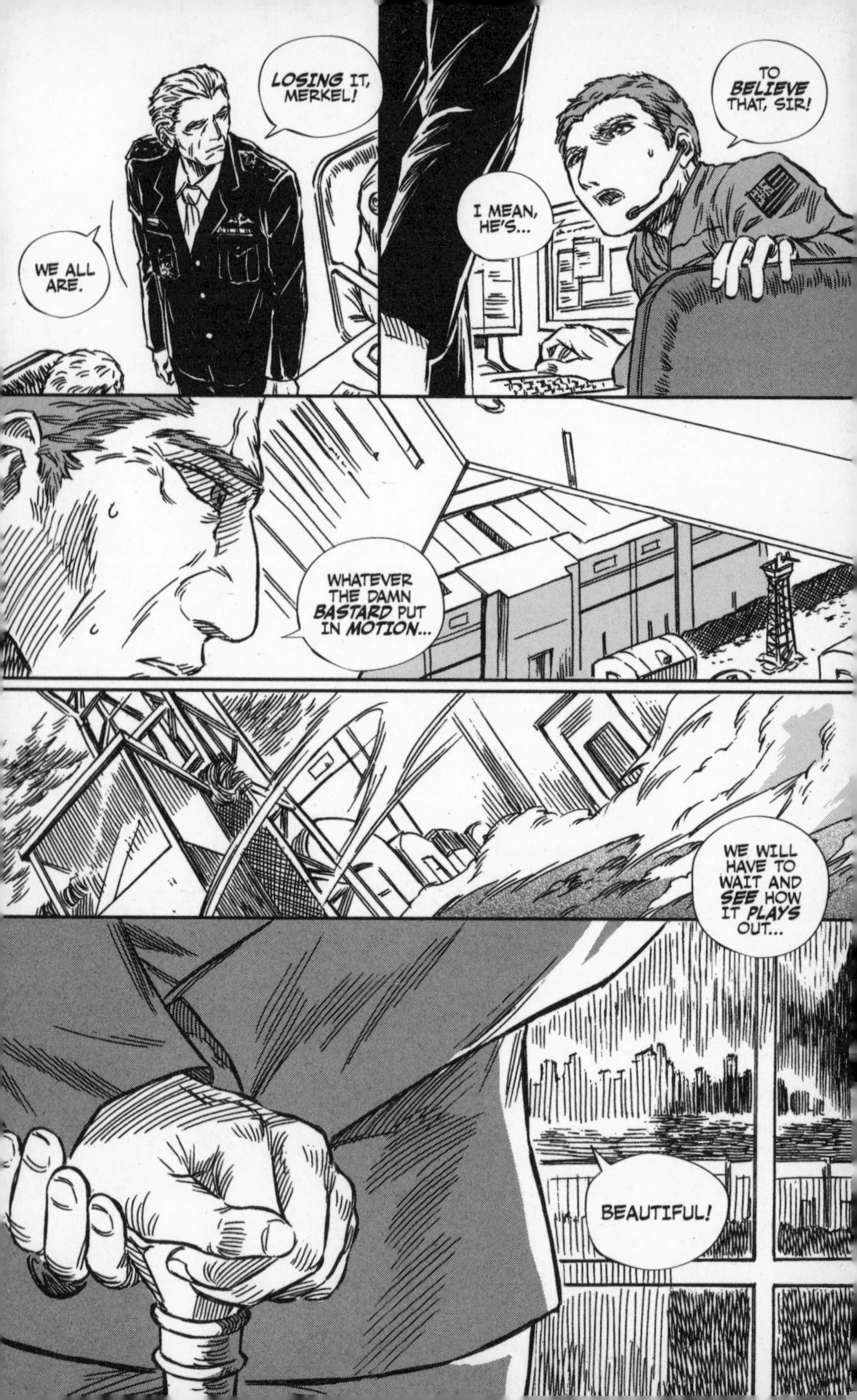
TO BELIEVE THAT, SIR!
I MEAN, HE'S...
LOSING IT, MERKEL!
WE ALL ARE.
WHATEVER THE DAMN BASTARD PUT IN MOTION...
WE WILL HAVE TO WAIT AND SEE HOW IT PLAYS OUT...
BEAUTIFUL!

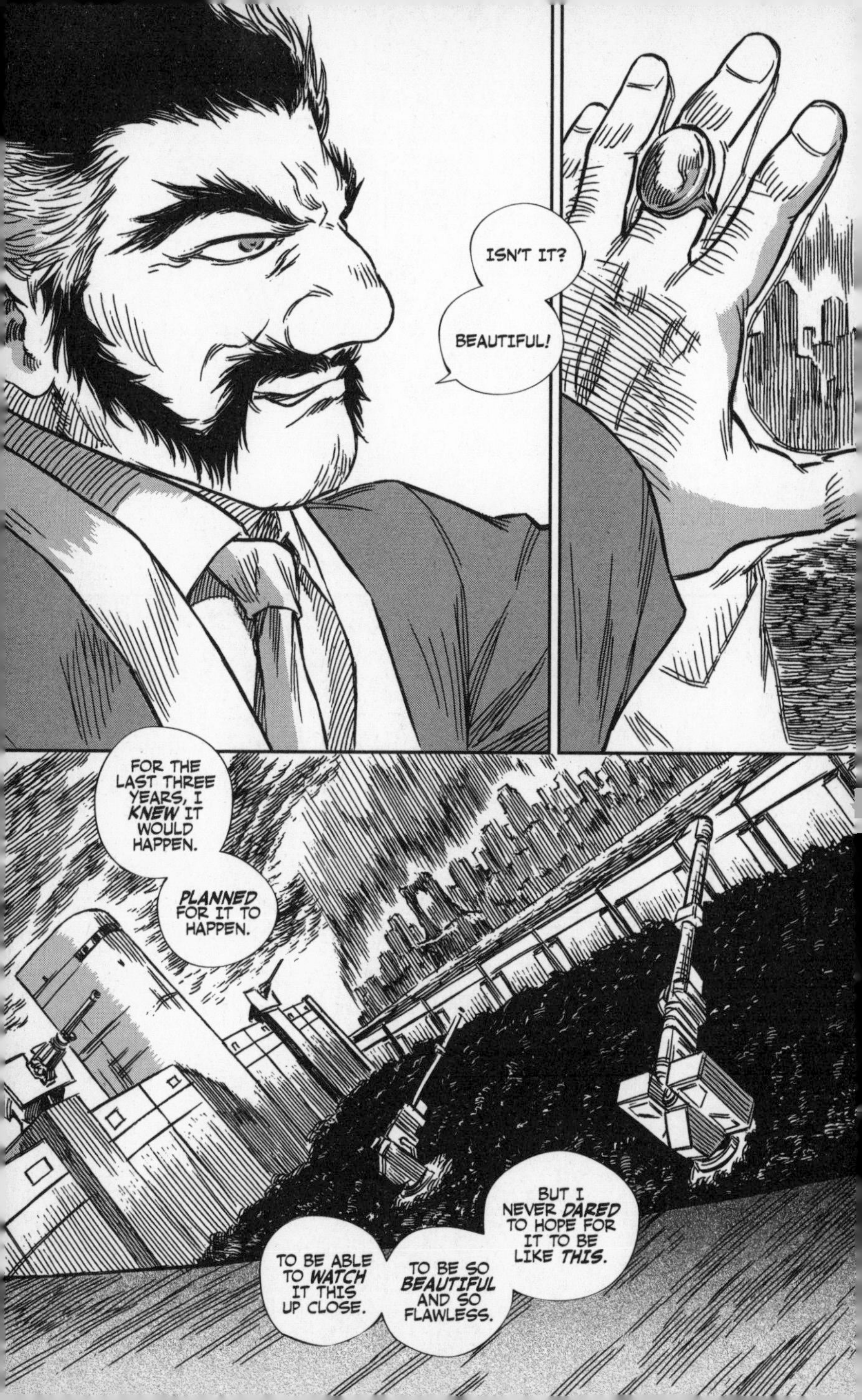
ISN'T IT?
BEAUTIFUL!
FOR THE LAST THREE YEARS, I *KNEW* IT WOULD HAPPEN.
PLANNED FOR IT TO HAPPEN.
BUT I NEVER *DARED* TO HOPE FOR IT TO BE LIKE *THIS*.
TO BE SO *BEAUTIFUL* AND SO FLAWLESS.
TO BE ABLE TO *WATCH* IT THIS UP CLOSE.

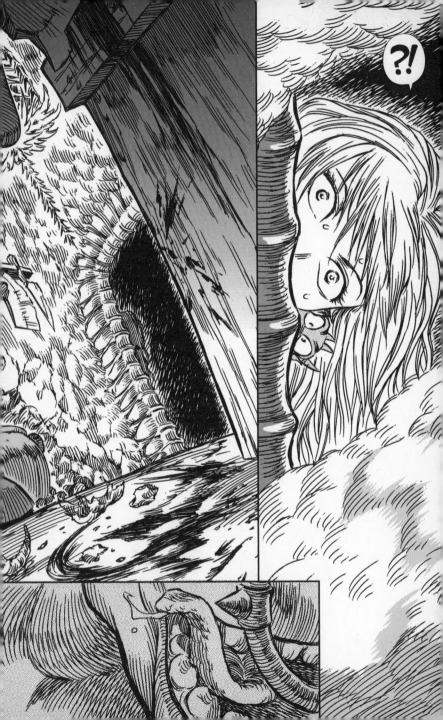

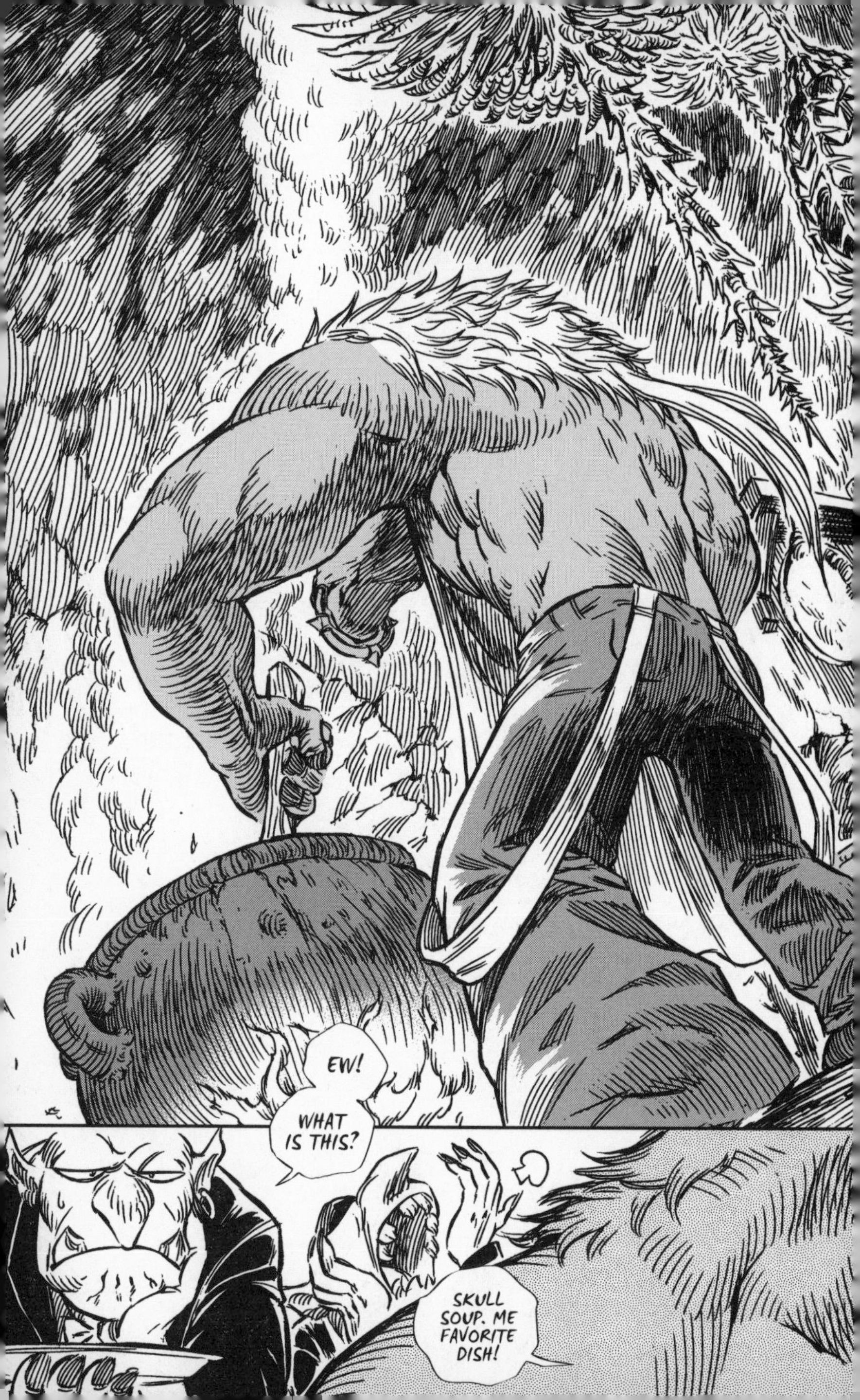
EW!
WHAT IS THIS?
SKULL SOUP. ME FAVORITE DISH!

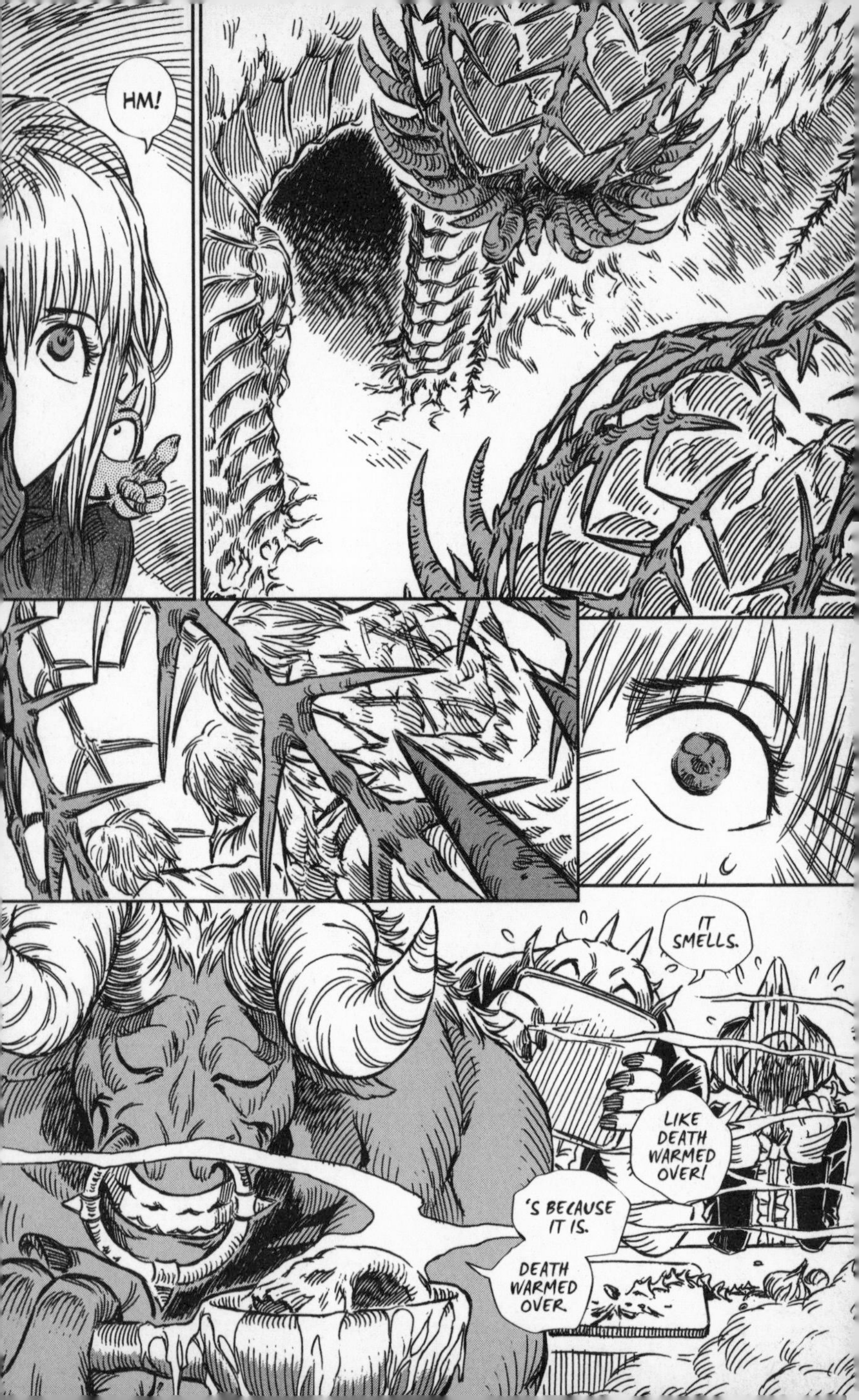
HM!
IT SMELLS.
LIKE DEATH WARMED OVER!
'S BECAUSE IT IS.
DEATH WARMED OVER.

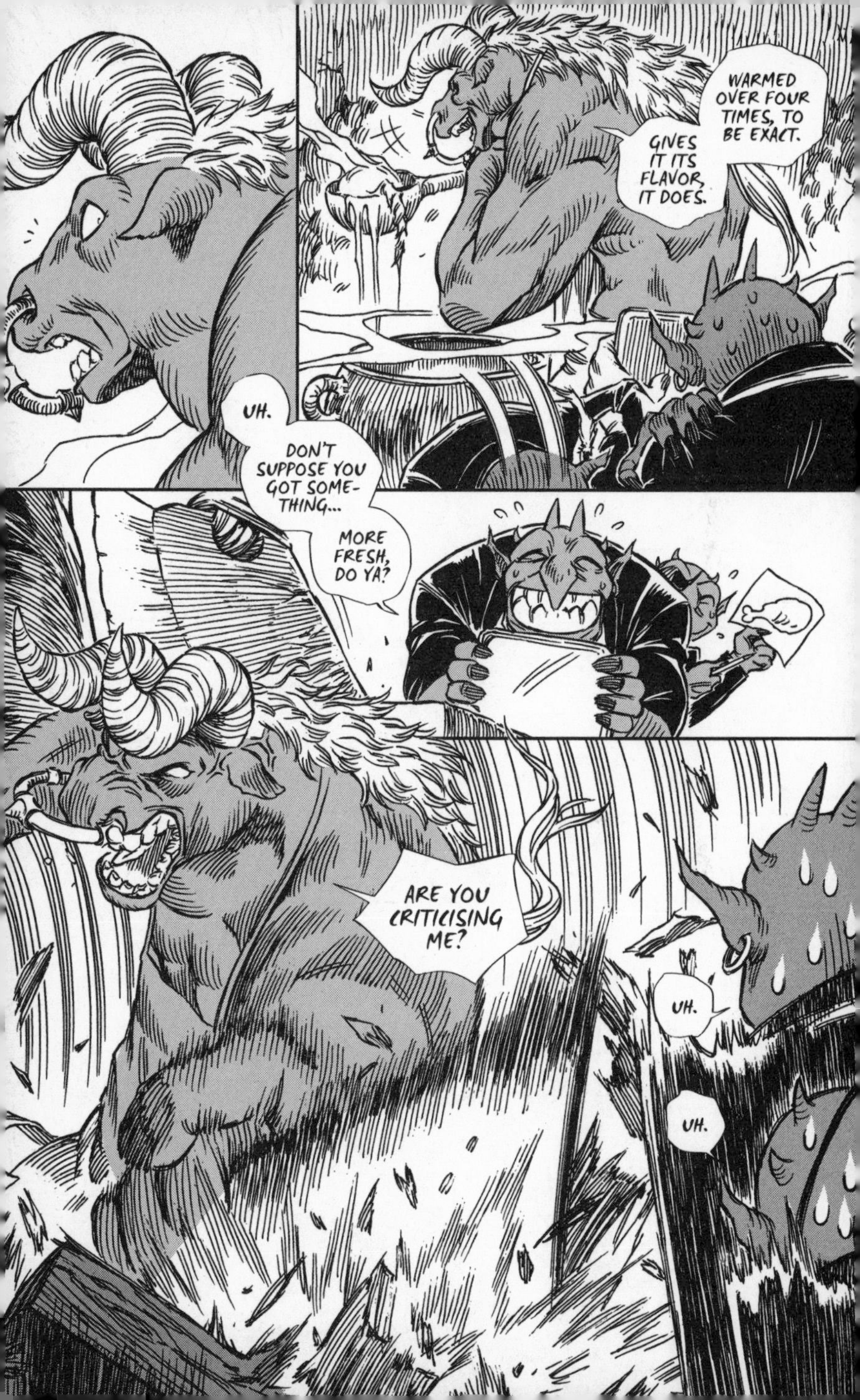
WARMED OVER FOUR TIMES, TO BE EXACT.
GIVES IT ITS FLAVOR, IT DOES.
UH.
DON'T SUPPOSE YOU GOT SOME-THING...
MORE FRESH, DO YA?
ARE YOU CRITICISING ME?
UH.
UH.

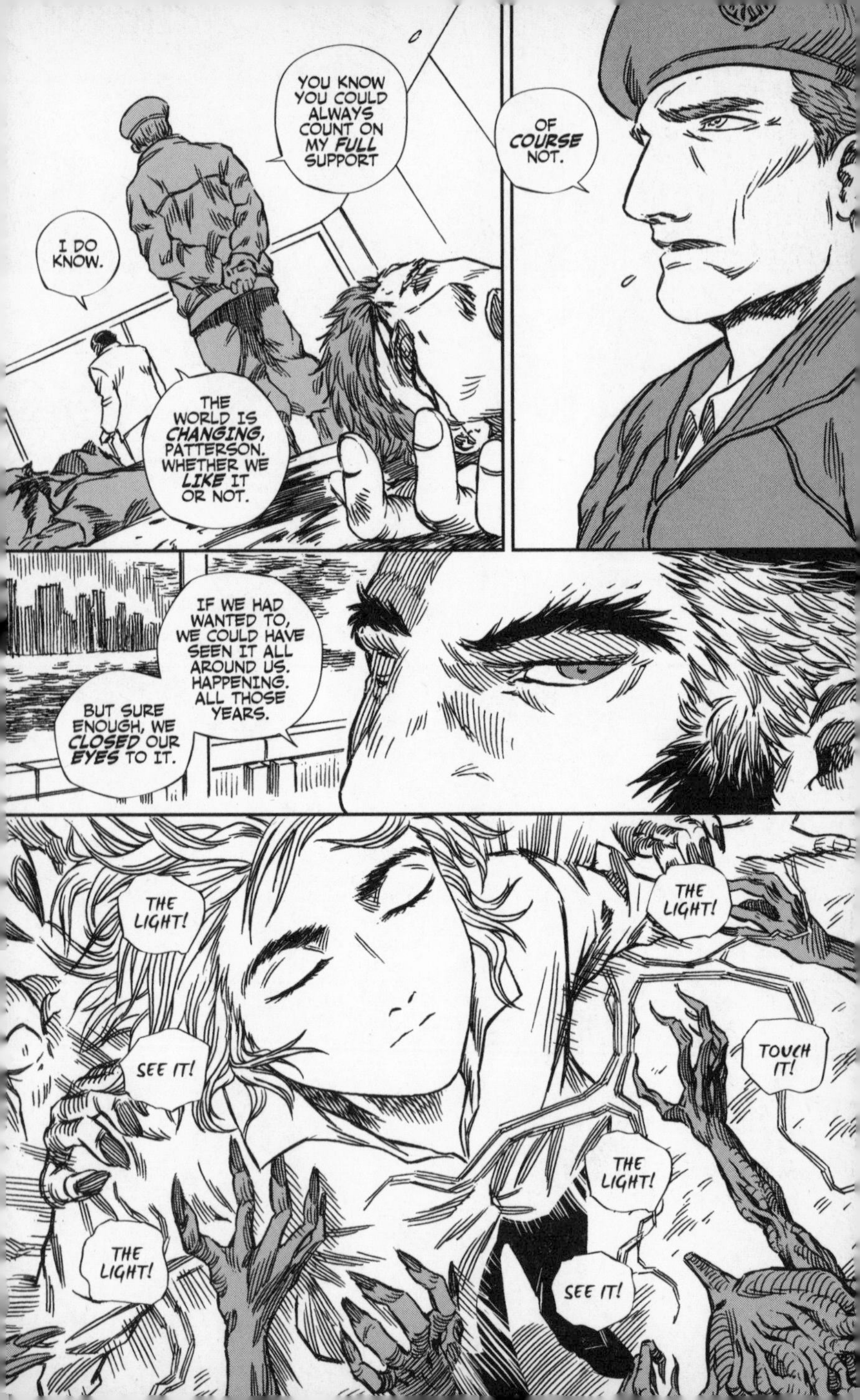
OF COURSE NOT.
YOU KNOW YOU COULD ALWAYS COUNT ON MY FULL SUPPORT
I DO KNOW.
THE WORLD IS CHANGING, PATTERSON. WHETHER WE LIKE IT OR NOT.
IF WE HAD WANTED TO, WE COULD HAVE SEEN IT ALL AROUND US. HAPPENING. ALL THOSE YEARS.
BUT SURE ENOUGH, WE CLOSED OUR EYES TO IT.
THE LIGHT!
THE LIGHT!
TOUCH IT!
SEE IT!
THE LIGHT!
SEE IT!
THE LIGHT!

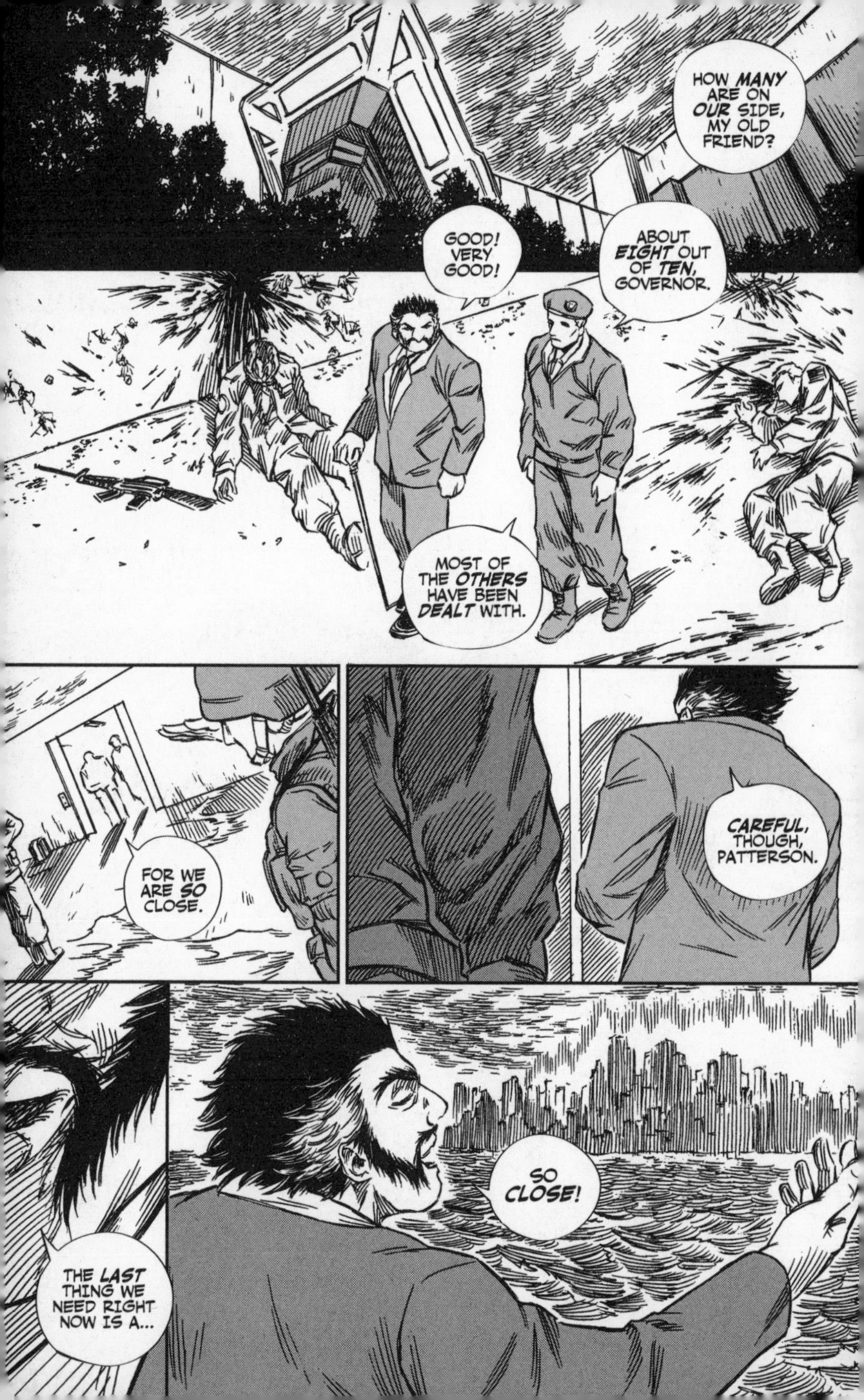
HOW MANY ARE ON OUR SIDE, MY OLD FRIEND?
ABOUT EIGHT OUT OF TEN, GOVERNOR.
GOOD! VERY GOOD!
MOST OF THE OTHERS HAVE BEEN DEALT WITH.
CAREFUL, THOUGH, PATTERSON.
FOR WE ARE SO CLOSE.
SO CLOSE!
THE LAST THING WE NEED RIGHT NOW IS A...

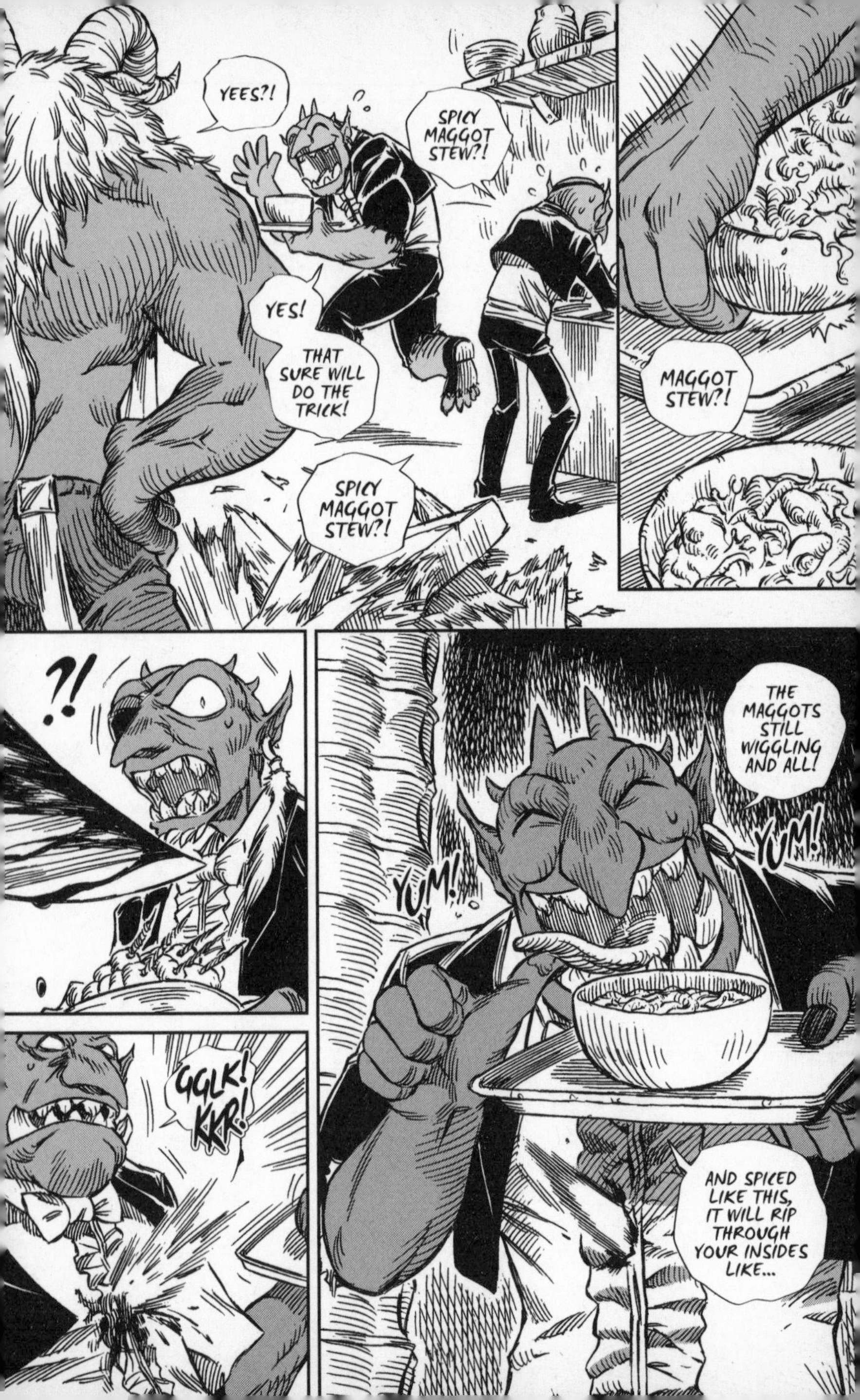
MAGGOT STEW?!
YEES?!
SPICY MAGGOT STEW?!
YES!
THAT SURE WILL DO THE TRICK!
SPICY MAGGOT STEW?!
THE MAGGOTS STILL WIGGLING AND ALL!
YUM!
YUM!
AND SPICED LIKE THIS, IT WILL RIP THROUGH YOUR INSIDES LIKE...
?!
GGLK! KKR!

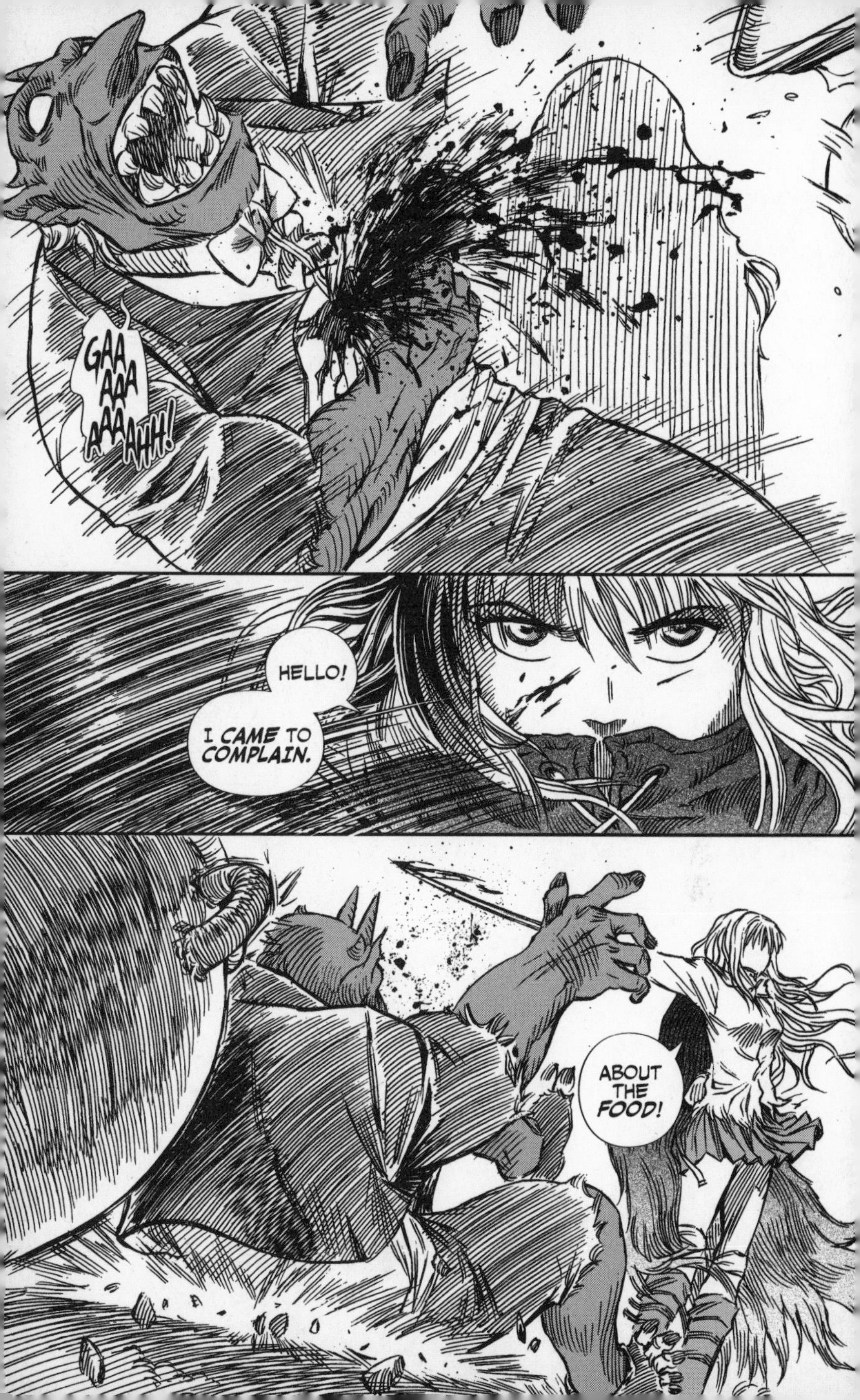
GAAAAAAAAAAHH!
HELLO!
I CAME TO COMPLAIN.
ABOUT THE FOOD!

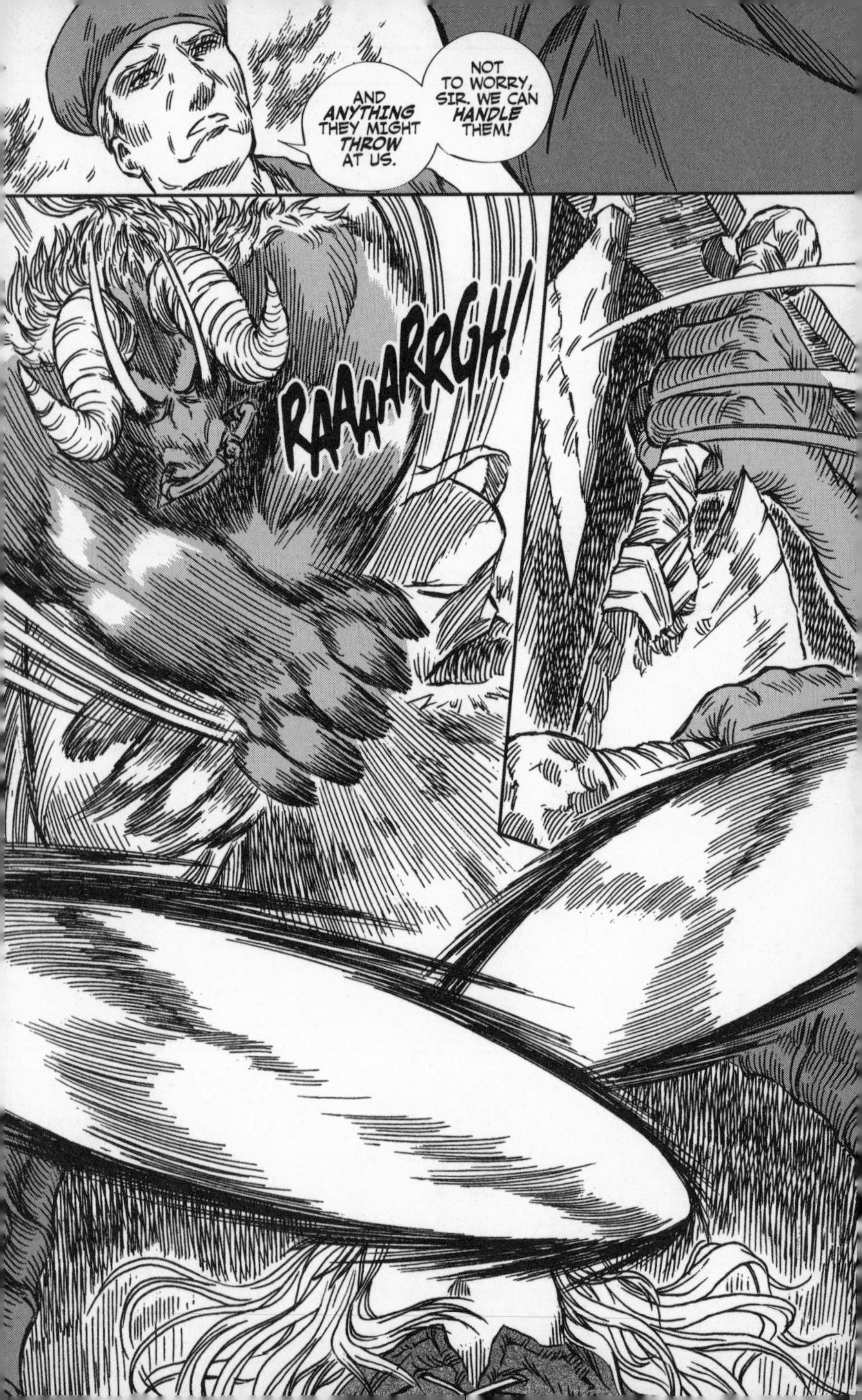
NOT TO WORRY, SIR. WE CAN *HANDLE* THEM!
AND *ANYTHING* THEY MIGHT *THROW* AT US.
RAAAARRGH!

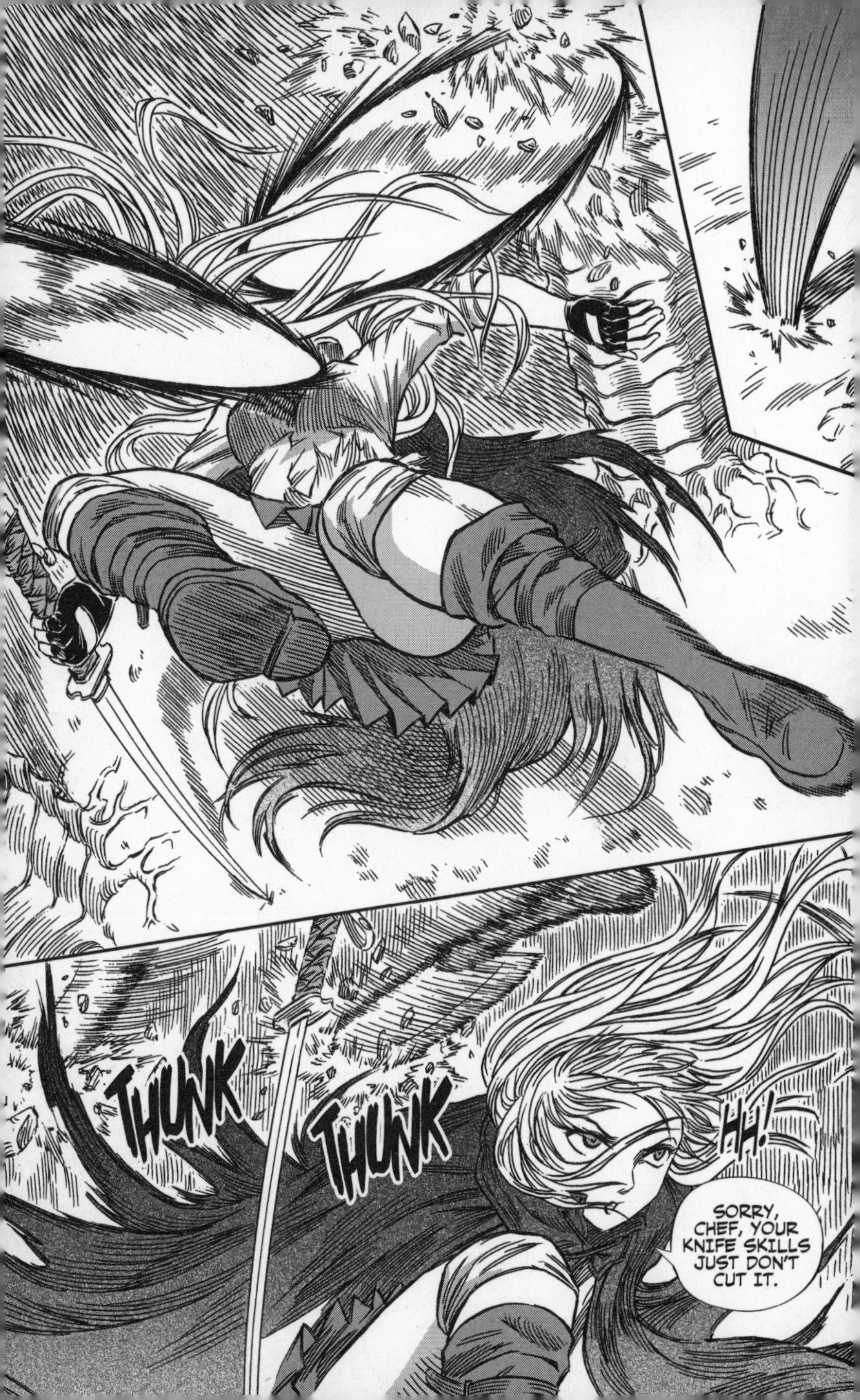
HH!
THUNK
THUNK
SORRY, CHEF, YOUR KNIFE SKILLS JUST DON'T CUT IT.

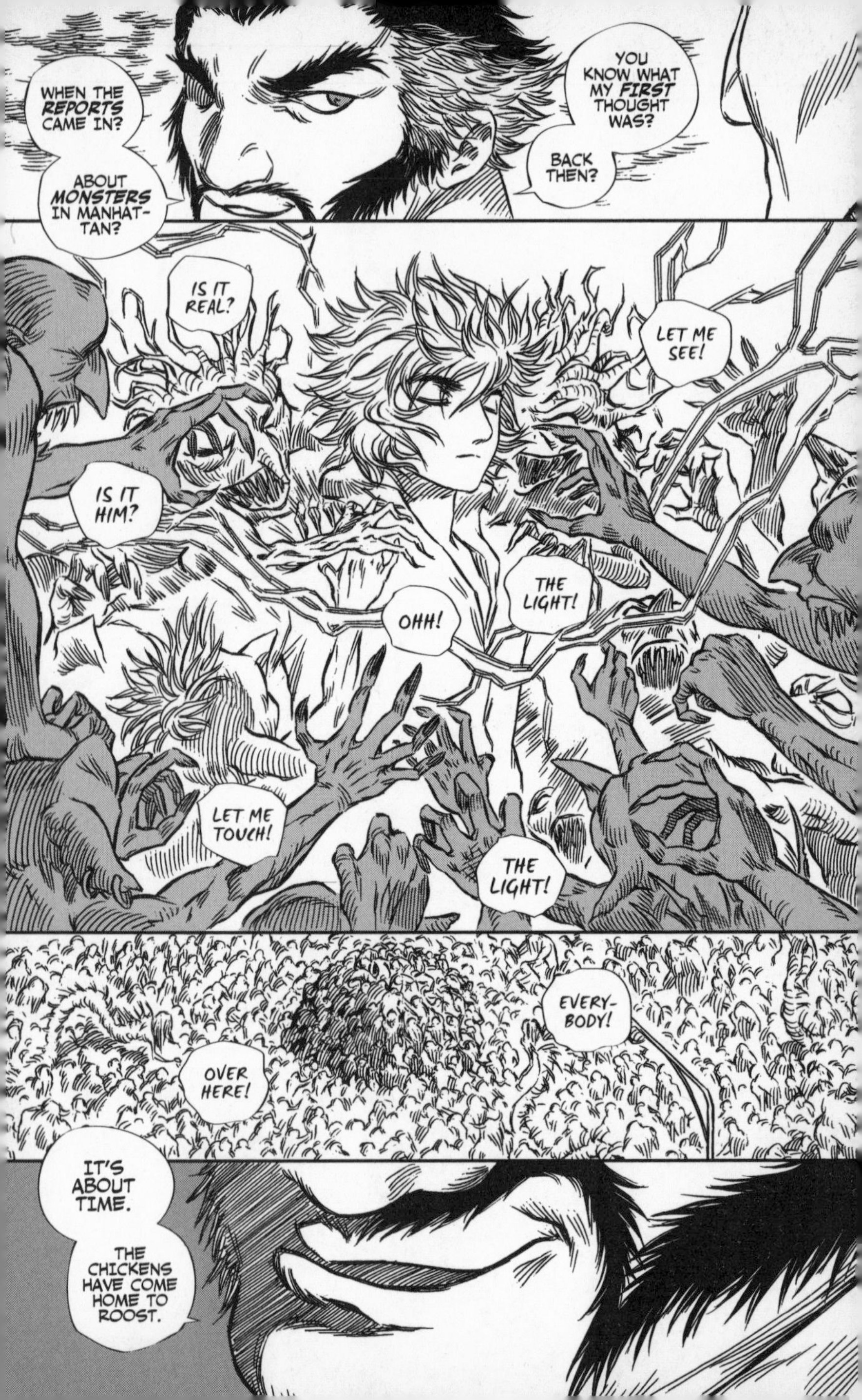
WHEN THE *REPORTS* CAME IN?
ABOUT *MONSTERS* IN MANHAT-TAN?
YOU KNOW WHAT MY *FIRST* THOUGHT WAS?
BACK THEN?
IS IT REAL?
LET ME SEE!
IS IT HIM?
THE LIGHT!
OHH!
LET ME TOUCH!
THE LIGHT!
EVERY-BODY!
OVER HERE!
IT'S ABOUT TIME.
THE CHICKENS HAVE COME HOME TO ROOST.

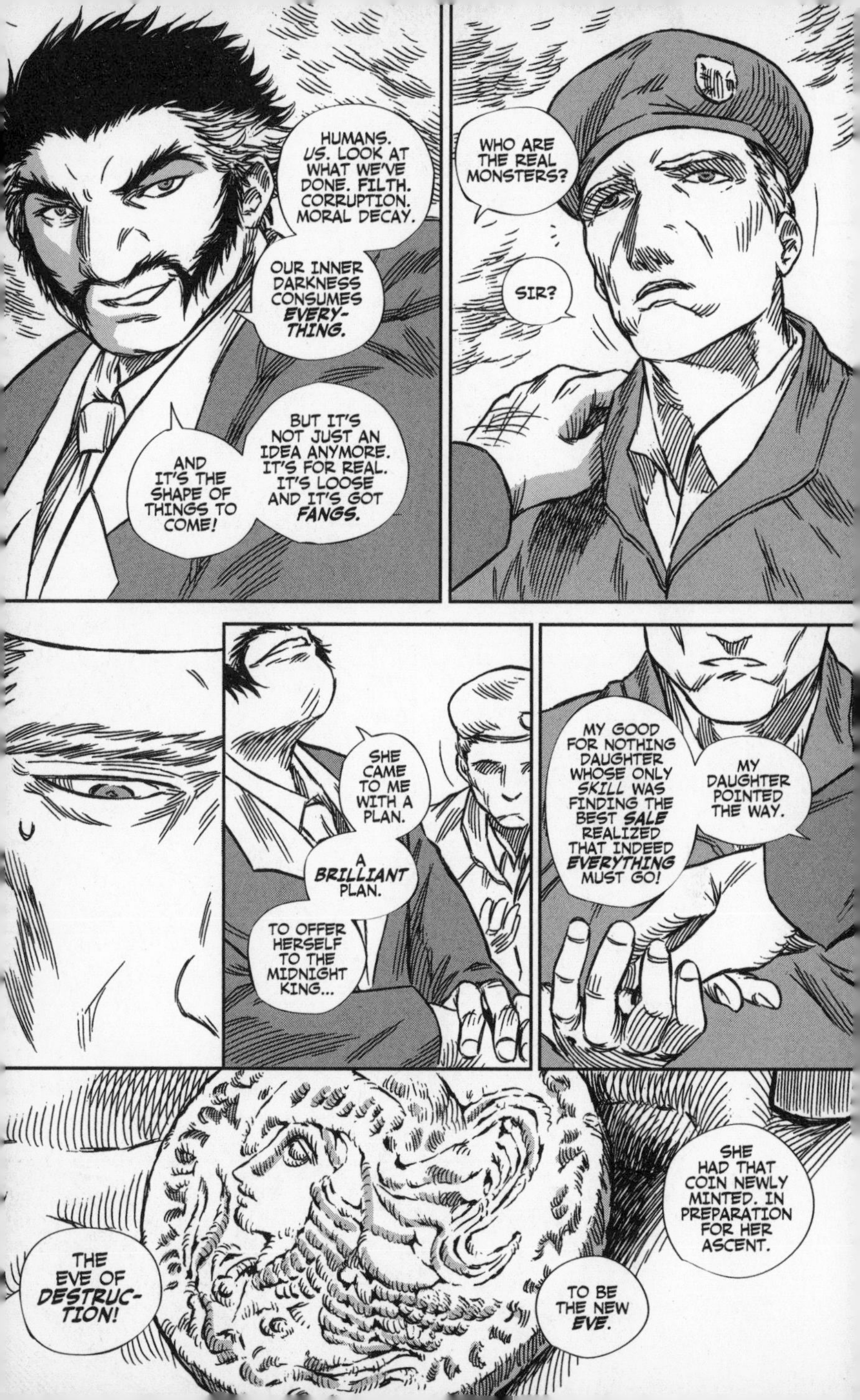
WHO ARE THE REAL MONSTERS?
SIR?
HUMANS. US. LOOK AT WHAT WE'VE DONE. FILTH. CORRUPTION. MORAL DECAY.
OUR INNER DARKNESS CONSUMES EVERY-THING.
BUT IT'S NOT JUST AN IDEA ANYMORE. IT'S FOR REAL. IT'S LOOSE AND IT'S GOT FANGS.
AND IT'S THE SHAPE OF THINGS TO COME!
MY DAUGHTER POINTED THE WAY.
MY GOOD FOR NOTHING DAUGHTER WHOSE ONLY SKILL WAS FINDING THE BEST SALE REALIZED THAT INDEED EVERYTHING MUST GO!
SHE CAME TO ME WITH A PLAN.
A BRILLIANT PLAN.
TO OFFER HERSELF TO THE MIDNIGHT KING...
SHE HAD THAT COIN NEWLY MINTED. IN PREPARATION FOR HER ASCENT.
TO BE THE NEW EVE.
THE EVE OF DESTRUC-TION!

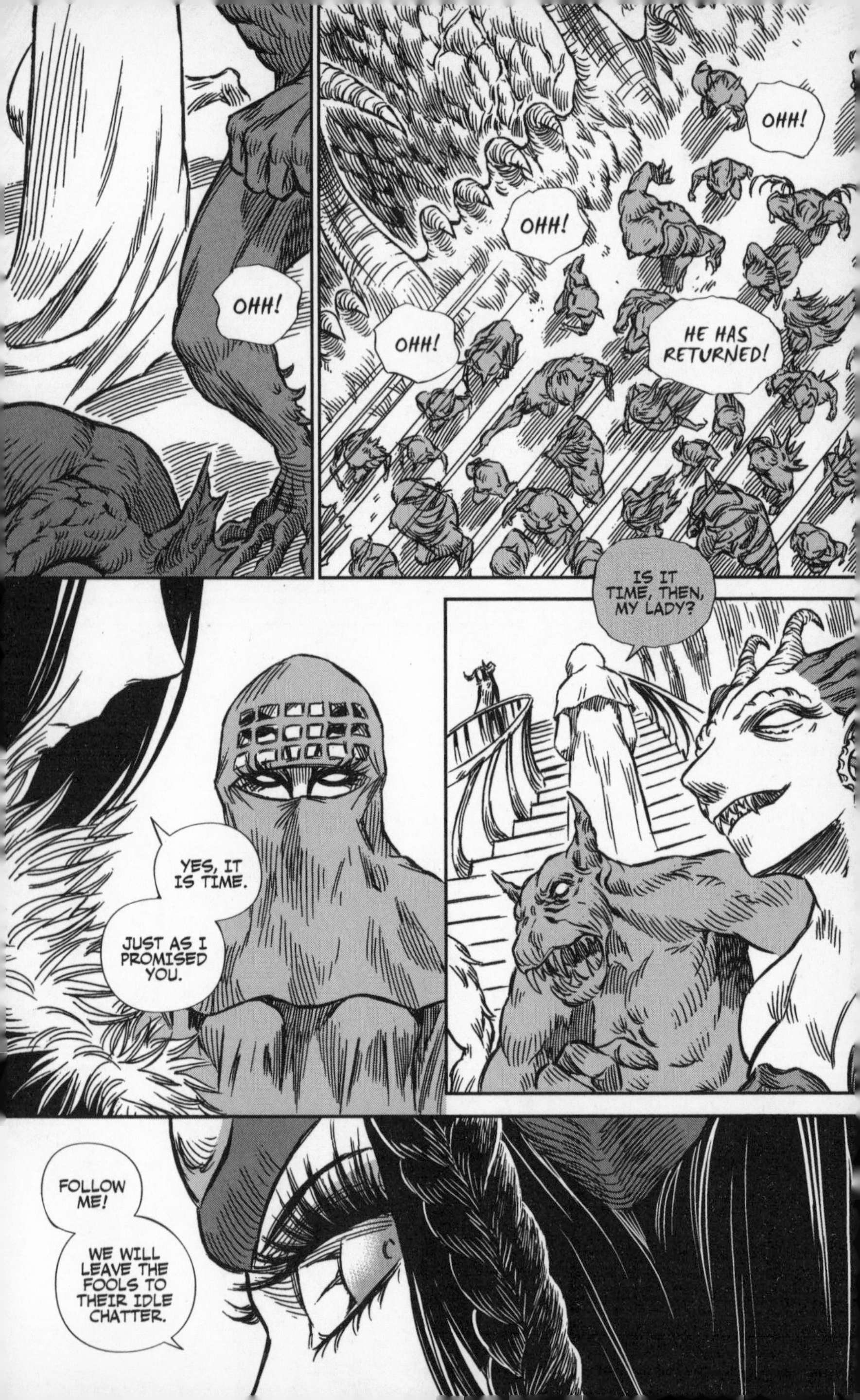
OHH!
OHH!
HE HAS RETURNED!
OHH!
OHH!
IS IT TIME, THEN, MY LADY?
YES, IT IS TIME.
JUST AS I PROMISED YOU.
FOLLOW ME!
WE WILL LEAVE THE FOOLS TO THEIR IDLE CHATTER.

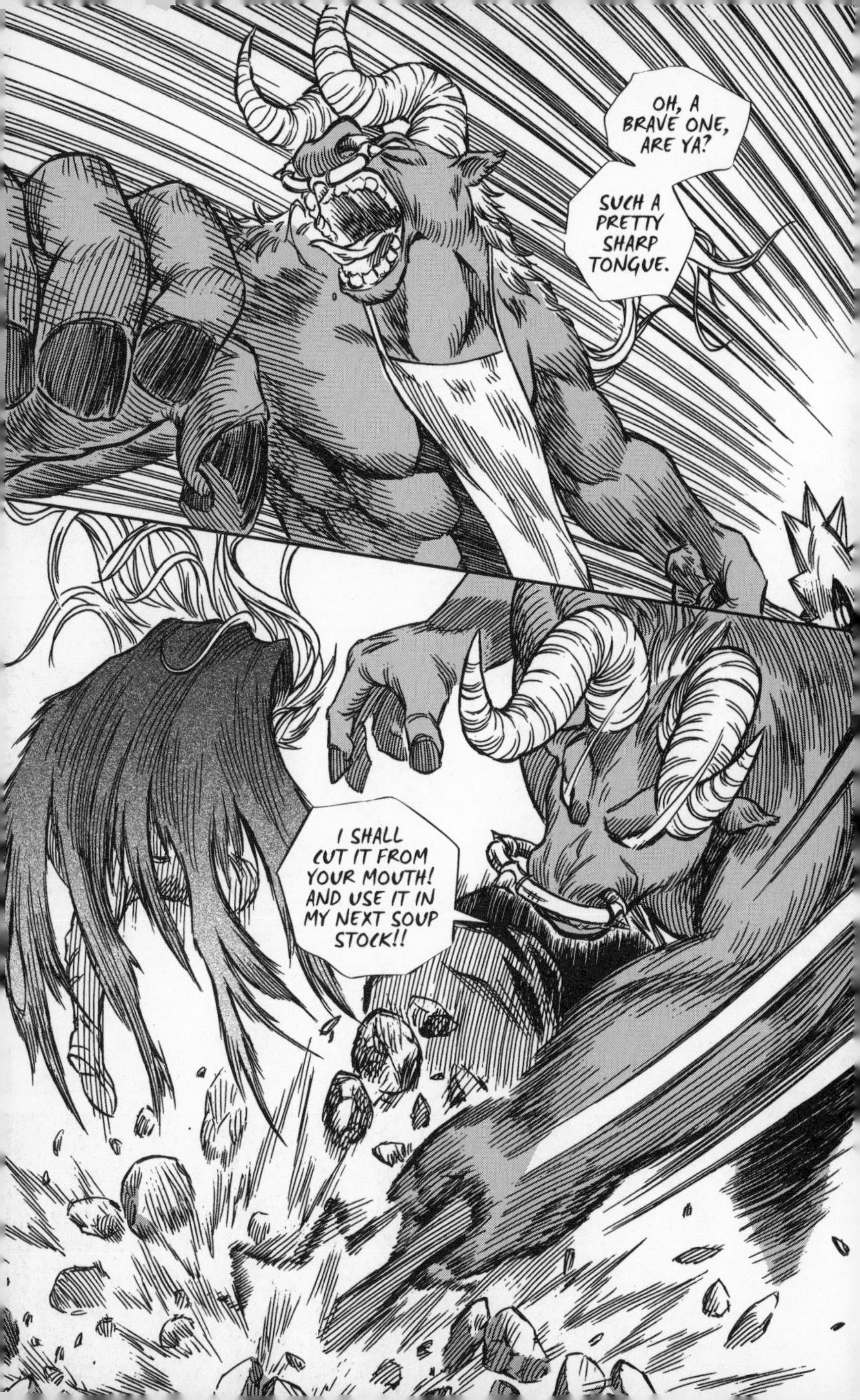
OH, A BRAVE ONE, ARE YA?
SUCH A PRETTY SHARP TONGUE.
I SHALL CUT IT FROM YOUR MOUTH! AND USE IT IN MY NEXT SOUP STOCK!!

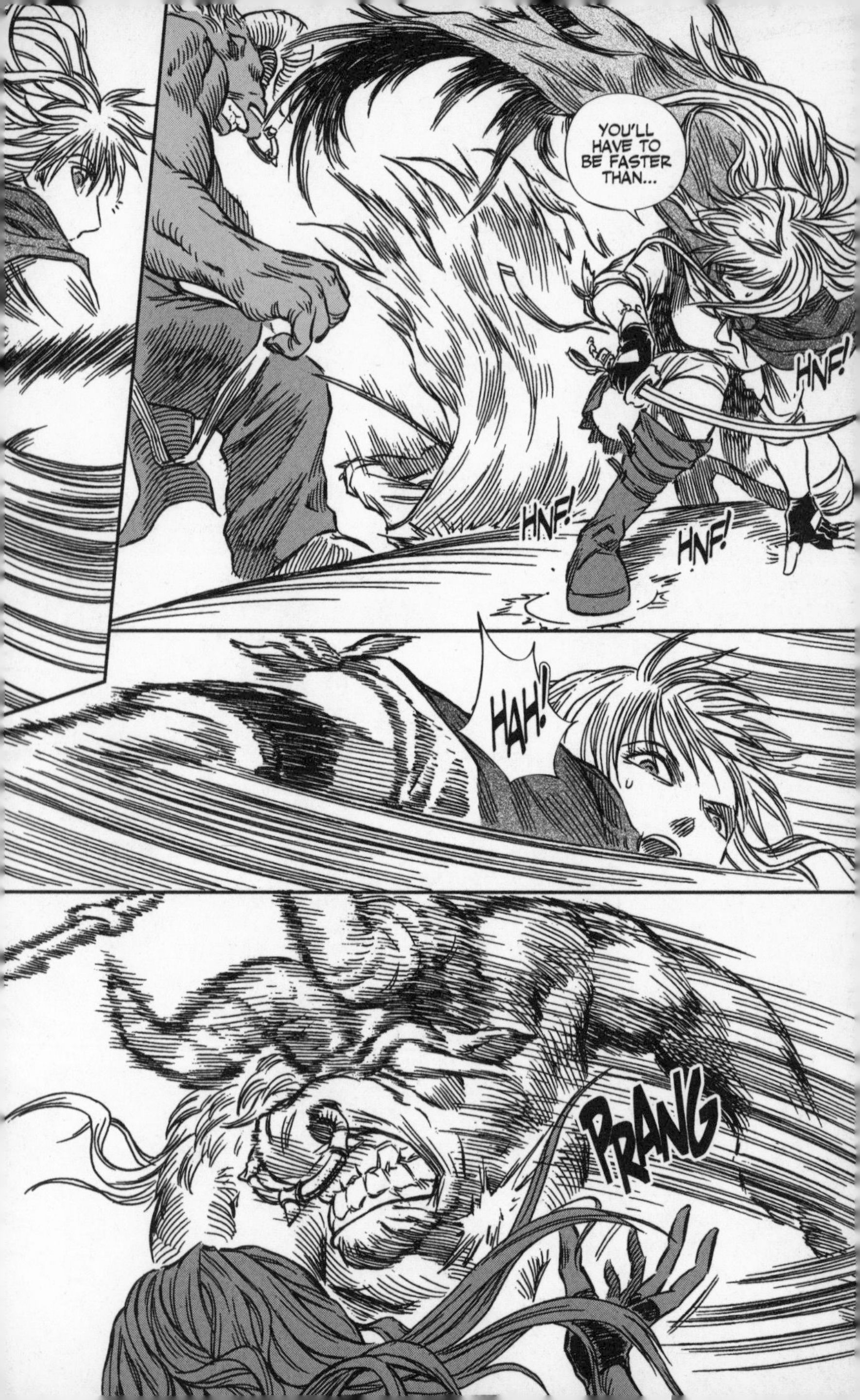
YOU'LL HAVE TO BE FASTER THAN...
HNF!
HNF!
HNF!
HAH!
PRANG

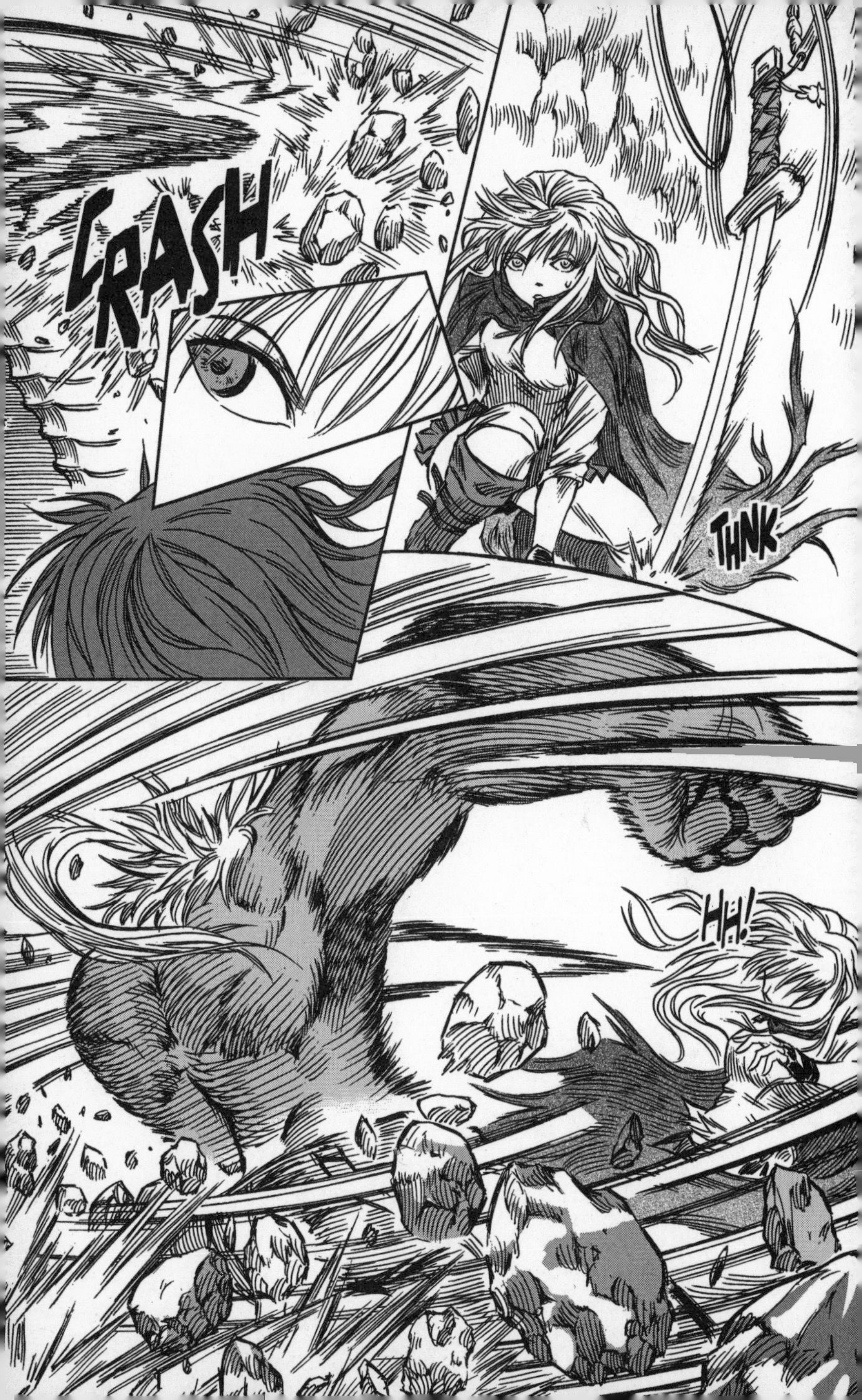
THNK
CRASH
HH!

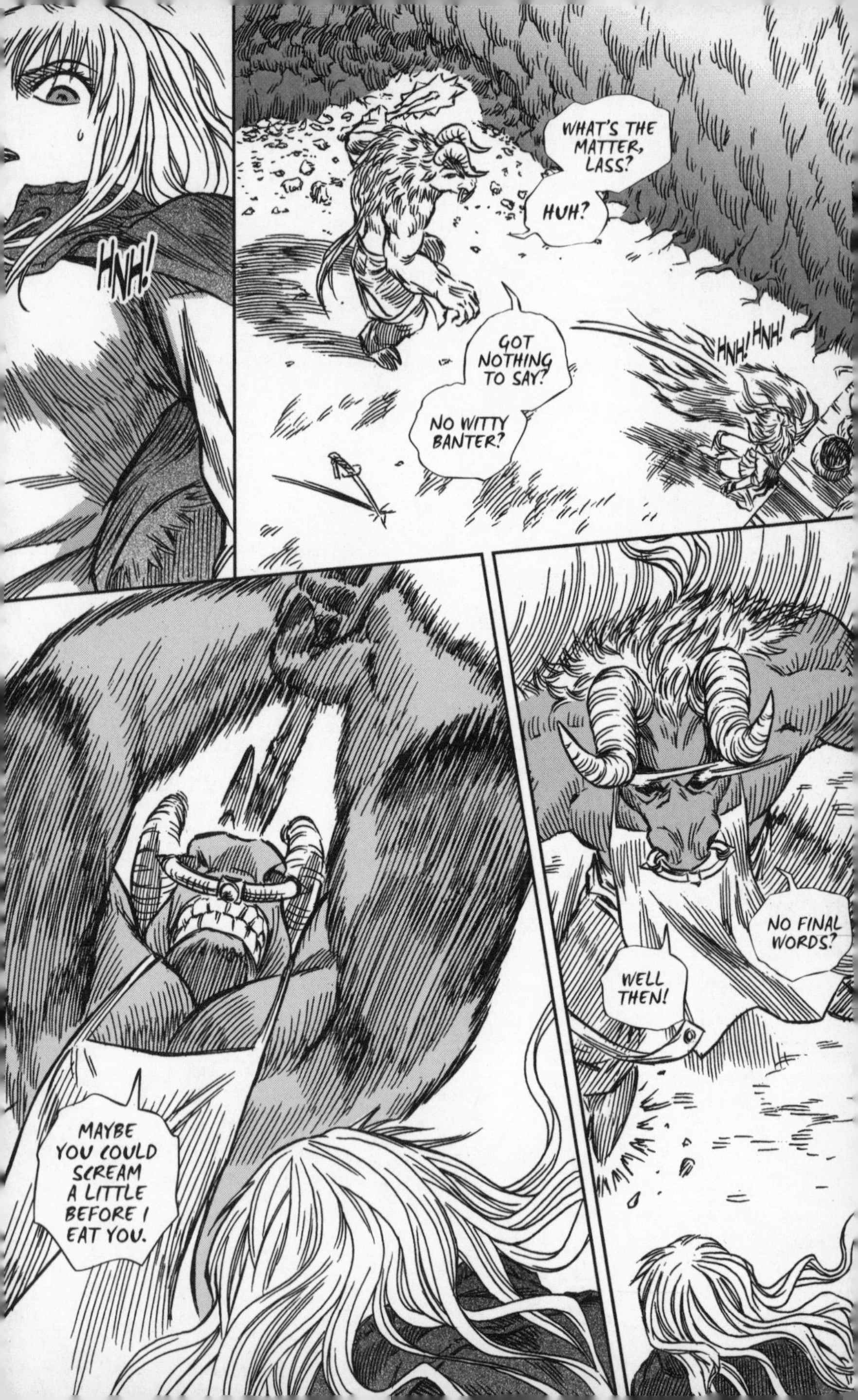
WHAT'S THE MATTER, LASS?
HUH?
HNH! HNH!
GOT NOTHING TO SAY?
NO WITTY BANTER?
HNH!
NO FINAL WORDS?
WELL THEN!
MAYBE YOU COULD SCREAM A LITTLE BEFORE I EAT YOU.

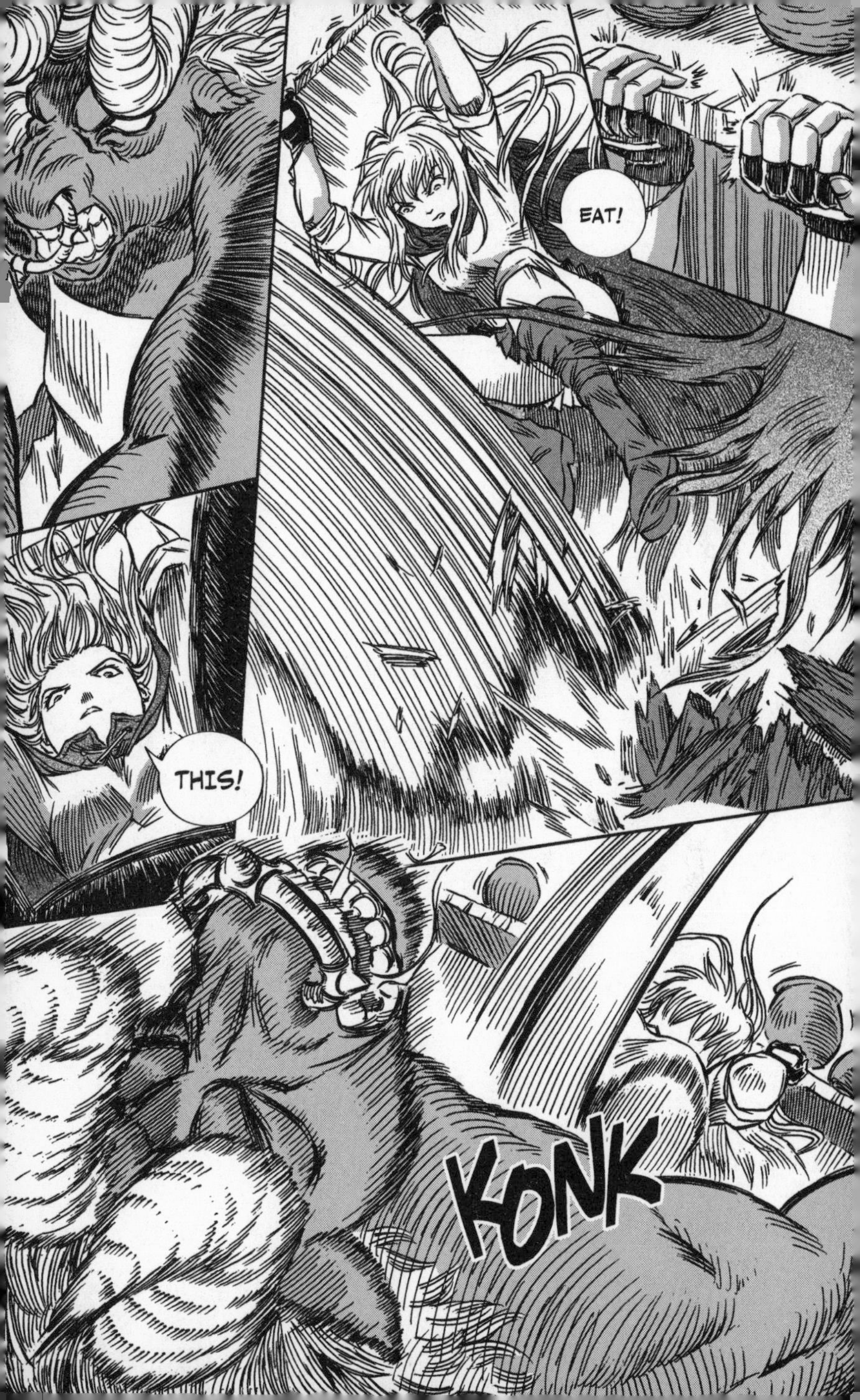
EAT!
THIS!
KONK

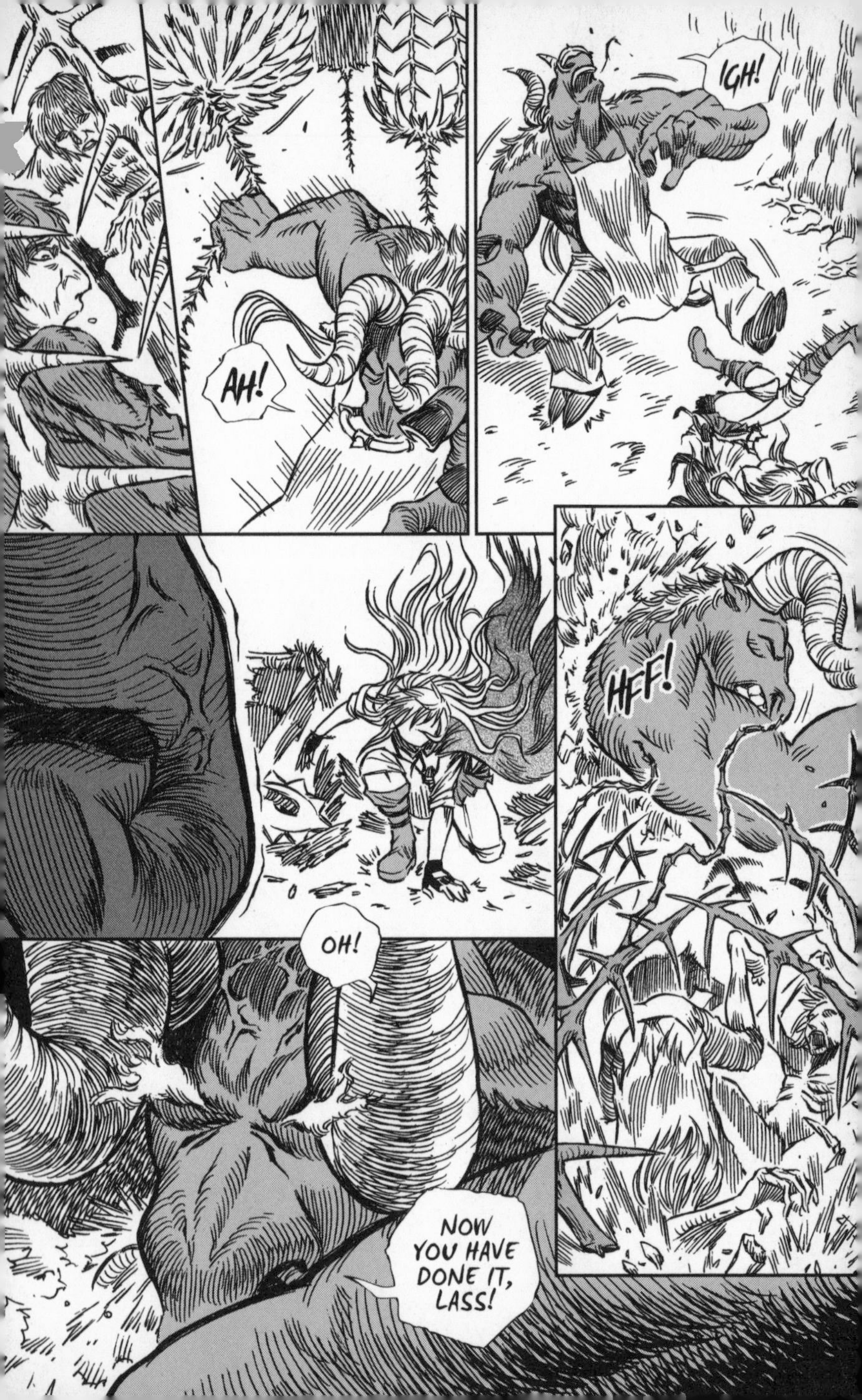
IGH!
AH!
HFF!
OH!
NOW YOU HAVE DONE IT, LASS!

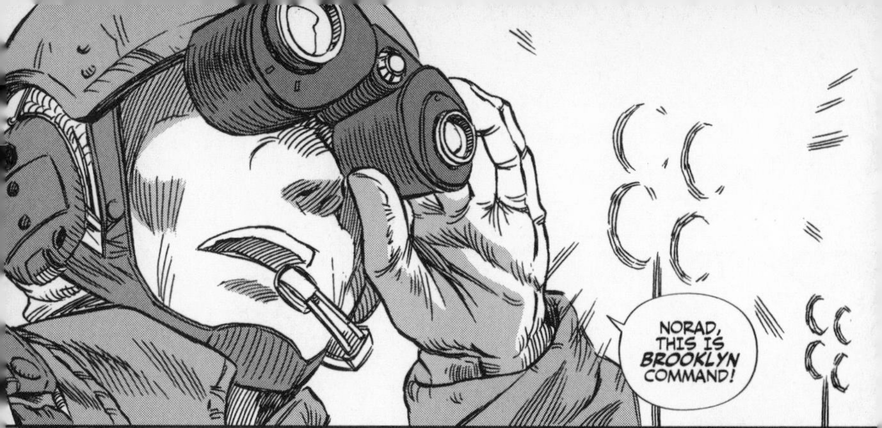
NORAD, THIS IS BROOKLYN COMMAND!

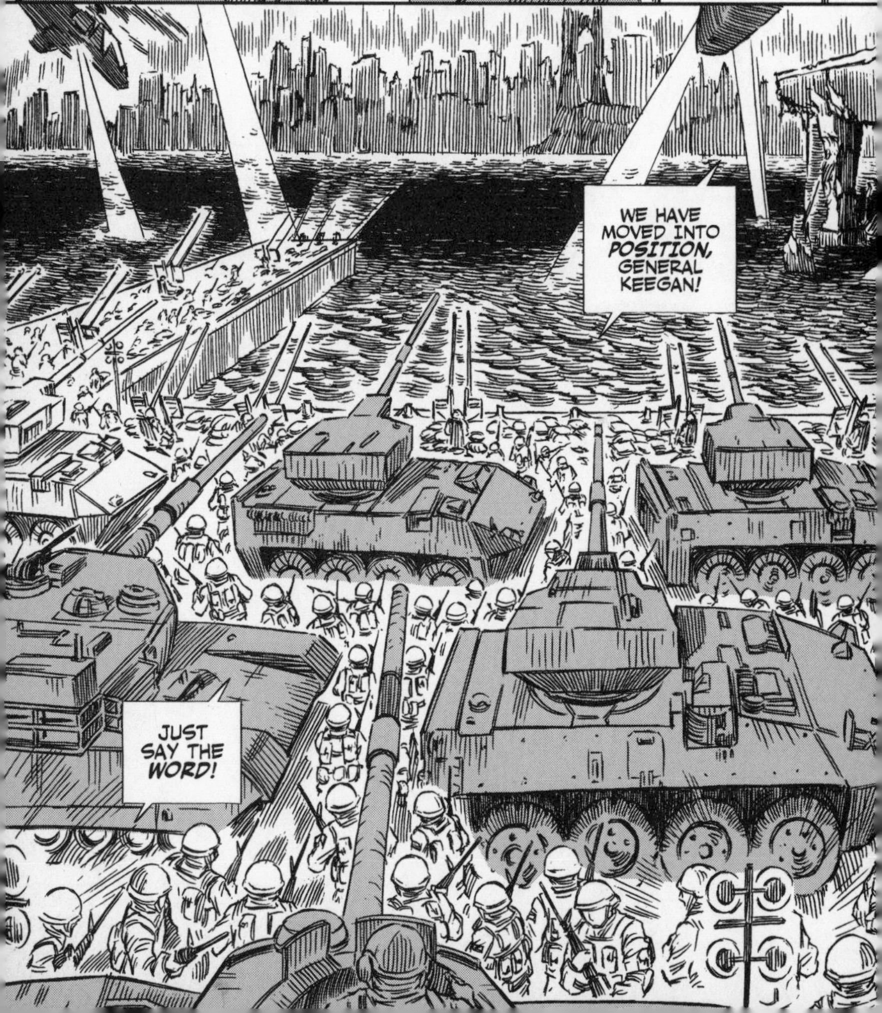
WE HAVE MOVED INTO POSITION, GENERAL KEEGAN!
JUST SAY THE WORD!

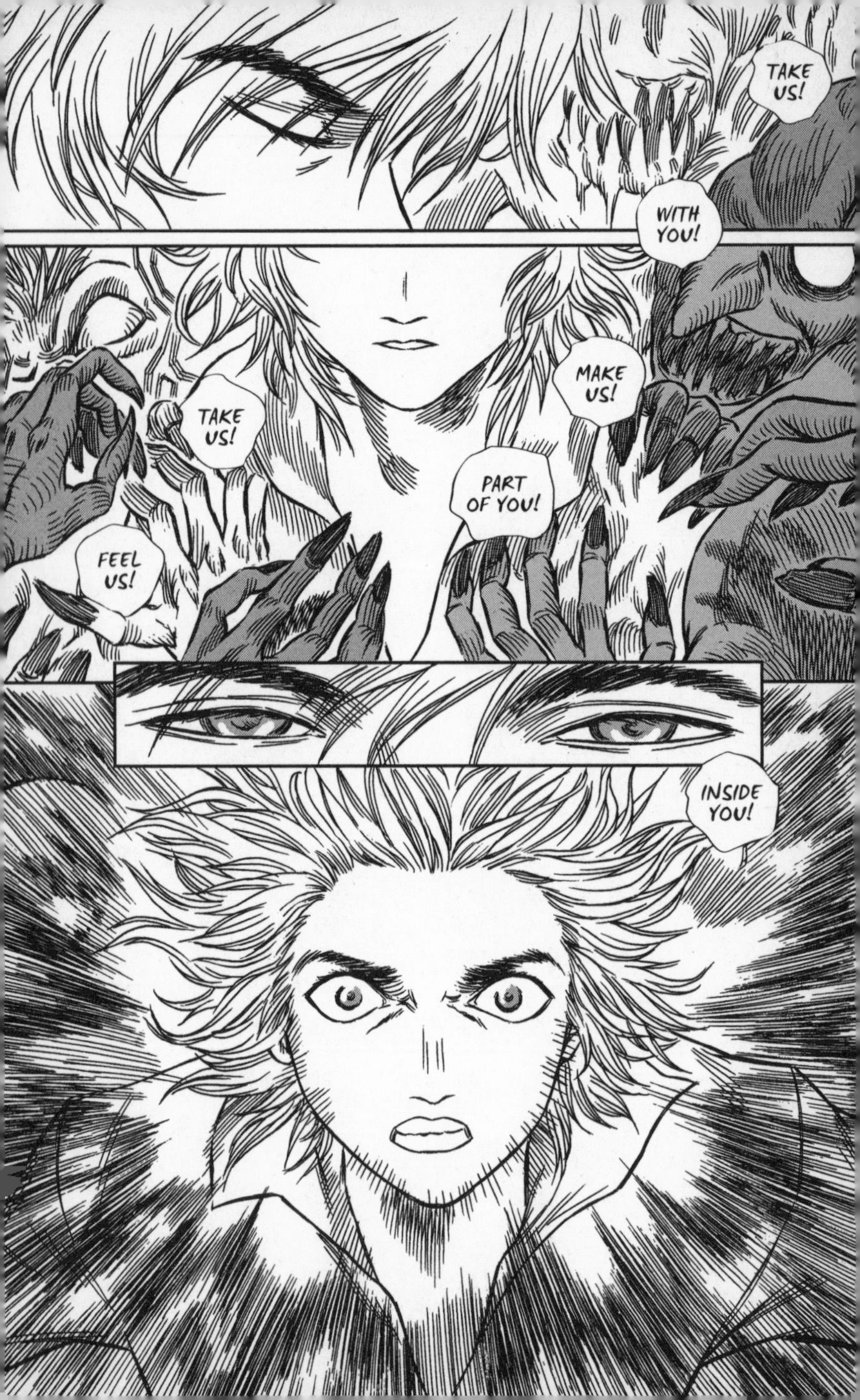
TAKE US!
WITH YOU!
MAKE US!
TAKE US!
PART OF YOU!
FEEL US!
INSIDE YOU!

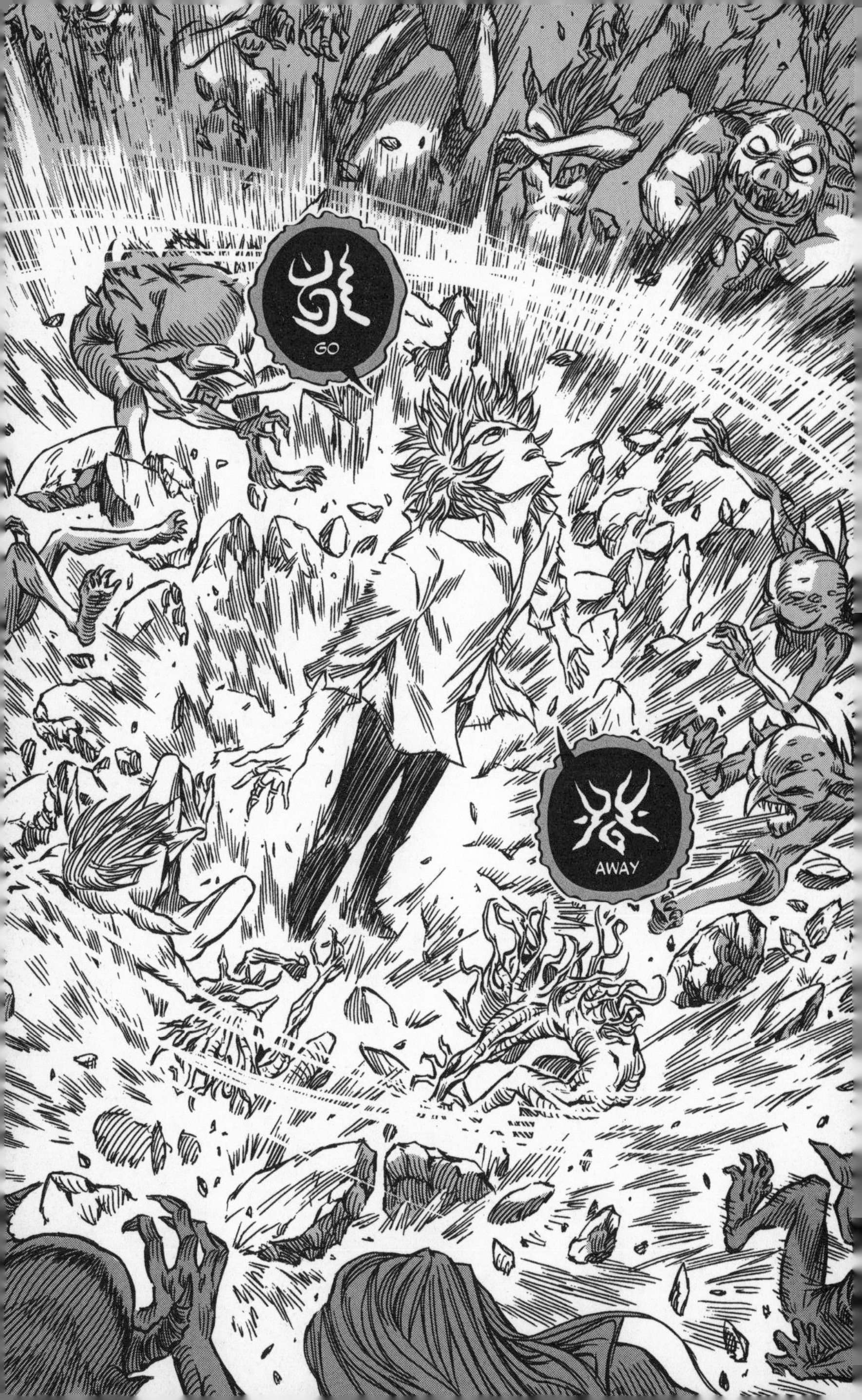
GO
AWAY

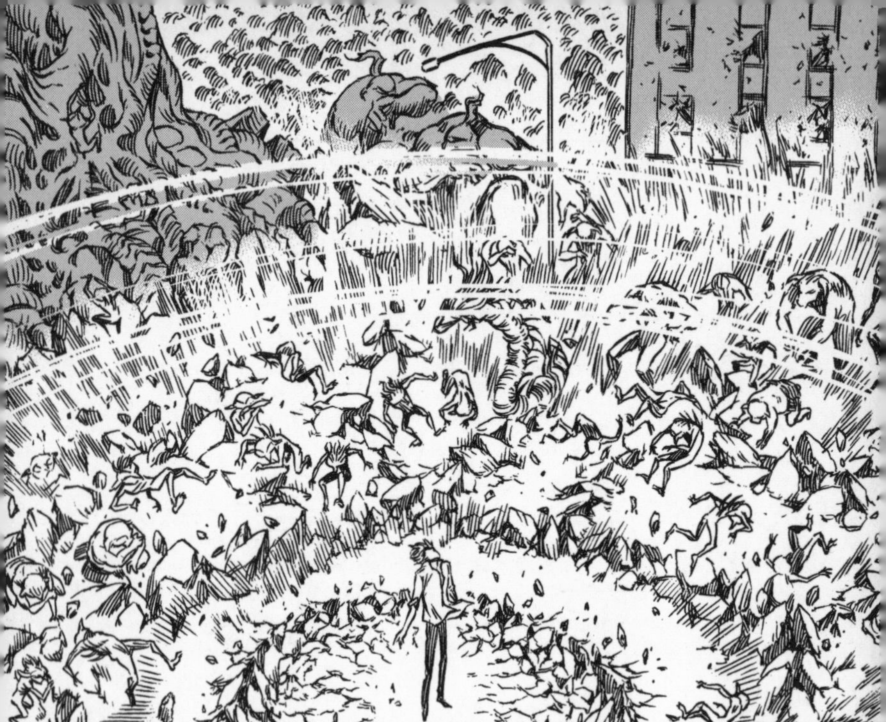
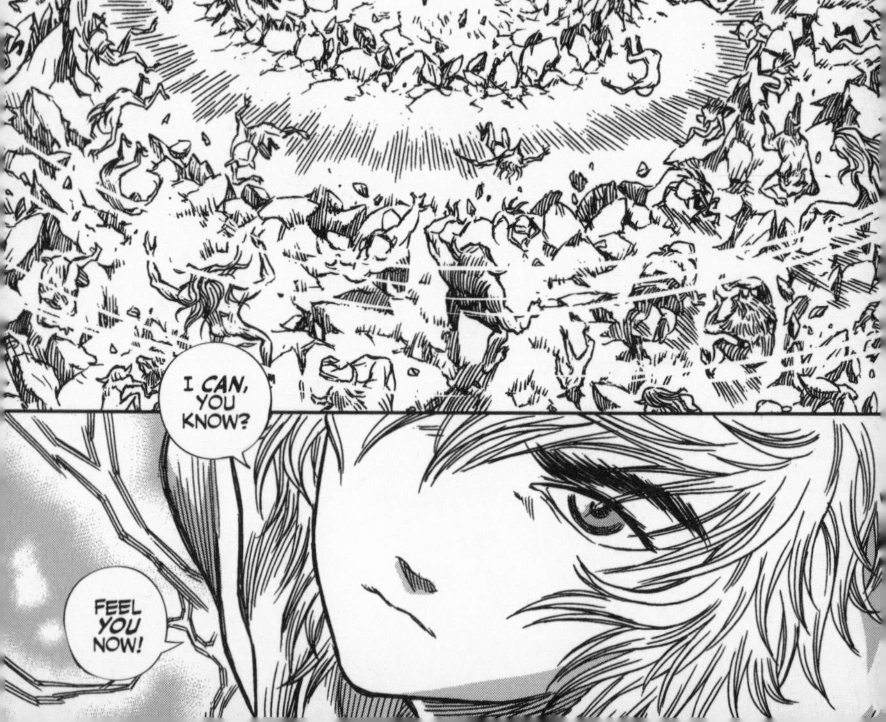
I *CAN,* YOU KNOW?
FEEL *YOU* NOW!

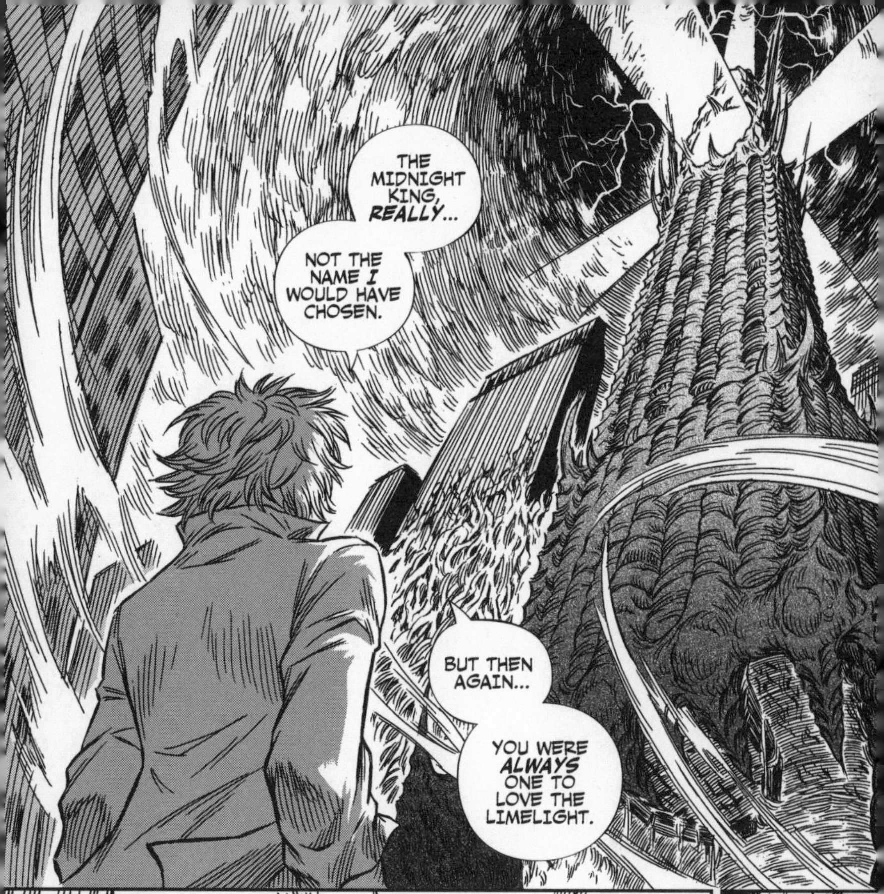
THE MIDNIGHT KING, REALLY...
NOT THE NAME I WOULD HAVE CHOSEN.
BUT THEN AGAIN...
YOU WERE ALWAYS ONE TO LOVE THE LIMELIGHT.
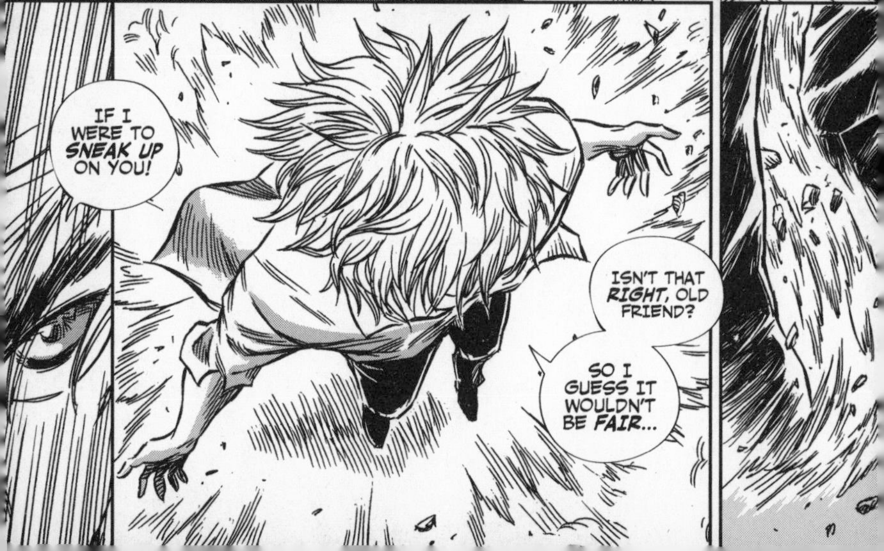
ISN'T THAT RIGHT, OLD FRIEND?
SO I GUESS IT WOULDN'T BE FAIR...
IF I WERE TO SNEAK UP ON YOU!

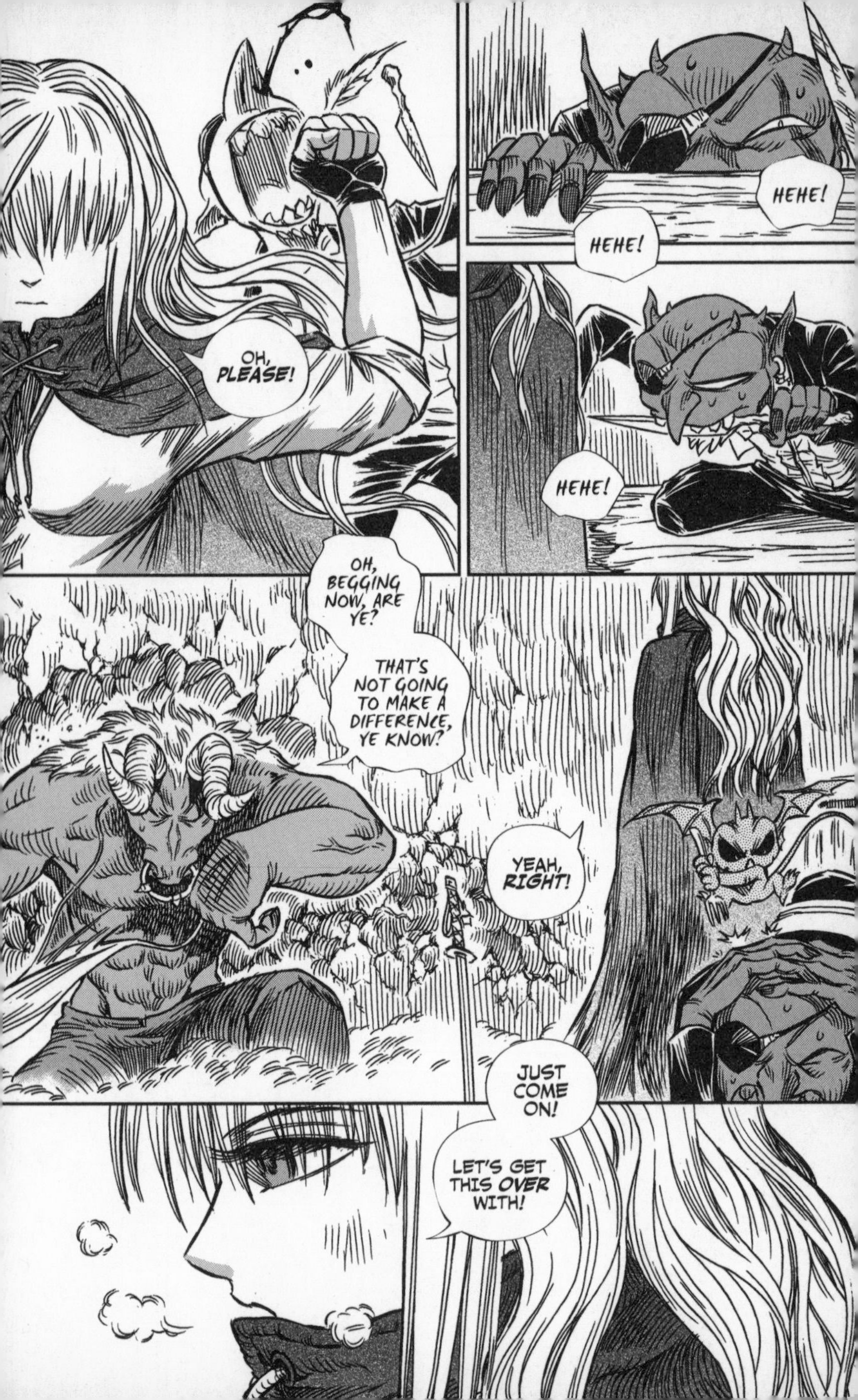
OH, PLEASE!
HEHE!
HEHE!
HEHE!
OH, BEGGING NOW, ARE YE?
THAT'S NOT GOING TO MAKE A DIFFERENCE, YE KNOW?
YEAH, RIGHT!
JUST COME ON!
LET'S GET THIS OVER WITH!

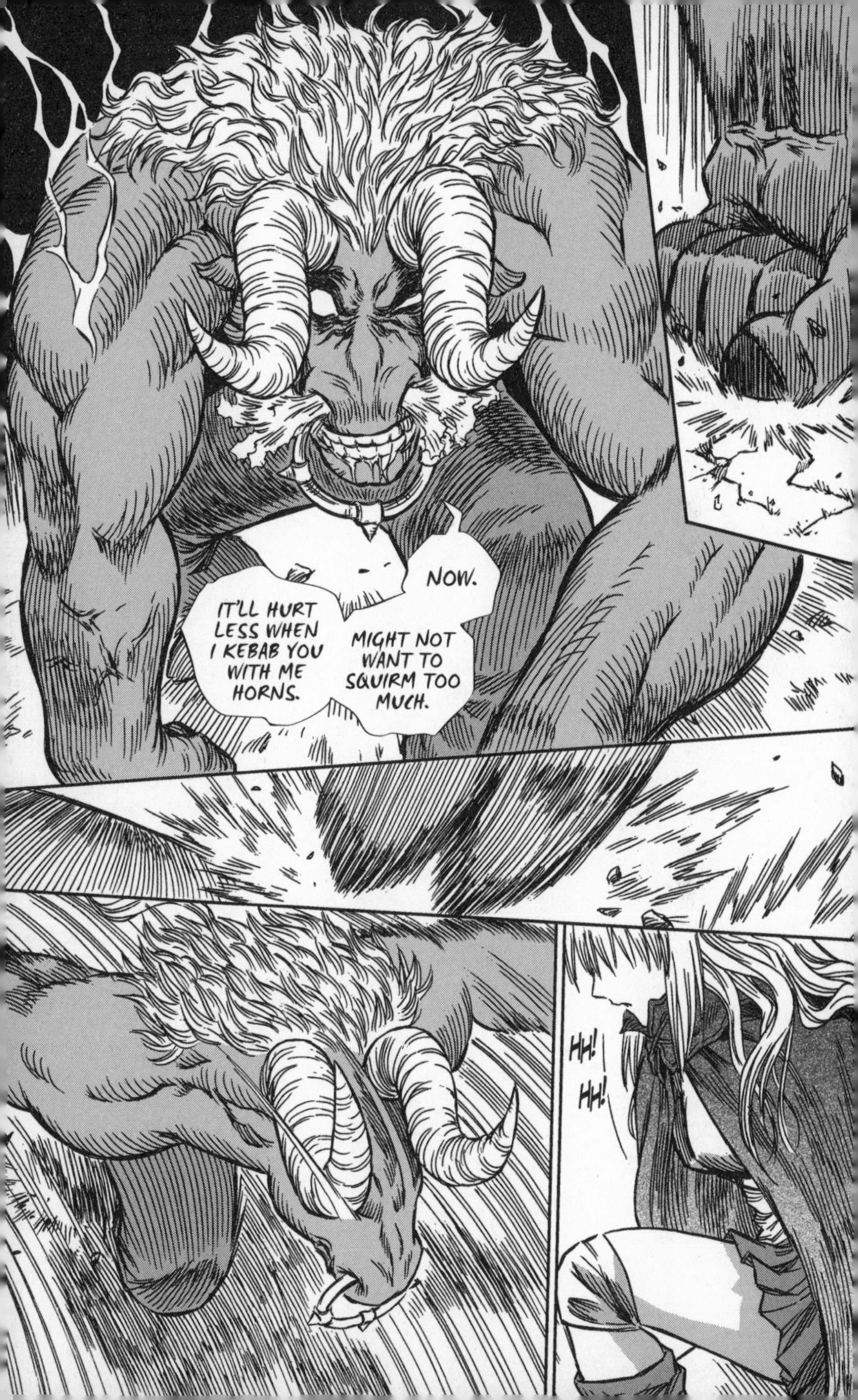
NOW.
MIGHT NOT WANT TO SQUIRM TOO MUCH.
IT'LL HURT LESS WHEN I KEBAB YOU WITH ME HORNS.
HH!
HH!

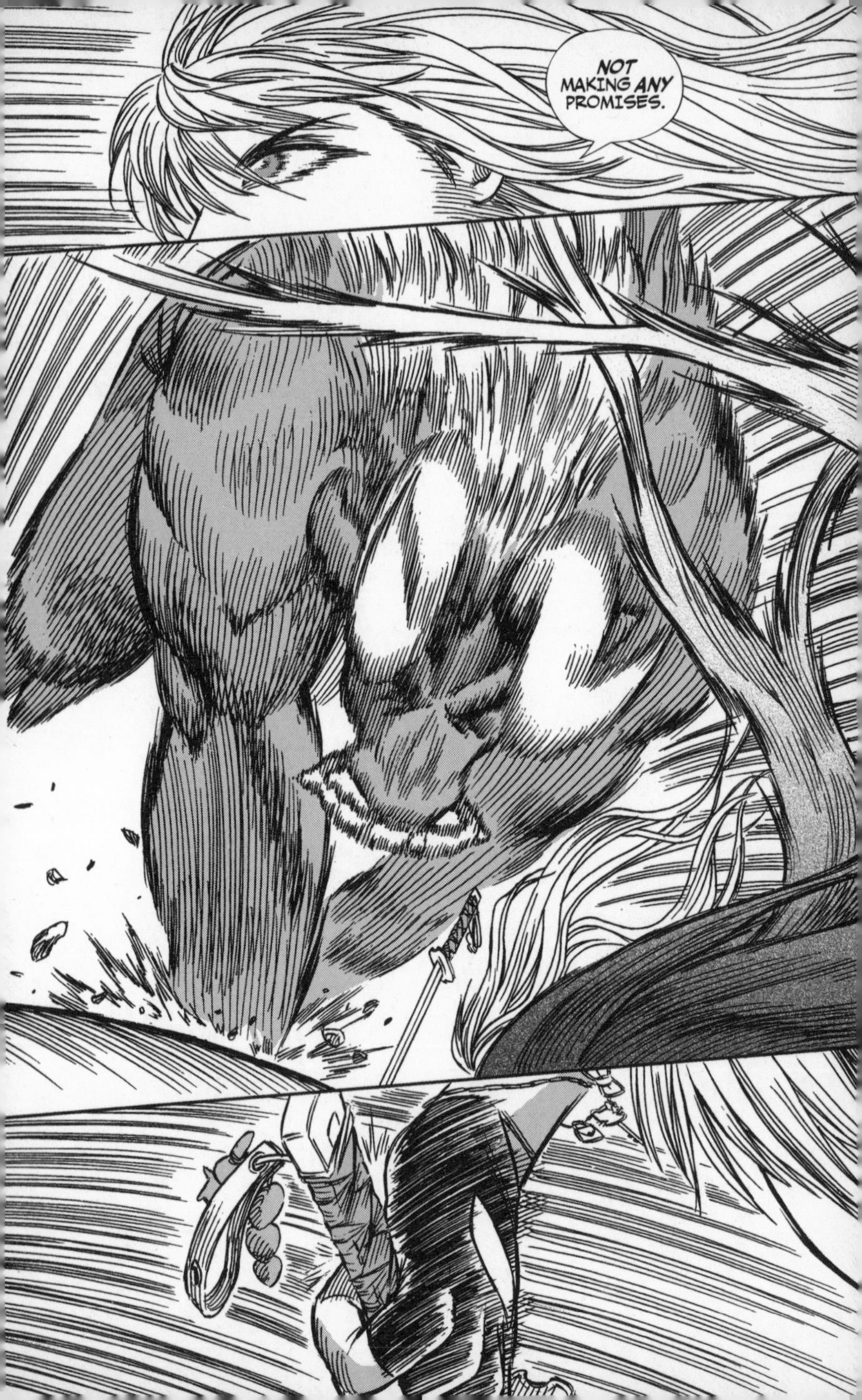
NOT MAKING ANY PROMISES.

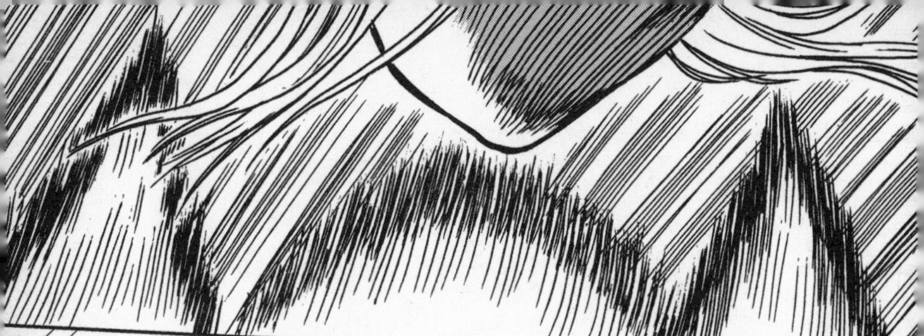

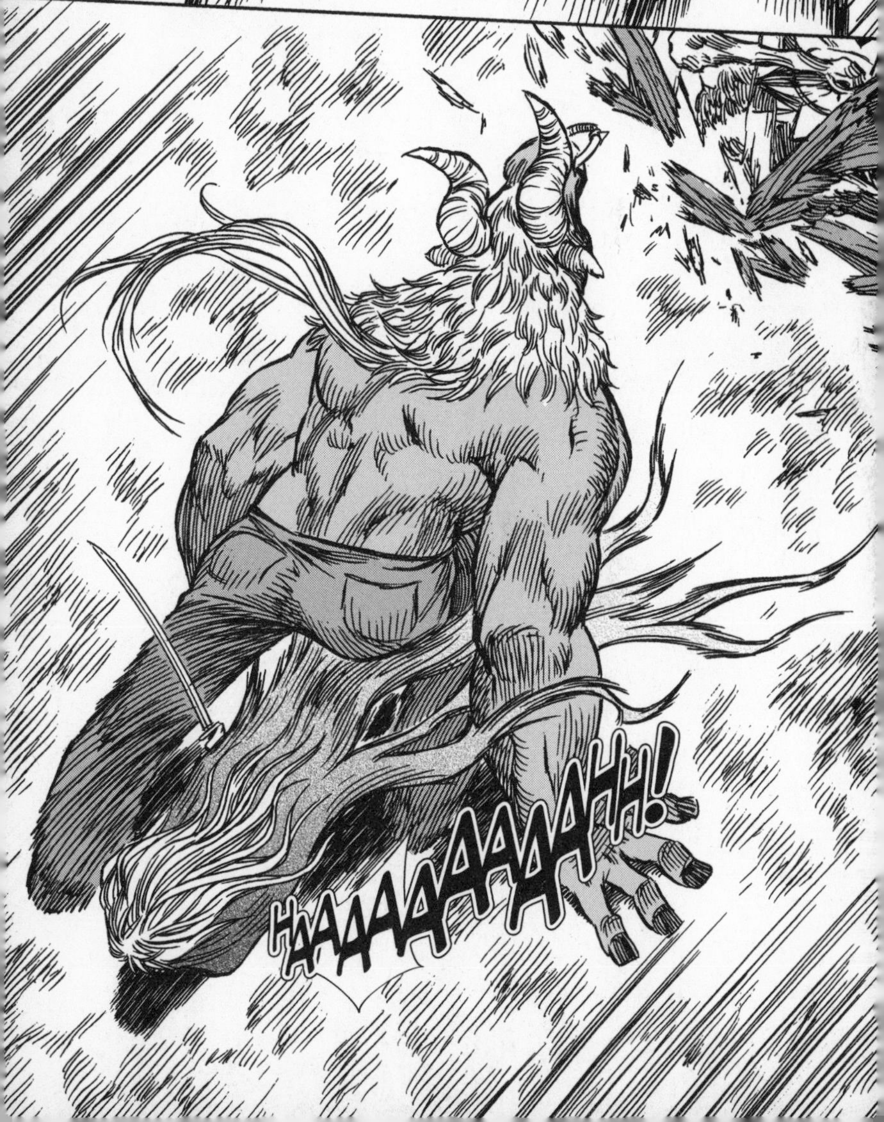
HAAAAAAAAHH!

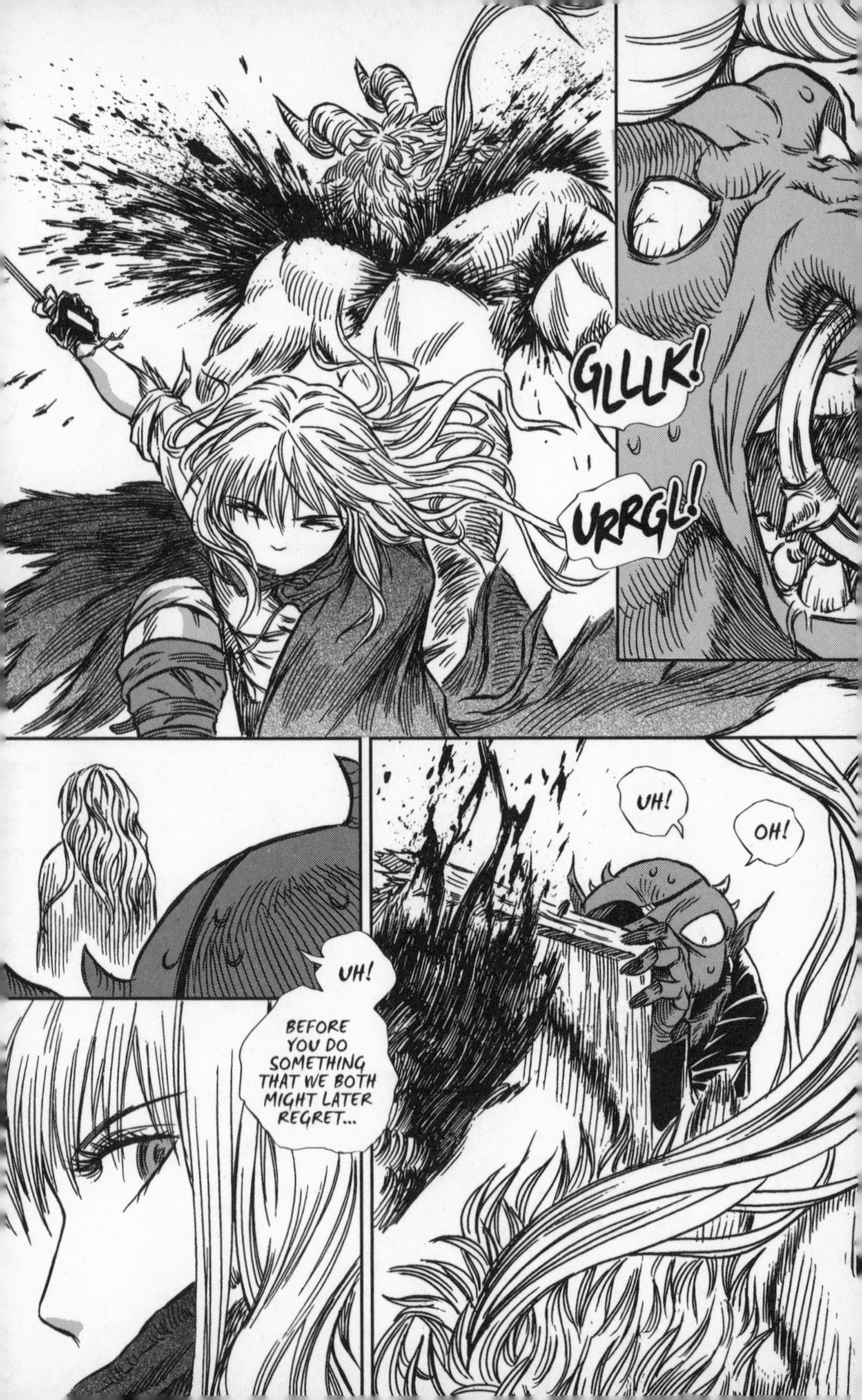
GLLLK!
URRGL!
OH!
UH!
UH!
BEFORE YOU DO SOMETHING THAT WE BOTH MIGHT LATER REGRET...

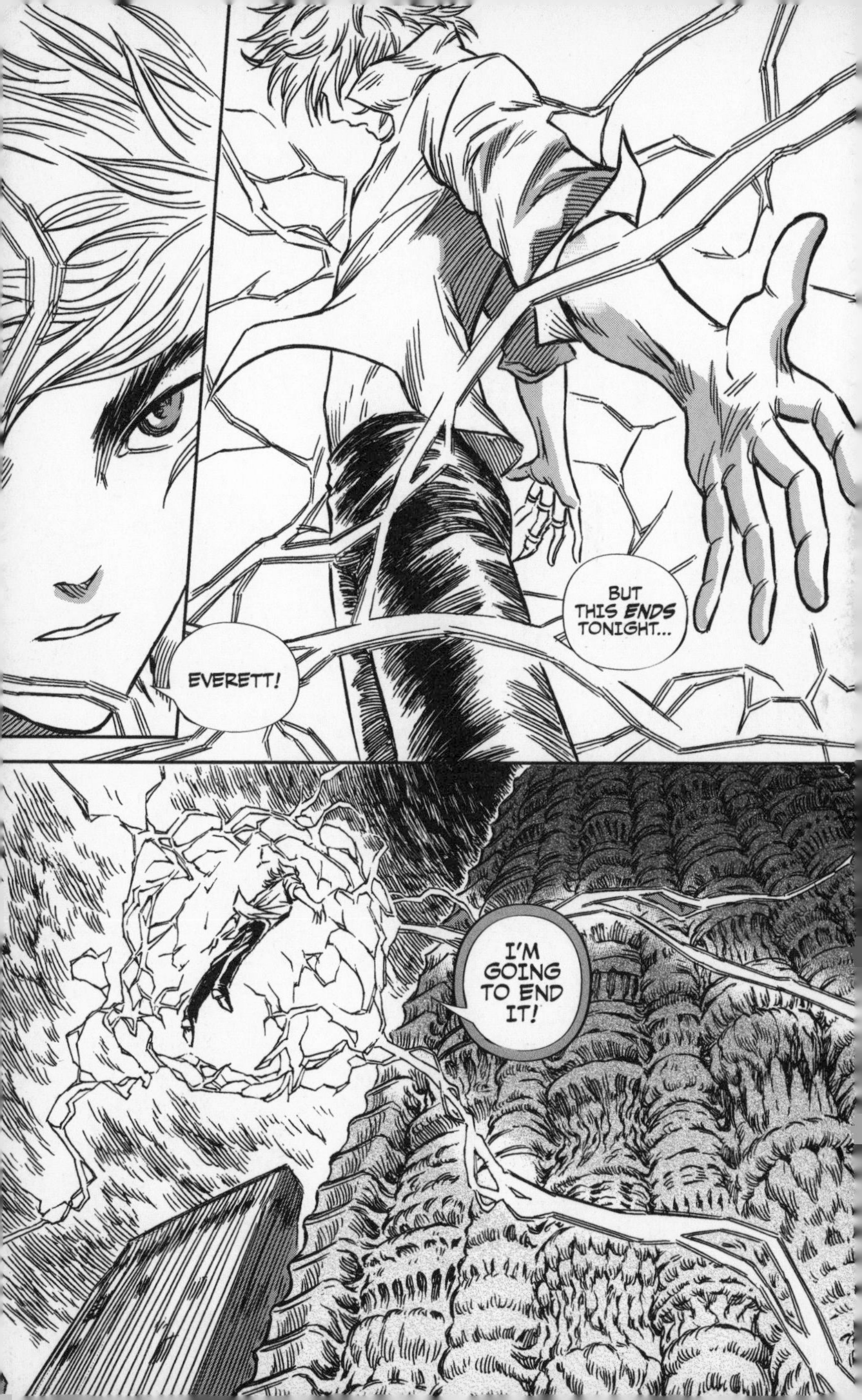
EVERETT!
BUT THIS *ENDS* TONIGHT...
I'M GOING TO END IT!

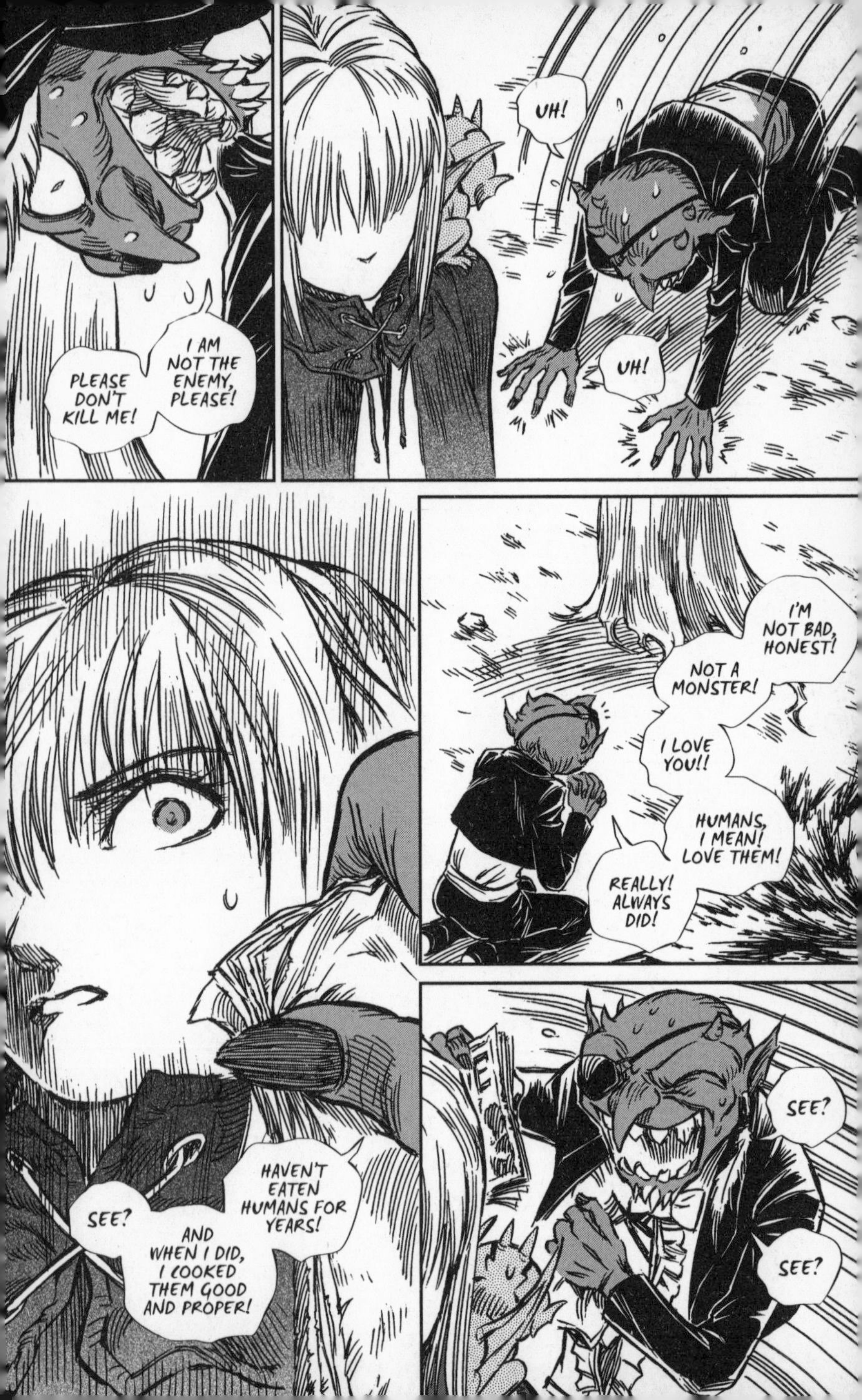
UH!
UH!
I AM NOT THE ENEMY, PLEASE!
PLEASE DON'T KILL ME!
I'M NOT BAD, HONEST!
NOT A MONSTER!
I LOVE YOU!!
HUMANS, I MEAN! LOVE THEM!
REALLY! ALWAYS DID!
SEE?
SEE?
HAVEN'T EATEN HUMANS FOR YEARS!
SEE?
AND WHEN I DID, I COOKED THEM GOOD AND PROPER!

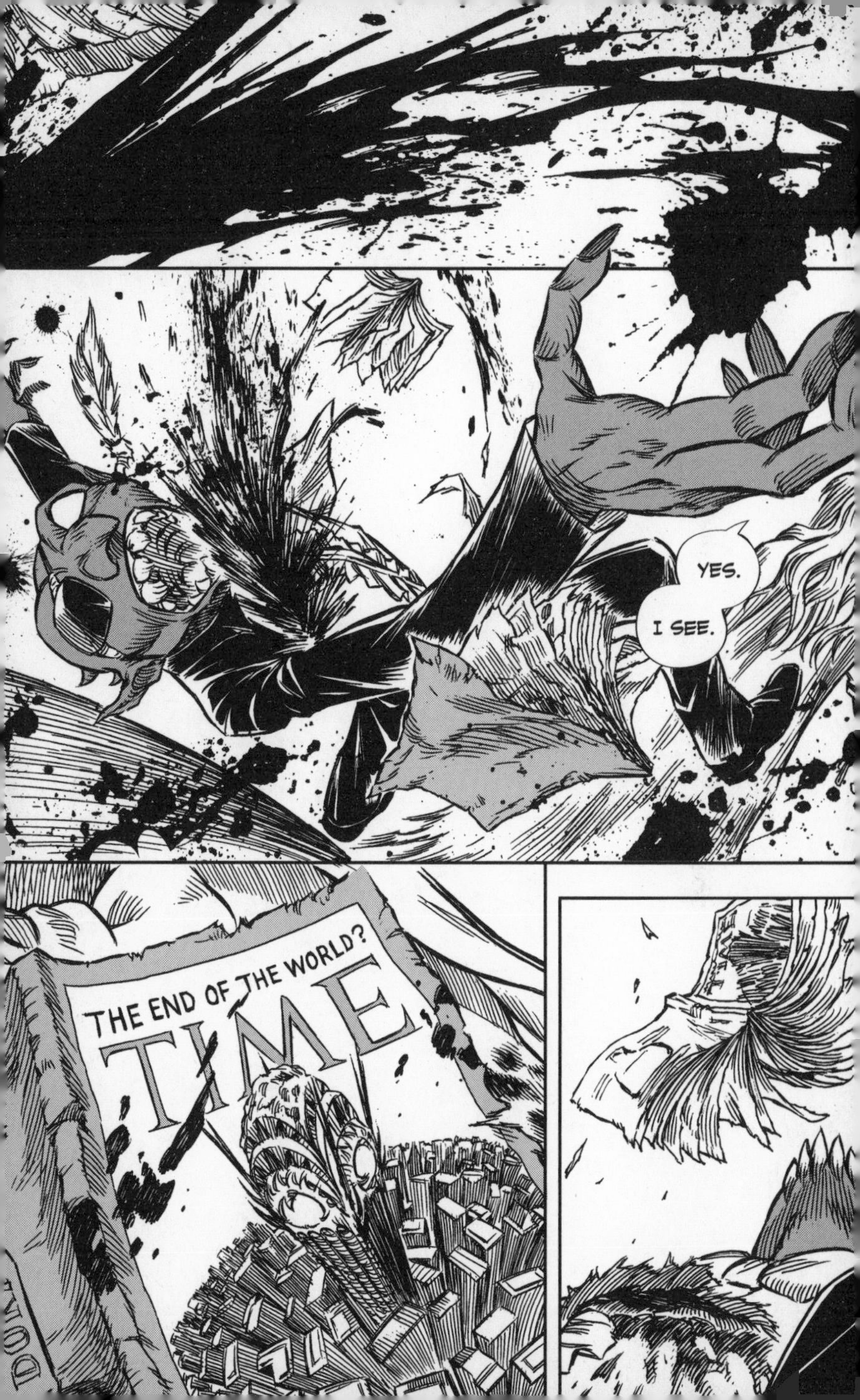
YES.
I SEE.
THE END OF THE WORLD?
TIME

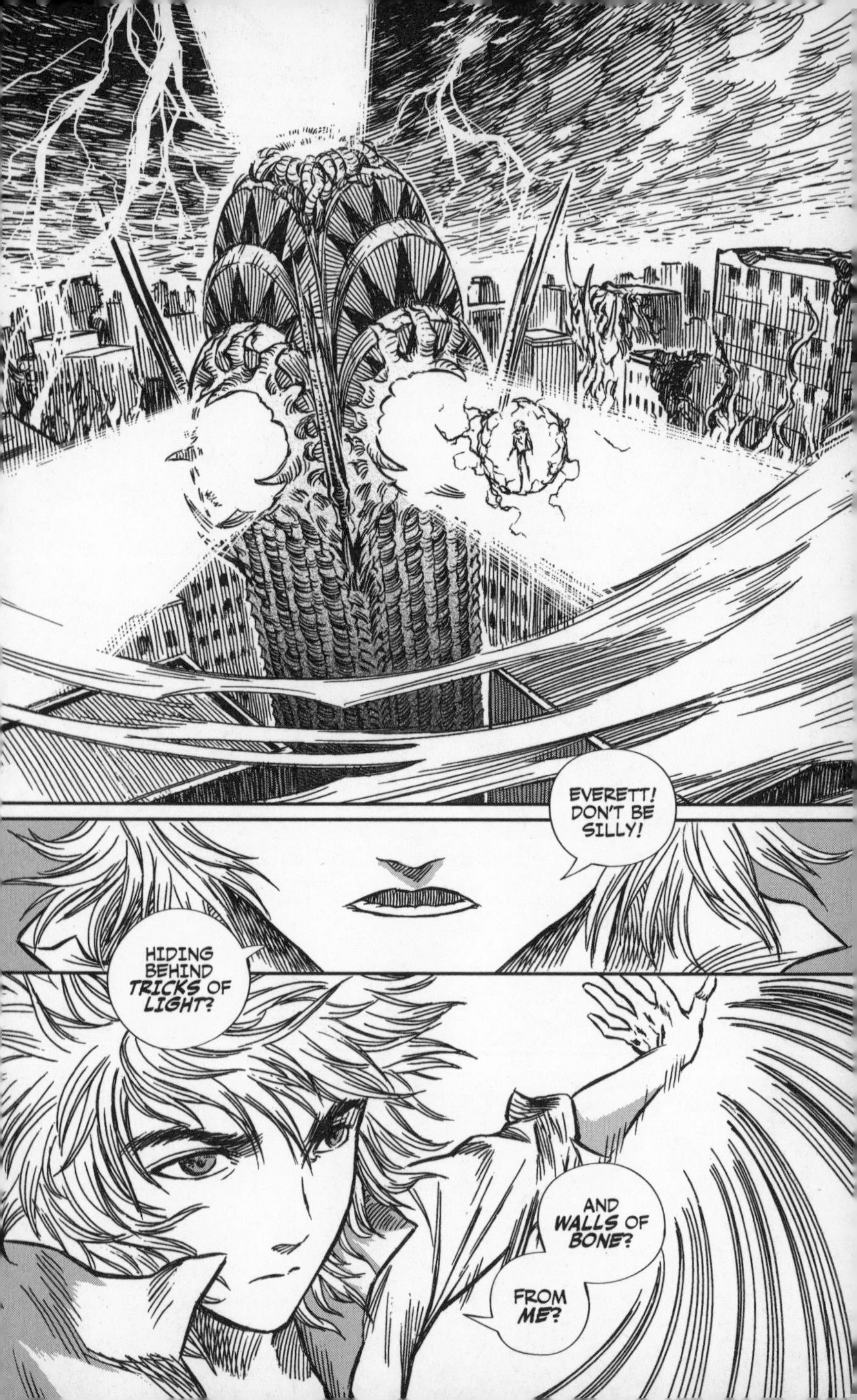
EVERETT! DON'T BE SILLY!
HIDING BEHIND *TRICKS* OF *LIGHT*?
AND *WALLS* OF *BONE*?
FROM *ME*?

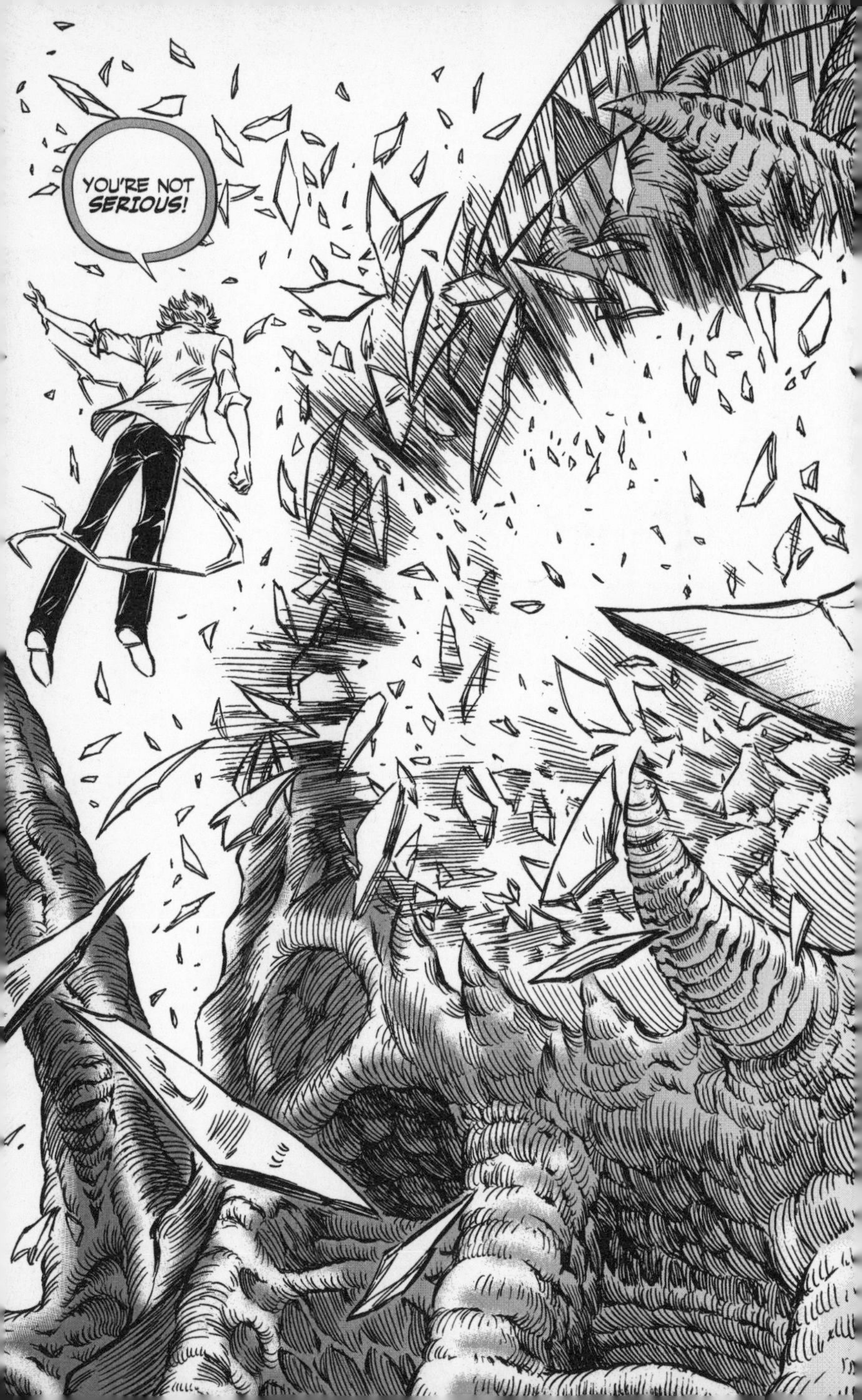
YOU'RE NOT SERIOUS!

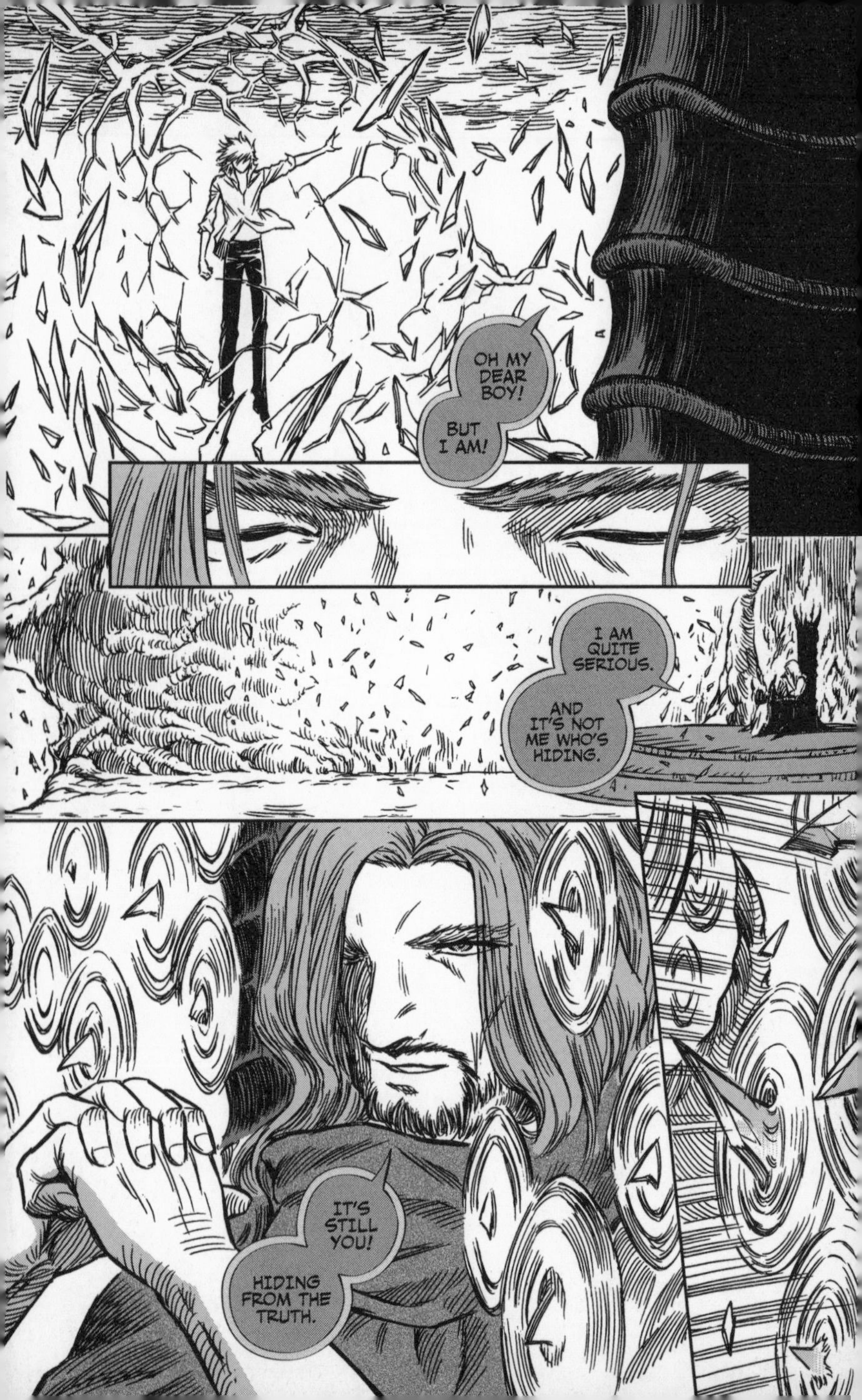
OH MY DEAR BOY!
BUT I AM!
I AM QUITE SERIOUS.
AND IT'S NOT ME WHO'S HIDING.
IT'S STILL YOU!
HIDING FROM THE TRUTH.

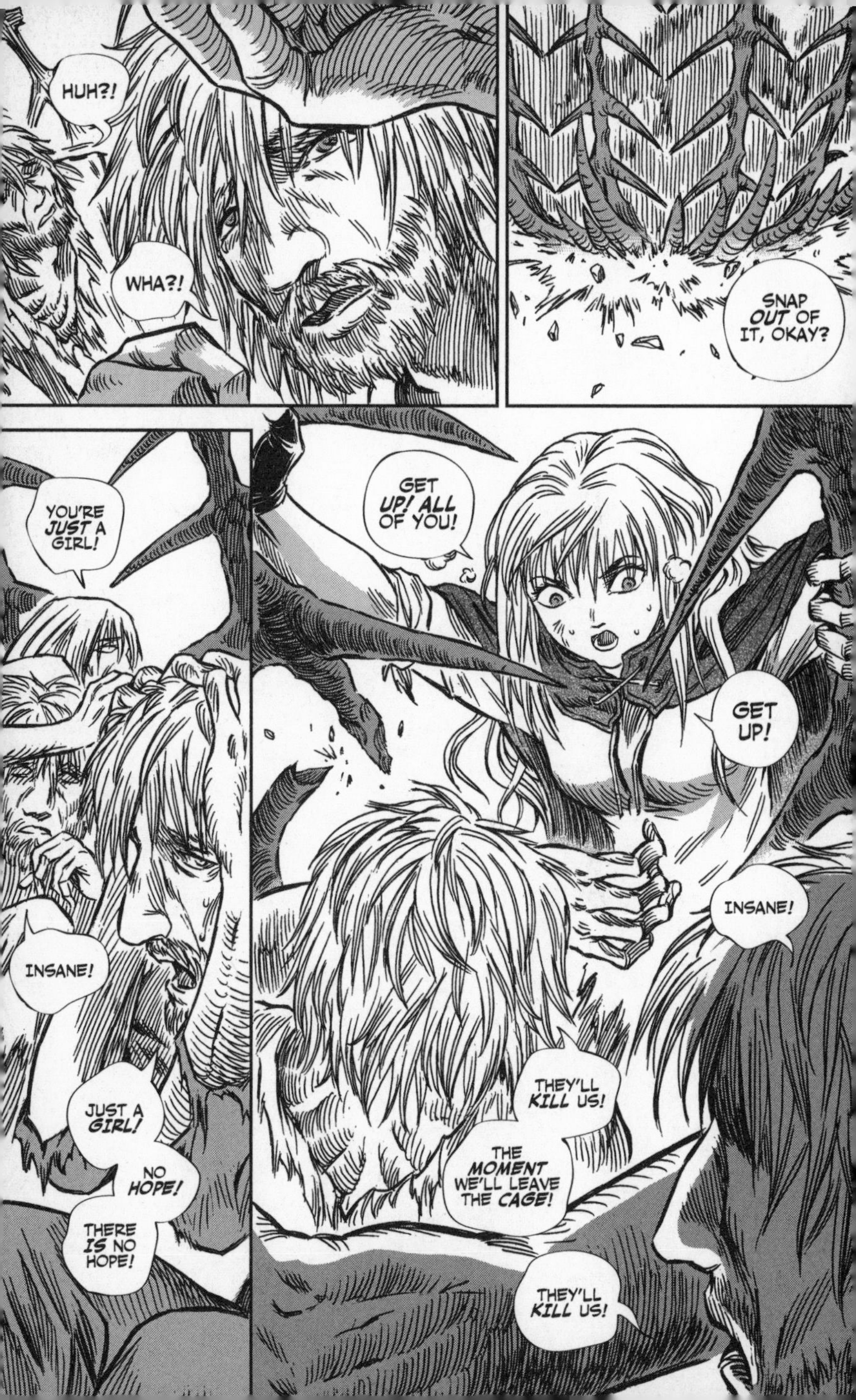
SNAP OUT OF IT, OKAY?
HUH?!
WHA?!
GET UP! ALL OF YOU!
GET UP!
INSANE!
THEY'LL KILL US!
THE MOMENT WE'LL LEAVE THE CAGE!
THEY'LL KILL US!
YOU'RE JUST A GIRL!
INSANE!
JUST A GIRL!
NO HOPE!
THERE IS NO HOPE!

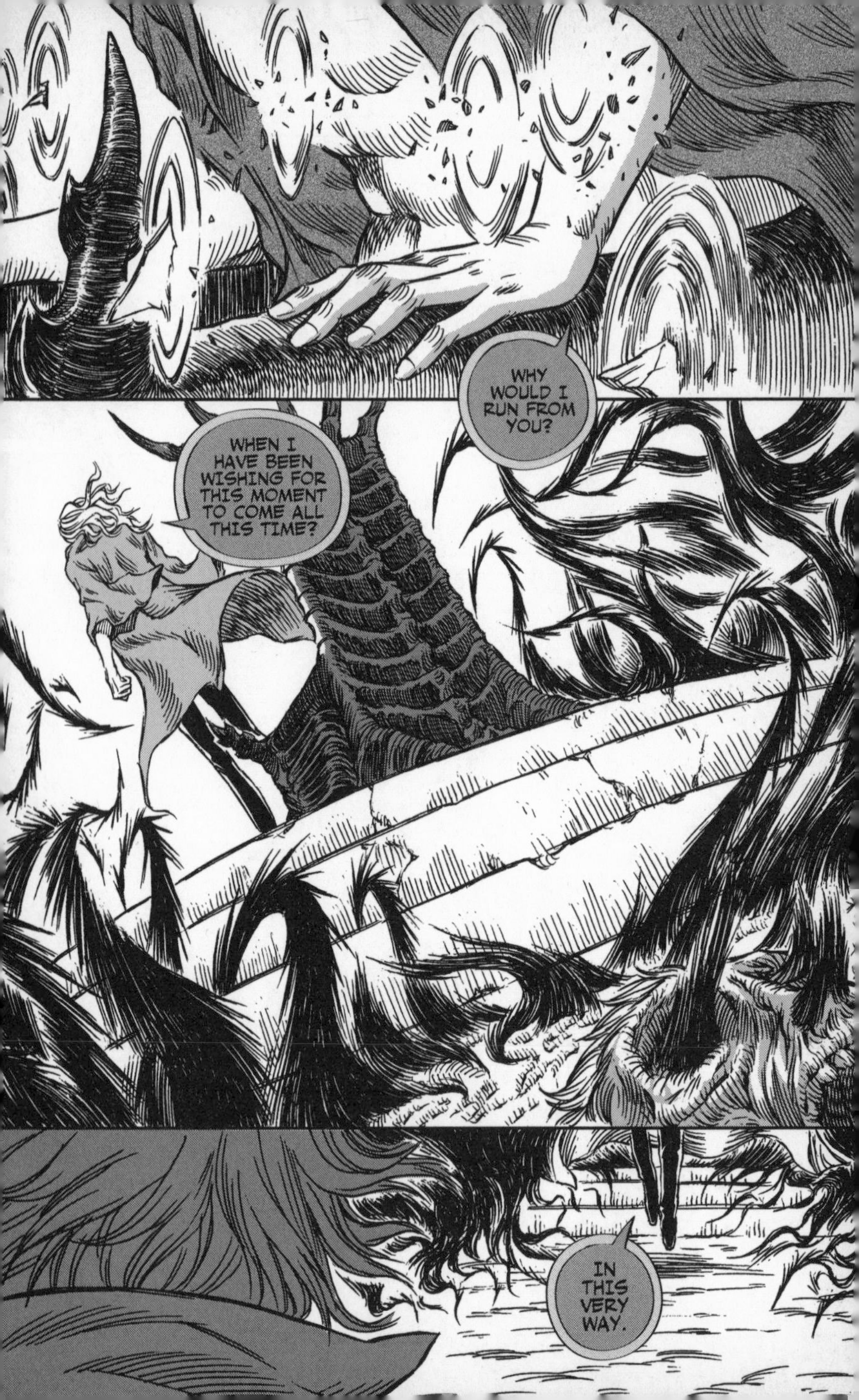
WHY WOULD I RUN FROM YOU?
WHEN I HAVE BEEN WISHING FOR THIS MOMENT TO COME ALL THIS TIME?
IN THIS VERY WAY.

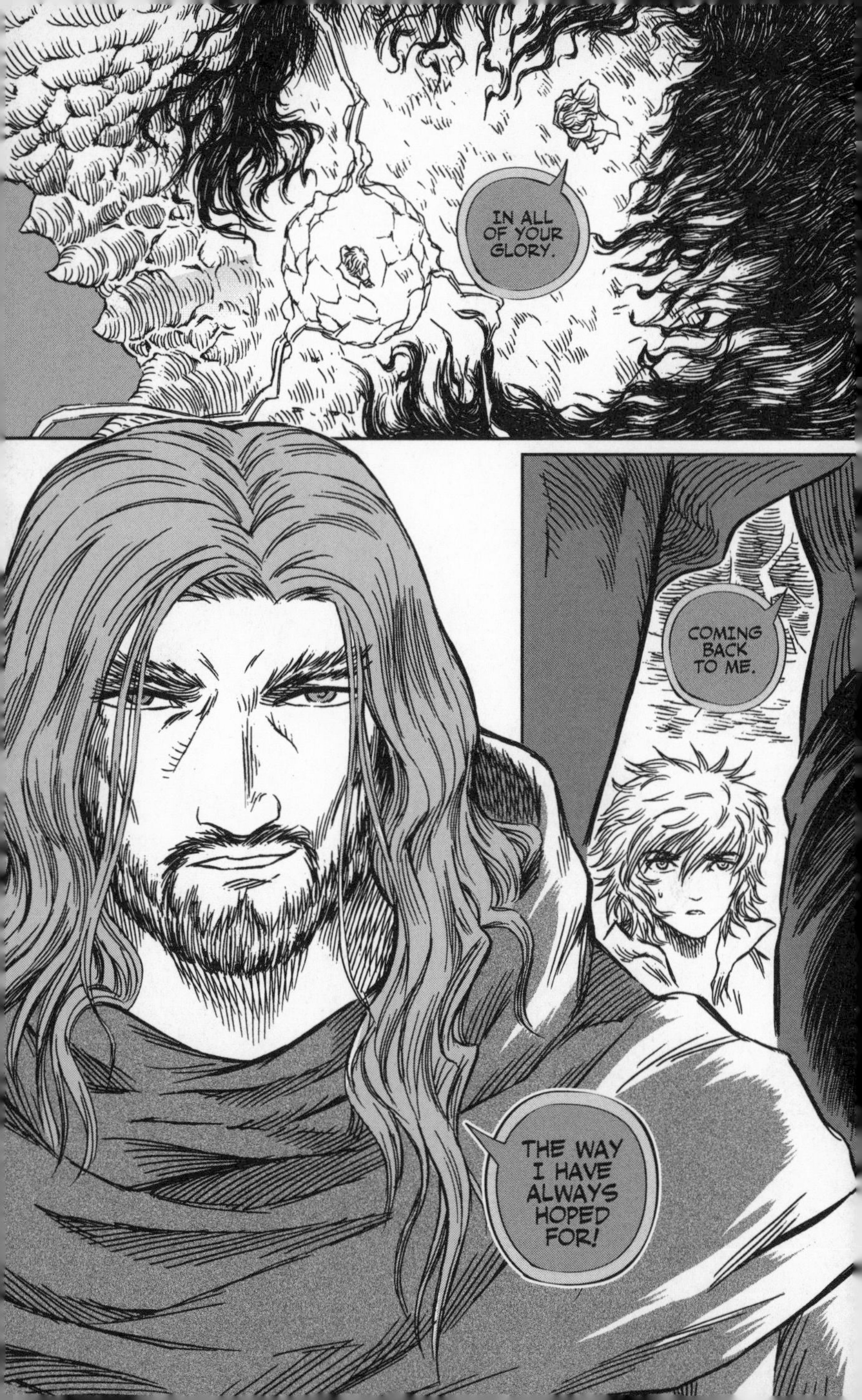
IN ALL OF YOUR GLORY.
COMING BACK TO ME.
THE WAY I HAVE ALWAYS HOPED FOR!

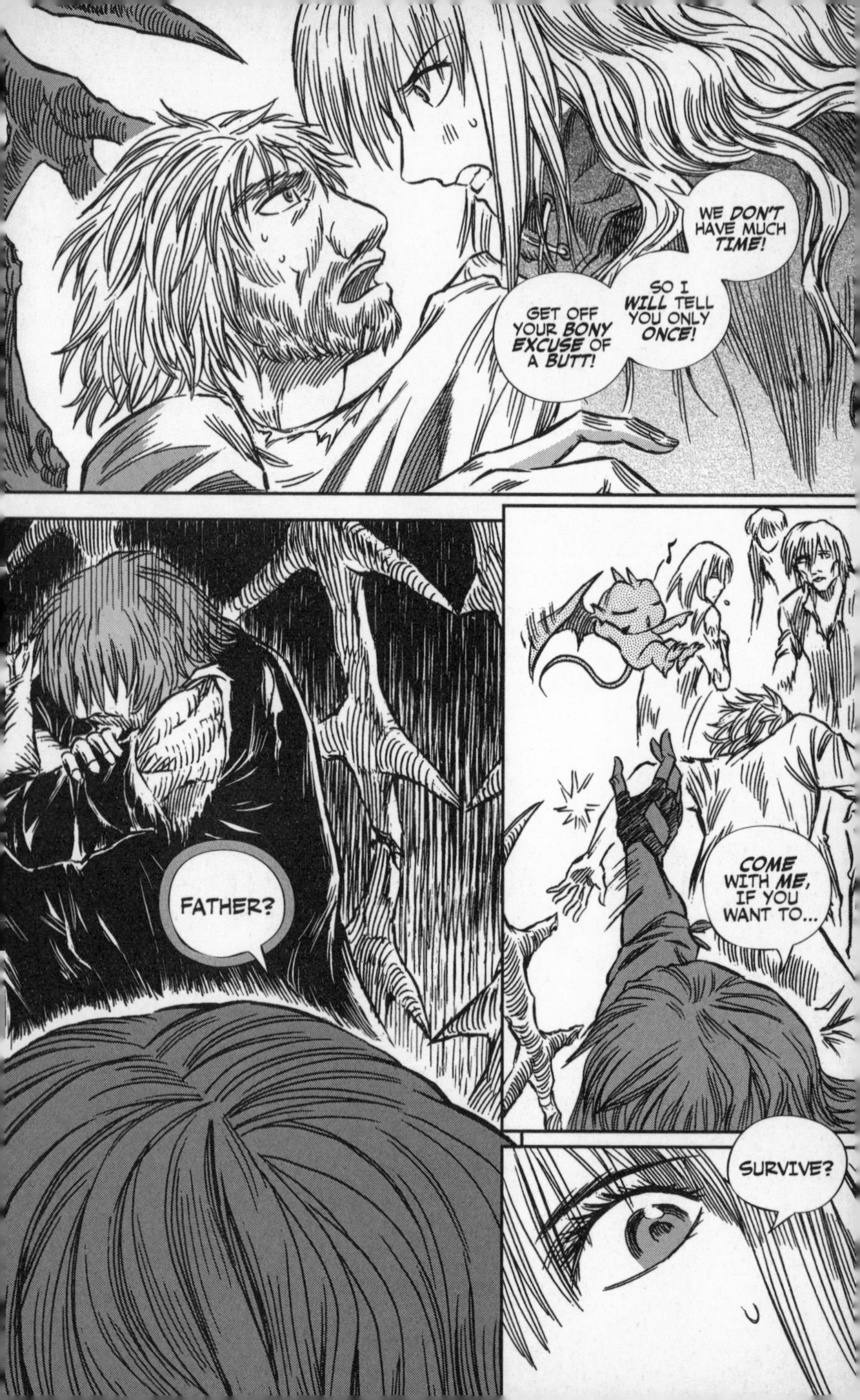
WE DON'T HAVE MUCH TIME!
SO I WILL TELL YOU ONLY ONCE!
GET OFF YOUR BONY EXCUSE OF A BUTT!
COME WITH ME, IF YOU WANT TO...
SURVIVE?
FATHER?

CHAPTER

TRUTHS BE TOLD

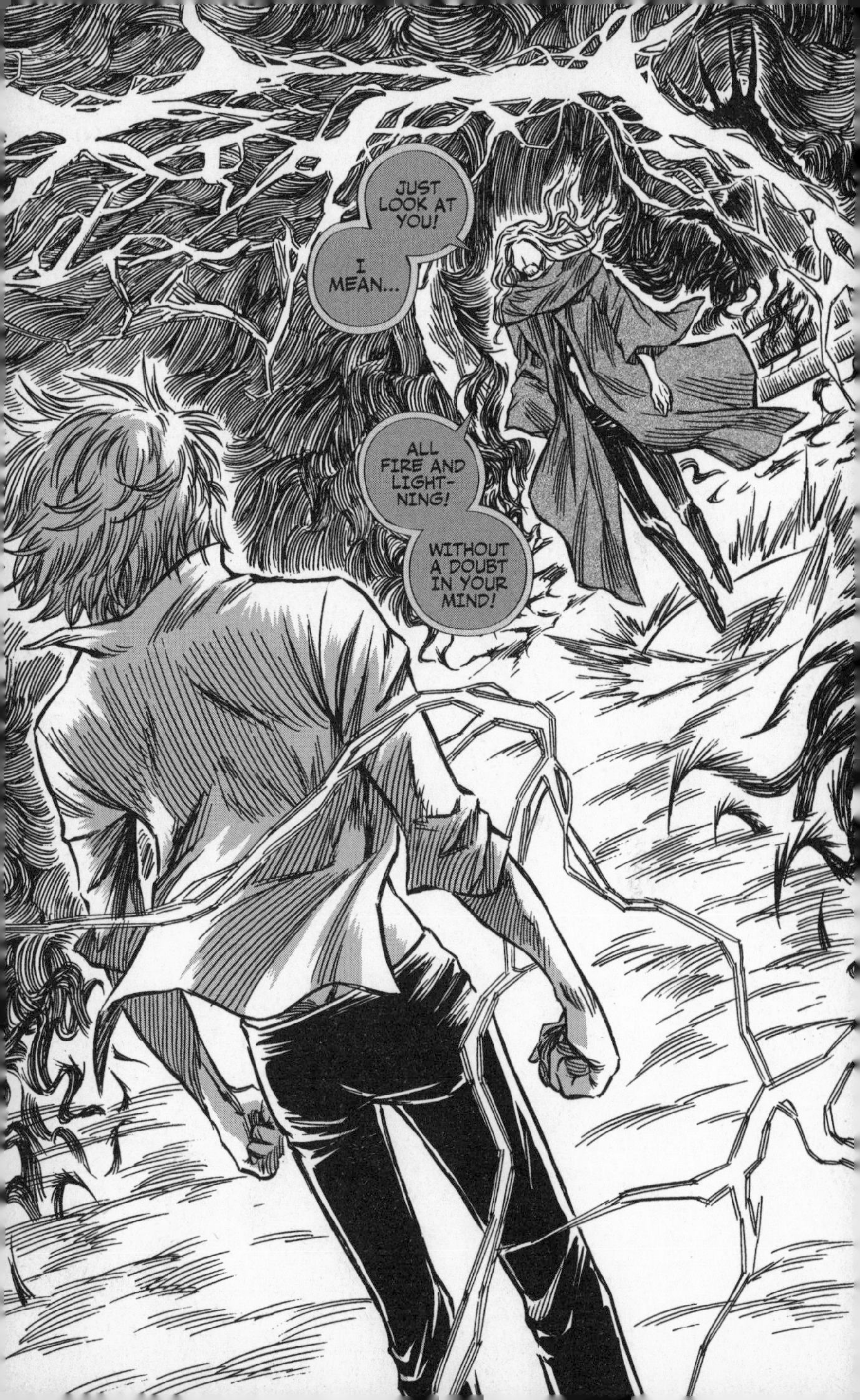
JUST LOOK AT YOU!
I MEAN...
ALL FIRE AND LIGHT-NING!
WITHOUT A DOUBT IN YOUR MIND!

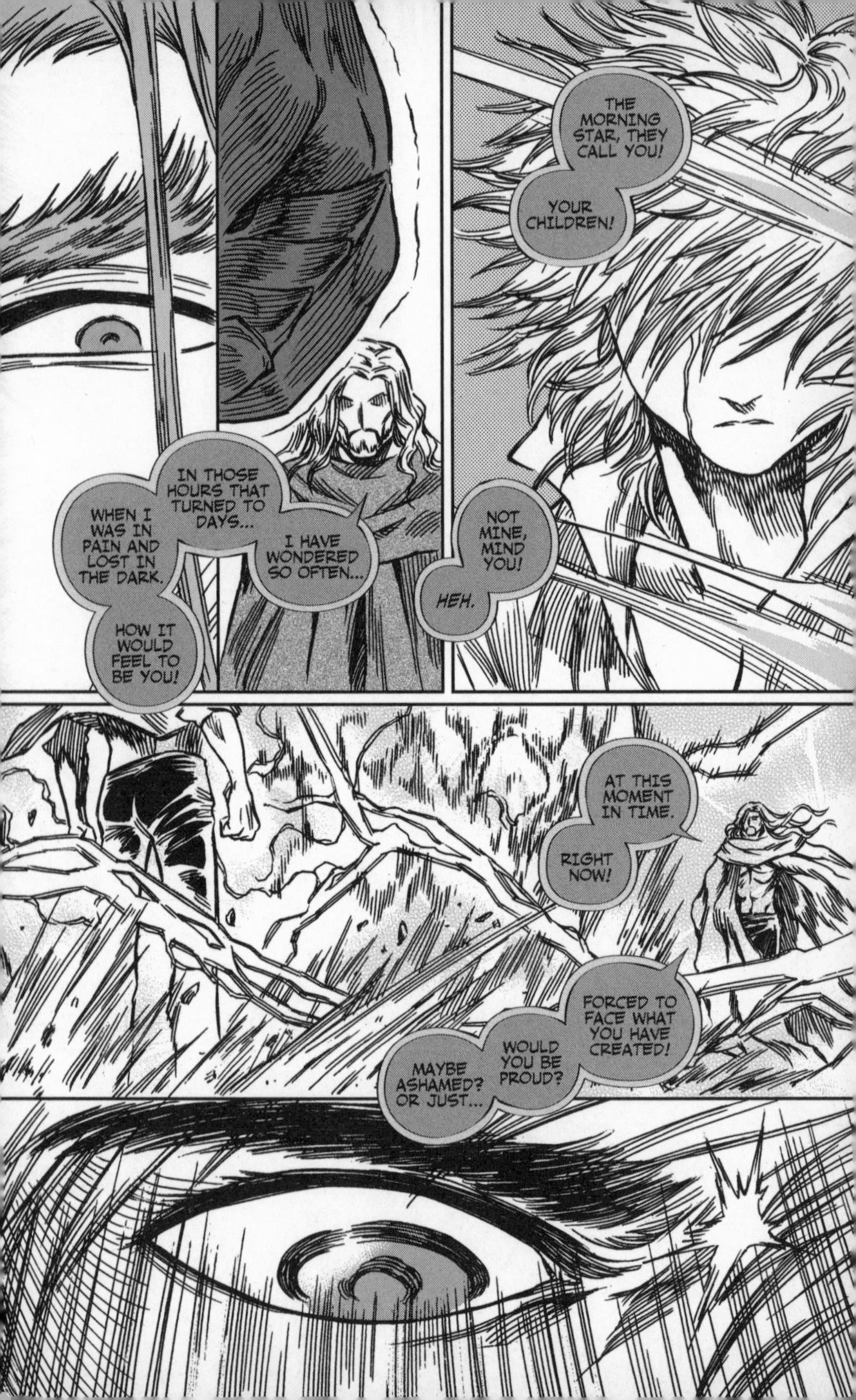
THE MORNING STAR, THEY CALL YOU!
YOUR CHILDREN!
NOT MINE, MIND YOU!
HEH.
IN THOSE HOURS THAT TURNED TO DAYS...
WHEN I WAS IN PAIN AND LOST IN THE DARK.
I HAVE WONDERED SO OFTEN...
HOW IT WOULD FEEL TO BE YOU!
AT THIS MOMENT IN TIME.
RIGHT NOW!
FORCED TO FACE WHAT YOU HAVE CREATED!
WOULD YOU BE PROUD?
MAYBE ASHAMED? OR JUST...

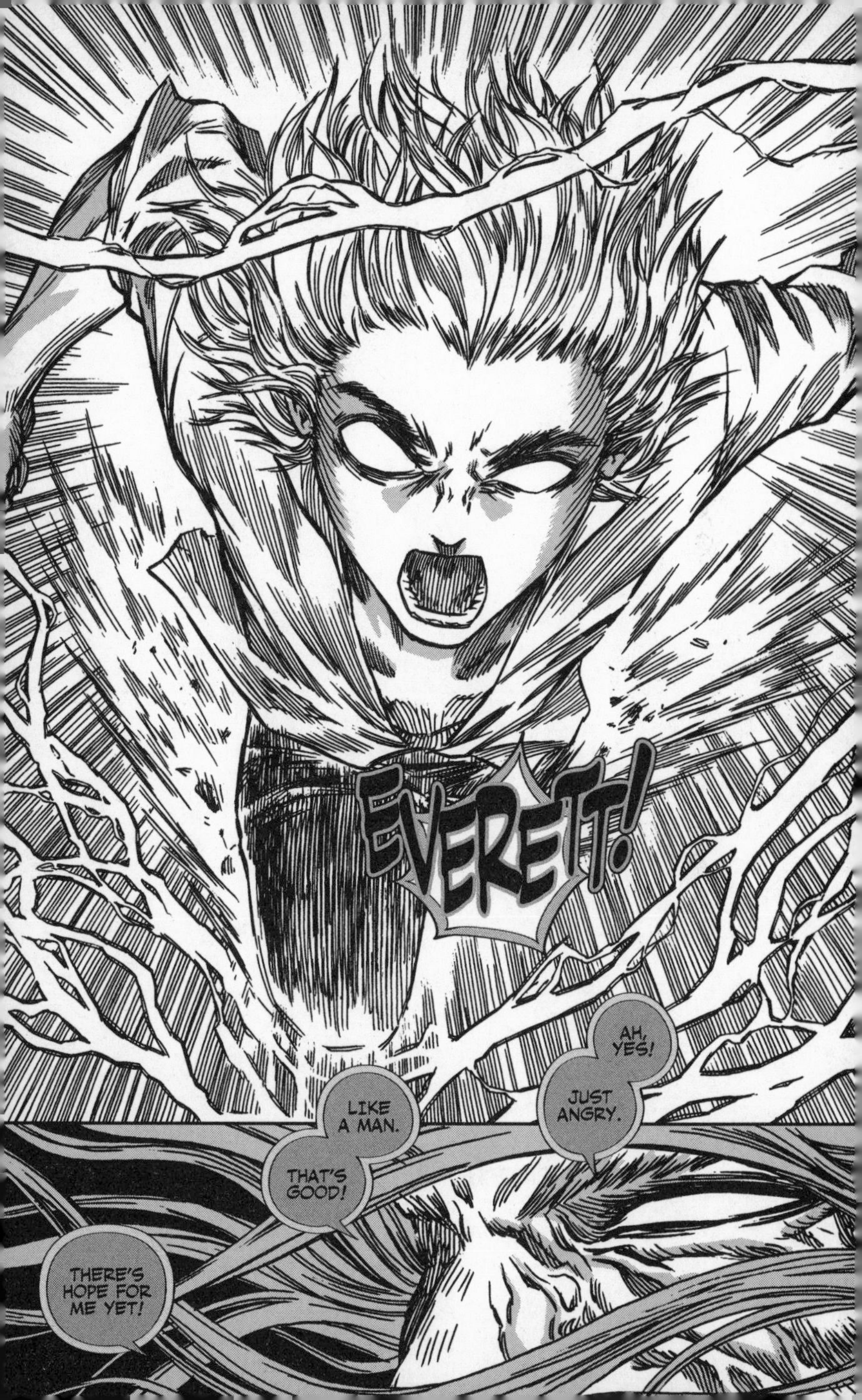
EVERETT!
AH, YES!
JUST ANGRY.
LIKE A MAN.
THAT'S GOOD!
THERE'S HOPE FOR ME YET!

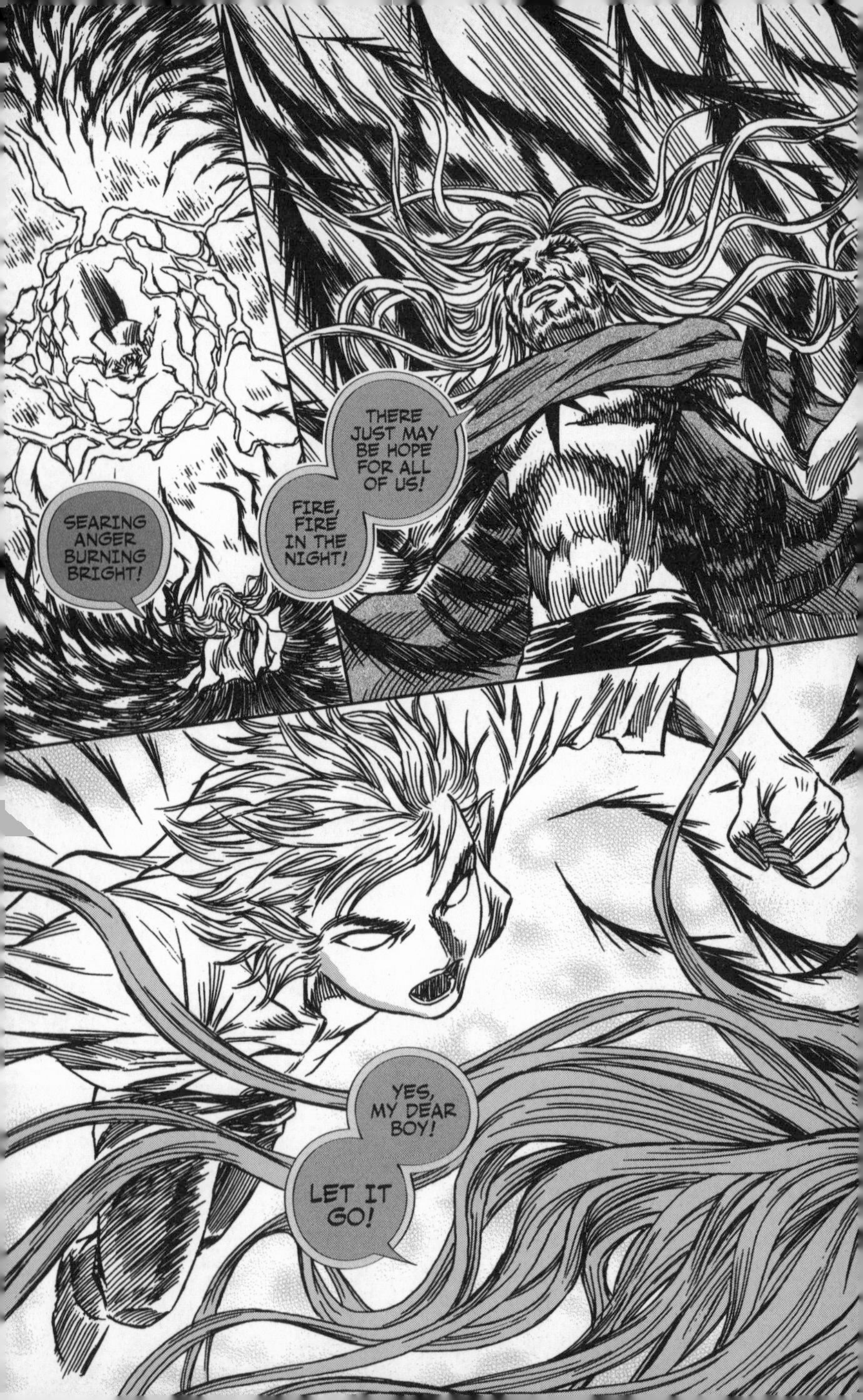
THERE JUST MAY BE HOPE FOR ALL OF US!
FIRE, FIRE IN THE NIGHT!
SEARING ANGER BURNING BRIGHT!
YES, MY DEAR BOY!
LET IT GO!

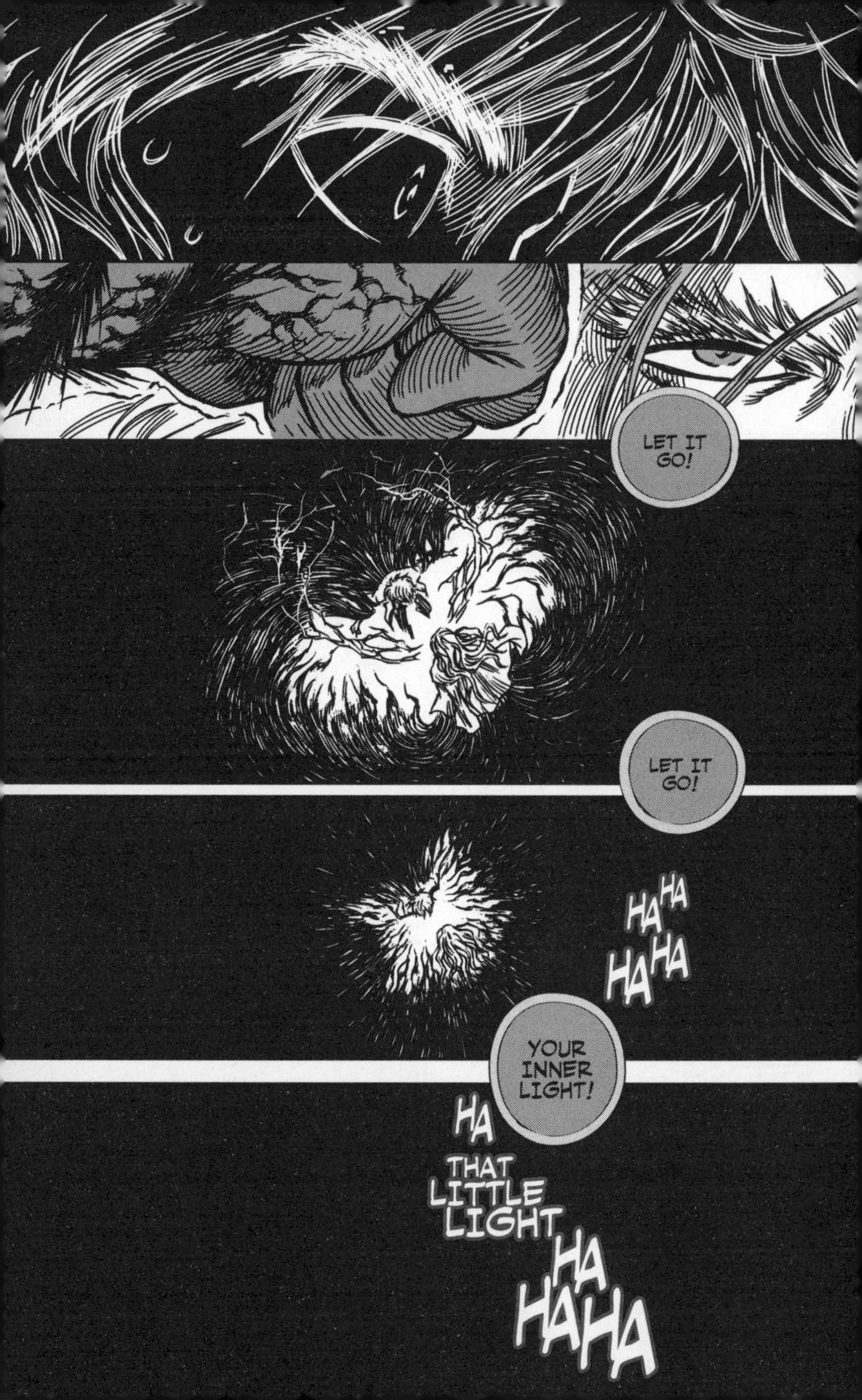
LET IT GO!
LET IT GO!
HA HA HA HA
YOUR INNER LIGHT!
HA
THAT LITTLE LIGHT
HA HA HA

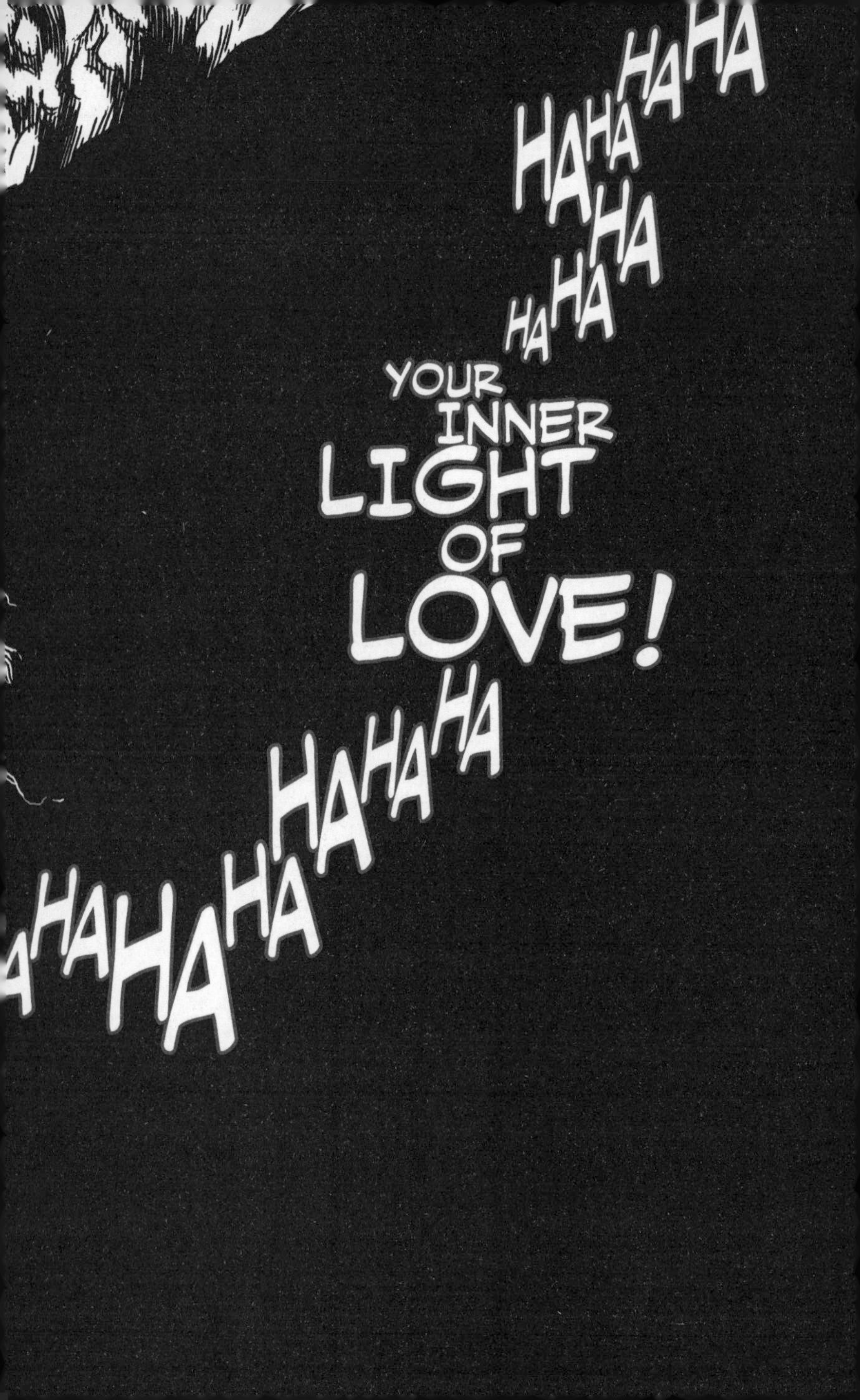
HAHAHAHA
HAHAHA
HAHA
YOUR INNER LIGHT OF LOVE!
HAHAHAHAHAHA
HAHAHAHA

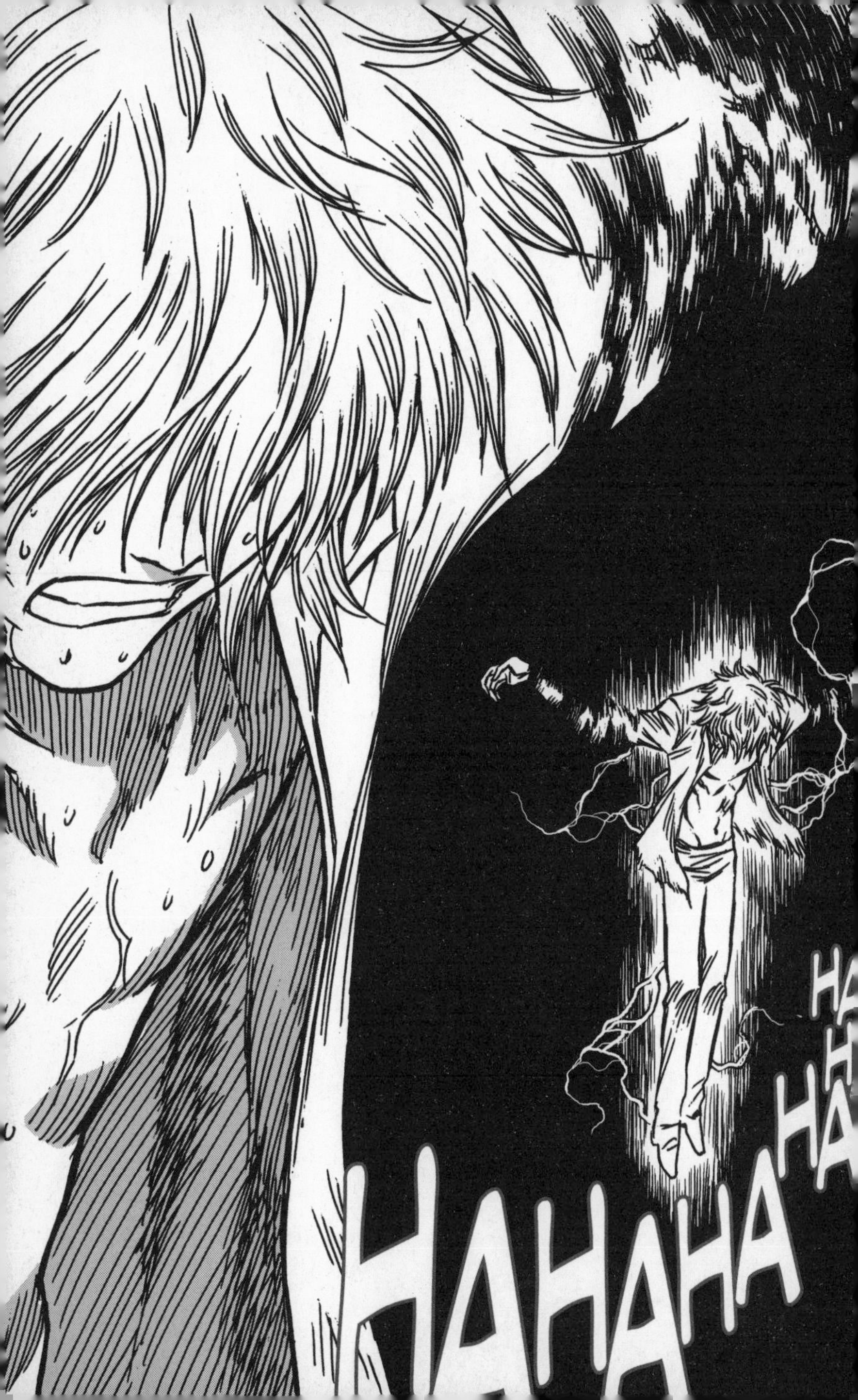
HAHAHAHAHAHA

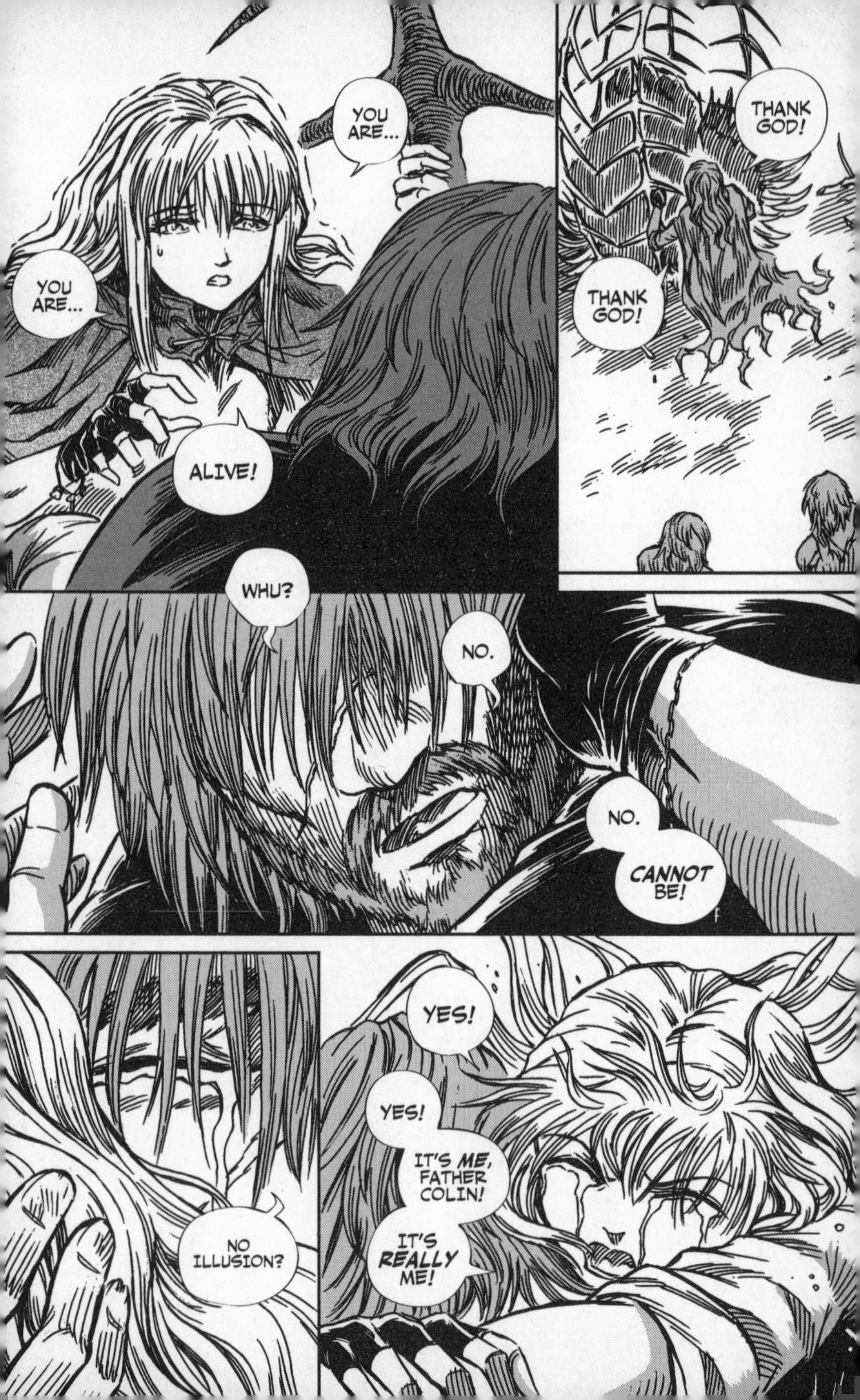
YOU ARE...
YOU ARE...
ALIVE!
THANK GOD!
THANK GOD!
WHU?
NO.
NO.
CANNOT BE!
NO ILLUSION?
YES!
YES!
IT'S ME, FATHER COLIN!
IT'S REALLY ME!

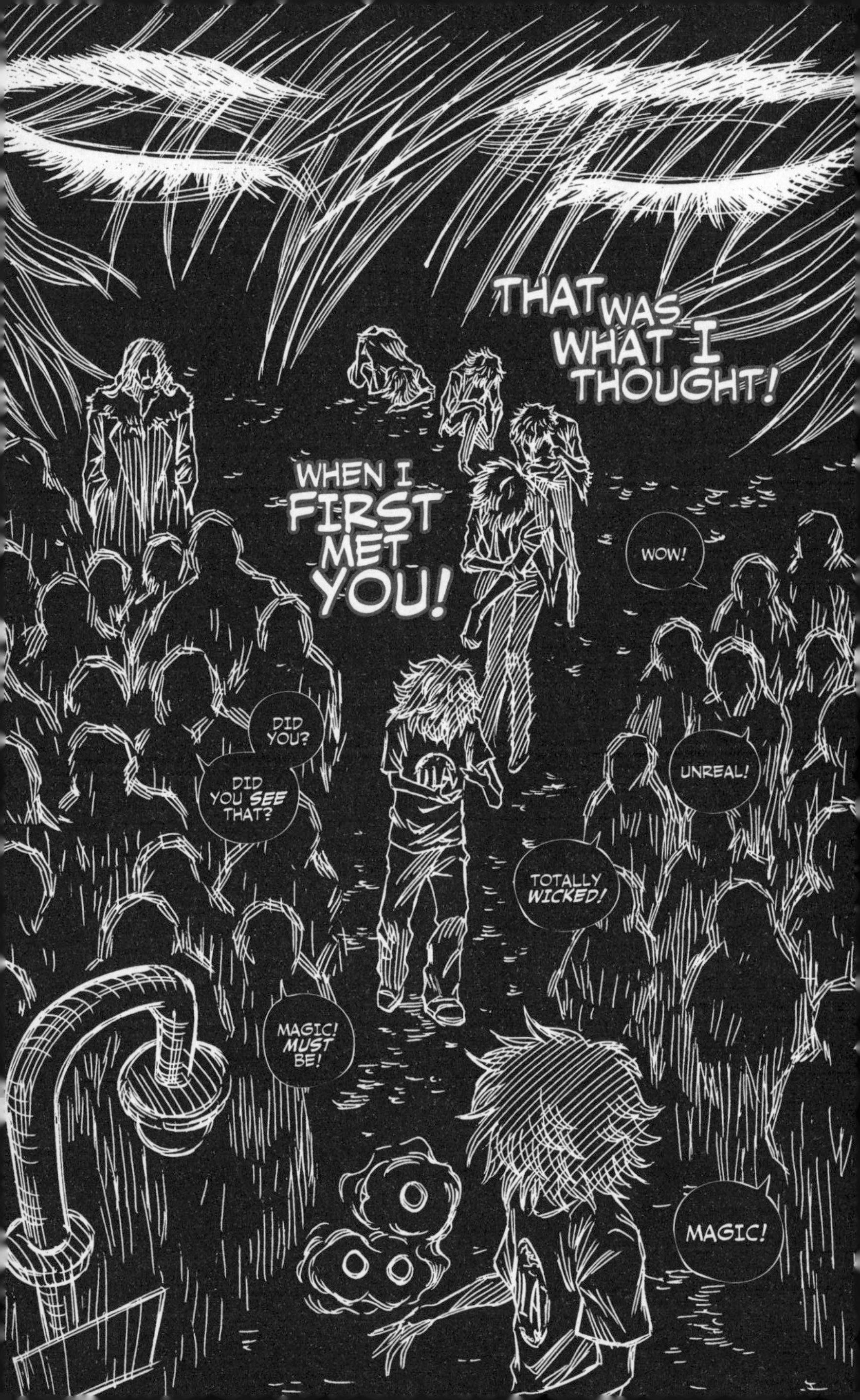
THAT WAS WHAT I THOUGHT!
WHEN I FIRST MET YOU!
WOW!
DID YOU?
UNREAL!
DID YOU SEE THAT?
TOTALLY WICKED!
MAGIC! MUST BE!
MAGIC!

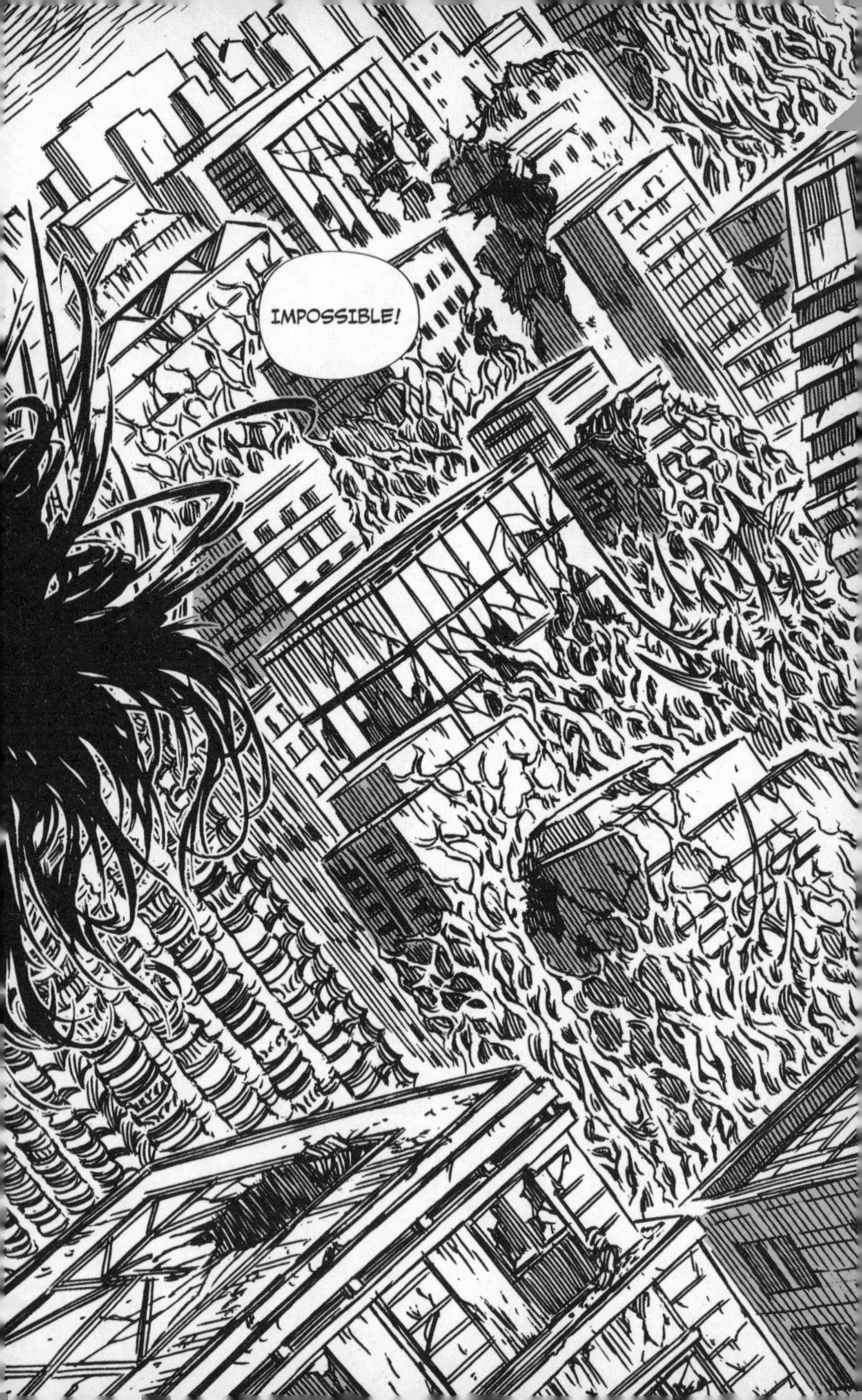
IMPOSSIBLE!

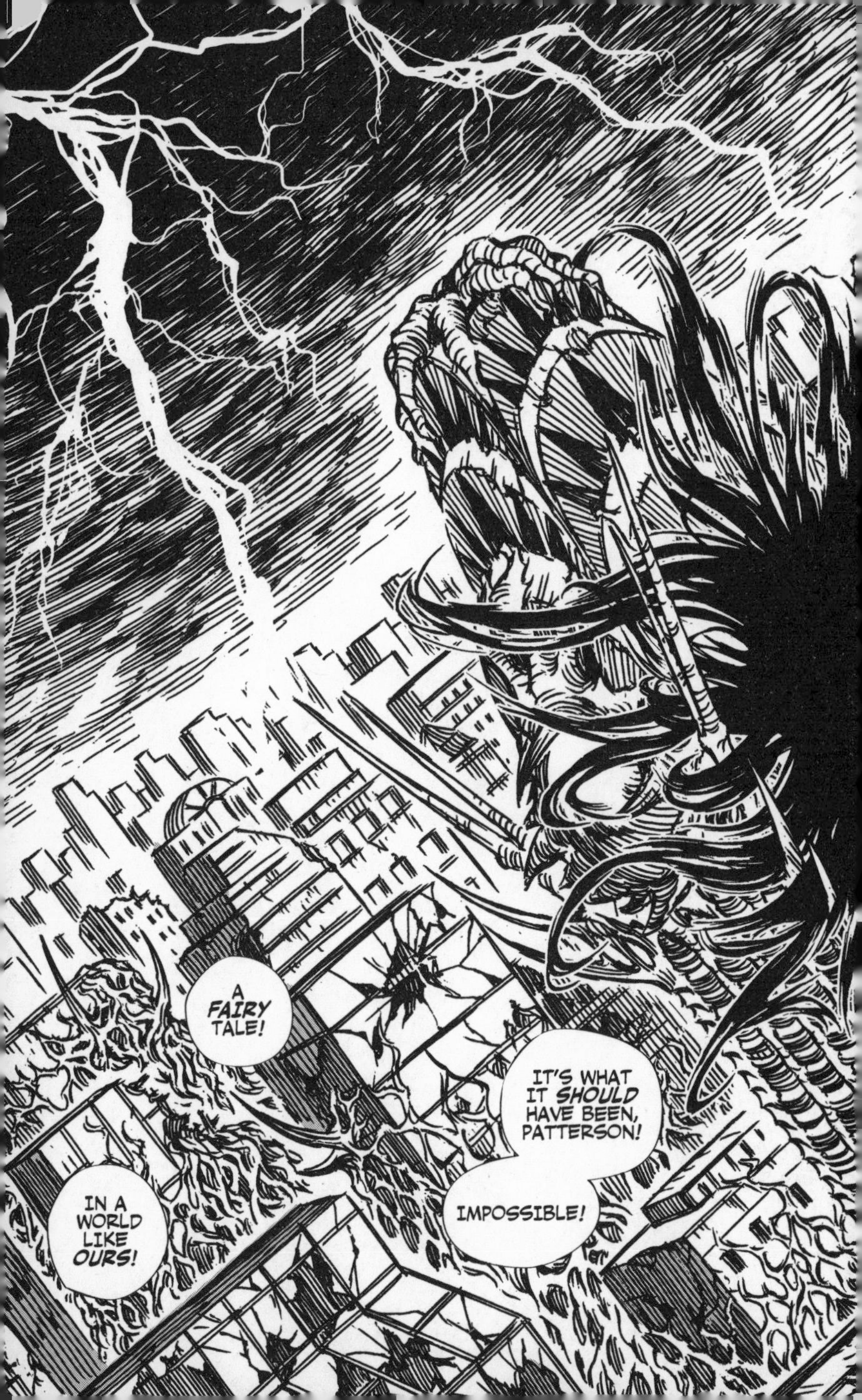
IT'S WHAT IT *SHOULD* HAVE BEEN, PATTERSON!
IMPOSSIBLE!
A *FAIRY* TALE!
IN A WORLD LIKE *OURS*!

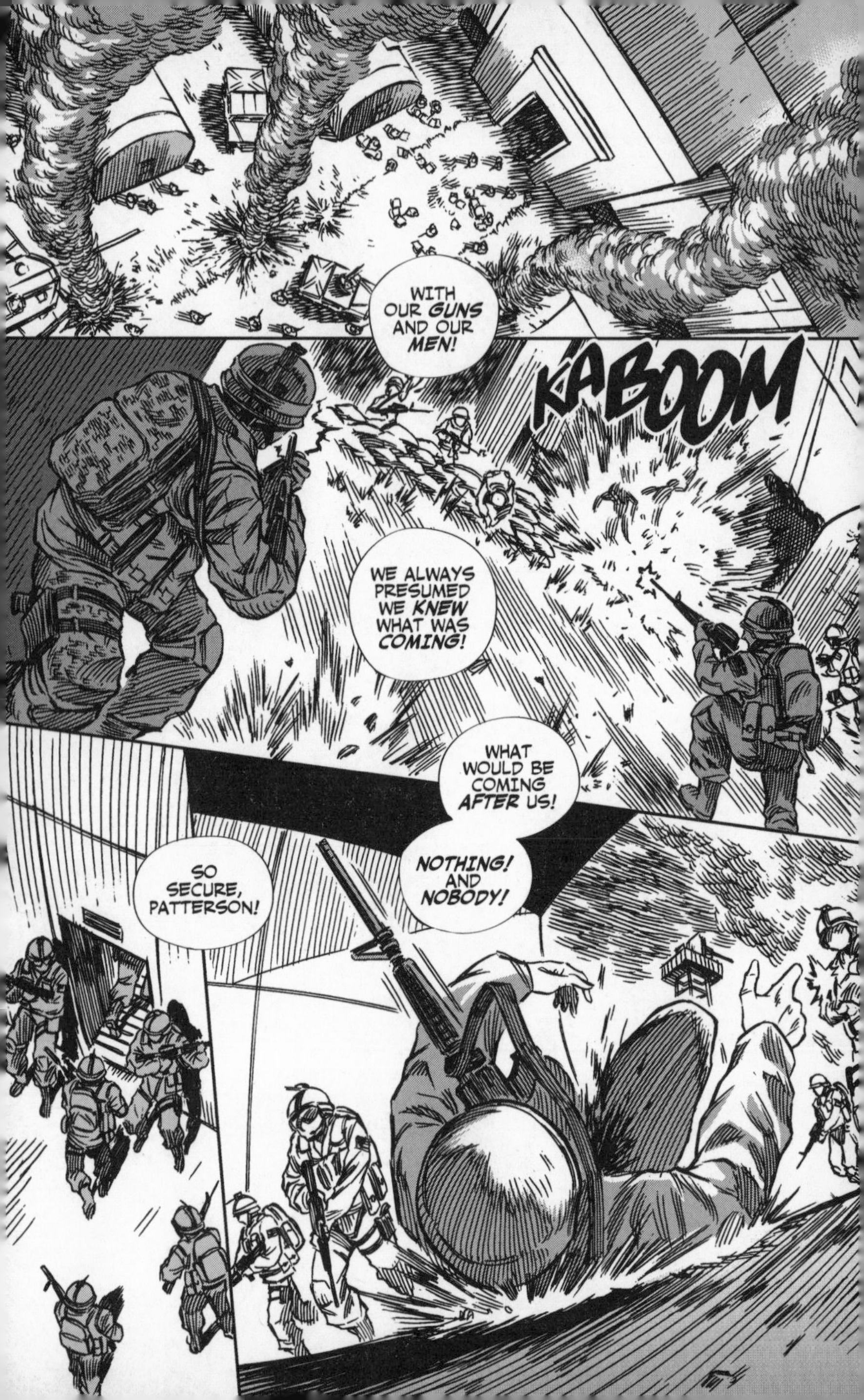
WITH OUR GUNS AND OUR MEN!
KABOOM
WE ALWAYS PRESUMED WE KNEW WHAT WAS COMING!
WHAT WOULD BE COMING AFTER US!
NOTHING! AND NOBODY!
SO SECURE, PATTERSON!

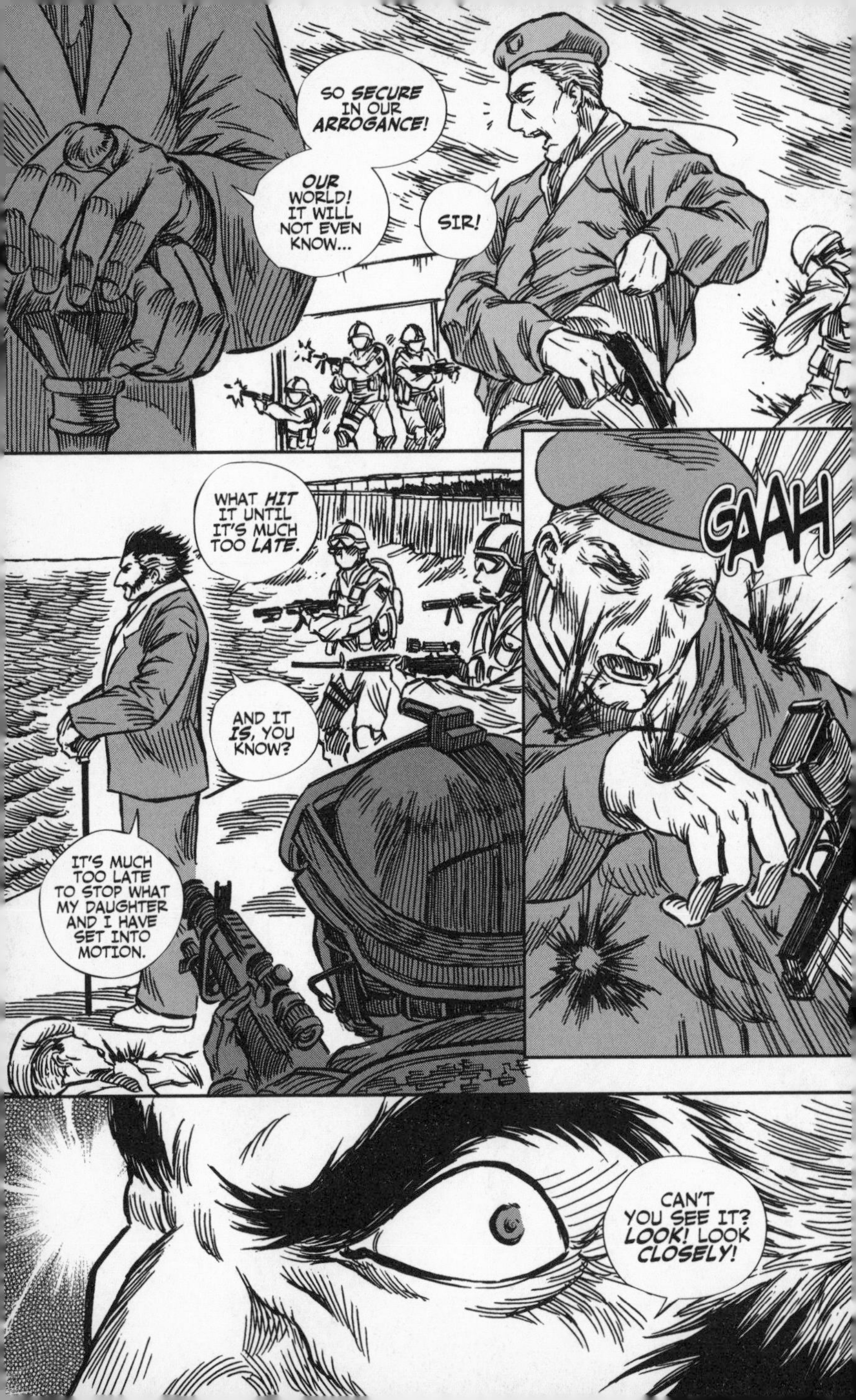
SO SECURE IN OUR ARROGANCE!
OUR WORLD! IT WILL NOT EVEN KNOW...
SIR!
WHAT HIT IT UNTIL IT'S MUCH TOO LATE.
AND IT IS, YOU KNOW?
IT'S MUCH TOO LATE TO STOP WHAT MY DAUGHTER AND I HAVE SET INTO MOTION.
GAAH
CAN'T YOU SEE IT? LOOK! LOOK CLOSELY!

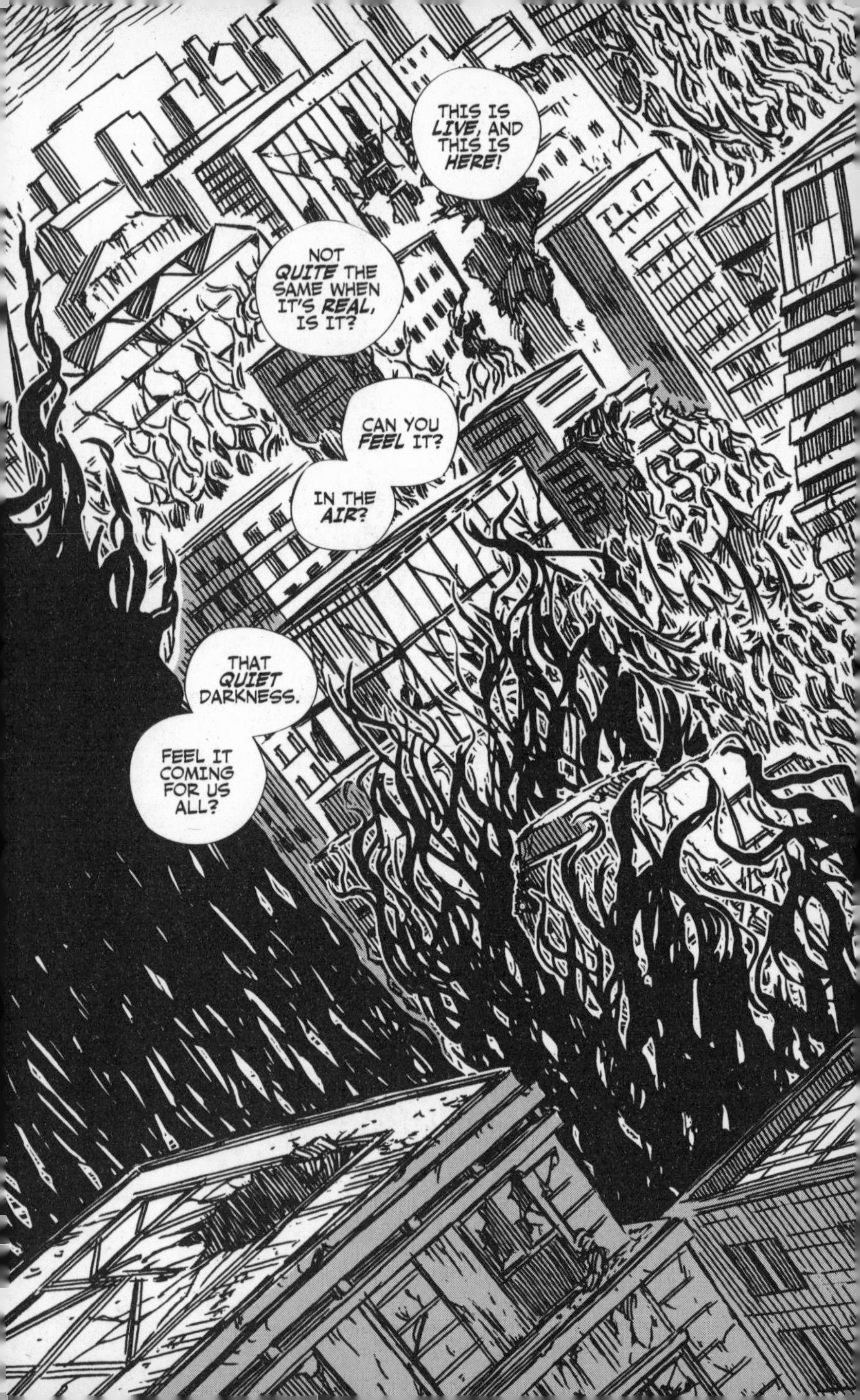
THIS IS LIVE, AND THIS IS HERE!
NOT QUITE THE SAME WHEN IT'S REAL, IS IT?
CAN YOU FEEL IT?
IN THE AIR?
THAT QUIET DARKNESS.
FEEL IT COMING FOR US ALL?

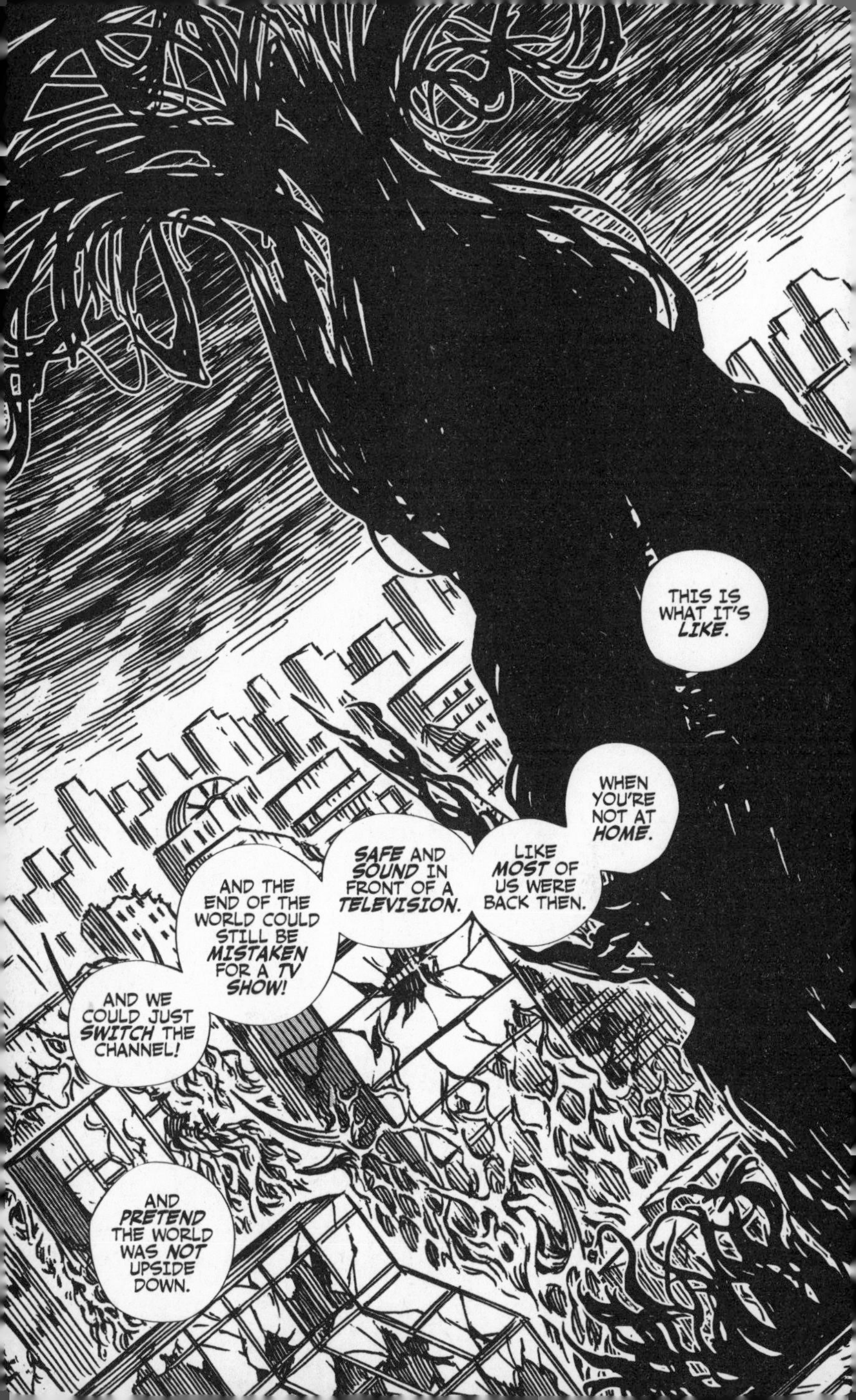
THIS IS WHAT IT'S LIKE.
WHEN YOU'RE NOT AT HOME.
LIKE MOST OF US WERE BACK THEN.
SAFE AND SOUND IN FRONT OF A TELEVISION.
AND THE END OF THE WORLD COULD STILL BE MISTAKEN FOR A TV SHOW!
AND WE COULD JUST SWITCH THE CHANNEL!
AND PRETEND THE WORLD WAS NOT UPSIDE DOWN.

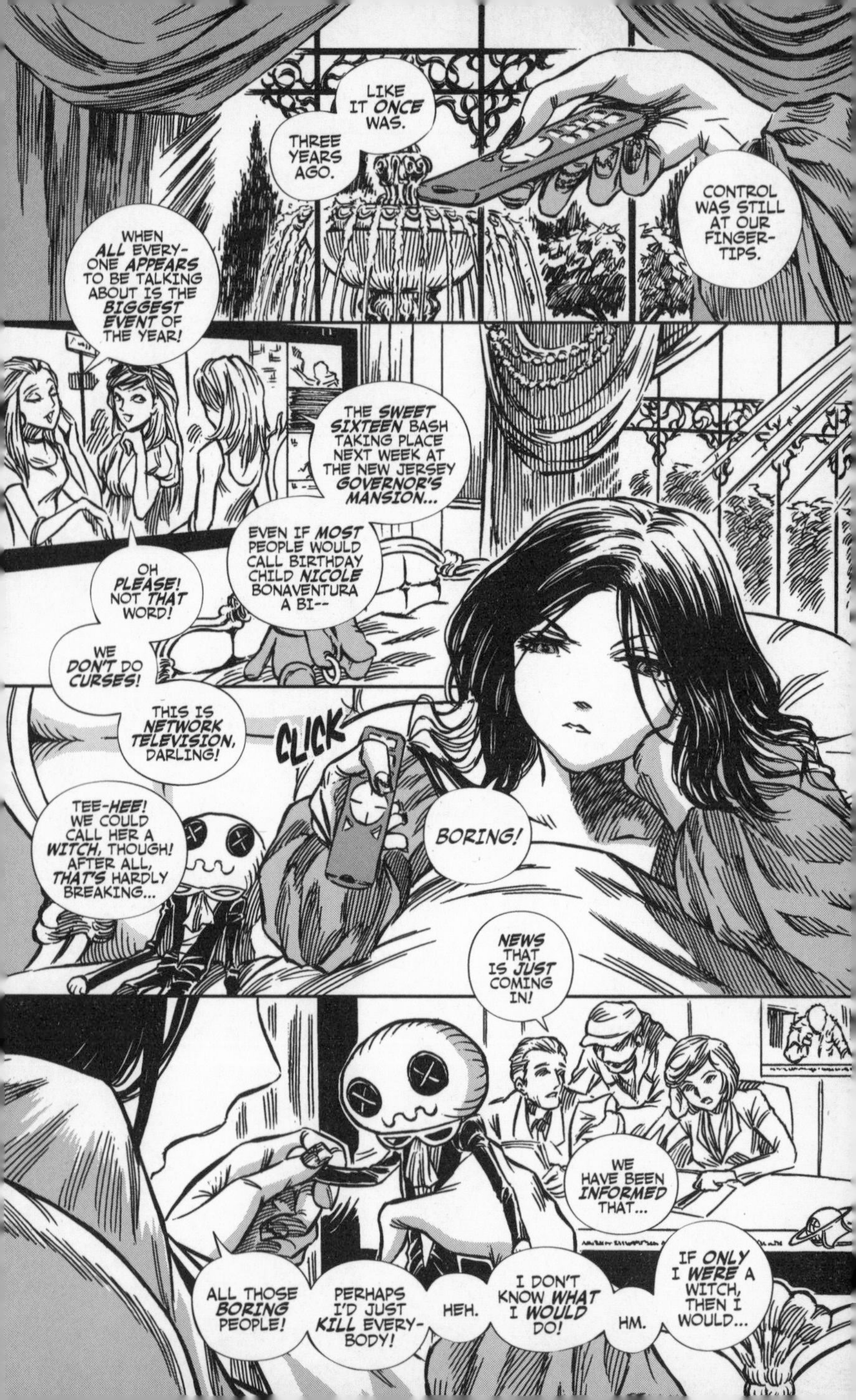
LIKE IT *ONCE* WAS.
THREE YEARS AGO.
CONTROL WAS STILL AT OUR FINGER-TIPS.
WHEN *ALL* EVERYONE *APPEARS* TO BE TALKING ABOUT IS THE *BIGGEST EVENT* OF THE YEAR!
THE *SWEET SIXTEEN* BASH TAKING PLACE NEXT WEEK AT THE NEW JERSEY *GOVERNOR'S MANSION*...
EVEN IF *MOST* PEOPLE WOULD CALL BIRTHDAY CHILD *NICOLE* BONAVENTURA A BI--
OH *PLEASE!* NOT *THAT* WORD!
WE *DON'T* DO *CURSES!*
THIS IS *NETWORK TELEVISION,* DARLING!
CLICK
TEE-*HEE!* WE COULD CALL HER A *WITCH,* THOUGH! AFTER ALL, *THAT'S* HARDLY BREAKING...
BORING!
NEWS THAT IS *JUST* COMING IN!
WE HAVE BEEN *INFORMED* THAT...
ALL THOSE *BORING* PEOPLE!
PERHAPS I'D JUST *KILL* EVERY-BODY!
HEH.
I DON'T KNOW *WHAT* I *WOULD* DO!
HM.
IF *ONLY* I *WERE* A WITCH, THEN I WOULD...

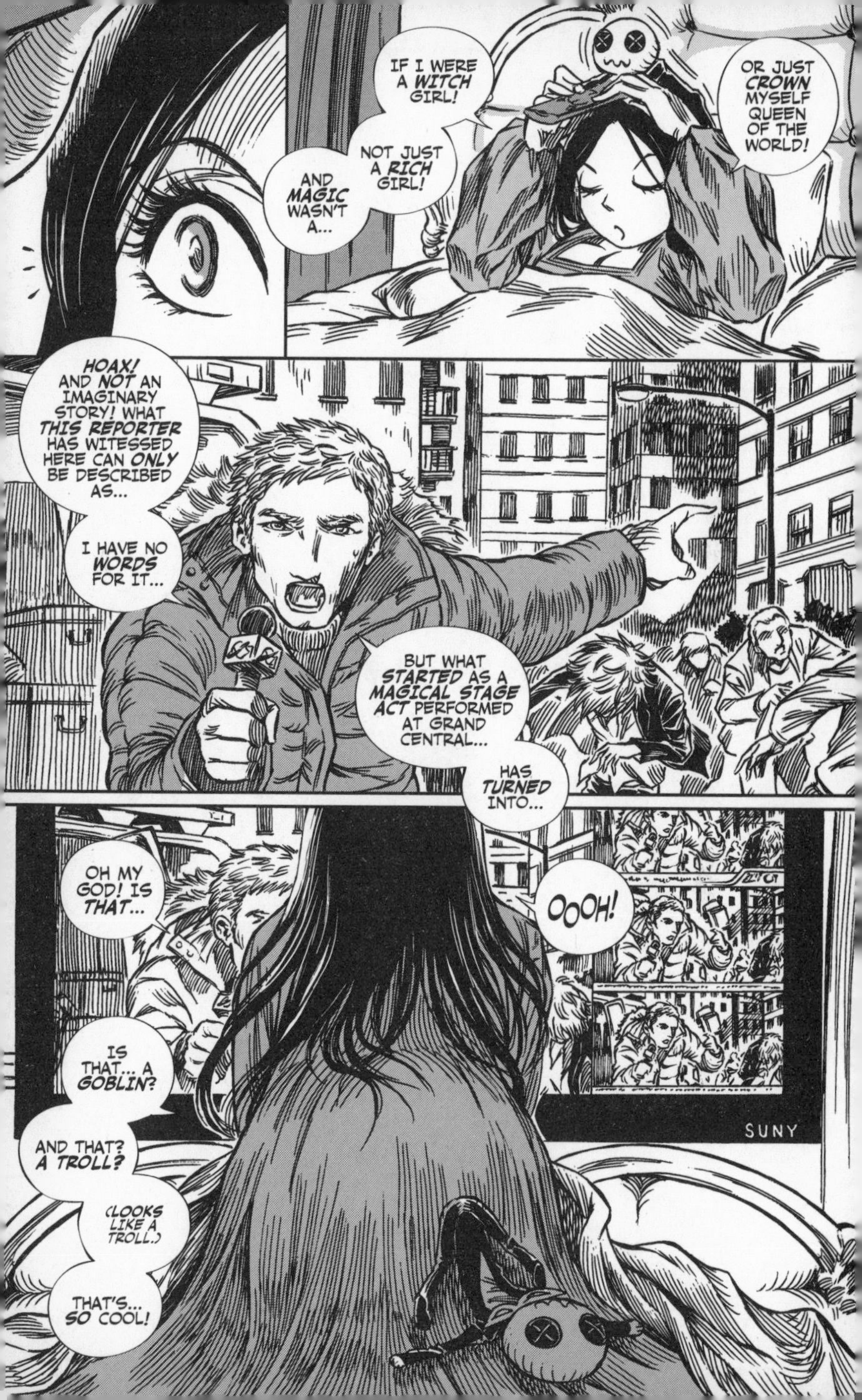
OR JUST CROWN MYSELF QUEEN OF THE WORLD!
IF I WERE A WITCH GIRL!
NOT JUST A RICH GIRL!
AND MAGIC WASN'T A...
HOAX! AND NOT AN IMAGINARY STORY! WHAT THIS REPORTER HAS WITESSED HERE CAN ONLY BE DESCRIBED AS...
I HAVE NO WORDS FOR IT...
BUT WHAT STARTED AS A MAGICAL STAGE ACT PERFORMED AT GRAND CENTRAL...
HAS TURNED INTO...
OOOH!
OH MY GOD! IS THAT...
IS THAT... A GOBLIN?
AND THAT? A TROLL?
(LOOKS LIKE A TROLL.)
THAT'S... SO COOL!
SUNY

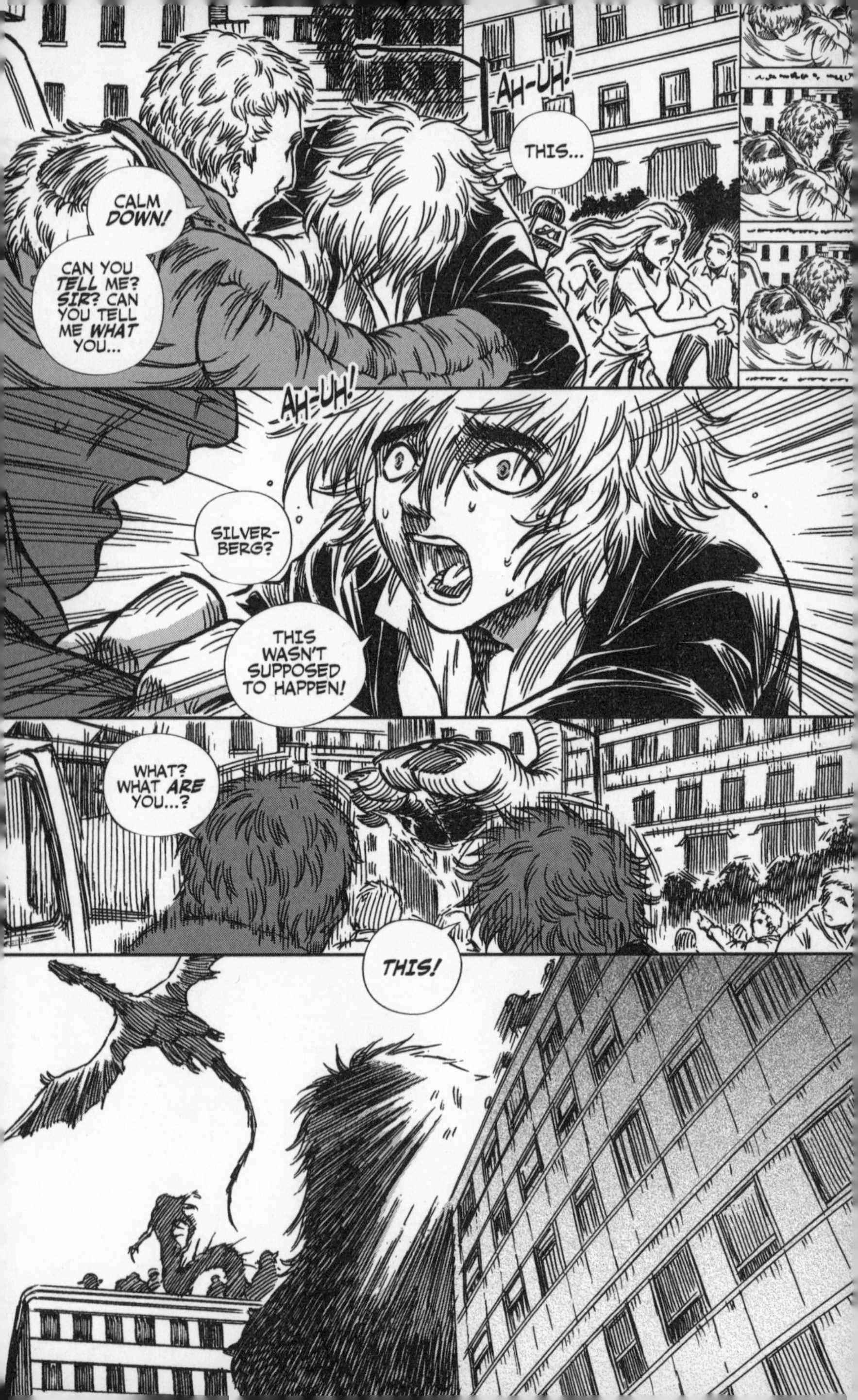
CALM DOWN!
CAN YOU TELL ME? SIR? CAN YOU TELL ME WHAT YOU...
AH-UH!
THIS...
AH-UH!
SILVER-BERG?
THIS WASN'T SUPPOSED TO HAPPEN!
WHAT? WHAT ARE YOU...?
THIS!

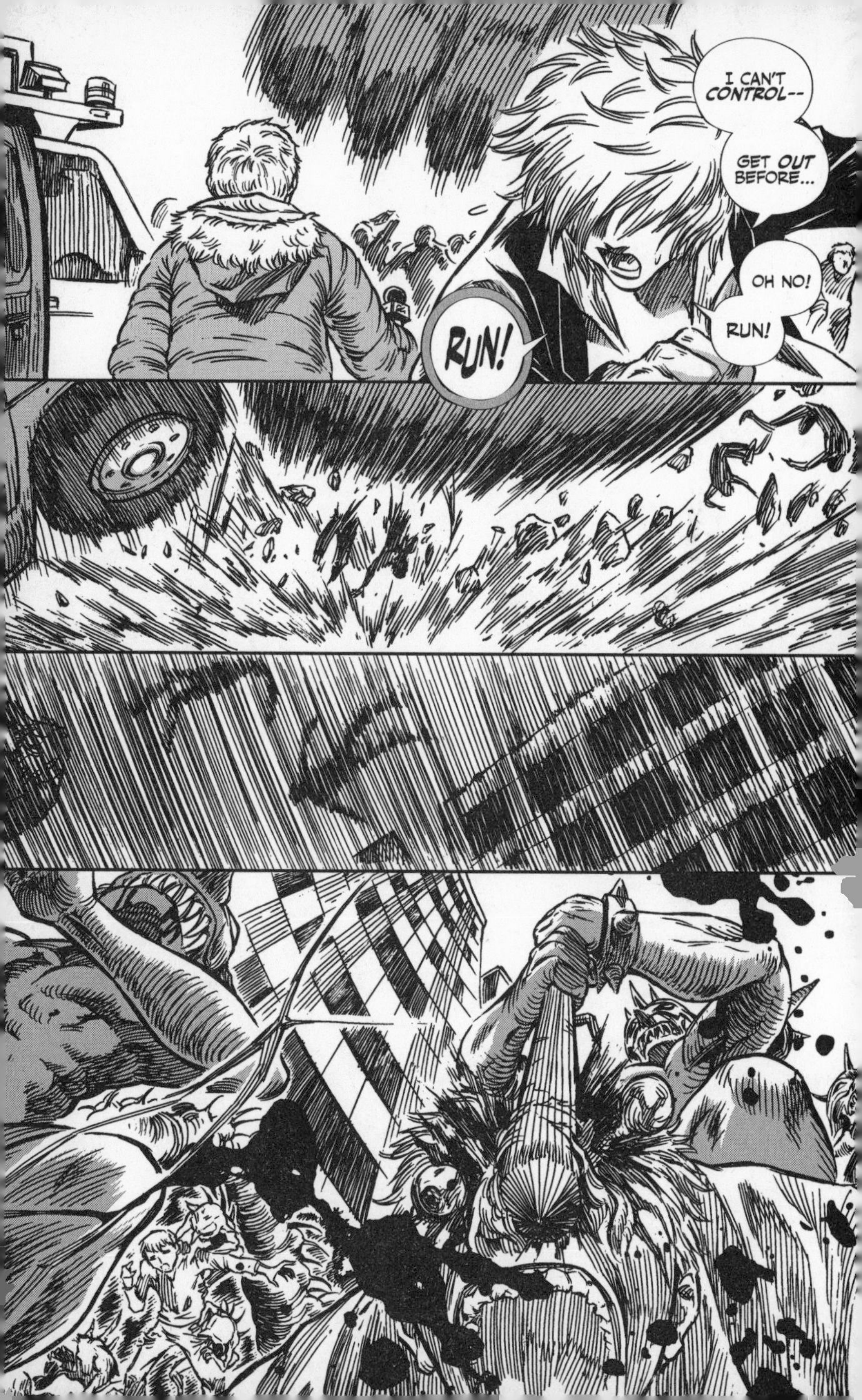
I CAN'T CONTROL--
GET OUT BEFORE...
OH NO!
RUN!
RUN!

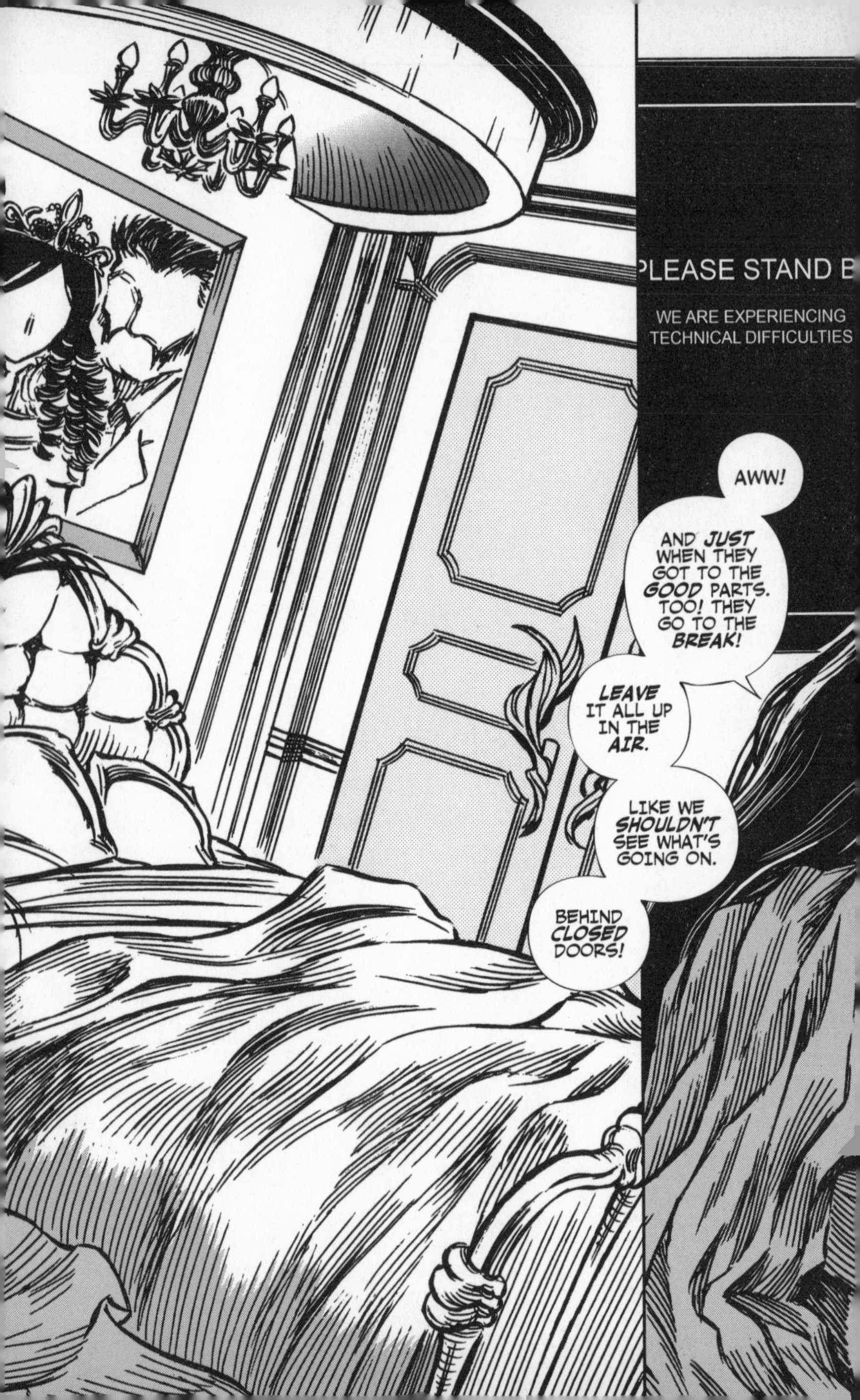
PLEASE STAND B
WE ARE EXPERIENCING TECHNICAL DIFFICULTIES
AWW!
AND JUST WHEN THEY GOT TO THE GOOD PARTS, TOO! THEY GO TO THE BREAK!
LEAVE IT ALL UP IN THE AIR.
LIKE WE SHOULDN'T SEE WHAT'S GOING ON.
BEHIND CLOSED DOORS!

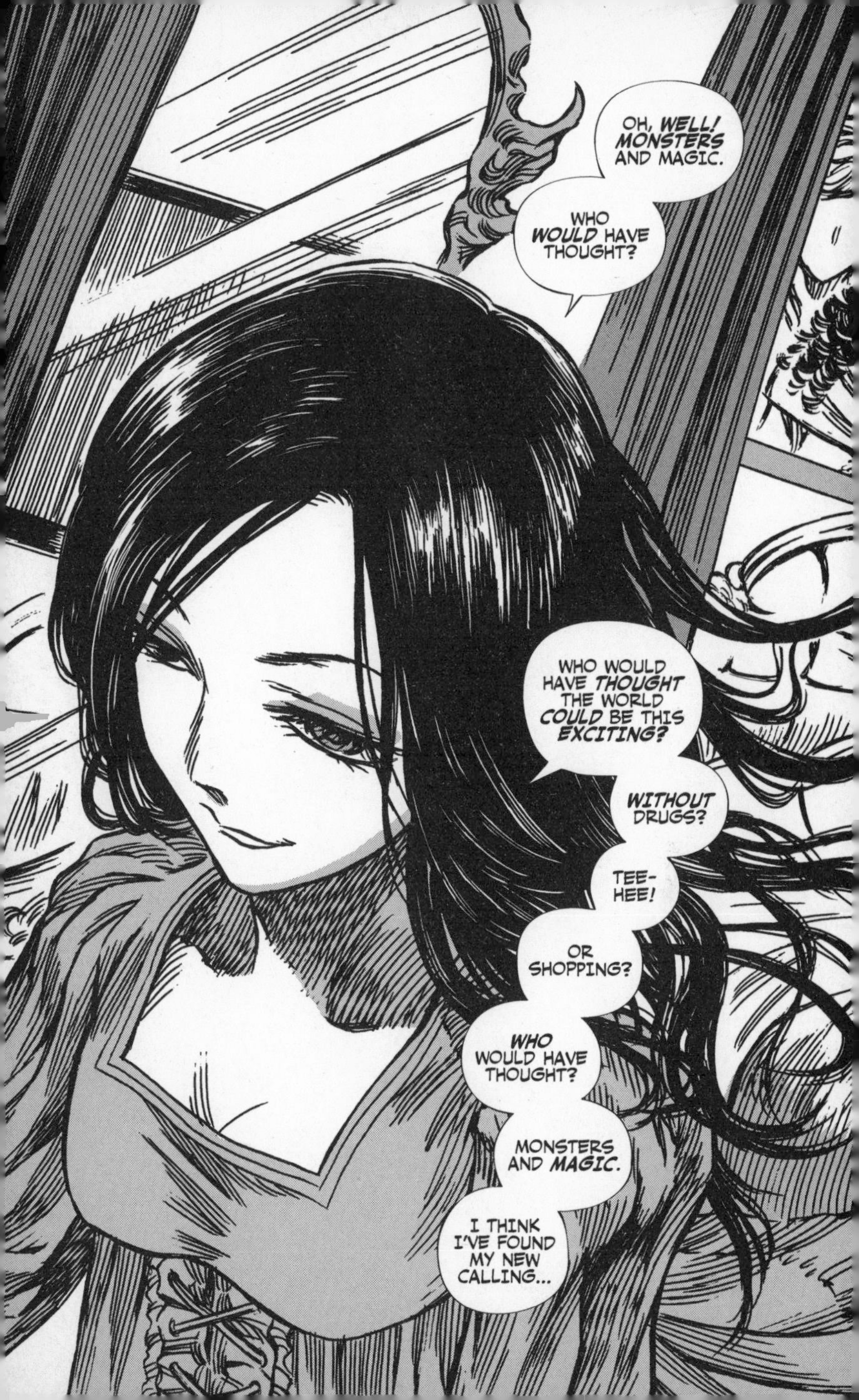
OH, WELL! MONSTERS AND MAGIC.
WHO WOULD HAVE THOUGHT?
WHO WOULD HAVE THOUGHT THE WORLD COULD BE THIS EXCITING?
WITHOUT DRUGS?
TEE-HEE!
OR SHOPPING?
WHO WOULD HAVE THOUGHT?
MONSTERS AND MAGIC.
I THINK I'VE FOUND MY NEW CALLING...

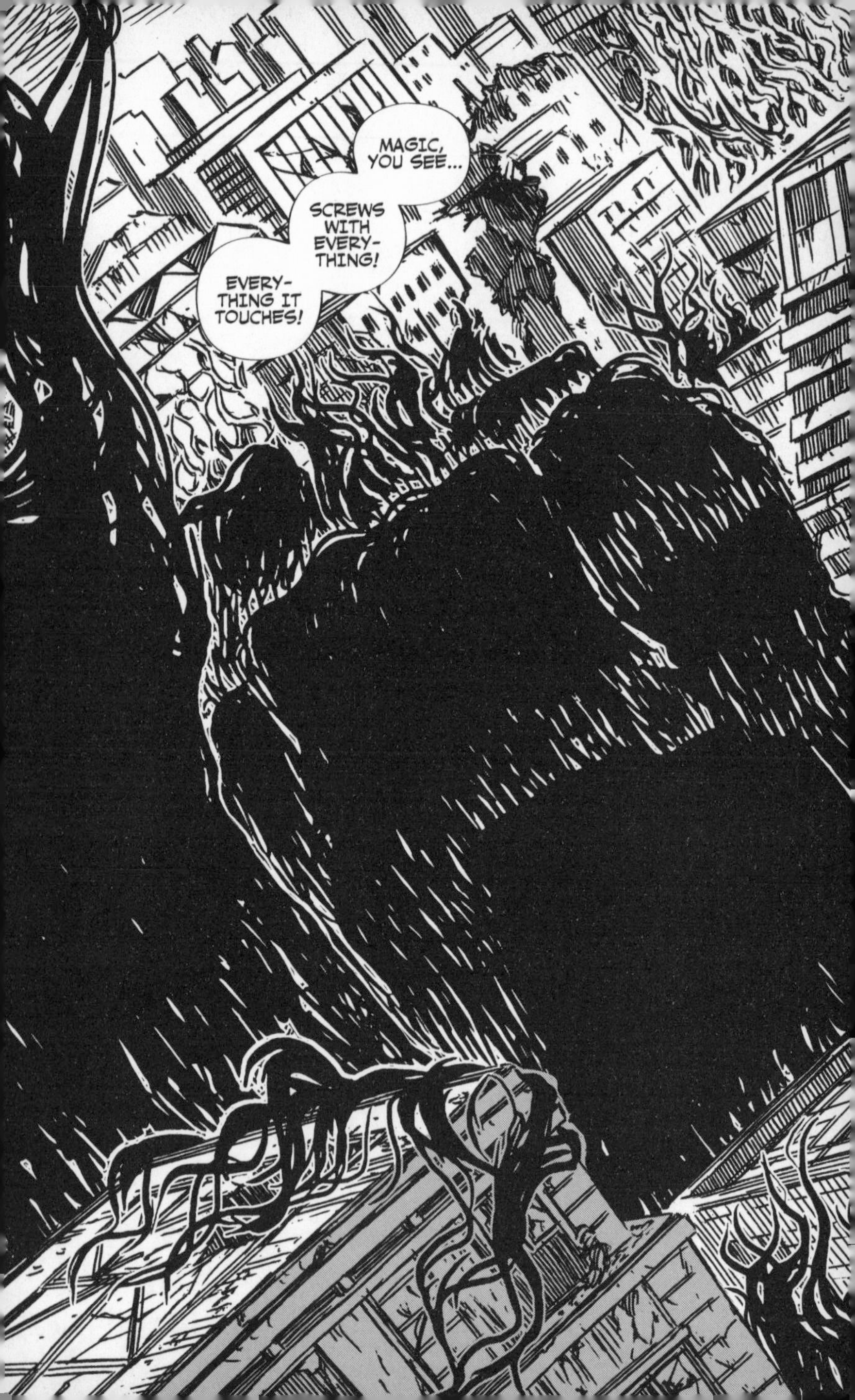
MAGIC, YOU SEE...
SCREWS WITH EVERY-THING!
EVERY-THING IT TOUCHES!

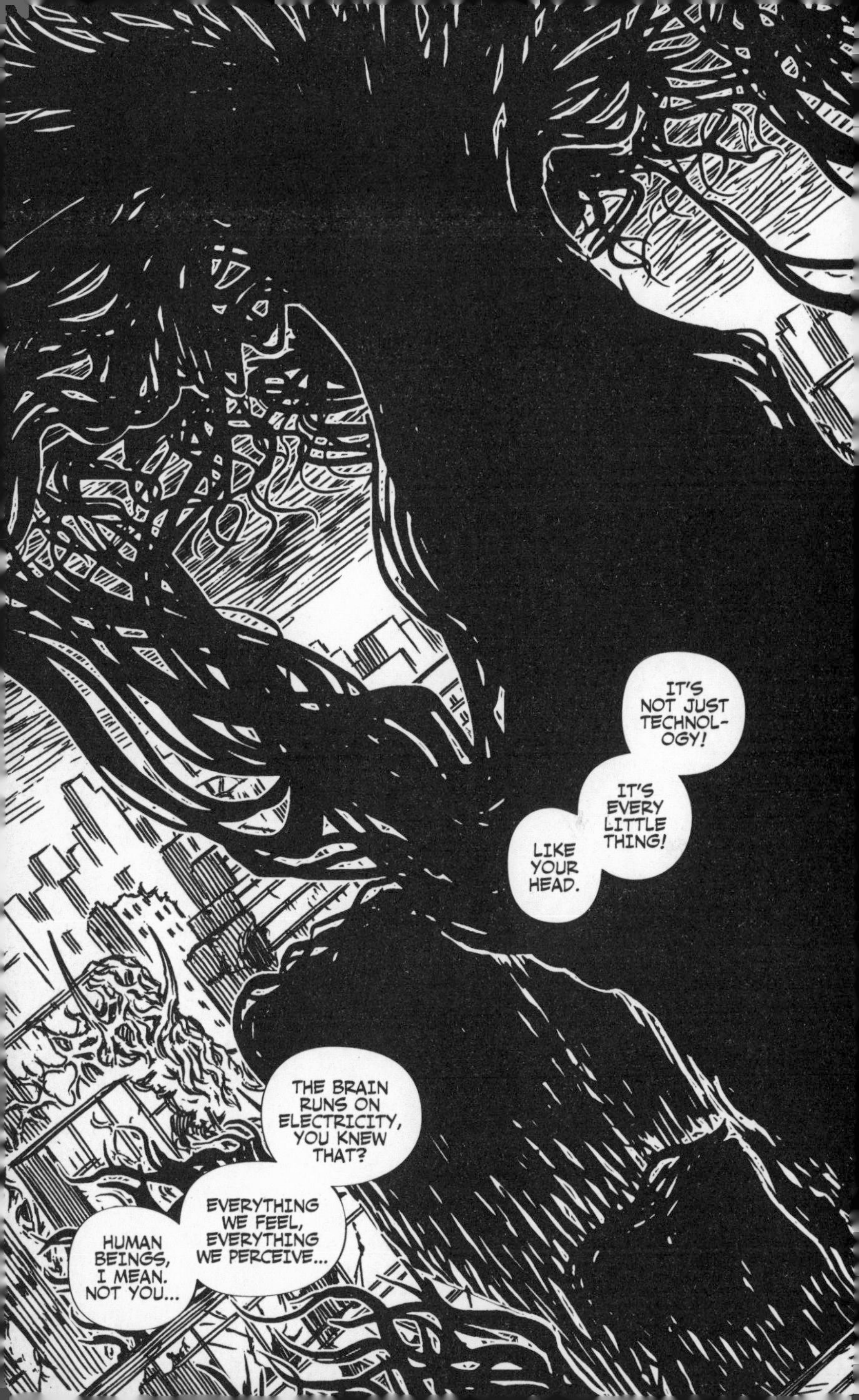
IT'S NOT JUST TECHNOL-OGY!
IT'S EVERY LITTLE THING!
LIKE YOUR HEAD.
THE BRAIN RUNS ON ELECTRICITY, YOU KNEW THAT?
EVERYTHING WE FEEL, EVERYTHING WE PERCEIVE...
HUMAN BEINGS, I MEAN. NOT YOU...

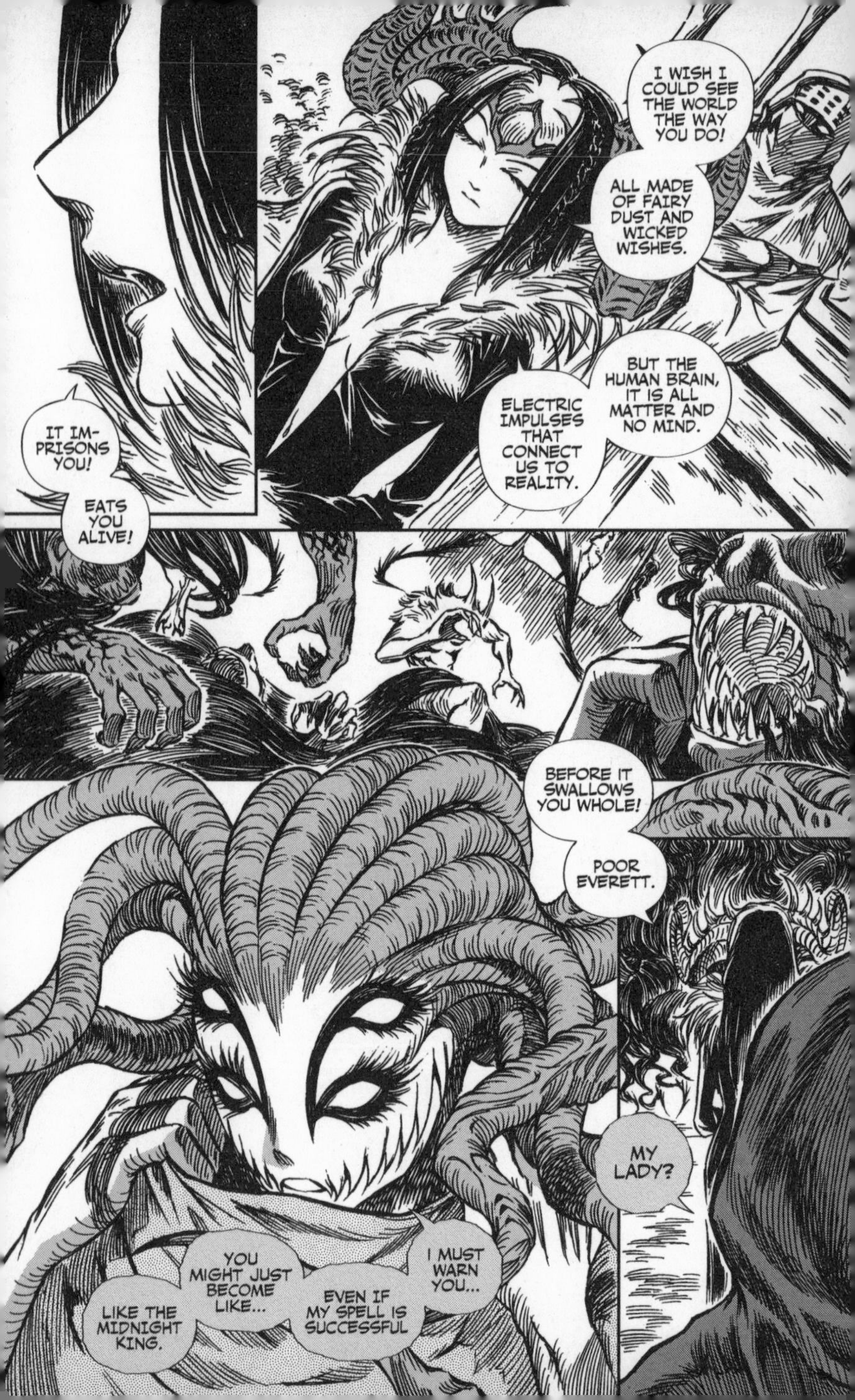
I WISH I COULD SEE THE WORLD THE WAY YOU DO!
ALL MADE OF FAIRY DUST AND WICKED WISHES.
BUT THE HUMAN BRAIN, IT IS ALL MATTER AND NO MIND.
ELECTRIC IMPULSES THAT CONNECT US TO REALITY.
IT IMPRISONS YOU!
EATS YOU ALIVE!
BEFORE IT SWALLOWS YOU WHOLE!
POOR EVERETT.
MY LADY?
I MUST WARN YOU...
EVEN IF MY SPELL IS SUCCESSFUL
YOU MIGHT JUST BECOME LIKE...
LIKE THE MIDNIGHT KING.

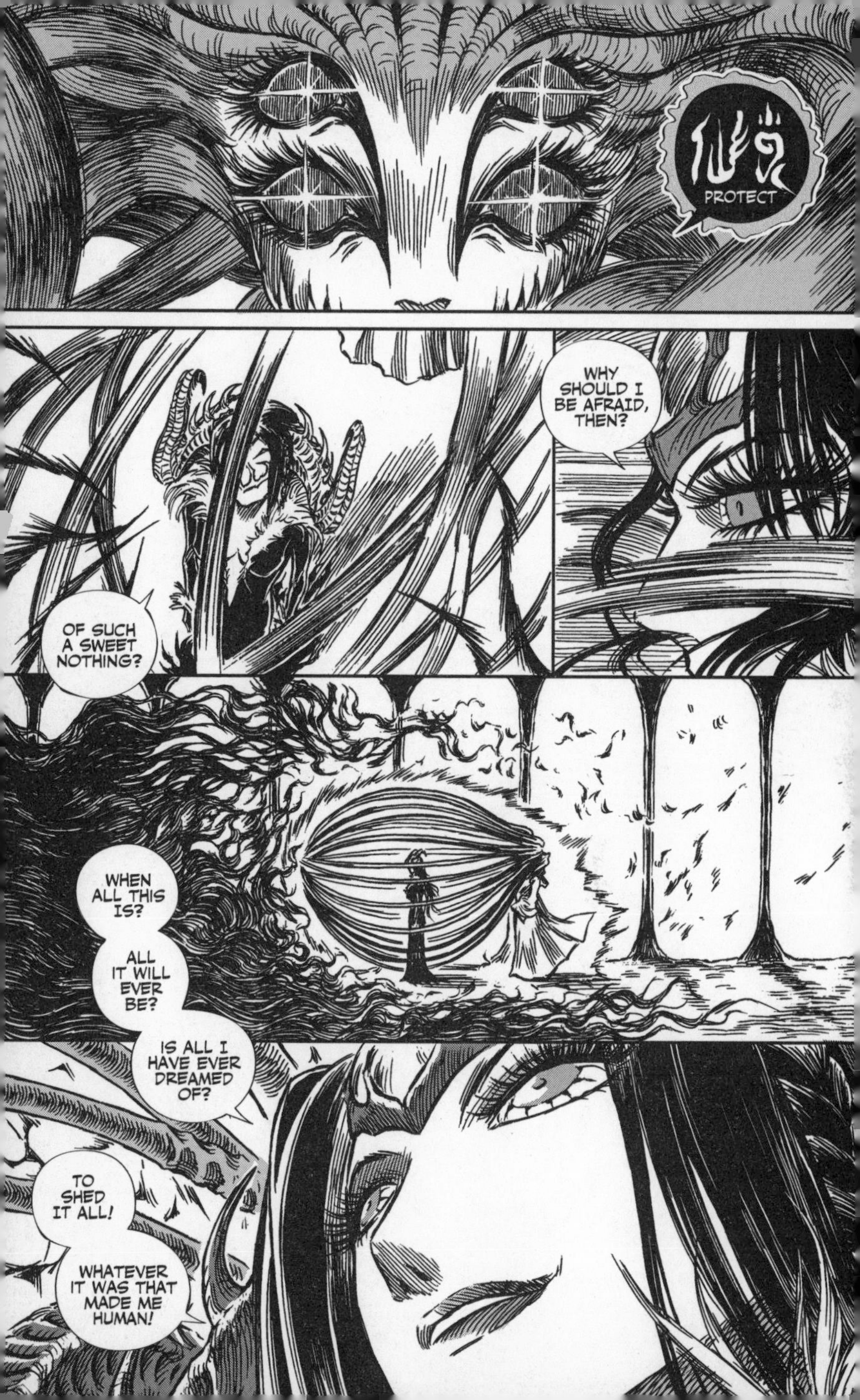
PROTECT
WHY SHOULD I BE AFRAID, THEN?
OF SUCH A SWEET NOTHING?
WHEN ALL THIS IS?
ALL IT WILL EVER BE?
IS ALL I HAVE EVER DREAMED OF?
TO SHED IT ALL!
WHATEVER IT WAS THAT MADE ME HUMAN!

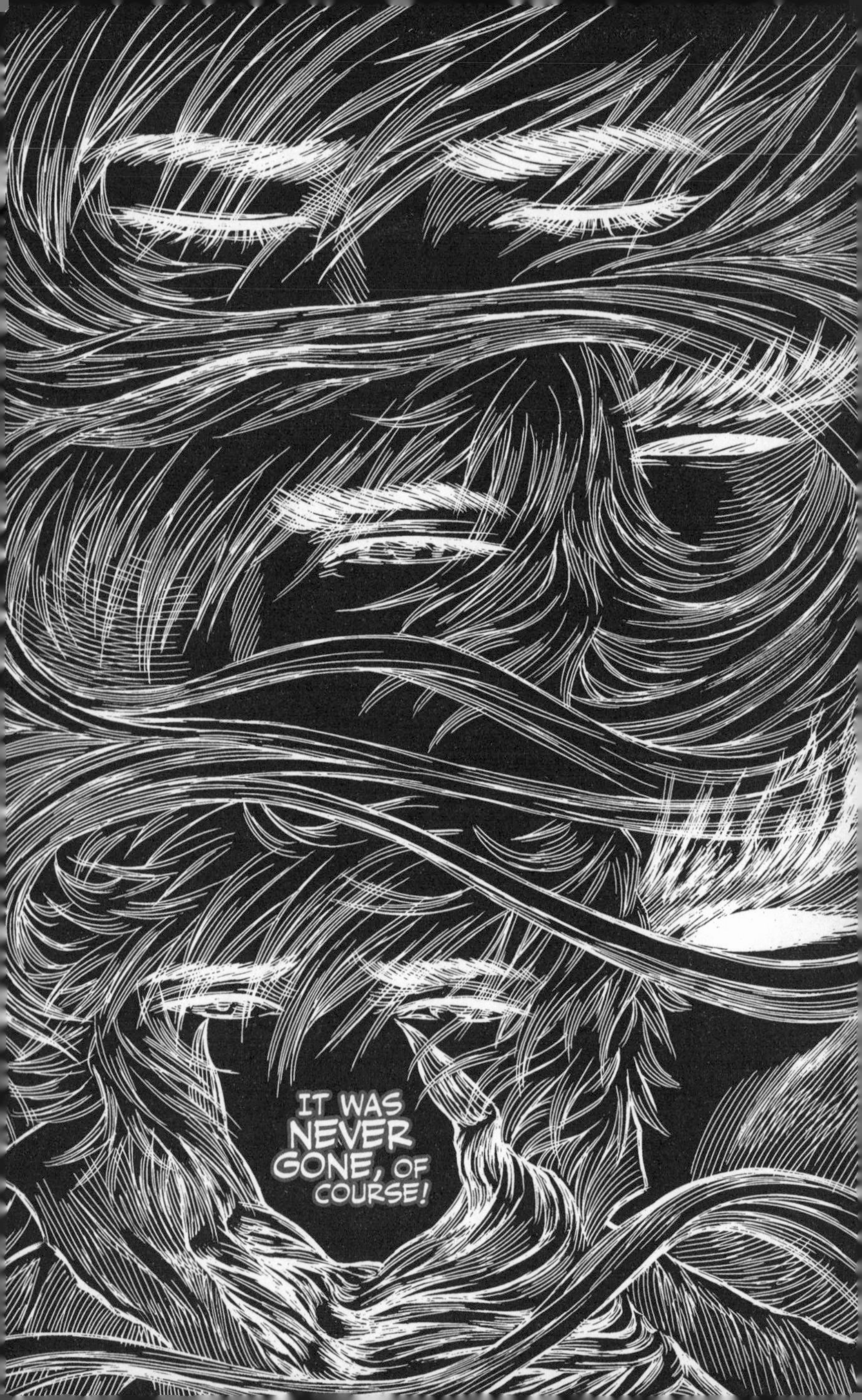
IT WAS NEVER GONE, OF COURSE!

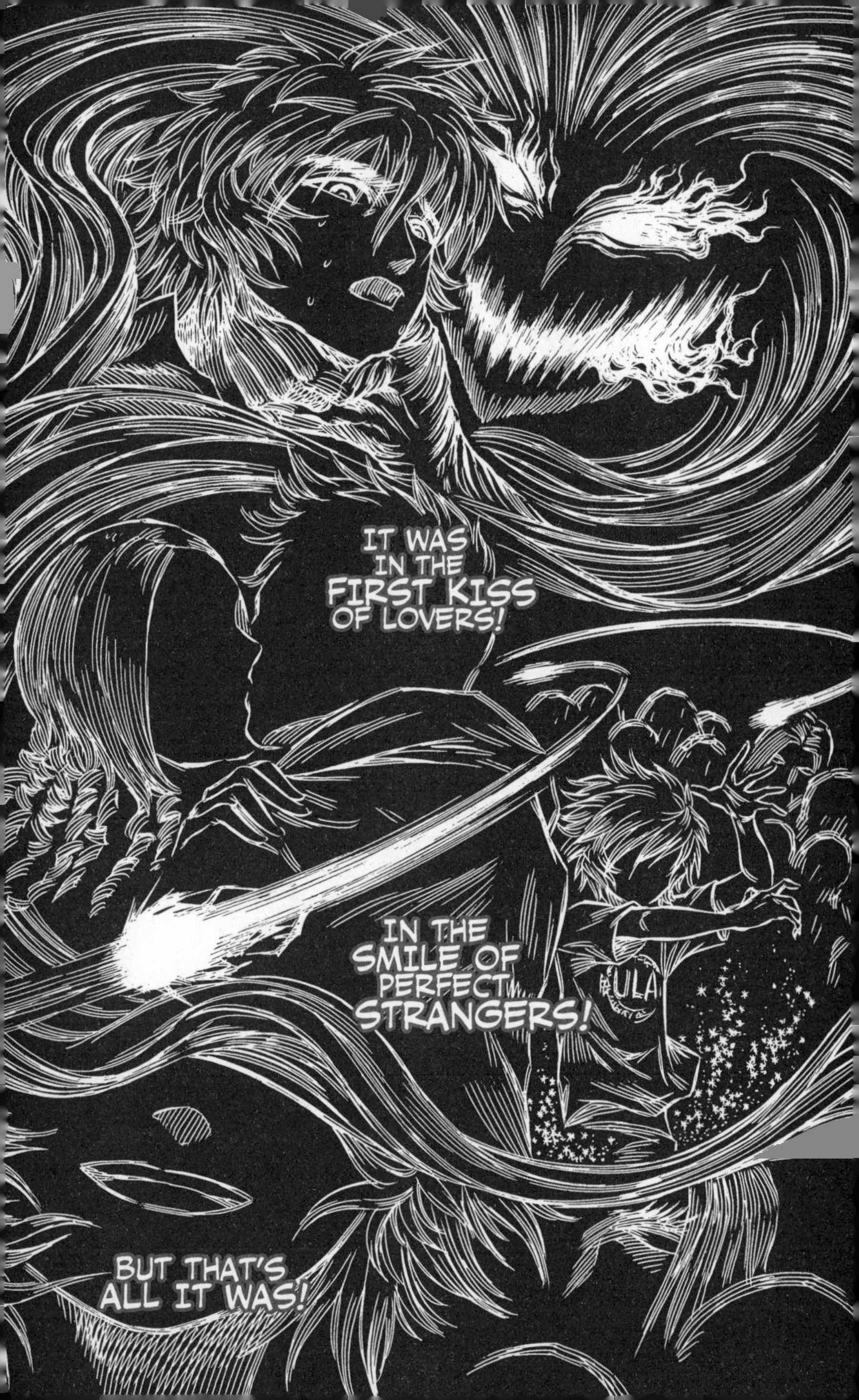
IT WAS IN THE FIRST KISS OF LOVERS!
IN THE SMILE OF PERFECT STRANGERS!
BUT THAT'S ALL IT WAS!

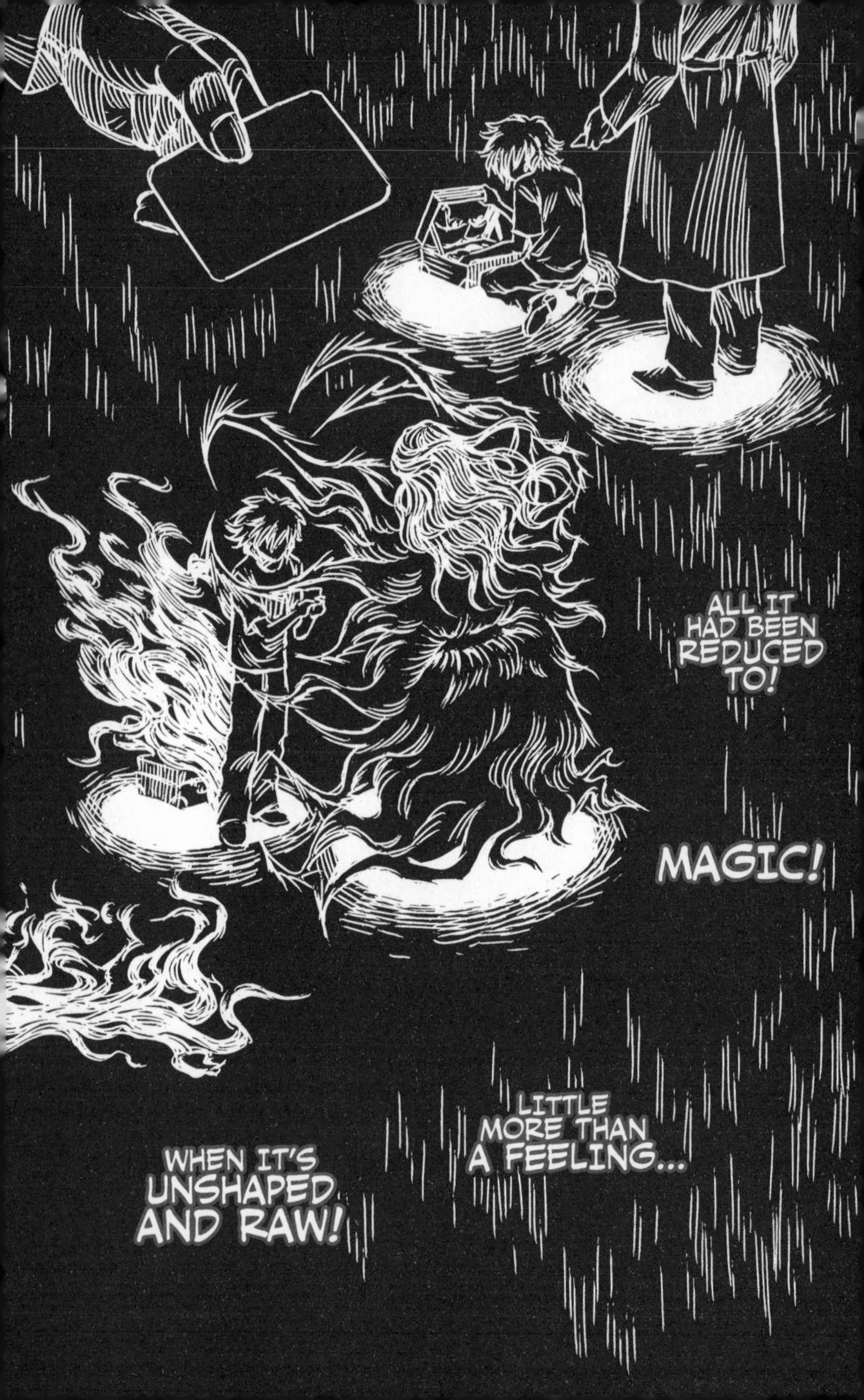
ALL IT HAD BEEN REDUCED TO!
MAGIC!
LITTLE MORE THAN A FEELING...
WHEN IT'S UNSHAPED AND RAW!

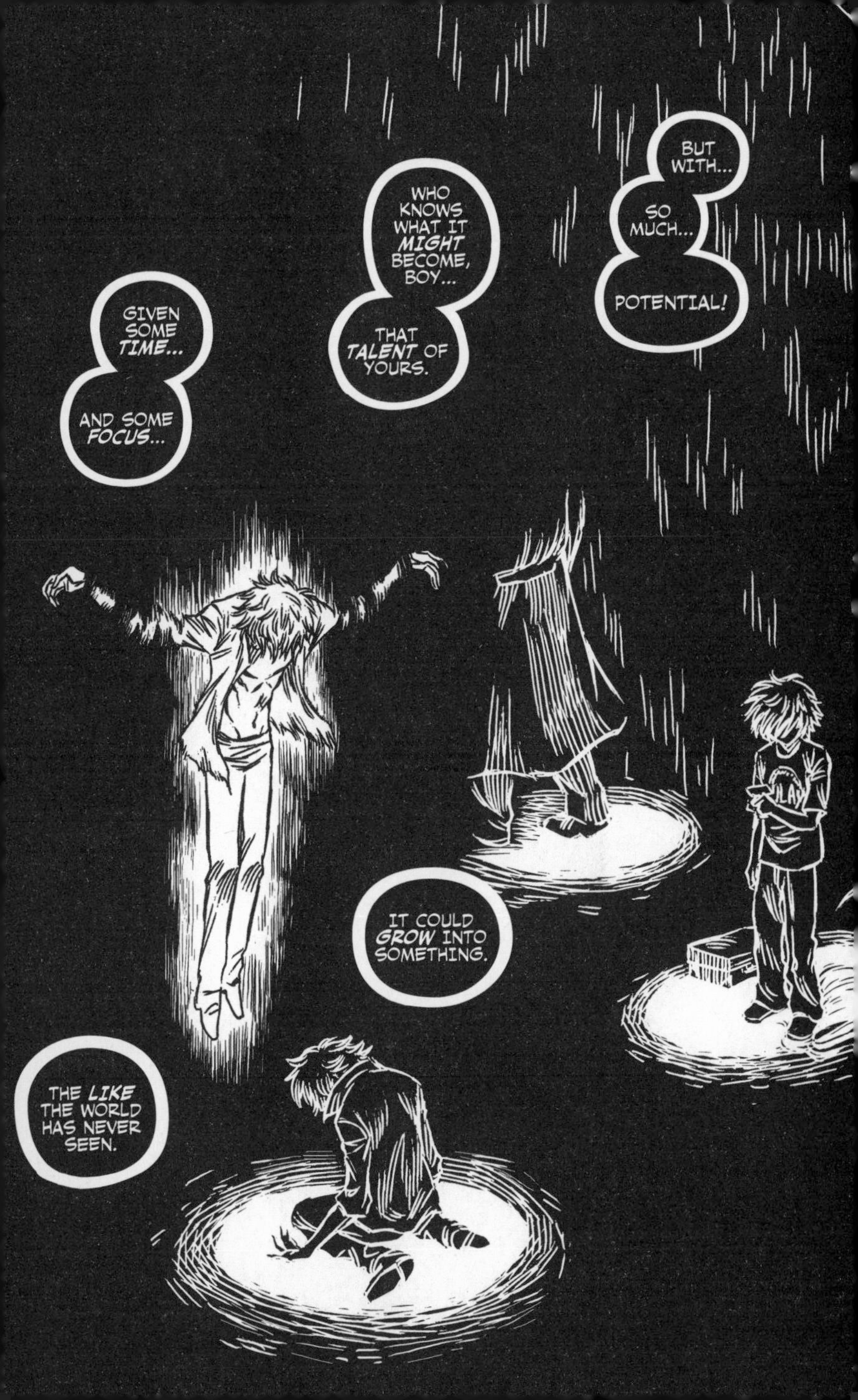
GIVEN SOME *TIME*...
AND SOME *FOCUS*...
WHO KNOWS WHAT IT *MIGHT* BECOME, BOY...
THAT *TALENT* OF YOURS.
BUT WITH...
SO MUCH...
POTENTIAL!
IT COULD *GROW* INTO SOMETHING.
THE *LIKE* THE WORLD HAS NEVER SEEN.

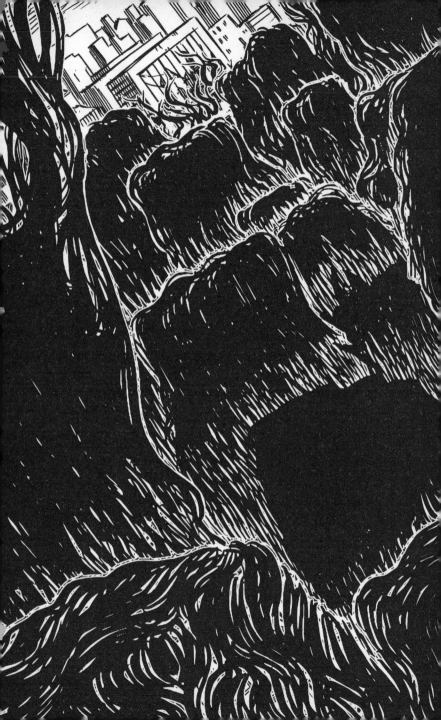

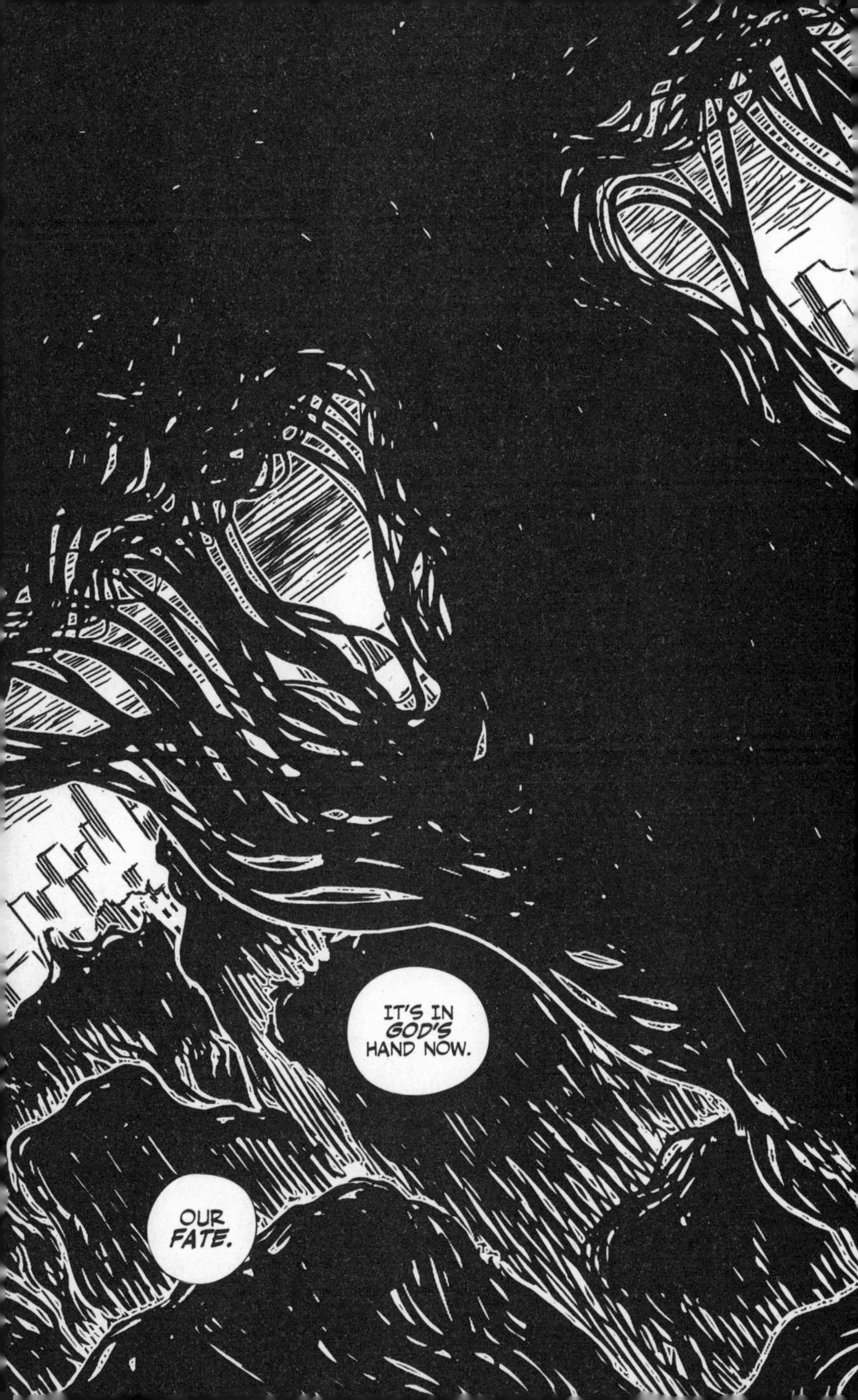
IT'S IN GOD'S HAND NOW.
OUR FATE.

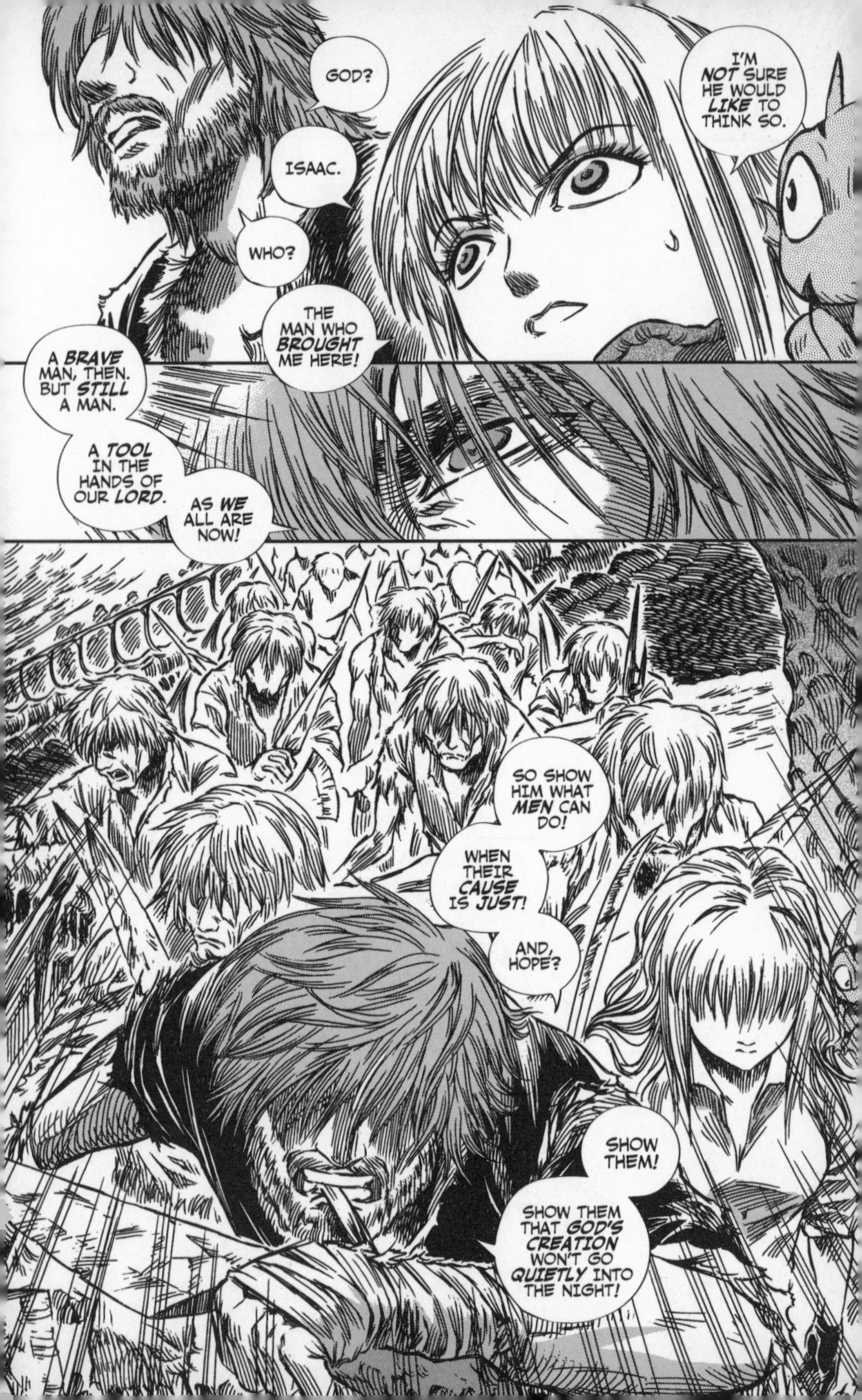
I'M NOT SURE HE WOULD LIKE TO THINK SO.
GOD?
ISAAC.
WHO?
THE MAN WHO BROUGHT ME HERE!
A BRAVE MAN, THEN. BUT STILL A MAN.
A TOOL IN THE HANDS OF OUR LORD.
AS WE ALL ARE NOW!
SO SHOW HIM WHAT MEN CAN DO!
WHEN THEIR CAUSE IS JUST!
AND, HOPE?
SHOW THEM!
SHOW THEM THAT GOD'S CREATION WON'T GO QUIETLY INTO THE NIGHT!

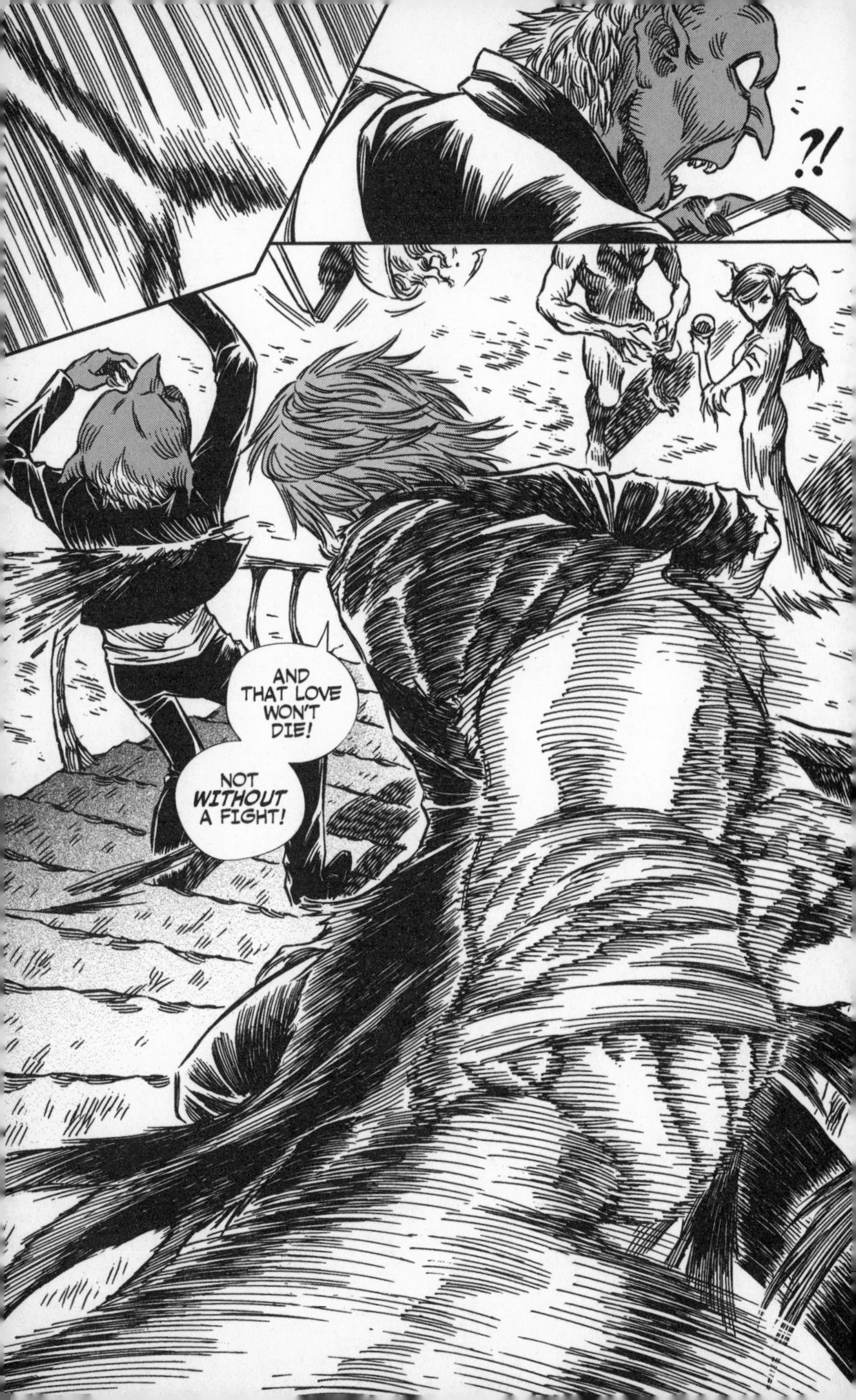
?!
AND THAT LOVE WON'T DIE!
NOT *WITHOUT* A FIGHT!

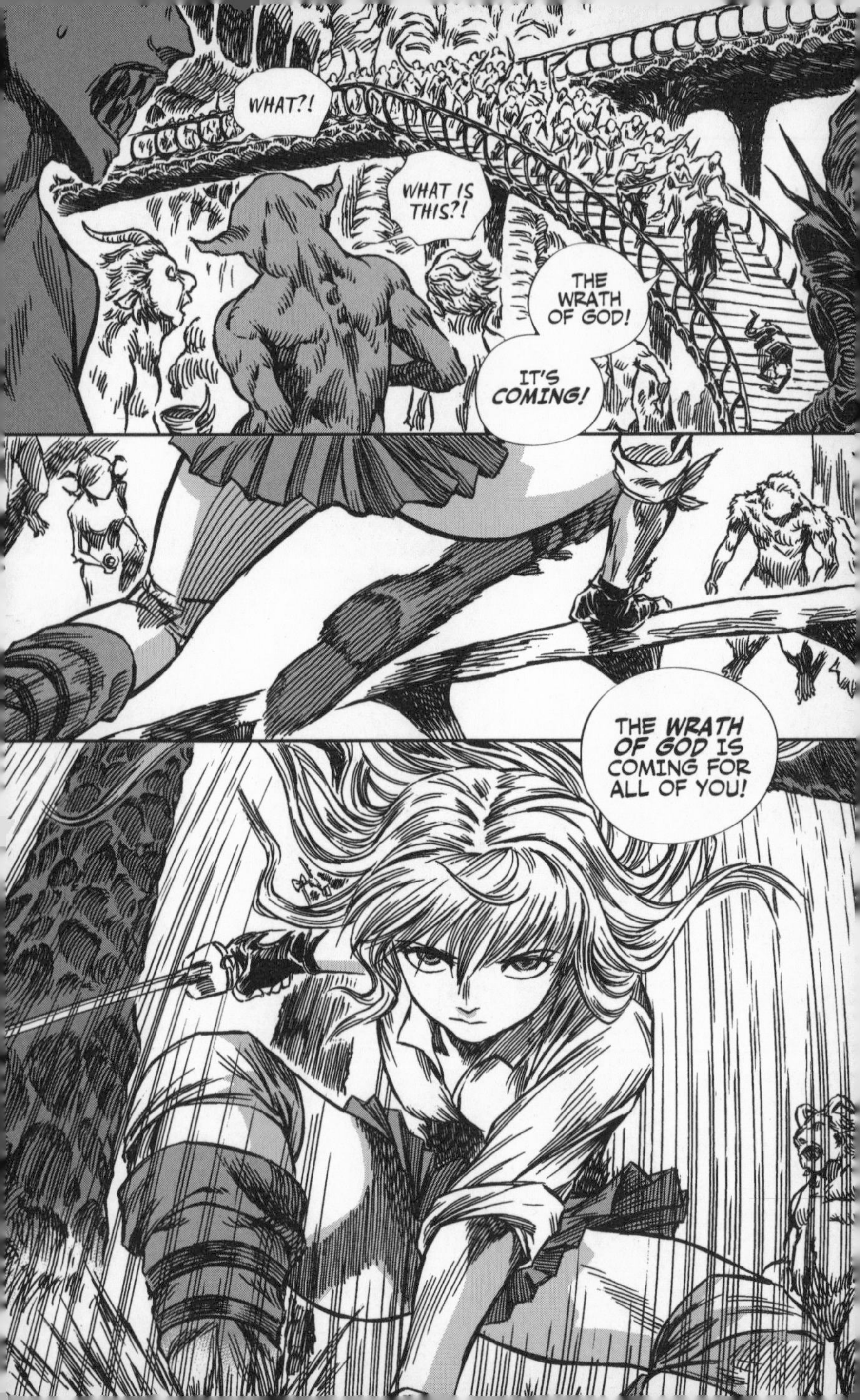
THE WRATH OF GOD!
IT'S COMING!
WHAT IS THIS?!
WHAT?!
THE WRATH OF GOD IS COMING FOR ALL OF YOU!

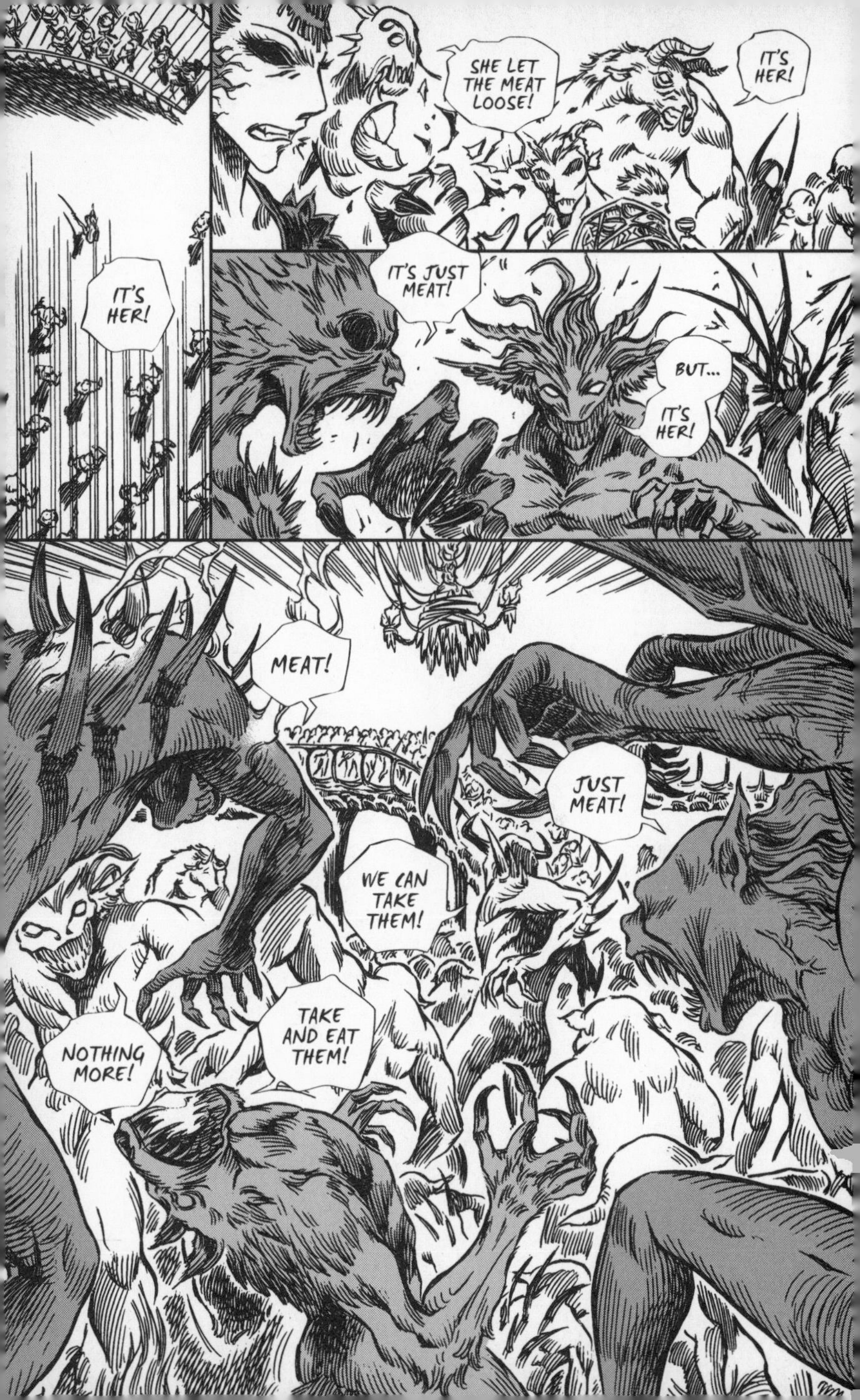
IT'S HER!
SHE LET THE MEAT LOOSE!
IT'S HER!
IT'S JUST MEAT!
BUT... IT'S HER!
MEAT!
JUST MEAT!
WE CAN TAKE THEM!
NOTHING MORE!
TAKE AND EAT THEM!

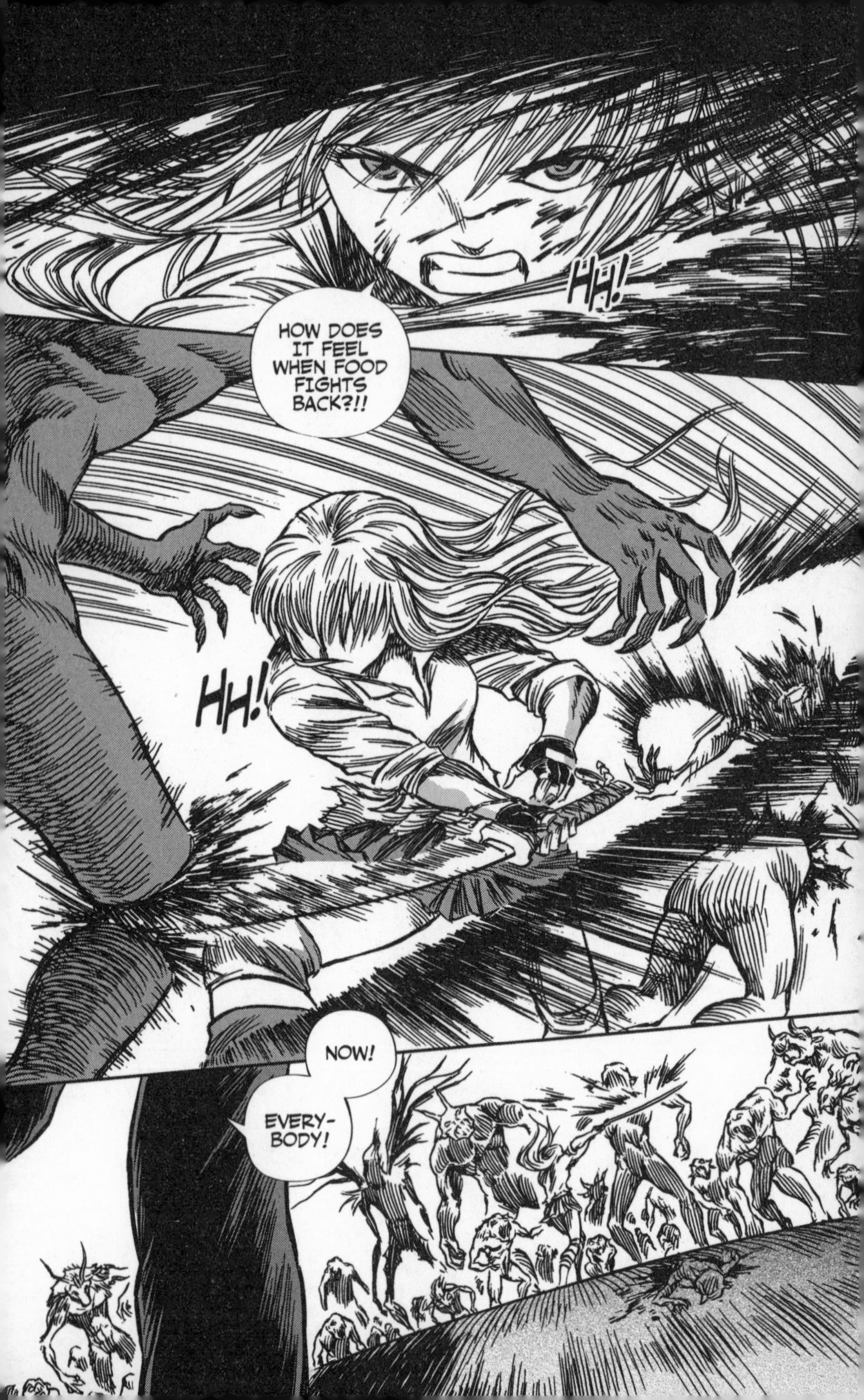
HH!
HOW DOES IT FEEL WHEN FOOD FIGHTS BACK?!!
HH!
NOW!
EVERY-BODY!

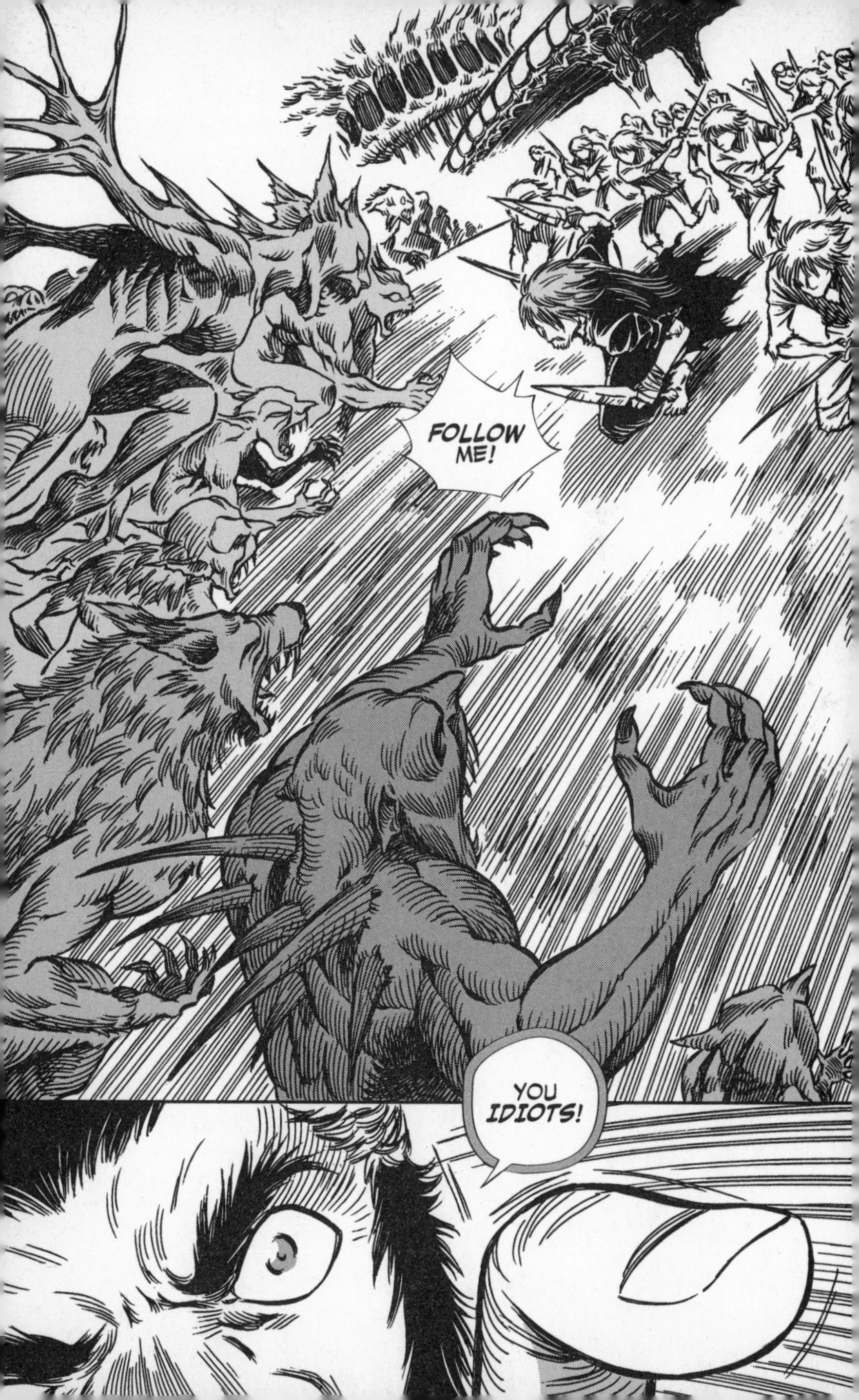
FOLLOW ME!
YOU IDIOTS!

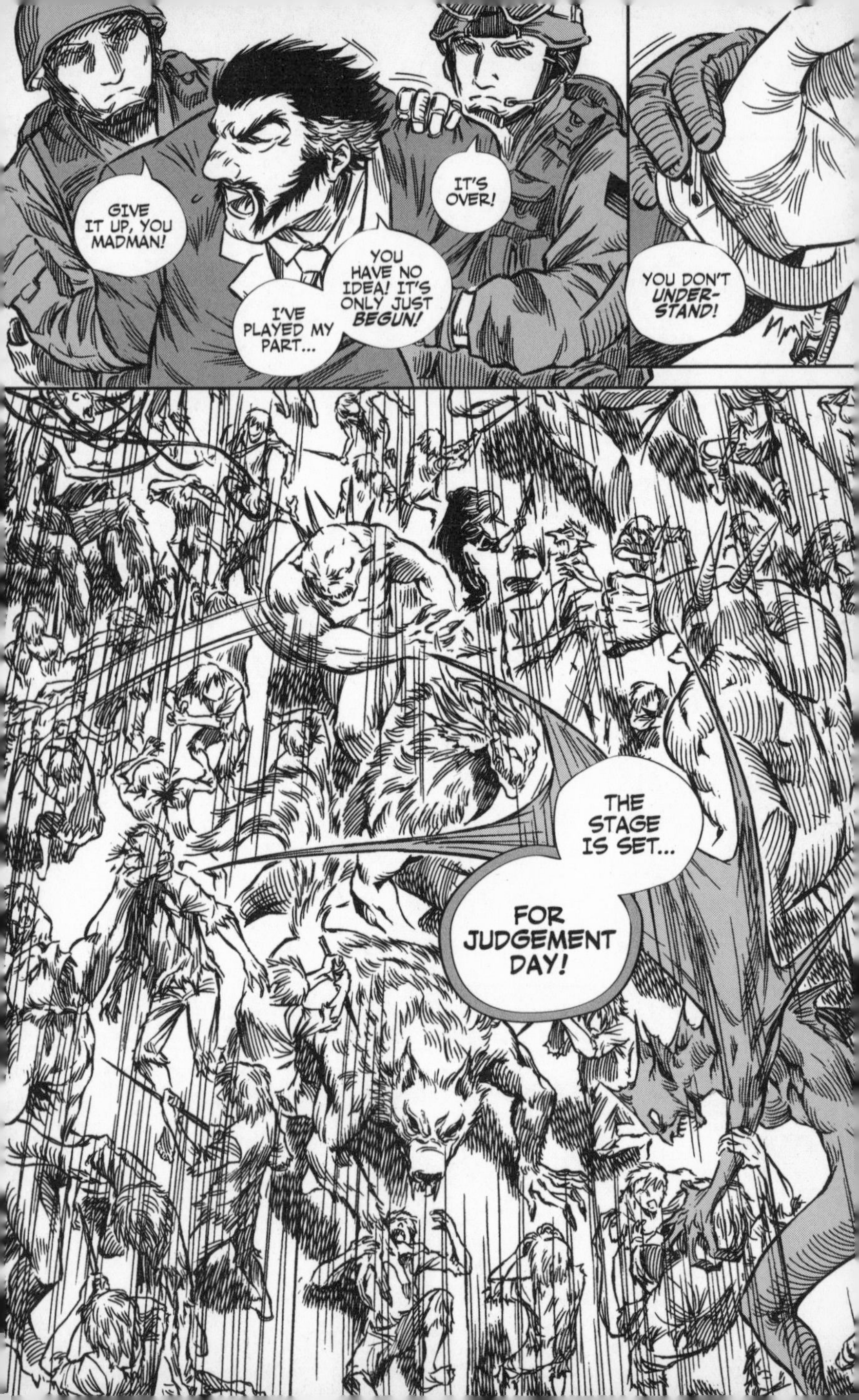
YOU DON'T UNDER-STAND!
IT'S OVER!
GIVE IT UP, YOU MADMAN!
YOU HAVE NO IDEA! IT'S ONLY JUST BEGUN!
I'VE PLAYED MY PART...
THE STAGE IS SET...
FOR JUDGEMENT DAY!

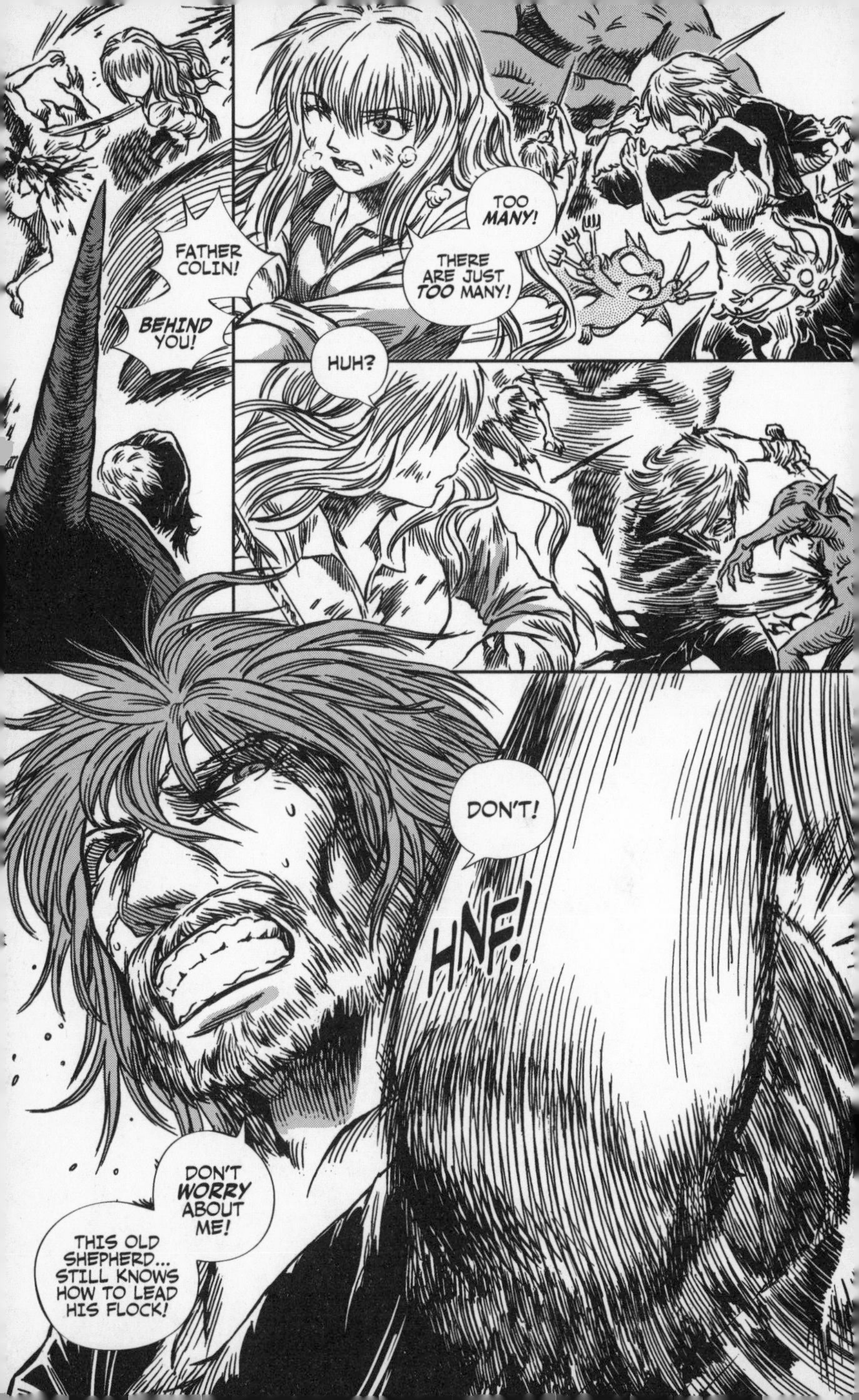
TOO MANY!
THERE ARE JUST TOO MANY!
FATHER COLIN!
BEHIND YOU!
HUH?
DON'T!
HNF!
DON'T WORRY ABOUT ME!
THIS OLD SHEPHERD... STILL KNOWS HOW TO LEAD HIS FLOCK!

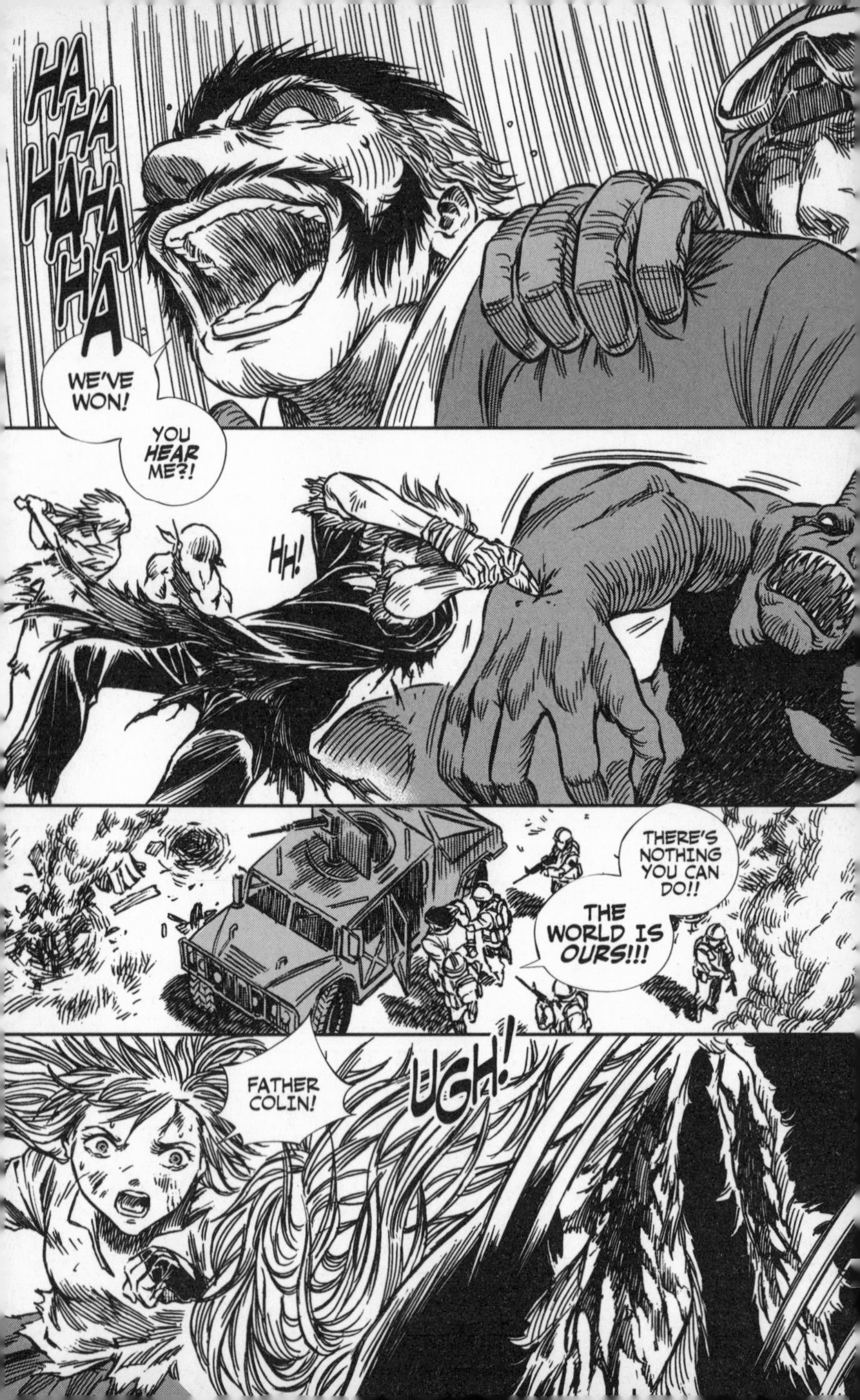
HAHAHAHAHAHAHA
WE'VE WON!
YOU HEAR ME?!
HH!
THERE'S NOTHING YOU CAN DO!!
THE WORLD IS OURS!!!
FATHER COLIN!
UGH!

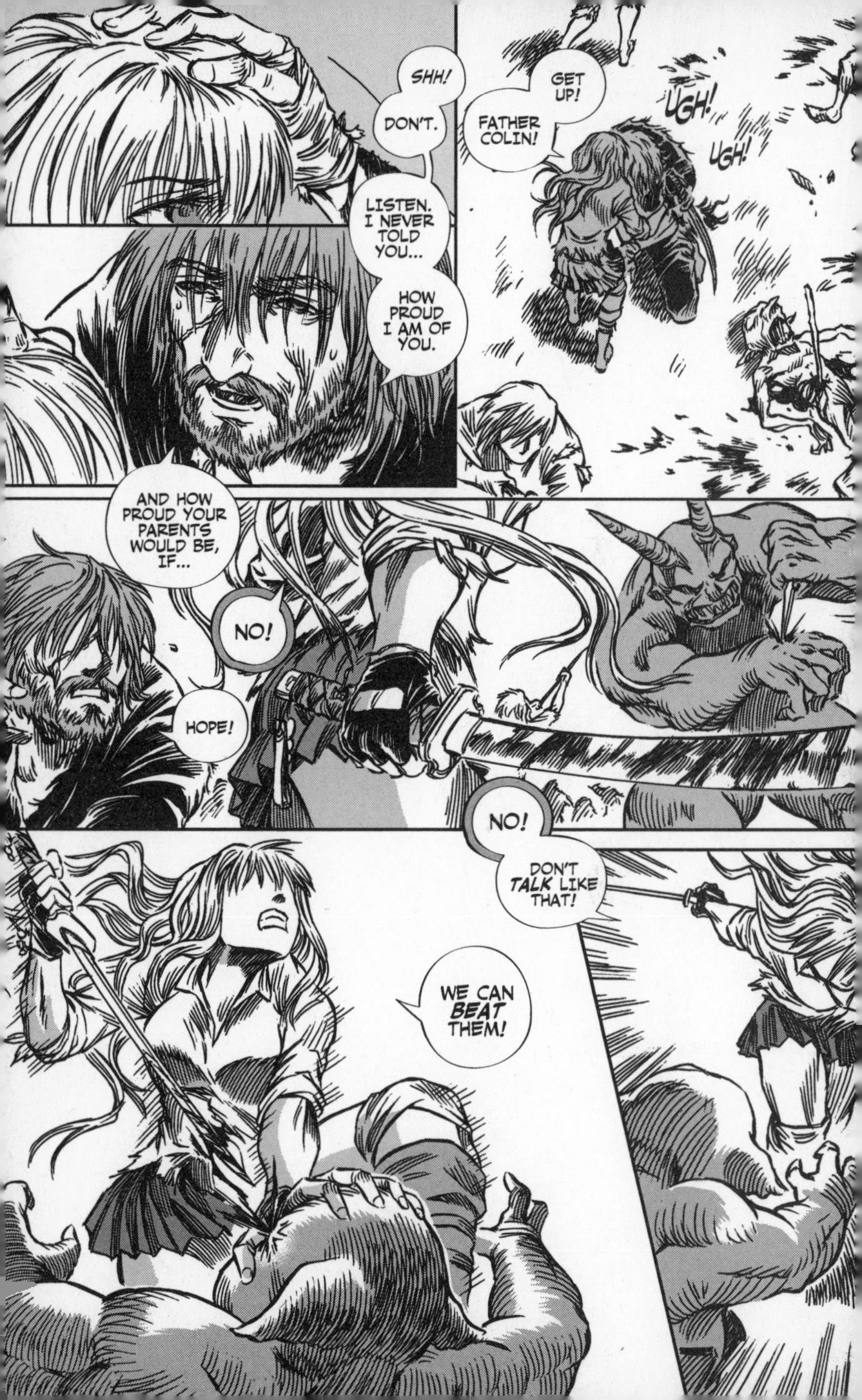
GET UP!
FATHER COLIN!
UGH!
UGH!
SHH!
DON'T.
LISTEN. I NEVER TOLD YOU...
HOW PROUD I AM OF YOU.
AND HOW PROUD YOUR PARENTS WOULD BE, IF...
NO!
HOPE!
NO!
DON'T *TALK* LIKE THAT!
WE CAN *BEAT* THEM!

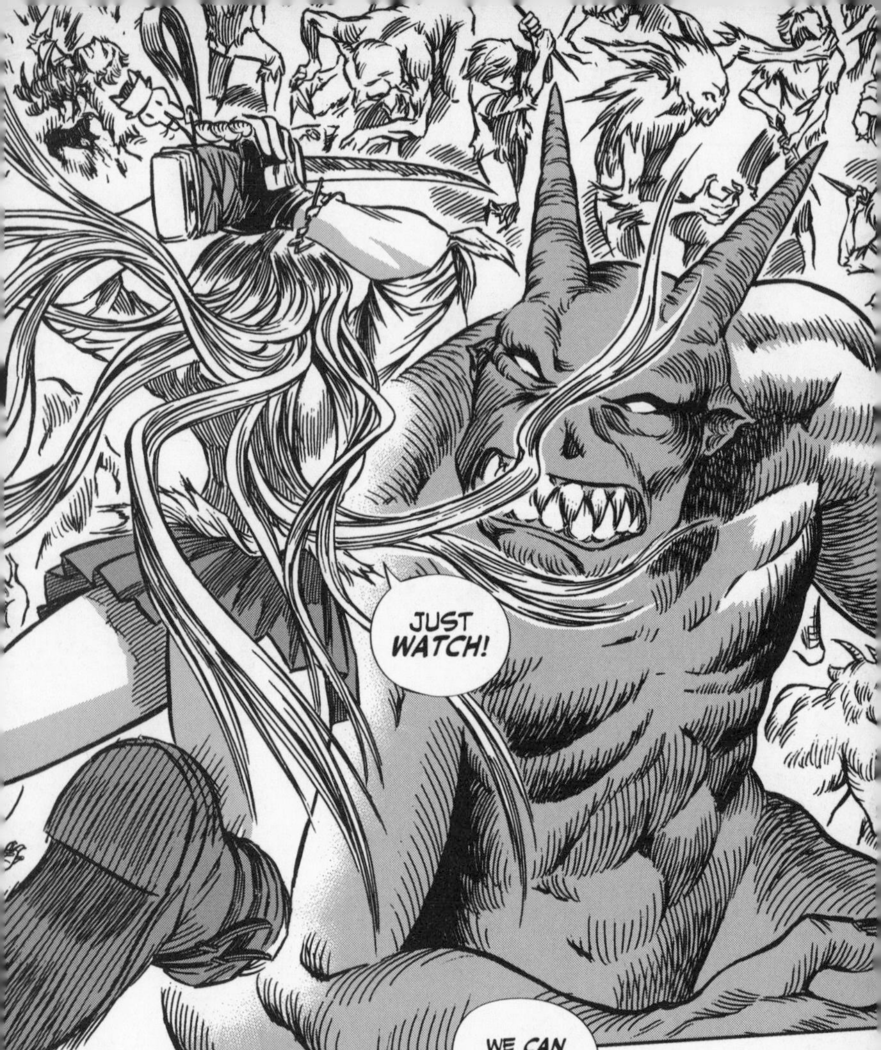
JUST WATCH!
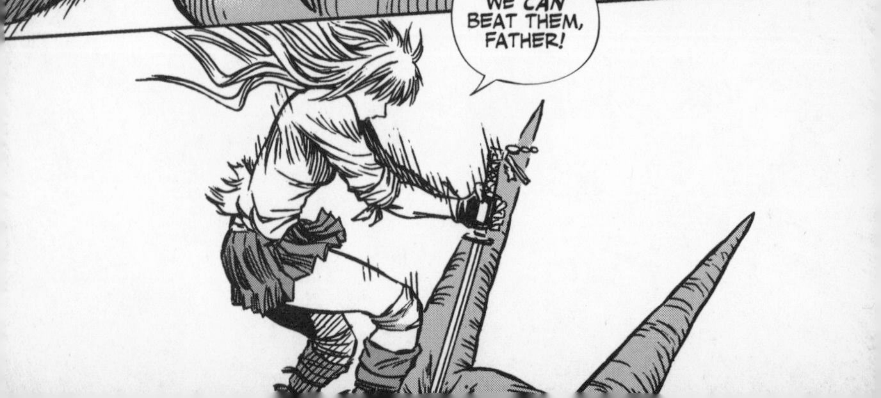
WE CAN BEAT THEM, FATHER!

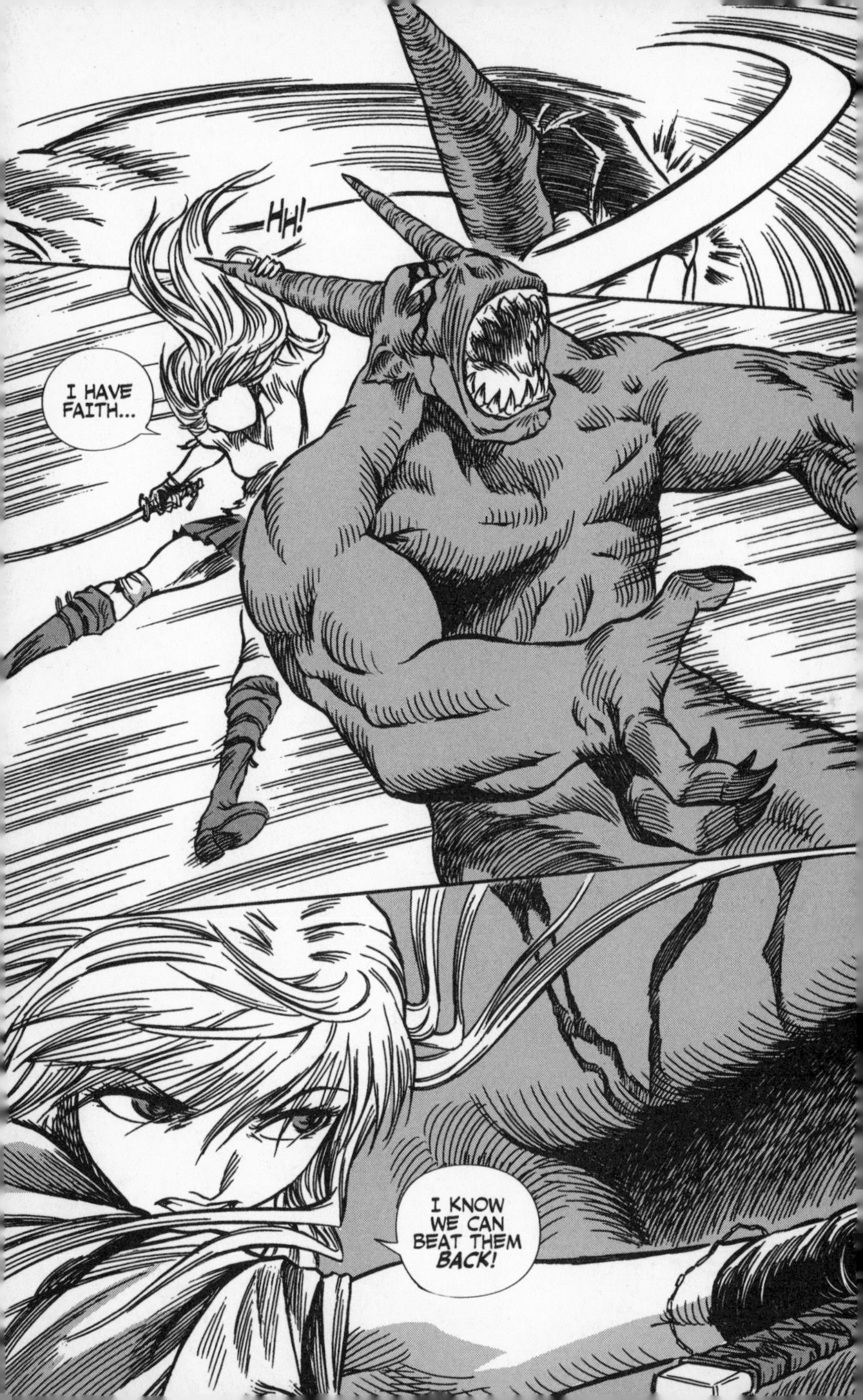
HH!
I HAVE FAITH...
I KNOW WE CAN BEAT THEM *BACK!*

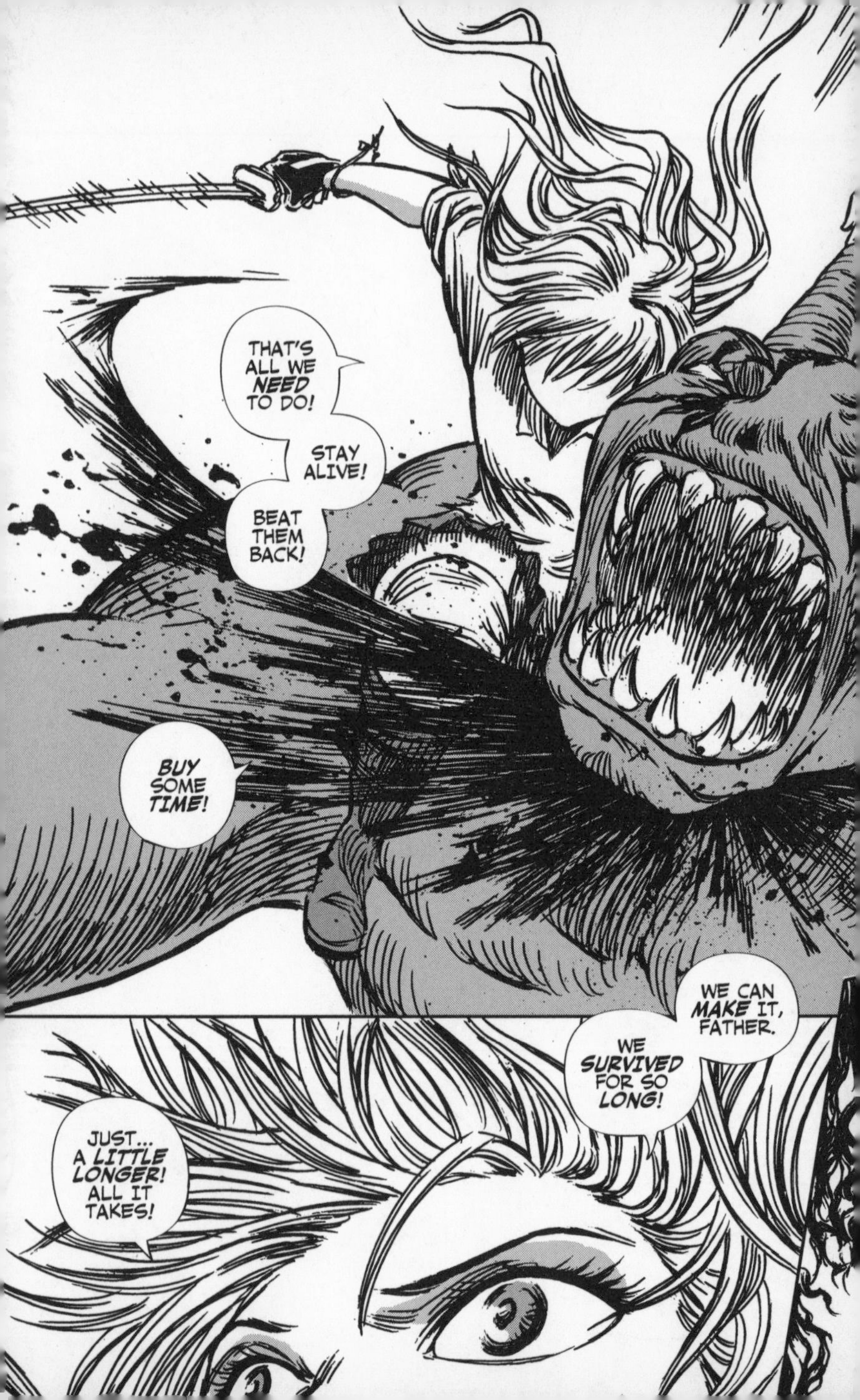
THAT'S ALL WE NEED TO DO!
STAY ALIVE!
BEAT THEM BACK!
BUY SOME TIME!
WE CAN MAKE IT, FATHER.
WE SURVIVED FOR SO LONG!
JUST... A LITTLE LONGER! ALL IT TAKES!

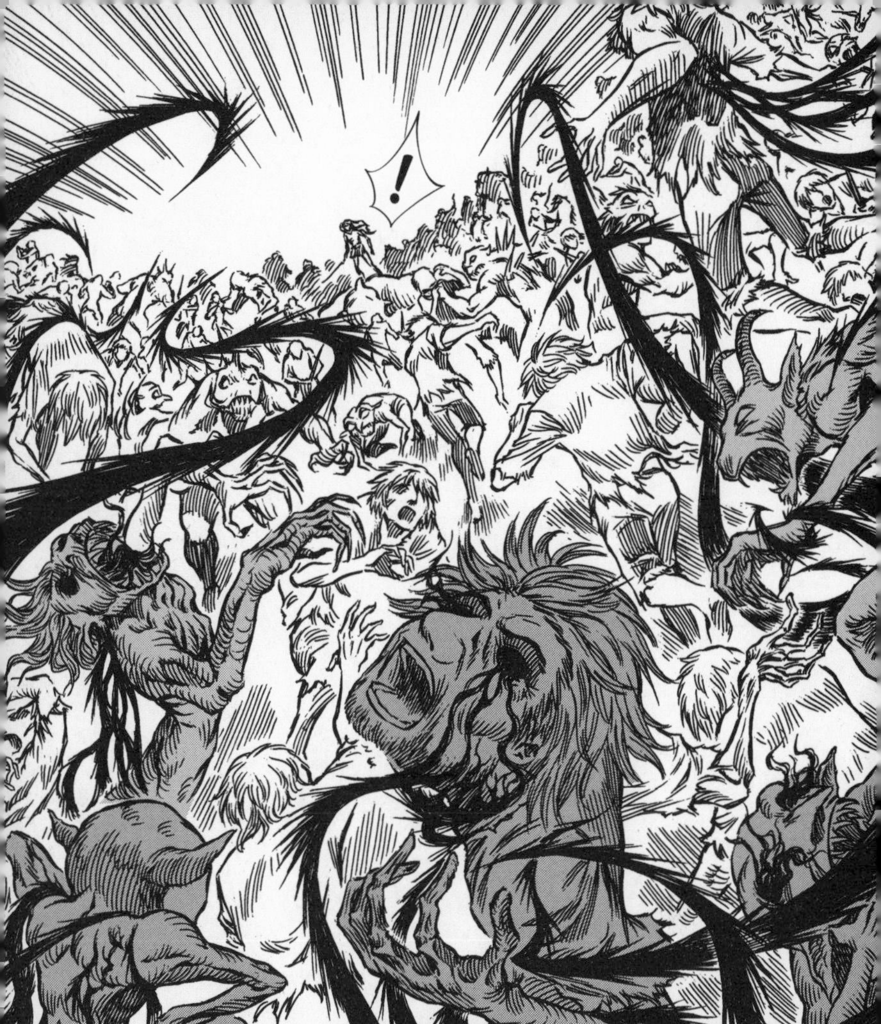
!
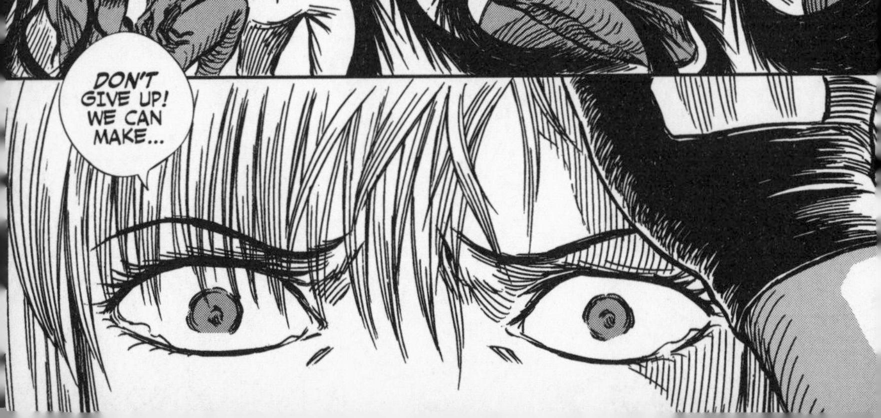
DON'T GIVE UP! WE CAN MAKE...

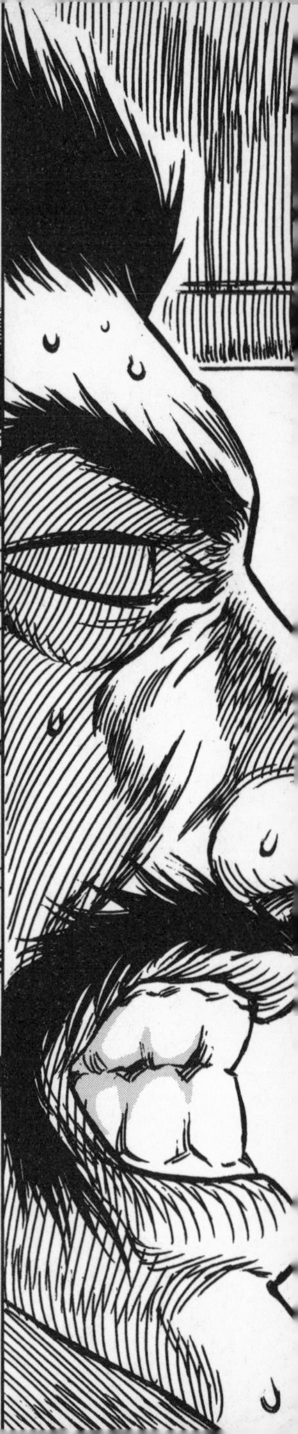
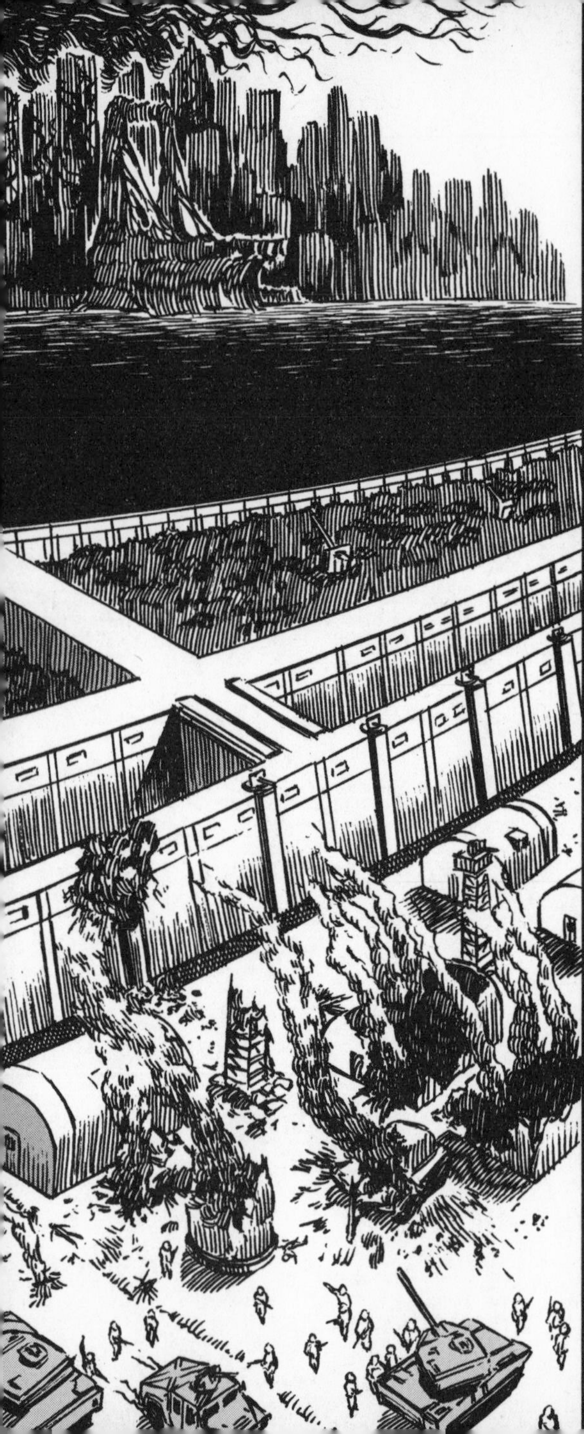

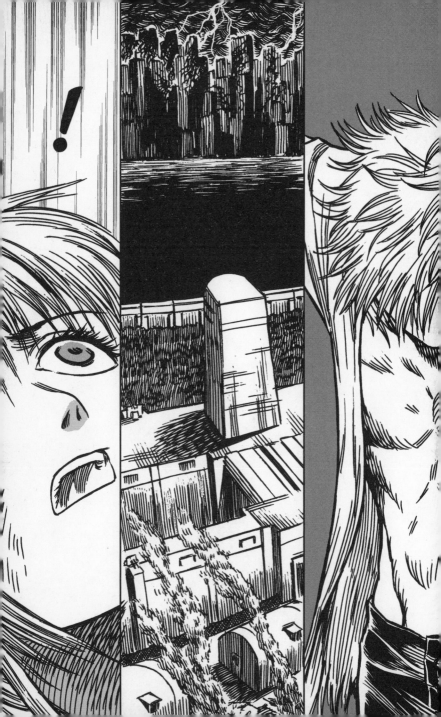

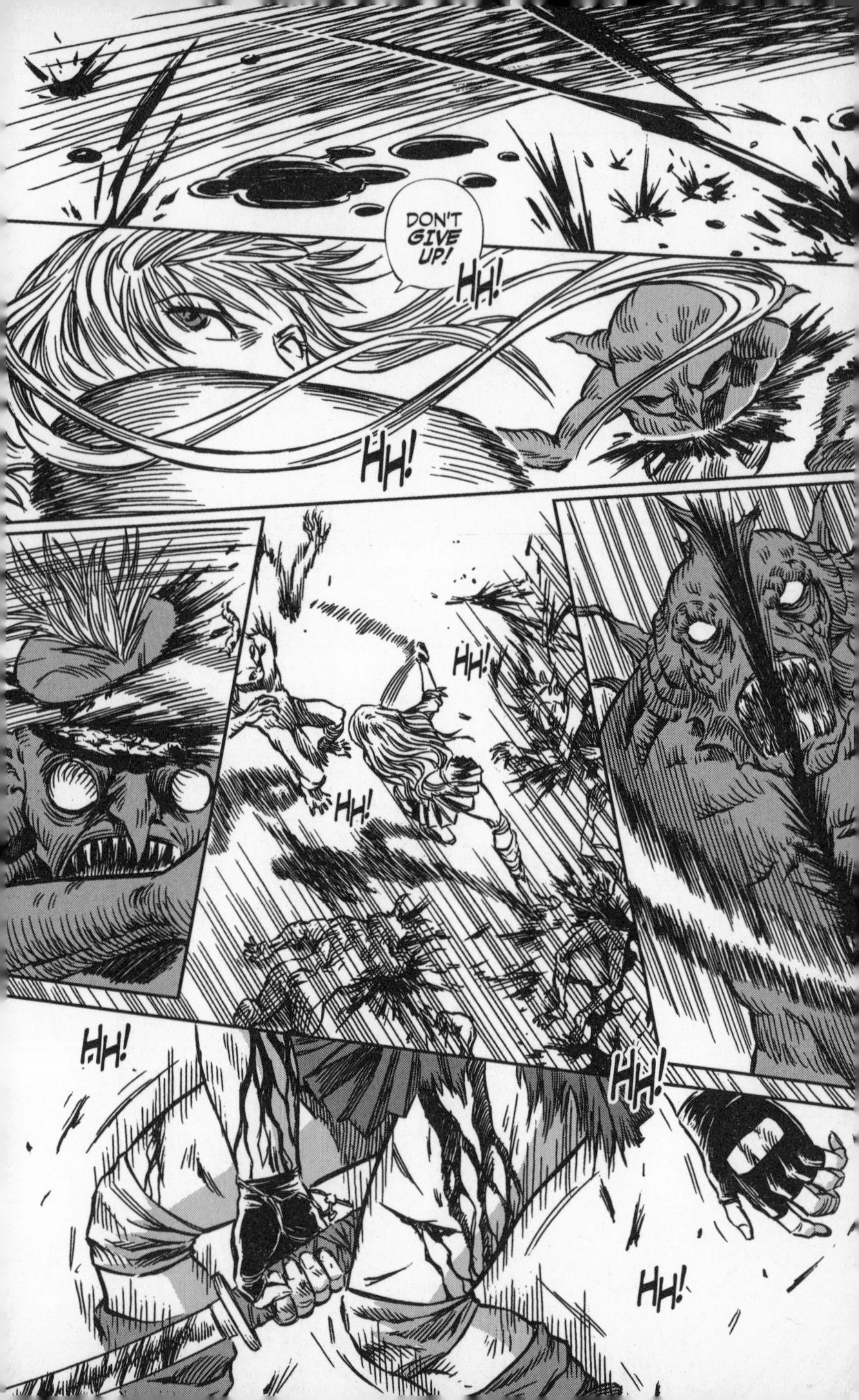
DON'T GIVE UP!
HH!
HH!
HH!
HH!
HH!
HH!
HH!

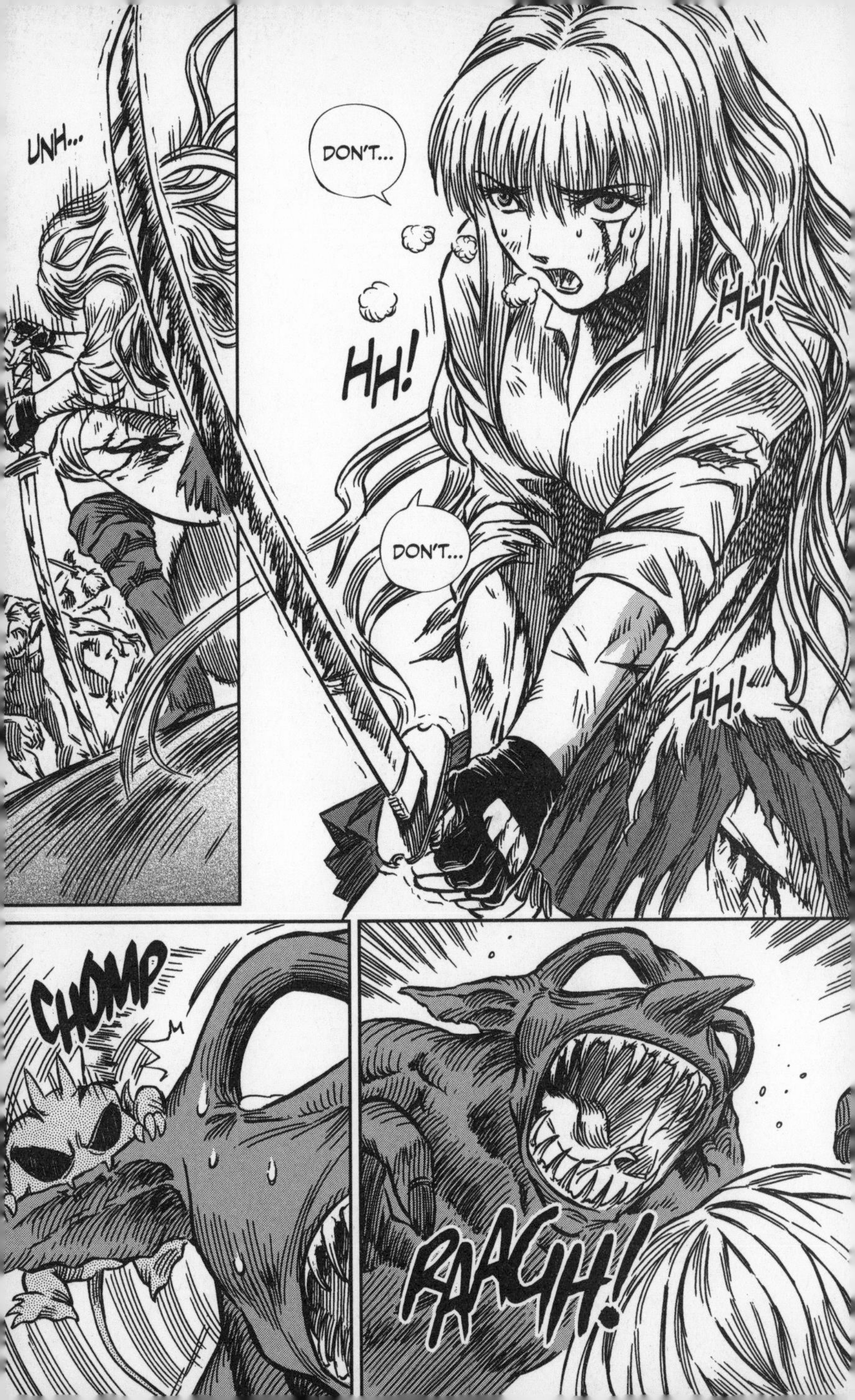
DON'T...
HH!
HH!
DON'T...
HH!
UNH...
RAAGH!
CHOMP

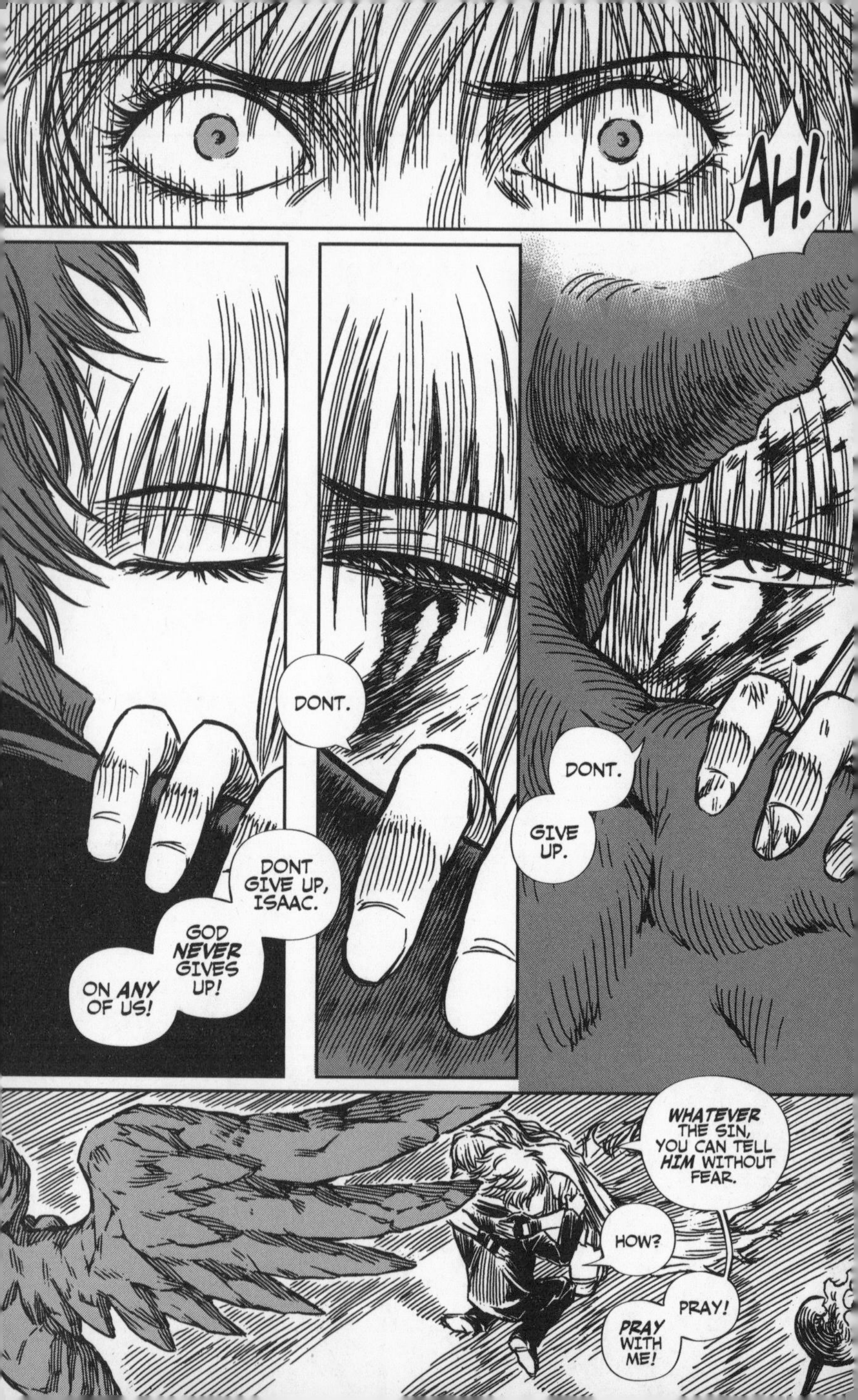
AH!
DONT.
GIVE UP.
DONT.
DONT GIVE UP, ISAAC.
GOD NEVER GIVES UP!
ON ANY OF US!
WHATEVER THE SIN, YOU CAN TELL HIM WITHOUT FEAR.
HOW?
PRAY!
PRAY WITH ME!

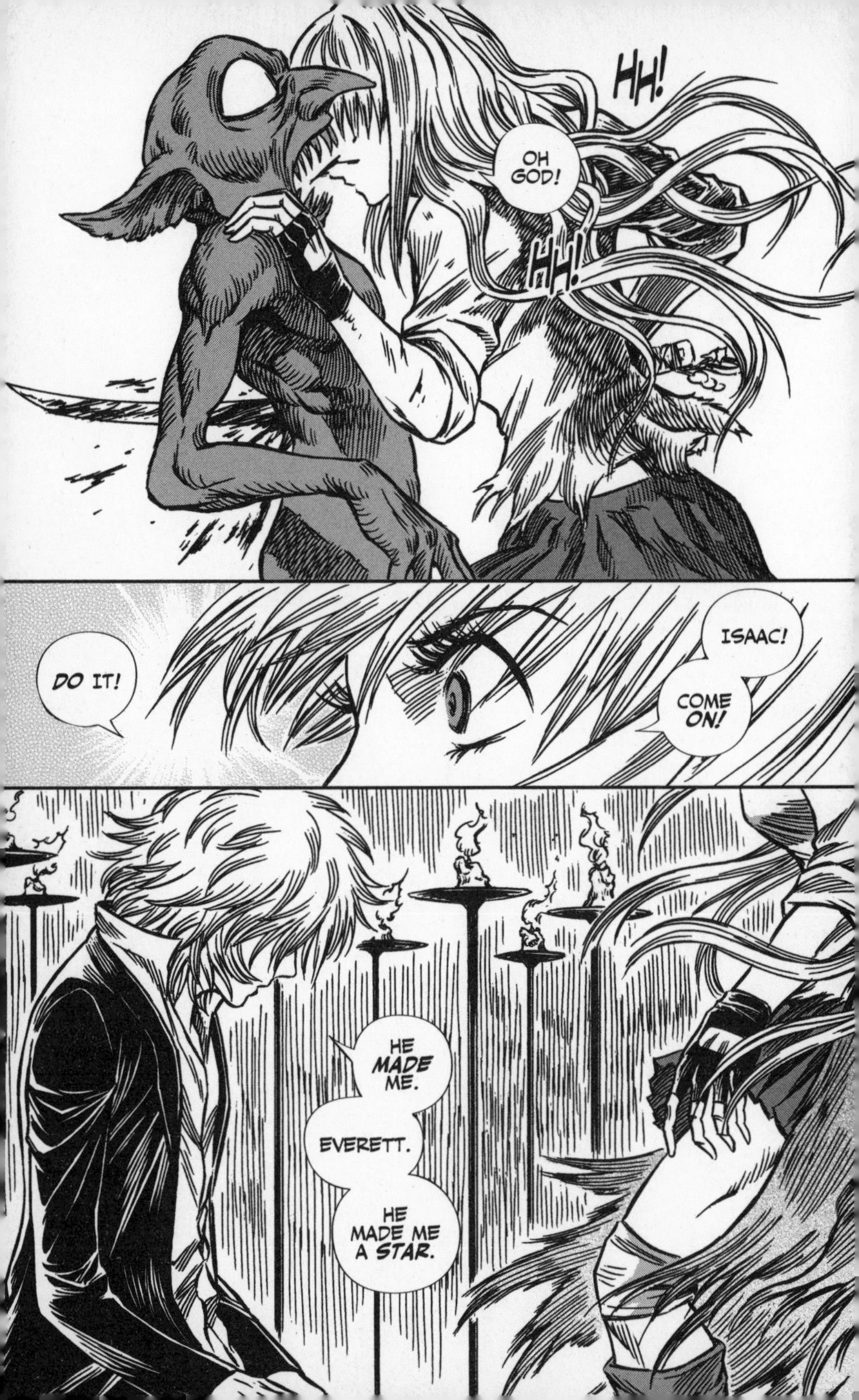
HH!
OH GOD!
HH!
ISAAC!
COME ON!
DO IT!
HE MADE ME.
EVERETT.
HE MADE ME A STAR.

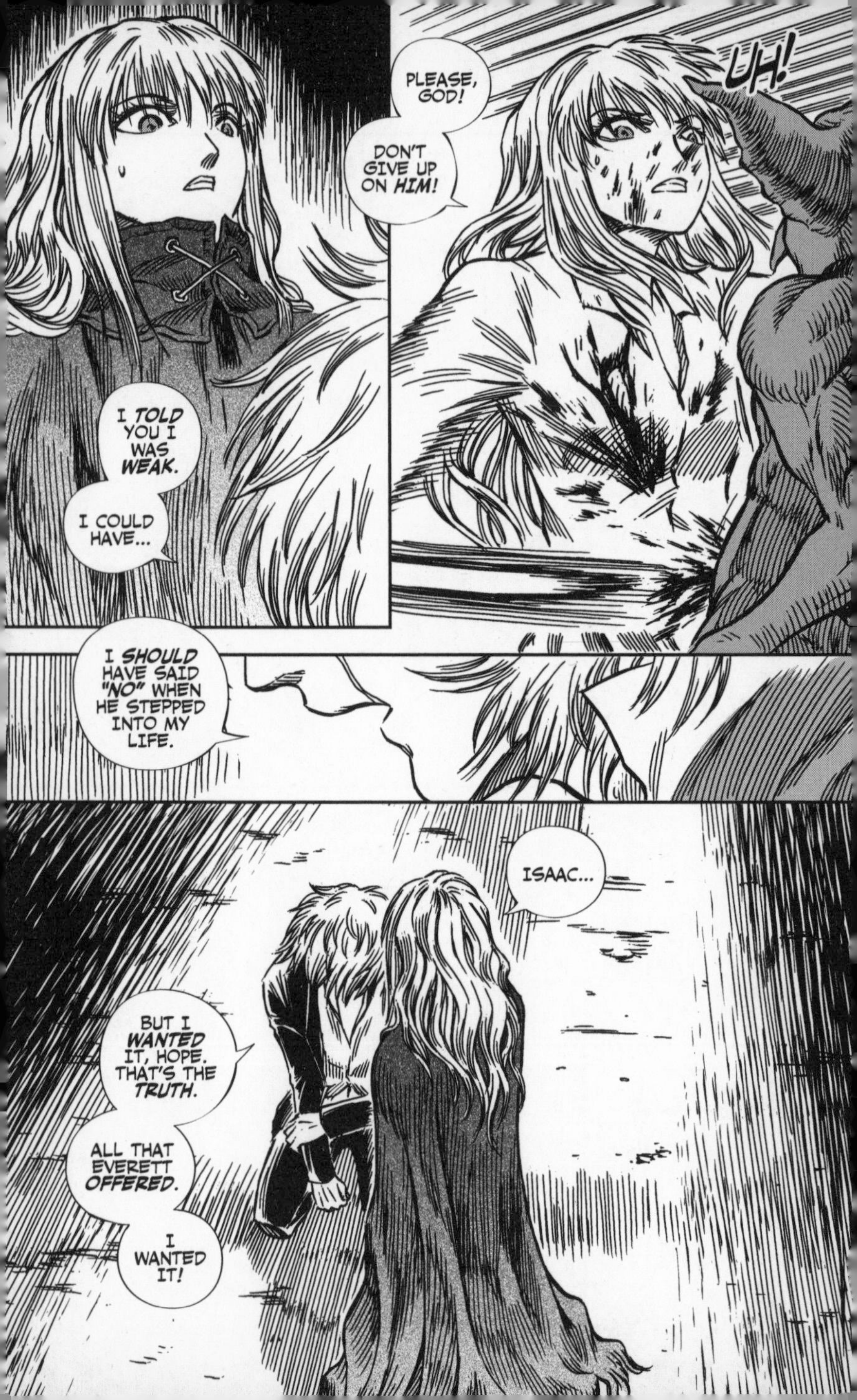
PLEASE, GOD!
DON'T GIVE UP ON *HIM!*
UH!
I *TOLD* YOU I WAS *WEAK.*
I COULD HAVE...
I *SHOULD* HAVE SAID *"NO"* WHEN HE STEPPED INTO MY LIFE.
ISAAC...
BUT I *WANTED* IT, HOPE. THAT'S THE *TRUTH.*
ALL THAT EVERETT *OFFERED.*
I WANTED IT!

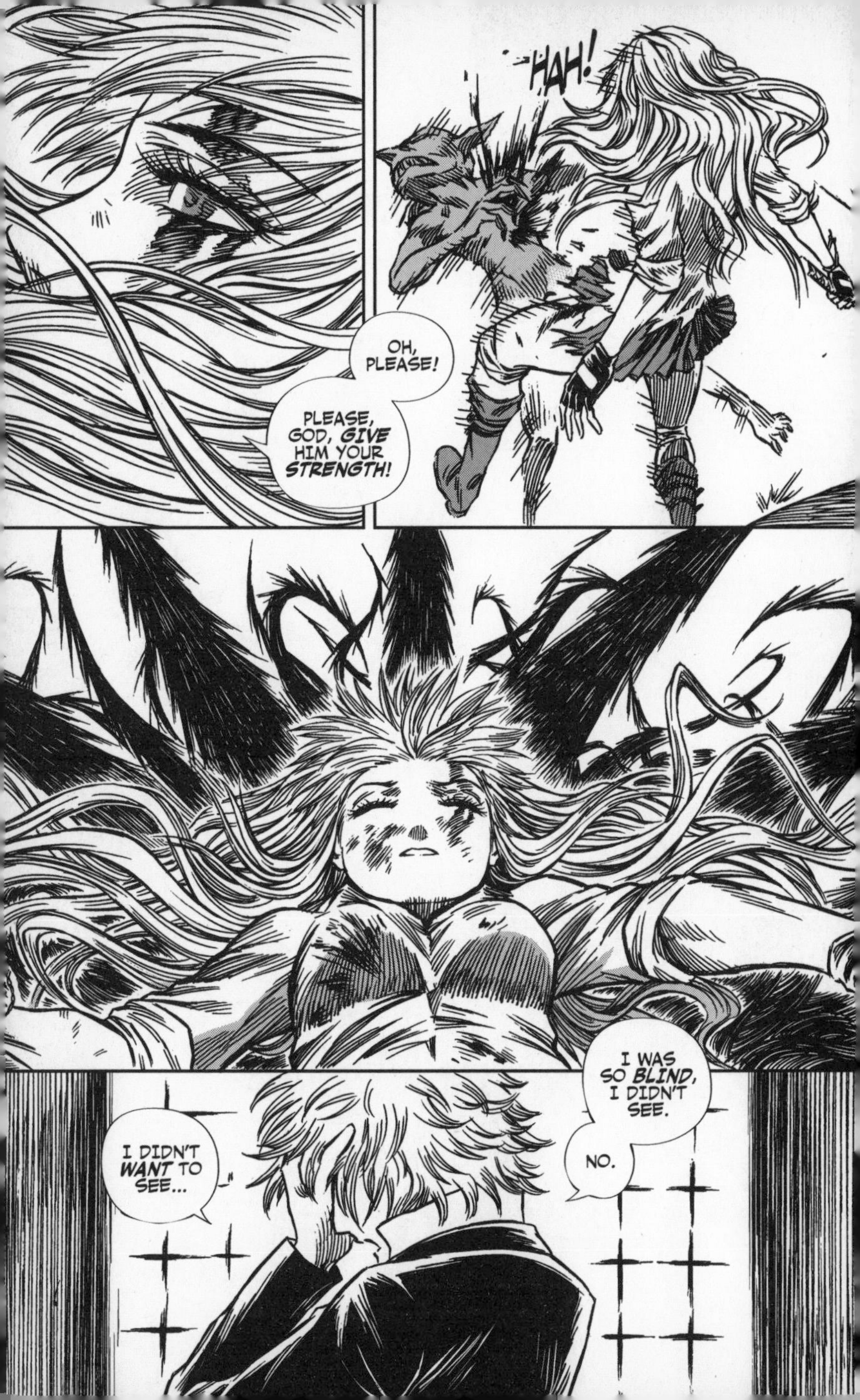
HAH!
OH, PLEASE!
PLEASE, GOD, GIVE HIM YOUR STRENGTH!
I WAS SO BLIND, I DIDN'T SEE.
NO.
I DIDN'T WANT TO SEE...

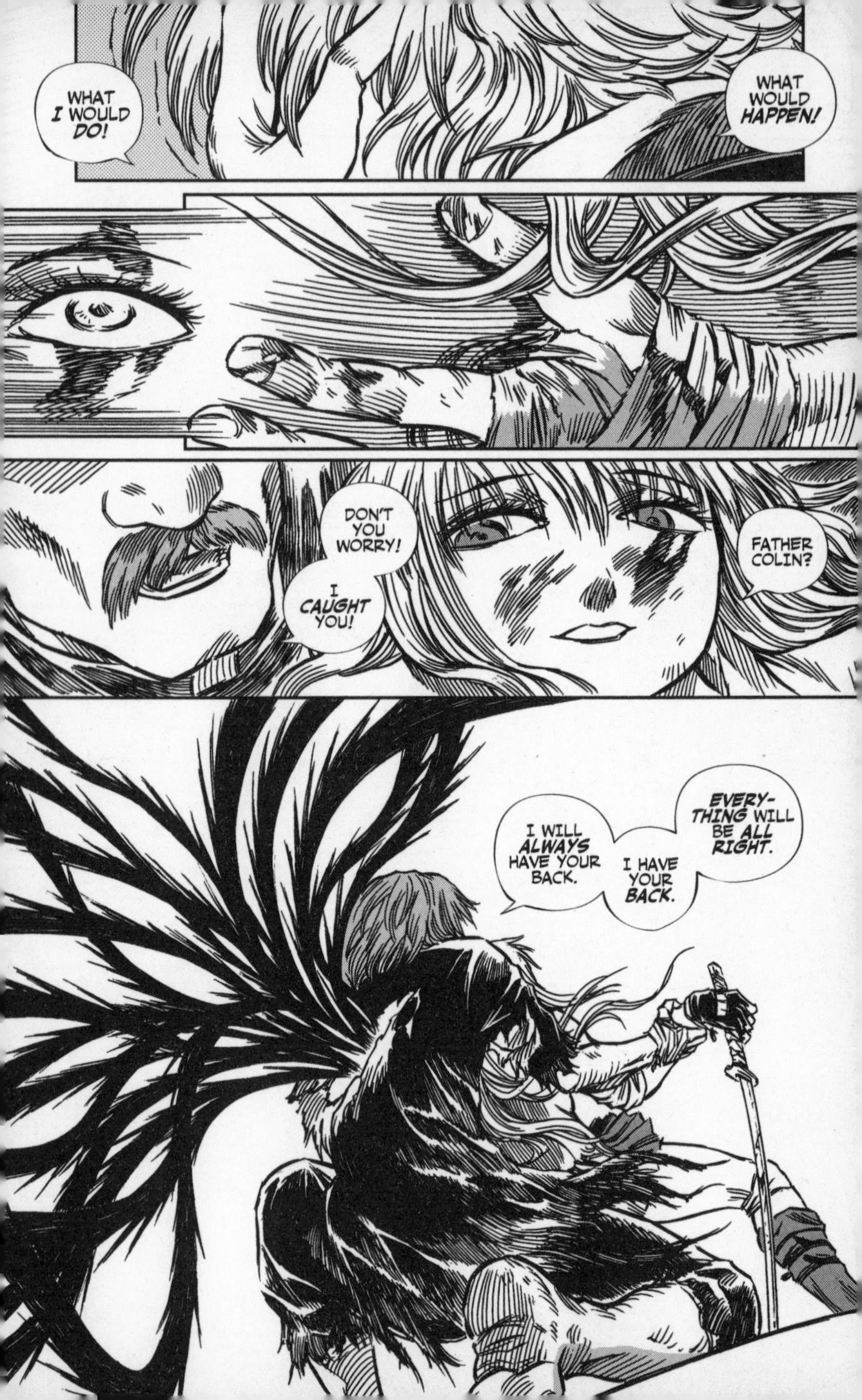
WHAT WOULD HAPPEN!
WHAT I WOULD DO!
FATHER COLIN?
DON'T YOU WORRY!
I CAUGHT YOU!
EVERYTHING WILL BE ALL RIGHT.
I HAVE YOUR BACK.
I WILL ALWAYS HAVE YOUR BACK.

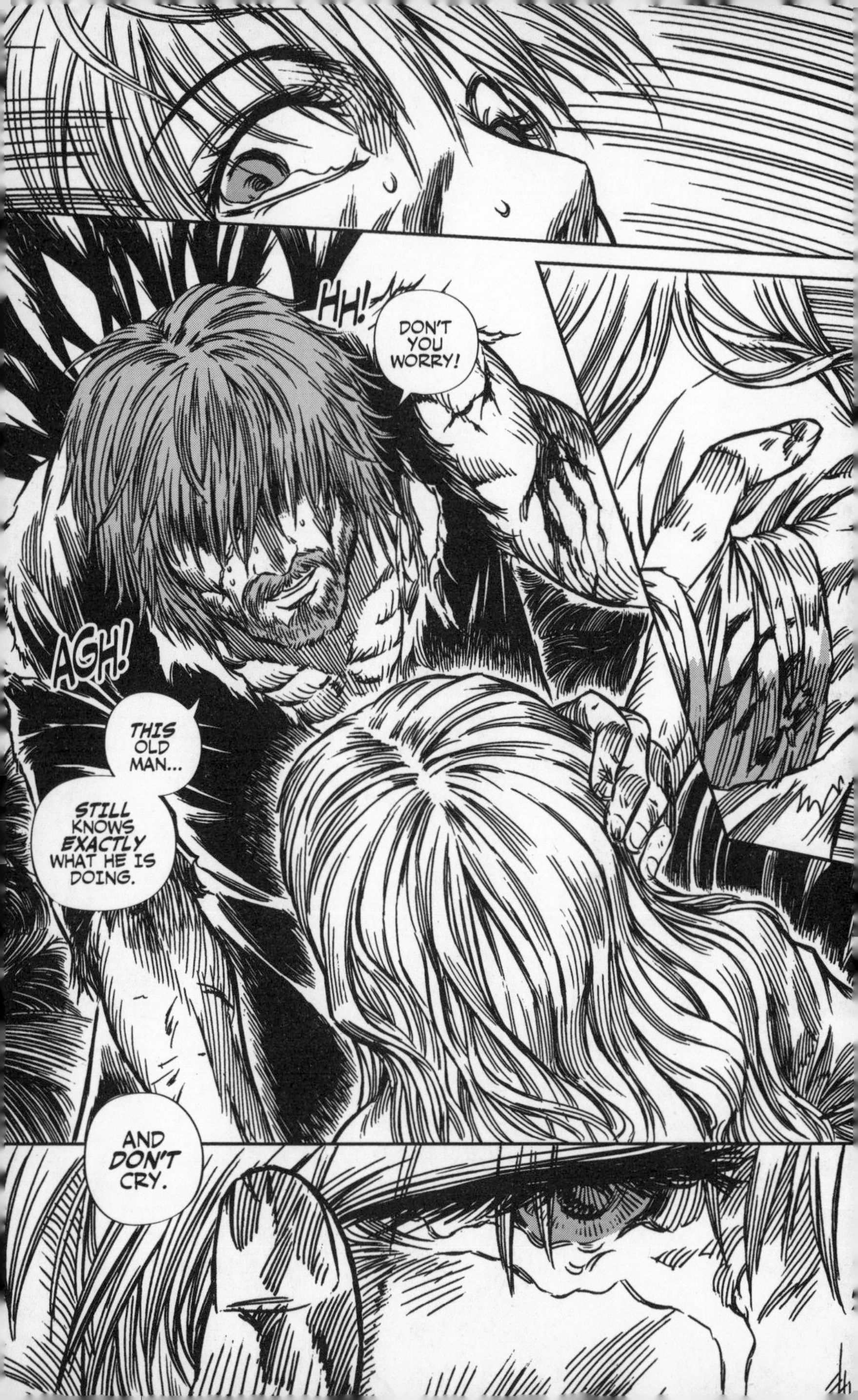
HH!
DON'T YOU WORRY!
AGH!
THIS OLD MAN...
STILL KNOWS EXACTLY WHAT HE IS DOING.
AND DON'T CRY.

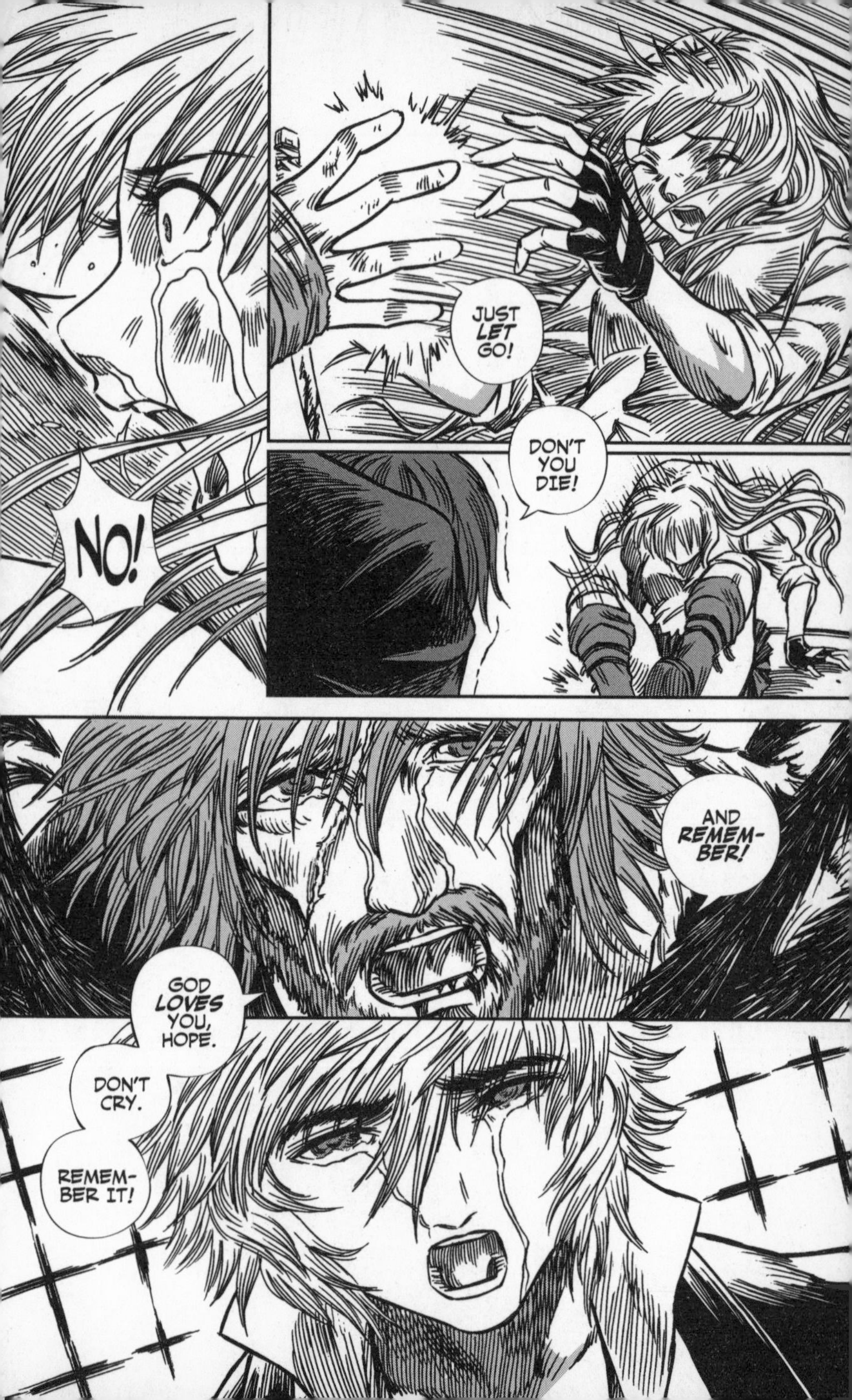
JUST *LET* GO!
DON'T YOU DIE!
NO!
AND *REMEMBER!*
GOD *LOVES* YOU, HOPE.
DON'T CRY.
REMEMBER IT!

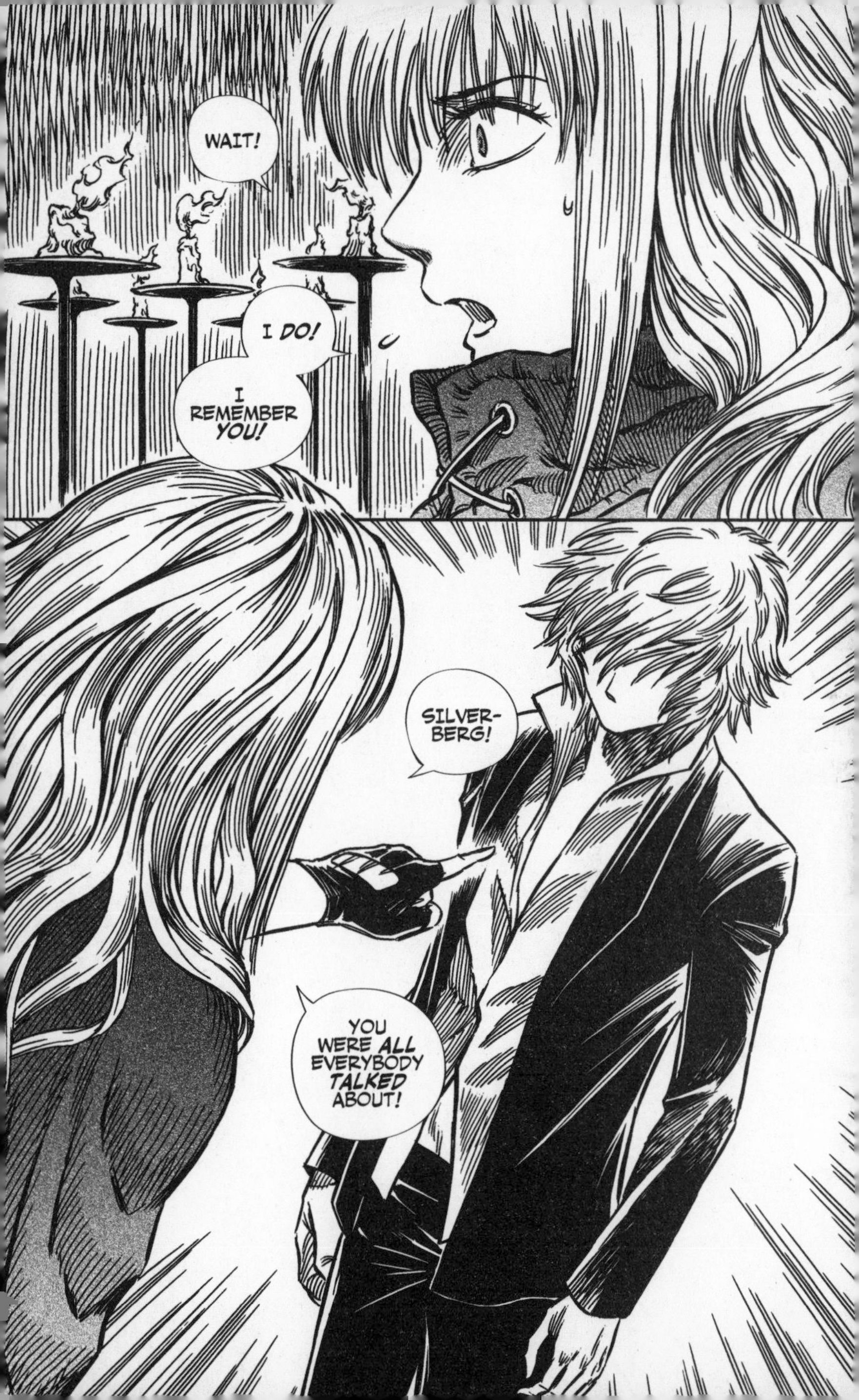
WAIT!
I DO!
I REMEMBER YOU!
SILVER-BERG!
YOU WERE ALL EVERYBODY TALKED ABOUT!

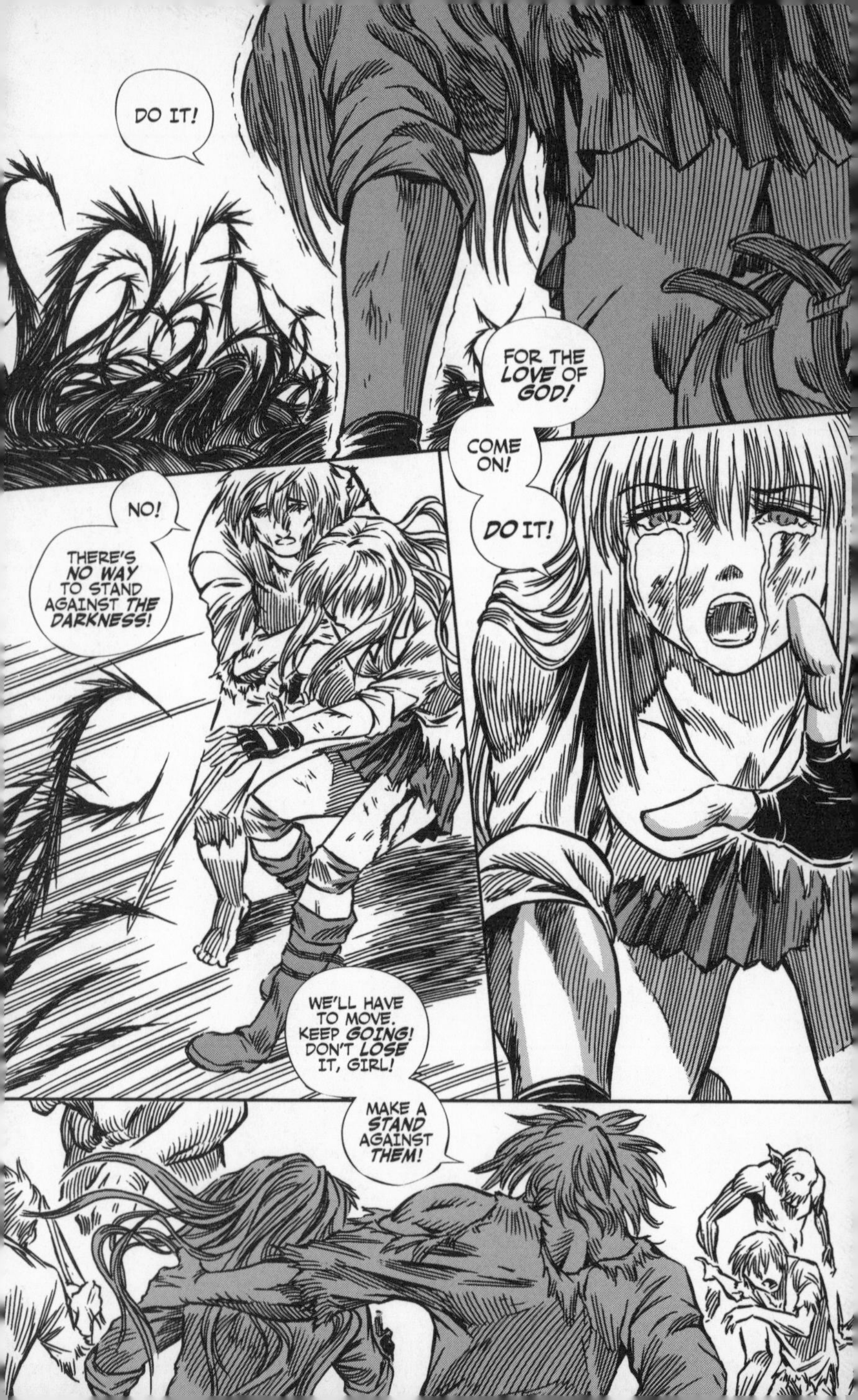
DO IT!
FOR THE LOVE OF GOD!
COME ON!
DO IT!
NO!
THERE'S NO WAY TO STAND AGAINST THE DARKNESS!
WE'LL HAVE TO MOVE. KEEP GOING! DON'T LOSE IT, GIRL!
MAKE A STAND AGAINST THEM!

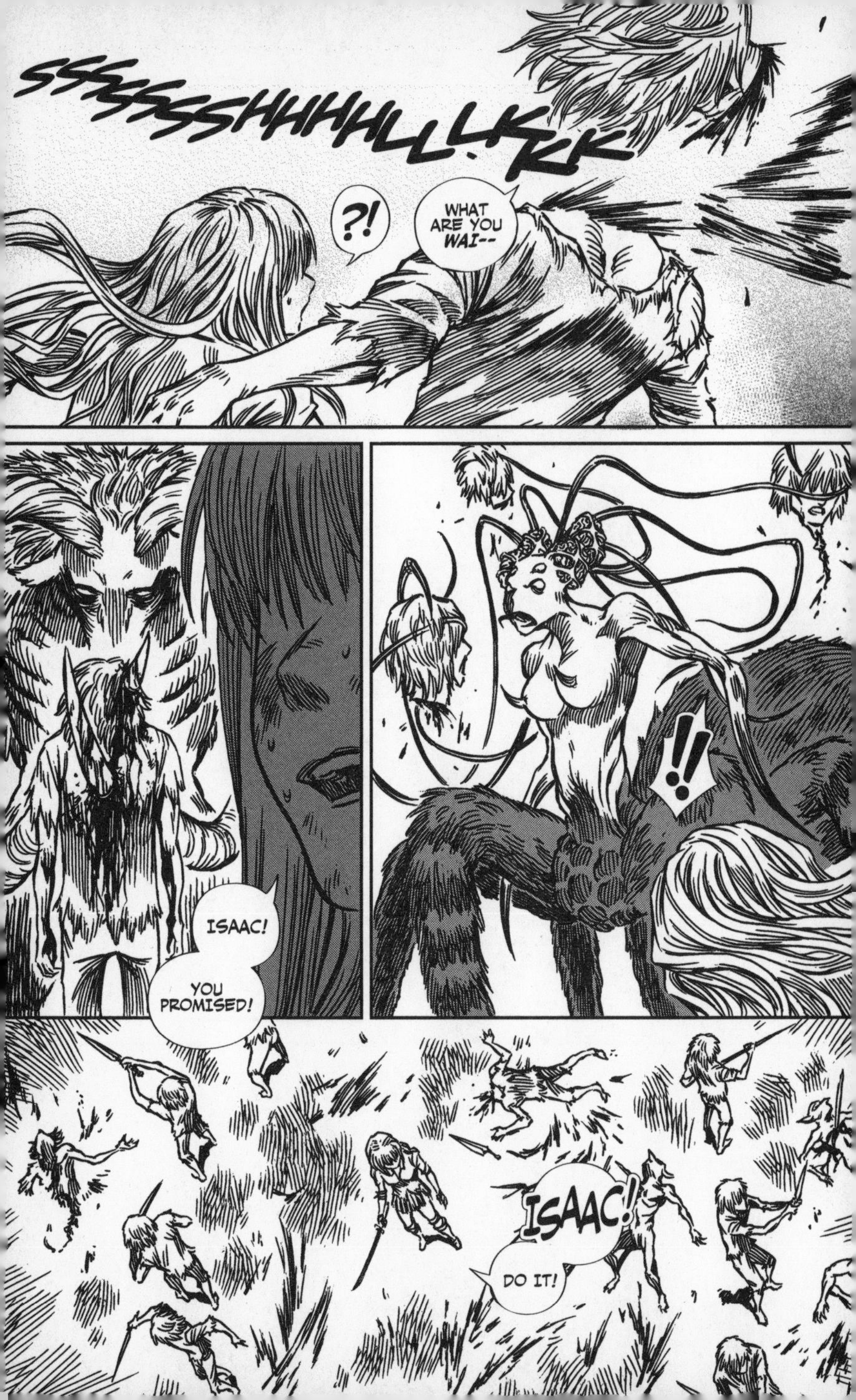
SSSSSSHHHHLLLKK
WHAT ARE YOU WAI--
?!
!!
ISAAC!
YOU PROMISED!
ISAAC!
DO IT!

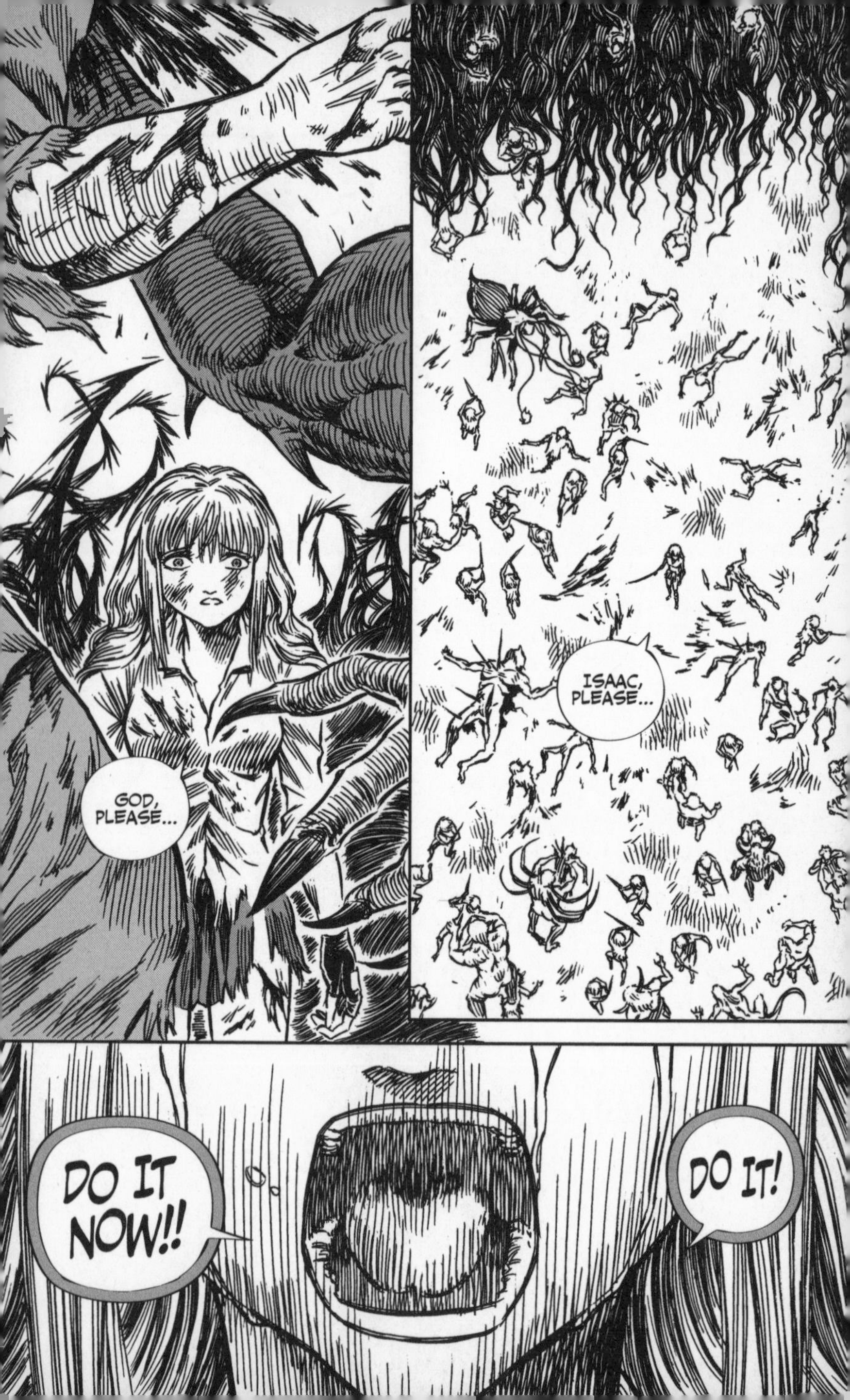
ISAAC, PLEASE...
GOD, PLEASE...
DO IT!
DO IT NOW!!

CHAPTER
9

AS WE KNOW IT

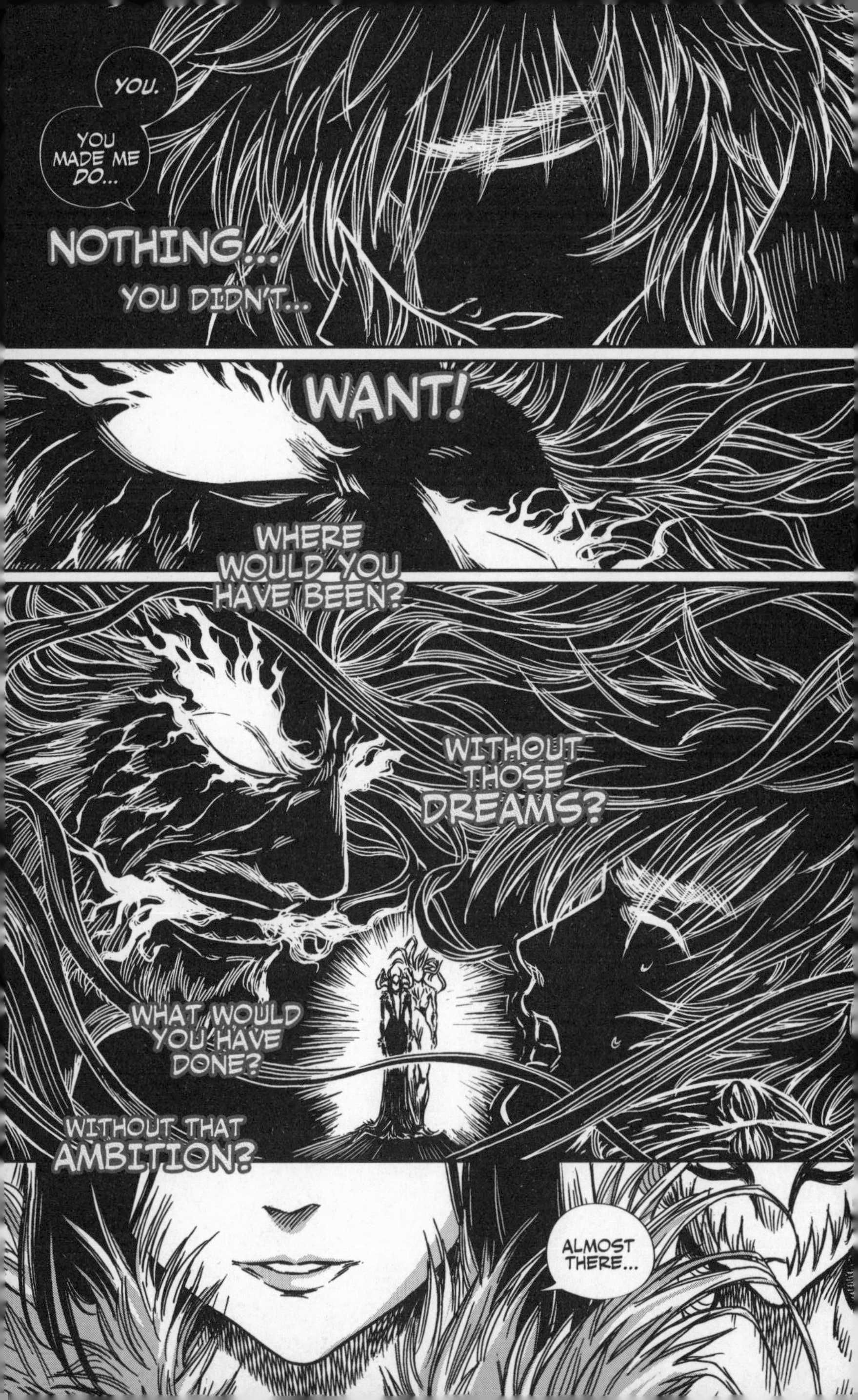
YOU.
YOU MADE ME DO...
NOTHING...
YOU DIDN'T...
WANT!
WHERE WOULD YOU HAVE BEEN?
WITHOUT THOSE DREAMS?
WHAT WOULD YOU HAVE DONE?
WITHOUT THAT AMBITION?
ALMOST THERE...

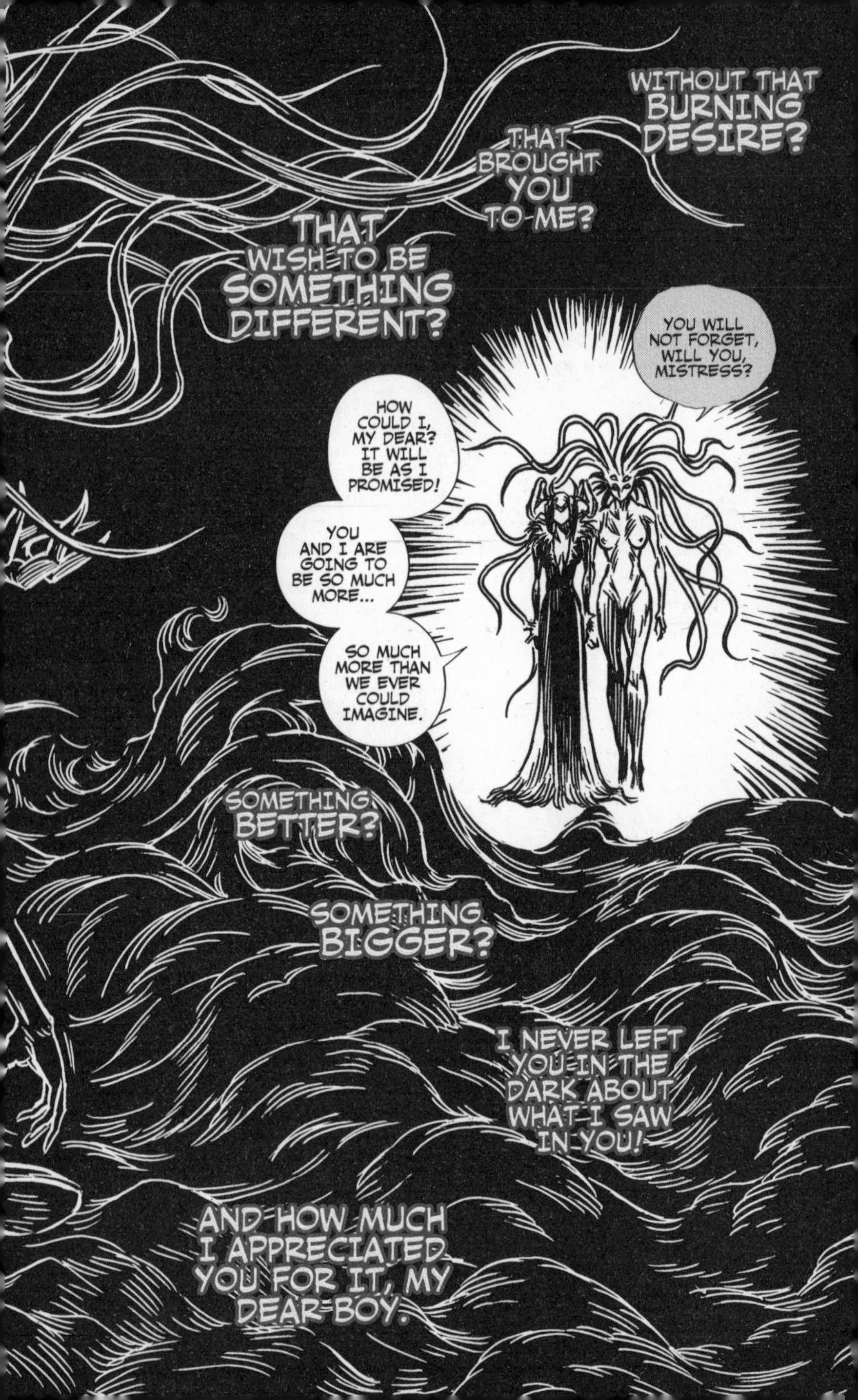
WITHOUT THAT BURNING DESIRE?
THAT BROUGHT YOU TO ME?
THAT WISH TO BE SOMETHING DIFFERENT?
YOU WILL NOT FORGET, WILL YOU, MISTRESS?
HOW COULD I, MY DEAR? IT WILL BE AS I PROMISED!
YOU AND I ARE GOING TO BE SO MUCH MORE...
SO MUCH MORE THAN WE EVER COULD IMAGINE.
SOMETHING BETTER?
SOMETHING BIGGER?
I NEVER LEFT YOU IN THE DARK ABOUT WHAT I SAW IN YOU!
AND HOW MUCH I APPRECIATED YOU FOR IT, MY DEAR BOY.

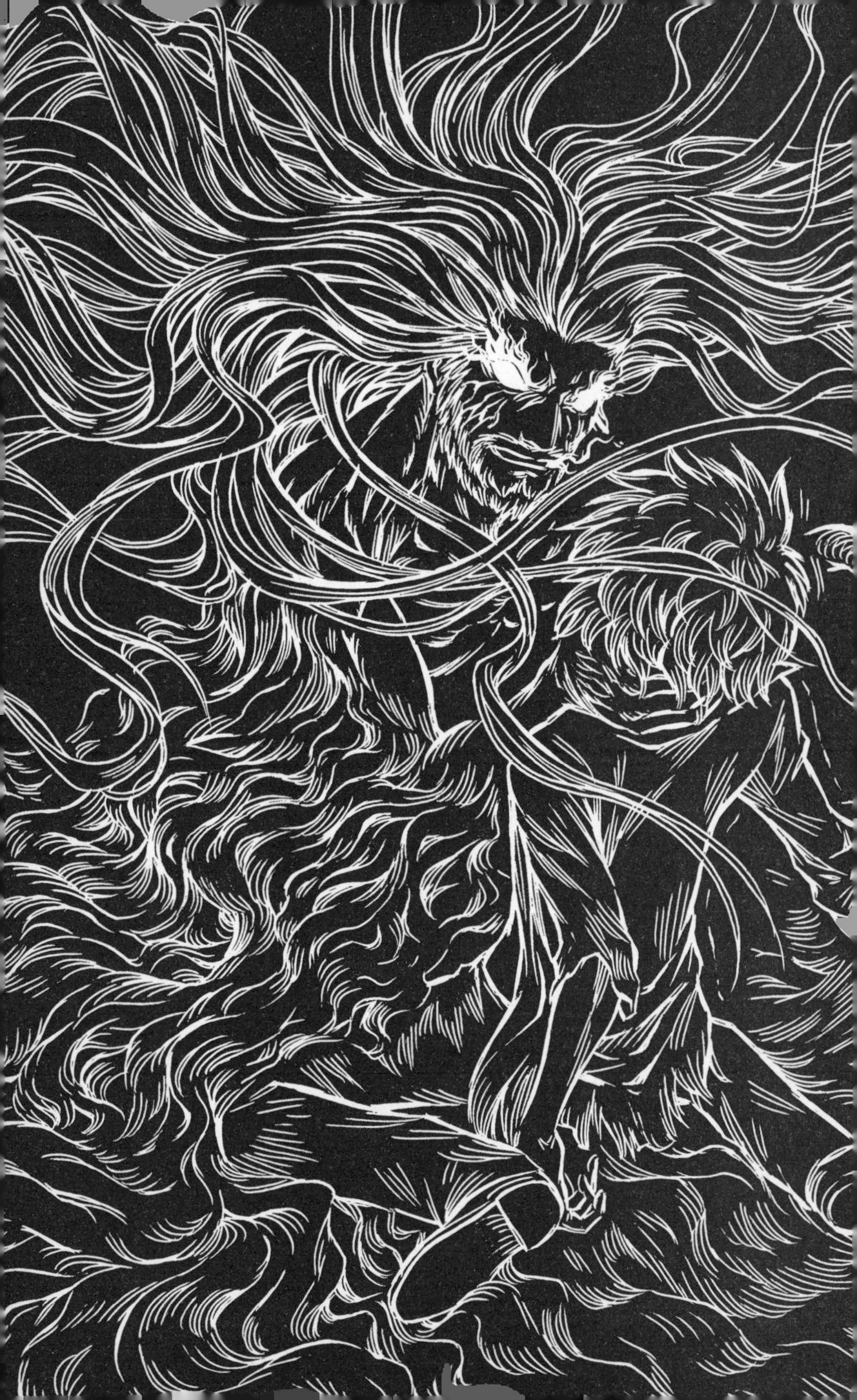

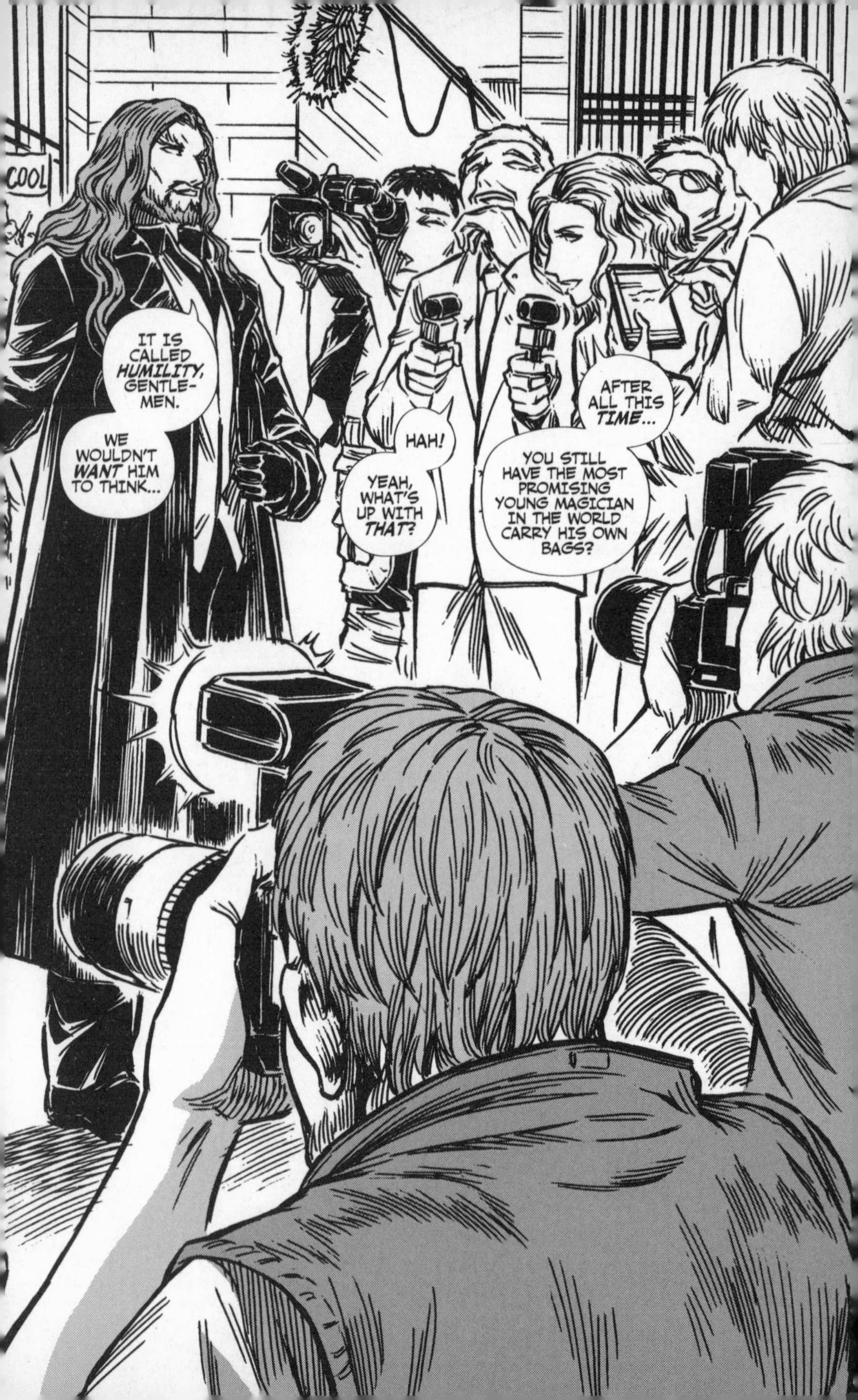
AFTER ALL THIS *TIME*...
YOU STILL HAVE THE MOST PROMISING YOUNG MAGICIAN IN THE WORLD CARRY HIS OWN BAGS?
HAH!
YEAH, WHAT'S UP WITH *THAT*?
IT IS CALLED *HUMILITY*, GENTLE-MEN.
WE WOULDN'T *WANT* HIM TO THINK...
COOL

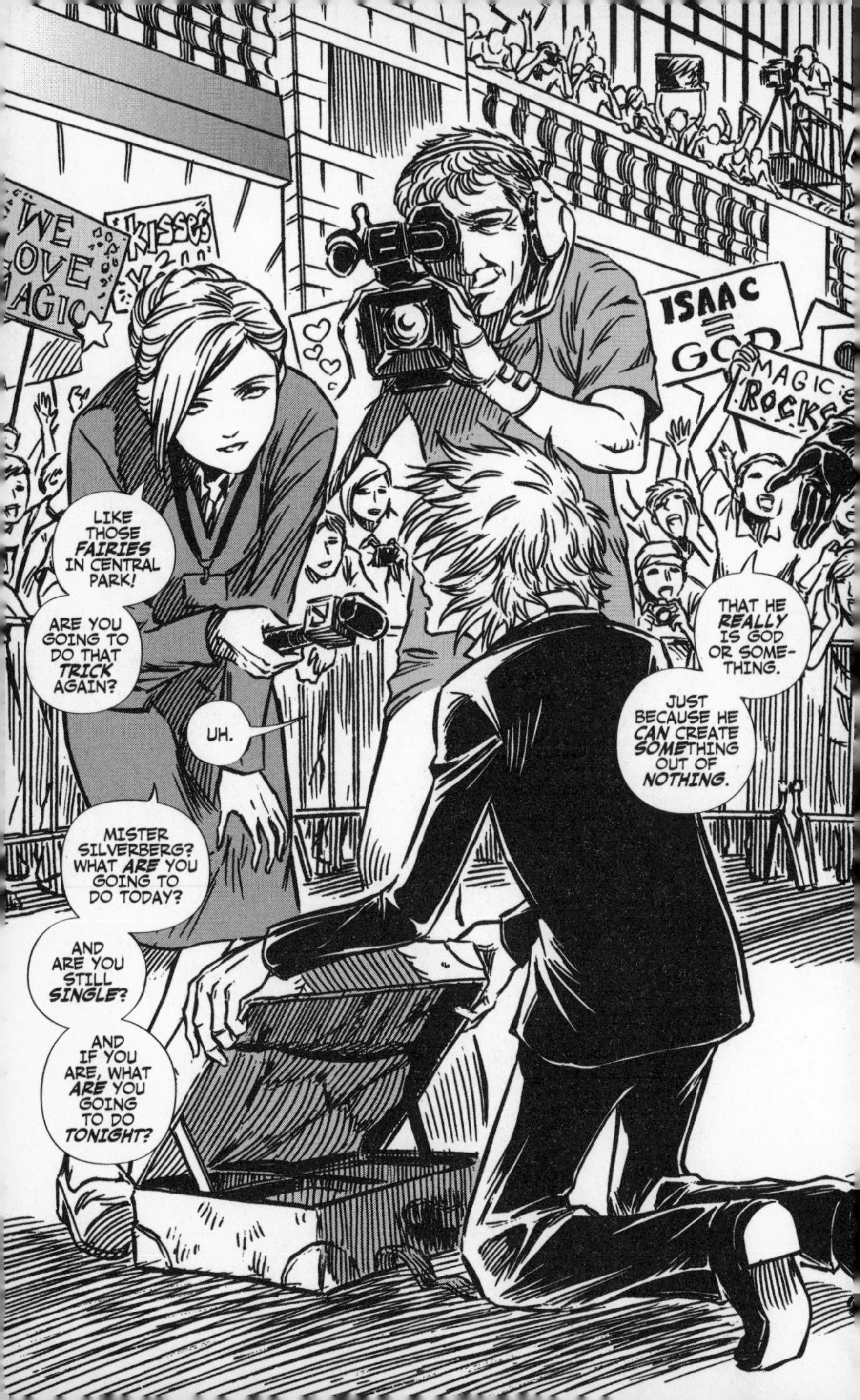
THAT HE REALLY IS GOD OR SOME-THING.
JUST BECAUSE HE CAN CREATE SOMETHING OUT OF NOTHING.
LIKE THOSE FAIRIES IN CENTRAL PARK!
ARE YOU GOING TO DO THAT TRICK AGAIN?
UH.
MISTER SILVERBERG? WHAT ARE YOU GOING TO DO TODAY?
AND ARE YOU STILL SINGLE?
AND IF YOU ARE, WHAT ARE YOU GOING TO DO TONIGHT?
ISAAC
MAGIC ROCKS

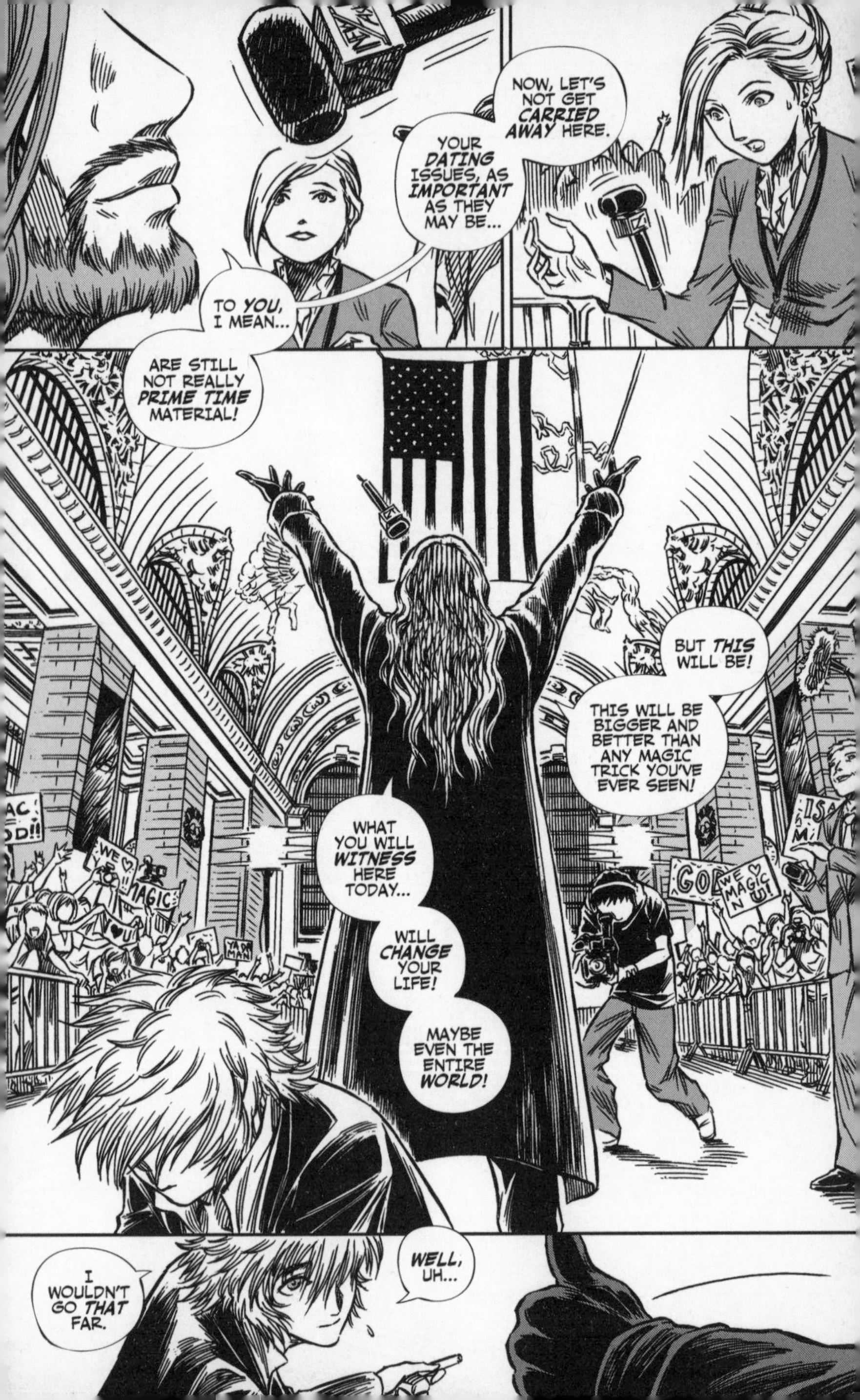
NOW, LET'S NOT GET CARRIED AWAY HERE.
YOUR DATING ISSUES, AS IMPORTANT AS THEY MAY BE...
TO YOU, I MEAN...
ARE STILL NOT REALLY PRIME TIME MATERIAL!
BUT THIS WILL BE!
THIS WILL BE BIGGER AND BETTER THAN ANY MAGIC TRICK YOU'VE EVER SEEN!
WHAT YOU WILL WITNESS HERE TODAY...
WILL CHANGE YOUR LIFE!
MAYBE EVEN THE ENTIRE WORLD!
WELL, UH...
I WOULDN'T GO THAT FAR.

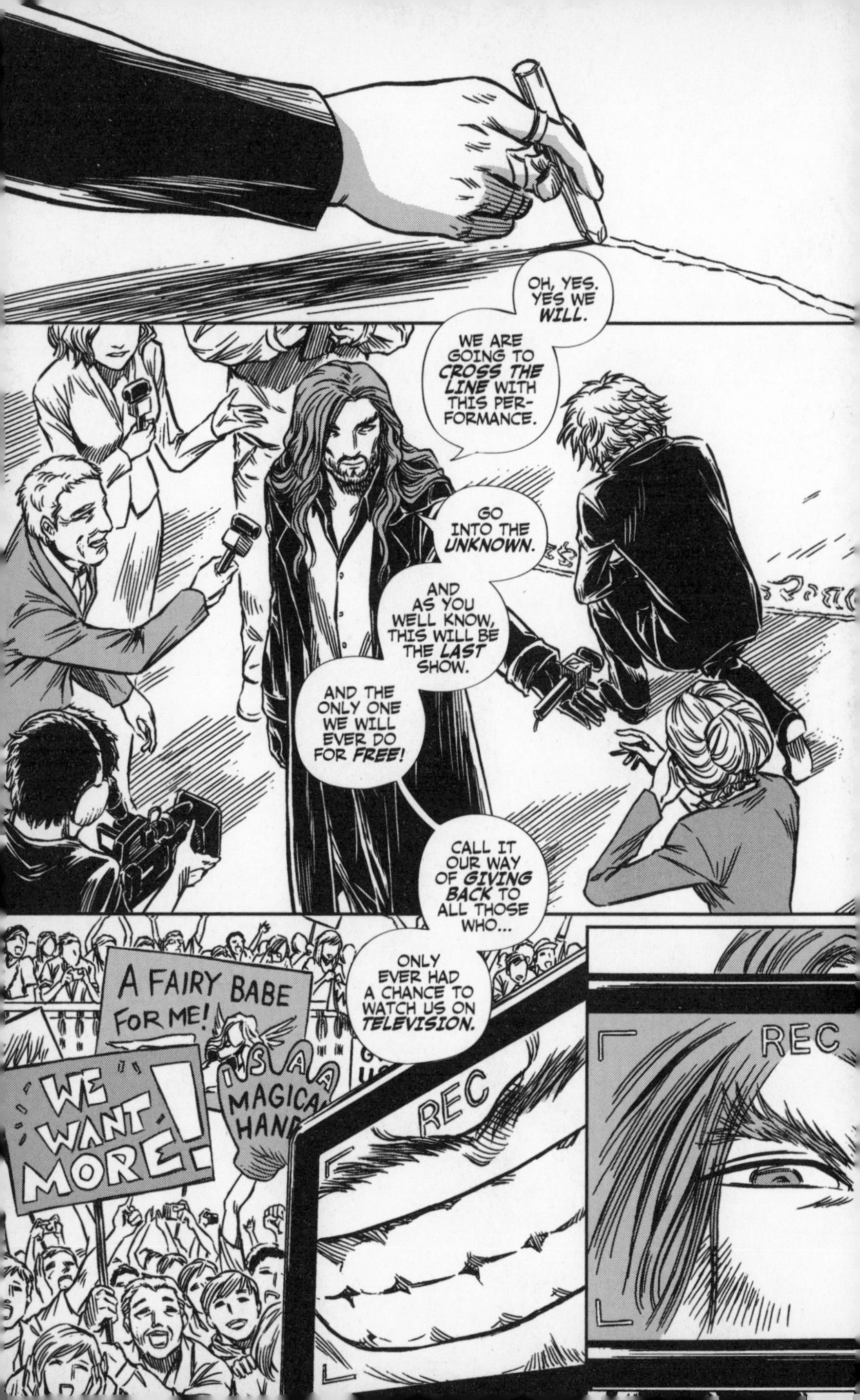
OH, YES. YES WE WILL.
WE ARE GOING TO CROSS THE LINE WITH THIS PERFORMANCE.
GO INTO THE UNKNOWN.
AND AS YOU WELL KNOW, THIS WILL BE THE LAST SHOW.
AND THE ONLY ONE WE WILL EVER DO FOR FREE!
CALL IT OUR WAY OF GIVING BACK TO ALL THOSE WHO...
ONLY EVER HAD A CHANCE TO WATCH US ON TELEVISION.
A FAIRY BABE FOR ME!
WE WANT MORE!
REC
REC

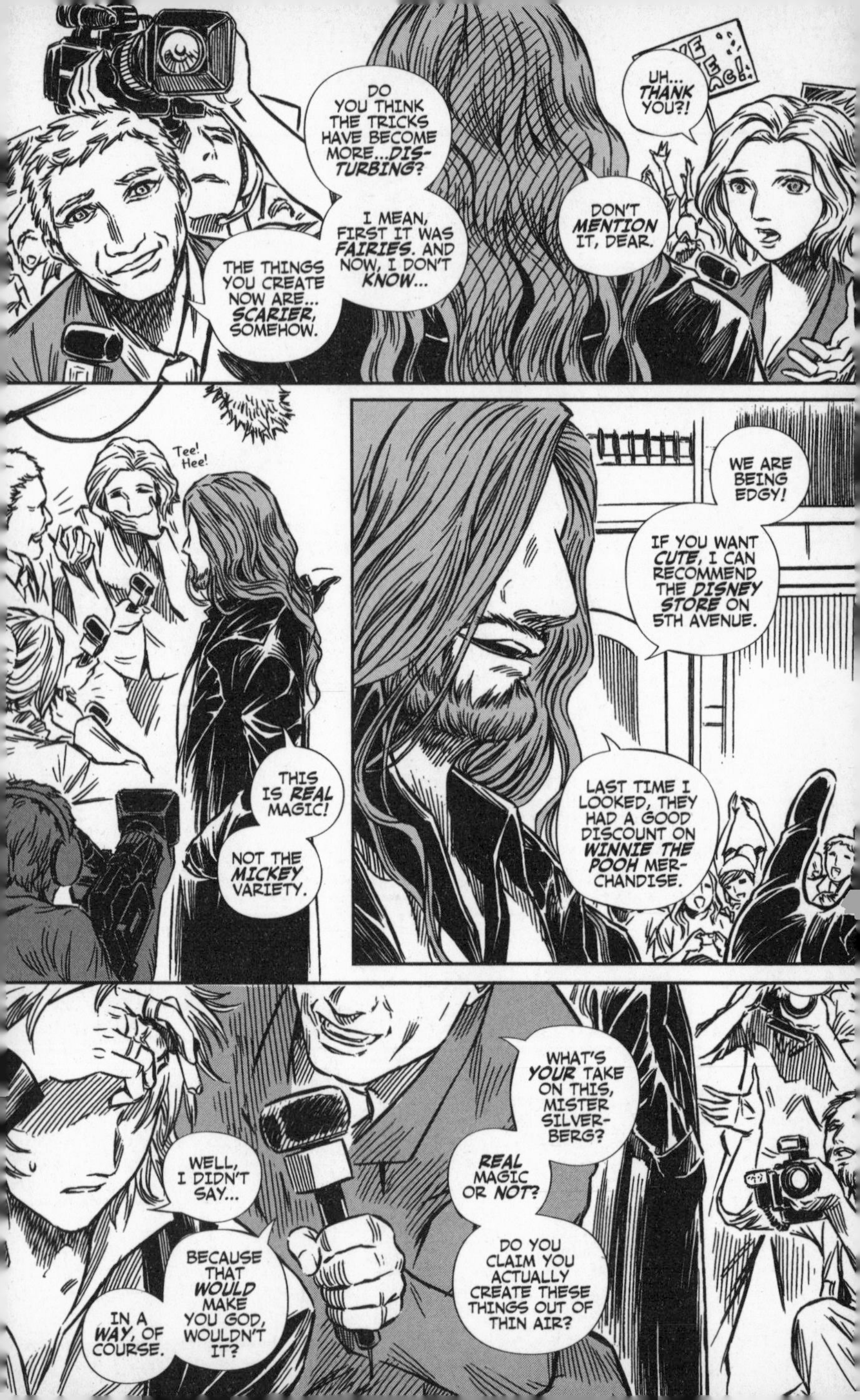
UH... THANK YOU?!
DON'T MENTION IT, DEAR.
DO YOU THINK THE TRICKS HAVE BECOME MORE...DISTURBING?
I MEAN, FIRST IT WAS FAIRIES. AND NOW, I DON'T KNOW...
THE THINGS YOU CREATE NOW ARE... SCARIER, SOMEHOW.
WE ARE BEING EDGY!
IF YOU WANT CUTE, I CAN RECOMMEND THE DISNEY STORE ON 5TH AVENUE.
LAST TIME I LOOKED, THEY HAD A GOOD DISCOUNT ON WINNIE THE POOH MERCHANDISE.
Tee! Hee!
THIS IS REAL MAGIC!
NOT THE MICKEY VARIETY.
WHAT'S YOUR TAKE ON THIS, MISTER SILVERBERG?
REAL MAGIC OR NOT?
DO YOU CLAIM YOU ACTUALLY CREATE THESE THINGS OUT OF THIN AIR?
WELL, I DIDN'T SAY...
BECAUSE THAT WOULD MAKE YOU GOD, WOULDN'T IT?
IN A WAY, OF COURSE.

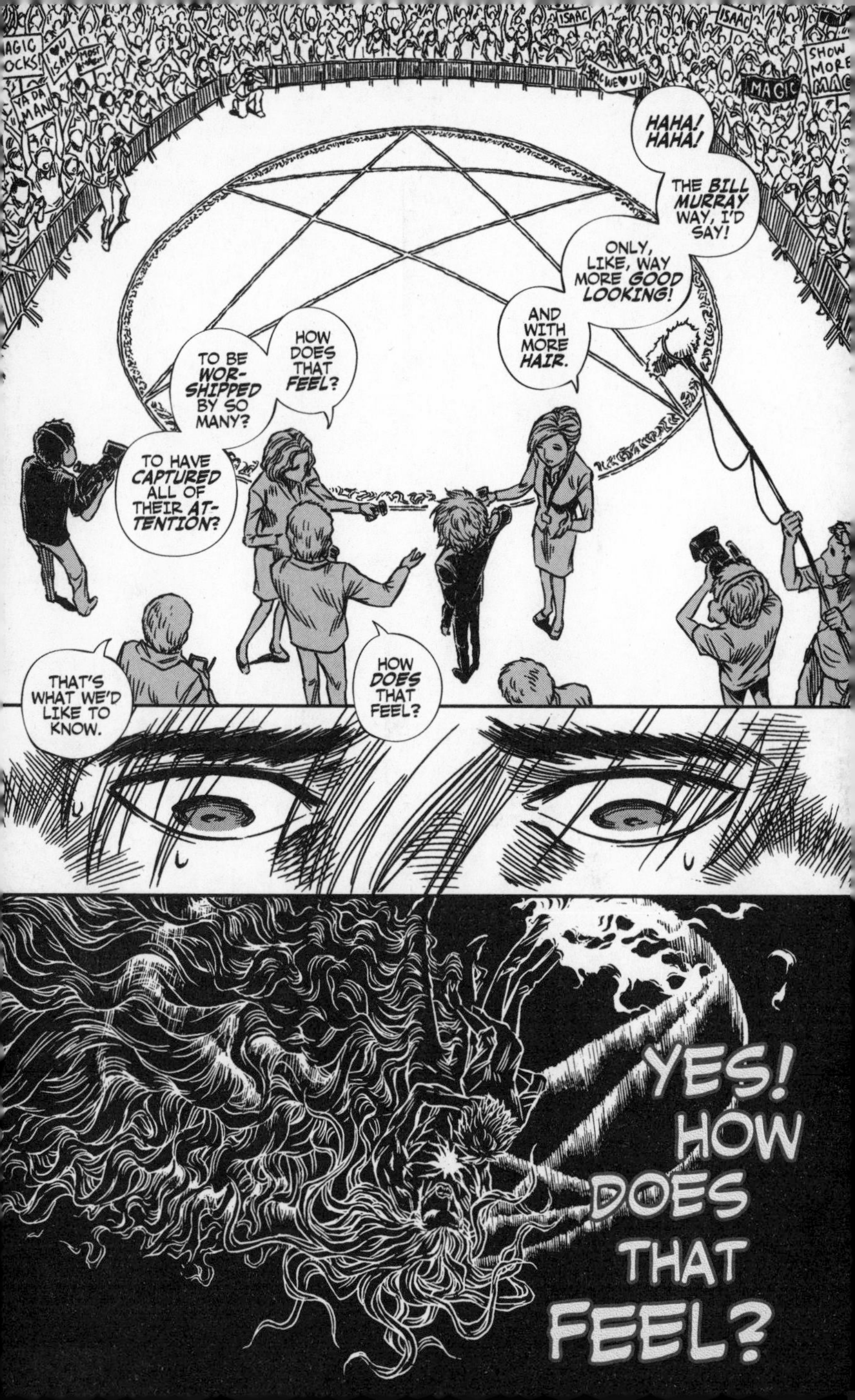
ISAAC
ISAAC
SHOW MORE
MAGIC
ISAAC WE ♥ U!
YA DA MAN
HAHA! HAHA!
THE BILL MURRAY WAY, I'D SAY!
ONLY, LIKE, WAY MORE GOOD LOOKING!
AND WITH MORE HAIR.
HOW DOES THAT FEEL?
TO BE WOR-SHIPPED BY SO MANY?
TO HAVE CAPTURED ALL OF THEIR AT-TENTION?
HOW DOES THAT FEEL?
THAT'S WHAT WE'D LIKE TO KNOW.
YES! HOW DOES THAT FEEL?

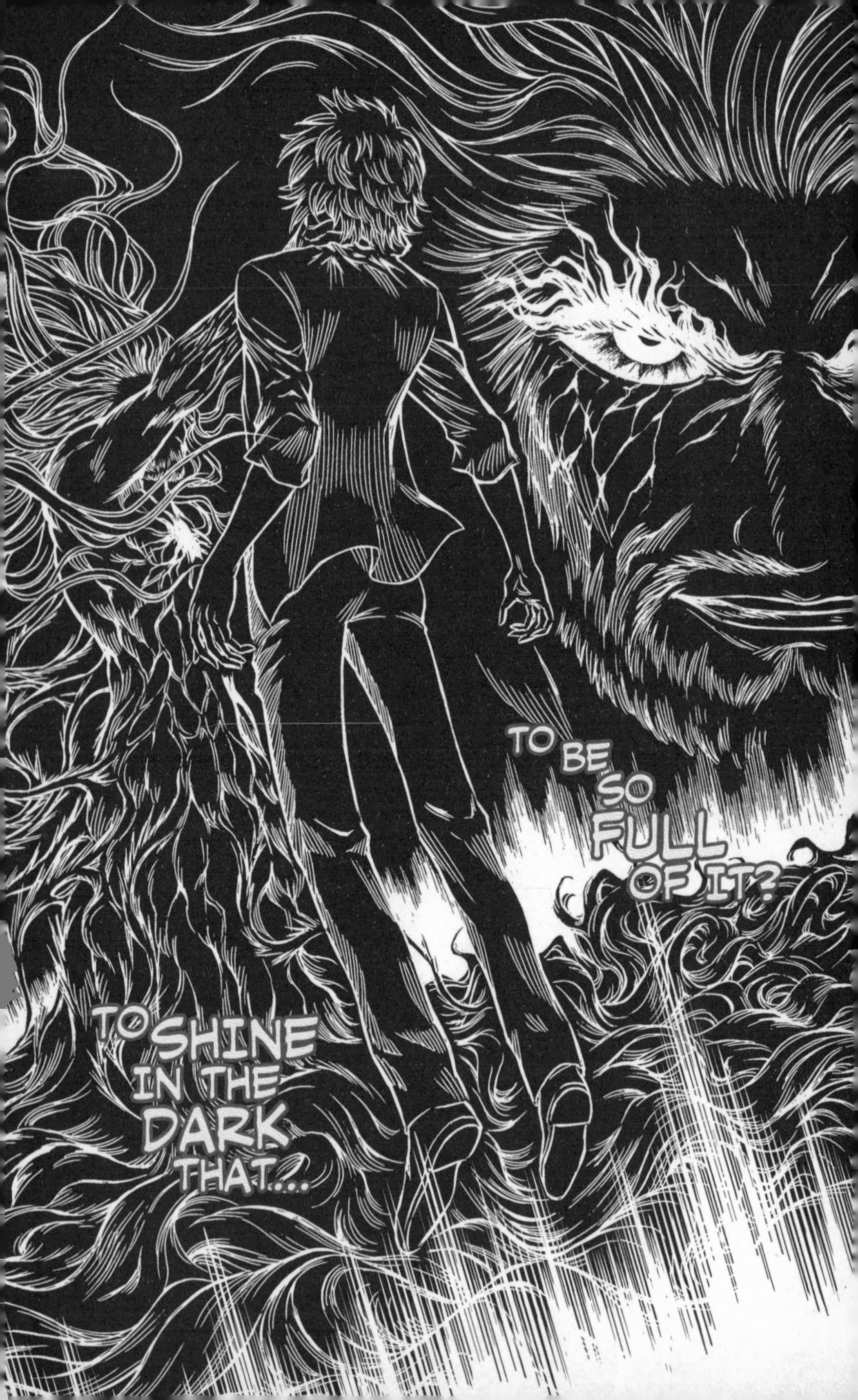
TO SHINE IN THE DARK THAT...
TO BE SO FULL OF IT?

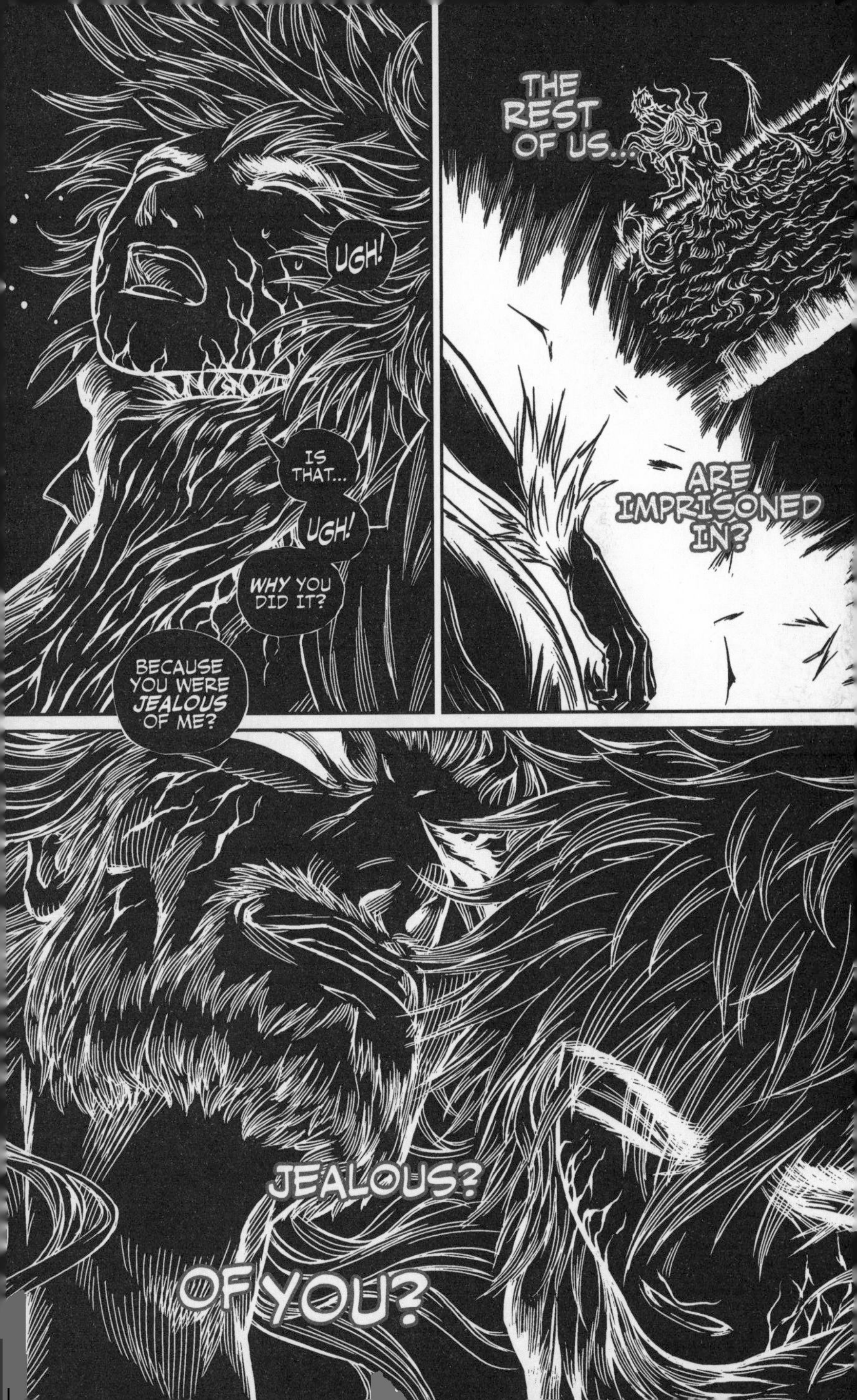
THE REST OF US...
ARE IMPRISONED IN?
UGH!
IS THAT...
UGH!
WHY YOU DID IT?
BECAUSE YOU WERE JEALOUS OF ME?
JEALOUS?
OF YOU?

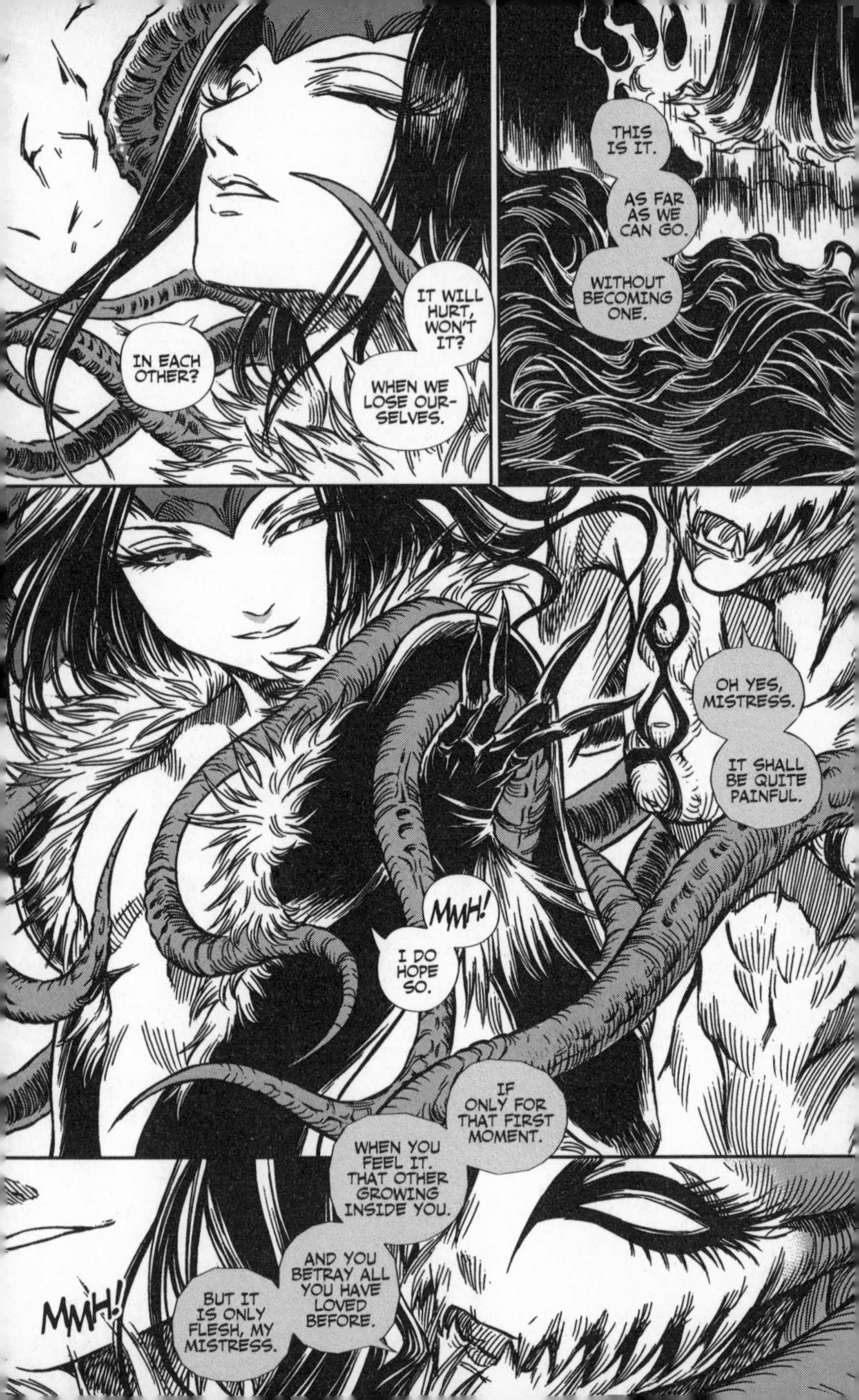
THIS IS IT.
AS FAR AS WE CAN GO.
WITHOUT BECOMING ONE.
IT WILL HURT, WON'T IT?
WHEN WE LOSE OUR-SELVES.
IN EACH OTHER?
OH YES, MISTRESS.
IT SHALL BE QUITE PAINFUL.
MMH!
I DO HOPE SO.
IF ONLY FOR THAT FIRST MOMENT.
WHEN YOU FEEL IT. THAT OTHER GROWING INSIDE YOU.
AND YOU BETRAY ALL YOU HAVE LOVED BEFORE.
BUT IT IS ONLY FLESH, MY MISTRESS.
MMH!

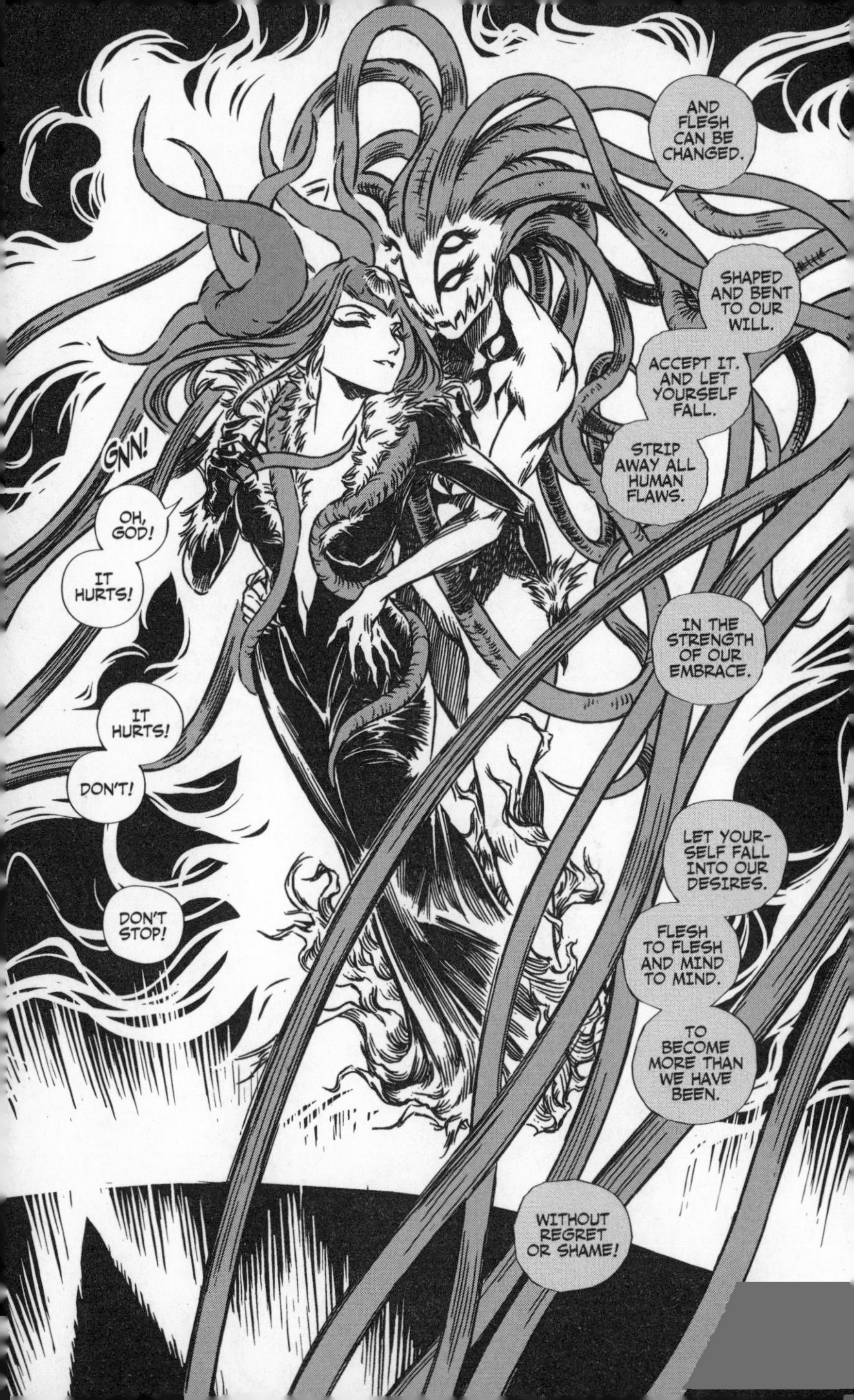
AND FLESH CAN BE CHANGED.
SHAPED AND BENT TO OUR WILL.
ACCEPT IT. AND LET YOURSELF FALL.
STRIP AWAY ALL HUMAN FLAWS.
GNN!
OH, GOD!
IT HURTS!
IN THE STRENGTH OF OUR EMBRACE.
IT HURTS!
DON'T!
LET YOURSELF FALL INTO OUR DESIRES.
DON'T STOP!
FLESH TO FLESH AND MIND TO MIND.
TO BECOME MORE THAN WE HAVE BEEN.
WITHOUT REGRET OR SHAME!

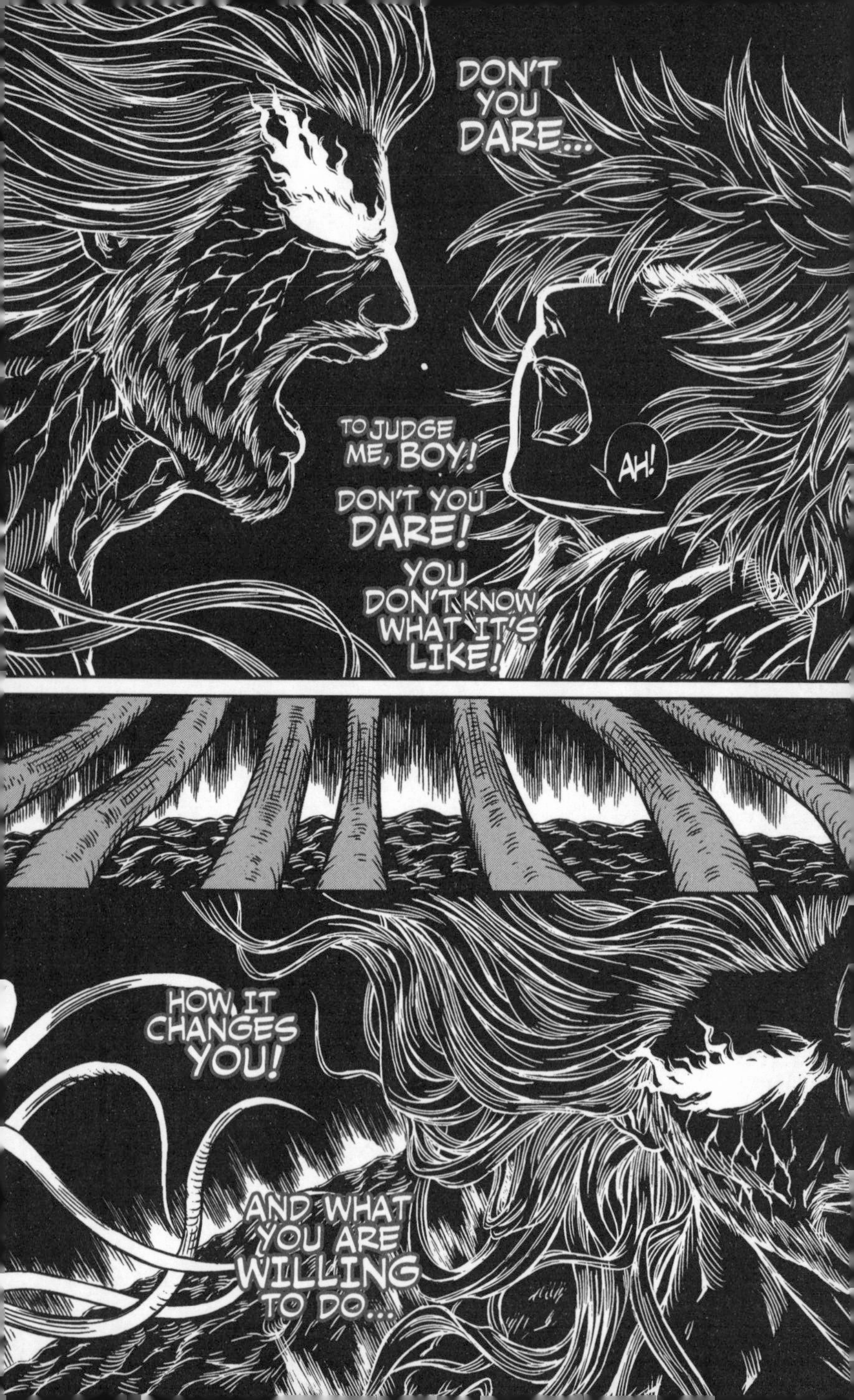
DON'T YOU DARE...
TO JUDGE ME, BOY!
AH!
DON'T YOU DARE!
YOU DON'T KNOW WHAT IT'S LIKE!
HOW IT CHANGES YOU!
AND WHAT YOU ARE WILLING TO DO...

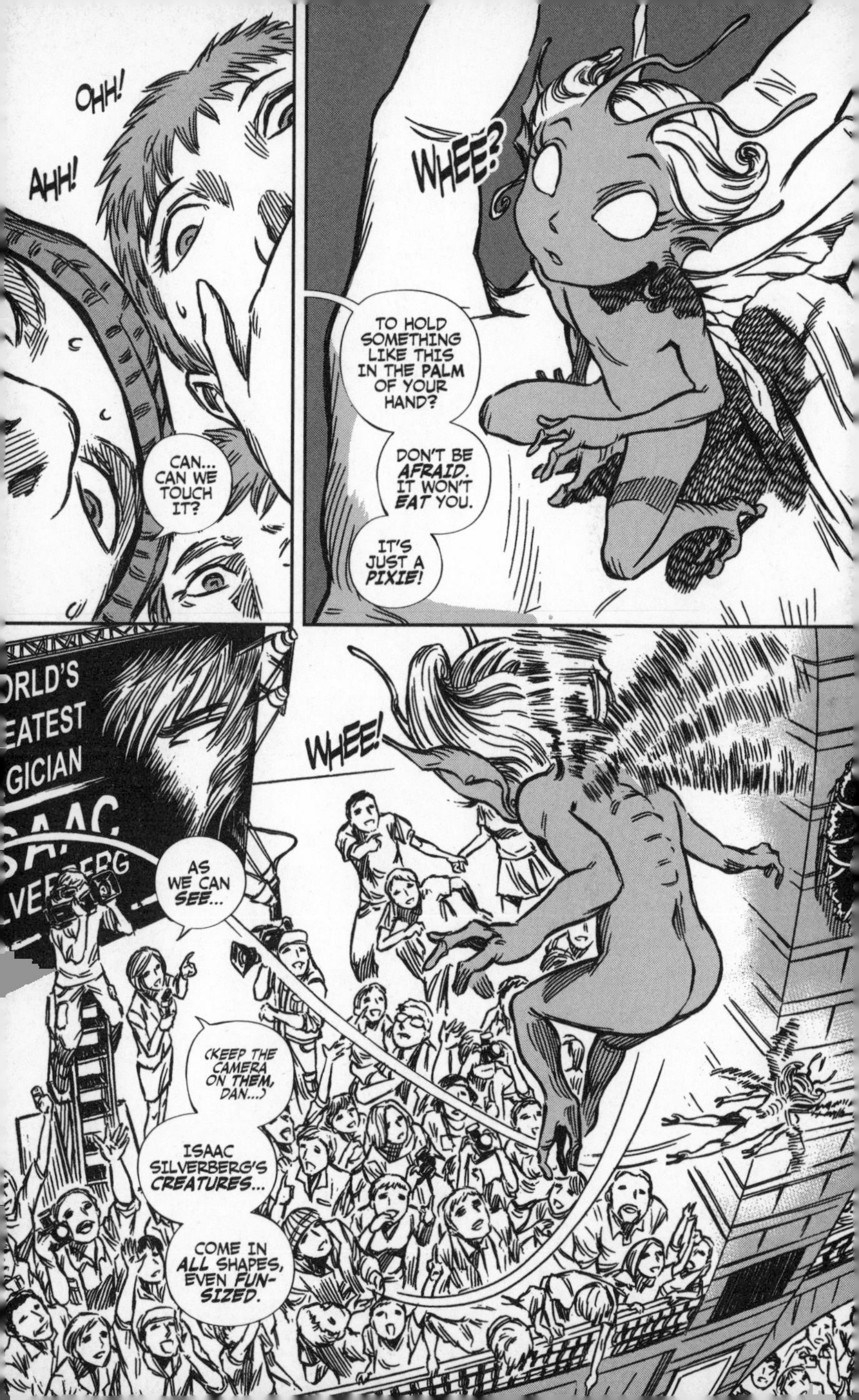
OHH!
AHH!
CAN... CAN WE TOUCH IT?
WHEE?
TO HOLD SOMETHING LIKE THIS IN THE PALM OF YOUR HAND?
DON'T BE AFRAID. IT WON'T EAT YOU.
IT'S JUST A PIXIE!
ORLD'S
EATEST
GICIAN
WHEE!
AS WE CAN SEE...
(KEEP THE CAMERA ON THEM, DAN...)
ISAAC SILVERBERG'S CREATURES...
COME IN ALL SHAPES, EVEN FUN-SIZED.

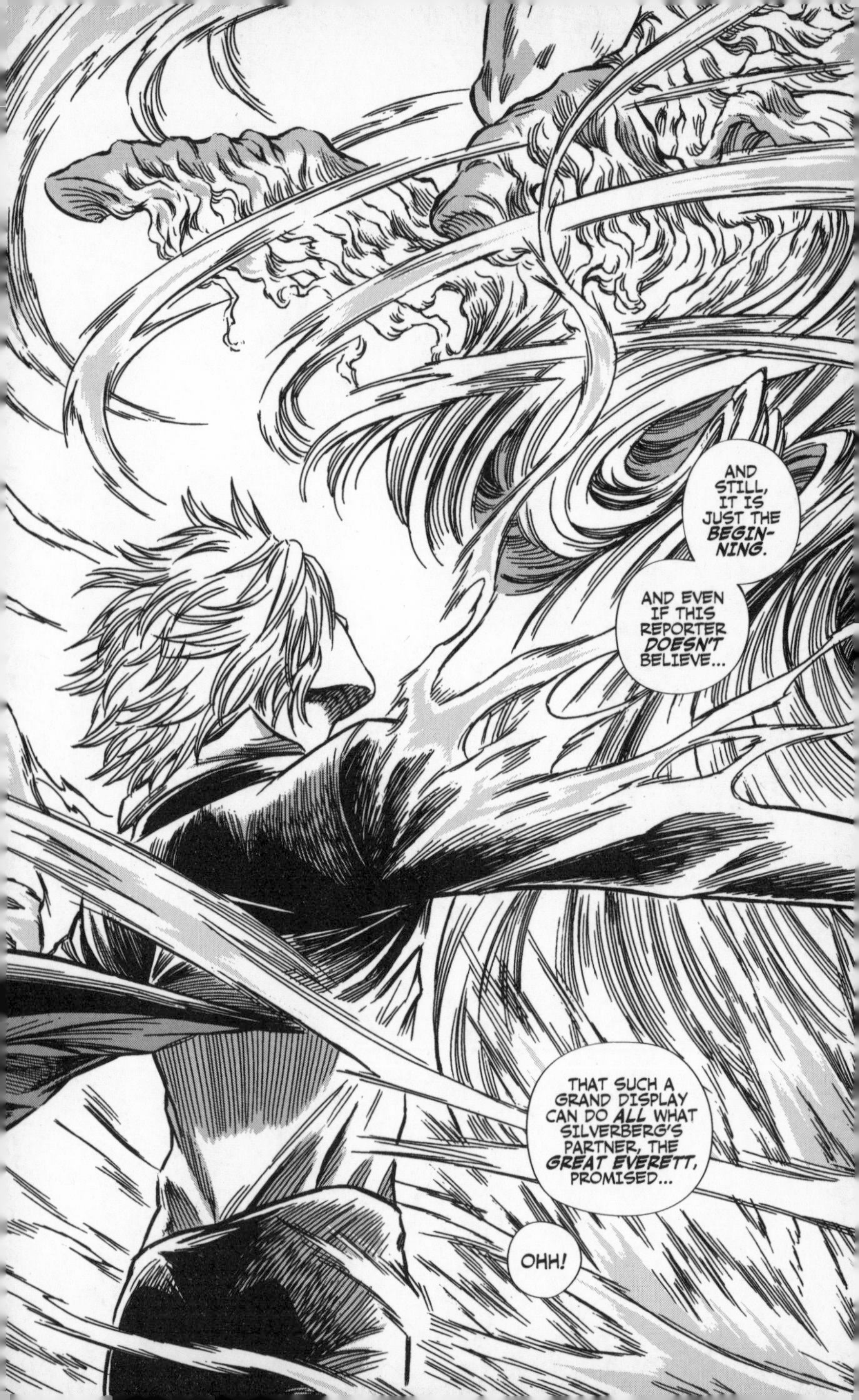
AND STILL, IT IS JUST THE BEGIN-NING.
AND EVEN IF THIS REPORTER DOESN'T BELIEVE...
THAT SUCH A GRAND DISPLAY CAN DO ALL WHAT SILVERBERG'S PARTNER, THE GREAT EVERETT, PROMISED...
OHH!

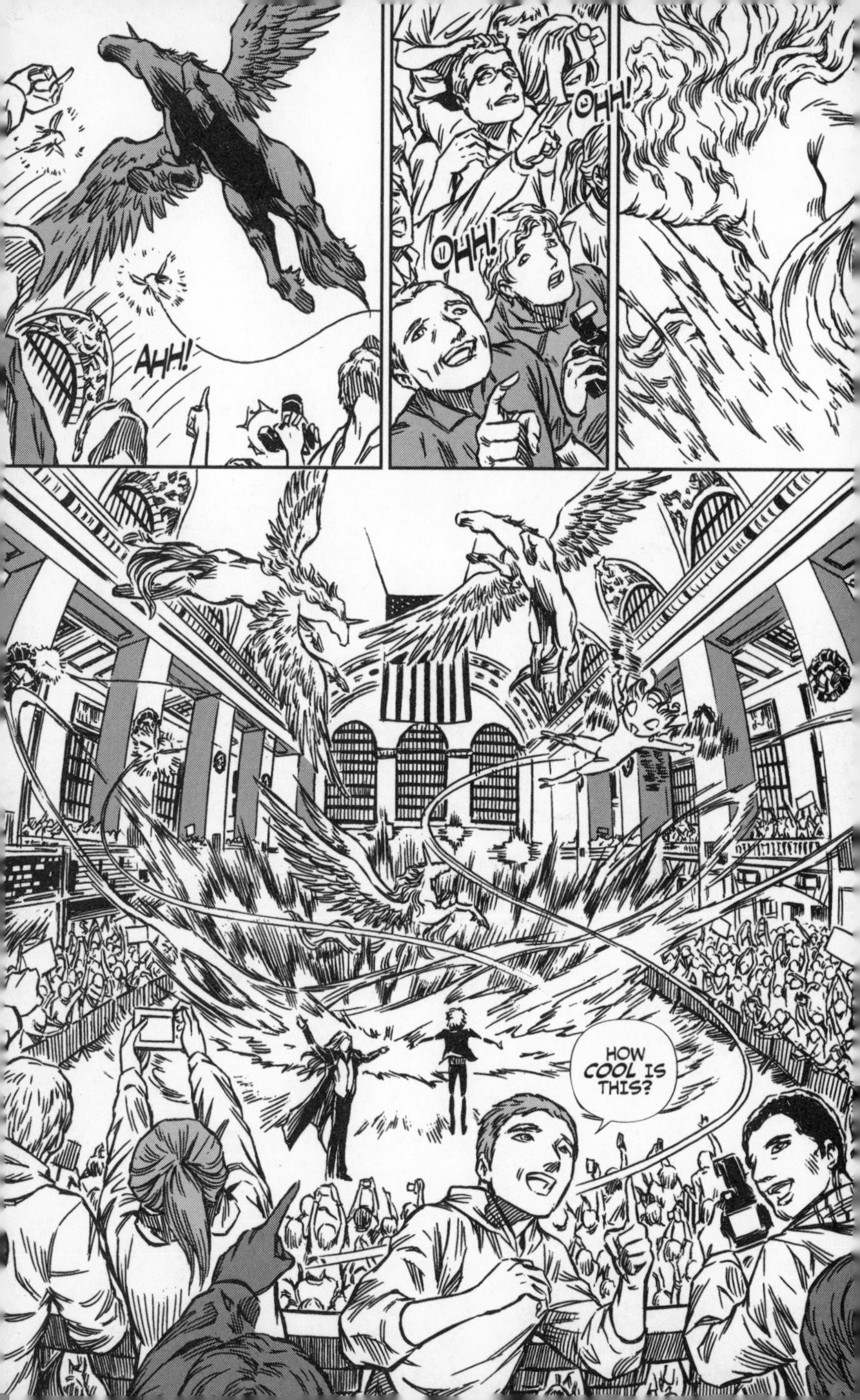
OHH!
OHH!
AHH!
HOW COOL IS THIS?

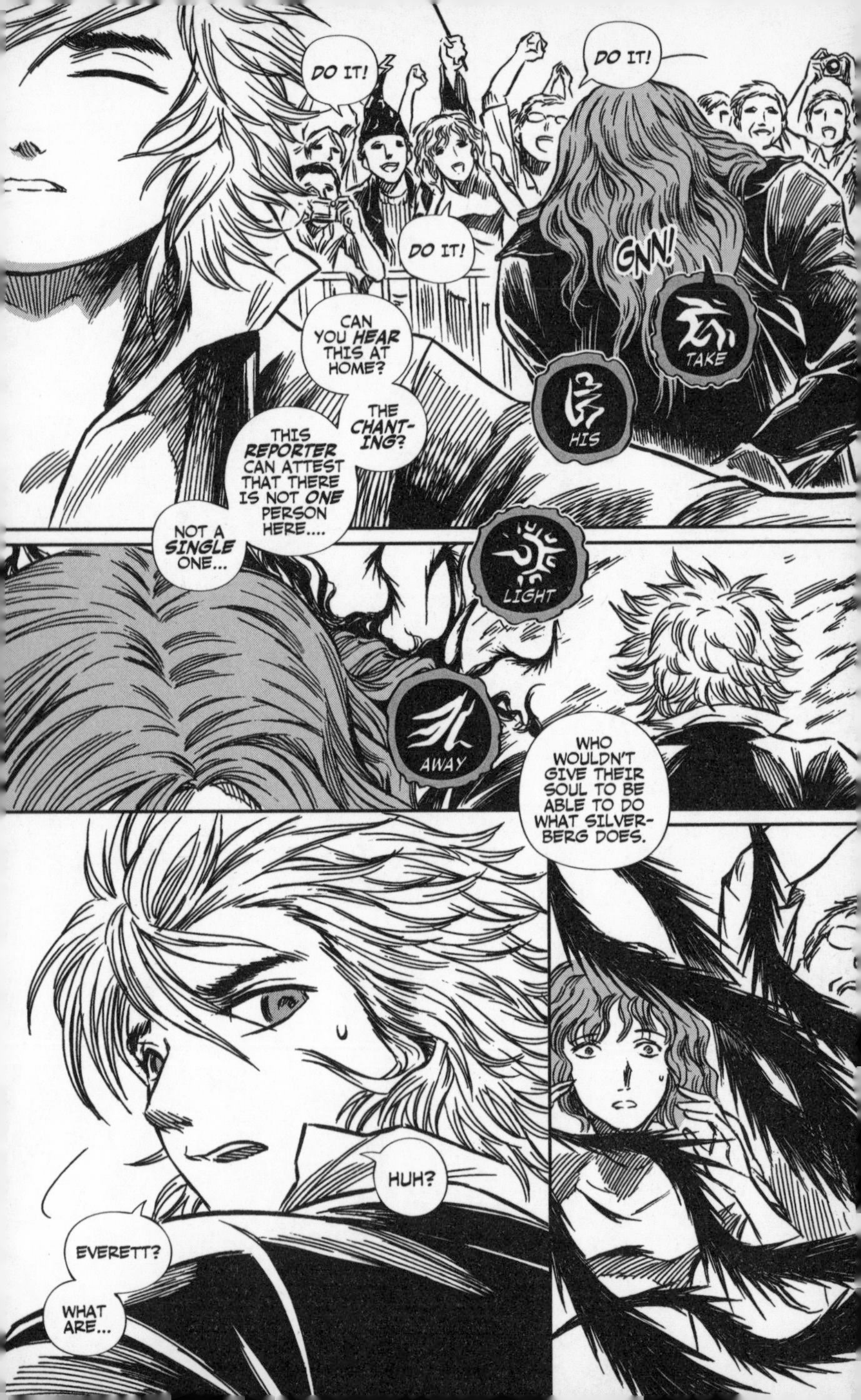
DO IT!
DO IT!
DO IT!
GNN!
TAKE
HIS
CAN YOU HEAR THIS AT HOME?
THE CHANTING?
THIS REPORTER CAN ATTEST THAT THERE IS NOT ONE PERSON HERE....
NOT A SINGLE ONE...
LIGHT
AWAY
WHO WOULDN'T GIVE THEIR SOUL TO BE ABLE TO DO WHAT SILVERBERG DOES.
HUH?
EVERETT?
WHAT ARE...

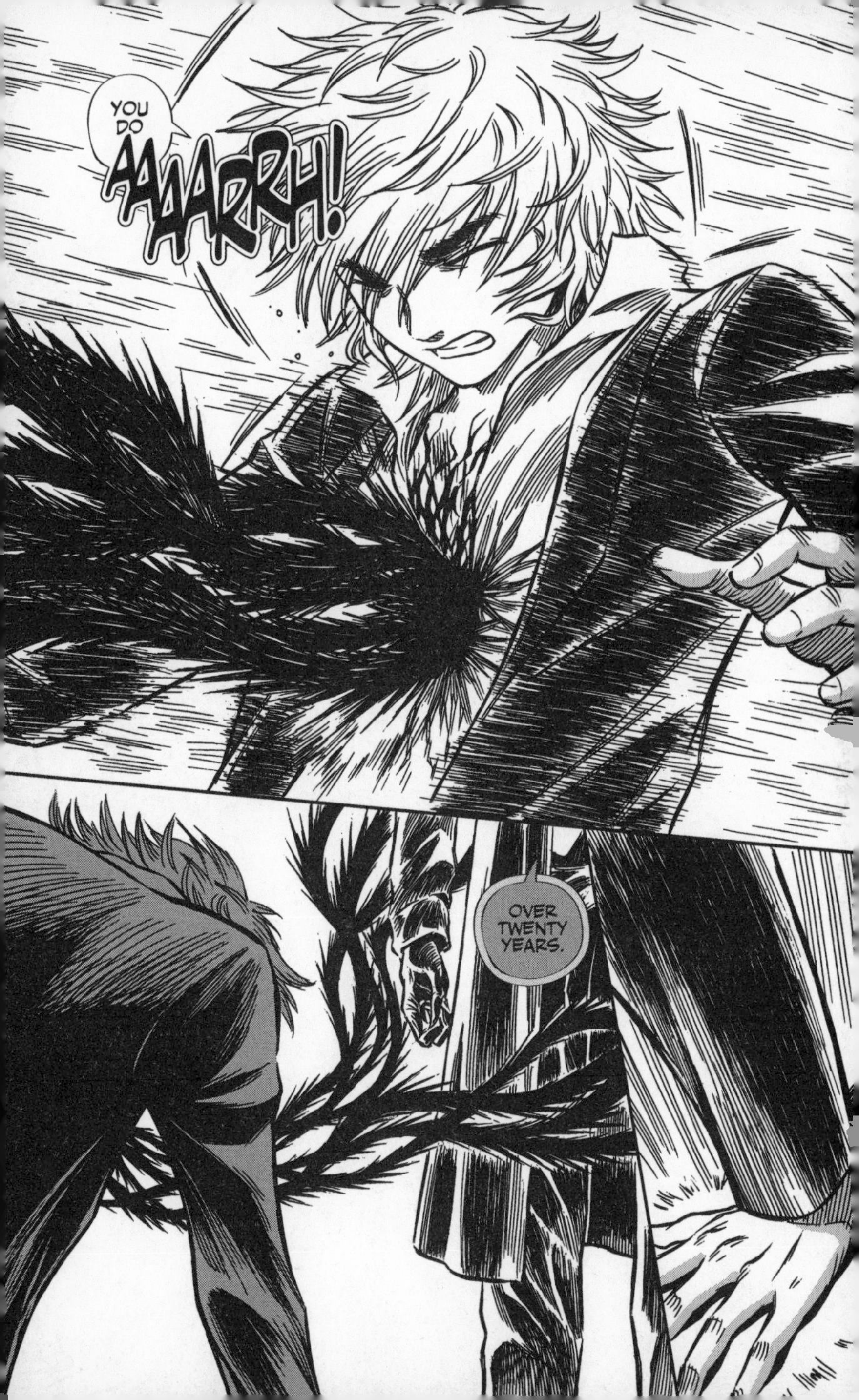
YOU DO
AAAARRH!
OVER TWENTY YEARS.

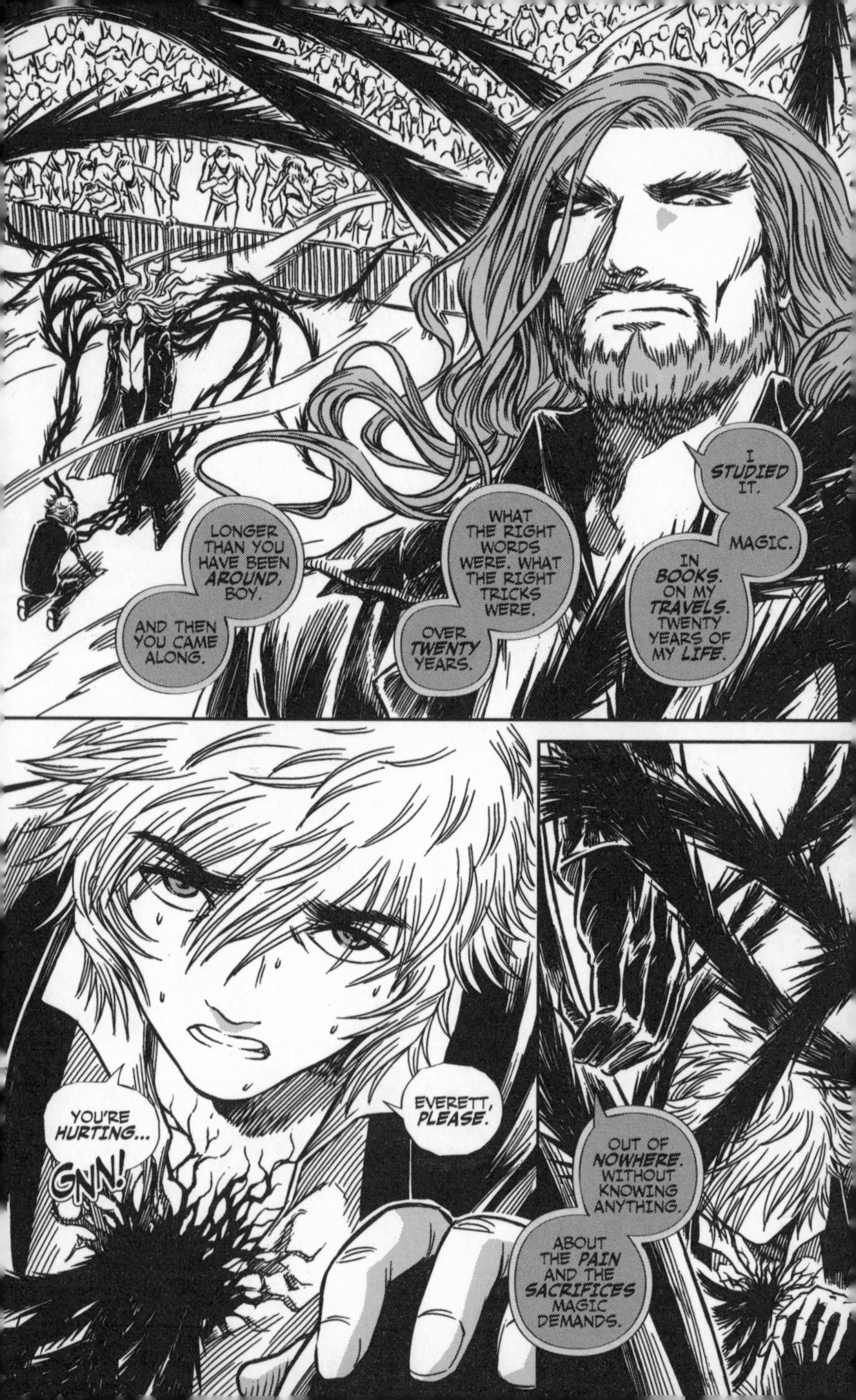
I STUDIED IT.
MAGIC.
IN BOOKS. ON MY TRAVELS. TWENTY YEARS OF MY LIFE.
WHAT THE RIGHT WORDS WERE. WHAT THE RIGHT TRICKS WERE.
OVER TWENTY YEARS.
LONGER THAN YOU HAVE BEEN AROUND, BOY.
AND THEN YOU CAME ALONG.
OUT OF NOWHERE. WITHOUT KNOWING ANYTHING.
ABOUT THE PAIN AND THE SACRIFICES MAGIC DEMANDS.
EVERETT, PLEASE.
YOU'RE HURTING...
GNN!

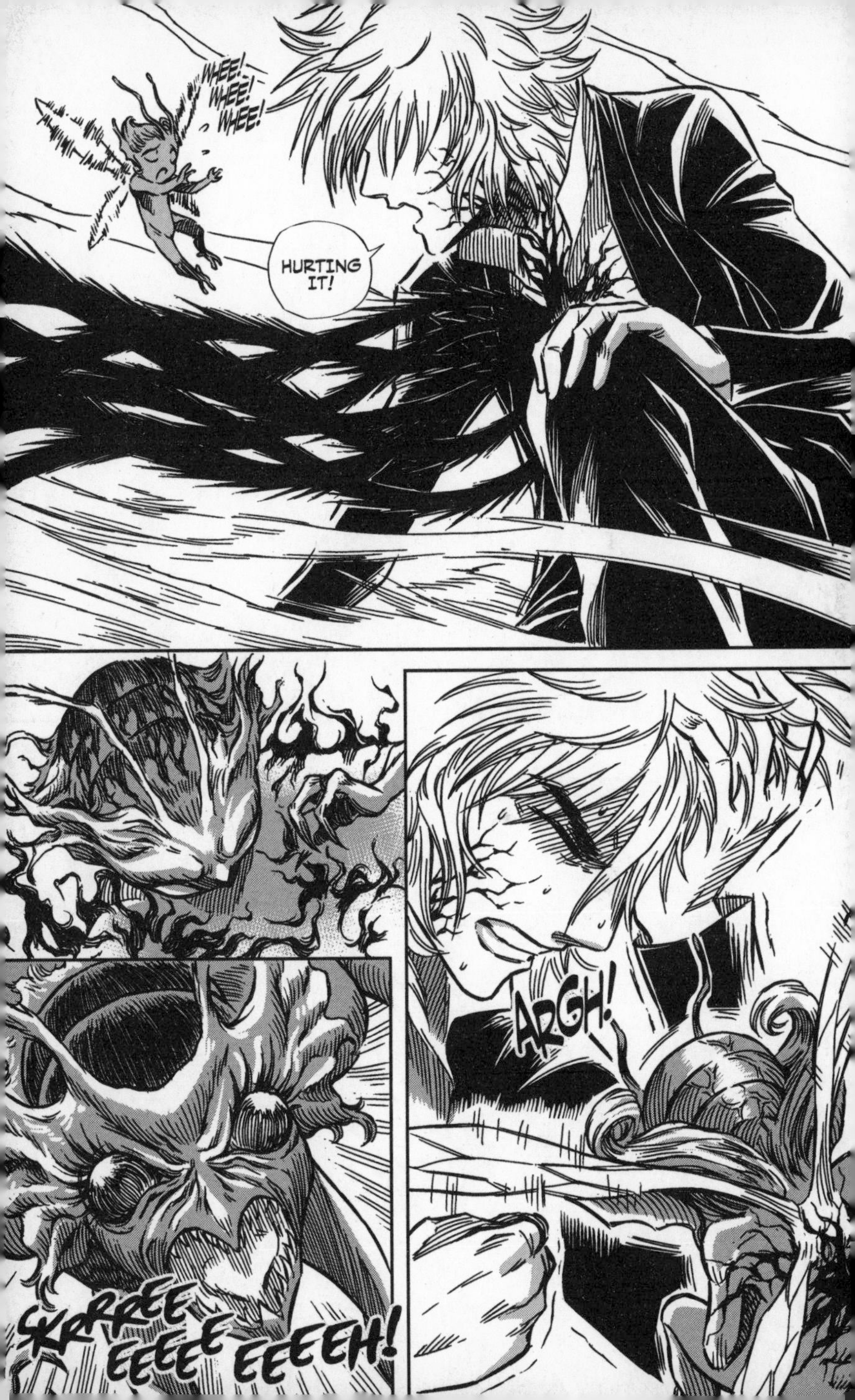
HURTING IT!
WHEE! WHEE! WHEE!
ARGH!
SKRREEE EEEEE EEEEEH!

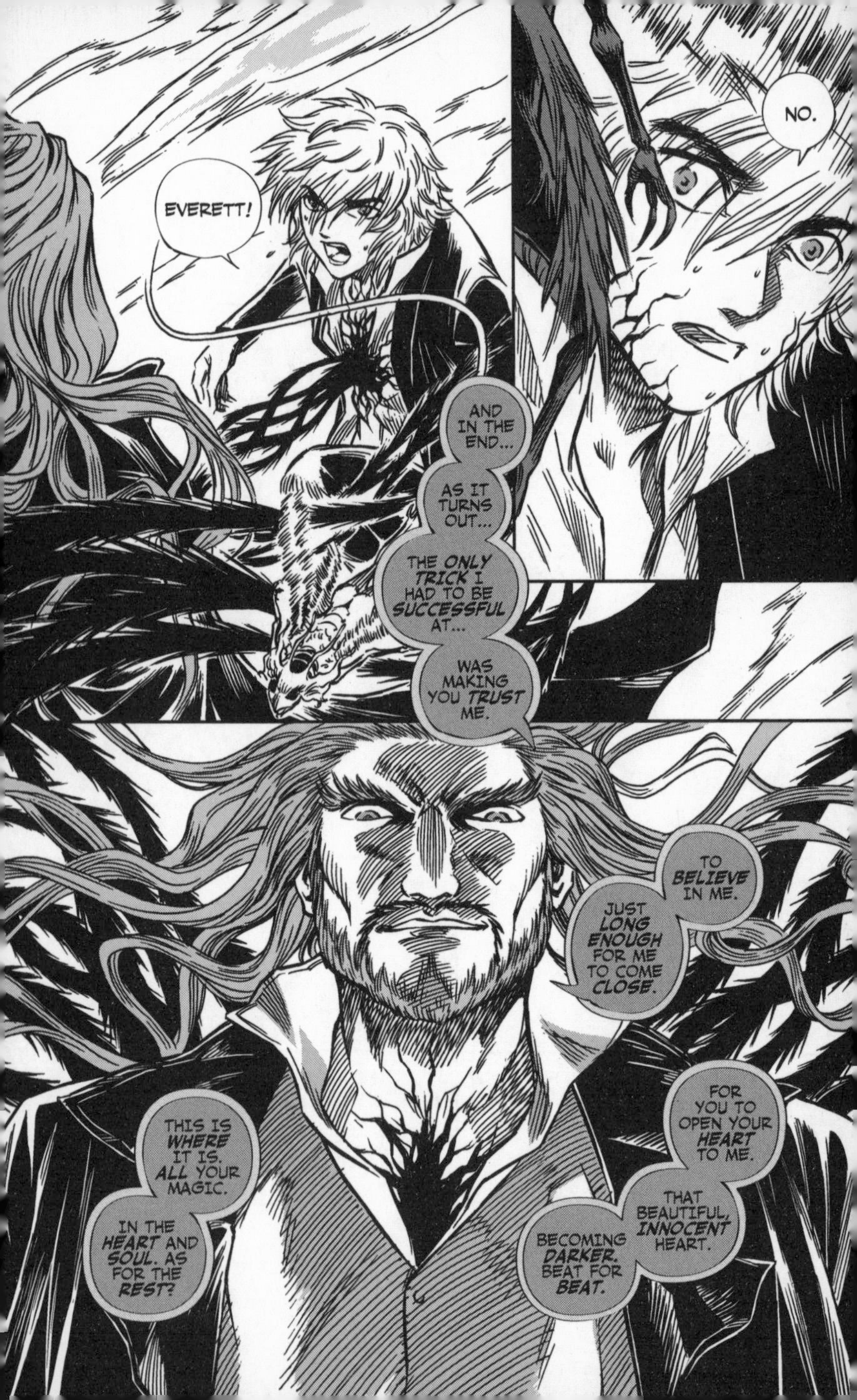
NO.
EVERETT!
AND IN THE END...
AS IT TURNS OUT...
THE ONLY TRICK I HAD TO BE SUCCESSFUL AT...
WAS MAKING YOU TRUST ME.
TO BELIEVE IN ME.
JUST LONG ENOUGH FOR ME TO COME CLOSE.
FOR YOU TO OPEN YOUR HEART TO ME.
THAT BEAUTIFUL, INNOCENT HEART.
BECOMING DARKER. BEAT FOR BEAT.
THIS IS WHERE IT IS. ALL YOUR MAGIC.
IN THE HEART AND SOUL. AS FOR THE REST?

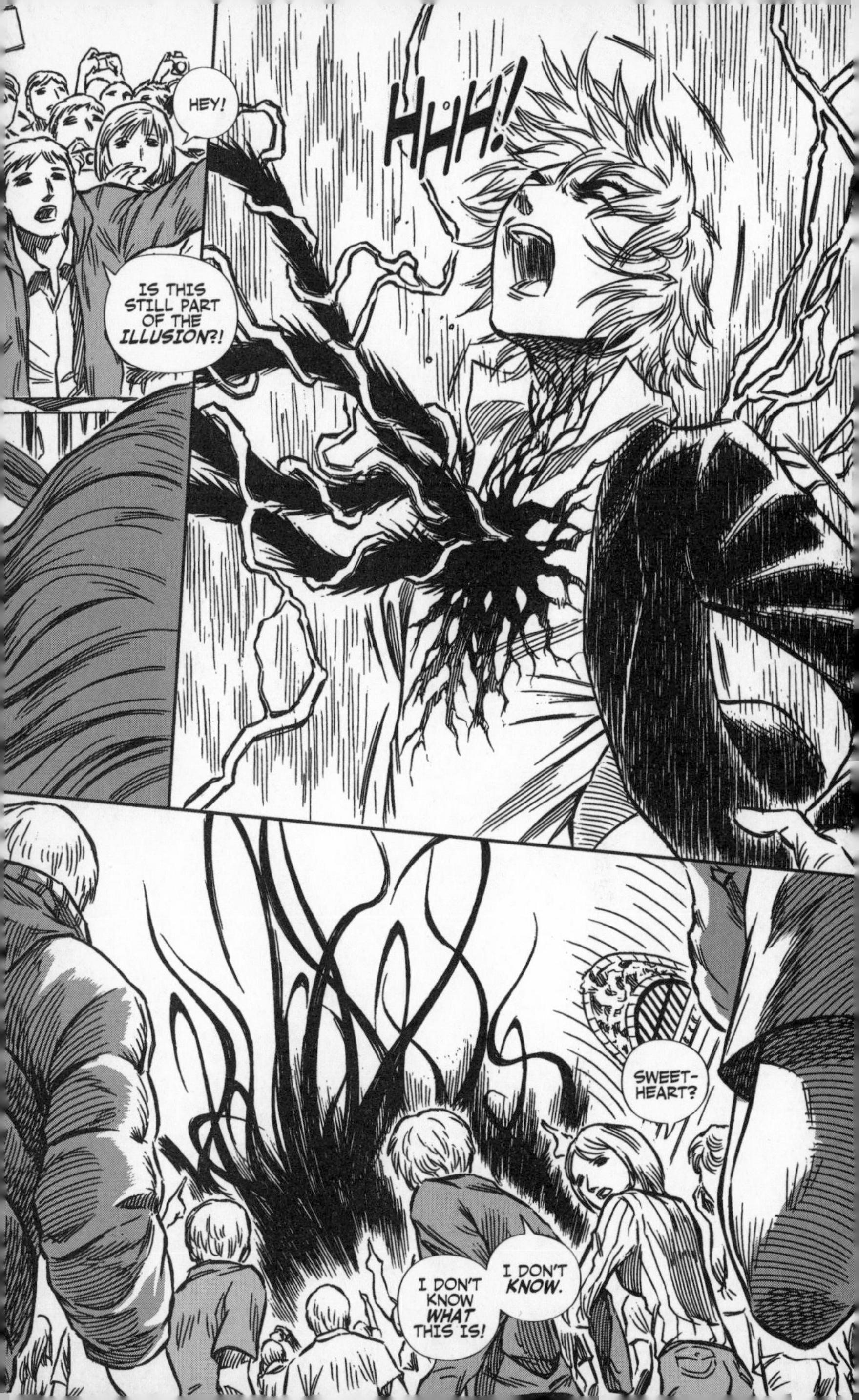
HHH!
HEY!
IS THIS STILL PART OF THE *ILLUSION*?!
SWEET-HEART?
I DON'T *KNOW*.
I DON'T KNOW *WHAT* THIS IS!

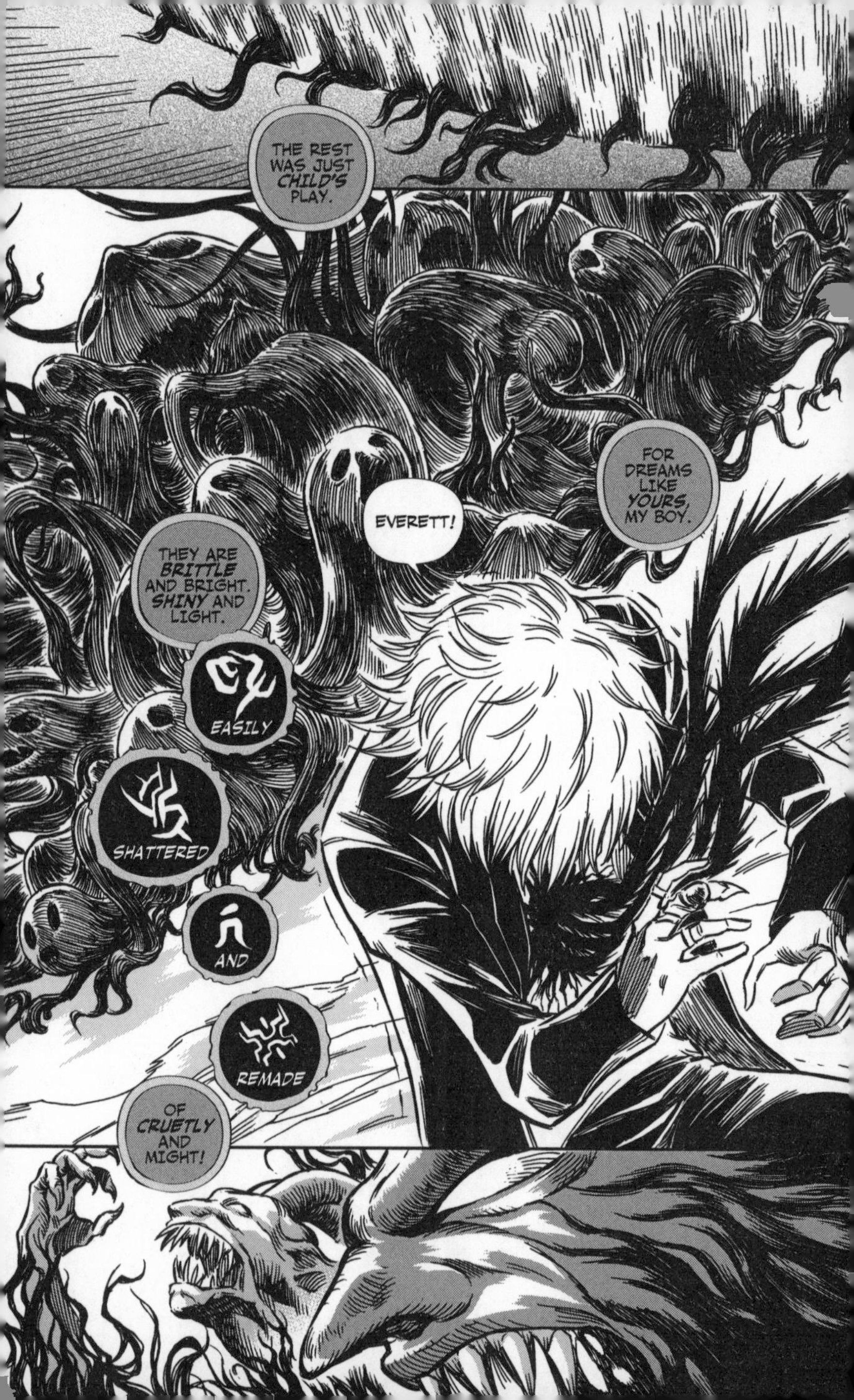
THE REST WAS JUST CHILD'S PLAY.
FOR DREAMS LIKE YOURS, MY BOY.
EVERETT!
THEY ARE BRITTLE AND BRIGHT. SHINY AND LIGHT.
EASILY
SHATTERED
AND
REMADE
OF CRUETLY AND MIGHT!

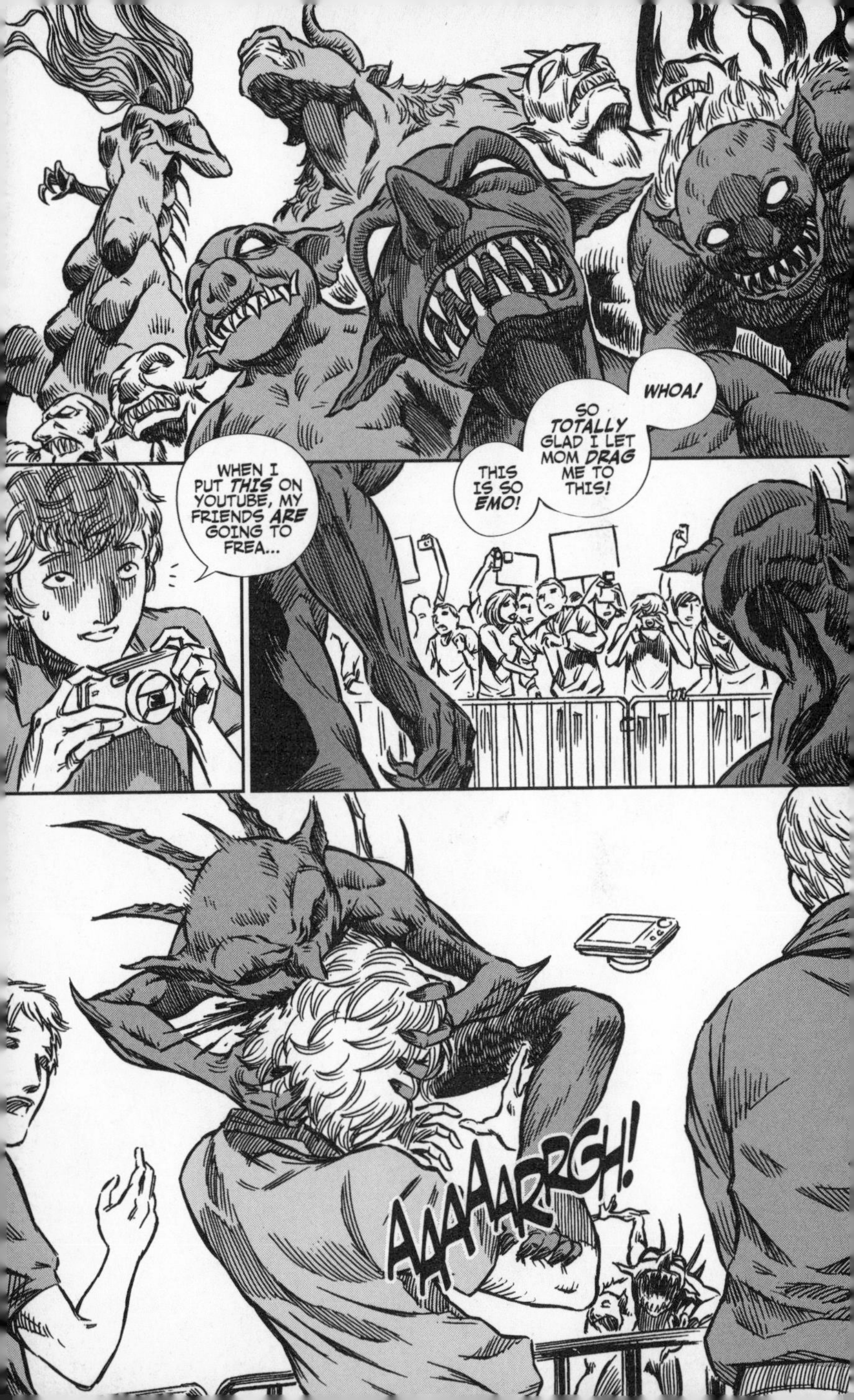
WHOA!
SO TOTALLY GLAD I LET MOM DRAG ME TO THIS!
THIS IS SO EMO!
WHEN I PUT THIS ON YOUTUBE, MY FRIENDS ARE GOING TO FREA...
AAAAARRGH!

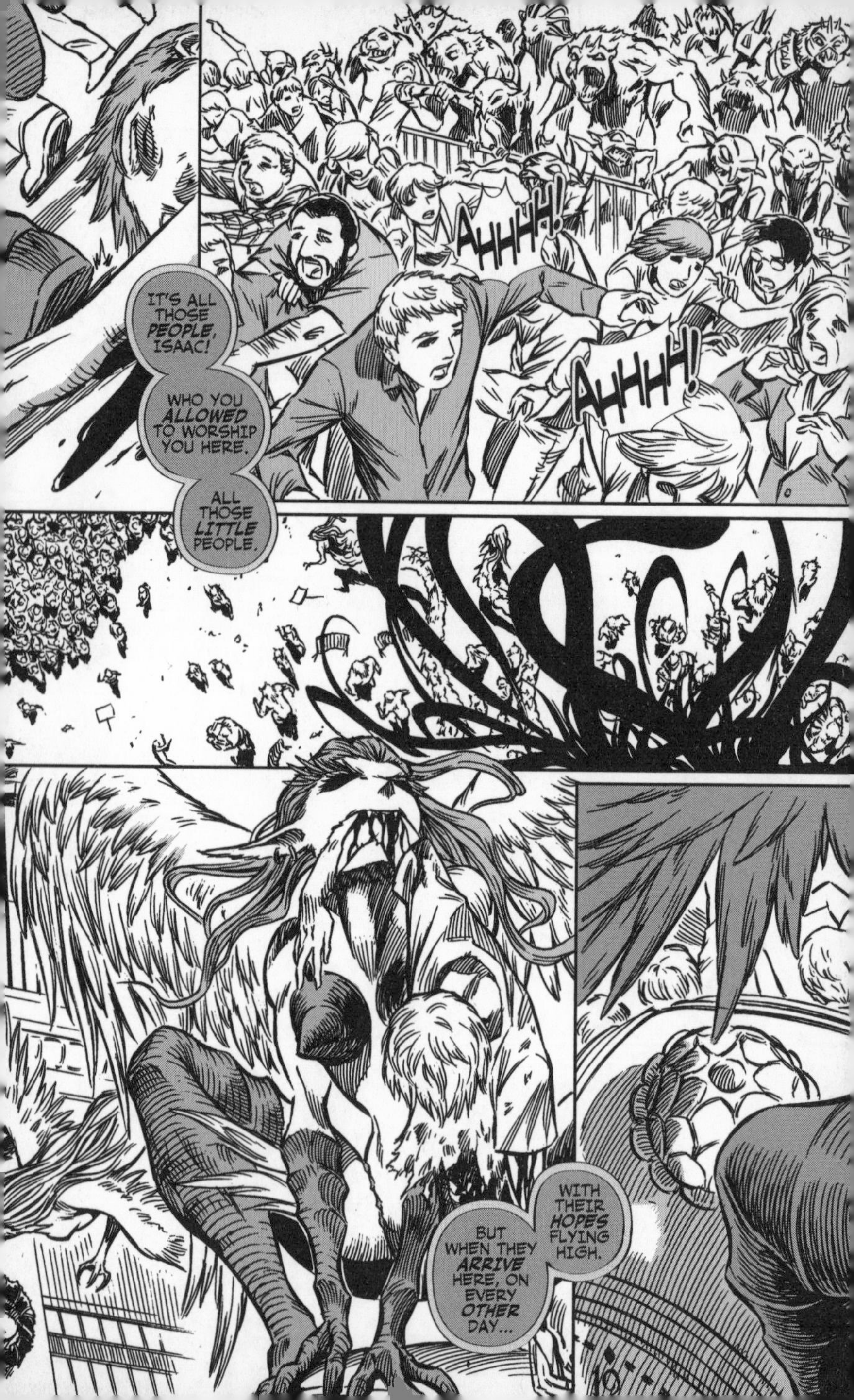
AHHHH!
IT'S ALL THOSE *PEOPLE*, ISAAC!
WHO YOU *ALLOWED* TO WORSHIP YOU HERE.
ALL THOSE *LITTLE* PEOPLE.
AHHHH!
WITH THEIR *HOPES* FLYING HIGH.
BUT WHEN THEY *ARRIVE* HERE, ON EVERY *OTHER* DAY...

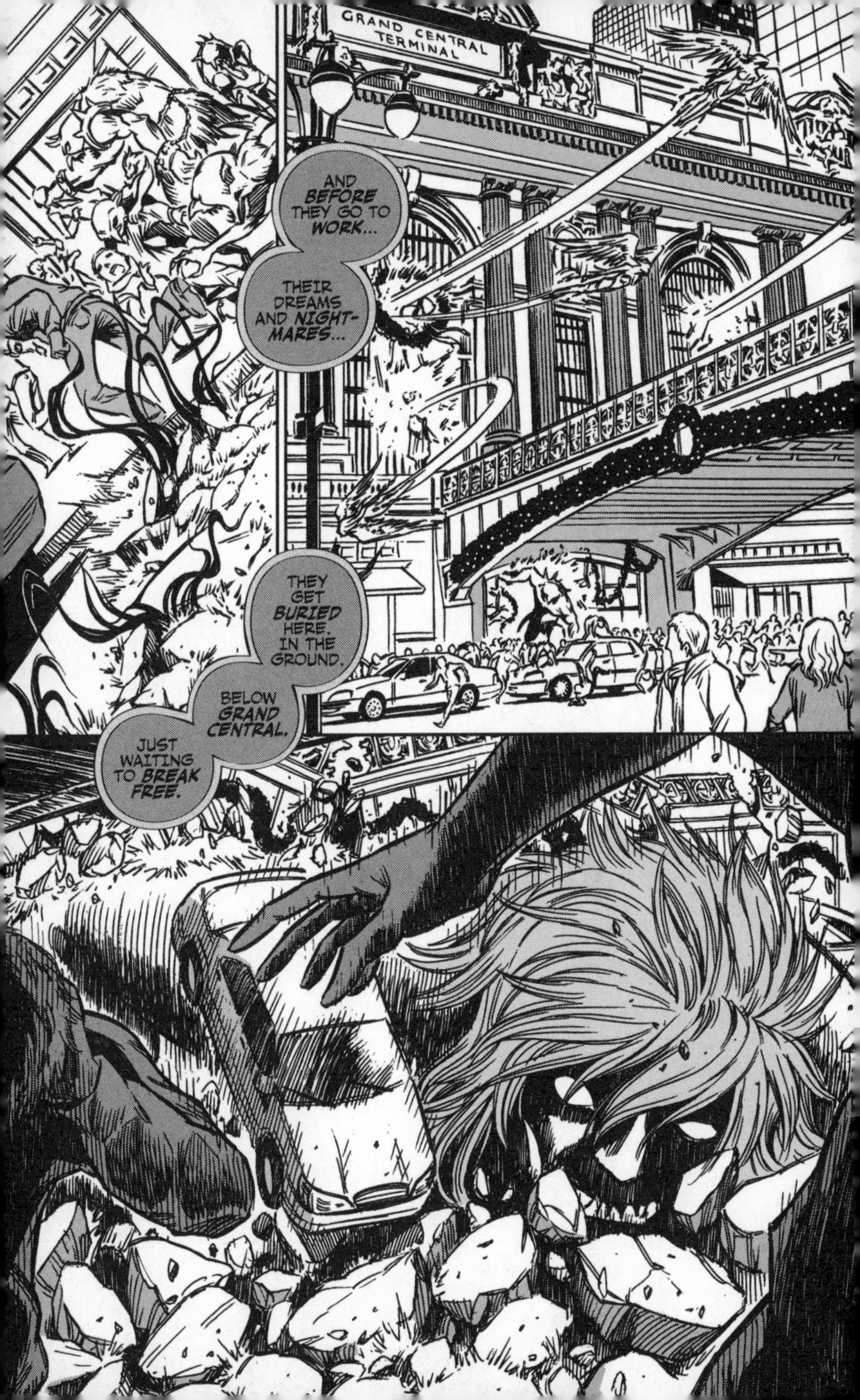
GRAND CENTRAL TERMINAL
AND BEFORE THEY GO TO WORK...
THEIR DREAMS AND NIGHT-MARES...
THEY GET BURIED HERE. IN THE GROUND.
BELOW GRAND CENTRAL.
JUST WAITING TO BREAK FREE.

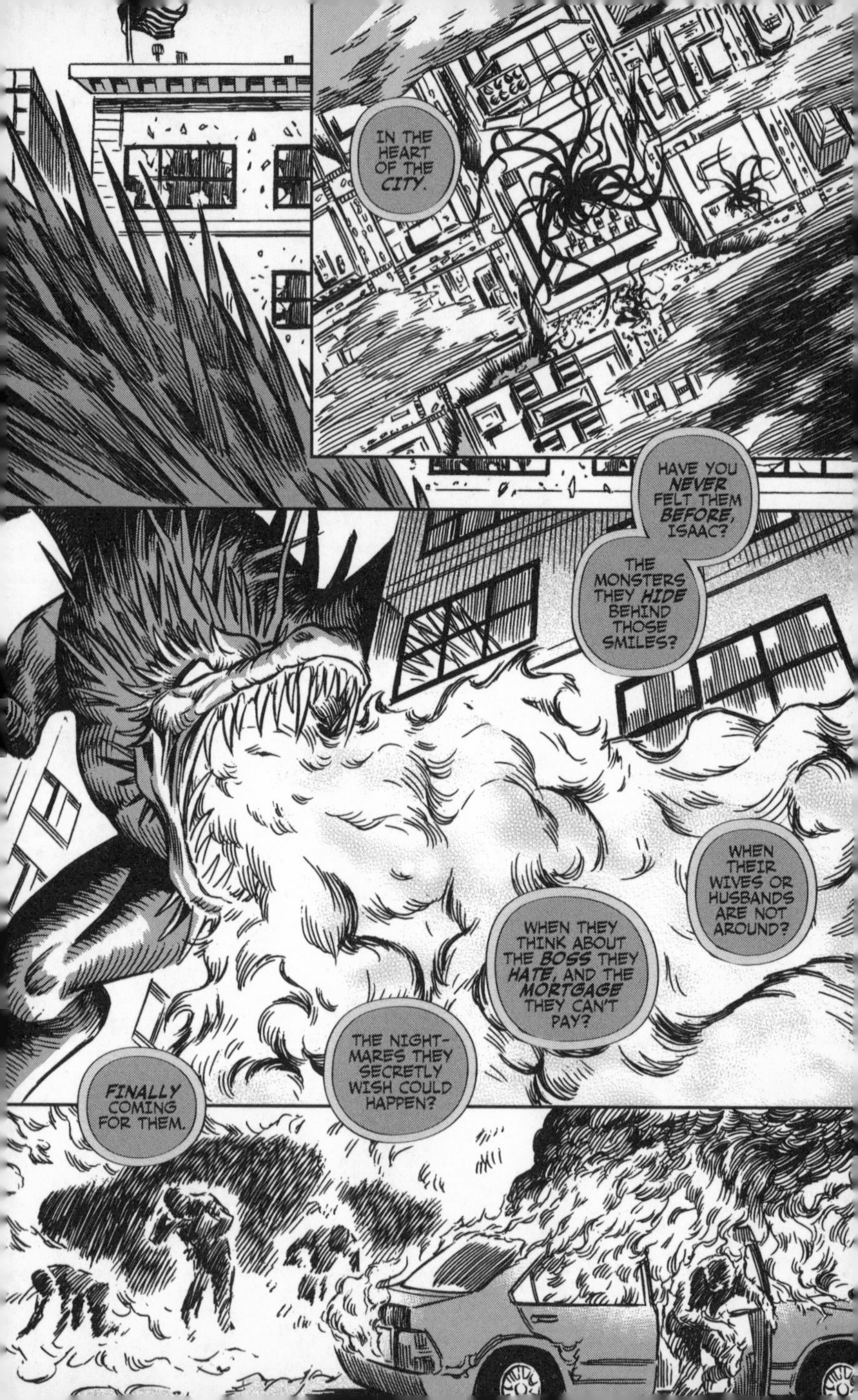
IN THE HEART OF THE *CITY*.
HAVE YOU *NEVER* FELT THEM *BEFORE*, ISAAC?
THE MONSTERS THEY *HIDE* BEHIND THOSE SMILES?
WHEN THEIR WIVES OR HUSBANDS ARE NOT AROUND?
WHEN THEY THINK ABOUT THE *BOSS* THEY *HATE*, AND THE *MORTGAGE* THEY CAN'T PAY?
THE NIGHT-MARES THEY SECRETLY WISH COULD HAPPEN?
FINALLY COMING FOR THEM.

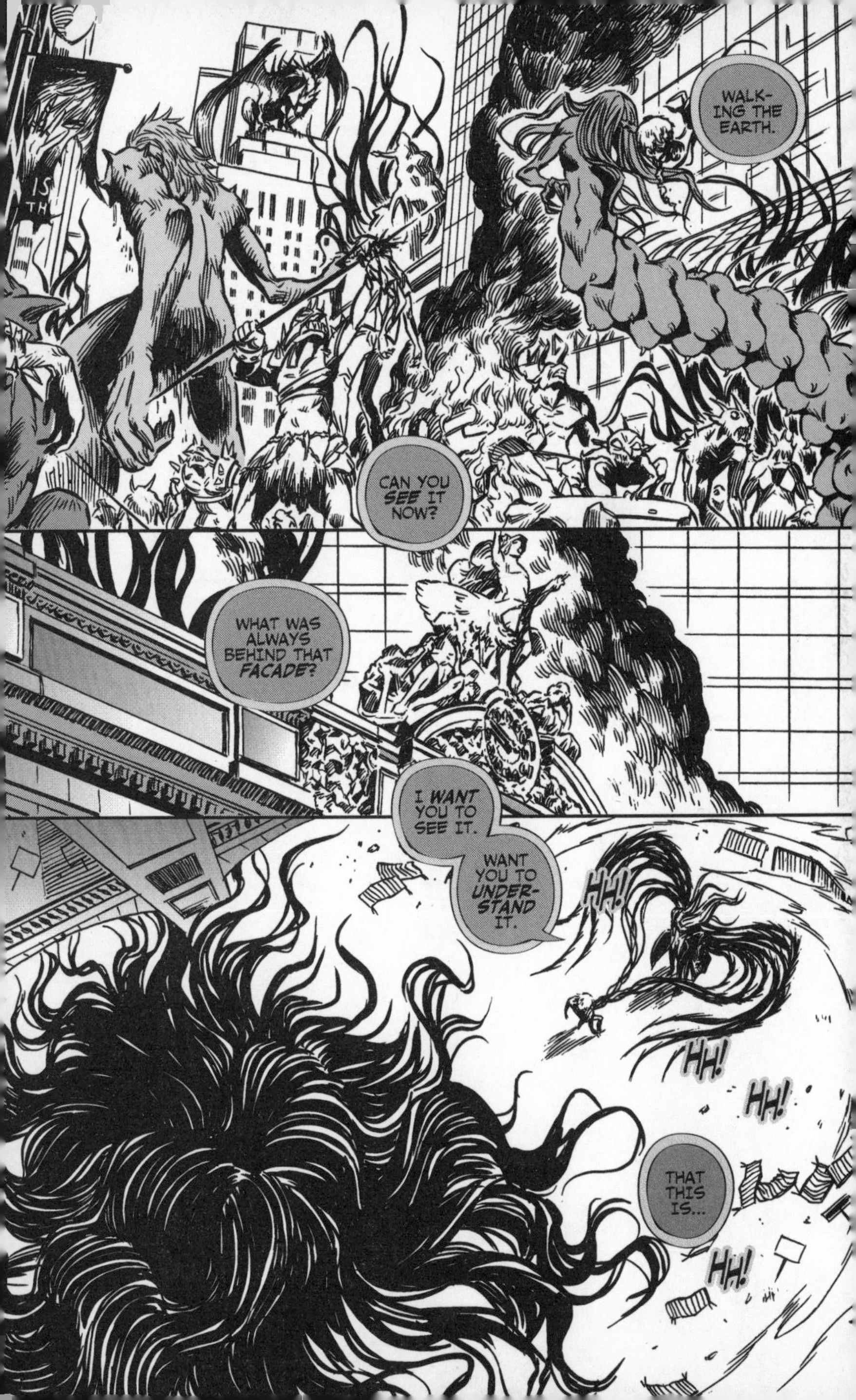
WALK-ING THE EARTH.
CAN YOU SEE IT NOW?
WHAT WAS ALWAYS BEHIND THAT FACADE?
I WANT YOU TO SEE IT.
WANT YOU TO UNDER-STAND IT.
HH!
HH!
HH!
THAT THIS IS...
HH!

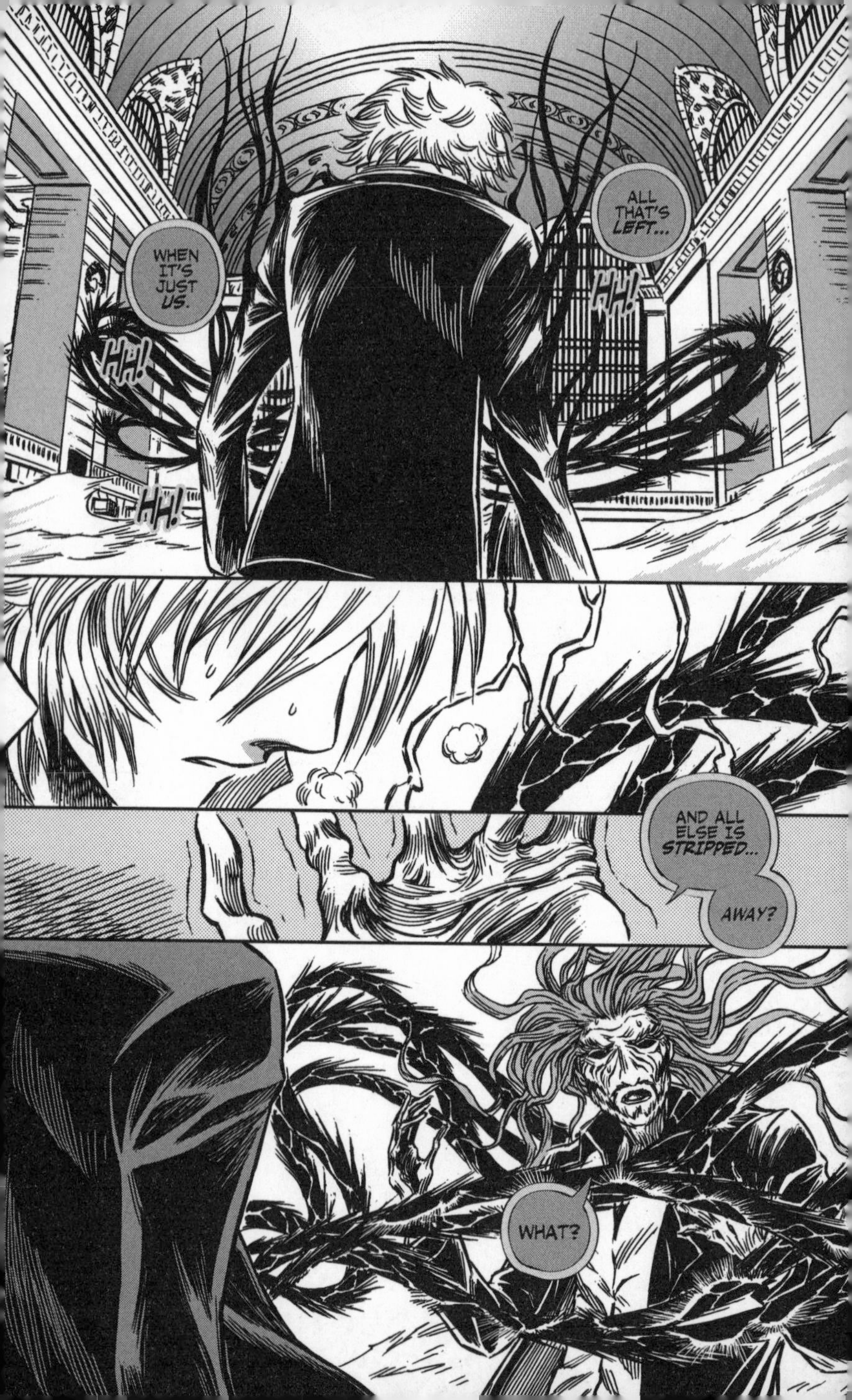
ALL THAT'S LEFT...
HH!
WHEN IT'S JUST US.
HH!
HH!
AND ALL ELSE IS STRIPPED...
AWAY?
WHAT?

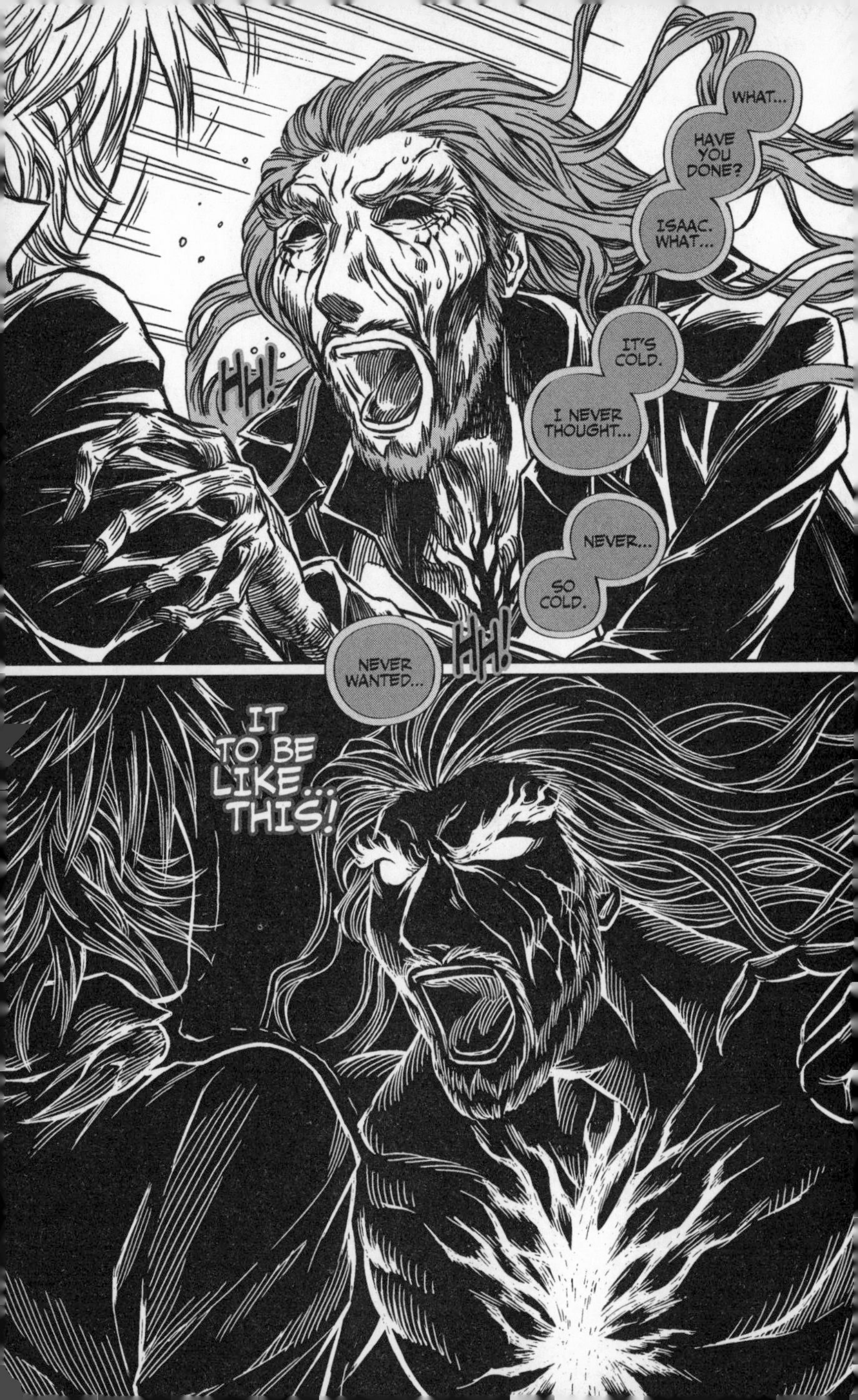
WHAT...
HAVE YOU DONE?
ISAAC. WHAT...
HH!
IT'S COLD.
I NEVER THOUGHT...
NEVER...
SO COLD.
HH!
NEVER WANTED...
IT TO BE LIKE... THIS!

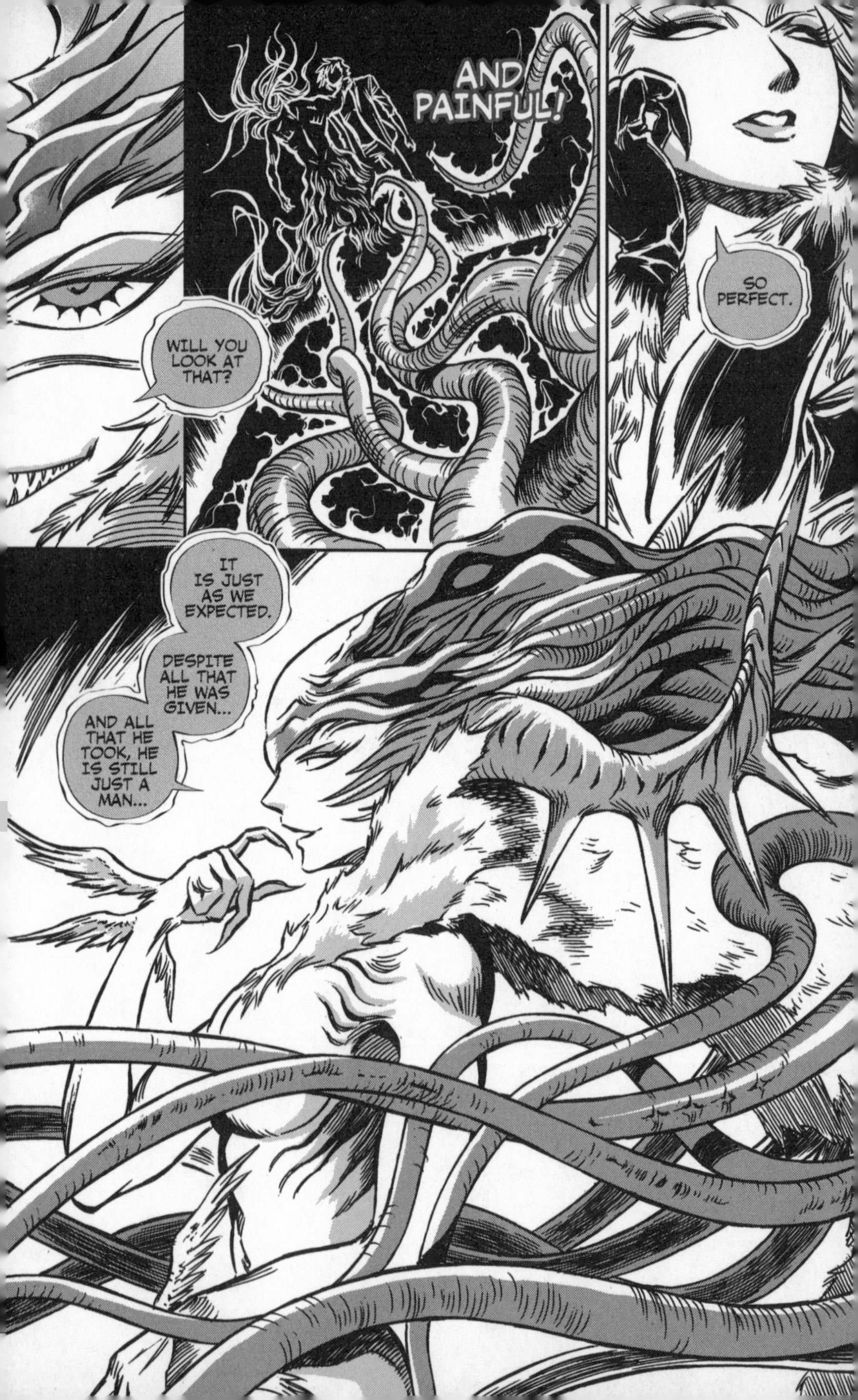
SO PERFECT.
AND PAINFUL!
WILL YOU LOOK AT THAT?
IT IS JUST AS WE EXPECTED.
DESPITE ALL THAT HE WAS GIVEN...
AND ALL THAT HE TOOK, HE IS STILL JUST A MAN...

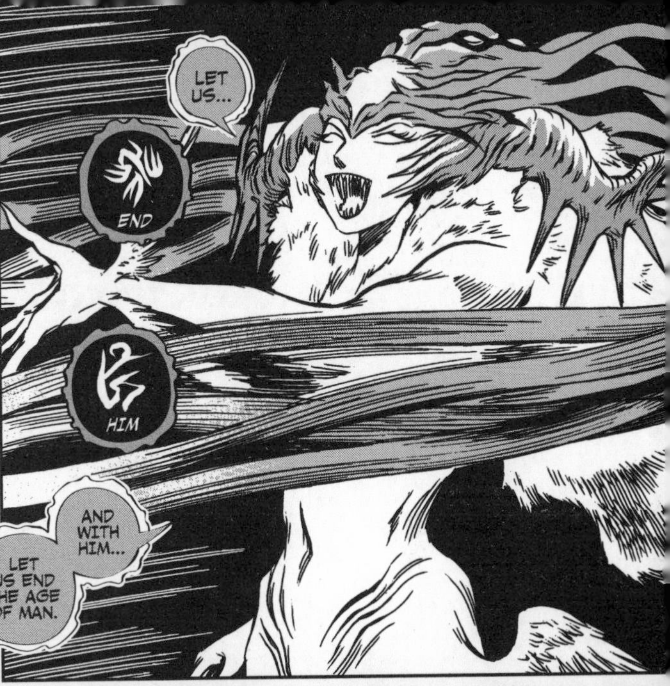
LET US...
END
HIM
AND WITH HIM...
LET US END THE AGE OF MAN.
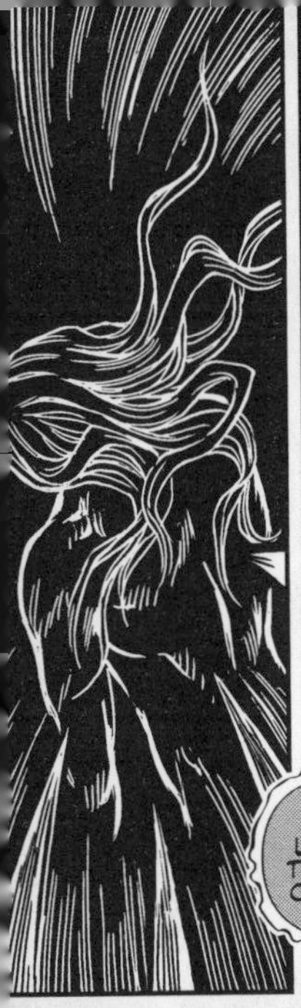
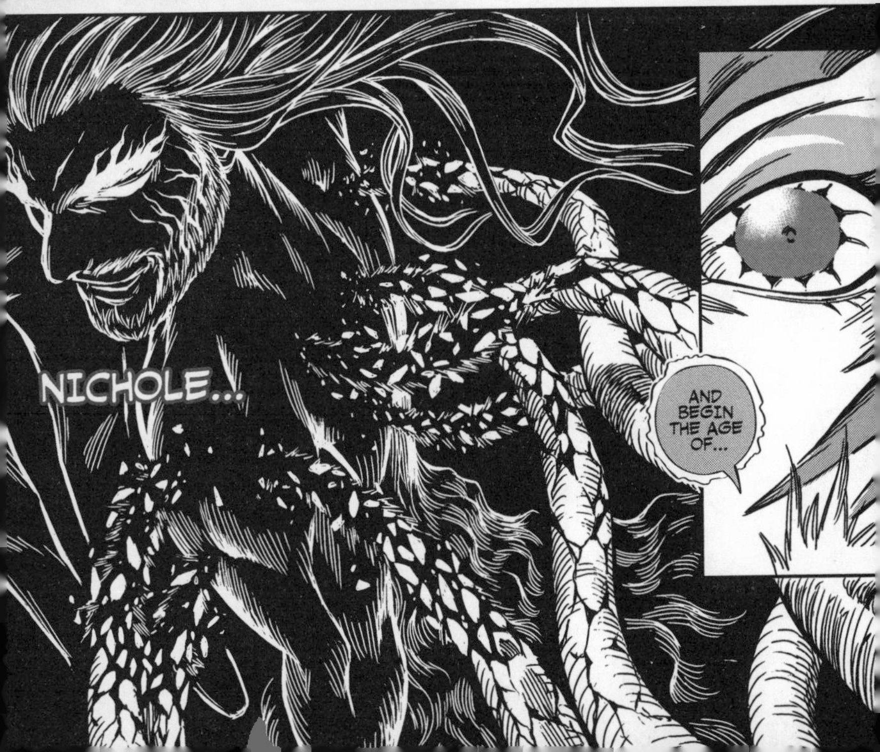
AND BEGIN THE AGE OF...
NICHOLE...

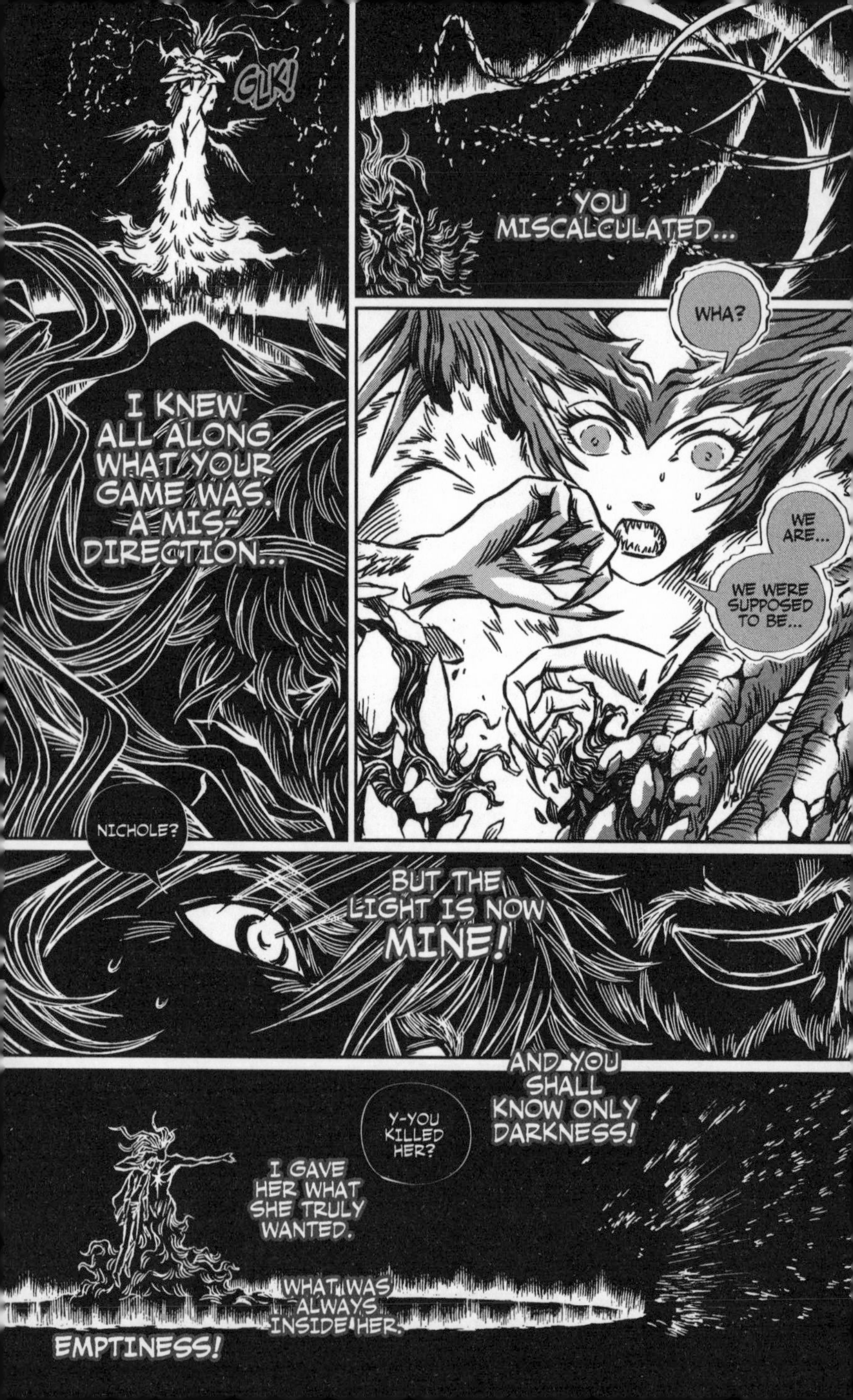
YOU MISCALCULATED...
WHA?
WE ARE...
WE WERE SUPPOSED TO BE...
GLK!
I KNEW ALL ALONG WHAT YOUR GAME WAS. A MIS-DIRECTION...
NICHOLE?
BUT THE LIGHT IS NOW MINE!
AND YOU SHALL KNOW ONLY DARKNESS!
Y-YOU KILLED HER?
I GAVE HER WHAT SHE TRULY WANTED.
WHAT WAS ALWAYS INSIDE HER.
EMPTINESS!

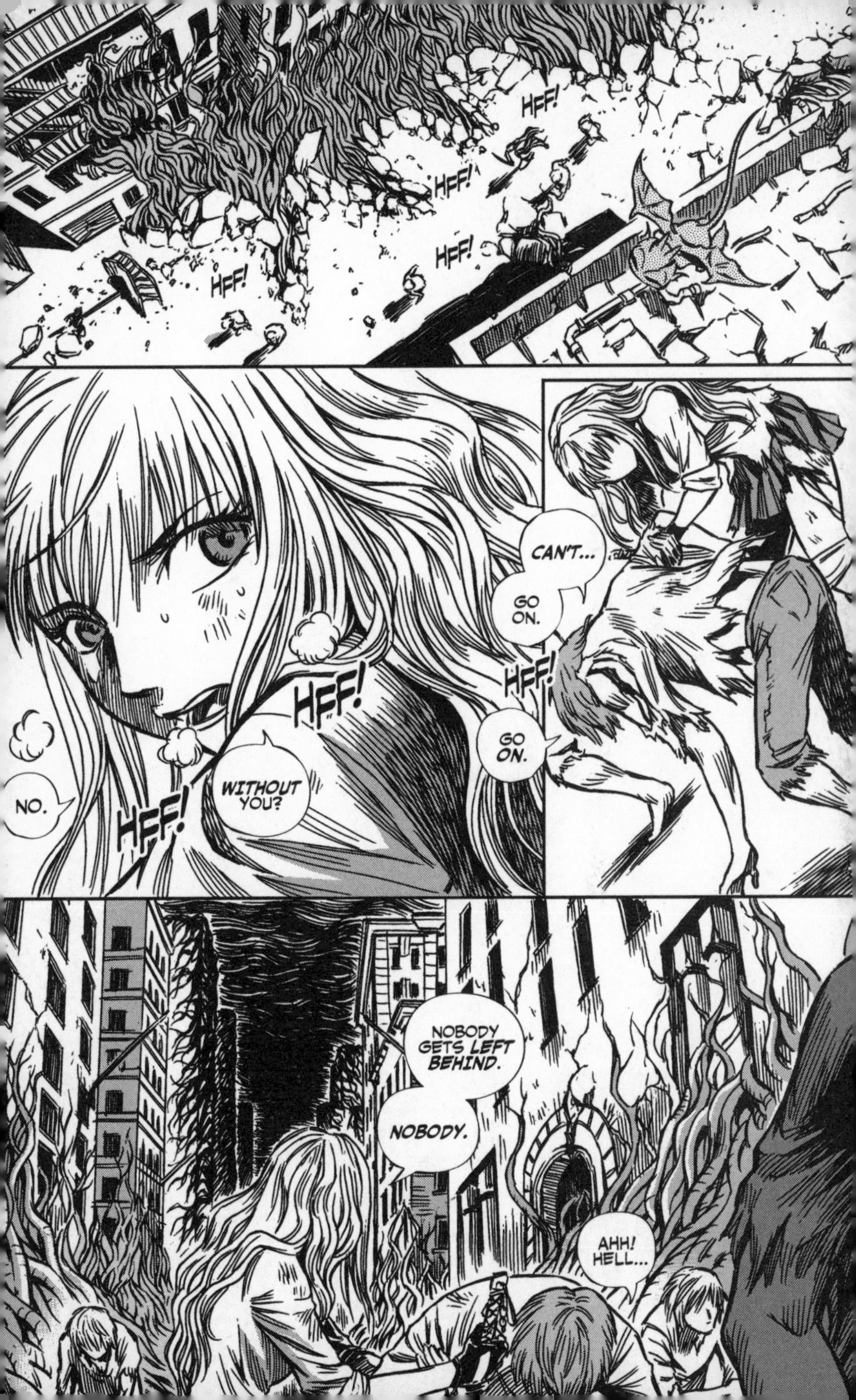
HFF!
HFF!
HFF!
HFF!
CAN'T...
GO ON.
HFF!
GO ON.
HFF!
WITHOUT YOU?
HFF!
NO.
NOBODY GETS LEFT BEHIND.
NOBODY.
AHH! HELL...

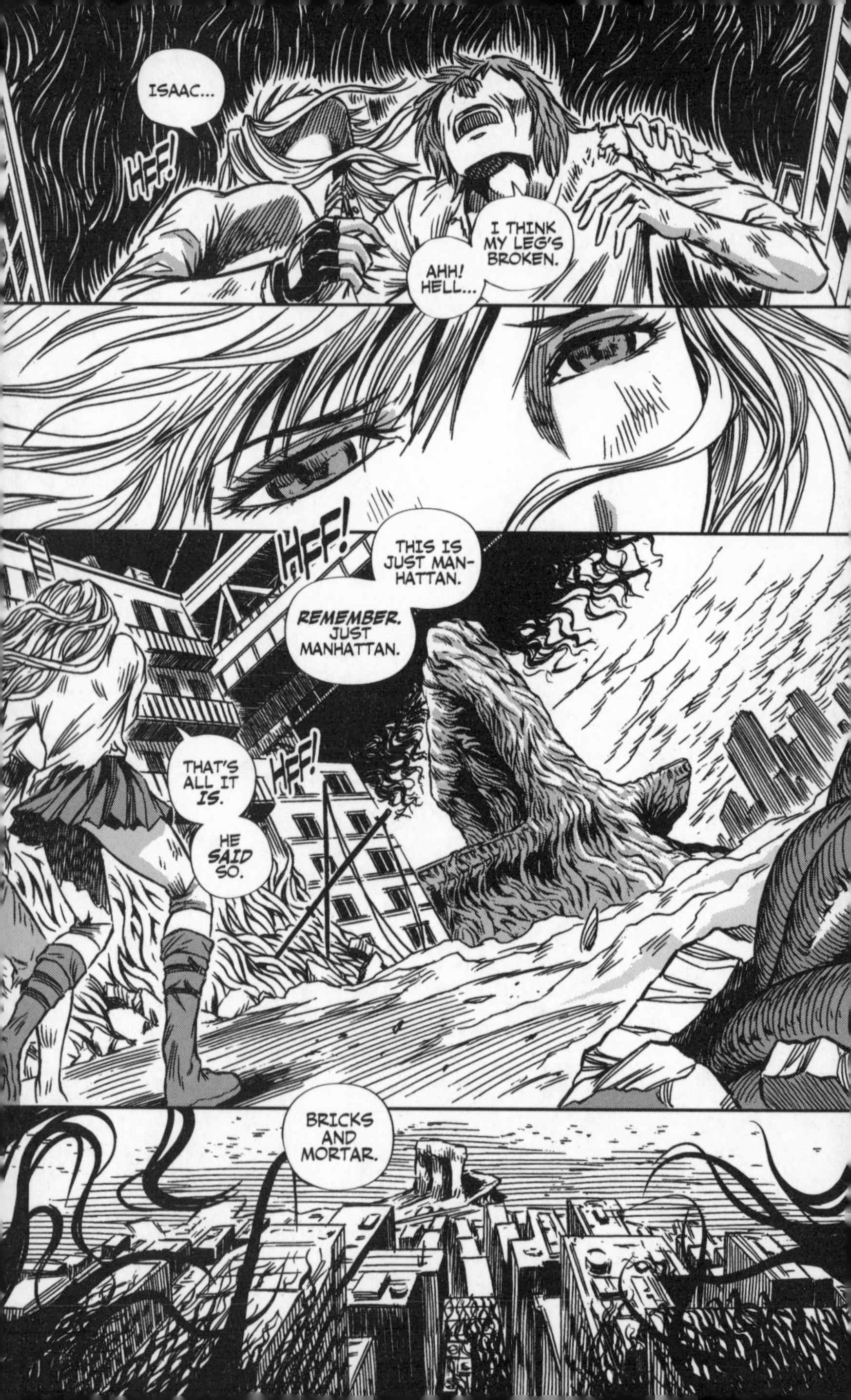
ISAAC...
HFF!
I THINK MY LEG'S BROKEN.
AHH! HELL...
HFF!
THIS IS JUST MAN-HATTAN.
REMEMBER. JUST MANHATTAN.
THAT'S ALL IT *IS.*
HFF!
HE *SAID* SO.
BRICKS AND MORTAR.

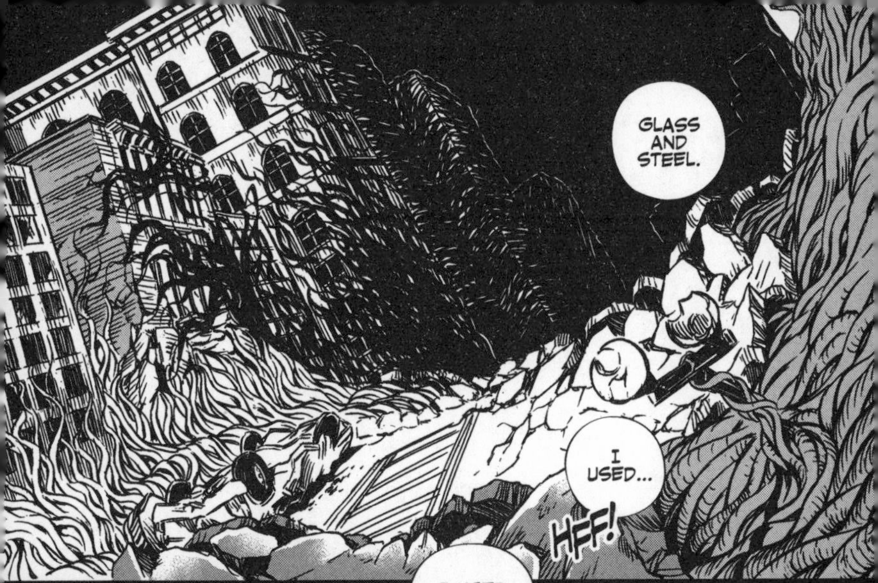
GLASS AND STEEL.
I USED...
HFF!
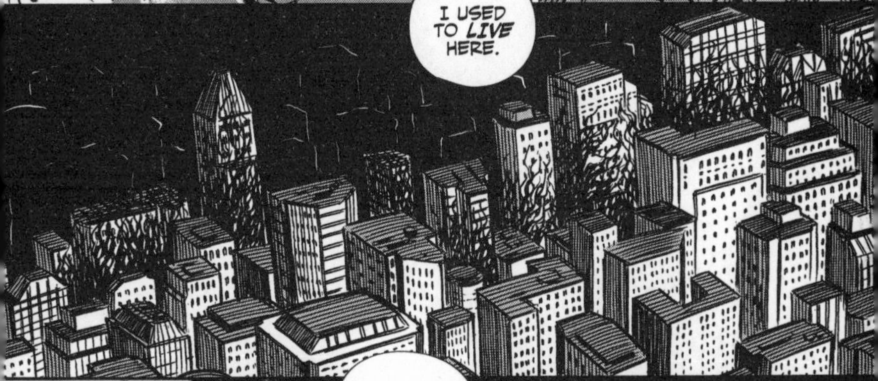
I USED TO *LIVE* HERE.
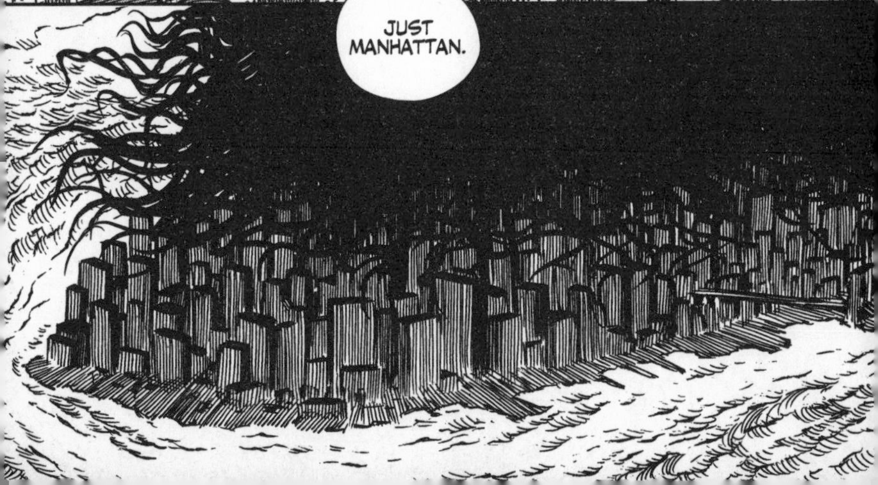
JUST MANHATTAN.

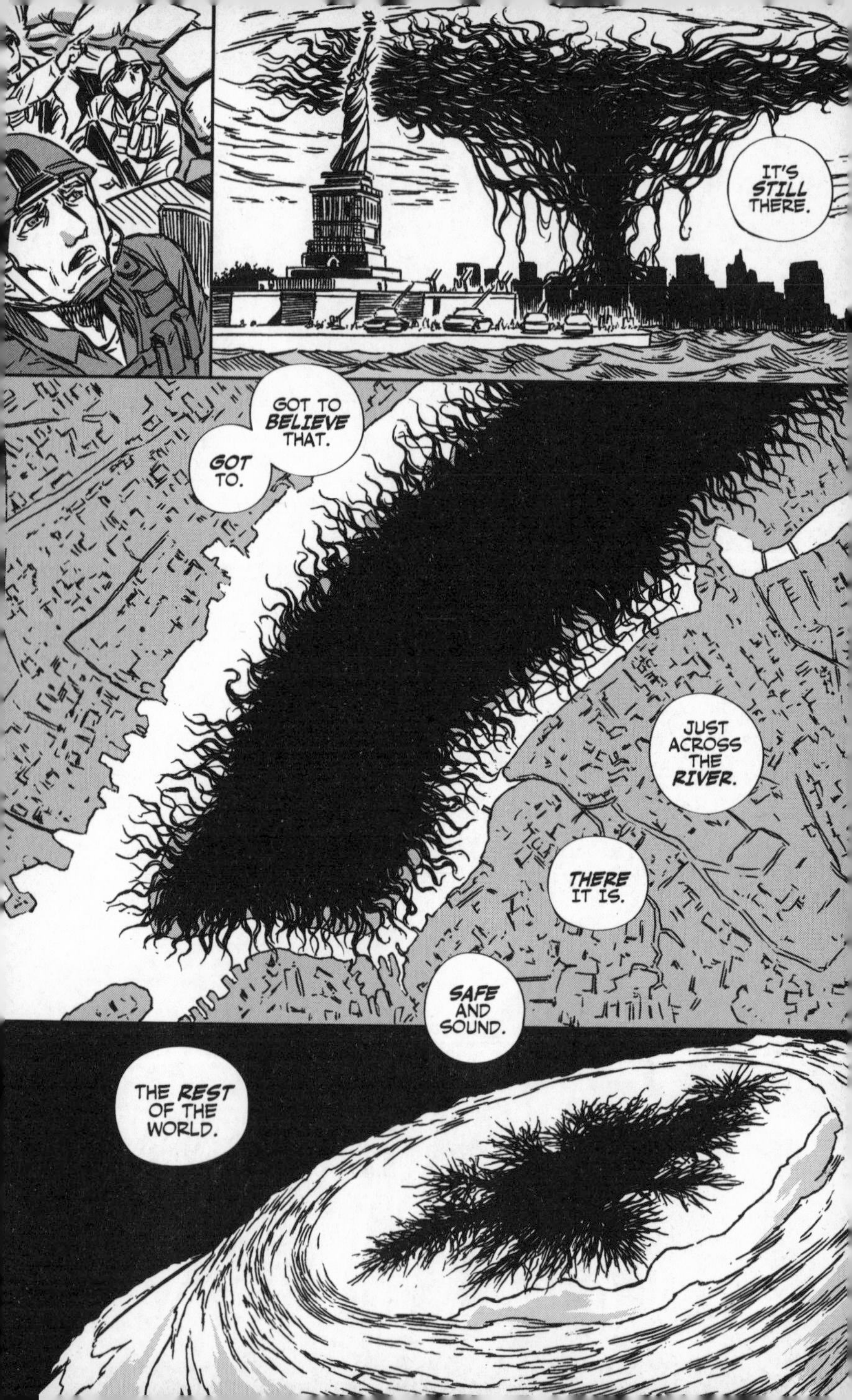
IT'S STILL THERE.
GOT TO BELIEVE THAT.
GOT TO.
JUST ACROSS THE RIVER.
THERE IT IS.
SAFE AND SOUND.
THE REST OF THE WORLD.

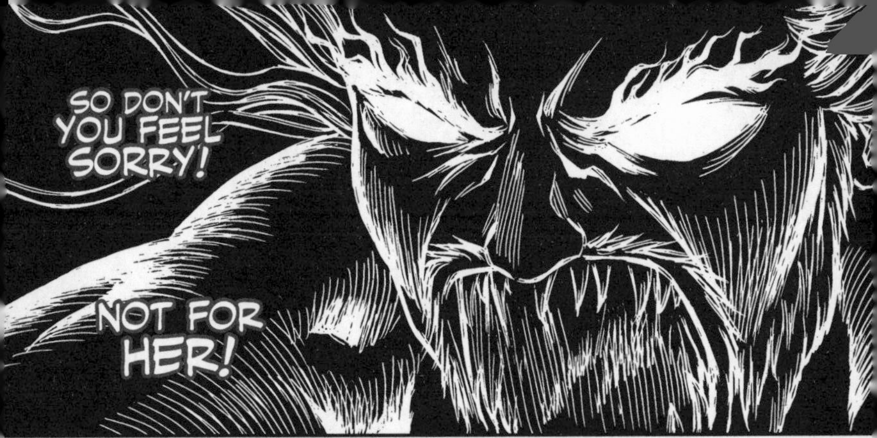
SO DON'T YOU FEEL SORRY!
NOT FOR HER!

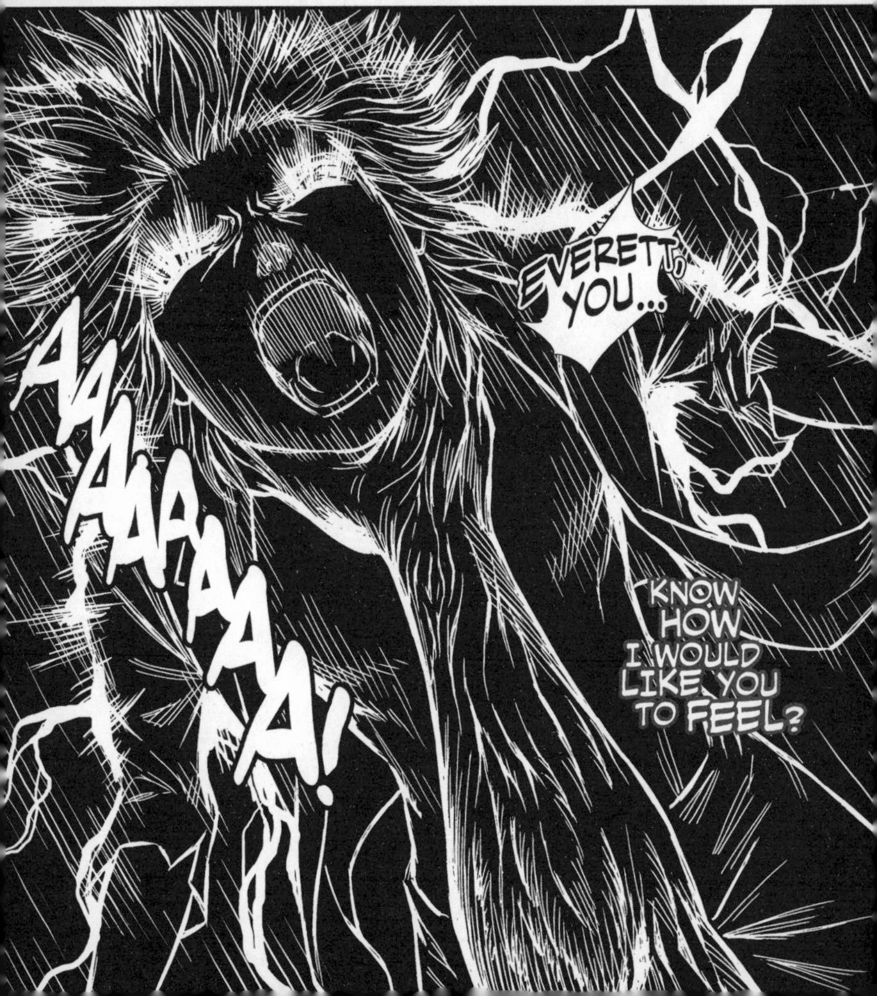
EVERETT, YOU...
KNOW HOW I WOULD LIKE YOU TO FEEL?
AAAAAAAAA!

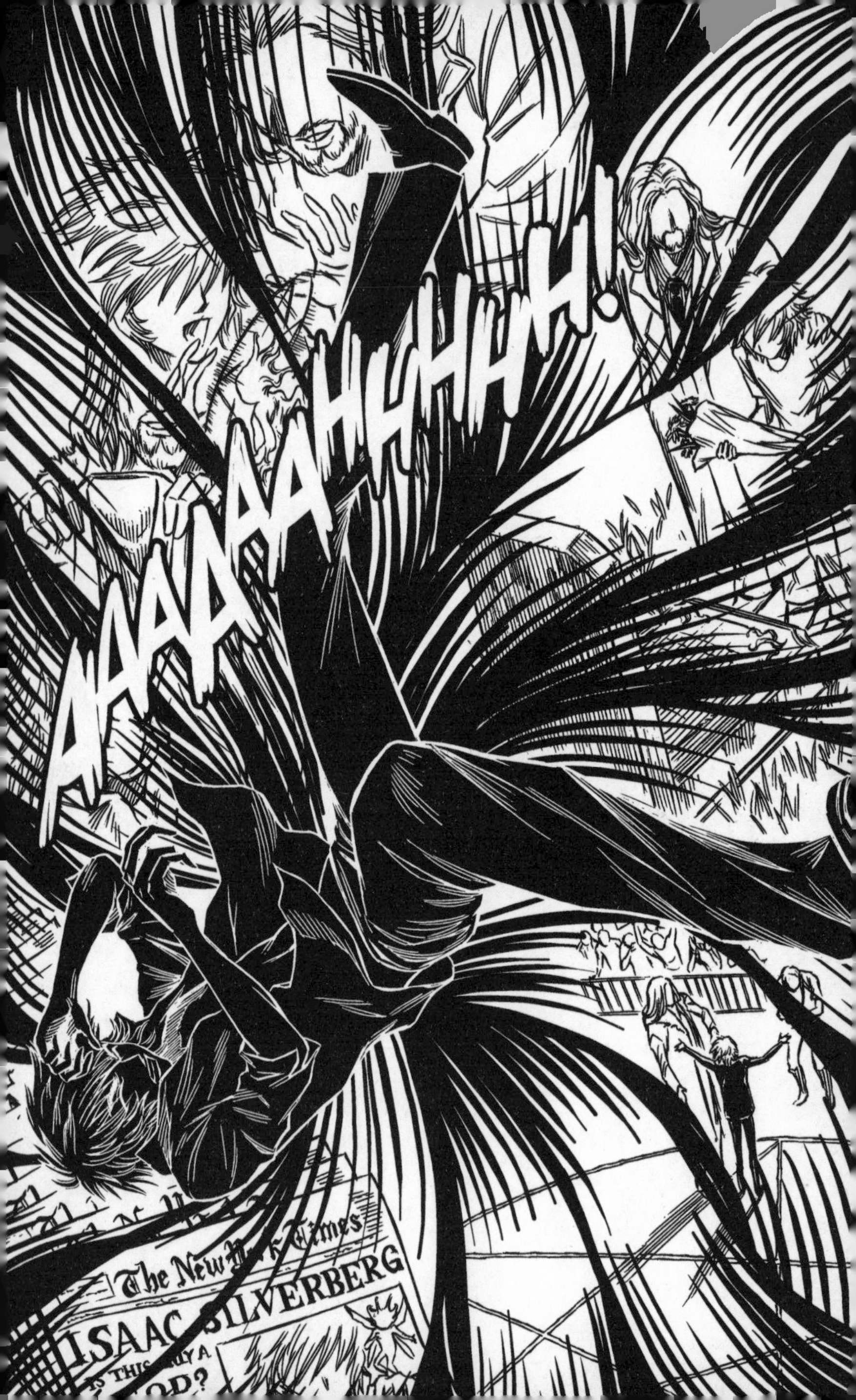
AAAAAHHHHHH!
The New
Times
ISAAC SILVERBERG

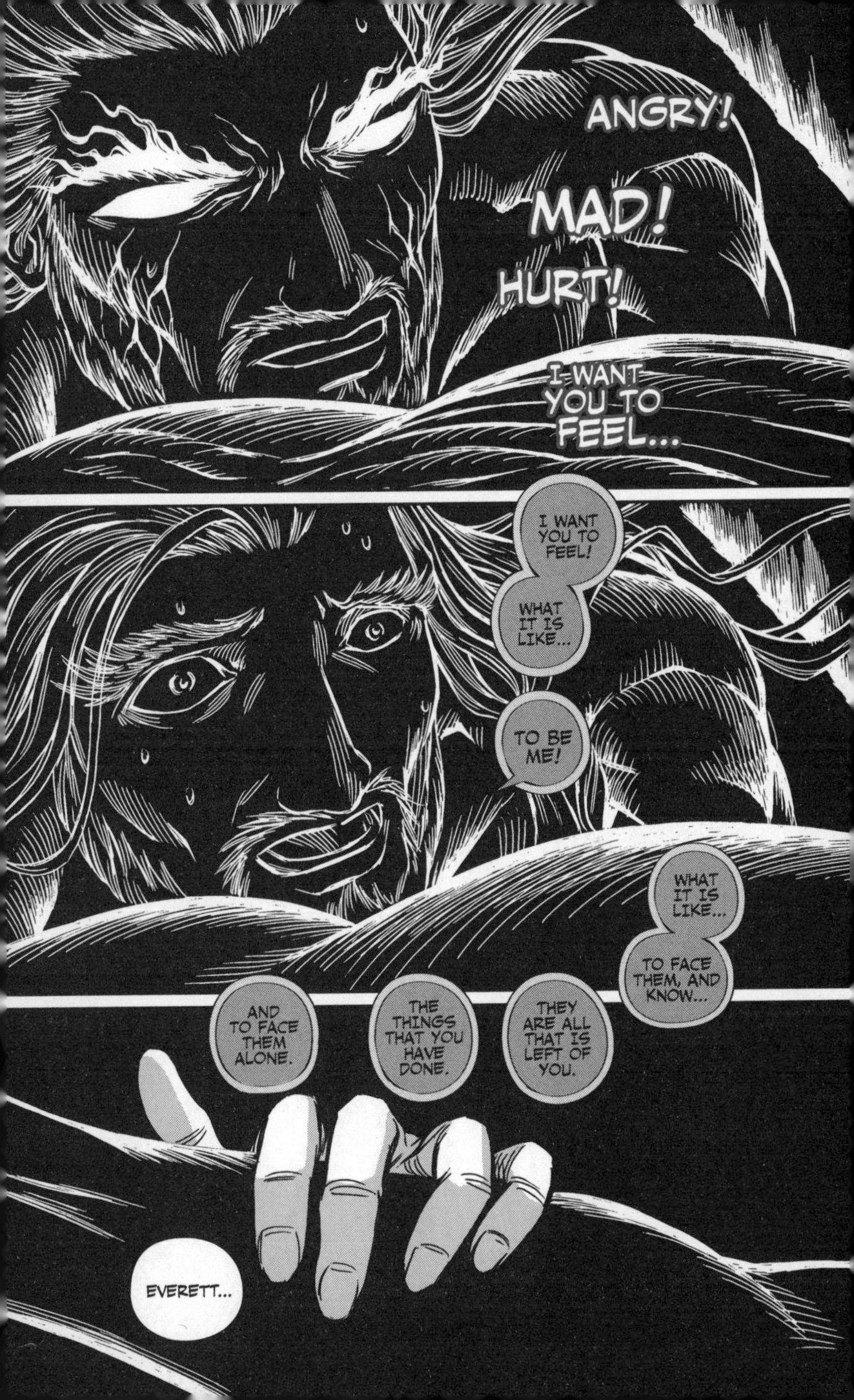
ANGRY!
MAD!
HURT!
I WANT YOU TO FEEL...
I WANT YOU TO FEEL!
WHAT IT IS LIKE...
TO BE ME!
WHAT IT IS LIKE...
TO FACE THEM, AND KNOW...
THEY ARE ALL THAT IS LEFT OF YOU.
THE THINGS THAT YOU HAVE DONE.
AND TO FACE THEM ALONE.
EVERETT...

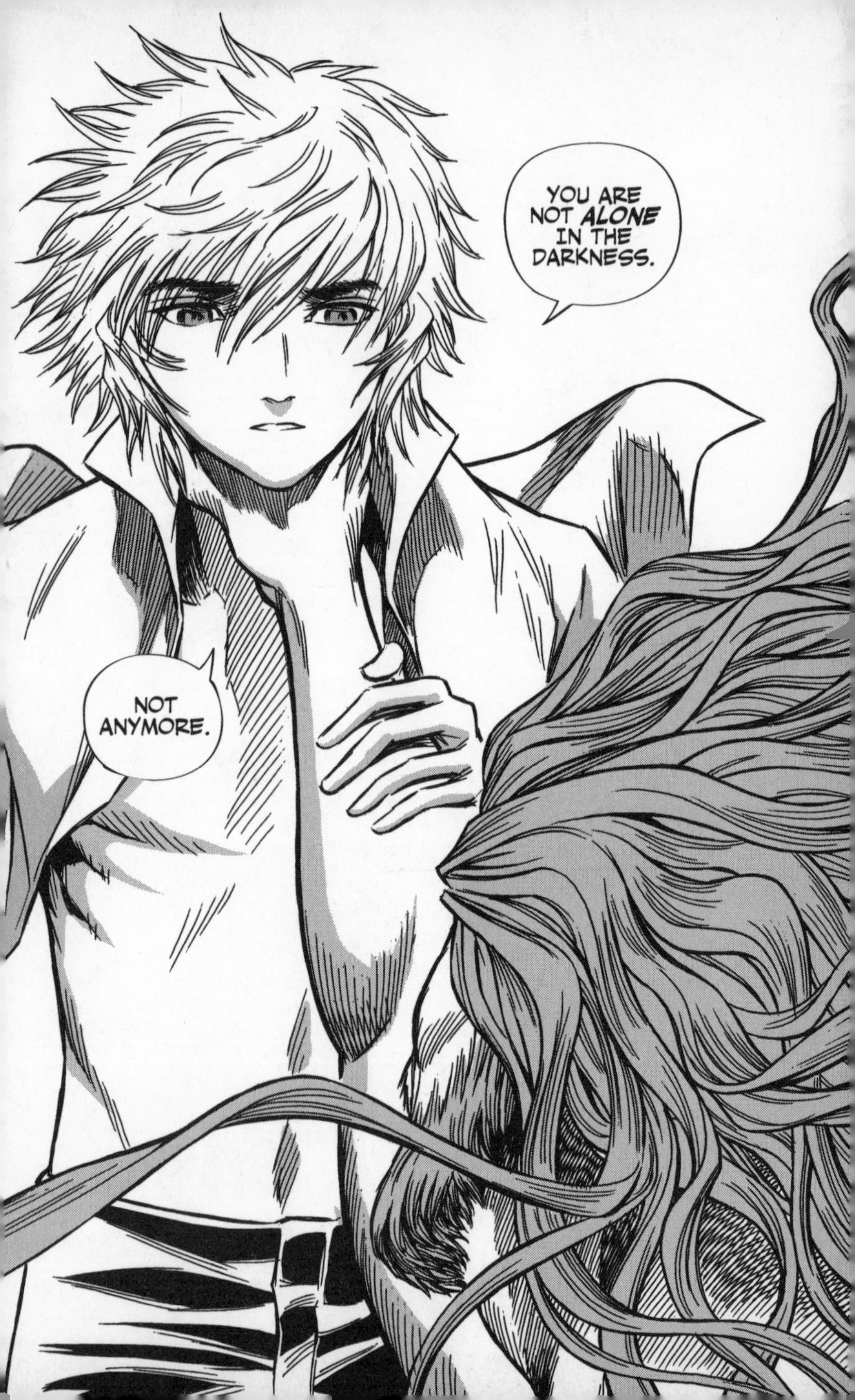
YOU ARE NOT *ALONE* IN THE DARKNESS.
NOT ANYMORE.

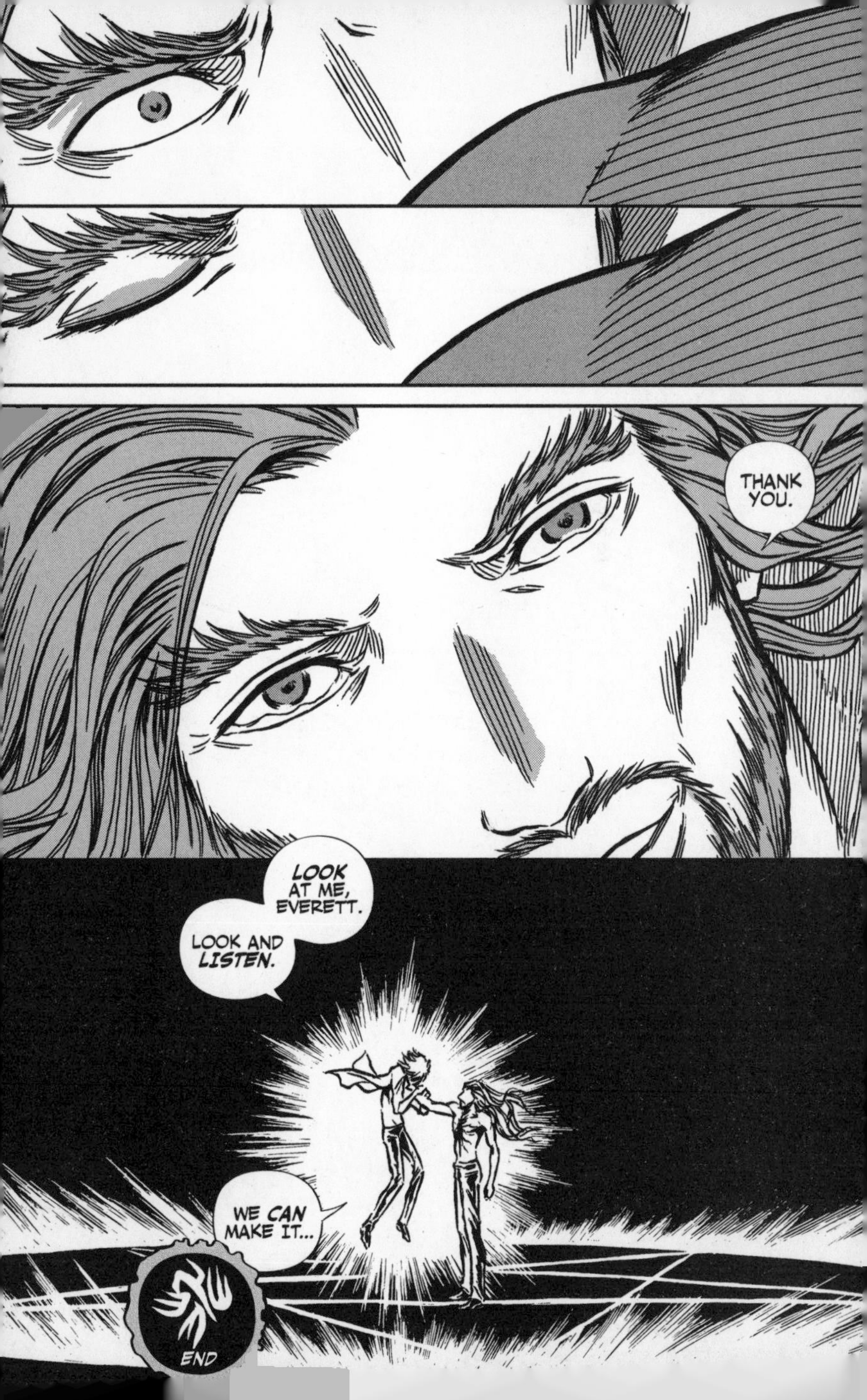
THANK YOU.
LOOK AT ME, EVERETT.
LOOK AND LISTEN.
WE CAN MAKE IT...
END

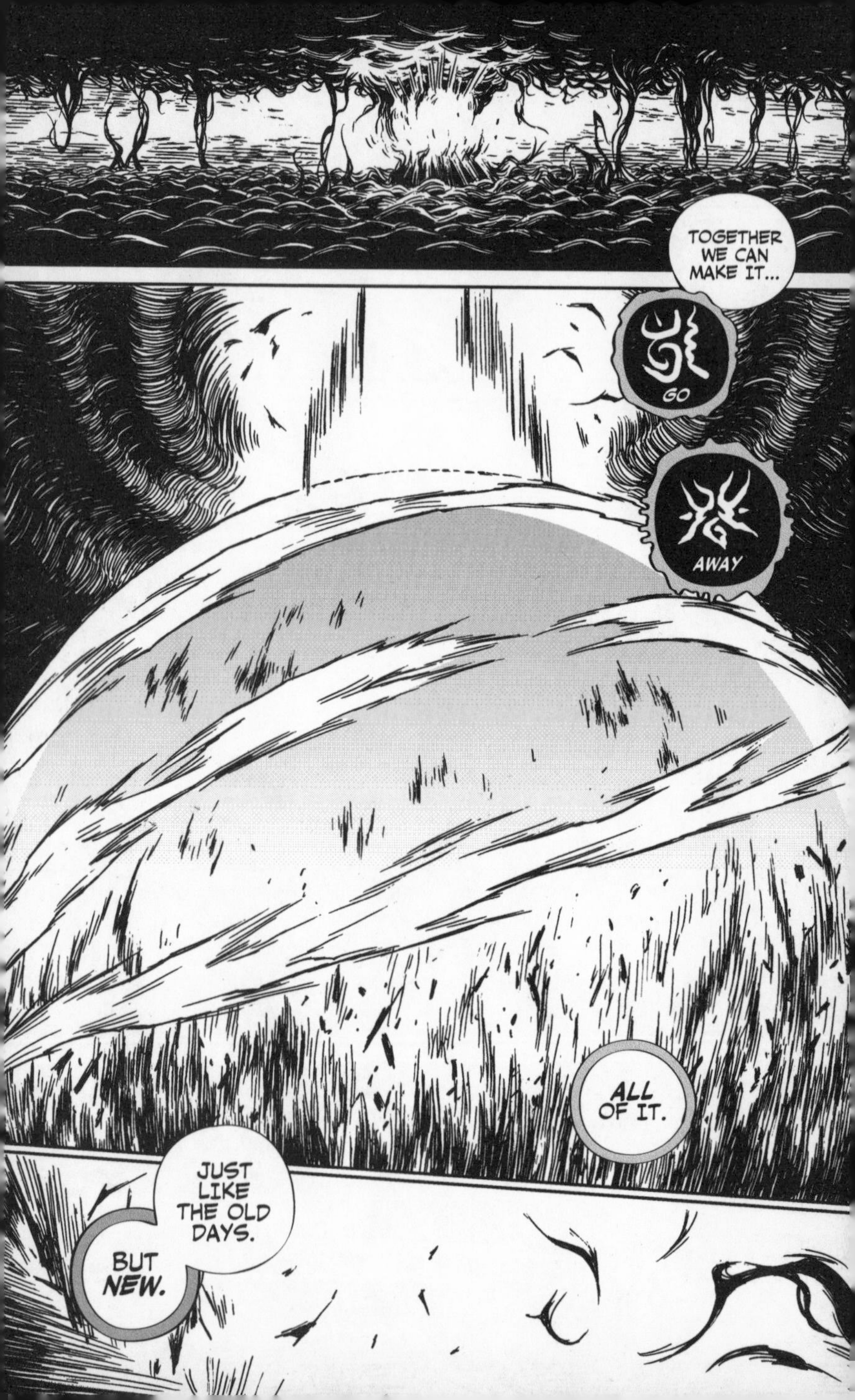
TOGETHER WE CAN MAKE IT...
GO
AWAY
ALL OF IT.
JUST LIKE THE OLD DAYS.
BUT NEW.

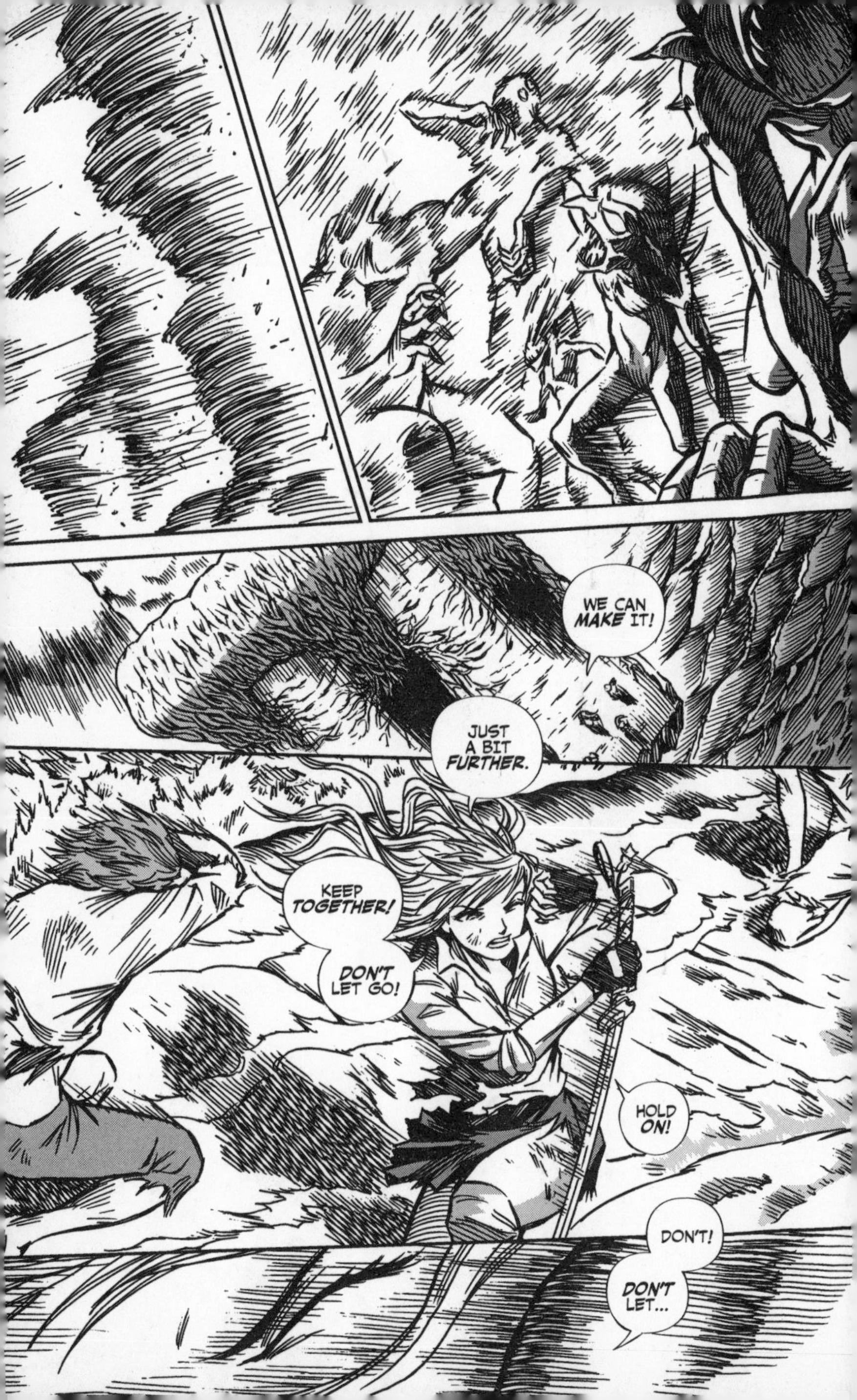
WE CAN *MAKE* IT!
JUST A BIT *FURTHER.*
KEEP *TOGETHER!*
DON'T LET GO!
HOLD *ON!*
DON'T!
DON'T LET...

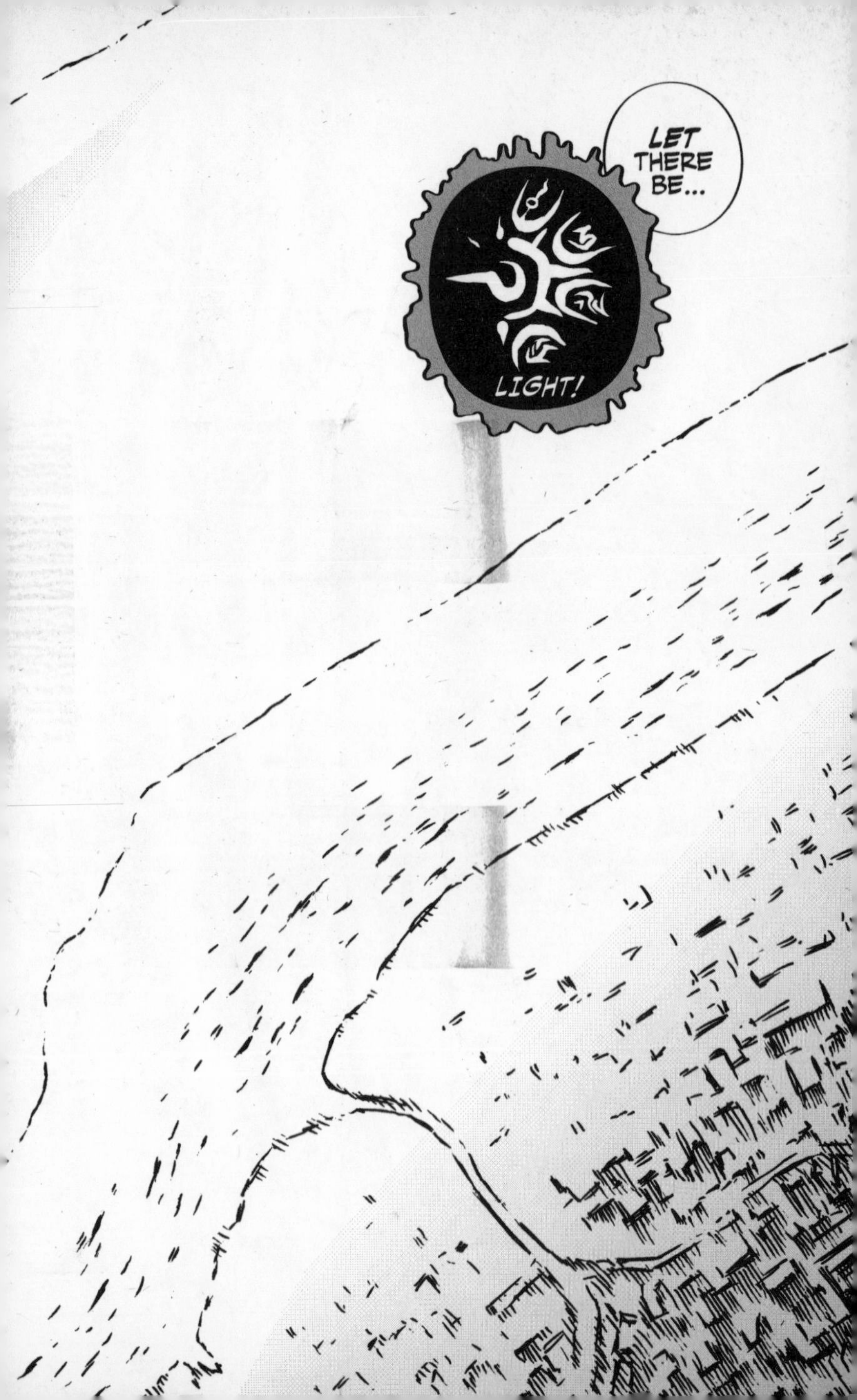
LET THERE BE...
LIGHT!

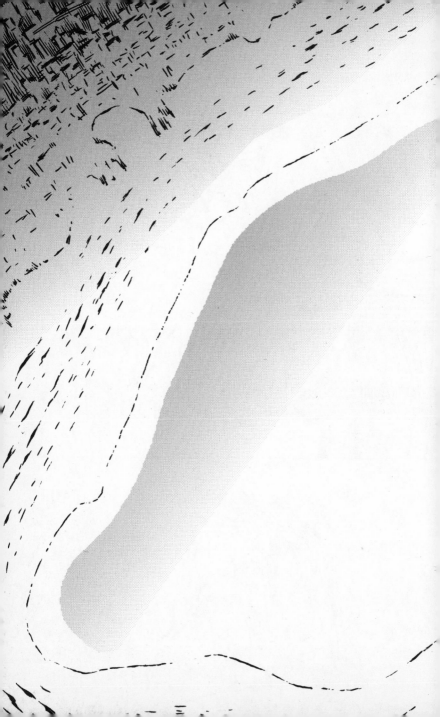

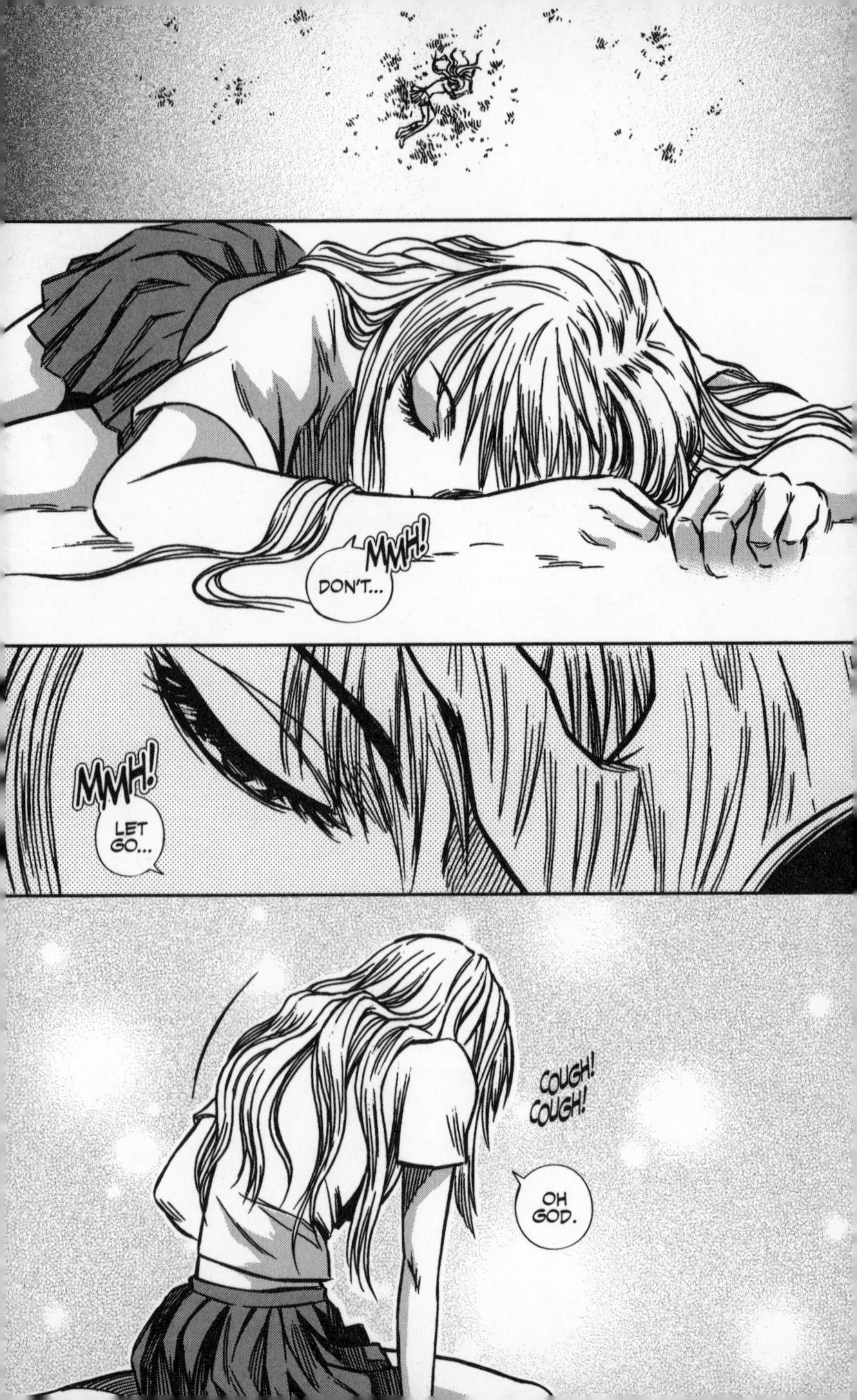
MMH!
DON'T...
MMH!
LET GO...
COUGH! COUGH!
OH GOD.

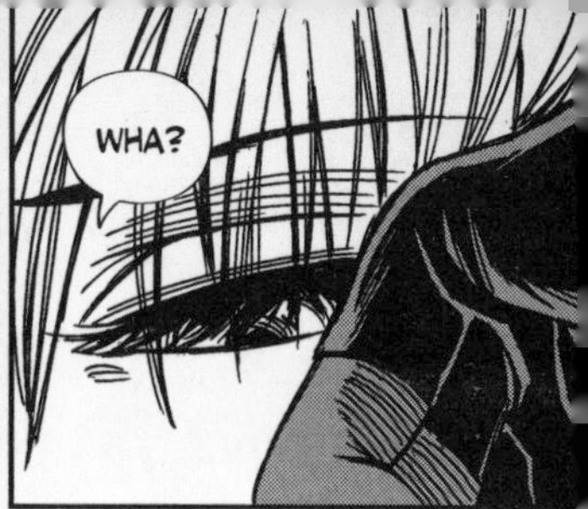
WHA?
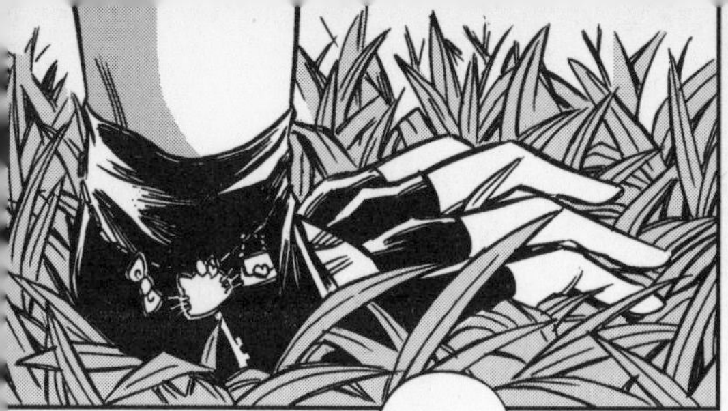
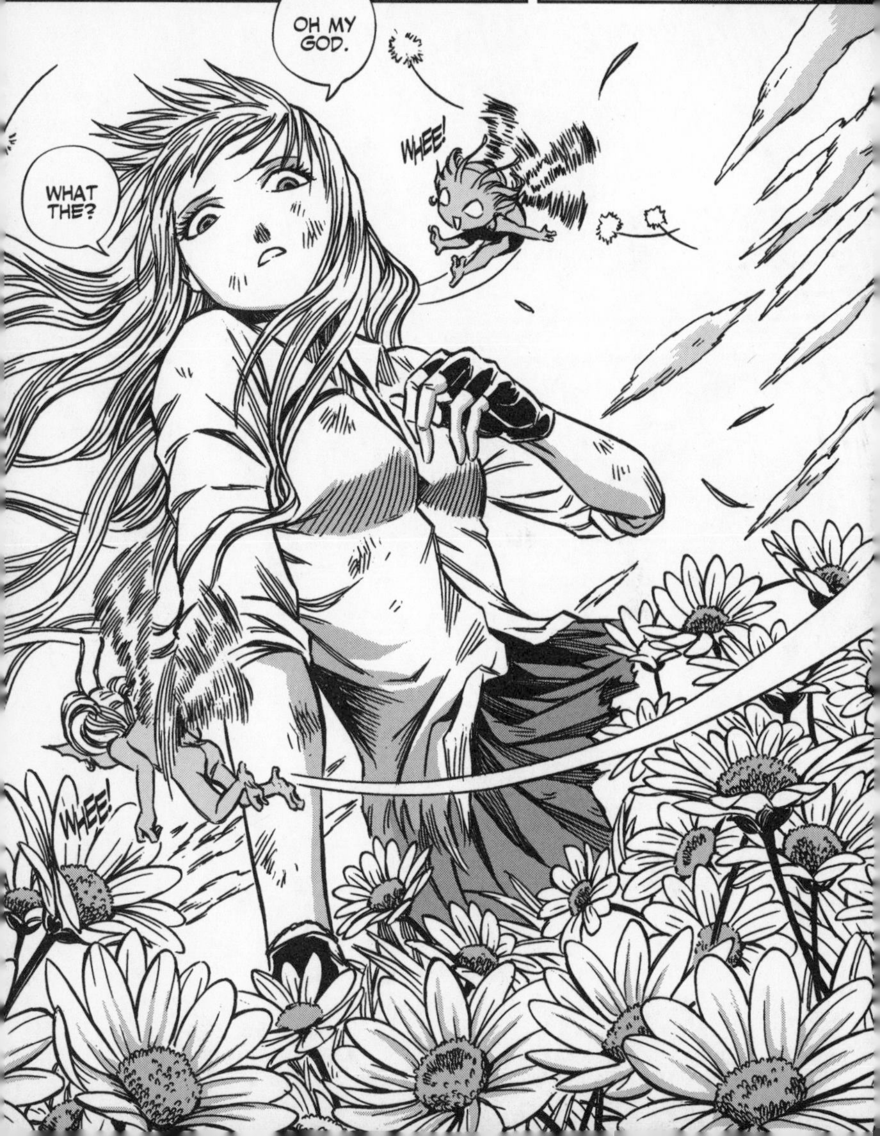
OH MY GOD.
WHEE!
WHAT THE?
WHEE!

IT'S A TRICK!
MUST BE!
ANY MOMENT NOW!
THEY'RE GOING TO TRY AND...
YOU JUST WATCH!
WATCH OUT!
JUST ANOTHER ILLUSION!

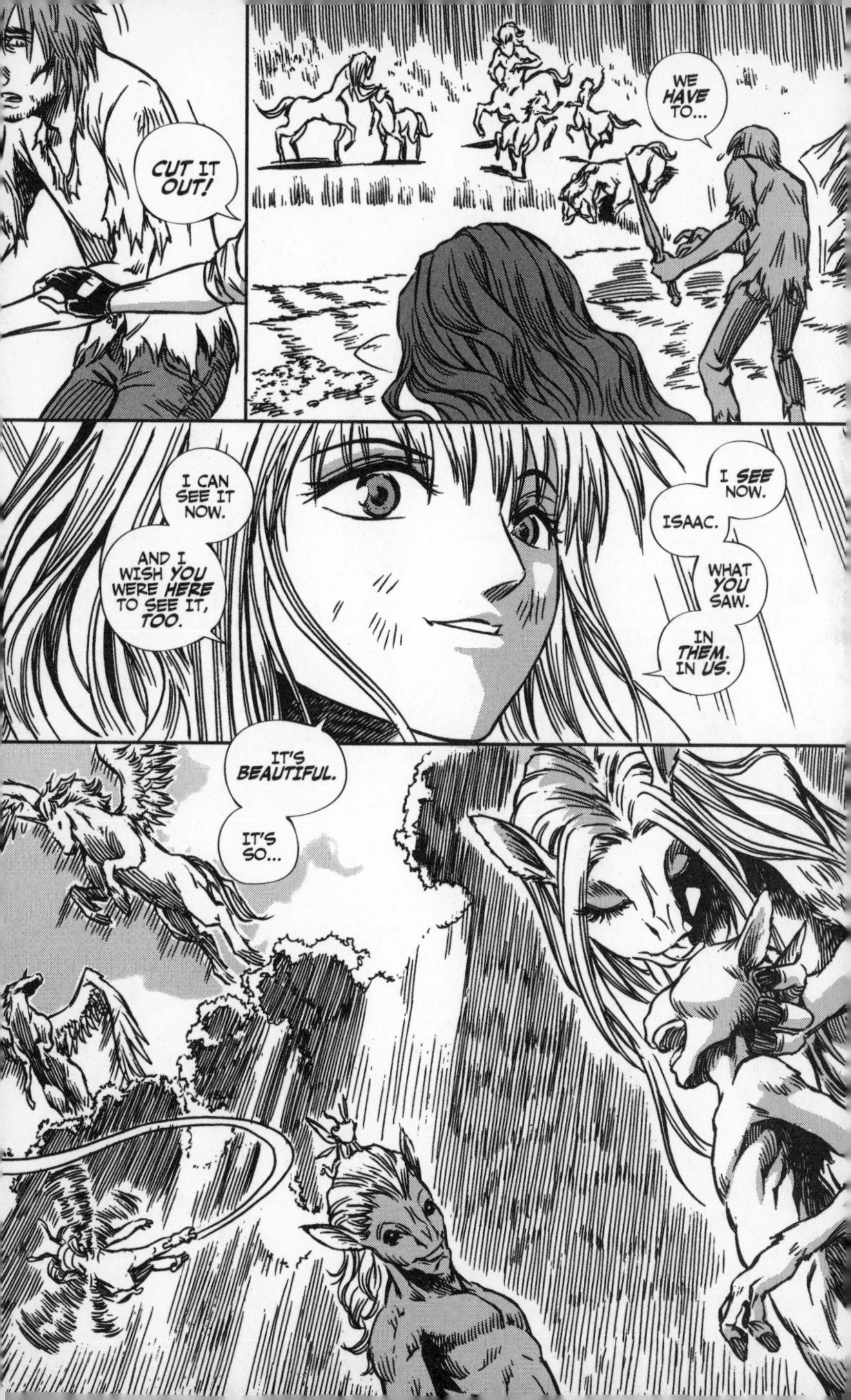
WE HAVE TO...
CUT IT OUT!
I SEE NOW.
ISAAC.
WHAT YOU SAW.
IN THEM. IN US.
I CAN SEE IT NOW.
AND I WISH YOU WERE HERE TO SEE IT, TOO.
IT'S BEAUTIFUL.
IT'S SO...

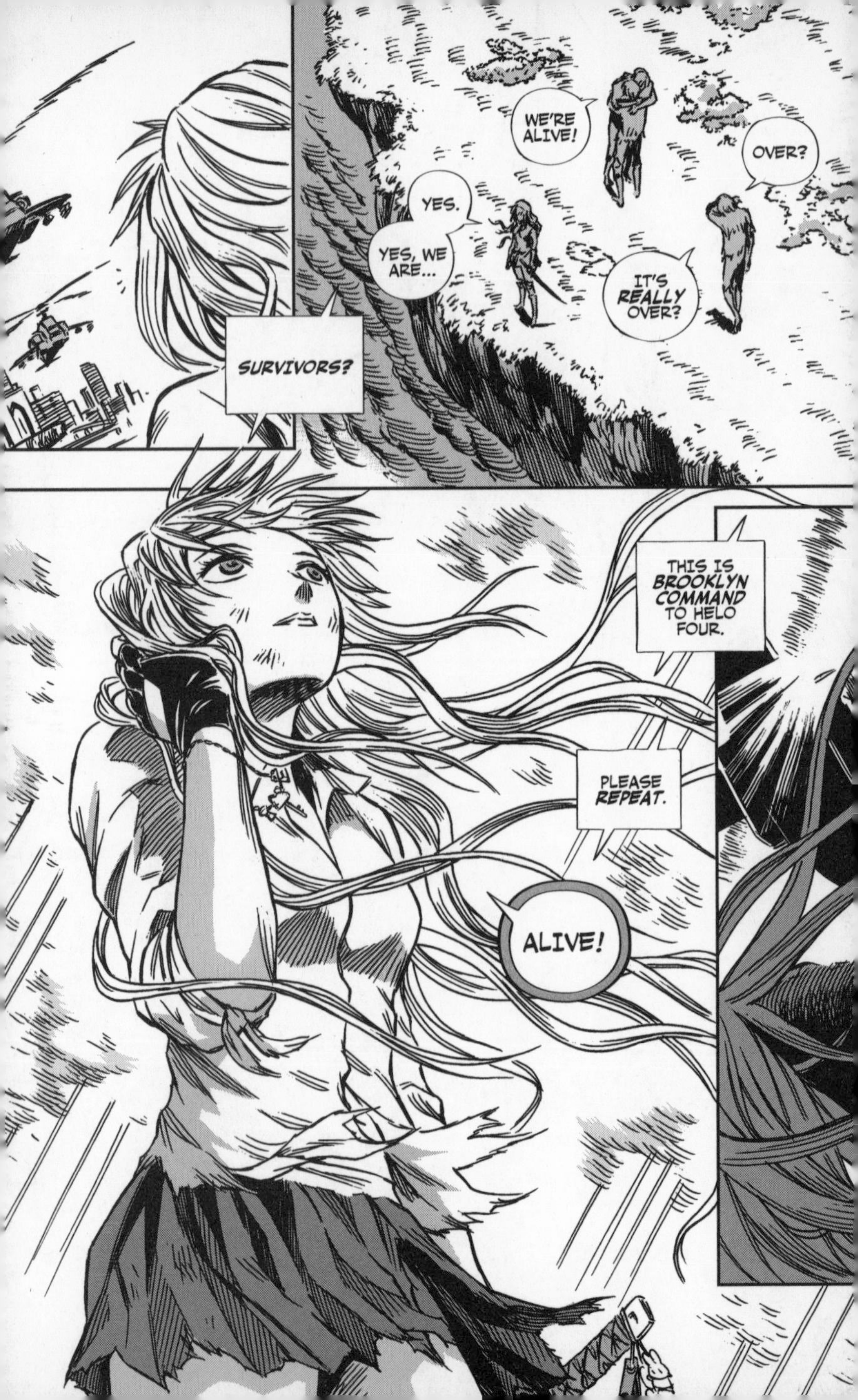
SURVIVORS?
WE'RE ALIVE!
OVER?
IT'S *REALLY* OVER?
YES.
YES, WE ARE...
THIS IS *BROOKLYN COMMAND* TO HELO FOUR.
PLEASE *REPEAT*.
ALIVE!

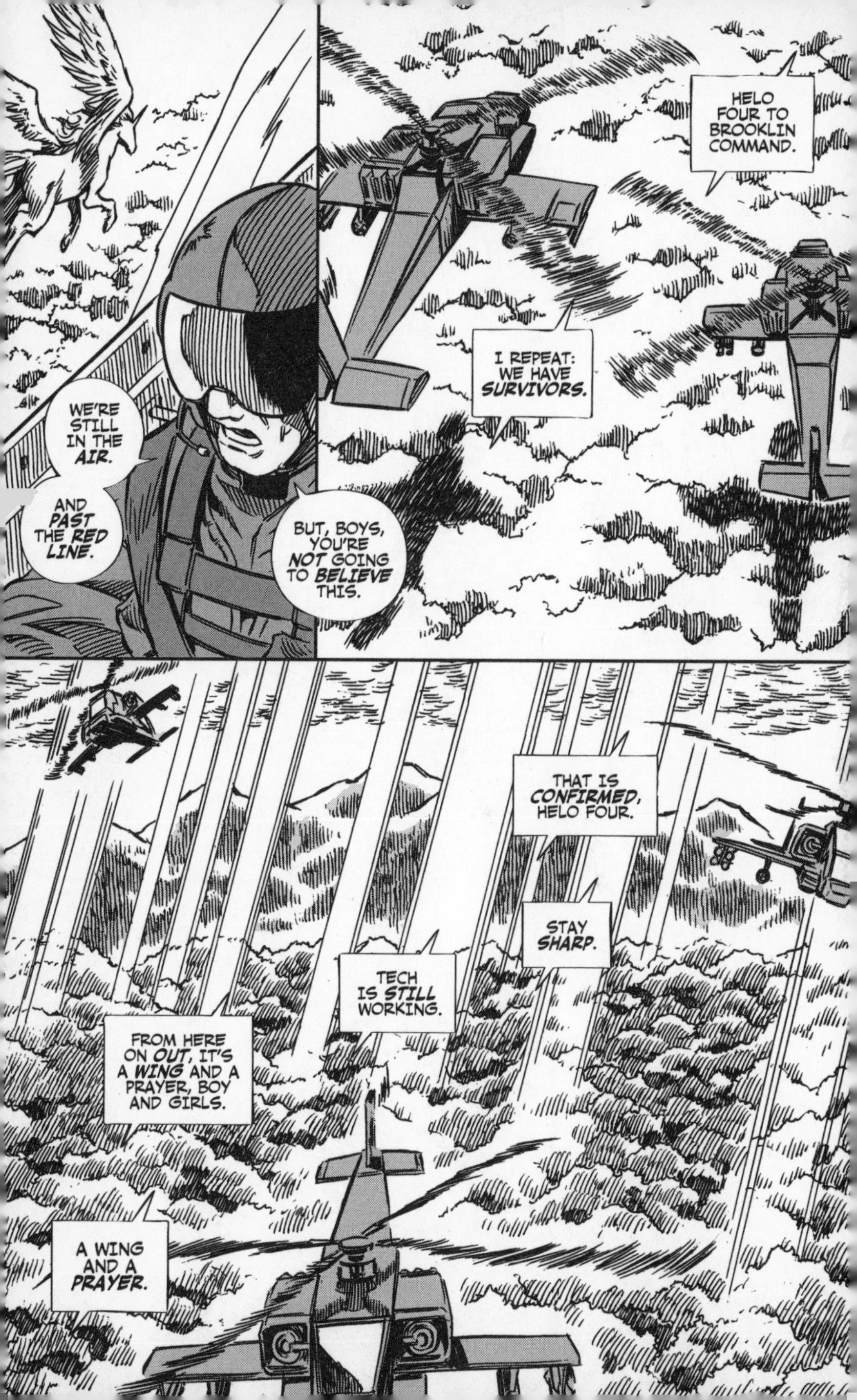
WE'RE STILL IN THE AIR.
AND PAST THE RED LINE.
BUT, BOYS, YOU'RE NOT GOING TO BELIEVE THIS.
HELO FOUR TO BROOKLIN COMMAND.
I REPEAT: WE HAVE SURVIVORS.
THAT IS CONFIRMED, HELO FOUR.
STAY SHARP.
TECH IS STILL WORKING.
FROM HERE ON OUT, IT'S A WING AND A PRAYER, BOY AND GIRLS.
A WING AND A PRAYER.

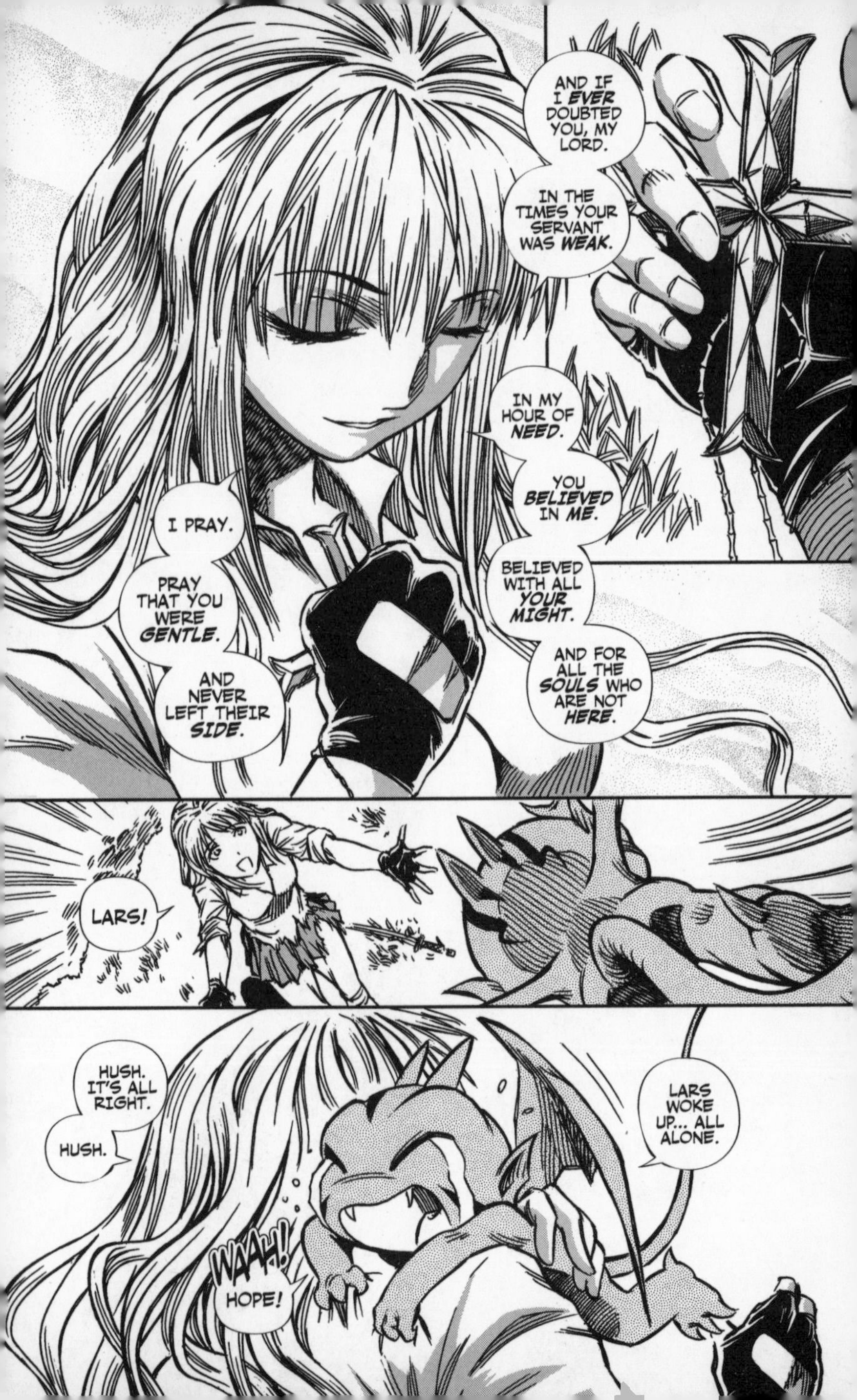
AND IF I EVER DOUBTED YOU, MY LORD.
IN THE TIMES YOUR SERVANT WAS WEAK.
IN MY HOUR OF NEED.
YOU BELIEVED IN ME.
BELIEVED WITH ALL YOUR MIGHT.
AND FOR ALL THE SOULS WHO ARE NOT HERE.
I PRAY.
PRAY THAT YOU WERE GENTLE.
AND NEVER LEFT THEIR SIDE.
LARS!
LARS WOKE UP... ALL ALONE.
HUSH. IT'S ALL RIGHT.
HUSH.
WAAH!
HOPE!

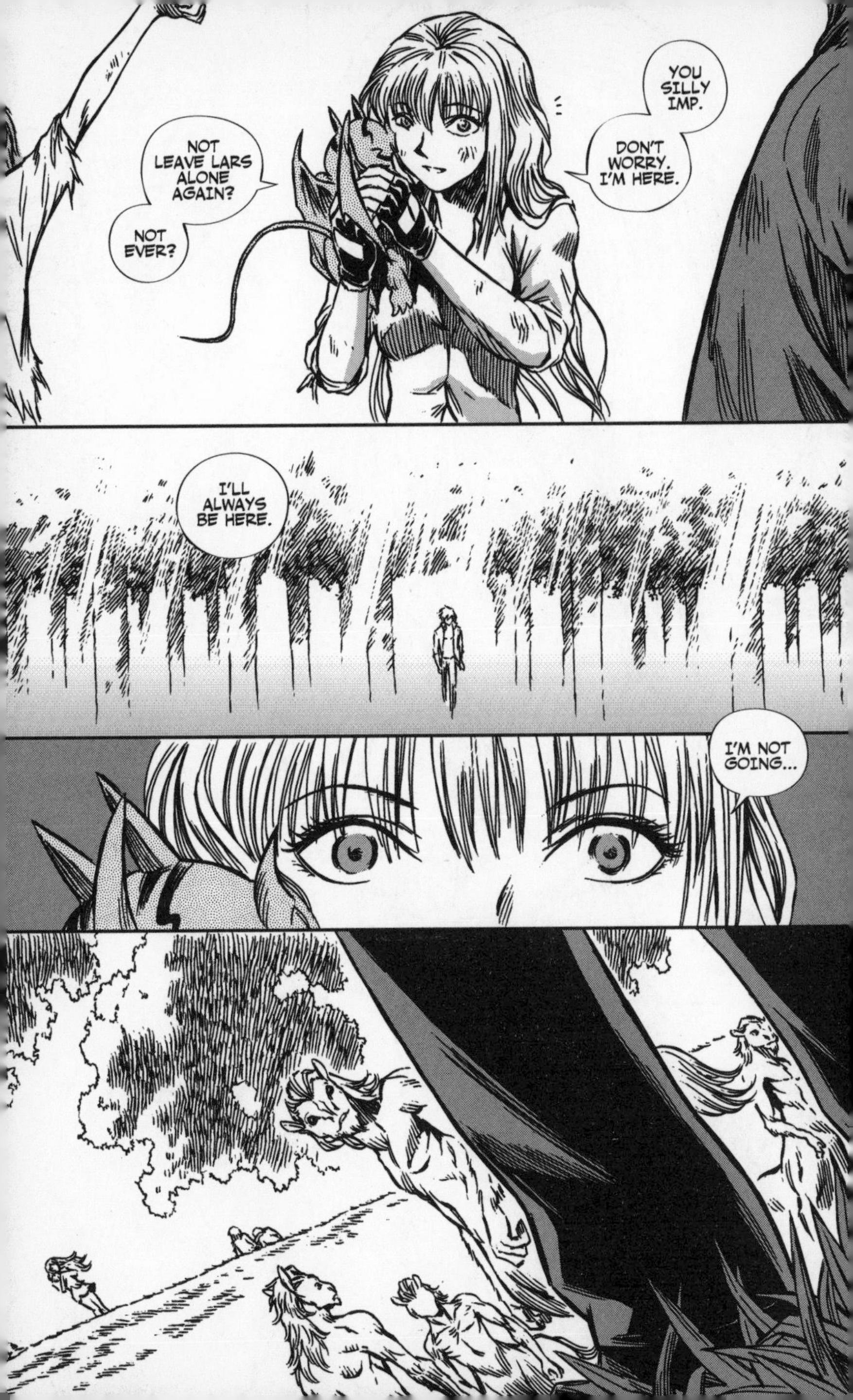
NOT LEAVE LARS ALONE AGAIN?
NOT EVER?
YOU SILLY IMP.
DON'T WORRY. I'M HERE.
I'LL ALWAYS BE HERE.
I'M NOT GOING...

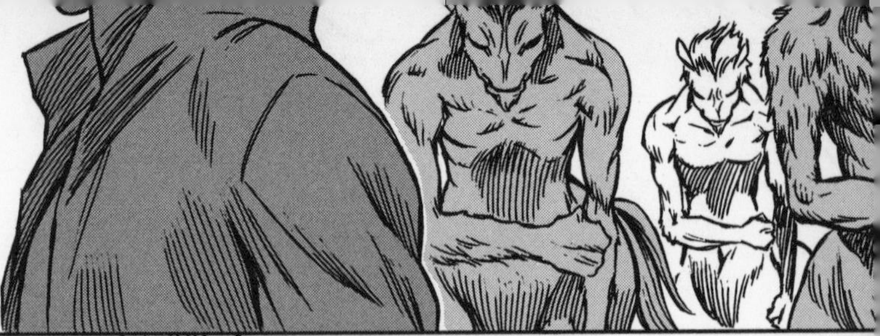
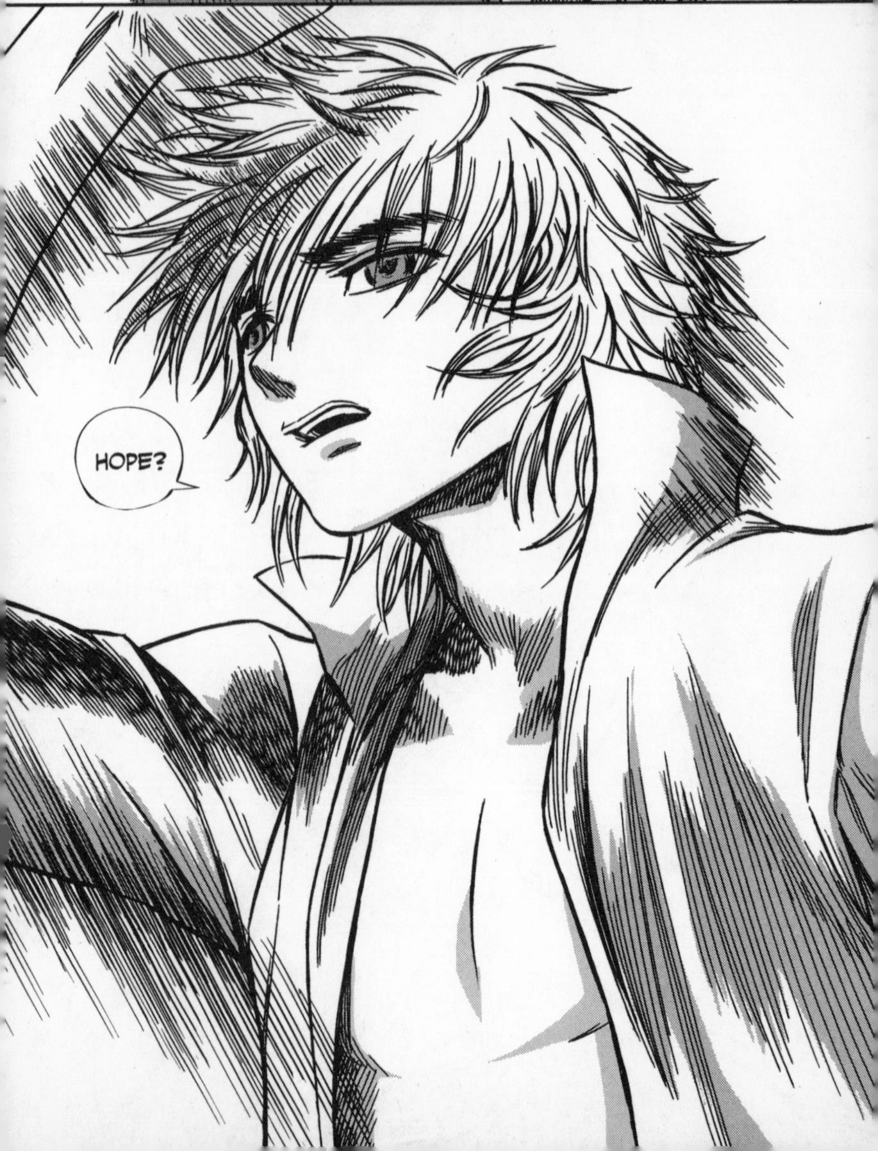
HOPE?

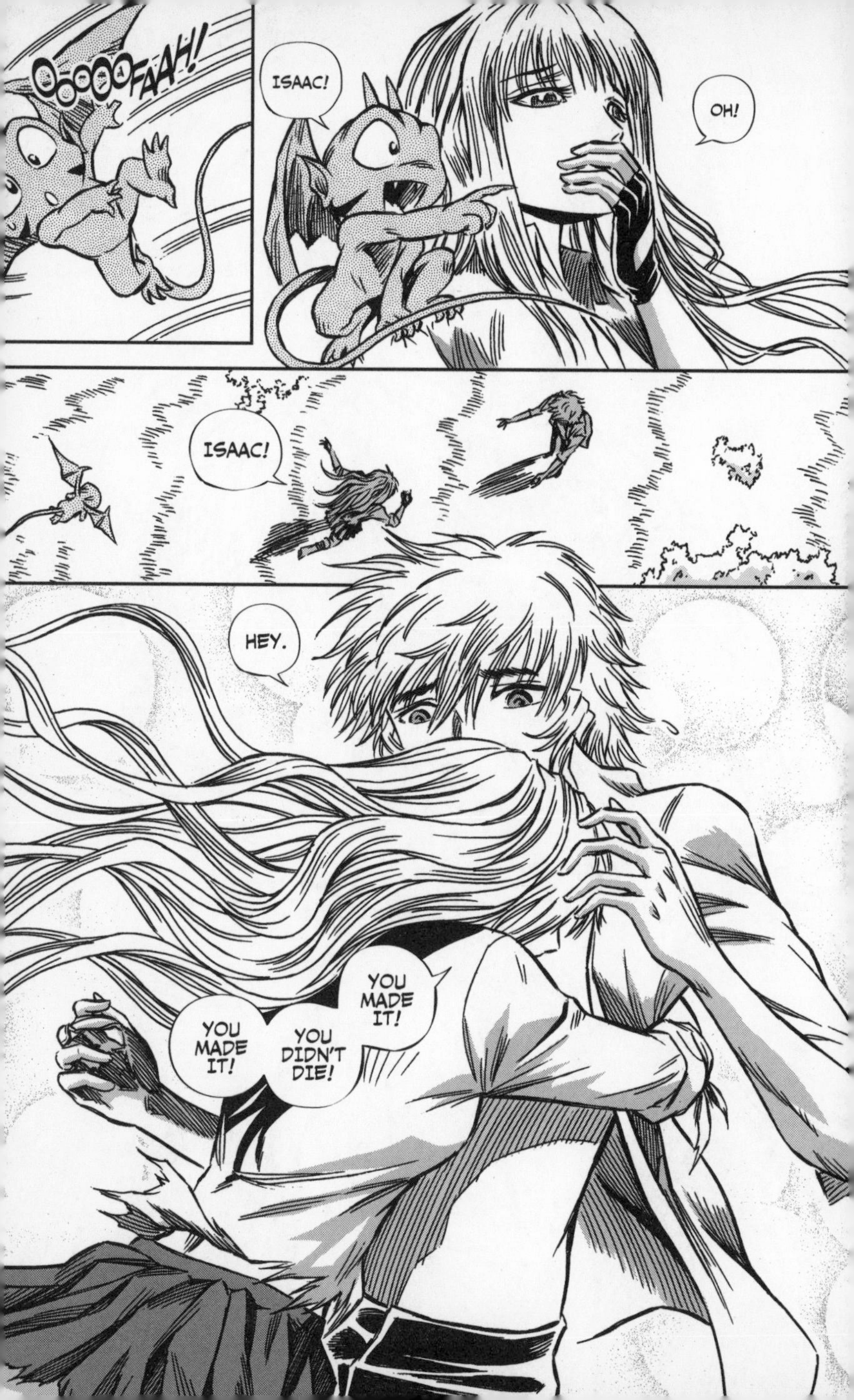
OH!
ISAAC!
OOOOOFAAH!
ISAAC!
HEY.
YOU MADE IT!
YOU DIDN'T DIE!
YOU MADE IT!

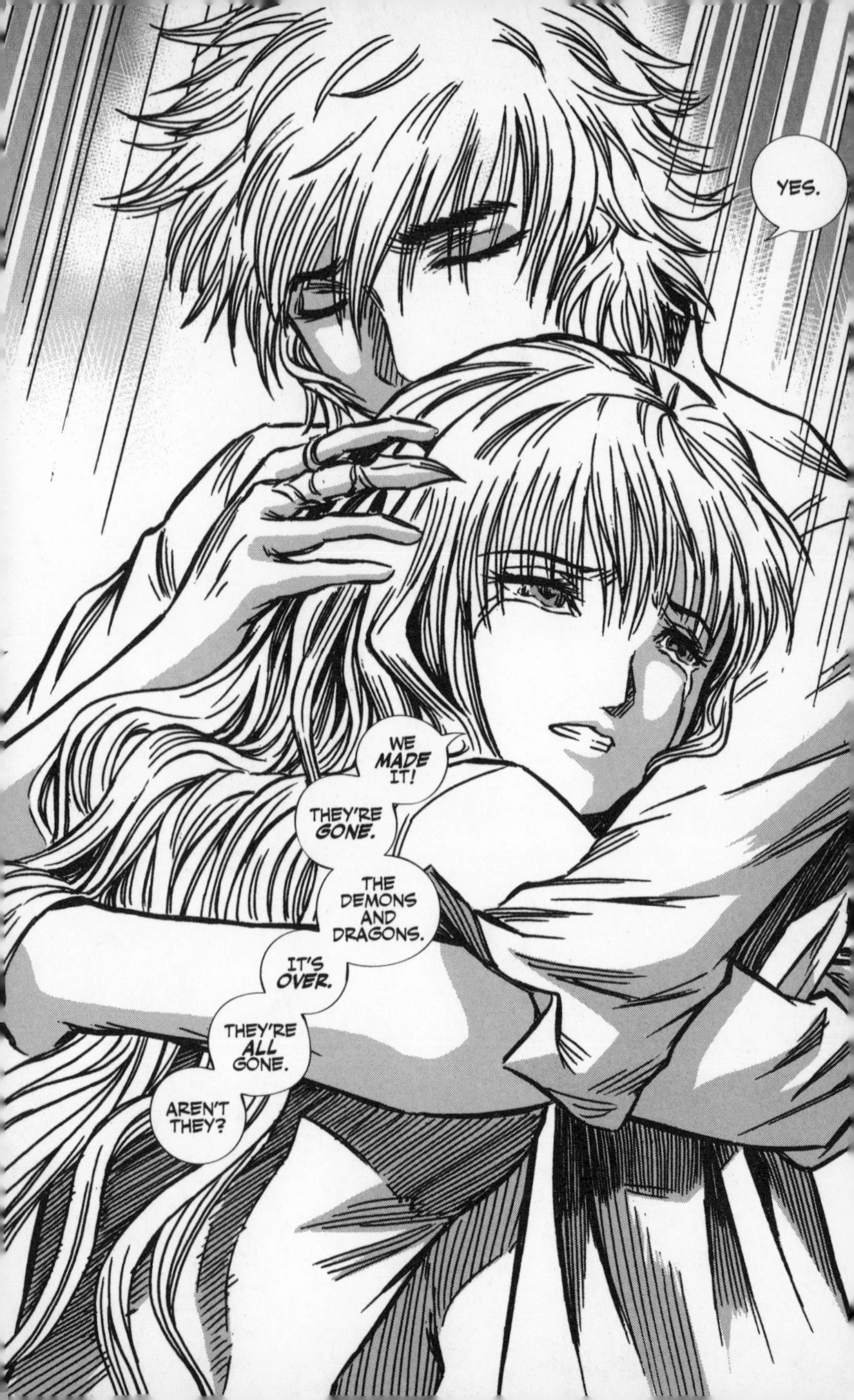
YES.
WE MADE IT!
THEY'RE GONE.
THE DEMONS AND DRAGONS.
IT'S OVER.
THEY'RE ALL GONE.
AREN'T THEY?

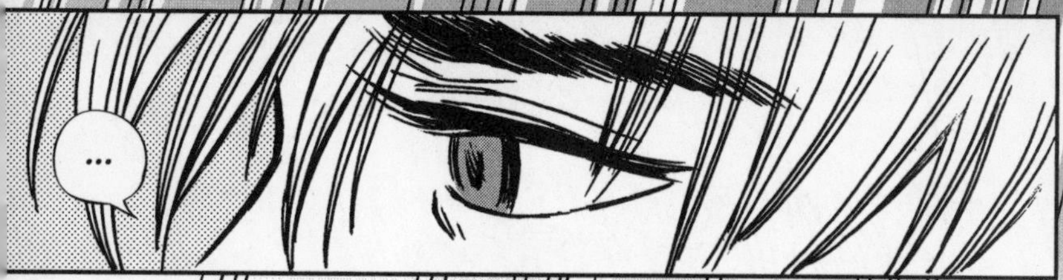
...
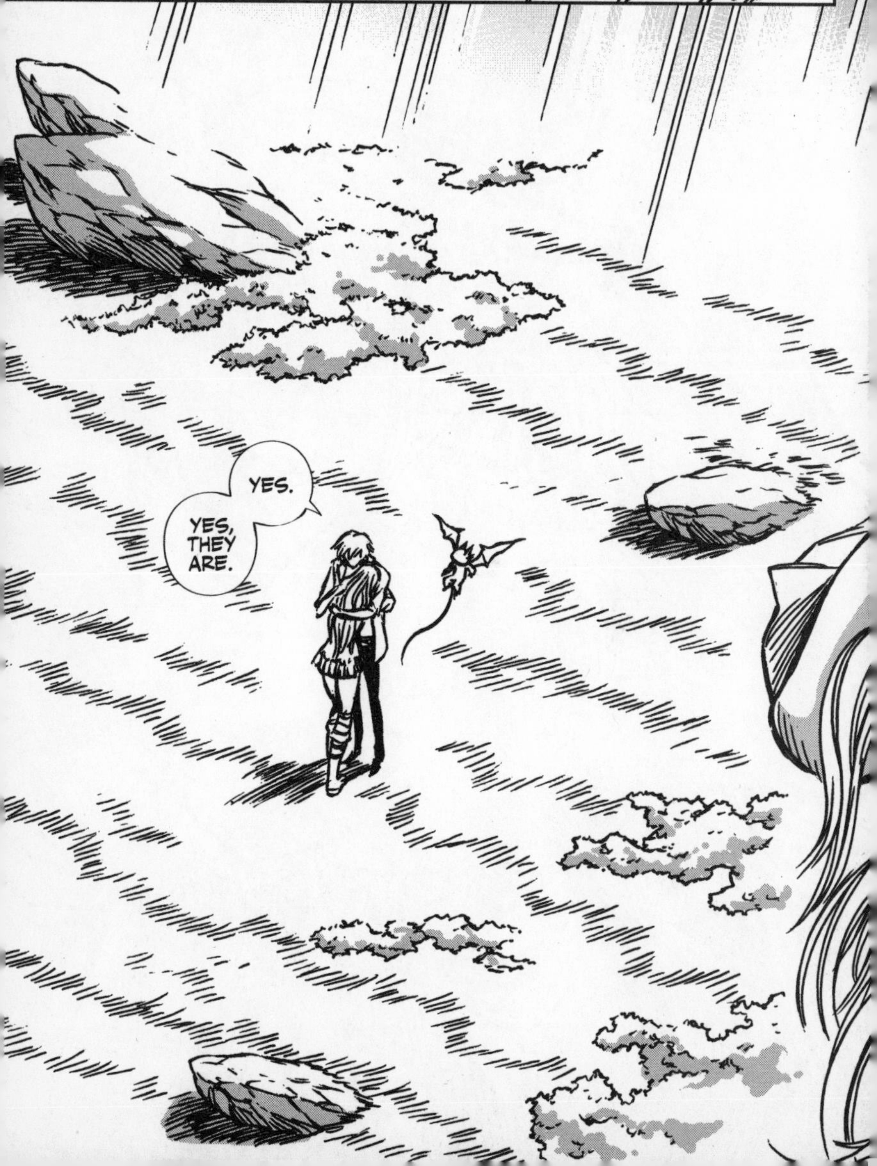
YES.
YES, THEY ARE.

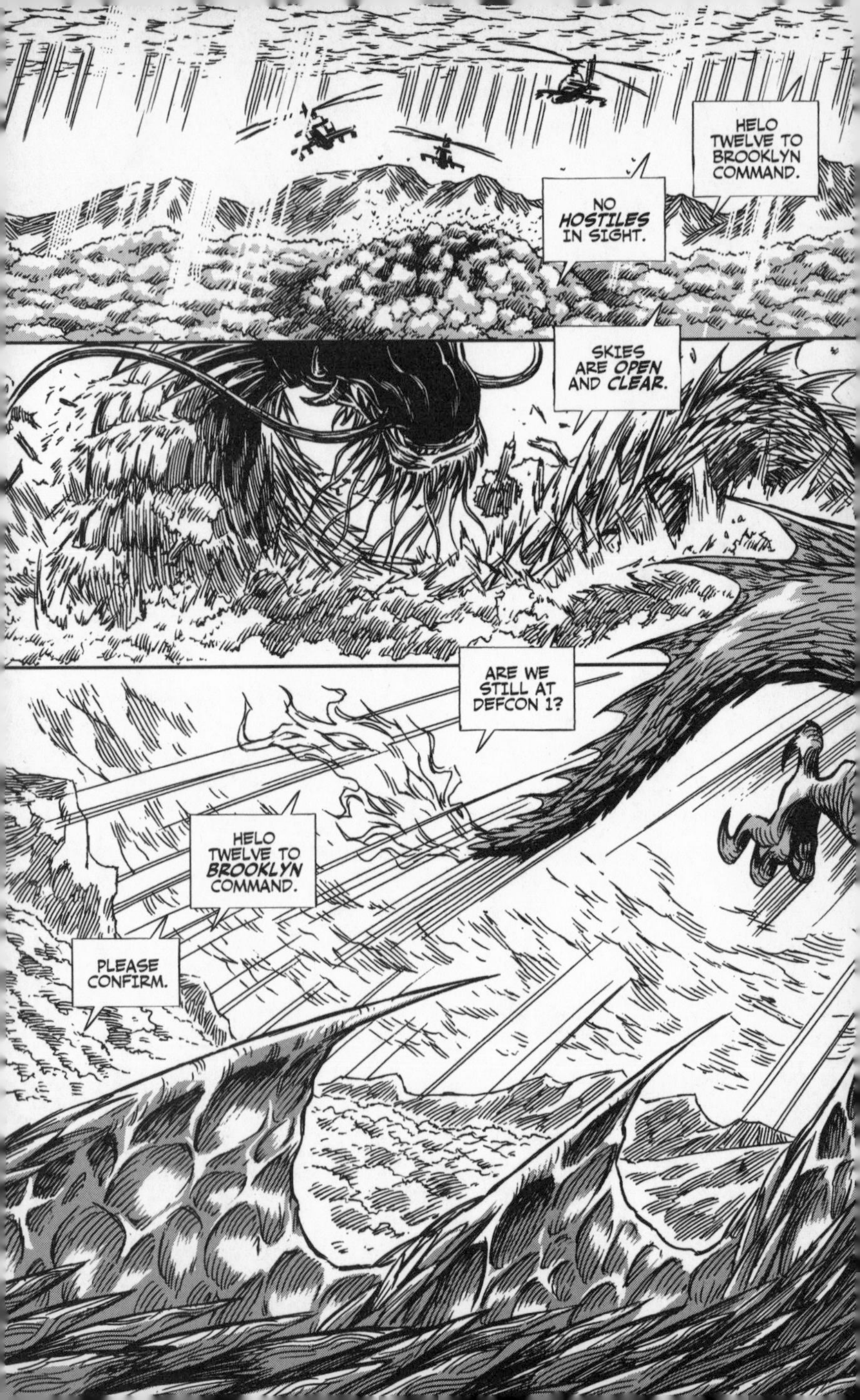
HELO TWELVE TO BROOKLYN COMMAND.
NO *HOSTILES* IN SIGHT.
SKIES ARE *OPEN* AND *CLEAR*.
ARE WE STILL AT DEFCON 1?
HELO TWELVE TO *BROOKLYN* COMMAND.
PLEASE CONFIRM.

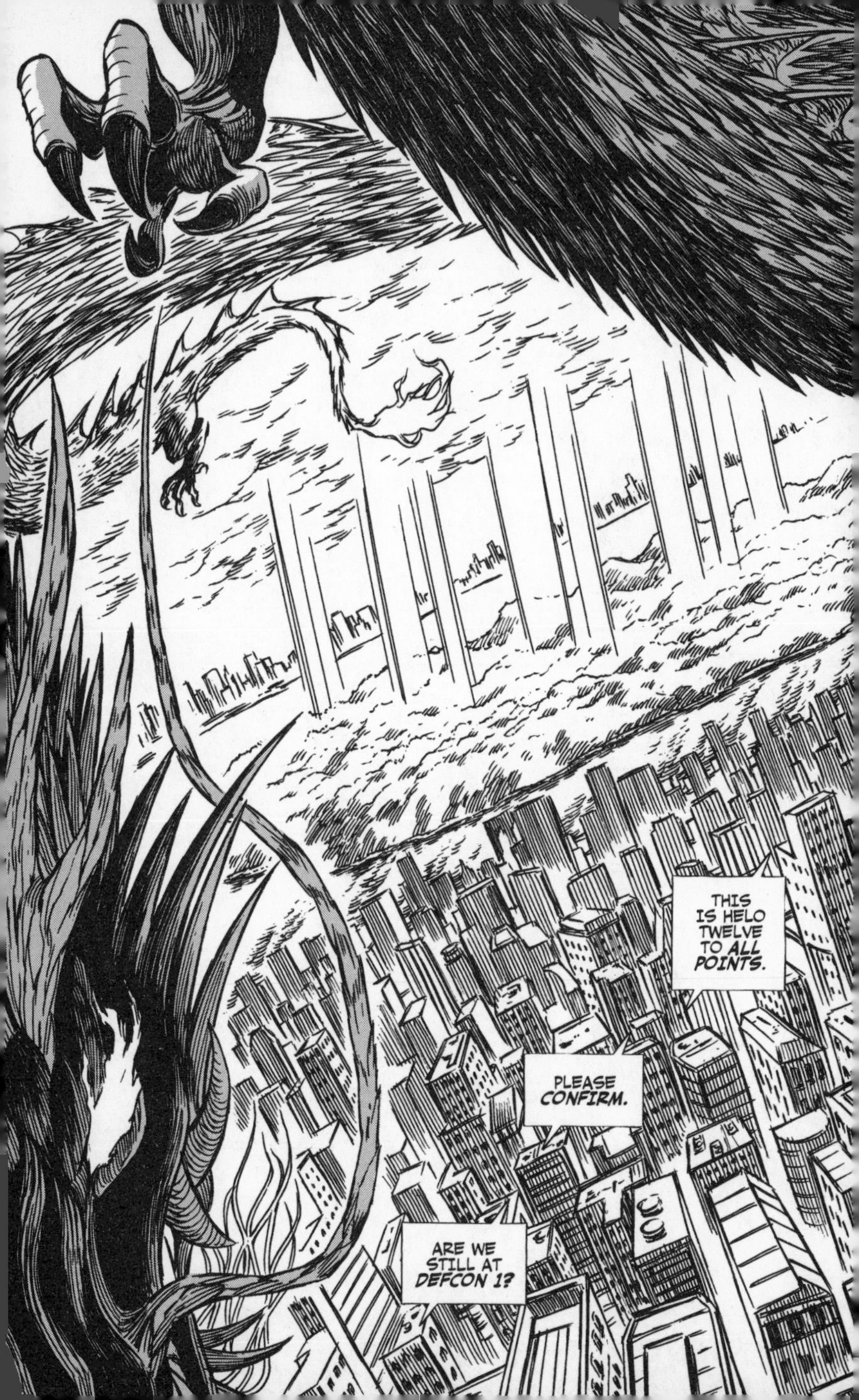
THIS IS HELO TWELVE TO *ALL POINTS*.
PLEASE *CONFIRM*.
ARE WE STILL AT *DEFCON 1*?

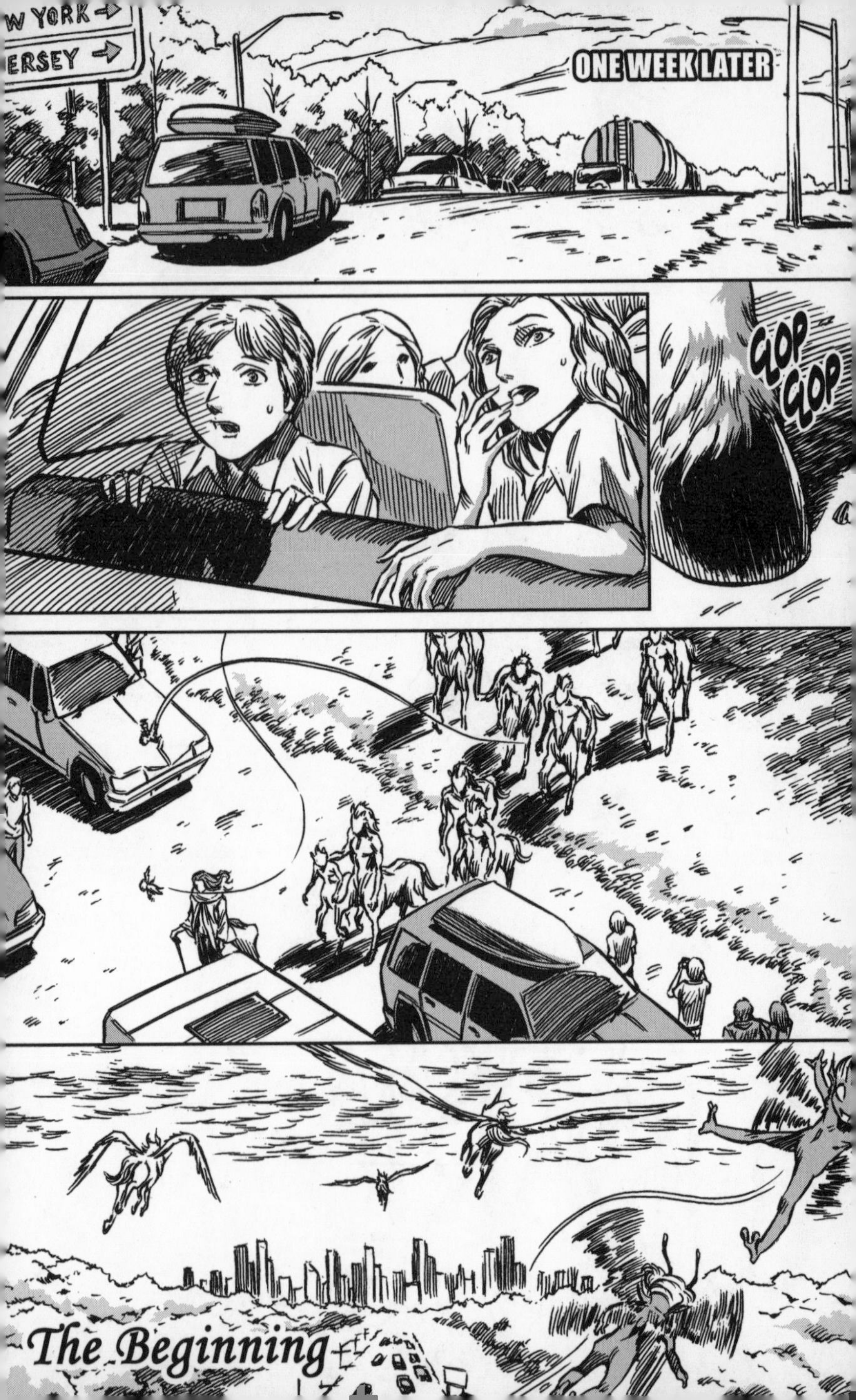
W YORK
ERSEY
ONE WEEK LATER
GLOP GLOP
The Beginning

YOU'RE READING THE WRONG WAY

This is the last page of
It Takes A Wizard

This book reads from right to left, Japanese style. To read from the beginning, flip the book over to the other side, start with the top right panel, and take it from there.

If this is your first time reading manga, just follow the diagram. It may seem backwards at first, but you'll get used to it! Have fun!

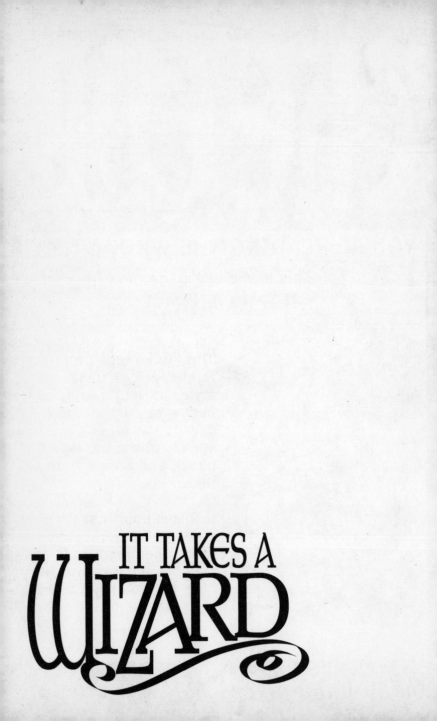

IT TAKES A
WIZARD